The 1987 Dow Jones-Irwin Business and Investment Almanac

The 1987 DOW JONES-IRWIN
Business and Investment Almanac

Edited by

Sumner N. Levine
State University of New York
at Stony Brook
and Editor
Financial Analyst's Handbook
and
The Investment Manager's Handbook

Executive Editor
Caroline Levine

DOW JONES-IRWIN
Homewood, Illinois 60430

© SUMNER N. LEVINE, 1987

ISBN 0–87094–915–2

Printed in the United States of America

1 2 3 4 5 6 7 8 9 0 K 3 2 1 0 9 8 7 6

Preface

This eleventh edition of the annual *Dow Jones-Irwin Business and Investment Almanac* contains a number of new features in response to the rapidly changing business and investment scene as well as updates on our standard features:

- Post World War II Bull Markets
- America's Most and Least Admired Corporations
- Federal Deficit Projections
- Acquisition and Takeover Glossary
- Summary of Provisions of the 1986 Tax Bill Affecting Business
- Summary of Provisions of the 1986 Tax Bill Affecting Individuals
- Major State Taxes and Rates
- State Business Assistance Centers

The editor and publisher are, of course, pleased with the acceptance of the *Dow Jones-Irwin Business and Investment Almanac* as a standard and unique reference for the business and investment community. As always, we continue to invite suggestions from our readers. All suggestions should be sent to: *Dow Jones-Irwin Business and Investment Almanac,* P.O. Box D, Setauket, New York 11733.

Sumner N. Levine
Editor

Contents

Business in Review

September 1985—September 1986

September 1985*

3 The U.S. trade deficit narrowed in July to $10.51 billion on a decline in imports. The narrowing was seen as temporary. Leading indicators rose 0.4%, but some analysts argued the rise overstated the economy's health.

A purchasing-managers' survey found the economy slumped in August, with a slight rise in output offset by lower prices and a fall in employment.

General Motors boosted most 1986 car prices in the range of 4% to 6%, an aggressive pricing tactic that comes even as GM is offering financing discounts on its 1985 models.

Federal budget deficits would narrow to $17.7 billion in 1990 from an estimated $211.3 billion this year, the administration projected. Projections were based on defense cuts proposed by Congress and large cuts in domestic programs proposed by Reagan—and largely rejected by Congress.

New construction contracts rose 16% in July to a seasonally adjusted annual rate of $231 billion, after a 12% drop in June, F. W. Dodge said.

The U.S. money supply's explosive growth this year sharply increases the odds of a surge in interest rates in coming months, according to many money managers and analysts.

4 The Farm Credit System is seeking a federal bailout of its $74 billion loan portfolio, a move that seems certain to dwarf Continental Illinois's record $4.5 billion rescue last year. As much as 15%, or $11.1 billion, of the system's loans are uncollectible, according to sources.

The dollar rose strongly for the third consecutive trading session, fueled in part by news that two western Canadian banks had failed.

New-construction spending rose 1.2% in July after falling a revised 0.6% in June. Analysts said the July rise, while reflecting a sharp decline in interest rates this year, wasn't as strong as they had expected.

* The cut-off date for Business in Review is usually the end of August because of our production schedule. Since the last entry in the previous Almanac was August 30, 1985, the current entry commences September 3, 1985.

Saudi Arabia is considering ways to boost oil sales by cutting prices, perhaps by $3 a barrel, below OPEC's official $28-a-barrel price, according to industry and government sources.

5 A bailout of the troubled Farm Credit System doesn't figure in the administration's immediate plans, officials said, despite warnings of a possible collapse. Treasury bond prices rose on speculation that the farm lending network's woes will keep the Fed from tightening credit.

6 The Farm Credit System will require "multibillions of dollars" in federal aid in 18 to 24 months, according to the system's chief regulator. But some bankers and farm economists believe help will be needed sooner.

Bond prices tumbled on news of surging new-car sales in late August. The strong showing sparked speculation the economy may finally be gaining momentum, which some analysts said could prompt the Fed to tighten credit soon. The dollar soared.

New-car sales soared 71% in the final 10 days of August, mainly because of low-interest rate sales incentives. U.S. auto makers sold 405,080 cars in the period, an annual rate of 13.5 million, the highest level since September 1973.

9 The jobless rate fell to 7% of the civilian work force in August, the lowest level in more than five years. The report, coupled with other recent data, suggests that the economy may be picking up steam as manufacturers' woes ease slightly.

The Bank Board is considering forming a quasi-governmental agency to buy billions of dollars of troubled assets from the beleaguered FSLIC (Federal Savings and Loan Insurance Corporation). The plan is part of a broad program to save the FSLIC without congressional intervention.

Some Texas banks are beginning to ask Farm Credit System banks to provide collateral for unsecured lines of credit. The system expects an increase of up to 55% in problem loans by the end of the third quarter.

10 The dollar rose again as dealers bought the U.S. currency in advance of what they expect to be a host of favorable economic reports, due Friday. In New York trading, the dollar settled at 2.9470 West German marks, up from 2.9225 marks late Friday.

Bond prices showed little change in lackluster trading. Many dealers and investors stayed out of the market, concerned that the economy is gaining momentum and that the Fed will decide to push up interest rates.

Wheat futures plunged as fresh signs appeared of a deterioration in world-wide demand for U.S. grain. Futures for September delivery tumbled 7.25 cents a bushel to $2.7575 on the Chicago Board of Trade.

The Rockefeller family will increase the size of the stake in Rockefeller Center it will offer to the public to 71.5% from the 60% originally planned. The common stock portion of the offer, which may begin this week, will total 37.5 million shares.

11 Citicorp and McGraw-Hill formed a joint venture to provide commodity traders with market information, and financial services, electronically. The service, which initially will focus on petroleum products, represents a significant expansion by Citicorp into the information-services business.

Moody's Investors Service is considering downgrading its double-A-1 rating on AT&T's debt and preferred stock. Moody's said the review was prompted by AT&T's "disappointing performance" in efforts to enter competitive high-technology markets.

The debt limit would be raised to $2.079 trillion if Congress approves an increase sought by the White House, more than double the level when Reagan took office in 1981. A Treasury official said the current ceiling of $1.824 trillion would be adequate only until September 30.

Metropolitan Life agreed to administer a plan, formally signed yesterday, to increase the return to holders of Baldwin-United annuities. Metropolitan will offer to swap its own annuities for those issued by Baldwin, but said it could take until next May before such an offer is made.

12 Volcker said the Fed is considering increasing capital requirements for banks and urged Congress to apply insurance premiums to foreign deposits. He also said the board is preparing standards on when bank holding companies should reduce or eliminate dividends.

Capital spending plans have been scaled back slightly by U.S. businesses. A government survey in July and August found that companies planned to spend 5.8% more on plant and equipment this year than in 1984, down from a 6.2% rise reported in a similar survey in April and May.

13 The Rockefeller family's public offering of 37.5 million shares, representing a stake in Rockefeller center, sold out at $20 a share.

Some congressmen are disputing former Attorney General Bell's conclusion that E. F. Hutton's senior managers didn't play a role in the firm's illegal bank overdrafts. Separately, regulators in four states plan to demand additional material from Hutton as part of their own probes.

16 Saudi Arabia has decided to boost oil production by one million barrels a day and cut prices, moves that could spark a global price war. Saudi Oil Minister Yamani warned that prices could fall to $18 a barrel by next spring unless other nations help stablize the market.

Retail sales surged 1.9% in August, paced by strong new-car sales, while industrial production rose 0.3%, the strongest signs yet that the economy is accelerating. Separately, producer prices last month fell 0.3%, the steepest drop in more than two years.

Sales of new cars soared 56.9% in the first 10 days of September, aided by low-interest financing. GM expects the sales momentum to continue but some industry experts expect a slowdown toward the end of the month.

17 The trade deficit swelled to $31.81 billion in the second quarter on a current account basis, confirming that the U.S. has become a net debtor nation for the first time since 1914. The first-half deficit totaled $62.14 billion, compared with the full-year record of $101.53 billion set in 1984.

The Eurobond market's largest borrowing ever, $2.5 billion of floating-rate notes, was issued by Britain in a move to shore up its dwindling foreign exchange reserves.

The dollar eased against most foreign currencies. Dealers cited the report that U.S. factory capacity utilization last month was only 80.5%, somewhat less than traders expected.

18 Phibro-Salomon is creating the first options market in oil. It plans to offer warrants outside the U.S. to investors seeking to lessen the effects of sudden oil-price swings, such as banks with large energy-loan portfolios.

Foreigners provided $352 million, or 27%, of the funds committed to private venture capital firms in the first half, up from 18% in 1984, according to Venture Capital Journal. Pension funds, the traditional source, provided 28%, down from 34% in 1984.

Stock prices tumbled broadly to their lowest levels in three months, with airline issues hardest hit. The Dow Jones Industrials fell 10.98 points to 1298.16 and the transportation index lost more than 13 points. Volume expanded to 111.9 million shares.

19 Apple Computer studied what actions, if any, to take against Steven P. Jobs, its former chairman and co-founder, who resigned after disclosing plans to start a new computer firm.

An insurance underwriter said it will stop insuring the launch of space satellites because of a growing number of mishaps. In the future, International Technology Underwriters will write policies only for satellites that have arrived safely in orbit.

The Farm Credit System's 37 principal banks agreed to seek a federal bailout. It was the first public acknowledgment at the operating level that the system can't withstand the huge losses it faces, barring a miraculous turnaround in farm income.

A Pentagon study found that more than 5,000 Soviet military research projects have benefited from technology obtained from the U.S. and its allies. Defense Secretary Weinberger said the flow of military technology was a "serious problem," and the U.S. was "subsidizing" Moscow's military buildup.

Housing starts jumped 6.2% in August, the sharpest rise in five months, to an annual rate of 1,749,000 units. Many analysts expect the increased activity to continue. Building permits issued last month rose 3.5%.

20 Consumer spending surged 1.2% in August, plunging the nation's savings rate to its lowest level in more than a quarter of a century. Many analysts said the low rate could retard future consumer spending and jeopardize growth. Personal income last month rose a modest 0.3%.

The FDIC (Federal Deposit Insurance Corporation) is unveiling a plan to charge banks risk-based premiums for deposit insurance. Banks in the "above normal risk" category would pay up to four times more for deposit insurance than they now pay.

The SEC (Securities and Exchange Commission) approved an experiment allowing specialist firms and market makers to trade options for over-the-counter stocks as well as the stocks themselves. Side-by-side trading will begin January 20 in six issues.

New textile-import quotas directed primarily at Asian nations were approved by a House subcommittee. The quotas wouldn't apply to textiles, apparel or man-made fibers from Canada or Common Market nations.

23 A major effort to lower the dollar against foreign currencies and head off a possible trade war was unveiled by the U.S. and four other nations. The plan involves U.S. intervention in financial markets, efforts to trim U.S. deficits and steps to spur growth in Europe and Japan.

Congressional leaders expressed relief at the initiative, but businessmen and economists were skeptical.

Interest rates may ease at first due to efforts to force the dollar down, but could eventually move higher, according to many bankers and analysts. A coordinated plan also reduces the possibility that the Fed will tighten credit soon, they said.

GNP growth has quickened to a 2.8% pace in the current quarter from a revised 1.9% second-quarter rate, the government estimated, suggesting a modest economic rebound. Separately, second-quarter corporate after-tax profits rose 0.3%, the first rise since the 1984 first quarter.

Ford Motor raised prices on most 1986-model cars 2.5% to 6.5%, generally in line with recent increases announced by GM. But analysts said both auto makers likely will return much of the increases to buyers in the form of incentive programs.

24 The dollar tumbled in its sharpest single-day drop ever, after the U.S. and four allies announced efforts to weaken the currency, and the Fed intervened in the foreign-exchange market. Stock prices soared and interest rates fell. Yields rose on long-term bonds.

Reagan announced a series of measures designed to combat unfair trading practices by other nations, including setting up a $300 million export-credit war chest. But the president said he will reject any efforts to close U.S. markets to imports.

The NASD (National Association of Securities Dealers) will enter the options market Friday with a stock-index contract based on 100 over-the-counter issues, opening the door to complex trading strategies that are growing rapidly in the listed market.

25 The dollar rebounded from its record fall Monday, as Japanese traders bought a record $4.73 billion of the U.S. currency. Their purchases stymied Japan's central bank, which sold $1.3 billion in a move to hold down the U.S. currency. The U.S. and West Germany also intervened.

General Foods received an unsolicited takeover bid that sent its stock soaring $16.625 a share to $101.50. The potential buyer wasn't identified, but speculation centered on Philip Morris. Unilever and Nestle also were mentioned. General Foods' board will discuss the proposal later this week.

Durable-goods orders rose a healthy 3.4% in August, further evidence of a resurgent economy. Consumer prices edged up only 0.2% for the fourth month in a row, a sign that inflation remains under control.

U.S. car sales jumped 32% in mid-September from a year earlier, but the sales pace is slowing as dealer stocks of 1985 models run low.

26 The dollar gave up Tuesday's gains after the U.S., Japan and West Germany intervened in foreign-currency markets for the third consecutive day. Added pressure came from a report that the Japanese intend to push the U.S. currency down to between 200 yen and 210 yen.

General Foods' stock rose again, amid speculation that the company's managers might propose a leveraged buyout to sidestep an anticipated takeover bid by Philip Morris. The stock rose $5.25 a share to $106.75, after surging $16.625 on Tuesday.

China will sign a $500 million agreement with Atlantic Richfield and a unit of Santa Fe International to develop a natural gas field in the South China Sea, industry sources said.

Reagan's top economic adviser may be pulling back from earlier forecasts that the economy will grow 5% in the second half. Beryl Sprinkel failed to mention that figure in congressional testimony, saying instead that the economy should meet a separate forecast of 4% growth in 1986.

27 Iranian oil exports from Kharg Island have been severely disrupted by Iraqi air raids, according to industry sources. Iran told several oil companies to delay purchases by as long as 20 days to allow crews to make emergency repairs, the sources said.

The dollar lost ground against the Japanese yen but firmed in relation to the West German mark yesterday, the first trading day since Monday that major central banks didn't intervene to any significant extent.

30 Philip Morris agreed to acquire General Foods for $120 a share, or $5.75 billion, the biggest non-oil merger ever. The combination will create the largest consumer-products firm in the U.S., with an-

nual sales of $23 billion. Many industry experts predict further mergers.

The trade deficit narrowed to $9.90 billion in August, the lowest level of the year, from $10.51 billion in July. The figures could help the administration's fight against protectionism.

China signed pacts with Atlantic Richfield and Santa Fe International for a $400 million offshore natural gas production platform and pipeline.

October 1985

1 The Bank Board is ordering many thrifts to set aside millions of dollars in reserves for potential losses on commercial real estate loans that were based on inflated appraisals. Separately, the board is seeking help from Congress to shore up its dwindling deposit insurance fund.

Oil prices were raised by Egypt and Algeria, following the abrupt suspension last week of Soviet oil deliveries to many Western European customers and recent Iraqi air attacks on Iran's Kharg Island terminal.

Leading indicators of the economy rose a healthy 0.7% in August for the second consecutive month, a strong signal of moderate growth in the future. Several economists said the strength of the report damps the notion that a recession may appear in the next year.

Salomon Brothers topped all underwriters of U.S. issues for the first three quarters, serving as lead underwriter on 218 issues that raised a total of $22.8 billion.

2 Revlon is negotiating to be taken private in a leveraged buyout to avoid Pantry Pride's hostile bid, sources said. They said the buyout group may offer $53 to $55 a share, giving the transaction a value of between $1.5 billion and $1.56 billion.

The dollar tumbled against foreign currencies, although most traders were unable to explain why. One analyst pointed to dispatches suggesting that the administration is committed to pushing the dollar lower.

Stock prices surged as corporate takeover speculation swept the trading floor. The Dow Jones Industrial Average rose 12.32 points to 1340.95 and volume expanded to 130.2 million shares. Oil issues posted strong gains for the second day in a row.

Richardson-Vicks accepted a $69-a-share, or $1.24 billion, takeover offer from Procter & Gamble, which prevailed despite an identical bid from Pfizer. P&G also will assume about $300 million in debt that Vicks took on in its effort to resist an unwanted takeover by Unilever.

Construction spending rose 1.1% in August, after falling a downward revised 1% in July. Analysts said the latest figures suggest a healthy but not robust construction market.

Takeover experts predict far-reaching effects from a court ruling that allowed Hanson Trust to continue buying shares of SCM Corp. without making a formal tender offer.

3 The Hunt family has sold "substantially all" of its $350 million silver hoard, incurring losses of about $1 billion. The sales are expected to remove a cloud that has hovered over the silver market since the Hunts accumulated their huge holdings in the late 1970s.

New factory-goods orders rose a moderate 0.9% in August, a further sign of economic improvement. Sales of single-family homes fell 5.6%, but a number of economists said the sales rate remains relatively high.

Hospital management stocks skidded after two of the industry's biggest firms made disappointing earnings statements. Hospital Corp. of America predicted flat 1986 earnings, while American Medical International said its fourth-quarter profit fell 38%.

4 Revlon agreed to go private by selling itself for $56 a share, or about $1.77 billion, to Forstmann Little and members of Revlon's management. That group, in turn, plans to sell Revlon's well-known beauty business and its consumer products and specialty chemicals units.

The dollar tumbled amid rumors that new steps to push the U.S. currency lower will be announced at next week's IMF (International Monetary Fund) meeting in Seoul. The dollar hit a four-and-a-half-year low against the Japanese yen and fell to its lowest point against the West German mark in over two years.

OPEC ministers split sharply over how much oil its member nations are entitled to sell. The dispute sparked a threat from Ecuador to become the first member to pull out of the cartel since it was founded 25 years ago.

Silver prices rose sharply following the disclosure that the Hunt family had sold most of its huge holdings. Silver for October delivery jumped 33.5 cents to $6.385, the biggest one-day rise since March. Some silver mining stocks rose as much as 10%.

New-car sales soared 59% in late September, continuing their recent strength. But auto makers expect a steep decline in October, due to sharply higher prices on new cars and the end of financing incentives.

7 Members of OPEC plan to move quickly to shore up their faltering economies by raising oil output, portending a sharp price drop by late winter. The move, following disarray at OPEC's meeting in Vienna, apparently means an end to the cartel's official price structure.

The jobless rate rose to 7.1% of the civilian work force in September from 7% in August, but there were signs of moderate growth during the month.

The economy showed dramatic improvement in September despite some softness in employment, a survey of purchasing managers found. New orders rebounded and production rose for the third month in a row.

U.S. auto makers are expected to hold to plans to build two million cars in the fourth quarter, as they push to replenish depleted inventories and ship new 1986 models. Separately, GM is adopting 8.8% financing on some 1985 and 1986 cars and trucks.

8 The dollar rose sharply despite intervention by the Japanese and West German central banks. Traders said the rise also was due to the failure of finance ministers meeting in Seoul to take additional steps to force the U.S. currency lower.

Pantry Pride sweetened its hostile bid for Revlon to $56.25 a share, or $1.78 billion, topping slightly Forstmann Little's leveraged buyout offer. Pantry Pride also will sue to block Revlon's chairman from collecting on a $20 million "golden parachute."

Chrysler and Mitsubishi formed a $500 million joint venture to build up to 180,000 subcompact cars a year at a new plant in Illinois. The first cars are expected in the 1989 model year.

9 The dollar strengthened for the second day in a row despite Japanese and West German intervention, leaving many traders convinced that the dollar's slide is over, at least for now. But Tokyo is ready to take further steps to push the dollar below the 200-yen level, a source said.

Chrysler agreed to acquire BankAmerica's consumer finance unit for $405 million, marking its entry into the nonautomotive consumer finance business and further expanding its financial-services operations. For BankAmerica, the sale will mean a much-needed infusion of capital.

10 Volkswagen of America plans to introduce a new, low-priced car in the 1987 model year aimed at the first-time buyer. The car, priced at under $6,000, will be built in Brazil.

The dollar rose again despite the third consecutive day of intervention by the Japanese central bank. Analysts said the dollar continued to strengthen despite the sale this week of at least $1.5 billion by Japan.

Bond activity was listless as investors waited for Congress to finish work on measures to raise the government's borrowing authority. Most of the attention was focused on the auction of 78-day Treasury bills, which sold at an average rate of 7.23%.

Japan disclosed it is considering a series of steps to help ease its international trade dispute. The steps, raised informally with U.S. officials, potentially include sizable additional purchases of U.S. manufactured goods and grain.

11 Major retailers reported generally disappointing September sales, raising fresh concerns about the important Christmas season. K mart said its sales fell 5.2% on a same-store basis, while Sears Roebuck posted a 0.4% decline. R. H. Macy's sales rose a slim 4%.

14 Producer prices tumbled 0.6% in September while retail sales jumped 2.7%, the sharpest rise since April. Both figures largely reflected special incentives to spur auto sales, leading many economists to question whether such strength can be sustained.

Several business leaders indicated they would accept a tax increase if accompanied by substantial spending cuts to reduce the deficit. Meanwhile, House-Senate conferees begin work this week on a measure calling for a balanced budget by fiscal 1991.

Farm Credit System officials may seek a direct Treasury loan of about $10 billion as the cornerstone of a federal bailout plan. But administration officials said they aren't convinced that a government rescue is needed and want to make their own review.

IBM's earnings fell 7% in the third quarter, its third consecutive quarterly decline. The results were at the low end of analysts' estimates, but the computer giant still hopes to post higher earnings for the full year.

15 The big three auto makers will report third-quarter earnings of about $1.15 billion, up 8.5% from a year earlier, despite costly sales incentives, analysts estimated. Both GM and Chrysler will post higher profits with only Ford expected to show a decline, they said.

Hewlett-Packard and Bechtel agreed to team up to build and equip automated factories for the electronics industry. Separately, GM will unveil next month its model of the automated factory of the future.

Japan unveiled a program designed to stimulate its economy and ease trade tensions with the U.S., but a number of Japanese economists said its impact is likely to be modest.

16 New-car sales plunged 10.2% in early October, marking the end of discount-financing incentives by dealers. The drop had been widely expected, but some analysts suggested that its magnitude could indicate weakening underlying demand for new cars.

Volcker strongly indicated that he doesn't plan to leave his post as Fed chairman soon, refuting speculation that he would step down to become president of the World Bank.

17 Kohlberg Kravis offered $45 a share in cash and stock, or nearly $4.91 billion, to take Beatrice Cos. private in what would be the largest leveraged buyout ever. Kohlberg is likely to promise that it won't break up the food and consumer products giant to pay for the buyout.

Stock prices soared as interest in takeover situations intensified. The Dow Jones Industrial Average jumped 17.69 points to 1368.50, surpassing the previous record of 1359.54 set July 19. But broader market barometers closed well below their July highs.

Industrial production fell 0.1% in September, suggesting that manufacturers still haven't broken out of their yearlong slump. The decline, coupled with August's drop in business inventories, could damp third-quarter GNP figures, due to be released today.

The Energy Department is seeking up to $500 million from Atlantic Richfield for alleged violations of oil price controls in the 1970s and early 1980s.

The Justice Department said AT&T improperly assigned hundreds of thousands of business telephone users to its long-distance service by relying on error-prone computer systems.

18 Economic growth accelerated to a 3.3% annual rate in the third quarter from the first half's sluggish 1.1% pace, but many economists predict only modest growth through year-end. Separately, housing starts fell 9.3% in September to their lowest rate in nearly a year.

The Bank Board plans to take over about 70 ailing thrifts, costing its insurance fund up to $1.5 billion. Chairman Gray conceded the fund would run out of money within a year if the board has to shore up other thrifts.

Bond prices rose after government reports on GNP and housing starts indicated that the economy's growth is far from robust. The dollar fell.

21 Beatrice Cos.' board unanimously rejected

a $4.91 billion leveraged buyout offer from Kohlberg Kravis as inadequate and reiterated that it wants to remain independent. The board said it decided to continue with its current restructuring program.

Pantry Pride raised its hostile bid for Revlon to $58 a share, or $1.83 billion, topping Forstmann Little's offer by 75 cents a share. Separately, investment banker Felix Rohatyn told Revlon recently it would be in a hopeless position if its plan to merge with Forstmann Little fell through.

Consumer spending surged 1.2% in September, far outpacing a 0.3% rise in personal income and pushing the nation's savings rate to a record low. Economists warn that the low savings rate could create problems for the economy in the fourth quarter.

Volcker is expected today to urge officials of the nation's 150 largest banks to make $20 billion in new loans to less-developed countries.

22 Fed Chairman Volcker urged major U.S. banks to increase their lending to developing countries, but rejected appeals from the bankers that federal regulators relax reserve requirements on such new loans.

Mobil had a loss of $116 million in the third quarter, reflecting write-offs as part of its plan to shed Montgomery Ward. Amoco's earnings fell 18%, Occidental Petroleum posted a rise in operating profit, and Ashland had a $46 million fourth-quarter profit compared with a year-earlier loss.

23 General Motors posted a $20.9 million loss from operations for the third quarter, the result of its low-interest rate incentive program. But the auto giant's net income jumped 24% to $516.5 million, reflecting tax credits and record earnings for its GMAC finance subsidiary.

Beatrice has been told by its advisers that Kohlberg Kravis will raise its buyout bid to between $48 and $50 a share from the $45-a-share, or $4.91 billion, offer that Beatrice turned down last Sunday, a source said.

Bond prices rose amid growing speculation that economic expansion in coming months will be lethargic, pushing interest rates lower. Treasury bond futures prices hit their highest levels in more than three months.

24 New-car sales fell 16.8% in mid-October, as the decline touched off by the end to sales incentives accelerated. Some analysts said the auto makers may have to cut production soon or offer renewed incentives.

Consumer prices rose a slim 0.2% in September for the fifth month in a row, indicating that inflation remains tightly under control. Durable goods orders fell 1.1%, but would have shown a rise except for a big drop in the volatile defense-goods sector.

Taxpayers will get a small tax cut as a result of the consumer price figures for fiscal 1985, which ended October 1. Social Security recipients will get a 3.1% cost-of-living increase.

The Farm Credit System had a third-quarter loss of $522.5 million and said it may face $3 billion or more of loan losses through 1987. Separately, the administration said it still believes the system has adequate reserves and doesn't need a federal bailout.

25 The International Tin Council threatened to crumble, raising fears of a price collapse that could depress other metals. The London Metal Exchange brought world-wide tin trading to a halt after the council said it couldn't afford to continue its four-year effort to prop up tin prices.

28 Japan's central bank is pushing interest rates higher to help drive up the yen's value. Bond dealers in the U.S. fear the action could lessen the appeal of dollar-denominated securities to Japanese investors.

Tin prices fell by as much as 17% in light trading as member nations of the International Tin Council tried to salvage their price-support pact.

29 Federal banking regulators decided to force U.S. banks to set aside special reserves for their loans to Peru, marking the first time U.S. regulators have taken such a step with a major Latin American debtor.

AT&T's plan to lay off 24,000 employees at its AT&T Information Systems unit was challenged by the Communications Workers of America. The union is seeking an injunction against the layoffs, which it claims would violate a prior agreement with AT&T.

Rockwell International will plead guilty to charges of submitting false bills to the Pentagon and has agreed to pay $1.5 million in fines and penalties, U.S. investigators said. The action is likely to sully Rockwell's image as it seeks billions of dollars of new defense work.

Chrysler posted record third-quarter profit of $316.2 million, despite the cost of subsidizing low-interest car loans. The auto maker's earnings from operations, more than double the year-earlier level, topped comparable results from GM and Ford Motor.

30 Bond prices soared in one of the strongest

rallies of the year, sparked by speculation the Fed may ease credit and push interest rates lower. Aiding the rally was heavy demand at yesterday's long-delayed Treasury note auction. Stock prices rose and the dollar fell sharply.

New-construction contracts rose 1% last month to a record annual rate of $233.75 billion, F. W. Dodge Co. said. The increase was led by a surge in nonresidential contracts.

U.S. Steel's profit fell 35% to $100 million in the third quarter. The company's Marathon Oil unit posted a 9.2% rise in pre-tax operating earnings, but steel operations showed a pre-tax operating loss of $4 million.

31 Bethlehem Steel's loss widened to $76.8 million in the third quarter, prompting the firm to omit its dividend for the first time in 46 years. The steelmaker also expects a loss in the current quarter and will try to restructure its labor contract.

Farm Credit System officials told Congress the system needs $5 billion to $6 billion in federal aid, far less than the $10 billion they had considered seeking. Without such assistance, they said, the system can't survive.

New-home sales dropped 2.6% in September to their slowest pace in five months, the latest sign that the industry may be weakening. The Commerce Department also said the median price of a new home rose 0.9%.

The Senate narrowly defeated an administration bid to trim farm subsidies starting in 1987. The measure would have cut U.S. price supports for wheat, corn and other crops.

The bond market rally continued as investors snapped up $6.27 billion of new Treasury notes at an average annual yield of 9.75%, the lowest in over six years. Prices of some long-term Treasury bonds surged.

Stock prices rose, reflecting the strong bond market and a continued drop in interest rates. The Dow Jones Industrials climbed 6.84 to 1375.57, eclipsing the record set October 17. Volume topped 120 million shares.

November 1985

1 The trade deficit swelled to a record $15.55 billion in September, despite the recent decline of the dollar. Meantime, leading economic indicators inched up 0.1% and factory orders fell 0.6%. The figures suggest the economy remains sluggish.

The House approved a $19.4 billion deficit-reduction measure that would make the federal cigarette tax permanent at 16 cents a pack and restrict reimbursements for medical bills to achieve Medicare savings.

Interest rates were little changed despite an $8.5 billion surge in the nation's money supply. The Treasury's sale of $4.76 billion of new bonds received a lukewarm reception, with the average yield set at 10.47%.

Inco asked the London Metal Exchange to suspend trading in nickel, saying the effects of last week's suspension of tin trading have affected other metal markets. Nickel, copper, zinc, lead and aluminum prices fell.

4 Corporate profits fell 5% in the third quarter despite a brisker economy, according to a Wall Street Journal survey of 501 companies. U.S. industrial concerns discounted prices heavily to meet import competition. Canadian corporate profits were little changed.

Pantry Pride won its fight to acquire Revlon. Revlon's anti-takeover defense was crippled by the Delaware Supreme Court, scuttling the firm's buyout pact with Forstmann Little.

The jobless rate was unchanged at 7.1% in October but business payrolls surged by 414,000 workers, helping send stock prices sharply higher. The Dow Jones Industrial Average rose 15.94 points to a record 1390.25.

Metal prices stabilized amid meetings involving the London Metal Exchange, the International Tin Council and banks. But the exchange said tin trading will remain suspended.

The nation's farm lenders continued to slide downhill, as the number of banks with more problem loans than capital rose to 146 in the second quarter from 135 in the first.

7 The dollar plunged to a 57-month low against the yen after a senior Japanese official said the yen should climb further. Foreign-currency futures surged, as traders also cited a proposal by oil nations to drop the dollar as a basis for pricing oil.

Nervousness about the outlook for the dollar helped push U.S. bond prices lower, ending a week-long rally.

IBM is cutting its U.S. workforce and delaying some capital spending because of the computer slump. It said the economy isn't improving as much as expected, but that it still sees strong fourth-quarter profit.

The Dow Jones Industrial Average closed at 1403.44 marking the first time it closed above 1400. However, the broader averages remained below their all-time high.

8 Big retailers reported disappointing sales in October, reflecting fierce competition and a consumer-spending slowdown. Same-store sales declined 2.6% for K mart, but rose 0.9% for Penney and 2.8% for Sears.

General Motors has reaffirmed its bullish U.S. production schedule for the fourth quarter, despite slowing sales and swelling inventories. Rivals fear that a surplus of unsold GM cars could spark another round of sales incentives before year's end.

U.S. companies expect to trim 1986 capital spending 1% to $380.69 billion, according to a McGraw-Hill Economics survey. The budget-cutting plans, the first reported in a non-recession period in the survey's 31-year history, were termed "disturbing."

The dollar's slide will force up prices for consumer electronics imports next year. The prospect may trigger a Christmas buying spree that would worsen the trade deficit. But many other industries are likely to feel effects of the currency upheaval only over the longer term.

11 A wave of borrowing is likely this week, possibly ending the powerful credit markets rally. The Treasury may borrow at least $18 billion, while state and local governments launch new issues. Meantime, the Fed disclosed it voted October 1 to continue slight pressure on credit.

The mutual-fund industry was warned by the SEC staff to end questionable advertising tactics or face strict regulation. The staff believes that some funds are misleading investors with claims of high yields.

Tin trading will resume next Monday on the London Metal Exchange. Traders and analysts expect prices to fall to as low as $5,600 a ton in coming weeks, down from over $11,000 a ton when trading was suspended October 24.

Bolivia may have to close half of its tin mines because of the crisis, according to its planning minister.

Baker is boycotting House Ways and Means panel hearings on tax overhaul. The Treasury secretary is upset over reports Chairman Rostenkowski agreed to keep state and local tax deductions, sources said.

E.S.M. Government Securities' customers would get 22 cents to 23 cents on the dollar under a proposed settlement. The state of Ohio would get $10 million on its $152 million claim, seven cents on the dollar.

Some major oil producers still believe prices will soften by spring, despite current firmness, followed by a possible price war. Saudi Arabia's oil minister told a Paris newspaper that prices could fall below an average $20 a barrel unless output is cut.

12 Stock prices soared, fueled by expectations of lower interest rates. The Dow Jones Industrial Average leaped more than 27 points to a record 1431.88. Broader market barometers also hit highs, including the S&P 500-stock index and the Big Board's composite index.

Lie-detector tests were given by the FBI to at least 15 Commerce Department employees in a move to find the source of apparent leaks of market-sensitive economic data. New procedures also were instituted to limit the possibility of future leaks.

13 The bond market rally gathered momentum amid growing speculation that interest rates will decline further. Prices of Treasury bonds spurted and yields moved close to a five-year low of below 10%. A broad cross section of buyers swarmed into the market.

Stock prices hit new highs, as volume swelled to 170.8 million shares, seventh heaviest ever. The Dow Jones Industrial Average rose 1.72 points to a record 1433.60, following Monday's surge of more than 27 points.

Britain will step up the pace of its program to sell state-owned companies. Parliament was told that the government plans to raise $6.75 billion in each of the next three fiscal years from the sale of state-owned assets.

14 A solution to the tin crisis was proposed by the International Tin Council's 16 creditors, including extending existing loans and negotiating new financing for the tottering cartel. Reaction to the proposals was divided.

U.S. auto sales fell 12.4% in early November, less than the average 15.5% drop in the two prior 10-day periods. The continuing decline reflects the end of incentive programs.

Consumer credit soared to a record $10.63 billion in September, boosted by a $7.4 billion rise in car loans. The September increase, 24.9% at an annual rate, topped the previous record of $9.09 billion set in May 1984.

15 Retail sales plunged 3.3% in October, the steepest decline since the government began reporting the statistics in 1967. Although a sharp drop in car sales caused the slump, the figures suggest that consumer spending will slow and remain sluggish through early 1986.

Beatrice's board accepted Kohlberg Kravis's sweetened $6.2 billion takeover bid after Kohlberg threatened to withdraw the offer. A broad restructuring of Beatrice is expected soon after the acquisition is completed, with many of its non-food companies being sold or spun off.

Congress extended the Treasury's borrowing authority, averting the threat of default by the government this morning. The measure raises the debt ceiling by $80 billion.

The Treasury will sell $61 billion of debt in seven auctions over the next two weeks, beginning today with $22 billion of short-term cash management bills. Bond prices tumbled.

Ford Motor will spend $1 billion to buy 20 million shares of its stock, calling it substantially undervalued. The automaker also is studying a restructuring that could involve separate classes of stock for acquisitions or spinning off operations to holders.

18 Producer prices jumped 0.9% in October, the sharpest rise since April 1981, but many analysts called the increase a fluke. Industrial production was flat last month, indicating manufacturers remain in a slump.

A torrent of borrowing by federal, state and local governments this week and next is expected to intensify pressures for higher interest rates.

19 Bond prices surged amid growing hope that interest rates will fall further despite the Treasury's massive financing plans. The euphoric mood helped push stock prices higher, with the Dow Jones Industrial Average rising 4.93 points to a record 1440.02. The dollar declined.

Oil prices will fall early next year as winter demand diminishes, executives of Exxon, Chevron and Shell said. Meanwhile, Kuwait's oil minister was reported to have warned that prices could skid to $15 a barrel.

20 Pennzoil was awarded $10.53 billion, the largest civil judgment in history, after a jury found that Texaco improperly seized ownership of Getty Oil from Pennzoil. But legal experts said the award likely would be reduced on appeal.

Merger experts were stunned by the size of the award, but predicted it wouldn't have a chilling effect on the recent wave of mergers.

Housing starts jumped 10.8% in October to an annual rate of 1,760,000 units, the highest level in six months. Many analysts predicted the rate will be sustained for several months.

Most interest rates fell, with the yield on the Treasury's 30-year bonds falling below the 10% level for the first time in more than five years.

21 Allied-Signal will spin off 28 diverse busi-

ness units into a new company to focus its attention on the aerospace, automotive, chemicals and electronics fields. As part of the plan, Allied-Signal will eliminate 3,000 jobs and take other steps aimed at saving $250 million a year.

The nation's economy grew at a 4.3% annual rate in the third quarter, the government said, well above the 3.3% rate it announced a month ago. But many analysts played down the significance of the revision. Separately, after-tax corporate profits jumped 5.3% in the third quarter.

Bond prices surged in late trading as speculation mounted that Congress is on the verge of requiring a balanced budget by 1991. Prices of some Treasury bonds jumped about $5 for each $1,000 face amount.

BankAmerica's debt ratings were lowered by Standard & Poor's. The rating agency said the firm continues to experience sizable loan losses and increasing nonperforming assets.

22 Consumer spending fell 0.9% in October, the sharpest drop in 25 years, following an auto-buying spree in September. The October decline appears to confirm the view that fourth-quarter spending will be sluggish. Personal income last month rose 0.4%.

Volcker warned that the sharp increase in debt in recent years is incompatible with economic stability. His statement came in a letter accompanying a Fed report concluding that debt expansion since 1981 has "vastly outpaced" economic growth.

The dollar dropped below key support levels against the Japanese yen and the West German mark, amid speculative selling and a growing perception of an economic slowdown.

Stock prices surged in heavy trading, with the Dow Jones Industrial Average jumping 23.05 points to a record 1462.27. Analysts cited hopes for lower interest rates, and investors' fears of missing the bull market. Big Board short interest, meanwhile, jumped 18% to record levels in the month ended November 15.

25 Beatrice's top six executives were granted golden parachutes totaling $23.5 million as a result of Kohlberg Kravis's pending $6.2 billion leveraged buyout, well above the average compensation package of this type.

Consumer prices rose 0.3% in October, or 3.8% at a compounded annual rate, up from 0.2% in each of the previous five months. Many analysts expect prices to rise next year at a pace slightly faster than this year's.

26 National Gypsum's managers offered to

take the company private in a leveraged buyout valued at $1.1 billion. The offer appears to have been triggered by rumors of an impending hostile takeover, although the firm's potential liability in asbestos suits might deter some suitors.

New-car sales plunged 27.2% in mid-November, the sharpest decline since the end of low-cost incentives. Analysts said the drop will put added pressure on auto makers to renew incentives or slash production.

The dollar was mixed in quiet trading. Separately, the head of West Germany's central bank disputed charges that Bonn isn't living up to agreements reached two months ago aimed at lowering the dollar's value.

The London Stock Exchange and the NASD plan to exchange quotation information on up to 580 issues, the first tangible step toward an international stock-trading link. The program could begin as early as March.

27 Texaco conceded that as a last resort it might have to file for Chapter 11 protection if a judge orders the oil giant to post a $12 billion bond in the Pennzoil case. The case also is likely to create other problems for Texaco, whose stock fell $2.125 a share to $32.125 in heavy trading.

Durable goods orders plummeted 2.1% in October from September, reflecting a big drop in defense orders. Orders for non-defense capital goods, an important indicator of future business activity, fell a sharp 7.4%.

Warner-Lambert will sell its hospital-equipment operations and take a $550 million charge against fourth-quarter earnings. The move will lead to the first full-year loss ever for the pharmaceutical maker, which will use proceeds from the sales to buy about eight million of its shares.

29 Chrysler resumed sales incentives, intensifying the auto industry's efforts to boost sagging sales. The rebates and cut-rate loans likely will prompt renewed discounting by other U.S. car makers, though GM and Ford said they had no immediate plans to follow suit.

Stock prices soared, sending the Dow Jones industrials up 18.92 points to a record 1475.69. Broader indexes also closed at records, but lagged the industrial average. The rally was helped by a strong bond market, as investors bid aggressively at the Treasury's $7.52 billion note auction.

Nissan will increase prices 4% on cars and trucks shipped to the U.S., effective Monday. The company cited the decline of the dollar's value against the yen. Toyota and Honda also are considering price boosts.

December 1985

2 The Tokyo Stock Exchange admitted its first six foreign member firms, including Merrill Lynch, Goldman Sachs, Morgan Stanley and a British affiliate of Citicorp. Meanwhile, yen bond futures trading, which began six weeks ago in Tokyo, is being closely watched by U.S. traders.

The economy improved again in November, suggesting continued strength in December, a survey of purchasing managers showed.

Foreign-exchange traders expect the West German mark to strengthen this week, reflecting Bonn's low 1.8% inflation rate and near-record October trade surplus. The yen has outpaced the mark in recent months.

3 A grand jury accused NASA's administrator, three General Dynamics officials and the firm itself with improperly charging cost overruns on a prototype of the Sgt. York antiaircraft gun. The NASA chief worked for General Dynamics at the time of the alleged conspiracy.

Japan's biggest microchip maker, NEC Corp., said it will increase prices on certain exports to the U.S. by as much as 20%. The announcement comes at a time when U.S. semiconductor makers are in a deep slump.

New construction spending rose 0.5% in October, fueled by a strong 1.6% increase in residential building. But the figures suggest that nonresidential construction isn't responding to recent interest-rate declines.

4 Sohio will take a $1.15 billion charge against fourth-quarter earnings, mainly to provide for writedowns of its copper, coal and oil shale interests. The announcement, which surprised analysts, drew a mildly positive reaction from Wall Street.

General Dynamics was suspended by the Pentagon from receiving new government contracts. The company, which was indicted Monday on charges of illegal cost overruns, has 30 days to challenge the suspension.

Leading economic indicators rose a modest 0.3% in October, the sixth consecutive monthly increase, suggesting moderate growth lies ahead. But new single-family home sales fell 5.5% to their slowest pace in six months.

5 GM offered 8.5% financing on some com-

pact car models in a fresh attempt to stimulate sales, following a similar move by Chrysler last week. New-car sales by the seven U.S. auto makers in late November slipped 1.2%.

Factory orders fell 1.1% in October following a 0.7% decline in September, indicating continuing problems for manufacturers. The October decline was sparked by a sharp drop in orders for defense goods.

6 OPEC ministers expressed concern over future oil prices as they gathered in Geneva for a weekend strategy session. Delegates fear prices will tumble next spring and summer after normally strong winter demand fades.

The nation's retailers reported mixed November sales. Several leading mass merchandisers posted declines, while department stores generally rang up gains of 9% or more. December sales also have been mixed so far, but merchants are resisting price-cutting.

A battery of Texaco lawyers challenged a $10.53 billion jury award against the oil giant. They told a Texas judge that the verdict violated the Constitution and would destroy the company's "life and blood."

9 GAF Corp. is expected to launch today a two-tiered bid for Union Carbide. GAF, which already holds about 10% of Carbide, is expected to offer $68 a share, or $1.84 billion, for an additional 40% stake, sources said. It would then offer a stock-and-debt package for the remaining shares.

OPEC is abandoning its four-year struggle to restrict oil production as a means of propping up prices. Instead, it will try to expand its share of the market, even if price wars follow.

The civilian jobless rate fell to 7% in November from 7.1% in October, the first decline in three months. But some analysts said the drop doesn't mean growing economic momentum.

The Fed proposed that margin regulations be applied to debt securities used in highly leveraged corporate takeovers. The proposal is widely viewed as an attempt to curb the use of "junk" securities, which have been blamed for the current explosion of hostile bids.

10 Union Carbide is the target of a $4.13 billion takeover bid by GAF Corp. Carbide may make a counteroffer for GAF, a source said, and also is mulling a leveraged buyout or seeking a friendly merger partner. Stock prices of both firms jumped, with GAF soaring $10 a share.

World oil prices fell more than a dollar a barrel following OPEC's weekend decision to abandon price supports. The cartel, in an apparent fight for survival, yesterday nearly declared the start of a price war.

Stock and bond prices surged, fueled by growing hopes of lower oil prices, as well as sharp cuts in the budget deficit. The Dow Jones Industrial Average leaped 19.84 points to a record 1497.02 in heavy trading. Energy and metal futures prices plummeted. The dollar firmed.

11 A Texas judge upheld an $11.1 billion judgment for Pennzoil against Texaco after Texaco failed in a last-minute move to focus attention on a possible settlement. But a settlement involving a transfer of assets remains a possibility.

Oil prices plummeted more than $2 a barrel amid the possibility of a price war between OPEC and other world oil producers. The price of West Texas Intermediate, the U.S. benchmark crude, fell to $25.20 a barrel.

Oil issues tumbled in heavy trading, but most other stocks rose. The Dow Jones Industrial Average moved above the 1500 level twice but closed at 1499.20, up 2.18 points.

Bond prices rose as speculation grew that the Fed will push interest rates still lower in coming weeks. State and local government bonds increased despite $1.8 billion in new issues that were offered yesterday.

12 RCA Corp.'s stock soared $10.75 a share to $63.50 amid indications it may be discussing a friendly merger with General Electric. Sources at RCA said GE had made an offer.

The Dow Jones Industrial Average closed above the 1500 level for the first time, rising 12.50 points to 1511.70. Broader indexes also set records. Big Board volume was 178.5 million shares, fifth heaviest ever.

Interest rates tumbled and bond prices soared amid signs that the Fed may be relaxing credit conditions, analysts said. A credit-easing move appeared more likely in view of the recent sharp drop in oil prices.

13 Retail sales rose 1.1% in November following a steep 4.2% tumble in October. Despite last month's rise, the figures suggest that sales have fallen back to last spring's levels. Some analysts warned of a mediocre Christmas selling season.

The SEC is investigating the explosive price rise in RCA Corp.'s stock and options prior to the announcement of its proposed merger with GE. Meanwhile, the companies have to work out a new management structure, arrange financing and figure out how to integrate their operations.

16 Japan raised the possibility of ending "voluntary" restraints on auto exports, leading several congressmen to promptly warn that such a step could lead to protectionist legislation.

Producer prices jumped 0.8% in November, the second sharp rise in as many months, but many economists brushed aside the idea that inflation is accelerating. Meantime, industrial production rose 0.4%, offsetting a revised 0.4% decline in October.

Union Carbide announced a $2 billion exchange offer for 35% of its common stock in a move to thwart GAF Corp.'s $68-a-share hostile offer. In rejecting the GAF offer, Carbide offered to swap a package of cash and debt securities valued at $85 a share for each of 23,550,000 shares.

17 Union Carbide set up "golden parachutes" for 42 of its executives if a hostile takeover for the company is successful. Meantime, GAF Corp. filed suit in New York to block Carbide's $85-a-share stock swap offer.

U.S. Steel Corp. will team up with South Korea's Pohang Iron & Steel Co. to make sheet and tin products at a U.S. Steel plant in California. The joint venture would have broad implications for the steel industry.

The operating rate for the nation's factories, mines and utilities rose slightly in November to 80.1% of capacity, indicating that there is still a lot of room to expand production.

18 Trans World Airlines is on the auction block again, as Carl Icahn continues to have problems arranging financing for the shares of the carrier he doesn't own. American Airlines, Northwest Airlines and Resorts International have been asked to submit bids for TWA, sources said.

Housing starts fell 12.2% in November to their lowest pace in more than two years. Many economists look for a pickup during the next few months, but expect activity in 1986 to trail this year's level slightly.

19 The dollar rose sharply after Japanese Prime Minister Nakasone called for lower interest rates in Japan. Meanwhile, a Bank of Japan governor said the yen has reached an "appropriate" level against the dollar and other foreign currencies.

Texaco obtained a temporary court order preventing Pennzoil from attaching liens on most of its assets until the record $11.1

billion judgment against Texaco is resolved.

The IRS will relax its rules for taxing employees' personal use of company-owned cars and planes, after getting a flood of complaints.

20 Capital spending will decline 1% in 1986 after rising an estimated 5.6% this year and 15.3% in 1984, according to a Commerce Department survey. The projected decline, reflecting concern over the economy and tax changes, would be a major drag on economic growth.

GM announced production cuts for the second time in two months, indicating that poor sales of some models may force changes in its robust output schedules. GM will close its Fiero assembly plant in Pontiac, Mich., for the first two weeks in January.

23 The economy grew at a 3.2% yearly rate in the fourth quarter, the Commerce Department estimated. Government figures indicate that GNP rose just 2.4% in 1985, and many economists say growth will remain sluggish. Separately, consumer prices rose 0.6% last month.

Texaco and Pennzoil held their first serious talks aimed at settling the $11.1 billion judgment against Texaco. That prompted a federal judge to adjourn a hearing without ruling on Texaco's suit to protect its assets from any liens by Pennzoil.

The Fed's policy arm agreed in early November not to change monetary policy, but the panel seemed more likely to favor a looser credit policy than a tighter one. Meantime, the latest economic figures mean the Fed could lower interest rates further, say many private analysts.

A new insurer was formed by 33 big U.S. concerns to remedy the liability-insurance shortage. They contributed nearly $300 million to the new firm, which can write $150 million of coverage for each participant.

24 Consumer spending jumped 0.9% in November, suggesting that Christmas shopping may be stronger than had been thought. The gain followed a 1.4% drop in October. November personal income rose 0.6%, the Commerce Department said.

R. J. Reynolds isn't liable for the death of a longtime smoker of the company's cigarettes, a jury ruled in Santa Barbara, California. It was the first jury verdict in a new wave of product-liability suits against tobacco firms.

Auto-safety regulators are reluctant to pursue reports that certain brake linings may be hazardous when installed in 1980

General Motors X-cars, consumer advo-
cates charged.

26 Westinghouse agreed to sell its Group W
cable-television unit for $1.6 billion to
a group including Time Inc. and Tele-
Communications Inc., two big cable operators. The divestiture would result in
further concentration in the industry.

Durable-goods orders rose 0.9% in November, reflecting a surge in military orders.
But a 1.4% drop in nondefense capital
goods orders showed that business investment likely will be slow in the first part
of 1986.

Livestock futures prices surged Tuesday,
reflecting signs that meat supplies may
shrink next year. The number of cattle
sent to feedlots in seven states fell 9%
in November.

27 Union Carbide's options appeared to be
narrowing in its attempts to defeat GAF
Corp.'s bid. GAF, which sweetened its
offer to $74 a share from $68, may be
able to foil some of Carbide's anti-takeover defenses.

GM and Ford announced 7.9% financing
on a number of car models in efforts to
spur sales, cutting the cost of buying an
auto. Sales plunged after the companies'
last round of incentives ended in early
October.

New construction contracts fell 5% in November, led by an 11% decline in nonresidential building, F. W. Dodge Co.
said. The drop ended a four-month period of record activity.

Retail chains reported a last-minute surge
in Christmas sales, resulting in generally
modest sales gains and stronger profits
for the season.

A new accounting standard was issued requiring corporations to disclose more
about unfunded pension costs. The con-
troversial rule requires about 20% of
public companies to increase reported liabilities.

30 The savings industry would post lower
profits under a rule that the FASB (Financial Accounting Standards Board) is
expected to propose. The accounting
board would require financial institutions
to defer the booking of most loan-related
fee income.

The property-casualty insurance industry
will likely report a $5.5 billion operating
loss for 1985, eclipsing last year's record.
The deficit will probably be narrowed
by tax credits and investment gains.

Japan announced a $267 billion govern-
ment budget aimed at shrinking the deficit. The plan calls for 5.4% growth in
defense spending.

Machine-tool orders fell 12% in November

to $186.2 million, reflecting order cancel-
lations. GM reportedly canceled or deferred certain orders because of lower
cash flow and changes in priorities and
schedules.

31 Leading indicators rose just 0.1% in November, suggesting that only modest
economic growth lies ahead. The increase stemmed from the stock market's
strength, which offset continued weakness in the manufacturing sector.

The Reagan administration forecast that
the economy will grow at a 4% annual
pace for the next three years, but slow
to a 3.5% rate by 1991. The projection
is rosier than those of most private forecasters.

Union Carbide shareholders are free to tender stock in the company's buyback program, a U.S. judge decided. But the ruling on Carbide's anti-takeover plan
apparently didn't derail GAF's hostile
bid. Separately, Carbide retrieved $509
million in surplus assets from its pension
fund.

January 1986

2 Occidental Petroleum agreed to acquire
MidCon for $3 billion in cash and stock.
The pact, valued at $72.38 a share, ex-
ceeds the hostile bid of Wagner & Brown
and Freeport-McMoRan. It would be the
first merger of a big oil company and a
big gas pipeline firm.

Union Carbide raised its credit line to $1.5
billion and agreed to sell assets for $253
million, swelling its resources for a possible sweetened buyback offer to fight GAF.
Carbide's board meets today. Separately,
a U.S. judge tomorrow will hear Carbide's
bid to move the Bhopal suits to India.

Interest rates are expected to drop slightly
early in 1986, but edge upward in the second half, according to a Wall Street Journal survey of 25 economists. Most also
think the economy will continue to grow.

Home mortgages held by savings institutions
have a higher market value than book
value for the first time since 1979, the
Bank Board said. But the improvement
won't ease pressure on the FSLIC's insurance fund.

Salomon Brothers was the leading underwriter of securities sold by U.S. issuers in
1985, capturing 20% of the market with
$34 billion of offerings.

3 Prudential-Bache was censured by the SEC
for allegedly failing to supervise employees. The agency said lack of oversight led
to fraudulent conduct at two branches.

The firm settled the charges, consenting to sanctions.

Factory orders rose 1% in November after two consecutive monthly declines. But durable-goods orders fell 0.3%, indicating that manufacturing remains sluggish. Meantime, new construction spending climbed 0.5%.

Union Carbide announced sweeping steps to resist a takeover after GAF Corp. sweetened its bid to $78 a share, or $5.06 billion. Carbide plans to sell its consumer products business, perhaps for $2 billion or more, and distribute some of the proceeds to stockholders.

6 Trans World Airlines named Carl Icahn chairman as he took control of its board. But the company's finances have continued to deteriorate, and he has huge paper losses on his 52% stake. He agreed not to sell TWA shares unless other holders can sell on the same terms.

The economy grew more slowly last month, reflecting seasonal factors, said a report by industrial purchasing agents. New orders, production and employment declined among 250 surveyed companies, and prices fell for the 13th month in a row.

Union Carbide's new buyback plan to fight off GAF will double Carbide's long-term debt and slash equity 79%. Still, the takeover battle has been a boon for shareholders. Carbide stock has risen to $75 a share from $63 the day GAF made its offer.

Mortgage rates fell to their lowest levels in nearly seven years during the past month. Analysts said rates may slip another half percentage point before leveling off.

Auto sales plunged nearly 16% in mid-December, continuing a slump that began in October when a round of sales incentives expired. Today car makers will post late-December sales, the first to reflect new financing incentives by GM and Ford.

7 Strong auto sales in the final 10 days of December were posted by GM and Chrysler, reflecting major new incentive programs. GM said its sales jumped 29.2% in the period while Chrysler had a 27% rise.

GAF Corp.'s stock skidded $4 a share as doubts grew that GAF will sweeten its hostile $74-a-share bid for Union Carbide. GAF had been widely expected to raise its offer yesterday, but didn't. Some sources said a sweetened bid might still come today.

Municipal bond prices surged, reflecting a recent sharp decline in the volume of new tax-exempt issues. Some actively traded state and local government issues rose by about $5 for each $1,000 face amount. Treasury bonds posted small declines.

The budget deficit for fiscal 1986 is running "well in excess" of $200 billion and could top last year's record $211.9 billion, according to internal Congressional Budget Office data.

8 Pennzoil rejected a proposal that it drop its $11.1 billion judgment against Texaco in exchange for a merger offer from Texaco intended to reward Pennzoil holders. The decision by the Pennzoil board signaled the possible renewal of hostilities between the companies. Pennzoil's stock soared $19.75 a share.

GAF Corp. is expected today to withdraw its $4.8 billion hostile offer for Union Carbide, Wall Street sources said. But many investment bankers and analysts believe GAF may return in a few months, perhaps with a lower offer or even a proxy fight.

Stock prices surged to new highs as Big Board volume swelled to more than 152.9 million shares. The Dow Jones Industrial Average rose 18.12 points to a record 1565.71. Bond prices rallied strongly amid renewed speculation that oil prices are headed for a sharp tumble in coming months.

Japanese auto exports to the U.S. aren't likely to increase sharply if current restraints are lifted at the end of March, Toyota's president said. Separately, imports captured more than 31% of the U.S. car market in December, up from 26% a year ago.

9 Stock prices plummeted in heavy trading, with the Dow Jones Industrial Average tumbling nearly 40 points, its biggest one-day drop ever. The skid was touched off by a sharp drop in bond prices after the government reported an unexpectedly large increase in employment.

The unemployment rate fell in December to 6.9% of the civilian work force, lowest since April 1980. Employment jumped by 320,000 jobs, suggesting a strengthening economy.

GAF's chairman conceded defeat in the month-long battle for control of Union Carbide, withdrawing the firm's $4.8 billion hostile takeover offer. He said GAF will keep its 10% stake in Carbide and may soon seek to acquire another chemical company.

Kohlberg Kravis modified the terms of its proposed $6.2 billion leveraged buyout of Beatrice Cos., lowering the amount of cash being offered. But indications were that the transaction still would go through.

Kodak lost a decisive round in a patent fight with Polaroid that forces it from the instant photography business. The federal appeals court decision likely means Kodak will write off tens of millions of dollars in plant and equipment. Polaroid could get a huge one-time gain from damages.

10 Bond prices tumbled again amid a growing conviction that the economy is finally accelerating and that the long decline in interest rates is over. Stock prices fell sharply in early trading following Wednesday's record drop but rebounded somewhat late in the session. Stocks plunged in Europe and Japan.

The dollar plunged amid rumors Arab nations were selling dollar-denominated instruments and going into other currencies in retaliation against Reagan's freeze on Libyan assets. Gold rose $3.90 an ounce to $338.30, its highest level in four months.

13 The Budget Office ordered many federal agencies to prepare across-the-board spending cuts of about 4.3%. The cuts, which will take effect March 1, represent the first step in the Gramm-Rudman deficit-reduction process. Officials report consternation over the cutbacks.

Texaco's bargaining position was strengthened by a federal judge's ruling that the company doesn't have to post a $12 billion appeal bond to continue its legal fight with Pennzoil.

Producer prices rose 0.4% in December, the third substantial increase in as many months. But as in the previous two months, the rise reflected a bulge in food and energy prices that most analysts believe is temporary.

14 Price supports for wheat and corn growers will be slashed by the maximum allowed under the new farm bill. The cuts are designed to make U.S. farmers more competitive, but they also will boost the government's farm-subsidy bill. Wheat and corn futures prices tumbled.

Pennzoil retained a Constitutional scholar to bolster its legal attack against a federal judge's decision to waive a Texas law requiring Texaco to post a $12 billion bond to continue its legal fight with Pennzoil.

15 Retail sales rose a strong 1.9% in December, further evidence the economy ended 1985 on solid footing. Much of the rise was due to a 5.7% gain in auto sales, aided by new incentive programs. Even without autos, retail sales rose 0.9%.

New-car sales slipped 8.3% in early January, leading some analysts to speculate that some sales that normally would have been recorded in January were counted in December.

16 Budget officials parcelled out $11.7 billion in spending cuts mandated by the new budget-balancing law, sending many agencies scrambling for ways to meet the reductions. There were signs lawmakers might try to head off the automatic cuts, set to take effect March 1.

Bond prices surged on speculation the U.S. will ask its major allies to help drive down interest rates, but U.S. officials denied the reports. Stocks also rose in active trading.

Gold futures prices soared amid continued Middle East tensions. Gold futures in New York jumped $9.70 an ounce to $350.70. Silver and platinum futures also posted sharp gains.

Business inventories rose a slim 0.2% in November while sales increased 1.5%, indicating that companies are maintaining lean stocks.

17 The price of gold soared to an 18-month high on near-record volume. Bullion for delivery this month surged to $380 an ounce in Europe, before falling back to close in New York to $356.60 an ounce, up $7.10.

Crude oil prices plummeted to their lowest levels in five years, as producers continue to pump more than demand dictates. Petroleum futures prices skidded. Oil issues fell, but gains in transportation companies, big fuel users, helped propel the stock market to broad gains.

Industrial output rose a strong 0.7% in December, its second consecutive solid increase, signaling the end of a year-long slump for manufacturers. Despite the strength, many analysts doubt production will continue to grow at such a rapid rate.

BankAmerica is under pressure to further reduce, or even eliminate, its dividend because of continuing high loan losses and new regulatory guidelines, industry sources said.

20 IBM's earnings dipped slightly in 1985 despite a 23% fourth-quarter rise, its first annual decline in six years. The computer giant issued a bleak 1986 forecast, bolstering the view that the industry has yet to rebound.

Housing starts leaped 17.5% in December to the highest level in eight months. Many analysts cited a drop in mortgage rates since October and said they expect the strength to persist for several months. Building permits last month rose a strong 11%.

21 Oil prices tumbled amid overproduction by OPEC and spring-like weather in Europe and parts of the U.S. In London, Brent crude for April delivery slid to $19.25 a barrel, cracking the psychological $20 level. The U.S. benchmark crude fell $2.25 a barrel to $21.25.

Stock prices fell in quiet trading, mainly because finance ministers from the U.S. and four major allies failed to take concerted action to push interest rates lower.

22 Oil prices plunged for the fourth consecutive day, raising fears that Mexico might default on interest payments to U.S. banks. Stock prices skidded, with oil and bank issues hardest hit. Gasoline prices could fall to as low as 75 cents a gallon later this year, one analyst said.

BankAmerica posted a $178 million fourth-quarter loss as its loan-loss provision surged to $591 million, prompting it to omit its dividend. Separately, the firm was fined a record $4.7 million on charges of failing to report large cash transactions.

AT&T abandoned its Net 1000 computer network, which it spent at least 10 years and $1 billion developing. The company said it might take a small charge on the visionary project, which never showed a profit.

Several bank holding companies issued mixed fourth-quarter profit reports. Citicorp, the nation's largest banking concern, reported a 7% decline. Gains were posted by Manufacturers Hanover, First Interstate, Wells Fargo and Mellon Bank.

23 The economy grew at a sluggish 2.4% annual rate in the fourth quarter, less than previously thought. GNP growth for all 1985 was 2.3%, the weakest showing since 1982. Consumer prices last month rose 0.4%, slightly more than the average 1985 monthly rise, but were up only 3.8% for the full year.

The Supreme Court ruled that the Fed exceeded its authority in trying to halt the spread of limited-service banks. The decision permits dozens of commercial firms to operate limited-service banks and will push regulators to act on requests by big banks to set up the so-called non-bank banks.

Bond prices swung wildly but wound up little changed. Analysts cited the GNP report and rumors Volcker told other finance ministers that he doesn't expect U.S. interest rates to decline further soon. A Fed spokesman denied the rumors.

27 Saudi Arabia appears to have devised an aggressive new oil-production policy designed to encourage greater consumption. Despite recent calls to other nations to hold down output, many experts believe that the Saudis have no real desire to cut their own production.

Many oil companies may cut exploration budgets amid tumbling prices, a move that could send some drilling firms reeling and force mergers among other. Worries are mounting at banks with big energy loans.

Gold prices could move higher in coming weeks as falling oil prices heighten concern over the stability of the banking system, some analysts believe. Gold jumped $6.60 an ounce, to $357.90, in New York Friday.

Durable goods orders surged 4.2% in December, reflecting a year-end bulge in aircraft orders rather than strength among other manufacturers.

28 Exxon lost a Supreme Court bid to avoid having to refund more than $2 billion for overpricing oil from a Texas field in the late 1970s. The judgment, to be distributed through state energy-conservation programs, is the largest to be upheld on appeal in American history.

Global Marine filed for Chapter 11 bankruptcy-law protection, making the giant offshore driller the biggest casualty yet in the current collapse of oil prices. The company listed about $1.8 billion in liabilities.

29 Lower earnings were posted by AT&T for the fourth quarter, surprising Wall Street. The 1.6% decline apparently was partly due to poor earnings from computer and telephone equipment lines. GTE reported a fourth-quarter loss, reflecting previously disclosed charges.

Thatcher dashed OPEC's hopes that Britain might reduce North Sea oil output to ease the glut of crude that has sent prices plummeting.

Stock prices surged despite the shock of the space shuttle tragedy. The Dow Jones Industrial rose 18.81 points to 1556.42, only about nine points below its record high. Bond prices continued to rally.

Beatrice's board again delayed a meeting to discuss Kohlberg Kravis's revised $6.2 billion leveraged-buyout offer, fueling speculation that the transaction may be snagged by suits over various parts of the plan.

30 The Bank of Japan cut its discount rate to 4.5% from 5% in an effort to stimulate the Japanese economy, but some analysts doubt that the move will provide enough stimulus.

Non-farm productivity fell at a 1.8% annual rate in the fourth quarter, the sharpest drop in four years. The decline, the first in a year, reflected sluggish growth in 1985.

The Treasury plans to raise a record $13.2 billion in new cash next week by selling $23 billion of notes and bonds to redeem $9.8 billion of maturing securities. Bond prices fell, snapping a two-day rally.

31 Leading indicators rose a strong 0.9% in December, the eighth consecutive monthly increase. But the nation's trade deficit widened to a record $17.37 billion, indicating trade problems will continue to restrain growth in the first half.

The dollar fell against most major currencies following the reports, while some foreign-currency futures surged to life-of-contract highs.

Cigna will take a $1.2 billion charge against fourth-quarter earnings to cover rising insurance claims, especially for professional liability. The firm expects a quarterly operating loss of more than $1 billion.

The SEC authorized the Philadelphia Stock Exchange to begin trading options on the European currency unit, one of the fastest-growing markets in international finance.

Japanese banks held $640 billion in international assets at the end of the 1985 third quarter, exceeding for the first time the total held by U.S. banks, according to a report from the Bank for International Settlements.

February 1986

3 Oil ministers from OPEC are scheduled to meet today in Vienna, but growing discord may severely limit their options in dealing with prices that threaten to plunge toward $15 a barrel soon. Over the weekend, Mexico, Venezuela and Norway announced price cuts averaging between $2.50 and $4 a barrel.

New-home sales climbed 1.7% in December to the highest level since July, and some analysts predicted the heightened tempo may last through midyear. Separately, a survey of purchasing managers found that the economy picked up in January.

PS Indiana will omit common and preferred dividends as part of a plan to write off its canceled $2.7 billion Marble Hill plant in return for an 8.2% rate increase. The size of the write-off wasn't disclosed, but it may be the largest ever by a utility.

4 Oil prices plummeted as several OPEC ministers called for a continued price war. Brent crude for March delivery fell to $16.75 a barrel, its lowest level in six years. Other oil prices also fell, as five OPEC ministers meeting in Vienna failed to resolve pricing and output disputes.

Stock prices surged, with the Dow Jones Industrials soaring 23.28 points to a record 1594.27. Bond prices rallied and the dollar rose against most currencies. Gold fell $5.10 an ounce to $343.70 and an index on nonfinancial futures hit an eight-year low.

Texaco may have problems borrowing $1

billion it needs by tomorrow to protect its assets from Pennzoil claims. But Texaco said it may be able to meet the court requirement by pledging its assets as security.

Construction contracts fell 2% in December, reflecting a drop in nonresidential building, F. W. Dodge said. But building awards for all 1985 rose 8% to a record $227.65 billion.

5 Opec ministers failed to agree on how to stem tumbling oil prices, amid signs that production is out of control. One OPEC official said a full-scale price war is underway. North Sea Brent crude fell to $15.55 a barrel, down from $16.75 on Monday and $18.50 last Friday.

The dramatic oil-price drop has left many forecasters stunned, curbing inflation expectations. Commodity prices have plunged 2.9% in just two days. The dollar rose yesterday but gold tumbled $9.60 an ounce to $334.10, its biggest drop in nine months.

Stock prices eased after showing early strength. The Dow Jones Industrial Average briefly broke through the 1600 level but closed at 1593.23, down 1.04 points. Big Board trading was a heavy 175.7 million shares.

U.S. auto makers reported a modest 1.2% rise in January sales despite discount financing on many vehicles. Sales in the final 10 days of the month fell 2.5% from a year earlier.

6 Congress reacted coolly to Reagan's fiscal 1987 budget, setting the stage for a renewed battle over spending and taxes. The $994 billion package, sent to Congress yesterday, calls for $38.2 billion in deficit-cuts and $6.3 billion in extra revenue, mainly from higher fees.

Many lawmakers hope to use the Gramm-Rudman deficit law to force Reagan to slow his defense buildup and raise taxes. But the law, with its automatic cuts, could make Congress less eager to reach a compromise.

The Veterans Administration will put strict, temporary curbs on its mortgage guarantees to avoid a midyear shutdown of a program used by nearly 200,000 veterans annually.

Bond prices slumped as foreign investors gave a cool reception to the Treasury's 10-year note sale, mainly due to the dollar's sharp decline. Stock prices closed mixed.

7 Stocks moved higher, with the Dow Jones Industrials closing above 1600 for the first time. Bond prices slumped as the Treasury completed a $24 billion financing operation.

Reagan's economic advisers urged the Federal Reserve to gradually tighten monetary policy to keep down inflation. The group also said Gramm-Rudman budget cuts wouldn't hurt the economy as long as the Fed keeps monetary growth "steady."

Corporate mergers could be sharply curtailed by a recent IRS regulation, accountants said. The rule could increase the tax bill for companies that acquire other firms by reducing both the value of acquired assets and the depreciation charges that can be deducted.

Major retailers reported sluggish sales for January, suggesting that debt-strapped consumers had exhausted their spending power, retail executives and analysts said.

Mortgage rates fell further in the past month, and analysts don't see any upturn soon. The rate on 30-year conventional fixed-rate mortgages eased to an average 10.89% last week from 11.09% a month earlier.

10 A federal court ruled that a key provision of the Gramm-Rudman budget law is unconstitutional. The decision, to be appealed to the Supreme Court, bolsters Reagan's hand in opposing higher taxes and poses problems for Congress and the Fed in handling budget deficits.

Wells Fargo will acquire Crocker National for $1.08 billion, creating one of the 10 biggest U.S. banks. The surprise move will give Wells Fargo a strong consumer bank operation and let the seller, Midland Bank, shed a disappointing investment.

Civilian unemployment fell to 6.7% of the labor force in January while business payrolls surged by 566,000 jobs. The figures added to evidence that the economy had an unexpectedly strong start this year. Many economists expect the momentum to continue through most of 1986.

11 Western Union said it will take a $300 million charge against fourth-quarter earnings to write down certain transmission and switching equipment, resulting in a $370 million loss for the year. The firm said the write-down is part of a major financial restructuring.

Accounting rule makers are debating whether to stem the recent flood of corporate write-offs. Critics say companies orchestrate the timing of such charges to take advantage of the ebullient stock market.

The U.S. dollar plunged, led by a sell-off in Europe as traders reacted to a federal court ruling that the Gramm-Rudman deficit-reduction law is unconstitutional.

12 Britain and France cut coal prices to keep them competitive with fuel oil. Meanwhile, U.S. bond prices rallied amid ex-

pectations that falling oil prices will keep inflation low.

Kodak plans to slash its staff 10% and trim costs an added 5% in a bid to reverse slumping profits. The firm indicated fiscal fourth-quarter net will be less than expected, partly due to an anticipated charge from its exit from the instant-camera market.

U.S. Steel's purchase of Texas Oil & Gas for $3 billion was approved by shareholders of both firms. The merger moves the No. 1 steelmaker deeper into the energy business and further away from steel.

The semiconductor industry's closely watched indicator of orders to sales rose for the fifth straight month, signaling the industry's worst slump ever is continuing to ease.

Pennzoil dropped its insistence that Texaco pledge a cash bond against the $11.1 billion judgment awarded by a Texas court. A lawyer for Pennzoil said the firm would be satisfied with liens and credit agreements.

13 Japan will extend its "voluntary" restraints on auto exports to the U.S. for a sixth year. Tokyo's decision, aimed at appeasing critics both in Japan and the U.S., would maintain Japanese shipments to America at their current level of 2.3 million cars a year.

Atlantic Richfield slashed its 1986 capital spending one-third, to $2 billion. The move, reflecting concern over falling crude prices, will sharply reduce the firm's oil and gas exploration and production in the U.S.

"Poison-put" bonds have become the latest takeover defense. The bonds allow investors to cash in their bonds if a hostile takeover threatens the firm that issued the debt.

14 Spot oil trading nearly halted in London after a Swiss firm alleged that traders couldn't deliver on a $75 million oil contract. Traders worried that the dispute, and other contested trades, could cause North Sea producers to turn elsewhere to sell oil, possibly causing the demise of the unregulated market.

The U.S. dollar fell broadly in volatile trading, tumbling 2.4% against the Japanese yen. Traders in Tokyo are pessimistic that the dollar will rally soon. Japanese firms, meanwhile, are boosting prices on exports to the U.S. due to the yen's recent surge.

Retail sales rose only 0.1% in January but economists suggested that solid growth is still likely. Recent gains in employment and personal income may encourage consumers to spend, one economist said.

18 Oil output by OPEC has fallen below 16

million barrels a day amid growing competition from noncartel producers, traders said. The development has forced Saudi Arabia to publicly retreat from efforts to lower prices by flooding the market with oil. The unstable market also has forced some traders to default.

Producer prices tumbled 0.7% in January, led by a sharp drop in oil prices. Industrial output, meanwhile, rose 0.3%, suggesting modest growth ahead for manufacturers.

Inflation fears are evaporating, setting the stage for further interest-rate declines, economists said. Stock and bond prices surged Friday on the inflation outlook. The yield on long-term Treasury bonds fell below 9% for the first time in 6½ years.

19 The dollar plunged after Treasury Secretary Baker voiced support for a further decline in the currency's value. In New York, the dollar fell below 180 yen for the first time since October 1978. Analysts are divided on what could halt the dollar's continued slide.

North Sea oil traders hope to prevent further defaults on contracts by placing stricter terms on trading in London. Crude oil prices, meanwhile, fell below $15 a barrel for the first time in seven years.

Bankers Trust was ordered by a federal court to stop its distribution of commercial paper. The ruling jeopardizes all big banks' business in the lucrative market.

The operating rate rose slightly at U.S. factories, mines and utilities last month, to 80.8% of capacity. The gain still left manufacturers considerable room to expand production.

20 Volcker indicated that the Fed isn't about to ease credit further. The Fed chairman told a House panel he is concerned about the dollar's recent slide, suggesting it eventually could worsen inflation. He also said the economy appears to be growing at a "reasonable" rate.

Stock and bond prices slumped following Volcker's testimony, while the dollar finished mixed in uneven trading. The Dow Jones Industrials tumbled 20.52 points, to 1658.26. Stocks also were hurt by profit-taking.

Housing starts jumped 15.7% in January to the highest rate in nearly two years. The surge, fueled by lower mortgage rates and mild weather, isn't likely to last. But analysts still expect a healthy pace for 1986.

The U.S. announced it will strictly enforce its ceiling on imports of European semifinished steel. The move is the latest in a bitter trade skirmish with the Common Market, which has called the steel quota illegal.

21 The economy grew at a meager 1.2% annual rate in the fourth quarter, half the Commerce Department's previous estimate. The revision reflected a worsening trade deficit and lower inventory investment. But economists expect sharper growth in the current quarter. GNP rose only 2.3% for all of 1985.

Texaco isn't required to post a $12 billion bond to pursue its legal battle with Pennzoil, a federal court ruled. But the court said Texaco must take the case back to Texas courts.

Oil futures prices dipped below $14 a barrel on rumors Saudi Arabia will boost oil output. The continued oil-price slide pushed bond and stock prices higher. The Dow Jones Industrials rose 14.56 points, to 1672.82.

Coca-Cola agreed to acquire Dr. Pepper, the nation's third-largest soft-drink maker, for $470 million. The move follows PepsiCo's plan to buy Seven-Up and continues a rapid consolidation of the industry.

Volcker urged Congress to consider tax changes to discourage corporate borrowing. The Fed chairman told a Senate panel he is worried about the rapid rise of business debt.

24 Consumer spending declined 0.4% in January and personal income fell 0.1%, raising questions on the economy's prospects. Bond prices soared, as analysts said the spending decline means inflation will remain low. Stocks rose, with the industrials climbing 24.89 to a record 1697.71.

Many foreign-exchange dealers say the dollar's decline will continue, despite Volcker's warning that it has fallen enough. The dollar rose against most major currencies Friday.

Corporate profits fell 13% in the fourth quarter, reflecting a wave of write-offs and lower productivity, according to a Wall Street Journal survey. It was the fourth consecutive quarterly decline, but analysts expect 1986 profits to improve.

Continental Illinois doubled its estimate of FDIC losses on loans the agency bought from the banking concern. The new estimate of between $1.16 billion and $1.56 billion seems to end hopes the FDIC would break even on its bailout of Continental.

25 Eastern Airlines agreed to be acquired by Texas Air after Eastern's management failed to win wage concessions from the machinists union. The merger would cre-

ate the nation's biggest airline operator and sharply change the competitive picture of the industry.

Ford and Mazda are discussing plans to give Mazda a major role in developing Ford's next generation of subcompact cars. The plan would replace two Ford models with Mazda-engineered cars by 1990.

GM began offering discount financing on most cars and trucks for an indefinite period. But the incentive program, the broadest in three years, mightn't be generous enough to reduce GM's swollen inventory.

The dollar resumed its steep decline, spurred by lower U.S. interest rates. The weak dollar helped spark a rally by gold, which rose $7.70 on the Comex to $348.70 an ounce.

26 Consumer prices rose a moderate 0.3% in January. But economists expect inflation will be pushed sharply lower in the next few months as the drop in oil prices is felt more by the economy. Separately, durable-goods orders rose 0.4% last month, largely due to military orders.

IBM lost out to Zenith Electronics Corp. for a laptop computer contract from the IRS. The $28 million award startled the personal computer industry, which had widely expected IBM to get the contract.

Car sales surged 11% in mid-February as consumers continued to take advantage of low-interest financing offered by auto makers. GM posted the sharpest gain of the Big Three, with its sales jumping 18.5%.

27 Bond prices soared on rumors that the U.S. and its major trading partners will soon cut interest rates. The yield on 30-year Treasury bonds fell below 8.5% for the first time in nearly 7½ years. Analysts expressed surprise over the market's explosive rally this month.

Precious metals contracts plunged on futures markets amid expectations of low U.S. inflation. Gold tumbled $11.30 on the Comex, to $336.40 an ounce. The dollar also fell.

28 Stock and bond prices rose sharply on expectations of lower inflation. The Dow Jones Industrials swept past 1700 for the first time, closing at 1713.99. Big Board volume jumped to the fifth-highest ever, while yields on 30-year Treasury bonds tumbled to eight-year lows.

British Petroleum took control of its 55%-owned Standard Oil Co. unit by replacing two top executives and naming a BP official as chief financial officer. BP cited "critical" times in the oil industry.

Non-farm productivity fell 0.2% last year,

the first decline since 1982. The figure was revised after fourth-quarter productivity was found to have tumbled at a 3.1% annual rate.

March 1986

3 BankAmerica's chief is likely to fight off a challenge to his job today. Samuel Armacost will defend his handling of the ailing bank before its board, which is considering a bid by Sanford Weill to unseat him. Meanwhile, Charles Schwab's job as head of the bank's discount brokerage unit may be in jeopardy, too.

The merchandise trade deficit swelled to a record $16.46 billion in January, suggesting the nation's trade problems will remain a blot on the economy for several months.

The economy strengthened further in February, according to a survey of purchasing managers. The report cited gains in new orders and output as well as lower prices.

4 Bond prices surged amid growing speculation that the U.S. and some allies will soon cut interest rates. Yields on 10-year Treasury notes fell below 8% for the first time in eight years. The bond rally accelerated as oil prices plunged to slightly more than $12 a barrel on spot and futures markets.

GM is repurchasing up to $1.95 billion of its three classes of common. The firm plans to use the shares for acquisitions and other purposes.

Construction spending rose 0.9% in January as lower interest rates spurred residential building. But a drop in nonresidential and public works construction caused new building contracts to plunge 14%.

5 Leading indicators fell 0.6% in January, the first decline in nine months. But many economists discounted the Commerce Department report, saying the economy is strong. The decline was paced by lower plant and equipment orders.

Auto sales plummeted 25.6% late last month. The decline, which compares with extremely strong year-earlier sales, indicates that consumers are reluctant to buy when auto makers don't offer strong incentives.

Bond prices posted strong gains, despite a flood of corporate debt issues totaling more than $2 billion. Stock prices closed mixed, as the Dow Jones Industrials fell 10.25 to 1686.42.

U.S. oil output is expected to fall this year for the first time since 1981, heralding greater dependence on imports. Due to tumbling oil prices, U.S. production may fall more than a million barrels a day in a year's time, according to some estimates.

6 New-home sales climbed 4.4% in January to the highest level in more than two years. Mortgage rates declined further in February, causing many analysts to predict that the housing boom will continue for most of this year.

Thrifts are expecting record profits for 1986 as falling rates prompt homeowners to refinance their mortgages. But the industry sees earnings being hurt eventually because of lower yields on the new loans.

Bond prices tumbled, snapping a month-long rally. The drop came as speculation eased about a cut in West German rates, which might lead the Fed to lower its discount rate.

7 Bond prices rallied on widespread speculation that the Fed would soon cut its discount rate. Hopes grew as West Germany's central bank lowered its discount rate. Japan is expected to make a similar cut today.

Retailers reported sluggish February sales as high consumer debt and bad weather discouraged shoppers. Sears and K mart had lower sales. Penney, Allied Stores and May Department Stores posted gains.

Mesa Partnership agreed to acquire Pioneer Corp. for an estimated $800 million. The accord calls for Mesa to issue partnership units to Pioneer shareholders and assume all the oil and gas firm's liabilities.

The tin crisis worsened as efforts to bail out the International Tin Council collapsed. Producing nations and some traders could face heavy losses. Tin prices fell in New York.

The Farmers Home Administration has run out of money for direct planting loans, sources said. The agency is being flooded by farmers' pleas for credit. Separately, a Treasury official reacted coolly to a proposed federal bailout of ailing farm banks.

10 The Fed lowered the discount rate half a point, to 7%, following similar cuts by West Germany and Japan. The moves signal a growing coordination of monetary policies among industrial nations. Major U.S. banks reacted by cutting their prime rates half a point, to 9%.

New worries about the economy may prompt the Fed to ease credit further in the next few months, many bankers and economists believe.

GM is cutting production further as it continues to struggle with huge inventories of unsold cars. The auto maker will temporarily close four plants later this month in addition to the one being idled this week.

Civilian unemployment jumped to 7.3% of the work force in February. The rise from January's 6.7% rate resulted mainly from statistical problems and unusual weather. But it still suggests the economy is weaker than many analysts had thought.

11 Bond prices surged again on speculation that the economy's weakness will lead to lower interest rates. Many analysts predicted that rates would drop even if the Fed doesn't ease credit further. Some actively traded 30-year Treasury bonds jumped almost two points.

States can't duplicate the federal Superfund law by taxing companies to pay for hazardous waste cleanups, the Supreme Court ruled. But the court said states can impose taxes to pay for costs the Superfund doesn't cover.

12 Rallies swept through the stock and bond markets, driven by continued expectations of lower interest rates. The Dow Jones Industrials jumped over 40 points in heavy trading to a record 1746.05. Several of the broader market indexes also set records. Yields on 30-year Treasury bonds dropped to 7.90%, the lowest since late 1977.

The semiconductor industry's most closely watched indicator posted its sixth straight monthly increase. The rise in the ratio of orders to sales suggests microchip makers are recovering from their worst slump ever.

Japanese investors continue to snap up U.S. securities despite the decline in the dollar and U.S. interest rates. The trend may add fuel to the rally in U.S. securities markets and help keep interest rates down.

13 The bond rally fizzled as investors became nervous over an unexpected rise in some short-term interest rates. Stocks, however, continued to gain ground as Big Board volume soared to its second-highest level ever.

The merchandise trade deficit grew to a record $39.48 billion in the fourth quarter, bringing the yearly total to a record $124.29 billion.

14 The FDIC is seeking broader powers to handle big bank failures. FDIC Chairman Seidman told a Senate panel that some major banks are in trouble and that the agency needs greater authority to prevent a big failure from triggering a crisis. Regulators said most of the troubled banks have substantial energy loans.

Plunging gasoline prices are putting billions of extra dollars in consumers' pockets and could lead to a decline in the Consumer Price Index for the first time since 1965.

Exxon is slashing capital spending 26% this year due to falling oil prices. U.S. Steel, meanwhile, expects a $260 million charge this quarter because of the dwindling value of its Marathon Oil unit's oil and gas inventories.

Japanese microchip producers were found for the second time this week to be selling at below-market prices in the U.S. The two types cited by the U.S. will make up the bulk of the chip market in coming years.

U.S. car sales fell 4% in early March from a year earlier. Dealers said financing and other incentives offered by the Big Three auto makers aren't attracting enough buyers.

February retail sales slipped 0.1%, the second straight monthly decline. But analysts see improvement ahead. Commerce Secretary Baldrige said declines in interest rates and inflation should boost consumer spending.

17 Producer prices tumbled a record 1.6% last month. The report helped fuel Friday's stock market rally, with the Dow Jones Industrial Average soaring over 39 points to a record 1792.74. Industrial output, meanwhile, slipped 0.6% in February, suggesting some manufacturers are still having problems.

More oil companies are announcing spending cuts and layoffs due to the sharp drop in crude prices. U.S. petroleum reserves, meanwhile, are eroding again as declining prices force firms to increase write-offs.

Accounting firms often do a sloppy job auditing the $100 billion in federal grants to states and cities each year, a GAO report says. The problem may require state action, the report adds.

The dollar plunged against the yen Friday, nearing its lowest point since World War II. Traders said an apparent Fed intervention stopped the dollar from sliding even further.

18 Members of OPEC failed to agree on a formula to prop up oil prices. The 13-member group, meeting in Geneva, discussed cutting production to reassert market control. But the talks were inconclusive.

Stock and bond prices sank, however, amid speculation that OPEC might agree to limit output and push oil prices higher. Energy futures rose sharply in uneasy trading.

Volcker initially opposed the Fed's recent cut in the discount rate, but was outvoted by other members. The incident may signal a shift in power at the central bank toward the four Fed members appointed by Reagan.

Banks are becoming more cautious about lending to companies that have trouble getting liability insurance. Bankers say they are less willing to offer unsecured loans to such firms and may make less credit available.

19 The dollar tumbled to a record low against the yen in Tokyo and New York. Reagan administration officials said the U.S. had no plans to stem the dollar's decline despite Japan's complaint that the strong yen is hurting its economy.

The current account deficit swelled to a record $36.56 billion in the fourth quarter. The growing gap in the broad trade measure shows U.S. producers were still being hurt by imports.

Exxon plans to trim operations overseas and at its New York headquarters. The restructuring is one of the first by a major energy company since oil prices began falling.

Housing starts fell 3.5% last month, but are still at relatively high levels. Economists expect construction will remain strong in the coming months as mortgage rates slip further.

20 Britain's new tax on U.K. shares trading in the U.S. may sharply curtail the lucrative ADR business of American banks and stockbrokers.

The economy grew at a 0.7% annual rate in the fourth quarter, far less than previous estimates. The revised figure meant GNP rose only 2.2% for all of 1985. But many analysts remain optimistic that the economy is beginning to rebound in the current quarter.

Japan has begun moving to slow the yen's sharp rise against the dollar. But sources said Tokyo's recent proposal to the U.S. for a joint intervention effort was rebuffed.

21 Stock prices surged in active trading as the Dow Industrials closed above 1800 for the first time. Buying programs related to arbitrage against stock-index futures accounted for much of the 16.29-point rise.

Personal income rose 0.6% last month, though partly because of special factors, the Commerce Department said. Consumer spending, meanwhile, edged up 0.3%, but the rise was limited to the services sector.

24 Preston Martin resigned from the Fed Board, but is likely to be replaced by another advocate of easier credit policy. Thus, Chairman Volcker still faces opposition from Reagan appointees to the board. They favor stimulating the economy over his policy of fighting inflation.

Blue-chip stocks plunged Friday (March 21)

sending the Dow Jones Industrials down 35.68 points. The market turned frantic as investors closed out positions in stock index futures, index options and stock options.

Morgan Stanley's success with its first stock offering Friday (March 21) may encourage other closely held securities firms to sell shares to the public.

25 The OPEC talks collapsed in Geneva, triggering a sharp drop in oil prices. Commodity futures prices plunged to an eight-year low, while the bond market and the U.S. dollar rallied. But bond prices lost some of their gains following reports of the U.S.-Libya confrontation.

26 Consumer prices fell 0.4% in February, the steepest monthly decline in over 30 years. The drop, reflecting the sharp slide in oil prices, is expected to continue for the next few months. It could set the stage for the lowest inflation rate since the early 1960s.

U.S. new-car sales plunged 17.2% in mid-March from a year earlier. Analysts said the weaker-than-expected results mean auto makers will have to offer stronger sales incentives or cut car production further.

The dollar rose sharply in response to the continued U.S.-Libyan conflict. Major foreign-currency futures fell for the second straight day. Gold, a traditional haven in times of international tensions, tumbled $7.30 on the Comex to $343.60 an ounce.

27 Electric utility bondholders may lose up to $100 million in the coming months as several utilities redeem their bonds at below-market prices.

The U.S. plans major changes in its trade strategy with Japan. Instead of seeking to open markets for specific goods, Reagan officials plan to press Tokyo for basic policy changes that would encourage purchases of all foreign products.

Stock prices surged, pushing the Dow Jones Industrials up 32.20 points to a record 1810.70. The bond market also rallied, fueled by expectations of lower interest rates. Treasury bond futures rose to contract highs for the second straight day.

Construction awards rebounded 11% last month, buoyed by a surge in public works projects that had been delayed. The rise followed a 14% decline during January.

28 General Motors raised prices on 1986 models an average 2.9% despite rising inventories. The price boost, the second within six months, stunned analysts and dealers. The auto maker has been offering incentives and cutting production recently to cope with its swollen stocks.

The U.S. trade deficit shrank to $12.49 billion in February due to slumping oil prices and other factors. But economists said the figure overstates the improvement in trade, which they believe will be slow.

31 Fed officials tomorrow probably will authorize easier credit to take effect if the economy remains sluggish, according to many economists. Meanwhile, leading economic indicators rose 0.7% in February, the Commerce Department said, bolstering forecasts of solid growth.

U.S.-Japanese talks on semiconductor trade broke down after the two sides proved unable to narrow their differences. The rift likely will increase pressure from Congress and American chip makers to retaliate against Japanese manufacturers.

The computer industry appears poised for a modest rebound. But this one will be based on cost reductions and wider profit margins, not on big increases in sales.

April 1986

1 Oil prices fell below $11 a barrel on spot and futures markets after the United Arab Emirates' oil minister predicted that crude could plunge to $5. Some analysts said prices may have to fall that far before OPEC can agree on production cuts.

Bond prices soared again, sparked by the slide in oil prices and speculation that the Fed will ease credit further. Gold tumbled $12 on the Comex in reaction to weak oil prices.

New-home sales unexpectedly fell 3.8% in February, but many economists believe lower mortgage rates will spark a rebound soon. Brisk home building, meanwhile, led McGraw-Hill to predict a record level of 1986 construction awards.

Tokyo stock prices continued to rally as Japan's fiscal year ended. The widely watched Nikkei stock average rose to a record for the fifth consecutive session. It has jumped 21% in the past three months.

Toyota was asked to voluntarily recall 74,000 1982–83 Cressidas after U.S. regulators said the cars could accelerate without warning. Toyota said it didn't intend to recall the cars.

2 Factory orders fell 1.4% in February, the steepest drop in nearly 1½ years. But the decline resulted from lower defense orders, which fluctuate widely month to month. Non-military orders rose 0.2%, suggesting the economy isn't weakening. Construction spending, meanwhile, rose 1.2% during the month.

Oil prices slipped below $10 a barrel, but rebounded sharply after Vice President Bush announced plans to discuss oil-price stability with Saudi Arabia. The unexpected recovery by oil caused an explosive rally in the bond market to fizzle.

Stock prices declined on profit-taking after the bond rally collapsed. The Dow Jones Industrials tumbled 28.50 points, to 1790.11.

3 The White House denied it was planning any effort to prop up oil prices. The free-market stance was meant to refute suggestions in recent days that the Reagan administration was changing its oil policy. Officials also denied that Vice President Bush intended to press Saudi Arabia to stablize the oil market.

Bond prices rallied following the White House statements, while a two-day rally by oil prices slowed. Stock prices also reacted to the news, reversing an early decline and closing mixed. The dollar strengthened.

Phillips Petroleum and Standard Oil became the latest energy companies to announce major cost-saving measures. Phillips plans to lay off up to 9.4% of its work force and suspend merit pay raises. Standard Oil will slash exploration spending 34%.

The Big Three auto makers will have to cut production further unless they can devise new buyer-incentive programs to boost lagging sales.

4 U.S. car sales plunged 21.5% at the end of March, resulting in a 15.6% decline for the entire month. Sales of imported cars, however, surged 22.9% last month despite higher prices caused by the weaker dollar.

Mutual funds gained an average 14.2% in the first quarter, the first time in nearly three years that they outperformed the S&P 500 index. The top gainers were aided by the bond market rally, while the big losers were hurt by sliding oil prices.

Mortgage rates continued to decline during March and are expected to move even lower soon. Fixed-rate loans fell the most, with 30-year conventional mortgages dropping to an average 10.1% last week from 10.51% a month earlier. Adjustable-rate loans also fell.

Oil refiners are seeing their profits sag as refined-product prices begin to fall in line with the drop in crude oil. Foreign oil producers, meanwhile, are buying up refineries in the U.S. to gain a marketing foothold.

7 Bush warned Saudi Arabia that the U.S. may abandon its free-market oil policy if prices drop too far and threaten the American oil industry. The vice president's message appeared to contradict a previous White House statement that Bush wouldn't pressure the Saudis to cut oil output and prop up prices.

Treasury Secretary Baker urged Congress to repeal the "windfall profits" tax on crude oil because of the sharp drop in prices. Energy Secretary Herrington, meanwhile, said he didn't think petroleum prices have fallen too low.

Civilian unemployment eased to 7.2% of the work force in March, indicating that the economy remains sluggish. A survey of purchasing agents showed that the economy is growing, but at a slower pace.

The Dow Jones Industrials tumbled a record 82.50 points last week, reflecting profit-taking as well as disappointment over the sluggish economy. The sharp swings in stock prices, meanwhile, are fueled by Major Market Index futures and options.

8 Union Carbide agreed to sell its battery products business to Ralston Purina for $1.42 billion. The chemical giant also plans to sell an additional $1 billion in assets, including its headquarters, and cut 1,200 more jobs. Carbide is trying to shrink its huge debt following the recent takeover battle with GAF Corp.

The White House again disputed Bush's suggestion that the U.S. might abandon its free-market oil policy. While denying any plans to intervene in oil markets, officials tried to distance President Reagan from Bush's comments in Saudi Arabia.

Confusion about U.S. oil policy caused bond prices to fluctuate widely before closing lower. Oil prices, meanwhile, surged to about $14 a barrel after a strike closed Norway's North Sea oil production.

9 Bond prices soared on speculation that the Federal Reserve would soon cut its discount rate to revive the sluggish U.S. economy. The rally was fueled by a sharp drop in oil prices. Some actively traded Treasury bonds jumped nearly three points, the biggest gain in 3½ years.

The plunge in oil prices was sparked by news that the Soviet Union was beginning to sell oil to Europe through netback transactions. The sales could add more than a million barrels a day to the world oil glut.

Stock prices rose sharply, spurred by the bond market rally and the renewed decline in crude-oil prices. The Dow Jones Industrials climbed 34.25 points to close at 1769.76.

10 Reagan said he hoped oil prices would stabilize soon, but emphasized that market forces should determine the price. The president also expressed concern that some oil producers may try to "play games" with the market. Confusion over U.S. oil policy recently has increased the volatility of the oil market.

Oil prices rebounded in reaction to a report indicating that motorists are using more gasoline. The rally also was fueled by Reagan's comments.

Oil inventories are rapidly drying up despite the glut on world oil markets. Many industries are delaying buying more oil because they expect crude prices to drop further.

TransCanada Pipelines said it would offer $3 billion for Hiram Walker if the firm supports the bid. Hiram's board, which has been trying to fend off a Gulf Canada takeover, is scheduled to meet today.

11 Ford Motor declared a 3-for-2 stock split and raised its quarterly cash dividend 18% on a pre-split basis. The auto maker cited improvement in its "underlying profitability." Ford's stock price has surged since the firm said last year that it would buy back up to 30 million shares.

The Soviet Union asked a West German bank to arrange a $427.4 million credit to help finance Western purchases. Moscow's hard-currency reserves have been depleted by the drop in oil prices.

The semiconductor industry continued to expand in March, based on the increased ratio of orders to sales.

Beryl Sprinkel indicated that he expects the Fed will soon lower its discount rate. The comment by Reagan's chief economic adviser suggests the White House favors a rate cut.

14 General Motors ordered further cost-cutting steps amid concern over bulging inventories and slumping sales. The auto maker also offered new financing incentives, but dealers worried that the program mightn't be attractive enough to offset recent price increases.

Producer prices tumbled 1.1% in March, reflecting steep declines in energy prices. Many economists expect the effects of the oil-price drop will continue spreading through the economy. Retail sales, meanwhile, fell 0.8% because of lower auto sales.

IBM's earnings rose 3.1% in the first quarter, though computer sales remained weak. The company again warned that the outlook for the year is uncertain. IBM, meanwhile, is starting to challenge Japan in the computer-printer market.

15 Oil prices tumbled in U.S. markets amid skepticism that OPEC will be able to agree on a plan to stabilize prices. As the oil ministers prepared to resume talks in Geneva today, several delegates said the group was unlikely to end its feuding. Oil analysts said prices were kept from falling further by worries about a U.S.-Libya conflict.

Business inventories were largely unchanged in February after edging up a revised 0.3% in January. Separately, consumer credit expanded by $4.97 billion during February, or at an 11% annual rate.

Bond prices rose as oil prices and short-term interest rates declined. The rate drop was prompted by continued speculation that the Fed will soon ease credit further.

16 Fed Chairman Volcker said the outlook for economic growth has improved because of falling oil prices and interest rates as well as greater efforts to shrink the budget deficit.

U.S. car sales increased 2.7% in early April. Analysts believe falling interest rates and fuel prices may boost car sales further. Chrysler, meanwhile, said it won't follow General Motors in raising prices.

Industrial output fell 0.5% in March, reflecting continued weakness in manufacturing and the overall economy. Most of the production drop came in oil and gas drilling, auto and truck assembly and steelmaking.

TransCanada PipeLines withdrew its $36.50-a-share (Canadian) bid for Hiram Walker following Gulf Canada's recent offer of $38 a share. But TransCanada didn't rule out the possibility of another bid.

17 Housing starts slipped 2.4% in March, though the pace remained strong. Economists expect declining mortgage rates will keep home building robust at least through summer.

U.S. businesses plan to increase spending on plant and equipment a meager 0.9% this year after inflation. Energy firms expect to slash capital spending, and falling oil prices may force even bigger reductions.

Stock and bond prices soared on expectations of further declines in interest rates and oil prices. The Dow Jones Industrials jumped more than 38 points to a record 1847.97. Bond prices posted the biggest single-day increase in 3½ years. The U.S. dollar tumbled.

Oil prices plunged as the OPEC talks in Geneva stalled again. A report showing increased U.S. refinery output contributed to the price slide on U.S. spot and futures markets.

18 Hiram Walker's board endorsed Gulf Canada's $2.38 billion takeover bid for the liquor and energy firm. But TransCanada PipeLines, which had dropped a rival offer, said it is still considering "its options."

China announced a slowdown in its soaring

industrial growth rate and predicted a rise in grain output. A government spokesman in Peking said, however, that prices were still rising rapidly and efficiency was deteriorating "in all industries."

The economy grew at a healthy 3.2% annual rate in the first quarter, aided by a rise in exports. The preliminary GNP estimate surprised economists because of recent indications that the economy was weak. A GNP-based price measure rose at a 2.5% annual rate, the smallest increase in almost 19 years.

21 The Fed may follow Friday's cut in the discount rate with other credit-easing moves. Bankers and economists said the half-point reduction, to 6½%, won't be enough to revive the sluggish U.S. economy. They believe the Fed has plenty of leeway to push rates lower because of falling oil prices and low inflation.

Japan lowered its discount rate on Saturday, capping the latest round of rate cuts by major industrial nations. The reductions were worked out informally at a recent IMF (International Monetary Fund) meeting.

Personal income rose only 0.2% in March, while consumer spending grew 0.3%. Lower oil prices are expected to boost consumers' purchasing power in the months ahead.

The U.S. dollar may fall even further despite its sharp drop last week, analysts said. They cited cheaper oil, a sluggish U.S. economy and the belief that the U.S. wants a weaker dollar to shrink the trade deficit.

22 The dollar continued to slide, partly on speculation that Reagan wants a weaker U.S. currency to help shrink the nation's trade deficit. The dollar reached a post-World War II low against the yen despite heavy intervention by Japan's central bank. In Chicago, futures in yen and Swiss francs hit contract highs.

Union Carbide will sell its home and auto product divisions to First Boston for $800 million. The sale completes Carbide's disposal of consumer product assets.

23 The dollar tumbled further on speculation that only a coordinated intervention can halt the currency's continued slide. Bond prices plunged amid fears that the weak dollar will reduce Japanese purchases of Treasury securities. Stocks also declined, with the Dow Jones Industrials falling 24.92 points, to 1830.98.

Consumer prices fell 0.4% in March, the same as in February. The two-month drop, the first in over 20 years, reflected tumbling oil prices. Separately, durable goods orders plunged 2.5% last month.

GM and Chrysler reported lower first-quarter earnings, reflecting a less robust U.S. auto market. GM's profit slipped 0.7%, while Chrysler's net income tumbled 30%.

24 Exxon offered 40,000 employees the option of early retirement or resigning with compensation, citing the pessimistic outlook for the oil industry. The request, which affects more than 25% of its work force, came as the oil giant reported a 37% rise in first-quarter profit.

Bond prices declined further amid worries about the dollar and an expected flood of Treasury borrowing. Stock prices also fell, though a late rally by blue chips pushed the Dow Jones Industrials back up to close at 1829.61, off just 1.37 points.

Fed Chairman Volcker said the rapid rise in public and private debt poses a serious threat to the economy. He also expressed some concern about the dollar's steep decline.

25 Kidder Peabody's directors approved GE's offer to buy about 80% of the securities firm for about $600 million, sources said. Kidder Peabody shareholders were expected to approve the takeover yesterday.

Bond prices tumbled for the third day in a row amid worries that the Japanese are reducing their U.S. bond holdings because of the dollar's slide. The dollar rebounded, though traders called it a technical correction.

West Germany and Japan signaled that they don't plan to take further steps to stimulate their economies, despite pressure from the U.S.

AT&T proposed steep rate cuts on long-distance service that will mostly benefit business customers. The move will increase pressure on its smaller long-distance competitors to offer similar reductions.

28 Three ad agencies agreed to merge, creating a company with combined billings of $5 billion a year. The three—BBDO International, Doyle Dane and Needham Harper—will swap stock, with BBDO holders getting 65% of the new agency.

GM announced more plant closings and layoffs, indicating that previous cutbacks haven't trimmed inventories enough. Separately, AMC's loss shrank to $18.9 million in the first quarter despite lower car sales.

General Electric plans to inject $130 million into Kidder Peabody when it buys 80% of the investment banking firm in about a month.

29 IBM has sharply cut hiring of U.S. college

graduates this year because of the continued slump in the computer industry. President John Akers told shareholders that the company expects "a demanding year ahead."

Non-farm productivity rebounded at a 3.4% annual rate in the first quarter, though the rise may not signify a trend. Also, new construction contracts fell 8% in March as the boom in office building slowed.

Outside bank auditors should report any fraud or other legal violations to federal regulators and not just to the bank, FDIC chairman William Seidman told a House panel.

30 Leading indicators rose 0.5% in March, suggesting solid economic growth ahead. But the gain came mainly from the rise in stock prices and money supply, masking some weak spots in the economy. New-home sales, meanwhile, soared 27.4% last month to a record level.

U.S. Steel posted a first-quarter loss of $249 million, reflecting a huge write-down of its Marathon Oil unit's petroleum assets. Bethlehem Steel said its loss widened to $91.8 million in the quarter and announced plans to sell its non-steel interests.

May 1986

1 Stock prices plunged amid concern about interest rates and the economy. The Dow Jones Industrials tumbled a record 41.91 points, to 1783.98. Meanwhile, farm commodity futures soared on speculation about damage to Soviet agriculture from the nuclear plant accident.

The dollar rose, partly on speculation that the disaster will boost purchases of the currency. West Germany signaled plans to intervene further to support the dollar.

Bond prices tumbled, ending a three-day rally. Prices fell as the Treasury unveiled plans to sell $27 billion of bonds and notes next week, more than analysts had expected.

The U.S. trade deficit widened to $14.52 billion in March as imports of manufactured goods rose sharply. Economists don't expect the weaker dollar will shrink the deficit much until later this year. Separately, factory orders tumbled 2.3% in March.

2 The Big Board is closer to dropping its rule that companies give shareholders equal voting rights. The exchange is under pressure to change because of the growth of unequal voting stock as a takeover defense.

Construction spending fell 1.2% in March as nonresidential building declined sharply. Economists, however, expect that robust residential construction in the months ahead will offset the weak commercial sector.

5 Ford and Chrysler raised prices on light trucks and minivans. Ford's increases ranged from 1.7% to 2.9%, while Chrysler's averaged 2.3%. The boosts came as the two companies publicized their refusal to follow General Motors and foreign auto makers in raising car prices.

Unemployment edged lower in April, to 7.1% from 7.2%. The Labor Department report indicated the economy has been growing only slowly, with manufacturing remaining weak.

Declines in production and inventories were reported in a monthly survey of corporate purchasing managers. But new orders were strong, portending higher output.

6 Saudi Arabia is offering oil companies cash discounts this month in an attempt to meet rising competition from other oil producers, sources said. The discounts range from 50 cents to $1.15 a barrel, depending on the size of the purchase.

First Boston was charged by the SEC with insider trading on Cigna Corp. stock and options. First Boston agreed to pay a fine and give back profits from the sale without admitting or denying guilt.

U.S. new-car sales improved in late April but were still down 5.9% from the strong year-earlier level. Imports surged 27% during the latest period despite higher prices caused by the weakened dollar.

The SEC's staff plans to recommend that the Big Board end its curbs on after-hours trading of listed stocks. SEC officials are concerned that the rule is driving trading volume to London and other foreign markets.

The U.S. dollar plunged, losing 2.3% of its value against the yen. Traders, meanwhile, reacted skeptically to the Tokyo agreement to monitor exchange rates. Many believe the U.S. still wants a lower dollar to shrink its huge trade deficit.

Bond prices soared amid speculation that the summit accord will lead to another round of interest-rate cuts. The bond rally helped lift stock prices, as the Dow Jones Industrials climbed 19.09 points, to 1793.77.

U.S. oil companies were ordered by Reagan to pull out of Libya by June 30. Most of the firms said ending their operations in the country won't hurt earnings significantly.

7 The SEC rejected a plan to let many ailing oil and gas firms delay writing down the

value of their reserves. The decision, which shocked the energy industry, may cause more companies to default on bank loans.

8   Burroughs plans to launch a $70-a-share tender offer for Sperry today. The computer firm said it is making the bid because its New York-based rival hadn't responded yet to an acquisition proposal.

Mortgage rates fell further in April, but at a slower pace. Rates on 30-year, conventional fixed mortgages eased to an average 9.9% last week from 9.99% a month earlier. Some analysts think the decline in rates may be starting to bottom out.

Oil prices jumped to a 10-week high of over $15 a barrel due to increased gasoline demand and Iraq's attack on an Iranian refinery. Some analysts speculated that oil prices could rise to the high teens.

9   House budget members endorsed a $35.2 billion cut in Reagan's defense request. The panel also backed $7.3 billion in new revenues to bring the deficit below Gramm-Rudman targets. The votes showed Democrats in control of the committee as it moved to complete its $994 billion budget plan.

Major retailers reported sluggish sales gains for April. The results reflect an early Easter, high consumer debt and the oil-industry slump. But industry officials expect sales to rebound sharply by August.

Sperry's stock price continued to surge as Burroughs launched its $70-a-share tender offer. The rise was fueled by renewed speculation that a higher offer will emerge for the New York computer company.

Farm futures prices rose broadly on a report that Moscow wants to boost food purchases from Western Europe because of contamination from the Chernobyl accident.

12 Reagan officials indicated they won't seek major changes in the Senate tax-overhaul bill. The president endorsed the plan even though it curtails tax benefits for IRAs and ends those for capital gains. Both Dole and Packwood expect it to clear the Senate largely intact.

Many big companies are backing the bill even though it would boost corporate taxes. Property developers and others may have a hard time fighting the measure.

Saatchi & Saatchi agreed to acquire Ted Bates Worldwide for $450 million, creating the world's largest advertising agency. The move highlights the scramble by agencies to forge international alliances.

GM plans to offer home mortgages to car-loan customers in Michigan. The pilot program, which will test GM's ability to broaden its financial services, is intended to compensate for cycles in the auto business.

The SEC's staff is considering tying the price of expiring stock options, stock-index options and futures to opening rather than closing prices. The aim is to make the markets less volatile on expiration Fridays.

13 Consumer credit grew at an 8.1% annual rate in March. The $3.71 billion rise, the smallest in nearly three years, follows a sharp increase in consumer debt last year.

The dollar plunged against the yen as Japan reported a record trade surplus with the U.S. for April. Bond prices tumbled partly in reaction to the dollar's sharp drop.

Oil drilling activity in the U.S. has fallen to a post-World War II low. Industry officials warned that the drop is causing the U.S. to become more dependent on foreign oil supplies.

Oil futures prices rose above $16 a barrel for the first time in nearly three months. But prices fell back by the close due to profit-taking.

14 The U.S. sought to slow the dollar's slide. Treasury Secretary Baker said currency traders overreacted to recent statements that the U.S. has "no target" for the dollar's value.

The dollar rose sharply within minutes after Baker's remarks, climbing 1.6% against the Japanese yen. Bond prices also rallied in reaction.

Prime Minister Nakasone ordered his government to draw up emergency measures to help export-oriented Japanese companies cope with the yen's sharp rise.

Retail sales rose 0.5% in April, the biggest gain since December. The increase resulted from strong auto sales, which tend to fluctuate from month to month. Sales of building materials also were robust.

Grain and livestock futures prices rose sharply amid renewed speculation that the Soviet nuclear accident would affect food supplies and trade. Sugar contracts declined.

15 U.S. car sales rose 9.1% in early May, mostly because auto makers lowered financing rates, analysts said. But there was disagreement on whether sales would remain strong.

Business inventories rose 0.4% in March as sales fell 1.6%, suggesting firms may be burdened with unwanted items. The growth in inventories, partly due to the auto industry, was the largest since October.

16 Industrial output rose 0.2% in April, reflecting an increase in auto production.

But the rise, the first since January, offered little evidence of a rebound by manufacturers.

Burroughs said it is ready to negotiate a "meaningful increase" in its $4.06 billion offer for Sperry. The computer maker's $70-a-share bid was rejected by Sperry on Wednesday (May 14).

Blue chip stocks reversed course and led the rest of the market lower. Sell programs late in the session helped push the Dow Jones Industrials down 33.60 points, to 1774.68.

The Amex and CBOE are investigating the heavy trading and price jumps in stock-index options on Wednesday (May 14). Traders said the activity, including program trading, was caused by firms and institutions.

19 Burroughs and Sperry said they are holding merger talks, indicating that Sperry had given up fighting a takeover. Some speculators believe the firms might settle on a price of $75 to $77 a share for Sperry.

The Fed isn't likely to ease credit further because of the weak dollar and the rapid growth in the money supply, many bankers and economists said. The Fed's Open Market panel meets tomorrow to plan credit strategy for the next few weeks.

Inflation and housing continued to improve last month. Producer prices fell 0.6%, the fourth consecutive monthly drop, while housing starts rose 4.1%. Other sectors of the economy remained weak, however. The nation's factories, mines and utilities operated at 79.3% of capacity, unchanged from March.

20 Burroughs raised its bid for Sperry to $75 a share, or $4.35 billion, after merger talks between the two computer makers broke down, sources said. Burroughs apparently plans to renew its hostile bid of $70 a share unless Sperry accepts the higher offer by tomorrow.

U.S. crude oil prices soared to a 14-week high of over $17 a barrel in record trading. The jump partly reflected rising demand by domestic refiners as gasoline use increases.

Bond prices tumbled in reaction to the surge in oil prices. Analysts said oil's rise could renew fears about inflation and discourage the Fed from easing credit further.

Johnson & Johnson may take its widely used spermicide birth-control products off the market following a recent $4.7 million damage award. The move could lead smaller firms to stop making such products.

21 The economy grew at a 3.7% annual rate in the first quarter, stronger than previous estimates. But economists said the GNP figure resulted from higher inventories and overstated the economy's strength. Corporate profits, meanwhile, fell 4.9%, but economists said earnings were better than the report shows.

The dollar rose sharply in reaction to the GNP report, climbing 1.4% against the West German mark. Traders speculated that a stronger economy would lead to higher interest rates and a stronger dollar.

Bond and stock prices rallied as a sharp drop in oil prices eased worries about inflation and interest rates. Some 30-year Treasury bonds surged about two points, while the Dow Jones Industrials rose 25.80, to 1783.98.

The mortgage insurance industry posted the first operating loss in its 29-year history due to defaults by home mortgage holders.

22 Consumer prices fell 0.3% in April, the third straight monthly decline. But the drop in the inflation index resulted mostly from lower energy prices, which some economists say won't last. Separately, personal income rose 1.2% last month, mainly from increased subsidies to farmers. Consumer spending was up 0.3%.

The dollar rallied sharply on the favorable economic news, climbing 1.3% against the West German mark. Traders expect the U.S. currency's rebound will continue.

23 Durable-goods orders fell 0.8% in April, reflecting continued weakness in the manufacturing sector. The three biggest categories—primary metals, machinery and transportation equipment—all posted declines.

27 Canada threatened to retaliate against the U.S. for imposing a 35% duty on imports of Canadian wood shingles and shakes. Prime Minister Mulroney will meet with his cabinet today to discuss the levy, which Reagan announced Thursday. It is the biggest trade dispute between the two countries in years.

The SEC plans to widen its search for possible accomplices of Dennis Levine, charged in a record insider-trading case. The agency is expected to subpoena scores of Wall Street investment bankers and others soon.

Mutual funds are expected to come under increased SEC pressure to better inform shareholders if investment funds are used to pay marketing costs. Meantime, more mutual funds are planning sales charges.

28 Bethlehem Steel signed a tentative con-

tract with the Steelworkers union that would cut labor costs about 10%. In return, Bethlehem agreed to pay stock and cash benefits and invest its labor savings in steel.

The U.S. Trade Commission ruled that Japanese firms sold a widely used computer chip in the U.S. at unfairly low prices. The decision will result in anti-dumping duties being levied on the Japanese semiconductors.

Several countries have raised gasoline and fuel-oil taxes to increase revenue while crude prices remain low. The move, which the U.S. is still debating, could frustrate OPEC's plans to revive oil consumption.

Sperry agreed to be acquired by Burroughs for $4.44 billion, or $76.50 a share, in cash and securities. The takeover, the largest in the computer industry, came after a weeks-long battle. Burroughs's chairman hopes the new company will provide tough competition for IBM.

IBM announced plans to buy less than 2% of its shares, currently valued at about $1.47 billion. The move is likely to give a short-term boost to the company's stock, which has lagged in the market recently.

29 Insider trading charges were brought against five people, who were accused of using data stolen from a law firm to trade in takeover stocks. The indictments are part of a continuing government crackdown on illegal use of inside information.

Burroughs said it expects to complete its $4.78 billion acquisition of Sperry in about two months. The Detroit-based computer maker, as expected, has assigned senior roles to Sperry's top two executives.

Stock prices continued to rally, pushing the Dow Jones Industrials up 25.25 points, to a record 1878.28. The broader S&P 500 and Big Board composite indexes also set new highs. Analysts, surprised by the surge, cited optimism on interest rates, inflation and the economy.

Bond prices slumped despite predictions that interest rates will continue to ease. Traders cited the poor reception for the Treasury's $7.76 billion note auction. Meanwhile, the U.S. dollar rose slightly.

Chrysler agreed to increase its stake in Maserati to 15%, with an option to buy up to 51% of the Italian car maker for $68.5 million.

30 Leading indicators rose a strong 1.5% in April, reflecting increases in stock prices and the money supply. It was the biggest

rise since October 1983. Non-farm productivity grew at a healthy rate of 3.6% in the first quarter.

Bond prices tumbled, while the dollar soared, as the economic report fueled speculation that interest rates will rise. Meanwhile, stock prices rose, sending the Dow Jones Industrials up 4.07, to 1882.35.

Rockwell plans to lay off about a quarter of its 27,400 workers in its B-1 bomber program. Some analysts suggested the move may have been timed to pressure Congress to reconsider phasing out the bomber.

Reagan promised to veto a House bill to toughen U.S. trade laws, calling it "kamikaze legislation" that would threaten the economy. The bill, which faces opposition in the Senate, would force the president to retaliate against unfair trade practices.

June 1986

2 Japan adopted several measures to help cushion the impact of the stronger yen on its economy. Because of the rising yen, the country's economy may face a turning point after 36 months of expansion.

The U.S. dollar Friday soared 1.5% against the yen and reached its highest level since mid-February against the West German mark.

The trade deficit narrowed to $12.07 billion in April, as imports fell 10%. But the figures suggest that a major improvement in the U.S. trade balance isn't likely soon.

The money supply's surge lowers chances of further easing by the Fed soon, economists say. The rise is seen as a sign that business activity will grow, and easing credit runs the risk of renewing inflation, they say.

3 Crude oil prices fell below $14 a barrel for the first time in a month, reflecting an increase in gasoline supplies and high refinery output.

The FHA faces another temporary closing of its popular mortgage-insurance program, and Congress apparently won't act quickly enough to head it off, officials said.

Canada imposed import levies on some products to retaliate against a planned U.S. tariff on Canadian shingles. Meanwhile, the Canadian dollar fell 1% against the U.S. dollar due to concern over the dispute.

Factory orders rose a slight 0.1% in April,

while strong residential building paced a 0.8% advance in construction spending. The increase in new orders doesn't signal a turnaround for manufacturers, many economists contend. Orders for durable goods declined 0.2%.

4 The tax bill was cleared for Senate debate today by the Budget Committee. But the panel warned that the bill would undermine Congress's chances of meeting Gramm-Rudman deficit targets because it would cause sharp swings in revenue in the coming years.

The Supreme Court ruled it is unconstitutional for New York to require that distillers charge the state's liquor wholesalers the lowest price they offer elsewhere in the nation. The decision affects 38 other states with similar liquor-price laws.

Bond prices rebounded from a four-day slump despite an increase in most short-term interest rates. Some long-term Treasury bonds rose more than a point in light trading.

Interferon will become available commercially for the first time. Hoffmann-LaRoche and Schering-Plough are expected to receive federal approval today to market the drug for a rare type of leukemia.

5 Oil prices tumbled to six-week lows on reports that U.S. inventories of gasoline and other refined products have grown sharply. Analysts and traders said it could be the start of another slide toward $10 a barrel. The growing oil glut is likely to set the tone for OPEC's planned meeting in three weeks.

Bond prices slumped amid fears the Fed would tighten credit and push interest rates higher. The decline, which spread to Treasury bond futures, was fueled by Volcker's remark that he is still concerned about inflation. Stock prices also fell.

Alpha interferon sales are expected to grow rapidly following the FDA's decision yesterday to allow commercial use of the cancer drug. The approval was a boost for biotechnology companies.

U.S. car sales tumbled 10.5% in late May, though the pace remained strong due to incentive programs. Sales of imports continued to surge, rising 7% during the month and capturing 26.6% of the U.S. market.

6 Dennis Levine pleaded guilty to four felony charges in the largest insider-trading case in history. The former investment banker also agreed to cooperate with U.S. authorities who are continuing to investigate the scheme. He faces up to 20 years in prison and $610,000 in fines.

Two former employees of Drexel Burnham and Marcus Schloss pleaded guilty to participating in an insider-trading ring. They also asserted that senior officials of the firms were aware of the trading. Both companies denied the allegations.

GE received government approval for its $6.46 billion takeover of RCA, the biggest non-oil merger in history. Analysts said GE is likely to sell some of RCA and cut its staff once the acquisition is completed.

Most major retailers had modest sales gains in May, suggesting slow improvement in consumers' finances. Some retailers believe it is too soon to predict a sharp rebound in sales for the second half of this year.

9 Federal authorities have widened their probe of the Levine insider-trading case to include a former executive who worked at both E. F. Hutton and Lazard Freres, attorneys said. Also under investigation are investment bankers at Lazard Freres and Goldman Sachs, an arbitrager and a takeover lawyer.

Anderson Clayton rejected a $655 million takeover bid by Bear Stearns and Gruss & Co. The investment firms plan legal action to block the food giant from executing a cash-and-securities offer to holders.

A sluggish economy helped push the civilian unemployment rate up to 7.3% in May from 7.1% in April. Manufacturing was particularly weak. Separately, consumer credit grew at a 9% annual rate in April.

The Fed won't tighten credit because of the weak economy, analysts contend. Some believe the Fed may even ease credit despite the explosive growth in the money supply.

10 Stock and bond prices tumbled amid renewed worries about the economy and interest rates. The broad sell-off was highlighted by a record 45.75-point drop in the Dow Jones Industrial Average, to 1840.15. Some actively traded Treasury bonds declined about a point.

Platinum prices soared $25 an ounce, pushing up other precious metals prices. The surge was prompted by renewed violence in South Africa, the leading platinum producer. On the Comex, gold jumped $9.60 an ounce, to $351.10.

The U.S. launched a major effort to discourage Mexico from limiting interest payments on its $97 billion foreign debt, over a quarter of which is owed to U.S. banks. Mexico is considering such a move because of the sharp drop in oil prices.

An offshore insurance firm was formed by

66 major corporations, reflecting the shortage in liability insurance. The companies have invested a total of $395 million in the venture and expect to receive up to $90 million in liability coverage each.

11 The housing market is being disrupted by the suspension of the FHA's mortgage-insurance program, which reached its credit limit Friday. Officials said the industry is entering its peak sales season plagued by delayed closings and mortgage backlogs. Congress is expected to extend the FHA program soon.

Anderson Clayton's recapitalization plan was delayed by a Delaware court, which may revive a $655 million takeover bid by Bear Stearns and Gruss & Co. The court said the food giant may have misled shareholders about its cash-and-stock offer.

Four more insurers have decided to stop writing new commercial policies in Florida. The move follows the state legislature's approval of a bill to sharply limit premiums.

U.S. Steel opens talks on a new labor contract tomorrow amid signs the No. 1 steelmaker could face its first walkout since 1959. Workers are bitter over U.S. Steel's diversification into oil and its planned partnership with a South Korean steel company.

12 U.S. auto makers are planning relatively high output for the third quarter despite a softening sales outlook. Analysts warn that inventories could swell even if car companies offer another round of sales incentives.

House-Senate conferees failed to reach a compromise on the fiscal 1987 budget and recessed the talks indefinitely. Senate Republicans tried to save higher defense spending amid a worsening deficit outlook and White House resistance to new taxes.

13 Fed member Manuel Johnson said the central bank will consider a discount rate cut if the economy doesn't pick up soon. Johnson is Reagan's nominee for Fed vice chairman.

Platinum futures soared on speculation that the unrest in South Africa will disrupt production of the metal. But other precious metals, which followed platinum's rise earlier in the week, declined on profit-taking.

Retail sales fell 0.1% in May, suggesting consumers remain cautious due to the sluggish economy. The drop surprised economists, who had expected lower energy prices to boost consumer spending. U.S. businesses, meanwhile, plan to re-duce capital spending 1.3% this year, the first drop since 1983.

Treasury bond prices climbed, partly in reaction to the retail sales report. Blue chip stocks ended lower, but the broader market posted a small gain in light trading.

16 Producer prices rose 0.6% in May after falling four consecutive months. Meanwhile, industry output fell a sharp 0.6% and business inventories rose 0.3%. But economists say inflation won't be a serious problem this year, and manufacturers' troubles appear far from over.

Prospects for lower interest rates caused bond prices to soar Friday. The stock market followed suit with the Dow Jones Industrials rising 36.06 points to close at 1874.19.

Beatrice is negotiating to sell its Coca-Cola bottling operation to Coca-Cola Co., sources said. Analysts valued the business at $1.1 billion. The sale of Beatrice's Tropicana line also is said to be imminent.

17 The Senate cleared one of the last major hurdles to approving the tax-overhaul bill this week. An amendment to help the real estate industry was quietly dismantled at the urging of Finance Committee Chairman Bob Packwood, who has led a coalition of senators against major changes in the bill.

Precious metals prices tumbled as speculation eased that the unrest in South Africa would disrupt its mining. Platinum futures fell $17.90 an ounce, while gold dropped $11.10, to $334.80.

18 Housing starts tumbled 7.4% in May, largely due to a slowdown in apartment building. Despite the drop, the biggest in a year, residential construction is expected to remain relatively high for the rest of 1986.

Allied Stores agreed to buy 10 Gimbels department stores from B.A.T Industries for up to $175 million. The sale portends the likely end of the famous chain that competed with Macy's for over a century.

Dome Petroleum will consider putting itself up for sale next year if it can quickly reschedule its $6 billion (Canadian) debt, chairman John Macdonald said. Dome is Canada's largest independent oil and gas company.

A resolution to retain the capital-gains tax break in the Senate tax bill was dropped due to an apparent lack of support. It was another sign that the bill is likely to be approved without major changes.

19 The U.S. economy grew at a 2.9% annual rate in the first quarter instead of 3.7%

estimated earlier, the Commerce Department said. Corporate profits fell 6.6%, rather than 4.9% reported previously, making it the biggest drop in four years.

IBM expects sales and profit to remain lackluster in the current quarter. But chairman John Akers said he sees encouraging signs for 1987 as the trade balance and economy improve.

20 Bristol-Myers recalled Excedrin capsules nationwide and said it is considering withdrawing all of its capsule products from the market. The action follows a second death in the Seattle area linked to cyanide poisoning.

Consumer spending rose a brisk 0.9% in May. But some economists, noting that personal income fell 0.1% last month, questioned whether the strength will last. Bond prices tumbled in reaction to the report.

The World Bank approved a $500 million loan to Brazil to help improve its electric power facilities.

23 May Stores proposed to acquire Associated Dry Goods in a stock swap valued at $2.7 billion. A merger of St. Louis-based May and New York-based Associated would create one of the largest retail chains in the country.

GNP growth has slowed to a lackluster 2.3% rate in the current quarter despite increased consumer spending, a Wall Street Journal survey of economists shows. Doubts are growing that the economy will pick up soon.

Consumer prices rose slightly last month, suggesting inflation will remain moderate for the year. The 0.2% increase in May, which followed three months of declines, reflected a slight rebound in energy prices.

The soft-drink industry's future has been thrown into limbo by the government's decision to oppose Coke's and Pepsi's acquisition plans. The move could open the door for smaller competitors to consolidate.

24 People Express said it is considering selling all or part of the airline. The carrier also said it is seeking ways to boost revenue and cut costs. The statement came in response to a sharp drop in People's stock price and frequent rumors about a possible sale.

Airline stocks soared in reaction to People's announcement. Analysts suggested that fare wars among the major carriers may be over.

Greyhound announced plans to dismiss 3,000 workers and sell or lease all of its 127 bus terminals. The firm also said it would have second-quarter charges of $52 million, but that these will be offset by an $87 million gain from the sale of its ConAgra stake.

The Supreme Court will review whether Texaco has to post a $12 billion bond to pursue its legal battle with Pennzoil. Separately, the court let stand a $9.6 million antitrust verdict against Kaiser Aluminum.

25 Japan's economic output fell 0.5% in the first quarter, the country's first GNP decline in 11 years. The drop was attributed to a sharply stronger yen, which caused Japanese exports to fall 4.9% during the quarter.

Congress passed an emergency bill to revive the FHA's mortgage-insurance program. But the renewal may last only until late July.

U.S. car sales rose 4.4% in mid-June from a weak year-earlier period. Analysts said the sales pace was in line with expectations because of buyer incentive programs, which are scheduled to end soon.

The Tax Bill swept through the Senate by a 97–3 vote. The measure now goes to a House-Senate committee, which will play a crucial role in deciding the final shape of the legislation. Despite some differences, both the House and Senate bills would slash individual tax rates, boost corporate taxes and reduce tax breaks.

Durable goods orders rose 0.4% in May, the first increase since January. But the gain resulted from a big jump in military orders, signaling continued weakness in manufacturing. The report helped fuel a bond rally.

26 ITT Corp. is negotiating to sell a major stake in its telecommunications-equipment business to a French company for about $2 billion, sources said. The sale would give ITT a major infusion of cash and narrow its focus to mainly service businesses.

The Fed voted to allow bank holding companies to expand into several non-banking businesses. It also decided to let banks underwrite certain types of insurance at the same rate as other providers.

Fruehauf agreed to be acquired by a management group and Merrill Lynch in a buyout they valued at $1.1 billion, or $48.50 a share. The truck trailer and auto parts firm rejected a $44-a-share bid by Asher Edelman.

May Department Stores launched a hostile $60-a-share offer for 51% of Associated Dry Goods. Analysts said the bid is intended to pressure Associated into accepting May's proposed stock swap, which is valued at $66 a share, or $2.7 billion.

27 Interest-rate cuts are likely soon in the U.S. and other industrial nations, some analysts predict. They contend that the Fed and other central banks are under pressure because of the sluggish world economy.

Shearson Lehman Brothers was named in an federal indictment accusing a former sales manager and six others of laundering proceeds from an illegal gambling operation.

Fruehauf received a sweetened bid of $49.50 a share from a group led by New York investor Asher Edelman. The bid appears to top a leveraged buyout offer of $48.50 a share that Fruehauf already has accepted.

30 The U.S. trade deficit totaled $14.21 billion in May, including the first agricultural deficit in 20 years. The report indicates that reviving U.S. farm exports will be more difficult than policymakers had expected.

West Germany plans to sell to the public its 19.4% stake in Volkswagen and its 25.6% interest in Veba AG. The holdings are valued at $2.26 billion, making the proposed stock offers the largest in German history.

Economists expect stronger growth and renewed inflation over the next six months, but without much change in interest rates, a Wall Street Journal survey shows. Separately, the dollar is expected to fall further this summer but rebound by year's end.

July 1986

1 Stock prices rose further, pushing the Dow Jones industrials up 7.46 points, to a record 1892.72. The advance was fueled by a bond rally as speculation grew that the Fed would soon drive interest rates lower.

OPEC ended a six-day meeting in Yugoslavia without any agreement on output or pricing. Oil prices fell on world markets in reaction.

U.S. Steel plans to change its name and restructure its troubled steel and iron ore assets into a separate unit. The moves reflect the company's retreat from steelmaking and growing involvement in the energy business.

Southwestern Bell agreed to buy Metromedia's cellular-telephone and paging operations for $1.65 billion. The acquisition suggests the regional Bell companies are moving to dominate the fledgling businesses, particularly in major metropolitan areas. The sale also marks a sudden turnaround for Metromedia.

New-home sales tumbled 11.6% in May, the biggest drop in over two years. But the sales pace remained relatively high, and many economists expect the strength to continue.

2 Leading indicators rose a slim 0.2% in May, casting further doubt that the economy will grow strongly in the second half of 1986. Separately, construction spending increased a brisk 0.8% during the month.

The Dow Jones industrials closed above 1900 for the first time, ending up 10.82 points, at 1903.54. The broader averages also set records, though analysts indicated the rally wasn't as strong as it seemed.

Oil prices tumbled for the second day in a row as traders continued to react to OPEC's failure to cut output. With the cartel in disarray, many expect prices to test the $10-a-barrel level before the end of summer.

Consumer-goods stocks were the big winners on Wall Street in the second quarter. But a sluggish economy hurt shares of firms that supply basic materials such as steel, cement, silver and electronic components.

3 ITT Corp. agreed with CGE of France to combine telecommunications and office-automation businesses. The joint venture, which still needs French government approval, would be the second biggest maker of telecommunications equipment.

The U.S. and Common Market agreed to a six-month truce to avert a trade war over farm products. The cease-fire is aimed at working out a dispute over increased Spanish and Portuguese tariffs on certain agricultural products from the U.S.

Canada is investigating whether it should impose duties on U.S. corn because of charges that American growers are heavily subsidized.

The Farm Credit System said it expects to report a second-quarter loss of about $600 million and another increase in bad assets. The lending agency's continued financial slide is heightening expectations that it will need government funds soon.

The FSLIC's reserves fell $1.1 billion last year as thrift failures remained high and the insurance fund's assets declined in value, a GAO audit says. The report likely will bolster the Reagan's administration's push to recapitalize the troubled fund.

Factory orders fell 0.1% in May despite a sharp increase in defense contracts. Orders for durable goods also fell 0.1% during the month. The latest figures suggest continued weakness in the manufacturing sector.

7 The economy remained weak in June, even though the civilian unemployment rate fell to 7.1% from 7.3%. The industrial sector posted declines in production, new orders and jobs, a survey of purchasing agents showed.

The Big Board agreed "reluctantly" to let companies list more than one class of common stock. The decision, which needs SEC approval, may prompt a review of Amex and NASD listing requirements.

U.S. auto sales jumped 21.6% in late June, capping a robust month and suggesting some unanticipated demand. But sales of Japanese cars slowed as the stronger yen pushed prices higher in the U.S.

The Fed faces intense pressure to drive down interest rates to prevent the economy from slumping into a recession. More economists and lawmakers are urging the central bank to act swiftly, even if West Germany and Japan leave their rates unchanged. The Fed's policy arm will review credit strategy this week.

The Alcoa strike ended after five weeks as two unions accepted a three-year contract that cuts benefits and freezes wages. The accord eases the threat of customer defections from the No. 1 aluminum producer.

China devalued its currency in a bid to revive exports, tourism and foreign investment. The devaluation, which ranges between 13% and 14% against major foreign currencies, is the sharpest in the past year.

8 Stock prices nosedived, sending the Dow Jones industrials down a record 61.87 points, or 3.25%, to close at 1839. The broad decline was attributed largely to worries about the economy and unexpected recommendations to sell stocks from some influential analysts.

Bond prices ended little changed after surging early in the session. One analyst said traders were waiting to see whether the Fed cuts its discount rate to help revive the economy.

Delta Air Lines may enter the bidding war surrounding People Express by offering to buy both Western Air and People's Frontier Airlines unit, sources said. Del-

ta's proposed offer for Western was valued at about $15 a share, or at least $675 million.

Oil prices tumbled to near $11 a barrel amid widespread predictions of further declines. The speculation was prompted by an industry report that OPEC is raising its output.

The dollar plunged to a post-World War II low against the yen in Tokyo trading following the landslide election victory by Japan's ruling party. But the dollar rallied later in Europe and the U.S. to finish higher.

Corn futures plummeted to 13-year lows of under $2 a bushel on dismal export demand and favorable growing conditions for the maturing bumper crop. Other agricultural futures led commodity prices lower.

9 Stock prices continued to lose ground as the Dow Jones industrials declined a further 18.27 points, to 1820.73. Monday's record 61.87-point drop also affected other financial markets in the U.S. and abroad. Gold rose $5.30 an ounce, to $349.70.

Mortgage rates began declining again last month after rising for seven weeks. The average rate on conventional fixed-rate loans fell to 10.61% last week. Analysts said rates soon may return to single digits.

10 The Fed will lower its discount rate soon even if West Germany and Japan don't cut their rates, a top Reagan official predicted. Renewed expectations of a discount rate cut pushed bond prices up sharply.

U.S. oil prices plunged to 15-week lows of less than $11 a barrel on signs Saudi Arabia is continuing to boost output. Analysts, meanwhile, expect world-wide inventories of crude and refined products to grow, damping hopes that prices will rebound.

11 The Fed Reduced its discount rate to 6% from 6½%, the lowest level in almost nine years. The widely expected move reflected the central bank's concern about the sluggish economy, though some economists had hoped for a full-point reduction. Bond traders reacted cautiously.

GE canceled plans by its new RCA unit to build a $200 million semiconductor plant with a Japanese firm. GE also outlined severance plans for 500 RCA employees and said second-quarter earnings rose 5%.

Reagan urged tax conferees not to raise individual rates above those contained in the Senate-passed bill. But most congressional tax writers believe the president will sign any tax bill they send him, even if the top rate is raised to 30% or higher. Farm states are pressing Reagan to expand agricultural export programs. The push by lawmakers and industry groups comes as U.S. farm trade continues to worsen.

14 General Motors is slashing capital spending plans for the next few years to improve profit margins and streamline operations. The cuts are said to reflect GM's concern over losing market share in the U.S. auto industry, which is expected to be far more competitive by 1990.

The Fed's discount-rate cut prompted major banks to lower their prime rates Friday to 8% from 8½%. Analysts say interest rates will have to decline further in the coming months to keep the economy afloat.

Producer prices were unchanged during June—indicating a slack, almost directionless economy, according to many analysts.

GE will restructure its unprofitable turbine business, cutting 1,800 jobs during the next 2½ years. GE said the move will result in a third-quarter charge and bring the business to at least the break-even point next year.

15 Mexico reached tentative agreement with the IMF on a plan to restructure the country's battered economy. The draft accord is a major departure from the austerity programs the IMF has previously required before lending to cash-squeezed nations. A detailed agreement could be signed next week.

IBM's profit fell 7.7% in the second quarter, damping hopes of a rebound in the computer industry this year. The latest decline makes it likely that IBM will post lower earnings for the second year in a row.

Honeywell's earnings slid 31% in the quarter, reflecting the weak U.S. computer market. NCR Corp., however, bucked the industry trend by posting an 18% rise in profit.

Stock prices fell further, partly on IBM's weaker-than-expected profit. The Dow Jones industrials tumbled 27.98 points to 1793.45. The decline by stocks and a gloomy economic outlook sent the U.S. dollar sharply lower, though bond prices rallied.

World oil prices skidded on a report that OPEC's oil production is at a 4½-year high. Prices in the U.S. recovered later after King Fahd urged Saudi oil minister Yamani to seek stability in world oil markets.

Budget Director Miller said the White

House miscalculated defense costs in February and that the budget deficit will grow to about $220 billion, a record, in the current fiscal year.

16 First Oklahoma's bank unit had such a poor loan portfolio that a federal rescue became a certainty several weeks ago. The big energy lender was closed Monday night.

Litton Industries agreed to pay a record $15 million in restitution and penalties after pleading guilty to defrauding the Pentagon.

U.S. car sales surged 8.9% in early July from a weak year-earlier period. Analysts said the gain reflected consumer confidence as well as cut-rate financing and other incentives.

Industrial output fell 0.5% in June, the fourth decline in five months. About half of the drop was due to strikes in several industries, though most sectors remained weak. Retail sales, meanwhile, rose 0.2%, encouraging some analysts.

Oil futures prices soared in record trading following Saudi King Fahd's statement urging stability in world oil markets. But many analysts, citing recent increases in Saudi oil output, expect the rally to fizzle soon.

17 BankAmerica posted a quarterly loss of $640 million, the second biggest in U.S. banking history. The surprisingly huge deficit revived speculation about chairman Samuel Armacost's future at the bank and the possibility that BankAmerica may become a takeover target again.

Soybean futures soared amid indications the Southeast heat wave is spreading to the southern Corn Belt. Wheat futures also surged on a report the U.S. may extend its export subsidy program to the Soviet Union.

Business sales plunged 1.8% in May, the steepest drop in over eight years, while inventories fell 0.3%, the first decline since August. Separately, the industrial operating rate fell to 78.3% of capacity in June as mining and manufacturing remained weak.

18 A bankruptcy petition was filed by LTV Corp., the largest industrial concern ever to seek Chapter 11 protection. LTV, which listed liabilities of $4.22 billion, cited worsening steel and energy operations as well as cash and credit woes. The surprise filing is likely to radically alter the nation's steel industry.

Housing starts fell 0.8% in June to their slowest pace since November. The drop was attributed to higher mortgage rates and a continued low level of apartment construction.

IBM is taking steps to improve earnings after reporting surprisingly weak results for the second quarter. But the moves might not bring any immediate relief.

House-Senate tax conferees began work on a final tax bill amid debate on whether the top individual rate should be set at 27%.

21 The Fed will ignore the basic money supply target this year, suggesting it is aiming policy at avoiding recession while risking rekindling inflation. Still, Fed officials appear to be relatively optimistic about the economic outlook for coming months, according to the Fed's midyear report to Congress.

BankAmerica has begun a plan to shrink its asset size to remain independent. The nation's second-largest bank firm, weakened by its big quarterly loss, is vulnerable to new takeover attempts, some bankers say.

22 The NRC will report in September that the containment shell on certain nuclear reactors designed by GE would fail in nine of 10 types of accidents, an agency official said.

LTV's attempt to reorganize around its successful aerospace and defense unit appears to have initial backing from some major creditors and bankruptcy lawyers. Meanwhile, Wheeling Steel, under Chapter 11, is making an uneven comeback.

23 Economic growth slowed sharply to a 1.1% annual rate in the second quarter from a revised 3.8% in the first period. The pace of real GNP, the weakest since 1982, was mostly due to a deterioration in the trade balance, a drop in nonresidential investment and a smaller accumulation of business inventories.

Bond prices tumbled, partly because of the upward revision in first-quarter GNP and a rise in consumer spending in the second period. The stock market reacted positively to that news, with the Dow Jones industrials rising 16.02, to 1795.13.

Oil prices are expected to drop to $6 to $8 a barrel if OPEC fails to agree on production restraints. Officials and analysts doubt the cartel will reach an accord at its meeting, which opens Monday.

General Motors is internally forecasting a third-quarter operating loss, as the No. 1 auto maker is expected to post flat or lower second-period earnings today. Company sources said GM still should have a third-period profit after gains from tax credits and earnings from its finance subsidiary.

24 Consumer prices rose a sharp 0.5% in June,

while durable goods orders gained 2.1% after four months of declines. Personal income was up 0.1% and consumer spending increased a strong 0.6%. Economists said the results indicate the economy is continuing its slow growth.

Bond prices slumped for the second consecutive day on the economic reports and speculation the Fed won't push interest rates lower soon.

Volcker indicated he has become less worried about a collapse in the dollar, suggesting the Fed may feel less constrained about cutting interest rates. But in testimony to Congress, the Fed chairman's assessment of the economy implied he sees few reasons to cut rates further right now.

GM posted a 16% drop in second-quarter profit and Chrysler's net fell 18%. The declines partly reflected lower vehicle shipments and, for GM, sharply higher costs. Separately, Chrysler said it called off its search to acquire a major high-tech firm.

U.S. auto makers reported a 7.8% decline in mid-July car sales, which was steeper than expected and came despite continuing incentives.

Exxon's operating profit fell 11% in the quarter, as refining and marketing profit buffered a plunge in exploration and production earnings. Meanwhile, Tenneco's net fell 47% on lower oil and gas prices.

25 The planned merger of Santa Fe and Southern Pacific railroads was rejected by the ICC. The decision, which stunned the industry, came after the commission voted that anti-competitive problems outweighed the public benefits. The agency ordered the railroads' parent to shed one or both units.

Ford's earnings jumped 54% in the second quarter, setting a record for any quarter and topping GM's profit for the period. But a current strike at one of the company's plants may hurt earnings in the third quarter.

PepsiCo agreed to acquire Kentucky Fried Chicken from RJR Nabisco for $850 million. The transaction would make PepsiCo the largest U.S. restaurant concern and free RJR to concentrate on packaged goods.

Standard Oil posted a $681 million second-quarter loss because of special charges mainly for write-downs of assets. The company said further write-downs aren't likely unless its oil prices stay below $10 a barrel.

Three oil companies posted sharply lower earnings, reflecting the plunge in oil prices. Texaco's profit was down 40%,

Phillips Petroleum's 93%, and Shell Oil's 35%.

28 Safeway stores agreed to be acquired by the investment firm Kohlberg Kravis Roberts for $69 a share in cash and securities, or $4.2 billion. The proposed leveraged buyout tops Dart Group's takeover bid of up to $64 a share in cash for the supermarket chain. Dart had no immediate comment on the accord.

Tax rates are likely to exceed the Senate's proposed 27% for individuals and 33% for corporations in the final tax-overhaul bill. House-Senate conferees may decide on higher rates in order to keep certain tax breaks.

The Fed is likely to ease credit further in the coming months to help stimulate the economy, many bankers and economists say. Meanwhile, machine tool orders fell 15% in June, ending a lackluster first half.

Future railroad mergers are in doubt following the ICC's rejection of the planned combination of Santa Fe and Southern Pacific. The industry now may be forced to cut costs by changing labor practices.

29 Stock and bond prices fell sharply, as did the U.S. dollar. The sell-off in stocks, blamed largely on slumping bond prices, sent the Dow Jones industrials skidding 36.14 points, to 1773.90, the seventh-biggest point drop ever. Bonds fell partly on the dollar's slide, which worsened as the other two markets declined.

Maxicare Health Plans said it agreed to acquire HealthAmerica for about $400 million. The move would roughly double the revenue and membership of the nation's biggest publicly-owned operator of HMOs.

Pay raises shrank in collective-bargaining agreements reached in the first half of this year, reflecting the continued economic slowdown.

30 Oil ministers of OPEC split sharply over opposing plans to halt the collapse of oil prices. A Saudi proposal for "voluntary" and modest production cuts was countered by Algeria, which urged sharp reductions and binding quotas. The dispute reinforced doubts that the group can work out an effective accord in Geneva.

World oil prices surged in frenetic trading after the Saudis indicated willingness to reverse their eight-month policy of increasing production. But analysts were divided on whether prices will continue rising.

USX Corp. posted sharply lower earnings for the second quarter, citing depressed prices for oil, natural gas and steel. Separately, Armco reported a loss of $384.7 million, including a charge for the possible closing of a joint mining venture with LTV.

GM probably will close three of its 26 car-assembly plants in the U.S. and Canada in the next four years, an official said. But some analysts believe GM may have to close up to six plants because of Asian competition.

Egypt has been so battered by sliding oil prices that it may need an IMF bailout soon to remain solvent. But President Mubarak is in a political bind over implied IMF demands that the government cut food subsidies.

31 United Steelworkers broke off contract talks with USX Corp., heightening prospects for the first nationwide strike against the No. 1 steelmaker since 1959. Separately, the union moved to widen its strike against LTV to a second plant, which could disrupt steel markets.

The U.S. trade deficit widened to $14.17 billion in June as exports rose but oil imports surged. The nation had a deficit in farm trade for the second consecutive month, highlighting the growing farm-policy crisis facing the Reagan administration and Congress.

Non-farm productivity grew at a 1.7% annual rate in the second quarter, compared with a revised 4.3% in the first period. Separately, new-home sales dropped 9.9% in June, the third consecutive monthly decline.

August 1986

1 Japan agreed to let U.S. semiconductor makers gain a far larger share of its market. It also vowed to prevent predatory pricing by Japanese producers. The five-year accord resolves a major trade dispute between the two countries and comes as U.S. chip makers begin to expand their production in Japan.

The dollar sank to a new low against the Japanese yen, helping to push gold up $10.70 an ounce on the Comex, to $362.70, its highest close in more than two years. Gold futures also surged in heavy trading.

Factory orders fell 0.3% in June, the fifth decline in six months. But excluding defense items, which fluctuate month to month, orders rose 0.3%. Meanwhile, purchasing agents said the economy weakened in July.

4 Farm prices rebounded in July, mainly reflecting higher prices for meat and potatoes. Analysts said the drought in the

Southeast contributed to higher poultry prices.

Corporate profits fell 5% in the second quarter, hurt by the sluggish economy and continued write-offs, a Wall Street Journal survey shows. Canadian company earnings were flat, due to weak commodity prices.

The economy is plodding along with few signs of either a recession or a major recovery, the latest figures indicate. The civilian jobless rate fell to 6.9% in July from 7.1% in June, while the index of leading indicators rose a modest 0.3% during June.

Chrysler is raising base prices on its 1987 model cars and trucks up to 5.7%. The increases include a hefty 5.5% price boost on the popular Omni and Horizon America models.

The USX Corp. strike enters its fourth day today amid growing signs that the walkout will be costly and prolonged. No new talks have been scheduled in the dispute.

U.S. computer chip makers reacted cautiously to last week's trade agreement with Japan. Some said the pact, designed to help them compete better against Japanese producers, will be difficult to enforce.

5   The U.S. reached a new textile-trade agreement with South Korea, completing accords with its three biggest foreign suppliers. The new pact allows South Korean textile shipments to the U.S. to grow only 0.8% annually during the next four years.

Reagan's decision to subsidize wheat sales to the Soviets will cost the U.S. about $52 million, the Agriculture Department said. Separately, most grain and soybean futures tumbled, partly because drought conditions were easing in the Southeast.

Members of OPEC approved an Iranian proposal to cut the group's oil output by nearly four million barrels a day. Though the pact still lacked Saudi Arabia's full support, industry officials said it could spark a sharp rebound in oil prices if OPEC adheres to the cuts. OPEC said it will meet today to discuss Saudi conditions for backing the plan.

Oil prices soared 15% in frenzied U.S. trading in reaction to OPEC's move to cut output. But some analysts and traders doubted that OPEC would stick to any agreement for long.

Bond prices rebounded from an early slump on reports Japan will ease curbs on purchases of foreign securities. But trading was light amid concerns about higher oil prices and the Treasury's borrowing needs. The rally helped lift stock prices.

The U.S. dollar firmed against most major currencies amid speculation that it is close to bottoming out, at least for the short run. Traders said Japan's central bank intervened heavily to bolster the dollar.

6   Oil prices rose further as OPEC formally agreed to cut its output for two months. On U.S. markets, prices soared to $15 a barrel, but analysts and traders differed on whether the OPEC accord would sustain higher prices over the long term. The agreement itself already is being strained by economic and political differences among the 13 members.

Stock prices were lifted by the OPEC pact, with oil issues leading the market. The Dow Jones industrial average closed up 7.03 points, at 1777.00. The U.S. dollar also rose.

U.S. auto sales rose 4.3% in late July as manufacturers continued to rely on financing incentives. But analysts were divided on whether demand is strong enough to maintain current production schedules.

7   Goldman Sachs is considering making Sumitomo Bank a limited partner in return for $500 million in capital. The talks illustrate the growing internationalization of securities markets, particularly Japan's drive to penetrate the U.S. market. They also reflect Wall Street's hunger for greater amounts of capital.

The Reagan administration projected a record $230.2 billion budget deficit for the current fiscal year. But it also expects a strong pickup in the economy to help narrow the gap to $171.5 billion in fiscal 1987.

8   Most big retailers reported increased sales for July, but much of the gains resulted from markdowns. Sentiment is growing that consumer spending won't be as strong in the second half as had been expected.

Beatrice agreed to sell its International Playtex division for about $1.25 billion to a group including management. The sale would further shrink Beatrice's debt and accelerate reported plans to go public again.

11   Two more steelmakers took advantage of an 11-day-old strike at USX, boosting some prices 3%. The moves by Bethlehem Steel and National Steel follow a similar rise by Inland Steel. Separately, USX stepped up preparations for a prolonged strike.

Senate approval of a debt-ceiling bill sets the stage for a debate with the House over attached amendments revising the Gramm-Rudman budget law. The changes would restore provisions for triggering automatic across-the-board spending cuts.

GM's robotics venture cut its revenue forecast for the year and plans to reduce its work force one-third. The troubles at GMFanuc reflect order cancellations from GM, which has slowed some automation projects.

Canada agreed with Japan on an auto import pact that paves the way for construction of a car plant in Canada by GM and Suzuki Motors.

12   Hammermill agreed to be acquired by International Paper in a "white knight" bid of $64.50 a share, or $1.1 billion. The offer tops an unwanted $52-a-share bid by a group led by investor Paul Bilzerian. The combination would create the nation's biggest paper concern.

Precious metals prices soared in hectic trading spurred by speculator buying and concerns over South Africa. Gold surged $15.80 an ounce, to $391.40, the sharpest daily advance since March 1985. Platinum futures rose $25 an ounce, to $548.10.

Wickes plans to launch a $74-a-share, or $2.1 billion, tender offer for Owens-Corning. Wickes last week offered to acquire Owens-Corning for $70 a share, but the firm didn't accept or reject that proposal.

13   Air Liquide agreed to acquire Big Three Industries for $1.05 billion, making the French firm a major U.S. industrial gas supplier. The $29-a-share bid is lower than expected, analysts said, but reflects the depressed state of the energy industry.

Stock prices climbed further, pushing the Dow Jones industrials up 24.33 points, to 1835.49. In Tokyo, expectations of lower interest rates helped the Nikkei stock average record its second-biggest point gain ever.

14   Retail sales edged up 0.1% in July, indicating that consumer spending won't continue to carry the economy in the second half. The gain, which followed a revised 0.1% drop in June, came despite plunging auto sales.

15   Money market fund assets plunged $1.25 billion in the week ended Wednesday, the first decline in six weeks. Analysts cited the rise in stock prices and seasonal factors.

The Soviet Union is considering joining such organizations as the IMF and World Bank. The change in attitude is believed part of Gorbachev's effort to modernize the Soviet economy and tap world credit markets.

18   Tax conferees approved a sweeping revision of the nation's tax code that dramatically cuts rates and curbs many loopholes. The bill sets a top corporate tax rate of 34% and a top individual rate of 28%. It raises corporate taxes about $120 billion over the next five years and gives individuals a similar tax cut. The House and Senate are expected to approve the measure next month.

Producer prices fell 0.4% in July, paced by an 11.9% drop in energy prices, and industrial output declined 0.1%. The figures suggest inflation continues to be well under control but manufacturers remain in a slump.

Military and domestic programs face across-the-board spending cuts of at least 5% and 7%, respectively, in fiscal 1987 unless new revenue measures are enacted, estimates show.

19   The new tax bill would take a heavy toll on many manufacturing firms, but could be beneficial for some service industries. Meanwhile, the compromise approved by House and Senate tax conferees contains dozens of transition rules that would benefit certain industries including steel and utilities.

The legislation is a possible boon for many states, which could see their income-tax revenue increase, but would hurt local governments.

The factory operating rate fell to 78.2% of capacity in July from a revised 78.4% in June, partly reflecting a sharp drop by auto producers.

20   The economy weakened in the second quarter, hurt by a worsening U.S. trade deficit. GNP grew only at a 0.6% annual rate, down from the 1.1% estimated earlier and first-quarter growth of 3.8%. Despite robust consumer spending, the economy isn't expected to improve much during the current half.

Bond prices surged on the GNP report, as did interest rate futures. Speculation grew that the Fed will drive rates lower to prevent a recession. The dollar fell sharply.

Seven big retailers posted mixed results for the fiscal second quarter, reflecting sluggish sales and price cutting. Most were in line with expectations, except for an 80% earnings drop at Associated Dry Goods.

21   The discount rate was cut by the Fed half a point, to 5½%, in a further attempt to bolster the economy. The reduction, the fourth this year, brought the central bank's loan fee to its lowest level in nine years. Bankers and economists said further rate declines are likely.

USX Corp. said Australian investor Robert

Holmes a Court intends to acquire up to 15% of the steelmaker. Analysts speculated that the financier may use the stake to force USX to sell him some oil and gas assets.

Housing starts sank 1.8% during July, the third consecutive monthly decline. The pace is expected to slow further in the months ahead. Meanwhile, personal income increased a solid 0.5% last month.

22 Consumer prices changed little during July, as lower energy prices offset higher food costs. Last month's performance followed a 0.5% surge in June. Economists generally expect consumer prices to increase modestly in the months ahead if energy prices stop declining.

U.S. multinationals are taking a hard look at their operations abroad because of the tax-overhaul bill. The measure will affect everything from how companies repatriate billions in foreign profits to where they build factories and create jobs.

Some taxpayers with rental real estate may find their marginal tax rate will remain high under the tax bill. And newly retired federal workers will lose a big benefit.

Short-term interest rates fell following the Fed's discount rate cut. Many analysts expect banks to lower their prime rates as early as today. The dollar drifted lower as traders waited for other nations to follow the Fed move. Stock prices closed mixed.

Platinum prices surged again despite the discovery of huge deposits in South Africa. Increased industrial and speculative demand has pushed the metal's price up over $47 an ounce, or 9%, in the past two days.

25 GM is offering white-collar employees in its North American auto operations "incentives" to resign. The auto maker, facing the highest costs among the Big Three, hopes to cut its white-collar staff 25% by 1989.

Durable goods orders rose 4.3% in July, indicating manufacturers aren't worse off but aren't improving much either. Last month's gain, following June's 0.1% increase, was largely due to sharply higher defense orders.

The Soviet Union offered to reduce oil exports to Western Europe, giving a boost to OPEC's efforts to control production. Moscow's unusual move follows other steps to broaden ties outside the Eastern bloc.

26 The energy drilling slump appears to have bottomed out in the U.S., though there aren't any clear signs of a recovery yet.

Analysts say the apparent firming reflects rising oil and gas prices, the new tax-overhaul bill and lower drilling costs.

Detroit Edison raised the estimated final cost for its troubled Fermi 2 nuclear plant to $4.23 billion. The utility said it plans to ask the state for additional rate relief to recover some of the new expense.

Precious metals surged again, supported by strong dealer buying in the spot bullion market. Platinum continued to lead the market, soaring $16.50 an ounce, to $588.20. On the Comex, October gold rose $7, to $382.80.

Tokyo stocks soared, pushing the Nikkei average up a record 432.78 points, or 2.4%, to 18565.61. Analysts attributed the rally to bargain-hunting that followed a steep decline over the previous three trading sessions.

Car sales were about flat for U.S. producers in mid-August, though analysts said the pace was healthy compared with a strong year-earlier period. Meanwhile, the new tax-overhaul bill is expected to give the domestic auto market a slight boost over the short term.

27 The prime rate was cut half a point, to 7½%, by most major banks, bringing it to the lowest level in about nine years. Other short-term rates also fell, while bond prices rose. The weak economy is expected to lead to even lower interest rates soon.

Stock prices surged in active trading. The Dow Jones industrials gained 32.48 points, to 1904.25, only five points below its high set in July. Some other market indicators set records.

The dollar rallied in response to an improved U.S. economic outlook by some analysts and speculation that the West German central bank will cut interest rates tomorrow.

28 Non-farm productivity fell at a 0.5% annual rate in the second quarter. It was the first drop in output and the smallest growth in hours worked since the depths of the recession in late 1982. Earlier, the rate was estimated to have grown 1.7%. Meanwhile, new construction contracts were nearly flat in July for the second month in a row.

GM is expected to announce a new sales incentive program today to reduce bloated inventories. The plan will include interest rates as low as 2.9% and rebates of up to $1,500.

Bond prices and the dollar slumped amid indications that West Germany and Japan won't cut their interest rates soon.

The drop by bonds accelerated on rumors that the July leading indicators, to be released today, will show a big increase.

Property and liability insurers reported strong first-half earnings, further evidence that the nation's insurance crisis is easing. Profits were buoyed by sharp premium increases and strong securities markets.

29   Frontier Airlines filed for bankruptcy-law protection after its parent, People Express, failed to find a buyer for the grounded carrier. The Chapter 11 petition cast a cloud over the future of People. Meanwhile, the airline pilots union came under criticism for blocking the sale of Frontier to United Air, which could have saved Frontier 4,700 jobs.

Leading indicators rose a sharp 1.1% in July, suggesting a pickup in the economy. But the gain followed a revised 0.4% drop in June, raising doubts about a significant improvement. An inquiry began into rumors the July index was leaked to traders.

Bond prices closed slightly higher after fluctuating widely on rumors about economic reports to be released either today or next week.

GM's new incentive program drew a quick response from consumers, who were lured by an unprecedented auto-loan rate of 2.9%. The program may reduce GM's swollen inventories, but it still leaves questions about long-term production strategy.

Platinum prices soared above $600 an ounce for the first time since 1980, boosted by speculation and hedging. October contracts jumped $21.90, to $614.60. The metal has gained over $163, or 36%, in the past month.

West Germany again defied U.S. pressure to stimulate its economy by cutting interest rates. But renewed speculation that a German rate cut is imminent sent the U.S. dollar higher in late trading.

GROWTH AND INFLATION IN THE INDUSTRIAL COUNTRIES, 1965–85 (average annual percentage change)

Indicator	1965–73	1973–80	1981	1982	1983	1984	1985[a]
Real GDP							
Canada	5.2	3.1	4.0	−4.4	2.8	5.4	4.0
France	5.5	3.1	0.5	1.9	0.7	1.3	1.0
Germany, Federal Republic of	4.7	2.7	0.1	−0.9	1.0	2.6	2.3
Italy	5.2	2.7	0.2	−0.5	−0.4	2.6	2.3
Japan	9.9	4.2	4.2	3.1	3.3	5.8	5.0
United Kingdom	2.8	1.2	−1.4	1.5	3.4	1.8	3.3
United States	3.2	3.0	3.4	−3.0	2.9	7.2	2.5
Industrial countries[b]	4.7	2.8	1.9	−0.6	2.3	4.6	2.8
GDP Deflator							
Canada	4.4	9.5	10.6	10.4	5.1	2.9	3.5
France	5.3	10.5	11.8	12.7	9.8	7.0	6.0
Germany, Federal Republic of	4.7	4.4	3.7	4.6	3.3	1.9	2.3
Italy	5.1	17.3	18.3	17.8	15.0	10.7	9.0
Japan	6.0	6.6	2.8	1.6	0.6	0.6	1.0
United Kingdom	6.2	16.2	11.9	7.4	5.0	4.4	5.0
United States	4.7	7.5	8.9	6.9	4.5	3.6	3.8
Industrial countries[b]	5.1	8.3	8.6	7.5	5.5	3.9	3.9

a. Preliminary.
b. The weights are the US-dollar GDP for each country, divided by the total US-dollar GDP for the industrial countries.

SOURCES: The World Bank and the OECD.

Source: *The World Bank Annual Report 1986.*

Industry Surveys*

The following provides information about a number of industries as well as financial data on companies in each industry. Financial Ratios are defined in the section *Investment and Financial Terms* (page 369).

EXPLANATIONS OF FINANCIAL AND STOCK MARKET INFORMATION

Revenue and Earnings

It should be noted that 12-month figures are trailing ones, calculated from figures shown in the latest interim reports and latest fiscal year reports, when appropriate. Fiscal figures are as reported by the company. Interim figures are based on cumulative data. All earnings per share figures are primary, and are reflected in all calculations. Earnings per share and total earnings figures show earnings from total operations. Earnings are before extraordinary items, but when this is not possible, special earnings footnotes are shown immediately to the right of the company name in the stock tables and these special footnotes are explained as follows:

◇—includes extraordinary gains
◆—includes extraordinary losses
□—excludes extraordinary gains
■—excludes extraordinary losses

5-Year Earnings Growth Rate The annual compound growth rate in primary earnings per share over the last five years computed by the least squares method using logarithms of the earnings per share data, brought up to date through the latest 12 months' earning per share by weighting the first and last points. The five-year earnings growth rate is calculated only for those companies which have all positive earnings per share data for each of the periods used in the calculation. An NC footnote will appear for all companies which do not have a positive earnings per share record for the five-year period. An NC footnote will appear for all companies which have an incomplete record of earnings per share for the five-year period.

Par Growth Rate Retained latest 12 months' earnings per share multiplied by latest 12 months return on common equity, as a percent of latest 12 months' earnings per share. Extra growth rate in EPS can be derived by subtracting par growth rate from 5-year EPS growth rate.

Dividends

Dividends are the latest indicated rate, and the yield is based on that amount and the latest close.

5-Year Growth Rate The figure is arrived at by the least squares method, using dividends actually paid for the first five years and the indicated rate for the sixth point.

Ratios

Profit Margin The profit margin of the company based on latest 12 months' revenue and earnings.

Asset Turnover The latest 12 months' return on total assets divided by the latest 12 months' profit margin.

Return on Common Equity The latest 12 months' earnings divided by stockholder equity from the latest balance sheet.

Return on Total Assets Based on the latest 12 months total earnings and the total asset as reported in the company's latest fiscal year balance sheet.

Leverage Ratio The latest 12 months' return on common equity divided by the latest 12 months' return on total assets.

Debt to Equity The total long-term debt of the company as a percentage of the total common equity of the company, both from the latest annual balance sheet.

Shareholdings

Market Value Latest reported shares outstanding times latest closing price per share of the common stock.

Latest Shares Outstanding Latest reported shares outstanding, adjusted for any subsequent stock splits or dividends.

Held by Banks-Funds The single figure here represents shares held by institutions with equity assets exceeding $100 million—banks, insurance companies, investment companies and managers, independent investment advisors and others. Shares held are adjusted for any stock splits or stock dividends that occur subsequent to the quarterly reporting date of the institutions covered. The data is furnished by Computer Directions Advisers, Inc.

Insider Net Trading Net change in insider holdings—purchases vs. sales—based on the latest SEC report in thousands of shares. 0 means there were no transactions or transactions netted to 0; +0 means transactions netted to purchases of fewer than 500 shares, and −0 means

* The financial data on companies in each industry come from the Media General *IndustriScope*, 301 East Grace Street, Richmond, VA 23219; June 30, 1986.

transactions netted to sales of fewer than 500 shares.

The most recent monthly period for insider transactions is February 11, 1986, to March 1, 1986.

Short Interest Ratio Short interest for the latest month reported, divided by average daily volume for the month corresponding to the report. The figure shows the number of days it would take to cover the short interest if the trading rate continued at the rate of the month covered by the report.

Short interest for the current issue is for the period May 15, 1986, through June 13, 1986.

GENERAL FOOTNOTES

*—As applied to beta figures, an asterisk denotes a co-efficient at least as large as its probable error (i.e., .6745 times the standard error of its mean).

G—Value calculated greater than allowed range.

L—Value calculated less than allowed range.

a—Under current dividend yield, an "a" indicates a stock dividend.

b—Indicates cash plus stock dividend when applied to dividend yield column.

NA—Item not applicable to this stock.

NE—Negative earnings invalidate calculation.

NC—Data required for calculation not available.

NS—Negative stockholder equity invalidates calculations.

NM—No meaningful figure

q—Based on first quarter information.

s—Based on second quarter information.

n—Based on third quarter information.

f—Based on fiscal year information.

*—When applied to 12-month earnings, an asterisk indicates an actual amount for an interim period, other than a quarterly multiple, resulting from a fiscal year change.

Aerospace

Recent Performance and Forecast: Aerospace (SIC 372,376)

(in millions of dollars except as noted)

	1982	1983	1984[1]	1985[2]	1986[3]	Percent Change			
						1982-83	1983-84	1984-85	1985-86
Industry Data									
Value of shipments[4]	66,466	74,823	77,672	89,250	96,582	12.6	3.8	14.9	8.2
Value of shipments (1982$)	66,466	70,876	69,212	75,826	78,600	6.6	-2.3	9.6	3.7
Total employment (000)	685	690	714	744	759	0.6	3.5	4.3	2.0
Production workers (000)	349	341	351	368	376	-2.2	2.9	5.1	2.2
Average hourly earnings ($)	12.23	13.08	13.79	14.12	—	7.0	—	—	—
Product Data									
Value of shipments[5]	60,024	66,229	68,682	79,340	85,930	10.3	3.7	15.5	8.3
Value of shipments (1982$)	60,024	62,631	61,058	67,205	69,699	4.3	-2.5	10.1	3.7
Shipments price index (1982=100)[6]	100.0	105.8	112.3	117.7	123.0	5.8	6.1	4.8	4.5

[1]Estimated.
[2]Estimated.
[3]Forecast.
[4]Value of all products and services sold by the Aerospace industry.
[5]Value of products classified in the Aerospace industry produced by all industries.
[6]Developed by the Office of Aerospace Policy and Analysis, ITA.

SOURCE: U.S. Department of Commerce: Bureau of the Census, Bureau of Economic Analysis, International Trade Administration (ITA). Estimates and forecasts by ITA.

Source: *U.S. Industrial Outlook 1986*, U.S. Department of Commerce.

Aerospace Manufacturing

Company	Revenue Pct. Change Last Qtr %	FY to Date %	Last 12 Mos %	Revenue Last 12 Mos $Mil	Earnings Per Share Last 12 Mos $	Pct. Change Qtr %	FY to Date %	Last 12 Mos %	5-Year Growth Rate %	Par Growth Rate %	Date of Report	Div. Current Rate Amt. $	Yield %	Div. 5-Year Growth Rate %	Payout Last FY %	Payout Last 5 Yrs %	Last X-Dvd Date	Profit Margin	Asset Turn-over	Return on Total Assets	Lever-age Ratio	Return on Equity	Debt to Eq-uity %	Curr-ent Ratio	Mar-ket Value $Mil	Latest Shares Out-standing 000	Held by Banks-Funds 000	Insider Net Trad-ing 000	Short Int-erest Ratio Days	Fiscal Year Ends Mo
																	= s/t x r/a = s/t x r/a x a/e = s/e													
Ind. Group	8.5	6.1	127.1	2,264.3	3.64	-4.4	-5.5	-15.3	5	9	---	1.25	2.3	1	29	29	---	1.6	3.25	5.2	2.58	13.4	18	1.3	32,507	606,865	298,396	+13	1.9	--
Boeing Co	20.2	20.2	27.0	604.0q	3.95	26.7	26.7	36.7	5	10	03-86	1.20	1.9	2	28	26	05-06-86	4.2	1.55	6.5	2.12	13.8	0	1.5	9,777	155,189	89,199	+22	0.8	12
Curtiss-Wright	12.4	12.4	14.4	-40.1q	-8.26	78.3	78.3	NE	NC	-26	03-86	1.20	2.3	5	NE	134	07-07-86	-23.0	.61	-14.1	1.58	-22.3	27	4.1	257	4,859	3,680	0	0.0	12
Fairchild Ind	12.3	12.3	-1.0	-152.2q	-12.07	NE	NE	NE	NC	0	03-86	.20	1.5	-5	NE	NE	06-24-86	-17.3	1.25	-21.7	.00	NM	370	1.6	180	13,714	5,389	+6	0.6	12
Gen Dynamics	2.7	2.7	925.2	365.7q	8.62	-25.1	-25.1	-1.5	29	24	03-86	1.00	1.3	11	11	16	07-14-86	.4	20.50	8.2	3.34	27.4	2	1.2	3,248	42,454	14,436	+10	1.1	12
Grumman Corp	8.9	8.9	13.7	74.6q	2.39	-28.9	-28.9	-34.9	10	7	03-86	1.00	3.4	10	38	26	05-05-86	2.4	1.96	4.7	2.64	12.4	44	1.9	930	31,647	9,579	-30	6.4	12
McDonnel Doug	11.0	11.0	13.9	315.1q	7.83	-33.8	-33.8	-9.9	18	9	03-86	2.08	2.7	16	21	21	06-03-86	2.7	1.59	4.3	2.79	12.0	19	1.1	3,140	40,320	13,430	+4	1.5	12
Northrop Corp	18.9	18.9	32.7	208.2q	4.50	-13.3	-13.3	14.5	41	17	03-86	1.20	2.4	14	26	33	05-27-86	4.0	2.23	8.9	2.61	23.2	4	.7	2,315	46,299	19,461	-9	2.9	12
Rockwell Intl	8.2	12.3	17.5	586.3s	3.92	1.9	-4.0	3.4	16	14	03-86	1.20	2.7	9	27	31	05-13-86	4.9	1.63	8.0	2.49	19.9	22	1.1	6,577	149,498	75,491	+13	1.3	09
Utd Technol	-2.9	-2.9	-7.2	302.7q	2.03	-8.8	-8.8	-58.7	-9	2	03-86	1.40	2.8	5	66	35	05-19-86	2.0	1.45	2.9	2.72	7.9	34	1.7	6,083	122,895	67,731	-2	2.5	12

Recent Performance and Forecast: Airlines (SIC 451)

Item	1982	1983	1984	1985[1]	1986[1]	Percent Change			
						1982-83	1983-84	1984-85	1985-86
Operating revenues (billions $)	36.4	39.0	43.8	47.7	51.5	7	12	9	8
Employees (thousands)	330	329	345	359	370	—	5	4	3
Revenue passenger miles (billions)	259	282	304	325	345	9	8	7	6

[1]Forecast.

SOURCE: Air Transport Association of America; forecasts by ITA.

Source: U.S. Industrial Outlook 1986, U.S. Department of Commerce.

Airlines

Ratio Analysis formula: $s/l \times r/a = s/a \times a/e = s/e$

Company	Rev %Chg Last Qtr	Rev %Chg FY to Date	Rev %Chg Last 12 Mos	Rev Last 12 Mos $Mil	EPS Last 12 Mos $	EPS %Chg Last Qtr	EPS %Chg FY to Date	EPS %Chg Last 12 Mos	EPS 5-Yr Gr Rate	Par Gr Rate	Date of Report	Div Amt	Div Yield	Div 5-Yr Gr Rate	Payout Last FY	Payout Last 5 Yrs	Last X-Dvd Date	Profit Margin	Asset Turnover	Return on Total Assets	Leverage Ratio	Return on Equity	Debt to Equity	Current Ratio	Mkt Value $Mil	Latest Shares Out 000	Held by Banks-Funds 000	Insider Net Trad 000	Short Int Ratio Days	Fiscal Yr Ends Mo
Ind. Group	9.3	11.1	19.8	574.1	.70	NE	-100.0	-40.4	NC	4	---	.16	.7		10	10	---	1.1	1.18	1.3	4.15	5.4	144	1.1	17,136	783,905	291,058	-.52	4.2	--
Air Wisconsin	62.6	62.6	81.9	1.3q	.17	-12.5	-12.5	-73.4	-25	2	03-86	.08		0	0	0	04-02-84	1.0	.70	.7	3.00	2.1	141	1.6	78	7,398	3,334	0	0.0	12
AirCal Inc	-4.5	13.4	13.4	5.1q	.21	-100.0	-61.1	-61.1	NC	7	12-85	.08		0	0	0	00-00-00	1.5	1.80	2.7	2.63	7.1	41	.9	74	8,526	220	0	19.7	12
Alaska AirGrp	19.2	19.2	20.3	19.5q	1.57	-100.0	-100.0	-35.4	16	11	03-86	.16	1.0	0	7	6	07-09-86	4.3	.84	3.6	3.36	12.1	145	2.1	202	12,361	5,449	+1	3.6	12
Aloha Inc	18.0	18.0	11.1	2.7q	1.34	-10.3	-10.3	NE	NC	12	03-86	.08	1.0	0	0	4	12-13-84	2.7	.81	2.2	5.27	11.6	256	1.1	40	1,999	97	0	32.1	12
Am West Airlns	-26.0	-26.0	54.7	7.0q	1.75	886.7	886.7	NE	NC	11	03-86	.08		0	0	0	00-00-00	3.1	.94	2.9	3.72	10.8	196	1.7	90	10,033	2,108	+17	0.0	12
AMR Corp	4.4	4.4	13.1	289.8q	4.86	-96.4	-96.4	11.5	13	13	03-86			0	0	0	01-28-80	4.7	.96	4.5	2.96	13.3	84	1.3	3,235	58,681	46,432	-4	1.5	12
Atlantic SE Air	44.5	44.5	60.7	10.0q	.94	-16.7	-16.7	46.9	84	35	08-86			0	0	0	08-26-85	12.2	1.06	12.9	2.72	35.1	100	1.8	124	10,633	2,158	0	0.0	12
Comair Inc	7.5	34.0	34.7	3.5q	.47	-100.0	-29.9	-29.9	52	17	03-86			0	0	0	08-14-85	5.6	2.00	11.2	1.53	17.1	19	2.0	59	7,700	2,623	0	0.0	03
Conti Airlines	21.7	21.7	34.7	9.00	.17	-100.0	-100.0	-89.3	NC	5	03-86			1	0	0	00-00-00	.5	1.40	.5	.00	NS	-769	1.6	381	24,007	1,804	0	0.1	03
Delta Air Lines	-5.2	-1.6	54.9	109.3q	2.74	-100.0	-85.6	-55.8	NC		03-86	1.00	2.4	1	11	30	05-02-86	2.4	1.25	3.0	2.83	8.5	42	.7	1,665	40,110	25,603	0	1.4	06
Eastern Airline	-6.8	-6.8	4.9	-127.3q	-1.77	-100.0	-67.5	NE	NC	-97	03-86	.08		0	NE	NE	00-00-00	-2.7	1.26	-3.4	28.41	-96.6	1738	.9	552	60,526	5,646	-5	3.0	12
HAL Inc	66.9	66.9	39.5	.30	.13	NE	NE	-67.5	NC	0	03-86	.08		0	NE	NE	00-00-00	1.0	1.00	1.0	8.00	1.6	308	1.0	24	1,871	114	-72	4.8	12
Jet Amer Arlns	3.5	3.5	11.9	-9.3q	-2.13	NE	NE	NE	NC	0	03-86	.08		0	0	0	00-00-00	-9.0	1.02	-9.2	.00	NM	1048	.4	11	4,352	276	0	0.7	12
KLM Airlines	41.1	42.7	42.7	121.9q	3.13	NE	44.9	44.9	62	27	03-86	.10		0	16	7	10-25-84	5.3	1.04	5.5	4.84	26.6	39	1.4	994	51,954	3,141	+1	0.6	03
Midway Airlines	91.5	91.5	38.1	1.3q	.12	NE	NE	NE	NC	3	03-86	.32	.8	0	0	0	00-00-00	.6	1.67	1.0	2.90	2.9	79	1.3	58	7,574	937		0.0	12
NWA Inc	10.6	10.6	9.5	55.9q	2.39	-100.0	-100.0	-35.9	70	-3	03-86	.90	1.8	2	28	23	06-10-86	2.1	1.14	2.4	2.46	5.9	52	.6	1,089	21,774	15,068	-1	1.9	12
Ozark Hldgs	-.7	-.7	1.2	-3.4q	-.29	NE	NE	-100.0	NC	11	03-86	.08			400	23	11-22-85	-.7	1.29	-.9	3.11	-2.8	96	.7	212	11,777	3,679	-1	18.7	12
Pan Am Corp	1.8	-5.4	-5.4	48.8q	.42	NE	NE	NE	NC	22	12-85			0	0	0	00-00-00	1.4	1.43	2.0	5.45	10.9	153	1.1	802	133,625	40,017	+17	3.1	12
People Express	68.9	68.9	64.9	49.3q	1.72	NE	NE	NE	NC	12	03-86	.10	1.5	0	NE	NE	04-25-86	4.4	1.05	4.6	5.09	23.4	257	.7	181	26,340	9,637	+17	0.0	12
Pied Aviation	0	0	11.6	66.7q	3.89	0	0	-7.4	5	5	03-86	.32	1.8	9	7	7	05-05-86	4.4	1.02	4.5	2.96	13.3	109	1.2	666	16,759	8,369	0	0.6	12
PSA Inc	25.0	25.0	16.2	15.4q	1.92	NE	NE	NE	NC	7	03-86	.60	2.4	4	15	32	04-15-86	1.9	.95	1.8	5.61	10.1	269	1.0	131	5,186	2,445	+4	0.4	12
Rep Air	9.9	9.9	15.1	45.4q	1.54	-100.0	-100.0	165.5	4	23	03-86			7	NE	NE	03-03-81	2.6	1.35	3.5	6.63	23.2	323	1.3	668	39,860	14,092	+9	3.7	12
SW Airlines	27.7	27.7	31.0	44.7q	1.44	-55.6	-55.6	-5.3	NC	4	03-86	.13	.6	0	8	9	06-06-86	6.2	.71	4.4	2.18	9.6	82	1.6	673	32,254	23,758	-5	1.3	12
Tex Air	24.3	24.3	33.8	36.3q	1.84	-100.0	-100.0	-9.4	NC	32	03-86	.08		0	0	0	07-06-83	1.8	1.06	1.9	16.58	31.5	616	2.4	702	21,423	9,172	0	5.3	12
Trans Wrld Air	-1.7	1.9	1.9	-208.4q	-6.54	NE	NE	-100.0	NC	-47	12-85			0	0	0	00-00-00	-5.6	1.34	-7.5	6.31	-47.3	286	.8	622	40,789	7,043	0	1.4	12
UAL Inc	23.2	23.2	-2.3	-151.1q	-4.38	NE	-100.0	-100.0	NC	-12	03-86	1.00	1.8	0	NE	NE	05-09-86	-2.2	.86	-1.9	5.11	-9.7	169	1.0	2,452	44,692	25,134	-13	1.6	12
USAir Grp	3.2	3.2	7.6	89.5q	3.30	-100.0	-100.0	-27.6	2	9	03-86	.12	.4	4	3	3	07-10-86	5.0	.92	4.6	2.04	9.4	47	1.7	858	26,905	19,048	+0	2.0	12
Wstn Air Lines	5.7	10.5	10.5	35.4q	.95	NE	NE	NE	NC	0	12-85			0	0	3	08-11-80	2.7	1.63	4.4	.00	NM	1355	.6	455	44,973	13,106	0	8.7	12
World Airways	3.9	3.9	10.0	5.5q	.68	NE	NE	NE	NC	0	03-86	.08		0	0	3	00-00-00	1.5	1.13	1.7	.00	NS	-714	.5	41	9,823	348	0	4.4	12

Recent Performance and Forecast: Apparel and Other Mill Products (SIC 23)
(in millions of dollars except as noted)

	1982	1983	1984[1]	1985[2]	Percent Change		
					1982-83	1983-84	1984-85
Industry Data							
Value of shipments[3]	53,403	55,480	56,055	55,171	3.9	1.0	-1.6
Value of shipments (1982$)	53,403	54,759	54,062	52,594	2.5	-1.3	-2.7
Total employment (000)	1,190	1,190	1,243	1,202	0.1	4.4	-3.3
Production workers (000)	1,010	1,003	1,059	1,021	-0.7	5.5	-3.6
Average hourly earnings ($)	4.90	5.07	—	—	3.5	—	—
Product Data							
Value of shipments[4]	46,692	49,549	48,680	47,999	6.1	-1.8	-1.4
Value of shipments (1982$)	46,692	49,096	47,079	45,802	5.1	-4.1	-2.7
Trade Data							
Value of imports	8,432	9,897	13,916	15,656	17.4	40.6	12.5
Value of exports	1,236	1,049	1,026	954	-15.1	-2.2	-7.0

[1]Estimated except for exports and imports.
[2]Estimated.
[3]Value of all products and services sold by the Apparel and Other Mill Products industry.
[4]Value of products classified in the Apparel and Other Mill Products industry produced by all industries.

SOURCE: U.S. Department of Commerce: Bureau of the Census, Bureau of Economic Analysis, International Trade Administration (ITA). Estimates by ITA.

Source: *U.S. Industrial Outlook 1986*, U.S. Department of Commerce.

Recent Performance and Forecast: Men's and Boys' Outerwear (SIC 231,2321,2327,2328)
(in millions of dollars except as noted)

	1982	1983	1984[1]	1985[2]	Percent Change		
					1982-83	1983-84	1984-85
Industry Data							
Value of shipments	13,364	14,007	14,125	14,153	4.8	0.8	0.2
2311 Men/Boys' Suits/Coats	3,060	3,046	3,253	3,165	-0.5	6.8	-2.7
2321 Men's Shirts/Nightwear	3,478	3,573	3,469	3,355	2.8	-2.9	-3.3
2327 Men's & Boys' Trousers	2,165	2,408	2,545	2,532	11.2	5.7	-0.5
2328 Men/Boys' Work Clothes	4,661	4,981	4,858	5,101	6.9	-2.5	5.0
Value of shipments (1982$)	13,364	13,782	13,474	13,236	3.1	-2.2	-1.8
2311 Men/Boys' Suits/Coats	3,060	2,951	3,069	2,875	-3.6	4.0	-6.3
2321 Men's Shirts/Nightwear	3,478	3,494	3,270	3,153	0.5	-6.4	-3.6
2327 Men's & Boys' Trousers	2,165	2,407	2,500	2,414	11.1	3.9	-3.5
2328 Men/Boys' Work Clothes	4,661	4,931	4,635	4,794	5.8	-6.0	3.4
Total employment (000)	312	307	318	310	-1.4	3.5	-2.5
2311 Men/Boys' Suits/Coats	75.0	70.8	72.5	70.3	-5.6	2.4	-3.0
2321 Men's Shirts/Nightwear	88.7	88.3	92.5	88.9	-0.5	4.8	-3.9
2327 Men's & Boys' Trousers	56.9	59.1	61.8	60.4	3.9	4.6	-2.3
2328 Men/Boys' Work Clothes	91.0	89.0	91.2	90.6	-2.2	2.5	-0.7
Production workers (000)	270	261	271	267	-3.3	4.0	-1.8
2311 Men/Boys' Suits/Coats	64.8	60.4	62.0	60.2	-6.8	2.6	-2.9
2321 Men's Shirts/Nightwear	76.0	74.7	78.8	75.5	-1.7	5.5	-4.2
2327 Men's & Boys' Trousers	49.4	48.7	51.1	50.3	-1.4	4.9	-1.6
2328 Men/Boys' Work Clothes	79.6	77.2	79.6	80.6	-3.0	3.1	1.3

Average hourly earnings ($)	4.96	5.03	—	—	1.5	—	—
2311 Men/Boys' Suits/Coats	5.65	5.94	6.15	6.44	5.3	3.4	4.7
2321 Men's Shirts/Nightwear	4.62	4.78	4.97	5.06	3.5	4.0	1.8
2327 Men's & Boys' Trousers	4.89	4.82	5.22	5.39	-1.5	8.4	3.3
2328 Men/Boys' Work Clothes	4.74	4.69	5.08	5.28	-1.1	8.3	3.9
Product Data							
Value of shipments	10,411	11,053	11,042	11,129	6.2	-0.1	0.8
2311 Men/Boys' Suits/Coats	2,439	2,602	2,699	2,513	6.7	3.7	-6.9
2321 Men's Shirts/Nightwear	2,644	2,701	2,535	2,560	2.2	-6.1	1.0
2327 Men's & Boys' Trousers	1,681	1,831	1,922	1,924	8.9	5.0	0.1
2328 Men/Boys' Work Clothes	3,647	3,919	3,886	4,132	7.5	-0.8	6.3
Value of shipments (1982$)	10,411	10,891	10,543	10,461	4.6	-3.2	-0.8
2311 Men/Boys' Suits/Coats	2,439	2,525	2,553	2,299	3.5	1.1	-10.0
2321 Men's Shirts/Nightwear	2,644	2,642	2,385	2,408	-0.1	-9.7	1.0
2327 Men's & Boys' Trousers	1,681	1,847	1,911	1,884	9.9	3.4	-1.4
2328 Men/Boys' Work Clothes	3,647	3,877	3,694	3,869	6.3	-4.7	4.7
Trade Data							
Value of imports	2,834	3,162	4,150	—	11.6	31.3	—
2311 Men/Boys' Suits/Coats	613	660	894	979	7.6	35.4	9.5
2321 Men's Shirts/Nightwear	1,707	1,882	2,455	2,627	10.2	30.5	7.0
2327 Men's & Boys' Trousers	0.0	0.0	0.0	—	—	—	—
2328 Men/Boys' Work Clothes	513	620	801	857	20.7	29.2	7.0
Value of exports	263	202	203	201	-23.1	0.2	-0.6
2311 Men/Boys' Suits/Coats	31.8	17.2	18.7	17.4	-45.9	8.7	-7.0
2321 Men's Shirts/Nightwear	139	99.3	81.1	79.5	-28.6	-18.3	-2.0
2327 Men's & Boys' Trousers	44.6	42.9	59.5	62.5	-3.8	38.7	5.0
2328 Men/Boys' Work Clothes	47.6	42.9	43.4	42.1	-9.9	1.2	-3.0

[1]Estimated except for exports and imports.
[2]Estimated.

SOURCE: U.S. Department of Commerce: Bureau of the Census, Bureau of Economic Analysis, International Trade Administration (ITA). Estimates by ITA.

Source: *U.S. Industrial Outlook 1986*, U.S. Department of Commerce.

Recent Performance and Forecast: Women's and Misses Outerwear (SIC 2331,2335,2337)

(in millions of dollars except as noted)

	1982	1983	1984[1]	1985[2]	Percent Change		
					1982-83	1983-84	1984-85
Industry Data							
Value of shipments[3]	13,406	13,482	12,930	12,285	0.6	-4.1	-5.0
2331 Women's/Misses' Blouses	3,896	3,804	3,442	3,291	-2.4	-9.5	-4.4
2335 Women's/Misses Dresses	4,623	4,859	4,886	4,544	5.1	0.6	-7.0
2337 Women's Suits & Coats	4,887	4,820	4,602	4,450	-1.4	-4.5	-3.3
Value of shipments (1982$)	13,406	13,194	12,503	11,788	-1.6	-5.2	-5.7
2331 Women's/Misses' Blouses	3,896	3,628	3,193	2,874	-6.9	-12.0	-10.0
2335 Women's/Misses Dresses	4,623	4,764	4,771	4,486	3.0	0.2	-6.0
2337 Women's Suits & Coats	4,887	4,802	4,538	4,428	-1.7	-5.5	-2.4
Total employment (000)	308	318	294	274	3.1	-7.6	-6.7
2331 Women's/Misses' Blouses	92.3	93.1	93.2	89.0	0.9	0.1	-4.5
2335 Women's/Misses Dresses	138	149	128	116	7.8	-14.2	-9.4
2337 Women's Suits & Coats	78.2	76.4	73.2	69.8	-2.3	-4.2	-4.6
Production workers (000)	263	271	246	227	3.2	-9.2	-7.6
2331 Women's/Misses' Blouses	79.4	79.3	79.5	74.8	-0.1	0.3	-5.9
2335 Women's/Misses Dresses	120	130	108	97.3	8.0	-16.4	-10.2
2337 Women's Suits & Coats	63.2	62.1	58.1	55.3	-1.7	-6.4	-4.8

Average hourly earnings ($)	4.53	4.97	—	—	9.6	—	—
2331 Women's/Misses' Blouses	4.42	4.62	4.69	4.80	4.5	1.5	2.3
2335 Women's/Misses' Dresses	4.56	5.18	4.94	5.08	13.6	-4.6	2.8
2337 Women's Suits & Coats	4.60	4.98	5.01	5.25	8.3	0.5	4.8
Product Data							
Value of shipments[4]	10,826	11,143	10,651	9,961	2.9	-4.4	-6.5
2331 Women's/Misses' Blouses	3,545	3,742	3,339	3,033	5.6	-10.8	-9.2
2335 Women's/Misses' Dresses	3,506	3,882	3,860	3,635	10.7	-0.6	-5.8
2337 Women's Suits & Coats	3,775	3,519	3,452	3,293	-6.8	-1.9	-4.6
Value of shipments (1982$)	10,826	10,949	10,373	9,662	1.1	-5.3	-6.9
2331 Women's/Misses' Blouses	3,545	3,553	3,086	2,610	0.2	-13.2	-15.4
2335 Women's/Misses' Dresses	3,506	3,836	3,814	3,650	9.4	-0.6	-4.3
2337 Women's Suits & Coats	3,775	3,559	3,473	3,402	-5.7	-2.4	-2.0
Trade Data							
Value of imports	1,800	2,167	2,778	—	20.4	28.2	—
2331 Women's/Misses' Blouses	1,022	1,282	1,679	1,941	25.5	31.0	15.6
2335 Women's/Misses' Dresses	0.0	0.0	0.0	—	—	—	—
2337 Women's Suits & Coats	779	885	1,099	1,192	13.6	24.2	8.5
Value of exports	119	96.7	92.5	80.7	-18.8	-4.3	-12.8
2331 Women's/Misses' Blouses	30.0	34.1	34.3	27.8	13.7	0.6	-19.0
2335 Women's/Misses' Dresses	55.0	32.4	31.0	26.4	-41.1	-4.3	-14.8
2337 Women's Suits & Coats	34.1	30.2	27.2	26.5	-11.4	-9.9	-2.6

[1] Estimated except for exports and imports.
[2] Estimated.
[3] Value of all products and services sold by the Women's and Misses Outerwear industry.
[4] Value of products classified in the Women's and Misses Outerwear industry produced by all industries.

SOURCE: U.S. Department of Commerce: Bureau of the Census, Bureau of Economic Analysis, International Trade Administration (ITA). Estimates by ITA.

Source: *U.S. Industrial Outlook 1986*, U.S. Department of Commerce.

Apparel

Ratio formula note (under Ratio Analysis headings): r/t × r/a = r/a = r/a × a/e = r/e

Company	Rev %Chg Last Qtr	Rev %Chg FY to Date	Rev %Chg Last 12 Mos	Rev Last 12 Mos $Mil	EPS Last 12 Mos $	EPS %Chg Last Qtr	EPS %Chg FY to Date	EPS %Chg Last 12 Mos	EPS Par Growth Rate	EPS Date of Report	EPS 5-Yr Growth Rate	Div Amt	Div Yield	Div 5-Yr Growth	Payout Last FY	Payout Last 5 Yrs	Last X-Dvd Date	Profit Margin	Asset Turnover	Return on Total Assets	Leverage Ratio	Return on Equity	Debt to Equity	Current Ratio	Market Value $Mil	Latest Shares Outstanding	Held by Banks-Funds	Insider Net Trading	Short Int Ratio	Fiscal Year Ends Mo
Ind. Group	-3.4	5.0	4.1	143.7	.77	253.9	74.9	11.0	0	—	7	.25	1.0	1	28	20	—	2.5	1.80	4.5	2.18	9.8	45	2.9	4,404	175,648	52,979	-150	6	—
Angelica	6.8	6.8	9.1	16.7	1.79	-11.4	NE	NE	.0	04-86	10	.60	2.0	16	32	29	06-10-86	6.1	1.49	9.1	1.57	14.3	23	4.1	274	9,292	3,771	0	1.0	01
Barco of Cal	7.5	-2.5	.0	-.4	-.15	NE	NE	NE	.0	05-07-84	-3	.00	.0		0			-1.8	1.50	-2.7	1.22	-3.3	18	4.4	10	2,106	31	0	0.0	06
Champ Prods	16.3	16.3	8.9	3.3	1.98	-100.0	-100.0	482.4	5	03-86	1	.72	2.0	0	50	69	04-29-86	2.7	2.07	5.6	1.50	8.4	18	4.1	60	1,645	539	-1	0.7	12
Eagle Clothes	36.3	19.1	13.2	-2.1	-.33	-41.9	-100.0	-33.6	19	04-86	-9	.00	.0	0	0	0	00-00-00	-1.9	2.00	-3.8	2.39	-9.1	38	2.7	16	6,321	1,409	0	0.2	07
Farah Mfg	19.3	21.4	19.6	8.7	1.46	-44.4	-44.4	-33.6	19	04-86	3	.88	3.5	0	49	20	07-29-86	2.5	1.80	4.5	2.69	12.1	38	1.6	145	5,849	1,354	-13	0.0	10
Garan Inc	-14.2	-25.4	-26.2	3.8	1.19	-10.5	NE	-63.4	-8	03-86	12	.60	2.2	12	70	37	05-19-86	3.1	1.29	4.0	1.45	5.8	14	4.1	81	2,972	1,007	-2	0.7	09
Genesco Inc	-3.8	-3.8	-2077.7	-34.3	-2.63	NE	NE	NE	.0	04-86	70	.00	.0	0	0	0	00-00-00	-6.4	1.88	-12.0	.00	NM	367	3.1	45	15,081	2,895	0	2.5	01
Hampton Ind	17.4	17.4	1.8	4.8	1.13	86.2	86.2	28.4	12	03-86	0	.00	.0	0	0	0	06-10-86	3.0	1.90	5.7	2.07	11.8	74	5.0	57	3,376	142	0	1.8	12
Johnston Ind	11.1	-1.2	13.5	2.7	2.74	23.6	23.6	28.6	37	04-86	0	.00	.0	0	0	0	00-00-00	3.7	1.60	12.3	3.05	37.5	115	2.8	59	3,212	187	-39	0.1	06
Kellwood Co	-45.4	-14.7	-14.7	19.2	3.03	4.7	19.8	19.8	60	04-86	28	.76	2.3	28	22	20	06-05-86	3.8	1.68	6.4	3.13	20.0	129	3.1	198	5,906	2,850	0	2.0	04
Kennington Ltd	2.9	2.9	-9.0	-7.6	-1.35	-100.0	NE	-100.0	-12	07-09-80	0	.00	.0	0	0	0	07-09-80	-25.3	.38	-9.5	1.22	-11.6	12	14.6	41	5,688	657	0	0.0	12
Littlefield Adam	15.0	15.0	.0	-.0	-.04	NE	NE	NE	.0	05-24-83	0	.00	.4	0	23	NE	05-24-83	.0	NC	.0	NC	.0	70	3.3	4	1,074	47	0	0.0	12
Liz Claiborne	40.5	40.5	37.5	66.5	1.56	35.9	35.9	38.1	52	03-86	1	.18	.4	12	12	12	04-08-86	10.8	2.77	29.9	1.37	40.9	6	4.4	2,015	42,666	20,624	-100	0.0	01
Manhattan Ind	-17.2	-17.2	-15.4	-2.3	-.50	NE	NE	NE	36	09-08-86	0	.20	1.2	0	NE	26	09-08-86	-.5	2.20	-1.1	2.91	-3.2	75	1.9	83	5,049	2,663	-6	4.0	01
Noel Industries	1.8	14.9	-3.2	.2	.21	NE	NE	NE	-4	04-86	1	.00	.0	0	0	0	00-00-00	.7	1.86	1.3	2.23	2.9	36	2.0	7	1,134	7	-5	0.3	10
Oxford Inds	-10.0	-6.8	-8.7	7.9	.72	250.0	12.9	-33.3	-1	02-86	19	.46	2.6	19	64	21	05-09-86	1.5	2.27	3.1	1.88	6.4	16	2.1	196	11,120	5,596	0	0.7	05
Phil-Van Heu	-13.3	-13.3	-9.3	17.1	2.73	46.3	46.3	21.3	22	08-15-86	7	.40	1.0	7	16	16	08-15-86	3.2	2.22	7.1	1.59	11.3	13	3.1	244	6,110	1,432	0	0.4	01
Pope Evan Rob	-76.4	-75.9	-133.0	-19.1	-2.33	-100.0	-100.0	8.3	-61	02-01-83	0	.00	.0	0	0	0	02-01-83	23.9	-1.07	-25.6	2.38	-61.0	103	3.4	24	7,902	1,021	0	0.0	06
Russ Togs	3.9	3.9	1.4	11.7	2.21	33.3	33.3	8.3	10	06-24-86	5	.76	2.3	5	37	35	06-24-86	4.2	1.98	8.3	1.51	12.5	2	2.8	163	5,023	2,811	0	0.6	01
Salant Corp	-4.2	-4.2	-22.2	3.6	1.09	NE	NE	NE	21	07-30-84	0	.00	.0	0	0	NE	07-30-84	2.5	1.56	3.9	5.44	21.2	0	7.4	55	3,309	485	0	0.2	11
Sanmark Star	16.2	22.1	22.0	2.9	.41	25.0	33.3	36.7	17	01-28-86	0	.00	.0	17	0	0	01-28-86	4.8	1.65	7.9	2.13	16.8	35	2.2	59	8,034	355	0	0.1	06
Sup Surgical	4.1	4.1	12.5	4.1	1.67	3.3	3.3	11.3	9	05-14-86	11	.40	1.8	9	22	21	05-14-86	4.1	1.80	7.4	1.65	12.2	29	4.0	53	2,431	708	+10	0.0	12
Tultex Cp	28.3	28.0	8.7	19.9	2.21	NE	1271.4	142.9	18	06-02-86	9	.48	1.1	18	33	26	06-02-86	6.9	1.65	11.4	2.04	23.2	49	3.5	387	9,009	837	+5	0.0	11
Wilson Bros	-14.1	-14.1	-10.1	-1.6	-.49	-100.0	-100.0	NE	-67	00-00-00	0	.00	.0	0	0	0	00-00-00	-2.6	1.50	-3.9	17.10	-66.7	913	2.2	4	3,321	22	0	0.0	12
Winter, Jack	21.6	21.6	-4.5	1.5	.41	27.3	27.3	NC	4	06-16-86	0	.20	2.5	0	0	NE	06-16-86	3.6	1.42	5.1	1.51	7.7	1	2.0	29	3,646	1,213	0	1.4	12
Wolf, Howard	8.7	-8.5	.0	-.2	-.25	100.0	-50.0	-100.0	4	08-09-84	0	.00	.0	0	0	NE	08-09-84	-2.2	1.27	-2.8	1.36	-3.8	12	4.4	6	1,081	19	+1	0.0	05
Work Wear Inc	3.4	3.4	7.0	10.4	3.35	52.4	52.4	70.1	19	01-28-86	26	.00	.0	1	17	25	01-28-86	4.3	1.60	6.9	2.81	19.4	111	3.1	87	3,091	297	0	0.7	12

Recent Performance and Forecast: Savings Institutions (SIC 603 and 612)
(in billions of dollars except as noted)

	1982	1983	1984	1985¹	1986²	Percent change		
						1983-84	1984-85	1985-86
Assets	867	1,008	1,185	1,265	1,379	17.6	6.8	9.0
Mortgages held	568	614	703	753	817	14.5	7.1	8.5
Mortgage-backed securities	76	111	128	125	137	15.3	-2.3	9.5
Deposits	710	840	968	1,040	1,134	15.2	7.4	9.0
Net Worth	34	43	49	49	69	14.0	18.4	19.0
New net savings	-17	64	51	-7	-40		-20.3	-113.7
Mortgages made	61	152	184	173	164	21.1	-6.0	-5.0
Number of institutions	3,767	3,571	3,550	3,625	3,752	-0.6	2.1	3.5
Number of offices	24,742	25,010	25,019	25,540	26,230	0.0	2.1	2.7
Employment (000)	343	368	391	435	470	6.3	11.3	8.0

SOURCE: Federal Home Loan Bank Board, National Council of Savings Institutions, Bureau of Labor Statistics.

¹Estimated
²Forecast

Source: *U.S. Industrial Outlook 1986*, U.S. Department of Commerce.

Recent Performance and Forecast: Commercial Banking (SIC 602)
(in billions of dollars except as noted)

	1982	1983¹	1984	1985²	1986³	Percent Change			
						1982-83	1983-84	1984-85	1985-86
Assets	1,820	2,094	2,277	2,527	2,754	15.1	8.7	11.0	9.0
Loans	1,001	1,249	1,464	1,684	1,852	24.8	17.2	15.0	10.0
Investments	370	431	378	416	466	16.5	-12.3	10.0	12.0
Deposits	1,362	1,504	1,631	1,843	1,990	10.8	8.1	13.0	8.0
Employment (000)	1,507	1,506	1,520	1,550	1,565	—	0.9	2.0	1.0

¹Revised Series.
²Estimated.
³Forecast.

SOURCE: Board of Governors of the Federal Reserve System. Estimates and forecasts by U.S. Department of Commerce, International Trade Administration.

Source: *U.S. Industrial Outlook 1986*, U.S. Department of Commerce.

Middle Atlantic Banks

Company	Revenue Last Qtr %	Revenue FY to Date %	Revenue Last 12 Mos %	Revenue Last 12 Mos $Mil	Earnings Per Share Last 12 Mos $	Earnings Last Qtr %	Earnings FY to Date %	Earnings Last 12 Mos %	5-Year Growth Rate %	Par Growth Rate %	Date of Report	Div Current Rate Amt $	Div Yield %	Div 5-Year Growth Rate %	Payout FY %	Payout Last 5 Yrs %	Last X-Dvd Date	Profit Margin	Asset Turnover	Return on Total Assets	Leverage Ratio	Return on Equity	Debt to Equity %	Current Ratio	Market Value $Mil	Latest Shares Outstndg 000	Held by Banks-Funds 000	Insider Net Trading 000	Short Interest Ratio Days	Fiscal Year Ends Mo
																		r/t x t/a = s/a x a/e = r/e												
Ind. Group	8.5	10.5	7.6	1,101.0	3.39	10.5	8.0	62.3	19	9	--	1.27	3.1	1	35	35	--	8.5	.09	8	18.75	15.0	43	NC	12,939	313,441	93,024	+38	.6	--
Citzns Fst Bcp	15.5	15.5	9.4	18.6q	1.48	41.0	-41.0	6.5	31	11	03-86	.60	2.7b	5	26	37	07-14-86	12.4	.10	1.2	15.92	19.1	1	NA	235	10,550	1,020	0	0.0	12
Contl Bancorp	3.3	3.3	11.6	53.2q	4.84	17.6	17.6	12.6	7	10	03-86	2.04	3.1b	7	42	46	05-27-86	11.1	.10	1.1	15.45	17.0	4	NA	724	10,983	956	+0	0.0	12
CoreStates Fnl	8.8	8.8	-2.8	101.5q	3.06	22.2	22.2	-6.1	13	9	03-86	1.24	3.2	10	38	35	06-02-86	9.5	.09	.9	15.89	14.3	35	NA	1,167	30,210	12,228	+33	0.0	12
Equimark Corp	-11.3	-11.3	-4.8	4.8q	.14	NE	NE	NE	NC	5	03-86	.00	.0	0	0	NE	09-04-81	1.6	.13	.2	25.00	5.0	138	NA	195	30,618	2,042	+1	0.7	12
Fidelcor Inc	-1.9	-1.9	-1.5	49.6q	4.18	-1.9	-1.9	8.0	19	11	03-86	1.40	3.1	47	31	26	04-24-86	7.6	.09	.7	23.43	16.4	45	NA	521	11,717	5,083	-7	0.0	12
Fst Fdl Bcp	12.1	12.1	1.8	99.9q	3.66	8.4	8.4	3.4	7	8	03-86	1.56	3.9	7	41	37	04-01-86	9.2	.09	.9	18.50	14.8	20	NA	1,029	25,963	6,884	0	4.2	12
Fst Jersey Natl	23.8	23.8	15.9	32.5q	4.48	.9	.9	3.2	11	9	03-86	1.80	3.2	6	40	41	03-03-86	9.1	.10	.9	16.78	15.1	19	NA	396	6,994	2,065	+0	0.0	12
Fst Penn Cp	-4.7	-4.7	-4.5	17.1q	-.11	NE	NE	NE	NC	11	03-86	.00	.0	0	0	0	03-03-80	3.1	.10	.3	36.33	10.9	97	NA	194	23,179	3,057	0	3.5	12
Horizon Bncp	10.3	10.3	4.6	32.4q	3.54	23.8	23.8	18.0	9	11	03-86	1.28	2.4	7	35	37	07-09-86	10.2	.11	1.1	16.36	18.0	7	NA	456	8,677	1,863	+2	0.0	12
HUBCO Inc	-27.8	-27.8	-15.9	4.2q	2.44	64.9	64.9	56.4	27	11	03-86	.76	2.2	12	32	40	05-19-86	11.4	.09	1.0	16.60	16.6	4	NA	59	1,725	26	0	0.0	12
Mellon Bank	0	0	1.8	201.7q	7.13	0	0	20.8	2	8	03-86	2.76	3.9	7	38	36	04-29-86	6.3	.10	.6	20.50	12.3	70	NA	1,894	27,109	15,781	+1	1.4	12
Meridian Bcp	13.2	29.4	29.2	57.6f	4.68	1.6	21.9	21.9	10	9	12-85	1.80	3.3	12	37	34	06-09-86	8.8	.10	.8	17.00	15.3	31	NA	667	12,290	4,195	-1	0.0	12
Midlantic Banks	34.1	34.1	39.7	98.7q	5.00	16.8	16.8	48.8	9	13	03-86	1.24	2.5	7	24	24	06-25-86	10.4	.10	1.0	17.00	17.0	37	NA	982	20,083	4,399	-4	0.0	12
Natl Cm Bk NJ	12.7	12.7	11.3	23.6q	9.13	22.3	22.3	27.5	29	13	03-86	3.00	2.7	4	34	47	06-09-86	12.6	.10	1.2	16.50	19.8	153	NA	292	2,580	93	0	0.0	12
Pennbancorp	52.8	52.8	14.3	23.7q	3.34	44.3	44.3	26.0	11	8	03-86	1.20	2.1	7	35	37	05-09-86	9.9	.08	.8	14.75	11.8	25	NA	492	8,742	2,198	+10	0.0	12
PNC Financial	12.0	12.0	16.0	197.9q	4.05	18.7	18.7	16.7	13	11	03-86	1.52	3.4	12	32	33	06-06-86	10.7	.10	1.1	15.45	17.0	4	NA	2,122	47,552	24,815	0	0.0	12
SW Bank	NA	NA	.0	NA	NA	NA	NA	NA	NA	NC	00-00	.00	.0	NA	NA	NA	00-00-00	NA	NC	NA	NC	NA	NA	NA	13	3,586	2	+1	NA	12
Union Natl Cp	.9	3.2	3.2	20.7f	2.63	29.8	19.0	19.0	5	7	12-85	1.14	2.5	7	39	41	05-19-86	8.2	.10	.8	15.00	12.0	21	NA	365	7,857	3,422	+1	0.9	12
Utd Jer Bk	27.9	27.9	9.0	40.0q	3.32	7.4	7.4	11.4	13	12	03-86	1.16	2.6	8	33	33	07-01-86	8.8	.10	.9	20.22	18.2	18	NA	639	14,564	2,738	0	0.0	12
Valley Natl Bcp	-18.5	28.2	28.5	23.3f	2.74	-31.1	-39.1	-39.1	36	12	12-85	1.27	2.2	0	39	33	05-29-86	17.3	.10	1.7	13.06	22.2	0	NA	499	8,462	157	+1	0.0	12

Banking

Ratio Analysis formula: $s/r \times r/a \times r/a \times a/e = r/e$

Units: Revenue & Earnings $Mil; Per Share $; growth/payout/yield %; Market Value $Mil; Shares/Held/Insider in 000; Short Interest Ratio in Days; Fiscal Year Ends in Mo.

Company	Rev %Chg Last Qtr	Rev %Chg FY to Date	Rev %Chg Last 12 Mos	Earn Last 12 Mos $Mil	EPS Last 12 Mos $	EPS %Chg Last Qtr	EPS %Chg Last FY to Date	EPS %Chg Last 12 Mos	Earn 5-Yr Growth	Par Growth	Date of Report	Div Amt $	Div Yield %	Div 5-Yr Growth	Payout Last FY	Payout Last 5 Yrs	Last X-Dvd Date	Profit Margin	Asset Turnover	Return on Total Assets	Leverage Ratio	Return on Equity	Debt to Eq	Curr Ratio	Market Value $Mil	Latest Shares Out	Held by Banks-Funds	Insider Net Trading	Short Int Ratio	Fiscal Yr Ends
New York Banks																														
Ind. Group	-30.0	-23.8	-7.1	3,995.6	6.46	12.1	11.6	17.8	8	10	--	2.12	3.9	1	31	33	--	6.5	.11	.7	21.00	14.7	136	NC	33,534	609,088	348,890	-307	2.4	--
Bank of NY Co	14.6	14.6	2.6	138.6q	6.69	18.0	18.0	3.1	11	11	03-86	2.28	3.6	8	33	33	04-14-86	8.4	.08	.7	24.14	16.9	52	NA	1,283	20,160	8,454	+6	3.5	12
Bankers Tr NY	4.8	4.8	-4.3	394.7q	5.66	19.7	19.7	14.3	7	12	03-86	1.49	3.1	10	25	27	06-25-86	8.3	.10	.8	21.00	16.8	69	NA	3,306	68,335	45,236	-803	1.2	12
Chase Manhttn	5.9	5.9	-1.6	574.6q	6.56	11.6	11.6	39.9	7	10	03-86	2.05	4.6	6	30	33	04-24-86	5.8	.12	.7	21.57	15.1	74	NA	3,501	78,904	51,982	+10	1.1	12
Chem NY Corp	3.5	3.5	-4.3	403.1q	7.58	14.9	14.9	15.2	7	11	03-86	2.60	5.1	10	33	34	06-09-86	7.1	.10	.7	23.00	16.1	64	NA	2,529	49,339	30,260		6.1	12
Citicorp	-99.9	-99.9	-19.3	721.3q	6.97	-7.4	-7.4	2.0	12	7	03-86	2.46	4.1	10	31	34	03-21-86	4.2	.10	.4	27.50	11.0	278	NA	7,730	129,377	88,620	+176	1.7	12
Irving Bk Cp	-2.6	-2.6	-5.9	119.1q	6.32	12.5	12.5	23.0	3	9	03-86	2.08	3.8	7	32	33	05-27-86	5.9	.10	.6	22.50	13.5	69	NA	971	17,855	6,225	+1	0.0	12
KeyCorp	38.8	38.8	39.8	72.4q	2.70	15.8	15.8	17.9	14	10	03-86	1.00	3.6	9	32	35	06-24-86	9.5	.11	1.0	15.30	15.3	34	NA	698	25,253	3,399	-3	0.0	12
Mfrs Hanover	-3.7	-3.7	-4.0	409.4q	8.32	-2.7	-2.7	11.8	5	9	03-86	3.24	6.3	5	38	38	06-26-86	4.9	.10	.5	28.20	14.1	272	NA	2,134	41,344	25,206	-1	3.4	12
Marine Midland	11.0	11.0	-.6	137.4q	6.60	40.0	40.0	47.7	7	9	03-86	2.04	3.9	15	28	29	06-02-86	5.4	.11	.6	21.00	12.6	81	NA	995	19,136	13,656	+2	4.1	12
Morgan, J.P.	9.8	9.8	1.6	774.7q	8.52	38.4	38.4	36.1	13	13	03-86	2.45	2.8	9	28	33	06-17-86	11.5	.12	1.1	17.00	18.7	34	NA	7,679	87,389	58,104	+64	1.7	12
Norstar Bncp	6.0	6.0	-3.7	96.7q	2.64	17.2	17.2	10.0	3	-3	03-86	1.28	4.3	13	46	45	06-03-86	12.5	.09	1.1	13.36	14.7	42	NA	1,031	34,367	6,872	+279	0.0	12
Rep NY	4.0	10.5	10.5	122.1†	3.98	19.3	8.7	8.7	2	7	12-85	1.12	2.4	2	27	26	03-10-86	9.8	.08	.8	20.13	16.1	113	NA	1,185	25,896	7,381	0	0.0	12
Sterling Bncp	-5.9	22.1	21.6	7.5†	1.40	17.1	22.8	22.8	3	12	12-85	.80	5.5	2	55	63	06-09-86	10.3	.09	.9	17.00	15.3	20	NA	80	5,491	1,040	-61	10.3	12
US Trust	5.1	5.5	6.9	24.0m	3.75	17.4	12.8	13.3	11	12	09-85	1.32	2.0	11	47	39	07-03-86	8.6	.12	1.0	18.30	18.3	23	NA	412	6,242	2,455	+23	0.0	12
Pacific States Banks																														
Ind. Group	-40.3	-32.2	-9.9	670.2	1.61	-11.9	-21	-49.2	-14	2	--	.96	2.8	1	47	43	--	2.3	.09	.2	27.50	5.5	122	NC	13,776	395,438	176,464	-0	1.0	--
Bancp Hawaii Inc	21.0	21.0	11.5	40.8q	4.54	22.8	22.8	13.5	11	11	03-86	1.36	2.5	6	30	31	05-19-86	8.5	.11	.9	17.33	15.6	14	NA	498	9,063	4,723	+1	0.0	12
BankAmerica	-99.9	-99.9	-27.3	-451.1q	-3.00	-50.8	-50.8	-100.0	-12	-12	03-86	.00	0.0	-3	NE	31	11-07-85	-4.3	.09	-.4	29.50	-11.8	54	NA	2,388	152,840	44,982	+7	1.7	12
BSD Bancorp	NA	NA	-6.5	NA	NA	NA	NA	NA	NC	NC	12-85	.00	0.0	NA	NA	NA	00-00-00	NA	NA	NA	NC	NA	NA	NA	10	2,954	0	0	NA	12
Calif Fst Bk	.7	1.8	1.6	25.6f	2.26	13.0	13.6	13.6	-5	5	12-85	1.08	3.5	1	48	54	06-09-86	4.7	.11	.5	18.20	9.1	93	NA	361	11,564	9,351	0	NA	12
City Natl	5.9	5.9	2.3	25.1q	2.74	16.7	16.7	23.4	10	9	03-86	1.04	2.3b	15	31	33	06-24-86	9.6	.10	.5	17.00	17.0		NA	410	9,158	1,836	-18	0.0	12
Fst Hawaiian	8.5	8.5	.6	28.6q	4.26	22.2	22.2	14.5	13	11	03-86	1.60	3.0	6	36	37	05-23-86	9.4	.11	.9	18.89	17.0	26	NA	361	6,692	2,039	+4	0.0	12
Fst Interstate	3.1	3.1	3.7	320.8q	6.98	8.9	8.9	10.6	3	8	03-86	2.66	4.3	6	36	37	06-12-86	6.1	.11	.7	19.14	13.4	125	NA	2,697	43,503	29,689	+8	0.5	12
Grt Amer First	15.6	15.6	18.8	53.9q	2.82	97.5	97.5	143.1	NC	12	06-85	.40	1.7	0	13	10	06-02-86	5.9	.12	.7	20.00	14.0	308	NA	438	18,853	9,550	-5	5.2	12
Orbanco Fnl Svcs	-9.3	-7.7	2.6	-33.5q	-11.36	NE	NE	NE	NC	41	06-85	.00	0.0	0	0	0	07-11-83	-21.5	.10	-2.5	16.36	-40.9	157	NA	44	2,962	318	0	0.0	12
Rainier Bcp	3.0	3.0	-.2	66.1q	3.28	2.7	2.7	2.8	9	9	03-86	1.08	2.9	10	31	31	04-30-86	8.0	.10	.8	16.50	13.2	47	NA	747	20,259	9,328	0	0.0	12
Security Pac °	8.9	8.9	4.4	337.2q	4.46	11.0	11.0	10.4	10	10	03-86	1.48	4.1	10	30	30	04-23-86	6.0	.10	.6	24.50	14.7	153	NA	2,794	76,548	41,896	-3	1.2	12
US Bcp	-.2	6.2	6.2	66.2q	3.33	32.4	32.4	9.2	1	8	03-86	1.00	2.5	8	30	29	03-03-86	8.1	.10	.8	14.38	11.5	54	NA	781	19,897	10,103	0	0.0	12
Wells Fargo	-1.0	1.2	1.2	190.0f	8.30	14.1	21.2	21.2	10	10	12-85	2.72	2.6	4	28	32	06-24-86	5.6	.10	.6	24.17	14.5	320	NA	2,246	21,135	12,649	+7	0.6	12

Value of Shipments by Selected Construction Materials Industries, 1984-86

SIC	Industry	Millions of 1982 Dollars			Percent Change		
		1984[1]	1985[1]	1986[2]	1983-84	1984-85	1985-86
3211	Flat glass	2,000	2,020	2,060	8	1	2
3241	Cement, hydraulic	4,015	4,055	4,155	10	1	2
3251	Brick and structural clay tile ...	830	840	880	7	7	5
3271	Concrete block and brick	1,635	1,700	1,790	5	4	5
3272	Concrete products, n.e.c.	4,185	4,415	4,600	14	6	4
3273	Ready-mixed concrete	10,120	10,675	11,240	14	5	6
3275	Gypsum products	1,700	1,680	1,750	10	−1	4
3441	Fabricated structural metal	9,180	9,172	9,310	13	0	2
3448	Prefabricated metal buildings and components	3,005	3,065	3,095	29	2	1

[1]Estimate.
[2]Forecast.

SOURCE: Bureau of Labor Statistics, and U.S. Department of Commerce: International Trade Administration.

Source: *U.S. Industrial Outlook 1986*, U.S. Department of Commerce.

Recent Performance and Forecast: Hydraulic Cement (SIC 3241)
(in millions of dollars except as noted)

	1982	1983	1984[1]	1985[2]	1986[3]	Percent Change			
						1982-83	1983-84	1984-85	1985-86
Industry Data									
Value of shipments[4]	3,542	3,683	4,150	4,365	—	4.0	12.7	5.2	—
Value of shipments (1982$)	3,542	3,666	4,015	4,055	4,155	3.5	9.5	1.0	2.5
Total employment (000)	24.6	23.1	24.0	24.5	—	-6.1	3.9	2.1	—
Production workers (000)	19.1	17.8	19.0	19.5	—	-6.8	6.7	2.6	—
Average hourly earnings ($)	12.98	13.50	13.87	13.63	—	4.0	2.7	-1.7	—
Product Data									
Value of shipments[5]	3,474	3,599	4,055	4,265	—	3.6	12.7	5.2	—
Value of shipments (1982$)	3,474	3,582	3,935	3,975	4,070	3.1	9.9	1.0	2.4
Shipments price index (1982=100)[6]	100.0	100.5	104.1	108.4	—	0.5	3.6	4.1	—
Trade Data									
Value of imports	111	162	294	480	—	45.8	81.9	63.2	—
Import/new supply ratio[7]	0.031	0.043	0.068	0.101	—	39.0	57.3	49.5	—
Value of exports	43.5	29.4	23.9	31.0	—	-32.4	-18.7	29.7	—
Export/shipments ratio	0.013	0.008	0.006	0.007	—	-34.7	-27.9	23.3	—

[1]Estimated except for exports and imports.
[2]Estimated.
[3]Forecast.
[4]Value of all products and services sold by the Hydraulic Cement industry.
[5]Value of products classified in the Hydraulic Cement industry produced by all industries.
[6]Developed by the Office of Industry Assessment, ITA.
[7]New supply is the sum of product shipments plus imports.
SOURCE: U.S. Department of Commerce: Bureau of the Census, Bureau of Economic Analysis, International Trade Administration (ITA). Estimates and forecasts by ITA.

Source: U.S. Industrial Outlook 1986, U.S. Department of Commerce.

Misc. Building Materials

Company	Rev Last Qtr %	Rev FY to Date %	Rev Last 12 Mos %	Rev 12 Mos $Mil	EPS Last 12 $	EPS Last Qtr %	EPS FY to Date %	EPS Last 12 Mos %	EPS 5-Yr Growth %	EPS Par Growth	Date of Report	Div Amt $	Div Yield %	Div 5-Yr Growth %	Payout Last FY %	Payout Last 5 Yrs %	Last X-Dvd Date	Profit Margin	Asset Turn-over	Return on Total Assets	Lever-age	Return on Equity %	Debt to Equity %	Cur-ent Ratio	Market Value $Mil	Latest Shares Out 000	Held by Banks-Funds 000	Insider Net Trad-ing 000	Short Int-erest Ratio Days	Fiscal Year Ends Mo
Ind. Group	10.1	10.8	6.3	622.2	2.29	7.9	6.8	-7.5	35	7	02-86	.87	2.5	0	31	36	---	4.3	1.30	5.6	2.05	11.5	27	2.3	8,967	253,223	100,706	-66	2.7	--
Ameron Inc	-.5	-.5	15.5	11.7q	2.45	-76.0	-76.0	9.9	4	10	03-86	.96	3.7	4	30	33	04-21-86	6.1	1.00	3.8	2.32	8.8	49	2.0	125	4,784	1,172	+2	0.7	11
Armstrng Wrld	14.4	14.4	11.0	105.9q	4.40	26.7	26.7	22.2	3	23	03-86	1.44	2.2	3	30	43	05-05-86	4.1	1.15	4.7	1.89	14.8	8	2.8	1,538	23,986	15,794	-5	1.1	12
Arundel Corp	33.6	33.6	16.2	3.5q	1.53	NE	NE	30.8	NC	9	03-86	.00	-	0	0	0	09-25-79	4.1			1.89	8.9	42	NA	55	2,287	381		1.1	12
Barnco Cp	6.7	6.7	7.4	20.4q	2.01	-27.5	-27.5	-20.9	8	5	05-30-86	.60	2.1	25	26	17	05-30-86	3.7	1.41	5.2	2.35	12.2	56	2.1	289	10,011	3,507	-5	0.8	12
Bird Inc	-17.8	-17.8	-34.6	2.3q	.18	NE	NE	NE	NC	5	12-14-81	.00	-	-	NE	NE	12-14-81	1.3	1.54	2.0	2.25	4.5	47	2.0	42	4,093	1,891	0	0.0	12
Butler Mfg	13.6	13.6	16.9	9.7q	1.83	NE	NE	161.4	2	8	03-86	1.32	4.3	1	66	119	06-10-86	1.9	2.00	3.8	1.84	7.0	28	2.9	157	5,121	1,039	+3	0.3	12
Certain-teed	.8	.8	-4.4	55.7q	2.88	36.6	36.6	35.2	NC	0	05-29-86	.90	2.5	0	26	39	05-29-86	5.0	1.46	7.3	1.66	12.1	25	2.7	688	18,971	4,901	0	0.3	12
Custom Energy	-35.1	-21.9	-19.3	-7.7n	-2.34	NE	NE	NE	NC	-6	00-00-00	.00	-	0	0	0	00-00-00	-30.8	.72	-22.1	.00	NM	957	1.2	2	4,808	82	0	21.9	06
Dallas Cp	1.2	1.2	2.3	-2.4q	-.32	-26.7	-26.7	-100.0	NC	-6	06-13-86	.66	4.3	-9	NE	85	06-13-86	-.6	1.50	.9	2.33	-2.1	58	2.4	113	7,284	4,330	0	1.7	12
Frantz Mfg	11.3	7.1	8.8	2.3	-2.69	87.1	87.1	-100.0	NC	12	03-18-86	1.00	2.4	13	NE	84	03-18-86	4.7	1.47	6.9	1.22	8.4	16	4.9	16	382	32	0	0.0	03
Hauserman Inc	25.0	-1.0	.0	4.7n	2.02	-11.4	-19.7	-27.6	NC	12	06-09-86	.50	2.0	-1	13	19	06-09-86	3.3	2.09	6.9	2.36	16.3	32	1.6	58	2,352	405	-2	0.0	06
Imperial Ind	-34.2	-12.8	-6.4	-5.2n	-1.20	-100.0	-100.0	-100.0	-66	12	09-85	.00	-	0	NE	NE	12-02-80	-5.1	2.02	-10.3	6.39	-65.8	248	1.8	2	4,727	110	0	3.7	06
Knape & Vogt Mfg	1.5	-2.5	-2.6	5.1n	3.89	.9	-4.1	-1.3	18	9	05-19-86	1.50	2.7	5	36	45	05-19-86	7.0	1.67	11.7	1.21	14.2	0	5.1	72	1,296	490	+1	0.0	06
Lawson Prod	6.1	6.1	4.8	13.2q	1.31	8.7	8.7	9.2	12	18	05-08-86	.00	.9	3	15	18	05-08-86	10.2	1.59	16.2	1.34	21.7	0	5.0	239	9,656	3,289	-2	0.2	12
Manville Co	5.1	5.1	3.5	-45.30q	-2.93	-4.0	-4.0	-100.0	NC	7	05-20-82	.00	-	0	NE	NE	05-20-82	-2.4	.79	-1.9	2.74	-5.2	10	2.9	66	24,000	7,378	-45	9.8	12
Owens Corning	27.7	27.7	16.2	126.1q	4.24	-18.9	-18.9	2.9	27	9	05-23-86	1.40	2.9	3	32	46	05-23-86	3.6	1.47	5.3	2.51	13.3	57	1.9	1,430	29,799	16,348	-4	3.2	12
Rep Gypsum	18.4	9.4	1.6	9.5n	.90	33.3	-4.5	-10.9	64	17	05-23-86	.36	3.0	42	30	29	05-23-86	15.6	1.09	17.0	1.62	27.5	41	5.2	127	10,657	1,274	-12	3.4	06
Susquehanna	-14.0	-14.0	-12.2	.28	.28	-85.7	-85.7	-68.9	NC	17	00-00-00	.00	-	0	0	0	00-00-00	2.5	1.28	3.2	1.53	4.9	22	3.3	47	9,580	974	0	9.6	12
USG Corp	5.7	5.7	5.5	233.0q	3.53	26.6	26.6	23.4	27	17	06-24-86	.96	2.3	0	25	29	06-24-86	9.1	1.48	13.5	1.76	23.7	19	1.7	2,649	64,812	33,610	-4	0.2	12
Vulcan Matls	-1.4	-1.4	-1.5	73.2q	6.33	41.9	41.9	-4.1	1	7	05-19-86	2.96	2.8	6	46	42	05-19-86	7.6	1.17	8.9	1.56	13.9	14	3.1	1,206	11,281	6,588	-45	0.0	12
Wolverine Alum	32.1	32.1	15.5	3.8q	1.14	NE	NE	153.3	NC	15	06-02-86	.24	1.6	0	15	13	06-02-86	4.3	2.19	9.4	2.06	19.4	55	2.8	46	3,136	111	0	0.0	12

Cement

Company	Rev Last Qtr %	Rev FY to Date %	Rev Last 12 Mos %	Rev 12 Mos $Mil	EPS Last 12 $	EPS Last Qtr %	EPS FY to Date %	EPS Last 12 Mos %	EPS 5-Yr Growth %	EPS Par Growth	Date of Report	Div Amt $	Div Yield %	Div 5-Yr Growth %	Payout Last FY %	Payout Last 5 Yrs %	Last X-Dvd Date	Profit Margin	Asset Turn-over	Return on Total Assets	Lever-age	Return on Equity %	Debt to Equity %	Cur-ent Ratio	Market Value $Mil	Latest Shares Out 000	Held by Banks-Funds 000	Insider Net Trad-ing 000	Short Int-erest Ratio Days	Fiscal Year Ends Mo
Ind. Group	14.8	29.0	4.5	-209.5	-2.05	NE	NE	-100.0	NC	-15	---	.52	2.6	0	41	64	---	-4.8	.90	-4.3	2.79	-12.0	69	1.3	2,369	116,817	29,682	-131	5.7	--
Calmat Co	2.3	2.3	33.7	39.7q	2.62	-19.4	-19.4	235.9	9	9	06-06-86	.68	1.9	-6	22	48	06-06-86	8.9	.85	7.6	1.55	11.8	11	2.6	525	15,014	3,832	-104	0.5	12
Fla Rock Ind	4.6	-1.2	.0	23.0q	5.03	2.2	-9.0	-1.2	18	15	06-24-86	.00	1.4	23	13	13	06-24-86	8.6	1.35	11.6	1.57	18.2	17	1.9	291	4,513	1,340	+0	0.7	09
Giant Grp	35.0	35.0	54.1	5.6q	1.38	NE	NE	NE	NC	25	00-00-00	.00	-	0	0	0	00-00-00	7.6	.79	6.0	4.18	25.1	203	4.3	66	3,240	935	0	10.1	12
Gifford Hill	-5.5	-.5	-3.7	5.8q	-4.23	NE	NE	-100.0	NC	-27	05-05-86	.52	2.2	0	NE	NE	05-05-86	-8.3	1.12	-9.3	2.56	-23.8	114	2.3	201	8,571	2,023	-13	0.7	12
Ideal Basic	-29.9	-29.9	-31.7	-36.2q	-25.31	NE	NE	NE	NC	-14	05-31-83	.00	-	0	NE	NE	05-31-83	NM	NC	NS	NC	NS	41	.2	31	13,802	6,488	0	9.5	12
Kaiser Cement	-16.1	-16.1	-4.7	-344.4q	.71	NE	NE	NE	NC	5	03-31-86	.20	1.4	-37	21	198	03-31-86	4.6	.57	2.6	2.81	7.3	88	1.5	102	7,326	3,543	0	9.8	12
Lafarge Cp	11.0	11.0	4.6	10.9q	.57	NE	NE	NE	NC	4	05-12-86	.20	1.9	0	65	NE	05-12-86	2.5	.96	2.4	2.67	6.4	74	1.6	399	37,513	1,804	+0	10.9	12
Lone Star	.8	.8	-10.6	23.6q	2.94	NE	NE	14.8	NC	-38	05-30-86	1.90	6.2	2	70	110	05-30-86	6.3	.67	4.2	2.64	11.1	52	1.7	440	14,247	7,320	-10	8.2	12
NWn St Port	1316.7	1316.7	58.6	55.1q	-11.42	NE	NE	NE	NC	6	03-11-83	.00	-	0	0	NE	03-11-83	-24.8	.91	-22.6	1.69	-38.1	64	1.4	8	994	44	-4	0.0	11
Puerto Rican C	-21	-21	-3.3	-11.4q	1.36	-7.5	-7.5	2.3	NC	6	07-10-86	.05	.4	0	0	0	07-10-86	4.7	.57	2.7	2.19	5.9	7	2.3	25	1,981	5	0	0.0	11
Slattery Grp	28.1	28.1	-.7	.0q	-.02	-100.0	-100.0	-100.0	NC	0	03-86	.00	-	0	82	19	02-11-85	.0	NC	NC	2.30	0	7	1.9	34	1,513	348	0	17.7	12
Tex Ind	153.4	102.5	74.7	21.9n	2.51	NE	NE	28.7	-9	8	02-86	.77	2.5b	7	36	30	04-28-86	3.7	1.43	5.3		12.2	74	2.5	247	8,103	1,999	0	0.7	05

Recent Performance and Forecast: Chemicals and Allied Products (SIC 28)
(in millions of dollars except as noted)

	1982	1983	1984[1]	1985[2]	1986[3]	Percent Change			
						1982-83	1983-84	1984-85	1985-86
Industry Data									
Value of shipments[4]	170,777	183,206	201,191	210,669	—	7.3	9.8	4.7	—
Value of shipments (1982$)	170,777	183,512	195,658	199,268	204,344	7.5	6.6	1.8	2.5
Total employment (000)	873	851	859	859	—	-2.5	1.0	-0.0	—
Production workers (000)	508	496	494	496	—	-2.5	-0.4	0.3	—
Average hourly earnings ($)	10.51	11.08	—	—	—	5.5	—	—	—
Product Data									
Value of shipments[5]	161,193	173,430	189,284	198,594	—	7.6	9.1	4.9	—
Value of shipments (1982$)	161,193	173,766	183,822	187,810	192,392	7.8	5.8	2.2	2.4
Shipments price index (1982=100)[6]	100.0	100.8	103.9	106.4	—	0.8	3.0	2.4	—
Trade Data									
Value of imports	7,600	9,333	11,927	13,332	15,328	22.8	27.8	11.8	15.0
Import/new supply ratio[7]	0.046	0.052	—	—	—	13.3	—	—	—
Value of exports	20,021	19,688	22,249	21,848	21,242	-1.7	13.0	-1.8	-2.8
Export/shipments ratio	0.123	0.112	—	—	—	-8.7	—	—	—

[1]Estimated except for exports and imports.
[2]Estimated.
[3]Forecast.
[4]Value of all products and services sold by the Chemicals and Allied Products industry.
[5]Value of products classified in the Chemicals and Allied Products industry produced by all industries.
[6]Developed by the Office of Industry Assessment, ITA.
[7]New supply is the sum of product shipments plus imports.

SOURCE: U.S. Department of Commerce: Bureau of the Census, Bureau of Economic Analysis, International Trade Administration (ITA). Estimates and forecasts by ITA.

Source: *U.S. Industrial Outlook 1986*, U.S. Department of Commerce.

Recent Performance and Forecast: Plastics Materials and Resins (SIC 2821)

(in millions of dollars except as noted)

	1982	1983	1984[1]	1985[2]	1986[3]	Percent Change			
						1982-83	1983-84	1984-85	1985-86
Industry Data									
Value of shipments[4]	15,814	18,936	20,830	21,562	—	19.7	10.0	3.5	—
Value of shipments (1982$)	15,814	18,568	19,413	20,189	20,997	17.4	4.6	4.0	4.0
Total employment (000)	54.7	53.2	56.3	53.9	—	-2.7	5.8	-4.3	—
Production workers (000)	32.8	32.7	34.1	34.1	—	-0.3	4.2	0.0	—
Average hourly earnings ($)	11.73	12.84	13.51	14.25	—	9.5	5.2	5.5	—
Product Data									
Value of shipments[5]	17,615	21,053	22,913	23,830	—	19.5	8.8	4.0	—
Value of shipments (1982$)	17,615	20,539	21,146	22,209	—	16.6	3.0	5.0	—
Shipments price index (1982=100)[6]	100.0	102.5	108.4	107.3	—	2.5	5.7	-1.0	—
Trade Data									
Value of imports (ITA)[7]	268	469	668	775	—	75.0	42.4	16.1	—
Import/new supply ratio[8]	0.015	0.022	0.028	0.032	—	45.4	30.0	11.8	—
Value of exports	2,472	2,510	2,655	2,546	—	1.5	5.8	-4.1	—
Export/shipments ratio	0.140	0.119	0.116	0.107	—	-15.1	-2.8	-7.8	—

[1]Estimated except for exports and imports.
[2]Estimated.
[3]Forecast.
[4]Value of all products and services sold by the Plastics Materials and Resins industry.
[5]Value of products classified in the Plastics Materials and Resins industry produced by all industries.
[6]Developed by the Office of Industry Assessment, ITA.
[7]Import data are developed by the chapter author.
[8]New supply is the sum of product shipments plus imports.
SOURCE: U.S. Department of Commerce: Bureau of the Census, Bureau of Economic Analysis, International Trade Administration (ITA). Estimates and forecasts by ITA.

Source: U.S. Industrial Outlook 1986, U.S. Department of Commerce.

Recent Performance and Forecast: Synthetic Rubber (SIC 2822)
(in millions of dollars except as noted)

	1982	1983	1984[1]	1985[2]	1986[3]	Percent Change			
						1982-83	1983-84	1984-85	1985-86
Industry Data									
Value of shipments[4]	3,139	3,149	3,350	3,140	—	0.3	6.4	-6.3	—
Value of shipments (1982$)	3,139	3,274	3,490	3,237	3,135	4.3	6.6	-7.2	-3.2
Total employment (000)	11.8	11.1	11.1	10.7	—	-5.9	0.1	-4.1	—
Production workers (000)	7.6	7.1	7.2	7.0	—	-6.6	1.7	-3.4	—
Average hourly earnings ($)	13.28	14.35	15.10	16.07	—	8.1	5.2	6.4	—
Product Data									
Value of shipments[5]	3,212	3,276	3,480	3,270	—	2.0	6.2	-6.0	—
Value of shipments (1982$)	3,212	3,407	3,625	3,371	3,347	6.1	6.4	-7.0	-0.7
Shipments price index (1982=100)[6]	100.0	96.2	96.0	97.0	—	-3.8	-0.2	1.1	—
Trade Data									
Value of imports	212	269	335	390	400	26.6	24.5	16.6	2.6
Import/new supply ratio[7]	0.062	0.076	0.088	0.107	—	22.3	15.7	21.5	—
Value of exports	590	590	674	655	675	-0.1	14.3	-2.8	3.1
Export/shipments ratio	0.184	0.180	0.194	0.200	—	-2.0	7.6	3.4	—

[1]Estimated except for exports and imports.
[2]Estimated.
[3]Forecast.
[4]Value of all products and services sold by the Synthetic Rubber industry.
[5]Value of products classified in the Synthetic Rubber industry produced by all industries.
[6]Developed by the Office of Industry Assessment, ITA.
[7]New supply is the sum of product shipments plus imports.
SOURCE: U.S. Department of Commerce: Bureau of the Census, Bureau of Economic Analysis, International Trade Administration (ITA). Estimates and forecasts by ITA.

Source: *U.S. Industrial Outlook 1986*, U.S. Department of Commerce.

Recent Performance and Forecast: Tires and Inner Tubes (SIC 3011)
(in millions of dollars except as noted)

	1982	1983	1984[1]	1985[2]	1986[3]	Percent Change			
						1982-83	1983-84	1984-85	1985-86
Industry Data									
Value of shipments[4]	9,340	10,165	11,245	10,700	—	8.8	10.6	-4.8	—
Value of shipments (1982$)	9,340	10,585	11,812	11,300	11,000	13.3	11.6	-4.3	-2.7
Total employment (000)	70.3	66.9	67.0	66.5	—	-4.8	0.2	-0.8	—
Production workers (000)	54.6	52.2	51.0	50.5	—	-4.4	-2.2	-1.1	—
Average hourly earnings ($)	12.72	13.50	14.14	14.37	—	6.2	4.8	1.6	—
Product Data									
Value of shipments[5]	9,047	9,893	10,940	10,425	—	9.3	10.6	-4.7	—
Value of shipments (1982$)	9,047	10,301	11,495	11,000	10,725	13.9	11.6	-4.3	-2.5
Shipments price index (1982=100)[6]	100.0	96.1	95.2	95.0	—	-3.9	-0.9	-0.3	—
Trade Data									
Value of imports	1,216	1,375	1,792	1,970	2,000	13.0	30.3	10.0	1.5
Import/new supply ratio[7]	0.125	0.128	0.147	0.166	—	2.6	15.2	12.8	—
Value of exports	372	304	392	380	400	-18.3	29.0	-3.0	5.3
Export/shipments ratio	0.041	0.031	0.036	0.036	—	-25.3	16.6	1.8	—

[1]Estimated except for exports and imports.
[2]Estimated.
[3]Forecast.
[4]Value of all products and services sold by the Tires and Inner Tubes industry.
[5]Value of products classified in the Tires and Inner Tubes industry produced by all industries.
[6]Developed by the Office of Industry Assessment, ITA.
[7]New supply is the sum of product shipments plus imports.
SOURCE: U.S. Department of Commerce: Bureau of the Census, Bureau of Economic Analysis, International Trade Administration (ITA). Estimates and forecasts by ITA.

Source: *U.S. Industrial Outlook 1986*, U.S. Department of Commerce.

Chemicals and Synthetics

Company	Rev %Chg Last Qtr	Rev %Chg FY to Date	Rev %Chg Last 12 Mos	Earn Last 12 Mos $Mil	EPS Last 12 Mos $	EPS %Chg Last Qtr	EPS %Chg FY to Date	EPS %Chg Last 12 Mos	EPS 5-Yr Grth	Par Grth	Date of Report	Div Current Rate Amt	Div Yield	Div 5-Yr Grth	Payout Last FY	Payout Last 5 Yrs	Last X-Dvd Date	Profit Margin	Asset Turn over	Return on Total Assets	Lever age Ratio	Return on Equity	Debt to Eq uity	Curr ent Ratio	Mar ket Value $Mil	Latest Shares Out stndg 000	Held by Banks Funds 000	Insider Net Trad ing 000	Short Int erest Ratio Days	Fiscal Year Ends Mo
Ind. Group	-.4	-.2	-1.7	2,757.3	1.67	40.4	40.4	45.2	-11	0	—	1.78	3.4	0	94	58	—	2.7	1.07	2.9	2.24	6.5	42	1.6	74,836	1,417,177	624,192	+42	2.4	—
Air Pd & Chem	11.2	10.2	9.1	149.3s	2.52	13.8	12.6	12.0	4	9	03-86	.80	2.3	8	25	22	06-06-86	7.8	.74	5.8	2.21	12.8	45	1.3	2,067	59,070	39,814	-2	0.9	09
Am Cyanamid	4.0	4.0	-6.0	132.4q	2.79	11.7	11.7	-33.6	-3	3	03-86	1.90	2.5	3	71	51	05-19-86	3.7	1.05	3.9	2.08	8.1	35	2.0	3,635	46,906	29,128	-2	0.8	12
Ausimont Comp	NA	NA	417.2	NA	NA	NA	NA	NA	NA	NC	03-86	.10	.3	NA	211	61	06-16-86	1.0	NA	NA	NA	NC	NA	NA	747	25,121	844	0	NA	12
Big Three Ind	3.8	3.8	7.8	16.9q	.46	26.7	26.7	-66.4	NA	-3	03-86	.88	3.4	12	50	48	06-27-86	2.0	.80	1.6	2.06	3.3	38	2.4	975	37,675	19,900	-0	0.2	12
Cabot Corp	6	-1.5	-12.2	59.8s	2.01	14.5	13.6	-33.2	-28	5	03-86	.92	3.1	5	33	35	05-21-86	4.3	.86	3.7	2.59	9.6	61	1.9	838	28,666	16,450	+0	0.1	09
Celanese Corp	-.1	-.1	-5.9	193.0q	15.23	58.8	58.8	41.9	-9	14	03-86	4.80	2.1	4	581	54	05-23-86	6.3	1.10	6.9	3.01	20.8	47	1.3	2,747	12,021	6,347	-11	2.3	12
Dow Chemical	3.6	3.6	3.3	123.0q	.65	58.6	58.6	-76.7	NC	-5	03-86	1.80	3.1	2	65	96	07-01-86	1.1	.91	1.0	2.60	2.6	67	1.5	10,910	190,160	92,532	+21	2.2	12
DuPont	-.7	-.7	-13.1	1379.0q	5.69	183.1	183.1	14.5	-31	5	03-86	3.00	3.6	11	38	55	05-09-86	4.7	1.17	5.5	2.02	11.1	26	1.7	20,028	240,580	89,607	+24	2.6	12
Essex Chemical	11.4	11.4	10.1	8.6q	1.77	4.0	4.0	14.5	1	10	03-86	.70	2.0	7	29	39	07-03-86	4.4	1.39	6.1	2.72	16.6	82	2.3	169	4,759	1,164	+1	0.0	12
Ethyl Corp	.2	-.2	-5.2	120.9q	.95	13.6	13.6	12.7	5	12	03-86	.32	1.5	7	29	30	06-10-86	7.8	1.00	7.8	1.96	15.3	51	2.1	2,622	125,590	42,084	+37	0.5	12
Genex Cp	-81.3	-81.3	-53.8	-13.7q	-1.08	NE	NE	NE	-17	-93	03-86	.00	0	0	99	NE	00-00-00	NM	NC	NC	NC	-92.6	70	1.4	38	12,768	1,009	0	0.0	12
Grace W R	-20.9	-20.9	1.7	108.3q	2.02	-100.0	-100.0	-46.8	0	-2	03-86	2.80	5.2	5	67	61	04-25-86	1.6	1.25	2.0	2.25	4.5	64	2.0	2,930	54,391	21,485	-3	3.2	12
Hercules Inc	2.5	2.5	.4	142.8q	2.56	24.6	24.6	-23.1	3	0	03-86	1.76	3.3	6	182	53	06-02-86	5.5	.98	5.4	1.80	9.7	36	2.5	2,882	54,246	34,742	-3	3.9	12
Imperial Chem	11.6	11.6	28.4	856.8q	1.11	-11.5	-11.5	-74.7	-3	-21	03-86	2.46	4.0	11	59	54	03-04-86	5.8	1.22	7.1	2.39	17.0	37	1.7	9,498	154,750	19,568	0	0.5	12
Intl Flav Frag	22.0	22.0	11.1	74.2q	2.00	22.9	22.9	7.5	2	7	03-86	1.16	2.4	5	66	56	06-18-86	14.1	.94	13.3	1.31	17.4	0	4.2	1,757	36,900	16,747	0	1.4	12
Koppers Co	-26.0	-26.0	-28.1	-88.7q	-3.29	NE	NE	11.0	-26	-26	03-86	1.60	2.7	-13	NE	NE	05-12-86	-6.8	1.22	-8.3	2.54	-21.1	51	2.2	832	28,577	15,335	-4	0.9	12
Liquid Air Cp	4.7	4.7	7.2	32.5q	2.42	0	0	11.0	4	-8	03-86	1.60	4.6	2	66	70	06-16-86	5.9	.86	5.1	2.43	12.4	54	1.2	446	12,923	161	-1	0.0	12
Monsanto Co	7.5	7.5	4.3	-97.0q	-1.27	35.7	35.7	-100.0	NC	-9	03-86	2.60	3.5	7	NE	NE	05-06-86	-1.4	.79	-1.1	2.55	-2.8	61	1.4	5,728	76,753	49,849	+2	1.1	12
Pennwalt Corp	7.9	7.9	7.9	-13.5q	-2.33	85.7	85.7	-100.0	NC	-8	03-86	2.20	3.8	0	NE	98	06-27-86	-1.3	1.08	-1.4	2.79	-3.9	43	1.7	586	10,068	5,927	-1	1.8	12
Publicker Ind	-65.8	-65.8	-39.4	-3.4q	-.31	NE	NE	NE	NC	-26	03-86	.00	0	0	0	0	00-00-00	-14.8	.68	-10.1	2.61	-26.4	11	.9	46	12,613	809	0	2.1	12
Regal Intl	-41.4	-41.4	-30.7	-1.4q	-.14	NE	NE	-100.0	NC	-13	03-86	.00	0	11	NE	NE	00-00-00	-15.6	.69	-10.7	1.18	-12.6	3	5.5	6	10,264	592	-6	10.6	12
Reichhold Chm	13.3	13.3	9.0	-29.9q	4.48	-81.8	-81.8	-2.4	NC	-20	03-86	.80	2.1	13	35	33	05-06-86	-3.5	1.71	-6.0	2.78	-16.7	58	1.3	280	7,403	5,585	+5	2.2	12
Rohm & Haas	-2.2	-2.2	1.6	139.0q	2.01	1.8	1.8	48.7	5	9	03-86	.80	2.4	8	37	33	06-13-86	6.8	1.18	8.0	1.86	14.9	26	2.1	2,233	68,952	30,895	0	0.6	12
Stepan Co	11.4	11.4	7.8	6.7q	2.32	159.3	159.3	159.3	10	9	03-86	.72	2.1	2	78	37	05-23-86	2.8	1.71	4.8	2.81	13.5	75	1.3	100	2,897	331	0	5.3	12
Union Carbide	-20.9	-20.9	-7.8	-627.0q	-2.82	11.8	11.8	-100.0	NC	-24	03-86	1.50	7.1	6	NE	126	03-04-86	-7.3	.81	-5.9	2.64	-15.6	44	1.6	1,868	88,443	75,958	0	18.4	12
Witco Chemical	-5.9	-5.9	-4.4	59.9q	4.05	26.7	26.7	-.5	10	9	03-86	1.68	3.1	2	39	40	06-23-86	4.2	1.88	7.9	2.03	16.0	38	2.2	806	14,681	7,329	-15	0.2	12

Specialty Chemicals

Company	Rev %Chg Last Qtr	Rev %Chg FY to Date	Rev %Chg Last 12 Mos	Rev Last 12 Mos $Mil	EPS Last 12 Mos $	EPS %Chg Last Qtr	EPS %Chg FY to Date	EPS %Chg Last 12 Mos	EPS 5-Yr Growth %	Par Growth %	Date of Report	Div Amt	Div Yield %	Div 5-Yr Growth %	Payout FY %	Payout 5 Yrs %	Last X-Dvd Date	Profit Margin	Asset Turnover	Return on Tot Assets	Leverage Ratio	Return on Equity	Debt to Equity %	Current Ratio	Mkt Value $Mil	Latest Shares Out 000	Held by Banks-Funds 000	Insider Net Trading 000	Short Int Ratio Days	Fiscal Year Ends Mo
Ind. Group	8.2	8.4	4.2	491.2	1.43	-29.4	-17.9	-28.9	2	5	–	.79	2.5	1	48	45	–	4.6	1.43	6.6	1.85	12.2	23	2.1	10,809	343,059	165,398	+1614	4	–
Betz Laboratories	8.5	8.5	6.1	37.0q	2.34	1.7	1.7	-.4	8	8	03-86	1.40	3.3	17	54	46	07-25-86	11.3	1.29	14.6	1.30	19.0	0	2.3	670	15,865	9,334	-3	.0	12
Bio-Rad Labs	21.0	21.0	21.3	4.9q	1.09	42.3	42.3	65.2	10	16	03-86	.00	–	0	0	0	06-11-86	4.5	1.53	6.9	2.38	16.4	55	2.3	96	4,692	55	0	.3	12
Chemed Cp	6.3	6.3	6.7	22.0q	2.50	2.2	2.2	14.2	23	9	03-86	1.56	4.1	8	61	69	05-19-86	5.8	1.66	9.6	2.53	24.3	63	1.8	337	8,859	6,462	-2	.0	12
Crompt & Knwl	11.5	11.5	5.3	8.4q	2.44	70.6	70.6	15.1	1	9	03-86	1.28	3.8	8	55	52	05-05-86	3.5	1.86	6.5	1.86	12.1	28	2.7	110	3,234	815	+0	1.1	12
Dexter Cp	1.7	1.7	1.1	29.6q	1.78	11.4	11.4	-6.3	2	7	03-86	.80	2.3	6	46	41	06-09-86	4.7	1.30	6.1	2.08	12.7	28	2.0	566	16,533	9,882	+2	.2	12
Diam Crystal	12.3	21.3	21.2	.3	.13	-100.0	-94.2	-94.2	-24	-2	03-86	.80	2.4	7	615	43	05-19-86	1.6	1.00	.3	1.33	.4	1	4.3	86	2,566	498	0	.0	03
Ferro Corp	8.6	8.6	1.2	10.8q	1.60	70.0	70.0	-25.6	-14	1	03-86	1.20	3.0	0	22	51	05-09-86	1.6	1.69	2.7	2.04	5.5	35	2.1	289	6,746	2,749	+0	.2	12
Fuller H B Co	14.8	12.3	8.0	16.2q	1.73	47.4	50.9	28.1	6	11	05-86	.36	1.3	10	22	21	04-25-86	3.3	1.94	6.4	2.23	14.3	39	2.0	256	9,210	3,819	0	.0	11
Grt Lks Chem	5.1	5.1	-3.7	25.5q	1.71	-38.6	-38.6	-29.0	12	9	03-86	.52	1.4	17	23	21	06-26-86	9.1	.87	7.9	1.66	13.1	19	2.3	571	14,976	8,993	0	1.1	12
Kinark Cp	5.8	5.8	1.0	-2.0q	-.58	NE	NE	NE	NC	-12	03-86	.00	0	0	0	0	00-00-00	-7.7	.65	-5.0	2.36	-11.8	79	1.4	14	3,482	543	0	.2	12
Lawter Int	6.8	6.8	1.0	-5.2q	-.30	6.3	6.3	-100.0	-7	31	03-86	.56	3.8	6	NE	99	05-09-86	-5.3	1.17	-6.2	1.76	-10.9	10	3.5	257	17,443	5,574	+8	1.7	12
LeaRonal Inc	-9.9	-19.5	-19.8	6.0q	.64	-64.3	-40.2	-40.2	12	5	02-86	.40	2.6	9	50	31	06-18-86	5.7	1.88	10.7	1.23	13.2	5	7.6	117	7,494	2,455	0	.0	02
Loctite Cp	23.7	12.4	7.6	19.7h	2.18	10.4	-3.5	-13.5	9	4	03-86	.80	1.9	8	34	33	06-03-86	7.8	1.15	9.0	1.74	15.7	12	2.0	412	9,046	3,661	-8	.4	06
Lubrizol Corp	9.4	9.4	9.4	6.3q	1.73	5.1	5.1	-2.3	-5	4	03-86	1.16	3.4	5	78	66	05-05-86	7.4	1.09	8.1	1.64	13.3	14	2.5	1,348	39,654	24,037	-8	1.5	12
MacDermid Inc	-.4	-9.3	-9.4	3.8	1.04	-7.4	-40.6	-40.6	8	6	03-86	.52	2.0	3	50	36	06-09-86	4.4	1.59	7.0	1.77	12.4	6	1.7	93	3,630	1,580	0	.0	03
Morton Thiokol	5.4	5.6	5.8	55.6q	1.26	-65.1	-36.4	-67.9	13	4	03-86	.70	1.9	6	25	32	05-19-86	2.9	1.41	4.1	1.93	7.9	22	1.8	1,708	47,122	27,267	-5	.5	06
Nalco Chem	30.3	30.3	15.6	71.1q	1.81	-13.3	-13.3	-6.2	4	6	03-86	1.20	4.3	8	64	62	05-23-86	9.8	1.34	13.3	1.41	18.5	6	1.9	1,099	39,106	27,408	+18	.0	12
NCH Corp	7.5	7.8	7.7	17.1q	1.77	15.2	11.3	11.3	-3	7	04-86	.72	2.4	0	41	44	04-06-86	4.6	1.52	7.0	1.57	11.0	8	3.6	279	9,190	2,689	0	1.0	04
Nuclear Metals	3.1	-6.7	-7.5	2.0s	.73	10.0	-17.5	-2.7	-3	5	03-86	.00	0	0	0	0	11-18-80	5.4	.54	2.9	1.76	5.1	32	3.3	47	2,701	625	0	.0	09
Oakite Products	-.5	-.5	-2.4	3.4q	2.12	-20.0	-20.0	-23.7	-2	4	03-86	1.52	5.2	3	68	67	05-14-86	4.2	2.00	8.4	1.55	13.0	0	2.5	48	1,619	502	0	2.3	12
Park Chemical	8.0	8.0	15.0	2.1q	-3.11	5.8	5.8	30.1	22	10	03-86	1.75	5.1	29	50	46	05-19-86	9.1	2.04	18.6	1.25	23.3	0	4.1	24	697	111	0	.0	10
Petrolite Corp	-3.0	-2.6	12.8	20.4s	1.75	-10.7	-13.8	-24.9	4	4	04-86	1.12	4.4	12	59	45	07-07-86	6.7	1.33	8.9	1.37	12.2	4	3.5	296	11,715	2,397	+0	.0	10
Prod Research	14.2	12.8	6.8	6.7s	.71	20.0	20.7	20.3	11	11	03-86	.48	1.6	11	43	43	05-12-86	7.6	1.53	11.6	1.28	14.8	5	3.7	163	9,459	3,456	-28	.3	09
Quaker Chemical	9.9	9.9	7.6	7.9q	1.14	17.9	17.9	14.0	14	8	03-86	.42	2.9	12	35	23	04-14-86	6.3	1.33	8.4	1.58	13.3	15	3.0	101	6,960	2,781	-94	.0	12
Sigma-Aldrich	15.9	15.9	18.6	30.0q	1.19	22.2	22.2	21.4	17	19	03-86	.24	.6	17	18	18	05-23-86	13.5	1.19	16.1	1.48	23.8	11	3.7	945	24,543	10,108	+1760	.0	12
Spectrum Grp	15.2	32.4	96.7	4.3s	.90	12.9	-8.0	30.4	NC	39	03-86	.08	.7	0	0	0	12-03-85	7.0	2.20	15.4	2.56	39.4	37	1.4	88	5,604	460	0	.1	09
Sun Chem Cp	7.8	7.8	2.0	3.5q	.45	-11.3	-87.3	-87.3	-23	-23	03-86	.07	–	3	92	26	06-09-86	.4	1.25	.5	3.60	1.8	104	1.4	560	7,806	2,770	-2	.1	12
Univar Cp	1.5	1.3	1.3	10.7q	1.90	-68.6	-33.3	-33.3	-1	10	02-86	.20	1.7	9	41	33	05-09-86	1.1	3.18	3.5	3.20	11.2	64	1.5	65	5,603	2,872	-30	.6	02
WD Forty Co	4.7	16.8	14.2	10.5n	1.39	9.7	15.6	6.9	6	9	05-86	1.04	4.0	12	72	63	04-04-86	16.4	1.95	31.9	1.15	36.7	0	7.2	193	7,504	1,555	0	.0	08

Tires and Inner Tubes

Company	Rev % Last Qtr	Rev % FY to Date	Rev % Last 12 Mos	Last 12 Mos $Mil	EPS Last 12 Mos $	EPS % Last Qtr	EPS % FY to Date	EPS % Last 12 Mos	5-Yr Growth Rate %	Par Growth Rate %	Date of Report	Div Cur Rate Amt $	Div Yield %	Div Date	Div 5-Yr Growth %	Payout Last FY %	Payout Last 5 Yrs %	Last X-Dvd Date	Profit Margin %	Asset Turnover	Return on Total Assets	Leverage Ratio	Return on Equity %	Debt to Eq %	Current Ratio	Mkt Value $Mil	Shares Outstndg 000	Held by Banks-Funds 000	Insider Net Trading 000	Short Int Ratio Days	Fiscal Yr Ends Mo
Ind. Group	-3.3	-2.7	-3.4	412.3	1.90	-96.0	-80.6	-37.7	-.5	2	---	1.25	3.5	---	1	47	40	---	2.3	1.39	3.2	2.06	6.6	28	1.7	7,355	206,150	116,813	-33	1.8	--
Alliance Tire	229.2	-4.4	11.9	-7.1n	-1.09	NE	NE	NE	NC	0	09-85	.00	.0	00-00	0	0	0	06-30-83	-15.1	.81	-12.3	.00	NM	971	1.1	18	6,509	20	-3	0.0	12
Armstrong Rub	-1.1	8.5	13.6	10.0s	.92	9.5	-61.9	-59.3	NC	20	03-86	.48	3.3	05-29-86	10	32	24	05-29-86	1.3	1.31	1.7	2.47	4.2	75	2.4	157	10,744	5,192	-3	6.6	09
Bandag Inc	15.3	15.3	7.9	44.6q	5.15	16.3	16.3	6.6	16	8	03-86	1.30	1.6	06-16-86	12	24	25	06-16-86	13.1	1.37	17.9	1.52	27.2	6	2.9	691	8,629	3,291	0	0.7	12
Cooper Tire	4.5	4.5	-2.0	18.1q	1.80	-10.5	-10.5	-25.6	1	-5	03-86	.40	1.7	06-02-86	14	22	16	06-02-86	3.4	1.79	6.1	1.69	10.3	24	2.8	242	10,085	5,258	+6	0.3	12
Firestone Tire	-7.3	-6.0	-5.0	-14.0s	-.26	-28.9	-14.3	-100.0	NC	3	04-86	.80	3.2	06-27-86	18	NE	50	06-27-86	-.4	1.50	-.6	2.00	-1.2	20	1.4	1,008	39,725	19,809	+2	3.5	10
GenCorp	-1.0	-1.4	4.8	95.0s	3.11	5.7	54.6	-1.9	2	4	05-86	1.50	2.0	07-31-86	2	66	53	07-31-86	3.2	1.44	4.6	2.17	10.0	27	2.0	1,671	22,348	11,411	-34	0.9	11
Goodyear Tire	-3.8	-3.8	-6.8	265.7q	2.48	-100.0	-100.0	-31.5	4	3	03-86	1.60	4.8	05-12-86	4	42	41	05-12-86	2.8	1.36	3.8	2.00	7.6	28	1.6	3,568	108,110	71,832	-4	0.6	12

Rubber and Plastic Products

Company	Rev % Last Qtr	Rev % FY to Date	Rev % Last 12 Mos	Last 12 Mos $Mil	EPS Last 12 Mos $	EPS % Last Qtr	EPS % FY to Date	EPS % Last 12 Mos	5-Yr Growth Rate %	Par Growth Rate %	Date of Report	Div Cur Rate Amt $	Div Yield %	Div Date	Div 5-Yr Growth %	Payout Last FY %	Payout Last 5 Yrs %	Last X-Dvd Date	Profit Margin %	Asset Turnover	Return on Total Assets	Leverage Ratio	Return on Equity %	Debt to Eq %	Current Ratio	Mkt Value $Mil	Shares Outstndg 000	Held by Banks-Funds 000	Insider Net Trading 000	Short Int Ratio Days	Fiscal Yr Ends Mo
Ind. Group	8.4	22.5	3.1	99.8	.46	-38.1	-24.2	568.0	1	5	---	.20	1.1	---	1	25	27	---	2.0	1.45	2.9	2.86	8.3	53	1.4	4,287	229,885	45,128	-3	1.8	--
Alpine Grp	-1.3	-2.6	34.7	.8n	.24	-100.0	-100.0	NC	NC	20	01-86	.00	.0	00-00-00	0	0	0	00-00-00	2.6	1.81	4.7	4.26	20.0	138	1.9	30	3,429	1	0	0.0	04
Am Biltrite	8.3	8.3	11.3	2.5q	1.05	-9.5	-9.5	-1.9	NC	9	03-86	.15	1.0	06-23-86	-18	14	39	06-23-86	2.6	1.73	4.5	2.22	10.0	10	1.5	36	2,389	565	0	0.0	12
Carlisle Corp	-7.1	-7.1	-9.9	21.3q	2.31	-37.5	-37.5	-33.4	-3	6	03-86	1.08	3.1	05-13-86	13	40	31	05-13-86	4.5	1.51	6.8	1.59	10.8	22	3.7	324	9,157	3,036	0	0.0	12
Chelsea Indus	-4.6	-5.2	-10.0	6.8s	2.64	5.9	15.7	11.4	14	10	03-86	.72	2.6	05-23-86	4	28	32	05-23-86	3.8	1.84	7.0	1.91	13.4	35	2.7	71	2,574	617	0	1.6	09
Crest-Foam	24.2	24.2	12.5	1.6q	1.22	42.9	42.9	.8	29	57	02-86	.15	1.0	12-13-85	15	11	11	12-13-85	3.6	2.36	8.5	1.60	13.6	8	2.5	19	1,293	76	0	0.0	11
Dayco Corp	2.6	-.1	.4	15.5s	2.09	7.9	7.4	9.4	19	8	04-86	.24	1.3	07-28-86	-20	12	24	07-28-86	1.7	1.88	3.2	2.72	8.7	75	2.0	134	7,105	3,196	+0	12.5	10
Fluorocarbon Co	-20.2	-20.2	-19.0	5.6q	1.28	-37.5	-37.5	-.8	14	12	04-86	.28	1.9	04-09-86	9	17	24	04-09-86	5.7	1.51	8.6	1.83	15.7	37	2.9	65	4,305	1,326	0	0.0	01
Kleer-Vu Ind	14.0	14.0	9.3	1.1q	.16	NE	NE	NE	-10	7	03-86	.03	1.50	12-16-85	0	30	21	12-16-85	3.1	1.16	3.6	2.36	8.5	53	1.5	22	6,121	329	0	1.0	08
Kroy Inc	-15.3	-9.8	3.1	3.1f	.53	-24.3	-24.3	-24.3	NC	57	03-86	.06	.6	12-10-85	0	7	7	12-10-85	5.2	1.13	5.9	1.41	8.3	9	3.8	56	5,764	720	0	0.0	03
Mark IV Ind	614.0	614.0	269.2	6.0q	1.21	100.0	100.0	75.4	NC	57	05-86	.00	.0	06-09-86	0	0	0	06-09-86	4.2	5.48	23.0	2.48	57.1	84	2.2	135	5,670	171	0	0.3	02
Martin Process	11.2	11.2	26.8	1.5q	.31	71.4	71.4	-6.1	NC	5	03-86	.04	.3	09-09-86	0	5	5	09-09-86	2.9	1.21	3.5	1.51	5.3	18	2.4	77	4,970	465	0	18.9	12
NVF Co	-11.5	-11.5	-10.1	-63.9q	-.69	NE	NE	NE	NC	20	03-86	.00	.0	01-25-82	0	0	NE	01-25-82	-5.5	1.25	-6.9	.00	NS	-186	.6	44	93,428	8,768	0	0.4	12
O'Sullivan	17.5	17.5	12.6	11.4q	1.13	10.3	10.3	.0	23	16	03-86	.32	1.3	06-09-86	28	27	23	06-09-86	7.5	2.03	15.2	1.48	22.5	0	2.0	242	10,088	707	0	0.3	12
Pantasote Inc	-30.0	-30.0	-12.6	-12.4q	-3.16	-100.0	NE	-100.0	NC	-65	02-86	.00	.0	11-02-81	0	0	NE	11-02-81	-10.0	2.04	-20.4	3.18	-64.9	52	1.6	47	3,917	240	0	1.2	12
Plymth Rub A	-19.4	-19.4	-16.9	-.1q	-.03	NE	NE	NE	NE	-2	02-86	.00	.0	00-00-00	0	0	0	00-00-00	-.2	2.50	-.5	3.00	-1.5	57	1.3	3	815	0	0	0.0	11
Porex Tech	64.6	76.1	76.3	8.0n	.72	37.5	30.2	-19.1	19	8	03-86	.00	.0	00-00-00	0	0	0	00-00-00	6.0	.47	2.8	2.71	7.6	105	3.1	375	10,978	2,359	-5	0.0	06
Rubbermaid	30.6	30.6	25.2	61.1q	1.66	22.9	22.9	16.9	19	14	03-86	.48	.9	05-12-86	13	28	30	05-12-86	8.5	1.49	12.7	1.60	20.3	11	2.3	1,949	36,175	15,600	+1	1.6	12
Schulman, A Inc	35.0	28.6	28.6	13.4s	2.20	25.5	21.5	11.1	40	12	02-86	.44	1.00	04-22-86	12	20	20	04-22-86	3.7	2.51	9.3	1.94	18.0	16	2.1	260	5,874	2,151	0	0.0	08
Sealed Air	12.7	12.7	11.1	14.4q	2.01	13.0	13.0	12.9	40	14	03-86	.48	1.2	06-02-86	11	22	25	06-02-86	7.6	1.28	9.7	1.60	15.5	16	2.4	296	7,211	3,005	+1	0.7	12
Velcro Industries	11.9	-30.1	0	6.0q	2.00	-28.6	-51.9	-28.6	NC	5	03-86	.92	3.2	05-27-86	8	46	36	05-27-86	NC	NC	.0	NC	.0	40	1.0	87	3,010	446	+1	0.0	09
Voplex Corp	-2.9	-2.9	-23.0	2.1q	.79	-23.3	-23.3	-9.2	44	5	03-86	.40	4.2	04-28-86	8	44	48	04-28-86	3.5	1.46	5.1	1.84	9.4	35	2.3	25	2,612	550	+0	0.0	12

Recent Performance and Forecast: Electronic Computing Equipment (SIC 3573)
(in millions of dollars except as noted)

	1982	1983	1984[1]	1985[2]	1986[3]	Percent Change			
						1982-83	1983-84	1984-85	1985-86
Industry Data									
Value of shipments[4]	36,704	41,977	52,500	56,700	65,800	14.4	25.1	8.0	16.0
Total employment (000)	336	354	388	388	404	5.4	9.5	0.0	4.1
Production workers (000)	140	150	161	148	143	7.4	7.3	-8.1	0.0
Average hourly earnings ($)	8.60	9.04	9.48	9.81	—	5.1	4.9	3.5	—
Product Data									
Value of shipments[5]	34,751	39,529	49,490	53,400	62,000	13.7	25.2	8.0	16.0
Trade Data									
Value of imports (ITA)[6]	2,354	4,499	7,834	8,615	11,200	91.1	74.1	10.0	30.0
Value of exports (ITA)[7]	9,118	10,569	13,511	15,400	17,860	15.9	27.8	14.0	16.0
Export/shipments ratio	0.262	0.267	0.273	0.288	0.283	-1.9	2.2	5.5	10.3

[1]Estimated except for exports and imports.
[2]Estimated.
[3]Forecast.
[4]Value of all products and services sold by the Electronic Computing Equipment industry.
[5]Value of products classified in the Electronic Computing Equipment industry produced by all industries.
[6]Import data, developed by the chapter author, are on a C.I.F. valuation basis.
[7]Export data are developed by the chapter author.
SOURCE: U.S. Department of Commerce: Bureau of the Census, Bureau of Economic Analysis, International Trade Administration (ITA). Estimates and forecasts by ITA.

Source: *U.S. Industrial Outlook 1986*, U.S. Department of Commerce.

Computers, Subsystems and Peripherals

Company	Rev Pct Chg Last Qtr	Rev Pct Chg FY to Date	Rev Pct Chg Last 12 Mos	Rev Last 12 Mos $Mil	EPS Per Share Last 12 Mos $	Earn Last 12 Mos $Mil	EPS Pct Chg Last Qtr	EPS Pct Chg FY to Date	EPS Pct Chg Last 12 Mos	5-Yr Growth Rate	Par Growth Rate	Date of Report	Div Current Rate Amt	Div Yield	Div 5-Yr Growth Rate	Payout Last FY	Payout Last 5 Yrs	Last X-Dvd Date	Profit Margin	Asset Turnover	Return on Total Assets	Leverage Ratio	Return on Equity	Debt to Equity	Current Ratio	Market Value $Mil	Latest Shares Outstndng 000	Held by Banks-Funds 000	Insider Net Trading 000	Short Interest Ratio Days	Fiscal Year Ends Mo
Ind. Group	4.7	4.8	1.4	7,522.6	2.50		12.4	-9.2	-17.3	4	7	--	1.09	2.1	1	11	4		6.6	1.02	6.7	1.75	11.7	18	2.4	157,100	3,062,925	G	-2856	.9	--
Amdahl Corp	12.7	12.7	13.1	22.7q	.47		-44.4	-44.4	-41.3	10	3	03-86	.20	1.1	0	39	33	05-13-86	2.6	.96	2.5	2.00	5.0	24	2.1	829	47,385	12,337	+2	4.7	12
Anderson Jacob	-14.9	-16.3	-17.0	-3.2q	-1.18		NE	NE	NE	NC	-29	03-86	.08		0	0	0	11-25-83	-8.2	1.34	-11.0	2.67	-29.4	43	1.2	6	2,702	131	-307	2.1	03
Apollo Cptr	-.1	-.1	13.4	-9.8q	-.28		-92.3	-92.3	-100.0	10	-6	03-86	.00		0	0	0	03-01-84	-3.3	1.15	-3.8	1.47	-5.6	17	3.5	417	34,383	16,692	-307	0.0	12
Apple Cptr	-6.1	-16.8	-15.0	93.8q	1.48		206.3	53.8	-13.5	20	17	03-86	.00		-14	0	0	00-00-00	5.4	1.85	10.0	1.70	17.0	0	2.8	2,248	62,650	17,856	-451	0.0	09
Appld Magnet	-2.2	-1.7	-11.7	1.9q	.29		-6.7	100.0	NE	NC	2	03-86	.00		0	0	0	02-14-84	1.6	.94	1.5	1.33	2.0	8	2.7	99	6,312	1,235	-10	1.1	09
AST Research	10.1	37.5	45.8	29.8q	2.62		-5.2	47.4	69.0	NC	52	03-86	.00		0	0	0	00-00-00	17.0	2.31	39.2	1.33	52.3	0	3.9	156	11,370	2,535	0	0.0	06
Audiotronics Cp	-178.6	-62.6	-58.8	-2.6q	-2.17		NE	NE	NE	NC	-65	03-86	.00		0	NE	NE	07-10-84	-37.1	1.02	-37.7	1.72	-65.0	40	4.5	3	1,189	25	0	0.0	06
Barry Wright	1.0	1.0	-2.4	11.2q	1.24		33.3	33.3	-15.6	-1	5	03-86	.60	2.9	16	52	32	04-14-86	5.7	1.32	7.5	1.39	10.4	0	3.0	191	9,141	3,357	+0	0.6	12
Burroughs Cp	-2.7	-2.7	2.3	217.6q	4.78		-66.0	-66.0	-12.8	20	4	03-86	2.60	4.2	1	48	61	06-30-86	4.3	1.12	4.8	1.81	8.7	32	2.3	2,802	45,555	32,574	+3	1.8	12
C 3 Inc	-41.3	4.1	18.1	-.6q	-.08		-100.0	-47.2	-100.0	NC	-1	12-85	.00		0	0	0	07-14-81	-.8	.75	-.6	1.33	-.8	0	3.4		9,648	2,226	0	0.8	12
C COR Electronics	-22.7	-19.1	-11.1	-4.9q	-1.61		NE	NE	NE	NC	-22	03-86	.00		0	0	0	00-00-00	-20.4	.93	-18.9	1.16	-22.0	4	7.5	22	3,015	118	0	0.0	06
Centronics Data	-16.7	-16.7	11.2	1.9q	.16		-73.0	-67.2	NE	NC	3	03-86	.00		0	0	0	12-22-80	.9	1.56	1.4	2.43	3.4	83	3.0	73	11,975	1,215	-12	0.7	12
Cipher Data	-9.5	-15.6	-11.9	5.4q	.38		-60.0	-73.0	NE	NC	5	03-86	.00		0	0	0	05-25-83	3.6	1.03	3.7	1.19	4.4	0	6.4	215	14,246	9,839	-12	0.0	06
Comdisco Inc	64.6	55.3	34.7	72.9q	1.77		100.0	59.0	77.0	83	24	03-86	.16	.7	24	9	11	03-11-86	9.5	.72	6.8	3.94	26.8	75	NA	882	40,300	8,885	+28	2.1	09
Compaq Cptr	48.5	48.5	51.7	30.3q	1.10		76.5	76.5	111.5	NC	32	03-86	.00		0	0	0	00-00-00	5.5	1.76	9.7	2.29	22.2	55	2.4	375	26,348	9,321	0	6.7	12
CompuScan	-40.0	-22.3	-19.0	-1.5q	-.27		NE	-100.0	-100.0	NC	-11	02-86	.00		0	0	0	06-22-81	-8.8	1.02	-9.0	1.17	-10.5	1	5.4	9	5,646	443	0	0.0	05
Comp Automation	-64.8	-63.5	-72.2	-12.5q	-6.01		NE	NE	NE	NC	-51	03-86	.00		0	0	0	09-09-85	-83.3	.66	-54.8	.00	NM	15	1.4	7	2,059	628	0	0.0	06
Comp Consoles	-18.5	-18.5	-17.6	-42.0q	-3.60		NE	400.0	NE	NC	0	03-86	.00		0	0	0	07-01-83	-39.3	.57	-22.4	1.40	NM	388	.8	108	11,485	2,915	+15	0.8	03
Comp Memories	9.9	61.0	86.4	-11.0q	-.99		-66.7	-66.7	NE	NC	-23	12-85	.00		0	0	0	06-01-83	-7.3	2.23	-16.3	1.40	-22.9	0	3.0	21	11,109	510	-10	0.0	03
Comp Prods	30.0	30.0	7.9	-2.8q	-.15		-2.9	-2.9	-100.0	NC	22	03-86	.00		0	0	0	04-01-85	-2.9	.72	-2.1	2.33	-4.9	90	3.5	106	19,716	10,143	-28	0.0	12
Computervision	6.6	6.6	-17.0	-69.0q	-2.69		NE	NE	-100.0	NC	-37	03-86	.00		19	0	0	00-00-00	-15.4	1.02	-15.7	2.36	-37.1	78	2.3	399	28,725	11,876	-7	5.2	12
Control Data	-10.6	-10.6	-24.1	-604.0q	-14.98		NE	NE	NE	NC	-51	03-86	.00		0	NE	NE	06-15-83	-16.8	1.17	-19.7	2.57	-50.7	20	NA	917	40,764	19,217	-1	1.4	12
Convergent Tech	-20.6	-20.6	-8.0	13.2q	.36		400.0	400.0	-6	NC	-6	03-86	.00		0	0	0	00-00-00	3.5	1.37	4.8	1.21	5.8	0	4.6	264	36,359	13,515	-1	0.0	12
Corvus Systs	5.6	5.6	6.0	-6.7q	-.66		-66.7	-66.7	NE	NC	-27	03-85	.00		0	0	0	00-00-00	-12.4	1.50	-18.6	1.42	-26.5	6	3.2	80	24,084	1,229	0	0.0	05
Cray Research	19.6	19.6	33.3	75.7q	2.46		-2.9	-2.9	4.2	38	25	03-86	.00		0	0	0	08-19-85	18.7	.91	17.1	1.45	24.8	4	3.2	2,880	29,807	21,296	-17	2.7	12
Data General	-.4	-6.3	-11.0	-4.6q	-.17		-76.5	-76.5	-39.4	42	-37	03-86	.00		0	0	0	11-21-83	-.4	1.00	-.7	1.75	-.7	45	3.0	901	26,035	18,747	+0	7.5	09
Data Switch Cp	26.4	26.4	20.0	-1.5q	-.18		NE	NE	-5.2	2	-5	06-85	.00		0	0	0	06-15-83	4.3	.91	-3.9	1.21	-4.7	1	4.2	58	8,995	1,361	+4	0.0	03
Datapoint Cp	-34.3	-40.2	-35.5	-21.2q	-1.34		NE	NE	-13.3	36	-8	04-86	.00		0	0	0	02-09-81	-5.9	.71	-4.2	1.83	-7.7	38	2.3	144	17,764	5,888	+1	0.5	07
Dataproducts	-14.8	-25.0	-25.0	-26.8q	-1.29		NE	116.7	-100.0	NC	2	03-86	.00		0	0	0	06-02-86	-7.6	.95	-7.2	1.53	-11.0	5	2.7	292	20,860	11,314	0	1.6	03
Dataram Cp	-30.2	-4.9	62.3	4.2q	2.07		NE	NE	NE	NC	50	04-86	.16	1.1	0	NE	33	05-12-80	8.3	1.52	12.6	1.42	50.0	0	3.6	18	1,983	96	0	1.0	04
Decision Ind	18.0	12.7	22.8	5.7s	.60		-17.4	-17.4	-39.4	42	7	05-86	.00		0	0	0	00-00-00	3.1	1.48	4.6	1.43	6.6	1	2.9	131	9,349	3,332	+0	0.0	11
Digital Equip	14.0	12.0	11.9	479.3n	3.82		71.4	71.4	-5.2	2	11	03-86	.00		0	0	0	05-12-86	6.6	1.14	7.5	1.40	10.5	18	4.9	10,200	118,956	103,080	+4	2.8	06
Educ Computer	0	11.4	18.1	2.7n	.60		-13.3	-6.5	13.2	3	11	03-86	.16	1.2	14	8	0	06-16-86	8.4	.81	8.4	1.75	14.7	17	4.7	58	4,455	1,361	+1	0.0	06
Electron Assoc	-40.4	-40.4	-23.0	.4q	.12		0	0	NE	NC	4	03-86	.00		0	0	0	00-00-00	1.3	1.85	2.4	1.79	4.3	4	2.3	15	2,846	289	0	0.1	12
Elron Electronic	-3.9	-3.9	62.3	1.8q	.17		-88.5	-88.5	-91.5	44	2	06-85	.00		0	0	0	01-18-83	1.2	.75	.9	2.11	1.9	29	1.7	64	10,739	324	0	0.0	03

Computers, Subsystems and Peripherals

Company	Rev %Qtr	Rev %FY to Date	Rev %12Mo	Rev Last 12 Mos $Mil	EPS Last 12 Mos $	Earn %Qtr	Earn %FY to Date	Earn %12Mo	5-Yr Gr	Par Gr	Rpt Date	Div Amt $	Div Yield %	Div 5-Yr Gr	Payout FY %	Payout 5Yr %	Last X-Dvd Date	Prof Mgn	Asset Turn	ROTA	Leverage	ROE	Debt/Eq %	Cur Ratio	Mkt Value $Mil	Shares Out 000	Held by Banks/Funds 000	Insider Trad 000	Short Int Ratio Days	FY Ends Mo
Ind. Group	4.7	4.8	1.4	7,522.6	2.50	12.4	-9.2	-17.3	4	7	---	1.09	2.1	1	11	4	---	6.6	1.02	6.7	1.75	11.7	18	2.4	157,100	3,062,925	G	-2856	.9	--
Emulex Cp	-.4	-2.2	-1.9	6.2n	.48	33.3	-22.0	-27.3	33	12	03-86	.00	.00	0	0	0	02-29-84	6.1	1.44	8.8	1.35	11.9	2	3.2	82	13,128	6,059	-59	0.0	06
Esprit Syst	5.2	-19.3	-16.1	-5.1n	-1.29	NE	NE	NE	NC	0	02-86	.00	.00	0	0	0	00-00-00	-19.6	1.57	-30.7	.00	NM	17	1.2	16	7,628	0	0	0.0	05
Fortune Systs	9.2	9.2	-26.1	-19.6q	-.93	NE	NE	NE	NC	-46	03-86	.00	.00	0	0	0	00-00-00	-40.8	.83	-33.7	1.37	-46.3	3	3.5	49	21,192	3,204	0	0.0	12
Gandalf Tech	31.3	26.6	24.3	.26	.26	400.0	-22.2	-46.9	-13	0	04-86	.00	NA	0	0	0	00-00-00	2.5	1.40	5.2	1.49	5.2	11	2.7	66	9,939	1,052	-1	0.0	07
Genisco Tech	19.5	15.0	25.8	.5s	.19	NE	NE	NE	5	3	03-86	.00	.00	0	0	0	03-10-81	1.3	1.31	1.7	1.88	3.2	44	3.4	15	2,667	505	0	2.3	09
Gould Inc	-.5	-.5	2.7	-180.4q	-4.05	-26.8	-26.8	-100.0	NC	-31	03-86	.68	3.1	-19	NE	328	06-09-86	-12.7	1.02	-13.0	2.06	-26.8	52	2.6	970	44,358	20,234	-3	0.6	12
Hewlett-Pack	6.0	5.2	4.2	480.0s	1.87	-3.9	-4.2	-28.9	12	11	04-86	.22	.7	18	NE	12	06-12-86	7.2	1.18	8.5	1.42	12.1	3	2.4	10,534	256,916	116,729	-3	1.8	10
Honeywell Inc	1.5	1.5	7.5	255.4q	5.59	-3.0	-43.0	-15.8	1	6	03-86	2.00	2.6	6	32	32	05-23-86	3.8	1.34	5.1	1.94	9.9	25	1.7	3,467	45,775	31,599	+1	0.8	12
Info International	-18.1	4.9	7.1	.6f	.22	-37.0	-37.0	-78.6	-6	1	03-86	.20	1.3	2	91	24	01-09-87	3.0	.90	1.8	1.33	2.4	0	3.9	39	2,481	543	+10	0.0	04
Intoltron Syst	4.4	4.4	.0	22g	.44	-80.0	-80.0	-72.2	17	4	03-86	.00	.0	0	0	0	00-00-00	2.0	.87	1.8	1.35	3.5	1	2.7	77	5,141	3,191	+9	0.0	12
Intecom Inc	-31.8	-31.8	-19.1	-13.4q	-.41	NE	NE	NE	-9	-9	03-86	.00	.0	0	0	0	09-22-83	-11.8	.63	-7.4	1.15	-8.5	0	6.1	167	32,673	12,365	-15	0.0	12
Integrated Soft	10.4	10.4	17.1	4.5q	.80	-12.5	-12.5	-3.6	NC	11	03-86	.00	.0	0	0	0	00-00-00	11.0	.75	8.2	1.39	11.4	3	3.1	58	5,500	2,648	0	0.0	12
Intelligent Sys	8.7	1.3	1.6	.0f	.00	-100.0	-100.0	-100.0	NC	NC	03-86	.00	.0	0	0	0	03-07-83	11.0	NC	NC	NC	0	3	2.2	60	10,850	2,699	0	0.0	03
Intergraph Cp	34.9	34.9	29.9	71.5q	1.29	14.3	14.3	-.8	50	18	03-86	.00	.0	0	0	0	06-17-85	12.7	1.10	14.0	1.26	17.7	3	4.4	1,449	55,733	29,662	-61	0.0	03
Intermec Cp	-1.9	7.2	7.5	1.5f	.28	-60.9	-65.0	-65.0	10	5	03-86	.00	.0	0	0	0	03-09-83	3.5	.97	3.4	1.32	4.5	0	3.6	84	5,482	1,575	0	0.0	03
Intl Bus Mach	3.7	3.7	9.3	6586.0q	10.71	2.5	2.9	2.9	14	12	03-86	4.40	3.0	5	41	43	05-08-86	13.1	.95	12.5	1.65	20.6	12	2.3	90,159	615,418	306,550	+1	0.8	12
Iomega Cp	50.2	50.2	86.7	9.8q	.64	110.0	110.0	113.3	NC	5	03-86	.00	.0	0	0	0	00-00-00	7.7	1.69	13.0	1.48	19.3	12	3.0	191	15,006	2,566	0	1.2	12
ISC Systems	8.7	14.1	-7.7	12.9n	.86	60.0	93.9	65.4	27	19	03-86	.00	.0	0	0	0	06-18-81	9.8	1.15	11.3	1.69	19.1	31	3.3	251	15,949	4,734	-150	0.0	07
Kaypro Cp	9.1	-21.4	-33.3	-17.4s	-.48	NE	NE	NE	NC	-72	02-86	.00	.0	0	0	0	00-00-00	-26.4	1.68	-44.4	1.62	-71.9	4	2.2	65	36,000	326	-58	0.0	08
Key Tronic	-9.0	-14.8	-18.1	.0n	.00	167	167	-100.0	NC	18	03-86	.00	.0	0	0	0	00-00-00	.0	NC	NC	NC	0	7	3.3	93	8,832	1,756	-58	0.0	06
Lee Data	17.4	2.2	2.1	2.1f	.15	NE	NE	NE	NC	2	03-86	.00	.0	0	0	0	00-00-00	2.3	.83	1.9	1.26	2.4	6	8.2	95	14,058	3,375	-30	0.0	03
LSI Logic	46.5	46.5	52.4	11.3q	.29	75.0	75.0	-17.1	NC	5	03-86	.00	.0	0	0	0	03-17-86	7.3	.41	-9.1	1.63	4.9	35	7.5	384	38,861	17,040	-14	0.0	12
LTX	-22.9	-35.4	-30.4	-10.6n	-1.17	-100.0	-100.0	-100.0	NC	-16	04-86	.00	.0	0	0	0	03-22-83	-11.0	.83	-9.1	1.74	-15.8	47	4.4	91	8,650	3,669	0	0.8	07
Maxstor Sys	-46.7	-46.7	-27.5	-10.7q	-.66	NE	NE	NE	NC	-48	02-86	.00	.0	0	0	0	00-00-00	-51.0	.65	-33.3	1.43	-47.6	17	4.7	33	15,970	2,057	0	0.0	12
Maxtor Cp	61.6	95.9	93.1	7.8f	.57	-12.5	-12.5	NC	NC	18	04-86	.16	.7	34	22	21	06-13-86	9.2	1.38	12.7	1.42	18.0	8	3.4	209	14,638	3,400	-29	0.0	03
Micom Syst	-27.1	-2.0	-1.5	10.7l	.61	-59.1	-59.1	-57.9	18	7	03-86	.00	.0	0	0	0	00-00-00	5.6	1.11	6.2	1.19	7.4	5	5.2	200	17,271	7,107	-1	0.0	03
Miniscribe Cp	68.6	68.6	14.0	1.1n	-.07	NE	NE	NE	NC	0	03-86	.00	.0	0	0	0	00-00-00	.3	1.67	1.0	2.00	1.0	52	3.0	144	19,192	2,440	+17	2.3	12
Mohawk Data	-40.1	-33.9	-30.5	-139.5n	-9.50	NE	NE	NE	NC	0	01-86	.00	.0	0	0	0	00-00-00	-52.4	1.04	-54.7	.00	NS	-326	NA	91	14,983	2,321	-14	0.0	04
MSI Data	10.8	11.2	12.5	.07	.07	NE	NE	NE	NC	0	03-86	.00	.0	0	0	0	00-00-00	.3	1.67	.5	1.60	.8	9	2.9	33	2,536	483	0	0.8	03
Natl Comcf Sys	33.0	33.0	59.3	16.1q	.93	25.0	25.0	36.8	33	27	04-86	.16	.7	34	22	21	06-09-86	7.0	2.53	17.7	1.85	32.8	34	2.3	373	17,145	8,291	-29	0.0	01
Natl Micronetics --- a	-21.2	-18.5	-26.7	-39.0n	-2.18	NE	NE	NE	NC	0	03-86	.00	.0	0	0	0	07-01-83	-95.1	.95	-90.1	.00	NM	32	1.0	21	9,187	1,980	-1	0.0	03
NBI Inc	23.8	37.5	36.3	1.1n	.08	-100.0	-100.0	-95.0	-16	0	03-86	.00	2.00	0	0	0	03-10-81	.4	1.25	.5	2.00	1.0	99	2.4	144	9,525	3,762	+17	2.3	06
NCR	14.0	14.0	-96.9	3.23	3.23	18.6	18.6	-8.3	10	7	06-09-86	.92	1.8	12	27	26	06-09-86	5.7	.04	.5	1.50	NS	10	2.1	5,029	97,895	63,276	-5	1.0	12
Netwk Systems	20.6	20.6	20.5	16.8q	.58	-8.3	-8.3	-3.3	47	11	03-86	.00	.0	0	0	0	04-16-85	17.9	.54	9.7	1.15	11.2	1	8.1	372	28,898	17,080	+2	0.0	12
Novell Inc	128.6	158.5	173.6	7.0s	.64	125.0	153.3	220.0	NC	0	04-86	.00	.0	0	0	0	00-00-00	13.5	3.35	45.2	.00	NM	18	1.5	219	10,972	883	0	0.0	10

Par Tech Cp	2.7	-15.0	11.9	-11.9	33.3
Priam Cp	2.7	25.2	11.9	-11.1	33.8
Prime Computer	14.5	21.3	17.5	-10.8	30.9
Printronix					
QMS Inc					
Quantum Cp	-16.4	48.9	22.2		
Recog Equip	55.2	-10.9	4.3		
SCI Systs Inc	-24.2	12.9	14.2		
Seagate Tech	214.4		18.8		
Sperry Corp	-.3	.9	46.8		
Storage Technl	-.3	-14.9	-27.2		
Stratus Cptr	77.0	84.0	10.2		
System Indus	7.2	-9.2	.4		
System Integ	.6	2.0	8.0		
Tab Products	-1.0	1.5	5.2		
Tandem Cpt	20.4	13.2	10.4	37.6	
Tandon Cp	-4.9	-30.2	-37.0	-97.9	
TEC Inc	-34.1	-24.1	-11.7	-.1	
TeleVideo Sys	-20.0	-18.2	-24.1	-10.1	
Telex Corp	17.0	20.0	19.9	67.5	
Tekon Cp	21.6	28.3	28.1	7.9	
Three Com	64.1	38.0	55.2	6.2	
Titan Cp	20.6	20.6	15.7	-7.9	
TRW Inc	3.8	3.8	-.9	139.2	
Ultimate Cp	54.9	37.6	37.2	14.4	
Ungemann Bass	117.5	117.5	59.2	5.0	
Valid Logic	-8.9	-8.9	.3	.01	
Ventron Resch	-52.0	-52.0	-40.0	-2.0	
Venritron Cp	-17.1	-17.1	-13.4	-3.8	
Visual Tech	-9.8	-9.8	-340.0	-29.7	
Wang Labs	24.0	12.2	5.3	-58.8	
Wells American	-100.0	-76.9	-75.0	-9.3	
Wespercorp	-72.2	54.3	200.0	-.6	
Wicat Systs	6.6	34.9	34.4	.4	
Wyse Technology	267.0	114.4	112.8	12.8	
Xebec	-46.9	-39.5	-33.9	-24.8	
Zentec	-16.4	-16.4	-26.0	-4.5	
Zycad Cp	-29.2	-29.2	25.0	-.2	

Value of New Construction Put in Place
(in billions of 1977 dollars except as noted)

Type of Construction	1972	1977	1982	1983	1984	1985[1]	1986[2]	Percent Change 1984 – 85	Percent Change 1985 – 86
Total new construction	194.0	173.4	153.6	170.9	191.2	201.8	212.9	6	6
Private residential	86.8	80.7	51.0	74.9	85.7	86.3	93.2	1	8
Single unit houses	44.1	55.0	26.2	44.6	50.3	50.0	56.0	-1	12
Multi – unit houses	27.6	10.5	10.3	14.5	17.4	17.5	17.5	1	0
Additions & alterations	11.9	14.2	11.8	12.5	13.9	14.5	15.2	4	5
Nonhousekeeping	3.2	1.0	2.7	3.3	4.1	4.3	4.5	5	5
Private nonresidential	60.8	54.5	69.1	62.6	70.4	77.2	79.9	10	4
Manufacturing facilities	6.9	7.7	11.1	8.2	8.4	9.5	10.5	13	10
Office buildings	7.7	5.3	14.8	13.2	15.9	19.0	19.8	20	4.0
Other commercial	12.0	9.5	9.1	9.5	13.6	16.2	17.8	19	10
Private electric utilities	12.7	12.4	14.9	13.1	12.7	12.0	11.2	-6	-7
Gas utilities	2.8	1.6	2.3	1.5	2.1	2.4	2.6	14	10
Telephone & telegraph	4.9	4.3	4.9	4.3	4.7	4.9	5.0	4	2
Private hospitals	4.7	3.3	3.8	4.2	3.9	3.4	3.2	-13	-5
Farm nonresidential	2.6	4.4	2.4	2.1	1.8	1.5	1.3	-17	-15
Railroads	0.6	0.7	1.7	2.0	2.4	2.5	(³)	4	(³)
Petroleum pipelines	0.5	1.2	0.3	0.3	0.2	0.2	(³)	0	(³)
Religious buildings	1.2	1.0	1.0	1.1	1.3	1.4	(³)	8	(³)
Private educational	1.4	0.7	0.9	0.9	0.9	1.0	(³)	11	(³)
Misc. buildings	1.3	1.2	1.1	1.2	1.5	1.6	(³)	7	(³)
Misc. construction	1.5	1.3	0.8	1.0	1.0	1.6	(³)	60	(³)
Public	46.4	38.1	33.5	33.4	35.1	38.3	39.8	9	4
Highways and bridges	16.5	9.3	9.0	9.7	10.7	12.0	12.8	12	7
Public educational	8.4	5.5	3.8	3.4	3.4	4.0	4.2	18	5
Sewer systems	2.7	5.4	3.7	3.5	4.0	4.2	4.2	5	0
Water supply systems	1.8	1.8	2.0	1.4	1.7	2.0	2.2	18	10
Conservation & development	3.4	3.9	3.3	3.2	3.0	3.2	3.4	7	7
Military facilities	1.7	1.4	1.4	1.6	1.8	2.0	2.3	11	15
Public hospitals	1.5	1.7	1.3	1.3	1.2	1.2	1.1	0	-8
Federal industrial	0.8	1.1	1.0	1.1	1.1	1.2	1.0	9	-20
Housing & redevelopment	1.4	0.9	1.0	1.1	1.0	0.9	(³)	-10	(³)
Other public buildings	4.9	3.6	3.7	4.0	4.2	4.6	(³)	10	(³)
Misc. public construction	3.3	3.5	3.3	3.1	3.0	3.0	(³)	0	(³)

[1] Estimated.
[2] Forecast.
[3] Value for this category not estimated separately, but included in totals.

SOURCE: U.S. Department of Commerce: Bureau of the Census, and International Trade Administration (ITA). Estimate and forecasts by ITA.

Source: *U.S. Industrial Outlook 1986*, U.S. Department of Commerce.

Residential Construction

Company	Rev Pct Chg Last Qtr %	Rev Pct Chg FY to Date %	Rev Pct Chg Last 12 Mos %	Rev Last 12 Mos $Mil	EPS Last 12 Mos $	EPS Pct Chg Last Qtr %	EPS Pct Chg FY to Date %	EPS Pct Chg Last 12 Mos %	EPS 5-Yr Growth Rate %	Par Growth Rate %	Date of Report	Div Amt $	Div Yield %	Div 5-Yr Growth Rate %	Payout Last FY %	Payout Last 5 Yrs %	Last X-Dvd Date	Profit Margin	Asset Turnover	Return on Total Assets	Leverage Ratio	Return on Equity	Debt to Equity %	Curr Ratio	Market Value $Mil	Latest Shares Outstndg 000	Held by Banks-Funds 000	Insider Net Trading 000	Short Interest Ratio Days	Fiscal Year Ends Mo
Ind. Group	-44.7	4.7	-7.9	278.4	1.48	-28.6	-5.4	40.0	42	8	03-86	.52	2.2	0	18	30	---	3.9	.64	2.5	4.64	11.6	135	2.7	4,292	179,473	56,575	-47	4.9	--
An Continental	43.7	43.7	2.3	43.7q	2.86	65.2	65.2	177.7	81	52	03-86	.10	.8	0	18	30	05-19-86	6.2	.18	1.1	48.64	53.5	1639	NA	160	12,228	2,063	0	0.0	12
Anthony Ind	27.2	27.2	12.1	3.50	.98	-10.5	-10.5	-35.1	11	5	03-86	.44	2.7b	6	41	33	05-27-86	1.5	.18	2.6	3.23	8.4	74	1.8	55	3,415	1,652	0	55.0	12
Calprop Cp	220.0	220.0	28.5	1.8q	.78	225.0	225.0	-51.3	8	10	03-86	.00	.0	0	0	2	11-14-85	10.0	1.73	5.4	1.78	9.6	0	NA	29	2,352	150	0	0.3	12
Centex Cp	16.9	17.4	17.4	47.6l	2.62	19.6	19.1	19.1	NC	13	03-86	.25	.7	0	10	11	06-10-86	3.3	1.58	5.2	2.79	14.5	37	.0	617	17,824	9,519	-18	0.3	03
Gen Homes	43.8	29.0		15.9s	1.06	NE	NE	100.0	42	12	03-86	.00	.0	0	0	11	00-00-00	4.0	.75	3.0	3.83	11.5	36	NA	201	15,000	691	0	2.9	09
Hovnanian Ent	106.8	40.3	40.2	11.5f	1.72	75.5	75.5	75.5	31	29	02-86	.00	.0	0	0	0	03-10-86	5.0	.98	4.9	5.84	28.6	119	NA	208	6,720	520	0	1.3	02
Key Company	61.3	58.3	39.2	.9s	.30	18.2	-10.5	-86.5	0	1	04-86	.25	4.4	7	141	29	06-23-86	2.3	2.09	4.8	1.83	8.8	0	1.7	6	1,128	53	0	1.0	10
Lennar Corp	-9.8	-9.8	37.5	9.9q	1.10	-50.0	-50.0	34.1	-12	6	02-86	.20	1.1	2	15	0	04-29-86	4.4	.68	3.0	2.33	7.0	40	NA	159	8,839	1,899	0	1.3	11
Levitt Cp	-23.6	-23.6	-16.8	1.5q	.42	-70.0	-70.0	-46.2	NC	7	03-86	.00	.0	0	0	0	00-00-00	2.2	.77	1.7	3.88	6.6	162	.0	34	3,400	75	0	0.0	12
Natl Enterpr	48.0	48.0	1.4	.9q	.10	NE	NE	NE	NC	5	03-86	.00	.0	0	0	0	00-00-00	1.3	1.00	1.3	4.15	5.4	190	1.3	42	7,027	436	0	0.3	12
Oriole Homes	13.8	13.8	33.3	3.1q	.80	NE	NE	2566.7	-21	6	03-86	.15	1.8	-15	25	75	03-11-86	4.1	.59	2.4	3.21	7.7	99	NA	17	2,016	108	0	20.5	12
Ryan Homes	.4	.4	-.5	22.4q	1.9	1.9	1.9	70.4	9	9	03-86	1.20	3.5	-5	32	60	07-01-86	4.0	1.58	6.3	2.37	14.9	12	2.7	238	6,857	4,608	-18	0.3	12
Ryland Grp	53.6	53.6	32.7	17.8q	2.80	185.7	185.7	91.8	31	16	03-86	.80	1.7	17	25	31	07-09-86	3.3	3.12	10.3	2.14	22.0	18	4.8	298	6,186	4,010	-3	1.9	12
Std-Pacific	13.2	13.2	33.0	22.2q	1.92	96.0	96.0	53.6	35	17	03-86	.40	1.2	-2	22	22	06-25-86	8.3	1.04	8.6	2.51	21.6	69	3.1	378	11,512	5,586	-7	0.1	12
US Home	-13.8	-13.8	-14.6	-7.3q	-.21	NE	NE	NE	NC	-3	03-86	.00	.0	0	0	NE	08-27-84	-.8	1.13	-.9	2.89	-2.6	110	NA	259	36,372	5,039	0	0.5	12
UDC Univ Dev	.0	.0	.0	0	NC	NE	NE	NC	NC	NC	00-00	4.00	11.9	-5	0	0	03-10-86	NC	NC	NC	NC	NC	0	.0	218	6,491	1,229	0	0.6	NA
Walter, Jim	-178.0	-62.3	-45.9	76.9n	2.66	-100.0	-100.0	-32.3	NC	4	05-86	1.40	3.1	0	25	38	04-14-86	6.1	.44	2.7	3.15	8.5	117	NA	1,305	28,994	18,678	-0	0.3	08
Wash Homes	61.3	26.2	25.4	6.1n	2.14	160.0	138.7	118.4	NC	47	04-86	.00	.0	0	0	0	01-21-86	8.2	1.63	13.4	3.50	46.9	174	NA	65	3,112	259	0	2.1	07

General Contractors

Company	Revenue Pct. Change Last Qtr %	Rev FY to Date %	Rev Last 12 Mos %	Last 12 Mos $Mil	EPS Per Share Last 12 Mos $	EPS Pct Change Last Qtr %	EPS FY to Date %	EPS Last 12 Mos %	5-Year Growth Rate %	Par Growth Rate %	Date of Report	Div Current Rate Amt $	Yield %	Div 5-Year Growth Rate %	Payout Last FY %	Payout Last 5 Yrs %	Last X-Dvd Date	Profit Margin %	Asset Turnover	Return on Total Assets %	Leverage Ratio	Return on Equity %	Debt to Eq. %	Current Ratio	Mkt Value $Mil	Latest Shares Outstndg 000	Held by Banks Funds 000	Insider Net Trading 000	Short Int. Ratio Days	Fiscal Year Ends Mo
Ind. Group	10.8	12.2	9.4	-456.3	-2.43	NE	-100.0	-100.0	NC	-20	—	.51	2.8		78	49	—	-3.2	1.78	-5.7	2.91	-16.6	30	1.3	3,529	190,850	70,314	-36	2.2	—
Am Med Bldg	56.7	11.8	7.1	-.3	-.19	NE	NE	-100.0	NC	0	12-85	.00	.0	0	0	0	07-20-83	-2.0	1.85	-3.7	.00	NS	-35	1.1	33	7,281	725	0	4.5	12
Blount Inc	-13.0	-13.0	24.4	-1.5q	-.13	-97.6	-97.6	-100.0	NC	-5	05-86	.45	3.1	21	167	26	06-09-86	-.1	2.00	-.2	5.50	-1.1	165	1.3	175	11,889	2,439	+0	12.1	02
Drevo Corp	-2.1	-2.1	3.4	4.0q	.27	NE	NE	NE	NC	-2	03-86	.50	3.1	-14	238	NE	04-29-86	.7	1.75	.7	2.86	2.0	27	1.4	221	13,561	6,938	0	.5	12
Dynalectron Cp	14.3	14.3	3.2	7.0q	.40	120.0	120.0	120.0	-16	2	03-86	.27	1.5	30	79	18	03-13-86	1.1	2.27	2.5	2.72	6.8	22	1.6	175	9,578	2,158	0	1.5	12
Elcor Cp	-19.2	-39.3	-41.9	-7.7n	-2.16	-67.7	NE	-67.7	NC	-43	04-86	.36	2.4	-8	NE	NE	04-07-86	-5.7	1.54	-8.8	4.18	-36.8	188	1.5	53	3,314	655	+0	1.2	06
Fluor Corp	21.0	23.0	10.9	-550.0s	-6.95	NE	NE	NE	NC	-56	04-86	.40	2.5	-9	NE	NE	06-27-86	-11.8	1.67	-19.7	2.70	-53.2	25	1.0	1,288	79,244	32,222	0	.9	10
Foster Wheeler	11.0	11.0	-.5	24.7q	.72	-15.4	-15.4	-30.8	-17	2	04-86	.44	3.3	1	58	33	05-09-86	2.0	1.20	2.4	2.50	6.0	30	1.7	465	34,459	16,522	-16	.6	12
Jacobs Eng	-6.5	-9.9	1.9	1.6q	.37	-78.6	-78.6	NE	NC	6	03-86	.00	.0	0	0	NE	11-15-83	.8	2.00	1.6	3.75	6.0	6	1.1	40	4,271	359	-3	.0	09
Morrison Knuds	5.6	5.6	7.1	41.9q	3.88	4.2	4.2	NE	2	6	03-86	1.48	3.2	10	38	33	05-06-86	.8	2.25	4.5	2.38	10.7	11	1.4	466	10,393	5,694	-13	.0	12
Perini Corp	-6.9	-3.3	-3.3	-17.9r	-5.64	-6.1	-6.1	-100.0	NC	-25	12-85	.80	2.6	35	80	49	08-18-86	-2.2	2.50	-5.5	3.96	-21.8	46	1.2	99	3,200	903	0	.5	12
Seligman&Assc	64.7	222.2	166.6	1.7n	.92	-100.0	-100.0	-100.0	NC	21	04-86	.00	.0	0	0	0	00-00-00	10.6	.79	8.4	2.44	20.5	114	.0	18	1,804	30	0	1.2	07
Stone & Web	-10.2	-10.2	-11.9	29.8q	4.19	113.9	113.9	109.1	-2	6	03-86	1.60	3.2	0	33	34	06-25-86	10.7	.53	5.7	1.84	10.5	2	1.6	370	7,335	1,079	-20	.0	12
Turner Cp	26.2	26.2	29.6	10.4q	2.47	-29.3	-29.3	-17.9	7	8	03-86	1.30	4.9	16	45	36	05-19-86	.5	2.80	1.4	11.36	15.9	11	1.1	105	3,931	590	+16	3.7	12

Other Building - Heavy

Company	Revenue Pct. Change Last Qtr %	Rev FY to Date %	Rev Last 12 Mos %	Last 12 Mos $Mil	EPS Per Share Last 12 Mos $	EPS Pct Change Last Qtr %	EPS FY to Date %	EPS Last 12 Mos %	5-Year Growth Rate %	Par Growth Rate %	Date of Report	Div Current Rate Amt $	Yield %	Div 5-Year Growth Rate %	Payout Last FY %	Payout Last 5 Yrs %	Last X-Dvd Date	Profit Margin %	Asset Turnover	Return on Total Assets %	Leverage Ratio	Return on Equity %	Debt to Eq. %	Current Ratio	Mkt Value $Mil	Latest Shares Outstndg 000	Held by Banks Funds 000	Insider Net Trading 000	Short Int. Ratio Days	Fiscal Year Ends Mo
Ind. Group	-.1	10.1	4.0	-4.6	-.05	NE	NE	NE	NC	-3	—	.59	4.5	-1	76	59	—	-.1	1.00	-.1	2.00	-.2	53	1.3	1,785	135,141	34,402	-6	2.8	—
ACMAT Corp	-50.0	-50.0	-57.4	-1.7q	-1.55	NE	NE	NE	NC	-61	03-86	.00	.0	0	0	0	00-00-00	-8.5	1.00	-8.5	7.14	-60.7	186	1.3	19	1,030	16	-2	.0	12
Am Ship Bldg	-50.0	-39.8	-14.9	8.0s	1.36	8.3	-51.3	-89.7	NC	7	03-86	.00	7.0	6	63	112	05-14-86	5.2	1.29	6.7	2.51	16.8	39	1.5	68	5,998	702	0	1.5	09
Banister Contl	-46.3	-46.3	-40.7	3.4n	.03	12.5	NE	89.8	NC	7	03-86	.80	7.0	0	112	261	09-17-79	-.2	1.00	-.5	2.50	-.5	4	1.1	35	5,038	290	+10	1.3	12
Bk Bldg Equip	1.1	-5.4	-2.5	1.8s	1.12	62.5	36.4	89.8	NC	11	04-86	.40	NA	0	40	190	05-13-86	1.6	3.06	4.9	3.47	17.0	9	1.2	15	1,624	175	0	.3	10
Burnup & Sims Inc	-.2	2.4	-2.6	.1n	.02	-100.0	-100.0	-98.2	NC	0	01-86	.00	4.3	-19	40	17	08-03-81		1.00		2.00		63	2.5	54	8,961	1,616	0	.0	04
Fischbach Cp	29.5	12.3	12.1	-13.6q	-3.50	NE	NE	NE	NC	-8	03-86	.00	.0	-1	NE	45	08-19-85	-1.2	2.17	-2.6	3.23	-8.4	19	1.5	103	3,911	2,735	0	8.6	09
Goldfield Cp	228.6	228.6	20.0	-2.6q	-.11	NE	NE	NE	NC	0	03-86	.00	.0	0	0	0	00-00-00	-43.3	.69	-29.9	.00	NM	58	.5	12	24,736	669	0	15.9	12
Kasler Cp	17.4	38.3	33.6	-6.9q	-1.38	NE	NE	NE	NC	49	04-86	.00	.0	0	NE	81	06-24-85	-4.7	2.66	-12.5	3.89	-48.6	80	1.3	50	5,026	1,906	0	.0	10
KOI Cp	13.8	13.8	12.1	10.0q	1.08	500.0	500.0	38.5	17	15	03-86	.24	1.6	0	14	30	05-28-86	3.7	1.89	7.0	2.73	19.1	81	2.3	132	8,729	1,254	0	.3	03
McDermott Intl	-4.3	.7		56.3l	1.52	NE	198.0	198.0	-18	-1	06-86	1.80	8.5	-12	30	57	06-10-86	3.7	.76	1.3	3.62	4.7	61	1.1	786	36,973	20,629	-3	1.6	03
McDowell Ent	-52.9	-52.9	-38.2	-3.6q	-1.48	NE	NE	NE	NC	-28	03-86	.00	.0	0	0	0	08-31-81	-7.2	1.36	-9.8	2.81	-27.5	5	1.1	10	2,452	149	0	.0	12
Myers LE Grp	-64.0	-64.0	-50.0	-13.9q	-6.12	NE	NE	NE	NC	-72	03-86	.00	.0	0	0	0	03-08-82	-15.4	2.29	-35.2	2.05	-72.0	41	3.3	9	2,261	19	0	1.9	12
Newberry Cp	21.3	13.6	13.8	-3.4l	-1.82	NE	NE	-100.0	NC	-31	02-86	.00	.0	0	0	NE	08-26-65	-4.1	2.27	-9.3	3.32	-30.9	85	1.4	11	1,883	41	0	.6	03
Std Shares	-3.0	116.4	116.6	19.5l	7.41	51.6	51.6	19.7	3	12	02-86	.00	.0	0	277	52	09-27-79	3.4	1.26	4.3	2.77	11.9	8	2.2	255	2,626	725	0	.3	02
Tacoma Bbldg	2.3	2.3	14.1	-60.0q	-5.22	NE	NE	NE	NC	3	03-86	.00	.0	0	0	0	12-07-82	-53.1	1.26	-67.0	.00	NS	0	1.1	11	11,911	199	0	4.9	12
Todd Shipyards	9.9	-18.4	-18.3	-2.3l	-.56	-65.1	-65.1	-100.0	NC	-5	03-86	1.32	4.8	18	NE	28	04-29-86	-.6	1.00	-.6	2.67	-1.6	39	1.6	116	4,194	1,791	-2	11.0	03
Ultrasystems	18.1	18.1	4.7	7.5q	.97	54.5	54.5	NE	13	17	04-86	.08	.7	0	7	10	02-10-86	4.8	1.63	7.8	2.31	18.0	77	2.7	92	7,798	1,486	-10	.0	01

Data Processing and Computer Software

World Computer Market Growth Outlook by Region
(in billions of dollars)

Region	Sales 1984	Sales 1987	Compound Annual Growth Rate 1984-87
North America			
United States	43.8	72.0	18
Canada	2.5	4.2	19
Total	46.3	76.2	18
Western Europe			
West Germany	6.8	9.8	13
United Kingdom	5.1	8.8	20
France	5.1	7.8	15
Italy	2.6	4.4	20
Sweden	1.8	3.2	20
Finland	1.3	1.8	13
Netherlands	1.1	1.8	17
Switzerland	0.9	1.4	16
Denmark	0.6	0.9	26
Spain	0.6	0.9	14
Belgium	0.5	0.9	18
Norway	0.5	0.7	17
Portugal	0.1	0.2	18
Total	27.0	42.9	18
East Asia & Pacific			
Japan	11.3	16.8	14
Australia	2.6	3.3	10
China	0.9	5.4	80
South Korea	0.2	0.5	24
New Zealand	0.2	0.5	31
Taiwan	0.2	0.4	23
Singapore	0.2	0.5	34
Hong Kong	0.1	0.3	30
Malaysia	0.1	0.4	43
Total	15.8	28.1	21
Central-South America			
Brazil	0.9	3.7	60
Mexico	0.4	0.7	19
Total	1.3	4.4	50
Africa			
South Africa	0.9	1.7	22
Total	0.9	1.7	22
Near East			
Israel	0.5	0.9	19
Saudi Arabia	0.2	0.3	20
Total	0.7	1.2	20
South Asia			
India	0.3	0.8	38
Total	0.3	0.8	38
TOTAL ALL REGIONS	92.3	155.3	19

SOURCE: Country Market Survey (CMS) and Post Country Action Plans (PCAP), International Trade Administration, U.S. Department of Commerce.

Source: *U.S. Industrial Outlook 1986*, U.S. Department of Commerce.

Computer Software, Data Processing

Company	Rev % Chg Last Qtr	Rev % Chg FY to Date	Rev % Chg Last 12 Mos	Rev Last 12 Mos $Mil	EPS Last 12 Mos $	Earn % Chg Last Qtr	Earn % Chg FY to Date	Earn % Chg Last 12 Mos	Earn 5-Yr Growth Rate	Par Growth Rate	Date of Report	Div Amt $	Div Yield %	Div 5-Yr Growth	Payout Last FY	Payout Last 5 Yrs	Last X-Dvd Date	Profit Margin %	Asset Turnover	Return on Total Assets	Leverage Ratio	Return on Equity	Debt to Equity %	Current Ratio	Market Value $Mil	Latest Shares Out 000	Held by Banks-Funds 000	Insider Net Trad 000	Short Int Ratio Days	Fiscal Yr End Mo
Ind. Group	14.8	45.2	19.8	512.5	.83	17.1	16.3	94.8	19	14	---	.10	.5	1	12	13	---	7.3	1.10	8.0	1.93	15.4	20	2.3	12,773	616,692	225,681	-1899	7	--
AGS Cptr	25.7	25.7	26.4	7.2q	1.36	-18.9	-18.9	15.3	37	15	03-86	.00	.0	0	0	•	00-00-00	2.4	2.71	6.5	2.26	14.7	31	1.5	110	5,253	1,329	0	2.1	12
Altos Cptr Syst	-19.7	-58.4	-42.7	16.7m	1.17	277.8	85.5	48.1	35	17	03-86	.00	.0	0	0	•	00-00-00	23.5	.59	13.9	1.20	16.7	1	5.2	219	14,012	4,137	+48	0.0	06
Am Managemnt	11.7	11.7	11.6	4.1q	.81	63.6	63.6	37.3	NC	18	03-86	.00	.0	0	0	•	06-10-86	3.6	2.31	8.3	2.18	18.1	22	1.8	80	4,752	1,152	0	0.0	12
Anacomp Inc	-5.7	-7.9	-5.6	-3.5s	-.19	-93.5	-86.7	NE	NC	0	03-86	.00	.0	0	0	NE	07-14-83	-3.0	1.27	-3.8	.00	NS	-1828	1.4	173	29,476	3,094	0	7.8	09
Ashton Tate	71.7	71.7	46.3	19.4q	1.92	88.0	88.0	106.5	NC	36	04-86	.00	.0	0	0	•	00-00-00	14.0	1.56	21.9	1.66	36.3	9	1.8	328	11,376	4,366	+23	0.0	01
ASK Cptr Systs	-8.3	-15.6	-11.3	6.2n	.49	-21.4	-34.0	-18.3	28	10	03-86	.00	.0	0	0	•	00-00-00	8.9	.84	7.5	1.27	9.5	2	4.5	141	12,804	7,817	-185	0.0	06
Autodesk Inc	115.7	115.7	150.0	7.8q	1.18	75.0	75.0	156.5	NC	NC	04-86	.00	.0	0	0	•	00-00-00	22.3	7.14	59.2	.00	NM		1.5	277	6,890	1,675	0	0.6	01
Autom Data Pr	18.6	16.0	15.5	101.3n	1.40	19.4	18.4	18.6	13	13	03-86	.38	1.1	14	25	26	06-13-86	8.8	1.14	10.0	1.81	18.1	29	1.9	2,588	73,150	48,680	0	0.6	06
BPI Systs Inc	39.1	17.2	22.2	.4l	.06	NE	NE	NE	NC	7	03-86	.00	.0	0	0	•	03-02-83	3.6	.78	2.8	2.54	7.1	93	2.5	16	5,680	714	0	0.0	03
CMX Co	-180.0	-50.5	-50.0	.2l	.05	NE	NE	NE	NC	10	12-85	.00	.0	0	0	•	00-00-00	4.0	.58	2.3	4.35	-10.0	100	1.6	6	3,793	14	0	0.0	12
Comp Assoc	109.2	48.2	48.0	18.5l	.83	35.3	36.1	36.1	38	18	03-86	.00	.0	0	0	•	05-09-86	9.7	1.29	12.5	1.41	17.6	8	3.0	588	24,498	12,120	-722	0.0	03
Comp Factory	60.4	73.7	81.3	1.6s	.78	30.8	71.4	66.0	30	16	03-86	.12	1.6	0	35	11	00-00-00	2.1	3.62	7.6	2.14	16.3	31	2.3	61	3,076	373	-9	0.0	09
Comp Language	-8.5	-8.5	-4.0	2.5q	.19	-28.8	-28.8	-61.2	-6	2	03-86	.00	.0	0	0	•	06-11-86	2.6	1.35	3.5	1.57	5.5	12	1.9	103	13,745	593	0	6.5	12
Comp Sciences	19.1	15.9	15.8	23.9l	1.69	15.1	-16.3	-16.3	3	13	04-86	.00	.0	0	0	•	00-00-00	2.8	1.96	5.5	2.33	12.8	26	1.5	548	13,916	7,896	-12	0.0	03
Computone Syst	64.6	75.3	92.5	-.2s	-.06	-100.0	-100.0	NE	NC	-1	11-85	.00	.0	0	0	•	00-00-00	-.3	2.00	-.6	1.50	-.9	1	2.4	12	3,547	1,052	0		05
Compurac	26.3	26.3	26.5	1.3q	.52	87.5	87.5	116.7	31	6	03-86	.00	.0	0	0	•	04-08-86	14.4	1.61	23.2	1.34	31.0		3.4	35	2,955	219	0	0.3	01
Comshare Inc	14.2	13.0	4.6	1.2n	.53	93.8	NE	NE	NC	-16	03-86	.00	.0	36	NE	13	00-00-00	1.8	1.72	3.1	1.90	5.9	7	1.3	35	2,684	424	+1	0.0	06
Continuum Co	-30.9	8.9	10.4	-1.8l	-.42	-100.0	-100.0	-100.0	NC	12	03-86	.00	.0	0	0	•	03-24-86	-3.4	1.29	-4.4	3.68	-16.2	94	1.3	31	4,322	942	0	0.0	03
Cullinet Softwr	2.8	.1	.3	15.3l	-.50	-45.5	-38.3	-38.3	27	10	04-86	.00	.0	0	0	•	01-22-85	8.3	.95	7.9	1.57	12.4	0	2.0	387	30,052	13,643	+11	0.7	04
Daisy Syst	-22.4	8.4	33.6	14.2s	.79	-100.0	-92.7	-15.1	NC	10	03-86	.00	.0	0	0	•	00-00-00	11.2	.73	8.2	1.16	9.5		6.8	191	17,327	10,425	-5		09

Data I O	15.8	15.8	5.4	3.9q	38	-25.0	-25.0	-39.7	4	03-86	6	00	0	0	0	08-22-83	6.7	78	5.2	1.13	5.9	0	6.4	100	9,989	2,201	-203	0.0	12
DST Syst Inc	43.1	43.1	25.0	7.6q	79	-26.9	-26.9	-23.3	17	03-86	8	00	23	0	6	06-09-96	10.1	53	5.4	1.96	10.6	47	1.3	192	9,723	464	0	0.0	12
Dyatron	-19.8	-19.8	-7.3	.5q	10	-50.0	-50.0	-23.1	NC	03-86	7	00	0	0	NE	03-16-81	1.3	200	2.6	2.69	7.0	24	1.1	23	4,670	173	0	0.0	12
Evans & Suth	49.4	49.4	19.1	7.1q	83	275.0	275.0	-12.2	4	03-86	11	00	0	0	0	06-10-81	8.2	79	6.5	1.68	10.9	8	2.0	178	8,070	2,727	-301	0.0	12
Fidsta Cp	-50.9	-50.9	-26.5	11.8q	2.64	7700.0	7700.0	NE	NC	03-86	33	00	0	NE	NE	08-31-81	10.9	16	1.7	19.41	33.0	6	NA	31	4,429	605	0	0.1	12
GTECH Corp	17.6	75.9	73.9	2.0f	21	-100.0	-100.0	-55.3	NC	02-86	6	00	0	0	NE	00-00-00	2.5	64	1.6	3.56	5.7	180	2.2	274	9,238	456	-34	0.0	02
HBO Co	0	0	67.2	20.8q	90	0	0	-1.1	30	03-86	20	00	21	0	27	03-24-86	11.0	1.40	15.4	1.66	25.5	5	3.1	346	22,851	11,734	+15	0.0	12
Hogan Systs	28.6	-4.3	-3.5	-6.9f	-.52	NE	NE	NE	30	03-86	-22	00	0	0	0	12-05-83	-25.6	.55	-14.1	1.58	-22.3	0	2.4	138	13,158	3,787	-50	0.0	03
Kalvar Corp	-16.1	-10.2	-13.0	.3f	.02	NE	NE	NE	NC	03-86	8	00	0	0	0	00-00-00	-1.5	1.60	.24	.00	NS	-700	1.1	8	4,167	167	0	0.0	03
Logicon Inc	36.5	20.8	21.0	10.0f	2.10	12.5	17.3	17.3	29	03-86	22	00	10	0	11	06-16-86	5.0	3.22	16.1	1.51	24.3	0	2.8	156	4,659	1,862	-12	7.6	06
Lotus Development	55.0	55.0	44.5	40.0q	2.43	20.7	20.7	3.4	NC	03-86	29	00	0	0	0	00-00-00	16.0	1.34	21.5	1.34	28.9	0	3.1	599	16,193	7,296	0	0.0	06
MacNeal Sch	34.8	34.8	35.2	3.2q	.51	50.0	50.0	-16.4	21	04-86	9	00	38	0	18	08-25-86	13.9	.95	13.2	1.14	15.0	0	6.4	188	6,090	3,157	0	0.1	01
Mgmt Sci Amer	22.5	22.5	19.8	9.2q	.53	NE	NE	NE	-20	03-86	7	00	0	0	0	12-20-82	5.9	.86	5.1	1.39	7.1	0	2.9	239	17,209	7,281	-25	0.0	12
Mentor Graphics	14.9	14.9	33.9	6.8q	.42	-45.5	-45.5	-40.0	NC	03-86	5	00	0	0	0	00-00-00	4.8	.73	3.5	1.40	4.9	0	3.1	240	15,756	7,600	-26	0.0	12
Microsoft	43.9	28.8	31.5	33.7n	1.40	61.5	46.2	NC	62	03-86	52	00	0	0	0	00-00-00	19.7	2.63	51.8	1.19	61.9	0	4.9	760	24,715	0	0	0.0	06
Natl Data Cp	6.8	8.7	7.9	10.4n	.94	30.0	53.3	25.3	9	02-86	9	44	65	26	39	05-13-86	6.9	1.36	9.4	1.70	16.0	5	1.4	225	11,128	4,960	-9	0.0	05
Pansophic Sys	21.7	21.0	20.8	14.3l	1.69	20.5	20.7	20.7	20	04-86	20	00	0	0	0	00-00-00	17.7	.94	16.7	1.17	19.5	1	8.2	254	8,466	2,895	-16	1.3	04
Policy Mgmt	28.0	28.0	20.8	13.7q	.84	-20.8	-20.8	-6.7	48	03-86	13	00	0	0	0	10-03-83	12.5	.79	9.9	1.30	12.9	9	3.0	313	16,234	9,530	0	0.0	12
Safeguard Bus	17.1	17.1	14.2	8.3q	.66	-100.0	-100.0	-39.4	8	03-86	6	00	30	12	24	06-13-86	3.6	.56	5.6	1.89	10.6	35	2.2	228	12,639	4,989	-2	0.4	12
SEI Corp	14.8	14.8	13.5	4.1q	.71	33.3	33.3	914.3	-7	03-86	10	00	0	0	0	02-23-83	3.8	1.18	4.5	2.16	9.7	73	1.7	102	5,740	1,772	0	0.0	12
Shared Med Systs	20.1	20.1	21.1	43.8q	1.74	21.1	21.1	20.8	24	03-86	18	00	9	0	31	06-24-86	13.4	1.30	17.4	1.57	27.4	6	2.3	848	25,037	12,318	-23	0.0	02
Software AG Syst	20.7	28.1	28.5	8.3n	1.41	22.7	34.9	25.9	49	02-86	25	00	0	2	0	00-00-00	12.9	1.29	17.0	1.48	25.1	2	3.1	107	5,783	995	+4	0.0	05
Sterling Sftwr	881.7	1078.0	790.0	6.1s	.63	21.4	65.0	90.9	NC	03-86	12	00	30	0	9	06-12-85	3.4	.76	2.6	6.42	16.7	283	1.7	92	4,954	188	-338	0.0	09
Symbolics	-214.4	-35.5	-13.3	4.0n	.16	-66.7	71.4	100.0	NC	03-86	6	00	.18	0	0	00-00-00	7.7	.53	4.1	1.34	5.5	6	5.2	274	25,505	11,041	-45	0.0	08
TERA Co	22.6	7.8	8.6	-2.8n	-.33	NE	NE	NE	-15	03-86	-15	00	0	0	0	00-00-00	-11.2	.86	-9.6	1.53	-14.7	0	2.6	37	7,354	814	0	0.0	06
Total Systs	40.0	40.0	40.9	4.5q	.30	40.0	40.0	42.9	24	03-86	23	00	0	0	0	05-02-86	14.5	1.41	20.5	1.13	23.2	1	3.8	446	15,916	224	0	0.0	12
Triad System	14.3	15.1	2.7	.7s	.08	NE	NE	NE	1	03-86	1	00	0	0	16	00-00-00	.6	1.00	.6	1.83	1.1	16	1.9	92	7,471	3,552	+4	0.0	09
UCCEL Cp	-18.4	-18.4	8.2	10.8q	.66	-22.2	-22.2	22.2	8	03-86	10	00	0	0	12	00-00-00	5.5	.91	5.0	1.98	9.9	12	2.1	355	16,240	2,228	+5	0.9	12

Drugs and Cosmetics

Recent Performance and Forecast: Drugs (SIC 283)
(in millions of dollars except as noted)

	1982	1983	1984[1]	1985[2]	1986[3]	Percent Change			
						1982-83	1983-84	1984-85	1985-86
Industry Data									
Value of shipments[4]	24,695	27,410	29,960	32,525	—	11.0	9.3	8.6	3.8
2831 Biological Products	2,300	2,817	3,220	3,400	—	22.5	14.3	5.6	2.6
2833 Medicinals & Botanicals	3,398	3,371	3,340	3,325	—	-0.8	-0.9	-0.4	3.8
2834 Pharmaceutical Preps	18,998	21,222	23,400	25,800	—	11.7	10.3	10.3	3.9
Value of shipments (1982$)	24,695	25,703	27,213	28,204	29,265	4.1	5.9	3.6	—
2831 Biological Products	2,300	2,731	3,058	3,071	3,150	18.8	12.0	0.4	—
2833 Medicinals & Botanicals	3,398	3,415	3,611	3,757	3,900	0.5	5.7	4.1	—
2834 Pharmaceutical Preps	18,998	19,556	20,544	21,375	22,215	2.9	5.1	4.0	—
Total employment (000)	166	168	173	172	—	1.4	2.8	-0.3	—
2831 Biological Products	23.5	26.6	26.4	25.8	—	13.2	-0.8	-2.3	—
2833 Medicinals & Botanicals	17.8	17.7	17.9	17.9	—	-0.6	1.1	0.0	—
2834 Pharmaceutical Preps	124	124	128	129	—	-0.6	3.8	0.1	—
Production workers (000)	84.1	84.2	84.5	84.5	—	0.1	0.4	0.0	—
2831 Biological Products	11.7	12.5	12.0	11.8	—	6.8	-4.0	-1.7	—
2833 Medicinals & Botanicals	10.2	9.8	10.1	10.2	—	-3.9	3.1	1.0	—
2834 Pharmaceutical Preps	62.2	61.9	62.4	62.5	—	-0.5	0.8	0.2	—
Average hourly earnings ($)	9.54	10.09	—	—	—	5.8	—	—	—
2831 Biological Products	7.39	7.82	8.06	8.28	—	5.8	3.1	2.7	—
2833 Medicinals & Botanicals	10.95	12.14	12.49	12.87	—	10.9	2.9	3.0	—
2834 Pharmaceutical Preps	9.69	10.22	10.83	11.35	—	5.4	6.0	4.8	—
Product Data									
Value of shipments[5]	22,840	25,017	26,990	29,431	—	9.5	7.9	9.0	—
2831 Biological Products	2,417	2,532	2,650	2,856	—	4.8	4.7	7.8	—
2833 Medicinals & Botanicals	3,733	3,505	3,470	3,460	—	-6.1	-1.0	-0.3	—
2834 Pharmaceutical Preps	16,691	18,980	20,870	23,115	—	13.7	10.0	10.8	—

Value of shipments (1982$)	22,840	23,432	24,432	25,390	26,340	2.6	4.3	3.9	3.7
2831 Biological Products	2,417	2,455	2,517	2,580	2,650	1.6	2.5	2.5	2.7
2833 Medicinals & Botanicals	3,733	3,551	3,751	3,910	4,050	-4.9	5.6	4.2	3.6
2834 Pharmaceutical Preps	16,691	17,427	18,164	18,900	19,640	4.4	4.2	4.1	3.9
Shipments price index (1982=100)[6]	100.0	106.7	110.5	116.2	—	6.7	3.6	5.1	—
2831 Biological Products	100.0	103.3	105.8	111.4	—	3.3	2.4	5.3	—
2833 Medicinals & Botanicals	100.0	98.7	92.6	88.7	—	-1.3	-6.2	-4.2	—
2834 Pharmaceutical Preps	100.0	109.0	115.2	123.0	—	9.0	5.7	6.8	—
Trade Data									
Value of imports	1,051	1,312	1,665	1,964	2,405	24.8	26.9	18.0	22.5
2831 Biological Products	33.9	47.7	76.8	185	380	40.7	61.0	140.9	105.4
2833 Medicinals & Botanicals	977	1,124	1,341	1,454	1,600	15.1	19.3	8.4	10.0
2834 Pharmaceutical Preps	40.7	141	247	325	425	245.5	75.7	31.5	30.8
Import/new supply ratio[7]	0.044	0.050	0.058	0.063	—	13.3	16.6	7.7	—
2831 Biological Products	0.014	0.018	0.028	0.061	—	33.7	52.3	160.0	—
2833 Medicinals & Botanicals	0.207	0.243	0.279	0.296	—	17.1	14.8	6.1	—
2834 Pharmaceutical Preps	0.002	0.007	0.012	0.014	—	202.3	59.1	18.5	—
Value of exports	2,298	2,533	2,637	2,840	3,095	10.2	4.1	7.7	9.0
2831 Biological Products	452	459	456	537	620	1.4	-0.6	17.8	15.5
2833 Medicinals & Botanicals	1,283	1,405	1,497	1,530	1,600	9.4	6.6	2.2	4.6
2834 Pharmaceutical Preps	563	670	684	773	875	19.0	2.1	12.9	13.2
Export/shipments ratio	0.101	0.101	0.098	0.096	—	0.6	4.1	-1.3	—
2831 Biological Products	0.187	0.181	0.172	0.188	—	-3.2	-5.0	9.3	—
2833 Medicinals & Botanicals	0.344	0.401	0.431	0.442	—	16.5	7.7	2.5	—
2834 Pharmaceutical Preps	0.034	0.035	0.033	0.033	—	4.7	-7.1	2.0	—

[1]Estimated except for exports and imports.
[2]Estimated.
[3]Forecast.
[4]Value of all products and services sold by the Drugs industry.
[5]Value of products classified in the Drugs industry produced by all industries.
[6]Developed by the Office of Industry Assessment, ITA.
[7]New supply is the sum of product shipments plus imports.
SOURCE: U.S. Department of Commerce: Bureau of the Census, Bureau of Economic Analysis, International Trade Administration (ITA). Estimates and forecasts by ITA.

Source: U.S. Industrial Outlook 1986, U.S. Department of Commerce.

Recent Performance and Forecast: Soap, Cleaners, and Toilet Goods (SIC 284)

(in millions of dollars except as noted)

	1982	1983	1984[1]	1985[2]	1986[3]	Percent Change			
						1982-83	1983-84	1984-85	1985-86
Industry Data									
Value of shipments[4]	26,037	27,034	28,537	30,628	—	3.8	5.6	7.3	—
2841 Soap & Other Detergents	9,167	9,117	9,550	10,028	—	−0.6	4.8	5.0	—
2842 Polishes/Sanitation Gds	4,626	4,717	5,092	5,300	—	2.0	7.9	4.1	—
2843 Surface Active Agents	2,060	2,276	2,430	2,520	—	10.5	6.8	3.7	—
2844 Toilet Preparations	10,183	10,925	11,465	12,780	—	7.3	4.9	11.5	—
Value of shipments (1982$)	26,037	26,148	26,965	27,663	28,360	0.4	3.1	2.6	2.5
2841 Soap & Other Detergents	9,167	8,796	9,001	9,200	9,400	−4.0	2.3	2.2	2.2
2842 Polishes/Sanitation Gds	4,626	4,595	4,764	4,840	4,940	−0.7	3.7	1.6	2.1
2843 Surface Active Agents	2,060	2,252	2,364	2,451	2,540	9.3	5.0	3.7	3.6
2844 Toilet Preparations	10,183	10,505	10,836	11,171	11,480	3.2	3.2	3.1	2.8
Total employment (000)	127	127	129	129	—	−0.3	1.8	0.2	—
2841 Soap & Other Detergents	35.4	35.5	35.2	35.4	—	0.3	−0.8	0.6	—
2842 Polishes/Sanitation Gds	23.0	21.2	23.0	23.1	23.0	−7.8	8.5	0.4	−0.4
2843 Surface Active Agents	8.5	9.3	7.1	7.2	—	9.4	−23.7	1.4	—
2844 Toilet Preparations	60.4	60.9	63.9	63.8	—	0.8	4.9	−0.2	—
Production workers (000)	75.4	75.3	76.2	76.7	—	−0.1	1.2	0.7	—
2841 Soap & Other Detergents	21.2	21.3	20.9	21.0	—	0.5	−1.9	0.5	—
2842 Polishes/Sanitation Gds	14.6	13.4	14.8	14.7	14.7	−8.2	10.4	−0.7	0.0
2843 Surface Active Agents	3.8	4.3	3.6	3.5	—	13.2	−16.3	−2.8	—
2844 Toilet Preparations	35.8	36.3	36.9	37.5	—	1.4	1.7	1.6	—
Average hourly earnings ($)	8.73	9.11	—	—	—	4.5			
2841 Soap & Other Detergents	10.76	11.44	11.84	12.04	—	6.3	3.5	1.7	—
2842 Polishes/Sanitation Gds	8.13	8.69	8.62	9.32	—	6.9	−0.8	8.1	—
2843 Surface Active Agents	9.87	10.52	9.85	11.27	—	6.5	−6.3	14.5	—
2844 Toilet Preparations	7.59	7.68	7.90	8.15	—	1.1	2.9	3.2	—
Product Data									
Value of shipments[5]	24,832	25,934	27,313	29,380	—	4.4	5.3	7.6	—
2841 Soap & Other Detergents	7,852	7,890	8,270	8,690	—	0.5	4.8	5.1	—
2842 Polishes/Sanitation Gds	4,047	4,248	4,543	4,750	—	5.0	6.9	4.6	—
2843 Surface Active Agents	2,496	2,548	2,700	2,790	—	2.1	6.0	3.3	—
2844 Toilet Preparations	10,437	11,248	11,800	13,150	—	7.8	4.9	11.4	—

	1982	1983	1984	1985[1]	1986[3]	Percent Change 1982-83	1983-84	1984-85	1985-86
Value of shipments (1982$)	24,832	25,112	25,803	26,491	27,170	1.1	2.8	2.7	2.6
2841 Soap & Other Detergents	7,852	7,639	7,802	7,972	8,150	-2.7	2.1	2.2	2.2
2842 Polishes/Sanitation Gds	4,047	4,136	4,222	4,300	4,390	2.2	2.1	1.8	2.1
2843 Surface Active Agents	2,496	2,522	2,626	2,714	2,800	1.0	4.2	3.3	3.2
2844 Toilet Preparations	10,437	10,815	11,153	11,505	11,830	3.6	3.1	3.2	2.8
Shipments price index (1982=100)[6]	100.0	108.5	111.6	115.7	—	8.5	2.9	3.7	27.1
2841 Soap & Other Detergents	100.0	103.3	104.2	105.9	—	3.3	0.9	1.7	21.4
2842 Polishes/Sanitation Gds	100.0	102.7	108.2	110.6	—	2.7	5.3	2.2	12.0
2843 Surface Active Agents	100.0	101.1	101.4	108.7	—	1.1	0.4	7.2	30.7
2844 Toilet Preparations	100.0	116.4	120.8	126.8	—	16.4	3.8	4.9	27.8
Trade Data									
Value of imports	245	307	470	561	713	25.1	53.3	19.3	27.1
2841 Soap & Other Detergents	48.8	52.1	68.9	70.0	85.0	6.8	32.2	1.6	21.4
2842 Polishes/Sanitation Gds	14.1	17.1	23.1	25.0	28.0	21.3	35.1	8.2	12.0
2843 Surface Active Agents	58.7	65.4	95.8	153	200	11.4	46.5	59.7	30.7
2844 Toilet Preparations	124	172	282	313	400	39.2	64.1	10.8	27.8
Import/new supply ratio[7]	0.010	0.012	0.017	0.019	—	19.5	45.2	10.7	—
2841 Soap & Other Detergents	0.004	0.005	0.006	0.006	—	4.8	26.0	-3.3	—
2842 Polishes/Sanitation Gds	0.018	0.020	0.025	0.026	—	14.5	25.7	3.3	—
2843 Surface Active Agents	0.023	0.025	0.034	0.052	—	8.9	36.9	51.7	—
2844 Toilet Preparations	0.012	0.016	0.024	0.024	—	28.7	55.0	-0.5	—
Value of exports	733	681	715	687	674	-7.1	4.9	-3.9	-1.9
2841 Soap & Other Detergents	128	122	144	164	190	-5.1	18.3	13.8	15.9
2842 Polishes/Sanitation Gds	96.1	86.4	85.7	71.0	64.0	-10.1	-0.8	-17.2	-9.9
2843 Surface Active Agents	156	145	155	143	130	-6.8	6.4	-7.5	-9.1
2844 Toilet Preparations	353	328	331	309	290	-7.0	0.8	-6.5	-6.1
Export/shipments ratio	0.030	0.026	0.026	0.023	—	-11.0	-0.4	-10.7	—
2841 Soap & Other Detergents	0.016	0.015	0.017	0.019	—	-5.6	12.9	8.3	—
2842 Polishes/Sanitation Gds	0.024	0.020	0.019	0.015	—	-14.3	-7.3	-20.8	—
2843 Surface Active Agents	0.062	0.057	0.057	0.051	—	-8.7	0.4	-10.5	—
2844 Toilet Preparations	0.034	0.029	0.028	0.023	—	-13.7	-3.9	-16.1	—

[1]Estimated except for exports and imports.
[2]Estimated.
[3]Forecast.
[4]Value of all products and services sold by the Soap, Cleaners, and Toilet Goods industry.
[5]Value of products classified in the Soap, Cleaners, and Toilet Goods industry produced by all industries.
[6]Developed by the Office of Industry Assessment, ITA.
[7]New supply is the sum of product shipments plus imports.

SOURCE: U.S. Department of Commerce: Bureau of the Census, Bureau of Economic Analysis, International Trade Administration (ITA). Estimates and forecasts by ITA.

Source: U.S. Industrial Outlook 1986, U.S. Department of Commerce.

Ethical Drugs

Company	Rev % Last Qtr	Rev % FY to Date	Rev % Last 12 Mos	Rev Last 12 Mos $Mil	EPS Last 12 Mos $	EPS % Last Qtr	EPS % FY to Date	EPS % Last 12 Mos	EPS 5-Yr Growth	Par Growth Rate	Date of Report	Div Amt	Div Yield	Div 5-Yr Growth	Payout Last FY	Payout 5 Yrs	Last X-Dvd Date	Profit Margin %	Asset Turnover	Return Total Assets	Return on Equity	Leverage Ratio	Debt to Equity %	Current Ratio	Market Value $Mil	Latest Shares Out 000	Held by Banks-Funds 000	Insider Net Trading 000	Short Int Ratio Days	Fiscal Yr Ends Mo
Ind. Group	11.1	12.3	7.1	4,869.1	2.69	14.9	14.9	18.4	17.2	10	---	1.37	2.0	1	45	45	---	11.5	.97	11.2	19.5	1.74	12	2.1	124,276	1,848,568	916,613	+1807	3.0	--
A L Labs	12.1	12.1	10.2	5.6q	.92	9.1	9.1	17.9	104	12	03-86	.18	.8		16	8	06-12-86	5.8	1.05	6.1	14.6	2.39	28	1.5	140	6,076	1,311	0	8.0	12
Abbott Labs	14.5	14.5	10.5	468.6q	2.03	20.9	20.9	17.3	17	15	03-86	.84	1.6	18	35	35	06-02-86	14.0	1.00	14.0	26.0	1.86	24	2.1	12,856	239,190	114,154	-252	9.0	12
Alco Hlth	29.4	27.1	24.5	14.8q	1.19	19.0	18.0	NC	NC	15	03-86	.00	.0	0	0	0	00-00-00	1.4	4.86	6.8	14.7	2.16	1	1.7	310	13,055	2,100		0.0	09
Alza Cp A	78.8	78.8	69.5	5.9q	.42	50.0	50.0	55.6	10	15	03-86	.00	.0	0	0	0	00-00-00	15.1	.25	3.7	7.5	2.03	32	2.5	722	14,519	4,359	-5	0.5	12
Am Home Prod	4.7	4.7	4.1	733.1q	4.82	10.2	10.2	8.1	10	11	03-86	3.10	3.4	11	62	60	05-07-86	15.5	1.39	21.6	32.0	1.48		3.4	13,580	150,889	80,958	+9	1.8	12
Amgen	207.1	229.6	228.5	.5	NA	NE	NE	NE	NC	1	03-86	.00	.0	0	NA	NA	00-00-00	2.2	.45	1.0	1.3	1.30	22	12.5	330	13,274	1,292	0	0.0	03
Biocraft Labs	NA	NA	72.0	28.7	NA	NA	NA	NA	NA		03-86	.00	.0	0	NA	NA	01-16-86		NA	1.0		NC	NA		236	12,261	994	+0	NA	NA
Block Drugs Co	21.4	10.7	10.4	7.9q	1.84	0	8.2	8.2	12	12	03-86	.50	2.0b	2	27	31	06-03-86	10.5	1.12	11.8	16.9	1.43	15	2.4	398	15,606	2,077	-364	0.0	03
Bolar Pharm	34.7	34.7	31.2	7.9q	.82	61.1	61.1	26.2	21	17	03-86	.05	.2	-4	4	4	02-24-86	18.8	.88	16.5	18.6	1.13	0	6.5	302	9,618	2,921	+12	32.0	03
Bristol-Myers	10.3	10.3	7.0	551.4q	3.97	12.1	12.1	11.8	13	12	03-86	2.20	2.6	18	47	42	06-27-86	12.1	1.22	14.8	22.5	1.52	5	2.5	11,872	138,048	73,137		3.4	12
Carter-Wallace	19.3	14.7	14.6	27.6q	3.63	85.7	85.7	146.2	22	13	03-86	.60	.9	7	16	19	04-14-86	10.1	1.46	15.4	21.1	1.52	4	2.2	535	7,582	1,526	0	1.1	03
Centocor Inc	87.2	87.2	91.6	2.7q	.32	NE	NE	NE	6		03-86	.00	.0	0	0	0	00-00-00	11.7	.42	5.5	5.5	1.31	2	16.7	350	8,234	2,915	-9	0.0	08
Collaborative Rsh	528.6	74.0	57.1	-5.3n	-.52	NE	NE	NE	-27		04-86	.00	.0	0	0	0	00-00-00	-48.2	.50	-24.0	-26.6	1.11	0	9.6	73	10,067	381		0.0	08
Cooper Develop	-8.5	-4.3	-3.4	-9.9s	-.33	NE	NE	NE	-17		03-86	.00	.0	0	0	0	00-00-00	-11.8	.81	-9.5	-16.7	1.76	21	1.5	75	25,071	2,389	0	0.0	10
Diagnostic Prods	26.9	26.9	26.3	4.4q	.82	60.0	60.0	36.7	23	12	03-86	1.80	2.2		0	C	09-27-83	18.3	1.05	19.2	21.2	1.10	0	7.8	132	5,380	689	0	0.0	12
Forest Labs	83.6	75.9	75.0	6.8q	.98	350.0	164.9	164.9	28	10	05-86	.00	.0	0	0	0	05-16-86	16.2	.86	13.9	21.1	1.52	4	4.5	275	13,942	5,020	+74	1.9	03
Genentech	43.6	43.6	25.0	6.7q	.20	66.7	66.7	81.8	84	23	03-86	.20	.4	7	26	3	03-03-86	7.4	.38	3.3	3.3	1.18	3	4.9	2,958	32,826	9,492	-345	0.0	12
ICN Pharm	78.7	78.7	48.0	-17.5q	-2.06	50.0	50.0	-100.0	-61		02-86	.00	.0	0	0	C	00-00-00	-23.6	.53	-12.4	-60.6	4.89	170	2.7	98	9,682	1,538	+257	1.1	11
Key Pharm	24.4	24.4	3.8	1.4q	.04	46.2	46.2	-93.4	NC	12	09-85	.00	.0	64	0	0	09-09-85	.8	.89	.7	2.7	3.38	180	3.3	798	35,454	4,066	-3	4.1	11
Lilly Eli Co	8.7	8.7	7.2	529.3q	3.79	8.8	8.8	7.7	10	12	03-86	1.80	2.2	8	43	45	09-06-85	15.8	.85	13.4	21.2	1.66	10	1.9	11,282	139,499	97,896	+2232	4.2	12
Lyphomed Inc	160.5	160.5	141.6	9.0q	.34	140.0	140.0	100.0	10	8	03-86	.00	.0	0	0	0	06-23-86	10.3	.58	6.0	10.1	1.68	6	1.7	665	28,595	9,833	+56	0.0	12
Marion Labs	26.6	32.9	30.8	51.0n	.65	50.0	52.9	51.2	41	37	06-86	.20	.4	7	26	26	06-16-86	14.0	1.64	22.9	33.2	1.45	0	2.1	3,314	74,066	33,982	-7	1.4	06
Merck & Co	7.6	7.6	7.8	566.2q	4.00	22.8	22.8	16.6	7	6	06-86	1.80	1.7	6	42	46	05-27-86	15.7	.73	11.5	21.5	1.87	6	1.9	14,666	140,346	86,784		2.3	12
Mylan Labs	33.6	50.7	50.0	20.7q	.86	25.0	65.4	65.4	63	63	03-86	.10	.4	10	12	10	06-24-86	25.6	2.20	56.4	70.9	1.26	13	5.9	593	24,221	2,749	0	13.5	03
Newport Pharm	46.2	-1.3	0	-.4n	-.06	0	-100.0	-100.0	-67		01-86	.80	.0	0	0	0	05-23-85	-4.0	.68	-2.7	-4.7	1.74	22	3.2	63	9,071	697	0	0.0	04
NMS	25.0	18.2	43.9	-2.0n	-.34	NE	NE	NE	NC	-27	02-86	.00	.0	0	0	0	12-15-80	NM	NC	NC	-26.7	1.50	15	12.7	29	5,905	112	+71	0.0	05
Novo Industri	21.3	21.3	5.9	65.6q	2.58	-14.1	-14.1	7.9	8	11	04-86	.31	.9	27	97	30	04-21-86	-20.7	.59	8.0	12.0	1.52	11	6.8	844	25,487	7,394	0	6.8	12
Pfizer Inc	9.1	9.1	13.8	601.3q	3.55	12.4	12.4	10.9	11	11	03-86	1.64	2.3	16	43	43	05-14-86	14.6	.92	13.5	20.5	1.52	-16	2.2	11,715	163,853	91,236	+19	3.3	12
Robins, AH	15.0	15.0	-7.6	62.3q	2.58	5.7	5.7	10.1	16	6	03-86	.00	.0	0	0	0	11-19-84	8.0	1.04	8.8	NS	1.68	-16	3.8	275	24,161	12,563		3.2	12
Rorer Group	1621	1621	0	40.0q	1.87	51.7	51.7	-10.1	1	6	03-86	1.12	2.7	5	65	55	05-05-86	9.0	1.00	9.0	15.1	1.68	14	1.5	913	21,614	7,084	0	2.6	12
Scher Plough	15.5	15.5	6.7	203.5q	3.95	16.8	16.8	12.2	8	7	03-86	1.80	2.1	1	45	48	04-28-86	10.2	.72	7.3	13.8	1.89	14	1.6	4,365	51,730	31,091	+1	4.8	12
Smith Labs	-14.6	-10.1	-12.5	-2.9s	-.21	NC	NC	-100.0	-7	7	04-86	.00	.0	0	0	0	00-00-00	-20.7	-.57	-5.7	-7.0	1.23	12	7.9	45	13,297	1,366	+4	0.0	10
Smithkline Beck	12.1	12.1	11.6	499.0q	6.41	-9.0	-9.0	2.1	8	7	03-86	3.00	3.0	10	43	41	05-06-86	14.9	.90	13.4	22.0	1.64	5	1.9	7,775	77,561	51,187	+6	1.9	12
Squibb Corp	23.4	23.4	12.4	237.9q	4.41	26.9	26.9	17.0	8	26	03-86	2.00	1.8	8	41	47	05-12-86	11.1	.87	9.7	16.2	1.67	13	2.1	6,063	53,418	36,328	+6	0.9	12
Syntex Corp	12.0	9.5	9.7	213.2n	5.37	43.9	43.6	160.7	30	24	04-86	1.20	1.7	26	20	20	05-12-86	21.0	.83	17.4	30.6	1.76	26	2.3	4,576	64,447	36,511	+33	1.8	07
TechAmerica	0	0	0	-2.9q	-.34	NE	NE	NE	-15		03-86	.00	.0	0	0	0	00-00-00	-8.3	1.04	-15.4	-17.4	1.79	21	1.9	29	8,377	1,408	0	0.0	12
Unimed Inc	0	1000.0	0	-.48	-.18	NE	NE	NE	9		03-02-81	.00	.0	0	0	0	03-02-81	-20.0	.29	-5.8	-8.7	1.50	11	7.2	33	2,508	57	0	0.0	09
Upjohn Co	-1.5	-1.5	-7.0	314.4q	3.46	20.2	20.2	32.6	3	7	05-86	1.52	1.6	9	40	42	05-02-86	10.7	.84	9.0	16.6	1.84	29	2.1	5,864	61,956	41,853	+10	2.2	12
Warner-Lambert	-6.0	-6.0	-13.8	-310.4q	-3.94	14.5	14.5	-100.0	NC	49	05-86	1.56	2.5	3	NE	139	05-05-86	-9.8	1.35	-13.2	-34.8	2.64	40	1.4	4,743	76,648	45,565	-1	2.7	12
Zenith Labs	4.4	4.4	76.0	16.5q	.76	23.1	23.1	216.7	43		03-86	.05	.3		0	0	06-19-86	20.4	1.72	35.0	46.3	1.32	5	3.7	337	20,784	9,568		6.2	12

Cosmetics and Grooming Aids

Ratio Analysis key: p/t × t/a × a/e = s/e

Company	Rev %Chg Last Qtr	Rev %Chg FY to Date	Rev %Chg Last 12 Mos	Rev Last 12 Mos $Mil	Earn Last 12 Mos $Mil	Earn/Sh Last 12 Mos $	Earn %Chg Last Qtr	Earn %Chg FY to Date	Earn %Chg Last 12 Mos	Earn 5-Yr Growth Rate	Par Growth Rate	Date of Report	Div Cur Rate Amt	Div Yield	Div 5-Yr Growth Rate	Payout Last FY	Payout Last 5 Yrs	Last X-Dvd Date	Profit Margin	Asset Turnover	Return on Total Assets	Leverage Ratio	Return on Equity	Debt to Equity	Current Ratio	Market Value $Mil	Latest Shares Outstdng 000	Held by Banks-Funds 000	Insider Net Trading 000	Short Interest Ratio Days	Fiscal Year Ends Mo
Ind. Group	22.8	32.7	9.6		501.1	2.04	27.9	29.2	-2.8	-3	6	---	1.34	3.4	0	68	62	05-05-86	5.1	1.14	5.8	2.88	16.7	77	1.8	9,560	242,037	116,239	+1356	1.1	--
Alberto-Culver	20.8	19.3	12.9		4.4s	.37	171.4	105.6	1133.3	NC	3	03-86	.21	.9	9	106	54	02-20-86	1.1	2.09	2.3	2.74	6.3	43	1.6	261	11,578	2,103	-71	3.0	09
Alfin Frag	162.5	48.9	42.8		5.6n	.75	92.9	19.0	19.0	110	33	04-86	.00	.0	0	0	0	05-09-86	18.7	1.22	22.9	1.44	32.9	11	3.5	158	6,626	184	+1392	3.5	07
Avon Products	-9.1	-9.1	-21.9		155.7q	1.97	-27.6	-27.6	-6.2	-13	0	03-86	2.00	5.6	-9	98	90	05-09-86	6.5	1.05	6.8	2.47	16.8	67	1.6	2,485	69,500	46,197		1.7	12
Chesbgh-Pnds	89.2	89.2	64.8		105.3q	2.92	98.3	98.3	-15.6	-4	5	03-86	2.00	3.9	9	85	55	05-29-86	3.4	1.03	3.5	4.43	15.5	173	1.8	2,143	41,320	20,536	+13	2.8	12
Del Labs	11.9	11.9	14.2		3.8q	2.52	15.0	15.0	1.2	11	11	03-86	.39	1.2	9	16	18	03-27-86	3.7	1.41	5.2	2.48	12.9	81	2.3	45	1,375	133	0	0.0	12
Gilette Co	17.5	17.5	7.5		166.1q	2.69	15.9	15.9	1.9	5	9	03-86	1.36	2.8	7	50	49	05-27-86	6.6	1.05	6.9	2.68	18.5	49	1.7	3,038	61,838	35,378	+45	2.5	12
Helene Curtis	1.1	-2.6	-2.4		11.0f	3.01	61.5	312.3	312.3	13	15	02-86	.15	.5	0	0	0	07-28-86	3.0	2.10	6.3	2.59	16.3	44	1.7	126	3,920	755	0	1.1	02
Johnson Prdts	-23.1	-20.0	0		0	-1.13	NE	NE	NE	NC	0	02-86	.00	.0	0	0	0	04-30-80	NC	NC	NC	NC	.0	1	1.3	10	3,985	244	0	0.0	08
Lamaur Inc	338.5	22.1	5.1		3.1q	.53	50.0	50.0	-33.8	12	6	03-86	.24	1.5	45	51	24	05-29-86	2.5	2.80	7.0	1.50	10.5	3	2.6	92	5,905	1,005	0	0.0	12
Lee Pharm		262.0	177.7		1.2s	.58	141.7	69.2	87.1	NC	25	03-86	.00	.0	0	0	0	00-00-00	4.8	3.85	18.5	1.32	24.5	0	3.1	59	1,968	160	0	0.9	09
MEM Co	3.3	3.3	1.3		2.4q	.92	NE	50.0	-31.3	0	2	03-86	.60	3.1	3	61	49	06-24-86	3.1	1.68	5.2	1.21	6.3	1	5.0	52	2,625	733	0	0.0	12
Minnetonka	-3.0	-3.0	24.0		4.8q	.56	50.0	50.0	194.7	16	16	03-86	.00	.0	0	0	0	02-13-81	3.9	2.44	9.5	1.69	16.1	5	2.4	135	8,413	2,170	+6	0.0	12
Noxell Cp	8.6	8.6	8.9		33.6q	1.68	9.8	9.8	12.0	17	14	03-86	.58	1.3	14	31	31	06-11-86	8.6	1.95	16.8	1.30	21.9	0	3.4	885	20,000	6,158	-28	0.0	12
Redken Labs	-12.4	-7.1	-2.8		4.1n	1.35	-91.3	-72.4	-46.9	4	7	04-86	.20	.80	19	21	18	04-01-86	4.0	1.18	4.7	1.66	7.8	23	2.7	72	2,984	483	-1	0.0	07

Electronic Components and Equipment

Recent Performance and Forecast: Electronic Components and Accessories (SIC 367)

(in millions of dollars except as noted)

	1982	1983	1984[1]	1985[2]	1986[3]	Percent Change			
						1982-83	1983-84	1984-85	1985-86
Industry Data									
Value of shipments[4]	34,517	37,194	47,546	43,617	47,073	7.8	27.8	−8.3	7.9
Value of shipments (1982$)	34,517	36,874	47,898	51,313	59,938	6.8	29.9	7.1	16.8
Total employment (000)	516	515	574	561	569	−0.2	11.4	−2.2	1.4
Production workers (000)	325	329	359	348	353	1.3	9.2	−3.1	1.5
Average hourly earnings ($)	7.42	7.81	—	—	—	5.3	—	—	—
Product Data									
Value of shipments[5]	32,158	35,353	44,067	40,143	43,132	9.9	24.6	−8.9	7.4
Value of shipments (1982$)	32,158	35,123	44,249	47,542	55,561	9.2	26.0	7.4	16.9
Shipments price index (1982=100)[6]	100.0	100.9	101.3	93.7	92.9	0.9	0.4	−7.5	−0.9
Trade Data									
Value of imports (ITA)[7]	5,742	6,750	10,220	9,584	11,125	17.6	51.4	−6.2	16.1
Value of exports (ITA)[8]	5,487	5,953	7,252	6,850	7,804	8.5	21.8	−5.5	13.9

[1]Estimated except for exports and imports.
[2]Estimated.
[3]Forecast.
[4]Value of all products and services sold by the Electronic Components and Accessories industry.
[5]Value of products classified in the Electronic Components and Accessories industry produced by all industries.
[6]Developed by the Office of Microelectronics and Instrumentation, ITA .
[7]Import data are developed by the chapter author.
[8]Export data are developed by the chapter author.

SOURCE: U.S. Department of Commerce: Bureau of the Census, Bureau of Economic Analysis, International Trade Administration (ITA). Estimates and forecasts by ITA.

Source: *U.S. Industrial Outlook 1986*, U.S. Department of Commerce.

Recent Performance and Forecast: Radio and TV Communication Equipment (SIC 3662)

(in millions of dollars except as noted)

	1982	1983	1984[1]	1985[2]	1986[3]	Percent Change			
						1982-83	1983-84	1984-85	1985-86
Industry Data									
Value of shipments[4]	33,028	36,404	39,800	43,500	48,000	10.2	9.3	9.3	10.3
Value of shipments (1982$)	33,028	34,555	36,480	38,598	40,991	4.6	5.6	5.8	6.2
Total employment (000)	464	478	520	573	620	3.0	8.8	10.2	8.1
Production workers (000)	228	225	246	269	—	-1.5	9.3	9.5	—
Average hourly earnings ($)	9.64	10.35	10.91	11.58	—	7.4	5.4	6.2	—
Product Data									
Value of shipments[5]	32,217	36,007	39,100	42,700	47,000	11.8	8.6	9.2	10.1
Value of shipments (1982$)	32,217	34,179	35,839	37,888	40,137	6.1	4.9	5.7	5.9
Shipments price index (1982=100)[6]	100.0	105.4	109.1	112.7	117.1	5.4	3.6	3.3	3.9
Trade Data									
Value of imports (ITA)[7]	2,022	2,060	2,664	3,000	3,300	1.9	29.3	12.6	10.0
Import/new supply ratio[8]	0.059	0.054	0.064	0.066	—	-8.4	17.9	2.9	—
Value of exports (ITA)[9]	2,402	2,534	2,768	3,000	3,200	5.5	9.2	8.4	6.7
Export/shipments ratio	0.075	0.070	0.071	0.070	—	-5.6	0.6	-0.8	—

[1]Estimated except for exports and imports.
[2]Estimated.
[3]Forecast.
[4]Value of all products and services sold by the Radio and TV Communication Equipment industry.
[5]Value of products classified in the Radio and TV Communication Equipment industry produced by all industries.
[6]Developed by the Office of Industry Assessment, ITA.
[7]Import data are developed by the chapter author.
[8]New supply is the sum of product shipments plus imports.
[9]Export data are developed by the chapter author.

SOURCE: U.S. Department of Commerce: Bureau of the Census, Bureau of Economic Analysis, International Trade Administration (ITA). Estimates and forecasts by ITA.

Source: U.S. Industrial Outlook 1986, U.S. Department of Commerce.

Electronic Devices

Company	Revenue Pct Change Last Qtr %	FY to Date %	Last 12 Mos %	Last 12 Mos $Mil	Earnings Per Share Last 12 Mos $	Pct Change Last Qtr %	FY to Date %	Last 12 Mos %	5-Year Growth Rate %	Par Growth Rate %	Date of Report	Div Current Rate Amt $	Yield %	5-Year Growth Rate %	Payout Last FY %	Last 5 Yrs %	Last X-Dvd Date	Profit Margin %	Asset Turnover	Return on Total Assets	Leverage Ratio	Return on Equity	Debt to Equity %	Current Ratio	Market Value $Mil	Latest Shares stndg 000	Held by Banks-Funds 000	Insider Net Trading 000	Short Int Ratio Days	Fiscal Year Ends Mo
Ind. Group	-11.8	-11.8	-3.6	186.1	.13	-100.0	-100.0	-100.0	-91.5	-27	—	.30	1.3	1	26	23	—	1.0	1.30	1.3	1.85	2.4	20	2.3	13,201	565,517	187,175	-153	1.1	—
Anaren Micrwve	12.0	14.8	14.2	3.1n	.73	25.0	31.7	32.7	29	14	03-86	.00	.3	0	0	0	03-30-81	9.7	.96	9.3	1.53	14.2	25	4.7	53	4,209	1,602	0	.0	06
Anthem Elects	3.3	-12.6	-12.5	3.1f	.44	-14.8	-48.2	-48.2	17	7	03-86	.00	.3	9	9	6	03-10-86	3.0	2.17	6.5	1.23	8.0	4	6.4	113	7,210	4,328	0	.0	03
Arvet Inc	-.2	-12.6	-15.9	29.8n	.84	-14.8	-47.0	-54.3	-8	-2	03-86	.50	1.7	5	36	29	05-28-86	2.2	1.50	3.3	1.42	4.7	18	4.7	1,026	35,546	25,354	0	1.3	06
AVX Corp	-4.7	-4.7	-21.7	-14.9q	-1.44	-100.0	-100.0	-100.0	NC	-12	03-86	.00	.0	6	NE	81	08-06-85	-8.5	.64	-5.4	2.15	-11.6	87	6.8	138	10,935	5,696	0	.2	03
Birdview Satellite	-21.6	40.8	60.4	-3.3n	-.35	-100.0	-100.0	-100.0	NC	-41	12-85	.00	.0	6	NE	—	09-09-33	-4.8	2.90	-13.9	2.97	-41.3	40	1.1	5	9,191	117	0	.0	03
Burr-Brown	11.7	11.7	6.5	4.4q	.56	-30.0	-30.0	-33.3	13	8	03-86	.00	.0	0	0	0	01-21-86	4.5	.98	4.4	1.89	8.3	51	3.1	121	7,452	1,843	0	.0	12
Celsc Corp	-4.9	-4.9	-48.4	-1.4q	-.62	-35.7	-35.7	-100.0	NC	-14	03-86	.20	2.8	12	NE	48	04-28-86	-4.2	1.33	-5.6	1.86	-10.4	44	3.7	15	2,078	478	0	.2	12
Condial Cp	7.9	7.9	-21.6	-28.5q	-1.35	NE	NE	NE	NC	8	03-86	.00	.0	0	0	0	00-00-00	-32.8	1.13	-37.0	.00	NM	9	.8	32	16,597	381	0	.0	12
E Systems	17.7	17.7	15.0	44.8q	1.46	-2.1	-2.1	-26.3	23	9	03-86	.50	1.4	18	34	27	06-09-86	4.6	2.04	9.4	1.49	14.0	6	2.9	1,049	29,979	12,847	+2	1.0	12
EDO Cp	-17.6	-17.6	60.9	7.7q	.99	-8.0	-8.0	-24.4	NC	9	03-86	.28	1.8	23	26	24	06-03-86	6.9	.80	5.5	2.38	13.1	8	1.9	108	7,106	1,847	0	.3	12
Equatorial Commun	106.6	106.6	60.9	-1.8q	-.15	-100.0	-100.0	-100.0	-2	NC	03-86	.00	.0	0	0	0	09-25-85	-2.7	.56	-1.5	1.20	-1.8	5	4.6	112	14,638	5,336	-32	.0	12
GenRad	-19.4	-19.4	-20.9	-60.9q	-3.79	-100.0	-100.0	-100.0	19	-46	03-86	.00	.0	0	NE	0	09-25-85	-29.4	.91	-26.8	1.72	-46.0	23	2.1	142	16,193	8,368	-4	3.5	12
Infight Svc	-3.9	-15.5	-12.1	-6.6q	-2.13	-100.0	-100.0	-100.0	NC	-72	04-86	.00	.0	0	0	19	10-21-85	-18.3	1.15	-21.0	3.41	-71.7	53	1.5	9	3,080	399	+4	.4	06
Jetronic Ind	20.3	20.3	11.3	1.6q	.72	36.4	36.4	35.8	NC	17	04-86	.00	.0	0	0	0	06-11-85	3.0	1.80	5.4	3.09	16.7	41	1.6	20	2,227	90	0	.3	01
KLA Instruments	27.2	29.0	26.6	9.6n	.55	16.7	13.5	14.6	50	15	03-86	.00	.0	0	0	24	12-17-84	12.6	.94	11.9	1.29	15.3	0	3.4	304	16,901	7,103	-20	.0	06
Knogo Cp	-13.3	7.5	5.8	5.8	1.19	44.4	35.2	35.2	NC	19	02-86	.00	.0	0	0	0	09-22-80	16.1	.47	7.6	2.43	18.5	114	NA	136	4,808	1,281	0	.1	02
Lynch Com Sys	-37.9	-37.9	-18.5	3.6q	.49	-79.1	-79.1	-68.0	NC	3	07-86	.00	.0	22	16	16	07-25-86	4.1	.93	3.8	1.24	4.7	6	5.6	101	7,063	766	+5	1.3	12
Mitel Cp	8.7	11.4	13.7	-97.4f	-2.56	NE	NE	NE	NC	-27	02-86	.00	.0	0	0	0	00-00-00	-23.6	.51	-12.1	2.26	-27.4	76	5.9	385	78,951	7,007	-160	4.1	12
North Telecom	-26.8	-.5	13.7	377.8q	2.97	-43.1	-43.1	2.1	-4	14	03-86	.40	NA	8	15	19	06-05-86	6.9	1.12	7.7	2.17	16.7	7	2.0	3,462	16,363	16,045	+2	4.6	12
Pac Scientific	.5	.5	-5.4	5.3q	.98	-25.0	-25.0	-25.8	NC	5	03-86	.40	2.4	13	38	24	06-06-96	6.2	.85	5.3	1.74	9.2	50	8.0	91	5,399	1,966	0	1.5	12
Paradyne Cp	-3.5	-3.5	-16.1	-30.7q	-1.36	200.0	200.0	35.2	NC	-17	03-86	.00	.0	0	0	0	03-22-83	-12.3	.78	-9.6	1.74	-16.7	56	6.1	187	22,643	14,481	0	.1	02
Plantronics	12.4	6.2	6.2	.82	.82	255.6	67.7	86.4	NC	0	03-85	.16	.9	20	0	20	07-31-86	NC	NC	3.8	1.96	-4.5	11	2.1	109	6,388	3,805	0	1.7	06
Regency Electro	-29.7	-19.4	-16.2	-2.1n	-.20	-100.0	-100.0	-100.0	NC	-9	03-86	.00	.0	50	41	50	05-06-86	-2.1	1.10	-2.3	1.96	7.1	4	3.1	67	10,730	2,671	0	.0	06
Sci-Atlanta	9.2	5.1	5.1	13.4n	.57	-88.9	-28.0	-12.3	-1	6	03-86	.20	1.2	18	20	17	07-25-86	-1.0	1.60	1.48	1.48	7.1	4	1.7	243	23,438	5,589	-11	1.0	06
Scope Inc	-126.4	44.4	0	1.9n	-.82	NE	NE	-100.0	NC	0	02-86	.00	.0	0	NE	NE	12-03-85	NC	NC	NC	NC	NC	0	1.7	13	1,459	150	+6	.0	08
Semtech Cp	45.8	19.3	18.1	-.9f	-.47	NE	NE	NE	1	-18	01-86	.00	.0	0	0	0	01-06	-6.9	1.71	-11.8	1.56	-18.4	0	2.2	5	1,831	929	+32	2.6	01
Servo Cp Am	27.8	35.8	30.7	1.0s	1.35	184.6	184.6	800.0	NC	18	04-86	.00	.0	0	0	0	00-00-00	3.0	1.51	8.9	2.04	18.2	5	1.9	15	694	4	+21	.0	02
Solitron Device	20.9	8.7	8.6	3.3f	.67	7.1	7.1	11.7	NC	12	02-86	.00	.0	0	NE	0	00-00-00	6.6	.77	5.1	2.37	12.1	57	2.1	42	4,866	415	0	.1	02
Sun Electric	-9.3	-42.5	-21.5	-8.4s	-1.28	-25.0	-25.0	NE	NC	-13	04-86	.00	.0	0	0	0	00-00-00	-6.4	.89	-5.7	2.28	-13.0	55	2.3	55	6,556	3,858	0	1.3	10
Tektronx Inc	-8.7	-5.2	-4.0	61.8n	3.03	-32.5	-46.6	-52.7	-2	5	03-86	1.00	1.7	4	23	22	07-14-86	4.5	1.11	5.0	1.44	7.2	11	3.4	1,185	19,792	12,481	0	4.4	05
TeleConcepts	-10.0	-10.0	-6.2	-3.5q	-1.07	NE	NE	NE	-53	0	03-86	.00	.0	0	0	0	02-15-83	-23.3	1.13	-26.3	2.02	-53.0	62	4.1	10	3,286	156	0	3.2	12
TeleSciences	-42.4	-42.4	-34.4	-1.3q	-.41	-100.0	-100.0	-100.0	-6	0	03-86	.00	.0	0	NE	0	10-30-79	-3.3	.94	-3.1	1.81	-5.6	25	2.7	30	3,338	1,078	0	.1	12
Tex Inst	-11.1	-11.1	-15.9	-140.8q	-5.68	-100.0	-100.0	-100.0	NC	-13	04-86	2.00	1.7	NE	77	77	04-02-86	-2.9	1.59	-4.6	2.15	-9.9	27	1.4	3,004	25,168	19,365	+2	2.9	12
Torotel Inc	-28.0	-18.4	-9.3	-.8s	-.31	-62.5	-100.0	-100.0	NC	3	10-85	.00	.0	0	0	0	04-24-85	-2.8	1.18	-3.3	2.76	-9.1	115	3.5	7	2,521	131	-1	1.2	03
Varian Assoc	-7.5	-5.9	-3.6	15.2s	1.94	-100.0	-100.0	-86.0	6	3	03-86	.26	1.0	2	11	11	04-14-86	1.6	1.25	2.0	1.75	3.5	11	1.9	549	21,313	14,035	-1	1.4	09
Vishay Inter	4.8	5.0	5.3	11.1n	1.37	17.6	17.2	20.2	29	23	03-86	.00	.0	0	0	0	12-31-85	18.8	.87	16.3	1.39	22.6	10	3.6	149	6,491	1,135	0	.0	12
Wavetek	-9.3	-9.7	-12.1	-13.0s	-1.43	NE	NC	-100.0	NC	-22	03-86	.00	.0	0	0	0	03-25-83	-18.1	.96	-17.4	1.24	-21.5	5	5.4	83	9,077	4,048	0	.0	09

Ratio Analysis formula: $\pi/I \times I/a = \pi/a \times a/e = \pi/e$

Company	Revenue Pct. Change Last Qtr %	FY to Date %	Last 12 Mos %	Revenue Last 12 Mos $Mil	Earnings Per Share Last 12 Mos	Last Qtr	Pct. Change Last Qtr %	FY to Date %	Last 12 Mos %	5-Yr Growth %	Par Growth %	Date of Report	Dividends Current Rate Amt	Yield %	5-Yr Growth %	Payout Last FY %	5 Yrs %	Last X-Dvd Date	Ratio Profit Margin	Asset Turn-over	Return on Total Assets	Lever-age	Return on Equity	Debt to Equity %	Curr. Ratio	Mkt Value $Mil	Shareholdings Latest Shares Out-strong 000	Held by Banks-Funds 000	Insider Net Trading 000	Short Int. Ratio Days	Fiscal Year Ends Mo
Ind. Group	2.0	8.7	8.6	202.7	.72		-38.1	-18.7	-40.7	-.2	8	----	.15	.6	1	24	21	----	3.5	1.31	4.6	2.07	9.5	27	2.0	6,499	275,596	67,028	+7	1.2	--
Electronic Systems																															
Adams Russell	25.3	20.0	17.5	9.8s	1.56	.29	5.7	-38.7	8.3	15	14	03-86	.15	.6	4	16	9	05-02-86	7.0	.97	6.8	2.31	15.7	75	2.7	256	6,193	2,429	+0	0.9	09
ArgoSysts Inc	20.1	21.4	19.0	5.1n	.75		-100.0	-24.2	26	13	03-86	.00	.0		0	0	05-13-83	6.8	1.22	8.3	1.51	12.5	0	2.4	144	6,660	2,488	+0	0.0	06
Cohu Inc	-0-	-0-	20.0	.9q	.49		-50.0	-52.9	3	4	03-86	.20	2.4	33	27		05-28-86	3.0	1.43	4.3	1.47	6.3	0	2.4	15	1,799	91	+13	0.0	12
Cubic Corp	3.9	8.3	17.3	8.5s	1.10		-90.2	-79.4	-36.4	3	3	03-86	.00	2.2	21	18	03-10-86	2.5	1.68	4.2	1.83	7.7	20	2.5	141	7,784	1,555	+1	1.4	09
DSC Commun	-3.7	-3.7	-21.2	-60.1q	-1.51		-83.3	-83.3	-83.3	-34		03-86	.00			0	0	05-24-83	-21.1	.72	-15.2	2.24	-34.1	89	3.9	497	39,743	14,114	+0	0.0	12
EECO Inc	9.7	9.7	14.2	2.2q	.90		NE	NE	143.2	NC	7	03-86	.32	1.6	9	50	84	05-06-86	3.9	1.49	5.8	1.74	10.1	28	2.4	50	2,539	229	+0	0.0	12
EG & G Inc	5.0	5.0	6.3	56.2q	2.08		2.1	2.1	6.1	15	21	03-86	.52	1.5	18	23	22	07-14-86	4.8	2.73	13.1	2.11	27.6	8	1.5	922	27,219	11,458	+1	0.3	12
Gen Datacomm	-11.2	-10.6	-1.1	5.2s	.34		-88.5	-74.0	-63.8	NC	21	03-86	.00		9	0	0	05-25-84	3.0	.93	2.8	2.29	6.4	83	4.5	185	15,141	3,562	-0	0.4	09
Hazeltine Corp	-6.0	-6.0	1.7	8.4q	1.35		-73.0	-73.0	-22.4	40	10	03-86	.40	2.0	9	24	30	05-12-86	4.8	1.27	6.1	2.23	13.6	0	1.5	128	6,298	1,403	-0	0.4	12
Plessey Co Ltd	6.6	20.9	20.8	147.2t	2.00		56.5	27.4	27.4	2	22	03-86	.07	.2	-6	30	29	03-14-86	6.9	1.35	9.3	2.43	22.6	25	1.8	2,581	73,730	224	0	9.6	03
Porta Syst	5.7	5.7	28.1	2.9q	.54		20.0	20.0	145.5	13	13	03-86	.00		0	0	0	07-01-83	7.1	.85	6.0	2.23	13.4	88	5.3	66	5,450	1,158	0	2.1	12
Ramtek Corp	-22.8	-26.9	-14.6	.3n	-1.57		-100.0	-100.0	3,453	676	0	.6	2.83	1.7	6			19													
Sanders Assoc	-12.8	-3.9	-.5	20.9n	1.07		-72.0	-45.4	1	17	3	04-86	.60	1.1	29	21	03-10-86	2.4	1.42	3.4	1.76	6.0	5	1.7	1,054	19,606	11,380	0	0.3	07
Sensormatic Elec	-1.0	-7.7	-4.7n	-.17	-100.0	-100.0	-100.0	NC	-3	02-86	.05	.5	22	19	05-30-86	-5.2	.37	-1.9	1.32	-2.5	6	NA	262	27,953	9,721	-1	0.0	05
Silicon Gen	-22.6	-40.0	-26.0	-1.1s	-.11		-100.0	-100.0	-100.0	NC	-3	12-85	.00		0	0	06-15-83	-3.0	.50	-1.5	1.80	-2.7	25	1.8	47	11,823	3,344	0	0.0	09
Technol for Comm	35.3	68.8	117.6	2.7s	.84		NE	122.2	265.2	14	4	03-86	.00		0	0	0	00-00-00	7.3	.86	6.3	2.17	13.7	5	1.8	47	3,055	461	+20	7.9	09
Trans-Lux Cp	-10.5	-10.5		.9q	.50		-100.0	-100.0	-47.9	-7	-6	03-86	.08	.60	7			03-17-86	3.0	.60	1.8	2.00	3.6	83	6.8	21	1,525	266	+11	0.0	12
Vicon Ind	-1.2	1.9		-.8s	-.35		-75.7	-100.0	-100.0	NC	-9	03-86	.00		0	0	07-05-83	-2.6	.85	2.2	2.68	-5.9	85	2.4	14	2,348	768	-0	0.0	09
VMX Inc	40.0	3.1	10.0	-1.8n	-.14		NE	NE	-100.0	NC	-5	03-86	.00		-6	0	0	00-00-00	-5.5	.78	-4.3	1.14	-4.9	0	8.0	50	12,977	1,701	-37	0.0	06
Ind. Group	12.0	14.7	5.2	450.6	.92		14.8	24.1	-39.4	-1	5	----	.28	1.1	0	29	23	----	2.6	1.27	3.3	2.12	7.0	25	1.7	12,659	486,896	99,922	+571	7.7	--
Radio - TV Manufacture																															
Andrea Radio	30.0	30.0	-20.0	-.2q	.43		35.3	35.3	-43.4	-8	-1	03-86	.54	4.6	10	146	80	04-16-86	5.0	1.06	5.3	1.06	5.6	0	16.5	6	508	3	0	0.0	12
Amatron Intl	-24.1	-2.5	-9.2	-2.8s	-3.83		NE	NE	NE	NC	-17	03-86	.00	.0	0	0	0	00-00-00	-4.7	1.00	-4.7	3.60	-16.9	99	1.4	2	2,551	166	0	28.5	09
Compact Video	-264.1	-78.0		0	.10		-100.0	NE	NC	NC	03-86	.00	.0	0	0	0	00-00-00	NC	NC	NC	NC	0	1.2	24	4,333	133	0	0.0	06				
Craig Corp	-20.5	-30.9	-29.1	1.0n	.55		20.0	110.5	NE	NC	0	03-86	.00	.0	0	0	0	00-00-00	5.9	1.02	6.0	1.20	7.2	64	6.4	30	1,769	276	+4	5.9	03
Emerson Radio	70.3	58.4	58.1	12.9t	.74		125.0	-2.6	-2.6	28	-1	03-86	.00	.0	0	0	0	12-21-79	3.0	3.61	3.3	3.34	27.7	61	2.0	319	17,505	2,739	+49	0.6	03
Esquire Radio	700.0	700.0	400.0	-.1q	-.11		NE	0	-100.0	NC	-4	03-86	.72	1.8	7	NE	22	03-21-86	-2.0	.20	-.4	1.25	-.5	0	4.3	19	483	95	0	17.1	12
Maranti Co	120.3	120.3	40.4	-1.8q	-.80		NE	NE	NE	NC	-12	03-86	.00	.0	0	0	0	00-00-00	-3.1	1.68	-5.2	2.33	-12.1	1	1.6	17	2,308	189	0	0.2	10
Microdyne	-3.0	8.1	7.4	.3s	.05		-100.0	-100.0	-63.8	-42	0	04-86	.06	1.2	-4	50	15	05-16-86	.8	.80	.6	1.13	.9	0	9.9	23	4,528	457	0	0.0	12
Motorola Inc	1.3	1.3	-18.8	76.0q	.63		5.7	5.7	-78.7	-12	0	03-86	.64	1.6	5	105	31	06-16-86	1.4	1.21	1.7	1.94	3.3	31	1.8	5,036	126,300	70,308	+517	1.5	12
Pioneer Elec	21.6	27.6	31.2	3.4s	.05		NE	NE	NE	NC	-1	03-86	.10	.4	-7	NE	85	09-23-85	.2	1.50	.3	1.67	.5	3	1.8	1,934	68,749	323	0	1.8	09
Sony Corp	20.6	21.1	27.7	381.6s	1.66		21.6	23.0	24.8	7	12	04-86	.20	1.0	5	10	14	04-23-86	5.1	1.10	5.6	2.41	13.5	22	1.5	4,652	231,148	16,264	0	10.3	10
Wells Gard El	29.4	3.9	3.9	-.3q	-.11		NE	NE	NE	NC	12	03-86	.00	.0	5	0	0	08-26-83	-1.6	1.31	-2.3	1.10	-2.3	0	8.6	14	3,591	302	0	33.2	12
Zenith Elms	-4.6	-4.6	-9.0	-19.8q	-.87		-100.0	-100.0	-100.0	NC	-5	03-86	.00	.0	-7	0	0	06-07-82	-1.2	1.75	-2.1	2.14	-4.5	38	2.4	572	23,123	8,667	0	1.4	12

Electronic Controls

Recent Performance and Forecast: Measuring and Controlling Instruments (SIC 3822,3823,3824,3829)

(in millions of dollars except as noted)

	1982	1983	1984[1]	1985[2]	1986[3]	Percent Change 1982-83	1983-84	1984-85	1985-86
Industry Data									
Value of shipments[4]	8,476	8,577	10,001	10,653	—	1.2	16.6	6.5	—
3822 Environmental Controls	1,549	1,745	1,871	1,990	—	12.7	7.2	6.4	—
3823 Control Instruments	4,006	3,782	4,023	4,409	—	−5.6	6.4	9.6	—
3824 Fluid Meters & Devices	727	692	807	759	—	−4.7	16.6	−5.9	—
3829 Instruments, nec	2,195	2,358	3,300	3,495	—	7.5	39.9	5.9	—
Value of shipments (1982$)	8,476	8,168	9,250	9,543	9,901	−3.6	13.2	3.2	3.8
3822 Environmental Controls	1,549	1,662	1,770	1,819	1,855	7.3	6.5	2.8	2.0
3823 Control Instruments	4,006	3,601	3,701	3,891	4,083	−10.1	2.8	5.1	5.0
3824 Fluid Meters & Devices	727	659	743	684	684	−9.3	12.7	−7.9	0.0
3829 Instruments, nec	2,195	2,246	3,036	3,149	3,275	2.3	35.2	3.7	4.0
Total employment (000)	137	133	142	147	—	−3.1	6.5	3.6	—
Production workers (000)	74.9	70.9	75.3	78.1	—	−5.3	6.2	3.8	—
Average hourly earnings ($)	8.36	9.13	9.24	—	—	9.3	1.2	—	—
Product Data									
Value of shipments[5]	8,320	8,320	9,627	10,235	—	0.0	15.7	6.3	—
3822 Environmental Controls	1,545	1,754	1,881	2,000	—	13.6	7.2	6.3	—
3823 Control Instruments	3,915	3,718	3,955	4,335	—	−5.0	6.4	9.6	—
3824 Fluid Meters & Devices	787	829	967	909	—	5.4	16.6	−6.0	—
3829 Instruments, nec	2,073	2,018	2,824	2,991	—	−2.7	39.9	5.9	—

Value of shipments (1982$)	8,320	7,923	8,905	9,167	9,503	-4.8	12.4	2.9	3.7
3822 Environmental Controls	1,545	1,671	1,779	1,828	1,865	8.2	6.5	2.8	2.0
3823 Control Instruments	3,915	3,541	3,639	3,826	4,017	-9.6	2.8	5.1	5.0
3824 Fluid Meters & Devices	787	790	889	819	819	0.3	12.6	-7.9	0.0
3829 Instruments, nec	2,073	1,922	2,598	2,694	2,802	-7.3	35.2	3.7	4.0
Shipments price index (1982=100)[6]	100.0	105.0	108.2	111.8	—	5.0	3.0	3.3	—
3822 Environmental Controls	100.0	105.0	105.7	109.4	—	5.0	0.7	3.5	—
3823 Control Instruments	100.0	105.0	108.7	113.3	—	5.0	3.5	4.2	—
3824 Fluid Meters & Devices	100.0	105.0	108.7	111.0	—	5.0	3.5	2.1	—
3829 Instruments, nec	100.0	105.0	108.7	111.0	—	5.0	3.5	2.1	—
Trade Data									
Value of imports (ITA)[7]	284	328	481	568	—	15.6	46.6	18.1	—
Import/new supply ratio[8]	0.033	0.038	0.048	0.053	—	15.0	25.4	10.5	—
Value of exports (ITA)[9]	1,549	1,463	1,526	1,633	—	-5.5	4.3	7.0	—
Export/shipments ratio	0.186	0.176	0.159	0.160	—	-5.5	-9.9	0.7	—

[1]Estimated except for exports and imports.
[2]Estimated.
[3]Forecast.
[4]Value of all products and services sold by the Measuring and Controlling Instruments industry.
[5]Value of products classified in the Measuring and Controlling Instruments industry produced by all industries.
[6]Developed by the Office of Industry Assessment, ITA.
[7]Import data are developed by the chapter author.
[8]New supply is the sum of product shipments plus imports.
[9]Export data are developed by the chapter author.
SOURCE: U.S. Department of Commerce: Bureau of the Census, Bureau of Economic Analysis, International Trade Administration (ITA). Estimates and forecasts by ITA.

Source: *U.S. Industrial Outlook 1986*, U.S. Department of Commerce.

Electronic Controls and Instruments

Company	Revenue Pct. Change Last Qtr %	FY to Date %	Last 12 Mos %	Earnings Last 12 Mos $Mil	Per Share Last 12 Mos $	Last Qtr $	Pct. Change Last Qtr %	FY to Date %	Last 12 Mos %	5-Year Growth Rate %	Par Growth Rate %	Date of Report	Dividends Current Rate Amt $	Yield %	5-Year Growth Rate %	Payout Last FY %	Last 5 Yrs	Last X-Dvd Date	Ratio Analysis Profit Margin %	Asset Turnover	Return on Total Assets %	Leverage Ratio	Return on Equity %	Debt to Equity %	Curr-ent Ratio	Shareholdings Market Value $Mil	Latest Shares Out-strding 000	Held by Banks/Funds 000	Insider Net Trading 000	Short Interest Ratio Days	Fiscal Year Ends Mo
Ind. Group	24.2	34.7	16.1	217.1	1.06	-40.9	-32.1	-27.4	3	5	--	.45	1.8	1	29	27	--	3.4	1.29	4.4	1.93	8.5	21	1.9	4,982	200,326	65,279	-51	1.9	--
AccuRay Cp	-1.3	-1.3	11.1	7.1q	1.69	45.7	45.7	-5.6	21	11	03-86	.24	.9	0	29	11	12-24-85	4.7	1.32	6.2	2.13	13.2	39	2.9	110	4,212	1,264	-6	0.0	12
Ametek Inc	17.8	17.8	4.8	35.2q	1.60	2.4	2.4	-16.2	10	6	03-86	1.00	3.3	12	53	46	06-10-86	6.7	1.31	8.8	1.82	16.0	18	2.0	658	22,011	6,805	+2	1.5	12
Bowmar Instr	-85.7	-41.3	-12.8	1.3s	.28	-33.3	-23.1	21.7	NC	17	03-86	.00	.0	0	0	0	00-00-00	3.8	1.39	5.3	3.19	16.9	145	3.4	21	4,629	267	-1	4.8	09
Clarostat Mfg	2.9	2.9	-3.5	1.9q	.24	27.3	27.3	9.0	36	22	03-86	1.00	2.0	0	22	17	05-21-86	7.0	1.89	13.2	1.21	16.0	612	6.4	24	476	34	-1	19.8	12
CompuDyne	7.0	12.5	13.7	1.1s	.50	NE	NE	NE	NC	22	03-86	.00	.0	0	0	0	00-00-00	.9	1.89	1.7	1.94	22.0		1.6	24	1,026	37	+23	3.1	09
Conrac Corp	-5.6	-5.6	-4.5	7.4q	1.22	13.6	13.6	34.1	4	5	03-86	.40	2.5b	2	34	35	05-07-86	5.0	1.14	5.7	1.40	8.0	5	2.7	107	6,634	1,155	-4	0.9	12
Daniel Inds	-15.8	-12.8	-6.5	1.8s	.17	NE	NE	NE	20	5	03-86	.18	2.6	8	850	23	05-30-86	1.4	.93	1.3	1.46	1.9	16	3.6	71	10,160	1,546	-1	1.2	09
Diagnostic Ret	14.4	7.8	9.0	.8f	.15	100.0	-34.8	-34.8	-16	3	03-86	.00	.0	0	0	0	07-18-83	2.2	.59	1.3	2.62	3.4	110	3.8	36	3,601	529	-80	1.4	08
Dranetz Tech	-20.3	-20.3	-7.4	3.3q	.70	-35.0	-35.0	-30.0	16	2	03-86	.20	1.6	56	26	12	05-19-86	13.2	1.08	14.2	1.14	16.2	70	8.8	60	4,718	697	0	0.0	12
Dynascan Cp	2.4	2.4	7.5	1.1s	.43	NE	NE	NE	NC	6	03-86	.00	.0	0	0	0	05-08-84	1.5	1.80	2.7	2.26	6.1	0	3.3	43	4,541	626	-1	0.0	09
EIP Microwave	1.9	-3.9	-9.0	.3s	.11	-57.1	-71.9	-86.9	17	0	03-86	.12	1.5	30	35	15	05-09-86	1.5	1.60	2.4	2.04	4.9	8	1.6	18	2,182	325	0	0.0	09
Electron Cp A	9.2	9.2	8.3	4.8q	2.58	9.0	9.0	32.3	NC	8	03-86	1.40	4.6	6	56	87	03-03-86	9.2	.95	8.7	2.07	18.0	55	4.5	56	1,827	117	0	0.7	12
Energy Conv Dev	-8.2	-27.2	-18.5	-27.7n	-6.18	NE	NE	NE	NC	8	03-86	.00	.0	0	0	0	00-00-00	NM	NC	NC	NC	NM	6	1.2	86	4,462	1,048	0	0.0	06
Fischer & Port	11.6	11.6	10.7	4.8q	1.11	-36.8	-36.8	32.1	27	8	03-86	.00	.0	0	0	0	03-17-86	2.7	1.44	3.9	2.03	7.9	16	2.6	62	3,334	1,417	0	1.7	12
Fluke, John	-4.7	-4.0	12.4	13.8s	1.63	-14.3	-14.6	-39.0	14	8	03-86	.00	.0	0	0	0	02-10-86	6.5	1.29	8.4	1.48	12.4	17	4.4	210	8,442	3,269	-4	0.4	09
Frequency Elec	40.4	31.0	36.3	4.6n	1.00	17.4	20.6	22.0	11	13	01-86	.00	.0	0	0	0	05-27-86	15.3	.65	10.0	1.27	12.7	10	8.8	97	4,576	1,420	0	0.1	04
Instron Corp	17.5	17.5	18.8	4.0q	.65	25.0	25.0	441.7	20	14	03-86	.12	.9	13	16	3	06-12-86	7.3	1.49	7.3	2.30	16.8	12	1.9	81	5,998	1,122	0	0.0	12
Johnson Contr	92.4	86.7	61.2	89.0s	4.61	-36.5	-8.2	-4.2	10	7	06-09-86	2.00	3.1	9	39	37	06-09-86	3.7	1.35	5.0	2.32	11.6	18	1.2	1,206	18,842	8,368	+8	1.1	09
Kollmorgen Cp	10.4	10.4	-1.8	-7.5q	-.75	-100.0	-100.0	-100.0	-11	14	05-19-86	.32	2.2	2	NE	7	05-19-86	-2.4	1.33	-3.2	2.34	-7.5	70	2.2	148	10,017	3,304	-2	5.4	12
Liebert Cp	9.1	7.8	12.4	18.4s	1.24	76.5	47.4	31.9	25	15	03-86	.09	.3	0	7	4	12-02-85	6.5	1.71	8.4	1.50	16.7	14	3.4	392	14,731	3,177	-4	0.0	09
Mangood Corp	8.5	8.5	1.6	-6.2q	-9.95	-100.0	-100.0	NE	NC	0	03-86	.00	.0	0	0	0	02-07-94	-10.0	1.51	-15.1	.00	NS	-331	1.0	7	629	51	+2	6.9	12
Measurex Corp	7.2	4.4	3.4	19.4s	2.08	12.5	16.3	17.5	NC	11	05-86	.36	1.0	0	0	0	06-26-86	10.7	.93	10.0	1.51	15.1	5	3.4	332	9,001	4,815	+3	1.2	11
MTS Systems Cp	4.9	10.0	20.4	5.1s	1.80	-12.8	1.3	17.6	8	11	05-86	.36	.9	6	13	2	06-09-86	5.1	1.16	5.9	2.15	12.7	28	1.8	84	2,747	902	0	0.0	09
Nicolet Instr	2.0	1.2		2.9s	.44	-10.0	-60.7	-60.7	4	4	02-86	.12	.7	-31	7	15	05-02-86	2.5	1.28	3.2	1.53	4.9	15	3.1	115	6,547	2,674	0	1.0	12
Nuclear Data	-25.6	-19.1	-18.4	-1.6f	-.86	-100.0	-100.0	-100.0	NC	-10	02-86	.00	.0	0	0	0	04-13-81	-45.7	.89	-10.1	2.35	-10.1	71	2.3		1,848	121	0	0.0	08
Robertshaw	4.0	4.0	.9	22.9q	4.21	-11.6	-11.6	-1.2	12	11	03-86	1.20	2.5	4	26	35	06-02-86	5.5	1.76	9.7	1.52	14.7	15	3.1	259	5,457	1,051	0	0.0	12
Tenney Engr	1.9	1.9	4.5	.9q	.28	-62.5	-62.5	-28.2	10	11	03-86	.00	.0	0	0	0	05-25-84	3.9	1.31	5.1	2.16	11.0	56	2.7	14	3,496	457	0	0.2	11
Teradyne Inc	-23.6	-23.6	-22.1	4.7q	.20	-100.0	-90.7	-90.7	20	11	03-86	.00	.0	0	0	0	08-01-83	1.4	.93	1.4	1.36	1.9	5	3.7	498	22,654	15,651	+8	0.8	12
Tesdata Sys	68.8	-23.0	-22.2	-3.2n	-2.49	NE	NE	NE	NC	-64	09-85	.00	.0	0	0	0	00-00-00	-40.5	.89	-64.0	1.58	-64.0	5	2.3	0	1,316	192	0	0.0	12
Veeco Instrs	1.8	-1.6	-6.7	5.9s	.62	-45.2	-55.0	-58.4	-3	2	03-86	.40	2.5	14	40	24	05-06-86	3.9	1.05	4.1	1.68	6.9	18	3.1	156	9,612	2,838	0	5.5	09

Energy: Coal, Oil, and Gas

CONSUMPTION BY FUEL TYPE AND SECTOR 1973–1984 [Quadrillon (10^{15}) BTU]

Residential and Commercial*				Transportation*			
Total	Coal	Natural Gas[1]	Petroleum	Total	Coal	Natural Gas[3]	Petroleum
1973	0.254	7.626	4.391	1973	0.003	0.743	17.821
1974	0.257	7.518	3.996	1974	0.002	0.685	17.396
1975	0.209	7.581	3.805	1975	0.001	0.595	17.610
1976	0.203	7.866	4.181	1976	([2])	0.559	18.499
1977	0.205	7.461	4.206	1977	([2])	0.543	19.230
1978	0.214	7.624	4.070	1978	([2])	0.539	20.019
1979	0.187	7.891	3.448	1979	([2])	0.612	19.817
1980	0.145	7.539	3.035	1980	([2])	0.648	19.009
1981	0.168	7.242	2.634	1981	([2])	R0.657	18.800
1982	0.188	7.433	2.449	1982	([2])	0.613	18.417
1983	0.196	7.025	2.499	1983	([2])	0.504	18.591
1984	0.212	7.292	2.582	1984	([2])	0.545	R19.295
1985	0.184	7.049	2.598	1985	([2])	0.522	19.446

* Geographic coverage: the 50 United States and District of Columbia.
The Residential and Commercial Sector consists of housing units, non-manufacturing business establishments (e.g., wholesale and retail businesses), health and educational institutions, and government office buildings.
R = Revised data.
· Totals may not equal sum of components due to independent rounding.
The Transportation Sector consists of both private and public passenger and freight transportation, as well as government transportation, including military operations.
[1] Includes supplemental gaseous fuels.
[2] Since 1976 coal use by transportation section has been negligible.
[3] Pipeline fuel only, including supplemental gaseous fuels.

Industrial*				Electric Utilities*			
Total	Coal	Natural Gas[1]	Petroleum	Total	Coal	Natural Gas[1]	Petroleum[2]
1973	4.057	10.388	9.113	1973	8.658	3.748	3.515
1974	3.870	10.003	8.698	1974	8.534	3.519	3.365
1975	3.667	8.532	8.151	1975	8.786	3.240	3.166
1976	3.661	8.761	9.018	1976	9.720	3.152	3.477
1977	3.454	8.636	9.786	1977	10.262	3.284	4.901
1978	3.314	8.539	9.890	1978	10.238	3.297	3.987
1979	3.593	8.549	10.576	1979	11.260	3.613	3.283
1980	3.155	8.394	9.524	1980	12.123	3.810	2.634
1981	3.157	8.257	8.295	1981	12.583	3.768	2.202
1982	2.552	7.116	7.798	1982	12.582	3.342	1.568
1983	2.490	6.821	7.421	1983	13.213	2.998	1.544
1984	2.842	7.448	7.889	1984	14.020	3.206	1.286
1985	2.775	7.053	7.718	1985	14.540	3.136	1.090

* Geographic coverage: the 50 United States and District of Columbia.
The Industrial Sector is made up of construction, manufacturing, agriculture, and mining establishments.
R = Revised data.
· Totals may not equal sum of components due to independent rounding.
[1] Includes supplemental gaseous fuels.
[2] Includes petroleum products reported as "oil consumed at steam units" through 1979 and "heavy oil" from 1980 forward, which are assumed to be residual fuel oil; petroleum products reported as "oil consumed by gas turbine and internal combustion units" through 1979 and "light oil" from 1980 forward, which are assumed to be distillate fuel oil and kerosene; and petroleum coke.
Source: *Monthly Energy Review*, U.S. Department of Energy, Energy Information Administration, March 1986.

PETROLEUM—CRUDE OIL[1] SUPPLY AND DISPOSITION

		Field Production		Supply		
				Imports		
		Total Domestic	Alaskan	Total	SPR[2]	Other
		Thousand barrels per day				
1973	AVERAGE	9,208	198	3,244		3,244
1974	AVERAGE	8,774	193	3,477		3,477
1975	AVERAGE	8,375	191	4,105		4,105
1976	AVERAGE	8,132	173	5,287		5,287
1977	AVERAGE	8,245	464	6,615	21	6,594
1978	AVERAGE	8,707	1,229	6,356	162	6,195
1979	AVERAGE	8,552	1,401	6,519	67	6,452
1980	AVERAGE	8,597	1,617	5,263	44	5,219
1981	AVERAGE	8,572	1,609	4,396	256	4,141
1982	AVERAGE	8,649	1,696	3,488	165	3,323
1983	AVERAGE	8,688	1,714	3,329	234	3,096
1984	AVERAGE	8,879	1,722	3,426	197	3,229
1985	AVERAGE	8,920	1,799	3,216	118	3,098
1986	AVERAGE	8,942[3]	1,822[3]	3,315[3]	58[3]	3,257[3]

Geographic coverage: the 50 United States and the District of Columbia.
* Totals may not equal sum of components due to independent rounding.
[1] Includes lease condensate.
[2] Strategic Petroleum Reserve.
[3] Estimates based on preliminary data.
Source: *Monthly Energy Review*, U.S. Department of Energy, Energy Information Administration, March 1986.

Oil, Natural Gas Producers

Company	Revenue Pct Change Last Qtr %	Rev FY to Date %	Rev Last 12 Mos %	Rev Last 12 Mos $Mil	Earn Per Share Last Qtr $	Earn Per Share Last 12 Mos $	Earn Pct Change FY to Date %	Earn Pct Change Last Qtr %	Earn Pct Change Last 12 Mos %	5-Year Growth Rate %	Par Growth Rate %	Date of Report	Div Current Rate Amt $	Div Yield %	Div 5-Year Growth Rate %	Payout Last FY %	Payout Last 5 Yrs %	Last X-Dvd Date	Pro-fit Mar-gin	Asset Turn-over	Return on Total Assets	Lever-age Ratio	Return on Equity	Debt to Eq-uity %	Curr-ent Ratio	Mar-ket Value $Mil	Latest Shares Out-stndng 000	Held by Banks 000	Insider Net Trad-ing 000	Short Int-erest Ratio Days	Fiscal Year Ends Mo
Ind. Group	-3.9	-.5	-1.8	420.6	-.42	-1.00.0	NE	NE	NE	NC	-11	--	.49	5.0	0	51	40	--	-.12	.75	-.9	5.89	-5.3	243	1.1	10,303	1,064,014	162,380	+883	3.7	--
Allegheny & Wstrn	-16.7	-10.9	-10.9	.0	1.81	3.8	17.2	293.5	NE	NC	0	05-09-86	.49	.9	0	3	2	NC	NC	NC	NC	5.89	NS	171	1.3	219	7,971	1,215	0	0.0	06
Argo Pet	-26.5	-16.1	-15.3	-36.88	-4.77		-100.0			NC	0	12-85	.00		0	0	0	01-21-81	NM	NM	NC	NC	NS	-36	.1	6	7,721	1,602	0	5.8	12
Asamera Inc	-11.8	-11.8	1.3	7.8q	.17		-100.0			-1	03-86	3.1	3.6	6	36	NE	03-25-86	2.1	1.33	2.8	2.32	6.5	34	1.5	215	33,039	3,787	0	1.1	12
Barnwell Indus	-31.0	-9.9	16.6	-3.1s	-.25		-100.0		-59.0	4	03-86	4.0		0	NE	0	03-10-86	-22.1	.63	-14.0	.00	-174		1.1	7	1,373	36	0	0.0	09
Baruch-Foster	-18.2	-18.2		.7q			NE			-18	03-86	NA		0	0	0	07-08-85	4.7	.51	2.4	1.71	4.1	46	1.6	23	2,718	303	+3	0.7	12
Cdn Occid Pet	-23.3	-23.3	-13.5	88.6q	2.63		-70.9	-27.9		22	03-86	.64	NA	16	18	19	06-02-86	14.8	.47	6.9	1.96	13.5	10	1.2	429	33,343	382	0	0.0	12
Coastal Corp	26.7	26.7	29.3	54.0q	.78		-67.2		-67.2	NC	10	03-86	.40	1.2	6	9	16	05-23-86	.7	1.00	7.0	10.00	7.0	509	1.0	941	29,282	10,816	-5	7.7	12
Consol O & G	3.0	3.0	-3.4	-4.0q	-.51		-100.0	-100.0		-50	03-86	.00	.0	1	0	0	05-28-80	-14.3	.18	-2.6	19.23	-50.0	1471	NA	12	5,748	1,005	+35	9.6	11
Damson Oil	-51.9	-40.4	-44.0	-61.6s	-8.12		-100.0		-100.0	-76	03-86	.00	.0	0	0	0	00-00-00	NM	NC	NC	NC	-76.0	122	1.0	6	7,977	457	+5	38.6	08
Devon Resourc	NA	NA	NA	NA	NA		NA	NA	NA	NC	NA	00-00	1.20	16.8	0	NA	NA	05-12-86	NM	NC	NC	NC	NA	NA	NA	24	3,334	0	0	NA	NA
Dome Petrol	7.9	2.7	7.0	-93.4n	-.43		NE	NE	NE	NC	-11	09-45	.00	NA	0	0	0	06-03-81	-3.8	.32	-1.2	.00	NS	-1153	.9	256	292,088	22,140	-8	0.4	12
Enserco Inc	-5.3	-5.3	-5.3	-42.4q	-12.52		-100.0	-100.0		-94	09-45	.00	.0	0	0	0	05-15-86	-33.1	.31	-25.4	3.71	-94.2	144	.9	24	3,370	245	+13	0.0	12
Equity Oil	-16.7	-16.7	-9.5	3.4q	.30		-57.1	-31.8		9	09-09-85	.00	.0	1	59	49	09-09-85	17.9	.32	5.8	1.47	8.5	0	3.0	69	11,684	3,377	0	0.0	12
Forest Oil	-28.6	-28.6	-19.7	6.9q	.26		-100.0	-87.9		12	05-21-86	1.10	9.8	-4	108	80	05-21-86	5.7	.23	1.3	5.85	7.6	279	.9	71	6,397	933	-58	0.0	12
Free Mc. Egy	NA	NA	NA	NA	NA		NA	NA	NA	NA	16	03-24-86	2.20	14.4	NA	NA	NA	05-14-86	2.20	.23	NM	3.66	NM	NA	NA	727	47,691	779	0	NA	NA
Gulf Appld Tech	96.3	96.3	36.3	-3.3q	-1.03		NE	NE	NE	NE	-11	06-29-94	.00	NA	0	0	NE	06-29-94	-22.0	.38	-8.3	1.33	-11.0	9	3.9	23	3,269	347	0	0.0	12
Hamilton Oil	117.4	117.4	63.8	31.9q	1.16		123.5	78.5		-12	03-10-86	.00	.0	0	0	9	03-10-86	9.6	.34	3.3	3.36	11.1	134	1.2	270	25,429	849	-1285	0.0	12
Howell Corp	-20.0	-20.0	-26.8	2.9q	.60		-93.3	-29.4		NC	11	05-27-86	.28	3.0	4	54	87	05-27-86	2.9	.55	1.6	2.44	3.9	62	1.0	45	4,791	318	0	0.2	12
Inexco Oil	-27.4	-27.4	-24.9	-128.0q	-5.20		-100.0		-100.0	-67	03-25-86	.00	.0	-4	NE	NE	03-25-86	-96.2	.23	-19.1	3.50	-66.8	175	.6	117	24,586	4,107	0	0.4	12
MAPCO	-9.2	-9.2	-3.6	97.5q	3.61		1.2	-34.0		16	05-14-86	1.00	2.2	-12	28	41	05-14-86	5.2	1.17	6.1	3.66	22.3	93	1.1	985	21,291	13,217	+5	2.4	12
May Petrol	3.0	3.0	-13.3	-33.4q	-3.48		-100.0	NE		-61	10-22-80	.00	.0	0	0	NE	10-22-80	NM	-60.9	NM	NC	29	1.3	26	12,612	1,729	0	0.0	12
Maynard Oil	-36.4	-36.4	-18.7	4.0q	.57		NE	NE		13	00-00-00	.00	.0	0	0	9	00-00-00	15.4	.53	8.1	1.56	12.6	24	2.8	24	6,139	849	0	0.0	12
MCO Holding	-32.6	-32.6	-48.0	1.7q	.15		-93.6		-93.6	-5	00-00-00	.00	.0	0	0	0	06-06-86	2.2	.14	2.0	6.00	1.8	226	.7	82	5,899	673	-3	3.7	01
Mitchell Energy	-13.2	-13.2	-9.5	42.0q	.88		-59.1	46.7		-19	00-00-00	.24	2.1	12	24	16	05-06-86	5.1	.39	2.0	3.65	7.3	159	1.1	556	47,863	9,967	-3	3.7	01
N Cdn Oils	1.5	1.5	61.2	20.6q	.82		-48.1	-64.7		15	08-23-85	.00	NA	0	0	0	08-23-85	13.7	.19	2.6	5.85	15.2	242	6.6	78	10,822	223	+1526	0.0	12
Numac O & G	-25.0	-25.0	-8.3	18.0q	.78		-29.4	25.8		20	12-12-83	.00	NA	0	0	5	12-12-83	27.3	.26	7.1	1.83	13.0	32	1.7	136	22,731	2,336	+423	2.5	12
Occidental Pet	-1.8	-1.8	-5.1	446.4q	2.55		283.3	-14.4		-19	04-04-86	2.50	9.3	0	113	84	04-04-86	26.3	1.26	6.9	3.49	22.9	117	1.2	2,936	109,762	49,581	+15	7.4	12
Pauley Petro	-7.2	-4.2	-3.9	5.2s	1.78		-93.3	-29.4		23	02-86	.00	.0	0	0	0	07-14-33	2.7	2.56	6.9	3.32	22.9	109	1.2	44	2,893	104	0	6.0	08
Petro-Lewis	-40.1	-40.1	-10.7	-354.1n	-14.24		-100.0		-2.8	0	07-14-33	.00	.0	0	0	33	07-14-33	NM	NC	NM	NC	NM	385	NA	15	25,559	4,576	0	21.8	06
Plains Petrol	-13.0	-13.0	240.0	3.9q	.42		-41.2	-16.1		NC	04-86	.00	.0	0	0	0	00-00-00	22.9	.69	15.7	2.07	32.5	53	1.3	216	9,047	3,485	+10	0.0	12
Prairie Oil Roy	11.1	11.1	-5.0	6.6q	.83		-4.5	5.1		17	01-00-85	.00	NA	0	0	0	01-00-85	34.7	.35	13.0	1.63	13.0	0	3.3	38	7,846	361	0	0.0	12
Ranger Oil	-3.1	-3.1	8.4	-22.1q	-.33		40.0	NE		-11	11-25-80	.00	NA	0	0	NE	11-25-80	-17.1	.26	-4.4	2.39	-10.5	24	3.2	277	69,304	3,814	+2	1.1	09
Scephre Rscs	13.0	13.0	15.4	15.4q	.33		-70.8	-48.4		12	00-00-00	.50		12	0	0	00-00-00	19.3	.31	6.0	.00	15.8	1834	1.3	52	25,776	341	+87	12.0	12
Scurry Rainbow	10.6	10.2	15.1	27.8s	2.07		-26.8	-2.8		23	06-02-86	.00	NA	0	23	20	06-02-86	28.1	.36	8.9	1.78	15.8	2	2.5	188	13,662	87	0	0.0	10
Slatex Pet	-17.9	-17.9	-20.0	-5.0s	-1.90		NE	NE		-31	04-86	NA		0	NE	NE	04-86	-31.3		-11.4	2.73	-31.1	71	1.5	21	2,938	250	+3	0.0	12
Summit En	-16.7	-16.7	-5.0	-4.6q	-2.27		NE	NE		-28	03-11-82	.00	NA	0	NE	NE	03-11-82	-63.7	.35	-22.9	1.22	-28.0	0	.4	38	2,715	96	0	0.0	07
Tesoro Petrol	42.0	42.0	-35.0	-149.4s	-11.55		NE	NE		-6	05-06-86	.40	4.2	11	NE	45	05-06-86	-8.1	2.05	-4.5	2.68	-44.5	53	1.3	132	13,729	4,164	0	4.1	09
Tex Am Energy	-31.7	-31.7	-17.3	-30.5q	-4.68		-66.7			-90	08-29-85	.00	.0	0	23	20	08-29-85	-18.8	.88	-16.5	5.44	-89.7	253		23	8,315	597	+21	15.5	12
Ter Pacific	-23.8	-23.8	15.1	6.7q	1.71		-22.2	6.2		29	02-26-86	.40	1.3	9	0	NE	02-26-86	55.8	.49	27.6	1.36	37.4	-226	NA	117	3,852	485	-2	1.6	12
Tesse Corp	-50.3	-50.3	-30.4	-66.8q	-2.73		NE	NE		-12	07-06-82	.00	.0	17	NE	NE	07-06-82	-5.1	2.08	-10.6	.00	NS		1.3	94	25,017	2,291	-2	0.8	12

Column key — Revenue: Pct Change (Last Qtr %, FY to Date %, Last 12 Mos %), Last 12 Mos $Mil. Earnings Per Share: Last 12 Mos $, Pct Change (Last Qtr %, FY to Date %, Last 12 Mos %), 5-Year Growth Rate %, Par Growth Rate %, Date of Report. Dividends: Current Rate (Amt $, Yield %), 5-Year Growth Rate %, Payout (Last FY %, Last 5 Yrs %), Last X-Dvd Date. Ratio Analysis (s/l × r/a × a/e = r/e): Profit Margin %, Asset Turnover, Return on Total Assets %, Leverage Ratio, Return on Equity %, Debt to Equity %, Current Ratio. Shareholdings: Market Value $Mil, Latest Shares Outstdng (000), Held by Banks/Funds (000), Insider Net Trading (000), Short Interest Ratio (Days), Fiscal Year Ends (Mo).

Oil, Natural Gas Producers

Company	Rev LQ %	Rev FY %	Rev 12M %	Rev 12M $Mil	EPS 12M $	EPS LQ %	EPS FY %	EPS 12M %	EPS 5-Yr %	Par %	Date	Div Amt	Yield	Div 5-Yr %	Payout FY	Payout 5Yr	X-Dvd	Prof Mgn	Asset T/O	Ret Tot Assets	Lever	Ret Equity	Debt/Eq	Curr	Mkt Val	Shares	Banks/Funds	Insider	Short	FY
Total Petro NA	-18.8	-18.8	-1.5	74.7q	2.89	-31.3	-31.3	217.6	NC	23	03-86	.36	1.8	-14	8	NE	05-23-86	3.3	2.30	7.6	3.42	26.0	106	1.0	427	21,747	4,134	+203	0.9	12
Unimar Co	NA	NA	0	NA	NA	NA	NA	NA	NC	NC	00-00	2.21	26.8	NA	0	NA	05-09-86	NA	NC	NC	NC	NA	NA	NA	99	12,051	2,053	0	NA	NA
Univ Resours	-43.9	-27.8	-17.3	-54.7s	-5.39	-100.0	-100.0	-100.0	NC	47	04-86	.00	.0	0	0	18	09-13-82	-33.8	.65	-22.1	NC	-46.8	54	1.1	48	10,142	1,989	-12	0.3	10
Wichita Indus	5.4	5.4	23.0	-5.4g	-1.94	-75.0	-75.0	-45.5	-5	-76	12-85	.24	1.6b	0	21	18	11-02-81	NM	.18	-22.1	3.44	-76.1	149	1.0	4	2,870	136	+4	0.0	12
Wilshire Oil	-51.2	-32.6	-29.4	2.0t	.24	NE	NE	-1.2	NC	6	03-86	.10	1.6b	0	21	18	01-06-86	16.7	.18	3.0	3.33	10.0	101	1.5	52	8,352	560	0	0.0	12
Wiser Oil	-8.3	-8.3	-11.7	7.4q	.81	-32.4	-45.5	-45.5	-15	4	03-86	.40	2.6	1	73	68	05-09-86	16.4	.39	6.4	1.23	7.9	1	5.4	138	9,069	2,433	-7	0.0	12

Ind. Group

Company	Rev LQ %	Rev FY %	Rev 12M %	Rev 12M $Mil	EPS 12M $	EPS LQ %	EPS FY %	EPS 12M %	EPS 5-Yr %	Par %	Date	Div Amt	Yield	Div 5-Yr %	Payout FY	Payout 5Yr	X-Dvd	Prof Mgn	Asset T/O	Ret Tot Assets	Lever	Ret Equity	Debt/Eq	Curr	Mkt Val	Shares	Banks/Funds	Insider	Short	FY
Ind. Group	-9.2		-4	20,122.1	3.87	-10.8	-3.5	-1.6		-5		2.30	5.7	0	30	27		4.3	.93	4.0	2.90	11.6	44	1.1	198,436	4,943,394	G	+60	2.6	12

Oil Refining and Marketing

Company	Rev LQ %	Rev FY %	Rev 12M %	Rev 12M $Mil	EPS 12M $	EPS LQ %	EPS FY %	EPS 12M %	EPS 5-Yr %	Par %	Date	Div Amt	Yield	Div 5-Yr %	Payout FY	Payout 5Yr	X-Dvd	Prof Mgn	Asset T/O	Ret Tot Assets	Lever	Ret Equity	Debt/Eq	Curr	Mkt Val	Shares	Banks/Funds	Insider	Short	FY
Adam Rsc En	-27.1	-27.1	-11.2	1.3q	.15	-90.9	-90.9	-65.1	0	0	03-86	.00	.0	NA	0	NE	00-00-00	1.1	4.64	5.1	.00	NS	-127	1.0	14	6,908	343	0	0.6	12
Adobe Rscs	NA	NA	56.8	15.4n	-7.54	NA	NA	NA	NA	NC	03-86	.00	.0	NA	0	NE	00-00-00	NA	NC	NC	NC	NS	NA	NA	171	20,716	1,348	0	NA	12
Amerada Hess	-31.2	-31.2	-10.9	-636.9g	-4.36	-100.0	-100.0	-100.0	4	-28	03-86	.00	.0	-5	84	18	12-10-85	-9.0	1.13	-10.2	2.76	-28.2	74	1.3	1,659	82,969	42,440	-34	0.3	12
Am Petrolina	-11.0	-11.0	8.9	-52.4q	6.94	-27.3	-27.3	-6.6	3	8	03-86	.00	.0	0	0	NE	08-28-85	-2.2	1.32	-2.9	2.90	-8.4	76	1.1	575	11,978	128	+1	0.5	12
Amoco Cp	-22.1	-22.1	-7.9	1811.0q	5.81	438.1	198.8	NE	3	8	03-86	3.30	5.5	5	44	43	05-01-86	7.5	.96	7.2	2.17	15.6	27	.9	15,588	258,727	92,441	0	2.1	12
Ashland Oil	-8.9	-5.5	-6.7	194.2s	-.86	7.5	7.5	-100.0	14	NE	03-86	1.80	3.3	9	39	158	05-20-86	2.5	1.96	4.9	4.27	20.9	66	1.1	1,733	32,012	12,790	+4	1.8	09
Atlantic Richfld	-23.1	-23.1	-11.4	-266.0q	3.72	-95.0	7.5	-4.1	-17	-27	04-86	4.00	7.7	14	67	110	05-12-86	-1.3	1.00	-1.3	3.69	-4.8	110	.6	9,438	181,500	91,638	0	1.0	12
Brit Petrol	-14.2	-14.2	25.3	2736.8q	-2.56	-95.0	-95.0	-4.1	-17	7	03-86	2.36	6.4	7	40	48	03-10-86	4.8	1.31	6.3	3.03	19.1	38	1.4	17,134	464,642	4,211	0	8.1	12
Charter Co	-21.4	-21.4	-42.8	-27.9q	4.53	1.0	1.0	27	5	8	03-86	.00	.0	5	53	NE	00-00-00	-1.9	2.26	-4.3	.00	NS	-9	2.3	45	16,453	448	-3	8.7	12
Chevron Cp	-24.9	-24.9	21.6	1549.0q	.46	-96.6	-96.6	NE	0	5	12-85	2.40	6.3	0	53	48	05-05-86	4.0	1.00	4.0	2.50	10.0	23	1.1	13,128	342,109	158,285	-3	3.5	12
Crown Ctrl Pet	8.3	-8.5	-8.5	.46	-5.65	NE	NE	NE	0	2	12-85	.00	.0	0	0	153	04-03-84	.3	2.67	.8	2.63	2.1	49	1.4	110	4,817	393	0	1.1	12
Diam Sham	-.5	-.5	-4.6	-673.8q	-5.65	-100.0	-100.0	-100.0	0	-47	03-86	1.19	10.9	0	NE	432	05-05-86	-16.4	.89	-14.6	2.67	-39.0	85	1.1	1,284	118,114	33,380	+4	4.7	12
Diam Sham Off	NA	NA	0	NA	7.10	37.4	37.4	5.5	NA	9	03-86	2.80	18.7	NA	NE	54	05-05-86	NA	NC	NC	NC	NA	NA	.9	638	42,500	381	0	4.4	12
Exxon	2.8	2.8	-2.2	5255.0q	1.96	447.1	447.1	NE	5	34	04-86	3.60	4b	-2	53	54	05-07-86	6.0	1.27	7.6	2.38	18.1	17	.9	44,500	731,000	235,567	+16	3.6	01
Getty Petro	-10.5	-10.5	22.0	19.3q	1.96	NE	NE	NE	-2	34	04-86	.12	4b	9	34	34	04-22-86	1.5	5.60	8.4	4.29	36.0	187	1.5	305	10,044	529	0	3.6	01
Gulf Canada	-17.2	-17.2	-45.3	270.0q	1.17	-74.4	-74.4	-19.9	5	8	03-86	.52	NA	35	45	39	05-23-86	9.5	.44	4.2	2.33	9.8	47	2.1	1,841	171,294	9,397	+7	0.5	12
Holly Corp	-28.0	-6.7	-2.5	15.4n	3.55	-1.2	91.7	181.7	28	10	04-86	.00	.0	9	30	10	09-24-85	4.0	2.13	8.5	3.24	27.5	0	1.2	82	4,127	1,838	+1	0.4	07
Husky Oil Ltd	-11.3	-11.3	-34.3	107.0q	1.16	-88.8	-68.8	-8.7	13	7	06-86	.20	NA	25	14	26	06-09-86	12.6	.43	5.4	2.24	12.1	25	.7	553	94,078	2,333	+1	0.7	12
Imperial Oil	-10.9	-10.9	-.4	650.0q	4.00	-27.2	-27.2	13.3	-2	4	03-86	1.65	NA	17	28	47	05-28-86	8.0	.89	7.1	1.82	12.9	23	2.2	4,487	163,181	2,129	0	1.8	12
Ker-McGee	-11.2	-11.2	-5.5	130.7q	2.53	-16.7	-16.7	153.0	4	4	03-86	1.10	6.2	4	42	42	06-02-86	4.0	.88	3.5	2.17	7.6	33	.8	1,361	49,699	28,019	-29	0.8	12
Mobil Corp	-1.8	-1.8	-4.6	1160.0q	2.85	38.5	38.5	-3.7	4	2	04-86	2.20	7.0	4	86	58	04-29-86	2.1	1.33	2.8	2.93	8.2	69	1.0	12,912	408,292	154,642	+7	1.8	12
Murphy Oil	-94.7	-94.7	-18.0	60.6q	1.77	-85.7	-85.7	-6.3	13	11	06-86	1.00	4.3	4	44	29	05-09-86	3.6	.64	2.3	2.61	6.0	25	1.2	807	34,918	14,722	+1	7.9	12
Pac Resources	-37.2	-37.2	-20.1	17.4q	.87	-70.3	-70.3	335.0	0	-2	00-00	.00	.0	1	0	29	11-27-84	1.4	2.32	3.2	3.53	11.3	78	1.4	232	14,307	1,942	-228	4.3	12
Pennzoil Co	-11.5	-11.5	-3.5	98.1q	1.93	-22.5	-22.5	-16.1	1	15	03-86	2.20	4.1	7	100	72	05-23-86	4.5	.67	3.0	4.33	13.0	169	1.2	2,222	41,344	18,734	0	1.8	12
Phillips Petrol	-21.9	-21.9	-4.0	408.0q	1.59	62.5	62.5	1.3	7	15	03-86	.60	6.2	-6	66	51	05-01-86	2.8	1.04	2.8	8.55	24.8	398	1.0	2,196	227,144	119,446	+444	2.9	12
Quaker St Oil	2.7	2.7	7.1	48.3q	1.99	23.5	23.5	37.2	8	8	03-86	.85	3.1	5	45	45	05-09-86	4.9	1.51	7.4	2.09	15.5	36	1.7	654	23,890	7,088	+3	6.6	12
Royal Dutch	11.7	11.7	11.7	2681.8t	10.01	12.1	11.8	11.8	10	9	12-84	3.29	4.1	10	30	31	09-17-85	99.8	.15	14.7	1.03	15.1	0	1.0	21,577	266,037	70,501	-135	1.4	07
Salomon Inc	15.8	15.8	1.5	606.0q	4.10	33.3	33.3	30.2	13	17	06-86	.64	1.3	25	14	17	06-10-86	2.1	.33	.7	29.29	20.5	144	NA	7,197	148,000	80,787	0	0.7	12
Shell Transport	5.9	5.9	5.8	1633.8t	5.91	6.5	5.9	5.9	4	7	12-84	2.45	4.9	3	26	44	04-11-86	99.7	.71	.7	1.03	13.8	0	1.1	13,672	276,209	17,547	+4	3.1	12
Std Oil Ohio	-3.0	-3.0	4.5	218.0q	2.53	-26.0	-26.0	-84.7	12	-28	03-86	2.80	6.2	12	214	44	05-13-86	1.7	.71	1.2	2.25	2.7	41	1.1	4,906	108,715	52,552	+4	4b	12
Sun Co Inc	-.2	.2	1.3	546.0q	4.94	19.6	19.6	8.3	4	4	03-86	3.00	6.3	2	47	49	05-05-86	4.7	1.05	4.8	2.45	10.3	33	1.2	5,259	110,144	46,639	0	2.3	12
Texaco Canada	-26.7	-26.7	-.7	321.0q	2.63	-13.6	-13.6	-19.3	-3	4	03-86	1.20	NA	15	44	60	05-06-86	8.2	1.07	8.8	1.60	14.1	0	2.2	2,355	120,768	817	+1	1.0	12
Texaco	-17.6	-17.6	-8.1	1241.0q	5.20	7.0	7.0	390.6	19	4	03-86	3.00	9.5	8	59	60	04-30-86	2.8	1.18	3.3	2.76	9.1	56	1.0	7,516	238,589	98,047	0	2.2	12
Unocal Cp	-12.2	-12.2	-4.6	214.5q	1.92	-42.3	-42.3	-52.4	-10	5	03-86	1.20	6.1	8	49	26	04-04-86	2.1	.95	2.0	6.60	13.2	347	1.4	2,294	116,169	105,587	+4	0.6	12

Recent Performance and Forecast: Health and Medical Services (SIC 80)
(in billions of dollars)

Item	1982	1983	1984	1985[1]	1986[2]	Percent Change			
						1982-83	1983-84	1984-85	1985-86
TOTAL EXPENDITURES	321.2	355.1	387.4	423.8	466.0	10.6	9.1	9.4	10.0
Health services and supplies	307.0	339.8	371.6	406.6	448.1	10.7	9.4	9.4	10.2
Personal health care	284.9	315.2	341.8	376.0	413.2	10.6	8.4	10.0	9.9
Hospital care	134.7	148.8	157.9	171.6	186.1	10.5	6.1	8.8	8.4
Physicians' services	61.8	68.4	75.4	83.5	92.5	10.7	10.2	10.7	10.8
Dentists' services	19.5	21.8	25.1	28.3	32.0	11.8	15.1	12.7	13.1
Other professional services	7.1	8.0	8.8	9.8	11.0	12.7	10.0	11.4	12.2
Drugs and medical sundries[3]	21.8	23.6	25.8	28.5	31.2	8.3	9.3	10.5	9.5
Eyeglasses and appliances	5.6	6.5	7.4	8.3	9.3	16.1	13.8	12.2	12.0
Nursing home care	26.9	29.4	32.0	35.2	39.3	9.3	8.8	10.0	11.6
Other health services	7.6	8.6	9.4	10.8	11.8	13.2	9.3	14.9	9.3
Program administration and net cost of insurance	12.8	14.5	19.1	19.1	22.8	13.3	31.7	0.0	19.4
Government public health activities	9.3	10.1	10.7	11.5	12.1	8.6	5.9	7.5	5.2
Research and construction of medical facilities	14.2	15.3	15.8	17.2	18.1	7.7	3.3	8.9	5.2
Research[4]	5.9	6.2	6.8	7.3	7.8	5.1	9.7	7.4	6.8
Construction	8.3	9.1	9.0	9.9	10.3	9.6	-1.1	10.0	4.0

[1]Estimated by U.S. Department of Commerce, International Trade Administration, (ITA).
[2]Forecast by U.S. Department of Commerce, ITA.
[3]Includes only expenditures for prescription drugs, over-the-counter drugs, and medical sundries dispensed through retail channels. Spending for drugs dispensed in hospitals and by physicians is reported within those cost categories.
[4]Research expenditures of drug companies and other manufacturers and providers of medical equipment and supplies are included in the expenditure class in which the product falls.

SOURCE: Bureau of Data Management and Strategy, Health Care Financing Administration.

Source: U.S. Industrial Outlook 1986, U.S. Department of Commerce.

Recent Performance and Forecast: X-ray Apparatus and Tubes (SIC 3693)
(in millions of dollars except as noted)

Item	1982	1983	1984[1]	1985[2]	1986[3]	Percent Change			
						1982-83	1983-84	1984-85	1985-86
Industry Data									
Value of shipments[4]	4,261	4,565	4,661	4,926	5,621	7.1	2.1	5.7	14.1
Value of shipments (1982$)	4,261	4,366	4,308	4,430	4,866	2.5	-1.3	2.8	9.9
Total employment (000)	47.7	45.7	48.8	47.7	—	-4.2	6.7	-2.2	—
Production workers (000)	22.9	22.2	23.8	23.0	—	-3.1	7.1	-3.3	—
Average hourly earnings ($)	7.98	8.40	8.87	9.19	—	5.2	5.6	3.6	—
Product Data									
Value of shipments[5]	3,834	4,017	4,101	4,334	4,945	4.8	2.1	5.7	14.1
Value of shipments (1982$)	3,834	3,842	3,790	3,898	4,282	0.2	-1.3	2.8	9.9
Shipments price index (1982=100)[6]	100.0	104.6	108.2	111.2	115.5	4.6	3.5	2.8	3.9
Trade Data									
Value of imports (ITA)[7]	487	673	840	910	1,014	38.2	24.8	8.3	11.5
Import/new supply ratio[8]	0.113	0.144	0.170	0.174	0.170	27.3	18.5	2.1	-1.9
Value of exports (ITA)[9]	1,025	1,086	1,099	1,200	1,350	5.9	1.2	9.2	12.5
Export/shipments ratio	0.267	0.270	0.268	0.277	0.273	1.1	-0.8	3.3	-1.4

[1]Estimated except for exports and imports.
[2]Estimated.
[3]Forecast.
[4]Value of all products and services sold by the X-ray Apparatus and Tubes industry.
[5]Value of products classified in the X-ray Apparatus and Tubes industry produced by all industries.
[6]Developed by the Office of Industry Assessment, ITA.
[7]Import data are developed by the chapter author.
[8]New supply is the sum of product shipments plus imports.
[9]Export data are developed by the chapter author.
SOURCE: U.S. Department of Commerce: Bureau of the Census, Bureau of Economic Analysis, International Trade Administration (ITA). Estimates and forecasts by ITA.

Source: U.S. Industrial Outlook 1986, U.S. Department of Commerce.

Recent Performance and Forecast: Surgical and Medical Instruments (SIC 3841)

(in millions of dollars except as noted)

	1982	1983	1984[1]	1985[2]	1986[3]	Percent Change			
						1982-83	1983-84	1984-85	1985-86
Industry Data									
Value of shipments[4]	4,085	4,343	4,495	4,617	4,857	6.3	3.5	2.7	5.2
Value of shipments (1982$)	4,085	4,167	4,273	4,327	4,423	2.0	2.5	1.3	2.2
Total employment (000)	56.9	60.2	60.4	58.9	—	5.8	0.4	−2.6	—
Production workers (000)	38.5	40.1	39.5	37.2	—	4.2	−1.4	−5.8	—
Average hourly earnings ($)	6.97	7.44	7.87	8.32	—	6.9	5.8	5.6	—
Product Data									
Value of shipments[5]	4,272	4,592	4,751	4,883	5,137	7.5	3.5	2.8	5.2
Value of shipments (1982$)	4,272	4,405	4,516	4,576	4,679	3.1	2.5	1.3	2.2
Shipments price index (1982=100)[6]	100.0	104.2	105.2	106.7	109.8	4.2	0.9	1.4	2.9
Trade Data									
Value of imports (ITA)[7]	222	258	337	395	450	16.4	30.7	17.0	14.0
Import/new supply ratio[8]	0.049	0.053	0.066	0.075	0.080	7.8	24.6	12.8	7.7
Value of exports (ITA)[9]	605	579	618	662	744	−4.4	6.8	7.1	12.3
Export/shipments ratio	0.142	0.126	0.130	0.136	0.145	−11.0	3.3	4.2	6.8

[1]Estimated except for exports and imports.
[2]Estimated.
[3]Forecast.
[4]Value of all products and services sold by the Surgical and Medical Instruments industry.
[5]Value of products classified in the Surgical and Medical Instruments industry produced by all industries.
[6]Developed by the Office of Industry Assessment, ITA.
[7]Import data are developed by the chapter author.
[8]New supply is the sum of product shipments plus imports.
[9]Export data are developed by the chapter author.
SOURCE: U.S. Department of Commerce: Bureau of the Census, Bureau of Economic Analysis, International Trade Administration (ITA). Estimates and forecasts by ITA.

Source: *U.S. Industrial Outlook 1986*, U.S. Department of Commerce.

Recent Performance and Forecast: Dental Equipment and Supplies (SIC 3843)

(in millions of dollars except as noted)

Item	1982	1983	1984[1]	1985[2]	1986[3]	Percent Change			
						1982-83	1983-84	1984-85	1985-86
Industry Data									
Value of shipments[4]	1,112	1,117	1,147	1,178	1,213	0.5	2.7	2.7	3.0
Value of shipments (1982$)	1,112	1,078	1,086	1,091	1,098	-3.0	0.7	0.4	0.6
Total employment (000)	15.5	14.4	14.7	14.5	—	-7.1	2.4	-1.4	—
Production workers (000)	9.8	9.0	9.2	8.9	—	-8.2	1.8	-2.4	—
Average hourly earnings ($)	7.02	7.11	7.47	7.79	—	1.3	5.0	4.3	—
Product Data									
Value of shipments[5]	957	955	980	1,007	1,037	-0.2	2.7	2.7	3.0
Value of shipments (1982$)	957	922	928	932	938	-3.7	0.7	0.4	0.7
Shipments price index (1982=100)[6]	100.0	103.6	105.6	108.0	110.5	3.6	1.9	2.3	2.3
Trade Data									
Value of imports (ITA)[7]	49.9	55.4	66.3	74.1	79.9	11.0	19.7	11.8	7.8
Import/new supply ratio[8]	0.050	0.055	0.063	0.069	0.072	10.6	15.6	8.2	4.4
Value of exports (ITA)[9]	143	146	137	144	154	1.8	-5.9	4.5	7.2
Export/shipments ratio	0.150	0.153	0.140	0.143	0.148	2.0	-8.3	1.8	4.1

[1]Estimated except for exports and imports.
[2]Estimated.
[3]Forecast.
[4]Value of all products and services sold by the Dental Equipment and Supplies industry.
[5]Value of products classified in the Dental Equipment and Supplies industry produced by all industries.
[6]Developed by the Office of Industry Assessment, ITA.
[7]Import data are developed by the chapter author.
[8]New supply is the sum of product shipments plus imports.
[9]Export data are developed by the chapter author.
SOURCE: U.S. Department of Commerce: Bureau of the Census, Bureau of Economic Analysis, International Trade Administration (ITA). Estimates and forecasts by ITA.

Source: U.S. Industrial Outlook 1986, U.S. Department of Commerce.

Hospital and Laboratory Instruments

Company	Rev Pct Chg Last Qtr	Rev Pct Chg FY to Date	Rev Pct Chg Last 12 Mos	Rev Last 12 Mos $Mil	EPS Last 12 Mos $	EPS Pct Chg Last Qtr	EPS Pct Chg FY to Date	EPS Pct Chg Last 12 Mos	EPS 5-Yr Growth Rate	Par Growth Rate	Date of Report	Div Current Rate Amt	Div Yield	Div 5-Yr Growth Rate	Payout Last FY	Payout Last 5 Yrs	Last X-Dvd Date	Profit Margin	Asset Turnover	Return on Total Assets	Leverage Ratio	Return on Equity	Debt to Equity	Current Ratio	Mkt Value $Mil	Latest Shares Outstanding 000	Held by Banks-Funds 000	Insider Net Trading 000	Short Int Ratio Days	Fiscal Year Ends Mo
Ind. Group	15.1	20.0	10.6	11.1	.05	-5.0	7.5	-8.4	-.42	0	---	.08	.5	1	15	10	----	.4	1.00	.4	2.00	.8	26	2.1	4,144	254,813	64,598	+147	.4	--
ADAC Labs	-40.0	-32.1	-28.1	-42.4s	-4.43	-100.0	-100.0	NE	NC	0	03-86	.08	.0	0	0	0	11-22-82	-92.2	.99	-91.0	.00	NM	61	1.3	12	9,606	1,305	-15	0.0	09
Biomet	41.0	32.0	46.4	4.8n	.47	55.6	54.2	62.1	85	24	02-86	.00	.0	0	0	0	05-01-86	11.7	1.62	18.9	1.24	23.5	2	5.4	165	10,284	2,856	0	0.0	05
Cobe Labs	16.4	16.4	18.7	8.4q	1.29	21.4	21.4	108.1	1	12	03-86	.00	.0	0	0	0	01-23-86	5.3	1.45	7.7	1.52	11.7	22	3.7	162	6,482	1,718	-15	0.0	12
Coherent Inc	6.2	16.4	14.8	4.8s	.60	-73.7	-52.5	-50.4	NC	6	03-86	.00	.0	0	0	0	10-01-84	3.5	1.06	3.7	1.62	6.0	4	2.8	98	7,865	3,033	-4	0.0	09
Cordis Cp	-10.2	-7.6	-5.9	1.2n	.09	-100.0	-100.0	-84.2	NC	1	03-86	.00	.0	0	0	0	07-21-83	-.7	1.00	-.6	1.83	1.1	58	3.9	180	13,230	7,629	-6	0.0	06
Damon Corp	21.1	15.3	6.9	-1.0s	-.16	NE	NE	NE	NC	4	02-86	.20	1.1		NE	NE	04-28-86	-.7	1.14	-.8	2.25	-1.8	53	3.7	115	6,466	2,375	0	0.8	08
Datascope Cp	30.6	33.3	31.9	2.5n	.98	65.0	120.0	78.2	-4	12	02-86	.00	.0	0	0	0	09-26-80	4.0	1.30	5.2	2.27	11.8	57	2.9	79	2,407	603	0	0.0	06
Diasonics Inc	33.9	33.9	28.2	4.2q	.06	0	0	NE	NC	5	03-86	.00	.0	0	0	0	00-00-00	2.5	.92	2.3	2.35	5.4	19	1.6	238	55,973	11,887	0	0.0	12
Dynatech Cp	21.9	25.5	25.3	20.4f	1.95	8.9	17.5	17.5	29	29	03-86	.00	.0	0	0	0	03-02-84	7.9	1.94	15.3	1.92	29.3	38	2.8	349	10,488	4,956	0	0.0	03
Electro Biology	22.4	22.4	25.0	4.2q	.70	5.9	5.9	11.1	16	16	03-86	.00	.0	0	0	0	04-04-83	12.0	1.13	13.6	1.13	16.4	1	5.3	46	5,874	1,840	+5	0.0	12
Elscint Ltd	-22.5	-22.5	-2.1	-50.8q	-3.09	-100.0	-100.0	-100.0	NC	-80	06-85	.00	.0	0	0	0	00-00-00	-36.5	.45	-16.6	4.80	-79.6	53	1.1	33	16,377	369	0	0.0	03
Fonar Cp	350.0	355.9	328.5	-1.8n	-.12	NE	NE	NE	NC	-9	03-86	.00	.0	0	0	0	12-31-80	-6.0	2.18	-13.1	.00	NS	0	.7	180	16,372	507	0	0.0	06
Gelman Sci	-2.3	3.4	4.3	-1.4n	-.55	-100.0	-100.0	-100.0	NC	-8	03-86	.00	.0	0	0	0	05-26-83	-2.9	1.28	-3.7	2.16	-8.0	68	2.9	38	2,476	343	+3	4.6	07
Healthdyne	-3.4	-3.4	-6.9	-.5q	.03	-100.0	-100.0	NE	NC	1	03-86	.00	.0	0	0	0	00-00-00	.4	.75	.3	1.67	.5	30	3.8	74	14,465	1,397	0	0.0	12
Intermedics Inc	-8.3	-8.3	-2.7	-18.3q	-1.78	NE	NE	-100.0	NC	-25	01-86	.00	.0	0	0	0	08-29-80	-8.6	1.14	-9.8	2.55	-25.0	6	1.3	139	10,285	2,054	0	2.4	10
Laser Indus	20.8	25.7	26.3	2.6n	.70	200.0	314.3	191.7	0	27	12-85	.00	.0	0	0	0	00-00-00	10.8	.79	8.5	3.15	26.8	10	1.3	73	4,431	643	0	1.3	12
Medtronic Inc	32.1	6.3	6.3	53.4f	3.65	753.8	47.2	47.2	3	3	04-86	.88	1.2	NE	27	23	07-03-86	13.3	.86	11.4	1.43	16.3	3	3.2	1,097	14,393	8,667	-0	0.9	04
Mtn Med Equip	115.9	26.7	28.5	2.2f	.42	18.2	23.5	23.5	5	11	02-86	.00	.0	0	0	0	02-28-83	6.1	.85	5.2	2.10	10.9	14	2.1	33	5,428	390	+3	0.0	03
Newport Cp	10.2	10.0	10.0	6.8n	.72	-18.2	-19.7	-13.3	19	11	04-86	.06	.3	31	7	7	05-16-86	17.0	.64	10.8	1.08	11.7	0	11.0	185	9,374	4,604	-10	0.0	07
Patient Tech	102.8	102.8	56.2	-10.9q	-1.80	NE	NE	NE	NC	-90	03-86	.00	.0	0	0	0	06-20-83	-43.6	.48	-21.0	4.29	-90.1	187	1.4	27	4,561	146	0	0.6	12
St Jude Med	390.9	390.9	34.4	3.0q	.62	NE	NE	6.9	NC	9	03-86	.00	.0	0	0	0	03-13-80	7.7	.99	7.6	1.12	8.5	0	10.4	158	4,652	974	0	0.0	12
Stryker Cp	20.4	20.4	21.5	8.9q	1.18	19.4	19.4	20.4	20	18	03-86	.00	.0	0	0	0	09-17-85	8.3	1.52	12.6	1.46	18.4	9	3.2	311	7,484	1,846	0	0.0	12
Survival Tech	18.8	36.7	21.4	.7n	.90	10.0	NE	NE	NC	11	04-86	.00	.0	0	0	0	00-00-00	2.1	1.62	3.4	3.32	11.3	85	1.5	62	2,684	82	-11	0.0	07
US Surgical	13.2	13.2	12.4	9.8q	.79	12.0	12.0	-36.8	NC	5	03-86	.40	1.7		53	21	05-30-86	5.2	.94	4.9	1.96	9.6	68	2.6	288	12,122	4,347	+201	0.0	12
USR Ind	-50.0	-50.0	-100.0	-.7q	-.79	NE	NE	NE	NC	-15	03-86	.00	.0	0	0	0	00-00-00	NC	NC	NC	NC	-14.9	0	5.3	3	1,034	27	0	0.0	12

Hospital and Laboratory Supplies

Company	Rev Last Qtr %	Rev FY to Date %	Rev Last 12 Mos %	Earn Last 12 Mos $Mil	EPS Last 12 Mos $	Earn Pct Chg Last Qtr %	Earn Pct Chg FY to Date %	Earn Pct Chg Last 12 Mos %	Earn 5-Yr Growth %	Earn Par Growth %	Date of Report	Div Current Rate Amt $	Div Yield %	Div 5-Yr Growth %	Payout Last FY %	Payout Last 5 Yrs %	Last X-Dvd Date	Profit Margin %	Asset Turnover	Return on Total Assets	Leverage Ratio	Return on Equity	Debt to Equity %	Current Ratio	Mkt Value $Mil	Latest Shares Outstanding 000	Held by Banks-Funds 000	Insider Net Trading 000	Short Interest Ratio Days	Fiscal Year Ends Mo
Ind. Group	38.2	48.4	18.5	1,077.0	1.58	-23.3	-20.6	18.1	1	7	---	.70	1.8	1	37	35	---	6.9	.88	6.1	2.13	13.0	49	2.3	26,294	679,668	303,335	-622	3.5	--
Acme United	-6.6	-6.6	-5.2	1.0q	.32	-85.7	-85.7	-38.5	-16	0	03-86	.32	3.1	8	84	39	05-09-86	2.8	1.18	3.3	1.42	4.7	28	8.8	33	3,220	1,256	0	0.0	12
Bard C R	15.5	15.5	14.4	43.9q	1.46	21.2	21.2	21.7	17	13	03-86	.32	.9	8	18	19	06-02-86	9.1	1.25	11.4	1.50	17.1	15	3.1	1,053	30,184	16,468	+4	4.7	12
Bausch Lomb	12.9	12.9	12.2	68.0q	2.27	10.8	10.8	12.4	2	2	03-86	.78	2.0	5	35	42	05-27-86	11.1	.97	10.8	1.55	16.7	23	3.3	1,154	29,593	19,037	+0	0.3	12
Baxter Travenol	181.3	181.3	71.5	146.3q	.72	-46.4	-46.4	200.0	-13	3	03-86	.40	2.1	24	42	27	06-10-86	4.5	.47	2.1	3.33	7.0	124	1.9	3,317	207,539	90,687	-18	10.1	12
Becton, Dick	11.1	8.2	5.6	100.2s	2.36	35.8	29.5	32.6	4	11	03-86	.66	1.2	5	29	34	06-03-86	8.4	.96	8.1	1.81	14.7	32	2.0	2,248	40,771	22,962	+2	1.4	09
Collagen Cp	58.1	27.9	17.6	1.2n	.22	175.0	175.0	10.0	NC	3	03-86	.00		0	0	0	00-00-00	6.0	.52	3.1	1.06	3.3	1	13.3	134	5,661	1,230	0	0.0	06
CooperVision	74.2	52.7	45.5	14.6s	.71	-100.0	-100.0	-51.0	24	3	04-86	.40	1.7	0	24	12	06-11-86	3.6	.75	2.7	2.67	7.2	110	3.2	519	21,640	7,176	0	0.4	10
Delmed Inc □	54.7	2.3	25.6	-38.8	-1.92	NE	NE	NE	NC	3	12-85	.00		0	0	0	00-00-00	-60.8	.51	-40.9	.00	NM	454	2.3	29	21,351	1,579	0	19.3	12
Durr Fillauer	23.5	23.5	5.8	6.3q	.80	11.8	11.8	1.3	18	10	03-86	.16	.7	18	18	17	05-19-86	1.4	3.29	4.6	2.61	12.0	79	2.7	125	7,842	2,267	0	0.0	12
Everest & Jen ◇	16.2	16.2	16.2	4.5q	.56	NE	NE	250.0	12	6	04-21-86	.10	.8	3	NE	83	04-21-86	2.5	1.20	3.0	2.33	7.0	72	2.2	29	2,355	87	0	0.0	12
Figtronics	6.2	5.6	5.5	2.7n	.84	-22.2	-22.2	-49.7	-10	2	02-86	.60	2.0	22	105	33	06-23-86	2.0	1.90	3.8	1.66	6.3	21	2.5	99	3,230	430	+3	4.4	05
Health-Chem	14.8	14.8	11.5	-1.7q	-.23	NE	NE	86.7	-7	-7	02-86	.00		0	0	0	10-16-80	-5.9	.44	-2.6	2.73	-7.1	87	4.1	81	7,355	908	0	0.4	12
Hillenbrand Ind	29.5	29.5	10.3	37.8q	1.95	86.7	86.7	9.6	NC	10	02-86	.56	1.3	11	32	27	04-21-86	1.00	1.00	11.1	2.10	14.7	48	1.8	853	19,437	6,668	0	0.5	11
Intl Hydron	33.6	33.6	14.2	-.1q	.00	-50.0	-50.0	-100.0	NC	NC	02-86	.00		0	0	0	00-00-00	-.2	.50	-.1	3.00	-.3	83	3.9	76	11,240	260	0	19.7	12
IPCO Corp ◇	-.2	2.1	3.3	6.1n	1.14	9.1	34.9	22.6	NC	-22	07-03-86	.36	2.9	26	37	28	07-03-86	2.9	1.83	5.3	1.85	9.8	38	2.2	66	5,272	1,711	0	0.6	06
Johnson & John	9.7	9.7	6.2	578.9q	3.17	-20.2	-20.2	8.9	7	10	03-86	1.40	1.9	12	38	36	05-23-86	8.8	1.30	11.4	1.52	17.3	6	2.5	13,280	182,852	111,359	0	1.8	12
Lunex	36.1	36.1	26.0	3.3q	.85	300.0	300.0	63.5	7	7	03-86	.08	.3	23	11	10	07-14-86	5.2	1.42	7.4	1.76	13.0	44	4.3	95	3,806	593	0	15.5	12
Medex Inc	18.6	30.0	35.7	1.8n	.46	8.3	3.0	4.5	12	13	03-86	.05	.6	34	9	9	09-16-85	9.5	1.17	11.1	1.32	14.6	13	6.3	32	3,724	325	0	0.0	06
Medig ○	39.9	36.6	44.3	8.9s	.87	25.0	24.1	22.5	26	20	03-86	.16	2.2	0	16	11	03-10-86	5.4	1.13	6.1	3.95	24.1	173	2.0	89	12,104	1,947	+22	0.3	12
Natl Patent	55.6	55.6	24.0	-12.8q	-1.19	NE	NE	-100.0	NC	-22	03-86	.10	.6	0	NE	16	06-25-86	-9.6	.61	-5.9	3.42	-20.2	181	4.7	192	11,042	1,198	-9	4.8	12
Puritan Bennett	10.0	10.0	5.8	5.5q	.95	177.8	177.8	NE	NC	7	03-86	.20	.8	0	25	81	05-29-86	4.3	1.42	6.1	1.43	8.7	3	2.7	155	6,332	2,672	-81	0.0	12
Sci Leasing	36.3	22.8	25.7	3.8n	1.24	-48.4	-38.3	-38.3	37	8	03-86	.00		0	0	0	00-00-00	8.6	.21	1.8	4.17	7.5	226	NA	43	3,012	899	0	1.1	06
Tambrands Inc	19.2	19.2	16.1	63.5q	5.74	8.6	8.6	11.9	11	11	03-86	3.40	3.0	5	58	63	05-23-86	14.5	1.34	19.4	1.45	28.1	0	2.2	1,271	11,079	6,403	+2	0.0	12
Themedics	61.5	61.5	100.0	-.6q	-.08	NE	NE	NE	NE	-6	03-86	.00		0	0	0	00-00-00	-10.0	.52	-5.2	1.12	-5.8	0	8.6	232	9,028	141	+1	0.0	12
Utd Industrial	-6.0	-6.0	12.7	18.0q	1.49	-16.0	-16.0	2.1	16	9	07-30-86	.64	3.1b	24	33	28	07-30-86	6.8	1.12	7.6	2.16	16.4	13	1.3	249	12,075	3,080	+251	0.7	12
West Co	7.7	7.7	5.4	14.7q	1.86	-16.0	-16.0	6.3	16	9	03-86	.48	1.6	14	24	21	04-11-86	7.6	1.08	8.2	1.50	12.3	22	3.5	238	7,924	1,972	0	5.8	12

Ratio Analysis formula: s/l × r/a = s/a × r/a × a/e = r/e

Hospitals and Laboratories

Company	Rev %Chg Last Qtr	Rev %Chg FY to Date	Rev %Chg Last 12 Mos	Rev Last 12 Mos $Mil	EPS Last 12 Mos $	EPS %Chg Last Qtr	EPS %Chg FY to Date	EPS %Chg Last 12 Mos	EPS 5-Yr Growth	Par Growth	Date of Report	Div Amt	Div Yield	Div 5-Yr Growth	Payout Last FY	Payout Last 5 Yrs	Last X-Dvd Date	Profit Margin	Asset Turnover	Return Total Assets	Leverage	Return on Equity	Debt/Equity	Current Ratio	Mkt Value $Mil	Shares Outstndg 000	Held Banks/Funds 000	Insider Net Trading 000	Short Int Ratio Days	Fiscal Yr Ends Mo
Ind. Group	28.5	33.8	29.8	881.0	1.35	-41.0	-26.0	-18.0	13	9	---	.42	1.8	2	23	21	---	4.7	.94	4.4	3.00	13.2	133	1.6	14,264	624,569	255,335	-248	1.4	--
Am Hithcare	68.7	68.7	60.9	6.0q	.49	-25.0	-25.0	-38.0	38	7	03-86	.00	.0	0	0	0	00-00-00	1.5	.73	1.1	6.55	7.2	494	2.1	62	12,008	754	-30	0.8	12
Am Med Intl	84.4	56.4	39.2	24.9s	.30	-100.0	-100.0	-85.3	4	4	02-86	.32	4.1	13	34	29	07-08-86	.9	.78	.7	3.57	2.5	158	1.6	1,506	86,653	34,794	-1	7.3	08
Cetus Corp	101.0	.8	-4.1	1.6n	.06	0	0	20.0	NC	1	03-86	.00	.0	0	0	0	00-00-00	3.5	.31	1.1	1.00	1.1	1	21.6	939	25,713	8,288	+38	0.0	08
Charter Med	23.8	24.1	35.9	41.3s	1.34	0	33.3	3.9	33	18	03-86	.20	.9	0	11	8	05-09-86	5.8	.98	5.7	3.81	21.7	203	1.5	462	21,382	10,005	+1	1.5	09
Chemex Pharma	.0	.0	.0	-2.4s	-.30	NE	NE	NE	NC	0	09-85	.00	.0	0	0	0	00-00-00	NC	NC	NC	NC	NS	0	.0	76	7,968	596	0	0.0	03
Commun Psych	19.8	19.2	16.5	48.9s	1.64	17.1	16.7	18.8	29	17	05-86	.32	1.1	23	17	19	06-04-86	21.7	.81	17.6	1.22	21.4	5	2.8	910	30,197	15,912	-4	4.3	11
Comphen Care	27.3	32.6	36.4	17.7n	1.15	-12.0	2.5	6.5	22	10	02-86	.36	2.7	27	27	23	07-25-86	9.5	.86	8.2	1.74	14.3	48	4.3	199	15,178	5,967	-1	0.0	05
DDI Pharm	-50.0	-50.0	-60.0	-.3n	-.07	-100.0	-100.0	-100.0	NC	-10	12-85	.00	.0	0	0	0	00-00-00	-15.0	.63	-9.4	1.03	-9.7	0	28.0	42	4,983	15	0	0.0	12
Enzo Biochem	44.4	45.7	16.6	1.3n	.14	-20.0	0	-6.7	NC	6	04-86	.00	.0	0	0	0	06-15-83	18.6	.30	5.5	1.04	5.7	0	26.8	113	8,985	407	0	7.1	07
Hazleton Labs	12.7	2.2	-19.7	3.3n	.89	58.3	97.3	111.9	NC	5	03-86	.32	1.4	15	60	48	06-24-86	5.8	.72	4.2	1.74	7.3	28	1.5	81	3,491	1,089	0	0.0	06
HealthAmer	56.4	56.4	114.7	9.8q	.43	-41.2	-41.2	-29.5	NC	10	03-86	.00	.0	0	0	0	07-10-84	1.9	2.47	4.7	2.19	10.3	25	1.2	302	23,239	2,900	0	0.6	12
Healthcare USA	-410.3	-33.3	0	0	-2.57	NE	NE	-100.0	NC	0	03-86	.00	.0	0	0	0	00-00-00	NC	NC	NC	NC	0	275	.7	64	5,111	3,091	+0	1.7	12
Hosp Cp Am	27.2	27.2	39.8	273.6q	3.08	-5.2	-5.2	-12.7	24	12	03-86	.66	1.7	24	18	15	06-27-86	5.1	.86	4.4	2.98	13.1	132	1.5	3,262	85,844	49,601	+45	1.2	12
Humana Inc	19.7	20.4	-.3	214.8n	2.17	-1.2	-1.2	1.9	36	15	03-86	.76	3.0	36	30	29	06-10-86	8.2	.96	7.9	3.01	23.8	134	1.5	2,469	97,299	45,605	-195	2.8	08
Intl Clim Lab	14.6	16.3	19.1	3.5n	.47	14.3	4.5	-14.5	0	5	05-86	.00	.0	0	0	0	01-03-83	2.2	1.00	2.2	2.27	5.0	72	1.5	124	7,521	2,032	-10	0.0	08
Maxicare Hlth	61.6	61.6	65.1	24.9q	.84	60.0	60.0	71.4	0	11	03-86	.00	.0	0	0	0	07-09-85	4.3	1.35	5.8	1.93	11.2	56	3.9	909	32,324	26,983	-100	0.0	12
Medicore Inc	-34.6	-34.6	-47.3	.3q	.21	-79.2	-79.2	-12.5	0	3	03-86	.00	.0	0	0	0	10-24-85	3.0	.53	1.6	2.00	3.2	28	2.4	31	4,154	0	0	0.0	12
Natl Med Ent	16.6	19.0	24.9	153.0m	1.97	10.9	-.7	2.6	27	12	02-86	.56	2.4	27	24	24	05-19-86	4.4	1.23	5.4	3.02	16.3	132	1.8	1,834	78,443	34,670	+45	4.5	05
Nelson Rsch Dev	.0	.0	.0	-2.5q	-.27	NE	NE	NE	0	-10	03-86	.00	.0	0	0	0	09-02-83	NM	NC	NC	NC	-10.3	0	27.5	48	9,226	1,017	0	0.0	12
Rep Health	-1.5	-1.5	4.4	18.9q	.94	-43.9	-43.9	-20.3	0	11	03-86	.00	.0	0	0	0	00-00-00	3.5	.71	2.5	4.24	10.6	258	1.5	325	17,451	3,212	+10	0.0	11
Summit Hlth	-48.3	22.0	25.7	19.1n	.62	4.3	-16.7	6.9	12	19	03-86	.12	1.4	0	12	5	06-17-86	6.0	.85	5.1	4.63	23.6	93	1.1	266	31,250	3,664	0	0.0	06
Univ Health	128.1	128.1	77.2	23.3q	1.23	0	0	7.9	0	13	03-86	.00	.0	0	0	0	07-05-83	3.9	.90	3.5	3.83	13.4	209	1.1	262	16,149	4,733	0	0.0	12

$s/r \times r/a = s/a \times a/e = r/e$

Household Appliances and Furniture

Recent Performance and Forecast: Household Appliances (SIC 363)

(in millions of dollars except as noted)

	1982	1983	1984[1]	1985[2]	1986[3]	Percent Change 1982-83	Percent Change 1983-84	Percent Change 1984-85	Percent Change 1985-86
Industry Data									
Value of shipments[4]	12,671	14,487	15,952	16,014	—	14.3	10.1	0.4	—
3631 Household Cooking Equip	2,415	3,076	3,542	3,538	—	27.4	15.2	-0.1	—
3632 Household Refrigerators	2,471	2,821	3,150	3,115	—	14.2	11.7	-1.1	—
3633 Household Laundry Equip	2,122	2,369	2,625	2,738	—	11.6	10.8	4.3	—
3634 Elect Housewares & Fans	3,156	3,186	3,314	3,286	—	1.0	4.0	-0.8	—
3635 Household Vacuums	776	971	971	982	—	25.1	0.0	1.1	—
3636 Sewing Machines	300	185	183	183	—	-38.2	-1.1	0.0	—
3639 Home Appliances, nec	1,432	1,879	2,167	2,172	—	31.2	15.3	0.2	—
Value of shipments (1982$)	12,671	13,929	15,049	14,935	14,657	9.9	8.0	-0.8	-1.9
3631 Household Cooking Equip	2,415	2,876	3,244	3,185	3,090	19.1	12.8	-1.8	-3.0
3632 Household Refrigerators	2,471	2,715	2,952	2,890	2,830	9.9	8.7	-2.1	-2.1
3633 Household Laundry Equip	2,122	2,324	2,529	2,615	2,590	9.5	8.8	3.4	-1.0
3634 Elect Housewares & Fans	3,156	3,086	3,193	3,160	3,097	-2.2	3.5	-1.0	-2.0
3635 Household Vacuums	776	942	920	910	900	21.4	-2.3	-1.1	-1.1
3636 Sewing Machines	300	183	180	175	170	-38.8	-1.9	-2.8	-2.9
3639 Home Appliances, nec	1,432	1,804	2,031	2,000	1,980	26.0	12.6	-1.5	-1.0
Total employment (000)	129	128	138	131	128	-0.7	7.5	-4.9	-3.0
Production workers (000)	98.1	101	110	104	100	2.7	9.2	-5.7	-3.6
Average hourly earnings ($)	8.50	8.93	9.34	9.61	—	5.1	4.5	2.9	—

	1982	1983	1984	1985[1]	1986[2]	Percent Change 1982–83	1983–84	1984–85	1985–86[3]
Product Data									
Value of shipments[5]	11,872	13,735	15,120	15,165	—	15.7	10.1	0.3	—
3631 Household Cooking Equip	2,346	2,998	3,452	3,444	—	27.8	15.1	-0.2	—
3632 Household Refrigerators	2,202	2,662	2,972	2,937	—	20.9	11.6	-1.2	—
3633 Household Laundry Equip	1,800	2,154	2,387	2,490	—	19.6	10.8	4.3	—
3634 Elect Housewares & Fans	2,846	2,896	3,012	2,985	—	1.8	4.0	-0.9	—
3635 Household Vacuums	906	1,013	1,013	1,025	—	11.8	0.0	1.2	—
3636 Sewing Machines	231	212	209	204	—	-8.1	-1.6	-2.4	—
3639 Home Appliances, nec	1,541	1,799	2,075	2,080	—	16.8	15.3	0.2	—
Value of shipments (1982$)	11,872	13,202	14,258	14,133	13,865	11.2	8.0	-0.9	-1.9
3631 Household Cooking Equip	2,346	2,803	3,161	3,100	3,000	19.5	12.8	-1.9	-3.2
3632 Household Refrigerators	2,202	2,562	2,785	2,725	2,675	16.3	8.7	-2.2	-1.8
3633 Household Laundry Equip	1,800	2,112	2,300	2,378	2,355	17.3	8.9	3.4	-1.0
3634 Elect Housewares & Fans	2,846	2,804	2,902	2,870	2,810	-1.4	3.5	-1.1	-2.1
3635 Household Vacuums	906	983	960	950	940	8.5	-2.3	-1.0	-1.1
3636 Sewing Machines	231	210	205	195	190	-8.9	-2.6	-4.9	-2.6
3639 Home Appliances, nec	1,541	1,728	1,945	1,915	1,895	12.1	12.6	-1.5	-1.0
Shipments price index (1982=100)[6]	100.0	104.0	105.9	107.1	—	4.0	1.8	1.2	—
Trade Data									
Value of imports	1,180	1,539	2,099	2,575	2,850	30.4	36.4	22.7	10.7
Import/new supply ratio[7]	0.096	0.109	0.122	0.145	—	14.3	11.4	18.9	—
Value of exports	1,115	994	990	875	900	-10.9	-0.4	-11.6	2.9
Export/shipments ratio	0.081	0.064	0.065	0.058	—	-21.3	1.9	-10.8	—

[1] Estimated except for exports and imports.
[2] Estimated.
[3] Forecast.
[4] Value of all products and services sold by the Household Appliances industry.
[5] Value of products classified in the Household Appliances industry produced by all industries.
[6] Developed by the Office of Industry Assessment, ITA.
[7] New supply is the sum of product shipments plus imports.
SOURCE: U.S. Department of Commerce: Bureau of the Census, Bureau of Economic Analysis, International Trade Administration (ITA). Estimates and forecasts by ITA.

Source: *U.S. Industrial Outlook 1986*, U.S. Department of Commerce.

Recent Performance and Forecast: Household Furniture (SIC 251)
(in millions of dollars except as noted)

	1982	1983	1984[1]	1985[2]	1986[3]	Percent Change			
						1982-83	1983-84	1984-85	1985-86
Industry Data									
Value of shipments[4]	12,776	14,191	15,967	16,908	—	11.1	12.5	5.9	—
2511 Wood Furniture, House	5,057	5,702	6,497	6,831	—	12.8	13.9	5.1	—
2512 Upholstered Furn, House	3,505	3,990	4,610	4,962	—	13.8	15.5	7.6	—
2514 Metal Furniture, House	1,591	1,701	1,821	1,900	—	6.9	7.1	4.3	—
2515 Mattresses & Bedsprings	1,935	2,026	2,169	2,297	—	4.7	7.1	5.9	—
Value of shipments (1982$)	12,776	13,853	15,105	15,487	15,800	8.4	9.0	2.5	2.0
2511 Wood Furniture, House	5,057	5,465	5,932	6,021	6,111	8.1	8.6	1.5	1.5
2512 Upholstered Furn, House	3,505	3,899	4,388	4,563	4,677	11.2	12.6	4.0	2.5
2514 Metal Furniture, House	1,591	1,694	1,804	1,850	1,877	6.5	6.5	2.5	1.5
2515 Mattresses & Bedsprings	1,935	2,043	2,165	2,219	2,286	5.5	6.0	2.5	3.0
Total employment (000)	263	266	281	280	—	1.1	5.7	-0.2	—
Production workers (000)	221	226	241	241	—	2.3	6.7	-0.1	—
Average hourly earnings ($)	5.74	5.97	6.17	6.42	—	4.0	3.4	4.1	—
Product Data									
Value of shipments[5]	12,353	13,720	15,423	16,333	—	11.1	12.4	5.9	—
2511 Wood Furniture, House	4,846	5,457	6,217	6,538	—	12.6	13.9	5.2	—
2512 Upholstered Furn, House	3,320	3,773	4,359	4,692	—	13.6	15.5	7.6	—
2514 Metal Furniture, House	1,517	1,604	1,717	1,792	—	5.7	7.0	4.4	—
2515 Mattresses & Bedsprings	2,043	2,146	2,297	2,432	—	5.1	7.0	5.9	—

Value of shipments (1982$)	12,353	13,398	14,609	14,975	15,282	8.5	9.0	2.5	2.1
2511 Wood Furniture, House	4,846	5,230	5,677	5,762	5,849	7.9	8.5	1.5	1.5
2512 Upholstered Furn, House	3,320	3,687	4,149	4,315	4,423	11.0	12.5	4.0	2.5
2514 Metal Furniture, House	1,517	1,597	1,709	1,751	1,778	5.3	7.0	2.5	1.5
2515 Mattresses & Bedsprings	2,043	2,163	2,293	2,350	2,421	5.9	6.0	2.5	3.0
Shipments price index (1982=100)[6]	100.0	102.4	105.6	109.0	—	2.4	3.1	3.3	—
2511 Wood Furniture, House	100.0	104.4	109.5	113.5	—	4.4	5.0	3.6	—
2512 Upholstered Furn, House	100.0	102.3	105.1	108.7	—	2.3	2.7	3.4	—
2514 Metal Furniture, House	100.0	100.4	100.5	102.3	—	0.4	0.1	1.8	—
2515 Mattresses & Bedsprings	100.0	99.2	100.2	103.5	—	-0.8	1.0	3.3	—
Trade Data									
Value of imports (ITA)[7]	1,079	1,435	2,010	2,610	—	33.0	40.1	29.9	—
Import/new supply ratio[8]	0.080	0.095	0.115	0.138	—	18.8	21.1	20.0	—
Value of exports (ITA)[9]	239	204	208	177	—	-14.6	2.0	-14.9	—
Export/shipments ratio	0.019	0.015	0.011	0.012	—	-21.1	-26.7	9.1	—

[1]Estimated except for exports and imports.
[2]Estimated.
[3]Forecast.
[4]Value of all products and services sold by the Household Furniture industry.
[5]Value of products classified in the Household Furniture industry produced by all industries.
[6]Developed by the Office of Industry Assessment, ITA.
[7]Import data, developed by the chapter author, includes an indeterminate amount of office furniture.
[8]New supply is the sum of product shipments plus imports.
[9]Export data are developed by the chapter author.
SOURCE: U.S. Department of Commerce: Bureau of the Census, Bureau of Economic Analysis, International Trade Administration (ITA). Estimates and forecasts by ITA.

Source: U.S. Industrial Outlook 1986, U.S. Department of Commerce.

Furniture, Home Furnishings

Company	Rev Last Qtr %	Rev FY to Date %	Rev Last 12 Mos %	Rev Last 12 Mos $Mil	EPS Last 12 Mos $	EPS Last Qtr %	EPS FY to Date %	EPS Last 12 Mos %	5-Year Growth Rate %	Par Growth Rate %	Date of Report	Div Amt $	Div Yield %	Div 5-Year Growth Rate %	Payout Last FY %	Payout Last 5 Yrs %	Last X-Dvd Date	Profit Margin %	Asset Turnover	Return on Total Assets %	Leverage Ratio	Return on Equity %	Debt to Equity %	Current Ratio	Mkt Value $Mil	Latest Shares Out 000	Held by Banks-Funds 000	Insider Net Trading 000	Short Interest Ratio Days	Fiscal Year Ends Mo
																		$r/t \times r/a = r/a \times a/e = r/e$												
Ind. Group	10.4	10.9	10.4	160.2	1.67	.4	1.6	-.7	14	9	--	.55	1.8	1	31	29	--	5.6	1.75	9.8	1.39	13.6	11	3.9	2,912	95,769	27,399	-.77	.1	--
Am Furniture	-1.9	-1.9	4.3	2.4q	1.00	-90.0	-90.0	-9.9	40	5	02-86	.28	1.9	9	24	25	06-02-86	2.5	1.64	4.1	1.85	7.6	46	3.7	36	2,459	324	0	0.0	11
Bassett Furniture	8.5	8.5	3.2	24.7q	2.95	-10.5	-10.5	-14.2	5	6	02-86	1.20	2.6	11	45	39	05-08-86	5.9	1.58	9.3	1.12	10.4	0	6.9	384	8,345	2,014	0	0.0	11
Berkline Corp	4.2	.2	-1.1	.9n	.57	12.5	8.8	-50.9	6		03-86	.50	3.2	0	100	76	06-25-86	1.0	2.60	2.6	1.62	4.2	12	2.6	24	1,518	147	0	0.0	08
Bush Industries	NA	NA	0	NA	NA	NA	NA	NA	NA	NC	00-00	.00	.0	NA	NA	NA	00-00-00	NA	NC	NA	NC	NA	NA	NA	42	2,000	177	-273	NA	NA
Flexsteel Ind	17.2	9.7	6.3	5.0n	1.02	13.0	-14.3	-23.9	4	5	03-86	.48	2.4	13	42	32	05-21-86	3.7	2.00	7.4	1.35	10.0	14	5.7	95	4,799	846	0	0.0	06
Henredon Furn	-7.8	-7.8	-10.0	9.5q	1.85	-32.9	-32.9	-36.0	-5	3	03-86	1.12	1.9	12	48	32	07-07-86	7.6	.95	7.2	1.18	8.5	4	9.2	297	5,151	2,106	0	0.0	12
La-Z Boy Chair	26.9	20.9	20.8	23.0f	5.02	4.8	7.5	7.5	25	13	04-86	1.40	2.0	16	28	27	05-13-86	6.7	1.78	11.9	1.50	17.8	9	3.1	324	4,591	346	-40	0.0	04
Ladd Furniture	7.6	7.6	23.5	18.9q	1.99	13.0	13.0	26.8	NC	24	03-86	.33	1.2	0	19	11	04-25-86	7.5	2.37	17.8	1.65	29.3	24	3.0	266	9,550	3,203	0	0.0	12
Lane Co Inc	1.4	1.4	9.1	27.5q	3.47	.0	.0	13.4	21	11	03-86	1.20	2.4	22	34	26	03-24-86	8.5	1.68	14.3	1.15	16.5	0	6.4	396	7,951	3,175	+191	0.0	12
Leggett Platt	16.9	16.9	15.5	26.3q	1.85	24.3	24.3	20.9	18	13	03-86	.40	1.2	14	19	20	03-17-86	5.3	1.83	9.7	1.77	17.2	34	2.5	457	13,730	5,079	0	0.6	12
Ohio Mattress	-6.8	.2	-1.4	9.1s	.58	.0	3.4	-24.7	13	2	05-86	.40	2.7	23	70	53	04-15-86	3.4	1.68	5.7	1.39	7.9	13	3.0	237	16,210	6,769	+2	0.0	11
Rowe Furniture	15.9	15.9	12.3	3.5q	1.47	12.9	12.9	-1.3	NC	15	02-86	.26	1.6	23	15	16	06-19-86	4.3	1.72	7.4	1.92	14.2	40	2.6	41	2,434	282	+0	0.0	11
Shelby Wms	9.8	9.8	16.3	8.7q	.85	23.1	23.1	30.8	21	15	03-86	.16	.6	0	15	7	04-25-86	7.2	1.88	13.5	1.39	18.8	3	3.0	273	10,306	2,321	+4	0.0	12
Sierra Hlth	100.0	100.0	109.0	.9q	.14	-20.0	-20.0	-26.3	NC	5	03-86	.00	.0	0	0	0	00-00-00	1.3	2.15	2.8	1.64	4.6	7	NA	36	5,525	589	0	0.5	12
Triangle Home	-6.3	-6.3	-6.8	-.2q	-.21	-100.0	-100.0	-100.0	NC	-3	03-86	.00	.0	0	0	0	00-00-00	-.7	3.14	-2.2	1.36	-3.0	10	3.8	5	1,200	21	0	0.0	12

Appliances

Company	Rev Last Qtr %	Rev FY to Date %	Rev Last 12 Mos %	Rev Last 12 Mos $Mil	EPS Last 12 Mos $	EPS Last Qtr %	EPS FY to Date %	EPS Last 12 Mos %	5-Year Growth Rate %	Par Growth Rate %	Date of Report	Div Amt $	Div Yield %	Div 5-Year Growth Rate %	Payout Last FY %	Payout Last 5 Yrs %	Last X-Dvd Date	Profit Margin %	Asset Turnover	Return on Total Assets %	Leverage Ratio	Return on Equity %	Debt to Equity %	Current Ratio	Mkt Value $Mil	Latest Shares Out 000	Held by Banks-Funds 000	Insider Net Trading 000	Short Interest Ratio Days	Fiscal Year Ends Mo
Ind. Group	9.0	9.5	10.2	302.0	3.25	31.1	30.9	10.4	7	8	--	1.55	2.9	1	45	44	--	5.4	1.83	9.9	1.61	15.9	12	2.4	5,016	92,924	44,261	-22	.6	--
Dynamics Amer	-.8	-.8	3.4	15.2q	3.57	-16.7	-16.7	74.1	30	16	03-86	.20	.6	7	5	10	02-10-86	10.3	1.13	11.6	1.42	16.5	3	3.1	135	4,274	1,026	0	0.0	12
Health-Mor	-5.8	-5.8	-6.8	2.2q	1.27	-25.0	-25.0	-18.6	1	4	03-86	.68	4.0	12	46	68	06-12-86	8.1	.98	7.9	1.22	9.6	7	5.9	30	1,769	421	0	0.0	12
Maytag Co	10.2	10.2	9.1	76.2q	2.82	25.4	19.0	19.0	17	8	03-86	2.05	3.8	10	62	68	05-23-86	10.9	1.92	20.9	1.42	29.7	9	3.4	1,452	27,137	11,532	0	3.7	12
Mor-Flo Inds	.0	.0	.9	3.2q	1.28	-56.9	-56.9	-51.3	22	8	03-86	.01	.1	0	1	1	12-02-85	1.6	1.69	2.7	3.00	8.1	91	2.4	42	2,534	227	0	0.0	12
Natl Presto	6.1	6.1	10.2	16.5q	2.23	.0	.0	-1.3	-8	5	03-86	1.14	3.4	7	46	31	06-02-86	17.0	.49	8.3	1.22	10.1	4	6.7	250	7,371	2,565	0	1.2	12
Preway Inc	-18.6	20.2	19.4	-13.9f	-3.65	NE	NE	NE	NC	9	12-85	.00	.0	0	0	NE	08-29-84	-10.8	1.35	-14.6	.00	NM	614	1.8	7	3,813	166	-28	0.0	12
Rangaire	7.2	2.1	-1.2	3.6n	.91	NC	200.0	167.6	8	0	04-86	.24	2.4b	4	47	51	05-16-86	4.6	1.43	6.6	1.77	11.7	28	1.9	40	3,921	307	+1	0.0	07
Roper Corp	11.8	10.3	4.6	6.3n	1.12	135.8	NE	27.3	NC	3	04-86	.64	1.7	6	NE	47	08-18-86	1.0	2.20	2.2	3.45	7.6	58	1.3	206	5,443	3,255	+1	0.3	07
Whirlpool Cp	10.2	10.2	12.3	192.7q	5.26	26.4	26.4	9.8	11	10	03-86	2.00	2.6	8	40	41	05-15-86	5.4	2.02	10.9	1.47	16.0	4	2.3	2,855	36,662	24,762	+1	0.4	12

Insurance

Recent Performance And Forecast: Life Insurance (SIC 6311)

(in billions of dollars except as noted)

	1982	1983	1984	1985[1]	1986[2]	Percent Change			
						1982-83	1983-84	1984-85	1985-86
Premium receipts	120.4	119.0	134.8	148.3	163.1	−1.2	13.3	10.0	10.0
New life insurance purchases[3]	837.9	1,026.4	1,114.8	1,226.3	1,348.9	22.5	8.6	10.0	10.0
Life insurance in force[3]	4,476.7	4,965.9	5,500.0	5,940.0	6,415.2	10.9	10.8	8.0	8.0
Total benefits paid	48.0	51.9	60.4	67.6	75.8	8.1	16.5	11.9	12.1
Life insurance assets	588.2	654.9	723.0	788.1	856.0	11.4	10.4	9.0	8.6
Total employment (000)[4]	546.1	539.9	532.0	532.0	532.0	−1.1	−1.5	0.0	0.0

[1]Estimated.
[2]Forecast.
[3]Excludes foreign business.
[4]Home office personnel only.
SOURCE: American Council of Life Insurance; estimates and forecasts by U.S. Department of Commerce, International Trade Administration.

Source: U.S. Industrial Outlook 1986, U.S. Department of Commerce.

Recent Performance and Forecast: Property/Casualty Insurance (SIC 6331)

(in billions of dollars except as noted)

Industry data	1982	1983	1984	1985[1]	1986[2]	Percent Change			
						1982-83	1983-84	1984-85	1985-86
Net premiums written	104.0	106.2	115.9	135.0	155.3	2.1	9.1	16.5	15.0
Underwriting gain (loss)	−10.3	−13.0	−20.5	−20.0	−22.0	−26.2	−57.6	—	−10.0
Net investment income	14.9	18.1	17.6	22.0	25.0	21.5	−2.8	25.0	13.6
Operating earnings after taxes	5.3	6.0	1.9	2.0	3.0	13.2	−68.3	5.3	50.0

[1]Estimated.
[2]Forecast.
SOURCE: Insurance Information Institute; estimates and forecasts by U.S. Department of Commerce, International Trade Administration.

Source: U.S. Industrial Outlook 1986, U.S. Department of Commerce.

820 Life, Accid., Health Ins.

Company	Revenue Pct Change Last Qtr	FY to Date	Last 12 Mos	Last 12 Mos $Mil	EPS Last 12 $	Pct Chg Last Qtr	Pct Chg FY to Date	Last 12 Mos	5-Yr Growth	Par Growth	Date of Report	Div Amt	Yield	5-Yr Growth	Payout Last FY	Payout Last 5 Yrs	Last X-Dvd Date	Profit Margin	Asset Turnover	Return on Total Assets	Leverage	Return on Equity	Debt to Eq	Current Ratio	Mkt Value $Mil	Latest Shares Out 000	Held by Banks-Funds 000	Insider Net Trading 000	Short Int Ratio Days	Fiscal Year Ends Mo
Ind. Group	6.7	11.3	13.9	2,049.2	1.56	-100.0	-100.0	-30.2	-7	2	--	1.14	2.8	1	45	44	--	2.5	.32	.8	8.88	7.1	15	2.6	44,790	1,106,584	503,339	+419	.8	--
												s/t x r/a = s/a x a/e = s/e																		
Academy Ins Grp	13.4	1.1	.8	-47.6	-2.85	NE	NE	NE	NC	0	12-85	.00	-	0	NE	NE	06-24-85	-38.7	.39	-14.9	.00	NM	120	NA	57	16,502	2,933	+1093	0.0	12
Aetna Life Cas	13.9	13.9	20.0	513.9q	4.54	137.3	137.3	130.5	-14	5	03-86	2.64	4.4	5	69	70	07-03-86	2.7	.39	.9	12.44	11.2	9	NA	6,709	110,663	71,021	+20	1.3	12
Alleghany Corp	73.8	73.8	96.8	109.2q	13.22	48.3	48.3	327.8	11	20	03-86	.00	.0	0	NE	10	01-27-86	21.6	.42	9.0	2.17	19.5	17	NA	632	6,425	2,653	0	0.0	12
Am Family Cp	25.7	15.9	15.8	54.2q	1.35	28.1	25.0	25.0	25	11	12-85	.40	1.2	8	26	32	05-09-86	5.7	.42	2.4	6.67	16.0	12	NA	1,321	39,873	10,540	+12	0.6	12
Am Heritage Lf	22.1	14.0	13.7	8.41	2.67	-55.1	-19.8	-19.8	8	5	12-85	1.32	3.1	16	43	36	07-08-86	4.4	.50	2.2	4.41	9.7	0	NA	133	3,130	207	+48	0.0	12
Am Income Life	-.7	-.5	.0	18.5r	1.37	-14.3	-4.9	-4.9	6	8	12-85	.40	2.9	0	15	10	06-05-86	15.4	.29	4.5	2.67	12.0	0	NA	187	13,470	4,078	0	0.0	12
Am Nat'l Ins	-.5	-.5	2.8	87.8q	3.04	-9.3	-9.3	-4.4	8	4	03-86	1.20	3.1	12	35	32	06-10-86	11.1	.21	2.3	2.87	6.6	2	NA	1,107	28,931	4,158	0	0.0	12
Bush Mens Assur	-5.2	-5.2	.7	17.6q	1.66	-100.0	-100.0	-54.4	2	2	03-86	1.10	3.8	5	48	35	05-20-86	4.3	.37	1.6	3.50	5.6	10	NA	307	10,581	3,449	+2	0.3	12
Capital Holdg	13.0	13.0	23.4	143.1q	2.65	13.0	13.0	12.3	9	10	03-86	.82	2.2	5	30	32	08-25-86	6.4	.34	2.2	6.36	14.0	27	NA	1,913	50,665	30,459	+2	0.3	12
CIGNA Cp	2.9	9.6	9.6	-854.6r	-12.46	-100.0	-100.0	-100.0	NC	-28	12-85	2.60	4.1	0	NE	146	06-06-86	-5.3	.36	-1.9	12.00	-22.8	9	NA	4,947	78,059	54,682	-3	0.3	12
Combined Intl	8.9	8.9	6.7	165.7q	4.98	13.7	13.7	-2.2	9	9	03-86	2.24	3.7	19	44	47	04-25-86	11.9	.44	5.2	3.27	17.0	9	NA	1,966	32,488	14,272	+9	0.5	12
Durham Cp	7.2	7.2	3.0	21.2q	3.72	14.5	14.5	-30.5	15	7	03-86	1.36	3.0	9	35	34	05-20-86	8.9	.38	3.4	3.06	10.4	0	NA	263	5,719	504	0	0.0	12
Equitable of Iowa	-6.5	-6.5	-5.1	16.8q	1.92	NE	NE	3.8	-5	2	03-86	1.28	4.5	1	72	60	05-09-86	3.8	.26	1.0	7.00	7.0	11	NA	201	7,048	708	-4	0.0	12
Fst Executive	-4.8	-4.8	27.7	106.4q	1.61	29.4	29.4	29.8	34	13	03-86	.00	.0	0	0	0	00-00-00	3.7	.32	1.2	10.83	13.0	0	NA	1,271	45,810	19,928	0	0.0	12
Home Beneficial	7.5	7.5	4.5	44.1q	3.57	9.5	9.5	-11.4	13	9	03-86	.96	2.1	11	25	24	05-14-86	23.8	.19	4.5	2.71	12.2	0	NA	566	12,312	4,076	+28	0.0	12
Home Grp	NA	NA	NA	NA	NA	NA	NA	NA	45	29	00-00	.08	.0	NA	NA	NA	00-00-00	NA	NA	NA	NA	NA	NA	NA	990	37,908	22,710	+0	NA	NA
ICH Corp	1.3	1.3	72.9	108.6q	2.33	3.1	3.1	53.3	45	7	03-86	.08	.3	0	2	3	05-20-86	7.1	.41	2.9	10.38	30.1	172	NA	1,466	47,115	4,751	+0	1.3	12
Indep Ins Grp	4.9	4.9	2.6	27.3q	4.36	65.4	65.4	-39.1	14	7	03-86	1.40	3.5	4	36	30	05-06-86	6.3	.38	2.4	4.25	10.2	13	NA	290	7,351	850	0	0.0	12
Jackson Nat'l Lf	74.3	74.3	67.2	27.3q	2.43	18.2	18.2	-45.9	34	14	03-86	.00	.0	0	0	1	03-10-86	3.4	.47	1.6	8.88	14.2	2	NA	470	11,681	6,072	0	0.0	12
Jefferson Pilot	1.8	1.8	2.8	117.5q	2.96	7.8	7.8	13.8	10	6	03-86	1.12	2.8	10	34	35	06-27-86	11.5	.28	3.2	3.09	9.9	2	NA	1,693	41,800	17,351	0	0.5	12

Kansas City Life	1.9	1.9	2.4	26.9q	3.57	43.6	43.6	24.4	1	7	03-86	.96	2.7	7	28	28	05-06-86	10.6	.18	1.9	5.26	10.0	4	NA	277	7,704	1,422	0	0.0	12
Kaufman Broad	29.4	29.4	52.3	30.2q	1.37	13.3	13.3	-16.5	12	12	02-86	.33	1.3	14	0	38	05-13-86	3.1	.45	1.4	10.86	15.2	130	NA	427	16,757	3,634	-22	7.1	11
Laurentian Cap	3380.0	3380.0	940.0	-.3q	.15	-100.0	-100.0	-73.2	-1	-1	03-86	.00	.0	0	0	0	00-00-00	-.6	.33	-.2	6.50	-1.3	18	NA	9	1,280	63	0	0.0	12
Liberty Corp	6.2	6.2	10.0	24.0q	2.37	-4.2	-4.2	10.7	2	6	03-86	.72	1.7	4	30	34	06-10-86	6.7	.37	2.5	3.52	8.8	13	NA	424	10,090	3,318	+9	0.0	12
Life Inv Inc	24.3	24.3	18.1	38.6q	4.11	6.2	6.2	10.5	20	10	03-86	.24	.5	0	6	8	07-16-85	4.4	.39	1.7	6.35	10.8	11	NA	456	9,268	24	0	0.0	12
Lincoln Natl	13.2	13.2	13.2	222.7q	4.30	10.1	10.1	12.3	6	7	03-86	2.00	3.8	5	45	45	07-03-86	4.4	.36	1.6	7.75	12.4	12	NA	2,335	44,159	22,810	+3	0.4	12
Manhattan Natl	-22.6	-22.6	-16.7	-1.2q	-.18	-93.3	-93.3	NE	NC	-4	03-86	.32	3.2	0	0	4	04-29-86	-.4	.25	-.1	15.00	-1.5	0	NA	52	5,108	882	0	2.5	12
Midland Co	6.8	6.8	-6.6	3.2q	1.81	2.0	2.0	-43.3	-5	-4	03-86	.40	1.2	6	22	16	06-16-86	2.8	.61	1.7	3.18	5.4	44	NA	59	1,753	153	-62	12.0	12
Monarch Cap	6.9	6.9	13.0	46.1q	5.38	0	0	25.4	12	16	03-86	.00	.0	-2	20	35	05-24-85	4.8	.40	1.9	8.42	16.0	0	NA	533	7,303	3,280	+0	0.8	12
Monumental Cp	12.6	12.6	11.4	18.4q	2.81	-20.9	-20.9	10.2	4	4	03-86	1.40	2.6	7	46	50	06-09-86	7.3	.25	1.8	4.72	8.5	7	NA	358	6,539	1,591	0	0.0	12
NWn Natl Life	5.0	5.0	2.5	30.7q	2.28	53.1	53.1	-45.5	5	7	03-86	.86	2.8	5	40	33	04-21-86	1.7	.35	.6	18.17	10.9	34	NA	292	9,340	6,415	0	0.0	12
Old Rep Intl	11.2	11.2	71.4	49.9q	2.77	-33.1	-33.1	-33.1	3	9	12-85	.78	2.1	1	26	21	05-27-86	5.6	.39	2.2	5.95	13.1	30	NA	511	14,012	7,444	-2	0.0	12
Orion Cap Cp	14.2	14.2	30.6	-30.6q	-5.77	NE	NE	NE	NC	-27	03-86	.76	2.2	14	NE	NE	06-10-86	-5.6	.59	-3.3	7.30	-24.1	85	NA	200	5,727	2,063	0	2.6	12
Peak Hlth Care	22.7	22.7	85.2	2.5q	.48	-63.6	-63.6	-37.7	NC	9	03-86	.00	.0	9	0	0	00-00-00	4.0	1.70	6.8	1.32	9.0	6	4.3	77	5,209	1,464	0	0.0	12
Protective Life	9.0	9.0	9.6	26.0q	1.83	32.3	32.3	-35.6	8	7	03-86	1.40	2.9	9	38	29	05-12-86	8.8	.31	2.7	4.44	12.0	0	NA	351	14,456	6,350	0	0.0	12
Provident Lf Acc	29.2	29.2	23.9	116.0q	2.87	-3.0	-3.0	-19.8	13	9	03-86	.84	2.8	13	30	27	05-23-86	6.5	.31	2.0	6.45	12.9	0	NA	1,104	37,282	17,536	0	0.0	12
Southland Fincl	-51.7	-51.7	-21.0	-18.0q	-1.30	-100.0	NE	NE	NC	-12	03-86	.52	2.6	0	NE	NE	08-04-86	-16.5	.10	-1.7	5.12	-8.7	355	NA	335	16,747	4,114	-648	0.0	12
Torchmark Cp	20.2	20.2	21.3	177.0q	1.83	-35.8	-35.8	-17.2	20	12	03-86	.60	1.6	11	24	30	04-04-86	12.4	.38	4.7	3.89	18.3	17	NA	2,628	70,549	28,900	-36	1.6	12
Travelers Corp	-11.8	-11.8	.7	408.1q	4.42	48.8	48.8	6.5	0	6	03-86	2.16	4.3	10	51	44	04-24-86	2.9	.34	1.0	10.90	10.9	2	NA	4,558	91,153	63,283	-1	0.4	12
US Hlthcare	59.7	59.7	71.5	28.3q	.58	70.0	70.0	93.3	NC	17	03-86	.12	.6	0	8	5	06-12-86	6.9	2.09	14.4	1.46	21.0	1	2.4	933	50,424	29,348	+33	0.0	12
Utd Cos Fincl	5.5	5.5	4.3	10.0q	3.36	1.6	1.6	10.9	21	17	03-86	.50	2.0	11	15	20	06-02-86	7.0	.14	1.4	13.86	19.4	281	NA	89	3,600	251	0	0.0	12
USLICO	68.0	68.0	51.3	18.9q	1.95	-16.4	-16.4	-43.1	10	5	03-86	.80	2.9	1	39	27	05-06-86	4.9	.22	1.1	7.45	8.2	45	NA	313	11,498	1,708	-2	0.0	12
USLIFE Cp	15.5	15.5	14.7	86.9q	4.27	72.2	72.2	-.5	0	8	03-86	1.12	2.3	8	29	29	04-29-86	8.2	.32	2.6	4.04	10.5	37	0	931	19,301	9,950	+1	0.3	12
Wash Natl Cp	-4.4	-4.4	-5.8	25.5q	2.22	-29.2	-29.2	-40.6	3	3	03-86	1.08	3.1	2	44	43	06-10-86	3.4	.21	.7	9.29	6.5	2	0	378	10,872	4,570	+2	0.2	12
Westbridge Cap	-14.9	-14.9	-2.2	4.0q	.93	164.3	164.3	40.9	5	12	03-86	.00	.0	0	0	0	08-25-83	4.7	.79	3.7	3.24	12.0	0	0	33	4,200	283	0	3.8	12
Williams A L	60.1	60.1	56.8	20.0q	.81	60.0	60.0	62.0	NC	22	03-86	.00	.0	0	0	0	09-16-83	13.4	.72	9.6	2.30	22.1	0	NA	637	24,722	7,081	+1	0.0	12

Lumber and Wood Products

Recent Performance and Forecast: Sawmills and Planing Mills - General (SIC 2421)
(in millions of dollars except as noted)

	1982	1983	1984[1]	1985[2]	1986[3]	Percent Change 1982-83	1983-84	1984-85	1985-86
Industry Data									
Value of shipments[4]	10,065	12,664	13,468	12,984	—	25.8	6.3	-3.6	—
Value of shipments (1982$)	10,065	11,021	11,835	11,956	11,836	9.5	7.4	1.0	-1.0
Total employment (000)	132	143	149	144	—	8.3	4.1	-3.1	—
Production workers (000)	114	125	131	126	—	9.7	4.5	-3.6	—
Average hourly earnings ($)	7.52	7.86	8.07	8.11	—	4.5	2.7	0.5	—
Product Data									
Value of shipments[5]	9,889	12,412	12,639	12,390	—	25.5	1.8	-2.0	—
Value of shipments (1982$)	9,889	10,771	11,097	11,184	11,404	8.9	3.0	3.0	-0.2
Shipments price index (1982=100)[6]	100.0	115.3	114.1	108.9	—	15.3	-1.0	-4.6	—
Quantity shipped (Million Board Feet)	28,935	35,158	36,765	37,200	—	21.5	4.6	1.2	—
Trade Data									
Value of imports	1,770	2,743	2,866	2,725	—	54.9	4.5	-4.9	—
Import/new supply ratio[7]	0.152	0.181	0.184	0.179	—	19.2	1.5	-2.5	—
Value of exports	1,027	1,066	983	1,045	—	3.8	-7.8	6.3	—
Export/shipments ratio	0.104	0.086	0.077	0.084	—	-17.3	-10.2	8.4	—

[1]Estimated except for exports and imports.
[2]Estimated.
[3]Forecast.
[4]Value of all products and services sold by the Sawmills and Planing Mills - General industry.
[5]Value of products classified in the Sawmills and Planing Mills - General industry produced by all industries.
[6]Developed by the Office of Industry Assessment, ITA.
[7]New supply is the sum of product shipments plus imports.
SOURCE: U.S. Department of Commerce: Bureau of the Census, Bureau of Economic Analysis, International Trade Administration (ITA). Estimates and forecasts by ITA.

Source: U.S. Industrial Outlook 1986, U.S. Department of Commerce.

Lumber and Wood Products

Company	Rev Pct Chg Last Qtr %	Rev Pct Chg FY to Date %	Rev Pct Chg Last 12 Mos %	Rev Last 12 Mos $Mil	Earn PS Last 12 Mos $	Earn Pct Chg FY to Date %	Earn Pct Chg Last 12 Mos %	Earn 5-Year Growth Rate %	Earn Last 12 Mos	Par Growth Rate %	Date of Report	Div Current Rate Amt $	Div Yield %	Div 5-Year Growth Rate %	Payout Last FY %	Payout Last 5 Yrs %	Last X-Dvd Date	Profit Margin %	Asset Turnover	Return on Total Assets	Leverage Ratio	Return on Equity	Debt to Equity %	Current Ratio	Market Value $Mil	Latest Shares Outstndg 000	Held by Banks-Funds 000	Insider Trading 000	Net Trading 000	Short Int Ratio Days	Fiscal Year Ends Mo
Ind. Group	-.72	-3.9	-2.6	821.1	1.27	-14.2	-13.1	33.4	9	2	---	.94	3.0	0	70	85	----	3.2	1.00	3.2	2.28	7.3	55	1.5	16,136	517,993	220,954	-838		2.4	--
Bohemia Inc	15.6	20.8	8.0	-2.2h	-.46	-25.9	-25.9	NE	NC	-3	01-66	.10	.6b	-12	NE	NE	11-29-85	-1.2	.75	-.9	2.78	-2.5	53	1.8	73	4,442	1,611	-3	+4	0.0	04
Boise Cascade	-4.3	-4.3	-3.3	96.0q	3.16	-53.5	-53.5	31.7	0	3	03-86	1.90	3.3	2	55	77	06-09-86	2.6	1.12	2.9	2.45	7.1	76	1.4	1,570	27,063	15,231	+4		1.8	12
Champ Intl	-31.8	-31.8	-6.6	141.3q	1.36	-53.5	-74.3	NE	NC	4	03-86	.52	2.1	-26	27	82	06-11-86	2.7	.85	2.3	2.52	5.8	70	.9	2,287	92,868	53,942	+0		0.7	12
Ecz Lavud Ltd	-50.6	-41.0	-41.1	1.3q	.74	-88.0	-74.3	-57.5	65	18	09-84	.11	.8	9	13	11	09-17-85	6.5	.66	4.3	4.95	21.3	61	1.2	23	1,724	5	0		0.0	08
Georgia-Pacific	1.5	1.5	-.5	158.0q	1.36	-41.9	-41.9	32.0	-4	3	03-86	.80	2.5	-11	53	80	05-12-86	2.3	1.39	3.2	2.31	7.4	59	1.8	3,239	103,225	59,316	-17	-17	1.5	12
Hines Ed Lumber □	-47.5	-12.0	-12.0	2.5f	1.46	NA	NA	NA	NC	7	12-85	.00	.0	0	68	264	06-14-85	1.0	3.70	3.7	1.92	7.1	0	NA	6	1,470	300	+1		0.0	12
IP Timberlands	NA	NA	1216.6	NA	NA	NA	NA	NA	NA	NC	03-86	.80	.0	NA	NA	NA	00-00-00	NA	NA	NA	NC	NA	NA	NA	1,071	45,332	351	0		NA	NA
La Pacific	19.0	19.0	10.1	24.5q	.69	-42.9	-42.9	-36.1	NC	NC	03-86	.80	3.0b	6	110	123	05-14-86	1.9	.95	1.8	1.78	3.2	28	1.7	973	36,553	10,706	0		1.1	12
Ply-Gem	24.3	24.3	8.6	5.1q	.72	30.0	30.0	-8.9	28	12	03-86	.12	.8	3	17	19	03-13-86	2.9	1.52	4.4	3.39	14.9	167	3.9	105	7,349	1,088	-745		29.2	12
Pope & Talbot	-10.8	-10.8	-2.1	4.0q	.65	-100.0	-100.0	NE	NC	-1	03-86	.80	4.0	73	72	82	04-22-86	1.3	1.46	1.9	2.05	3.9	41	1.5	120	5,996	1,678	-8		0.0	12
Potlatch Cp	-.6	-.6	-3.0	39.8q	2.47	41.8	41.8	-12.1	2	3	03-86	1.56	3.1	3	71	75	05-13-86	4.2	.83	3.5	2.40	8.4	71	1.6	659	12,986	3,389	0		0.6	12
Rayonier Timb	NA	NA	NA	4.9q	NA	NA	NA	NA	NA	NA	00-00	2.60	12.7	NA	NA	NA	00-00-00	NC	NC	NC	NC	NA	NA	NA	410	20,000	1,201	-10		NA	NA
Tins Joist Cp	11.6	11.6	9.6	211.9q	1.29	29.2	29.2	-37.1	-3	6	03-86	.48	1.4	8	32	20	05-23-86	3.6	1.33	4.8	2.06	9.9	57	3.1	129	3,667	1,195	0		0.0	12
Weyerhaeuser	2.4	2.4	-5.6	53.5q	1.39	29.2	29.2	-9.2	-6	0	04-28-86	1.30	3.7	0	98	96	04-28-86	4.0	.88	3.5	1.83	6.4	37	1.7	4,531	129,913	59,549	0		1.3	12
Willamette Inc	-5.5	-5.5	-4.2		2.11	-46.4	-46.4	-25.7	17	6	05-19-86	1.03	2.8	3	42	64	05-19-86	4.7	1.23	5.8	1.95	11.3	39	1.7	940	25,405	11,392	-58		0.0	12

Ratio Analysis: r/r × r/a = r/a × a/e = r/e

Recent Performance and Forecast: Metal-Cutting Machine Tools (SIC 3541)

(in millions of dollars except as noted)

	1982	1983	1984[1]	1985[2]	1986[3]	Percent Change			
						1982-83	1983-84	1984-85	1985-86
Industry Data									
Value of shipments[4]	4,440	2,881	3,150	3,150	2,899	-35.1	9.3	0.0	-8.0
Value of shipments (1982$)	4,440	2,839	3,038	2,922	2,660	-36.1	7.0	-3.8	-9.0
Total employment (000)	58.1	43.0	46.3	47.9	—	-26.0	7.7	3.3	—
Production workers (000)	33.7	24.5	27.9	30.2	—	-27.3	14.0	8.0	—
Average hourly earnings ($)	11.15	11.16	11.48	11.93	—	0.0	2.9	3.9	—
Product Data									
Value of shipments[5]	4,155	2,545	2,800	2,800	2,600	-38.7	10.0	0.0	-7.2
Value of shipments (1982$)	4,155	2,508	2,700	2,597	2,385	-39.6	7.7	-3.8	-8.2
Shipments price index (1982=100)[6]	100.0	101.6	104.0	108.1	—	1.6	2.4	3.9	—
Trade Data									
Value of imports	1,271	839	1,322	1,500	1,600	-34.0	57.5	13.5	6.7
Import/new supply ratio[7]	0.234	0.248	0.321	0.349	—	5.9	29.3	8.8	—
Value of exports	654	436	455	450	400	-33.4	4.4	-1.1	-11.1
Export/shipments ratio	0.157	0.171	0.163	0.161	—	8.8	-5.1	-1.1	—

[1]Estimated except for exports and imports.
[2]Estimated.
[3]Forecast.
[4]Value of all products and services sold by the Metal-Cutting Machine Tools industry.
[5]Value of products classified in the Metal-Cutting Machine Tools industry produced by all industries.
[6]Developed by the Office of Industry Assessment, ITA.
[7]New supply is the sum of product shipments plus imports.
SOURCE: U.S. Department of Commerce: Bureau of the Census, Bureau of Economic Analysis, International Trade Administration (ITA). Estimates and forecasts by ITA.

Source: U.S. Industrial Outlook 1986, U.S. Department of Commerce.

Recent Performance and Forecast: Metal-Forming Machine Tools (SIC 3542)
(in millions of dollars except as noted)

	1982	1983	1984[1]	1985[2]	1986[3]	Percent Change			
						1982-83	1983-84	1984-85	1985-86
Industry Data									
Value of shipments[4]	1,429	1,142	1,350	1,450	1,300	-20.0	18.2	7.4	-10.3
Value of shipments (1982$)	1,429	1,130	1,305	1,363	1,193	-20.9	15.5	4.4	-12.5
Total employment (000)	19.5	15.3	16.9	18.2	—	-21.5	10.5	7.4	—
Production workers (000)	12.1	9.6	11.2	12.3	—	-20.7	17.2	9.1	—
Average hourly earnings ($)	10.57	11.01	11.18	11.42	—	4.1	1.5	2.1	—
Product Data									
Value of shipments[5]	1,384	1,119	1,300	1,400	1,250	-19.1	16.2	7.7	-10.7
Value of shipments (1982$)	1,384	1,107	1,257	1,316	1,147	-20.0	13.5	4.7	-12.9
Shipments price index (1982=100)[6]	100.0	101.1	103.5	106.5	—	1.1	2.4	2.9	—
Trade Data									
Value of imports	229	254	330	350	360	11.1	29.8	6.2	2.9
Import/new supply ratio[7]	0.097	0.128	0.141	0.139	—	32.1	10.2	-1.2	—
Value of exports	372	261	289	300	310	-29.8	10.7	3.8	3.3
Export/shipments ratio	0.269	0.233	0.222	0.214	—	-13.2	-4.7	-3.6	—

[1]Estimated except for exports and imports.
[2]Estimated.
[3]Forecast.
[4]Value of all products and services sold by the Metal-Forming Machine Tools industry.
[5]Value of products classified in the Metal-Forming Machine Tools industry produced by all industries.
[6]Developed by the Office of Industry Assessment, ITA.
[7]New supply is the sum of product shipments plus imports.
SOURCE: U.S. Department of Commerce: Bureau of the Census, Bureau of Economic Analysis, International Trade Administration (ITA). Estimates and forecasts by ITA.

Source: U.S. Industrial Outlook 1986, U.S. Department of Commerce.

Machine Tools and Accessories

Company	Rev %Chg Last Qtr	Rev %Chg FY-to-Date	Rev %Chg Last 12 Mos	Earn Last 12 Mos $Mil	Earn Last 12 $	Earn %Chg Last Qtr	Earn %Chg FY-to-Date	Earn %Chg Last 12 Mos	Earn 5-Yr Grth Rate %	Par Grth Rate %	Date of Report	Div Cur Amt $	Div Yield %	Div 5-Yr Grth %	Payout Last FY %	Payout Last 5 Yrs %	Last X-Dvd Date	Profit Margin %	Asset Turnover	Return on Total Assets	Leverage Ratio	Return on Equity	Debt to Equity %	Current Ratio	Mkt Value $Mil	Shares Outstndg 000	Held by Banks-Funds 000	Insider Net Trading 000	Short Int Ratio Days	Fiscal Year Ends Mo
Ind. Group	4.5	5.2	2.6	99.1	.62	-40.8	-42.3	-53.5	-14	-1	---	.73	2.9	0	74	58	---	1.5	1.13	1.7	1.82	3.1	25	2.1	3,907	151,931	57,009	-18	.6	--
Acme-Cleveind	-24.3	-19.1	-9.9	-17.3s	-.27	-100.0	-100.0	NE	NC	-19	03-86	.40	3.4	-25	NE	NE	04-28-86	-8.7	.89	-7.7	2.25	-17.3	42	1.9	75	6,279	3,607	0	0.8	09
Barden Corp	-.5	1.4	7.3	4.7s	2.81	-21.1	-25.7	21.1	-6	6	04-86	1.00	3.9	2	32	32	05-28-86	6.4	1.20	7.7	1.25	9.6	3	5.0	42	1,662	513	0	0.0	10
Brenco Inc	-1.5	-1.5	-8.0	-3.2q	-.32	NE	NE	NE	NC	-11	03-86	.12	2.1	-26	NE	NE	06-16-86	-13.9	.55	-7.7	1.04	-8.0	0	11.3	57	9,885	2,382	0	0.0	12
Brown & Shrpe	32.3	32.3	6.6	8.0q	.23	NE	NE	-9.0	NC	8	03-86	.40	1.6	-37	11	157	05-12-86	6.2	.97	6.0	1.68	10.1	25	3.8	87	3,526	1,413	+2	1.9	12
Chi Pneu Tool	-.5	-.5	-.4	-10.9q	-2.42	-64.7	-64.7	-100.0	NC	-11	03-86	.00	.0	0	NE	NE	11-27-85	-2.7	1.52	-4.1	2.56	-10.5	50	1.9	161	4,281	1,932	-4	0.7	12
Cinn Milacron	12.4	12.4	12.2	2.5q	.09	26.7	26.7	-89.7	-7	-7	03-86	.72	3.4	1	1440	93	05-12-86	.3	1.33	.4	2.50	1.0	65	2.1	495	23,453	7,222	+1	0.9	12
Conchemco Inc	13.5	12.6	5.2	1.0s	1.65	72.2	17.0	57.1	0	7	04-86	.40	2.0	0	27	125	06-10-86	5.0	1.22	6.1	1.43	8.7	5	4.2	12	575	116	0	0.1	10
Cross Trecker	-4.5	3.0	7.7	8.0s	.65	-100.0	-69.8	-17.7	-30	-1	03-86	.80	4.2	7	84	48	05-05-86	1.9	1.11	2.1	1.81	3.8	6	2.0	238	12,365	7,234	0	0.5	09
Ex-Cell-O	10.7	6.9	7.7	56.5s	3.97	-5.0	-5.0	5.0	4	6	03-86	1.72	3.6	5	41	42	06-03-86	4.8	1.48	7.1	1.61	11.4	10	2.1	687	14,228	7,164	+6	0.5	11
Fedl Mogul	5.7	5.7	-.2	49.8q	3.76	-15.7	-15.7	9.9	8	8	03-86	1.60	3.7	5	40	47	05-20-86	5.5	1.33	7.3	2.01	14.7	37	2.5	554	12,956	5,605	-44	0.4	12
Gleason Cp	11.2	11.2	7.8	1.2q	.20	NC	NC	NE	NC	10	03-86	.00	.0	0	0	0	08-02-82	.5	1.20	.6	2.17	1.3	40	2.2	128	5,584	1,673	-1	0.6	12
Hein-Werner	-18.5	-18.5	-2.0	1.3q	.94	-28.6	-28.6	-10.5	NC	1	03-86	.00	.0	0	20	31	12-20-84	2.7	1.70	4.6	2.13	9.8	44	2.3	15	1,356	26	0	0.0	12
Kennametal	2.4	4.4	3.2	11.2h	.99	2.3	-48.1	-31.3	4	1	03-86	.88	3.8	1	52	59	05-05-86	3.2	1.06	3.4	1.53	5.2	16	3.3	232	10,080	4,525	-0	0.4	06
Lodge & Ship	-38.6	-38.6	-15.7	-4.1q	-1.17	NE	NE	NE	NC	-60	12-07-81	.00	.0	0	0	0		-25.6	.93	-23.8	2.53	-60.3	46	2.0	6	3,487	157	-4	0.0	12
Mestek Inc	12.8	12.8	183.3	.1q	-.01	NC	NC	NC	NC	11	03-86	.00	.0	0	0	0		.6	1.33	.8	13.88	11.1	567	2.5	11	1,743	61	+	0.0	12
Monarch Mach	-19.7	-19.7	2.7	2.5q	.67	-57.1	-57.1	-1.5	-35	-1	03-86	.80	5.0	1	113	48	05-15-86	3.3	.91	3.0	1.20	3.6	0	4.2	59	3,674	1,374	0	2.3	12
Newcor	16.1	24.1	-10.2	-3.1s	-1.08	NE	NE	-100.0	-21	-21	04-86	.32	3.1	12	NE	42	07-09-86	-4.4	1.11	-4.9	3.35	-16.4	119	2.4	29	2,816	490	+29	0.0	10
Ransburg Corp	10.9	8.3	8.9	4.7s	.58	-53.3	-53.3	625.0	0	7	05-86	.72	3.6	6	96	53	06-19-86	2.3	1.13	2.6	2.00	5.2	6	1.5	158	7,964	3,284	0	0.6	11
Regal-Beloit	38.8	38.8	5.1	3.6q	1.13	25.0	25.0	-12.4	8	7	06-24-86	.60	3.6	8	55	53		5.9	1.27	7.1	2.00	15.0	57	3.4	54	3,209	504	-	0.0	12
Spectra-Phys	14.7	16.1	15.7	2.1s	.32	NE	NE	NE	NC	2	03-86	.00	.0	0	0	0		1.0	1.10	1.1	1.45	1.6	25	4.3	203	7,260	1,594	-4	0.7	09
Timken Co	-.7	-.7	-5.4	-18.1q	-1.49	-100.0	-100.0	-100.0	-4	-4	03-86	1.00	2.1	-13	NE	NE	05-14-86	-1.7	.76	-1.3	1.77	-2.3	20	1.5	592	12,175	5,424	+0	4.3	12
Wedco Inc	12.5	4.8	13.3	-1.4n	-.42	-100.0	-100.0	-100.0	NC	-13	12-85	.00	.0	0	NE	NE	02-08-85	-8.2	.73	-6.0	2.12	-12.7	35	1.4	11	3,363	99	0	0.0	03

Recent Performance and Forecast: Steel Mill Products (SIC 3312,3315,3316,3317)

(in millions of dollars except as noted)

Item	1982	1983	1984[1]	1985[2]	1986[3]	Percent Change			
						1982-83	1983-84	1984-85	1985-86
Industry Data									
Value of shipments[4]	46,007	45,308	53,028	53,907	53,137	-1.5	17.0	1.7	—
Value of shipments (1982$)	46,007	45,377	51,785	52,134	—	-1.4	14.1	0.7	1.9
Total employment (000)	360	310	299	267	252	-14.0	-3.5	-10.5	-5.7
Production workers (000)	263	231	229	203	193	-11.9	-1.3	-11.0	-5.0
Average hourly earnings ($)	15.48	14.38	14.50	14.86	—	-7.1	0.8	2.5	—
Product Data									
Value of shipments[5]	43,006	42,660	49,846	50,673	53,695	-0.8	16.8	1.7	6.0
Value of shipments (1982$)	43,006	42,694	48,069	48,398	49,488	-0.7	12.6	0.7	2.3
Shipments price index (1982=100)[6]	100.0	100.1	103.7	104.7	108.5	0.1	3.6	1.0	3.6
Trade Data									
Value of imports	8,861	6,240	10,098	9,244	8,798	-29.6	61.8	-8.5	-4.8
Import/new supply ratio[7]	0.172	0.129	0.171	0.156	0.143	-25.1	32.2	-8.4	-8.7
Value of exports	1,562	977	869	903	940	-37.4	-11.1	3.9	4.1
Export/shipments ratio	0.037	0.023	0.018	0.018	0.018	-36.8	-23.7	2.2	-1.8

[1]Estimated except for exports and imports.
[2]Estimated.
[3]Forecast.
[4]Value of all products and services sold by the Steel Mill Products industry.
[5]Value of products classified in the Steel Mill Products industry produced by all industries.
[6]Developed by the Office of Industry Assessment, ITA.
[7]New supply is the sum of product shipments plus imports.

SOURCE: U.S. Department of Commerce: Bureau of the Census, Bureau of Economic Analysis, International Trade Administration (ITA). Estimates and forecasts by ITA.

Source: *U.S. Industrial Outlook 1986*, U.S. Department of Commerce.

Recent Performance and Forecast: Selected Nonferrous Metals (SIC 3331,3332,3333,3334)

(in millions of dollars except as noted)

	1982	1983	1984[1]	1985[2]	1986[3]	Percent Change			
						1982-83	1983-84	1984-85	1985-86
Industry Data									
Value of shipments[4]	9,008	10,445	9,675	7,682	8,485	16.0	-7.4	-20.6	10.5
3331 Primary Copper	3,078	3,467	3,085	2,930	2,930	12.7	-11.0	-5.0	0.0
3332 Primary Lead	559	515	430	500	500	-7.9	-16.5	16.3	0.0
3333 Primary Zinc	334	373	460	387	415	11.7	23.3	-15.9	7.2
3334 Primary Aluminum	5,037	6,090	5,700	3,865	4,640	20.9	-6.4	-32.2	20.1
Value of shipments (1982$)	9,008	10,226	9,597	8,161	8,611	13.5	-6.2	-15.0	5.5
3331 Primary Copper	3,078	3,271	3,327	3,306	3,307	6.3	1.7	-0.6	0.0
3332 Primary Lead	559	610	424	638	580	9.1	-30.5	50.4	-9.0
3333 Primary Zinc	334	358	375	347	363	7.1	4.8	-7.5	4.8
3334 Primary Aluminum	5,037	5,987	5,471	3,871	4,361	18.9	-8.6	-29.3	12.7
Total employment (000)	34.7	—	31.2	29.7	28.7	—	—	-4.7	-3.4
3331 Primary Copper	7.6	6.7	6.5	6.0	6.0	-11.8	-3.0	-7.7	0.0
3332 Primary Lead	2.2	—	2.0	1.9	1.9	—	—	-5.0	0.0
3333 Primary Zinc	2.0	1.6	1.7	1.8	1.8	-20.0	4.0	8.2	0.0
3334 Primary Aluminum	22.9	21.4	21.0	20.0	19.0	-6.6	-1.9	-4.8	-5.0
Production workers (000)	26.0	24.5	—	22.9	22.1	-5.8	—	—	-3.5
3331 Primary Copper	5.9	5.3	5.2	5.0	5.0	-10.2	-1.9	-3.8	0.0
3332 Primary Lead	1.7	1.6	—	1.6	1.5	-5.9	—	—	-6.2
3333 Primary Zinc	1.5	1.1	1.2	1.3	1.3	-26.7	5.6	11.9	0.0
3334 Primary Aluminum	16.9	16.5	15.8	15.0	14.3	-2.4	-4.2	-5.1	-4.7

Average hourly earnings ($)	15.30	—	—	—	—	—	—	—	—
3331 Primary Copper	14.08	14.22	14.40	15.08	—	1.0	1.3	4.7	—
3332 Primary Lead	13.18	—	—	—	—	—	—	—	—
3333 Primary Zinc	12.13	13.23	13.23	13.61	—	9.0	0.0	2.9	—
3334 Primary Aluminum	16.26	16.53	16.36	16.70	—	1.7	-1.0	2.1	—
Product Data									
Value of shipments[5]	11,743	13,631	13,900	14,360	14,374	16.1	2.0	3.3	0.1
3331 Primary Copper	3,875	4,305	4,520	4,650	4,420	11.1	5.0	2.9	-4.9
3332 Primary Lead	1,155	993	730	850	840	-14.0	-26.5	16.4	-1.2
3333 Primary Zinc	492	554	650	570	614	12.7	17.4	-12.3	7.7
3334 Primary Aluminum	6,222	7,779	8,000	8,290	8,500	25.0	2.8	3.6	2.5
Value of shipments (1982$)	11,743	13,138	13,472	15,008	14,363	11.9	2.5	11.4	-4.3
3331 Primary Copper	3,875	4,111	4,818	5,200	4,944	6.1	17.2	7.9	-4.9
3332 Primary Lead.	1,155	1,106	732	1,069	1,000	-4.3	-33.8	46.0	-6.5
3333 Primary Zinc	492	533	545	530	549	8.4	2.4	-2.9	3.6
3334 Primary Aluminum	6,222	7,388	7,376	8,209	7,870	18.7	-0.2	11.3	-4.1
Shipments price index (1982=100)[6]	100.0	103.9	103.1	96.4	99.8	3.9	-0.8	-6.6	3.6
3331 Primary Copper	100.0	104.8	91.9	92.3	96.2	4.8	-12.3	0.4	4.2
3332 Primary Lead	100.0	90.1	99.7	79.6	84.0	-9.9	10.6	-20.1	5.5
3333 Primary Zinc	100.0	103.9	119.4	107.7	111.9	3.9	14.8	-9.7	3.9
3334 Primary Aluminum	100.0	106.0	109.5	101.1	104.0	6.0	3.3	-7.7	2.9

[1]Estimated except for exports and imports.
[2]Estimated.
[3]Forecast.
[4]Value of all products and services sold by the Selected Nonferrous Metals industry.
[5]Value of products classified in the Selected Nonferrous Metals industry produced by all industries.
[6]Developed by the Office of Industry Assessment, ITA.

SOURCE: U.S. Department of Commerce: Bureau of the Census, Bureau of Economic Analysis, International Trade Administration (ITA). Estimates and forecasts by ITA.

Source: *U.S. Industrial Outlook 1986*, U.S. Department of Commerce.

Company	Rev %Chg Last Qtr	Rev %Chg FY to Date	Rev %Chg Last 12 Mos	Earn $Mil Last 12 Mos	Earn Per Share Last 12 Mos	Earn %Chg Last Qtr	Earn %Chg FY to Date	Earn %Chg Last 12 Mos	Earn 5-Yr Growth Rate	Par Growth Rate	Date of Report	Div Amt	Div Yield	Div 5-Yr Growth	Payout Last FY	Payout Last 5 Yrs	Last X-Dvd Date	Profit Margin	Asset Turnover	Return on Total Assets	Leverage Ratio	Return on Equity	Debt to Equity	Current Ratio	Mkt Value $Mil	Latest Shares Outstndg	Held by Banks/Funds	Insider Net Trading	Short Int (Days)	Fiscal Yr Ends (Mo)
Copper Mining and Refining																														
Ind. Group	2.4	6.1	-5.6	-147.4	-1.19	NE	NE	NE	NC	-.5	---	.15	1.1	-.2	146	69	---	-4.2	.52	-2.2	2.18	-4.8	46	1.5	2,765	205,264	40,725	-171	.9	--
ASARCO Inc	11.9	11.9	.9	-72.3q	-3.20	NE	NE	NE	NC	-11	03-86	.00	.0	0	0	NE	08-03-84	-6.0	.68	-4.1	2.76	-11.3	68	1.3	443	27,496	8,108	0	.8	12
Atlas Consol B	-39.8	-4.9	-4.8	-81.3q	-.97	NE	NE	NE	NC	0	12-85	.00	.0	0	0	NE	04-06-81	-59.3	.33	-19.7	.00	NM	316	.3	42	83,611	1,663	0	2.2	12
Campbell Rsc	-96.8	-48.9	-45.1	-14.4n	-.84	NE	NE	NE	NC	-19	03-86	.00	NA	0	0	NE	05-21-84	-25.3	.24	-6.0	3.18	-19.1	100	1.4	22	25,593	808	-126	.3	06
Newmont Mng	14.1	14.1	-6.9	21.0q	-1.27	-100.0	177.8	177.8	NC	3	03-86	1.00	2.1	-17	0	105	05-20-86	3.0	.33	1.0	1.50	1.5	17	1.5	1,421	30,325	11,665	0	.7	12
O'Okiep Copp	-90.0	-35.7	-36.6	-19.2q	-2.63	NE	NE	NE	NC	-19	12-84	.00	.0	0	0	NE	02-06-81	-48.4	.26	-12.5	1.50	-18.8	41	2.1	13	3,525	0	0	0.0	12
Phelps Dodge	3.3	3.3	1.2	26.3q	.49	NE	NE	NE	NC	3	03-86	.00	.0	0	0	NE	05-17-82	2.9	.55	1.6	2.13	3.4	57	1.8	663	27,200	17,032	-18	2.1	12
Revere Copper	-4.1	-4.1	-19.6	-17.5q	-2.56	NE	-100.0	-100.0	NC	-41	03-86	.00	.0	0	0	NE	11-25-81	-3.9	1.18	-4.6	8.98	-41.3	5	8.3	160	7,514	1,429	-27	.4	12
Aluminum Refining																														
Ind. Group	-7.4	-4.5	-10.1	-678.0	-2.75	228.4	230.5	NE	NC	-11	---	.79	2.5	-1	7735	88	04-30-86	-4.2	.81	-3.4	2.44	-8.3	69	1.9	8,039	252,948	133,703	+1548	1.6	--
Alcan Alum	4.5	4.5	6.4	-207.0q	-2.08	50.0	50.0	NE	NC	-10	03-86	.80	2.6	-7	NE	197	04-30-86	-3.6	.83	-3.0	2.50	-7.5	58	2.3	3,043	99,780	37,003	-1	.7	12
Alum Co Am	-10.4	-10.4	-9.9	-21.9q	-.30	-87.5	-87.5	NE	NC	-4	03-86	1.20	3.1	-8	NE	81	04-28-86	-.4	.75	-.3	2.33	-.7	48	2.1	3,115	81,707	56,454	-33	.6	12
Dw Industries	40.5	23.7	13.7	1.9q	.33	-74.3	-56.4	26.9	NC	5	04-86	.00	.0	0	0	NE	00-00-00	1.1	2.36	2.6	1.81	4.7	14	1.4	40	5,552	438		2.2	10
Kaiser Alum	-35.0	-35.0	-45.9	-160.8q	-3.75	NE	NE	NE	NC	-15	03-86	.00	.0	-30	NE	NE	02-04-85	-9.2	.53	-4.9	2.96	-14.5	111	1.6	811	44,121	25,914	+1601	.6	12
Reynolds Metal	3.1	3.1	-4.2	-290.2q	-13.72	-100.0	64.5	64.5	NC	-31	03-86	1.00	2.1	-19	0	NE	06-02-86	-8.4	.95	-8.0	3.64	-29.1	122	1.5	1,029	21,788	13,894	-18	3.9	12
Lead, Nck, Tn, Zn Mining & Refining																														
Ind. Group	-57.9	-51.0	-20.1	9.3	-.25	-100.0	-100.0	NE	NC	1	---	.11	1.0	0	37	136	---	.3	.67	.2	2.50	.5	90	1.7	2,100	182,077	51,391	0	1.8	--
Cominco Ltd	-14.6	-14.6	-9.2	-87.9q	-1.75	NE	NE	NE	NC	-14	03-86	.00	NA	-42	NE	4	12-02-85	-6.2	.69	-4.3	3.23	-13.9	107	1.2	635	64,304	824	0	5.1	12
Gulf Res & Ch	-40.1	-40.1	-58.2	57.0q	5.56	-100.0	-100.0	NE	NC	32	03-86	.00	.0	0	0	NE	00-00-00	52.3	.20	15.5	2.08	32.3	62	3.3	119	9,276	1,102	0	3.1	12
Inco Ltd	-99.9	-99.9	-25.2	40.1q	.15	-100.0	511.0	NE	NC	-1	03-86	.20	1.6	0	71	4	04-29-86	3.6	.36	1.3	3.15	4.1	87	2.0	1,313	102,009	48,879	0	.8	12
Utd Park City	0	0	-100.0	-.9q	-.16	NE	NE	NE	NC	-6	03-86	.00	.0	0	0	NE	00-00-00	NC	NC	NC	NC	-5.7	0	.3	18	5,401	491	0	0.0	12
Pac Tin Cons	-6.5	-6.5	0	1.0q	.96	-92.3	-92.3	NE	NC	3	03-86	.40	2.9	-20	30	NE	06-03-86	2.9	1.28	3.7	1.46	5.4	0	2.4	15	1,087	95	0	0.0	12

Motor Vehicles

Recent Performance and Forecast: Motor Vehicles and Car Bodies (SIC 3711)

(in millions of dollars except as noted)

	1982	1983	1984[1]	1985[2]	1986[3]	Percent Change			
						1982-83	1983-84	1984-85	1985-86
Industry Data									
Value of shipments[4]	70,740	95,931	98,594	101,984	99,873	35.6	2.8	3.4	-2.1
Value of shipments (1982$)	70,740	93,655	94,055	95,327	90,794	32.4	0.4	1.4	-4.8
Total employment (000)	240	261	262	266	253	8.6	0.5	1.5	-4.9
Production workers (000)	194	217	217	221	210	11.9	0.2	1.8	-5.0
Average hourly earnings ($)	14.45	14.75	15.59	16.53	—	2.1	5.7	6.0	—
Product Data									
Value of shipments[5]	66,706	90,935	93,459	97,029	94,673	36.3	2.8	3.8	-2.4
Value of shipments (1982$)	66,706	88,778	89,156	90,696	86,066	33.1	0.4	1.7	-5.1
Shipments price index (1982=100)[6]	100.0	102.4	104.8	107.0	—	2.4	2.4	2.0	—
Trade Data									
Value of imports (ITA)[7]	16,529	19,203	21,400	23,400	—	16.2	11.4	9.3	—
Import/new supply ratio[8]	0.197	0.173	0.157	0.159	—	-12.5	-9.1	1.2	—
Value of exports (ITA)[9]	3,360	2,339	1,700	1,800	—	-30.4	-27.3	5.9	—
Export/shipments ratio	0.050	0.025	0.015	0.015	—	-49.1	-41.9	-1.8	—

[1]Estimated except for exports and imports.
[2]Estimated.
[3]Forecast.
[4]Value of all products and services sold by the Motor Vehicles and Car Bodies industry.
[5]Value of products classified in the Motor Vehicles and Car Bodies industry produced by all industries.
[6]Developed by the Office of Industry Assessment, ITA.
[7]Import data are developed by the chapter author.
[8]New supply is the sum of product shipments plus imports.
[9]Export data are developed by the chapter author.

SOURCE: U.S. Department of Commerce: Bureau of the Census, Bureau of Economic Analysis, International Trade Administration (ITA). Estimates and forecasts by ITA.

Source: *U.S. Industrial Outlook 1986*, U.S. Department of Commerce.

Recent Performance and Forecast: Motor Vehicle Parts and Accessories (SIC 3714)

(in millions of dollars except as noted)

	1982	1983	1984[1]	1985[2]	1986[3]	Percent Change			
						1982-83	1983-84	1984-85	1985-86
Industry Data									
Value of shipments[4]	36,293	44,415	49,741	50,878	50,107	22.4	12.0	2.3	-1.5
Value of shipments (1982$)	36,293	43,689	48,814	49,783	49,028	20.4	11.7	2.0	-1.5
Total employment (000)	321	338	379	387	381	5.2	12.0	2.3	-1.5
Production workers (000)	251	267	306	313	308	6.5	14.3	2.3	-1.5
Average hourly earnings ($)	11.65	12.26	12.90	13.57	—	5.2	5.2	5.2	—
Product Data									
Value of shipments[5]	38,414	46,776	53,485	54,707	53,878	21.8	14.3	2.3	-1.5
Value of shipments (1982$)	38,414	46,011	52,488	53,529	52,718	19.8	14.1	2.0	-1.5
Shipments price index (1982=100)[6]	100.0	101.7	101.9	102.2	102.2	1.7	0.2	0.3	0.0
Trade Data									
Value of imports	6,045	8,102	11,380	12,612	13,977	34.0	40.5	10.8	10.8
Import/new supply ratio[7]	0.105	0.118	0.136	0.128	0.120	12.7	15.0	-6.0	-6.0
Value of exports	6,844	7,080	8,767	9,463	10,215	3.4	23.8	7.9	7.9
Export/shipments ratio	0.165	0.139	0.152	0.160	0.176	-15.9	9.0	5.5	9.6

[1]Estimated except for exports and imports.
[2]Estimated.
[3]Forecast.
[4]Value of all products and services sold by the Motor Vehicle Parts and Accessories industry.
[5]Value of products classified in the Motor Vehicle Parts and Accessories industry produced by all industries.
[6]Developed by the Office of Industry Assessment, ITA.
[7]New supply is the sum of product shipments plus imports.

SOURCE: U.S. Department of Commerce: Bureau of the Census, Bureau of Economic Analysis, International Trade Administration (ITA). Estimates and forecasts by ITA.

Source: *U.S. Industrial Outlook 1986*, U.S. Department of Commerce.

Auto Manufacture

Revenue & Earnings

Company	Rev Last Qtr %	Rev FY to Date %	Rev Last 12 Mos %	Earn Last 12 Mos $Mil	Per Share Last 12 Mos $	Earn Last Qtr %	Earn FY to Date %	Earn Last 12 Mos %	5-Year Growth Rate %	Par Growth Rate %	Date of Report
Ind. Group	18.0	13.0	13.9	8,788.1	4.34	-34.7	-59.4	-35.4	33	11	- - -
Am Motors	-.1	-.3	-.1	-115.2q	-1.15	NE	NE	NE	NC	-77	03-86
Chrysler Cp	6.8	7.8	6.8	1,484.5q	8.95	-15.4	-15.4	4.3	NC	31	03-86
ESI Ind	11.6	25.0	11.6	2.5q	.70	-14.3	-14.3	40.0	NC	18	03-86
Ford Motor Co	11.6	3.2	11.6	2,460.4q	8.99	-3.6	-3.6	-10.6	NC	15	03-86
Ford of Can	7.8	7.4	7.8	1,113.3q	13.42	-93.3	-93.3	-64.1	NC	1	03-86
Gen Motors	10.9	16.2	10.9	3,991.1q	12.13	-4.6	-4.6	-1.9	NC	8	03-86
Gen Motors E	NA	NA	NA	NA	NA	NA	NA	NA	NA	NC	00-00
Gen Motors H	NA	NA	NA	NA	NA	NA	NA	NA	NA	NC	00-00
Honda Motor	169.8	58.5	58.6	813.2q	.83	-78.5	-84.4	-84.4	-20	8	02-86
Mack Trucks	-27.9	-13.9	-27.9	-78.3q	-2.71	-100.0	-100.0	-100.0	NC	-15	03-86
Oshkosh Truck	-41.5	8.5	-13.8	18.2s	2.09	81.6	52.6	NC	NC	33	03-86
Pullman Pbdy	96.1	70.6	84.9	12.3s	.41	-9.1	-4.8	17.1	NC	32	03-86
Subaru of Amer	46.0	42.8	46.3	88.1s	1.79	27.0	30.1	31.6	29	28	04-86

Dividends

Company	Current Rate Amt $	Yield %	5-Year Growth Rate %	Payout Last FY %	Payout Last 5 Yrs %	Last X-Dvd Date
Ind. Group	1.47	2.5	1	31	21	- - - -
Am Motors	.00	.0	0	0	21	03-26-80
Chrysler Cp	1.00	2.6	0	7	9	06-10-86
ESI Ind	.00	.0	0	0	9	11-08-85
Ford Motor Co	2.20	4.0	27	21	20	06-03-86
Ford of Can	12.00	NA	0	58	42	03-10-86
Gen Motors	5.00	6.4	15	41	41	05-09-86
Gen Motors E	.30	.6	NA	NA	NA	05-09-86
Gen Motors H	.30	.7	NA	NA	NA	05-09-86
Honda Motor	.47	.7	2	54	11	02-21-86
Mack Trucks	.00	.0	0	0	0	00-00-00
Oshkosh Truck	.20	.6	6	0	0	07-09-86
Pullman Pbdy	.06	.6	6	0	0	03-18-86
Subaru of Amer	.29	.8	52	13	12	05-02-86

Ratio Analysis

Company	Profit Margin %	Asset Turnover	Return on Total Assets	Leverage Ratio	Return on Equity	Debt to Equity %	Current Ratio	Market Value $Mil
Ind. Group	4.1	1.73	7.1	2.38	16.9	18	1.1	118,819
Am Motors	-2.9	2.00	-5.8	13.31	-77.2	537	1.0	468
Chrysler Cp	6.9	1.71	11.8	2.98	35.2	56	1.1	6,420
ESI Ind	5.0	2.00	10.0	1.81	18.1	19	2.2	34
Ford Motor Co	4.5	1.73	7.8	2.58	20.1	18	1.1	15,380
Ford of Can	.8	4.63	3.7	2.81	10.4	1	1.3	991
Gen Motors	4.0	1.58	6.3	2.16	13.6	10	1.1	24,596
Gen Motors E	NA	NC	NA	NC	NA	NA	NA	3,109
Gen Motors H	NA	NC	NA	NC	NA	NA	NA	624
Honda Motor	5.0	1.74	8.7	2.21	19.2	28	1.3	64,381
Mack Trucks	-4.1	1.80	-7.4	1.99	-14.7	21	2.2	359
Oshkosh Truck	6.2	2.10	13.0	2.82	36.7	15	1.5	284
Pullman Pbdy	2.7	2.74	7.4	5.09	37.7	55	1.1	388
Subaru of Amer	4.9	4.27	20.9	1.58	33.0	5	3.0	1,785

r/t x t/a = r/e   t/t x r/a = r/t x t/a x a/e = r/e

Shareholdings

Company	Latest Shares Outstnding 000	Held by Banks-Funds 000	Insider Net Trading 000	Short Interest Ratio Days	Fiscal Year Ends Mo
Ind. Group	1,988,802	449,117	-22	1.9	--
Am Motors	110,077	6,079	+1	4.0	12
Chrysler Cp	168,392	95,301	-41	1.0	12
ESI Ind	3,476	677	+0	0.1	12
Ford Motor Co	279,010	165,252	+6	2.9	12
Ford of Can	8,291	61	0	0.0	12
Gen Motors	316,853	116,317	+44	1.5	12
Gen Motors E	63,774	17,996	+3	NA	NA
Gen Motors H	15,000	2,648	+9	NA	NA
Honda Motor	897,295	6,352	0	11.7	02
Mack Trucks	29,576	10,002	+7	0.0	12
Oshkosh Truck	9,008	1,884	-27	0.0	09
Pullman Pbdy	38,809	12,660	-8	1.3	09
Subaru of Amer	49,241	13,888	-16	0.0	10

Auto Parts and Accessories

Company	Rev Last Qtr %	Rev FY to Date %	Rev Last 12 Mos %	Rev Last 12 Mos $Mil	EPS Last 12 $	EPS Last Qtr %	EPS FY to Date %	EPS Last 12 Mos %	5-Year Growth Rate %	Par Growth Rate %	Date of Report	Div Amt $	Yield %	Div 5-Year Growth Rate %	Payout FY %	Payout Last 5 Yrs %	Last X-Dvd Date	Profit Margin %	Asset Turnover	Return on Total Assets %	Leverage Ratio	Return on Equity %	Debt to Equity %	Current Ratio	Market Value $Mil	Latest Shares Outstndg 000	Held by Banks Funds 000	Insider Net Trading 000	Short Interest Ratio Days	Fiscal Year Ends Mo
Ind. Group	3.7	5.5	4.5	762.1	1.96	-13.2	-11.5	-8.5	NC	8	03-86	.71	2.5	0	30	39	06-02-86	4.0	1.48	5.9	2.07	12.2	38	2.3	11,068	393,765	160,781	+1148	1.6	--
Allen Group	21.2	21.2	19.4	14.7q	1.60	-66.7	-66.7	55.3	NC	8	03-86	.56	2.8	-12	26	79	06-02-86	3.5	1.63	5.7	2.18	12.4	57	2.6	178	9,014	4,411	+2	1.8	12
Arvin Indus	4.4	4.4	3.4	39.(q)	2.36	36.6	36.6	18.6	35	12	03-86	.64	1.9	1	28	42	06-09-86	4.7	2.19	10.3	1.53	15.8	23	3.6	539	16,155	5,663	0	1.8	12
Barnes Group	-15.6	-15.6	-17.4	11.1q	1.59	-12.9	-12.9	-31.8	16	4	03-86	1.00	3.0	-2	51	61	05-23-86	2.7	1.63	4.4	2.20	9.7	26	1.6	218	6,448	3,216	+1	0.0	12
Buell Indus	-7.3	-2.6	-2.6	5.3s	2.19	7.9	-4.4	-9.1	49	13	04-86	.32	1.4	-	13	17	06-02-86	7.2	1.57	11.3	1.33	15.0	4	4.8	110	4,792	156	0	0.3	10
Champ Parts	10.9	10.9	-5.5	.2q	.06	NE	NE	-87.0	NC	-	03-86	-	-	-	-	138	07-02-85	.2	1.50	1.0	3.33	1.0	141	2.6	13	1,945	48	0	0.0	12
Champ Spark	2.0	2.0	1.0	5.7q	.15	-100.0	-100.0	-78.9	-16	-3	03-86	.40	3.9	-16	100	85	05-19-86	.7	1.29	.9	1.67	1.5	8	2.1	398	38,396	26,908	-1	0.3	12
Dana Corp	.9	.9	4.2	150.6q	2.73	-25.3	-25.3	-20.2	15	7	03-86	1.28	3.9	4	43	51	05-21-86	4.0	1.55	6.2	2.03	12.6	30	1.9	1,858	56,531	27,399	0	0.9	12
Donaldson	7.0	7.0	.3	15.7m	2.99	29.0	29.0	57.4	30	5	04-86	.80	1.8	2	30	46	05-22-86	5.9	1.73	10.2	1.60	16.3	18	2.9	197	5,278	2,687	0	0.7	07
Dyneer Corp	7.1	4.7	6.1	6.0n	1.71	-37.3	-37.3	-27.8	3	5	04-86	.80	3.0	7	33	40	03-25-86	2.7	1.67	4.5	2.09	9.4	36	2.1	88	3,370	692	0	0.4	07
Eaton Corp	-2.9	-2.9	1.2	215.1q	6.52	-24.4	-24.4	-18.6	NC	12	03-86	1.60	2.3	-9	19	42	04-29-86	5.9	1.29	7.6	2.03	15.4	31	3.2	2,241	32,829	17,616	+3	0.2	12
Echlin Inc	9.9	9.9	17.2	44.3n	1.05	16.7	16.7	-1.9	26	8	05-86	.50	2.6	11	37	41	03-26-86	5.1	1.51	7.7	1.99	15.3	41	2.3	910	47,286	26,045	+178	0.2	08
Excel Ind	72.0	72.0	72.0	3.2q	.96	100.0	100.0	6.7	NC	14	05-86	.40	2.6b	0	17	17	06-27-86	3.0	2.67	8.0	2.99	23.9	72	1.9	51	3,371	354	-48	0.0	12
Facet Entprs	2.9	3.7	4.3	.0s	-.04	-9.1	-9.1	-100.0	NC	8	03-86	.00	-	0	-	-	12-13-80	.0	NC	NC	NC	0	127	2.7	33	3,052	806	0	3.5	09
Fruehauf Cp	-2.7	-2.7	-7.2	58.4q	3.21	-34.4	-34.4	-25.9	NC	0	03-86	.80	1.4	-25	18	48	06-25-86	2.3	1.39	3.2	3.16	10.1	94	1.7	1,037	20,997	10,699	-4	6.0	12
Hastings Mfg	12.1	12.1	6.6	1.3q	3.01	-100.0	-100.0	-45.6	19	7	03-86	.45	1.2	8	21	20	05-21-86	2.3	1.65	3.3	2.36	7.8	73	2.8	16	420	48	0	0.0	12
Hayes Albion	0	-7.6	-8.9	4.8n	1.22	-32.2	-23.7	-24.7	NC	6	04-86	.40	3.5	-11	19	NE	06-03-86	2.3	2.13	4.9	1.78	8.7	18	1.7	44	3,824	1,042	0	1.2	07
Kysor Ind	-10.6	-10.6	-15.3	9.2q	2.87	-29.5	-29.5	-4.7	NC	12	03-86	.88	3.6	-	23	36	07-10-86	6.7	1.40	9.4	1.83	17.2	23	2.3	77	3,091	769	+2	0.0	12
Magna Intl	44.6	53.9	51.9	49.7n	2.07	5.0	5.0	6.7	NC	12	04-86	.48	2.0	0	18	18	08-11-86	5.2	1.48	7.7	2.17	16.7	35	1.3	581	23,968	4,351	-69	0.0	07
Modine Mfg	4.9	3.1	2.9	20.5f	2.67	30.0	30.0	-8.9	NC	13	03-86	.76	2.9	2	25	23	05-21-86	6.6	1.68	11.1	1.68	18.7	30	2.8	195	7,512	1,914	+2	0.0	03
Mr Gasket	-10.1	6.9	6.7	5.3f	.50	NE	NE	-3.8	NC	12	03-86	.00	.0	0	0	0	00-00-00	4.2	.95	4.0	2.93	11.7	152	4.5	81	10,629	1,636	0	0.0	03
Murphy Ind Inc	-31.4	-32.1	-8.9	0	-1.51	NE	NE	NE	NC	14	02-86	.00	-	0	0	0	03-31-80	NC	NC	NC	NC	NC	220	1.9	11	6,769	566	+131	0.0	08
Premier Ind	2.6	1.3	3.3	40.7m	1.38	16.7	16.7	.7	6	6	02-86	.40	1.3	13	27	25	07-17-86	9.3	1.71	15.9	1.25	19.8	1	5.8	896	29,607	4,784	0	0.9	05
Raymark Cp	4.8	4.8	23.9	-16.5q	-5.75	1000.0	1000.0	NE	NC	14	03-86	.00	.0	0	NE	NE	06-22-82	-14.5	.00	-19.8	.00	NM	647	1.1	29	2,361	605	0	4.4	12
Sealed Power	4.9	4.9	19.4	27.7q	2.26	-25.0	-25.0	-32.3	12	6	03-86	1.10	3.7	9	41	33	08-18-86	4.4	1.25	5.5	1.96	10.8	62	3.4	360	12,251	6,378	+2	0.5	12
Seaport Cp	-18.6	-18.6	-18.5	-.7q	-.34	NE	NE	NE	-16	-16	03-86	.00	.0	0	0	0	00-00-00	-3.2	1.44	-4.6	3.54	-16.3	37	1.1	3	2,073	10	0	2.3	12
Simpson Indust	32.5	24.3	19.8	9.1n	1.44	25.7	25.7	29.7	11	13	03-86	.56	3.0	-4	34	61	04-25-86	5.6	2.04	11.4	1.85	21.1	29	1.9	116	6,295	2,094	0	0.0	06
Smith AO	-.4	-.4	5.6	28.2q	3.57	3.0	3.0	NE	9	9	03-86	.80	2.8	-12	18	18	04-24-86	3.1	1.87	5.8	2.07	12.0	34	1.4	237	8,373	1,380	0	19.4	12
Sparton Corp	47.9	63.0	50.0	.1n	-.04	1066.7	1066.7	-100.0	NC	7	03-86	.52	3.0	15	NE	44	05-09-86	.1	1.00	.1	2.00	.2	2	1.9	139	7,896	1,997	+951	3.2	06
Std Motor Prd	10.1	10.1	6.8	12.5q	.95	93.8	93.8	-20.2	14	7	03-86	.32	1.6	16	40	22	05-08-86	5.0	1.44	7.2	1.43	10.3	15	4.0	260	13,169	4,638	0	0.3	12
Trico Prods	-.9	1.0	2.8	2.7n	1.21	-100.0	-100.0	-68.6	NC	-	09-85	1.00	2.3	0	44	-	05-27-86	1.9	1.37	2.6	1.23	3.2	0	2.5	81	1,847	164	0	0.0	12
Wynn's Intl	50.2	50.2	22.8	-1.8q	-.46	26.9	26.9	-100.0	NC	-6	03-86	.60	2.4	8	NE	36	06-09-86	-.7	1.43	-1.0	2.50	-2.5	57	2.1	91	3,716	1,705	0	0.4	12

Recent Performance and Forecast: Selected Merchandise Categories (SIC 52, 59, 5311, 56, 5812, 5813)

(in millions of dollars except as noted)

	1982	1983	1984	1985[1]	1986[2]	Percent change			
						1982-83	1983-84	1984-85	1985-86
Retail Trade (total)									
Sales	1,072,065	1,174,298	1,297,015	1,394,275	1,505,817	9.5	10.5	7.5	8.0
Employment (000)	15,258	15,281	16,261	16,586	16,917	.002	6.4	2.0	2.0
Department Stores									
Sales	107,163	116,562	129,284	138,980	149,404	8.8	10.9	7.5	7.5
Employment (000)	1,885	1,885	1,950	1,979	2,009	3.4	3.4	1.5	1.5
Apparel & Accessory Stores									
Sales	55,281	60,304	66,891	71,573	76,583	9.1	10.9	7.0	7.0
Employment (000)	970	951	978	991	1,004	-1.8	2.8	1.3	1.3
Eating & Drinking Places									
Sales	104,427	114,684	124,109	134,038	144,761	9.8	8.2	8.0	8.0
Employment (000)	4,781	4,888	5,212	5,472	5,746	2.2	6.6	5.0	5.0

[1] Estimated.
[2] Forecast.

Source: *U.S. Industrial Outlook 1986*, U.S. Department of Commerce.

SOURCE: U.S. Department of Commerce: Bureau of the Census, Bureau of Economic Analysis, and International Trade Administration (ITA). Estimates and forecasts by ITA.

Recent Performance and Forecast: Food Retailing (SIC54)
(in millions of dollars except as noted)

	1982	1983	1984	1985[1]	1986[2]	Percent Change			
						1982-83	1983-84	1984-85[1]	1985-86[2]
Industries Sales									
All Food retailing establishments	245,346	254,878	269,959	282,097	297,048	3.9	5.9	4.5	5.3
Chains with 11 or more establishments	135,499	141,314	148,957	155,660	163,443	4.3	5.4	4.5	5.0
Grocery stores	230,142	239,054	252,939	264,466	278,879	3.9	5.8	4.6	5.4
Chains with 11 or more establishments	133,587	139,385	146,983	153,968	161,743	4.3	5.5	4.8	5.0
Retail bakeries	3,669	3,877	4,135	4,148	4,154	5.7	0.7	0.3	0.1
Other retail food stores	11,535	11,947	12,885	13,483	14,015	3.6	7.9	4.6	3.9
Employment and earnings									
Total employment(000)	2,478	2,556	2,655	2,790	2,910	3.1	3.9	5.1	4.3
Non-supervisory employment(00) ...	2,294	2,374	2,467	2,596	2,709	3.5	3.9	5.2	4.4
Average hourly earnings, non-supervisory employmen($)	7.22	7.51	7.65	7.53	—	4.0	1.9	−1.6	—

[1]Estimated.
[2]Forecast.

SOURCE: U.S. Department of Commerce: Bureau of the Census, Bureau of Economic Analysis, and International Trade Administration (ITA). Estimates and forecasts by ITA.

Source: U.S. Industrial Outlook 1986, U.S. Department of Commerce.

Food Chain Stores

Company	Revenue Pct Change Last Qtr %	FY to Date %	Last 12 Mos %	Last 12 Mos $Mil	EPS Last 12 Mos $	Last Qtr %	FY to Date %	Last 12 Mos %	5-Year Growth Rate %	Par Growth Rate %	Date of Report	Dividends Current Rate Amt $	Yield %	5-Year Growth Rate %	Payout Last FY %	Payout Last 5 Yrs %	Last X-Dvd Date	Profit Margin	Asset Turn over	Return on Total Assets %	Leverage Ratio	Return on Equity %	Debt to Equity %	Current Ratio	Market Value $Mil	Latest Shares Out stndng 000	Held by Banks Funds 000	Insider Net Trad ing 000	Short Interest Ratio Days	Fiscal Year Ends Mo
Ind. Group	7.7	7.0	5.9	1,381.9	1.81	-29.4	-21.2	-.5	11	8	--	.72	2.1	1	32	36	--	1.3	3.77	4.9	2.80	13.7	64	1.3	25,263	735,322	241,976	+105	3.1	--
Albertson's Inc	6.3	6.3	6.8	91.4q	2.75	31.6	31.6	12.7	14	12	04-86	.84	1.8	15	29	27	08-04-86	1.8	4.50	8.1	2.17	17.6	64	1.6	1,553	33,220	12,458	0	0.4	01
Alld Supermkts	NA	NA	-.9	NA	NA	NA	NA	NA	NA	NC	00-00	.00	.0	NA	NA	0	00-00-00	NA	NC	NA	NC	NA	NA	1.6	69	7,859	996	+13	NA	NA
Arden Group Inc	.8	.8	-3.0	6.0q	2.41	NA	54.5	23.0	23	15	03-86	.00	.0	0	0	0	00-00-00	NA	3.29	4.6	3.17	NA	69	1.2	60	2,342	178	0	0.0	12
Big Bear	6.9	9.8	12.3	13.3q	1.95	-34.5	-24.0	12.7	22	20	03-86	.00	.0	0	0	0	01-27-86	1.5	4.20	6.3	3.24	20.4	60	1.3	148	6,815	1,741	+120	1.0	08
Big V Supmkt	3.0	3.0	2.5	5.9q	1.09	14.3	14.3	105.7	-7	8	03-86	.44	3.0	26	38	31	05-27-86	1.0	5.40	5.4	2.56	13.8	75	1.1	61	5,405	888	0	1.0	12
Borman's Inc	5.3	5.3	-1.7	6.0q	2.10	143.5	143.5	346.8	NC	19	04-86	.05	.2	0	NE	NE	05-13-86	.6	6.67	4.0	4.98	19.9	112	2.2	61	2,803	485	0	0.5	06
Bruno's Inc	9.5	15.7	16.7	29.2q	.75	5.0	5.0	15.4	22	35	05-86	.08	.6	18	20	22	05-05-86	2.9	4.24	12.3	1.55	19.1	10	1.5	818	39,404	8,205	0	0.0	06
Circle K Cp	21.0	25.5	25.5	39.8f	1.73	-40.0	-40.0	6.8	33	22	04-86	.56	1.6	2	29	44	06-09-86	1.9	3.63	6.9	4.71	32.5	220	1.5	745	21,441	10,063	-2	8.5	04
Cullum Companies	-5.7	-14.8	-16.8	18.1n	1.64	2.9	2.9	7.2	6	12	03-86	.50	2.0	10	27	20	06-24-86	.6	4.39	5.7	2.15	17.0	46	1.5	279	10,923	3,298	-3	0.0	06
Delchamps Inc	10.4	10.1	10.6	8.6n	1.23	-5.0	-4.9	-10.2	9	12	05-86	.28	1.6	0	23	13	05-01-86	.8	4.38	3.7	2.25	12.8	55	1.8	119	6,994	1,523	0	0.0	06
Fam Fresh	30.0	30.0	24.2	7.4q	.71	-14.3	-14.3	-31.7	14	9	06-18-84	.00	.0	0	0	0	06-18-84	1.6	2.13	3.4	2.53	8.6	104	2.6	154	10,529	3,390	0	0.0	12
Fisher Foods	27.5	27.5	6.9	2.7q	.54	NE	NE	NE	NC	4	11-15-85	.05	.3	-41	22	85	11-15-85	.6	3.40	1.7	2.59	4.4	53	1.4	69	4,187	2,465	+1	2.7	12
Food Lion	22.2	22.2	22.6	49.9q	.31	16.7	16.7	24.0	NC	25	06-19-86	.02	.2	8	7	13	06-19-86	2.6	4.35	11.3	2.13	24.1	28	1.4	1,347	79,255	5,432	0	0.0	12
Foodarama	10.9	9.2	9.2	2.7p	2.07	-13.4	-13.4	-11.5	11	11	09-17-79	.00	.0	0	0	0	09-17-79	.6	6.00	3.6	2.97	10.7	50	.9	27	1,341	85	0	0.0	10
Gen Host	28.1	28.1	11.4	32.2q	1.17	225.0	225.0	-29.9	18	11	06-10-86	.22	.9	19	19	28	06-10-86	5.2	1.04	3.4	2.56	13.8	96	1.8	671	26,830	11,388	0	0.3	01
Giant Food A	8.0	8.0	5.6	57.8q	1.93	7.1	7.1	24.5	26	15	05-06-86	.60	1.9	23	25	24	05-05-86	.8	3.72	9.3	2.29	21.3	47	1.3	927	30,024	8,312	+3	0.2	02
Grt A & P Tea	11.4	12.5	12.5	56.1f	1.48	9.6	9.6	9.6	12	15	04-09-86	.00	.0	0	0	0	04-09-86	.8	4.25	3.4	2.47	8.4	23	1.3	995	37,896	7,018	-3	0.3	02
Hannaford Bros	7.7	7.7	10.9	15.8q	1.86	42.9	42.9	26.5	14	11	06-09-86	.50	1.4	10	28	28	06-09-86	1.9	3.79	7.2	2.10	15.1	54	1.7	311	8,698	2,395	+0	48.2	12
Kroger	9.1	9.1	8.4	182.0q	4.13	5.7	5.7	9.5	-2	11	04-28-86	2.00	3.3	8	49	48	04-28-86	.9	4.40	4.4	3.48	15.3	60	1.2	2,603	43,467	16,664	-19	0.5	12
Lucky Stores	.6	.6	-.5	87.0q	1.61	-12.8	-12.8	-14.8	4	4	06-10-86	1.16	3.9	19	69	63	06-10-86	.9	4.78	4.3	3.07	13.2	60	1.2	1,517	51,000	26,321	0	0.9	01
Marsh Supermkt	13.9	14.4	14.4	6.4f	1.73	133.3	133.3	37.3	-3	9	07-14-86	.52	2.4	4	29	37	07-14-86	.4	4.89	4.4	3.07	13.5	105	1.4	72	3,336	430	+0	0.0	03
Mott's Super	-11.3	-11.3	-5.3	-5.7q	-2.03	-100.0	-100.0	-100.0	NC	NC	02-04-86	.00	.0	NE	NE	NE	02-04-86	-2.0	5.15	-10.3	2.17	-22.3	5	1.1	23	2,786	326	-13	0.0	12
Munford Inc	14.0	14.0	10.9	5.5q	1.41	NE	NE	-24.2	33	23	06-23-86	.54	2.3	0	39	30	06-23-86	1.2	2.67	3.2	3.28	10.5	106	1.8	89	3,764	1,293	+0	2.2	09
Natl Conv Str	9.3	10.9	10.7	7.2q	.32	-53.8	-54.9	-64.8	-4	-1	06-23-86	.36	3.2	19	46	37	06-23-86	.7	2.43	1.7	4.41	7.5	245	1.8	257	22,853	10,389	-12	0.3	06
Penn Traffic	-2.4	-2.4	-5.5	7.0q	3.36	31.1	31.1	66.3	3	7	07-03-86	1.36	3.1	14	38	47	07-03-86	1.4	4.00	5.6	2.16	12.1	56	1.5	92	2,069	270	+0	0.0	01
Pueblo Intl	18.0	18.0	18.9	5.8q	1.49	15.4	15.4	104.1	13	10	07-21-86	.16	.7	19	16	16	07-21-86	.16	3.78	NC	3.38	11.5	95	1.2	86	3,584	911	+6	9.5	01
Revlon Grp	190.5	123.8	--	0	-.30	NE	NE	NE	NC	0	00-00-00	.00	.0	0	0	0	00-00-00	NC	NC	NC	NC	NC	5	2.4	643	39,551	12,945	-5	0.7	07
Safeway Stores	-1.9	-1.9	-1.1	232.6q	3.84	NE	NE	20.8	11	8	05-14-86	1.70	3.2	5	43	47	05-14-86	1.2	4.00	4.8	2.98	14.3	81	1.2	3,267	60,778	33,488	0	0.5	12
Seaway Food Town	4.7	.0	-3.5	2.6q	1.49	2.3	2.3	-14.4	-9	4	07-09-86	.68	3.2	7	33	39	07-09-86	1.4	3.83	2.3	3.35	7.7	106	1.3	38	1,746	236	-1	0.4	09
Showell Inc	-15.7	-19.9	--	-2.08	-2.08	-100.0	-100.0	-100.0	NC	0	10-04-85	.00	.0	14	NE	95	10-04-85	NC	NC	NC	NC	0	101	1.0	65	2,108	153	+21	0.1	01
Southland Corp	9.1	9.1	5.3	123.0q	2.48	15.4	15.4	-20.8	10	5	05-23-86	1.12	2.0	10	23	23	05-23-86	1.0	3.30	3.3	2.73	9.0	50	1.7	2,600	47,496	21,173	+2	37.0	12
Stop & Shop	17.1	17.1	14.9	27.3q	1.98	-44.0	-44.0	-56.5	16	8	05-23-86	.70	.7	16	49	39	05-23-86	.7	3.57	2.5	2.68	6.7	56	1.2	766	13,810	8,701	+7	0.1	07
Sunshine-Jr	-.2	-.2	-1.0	2.5q	1.51	19.0	19.0	7.9	9	9	05-21-86	.48	1.9	3	33	33	05-21-86	1.4	4.43	6.2	1.92	11.9	34	1.3	43	1,702	455	-1	0.5	12
Supermkts Gen	10.0	10.0	12.1	64.2q	3.57	1.5	1.5	5.9	18	19	07-09-86	.56	.9	15	16	16	07-09-86	1.2	5.42	6.5	3.43	22.3	91	1.1	1,196	19,143	8,726	0	0.4	01
Victory Markets	4.2	4.2	2.7	3.7q	1.32	17.6	17.6	38.9	37	13	06-16-86	.05	.26	9	2	9	06-16-86	.9	5.33	4.8	3.52	0	101	1.1	98	2,764	526	-2	0.0	01
Waldbaum Inc	2.4	2.4	2.6	16.7q	2.93	-12.2	-12.2	23.1	9	13	06-09-86	.05	.26	0	2	20	06-09-86	.9	5.56	5.0	2.60	13.0	76	1.2	166	5,729	676	0	0.0	12
Wies Markets	10.2	10.2	7.8	61.6q	2.00	10.9	10.9	10.5	12	12	04-28-86	.54	1.4	12	20	20	04-28-86	5.9	2.44	14.4	1.17	16.8	0	5.3	1,211	30,755	13,473	+0	0.0	12
Winn-Dixie A	5.2	6.3	6.4	112.9n	2.76	6.3	6.3	2.6	4	6	06-05-86	1.74	3.5	3	50	37	06-05-86	1.4	6.50	9.1	1.92	17.5	15	1.6	2,025	40,915	4,500	+0	2.1	06

Department Stores

Company	Rev. Last Qtr %	Rev. FY to Date %	Rev. Last 12 Mos %	Rev. Last 12 Mos $Mil	EPS Last 12 Mos $	EPS Chg Last Qtr %	EPS Chg FY to Date %	EPS Chg Last 12 Mos %	EPS 5-Year Growth Rate %	Par Growth Rate %	Date of Report	Div. Current Amt $	Div. Yield %	Div. 5-Year Growth Rate %	Payout Last FY %	Payout Last 5 Yrs %	Last X-Div Date	Profit Margin %	Asset Turn over	Return on Total Assets	Lever age Ratio	Return on Equity	Debt to Eq uity %	Curr ent Ratio	Mar ket Value $Mil	Latest Shares Out strdng 000	Held by Banks Funds 000	Insider Net Trad ing 000	Short Int erest Ratio Days	Fiscal Year Ends Mo
																		s/r x r/a	= r/a	x a/e	= s/e									
Ind. Group	-2.1	1.3	3.8	3,450.4	3.65	8.9	9.0	-2.8	9	7	---	1.55	2.7	1	40	39	---	3.2	1.00	3.2	3.72	11.9	125	2.1	54,433	940,254	496,477	+354	1.7	--
Alexander's Inc ○	5.2	.5	.1	2.6n	.58	NE	-56.4	-48.2	NC	4	04-86	.00	0	0	0	4	08-20-80	.5	3.00	1.5	2.40	3.6	87	2.2	173	4,519	1,269	-40	1.3	07
Allied Stores	7.6	7.6	4.8	162.8q	.74	9.8	9.8	9.4	14	9	04-86	1.16	2.2	4	28	33	04-02-86	3.9	1.51	5.9	2.19	12.9	53	2.3	2,461	46,102	32,974	+30	4.4	01
Ames Dept St	103.2	103.2	100.7	41.5q	1.19	0	0	15.5	25	10	04-86	.10	.3	14	8	11	08-18-86	2.5	2.44	6.1	1.85	11.3	39	2.7	1,163	34,656	22,438	-63	0.3	01
Assoc Dry Gds	4.9	4.9	4.9	115.7q	2.90	-41.7	-41.7	-7.9	10	6	04-86	1.40	2.1	12	45	41	05-05-86	2.6	1.96	5.1	2.31	11.8	43	1.7	2,290	34,957	25,552	0	0.2	01
Carson Pirie	9.6	9.6	6.9	15.0q	1.53	-100.0	-100.0	-41.6	16	4	04-86	.70	2.0	0	32	36	08-25-86	1.1	2.27	2.5	2.84	7.1	67	1.6	353	10,081	6,074	+18	1.4	01
Carter Hawley	1.8	1.8	4.2	51.0q	1.06	66.7	66.7	NE	NC	-2	04-86	1.22	3.3	1	133	103	05-12-86	1.3	1.77	2.3	6.17	14.2	194	1.6	715	19,469	6,338	-555	2.4	01
Crowley Milner	4.5	4.5	9.3	1.3q	2.61	-100.0	-100.0	-45.6	11	11	04-86	1.00	2.7	15	35	25	04-09-86	1.2	2.00	2.4	2.67	6.4	90	1.9	19	509	74	0	0.0	01
Dayton Hudson	10.3	10.3	9.3	288.7q	2.98	17.6	17.6	9.2	15	11	04-86	.84	1.5	10	26	26	05-14-86	3.2	2.03	6.5	2.28	14.8	47	1.8	5,413	97,101	58,378	0	1.7	01
Dillard Dept	14.4	14.4	20.0	68.5q	2.33	11.4	11.4	20.1	39	18	04-86	.12	.3	16	4	5	06-24-86	4.2	1.90	8.0	2.36	18.9	55	1.6	1,333	31,824	10,612	+1	0.4	01
Elder Beerman Str	12.3	12.3	13.1	8.0q	2.26	0	0	2.7	37	12	04-86	.22	.9b	5	8	12	05-23-86	4.2	1.64	3.6	3.67	13.2	82	1.5	89	3,541	202	+1030	0.0	01
Federated Dep Str	-99.9	-99.9	-20.6	243.2q	5.96	9.0	9.0	-13.9	6	5	04-86	2.68	3.0	7	43	37	04-04-86	3.1	1.45	4.5	2.00	9.0	29	2.0	4,338	48,815	31,994	-0	1.1	01
Holmes, D.H.	-4.6	-4.6	-3.5	2.4q	.68	-100.0	-100.0	-68.5	-10	-2	04-86	1.00	3.6	5	100	46	06-09-86	.9	1.56	1.4	2.43	3.4	77	1.7	93	3,398	538	0	0.0	01
INTERCO Inc ◇	-1.7	-1.7	-2.6	95.5q	6.04	28.2	28.2	51.4	-5	4	05-86	3.08	3.3	3	53	49	06-13-86	3.8	1.61	6.1	1.49	9.1	18	4.7	1,350	14,300	9,835	+0	11.6	02
Macy, R.H. ◇	5.3	5.3	5.0	211.1n	4.28	18.4	18.4	4.9	16	6	04-86	1.16	1.7	19	30	23	03-06-86	3.0	1.92	9.4	1.80	16.9	14	1.4	3,501	51,484	27,338	0	1.6	07
May Dept Strs ◇	8.7	8.7	5.8	242.4q	5.54	21.1	21.1	8.8	16	8	04-86	2.80	3.4	12	34	34	05-23-86	4.7	1.49	7.0	2.44	17.1	45	2.1	3,562	42,984	21,977	0	1.8	01
Mercantile Strs	8.7	8.7	9.7	106.4q	7.22	22.7	22.7	20.9	17	12	04-86	1.50	1.3	14	18	19	08-25-86	5.6	1.64	9.2	1.71	15.7	31	3.5	1,711	14,738	4,679	0	2.4	01
Nordstrom	33.4	33.4	33.7	52.2q	1.36	25.0	25.0	18.3	16	6	04-86	.52	1.3	20	17	16	06-17-86	3.8	2.29	8.7	2.21	19.2	56	1.5	1,537	37,252	15,690	0	0.0	01
Penney, JC	8.7	8.7	3.6	434.0q	5.80	73.1	73.1	4.3	15	4	04-86	2.48	2.9	6	44	38	04-04-86	3.1	1.32	4.1	2.61	10.7	76	2.6	6,350	74,484	42,227	-66	1.3	01
Sears, Roebuck	7.1	7.1	4.6	1275.3q	3.45	-13.3	-13.3	-14.0	15	5	03-86	1.76	3.6	6	50	49	05-30-86	3.1	.61	1.9	5.79	11.0	236	NA	17,635	363,605	175,541	0	1.4	12
Strawbrid & Cloth •	9.2	9.2	8.3	22.8q	3.18	-37.5	-37.5	-2.5	21	11	04-86	.79	1.4b	15	19	18	05-28-86	3.3	1.52	5.0	3.00	15.0	110	2.4	346	6,235	2,797	-1	0.0	01

Discount and Variety Stores

Company	Rev %Chg Last Qtr	Rev %Chg FY to Date	Rev %Chg Last 12 Mos	Earn Last 12 Mos $Mil	EPS Last 12 Mos $	EPS %Chg Last Qtr	EPS %Chg FY to Date	EPS %Chg Last 12 Mos	EPS 5-Yr Growth %	Par Growth %	Date of Report	Div Amt $	Div Yield %	Div 5-Yr Growth %	Payout Last FY %	Payout Last 5 Yrs %	Last X-Dvd Date	Profit Margin %	Asset Turnover	Return on Total Assets %	Leverage Ratio	Return on Equity %	Debt to Equity %	Current Ratio	Market Value $Mil	Shares Out 000	Held by Banks-Funds 000	Insider Net Trading 000	Short Int Ratio Days	Fiscal Yr Ends Mo
Ind. Group	16.1	18.7	14.4	1,124.6	1.32	24.5	26.6	-.2	26	10	---	.36	.9	1	24	25	---	2.0	2.50	5.0	2.70	13.5	68	1.7	39,959	968,874	453,171	+2054	1.1	--
Best Products	.9	.9	-1.6	-1.4	-.06	NE	NE	-100.0	NC	-2	04-86	.24	1.7	NA	300	22	05-23-86	-.1	1.00	-.1	3.00	-.3	89	1.6	374	26,949	17,667	0	.1	01
Consol Store	NA	NA	.0	NA	NA	NE	NE	NA	NA	NC	00-00	.00	.0	0	0	NA	06-17-86	NA	NC	NA	3.00	NA	NA	NA	833	40,800	11,714	0	NA	
Cook Utd	-9.4	-18.6	-18.3	-30.8	-4.53	NE	NE	NE	NC	-9	01-86	.00	.0	0	0	NE	04-20-82	-12.6	2.57	-32.4	.00	NS	-48	1.7	8	6,815	517	0	4.3	01
Costco Wholesale	99.5	114.1	268.7	-2.3	-.20	-100.0	-100.0	NC	NC	10	02-86	.00	.0	0	0	0	00-00-00	-.4	6.00	-2.4	3.88	-9.3	98	1.4	363	21,489	2,435	0	0.0	08
Dollar General Cp	-5.9	-5.9	14.0	14.8	.79	NE	NE	-30.1	25	90	03-86	.20	.9	26	17	18	05-02-86	2.6	2.50	6.5	2.11	13.7	60	3.8	397	18,796	3,155	0	0.0	12
Family Dollar	19.5	18.4	16.8	29.1	1.02	6.9	8.2	12.1	28	19	02-86	.24	1.0	22	17	17	06-09-86	6.5	2.52	16.4	1.54	25.2	0	2.2	730	28,899	10,797	0	3.2	08
Hecks Inc	25.9	25.9	16.8	-7.6	-.86	NE	NE	NE	NC	-9	03-86	.04	.3	7	NE	181	05-05-86	-1.4	1.79	-2.5	3.36	-8.4	93	1.7	114	8,871	4,302	0	0.9	12
Home Shop	NA	NA	737.5	NA	NA	NA	NA	NA	NA	NC	02-86	.00	.0	NA	NA	NA	00-00-00	NA	NA	NA	NC	NA	NA	NA	1,167	12,231	0	0	NA	12
Jamesway Corp	14.5	14.5	9.1	9.2	1.29	-14.3	-14.3	-41.4	17	9	04-86	.12	.4	17	9	6	06-27-86	1.7	3.06	5.2	2.00	10.4	42	2.6	197	6,873	2,490	0	0.4	01
K mart Cp	4.6	4.6	3.3	254.3	1.97	52.2	52.2	-48.8	4	2	04-86	1.48	2.6	8	79	42	05-16-86	1.1	2.27	2.7	3.12	7.8	97	1.8	7,155	125,801	89,599	0	1.9	01
Marcade Grp	-5.6	5.7	3.2	-6.2	-.67	-50.0	100.0	NE	NC	0	04-86	.00	.0	0	0	0	00-00-00	-9.1	2.53	-23.0	.00	NS	-3	.6	10	9,274	1,100	0	0.0	12
Nichols, SE	5.7	5.7	3.2	4.1	.87	6.7	-50.0	-37.4	NC	8	04-86	.00	.0	0	0	0	12-31-30	1.3	2.54	3.3	2.48	8.2	91	3.4	51	4,665	782	0	2.9	01
Pic 'n Save	13.2	13.2	21.8	41.6	1.05	9.1	6.7	23.5	25	37	03-86	.00	.0	0	0	0	06-11-86	14.6	1.99	29.0	1.28	37.0	1	3.0	1,164	39,472	23,357	+29	0.0	12
Price Co	35.7	43.8	45.8	45.8	1.22	96.9	27.4	34.1	95	55	05-86	.00	.0	0	0	0	02-04-86	2.3	9.09	20.9	2.63	55.0	76	2.0	2,106	45,775	23,020	-5	0.0	08
Rose's Stores	20.2	20.2	10.5	23.5	2.29	NE	96.9	0	27	12	04-86	.38	.9	22	24	17	03-14-86	2.2	3.41	7.5	1.95	14.6	24	2.1	457	10,265	866	+87	0.0	01
Svc Merchandise	31.7	31.7	51.5	-14.6	-.44	60.0	NE	-100.0	NC	-5	03-86	.08	.7	3	25	7	05-19-86	-.6	1.67	-1.0	4.40	-4.4	150	1.3	408	33,315	17,506	0	0.0	12
Three D Depts	-70.5	-17.3	-8.7	1.2	.36	-11.1	60.0	3.4	27	16	04-86	.06	1.5	-5	22	13	04-15-86	2.3	2.00	4.6	1.87	8.6	29	2.8	7	1,595	208	+2	0.5	07
Toys R Us	13.0	13.0	13.3	117.9	.92	36.8	3.4	24.2	38	31	04-86	.00	.0	0	0	0	01-09-85	5.8	1.66	9.6	1.71	16.4	12	1.5	4,173	122,736	67,856	+1877	3.3	01
Wal-Mart Strs	41.6	41.6	33.9	349.2	1.23	36.8	36.8	24.2	NC	12	04-86	.17	.3	37	12	11	06-16-86	3.8	4.16	15.8	2.25	35.5	50	1.9	14,566	280,781	107,060	+91	2.0	01
Woolworth FW	9.8	9.8	5.4	184.0	5.61	122.2	122.2	147.1	28	13	04-86	1.12	2.3	2	18	91	06-02-86	4.0	2.43	7.3	2.07	15.1	29	1.8	3,068	63,916	35,852	-29	2.6	01
Zayre Corp	32.2	32.2	30.3	96.1	1.63	3.7	3.8	3.8	39	13	04-86	.32	.7	39	14	10	08-01-86	2.2	2.77	6.1	2.61	15.9	52	1.7	2,553	59,556	32,888	+2-	0.8	01

Recent Performance and Forecast: Textile Mill Products (SIC 22)
(in millions of dollars except as noted)

	1982	1983	1984[1]	1985[2]	Percent Change		
					1982-83	1983-84	1984-85
Industry Data							
Value of shipments[3]	47,585	53,358	56,293	57,982	12.1	5.5	3.0
Value of shipments (1982$)	47,585	52,709	54,128	54,907	10.8	2.7	1.4
Total employment (000)	718	723	737	707	0.8	1.8	-4.0
Production workers (000)	616	624	638	619	1.3	2.2	-3.0
Average hourly earnings ($)	5.99	6.32	6.57	6.81	5.6	3.9	3.7
Product Data							
Value of shipments[4]	44,916	50,297	52,150	54,132	12.0	3.7	3.8
Value of shipments (1982$)	44,916	49,706	50,289	51,505	10.7	1.2	2.4
Shipments price index (1982=100)[5]	100.0	101.3	—	—	1.3	—	—
Trade Data							
Value of imports	2,225	2,557	3,539	3,847	14.9	38.4	8.7
Value of exports	1,766	1,560	1,541	1,521	-11.7	-1.2	-1.3

[1]Estimated except for exports and imports.
[2]Estimated.
[3]Value of all products and services sold by the Textile Mill Products industry.
[4]Value of products classified in the Textile Mill Products industry produced by all industries.
[5]Developed by the Office of Industry Assessment, ITA.
SOURCE: U.S. Department of Commerce: Bureau of the Census, Bureau of Economic Analysis, International Trade Administration (ITA). Estimates by ITA.

Source: *U.S. Industrial Outlook 1986*, U.S. Department of Commerce.

Textile Mills

Company	Revenue Pct Change Last Qtr %	FY to Date %	Last 12 Mos %	Last 12 Mos $Mil	Earnings Per Share Last 12 Mos $	Pct Change Last Qtr %	FY to Date %	Last 12 Mos %	5-Year Growth Rate %	Par Growth Rate %	Date of Report	Dividends Current Rate Amt $	Yield %	5-Year Growth Rate %	Payout Last FY %	Last 5 Yrs %	Last X-Dvd Date	Profit Margin v/t	Asset Turnover x r/a	Return on Total Assets x	Leverage Ratio x a/e =	Return on Equity v/e	Debt to Equity %	Current Ratio	Market Value $Mil	Latest Shares Outstanding 000	Held by Banks-Funds 000	Insider Net Trading 000	Short Interest Ratio Days	Fiscal Year Ends Mo
Ind. Group	16.4	17.9	9.2	532.2	.87	38.4	42.8	9.9	9	6	--	.36	2.2	1	40	38	--	3.0	1.60	4.8	2.04	9.8	42	2.4	10,081	621,030	114,432	-209	9	--
Adams-Mills	11.6	11.6	8.1	5.5n	2.37	23.1	23.1	-3.7	30	10	03-86	.40	1.2	12	15	16	05-12-86	4.6	1.61	7.4	1.62	12.0	23	3.7	74	2,277	1,244	+2	0.0	12
Aileen Inc	-15.2	-14.4	-3.8	.3n	.05	0	NE	NE	NC	--	04-86	.00	.0	0	0	0	00-00-00	.6	1.17	.7	1.43	1.0	7	2.8	26	5,076	488	0	0.3	10
Alba-Waldens	4.2	4.2	-10.6	-2.2n	-1.25	-100.0	-100.0	-100.0	NC	-10	03-86	.00	.0	0	0	32	09-07-84	-5.2	1.29	-6.7	1.48	-9.9	13	3.4	16	1,861	190	0	0.0	11
Avondale Mills	25.6	30.4	22.3	5.4n	1.33	NE	NE	NE	NC	6	05-86	.00	.0	8	NE	62	12-16-85	1.9	1.63	3.1	1.81	5.6	39	2.7	112	4,005	677	0	0.0	08
Belding Hemin	0	0	-7.3	4.3n	1.57	4.8	4.8	-1.3	22	7	03-86	.40	1.9	7	26	29	05-27-86	3.8	1.42	5.4	1.69	9.1	14	2.3	57	2,736	310	0	3.1	12
Burlington Inds	-4.2	.1	-4.1	31.3s	1.10	288.9	194.1	205.6	-26	-1	03-86	1.64	4.2	3	373	67	04-22-86	1.1	1.36	1.5	1.80	2.7	33	2.5	1,114	28,476	14,752	-69	0.7	09
Chatham Mfg	1.1	1.1	-.8	3.5s	1.99	80.0	80.0	-5.7	17	4	03-86	.80	2.6	5	49	41	03-04-86	2.9	1.76	5.1	1.29	6.6	9	5.5	52	1,682	488	0	0.0	12
Collins & Aikm	6.9	6.9	8.2	66.8q	3.07	1.2	1.2	7.0	40	14	05-86	.80	2.0	14	22	24	05-05-86	6.0	1.80	10.8	1.81	19.5	30	2.8	851	21,686	11,616	-7	0.4	02
Concord Fab	-4.0	-1.9	-10.6	.7s	.40	1166.7	112.5	-66.1	NC	3	02-86	.07	1.5	0	0	0	00-00-00	.6	3.00	3.0	1.67	3.0	13	2.9	32	1,783	92	0	0.0	08
Courtaulds Ltd	29.6	20.2	20.2	167.9l	.44	85.7	46.7	46.7	NC	22	03-86		1.5	7	16	35	11-29-85	5.2	1.87	9.7	2.69	26.1	51	1.7	1,778	379,300	1,264	0	0.8	03
Crown Crafts	25.0	24.4	23.5	.6l	.89	NE	NE	NE	NC	8	03-86	.00	.0	0	0	0	05-08-80	1.4	2.07	2.9	2.79	8.1	89	2.3	11	712	2	0	1.2	03
Damon Creat	-14.5	-14.5	-6.5	-2.6q	-2.33	-100.0	-100.0	-100.0	NC	-23	03-86	.00	.0	9	0	0	00-00-00	-6.0	1.70	-10.2	2.22	-22.6	15	1.8	6	1,100	0	0	0.0	12
Fab Indus	10.4	10.4	-4.3	9.2q	2.54	28.8	28.8	-4.9	10	6	02-86	.50	1.5	9	17	15	12-04-85	8.4	1.02	8.6	1.51	13.0	2	4.1	122	3,632	1,213	-36	0.0	11
Fieldcrest Mill	70.6	70.6	19.1	6.8q	1.73	-100.0	-100.0	458.1	NC	2	03-86	1.00	1.2	-6	37	72	06-10-86	1.0	1.80	1.8	2.11	3.8	47	2.7	332	3,901	773	-87	0.0	12
Guilford Mills	21.8	19.7	14.7	16.5n	2.10	23.3	-6.8	-19.2	-2	7	03-86	.68	1.9	18	33	20	05-02-86	4.1	1.78	7.3	1.49	10.9	8	2.9	284	7,864	3,789	0	0.5	06
Ruddick Corp	-1.3	-3.2	-2.4	12.0s	2.47	8.0	-11.4	-10.2	NC	7	03-86	.85	2.5	9	28	28	06-09-86	1.4	3.57	5.0	2.22	11.1	41	1.6	165	4,804	432	0	1.0	10
Russell Cp	21.0	21.0	13.8	34.4q	1.72	92.3	92.3	22.9	6	13	03-86	.32	.8	9	20	21	04-29-86	8.6	1.24	10.7	1.47	15.7	19	5.3	759	19,779	5,860	+9	0.7	12
Springs Indus	79.4	79.4	27.5	14.8q	1.66	47.2	47.2	-53.5	-15	-27	03-86	1.52	2.8	7	102	40	06-09-86	1.3	1.15	1.5	2.20	3.3	70	3.1	473	8,833	1,957	0	0.7	12
Stanwood Cp	21.5	21.5	7.9	.7q	.42	-57.7	-57.7	82.6	NC	3	04-86	.00	.0	0	0	0	00-00-00	.6	1.67	1.0	2.70	2.7	56	1.9	21	1,533	176	0	3.5	12
Stevens JP	1.5	1.8	-9.2	-2.7s	-.16	182.5	182.5	-100.0	NC	4	04-86	1.20	3.3	0	NE	140	06-30-86	-.2	1.00	-.2	2.50	-.5	46	2.3	625	17,433	10,564	0	3.9	10
Texfi Ind	-16.1	-16.1	-6.2	-.9q	.10	-50.0	-50.0	NE	NC	-15	01-86	.00	.0	0	0	0	00-00-00	-.9	2.44	-2.2	6.82	-15.0	352	1.6	16	3,687	290	-32	0.0	10
Unifi Inc	12.3	6.7	3.5	12.0n	1.25	26.3	200.0	12.6	10	10	03-86	.00	.0	0	0	0	02-24-86	5.3	2.00	10.6	1.58	16.8	22	3.3	145	9,323	4,949	-5	0.0	06
Utd Mer Mfrs	-15.6	2.1	3.5	-39.5n	-4.39	-100.0	-100.0	-100.0	NC	-27	03-86	.00	.0	0	0	0	00-00-00	-4.9	1.10	-5.4	4.94	-26.7	248	2.5	166	8,839	5,451	-2	1.6	08
Vertipile Inc	-10.0	13.4	13.4	.9l	.55	NE	NE	NE	NC	9	03-86	.00	.0	0	0	0	10-30-84	.8	2.63	2.1	4.24	8.9	205	2.3	6	1,664	123	0	0.0	02
V.F. Corp	5.1	5.1	24.2	141.3q	2.28	7.9	7.9	18.8	28	9	03-86	.64	2.0	22	26	26	06-04-86	9.4	1.74	16.4	1.55	25.5	22	3.0	1,982	62,194	41,748	+5	0.4	12
West Point-P	59.4	41.5	29.8	.44.8n	3.75	-37.0	53.5	28.4	-5	4	05-86	2.20	3.9	9	80	45	04-18-86	2.8	2.04	5.7	1.70	9.7	20	2.4	840	14,738	5,705	+12	5.0	08
Wright Wm Co	-7.1	-4.5	-5.6	.4n	.15	NE	-100.0	-82.4	-23	-2	03-86	.38	3.0	9	55	30	06-09-86	.8	1.38	1.1	1.27	1.4	1	4.6	26	2,112	279	0	0.0	06

Recent Performance and Forecast: Telephone and Telegraph Services (SIC 4811 & 4821)
(in millions of dollars except as noted)

	1982	1983	1984[1]	1985[1]	1986[2]	Percent Change			
						1982-83	1983-84	1984-85	1985-86
Operating revenues									
Domestic telephone & telegraph ..	78,886	86,870	95,700	103,000	110,000	10.10	10.20	7.6	6.8
Int'l. telephone & telegraph	2,325	2,500	2,800	3,200	3,600	7.5	12.0	14.3	12.5
Operating Revenues (1982$)									
Domestic telephone & telegraph ..	78,886	83,288	88,858	93,297	96,407	5.6	6.8	4.9	3.3
Capital expenditures	22,525	21,125	21,400	24,300	25,000	-6.2	1.3	13.6	2.9
Gross cumulative plant investment[3]	202,350	216,925	231,690	244,497	258,000	7.2	6.8	5.5	5.5
Total employment (000)[4]	1,100	984	982	950	935	-10.5	-0.2	-3.3	-1.6
Production workers (000)[4]	790	720	731	707	690	-8.9	1.5	-3.3	-2.4
Average hourly earnings ($)	10.65	11.90	12.43	12.78	13.16	11.7	4.5	2.8	3.0
No. of telephones (000)	183,530	189,000	198,000	205,000	212,000	3.0	4.8	3.5	3.4
Industry price index (domestic)[5]	100.0	104.3	107.7	110.4	114.1	4.3	3.3	2.5	3.4

[1]Estimated. Includes independents, RBOC's, AT&T, Southern New England and Cincinnati telephone companies, Western Union Telegraph and IRC's.
[2]Forecast.
[3]Does not include domestic or international telegraph carriers.
[4]Includes both telephone and telegraph workers.
[5]Price indexes for international services have declined slightly since 1972.
SOURCE: U.S. Department of Commerce: Bureau of the Census; Bureau of Labor Statistics. Estimates and forecast by International Trade Administration.

Source: U.S. Industrial Outlook 1986, U.S. Department of Commerce.

Broadcasting

Company	Rev Last Qtr %	Rev FY to Date %	Rev Last 12 Mos %	Rev Last 12 Mos $Mil	EPS Last 12 Mos $	EPS Last Qtr %	EPS FY to Date %	EPS Last 12 Mos %	EPS 5-Year Growth %	Par Rate %	Date of Report	Div Amt $	Div Yield %	Div 5-Year Growth %	Payout Last FY %	Payout Last 5 Yrs %	Last X-Dvd Date	Profit Margin	Asset Turnover	Return on Total Assets	Leverage Ratio	Return on Equity	Debt to Eq %	Curr Ratio	Market Value $Mil	Latest Shares Outstndng 000	Held by Banks-Funds 000	Insider Net Trading 000	Short Int Ratio Days	Fiscal Year Ends Mo
																		r/t x r/a = r/a			x a/e = r/e									
Ind. Group	48.2	71.3	17.3	350.4	1.09	-100.0	-61.6	-24.8	-1	7	---	.33	.6	0	25	22	---	3.6	.69	2.5	3.84	9.6	131	1.6	19,223	350,412	135,107	+172	2.9	---
Acton Cp	8.1	14.9	-5.5	-10.8n	-1.86	NE	NE	NE	NC	0	09-85	.00	.0	0	0	NE	07-11-83	-63.5	.32	-20.1	.00	NS	-784	.2	13	5,884	945	0	0.1	12
Cap Cities/ABC	289.7	289.7	75.6	116.5q	8.86	-94.4	-94.4	-15.3	14	13	03-86	.20	.1	2	2	NE	06-24-86	6.9	.90	6.2	2.11	13.1	80	5.7	4,103	15,998	8,703	-4	5.8	12
CBS Inc	10.9	10.9	.1	26.9q	.81	.0	.0	-86.1	-29	-15	03-86	3.00	2.1	1	370	54	05-21-86	.6	1.33	.8	7.00	5.6	198	1.2	3,388	23,449	12,866	+96	2.5	12
Chris-Craft	1428.4	17.4	.0	0	2.53	NE	NE	NE	NC	-1	03-86	.00	.0	0	0	0	04-02-86	NC	NC	NC	NC	.0	632	1.3	469	6,398	2,953	+3	5.8	12
Comcast Cp	11.6	11.6	13.0	16.2q	.75	35.7	35.7	11.9	23	12	03-86	.12	.4	22	14	12	08-29-86	13.4	.34	4.5	3.13	14.1	170	7.1	594	21,298	8,683	0	.0	12
Heft Comm	9.9	9.9	17.5	7.4q	.43	-62.5	-62.5	-10.4	18	6	06-86	.04	.1	0	8	2	06-25-86	4.6	.46	2.1	3.14	6.6	130	1.2	471	17,379	7,086	+52	1.0	12
Jones Intercable	29.4	31.3	23.0	3.5n	.41	257.1	94.4	20.6	29	17	02-86	.00	.0	0	0	0	04-01-85	21.9	.24	5.3	3.19	16.9	176	NA	148	9,930	293	+20	.0	05
Lin Broadcasting	29.7	29.7	16.6	34.7q	1.31	-37.5	-37.5	-2.2	14	11	03-86	.00	.0	0	0	0	06-27-83	19.1	.48	9.1	1.21	11.0	0	3.3	1,301	26,409	19,157	+10	.0	12
Malrite Commun	21.7	21.7	33.8	4.3q	.22	-100.0	-100.0	-68.6	21	10	03-86	.00	.0	0	0	0	00-00-00	4.9	.53	2.6	3.73	9.7	155	1.6	190	12,655	779	0	.0	12
Park Commun	27.7	27.7	11.1	14.5q	1.05	-26.3	-26.3	1.0	16	12	03-86	.00	.0	0	0	0	09-03-85	12.1	.69	8.4	1.48	12.4	22	2.4	400	13,800	1,163	0	.0	12
Price Comm	359.5	205.1	200.0	-12.3l	-2.01	NE	NE	NE	NC	9	12-85	.00	.0	0	0	0	02-19-86	-29.3	.12	-3.6	.00	NM	3231	2.8	93	7,901	3,289	+0	6.6	12
Rollins Commun	13.4	13.1	14.5	13.2h	.90	14.0	14.0	25.0	3	9	03-86	.42	1.1	0	49	10	05-05-86	12.0	.96	11.5	1.55	17.8	5	.9	573	14,610	5,472	+0	.1	06
Scripps Howard	55.8	55.8	23.9	28.4q	2.75	-100.0	-100.0	61.8	10	15	03-86	.80	1.0	0	27	40	05-20-86	18.9	.60	11.4	1.89	21.5	21	1.3	806	10,328	475	0	.0	12
Taft Brdcast	64.6	26.0	26.1	19.4f	2.11	-59.6	-59.6	-59.6	-1	3	03-86	1.16	1.1	7	55	28	05-09-86	4.1	1.3	7.3	4.46	5.8	265	1.4	974	9,060	4,223	+42	.2	03
TCA Cable TV	13.2	13.5	30.5	6.1s	.56	-13.3	-13.3	-9.7	23	20	04-86	.16	.7	0	22	19	04-25-86	13.0	.56	7.3	3.78	27.6	202	NA	235	10,795	2,011	-50	.0	10
Tele Commun A	8.0	8.0	15.4	12.1q	.26	400.0	400.0	136.4	10	5	03-86	.00	.0	0	0	0	07-18-83	2.1	.38	.8	6.50	5.2	761	NA	2,631	48,050	27,407	0	.0	12
Turner Brdcst	28.5	28.5	26.1	11.1q	.50	NE	NE	4.2	NC	37	03-86	.00	.0	0	0	0	07-13-81	3.0	1.03	3.1	12.06	37.4	779	1.5	490	21,789	1,237	+3	1.4	12
Utd Cable TV	18.8	15.5	16.0	11.5n	.40	-41.7	-4.0	233.3	26	31	02-86	.08	.3	0	15	0	06-25-86	6.2	.52	3.2	10.25	32.8	160	NA	714	23,228	9,648	+3	33.6	05
Utd Television	-1.9	2.5	2.6	12.6f	1.14	NE	NE	NE	NC	4	12-85	.00	.0	0	0	0	00-00-00	16.4	.47	7.7	4.06	31.3	160	1.1	375	10,953	2,335	0	.0	12
Viacom Intl Ind	159.0	159.0	74.7	35.0q	1.03	-54.5	-54.5	-10.4	7	4	03-86	.28	.9	20	20	16	05-27-86	6.1	.36	2.2	2.64	5.8	95	1.4	1,235	40,498	16,382	0	1.2	12

Telephone Utility

Company	Revenue Pct Change Last Qtr	Rev Pct Chg FY to Date	Rev Pct Chg Last 12 Mos	Rev Last 12 Mos $Mil	Earn Per Share Last 12 Mos	Earn Per Share Last Qtr	Earn Pct Chg FY to Date	Earn Pct Chg Last 12 Mos	Earn 5-Yr Growth Rate	Par Growth Rate	Date of Report	Div Current Rate Amt	Div Yield	Div 5-Yr Growth Rate	Payout Last FY	Payout Last 5 Yrs	Last X-Dvd Date	Profit Margin	Return on Total Assets	Asset Turnover	Leverage Ratio	Return on Equity	Debt to Equity	Current Ratio	Mkt Value $Mil	Latest Shares Outstndg	Held by Banks-Funds	Insider Net Trading	Short Int Ratio	Fiscal Year Ends Mo
Ind. Group	7.8	8.2	9.3	11,113.4	2.60	-.4	-.3	-23.5	38	1	---	2.33	5.3	0	83	68	---	7.8	4.4	.56	3.00	13.2	81	1.1	167,193	3,766,785	946,692	-515	1.4	--
ADC Telecomm	13.9	17.0	22.7	10.3s	1.19	36.0	68.3	63.1	14	21	04-86	.00	.0	0	0	0	04-28-86	7.6	13.3	1.75	1.61	21.4	22	3.1	170	8,598	2,625	+3	0.0	10
ALLTEL Cp	7.0	7.0	5.5	73.2q	3.39	11.5	11.5	8.7	14	8	03-86	1.96	5.3	3	56	61	05-23-86	10.7	4.3	.43	3.37	15.5	139	1.0	763	20,757	3,089	-2	0.4	12
Am Tel & T	4.9	4.9	5.9	1732.8q	1.53	51.6	51.6	8.7	NC	3	03-86	1.20	4.7	0	88	92	06-24-86	4.9	4.3	.88	2.74	11.8	53	1.5	27,134	1,069,330	175,706	0	0.2	12
Ameritech Cp	3.5	3.5	6.6	1088.1q	11.15	4.6	4.6	12.5	NC	5	03-86	7.08	5.2	0	59	52	03-24-86	12.1	6.0	.50	2.43	14.6	61	.9	13,301	97,352	32,257	+1	2.9	12
Bell Atlantic	11.3	11.3	12.9	1127.5q	5.64	13.3	13.3	12.1	NC	5	03-86	3.60	5.2	0	61	55	04-18-86	12.0	5.7	.47	2.9	14.2	62	.9	13,886	199,800	64,704	+6	1.9	12
Bell Canada	6.7	6.7	20.0	1035.5q	4.12	-10.6	-10.6	-1.7	13	6	09-06-86	2.36	NA	5	54	52	09-06-86	7.7	5.0	.65	2.84	14.2	77	1.3	6,908	248,940	6,627	+2	12.6	12
BellSouth	29.6	29.6	14.8	1506.9q	4.96	24.5	24.5	11.5	NC	6	03-86	3.04	4.8	5	59	52	04-04-86	15.3	6.0	.39	2.47	14.8	63	1.0	19,019	303,099	73,175	+1	3.3	12
CTEC Cp	6.9	6.9	3.6	16.6q	2.34	62.3	62.3	30.7	18	9	03-86	.92	4.3	6	40	46	05-20-86	9.4	4.1	.43	3.76	15.4	142	1.4	57	2,670	336	0	0.0	12
Centel Cp	-2.4	-2.4	-4.1	128.3q	4.59	-1.8	-1.8	2.0	5	7	03-86	2.44	4.1	3	52	54	09-01-86	9.7	5.1	.53	2.98	15.2	91	1.1	1,646	27,670	11,450	+6	0.6	12
Century Tel	-21.0	-21.0	-21.0	16.1q	1.50	9.1	9.1	7.9	1	7	03-86	.84	5.2	2	54	58	05-23-86	8.7	3.7	.43	4.03	14.9	192	1.1	173	10,713	1,941	-11	0.5	12
Cinn Bell	9.0	9.0	5.7	52.4q	3.17	7.1	7.1	6.4	5	5	03-86	1.89	4.8	4	50	56	05-22-86	11.9	5.6	.53	2.38	13.3	53	1.1	638	16,192	4,574	+0	0.0	12
Contel Cp	20.4	20.4	15.4	246.6q	3.27	10.3	10.3	24.8	8	7	03-86	1.88	6.2	5	55	64	05-09-86	9.2	4.9	.53	3.57	17.5	125	.9	2,265	75,188	30,888	+0	3.9	12
Graphic Scanning	-20.2	-1.8	5.6	-22.6q	-.60	NE	NE	-100.0	NC	-49	03-86	.00	.0	0	0	0	11-01-83	-15.2	-10.9	.72	4.49	-48.9	239	1.3	357	37,100	5,079	-340	0.0	06
GTE Cp	8.3	8.3	8.7	-151.5q	-.95	-50.0	-50.0	-100.0	NC	-10	03-86	3.16	5.8	3	NE	79	05-16-86	-.9	-.6	.67	3.67	-2.2	121	.8	11,466	211,840	103,216	+6	1.3	12
Inter Tel	566.7	566.7	32.3	-.8q	-.11	-50.0	-50.0	NE	NC	-5	02-86	.00	.0	0	0	0	08-17-81	-1.8	-2.8	1.56	1.89	-5.3	41	2.6	10	8,545	102	0	0.0	11
Lincoln Telecom	2.2	2.2	.6	15.0q	3.47	-3.4	-3.4	-11.5	2	9	03-86	2.20	5.1	11	63	55	03-24-86	10.3	5.3	.51	2.43	12.9	67	1.4	180	4,149	844	+2	0.0	12
MCI Communicatn	43.6	43.6	35.8	119.0q	.50	52.9	52.9	28.2	25	9	03-86	.00	.0	0	0	0	08-22-83	4.3	2.6	.60	3.46	9.0	129	1.0	2,430	234,253	90,367	-221	0.0	12
Millicom Inc	100.0	100.0	.0	-1.44q	-.16	-100.0	-100.0	NA	NA	-78	03-86	.00	NE	0	0	0	00:00:00	NM	-.6	NA	NC	NC	456	.4	55	8,237	758	0	NA	12
NYNEX Cp	NA	NA	7.3	NA	NA	NA	NA	NA	NA	NC	03-86	3.48	5.2	NA	0	0	05-01-86	NM	NA	NA	NC	NA	100	NA	27,292	404,332	70,624	+2	NA	12
Pac Telecom	13.4	13.4	7.3	35.0q	.92	43.8	43.8	43.8	-7	NC	03-86	.80	5.7	15	87	52	05-12-86	7.4	3.9	.39	2.33	8.5	100	.9	541	38,313	1,519	0	0.0	12
Pac Telesis	8.1	8.1	8.0	973.5q	4.70	14.3	14.3	8.5	NC	5	03-86	3.04	5.4	0	62	55	06-10-86	11.3	5.0	.44	2.68	13.4	79	1.0	12,050	214,706	89,024	0	0.0	12
Philcp LD Tel	10.5	10.5	17.0	22.9s	1.05	61.9	61.9	-12.5	-12	22	06-85	.25	3.9	-11	30	42	03-10-86	10.1	2.7	.27	10.85	29.3	763	1.4	110	17,206	1,872	+0	0.2	12
Rochester Tele	12.6	12.6	11.7	40.0q	3.80	-11.8	-11.8	-1.8	5	5	03-86	2.56	5.3	8	71	61	07-09-86	9.6	7.1	.74	2.15	15.3	58	1.2	494	10,207	2,332	+0	0.6	12
So N Eng Tel	3.7	3.7	3.7	124.1q	3.94	13.7	13.7	.8	5	5	03-86	2.90	5.5	9	65	65	06-17-86	9.4	5.1	.54	2.57	13.1	61	1.1	1,552	30,205	5,928	+6	NA	12
Swtrn Bell	0	0	7.0	957.1q	9.60	-15.0	-15.0	-15.0	NC	4	03-86	6.40	5.8	4	59	53	04-04-86	12.1	5.0	.41	2.58	12.9	68	.9	10,998	99,620	35,437	+6	4.5	12
Telecom Plus	24.9	24.9	50.5	-18.0q	-.64	-100.0	-100.0	-100.0	NC	-9	03-86	.00	.0	0	46	0	08-01-83	-7.1	-4.5	.63	2.00	-9.0	3	2.6	221	30,018	5,009	0	0.0	12
Telephone Data	23.0	23.0	22.5	8.9q	.91	-8.3	-8.3	16.7	NC	22	03-86	.46	2.5	14	47	39	03-86	7.1	2.6	.53	4.23	11.0	216	1.4	164	8,838	2,460	0	0.0	12
TIE Comm	-6.8	-6.8	-32.5	-73.8q	-2.05	NE	NE	NE	NC	-35	03-86	.00	.0	0	0	0	07-19-83	-23.4	-22.4	.96	1.56	-34.9	35	6.9	215	35,832	5,520	0	0.8	12
US West	7.1	7.1	6.8	908.1q	4.76	-7.8	-7.8	3.5	NC	4	03-86	3.04	5.5	0	58	51	05-29-86	11.4	5.3	.46	2.58	13.7	73	1.0	10,473	189,986	71,066	+6	0.0	12
Utd Telecom	-23.9	-23.9	3.3	4.3q	.01	-26.6	-26.6	-99.6	NC	-57	03-86	1.92	7.0	0	1067	86	06-06-86	1.1	1.00	1.00	3.00	.3	115	.2	2,614	95,916	47,365	+25	2.6	12
Univ Commun	49.0	49.0	18.4	4.9h	.68	-11.8	-11.8	-28.6	NC	14	04-86	.00	.0	0	0	0	01-03-83	6.4	6.5	1.02	2.11	13.7	56	2.8	101	7,174	178	0	0.1	07

Purchasing Power of the Dollar: 1940 to 1984

[1967 = $1.00. Producer prices prior to 1961, and consumer prices prior to 1964, exclude Alaska and Hawaii. For 1940 and 1945, producer prices based on all commodities index; subsequent years based on finished goods index. Obtained by dividing the average price index for the 1967 base period (100.0) by the price index for a given period and expressing the result in dollars and cents. Annual figures are based on average of monthly data]

YEAR	ANNUAL AVERAGE AS MEASURED BY—		YEAR	ANNUAL AVERAGE AS MEASURED BY—		YEAR	ANNUAL AVERAGE AS MEASURED BY—	
	Producer prices	Consumer prices		Producer prices	Consumer prices		Producer prices	Consumer prices
1940	$2.469	$2.381	1959	$1.075	$1.145	1972	$.853	$.799
1945	1.832	1.855	1960	1.067	1.127	1973	.782	.751
1948	1.252	1.387	1961	1.067	1.116	1974	.678	.677
1949	1.289	1.401	1962	1.064	1.104	1975	.612	.620
1950	1.266	1.387	1963	1.067	1.091	1976	.586	.587
1951	1.156	1.285	1964	1.063	1.076	1977	.550	.551
1952	1.163	1.258	1965	1.045	1.058	1978	.510	.512
1953	1.175	1.248	1966	1.012	1.029	1979	.459	.460
1954	1.172	1.142	1967	1.000	1.000	1980	.405	.405
1955	1.170	1.247	1968	.972	.960	1981	.371	.367
1956	1.138	1.229	1969	.938	.911	1982	.356	.346
1957	1.098	1.186	1970	.907	.860	1983	.351	.335
1958	1.073	1.155	1971	.880	.824	1984	.344	.321

Source: U.S. Bureau of Labor Statistics. Monthly data in U.S. Bureau of Economic Analysis, *Survey of Current Business.*

Source: *Statistical Abstracts of the United States, 1986,* U.S. Department of Commerce.

Financial Statement Ratios by Industry

Many quantitative indicators are used to assess the financial strength of an enterprise and the success of its operations. The simplest is to assemble related financial items, such as sales and profits, and express the relationship in the form of a ratio. Using these ratios, various aspects of corporate operations may be compared with the performance of other corporations or groups of corporations of similar size or in a similar industry.

The Quarterly Financial Report's (QFR) ratio formatted income statement and selected balance sheet ratios are expressed as a percent of net sales and total assets, respectively. The operating and financial characteristics of the respective industries and asset size groups are thus reduced to a common denominator to facilitate analysis.

The ratio tables include the following additional basic operating ratios:

1. *Annual rate of profit on stockholders' equity at end of the period.* This ratio is obtained by multiplying income for the quarter before or after domestic taxes [including branch income (loss) and equity in the earnings of non-consolidated subsidiaries net of foreign taxes] by four, to put it on an annual basis, and then dividing by stockholders' equity at the end of the quarter. It measures the rate of return which accrues to stockholders on their investment.

2. *Annual rate of profit on total assets.* This ratio is obtained by multiplying income, as defined in deriving the rate of profit on stockholders' equity, both before and after taxes, by four and then dividing by total assets at the end of the quarter. This ratio measures the productivity of assets in terms of producing income.

3. *Total current assets to total current liabilities.* This ratio is obtained by dividing total current assets by total current liabilities. It measures the ability to discharge current maturing obligations from existing current assets.

4. *Total cash, U.S. government and other securities to current liabilities.* This ratio is obtained by dividing total cash, U.S. government and other securities by total current liabilities. It measures the ability to discharge current liabilities from liquid assets.

5. *Total stockholders' equity to total debt.* This ratio is obtained by dividing total stockholders' equity by the total of short-term loans, current installments on long-term debt, and long-term debt due in more than one year. It indicates the extent of leverage financing used.

DESCRIPTION OF THE SAMPLE

The sample on which the QFR estimates for mining, wholesale and retail trade are based is a composite sample selected from two mutually exclusive sampling frames. Prior to the third quarter 1977, the sample drawn for manufacturing estimates was similarly based. The frame from which the major portion of the sample continues to be selected consists of the Internal Revenue Service file of those corporate entities which are required to file Form 1120 or 1120-S and which also have as their principal industrial activity manufacturing, mining, or wholesale or retail trade. The IRS file is sampled once each year. At the time the sample is selected, the file does not contain those corporate entities whose first income tax return has not been processed. In addition, several months elapse between the selection of this sample and its introduction into the QFR program. To keep the mining and wholesale and retail trade QFR sample as up to date as possible, a separate sample is drawn each calendar quarter from a frame comprising applications for a Federal Social Security Employer's Identification Number filed with the Social Security Administration (SSA) during the previous quarter by new corporations. In processing the composite list of sample companies, a screening technique is used to insure that corporations drawn from the SSA frame could not have been drawn from the IRS frame.

Stratification is used in the sample selection process. In sampling from the IRS frame, stratification by industry and size is employed. In sampling from the SSA frame, stratification is by division and size alone. The measures of size used in the IRS frame are total assets and gross receipts while the measure of size used in the SSA frame is number of employees. Beginning with the third quarter 1977, the strata comprised of manufacturing firms with assets of less than $250,000 and the strata which contained corporations in the SSA frame are estimated by multivariate techniques. The sampling fractions applied to the other various industry-size strata vary according to both industry and size. They range from approximately one out of 850 to one out of one. Nearly all corporations whose operations are within the scope of the QFR and which have total assets greater than $50 million are included in the sample. Corporations whose total assets are between $10 million and $50

Source: *Quarterly Financial Report*, Bureau of the Census. The exhibits in this section are from the same publication.

million and whose receipts exceed the estimated average value for a corporation with $25 million in assets in its industry are also in the sample. Thus, for the most part, corporations with assets over $25 million are permanent sample members with a one out of one sampling fraction.

In those industry-size strata for which the sampling fraction is less than one out of one, a replacement scheme is utilized which provides that one eighth of the sample is replaced each quarter. Corporations removed are those that have been in the reporting group longest (usually eight quarters). Therefore, samples of small corporations for adjacent quarters are seven-eighths identical; for quarters ending nine months apart they are five-eighths identical; etc.

Industry Contents

TABLE 1—INCOME STATEMENT
FOR CORPORATIONS INCLUDED IN ESIC MAJOR GROUPS 20 AND 21

	Food and Kindred Products[1]				
	1Q 1985	2Q 1985	3Q 1985	4Q 1985	1Q 1986
	(percent of net sales)				
INCOME STATEMENT IN RATIO FORMAT					
Net sales, receipts, and operating revenues	100.0	100.0	100.0	100.0	100.0
Less: Depreciation, depletion, and amortization of property, plant and equipment	2.4	2.3	2.6	2.4	2.6
Less: All other operating costs and expenses	91.9	91.0	90.8	90.8	91.5
Income (or loss) from operations	5.7	6.7	6.7	6.8	5.9
Non-operating income (expense)	0.0	-0.2	0.9	0.5	-0.2
Income (or loss) before income taxes	5.7	6.5	7.6	7.2	5.7
Less: Provision for current and deferred domestic income taxes	2.3	2.6	3.0	2.6	2.1
Income (or loss) after income taxes	3.4	3.9	4.6	4.6	3.6
	(percent)				
OPERATING RATIOS (see explanatory notes)					
Annual rate of profit on stockholders' equity at end of period:					
Before income taxes	21.31	24.95	27.15	26.32	20.44
After taxes	12.77	14.96	16.46	16.90	12.94
Annual rate of profit on total assets:					
Before income taxes	9.26	10.97	11.97	11.05	8.38
After taxes	5.55	6.58	7.26	7.09	5.30
BALANCE SHEET RATIOS (based on succeeding table)					
Total current assets to total current liabilities	1.46	1.47	1.51	1.51	1.55
Total cash, U.S. Government and other securities to total current liabilities	0.18	0.20	0.23	0.21	0.25
Total stockholders' equity to total debt	1.40	1.45	1.43	1.31	1.21

[1] During the first quarter of 1986, a considerable number of companies were reclassified by industry. To provide comparability, the four quarters of 1985 have been restated to reflect these reclassifications.
[2] 1985 Data are Revised.
[3] Tobacco industry data have been collapsed into food industry data. Major merger and acquisition activity resulted in the reclassification of a significant portion of gross receipts and assets from tobacco to food. The remainder, comprised of data from highly specialized tobacco manufacturers, is too small to be considered publishable as a separate industry category.

TABLE 2—BALANCE SHEET
FOR CORPORATIONS INCLUDED IN ESIC MAJOR GROUPS 20 AND 21

	Food and Kindred Products[1]				
	1Q 1985	2Q 1985	3Q 1985	4Q 1985	1Q 1986
	(percent of total assets)				
SELECTED BALANCE SHEET RATIOS					
Total cash, U.S. Government and other securities	4.8	5.2	5.8	5.1	6.2
Trade accounts and trade notes receivable	13.1	12.8	12.4	11.9	12.1
Inventories	19.1	17.9	16.8	17.1	16.7
Total current assets	39.7	38.7	38.1	37.2	37.9
Net property, plant and equipment	34.4	34.7	33.4	32.3	34.5
Short-term debt including installments on long-term debt	9.4	8.3	7.6	6.3	7.1
Total current liabilities	27.3	26.3	25.2	24.6	24.4
Long-term debt	21.8	22.1	23.2	25.9	26.8
Total liabilities	56.5	56.0	55.9	58.0	59.0
Stockholders' equity	43.5	44.0	44.1	42.0	41.0

[1] During the first quarter of 1986, a considerable number of companies were reclassified by industry. To provide comparability, the four quarters of 1985 have been restated to reflect these reclassifications.
[2] 1985 Data are Revised.
[3] Tobacco industry data have been collapsed into food industry data. Major merger and acquisition activity resulted in the reclassification of a significant portion of gross receipts and assets from tobacco to food. The remainder, comprised of data from highly specialized tobacco manufacturers, is too small to be considered publishable as a separate industry category.

Food and Kindred Products[2] Assets Under $25 Million					Tobacco Manufactures[3]					Tobacco Manufactures[3] Assets Under $25 Million				
1Q 1985	2Q 1985	3Q 1985	4Q 1985	1Q 1986	1Q 1985	2Q 1985	3Q 1985	4Q 1985	1Q 1986	1Q 1985	2Q 1985	3Q 1985	4Q 1985	1Q 1986
(percent of net sales)					(percent of net sales)					(percent of net sales)				
100.0	100.0	100.0	100.0	100.0										
2.1	2.0	2.1	2.0	1.9										
94.8	95.9	94.8	96.3	95.3										
3.2	2.1	3.1	1.6	2.8										
-0.5	-0.5	-0.6	-0.3	-0.5										
2.7	1.6	2.5	1.3	2.3										
1.3	0.8	1.3	0.7	1.0										
1.4	0.9	1.2	0.7	1.3										
(percent)					(percent)					(percent)				
18.70	12.56	17.61	9.46	17.62										
9.90	6.75	8.65	4.60	9.88										
7.94	5.14	7.43	3.95	7.07										
4.20	2.76	3.65	1.92	3.96										
1.72	1.61	1.69	1.71	1.72										
0.27	0.24	0.30	0.30	0.27										
1.17	1.14	1.20	1.17	1.08										

Food and Kindred Products[2] Assets Under $25 Million					Tobacco Manufactures [3]					Tobacco Manufactures Assets Under $25 Million [3]				
1Q 1985	2Q 1965	3Q 1985	4Q 1985	1Q 1986	1Q 1985	2Q 1985	3Q 1985	4Q 1985	1Q 1986	1Q 1985	2Q 1985	3Q 1985	4Q 1985	1Q 1986
(percent of total assets)					(percent of total assets)					(percent of total assets)				
9.0	8.6	10.1	10.4	9.1										
21.4	22.3	21.6	22.1	23.2										
22.6	22.5	22.4	23.8	22.5										
57.1	56.9	57.5	59.1	57.7										
37.0	36.7	35.8	34.0	34.8										
13.2	13.8	12.7	13.5	12.9										
33.2	35.4	34.0	34.5	33.5										
23.0	22.2	22.4	22.3	24.2										
57.6	59.1	57.8	58.3	59.9										
42.4	40.9	42.2	41.7	40.1										

TABLE 3—INCOME STATEMENT
FOR CORPORATIONS INCLUDED IN ESIC MAJOR GROUPS 22 AND 26

	Textile Mill Products[1]				
	1Q 1985	2Q 1985	3Q 1985	4Q 1985	1Q 1986
	(percent of net sales)				
INCOME STATEMENT IN RATIO FORMAT					
Net sales, receipts, and operating revenues	100.0	100.0	100.0	100.0	100.0
Less: Depreciation, depletion, and amortization of property, plant and equipment	3.4	3.3	3.2	2.9	3.2
Less: All other operating costs and expenses	92.2	91.6	91.3	90.0	90.7
Income (or loss) from operations	4.4	5.1	5.4	7.1	6.2
Non-operating income (expense)	-1.0	-1.7	-1.9	-1.1	-0.9
Income (or loss) before income taxes	3.4	3.4	3.5	6.0	5.3
Less: Provision for current and deferred domestic income taxes	1.7	1.4	1.3	2.5	2.0
Income (or loss) after income taxes	1.7	2.1	2.2	3.5	3.3
	(percent)				
OPERATING RATIOS (see explanatory notes)					
Annual rate of profit on stockholders' equity at end of period:					
Before income taxes	11.41	12.19	12.60	23.08	19.33
After taxes	5.67	7.35	7.75	13.48	12.02
Annual rate of profit on total assets:					
Before income taxes	5.42	5.81	5.75	10.44	8.76
After taxes	2.69	3.50	3.54	6.10	5.45
BALANCE SHEET RATIOS (based on succeeding table)					
Total current assets to total current liabilities	2.34	2.32	2.19	2.30	2.34
Total cash, U.S. Government and other securities to total current liabilities	0.28	0.26	0.23	0.30	0.29
Total stockholders' equity to total debt	1.61	1.60	1.47	1.41	1.42

[1] During the first quarter of 1986, a considerable number of companies were reclassified by industry. To provide comparability, the four quarters of 1985 have been restated to reflect these reclassifications.

TABLE 4—BALANCE SHEET
FOR CORPORATIONS INCLUDED IN ESIC MAJOR GROUPS 22 AND 26

	Textile Mill Products[1]				
	1Q 1985	2Q 1985	3Q 1985	4Q 1985	1Q 1986
	(percent of total assets)				
SELECTED BALANCE SHEET RATIOS					
Total cash, U.S. Government and other securities	6.8	5.6	6.0	7.4	7.1
Trade accounts and trade notes receivable	21.6	23.1	24.6	24.1	23.8
Inventories	26.1	25.7	24.1	23.3	24.4
Total current assets	57.0	57.7	57.0	57.2	57.5
Net property, plant and equipment	34.2	34.4	32.6	31.4	32.2
Short-term debt including installments on long-term debt	6.9	7.4	8.2	7.7	7.3
Total current liabilities	24.4	24.9	26.0	24.9	24.6
Long-term debt	22.8	22.3	22.8	24.4	24.5
Total liabilities	52.5	52.4	54.4	54.8	54.7
Stockholders' equity	47.5	47.6	45.6	45.2	45.3

[1] During the first quarter of 1986, a considerable number of companies were reclassified by industry. To provide comparability, the four quarters of 1985 have been restated to reflect these reclassifications.

	Textile Mill Products Assets Under $25 Million					Paper and Allied Products[1]					Paper and Allied Products Assets Under $25 Million				
	1Q 1985	2Q 1985	3Q 1985	4Q 1985	1Q 1986	1Q 1985	2Q 1985	3Q 1985	4Q 1985	1Q 1986	1Q 1985	2Q 1985	3Q 1985	4Q 1985	1Q 1986
	(percent of net sales)					(percent of net sales)					(percent of net sales)				
	100.0	100.0	100.0	100.0	100.0	100.0	100.0	100.0	100.0	100.0	100.0	100.0	100.0	100.0	100.0
	2.9	3.1	2.9	2.6	2.7	4.3	4.2	4.5	4.4	4.7	2.6	2.3	2.7	2.4	2.4
	93.3	91.5	92.4	92.3	91.3	88.2	87.7	88.7	89.1	88.8	92.1	91.0	92.4	93.5	91.5
	3.8	5.4	4.7	5.2	6.0	7.5	8.1	6.8	6.5	6.6	5.3	6.7	4.8	4.2	6.1
	-0.8	-0.4	-0.7	-0.2	-0.3	-1.0	-0.7	-1.9	-0.8	-1.2	-0.3	-0.4	0.3	-0.4	-0.8
	3.0	5.0	3.9	5.0	5.7	6.5	7.4	4.9	5.7	5.4	5.1	6.3	5.1	3.8	5.3
	2.2	1.7	1.4	1.3	1.7	2.5	2.6	1.6	1.8	2.0	1.7	2.2	1.9	1.3	2.3
	0.8	3.3	2.5	3.7	4.0	4.0	4.8	3.3	3.9	3.4	3.4	4.0	3.2	2.5	3.0
	(percent)					(percent)					(percent)				
	13.07	21.12	18.15	25.06	27.61	15.85	18.21	11.88	13.62	12.59	26.56	33.72	25.54	21.32	26.89
	3.53	14.10	11.48	18.72	19.53	9.81	11.73	8.08	9.36	7.85	17.74	21.71	15.89	13.93	15.32
	6.35	10.42	8.43	11.49	12.93	7.56	8.81	5.65	6.47	5.91	12.02	15.59	12.02	8.85	12.06
	1.72	6.95	5.33	8.58	9.15	4.68	5.68	3.84	4.45	3.68	8.03	10.04	7.48	5.78	6.87
	2.03	2.10	1.95	2.13	2.08	1.65	1.65	1.66	1.55	1.69	1.95	2.02	2.02	1.86	2.13
	0.35	0.34	0.26	0.36	0.31	0.21	0.19	0.21	0.20	0.20	0.25	0.32	0.37	0.29	0.41
	1.81	1.74	1.56	1.40	1.49	1.67	1.73	1.66	1.68	1.60	1.50	1.57	1.72	1.37	1.42

	Textile Mill Products Assets Under $25 Million					Paper and Allied Products[1]					Paper and Allied Products Assets Under $25 Million				
	1Q 1985	2Q 1985	3Q 1985	4Q 1985	1Q 1986	1Q 1985	2Q 1985	3Q 1985	4Q 1985	1Q 1986	1Q 1985	2Q 1985	3Q 1985	4Q 1985	1Q 1985
	(percent of total assets)					(percent of total assets)					(percent of total assets)				
	11.5	10.5	8.8	12.0	10.0	4.1	3.5	3.8	3.6	3.3	8.3	10.2	11.7	10.1	11.9
	23.9	26.3	30.9	31.4	29.9	12.5	12.2	11.8	11.0	11.3	28.7	28.7	27.0	26.5	24.8
	28.2	25.2	25.3	24.7	23.9	12.4	12.1	11.7	11.6	11.5	22.7	22.5	21.3	22.9	21.1
	66.2	64.2	67.7	70.6	66.3	31.6	30.5	29.8	28.4	28.7	64.5	64.9	63.7	64.7	62.2
	30.2	30.4	28.3	26.4	31.1	59.1	59.9	60.5	62.1	62.0	29.1	30.4	31.0	30.7	31.8
	9.9	9.9	13.0	12.7	11.5	4.8	4.6	3.8	3.8	3.5	9.9	9.3	8.4	8.4	8.2
	32.6	30.5	34.7	33.2	31.8	19.2	18.5	17.9	18.3	17.0	33.1	32.0	31.5	34.7	29.2
	16.9	18.3	16.8	20.0	19.9	23.8	23.5	24.9	24.4	25.9	20.2	20.2	19.0	22.0	23.5
	51.4	50.7	53.6	54.2	53.2	52.3	51.6	52.4	52.5	53.1	54.7	53.8	52.9	58.5	55.1
	48.6	49.3	46.4	45.8	46.8	47.7	48.4	47.6	47.5	46.9	45.3	46.2	47.1	41.5	44.3

TABLE 5—INCOME STATEMENT
FOR CORPORATIONS INCLUDED IN ESIC MAJOR GROUPS 27 AND 28

	Printing and Publishing[1]				
	1Q 1985	2Q 1985	3Q 1985	4Q 1985	1Q 1986
	(percent of net sales)				
INCOME STATEMENT IN RATIO FORMAT					
Net sales, receipts, and operating revenues	100.0	100.0	100.0	100.0	100.0
Less: Depreciation, depletion, and amortization of property, plant and equipment	3.6	3.4	3.5	3.4	3.7
Less: All other operating costs and expenses	87.5	85.9	85.7	86.0	87.6
Income (or loss) from operations	8.9	10.7	10.8	10.6	8.7
Non-operating income (expense)	0.6	1.4	0.6	-0.6	1.0
Income (or loss) before income taxes	9.5	12.1	11.3	9.9	9.7
Less: Provision for current and deferred domestic income taxes	3.8	4.5	4.6	4.2	4.0
Income (or loss) after income taxes	5.8	7.6	6.7	5.7	5.7
	(percent)				
OPERATING RATIOS (see explanatory notes)					
Annual rate of profit on stockholders' equity at end of period:					
Before income taxes	26.76	35.72	34.53	31.03	27.77
After taxes	16.19	22.41	20.57	17.81	16.25
Annual rate of profit on total assets:					
Before income taxes	12.62	16.64	15.38	13.55	12.35
After taxes	7.63	10.44	9.16	7.78	7.22
BALANCE SHEET RATIOS (based on succeeding table)					
Total current assets to total current liabilities	1.85	1.86	1.80	1.72	1.82
Total cash, U.S. Government and other securities to total current liabilities	0.43	0.40	0.36	0.36	0.40
Total stockholders' equity to total debt	1.92	1.79	1.60	1.58	1.60

[1] During the first quarter of 1986, a considerable number of companies were reclassified by industry. To provide comparability, the four quarters of 1985 have been restated to reflect these reclassifications.

TABLE 6—BALANCE SHEET
FOR CORPORATIONS INCLUDED IN ESIC MAJOR GROUPS 27 AND 28

	Printing and Publishing[1]				
	1Q 1985	2Q 1985	3Q 1985	4Q 1985	1Q 1986
	(percent of total assets)				
SELECTED BALANCE SHEET RATIOS					
Total cash, U.S. Government and other securities	10.1	9.1	8.4	8.8	8.9
Trade accounts and trade notes receivable	18.6	18.8	19.8	19.7	18.2
Inventories	9.7	9.8	9.5	8.9	8.6
Total current assets	43.5	42.3	42.4	41.8	40.7
Net property, plant and equipment	31.2	31.7	32.0	31.4	32.1
Short-term debt including installments on long-term debt	4.3	4.3	4.9	4.8	4.1
Total current liabilities	23.5	22.8	23.6	24.2	22.3
Long-term debt	20.2	21.7	22.8	22.8	23.6
Total liabilities	52.9	53.4	55.5	56.3	55.5
Stockholders' equity	47.1	46.6	44.5	43.7	44.5

[1] During the first quarter of 1986, a considerable number of companies were reclassified by industry. To provide comparability, the four quarters of 1985 have been restated to reflect these reclassifications.

	Printing and Publishing Assets Under $25 Million					Chemicals and Allied Products[1]					Chemicals and Allied Products Assets Under $25 Million				
	1Q 1985	2Q 1985	3Q 1985	4Q 1985	1Q 1986	1Q 1985	2Q 1985	3Q 1985	4Q 1985	1Q 1986	1Q 1985	2Q 1985	3Q 1985	4Q 1985	1Q 1986
(percent of net sales)						*(percent of net sales)*					*(percent of net sales)*				
	100.0	100.0	100.0	100.0	100.0	100.0	100.0	100.0	100.0	100.0	100.0	100.0	100.0	100.0	100.0
	3.1	3.2	3.5	3.4	3.4	4.5	4.1	4.6	4.9	5.0	2.3	2.1	1.9	2.1	2.2
	90.5	90.5	90.6	90.4	90.7	88.3	88.3	88.4	90.9	87.6	92.0	90.4	93.2	94.9	96.5
	6.4	6.3	5.9	6.1	6.0	7.2	7.6	6.9	4.3	7.4	5.7	7.6	4.9	3.0	1.3
	-0.4	-0.4	-0.1	-0.7	-1.3	2.1	1.7	-0.6	-2.5	2.1	-0.1	-0.7	1.7	-0.2	0.1
	5.9	5.9	5.8	5.4	4.6	9.2	9.3	6.4	1.8	9.5	5.6	6.9	6.6	2.8	1.4
	2.2	2.2	2.1	1.8	1.7	2.9	2.8	1.9	0.2	3.4	2.3	2.3	2.7	1.9	1.7
	3.7	3.7	3.7	3.6	2.9	6.3	6.5	4.4	1.5	6.1	3.3	4.5	3.9	0.9	-0.3
(percent)						*(percent)*					*(percent)*				
	27.23	27.54	28.11	26.67	21.62	18.37	19.26	12.59	3.57	19.84	22.54	32.43	28.28	12.00	5.41
	17.16	17.10	17.87	17.94	13.70	12.52	13.43	8.74	3.08	12.78	13.30	21.36	16.87	3.83	-1.32
	11.77	12.02	11.46	10.98	9.12	9.44	9.97	6.27	1.74	9.17	10.98	15.47	14.16	5.92	2.53
	7.41	7.46	7.29	7.39	5.78	6.43	6.96	4.35	1.50	5.91	6.48	10.19	8.45	1.89	-0.62
	1.84	1.85	1.79	1.73	1.90	1.61	1.61	1.51	1.47	1.50	2.02	2.07	2.13	2.08	2.07
	0.42	0.39	0.36	0.35	0.39	0.19	0.18	0.18	0.20	0.20	0.24	0.26	0.34	0.36	0.32
	1.38	1.39	1.22	1.25	1.32	2.25	2.31	2.02	1.99	1.64	1.89	1.78	2.05	2.01	1.64

	Printing and Publishing Assets Under $25 Million					Chemicals and Allied Products[1]					Chemicals and Allied Products Assets Under $25 Million				
	1Q 1985	2Q 1985	3Q 1985	4Q 1985	1Q 1986	1Q 1985	2Q 1985	3Q 1985	4Q 1985	1Q 1986	1Q 1985	2Q 1985	3Q 1985	4Q 1985	1Q 1986
(percent of total assets)						*(percent of total assets)*					*(percent of total assets)*				
	12.8	11.6	11.2	11.2	11.7	4.4	4.2	4.4	4.8	4.7	7.8	8.5	10.8	11.6	10.2
	25.6	26.2	26.7	26.5	26.3	15.0	14.8	14.7	13.8	13.9	27.2	29.8	28.6	26.5	25.0
	12.5	12.2	12.0	12.3	12.3	14.6	14.4	13.9	13.9	13.6	25.7	23.9	23.4	23.6	24.6
	56.5	55.4	55.7	54.8	56.4	37.6	37.0	36.6	36.1	36.0	65.6	67.8	68.7	67.0	65.5
	23.4	35.6	35.1	36.0	36.2	39.3	39.2	38.3	37.6	36.6	28.3	26.1	25.0	27.1	25.8
	9.3	9.2	9.4	9.5	8.6	5.4	5.1	6.5	6.1	6.4	8.6	8.8	8.0	7.8	9.2
	30.7	29.9	31.1	31.7	29.6	23.4	23.0	24.3	24.5	24.0	32.5	32.7	32.2	32.3	31.6
	22.0	22.3	24.0	23.3	23.5	17.4	17.3	18.2	18.7	21.9	17.2	17.9	16.4	16.8	19.3
	56.8	56.4	59.2	58.8	57.8	48.6	48.2	50.2	51.1	53.8	51.3	52.3	49.9	50.6	53.1
	43.2	43.6	40.8	41.2	42.2	51.4	51.8	49.8	48.9	46.2	48.7	47.7	50.1	49.4	46.9

TABLE 7—INCOME STATEMENT
FOR CORPORATIONS INCLUDED IN ESIC MAJOR GROUPS 28.1 AND 28.3

	Industrial Chemicals and Synthetics[1][2]				
	1Q 1985	2Q 1985	3Q 1985	4Q 1985	1Q 1986
	(percent of net sales)				
INCOME STATEMENT IN RATIO FORMAT					
Net sales, receipts, and operating revenues	100.0	100.0	100.0	100.0	100.0
Less: Depreciation, depletion, and amortization of property, plant and equipment	6.3	6.1	6.9	6.9	7.1
Less: All other operating costs and expenses	88.2	87.2	89.1	88.8	85.4
Income (or loss) from operations	5.5	6.7	4.0	4.2	7.6
Non-operating income (expense)	0.2	0.9	-5.7	-6.5	2.5
Income (or loss) before income taxes	5.7	7.6	-1.7	-2.3	10.1
Less: Provision for current and deferred domestic income taxes	1.7	2.1	-1.4	-1.7	3.5
Income (or loss) after income taxes	4.0	5.5	-0.3	-0.5	6.6
	(percent)				
OPERATING RATIOS (see explanatory notes)					
Annual rate of profit on stockholders' equity at end of period:					
Before income taxes	10.83	15.14	-3.11	-4.50	21.33
After taxes	7.52	10.99	-0.57	-1.07	13.91
Annual rate of profit on total assets:					
Before income taxes	5.28	7.35	-1.43	-2.07	9.18
After taxes	3.66	5.33	-0.26	-0.49	5.98
BALANCE SHEET RATIOS (based on succeeding table)					
Total current assets to total current liabilities	1.49	1.49	1.29	1.36	1.35
Total cash, U.S. Government and other securities to total current liabilities	0.10	0.09	0.07	0.12	0.10
Total stockholders' equity to total debt	1.98	1.96	1.67	1.74	1.41

[1] Included in Chemicals and Allied Products.
[2] During the first quarter of 1986, a considerable number of companies were reclassified by industry. To provide comparability, the four quarters of 1985 have been restated to reflect these reclassifications.

TABLE 8—BALANCE SHEET
FOR CORPORATIONS INCLUDED IN ESIC MAJOR GROUPS 28.1 AND 28.3

	Industrial Chemicals and Synthetics[1][2]				
	1Q 1985	2Q 1985	3Q 1985	4Q 1985	1Q 1986
	(percent of total assets)				
SELECTED BALANCE SHEET RATIOS					
Total cash, U.S. Government and other securities	2.1	2.0	1.8	2.8	2.4
Trade accounts and trade notes receivable	15.1	14.8	14.5	13.9	14.4
Inventories	12.8	12.9	12.2	12.1	12.3
Total current assets	33.2	32.8	31.7	31.6	32.2
Net property, plant and equipment	46.2	46.1	44.3	43.9	43.5
Short-term debt including installments on long-term debt	4.4	4.2	6.7	4.9	6.3
Total current liabilities	22.3	22.0	24.6	23.2	23.9
Long-term debt	20.2	20.5	20.8	21.7	24.2
Total liabilities	51.3	51.5	53.9	54.1	57.0
Stockholders' equity	48.7	48.5	46.1	45.9	43.0

[1] Included in Chemicals and Allied Products.
[2] During the first quarter of 1986, a considerable number of companies were reclassified by industry. To provide comparability, the four quarters of 1985 have been restated to reflect these reclassifications.

Industrial Chemicals and Synthetics[1] Assets Under $25 Million					Drugs[1][2]					Drugs[1] Assets Under $25 Million				
1Q 1985	2Q 1985	3Q 1985	4Q 1985	1Q 1986	1Q 1985	2Q 1985	3Q 1985	4Q 1985	1Q 1986	1Q 1985	2Q 1985	3Q 1985	4Q 1985	1Q 1986
(percent of net sales)					(percent of net sales)					(percent of net sales)				
100.0	100.0	100.0	100.0	100.0	100.0	100.0	100.0	100.0	100.0	100.0	100.0	100.0	100.0	100.0
3.2	2.3	2.7	2.5	2.1	3.2	3.2	3.2	3.5	3.5	2.2	2.9	2.7	3.2	3.2
89.2	87.9	97.3	88.9	95.1	85.0	86.7	85.7	90.8	85.7	86.2	92.4	95.3	96.4	91.4
7.7	9.7	-0.0	8.6	2.8	11.8	10.1	11.0	5.7	10.8	11.6	4.7	1.9	0.4	5.4
-0.2	-0.6	-0.4	0.0	-0.1	6.7	7.2	6.6	-0.9	7.5	0.7	0.1	1.9	-0.5	-5.3
7.5	9.2	-0.4	8.6	2.8	18.5	17.3	17.6	4.8	18.3	12.2	4.8	3.8	-0.1	0.2
3.4	3.2	0.8	2.4	0.2	5.7	5.6	5.6	2.0	5.7	4.6	1.8	1.8	0.6	2.7
4.1	6.0	-1.2	6.2	2.6	12.8	11.7	12.0	2.8	12.6	7.6	2.9	2.0	-0.7	-2.6
(percent)					(percent)					(percent)				
27.50	37.74	-1.62	33.90	9.41	29.59	26.20	26.68	7.47	28.78	24.06	9.84	7.73	-0.12	0.55
15.15	24.45	-4.55	24.29	8.63	20.54	17.79	18.16	4.33	19.81	14.94	6.06	4.11	-1.48	-7.78
13.07	17.98	-0.80	18.08	5.46	17.08	15.14	15.34	4.21	15.39	16.33	5.84	4.51	-0.07	0.26
7.20	11.65	-2.24	12.95	5.00	11.85	10.28	10.44	2.44	10.59	10.13	3.60	2.40	-0.88	-3.62
2.11	2.19	2.29	2.50	2.57	1.58	1.55	1.49	1.53	1.54	3.42	3.02	2.49	2.41	1.88
0.29	0.24	0.32	0.55	0.38	0.26	0.26	0.22	0.24	0.27	0.70	0.67	0.55	0.28	0.20
1.54	1.71	1.88	2.08	2.68	3.16	3.10	3.16	3.28	2.55	4.94	2.75	2.61	2.59	1.54

Industrial Chemicals and Synthetics[1] Assets Under $25 Million					Drugs[1][2]					Drugs[1] Assets Under $25 Million				
1Q 1985	2Q 1985	3Q 1985	4Q 1985	1Q 1986	1Q 1985	2Q 1985	3Q 1985	4Q 1985	1Q 1986	1Q 1985	2Q 1985	3Q 1985	4Q 1985	1Q 1986
(percent of total assets)					(percent of total assets)					(percent of total assets)				
8.0	6.9	9.7	14.5	10.2	6.5	6.4	5.5	6.0	6.4	13.3	14.8	14.3	7.6	6.3
25.4	26.9	25.3	24.6	27.6	13.6	13.2	13.6	13.2	12.4	20.7	18.7	19.2	22.1	22.0
19.8	21.9	21.2	19.1	24.8	13.7	13.4	13.2	13.6	12.2	17.1	18.6	17.8	18.0	18.4
58.3	64.3	69.2	65.8	69.5	38.6	38.1	37.0	38.1	36.3	64.7	66.7	64.8	64.3	60.4
37.9	31.5	25.9	30.9	26.0	29.8	29.6	29.8	30.0	27.9	23.9	22.6	21.5	24.5	29.2
7.8	6.5	7.2	6.2	7.5	7.3	7.7	7.4	6.1	5.2	2.9	6.9	7.3	10.2	10.5
27.6	29.3	30.2	26.3	27.0	24.4	24.5	24.9	25.0	23.5	18.9	22.1	26.0	26.7	32.1
22.9	21.4	18.9	19.5	14.2	11.0	11.0	10.8	11.0	15.7	10.8	14.6	15.1	12.9	20.2
52.5	52.4	50.9	46.7	42.0	42.3	42.2	42.5	43.6	46.5	32.1	40.7	41.6	40.4	53.5
47.5	47.6	49.1	53.3	58.0	57.7	57.8	57.5	56.4	53.5	67.9	59.3	58.4	59.6	46.5

TABLE 9—INCOME STATEMENT
FOR CORPORATIONS INCLUDED IN ESIC MAJOR GROUPS 29 AND 30

	Petroleum and Coal Products[1]				
	1Q 1985	2Q 1985	3Q 1985	4Q 1985	1Q 1986
	(percent of net sales)				
INCOME STATEMENT IN RATIO FORMAT					
Net sales, receipts, and operating revenues	100.0	100.0	100.0	100.0	100.0
Less: Depreciation, depletion, and amortization of property, plant and equipment	6.8	6.5	7.2	7.1	8.2
Less: All other operating costs and expenses	86.8	87.9	86.6	88.3	86.6
Income (or loss) from operations	6.5	5.5	6.2	4.6	5.2
Non-operating income (expense)	0.8	-2.5	0.2	0.7	0.7
Income (or loss) before income taxes	7.2	3.0	6.4	5.4	5.9
Less: Provision for current and deferred domestic income taxes	2.0	0.7	2.1	1.3	1.8
Income (or loss) after income taxes	5.2	2.4	4.3	4.0	4.1
	(percent)				
OPERATING RATIOS (see explanatory notes)					
Annual rate of profit on stockholders' equity at end of period:					
Before income taxes	14.65	6.58	13.99	11.72	10.66
After taxes	10.52	5.15	9.33	8.83	7.47
Annual rate of profit on total assets:					
Before income taxes	6.46	2.78	5.90	4.90	4.46
After taxes	4.64	2.18	3.93	3.69	3.13
BALANCE SHEET RATIOS (based on succeeding table)					
Total current assets to total current liabilities	1.03	1.02	0.99	0.93	0.99
Total cash, U.S. Government and other securities to total current liabilities	0.13	0.10	0.12	0.12	0.20
Total stockholders' equity to total debt	1.72	1.55	1.60	1.63	1.56

[1] During the first quarter of 1986, a considerable number of companies were reclassified by industry. To provide comparability, the four quarters of 1985 have been restated to reflect these reclassifications.
[2] 1985 Data are Revised.

TABLE 10—BALANCE SHEET
FOR CORPORATIONS INCLUDED IN ESIC MAJOR GROUPS 29 AND 30

	Petroleum and Coal Products[1]				
	1Q 1985	2Q 1985	3Q 1985	4Q 1985	1Q 1985
	(percent of total assets)				
SELECTED BALANCE SHEET RATIOS					
Total cash, U.S. Government and other securities	2.3	1.9	2.2	2.5	3.5
Trade accounts and trade notes receivable	7.9	7.7	7.6	7.9	6.5
Inventories	6.3	6.4	6.1	6.0	5.8
Total current assets	18.3	18.1	18.1	18.7	17.7
Net property, plant and equipment	57.9	57.9	58.1	57.6	57.1
Short-term debt including installments on long-term debt	3.0	3.2	3.2	4.1	4.8
Total current liabilities	17.9	17.8	18.5	20.1	18.0
Long-term debt	22.7	24.0	23.3	21.5	22.0
Total liabilities	55.9	57.7	57.8	58.2	58.2
Stockholders' equity	44.1	42.3	42.2	41.8	41.8

[1] During the first quarter of 1986, a considerable number of companies were reclassified by industry. To provide comparability, the four quarters of 1985 have been restated to reflect these reclassifications.
[2] 1985 Data are Revised.

	Petroleum and Coal Products[2] Assets Under $25 Million					Rubber and Misc. Plastics Products[1]					Rubber and Misc. Plastics Products[2] Assets Under $25 Million				
	1Q 1985	2Q 1985	3Q 1985	4Q 1985	1Q 1986	1Q 1985	2Q 1985	3Q 1985	4Q 1985	1Q 1986	1Q 1985	2Q 1985	3Q 1985	4Q 1985	1Q 1985
(percent of net sales)															
	100.0	100.0	100.0	100.0	100.0	100.0	100.0	100.0	100.0	100.0	100.0	100.0	100.0	100.0	100.0
	2.4	2.3	2.0	2.3	3.4	3.1	2.9	3.0	3.1	3.4	2.7	2.5	2.8	3.1	2.9
	97.5	95.6	89.7	94.1	99.9	90.6	90.5	92.0	92.7	92.3	90.5	90.7	92.3	91.1	93.4
	0.1	2.1	8.3	3.7	-3.3	6.3	6.6	5.0	4.2	4.3	6.8	6.8	4.9	5.8	3.6
	0.0	0.9	2.7	-0.3	0.5	-0.5	-2.6	0.1	-1.0	-0.8	-0.6	-0.4	-1.2	-0.3	-0.4
	0.1	3.0	11.0	3.4	-2.9	5.9	4.0	5.1	3.2	3.5	6.2	6.4	3.7	5.5	3.2
	0.8	1.6	4.0	1.2	0.8	2.2	2.4	1.8	1.2	1.1	2.6	2.4	1.3	2.4	1.1
	-0.7	1.4	7.0	2.2	-3.6	3.6	1.6	3.3	2.0	2.4	3.6	4.1	2.4	3.1	2.1
(percent)															
	0.61	24.69	81.63	22.83	-14.61	20.11	15.07	18.40	12.06	12.58	31.97	32.83	19.57	26.52	16.77
	-3.29	11.76	51.79	14.99	-18.51	12.44	6.08	11.94	7.54	8.51	18.63	20.72	12.58	14.78	10.86
	0.24	7.55	28.99	8.61	-5.11	9.28	6.57	7.90	5.07	5.24	13.36	13.86	7.64	11.47	6.63
	-1.30	3.60	16.39	5.65	-6.47	5.74	2.65	5.13	3.17	3.54	7.78	8.75	4.31	6.39	4.29
	1.47	1.33	1.75	1.81	1.77	1.73	1.73	1.77	1.60	1.62	1.72	1.78	1.70	1.71	1.59
	0.46	0.30	0.40	0.41	0.52	0.20	0.19	0.19	0.20	0.17	0.23	0.27	0.21	0.25	0.18
	1.08	0.82	1.11	1.07	0.97	1.78	1.61	1.49	1.46	1.39	1.31	1.33	1.13	1.45	1.22

	Petroleum and Coal Products[2] Assets Under $25 Million					Rubber and Misc. Plastics Products[1]					Rubber and Misc. Plastics Products[2] Assets Under $25 Million				
	1Q 1985	2Q 1985	3Q 1985	4Q 1985	1Q 1986	1Q 1985	2Q 1985	3Q 1985	4Q 1985	1Q 1986	1Q 1985	2Q 1985	3Q 1985	4Q 1985	1Q 1986
(percent of total assets)															
	18.4	14.4	14.4	13.5	17.1	5.9	5.7	5.5	6.3	5.2	8.6	9.5	7.5	8.9	6.9
	21.6	32.5	31.9	30.0	22.4	23.1	23.0	22.0	21.7	21.1	29.2	28.0	26.2	26.3	26.0
	16.3	15.8	14.6	14.2	16.1	20.7	20.2	20.1	19.1	19.4	22.7	21.7	22.5	22.4	22.5
	58.6	64.2	63.5	59.9	58.3	51.9	52.1	50.7	49.8	48.6	63.2	63.2	59.9	61.0	59.2
	30.8	29.4	29.8	34.6	35.6	35.0	35.1	35.6	36.7	38.0	30.5	30.7	33.0	32.9	33.8
	17.1	18.6	7.9	10.3	9.0	7.7	7.8	6.4	7.9	7.5	11.5	10.9	10.6	10.6	10.7
	46.0	48.2	36.3	33.0	32.9	30.1	30.2	28.7	31.2	30.0	36.7	35.5	35.3	35.7	37.1
	19.4	19.0	24.3	25.1	27.2	18.2	19.3	22.5	20.9	22.5	20.4	20.9	23.9	19.1	21.7
	63.5	69.4	64.5	62.3	65.0	53.9	56.4	57.1	57.9	58.4	58.2	57.8	60.9	56.7	60.5
	35.5	30.6	35.5	37.7	35.0	46.1	43.6	42.9	42.1	41.6	41.8	42.2	39.1	43.3	39.5

TABLE 11—INCOME STATEMENT
FOR CORPORATIONS INCLUDED IN ESIC MAJOR GROUPS 32 AND 33

	Stone, Clay and Glass Products[1]				
	1Q 1985	2Q 1985	3Q 1985	4Q 1985	1Q 1986
	(percent of net sales)				
INCOME STATEMENT IN RATIO FORMAT					
Net sales, receipts, and operating revenues	100.0	100.0	100.0	100.0	100.0
Less: Depreciation, depletion, and amortization of property, plant and equipment	4.7	4.1	4.1	4.3	4.9
Less: All other operating costs and expenses	92.2	86.7	87.2	89.5	90.1
Income (or loss) from operations	3.1	9.1	8.7	6.2	5.1
Non-operating income (expense)	-0.5	-1.7	-2.3	-0.9	-1.1
Income (or loss) before income taxes	2.5	7.5	6.4	5.3	3.9
Less: Provision for current and deferred domestic income taxes	1.5	3.1	2.8	2.1	2.2
Income (or loss) after income taxes	1.0	4.4	3.6	3.2	1.7
	(percent)				
OPERATING RATIOS (see explanatory notes)					
Annual rate of profit on stockholders' equity at end of period:					
Before income taxes	5.78	19.68	17.16	13.53	8.78
After taxes	2.21	11.59	9.68	8.21	3.84
Annual rate of profit on total assets:					
Before income taxes	2.74	9.48	8.29	6.57	4.26
After taxes	1.05	5.59	4.68	3.98	1.86
BALANCE SHEET RATIOS (based on succeeding table)					
Total current assets to total current liabilities	1.88	1.91	1.89	1.84	1.83
Total cash, U.S. Government and other securities to total current liabilities	0.24	0.24	0.27	0.28	0.28
Total stockholders' equity to total debt	1.57	1.66	1.69	1.73	1.72

[1] During the first quarter of 1986, a considerable number of companies were reclassified by industry. To provide comparability, the four quarters of 1985 have been restated to reflect these reclassifications.
[2] 1985 Data are Revised.

TABLE 12—BALANCE SHEET
FOR CORPORATIONS INCLUDED IN ESIC MAJOR GROUPS 32 AND 33

	Stone, Clay and Glass Products[1]				
	1Q 1985	2Q 1985	3Q 1985	4Q 1985	1Q 1986
	(percent of total assets)				
SELECTED BALANCE SHEET RATIOS					
Total cash, U.S. Government and other securities	4.9	5.0	5.7	6.0	5.9
Trade accounts and trade notes receivable	16.3	17.6	18.3	16.2	16.0
Inventories	14.7	14.1	13.0	13.6	13.6
Total current assets	38.9	39.5	40.0	39.1	39.0
Net property, plant and equipment	45.8	45.1	45.0	46.4	46.2
Short-term debt including installments on long-term debt	5.7	5.7	5.9	5.9	5.4
Total current liabilities	20.7	20.7	21.2	21.3	21.3
Long-term debt	24.4	23.3	22.7	22.1	21.9
Total liabilities	52.6	51.8	51.7	51.5	51.5
Stockholders' equity	47.4	48.2	48.3	48.5	48.5

[1] During the first quarter of 1986, a considerable number of companies were reclassified by industry. To provide comparability, the four quarters of 1985 have been restated to reflect these reclassifications.
[2] 1985 Data are Revised.

	Stone, Clay and Glass Products Assets Under $25 Million					Primary Metal Industries [1]					Primary Metal Industries [2] Assets Under $25 Million				
	1Q 1985	2Q 1985	3Q 1985	4Q 1985	1Q 1986	1Q 1985	2Q 1985	3Q 1985	4Q 1985	1Q 1986	1Q 1985	2Q 1985	3Q 1985	4Q 1985	1Q 1986
(percent of net sales)						(percent of net sales)					(percent of net sales)				
	100.0	100.0	100.0	100.0	100.0	100.0	100.0	100.0	100.0	100.0	100.0	100.0	100.0	100.0	100.0
	3.8	3.0	3.1	3.4	4.2	3.8	3.7	3.8	4.0	4.0	2.9	3.1	3.0	3.4	3.0
	97.2	89.2	89.0	93.0	93.6	94.9	94.9	94.8	94.6	94.0	91.7	91.5	93.8	91.7	93.2
	-1.0	7.8	7.9	3.6	2.2	1.2	1.4	1.4	1.5	2.0	5.4	5.5	3.2	4.9	3.8
	0.1	-1.2	-0.5	-0.7	0.2	-1.7	-3.3	-3.3	-6.7	-2.1	-0.5	0.2	-0.5	0.0	-0.8
	-0.8	6.6	7.4	2.9	2.4	-0.4	-1.9	-1.9	-5.2	-0.2	4.9	5.7	2.7	4.9	3.0
	0.9	2.2	2.6	1.0	1.9	0.6	0.7	0.6	-0.9	0.7	2.1	1.6	1.2	1.4	1.3
	-1.7	4.4	4.8	1.9	0.5	-1.0	-2.6	-2.4	-4.3	-0.8	2.8	4.1	1.5	3.5	1.8
(percent)						(percent)					(percent)				
	-3.02	25.97	31.46	11.47	7.42	-1.28	-5.87	-5.61	-16.05	-0.55	19.67	23.64	11.22	19.88	12.80
	-6.20	17.45	20.39	7.56	1.67	-3.00	-8.07	-7.28	-13.32	-2.57	11.31	16.98	6.37	14.28	7.46
	-1.39	13.03	15.38	5.73	3.83	-0.48	-2.19	-2.10	-5.88	-0.20	9.49	11.12	5.00	8.96	5.72
	-2.85	8.76	9.97	3.78	0.86	-1.13	-3.02	-2.72	-4.88	-0.93	5.46	7.99	2.84	6.44	3.33
	1.90	2.01	1.90	1.95	1.99	1.59	1.63	1.63	1.57	1.58	2.00	1.97	1.81	1.90	1.84
	0.39	0.38	0.33	0.36	0.45	0.14	0.16	0.18	0.19	0.16	0.36	0.36	0.34	0.35	0.29
	1.40	1.74	1.65	1.72	1.92	1.18	1.17	1.16	1.12	1.07	1.78	1.62	1.47	1.49	1.45

	Stone, Clay and Glass Products Assets Under $25 Million					Primary Metal Industries [1]					Primary Metal Industries [2] Assets Under $25 Million				
	1Q 1985	2Q 1985	3Q 1985	4Q 1985	1Q 1986	1Q 1985	2Q 1985	3Q 1985	4Q 1985	1Q 1986	1Q 1985	2Q 1985	3Q 1985	4Q 1985	1Q 1986
(percent of total assets)						(percent of total assets)					(percent of total assets)				
	12.0	11.2	10.3	10.7	13.2	3.6	3.9	4.5	4.7	4.0	11.3	11.0	11.3	10.6	9.0
	24.9	26.7	28.9	25.3	24.2	16.3	16.0	16.0	15.2	16.1	27.0	26.8	25.6	24.3	26.0
	19.1	18.8	17.3	18.2	17.5	18.1	17.9	17.5	17.6	17.8	19.1	19.1	19.2	19.8	19.5
	58.8	59.4	59.5	57.6	58.4	40.0	39.7	39.7	39.1	39.7	62.2	61.1	60.0	58.3	57.7
	36.3	33.8	34.8	35.9	36.4	45.2	45.1	45.2	45.7	45.3	33.1	34.2	33.4	34.7	35.7
	10.7	9.5	10.9	10.3	9.7	5.9	5.5	5.6	5.7	6.1	8.9	10.2	10.9	8.9	9.5
	31.0	24.6	31.4	29.5	29.4	25.1	24.4	24.4	24.9	25.1	31.1	30.9	33.1	30.7	31.4
	22.1	19.3	18.7	18.8	17.2	26.2	26.4	26.8	27.0	27.7	18.1	18.8	19.4	21.2	21.3
	54.1	54.8	51.1	50.0	48.4	62.3	62.6	62.6	63.4	64.0	51.8	53.0	55.5	54.9	55.4
	45.9	50.2	48.9	50.0	51.6	37.7	37.4	37.4	36.6	36.0	48.2	47.0	44.5	45.1	44.6

TABLE 13—INCOME STATEMENT
FOR CORPORATIONS INCLUDED IN ESIC MAJOR GROUPS 33.1-2 AND 33.5-6

	Iron and Steel [1] [2]				
	1Q 1985	2Q 1985	3Q 1985	4Q 1985	1Q 1986
	(percent of net sales)				
INCOME STATEMENT IN RATIO FORMAT					
Net sales, receipts, and operating revenues	100.0	100.0	100.0	100.0	100.0
Less: Depreciation, depletion, and amortization of property, plant and equipment	3.8	3.6	3.7	3.8	4.0
Less: All other operating costs and expenses	95.7	96.8	95.0	95.2	95.8
Income (or loss) from operations	0.5	-0.4	1.3	1.0	0.2
Non-operating income (expense)	-1.8	-1.7	-2.1	-4.5	-2.7
Income (or loss) before income taxes	-1.4	-2.2	-0.9	-3.5	-2.5
Less: Provision for current and deferred domestic income taxes	0.8	0.8	1.3	-0.2	0.4
Income (or loss) after income taxes	-2.1	-2.9	-2.1	-3.3	-2.9
	(percent)				
OPERATING RATIOS (see explanatory notes)					
Annual rate of profit on stockholders' equity at end of period:					
Before income taxes	-5.28	-9.35	-3.62	-14.70	-10.74
After taxes	-8.36	-12.80	-8.95	-14.04	-12.58
Annual rate of profit on total assets:					
Before income taxes	-1.60	-2.71	-1.04	-4.16	-2.92
After taxes	-2.54	-3.71	-2.57	-3.98	-3.43
BALANCE SHEET RATIOS (based on succeeding table)					
Total current assets to total current liabilities	1.47	1.50	1.50	1.46	1.43
Total cash, U.S. Government and other securities to total current liabilities	0.13	0.15	0.17	0.16	0.14
Total stockholders' equity to total debt	0.89	0.85	0.83	0.80	0.74

[1] Included in Primary Metal Industries.

[2] During the first quarter of 1986, a considerable number of companies were reclassified by industry. To provide comparability, the four quarters of 1985 have been restated to reflect these reclassifications.

[3] 1985 Data are Revised.

TABLE 14—BALANCE SHEET
FOR CORPORATIONS INCLUDED IN ESIC MAJOR GROUPS 33.1-2 AND 33.5-6

	Iron and Steel [1] [2]				
	1Q 1985	2Q 1985	3Q 1985	4Q 1985	1Q 1986
	(percent of total assets)				
SELECTED BALANCE SHEET RATIOS					
Total cash, U.S. Government and other securities	3.9	4.2	4.8	4.7	4.0
Trade accounts and trade notes receivable	17.6	17.6	17.7	16.9	17.4
Inventories	20.0	20.0	19.5	19.6	19.4
Total current assets	42.9	43.0	43.0	42.3	42.1
Net property, plant and equipment	47.3	47.5	47.5	48.3	48.1
Short-term debt including installments on long-term debt	6.0	5.7	5.5	6.1	6.6
Total current liabilities	29.1	28.7	28.7	29.0	29.5
Long-term debt	28.1	28.4	27.0	29.3	30.2
Total liabilities	69.6	71.0	71.3	71.7	72.8
Stockholders' equity	30.4	29.0	28.7	28.3	27.2

[1] Included in Primary Metal Industries.

[2] During the first quarter of 1986, a considerable number of companies were reclassified by industry. To provide comparability, the four quarters of 1985 have been restated to reflect these reclassifications.

[3] 1985 Data are Revised.

	Iron and Steel[13] Assets Under $25 Million					Nonferrous Metals[12]					Nonferrous Metals[13] Assets Under $25 Million				
	1Q 1985	2Q 1985	3Q 1985	4Q 1985	1Q 1986	1Q 1985	2Q 1985	3Q 1985	4Q 1985	1Q 1986	1Q 1985	2Q 1985	3Q 1985	4Q 1985	1Q 1986
	(percent of net sales)					(percent of net sales)					(percent of net sales)				
	100.0	100.0	100.0	100.0	100.0	100.0	100.0	100.0	100.0	100.0	100.0	100.0	100.0	100.0	100.0
	3.7	4.0	3.8	4.5	4.0	3.9	3.8	3.9	4.2	4.0	2.3	2.5	2.4	2.7	2.4
	90.4	91.4	93.6	91.3	93.0	93.9	92.4	94.5	93.7	91.8	92.8	91.5	93.9	91.9	93.3
	5.9	4.6	2.6	4.2	3.0	2.2	3.8	1.6	2.1	4.2	5.0	6.0	3.7	5.4	4.3
	-0.8	-0.7	-1.1	-1.9	-1.0	-1.5	-5.3	-4.7	-9.6	-1.4	-0.2	0.8	-0.2	1.2	-0.6
	5.1	3.9	1.4	2.3	2.0	0.7	-1.5	-3.2	-7.4	2.7	4.8	6.9	3.5	6.6	3.7
	2.6	1.6	1.3	1.0	1.6	0.3	0.6	-0.4	-1.8	1.0	1.7	1.6	1.1	1.6	1.0
	2.5	2.3	0.1	1.3	0.4	0.4	-2.1	-2.8	-5.6	1.8	3.1	5.3	2.4	4.9	2.6
	(percent)					(percent)					(percent)				
	19.30	15.92	6.23	7.82	7.13	1.64	-3.47	-6.95	-16.98	6.06	19.99	29.10	14.29	29.80	17.77
	5.44	9.40	0.54	4.45	1.47	0.93	-4.83	-6.15	-12.83	3.94	12.94	22.34	9.96	22.36	12.69
	9.12	6.93	2.52	3.53	3.30	0.76	-1.62	-3.25	-7.78	2.77	9.83	14.52	6.78	13.43	7.69
	4.46	4.09	0.22	2.01	0.68	0.43	-2.26	-2.88	-5.88	1.80	6.36	11.15	4.73	10.08	5.49
	1.86	1.85	1.61	1.91	1.87	1.77	1.83	1.83	1.74	1.83	2.12	2.07	1.96	1.89	1.82
	0.35	0.39	0.31	0.40	0.34	0.16	0.18	0.21	0.23	0.20	0.37	0.33	0.36	0.31	0.25
	1.64	1.32	1.21	1.30	1.41	1.54	1.59	1.56	1.54	1.50	1.92	1.91	1.70	1.70	1.49

	Iron and Steel[13] Assets Under $25 Million					Nonferrous Metals[12]					Nonferrous Metals[13] Assets Under $25 Million				
	1Q 1985	2Q 1985	3Q 1985	4Q 1985	1Q 1986	1Q 1985	2Q 1985	3Q 1985	4Q 1985	1Q 1986	1Q 1985	2Q 1985	3Q 1985	4Q 1985	1Q 1986
	(percent of total assets)					(percent of total assets)					(percent of total assets)				
	10.4	11.6	10.6	11.0	9.3	3.3	3.6	4.2	4.6	4.0	12.1	10.5	11.8	10.4	8.8
	23.7	22.4	22.5	21.6	22.6	14.9	14.2	14.1	13.4	14.7	30.0	30.5	27.8	26.6	28.7
	18.5	18.5	19.5	17.9	16.9	16.0	15.4	15.3	15.4	16.1	19.7	19.5	19.1	21.4	21.6
	55.1	55.2	54.6	52.7	51.5	36.7	36.0	36.0	35.4	37.0	68.6	65.8	63.8	62.9	62.7
	40.4	41.0	41.3	40.9	42.1	42.9	42.4	42.6	42.9	42.3	26.4	28.7	27.6	29.6	30.4
	8.5	9.8	10.9	10.1	9.3	5.8	5.4	5.6	5.4	5.4	9.3	10.6	10.8	8.2	9.7
	29.7	29.8	33.8	27.6	27.5	20.7	19.7	19.7	20.3	20.2	32.4	31.8	32.6	33.3	34.5
	20.3	23.1	22.5	24.7	23.6	24.0	24.0	24.4	24.3	25.0	16.2	15.4	17.1	18.5	19.4
	52.8	56.5	59.5	54.9	53.7	54.1	53.3	53.1	54.2	54.4	50.9	50.1	52.5	55.9	56.7
	47.2	43.5	40.5	45.1	46.3	45.9	46.7	46.9	45.8	45.6	49.1	49.9	47.5	45.1	43.3

TABLE 15—INCOME STATEMENT
FOR CORPORATIONS INCLUDED IN ESIC MAJOR GROUPS 34 AND 35

	Fabricated Metal Products[1]				
	1Q 1985	2Q 1985	3Q 1985	4Q 1985	1Q 1986
	(percent of net sales)				
INCOME STATEMENT IN RATIO FORMAT					
Net sales, receipts, and operating revenues	100.0	100.0	100.0	100.0	100.0
Less: Depreciation, depletion, and amortization of property, plant and equipment	3.0	3.0	2.9	3.1	3.2
Less: All other operating costs and expenses	91.3	90.6	91.2	91.6	91.4
Income (or loss) from operations	5.7	6.4	5.9	5.3	5.4
Non-operating income (expense)	-0.6	-0.8	-1.4	-2.1	-0.3
Income (or loss) before income taxes	5.1	5.7	4.5	3.2	5.1
Less: Provision for current and deferred domestic income taxes	2.0	2.4	1.6	1.3	2.1
Income (or loss) after income taxes	3.1	3.3	2.9	1.9	3.1
	(percent)				
OPERATING RATIOS (see explanatory notes)					
Annual rate of profit on stockholders' equity at end of period:					
Before income taxes	16.41	19.60	14.79	10.37	15.82
After taxes	9.85	11.29	9.54	6.09	9.47
Annual rate of profit on total assets:					
Before income taxes	7.41	8.81	6.76	4.79	7.28
After taxes	4.44	5.08	4.36	2.81	4.36
BALANCE SHEET RATIOS (based on succeeding table)					
Total current assets to total current liabilities	1.90	1.90	1.93	1.98	2.02
Total cash, U.S. Government and other securities to total current liabilities	0.32	0.28	0.30	0.36	0.35
Total stockholders' equity to total debt	1.58	1.58	1.65	1.69	1.66

[1] During the first quarter of 1986, a considerable number of companies were reclassified by industry. To provide comparability, the four quarters of 1985 have been restated to reflect these reclassifications.
[2] 1985 Data are Revised.

TABLE 16—BALANCE SHEET
FOR CORPORATIONS INCLUDED IN ESIC MAJOR GROUPS 34 AND 35

	Fabricated Metal Products[1]				
	1Q 1985	2Q 1985	3Q 1985	4Q 1985	1Q 1986
	(percent of total assets)				
SELECTED BALANCE SHEET RATIOS					
Total cash, U.S. Government and other securities	9.5	8.1	8.5	9.7	9.3
Trade accounts and trade notes receivable	22.3	23.3	23.0	21.3	22.0
Inventories	21.6	20.8	20.1	19.5	20.0
Total current assets	56.0	54.9	54.2	53.6	54.2
Net property, plant and equipment	29.2	29.8	30.1	30.2	29.5
Short-term debt including installments on long-term debt	8.1	7.0	6.2	5.9	6.1
Total current liabilities	29.5	28.8	28.1	27.0	26.9
Long-term debt	20.5	21.4	21.3	21.5	21.5
Total liabilities	54.9	55.1	54.3	53.8	54.0
Stockholders' equity	45.1	44.9	45.7	46.2	46.0

[1] During the first quarter of 1986, a considerable number of companies were reclassified by industry. To provide comparability, the four quarters of 1985 have been restated to reflect these reclassifications.
[2] 1985 Data are Revised.

Fabricated Metal Products[2] Assets Under $25 Million					Machinery, Except Electrical[1]					Machinery, Except Electrical[2] Assets Under $25 Million				
1Q 1985	2Q 1985	3Q 1985	4Q 1985	1Q 1986	1Q 1985	2Q 1985	3Q 1985	4Q 1985	1Q 1986	1Q 1985	2Q 1985	3Q 1985	4Q 1985	1Q 1986
(percent of net sales)					(percent of net sales)					(percent of net sales)				
100.0	100.0	100.0	100.0	100.0	100.0	100.0	100.0	100.0	100.0	100.0	100.0	100.0	100.0	100.0
2.8	2.8	2.9	3.1	3.0	4.4	4.3	4.3	4.3	4.7	3.3	3.1	3.1	3.3	3.2
91.5	90.5	91.4	93.3	91.9	91.2	89.1	89.5	88.0	91.1	93.1	92.0	92.3	94.1	92.4
5.7	6.7	5.7	3.6	5.1	4.4	6.6	6.2	7.7	4.2	3.6	4.9	4.7	2.6	4.4
-0.8	-0.7	-0.5	-0.5	-1.3	1.3	0.9	0.6	0.9	0.5	-1.0	-1.4	-1.0	-0.7	-0.7
4.9	6.1	5.2	3.1	3.8	5.6	7.5	6.8	8.6	4.7	2.6	3.4	3.7	1.9	3.7
1.9	2.3	2.1	1.3	1.6	1.9	2.5	2.5	2.8	1.9	1.7	1.7	1.9	1.4	2.0
3.0	3.8	3.1	1.9	2.1	3.7	4.9	4.3	5.8	2.8	0.9	1.8	1.8	0.5	1.6
(percent)					(percent)					(percent)				
19.88	25.98	20.88	12.10	14.49	10.74	15.19	13.33	17.36	8.52	9.43	14.08	14.02	7.75	14.48
12.13	16.32	12.51	7.19	8.23	7.10	10.05	8.47	11.77	5.15	3.28	7.18	6.92	2.11	6.47
9.38	12.15	10.09	5.97	7.06	5.81	8.16	7.16	9.24	4.56	4.26	6.12	6.41	3.32	6.25
5.72	7.63	6.05	3.55	4.01	3.84	5.40	4.55	6.27	2.75	1.48	3.12	3.16	0.91	2.79
1.97	1.98	2.04	2.09	2.10	1.96	1.92	1.99	1.97	1.98	2.00	1.87	1.95	1.92	1.95
0.36	0.36	0.37	0.44	0.41	0.23	0.23	0.27	0.31	0.33	0.37	0.32	0.39	0.35	0.35
1.62	1.58	1.73	1.81	1.73	2.66	2.64	2.59	2.54	2.57	1.46	1.48	1.58	1.36	1.41

Fabricated Metal Products[2] Assets Under $25 Million					Machinery, Except Electrical[1]					Machinery, Except Electrical[2] Assets Under $25 Million				
1Q 1985	2Q 1985	3Q 1985	4Q 1985	1Q 1986	1Q 1985	2Q 1985	3Q 1985	4Q 1985	1Q 1986	1Q 1985	2Q 1985	3Q 1985	4Q 1985	1Q 1986
(percent of total assets)					(percent of total assets)					(percent of total assets)				
11.8	11.7	11.7	13.5	12.3	6.0	6.0	6.7	7.7	8.2	12.7	11.8	13.7	12.4	12.4
26.4	27.0	27.2	25.5	26.5	19.3	19.3	19.2	18.9	18.4	23.9	24.6	24.3	23.4	24.8
23.7	22.5	22.3	21.7	21.7	21.8	21.6	21.0	19.8	19.9	27.0	28.8	28.1	28.9	28.7
64.9	64.4	64.2	64.1	63.7	50.5	49.8	49.8	49.0	49.3	68.7	68.6	69.4	68.3	69.6
28.9	29.4	29.9	30.5	29.7	26.9	27.1	26.9	26.4	25.8	25.9	25.8	25.0	26.0	25.2
11.3	10.6	9.5	9.2	9.5	5.2	5.1	4.7	4.6	4.7	12.7	11.7	12.6	12.3	13.0
33.0	32.5	31.4	30.6	30.3	25.8	26.0	25.1	24.9	24.9	34.3	36.7	35.6	35.6	35.6
17.9	19.0	18.4	18.1	18.6	15.1	15.2	16.1	16.4	16.1	18.4	17.6	16.4	19.4	17.7
52.8	53.2	51.7	50.6	51.3	45.9	46.3	46.2	46.8	46.5	54.8	56.5	54.3	57.1	56.8
47.2	46.8	48.3	49.4	48.7	54.1	53.7	53.8	53.2	53.5	45.2	43.5	45.7	42.9	43.2

TABLE 17—INCOME STATEMENT
FOR CORPORATIONS INCLUDED IN ESIC MAJOR GROUPS 36 AND 37

	Electrical and Electronic Equipment [1]				
	1Q 1985	2Q 1985	3Q 1985	4Q 1985	1Q 1986
	(percent of net sales)				
INCOME STATEMENT IN RATIO FORMAT					
Net sales, receipts, and operating revenues	100.0	100.0	100.0	100.0	100.0
Less: Depreciation, depletion, and amortization of property, plant and equipment	3.8	3.7	3.7	3.7	4.1
Less: All other operating costs and expenses	90.3	90.7	91.3	91.3	90.5
Income (or loss) from operations	6.0	5.6	5.0	5.0	5.4
Non-operating income (expense)	0.3	0.4	-0.2	-0.6	0.6
Income (or loss) before income taxes	6.3	6.0	4.8	4.4	6.0
Less: Provision for current and deferred domestic income taxes	2.3	2.5	1.7	1.5	2.3
Income (or loss) after income taxes	4.0	3.5	3.1	2.9	3.7
	(percent)				
OPERATING RATIOS (see explanatory notes)					
Annual rate of profit on stockholders' equity at end of period:					
Before income taxes	15.24	15.71	11.72	11.10	13.50
After taxes	9.77	8.63	7.56	7.30	8.27
Annual rate of profit on total assets:					
Before income taxes	7.30	7.06	5.69	5.32	6.63
After taxes	4.68	4.14	3.67	3.50	4.06
BALANCE SHEET RATIOS (based on succeeding table)					
Total current assets to total current liabilities	1.59	1.59	1.60	1.59	1.66
Total cash, U.S. Government and other securities to total current liabilities	0.13	0.13	0.14	0.15	0.17
Total stockholders' equity to total debt	2.73	2.60	2.76	2.70	2.64

[1] During the first quarter of 1986, a considerable number of companies were reclassified by industry. To provide comparability, the four quarters of 1985 have been restated to reflect these reclassifications.
[2] 1985 Data are Revised.

TABLE 18—BALANCE SHEET
FOR CORPORATIONS INCLUDED IN ESIC MAJOR GROUPS 36 AND 37

	Electrical and Electronic Equipment [1]				
	1Q 1985	2Q 1985	3Q 1985	4Q 1985	1Q 1986
	(percent of total assets)				
SELECTED BALANCE SHEET RATIOS					
Total cash, U.S. Government and other securities	4.4	4.4	4.8	5.1	5.5
Trade accounts and trade notes receivable	21.8	21.1	21.3	21.5	19.
Inventories	23.3	23.2	22.5	21.3	22.
Total current assets	54.6	54.3	53.6	53.1	52.
Net property, plant and equipment	26.2	26.2	26.3	26.4	26.
Short-term debt including installments on long-term debt	5.6	6.4	5.6	5.2	5.
Total current liabilities	34.3	34.2	33.5	33.3	31.
Long-term debt	12.0	12.0	12.0	12.5	13.
Total liabilities	52.1	52.0	51.5	52.1	50.
Stockholders' equity	47.9	48.0	48.5	47.9	49.

[1] During the first quarter of 1986, a considerable number of companies were reclassified by industry. To provide comparability, the four quarters of 1985 have been restated to reflect these reclassifications.
[2] 1985 Data are Revised.

Electrical and Electronic Equipment Assets Under $25 Million					Transportation Equipment[1]					Transportation Equipment[2] Assets Under $25 Million				
1Q 1985	2Q 1985	3Q 1985	4Q 1985	1Q 1986	1Q 1985	2Q 1985	3Q 1985	4Q 1985	1Q 1986	1Q 1985	2Q 1985	3Q 1985	4Q 1985	1Q 1986
(percent of net sales)					(percent of net sales)					(percent of net sales)				
100.0	100.0	100.0	100.0	100.0	100.0	100.0	100.0	100.0	100.0	100.0	100.0	100.0	100.0	100.0
2.5	2.3	2.3	2.4	2.6	3.6	3.7	3.7	3.5	3.6	2.6	2.3	2.7	2.7	2.9
92.6	93.5	92.9	92.9	92.7	90.1	90.0	94.5	91.5	91.2	91.0	89.4	92.5	93.1	92.8
4.9	4.2	4.8	4.7	4.7	6.3	6.3	1.8	4.9	5.2	6.4	8.3	4.9	4.2	4.3
-0.8	-0.6	-0.4	0.0	-0.5	0.9	1.5	2.1	1.0	1.5	0.0	-0.3	-0.6	-0.8	-1.4
4.1	3.6	4.4	4.7	4.2	7.2	7.8	4.0	6.0	6.7	6.4	8.0	4.2	3.4	2.9
2.5	2.2	2.6	2.4	2.3	2.8	2.6	1.0	2.0	2.2	2.5	2.5	1.1	1.1	1.4
1.7	1.4	1.9	2.3	1.9	4.4	5.1	2.9	4.0	4.5	3.8	5.5	3.2	2.3	1.5
(percent)					(percent)					(percent)				
16.67	14.39	16.69	18.14	14.97	27.13	30.02	13.62	22.34	23.50	28.17	38.01	18.94	15.88	14.72
6.74	5.63	7.04	9.00	6.71	16.47	19.83	10.13	15.04	15.72	17.00	25.91	14.22	10.60	7.53
7.42	6.36	7.86	8.47	7.06	10.32	11.48	5.19	8.46	9.03	13.06	17.93	8.47	6.62	5.12
3.00	2.49	3.32	4.20	3.17	6.26	7.59	3.86	5.70	6.04	7.88	12.22	6.36	4.42	2.62
1.90	1.84	2.03	2.07	2.03	1.27	1.26	1.24	1.23	1.19	1.97	2.14	2.02	1.91	1.60
0.26	0.28	0.34	0.38	0.38	0.22	0.23	0.20	0.22	0.19	0.27	0.31	0.24	0.23	0.18
1.49	1.49	1.74	1.64	1.75	2.83	2.98	3.06	2.92	2.88	1.78	1.87	1.57	1.37	0.89

Electrical and Electronic Equipment Assets Under $25 Million					Transportation Equipment[1]					Transportation Equipment[2] Assets Under $25 Million				
1Q 1985	2Q 1985	3Q 1985	4Q 1985	1Q 1986	1Q 1985	2Q 1985	3Q 1985	4Q 1985	1Q 1986	1Q 1985	2Q 1985	3Q 1985	4Q 1985	1Q 1986
(percent of total assets)					(percent of total assets)					(percent of total assets)				
9.8	10.6	12.2	13.4	13.5	9.5	10.3	8.6	9.6	8.0	9.2	10.1	7.9	8.2	7.0
27.4	26.7	26.8	27.1	25.3	15.0	15.1	14.4	13.6	14.0	21.7	21.5	20.1	19.4	21.1
29.7	28.5	29.2	27.7	27.4	27.9	27.0	27.3	26.4	25.7	28.8	31.0	32.2	35.2	29.1
71.8	69.9	72.1	73.1	71.3	55.7	55.8	53.9	53.0	50.9	66.8	68.9	66.0	69.1	62.8
22.4	23.0	21.3	20.7	21.2	25.2	25.2	25.8	26.0	27.0	27.6	25.2	27.2	24.6	30.0
13.9	13.9	11.5	12.0	10.4	3.9	4.1	2.9	3.2	3.3	9.0	7.7	9.0	10.6	16.5
37.8	38.0	35.6	35.2	35.1	44.0	44.1	43.4	43.2	42.9	33.8	32.2	32.7	36.2	39.3
16.1	15.8	15.6	16.6	16.5	9.5	8.8	9.5	9.8	10.1	17.1	17.6	19.5	19.8	22.5
55.5	55.8	52.9	53.3	52.8	62.0	61.7	61.9	62.1	61.6	53.6	52.8	55.3	58.3	65.2
44.5	44.2	47.1	46.7	47.2	38.0	38.3	38.1	37.9	38.4	46.4	47.2	44.7	41.7	34.8

TABLE 19—INCOME STATEMENT
FOR CORPORATIONS INCLUDED IN ESIC MAJOR GROUPS 37.1 AND 37.7

	Motor Vehicles and Equipment [12]				
	1Q 1985	2Q 1985	3Q 1985	4Q 1985	1Q 1986
	(percent of net sales)				
INCOME STATEMENT IN RATIO FORMAT					
Net sales, receipts, and operating revenues	100.0	100.0	100.0	100.0	100.0
Less: Depreciation, depletion, and amortization of property, plant and equipment	4.1	4.2	4.1	4.0	3.9
Less: All other operating costs and expenses	89.3	89.2	94.3	91.5	91.2
Income (or loss) from operations	6.6	6.7	1.6	4.4	4.9
Non-operating income (expense)	1.3	2.2	2.1	2.9	2.3
Income (or loss) before income taxes	7.9	8.9	3.7	7.3	7.2
Less: Provision for current and deferred domestic income taxes	3.2	3.0	0.5	1.5	2.2
Income (or loss) after income taxes	4.8	5.9	3.2	5.8	5.0
	(percent)				
OPERATING RATIOS (see explanatory notes)					
Annual rate of profit on stockholders' equity at end of period:					
Before income taxes	30.79	34.61	12.37	26.20	25.48
After taxes	18.48	22.95	10.60	20.79	17.62
Annual rate of profit on total assets:					
Before income taxes	14.05	15.08	5.65	11.91	11.61
After taxes	8.43	10.65	4.84	9.46	8.03
BALANCE SHEET RATIOS (based on succeeding table)					
Total current assets to total current liabilities	1.34	1.36	1.31	1.29	1.16
Total cash, U.S. Government and other securities to total current liabilities	0.40	0.45	0.36	0.37	0.28
Total stockholders' equity to total debt	4.07	4.72	4.20	3.79	3.60

[1] Included in Transportation Equipment.
[2] During the first quarter of 1986, a considerable number of companies were reclassified by industry. To provide comparability, the four quarters of 1985 have been restated to reflect these reclassifications.
[3] 1985 Data are Revised.

TABLE 20—BALANCE SHEET
FOR CORPORATIONS INCLUDED IN ESIC MAJOR GROUPS 37.1 AND 37.7

	Motor Vehicles and Equipment [12]				
	1Q 1985	2Q 1985	3Q 1985	4Q 1985	1Q 1986
	(percent of total assets)				
SELECTED BALANCE SHEET RATIOS					
Total cash, U.S. Government and other securities	14.1	15.4	12.2	12.5	9.7
Trade accounts and trade notes receivable	14.5	14.2	13.3	12.5	13.1
Inventories	13.9	13.0	13.8	13.6	12.6
Total current assets	46.5	46.4	44.5	43.4	39.9
Net property, plant and equipment	29.3	29.2	30.0	30.0	31.8
Short-term debt including installments on long-term debt	3.2	2.5	2.6	3.0	3.3
Total current liabilities	34.8	34.1	34.0	33.6	34.3
Long-term debt	7.9	7.4	8.3	9.1	9.3
Total liabilities	54.4	53.5	54.3	54.5	54.4
Stockholders' equity	45.6	46.5	45.7	45.5	45.6

[1] Included in Transportation Equipment.
[2] During the first quarter of 1986, a considerable number of companies were reclassified by industry. To provide comparability, the four quarters of 1985 have been restated to reflect these reclassifications.
[3] 1985 Data are Revised.

Motor Vehicles and Equipment[1 3] Assets Under $25 Million					Aircraft, Guided Missiles and Parts[1 2]					Aircraft, Guided Missiles and Parts[1 3] Assets Under $25 Million				
1Q 1985	2Q 1985	3Q 1985	4Q 1985	1Q 1986	1Q 1985	2Q 1985	3Q 1985	4Q 1985	1Q 1986	1Q 1985	2Q 1985	3Q 1985	4Q 1985	1Q 1986
(percent of net sales)					(percent of net sales)					(percent of net sales)				
100.0	100.0	100.0	100.0	100.0	100.0	100.0	100.0	100.0	100.0	100.0	100.0	100.0	100.0	100.0
2.1	1.9	2.3	2.5	2.9	2.9	2.9	3.1	2.8	3.0	4.4	3.9	3.7	3.8	3.9
89.5	89.1	93.6	93.8	93.4	91.3	91.4	95.0	91.7	91.1	84.4	84.8	84.9	85.9	89.0
8.3	9.0	4.1	3.7	3.8	5.8	5.6	1.9	5.5	5.9	11.2	11.2	11.5	10.3	7.2
0.7	0.4	0.1	-0.2	-1.3	0.7	0.6	2.8	-1.3	0.5	-1.3	-2.0	-1.1	-1.2	-0.6
9.0	9.4	4.2	3.4	2.4	6.5	6.3	4.7	4.2	6.4	9.9	9.2	10.4	9.2	6.5
3.1	2.8	1.0	0.6	1.0	2.4	2.1	1.9	2.8	2.3	2.2	2.5	2.2	2.7	2.9
5.9	6.6	3.2	2.8	1.4	4.1	4.2	2.8	1.4	4.1	7.8	6.7	8.2	6.5	3.7
(percent)					(percent)					(percent)				
39.60	45.43	19.62	16.85	12.68	22.40	22.61	16.24	16.11	20.70	30.42	28.62	37.74	30.08	19.88
25.84	32.02	14.89	13.84	7.22	14.21	15.08	9.76	5.46	13.12	23.83	20.73	29.85	21.24	11.13
19.41	23.03	9.22	7.18	4.18	7.20	7.17	5.22	5.11	6.80	14.29	13.86	17.33	14.01	9.51
12.66	16.23	7.00	5.90	2.38	4.57	4.78	3.14	1.73	4.31	11.20	10.04	13.71	9.89	5.32
2.00	2.29	2.00	1.98	1.53	1.21	1.19	1.19	1.18	1.20	1.91	1.90	1.92	1.96	2.01
0.38	0.40	0.24	0.26	0.18	0.09	0.09	0.08	0.12	0.11	0.23	0.23	0.20	0.23	0.27
2.29	2.39	1.90	1.47	0.79	2.47	2.39	2.78	2.74	2.98	1.79	2.17	1.71	1.94	1.94

Motor Vehicles and Equipment[1 3] Assets Under $25 Million					Aircraft, Guided Missiles and Parts[1 2]					Aircraft, Guided Missiles and Parts[1 3] Assets Under $25 Million				
1Q 1985	2Q 1985	3Q 1985	4Q 1985	1Q 1986	1Q 1985	2Q 1985	3Q 1985	4Q 1985	1Q 1986	1Q 1985	2Q 1985	3Q 1985	4Q 1985	1Q 1986
(percent of total assets)					(percent of total assets)					(percent of total assets)				
2.2	12.3	7.8	9.7	7.3	4.7	5.0	4.5	6.7	6.0	7.6	7.9	6.5	7.5	8.6
2.1	21.6	20.8	18.2	21.2	13.5	14.3	13.8	13.0	12.8	17.2	17.6	14.7	17.9	18.7
4.3	29.8	31.1	35.4	27.3	44.3	43.2	43.7	41.6	42.2	34.7	35.5	38.6	37.6	34.0
5.2	70.8	66.0	72.1	62..1	65.2	65.7	63.8	63.0	62.7	64.5	64.1	62.6	64.3	63.5
7.6	22.0	24.9	20.4	28.5	20.1	20.1	20.6	20.8	20.9	29.6	29.9	31.2	27.4	30.4
7.1	6.3	7.7	10.7	19.6	4.1	5.5	2.8	3.2	2.4	9.7	7.8	9.0	7.3	7.7
2.6	30.9	32.9	36.4	40.5	53.8	55.1	53.5	53.4	52.4	33.8	33.7	32.6	32.8	31.6
4.3	14.9	17.0	18.3	22.1	8.9	7.8	8.8	8.4	8.6	16.6	14.6	17.9	16.6	16.9
1.0	49.3	53.0	57.4	67.1	67.8	68.3	67.8	68.3	67.1	53.0	51.6	54.1	53.4	52.2
9.0	50.7	47.0	42.6	32.9	32.2	31.7	32.2	31.7	32.9	47.0	48.4	45.9	46.6	47.8

TABLE 21—INCOME STATEMENT
FOR CORPORATIONS INCLUDED IN ESIC MAJOR GROUP 38
AND OTHER DURABLE MANUFACTURING INDUSTRIES

	Instruments and Related Products[1]				
	1Q 1985	2Q 1985	3Q 1985	4Q 1985	1Q 1986
	(percent of net sales)				
INCOME STATEMENT IN RATIO FORMAT					
Net sales, receipts, and operating revenues	100.0	100.0	100.0	100.0	100.0
Less: Depreciation, depletion, and amortization of property, plant and equipment	5.0	4.9	5.2	5.1	5.5
Less: All other operating costs and expenses	87.4	88.1	87.9	90.0	91.1
Income (or loss) from operations	7.6	7.0	6.9	4.9	3.3
Non-operating income (expense)	2.1	2.8	1.1	-0.9	-3.7
Income (or loss) before income taxes	9.8	9.8	8.0	4.0	-0.4
Less: Provision for current and deferred domestic income taxes	3.2	3.1	2.0	0.3	0.4
Income (or loss) after income taxes	6.6	6.6	6.0	3.7	-0.7
	(percent)				
OPERATING RATIOS (see explanatory notes)					
Annual rate of profit on stockholders' equity at end of period:					
Before income taxes	17.12	17.69	13.78	7.05	-0.65
After taxes	11 53	12.02	10.29	6.52	-1.26
Annual rate of profit on total assets:					
Before income taxes	10.06	10.38	8.22	4.11	-0.37
After taxes	6.77	7.06	6.14	3.80	-0.73
BALANCE SHEET RATIOS (based on succeeding table)					
Total current assets to total current liabilities	2.07	2.09	2.13	1.97	1.89
Total cash, U.S. Government and other securities to total current liabilities	0.24	0.22	0.24	0.26	0.24
Total stockholders' equity to total debt	3.48	3.37	3.54	3.43	3.38

[1] During the first quarter of 1986, a considerable number of companies were reclassified by industry. To provide comparability, the four quarters of 1985 have been restated to reflect these reclassifications.
[2] 1985 Data are Revised.

TABLE 22—BALANCE SHEET
FOR CORPORATIONS INCLUDED IN ESIC MAJOR GROUP 38
AND OTHER DURABLE MANUFACTURING INDUSTRIES

	Instruments and Related Products[1]				
	1Q 1985	2Q 1985	3Q 1985	4Q 1985	1Q 1986
	(percent of total assets)				
SELECTED BALANCE SHEET RATIOS					
Total cash, U.S. Government and other securities	5.7	5.1	5.3	6.2	5.9
Trade accounts and trade notes receivable	18.3	18.2	18.6	17.5	17.2
Inventories	20.3	20.3	19.5	18.9	18.9
Total current assets	48.7	48.0	47.6	47.6	47.1
Net property, plant and equipment	30.2	30.2	30.1	30.2	30.4
Short-term debt including installments on long-term debt	4.4	4.7	4.4	5.0	4.7
Total current liabilities	23.5	23.0	22.4	24.1	24.8
Long-term debt	12.5	12.7	12.4	12.1	12.4
Total liabilities	41.3	41.3	40.4	41.7	42.5
Stockholders' equity	58.7	58.7	59.6	58.3	57.5

[1] During the first quarter of 1986, a considerable number of companies were reclassified by industry. To provide comparability, the four quarters of 1985 have been restated to reflect these reclassifications.
[2] 1985 Data are Revised.

Instruments and Related Products[2] Assets Under $25 Million					Other Durable Mfg. Industries[1]					Other Durable Mfg. Industries[2] Assets Under $25 Million				
1Q 1985	2Q 1985	3Q 1985	4Q 1985	1Q 1986	1Q 1985	2Q 1985	3Q 1985	4Q 1985	1Q 1986	1Q 1985	2Q 1985	3Q 1985	4Q 1985	1Q 1985
(percent of net sales)					(percent of net sales)					(percent of net sales)				
100.0	100.0	100.0	100.0	100.0	100.0	100.0	100.0	100.0	100.0	100.0	100.0	100.0	100.0	100.0
2.6	2.4	2.6	2.3	2.8	3.0	2.7	2.7	2.8	3.1	2.5	2.2	2.2	2.3	2.5
92.3	92.0	91.3	93.2	92.5	92.3	90.8	90.8	91.5	92.5	94.2	92.8	92.3	93.4	94.1
5.1	5.6	6.1	4.6	4.7	4.7	6.5	6.4	5.7	4.4	3.3	5.1	5.3	4.3	3.4
-0.2	-0.4	0.7	-0.9	-1.7	-0.3	-0.6	-0.6	-0.7	-0.6	0.3	-0.7	-0.6	-0.8	-0.6
4.9	5.2	6.8	3.6	3.0	4.4	5.8	5.8	5.0	3.8	3.6	4.3	4.9	3.5	2.8
2.2	2.3	1.8	2.2	1.3	1.9	2.5	2.5	2.2	1.8	1.6	2.0	1.9	1.6	1.3
2.7	2.9	5.1	1.4	1.7	2.5	3.3	3.3	2.8	2.1	2.0	2.4	3.0	1.9	1.5
(percent)					(percent)					(percent)				
14.13	16.99	19.44	12.03	9.43	14.94	20.87	20.17	17.81	12.56	17.04	20.48	22.30	17.62	12.91
7.85	9.61	14.45	4.67	5.23	8.46	11.92	11.62	9.94	6.78	9.37	11.27	13.74	9.46	6.78
7.10	8.28	10.13	5.75	4.50	7.03	9.96	9.79	8.64	6.03	7.53	9.43	10.71	8.23	5.93
3.94	4.68	7.53	2.23	2.50	3.98	5.68	5.64	4.82	3.26	4.14	5.19	6.60	4.42	3.11
2.49	2.23	2.58	2.32	2.30	1.97	2.07	2.08	2.10	2.10	1.85	1.96	2.04	1.98	1.96
0.41	0.31	0.38	0.40	0.40	0.25	0.28	0.30	0.31	0.28	0.24	0.27	0.29	0.27	0.25
1.92	1.85	1.99	1.85	1.72	1.58	1.60	1.71	1.75	1.67	1.39	1.51	1.59	1.53	1.42

Instruments and Related Products[2] Assets Under $25 Million					Other Durable Mfg. Industries[1]					Other Durable Mfg. Industries[2] Assets Under $25 Million				
1Q 1985	2Q 1985	3Q 1985	4Q 1985	1Q 1986	1Q 1985	2Q 1985	3Q 1985	4Q 1985	1Q 1986	1Q 1985	2Q 1985	3Q 1985	4Q 1985	1Q 1986
(percent of total assets)					(percent of total assets)					(percent of total assets)				
11.7	9.9	10.5	12.6	12.4	7.0	7.5	7.8	8.0	7.3	8.7	9.4	9.7	9.2	8.5
26.5	28.1	25.6	26.0	25.4	21.0	20.8	21.2	20.4	20.3	26.8	25.5	26.0	26.4	25.6
29.4	29.9	29.5	29.1	30.3	22.1	22.1	21.4	21.2	21.8	28.1	29.2	28.4	27.1	28.1
71.6	72.4	70.2	72.5	71.8	54.4	54.6	54.9	54.3	54.4	67.2	67.5	67.8	66.6	66.3
20.8	21.5	21.6	21.5	22.7	36.3	35.5	35.9	36.5	36.1	27.3	26.3	26.6	27.7	28.0
7.7	10.3	7.2	7.5	8.3	9.5	8.9	8.9	8.0	8.8	14.1	13.0	13.1	12.7	13.9
28.8	32.4	27.3	31.2	31.2	27.6	26.4	26.3	25.8	25.9	36.4	34.5	33.2	33.6	33.8
18.5	16.0	19.0	18.4	19.4	20.2	20.9	19.6	19.7	20.0	17.7	17.6	17.0	17.8	18.4
49.8	51.3	47.9	52.2	52.3	53.0	52.3	51.5	51.5	52.0	55.8	53.9	52.0	53.3	54.1
50.2	48.7	52.1	47.8	47.7	47.0	47.7	48.5	48.5	48.0	44.2	46.1	48.0	46.7	45.9

TABLE 23—INCOME STATEMENT
FOR CORPORATIONS INCLUDED IN ESIC MAJOR GROUP 20,
ASSETS $25 MILLION AND OVER

	Food and Kindred Products[1]				
	1Q 1985	2Q 1985	3Q 1985	4Q 1985	1Q 1986
INCOME STATEMENT IN RATIO FORMAT	(percent of net sales)				
Net sales, receipts, and operating revenues	100.0	100.0	100.0	100.0	100.0
Less: Depreciation, depletion, and amortization of property, plant and equipment	2.5	2.4	2.7	2.5	2.7
Less: All other operating costs and expenses	91.2	89.9	89.9	89.7	90.6
Income (or loss) from operations	6.3	7.8	7.5	7.8	6.7
Non-operating income (expense)	-0.6	-1.1	-0.4	-0.3	-1.2
Income (or loss) before income taxes	5.6	6.7	7.1	7.5	5.4
Net income (or loss) of foreign branches and equity in earnings (losses) of non-consolidated subsidiaries (net of foreign taxes)	0.8	0.9	1.6	0.9	1.1
Less: Provision for current and deferred domestic income taxes	2.5	3.1	3.3	2.9	2.3
Income (or loss) after income taxes	3.9	4.6	5.3	5.5	4.2
OPERATING RATIOS (see explanatory notes)	(percent)				
Annual rate of profit on stockholders' equity at end of period:					
Before income taxes	21.60	26.26	28.11	27.95	20.71
After taxes	13.09	15.82	17.25	18.09	13.23
Annual rate of profit on total assets:					
Before income taxes	9.41	11.64	12.45	11.74	8.51
After taxes	5.70	7.01	7.64	7.60	5.43

[1] During the first quarter of 1986, a considerable number of companies were reclassified by industry. To provide comparability, the four quarters of 1985 have been restated to reflect these reclassifications.

TABLE 24—INCOME STATEMENT
FOR CORPORATIONS INCLUDED IN ESIC MAJOR GROUP 21,
ASSETS $25 MILLION AND OVER

	Tobacco Manufactures[1]				
	1Q 1985	2Q 1985	3Q 1985	4Q 1985	1Q 1986
INCOME STATEMENT IN RATIO FORMAT	(percent of net sales)				
Net sales, receipts, and operating revenues					
Less: Depreciation, depletion, and amortization of property, plant and equipment					
Less: All other operating costs and expenses					
Income (or loss) from operations					
Non-operating income (expense)					
Income (or loss) before income taxes					
Net income (or loss) of foreign branches and equity in earnings (losses) of non-consolidated subsidiaries (net of foreign taxes)					
Less: Provision for current and deferred domestic income taxes					
Income (or loss) after income taxes					
OPERATING RATIOS (see explanatory notes)	(percent)				
Annual rate of profit on stockholders' equity at end of period:					
Before income taxes					
After taxes					
Annual rate of profit on total assets:					
Before income taxes					
After taxes					

[1] Tobacco industry data have been collapsed into food industry data. Major merger and acquisition activity resulted in the reclassification of a significant portion of gross receipts and assets from tobacco to food. The remainder, consisting of data from highly specialized tobacco manufacturers, is too small to be considered publishable as a separate industry category.

TABLE 25—INCOME STATEMENT
FOR CORPORATIONS INCLUDED IN ESIC MAJOR GROUP 22,
ASSETS $25 MILLION AND OVER

	Textile Mill Products[1]				
	1Q 1985	2Q 1985	3Q 1985	4Q 1985	1Q 1986
INCOME STATEMENT IN RATIO FORMAT	(percent of net sales)				
Net sales, receipts, and operating revenues	100.0	100.0	100.0	100.0	100.0
Less: Depreciation, depletion, and amortization of property, plant and equipment	3.7	3.4	3.4	3.1	3.5
Less: All other operating costs and expenses	91.5	91.7	90.6	88.6	90.3
Income (or loss) from operations	4.7	4.9	5.9	8.2	6.2
Non-operating income (expense)	-1.2	-2.5	-2.7	-1.7	-1.4
Income (or loss) before income taxes	3.6	2.4	3.2	6.6	4.9
Net income (or loss) of foreign branches and equity in earnings (losses) of non-consolidated subsidiaries (net of foreign taxes)	0.1	0.0	0.0	0.1	0.2
Less: Provision for current and deferred domestic income taxes	1.4	1.2	1.3	3.3	2.3
Income (or loss) after income taxes	2.2	1.2	1.9	3.4	2.8
OPERATING RATIOS (see explanatory notes)	(percent)				
Annual rate of profit on stockholders' equity at end of period:					
Before income taxes	10.71	7.78	10.26	22.26	15.90
After taxes	6.57	4.02	6.18	11.35	8.91
Annual rate of profit on total assets:					
Before income taxes	5.04	3.65	4.64	10.02	7.11
After taxes	3.09	1.88	2.80	5.10	3.99

[1] During the first quarter of 1986, a considerable number of companies were reclassified by industry. To provide comparability, the four quarters of 1985 have been restated to reflect these reclassifications.

TABLE 26—INCOME STATEMENT
FOR CORPORATIONS INCLUDED IN ESIC MAJOR GROUP 26,
ASSETS $25 MILLION AND OVER

	Paper and Allied Products[1]				
	1Q 1985	2Q 1985	3Q 1985	4Q 1985	1Q 1986
INCOME STATEMENT IN RATIO FORMAT	(percent of net sales)				
Net sales, receipts, and operating revenues	100.0	100.0	100.0	100.0	100.0
Less: Depreciation, depletion, and amortization of property, plant and equipment	4.6	4.5	4.8	4.8	5.1
Less: All other operating costs and expenses	87.4	87.0	88.0	88.2	88.3
Income (or loss) from operations	7.9	8.4	7.2	7.0	6.7
Non-operating income (expense)	-1.5	-1.3	-2.8	-1.4	-1.6
Income (or loss) before income taxes	6.5	7.1	4.4	5.6	5.0
Net income (or loss) of foreign branches and equity in earnings (losses) of non-consolidated subsidiaries (net of foreign taxes)	0.3	0.5	0.5	0.5	0.4
Less: Provision for current and deferred domestic income taxes	2.6	2.7	1.5	1.9	1.9
Income (or loss) after income taxes	4.2	4.9	3.4	4.2	3.4
OPERATING RATIOS (see explanatory notes)	(percent)				
Annual rate of profit on stockholders' equity at end of period:					
Before income taxes	14.98	17.00	10.75	13.06	11.48
After taxes	9.17	10.95	7.43	9.03	7.27
Annual rate of profit on total assets:					
Before income taxes	7.18	8.25	5.12	6.27	5.41
After taxes	4.39	5.32	3.54	4.33	3.43

[1] During the first quarter of 1986, a considerable number of companies were reclassified by industry. To provide comparability, the four quarters of 1985 have been restated to reflect these reclassifications.

TABLE 27—INCOME STATEMENT
FOR CORPORATIONS INCLUDED IN ESIC MAJOR GROUP 27,
ASSETS $25 MILLION AND OVER

	Printing and Publishing [1]				
	1Q 1985	2Q 1985	3Q 1985	4Q 1985	1Q 1986
INCOME STATEMENT IN RATIO FORMAT	(percent of net sales)				
Net sales, receipts, and operating revenues	100.0	100.0	100.0	100.0	100.0
Less: Depreciation, depletion, and amortization of property, plant and equipment	3.8	3.5	3.6	3.4	3.9
Less: All other operating costs and expenses	85.9	83.4	83.1	83.7	85.8
Income (or loss) from operations	10.3	13.1	13.3	12.9	10.3
Non-operating income (expense)	1.7	1.4	0.2	-1.5	1.5
Income (or loss) before income taxes	12.0	14.5	13.5	11.4	11.8
Net income (or loss) of foreign branches and equity in earnings (losses) of non-consolidated subsidiaries (net of foreign taxes)	-0.6	1.0	0.7	0.9	0.8
Less: Provision for current and deferred domestic income taxes	4.7	5.8	5.9	5.6	5.4
Income (or loss) after income taxes	6.9	9.7	8.4	6.8	7.2
OPERATING RATIOS (see explanatory notes)	(percent)				
Annual rate of profit on stockholders' equity at end of period:					
Before income taxes	26.63	38.09	36.33	32.22	29.54
After taxes	15.93	23.95	21.32	17.77	16.98
Annual rate of profit on total assets:					
Before income taxes	12.87	18.09	16.61	14.31	13.34
After taxes	7.70	11.37	9.75	7.89	7.67

[1] During the first quarter of 1986, a considerable number of companies were reclassified by industry. To provide comparability, the four quarters of 1985 have been restated to reflect these reclassifications.

TABLE 28—INCOME STATEMENT
FOR CORPORATIONS INCLUDED IN ESIC MAJOR GROUP 28,
ASSETS $25 MILLION AND OVER

	Chemicals and Allied Products [1]				
	1Q 1985	2Q 1985	3Q 1985	4Q 1985	1Q 1986
INCOME STATEMENT IN RATIO FORMAT	(percent of net sales)				
Net sales, receipts, and operating revenues	100.0	100.0	100.0	100.0	100.0
Less: Depreciation, depletion, and amortization of property, plant and equipment	4.7	4.4	4.9	5.1	5.3
Less: All other operating costs and expenses	88.0	88.0	88.0	90.5	86.8
Income (or loss) from operations	7.3	7.6	7.1	4.4	8.0
Non-operating income (expense)	0.2	-0.3	-3.5	-5.6	-0.7
Income (or loss) before income taxes	7.5	7.3	3.6	-1.1	7.4
Net income (or loss) of foreign branches and equity in earnings (losses) of non-consolidated subsidiaries (net of foreign taxes)	2.1	2.3	2.7	2.8	2.9
Less: Provision for current and deferred domestic income taxes	3.0	2.9	1.9	0.1	3.5
Income (or loss) after income taxes	6.5	6.7	4.5	1.6	6.7
OPERATING RATIOS (see explanatory notes)	(percent)				
Annual rate of profit on stockholders' equity at end of period:					
Before income taxes	18.20	18.69	11.89	3.20	20.51
After taxes	12.49	13.09	8.37	3.04	13.44
Annual rate of profit on total assets:					
Before income taxes	9.37	9.72	5.92	1.56	9.48
After taxes	6.43	6.80	4.17	1.49	6.21

[1] During the first quarter of 1986, a considerable number of companies were reclassified by industry. To provide comparability, the four quarters of 1985 have been restated to reflect these reclassifications.

TABLE 29—INCOME STATEMENT
FOR CORPORATIONS INCLUDED IN ESIC MAJOR GROUP 28.1,
ASSETS $25 MILLION AND OVER

	Industrial Chemicals and Synthetics[1]				
	1Q 1985	2Q 1985	3Q 1985	4Q 1985	1Q 1986
INCOME STATEMENT IN RATIO FORMAT	(percent of net sales)				
Net sales, receipts, and operating revenues	100.0	100.0	100.0	100.0	100.0
Less: Depreciation, depletion, and amortization of property, plant and equipment	6.4	6.2	7.1	7.1	7.3
Less: All other operating costs and expenses	88.2	87.2	88.7	88.8	84.8
Income (or loss) from operations	5.4	6.6	4.2	4.0	7.8
Non-operating income (expense)	-0.7	-0.7	-7.9	-8.2	0.6
Income (or loss) before income taxes	4.7	5.9	-3.7	-4.2	8.4
Net income (or loss) of foreign branches and equity in earnings (losses) of non-consolidated subsidiaries (net of foreign taxes)	0.9	1.7	2.0	1.3	2.1
Less: Provision for current and deferred domestic income taxes	1.7	2.0	-1.5	-1.9	3.7
Income (or loss) after income taxes	4.0	5.5	-0.3	-0.9	6.8
OPERATING RATIOS (see explanatory notes)	(percent)				
Annual rate of profit on stockholders' equity at end of period:					
Before income taxes	10.51	14.63	-3.14	-5.41	21.72
After taxes	7.37	10.69	-0.48	-1.67	14.08
Annual rate of profit on total assets:					
Before income taxes	5.12	7.10	-1.44	-2.48	9.26
After taxes	3.59	5.19	-0.22	-0.77	6.01

[1] During the first quarter of 1986, a considerable number of companies were reclassified by industry. To provide comparability, the four quarters of 1985 have been restated to reflect these reclassifications.

TABLE 30—INCOME STATEMENT
FOR CORPORATIONS INCLUDED IN ESIC MAJOR GROUP 28.3,
ASSETS $25 MILLION AND OVER

	Drugs[1]				
	1Q 1985	2Q 1985	3Q 1985	4Q 1985	1Q 1986
INCOME STATEMENT IN RATIO FORMAT	(percent of net sales)				
Net sales, receipts, and operating revenues	100.0	100.0	100.0	100.0	100.0
Less: Depreciation, depletion, and amortization of property, plant and equipment	3.2	3.3	3.2	3.5	3.5
Less: All other operating costs and expenses	85.0	86.4	85.4	90.6	85.5
Income (or loss) from operations	11.8	10.3	11.3	5.9	10.9
Non-operating income (expense)	0.9	0.4	-0.2	-9.2	0.8
Income (or loss) before income taxes	12.7	10.7	11.2	-3.4	11.7
Net income (or loss) of foreign branches and equity in earnings (losses) of non-consolidated subsidiaries (net of foreign taxes)	6.0	7.0	6.9	8.4	7.2
Less: Provision for current and deferred domestic income taxes	5.7	5.7	5.8	2.1	5.8
Income (or loss) after income taxes	13.0	12.1	12.3	2.9	13.1
OPERATING RATIOS (see explanatory notes)	(percent)				
Annual rate of profit on stockholders' equity at end of period:					
Before income taxes	29.74	26.63	27.17	7.63	29.27
After taxes	20.69	18.10	18.52	4.45	20.29
Annual rate of profit on total assets:					
Before income taxes	17.09	15.38	15.61	4.30	15.70
After taxes	11.89	10.45	10.64	2.51	10.88

[1] During the first quarter of 1986, a considerable number of companies were reclassified by industry. To provide comparability, the four quarters of 1985 have been restated to reflect these reclassifications.

TABLE 31—INCOME STATEMENT
FOR CORPORATIONS INCLUDED IN ESIC MAJOR GROUP 29,
ASSETS $25 MILLION AND OVER

	Petroleum and Coal Products[1]				
	1Q 1985	2Q 1985	3Q 1985	4Q 1985	1Q 1986
INCOME STATEMENT IN RATIO FORMAT	(percent of net sales)				
Net sales, receipts, and operating revenues	100.0	100.0	100.0	100.0	100.0
Less: Depreciation, depletion, and amortization of property, plant and equipment ...	6.8	6.6	7.2	7.1	8.2
Less: All other operating costs and expenses	86.7	87.9	86.6	88.2	86.5
Income (or loss) from operations	6.5	5.5	6.2	4.7	5.3
Non-operating income (expense)	-1.1	-3.3	-1.2	-0.3	-1.4
Income (or loss) before income taxes	5.5	2.2	5.0	4.3	3.9
Net income (or loss) of foreign branches and equity in earnings (losses) of non-consolidated subsidiaries (net of foreign taxes)	1.8	0.8	1.3	1.1	2.1
Less: Provision for current and deferred domestic income taxes	2.0	0.7	2.1	1.3	1.7
Income (or loss) after income taxes	5.3	2.4	4.2	4.0	4.2
OPERATING RATIOS (see explanatory notes)	(percent)				
Annual rate of profit on stockholders' equity at end of period:					
Before income taxes	14.71	6.53	13.75	11.68	10.74
After taxes	10.57	5.13	9.17	8.80	7.55
Annual rate of profit on total assets:					
Before income taxes	6.49	2.76	5.80	4.89	4.50
After taxes	4.67	2.17	3.87	3.68	3.16

[1] During the first quarter of 1986, a considerable number of companies were reclassified by industry. To provide comparability, the four quarters of 1985 have been restated to reflect these reclassifications.

TABLE 32—INCOME STATEMENT
FOR CORPORATIONS INCLUDED IN ESIC MAJOR GROUP 30,
ASSETS $25 MILLION AND OVER

	Rubber and Misc. Plastics Products[1]				
	1Q 1985	2Q 1985	3Q 1985	4Q 1985	1Q 1986
INCOME STATEMENT IN RATIO FORMAT	(percent of net sales)				
Net sales, receipts, and operating revenues	100.0	100.0	100.0	100.0	100.0
Less: Depreciation, depletion, and amortization of property, plant and equipment ...	3.4	3.1	3.2	3.1	3.7
Less: All other operating costs and expenses	90.7	90.4	91.7	94.1	91.3
Income (or loss) from operations	5.9	6.4	5.0	2.8	5.0
Non-operating income (expense)	-0.8	-5.0	1.1	-2.1	-1.7
Income (or loss) before income taxes	5.0	1.5	6.2	0.7	3.2
Net income (or loss) of foreign branches and equity in earnings (losses) of non-consolidated subsidiaries (net of foreign taxes)	0.5	0.6	0.2	0.5	0.6
Less: Provision for current and deferred domestic income taxes	1.9	2.4	2.2	0.2	1.1
Income (or loss) after income taxes	3.6	-0.3	4.1	1.1	2.7
OPERATING RATIOS (see explanatory notes)	(percent)				
Annual rate of profit on stockholders' equity at end of period:					
Before income taxes	14.66	6.39	17.83	3.85	10.51
After taxes	9.59	-1.07	11.62	3.44	7.35
Annual rate of profit on total assets:					
Before income taxes	7.10	2.83	8.05	1.60	4.49
After taxes	4.65	-0.47	5.25	1.42	3.14

[1] During the first quarter of 1986, a considerable number of companies were reclassified by industry. To provide comparability, the four quarters of 1985 have been restated to reflect these reclassifications.

TABLE 33—INCOME STATEMENT
FOR CORPORATIONS INCLUDED IN ESIC MAJOR GROUP 32,
ASSETS $25 MILLION AND OVER

	Stone, Clay and Glass Products[1]				
	1Q 1985	2Q 1985	3Q 1985	4Q 1985	1Q 1986
INCOME STATEMENT IN RATIO FORMAT	(percent of net sales)				
Net sales, receipts, and operating revenues	100.0	100.0	100.0	100.0	100.0
Less: Depreciation, depletion, and amortization of property, plant and equipment	5.1	4.5	4.5	4.6	5.1
Less: All other operating costs and expenses	90.3	85.8	86.5	88.2	88.9
Income (or loss) from operations	4.6	9.6	9.0	7.2	6.0
Non-operating income (expense)	-1.1	-2.5	-2.0	-1.8	-1.8
Income (or loss) before income taxes	3.4	7.1	7.0	5.4	4.2
Net income (or loss) of foreign branches and equity in earnings (losses) of non-consolidated subsidiaries (net of foreign taxes)	0.4	0.7	-1.0	0.8	0.3
Less: Provision for current and deferred domestic income taxes	1.8	3.5	2.9	2.5	2.4
Income (or loss) after income taxes	2.0	4.4	3.1	3.7	2.1
OPERATING RATIOS (see explanatory notes)	(percent)				
Annual rate of profit on stockholders' equity at end of period:					
Before income taxes	7.67	18.30	14.10	13.94	9.07
After taxes	4.02	10.31	7.39	8.33	4.29
Annual rate of profit on total assets:					
Before income taxes	3.66	8.75	6.79	6.73	4.34
After taxes	1.92	4.93	3.56	4.02	2.05

[1] During the first quarter of 1986, a considerable number of companies were reclassified by industry. To provide comparability, the four quarters of 1985 have been restated to reflect these reclassifications.

TABLE 34—INCOME STATEMENT
FOR CORPORATIONS INCLUDED IN ESIC MAJOR GROUP 33,
ASSETS $25 MILLION AND OVER

	Primary Metal Industries[1]				
	1Q 1985	2Q 1985	3Q 1985	4Q 1985	1Q 1986
INCOME STATEMENT IN RATIO FORMAT	(percent of net sales)				
Net sales, receipts, and operating revenues	100.0	100.0	100.0	100.0	100.0
Less: Depreciation, depletion, and amortization of property, plant and equipment	4.0	3.8	4.0	4.1	4.2
Less: All other operating costs and expenses	95.5	95.5	95.0	95.1	94.2
Income (or loss) from operations	0.5	0.6	1.1	0.9	1.6
Non-operating income (expense)	-2.2	-3.9	-3.2	-7.0	-2.3
Income (or loss) before income taxes	-1.8	-3.3	-2.2	-6.1	-0.6
Net income (or loss) of foreign branches and equity in earnings (losses) of non-consolidated subsidiaries (net of foreign taxes)	0.4	0.1	-0.6	-1.0	-0.2
Less: Provision for current and deferred domestic income taxes	0.3	0.5	0.4	-1.3	0.5
Income (or loss) after income taxes	-1.7	-3.8	-3.2	-5.8	-1.3
OPERATING RATIOS (see explanatory notes)	(percent)				
Annual rate of profit on stockholders' equity at end of period:					
Before income taxes	-3.87	-9.70	-7.84	-20.88	-2.30
After taxes	-4.77	-11.33	-9.09	-17.03	-3.89
Annual rate of profit on total assets:					
Before income taxes	-1.42	-3.53	-2.87	-7.46	-0.81
After taxes	-1.75	-4.13	-3.32	-6.08	-1.37

[1] During the first quarter of 1986, a considerable number of companies were reclassified by industry. To provide comparability, the four quarters of 1985 have been restated to reflect these reclassifications.

TABLE 35—INCOME STATEMENT
FOR CORPORATIONS INCLUDED IN ESIC MAJOR GROUPS 33.1-2, ASSETS $25 MILLION AND OVER

	Iron and Steel [1]				
	1Q 1985	2Q 1985	3Q 1985	4Q 1985	1Q 1986
INCOME STATEMENT IN RATIO FORMAT	(percent of net sales)				
Net sales, receipts, and operating revenues	100.0	100.0	100.0	100.0	100.0
Less: Depreciation, depletion, and amortization of property, plant and equipment	3.8	3.6	2.7	3.7	4.0
Less: All other operating costs and expenses	96.4	97.4	95.1	95.7	96.2
Income (or loss) from operations	-0.2	-1.0	1.1	0.6	-0.2
Non-operating income (expense)	-2.1	-2.1	-2.4	-4.4	-2.9
Income (or loss) before income taxes	-2.3	-3.1	-1.3	-3.8	-3.1
Net income (or loss) of foreign branches and equity in earnings (losses) of non-consolidated subsidiaries (net of foreign taxes)	0.1	0.2	0.2	-0.4	0.1
Less: Provision for current and deferred domestic income taxes	0.5	0.7	1.3	-0.3	0.3
Income (or loss) after income taxes	-2.8	-3.6	-2.4	-3.9	-3.3
OPERATING RATIOS (see explanatory notes)	(percent)				
Annual rate of profit on stockholders' equity at end of period:					
Before income taxes	-8.64	-12.70	-4.85	-18.11	-13.58
After taxes	-10.80	-15.74	-10.13	-16.83	-14.82
Annual rate of profit on total assets:					
Before income taxes	-2.50	-3.53	-1.35	-4.86	-3.47
After taxes	-3.13	-4.37	-2.81	-4.51	-3.79

[1] During the first quarter of 1986, a considerable number of companies were reclassified by industry. To provide comparability, the four quarters of 1985 have been restated to reflect these reclassifications.

TABLE 36—INCOME STATEMENT
FOR CORPORATIONS INCLUDED IN ESIC MAJOR GROUPS 33.5-6, ASSETS $25 MILLION AND OVER

	Nonferrous Metals [1]				
	1Q 1985	2Q 1985	3Q 1985	4Q 1985	1Q 1986
INCOME STATEMENT IN RATIO FORMAT	(percent of net sales)				
Net sales, receipts, and operating revenues	100.0	100.0	100.0	100.0	100.0
Less: Depreciation, depletion, and amortization of property, plant and equipment	4.3	4.2	4.3	4.6	4.5
Less: All other operating costs and expenses	94.2	92.6	94.7	94.2	91.4
Income (or loss) from operations	1.6	3.1	1.0	1.3	4.1
Non-operating income (expense)	-2.5	-6.7	-4.4	-10.6	-1.1
Income (or loss) before income taxes	-0.9	-3.6	-3.4	-9.4	3.0
Net income (or loss) of foreign branches and equity in earnings (losses) of non-consolidated subsidiaries (net of foreign taxes)	0.7	-0.2	-1.7	-2.0	-0.6
Less: Provision for current and deferred domestic income taxes	0.0	0.3	-0.7	-2.8	0.9
Income (or loss) after income taxes	-0.2	-4.2	-4.3	-8.6	1.5
OPERATING RATIOS (see explanatory notes)	(percent)				
Annual rate of profit on stockholders' equity at end of period:					
Before income taxes	-0.44	-7.65	-9.88	-22.73	4.73
After taxes	-0.43	-8.32	-8.38	-17.16	2.94
Annual rate of profit on total assets:					
Before income taxes	-0.20	-3.54	-4.62	-10.44	2.17
After taxes	-0.20	-3.85	-3.92	-7.88	1.35

[1] During the first quarter of 1986, a considerable number of companies were reclassified by industry. To provide comparability, the four quarters of 1985 have been restated to reflect these reclassifications.

TABLE 37—INCOME STATEMENT
FOR CORPORATIONS INCLUDED IN ESIC MAJOR GROUP 34,
ASSETS $25 MILLION AND OVER

	Fabricated Metal Products[1]				
	1Q 1985	2Q 1985	3Q 1985	4Q 1985	1Q 1986
INCOME STATEMENT IN RATIO FORMAT	(percent of net sales)				
Net sales, receipts, and operating revenues	100.0	100.0	100.0	100.0	100.0
Less: Depreciation, depletion, and amortization of property, plant and equipment	3.2	3.2	3.0	3.2	3.4
Less: All other operating costs and expenses	91.2	90.7	91.0	89.6	90.9
Income (or loss) from operations	5.6	6.0	6.0	7.2	5.7
Non-operating income (expense)	-1.1	-1.2	-3.9	-4.6	-0.8
Income (or loss) before income taxes	4.5	4.9	2.0	2.5	4.9
Net income (or loss) of foreign branches and equity in earnings (losses) of non-consolidated subsidiaries (net of foreign taxes)	0.7	0.3	1.7	0.8	1.8
Less: Provision for current and deferred domestic income taxes	2.2	2.5	1.1	1.5	2.6
Income (or loss) after income taxes	3.1	2.6	2.6	2.0	4.1
OPERATING RATIOS (see explanatory notes)	(percent)				
Annual rate of profit on stockholders' equity at end of period:					
Before income taxes	13.83	14.81	10.19	9.04	16.83
After taxes	8.15	7.52	7.30	5.24	10.40
Annual rate of profit on total assets:					
Before income taxes	6.05	6.47	4.47	3.98	7.43
After taxes	3.56	3.28	3.20	2.31	4.59

[1] During the first quarter of 1986, a considerable number of companies were reclassified by industry. To provide comparability, the four quarters of 1985 have been restated to reflect these reclassifications.

TABLE 38—INCOME STATEMENT
FOR CORPORATIONS INCLUDED IN ESIC MAJOR GROUP 35,
ASSETS $25 MILLION AND OVER

	Machinery, Except Electrical[1]				
	1Q 1985	2Q 1985	3Q 1985	4Q 1985	1Q 1986
INCOME STATEMENT IN RATIO FORMAT	(percent of net sales)				
Net sales, receipts, and operating revenues	100.0	100.0	100.0	100.0	100.0
Less: Depreciation, depletion, and amortization of property, plant and equipment	4.7	4.6	4.7	4.6	5.1
Less: All other operating costs and expenses	90.7	88.3	88.6	86.3	90.7
Income (or loss) from operations	4.6	7.1	6.7	9.1	4.2
Non-operating income (expense)	-0.9	-1.3	-1.3	-3.1	-1.9
Income (or loss) before income taxes	3.6	5.8	5.4	6.0	2.3
Net income (or loss) of foreign branches and equity in earnings (losses) of non-consolidated subsidiaries (net of foreign taxes)	2.9	2.8	2.4	4.4	2.7
Less: Provision for current and deferred domestic income taxes	2.0	2.8	2.7	3.2	1.8
Income (or loss) after income taxes	4.5	5.9	5.1	7.3	3.2
OPERATING RATIOS (see explanatory notes)	(percent)				
Annual rate of profit on stockholders' equity at end of period:					
Before income taxes	10.91	15.33	13.23	18.57	7.78
After taxes	7.59	10.41	8.68	12.98	4.99
Annual rate of profit on total assets:					
Before income taxes	6.05	8.49	7.29	10.20	4.29
After taxes	4.21	5.76	4.78	7.13	2.75

[1] During the first quarter of 1986, a considerable number of companies were reclassified by industry. To provide comparability, the four quarters of 1985 have been restated to reflect these reclassifications.

TABLE 39—INCOME STATEMENT
FOR CORPORATIONS INCLUDED IN ESIC MAJOR GROUP 36,
ASSETS $25 MILLION AND OVER

	Electrical and Electronic Equipment[1]				
	1Q 1985	2Q 1985	3Q 1985	4Q 1985	1Q 1986
INCOME STATEMENT IN RATIO FORMAT	(percent of net sales)				
Net sales, receipts, and operating revenues	100.0	100.0	100.0	100.0	100.0
Less: Depreciation, depletion, and amortization of property, plant and equipment	4.0	4.0	3.9	3.9	4.3
Less: All other operating costs and expenses	89.9	90.2	91.1	91.1	90.2
Income (or loss) from operations	6.1	5.8	5.0	5.0	5.5
Non-operating income (expense)	-0.5	-0.6	-1.1	-1.8	-0.7
Income (or loss) before income taxes	5.6	5.2	4.0	3.2	4.9
Net income (or loss) of foreign branches and equity in earnings (losses) of non-consolidated subsidiaries (net of foreign taxes)	1.0	1.2	0.9	1.2	1.4
Less: Provision for current and deferred domestic income taxes	2.2	2.5	1.6	1.4	2.3
Income (or loss) after income taxes	4.5	3.9	3.3	3.0	4.0
OPERATING RATIOS (see explanatory notes)	(percent)				
Annual rate of profit on stockholders' equity at end of period:					
Before income taxes	15.10	14.75	11.23	10.45	13.36
After taxes	10.07	8.92	7.62	7.15	8.42
Annual rate of profit on total assets:					
Before income taxes	7.29	7.13	5.47	5.02	6.59
After taxes	4.86	4.31	3.71	3.43	4.15

[1] During the first quarter of 1986, a considerable number of companies were reclassified by industry. To provide comparability, the four quarters of 1985 have been restated to reflect these reclassifications.

TABLE 40—INCOME STATEMENT
FOR CORPORATIONS INCLUDED IN ESIC MAJOR GROUP 37,
ASSETS $25 MILLION AND OVER

	Transportation Equipment[1]				
	1Q 1985	2Q 1985	3Q 1985	4Q 1985	1Q 1986
INCOME STATEMENT IN RATIO FORMAT	(percent of net sales)				
Net sales, receipts, and operating revenues	100.0	100.0	100.0	100.0	100.0
Less: Depreciation, depletion, and amortization of property, plant and equipment	3.7	3.8	3.7	3.6	3.6
Less: All other operating costs and expenses	90.1	90.0	94.6	91.5	91.2
Income (or loss) from operations	6.2	6.2	1.7	5.0	5.2
Non-operating income (expense)	-0.5	-0.1	0.5	-1.0	-0.1
Income (or loss) before income taxes	5.8	6.0	2.2	4.0	5.1
Net income (or loss) of foreign branches and equity in earnings (losses) of non-consolidated subsidiaries (net of foreign taxes)	1.5	1.7	1.7	2.1	1.8
Less: Provision for current and deferred domestic income taxes	2.9	2.6	1.0	2.0	2.3
Income (or loss) after income taxes	4.4	5.1	2.9	4.1	4.6
OPERATING RATIOS (see explanatory notes)	(percent)				
Annual rate of profit on stockholders' equity at end of period:					
Before income taxes	27.09	29.66	13.43	22.55	23.78
After taxes	16.44	19.56	9.99	15.18	15.98
Annual rate of profit on total assets:					
Before income taxes	10.22	11.25	5.10	8.52	9.17
After taxes	6.20	7.42	3.79	5.73	6.16

[1] During the first quarter of 1986, a considerable number of companies were reclassified by industry. To provide comparability, the four quarters of 1985 have been restated to reflect these reclassifications.

TABLE 41—INCOME STATEMENT
FOR CORPORATIONS INCLUDED IN ESIC MAJOR GROUP 37.1, ASSETS $25 MILLION AND OVER

	Motor Vehicles and Equipment [1]				
	1Q 1985	2Q 1985	3Q 1985	4Q 1985	1Q 1986
INCOME STATEMENT IN RATIO FORMAT	(percent of net sales)				
Net sales, receipts, and operating revenues	100.0	100.0	100.0	100.0	100.0
Less: Depreciation, depletion, and amortization of property, plant and equipment	4.1	4.3	4.2	4.1	3.9
Less: All other operating costs and expenses	89.3	89.2	94.4	91.5	91.1
Income (or loss) from operations	6.6	6.6	1.5	4.5	5.0
Non-operating income (expense)	-0.6	0.0	0.0	0.2	0.1
Income (or loss) before income taxes	6.0	6.6	1.5	4.7	5.1
Net income (or loss) of foreign branches and equity in earnings (losses) of non-consolidated subsidiaries (net of foreign taxes)	1.9	2.2	2.2	2.8	2.3
Less: Provision for current and deferred domestic income taxes	3.2	3.0	0.5	1.5	2.2
Income (or loss) after income taxes	4.7	5.8	3.2	5.9	5.1
OPERATING RATIOS (see explanatory notes)	(percent)				
Annual rate of profit on stockholders' equity at end of period:					
Before income taxes	30.49	34.20	12.15	26.45	25.84
After taxes	18.23	22.60	10.47	20.98	17.90
Annual rate of profit on total assets:					
Before income taxes	13.88	15.84	5.54	12.05	11.90
After taxes	8.30	10.47	4.78	9.56	6.25

[1] During the first quarter of 1986, a considerable number of companies were reclassified by industry. To provide comparability, the four quarters of 1985 have been restated to reflect these reclassifications.

TABLE 42—INCOME STATEMENT
FOR CORPORATIONS INCLUDED IN ESIC MAJOR GROUP 37.7, ASSETS $25 MILLION AND OVER

	Aircraft, Guided Missiles and Parts[1]				
	1Q 1985	2Q 1985	3Q 1985	4Q 1985	1Q 1986
INCOME STATEMENT IN RATIO FORMAT	(percent of net sales)				
Net sales, receipts, and operating revenues	100.0	100.0	100.0	100.0	100.0
Less: Depreciation, depletion, and amortization of property, plant and equipment	2.9	2.9	3.0	2.8	3.0
Less: All other operating costs and expenses	91.4	91.6	95.2	91.8	91.2
Income (or loss) from operations	5.7	5.5	1.7	5.4	5.8
Non-operating income (expense)	-0.1	-0.2	1.9	-2.5	-0.4
Income (or loss) before income taxes	5.7	5.3	3.5	3.0	5.5
Net income (or loss) of foreign branches and equity in earnings (losses) of non-consolidated subsidiaries (net of foreign taxes)	0.8	0.9	1.0	1.1	0.9
Less: Provision for current and deferred domestic income taxes	2.4	2.1	1.8	2.8	2.4
Income (or loss) after income taxes	4.1	4.1	2.7	1.3	4.1
OPERATING RATIOS (see explanatory notes)	(percent)				
Annual rate of profit on stockholders' equity at end of period:					
Before income taxes	22.21	21.46	15.81	15.81	20.72
After taxes	13.98	14.94	9.35	5.12	13.17
Annual rate of profit on total assets:					
Before income taxes	7.09	7.06	5.05	4.98	6.76
After taxes	4.46	4.70	2.99	1.61	4.29

[1] During the first quarter of 1986, a considerable number of companies were reclassified by industry. To provide comparability, the four quarters of 1985 have been restated to reflect these reclassifications.

TABLE 43—INCOME STATEMENT
FOR CORPORATIONS INCLUDED IN MINING,
ALL WHOLESALE TRADE AND ESIC MAJOR GROUPS 50, 51,
ASSETS $25 MILLION AND OVER[1]

	All Mining[2]				
	1Q 1985	2Q 1985	3Q 1985	4Q 1985	1Q 1986
	(percent of net sales)				
INCOME STATEMENT IN RATIO FORMAT					
Net sales, receipts, and operating revenues	100.0	100.0	100.0	100.0	100.0
Less: Depreciation, depletion, and amortization of property, plant and equipment	15.1	14.1	14.7	15.9	15.3
Less: All other operating costs and expenses	78.6	80.1	80.2	88.5	90.5
Income (or loss) from operations	6.3	5.8	5.1	−4.3	−5.8
Non-operating income (expense)	−1.2	−5.5	−7.4	−12.0	−7.2
Income (or loss) before income taxes	5.1	0.4	−2.3	−16.3	−13.0
Less: Provision for current and deferred domestic income taxes	2.9	−0.8	1.2	−3.6	−2.3
Income (or loss) after income taxes	2.2	1.2	−3.5	−12.8	−10.7
	(percent)				
OPERATING RATIOS (see explanatory notes)					
Annual rate of profit on stockholders' equity at end of period:					
Before income taxes	6.24	0.44	−2.78	−20.37	−16.00
After taxes	2.75	1.41	−4.26	−15.92	−13.22
Annual rate of profit on total assets:					
Before income taxes	2.27	0.17	−1.05	−7.53	−6.25
After taxes	1.00	0.53	−1.61	−5.89	−5.17
BALANCE SHEET RATIOS (based on succeeding table)					
Total current assets to total current liabilities	1.13	1.22	1.19	1.19	1.33
Total cash, U.S. Government and other securities to total current liabilities	0.33	0.35	0.32	0.32	0.41
Total stockholders' equity to total debt	0.92	0.99	1.02	0.95	1.10

[1] This asset size cutoff can lead to inconsistencies when comparing data on a quarter-to quarter basis. Corporations that have exceeded the asset cutoff limit for the first time in the current quarter are not represented in previous quarter's data, and those falling below the cutoff are no longer represented.
[2] During the first quarter of 1986, a considerable number of companies were reclassified by industry. To provide comparability, the four quarters of 1985 have been restated to reflect these reclassifications.

TABLE 44—BALANCE SHEET
FOR CORPORATIONS INCLUDED IN MINING,
ALL WHOLESALE TRADE AND ESIC MAJOR GROUPS 50, 51,
ASSETS $25 MILLION AND OVER[1]

	All Mining[2]				
	1Q 1985	2Q 1985	3Q 1985	4Q 1985	1Q 1986
	(percent of total assets)				
SELECTED BALANCE SHEET RATIOS					
Total cash, U.S. Government and other securities	5.4	5.7	5.1	4.9	6.5
Trade accounts and trade notes receivable	7.6	7.9	8.0	8.0	8.1
Inventories	3.4	3.7	3.6	3.6	4.1
Total current assets	18.7	19.6	18.7	18.5	20.9
Net property, plant and equipment	61.0	61.2	61.9	60.7	62.0
Short-term debt including installments on long-term debt	5.0	4.4	4.1	4.4	4.1
Total current liabilities	16.6	16.1	15.8	15.6	15.7
Long-term debt	34.4	33.6	32.8	34.5	31.6
Total liabilities	63.6	62.5	62.3	63.0	60.9
Stockholders' equity	36.4	37.5	37.7	37.0	39.1

[1] This asset size cutoff can lead to inconsistencies when comparing data on a quarter-to-quarter basis. Corporations that have exceeded the asset cutoff limit for the first time in the current quarter are not represented in previous quarter's data, and those falling below the cutoff are no longer represented.
[2] During the first quarter of 1986, a considerable number of companies were reclassified by industry. To provide comparability, the four quarters of 1985 have been restated to reflect these reclassifications.

	All Wholesale Trade [2]					Wholesale Trade, Durable Goods [2]					Wholesale Trade, Nondurable Goods [2]			
1Q 1985	2Q 1985	3Q 1985	4Q 1985	1Q 1986	1Q 1985	2Q 1985	3Q 1985	4Q 1985	1Q 1986	1Q 1985	2Q 1985	3Q 1985	4Q 1985	1Q 1986
(percent of net sales)					(percent of net sales)					(percent of net sales)				
100.0	100.0	100.0	100.0	100.0	100.0	100.0	100.0	100.0	100.0	100.0	100.0	100.0	100.0	100.0
0.9	1.0	1.0	1.0	1.1	1.1	1.1	1.1	1.1	1.2	0.8	0.9	0.9	0.9	1.0
96.9	96.4	96.8	96.8	97.3	95.3	94.8	95.5	95.7	96.2	97.9	97.5	97.5	97.5	97.9
2.2	2.6	2.2	2.2	1.7	3.6	4.1	3.4	3.2	2.6	1.3	1.6	1.5	1.6	1.1
-0.3	-0.2	0.0	-0.9	-0.2	-0.4	-0.4	-0.3	-0.8	0.0	-0.2	0.0	0.2	-1.0	-0.3
1.9	2.4	2.2	1.3	1.5	3.2	3.7	3.0	2.4	2.6	1.1	1.6	1.7	0.7	0.8
0.9	1.0	1.0	0.9	0.7	1.6	1.8	1.6	1.4	1.2	0.4	0.5	0.6	0.6	0.5
1.0	1.4	1.2	0.4	0.8	1.5	1.9	1.4	1.0	1.5	0.7	1.1	1.1	0.1	0.3
(percent)					(percent)					(percent)				
15.10	20.36	18.35	11.49	12.52	21.35	25.55	21.31	16.90	17.76	11.31	15.80	15.92	6.60	7.52
8.65	11.85	10.32	3.80	6.41	10.24	12.93	10.23	7.06	9.88	7.21	10.90	10.39	0.86	3.10
5.51	6.99	6.16	3.79	4.22	7.56	8.80	7.05	5.82	6.40	3.75	5.40	5.41	2.10	2.39
2.96	4.07	3.46	1.25	2.16	3.62	4.45	3.38	2.43	3.57	2.39	3.73	3.53	0.27	0.98
1.40	1.39	1.37	1.38	1.41	1.52	1.48	1.45	1.49	1.57	1.29	1.30	1.30	1.27	1.27
0.18	0.18	0.18	0.19	0.18	0.17	0.19	0.20	0.23	0.23	0.15	0.16	0.16	0.15	0.14
1.01	1.00	0.99	0.97	0.95	1.09	0.99	0.97	1.03	1.10	0.95	1.00	1.02	0.93	0.83

	All Wholesale Trade [2]					Wholdsale Trade, Durable Goods [2]					Wholesale Trade, Nondurable Goods [2]			
1Q 1985	2Q 1985	3Q 1985	4Q 1985	1Q 1986	1Q 1985	2Q 1985	3Q 1985	4Q 1985	1Q 1986	1Q 1985	2Q 1985	3Q 1985	4Q 1985	1Q 1986
(percent of total assets)					(percent of total assets)					(percent of total assets)				
7.0	7.8	8.2	8.7	7.9	7.9	9.2	10.1	11.1	10.2	6.2	6.6	6.6	6.6	5.9
25.1	24.9	24.9	25.9	24.6	28.6	27.6	27.4	28.0	26.7	22.1	22.5	22.8	24.1	22.8
26.2	25.3	24.7	24.3	25.0	31.2	30.1	30.0	28.5	29.2	21.9	21.2	20.1	20.8	21.4
61.9	61.7	61.7	62.5	61.0	71.4	71.2	71.6	71.6	70.4	53.9	53.5	53.3	54.9	53.1
22.6	22.7	22.3	22.1	22.7	17.7	17.7	17.4	17.1	17.8	26.8	27.0	26.5	26.3	26.8
16.2	17.0	16.4	16.6	16.9	18.0	20.5	20.2	19.3	17.6	14.6	13.9	13.1	14.2	16.2
44.2	44.4	44.9	45.3	43.3	45.9	48.2	49.3	48.0	44.9	41.8	41.1	41.1	43.2	41.9
17.6	17.3	17.4	17.4	18.7	14.4	14.2	14.1	14.0	15.1	20.3	20.0	20.2	20.2	21.7
65.8	65.7	66.4	67.0	66.3	64.5	65.6	66.9	65.6	63.9	66.8	65.8	66.0	68.2	68.2
34.2	34.3	33.6	33.0	33.7	35.4	34.4	33.1	34.4	36.1	33.2	34.2	34.0	31.8	31.8

General Business and Economic Indicators

SELECTED BUSINESS STATISTICS

SEASONALLY ADJUSTED WHERE APPLICABLE

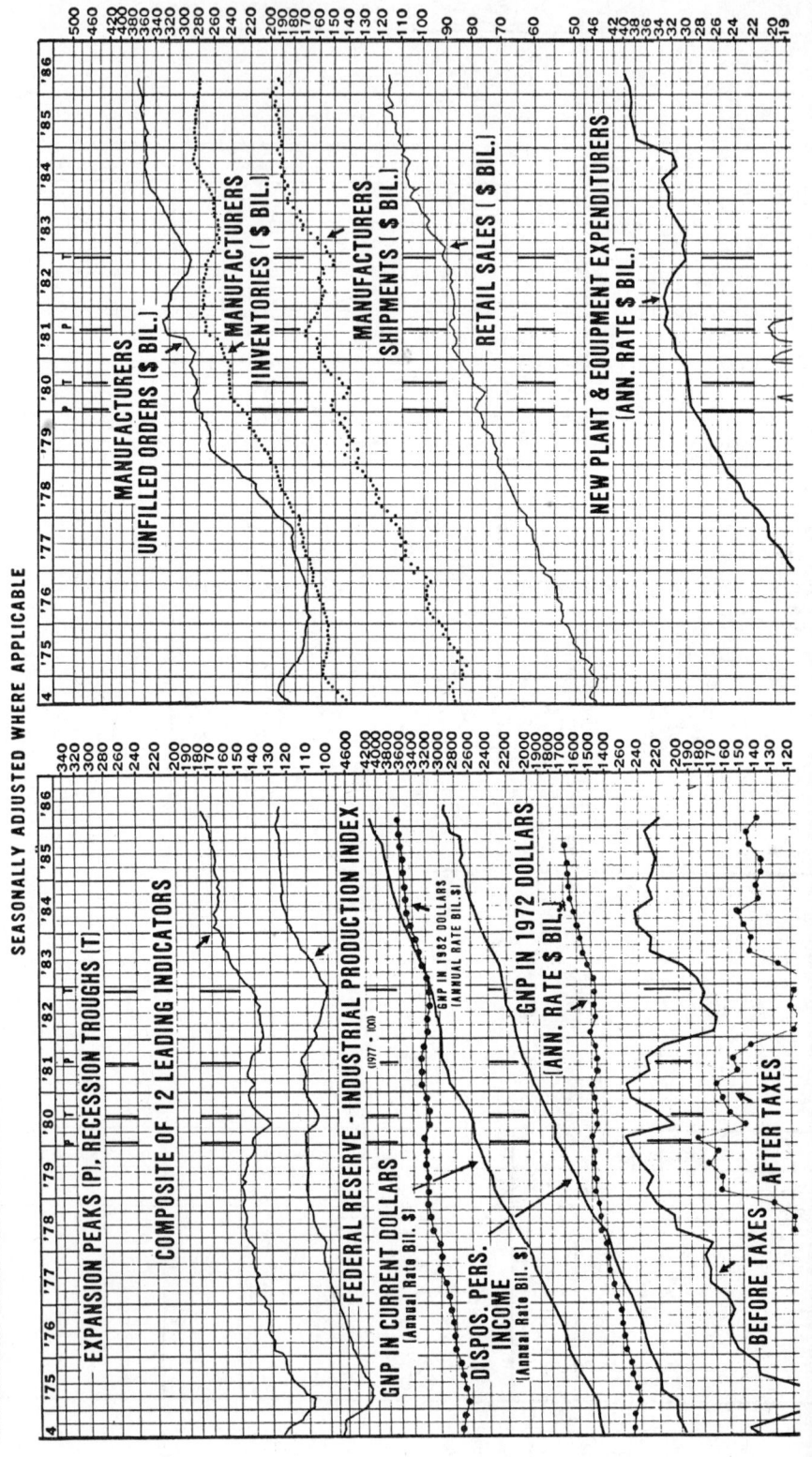

EXPANSION PEAKS (P), RECESSION TROUGHS (T)

COMPOSITE OF 12 LEADING INDICATORS

FEDERAL RESERVE - INDUSTRIAL PRODUCTION INDEX
(1977 = 100)

GNP IN CURRENT DOLLARS
(Annual Rate Bil. $)

GNP IN 1972 DOLLARS
(Ann. Rate $ Bil.)

GNP IN 1982 DOLLARS
(ANNUAL RATE BIL. $)

DISPOS. PERS. INCOME
(Annual Rate Bil. $)

BEFORE TAXES   AFTER TAXES

MANUFACTURERS UNFILLED ORDERS ($ BIL.)

MANUFACTURERS INVENTORIES ($ BIL.)

MANUFACTURERS SHIPMENTS ($ BIL.)

RETAIL SALES ($ BIL.)

NEW PLANT & EQUIPMENT EXPENDITURERS
(ANN. RATE $ BIL.)

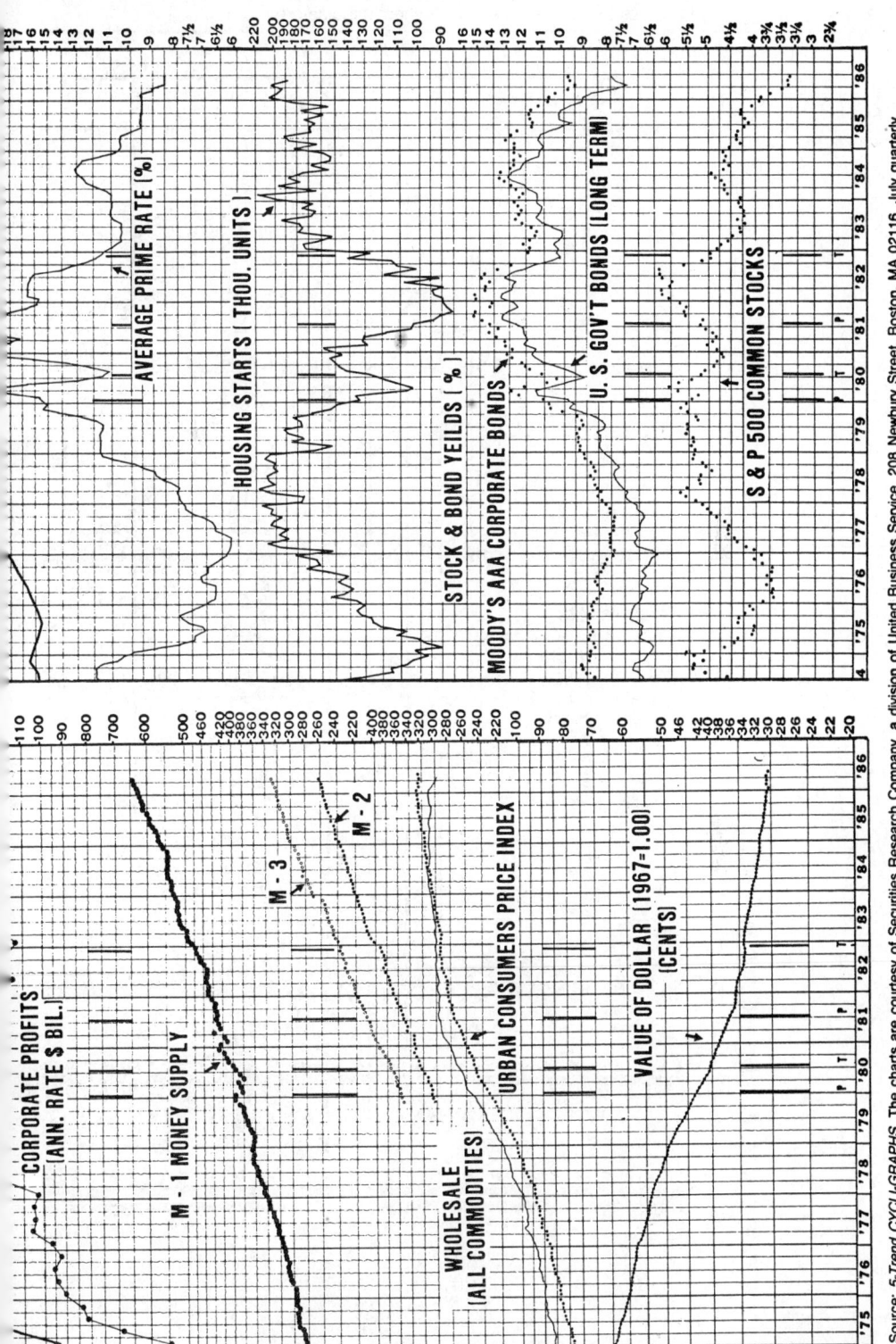

Source: *5-Trend CYCLI-GRAPHS.* The charts are courtesy of Securities Research Company, a division of United Business Service. 208 Newbury Street, Boston, MA 02116, July quarterly edition, 1986.

173

COMPOSITE INDEXES AND THEIR COMPONENTS

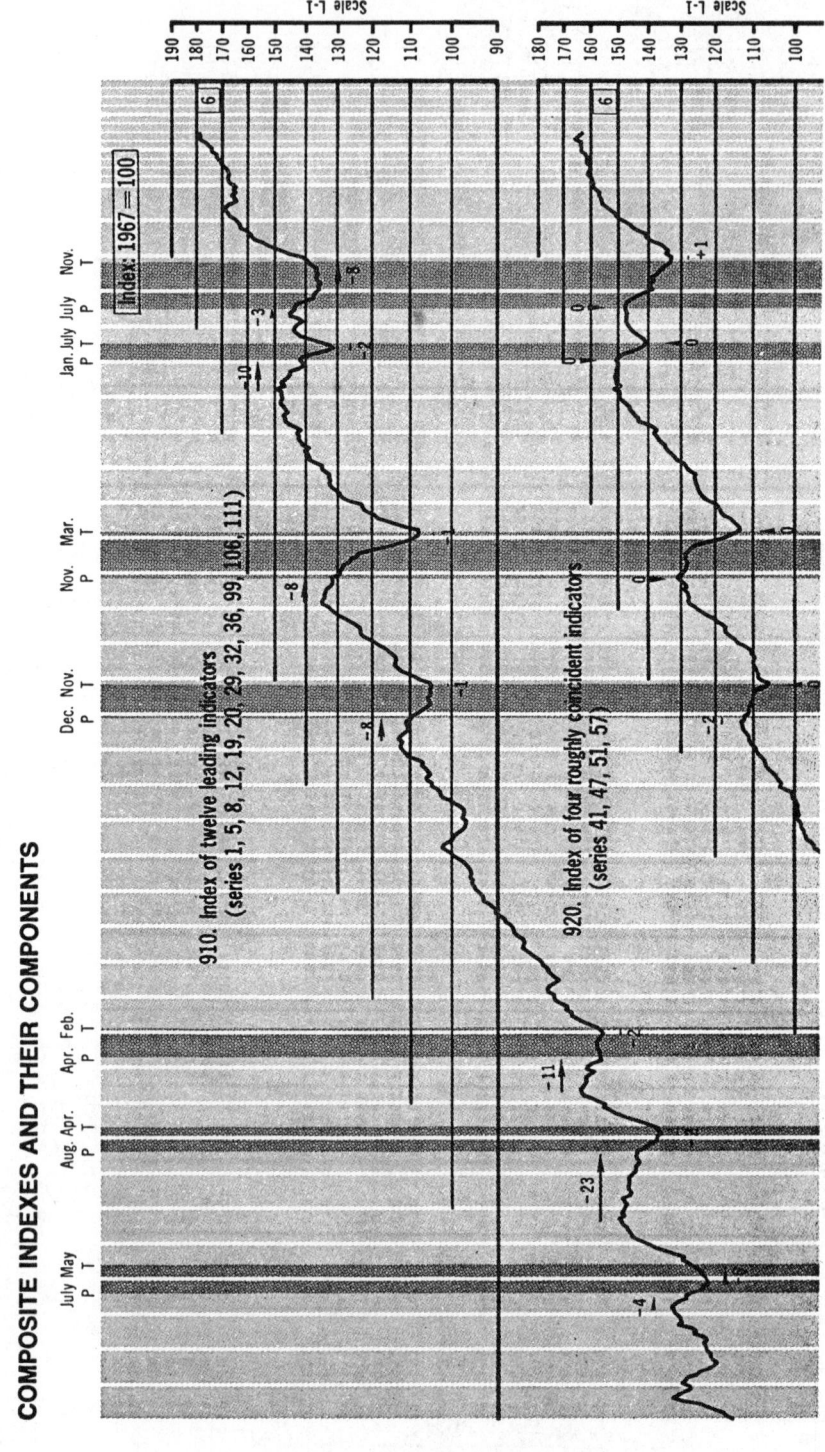

Index: 1967 = 100

910. Index of twelve leading indicators
(series 1, 5, 8, 12, 19, 20, 29, 32, 36, 99, 106, 111)

920. Index of four roughly coincident indicators
(series 41, 47, 51, 57)

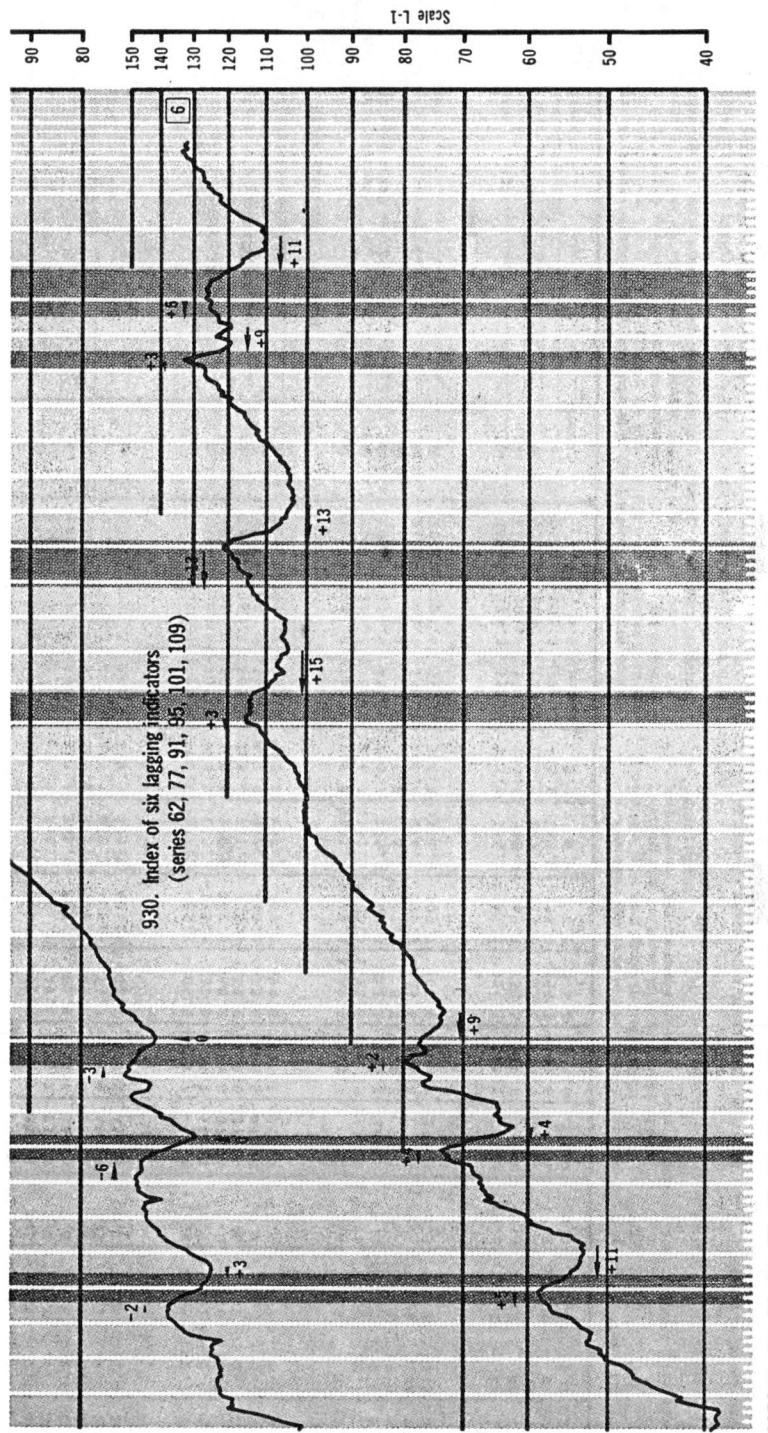

Scale L-1

930. Index of six lagging indicators
(series 62, 77, 91, 95, 101, 109)

6

NOTE: Numbers entered on the chart indicate length of leads (−) and lags (+) in months from reference turning dates.

Source: Business Conditions Digest, U.S. Department of Commerce, Bureau of Economic Analysis, July 1986.

Composition of Leading, Coincident, and Lagging Indicators

I. THE TWELVE LEADING INDICATORS

1. Average weekly hours paid to production or non-supervisory workers in manufacturing.
5. Average weekly claims for Unemployment Insurance (inversely related).
8. New orders for consumer goods and materials in 1972 dollars.
12. Monthly estimate of net formation of new businesses incorporated.
19. Index of 500 common stock prices.
20. Contracts and orders for new plant and equipment in 1972 dollars.
29. Index of new private housing starts.
32. Percentage of purchasing agents in greater Chicago area who experience slower deliveries in current month.
36. Change in manufacturing and trade inventories on hand and on order in 1972 dollars.
99. Change in index of 28 sensitive materials prices.
106. Money supply (M2 in 1972 dollars).

111. Change in business and consumer credit (consumer installment credit, business and real estate loans, etc.).

II. THE FOUR COINCIDENT INDICATORS

41. Employees on non-agricultural payrolls.
47. Index of industrial production, including all stages in manufacturing, mining, gas and electrical utilities.
51. Personal income less transfer payments in 1972 dollars.
57. Monthly volume of sales in manufacturing, wholesale, and retail in 1972 dollars.

III. THE SIX LAGGING INDICATORS

62. Index of labor costs per unit of manufacturing output.
77. Ratio of manufacturing and trade inventories to sales in 1972 dollars.
91. Average duration of unemployment in weeks (inversely related).
95. Ratio of consumer installment credit to personal income.
101. Commercial and industrial loans outstanding in 1972 dollars.
109. Average prime rate charged by banks.

NATIONAL INCOME

[Billions of dollars; quarterly data at seasonally adjusted annual rates]

Period	National income	Compensation of employees[1]	Proprietors' income with inventory valuation and capital consumption adjustments		Rental income of persons with capital consumption adjustment	Corporate profits with inventory valuation and capital consumption adjustments					Net interest
			Farm	Nonfarm		Total	Profits with inventory valuation adjustment and without capital consumption adjustment			Capital consumption adjustment	
							Total	Profits before tax	Inventory valuation adjustment		
1981	2,443.5	1,807.4	30.7	156.1	13.3	188.0	202.3	226.5	−24.2	−14.4	248.1
1982	2,518.4	1,907.0	24.6	150.9	13.6	150.0	159.2	169.6	−10.4	−9.2	272.3
1983 r	2,719.5	2,020.7	12.4	178.4	13.2	213.7	196.7	207.6	−10.9	17.0	281.0
1984 r	3,032.0	2,214.7	31.5	205.3	8.3	264.7	230.2	235.7	−5.5	34.5	307.4
1985 r	3,222.3	2,368.2	29.2	225.2	7.6	280.7	222.6	223.2	−.6	58.1	311.4
1982: III	2,528.4	1,918.4	22.9	151.7	12.0	154.3	161.6	171.6	−10.0	−7.3	269.1
IV	2,548.2	1,931.1	28.5	159.8	15.8	146.1	150.7	164.1	−13.4	−4.5	266.9
1983: I r	2,599.1	1,958.8	18.1	165.9	13.8	170.6	163.9	169.7	−5.9	6.7	272.1
II r	2,685.5	1,995.0	15.9	176.4	15.4	207.0	191.2	201.8	−10.6	15.8	275.8
III r	2,741.8	2,036.3	−3.5	183.0	11.2	228.9	208.5	227.5	−19.0	20.5	285.9
IV r	2,851.5	2,092.7	19.3	188.6	12.4	248.5	223.4	231.5	−8.1	25.1	290.2
1984: I r	2,963.2	2,153.7	44.5	198.0	12.1	262.5	235.7	249.3	−13.6	26.7	292.5
II r	3,010.3	2,195.4	26.4	203.2	8.4	271.7	241.5	246.5	−4.9	30.2	305.2
III r	3,052.3	2,234.7	24.7	209.9	7.1	259.8	223.3	225.1	−1.8	36.5	316.1
IV r	3,102.0	2,275.0	30.4	210.3	5.6	265.0	220.3	221.9	−1.6	44.7	315.7
1985: I r	3,157.0	2,316.3	32.9	217.8	6.8	266.4	213.3	213.8	−.5	53.2	316.8
II r	3,201.4	2,352.1	33.0	222.5	8.1	274.3	215.4	213.8	1.6	58.9	311.4
III r	3,243.4	2,380.9	21.6	227.7	7.3	296.3	235.3	229.2	6.1	61.0	309.7
IV r	3,287.3	2,423.6	29.4	232.7	8.3	285.6	226.4	235.8	−9.4	59.2	307.6
1986: I r	3,340.7	2,461.5	24.4	240.9	12.8	296.4	240.8	224.3	16.5	55.6	304.9
II p		2,478.8	39.1	249.0	15.1				5.9	51.4	299.1

Source: Department of Commerce, Bureau of Economic Analysis.

[1] Includes employer contributions for social insurance.

NOTE.—Series revised beginning 1983. See Survey of Current Business, July 1986.

Source: Economic Indicators, Council of Economic Advisers.

GROSS NATIONAL PRODUCT

BILLIONS OF DOLLARS (RATIO SCALE)

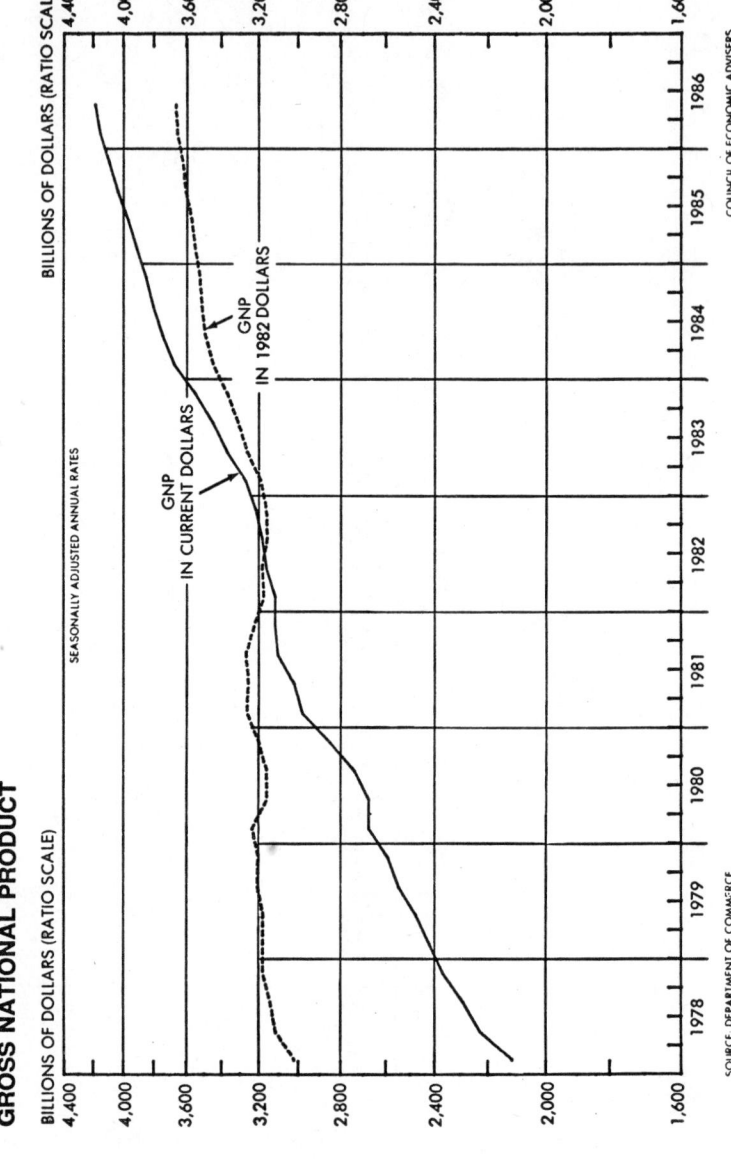

GNP
IN CURRENT DOLLARS

GNP
IN 1982 DOLLARS

SEASONALLY ADJUSTED ANNUAL RATES

BILLIONS OF DOLLARS (RATIO SCALE)

SOURCE: DEPARTMENT OF COMMERCE

COUNCIL OF ECONOMIC ADVISERS

[Billions of current dollars; quarterly data at seasonally adjusted annual rates]

Period	Gross national product	Personal consumption expenditures	Gross private domestic investment	Exports and imports of goods and services			Government purchases of goods and services					Final sales
				Net exports	Exports	Imports	Total	Federal Total	National defense	Non-defense	State and local	
1978	2,249.7	1,403.5	416.8	4.1	227.5	223.4	425.2	161.8	108.9	52.9	263.4	2,221.0
1979	2,508.2	1,566.8	454.8	18.8	291.2	272.5	467.8	178.0	121.9	56.1	289.9	2,495.2
1980	2,732.0	1,732.6	437.0	32.1	351.0	318.9	530.3	208.1	142.7	65.4	322.2	2,740.3
1981	3,052.6	1,915.1	515.5	33.9	382.8	348.9	588.1	242.2	167.5	74.8	345.9	3,028.6
1982	3,166.0	2,050.7	447.3	26.3	361.9	335.6	641.7	272.7	193.8	78.9	369.0	3,190.5
1983 r	3,405.7	2,234.5	502.3	−6.1	352.5	358.7	675.0	283.5	214.4	69.1	391.5	3,412.8
1984 r	3,765.0	2,428.2	662.1	−58.7	382.7	441.4	733.4	311.3	235.0	76.2	422.2	3,700.9
1985 r	3,998.1	2,600.5	661.1	−78.9	369.8	448.6	815.4	354.1	259.4	94.7	461.3	3,987.0
1982: III	3,179.4	2,065.6	452.2	14.5	359.9	345.4	647.1	275.3	197.3	78.0	371.8	3,188.4
IV	3,212.5	2,117.0	409.6	14.1	335.9	321.9	671.8	293.2	205.4	87.7	378.7	3,272.4
1983: I r	3,265.8	2,146.6	428.3	22.7	343.6	320.9	668.1	285.5	208.5	77.0	382.7	3,308.4
II r	3,367.4	2,213.0	481.3	−2.1	344.1	346.2	675.2	287.7	213.3	74.4	387.5	3,378.6
III r	3,443.9	2,262.8	519.7	−19.3	357.7	376.9	680.7	284.9	214.3	70.6	395.8	3,449.4
IV r	3,545.8	2,315.8	579.8	−25.8	364.7	390.5	676.1	276.1	221.5	54.6	400.0	3,514.8
1984: I r	3,670.9	2,363.8	659.5	−45.6	373.4	419.0	693.2	283.4	227.1	56.3	409.8	3,575.4
II r	3,743.8	2,416.1	657.5	−63.2	382.1	445.3	733.3	315.2	233.7	81.6	418.1	3,683.9
III r	3,799.7	2,445.6	670.3	−60.0	389.2	449.1	743.8	317.2	234.5	82.7	426.6	3,735.3
IV r	3,845.6	2,487.2	661.1	−66.1	386.2	452.2	763.4	329.1	244.9	84.2	434.3	3,808.9
1985: I r	3,909.3	2,530.9	650.6	−49.4	378.4	427.9	777.3	333.7	248.9	84.8	443.5	3,883.9
II r	3,965.0	2,576.0	667.1	−77.1	370.0	447.1	799.0	340.9	255.1	85.8	458.1	3,945.9
III r	4,030.5	2,627.1	657.4	−83.7	362.3	446.0	829.7	360.9	265.5	95.5	468.8	4,027.4
IV r	4,087.7	2,667.9	669.5	−105.3	368.2	473.6	855.6	380.9	268.0	112.9	474.7	4,090.8
1986: I r	4,149.2	2,697.9	708.3	−93.7	374.8	468.5	836.7	355.7	266.4	89.3	480.9	4,105.4
II p	4,182.3	2,730.1	691.4	−96.4	375.6	472.0	857.2	364.8	277.5	87.3	492.4	4,162.8

NOTE.—Series revised beginning 1983. See Survey of Current Business, July 1986.

Source: Department of Commerce, Bureau of Economic Analysis.

Source: Economic Indicators, Council of Economic Advisers.

GROSS NATIONAL PRODUCT IN 1982 DOLLARS

[Billions of 1982 dollars; quarterly data at seasonally adjusted annual rates]

Period	Gross national product	Personal consumption expenditures	Gross private domestic investment — Nonresidential fixed	Gross private domestic investment — Residential fixed	Gross private domestic investment — Change in business inventories	Net exports	Exports of goods and services — Exports	Exports of goods and services — Imports	Government purchases of goods and services — Total	Government purchases — Federal — Total	Government purchases — Federal — National defense	Government purchases — Federal — Non-defense	Government purchases — State and local	Final sales
1978	3,115.2	1,961.0	362.1	178.0	36.8	−26.8	312.6	339.4	604.1	233.7	160.7	73.0	370.4	3,078.4
1979	3,192.4	2,004.4	389.4	170.8	15.0	3.6	356.8	353.2	609.1	236.2	164.3	71.9	373.0	3,177.4
1980	3,187.1	2,000.4	379.2	137.0	−6.9	57.0	388.9	332.0	620.5	246.9	171.2	75.7	373.6	3,194.0
1981	3,248.8	2,024.2	395.2	126.5	23.9	49.4	392.7	343.4	629.7	259.6	180.3	79.3	370.1	3,225.0
1982	3,166.0	2,050.7	366.7	105.1	−24.5	26.3	361.9	335.6	641.7	272.7	193.8	78.9	369.0	3,190.5
1983 r	3,279.1	2,146.0	361.2	149.3	−6.4	−19.9	348.1	368.1	649.0	275.1	206.9	68.2	373.9	3,285.5
1984 r	3,489.9	2,246.3	422.2	170.6	59.2	−83.6	369.7	453.2	675.2	291.7	219.4	72.3	383.5	3,430.7
1985 r	3,585.2	2,324.5	461.4	177.2	9.0	−108.2	362.3	470.5	721.2	323.6	235.7	87.8	397.6	3,576.2
1982: III	3,154.5	2,051.8	358.0	100.1	−9.4	11.7	359.5	347.8	642.5	273.8	197.0	76.9	368.6	3,164.0
IV	3,159.3	2,078.7	352.3	115.8	−59.3	11.7	336.0	324.3	660.1	289.5	201.4	88.2	370.6	3,218.6
1983: I r	3,186.6	2,094.2	341.6	127.8	−42.3	16.1	342.5	326.4	649.2	278.2	203.2	75.1	371.0	3,228.9
II r	3,258.3	2,135.1	348.8	147.4	−9.3	−14.6	341.7	356.3	650.9	278.5	206.3	72.2	372.4	3,267.6
III r	3,306.4	2,163.0	363.9	161.9	−1.0	−35.0	352.8	387.8	653.6	277.6	206.5	71.1	376.0	3,307.4
IV r	3,365.1	2,191.9	390.4	159.9	27.0	−46.2	355.5	401.6	642.2	266.0	211.6	54.4	376.2	3,338.1
1984: I r	3,444.7	2,213.8	394.4	169.7	85.1	−68.6	361.3	429.9	650.2	271.2	214.4	56.8	379.0	3,359.6
II r	3,487.1	2,246.3	419.5	173.2	57.0	−87.2	367.0	454.2	678.2	296.3	219.0	77.3	381.8	3,430.0
III r	3,507.4	2,253.3	427.1	171.2	60.6	−85.7	375.5	461.2	681.0	295.6	218.4	77.1	385.4	3,446.8
IV r	3,520.4	2,271.7	447.6	168.3	33.9	−92.7	375.0	467.7	691.5	303.8	225.9	77.9	387.7	3,486.4
1985: I r	3,547.0	2,292.3	442.7	172.4	23.2	−78.8	369.4	448.2	695.3	305.6	228.0	77.8	389.5	3,523.9
II r	3,567.6	2,311.9	463.0	175.1	17.4	−108.1	361.2	469.3	708.3	311.4	233.5	77.9	396.9	3,550.2
III r	3,603.8	2,342.0	463.1	180.0	.7	−113.8	355.8	469.6	731.8	329.9	242.2	87.6	401.9	3,603.1
IV r	3,622.3	2,351.7	476.9	181.5	−5.2	−132.0	362.9	494.8	749.4	347.2	239.3	107.9	402.2	3,627.5
1986: I r	3,655.9	2,372.7	457.8	186.3	39.9	−125.9	369.2	495.1	725.2	320.4	238.7	81.7	404.8	3,616.1
II p	3,665.7	2,407.0	454.8	193.1	19.6	−146.3	371.9	518.3	737.5	325.1	247.5	77.5	412.4	3,646.1

NOTE.—Series revised beginning 1983. See *Survey of Current Business*, July 1986.

Source: Department of Commerce, Bureau of Economic Analysis.

Source: *Economic Indicators*, Council of Economic Advisers.

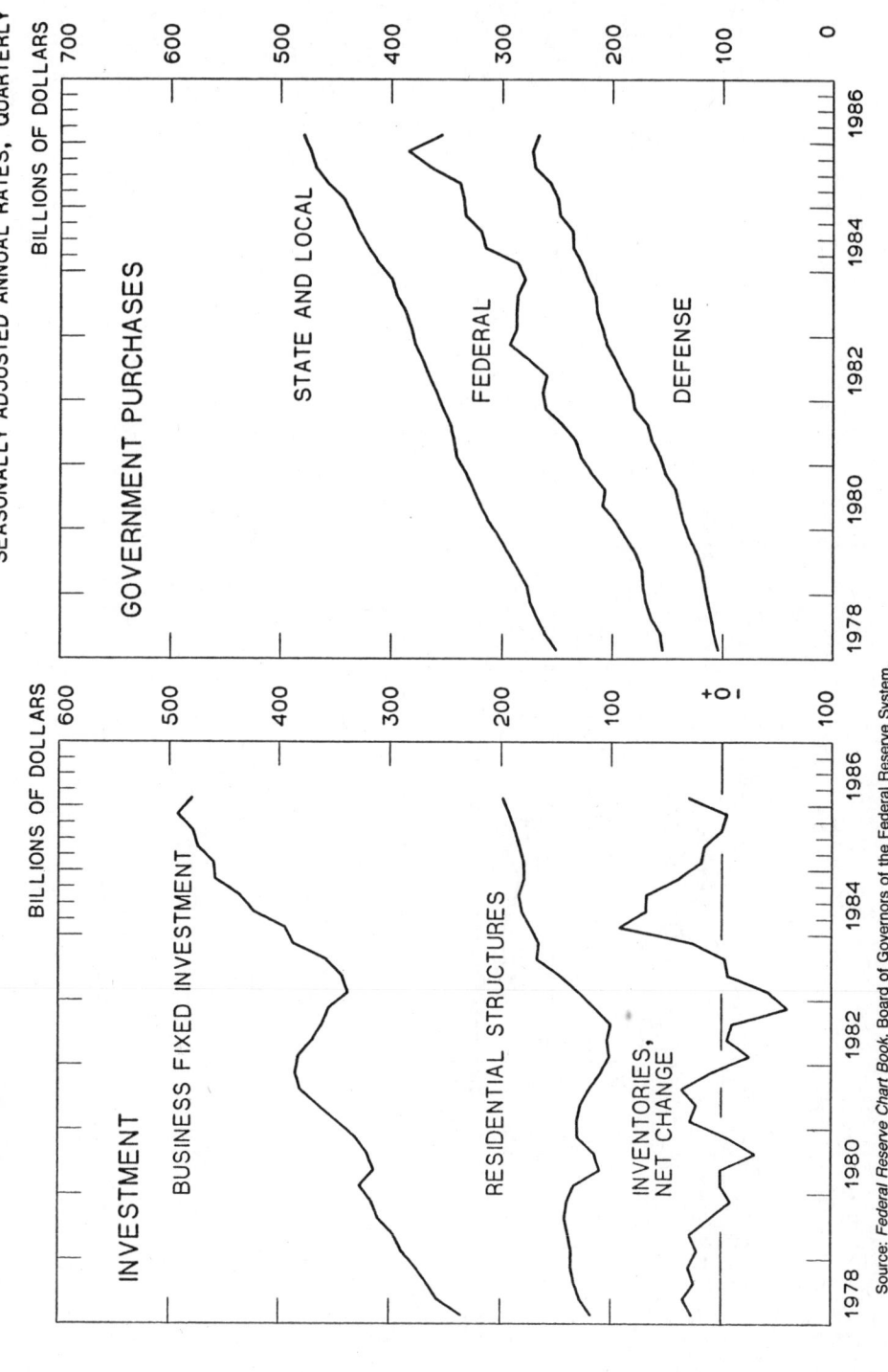

SELECTED COMPONENTS OF GNP

SEASONALLY ADJUSTED ANNUAL RATES, QUARTERLY

BILLIONS OF DOLLARS

GOVERNMENT PURCHASES

STATE AND LOCAL

FEDERAL

DEFENSE

BILLIONS OF DOLLARS

INVESTMENT

BUSINESS FIXED INVESTMENT

RESIDENTIAL STRUCTURES

INVENTORIES, NET CHANGE

Source: Federal Reserve Chart Book, Board of Governors of the Federal Reserve System.

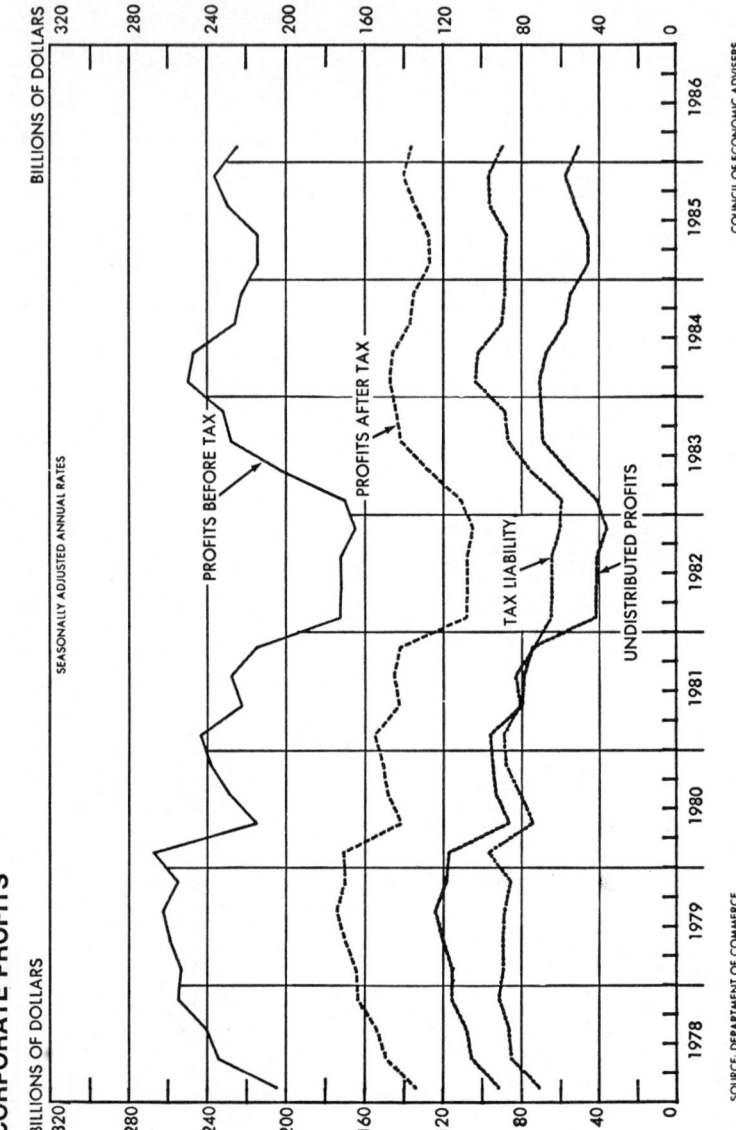

CORPORATE PROFITS

BILLIONS OF DOLLARS

SEASONALLY ADJUSTED ANNUAL RATES

BILLIONS OF DOLLARS

PROFITS BEFORE TAX

PROFITS AFTER TAX

TAX LIABILITY

UNDISTRIBUTED PROFITS

SOURCE: DEPARTMENT OF COMMERCE

COUNCIL OF ECONOMIC ADVISERS

[Billions of dollars; quarterly data at seasonally adjusted annual rates]

Period	Profits (before tax) with inventory valuation adjustment [1]						Profits before tax	Tax liability	Profits after tax			Inventory valuation adjustment
	Total [2]	Domestic industries							Total	Dividends	Undistributed profits	
		Total	Financial	Nonfinancial								
				Total [3]	Manufacturing	Wholesale and retail trade						
1980	194.0	159.6	21.0	138.6	77.1	21.6	237.1	84.8	152.3	54.7	97.6	−43.1
1981	202.3	173.8	16.5	157.3	88.5	32.5	226.5	81.1	145.4	63.6	81.8	−24.2
1982	159.2	131.2	11.8	119.4	58.0	34.6	169.6	63.1	106.5	66.9	39.6	−10.4
1983 ʳ	196.7	166.6	18.1	148.5	70.1	38.9	207.6	77.2	130.4	71.5	58.9	−10.9
1984 ʳ	230.2	199.2	15.4	183.8	87.4	49.7	235.7	95.4	140.3	78.3	62.0	−5.5
1985 ʳ	222.6	190.8	21.0	169.7	73.0	49.7	223.2	91.8	131.4	81.6	49.8	−.6
1982: III	161.6	133.0	12.4	120.6	64.3	32.9	171.6	64.3	107.3	66.6	40.7	−10.0
IV	150.7	121.6	18.7	102.9	46.8	33.6	164.1	59.8	104.3	68.5	35.8	−13.4
1983: I ʳ	163.9	135.7	19.4	116.3	51.2	32.5	169.7	59.1	110.6	69.8	40.8	−5.9
II ʳ	191.2	163.0	20.3	142.7	63.2	41.0	201.8	75.3	126.6	70.4	56.1	−10.6
III ʳ	208.5	176.8	17.2	159.6	77.7	39.0	227.5	86.5	141.0	72.0	69.0	−19.0
IV ʳ	223.4	190.7	15.5	175.2	88.6	43.1	231.5	88.1	143.4	73.9	69.5	−8.1
1984: I ʳ	235.7	205.2	16.6	188.6	95.0	46.2	249.3	102.9	146.4	76.0	70.4	−13.6
II ʳ	241.5	211.5	15.4	196.1	94.6	51.1	246.5	101.6	144.8	78.1	66.7	−4.9
III ʳ	223.3	191.3	13.4	177.8	81.3	51.0	225.1	89.3	135.8	79.0	56.8	−1.8
IV ʳ	220.3	188.8	16.1	172.6	78.9	50.7	221.9	87.8	134.1	80.1	54.0	−1.6
1985: I ʳ	213.3	182.6	18.2	164.4	70.4	48.8	213.8	87.8	126.0	80.9	45.1	−.5
II ʳ	215.4	183.8	21.1	162.7	68.2	51.1	213.8	87.1	126.7	81.4	45.3	1.6
III ʳ	235.3	205.3	21.7	183.6	79.0	54.2	229.2	95.8	133.4	81.6	51.8	6.1
IV ʳ	226.4	191.3	23.2	168.1	74.5	45.0	235.8	96.4	139.4	82.5	57.0	−9.4
1986: I ʳ	240.8	202.4	28.4	174.0	67.1	52.5	224.3	89.1	135.2	85.2	50.0	16.5
II ᵖ										87.5		5.9

[1] See p. 177 for profits with inventory valuation and capital consumption adjustments.
[2] Includes rest of the world, not shown separately.
[3] Includes industries not shown separately.

Source: *Economic Indicators*, Council of Economic Advisers.

NOTE.—Series revised beginning 1983. See *Survey of Current Business*, July 1986.

Source: Department of Commerce, Bureau of Economic Analysis.

Price Data

Definitions are applicable to the exhibit on pages 185 and 188.

Price data are gathered by the Bureau of Labor Statistics from retail and primary markets in the United States. Price indexes are given in relation to a base period (1967 = 100, unless otherwise noted).

DEFINITIONS

The **Consumer Price Index** (CPI) is a measure of the average change in the prices paid by urban consumers for a fixed market basket of goods and services. The CPI is calculated monthly for two population groups, one consisting only of urban households whose primary source of income is derived from the employment of wage earners and clerical workers, and the other consisting of all urban households. The wage earner index (CPI–W) is a continuation of the historic index that was introduced well over a half-century ago for use in wage negotiations. As new uses were developed for the CPI in recent years, the need for a broader and more representative index became apparent. The all urban consumer index (CPI–U) introduced in 1978 is representative of the 1972–73 buying habits of about 80 percent of the noninstitutional population of the United States at that time, compared with 40 percent represented in the CPI–W. In addition to wage earners and clerical workers, the CPI–U covers professional, managerial, and technical workers, the self-employed, short-term workers, the unemployed, retirees, and others not in the labor force.

The CPI is based on prices of food, clothing, shelter, fuel, drugs, transportation fares, doctor's and dentist's fees, and other goods and services that people buy for day-to-day living. The quantity and quality of these items are kept essentially unchanged between major revisions so that only price changes will be measured. All taxes directly associated with the purchase and use of items are included in the index.

Data are collected from more than 24,000 retail establishments and 24,000 tenants in 85 urban areas across the country and used to develop the "U.S. city average."

NOTES ON THE DATA

In January 1983, the Bureau changed the way in which homeownership costs are measured for the CPI–U. A rental equivalence method replaced the asset-price approach to homeownership costs for that series. In January 1985, the same change was made in the CPI–W. The central purpose of the change was to separate shelter costs from the investment component of homeownership so that the index would reflect only the cost of shelter services provided by owner-occupied homes.

Additional Sources of Information

For a discussion of the general method for computing the CPI, see *BLS Handbook of Methods, Volume II, The Consumer Price Index,* Bulletin 2134–2 (Bureau of Labor Statistics, 1984). The recent change in the measurement of homeownership costs is discussed in Robert Gillingham and Walter Lane, "Changing the treatment of shelter costs for homeowners in the CPI," *Monthly Labor Review,* June 1982, pp. 9–14.

Additional detailed CPI data and regular analyses of consumer price changes are provided in the *CPI Detailed Report,* a monthly publication of the Bureau. Historical data for the overall CPI and for selected groupings may be found in the *Handbook of Labor Statistics,* Bulletin 2217 (Bureau of Labor Statistics, 1985).

Source: *Monthly Labor Review,* U.S. Department of Labor, Bureau of Labor Statistics, July 1986.

CONSUMER PRICE INDEX FOR ALL URBAN CONSUMERS: U.S. CITY AVERAGE

(1967 = 100, unless otherwise indicated)

Series	Annual avg 1984	Annual avg 1985	1985 May	June	July	Aug.	Sept.	Oct.	Nov.	Dec.	1986 Jan.	Feb.	Mar.	Apr.	May
All items	311.1	322.2	321.3	322.3	322.8	323.5	324.5	325.5	326.6	327.4	328.4	327.5	326.0	325.3	326.3
Commodities	280.7	286.7	287.0	286.9	286.5	286.5	287.1	287.9	289.2	289.9	290.1	287.4	283.7	281.2	282.1
Food and beverages	295.1	302.0	301.0	301.4	301.6	301.8	302.1	302.5	303.6	305.6	307.9	307.7	307.8	308.5	309.4
Commodities less food and beverages	—	—	—	—	—	—	—	—	—	—	—	—	—	—	—
Nondurables less food and beverages	275.7	282.1	283.1	283.5	282.9	283.1	284.6	285.3	286.8	286.8	284.9	278.6	268.9	262.0	263.3
Apparel commodities	187.0	191.6	191.0	190.2	188.0	190.6	195.3	196.7	196.8	194.2	189.5	188.5	190.8	191.7	190.7
Nondurables less food, beverages, and apparel	325.8	333.3	335.1	336.2	336.4	335.4	335.3	335.6	337.8	339.1	338.7	329.5	313.6	302.6	305.2
Durables	266.5	270.7	271.6	271.4	269.3	268.6	268.7	270.2	271.5	271.4	271.4	270.5	269.7	269.2	269.6
Services	363.0	381.5	378.9	381.3	383.3	384.9	386.5	387.7	388.7	389.5	391.7	393.3	394.9	396.8	397.9
Rent of shelter	107.7	113.9	113.2	113.6	114.3	115.1	115.4	116.1	116.7	117.0	117.4	117.7	118.5	119.4	119.7
Household services less rent of shelter	108.1	111.2	110.9	112.7	113.2	113.2	113.5	112.1	110.8	110.8	111.4	111.8	111.6	111.6	112.3
Transportation services	321.1	337.0	334.5	335.3	337.0	337.4	337.1	341.1	344.7	346.1	349.0	351.0	352.4	353.2	353.4
Medical care services	410.3	435.1	430.9	433.0	435.8	438.6	440.5	443.0	445.8	448.0	451.9	456.2	460.1	462.3	464.2
Other services	296.0	314.1	310.7	312.0	313.0	313.8	319.7	321.4	322.5	322.9	324.8	326.1	326.6	327.6	328.2
Special indexes:															
All items less food	311.3	323.3	322.4	323.6	324.2	325.0	326.2	327.4	328.5	328.9	329.5	328.5	326.6	325.7	326.7
All items less shelter	295.1	303.9	303.4	304.3	304.4	304.6	305.7	306.3	307.2	307.9	308.8	307.4	305.2	303.6	304.7
All items less homeowners' costs	106.3	109.7	109.5	109.8	109.9	110.1	110.4	110.7	111.1	111.3	111.6	111.2	110.5	110.1	110.4
All items less medical care	307.3	317.7	317.0	317.9	318.4	318.9	319.9	320.8	321.9	322.6	323.4	322.2	320.5	319.7	320.6
Commodities less food	267.0	272.5	273.4	273.1	272.9	272.3	273.1	274.4	275.7	275.7	274.7	270.9	265.2	261.2	262.1
Nondurables less food	270.8	277.2	278.0	278.4	277.9	278.1	279.6	280.7	282.0	282.0	280.4	274.5	265.5	259.2	260.5
Nondurables less food and apparel	311.9	319.2	320.7	321.7	321.9	321.1	321.0	322.0	324.0	325.1	324.9	316.8	302.7	292.9	295.2
Nondurables	286.6	293.2	293.3	293.7	293.5	293.7	294.7	295.1	296.4	297.4	297.7	294.3	289.5	287.0	287.4
Services less rent of shelter	108.5	113.5	112.8	113.7	114.2	114.5	115.0	115.1	115.2	115.4	116.2	116.8	117.1	117.4	117.8
Services less medical care	355.6	373.3	370.9	373.3	375.2	376.7	378.3	379.3	380.1	380.8	382.7	384.0	385.4	387.2	388.3
Energy	423.6	426.5	431.7	436.8	437.1	433.8	432.6	427.1	425.1	426.5	424.7	408.9	381.3	361.8	367.6
All items less energy	302.9	314.8	313.3	313.9	314.5	315.6	316.8	318.4	319.8	320.5	321.8	322.3	323.6	324.4	325.0
All items less food and energy	301.2	314.4	312.8	313.4	314.1	315.3	316.9	318.9	320.4	320.7	321.6	322.3	323.6	324.8	325.3
Commodities less food and energy	253.1	259.7	259.6	259.0	258.2	258.8	260.2	262.0	262.7	262.2	261.8	261.6	262.0	262.1	262.2
Energy commodities	409.8	409.9	417.0	418.7	418.1	414.0	411.2	410.1	415.2	417.9	413.2	386.5	343.0	313.3	319.3
Services less energy	356.4	375.9	372.9	374.6	376.6	378.6	380.2	382.5	384.8	385.8	387.9	389.4	391.5	393.8	394.5
Purchasing power of the consumer dollar:															
1967=$1.00	32.1	31.0	31.1	31.0	31.0	30.9	30.8	30.7	30.6	30.5	30.5	30.5	30.7	30.7	30.6
1957-59=$1.00	27.6	26.7	26.8	26.7	26.6	26.6	26.5	26.4	26.3	26.3	26.2	26.3	26.4	26.4	26.4

Source: Monthly Labor Review, U.S. Department of Labor, Bureau of Labor Statistics, July, 1986.

CONSUMER PRICES—ALL URBAN CONSUMERS

INDEX, 1967 = 100 (RATIO SCALE)

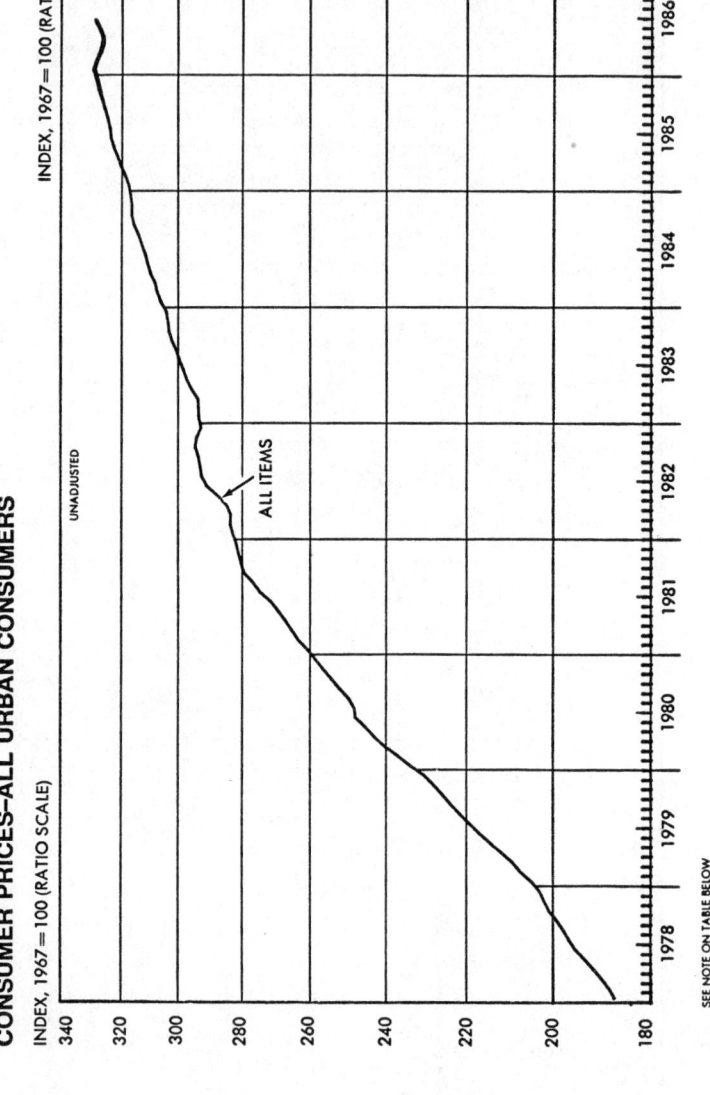

INDEX, 1967 = 100 (RATIO SCALE)

UNADJUSTED

ALL ITEMS

SEE NOTE ON TABLE BELOW
SOURCE: DEPARTMENT OF LABOR

COUNCIL OF ECONOMIC ADVISERS

[1967=100, except as noted; monthly data seasonally adjusted, except as noted by NSA]

Period	All items¹ (NSA)	Food	Housing Total¹	Housing — Shelter Total	Housing — Shelter Renters' costs (Dec. 1982=100)	Housing — Shelter Homeowners' costs (Dec. 1982=100)	Housing — Shelter Maintenance and repairs (NSA)	Housing Fuel and other utilities	Apparel and upkeep	Transportation Total¹	Transportation New cars	Transportation Motor fuel	Medical care	Energy²	All items less food, energy, and shelter
Rel. imp.³	100.0	18.5	37.9	22.3	7.3	14.4	0.5	8.1	5.0	21.4	3.4	5.5	6.5	11.3	48.0
1978	195.4	211.4	202.8	210.4			233.0	216.0	159.6	185.5	153.8	196.3	219.4	220.4	179.1
1979	217.4	234.5	227.6	239.7			256.4	239.3	166.6	212.0	166.0	265.6	239.7	275.9	191.5
1980	246.8	254.6	263.3	281.7			285.7	278.6	178.4	249.7	179.3	369.1	265.9	361.1	208.3
1981	272.4	274.6	293.5	314.7			314.4	319.2	186.9	280.0	190.2	410.9	294.5	410.0	228.1
1982	289.1	285.7	314.7	337.0			334.1	350.8	191.8	291.5	197.6	389.4	328.7	416.1	245.6
1983	298.4	291.7	323.1	344.8	103.0	102.5	346.3	370.3	196.5	298.4	202.6	376.4	357.3	419.3	258.4
1984	311.1	302.9	336.5	361.7	108.6	107.3	359.2	387.3	200.2	311.7	208.5	370.7	379.5	423.6	271.2
1985	322.2	309.8	349.9	382.0	115.4	113.1	363.5	393.6	206.0	319.9	215.2	373.8	403.1	426.5	281.6
1985: June	322.3	309.1	349.4	381.1	115.3	112.9	367.6	394.7	205.5	320.2	215.0	378.8	402.6	430.3	280.9
July	322.8	309.2	350.3	383.1	115.8	113.6	367.8	394.2	205.6	320.3	215.2	379.1	404.3	429.4	281.4
Aug	323.5	309.6	351.7	385.3	116.3	114.3	370.6	393.6	205.9	319.8	215.7	377.4	406.6	427.6	282.1
Sept	324.5	310.7	352.2	386.1	116.7	114.5	368.7	394.4	206.8	319.3	216.2	375.2	409.0	426.8	282.6
Oct	325.5	311.1	353.3	387.9	117.5	114.9	368.5	393.7	207.7	320.5	217.0	374.3	410.9	425.8	284.1
Nov	326.6	313.2	355.2	390.5	118.2	115.7	372.7	395.4	208.4	322.6	217.7	377.4	413.0	428.4	285.4
Dec	327.4	315.2	356.2	391.9	118.5	116.2	373.7	396.5	208.3	323.9	218.4	379.4	415.7	430.3	286.2
1986: Jan	328.4	315.9	357.1	393.3	118.8	116.6	379.1	397.2	207.7	325.5	218.6	380.1	417.5	430.8	287.5
Feb	327.5	313.8	356.8	394.8	119.2	117.0	379.6	392.4	206.6	320.9	219.5	357.2	420.4	414.3	288.0
Mar	326.0	314.1	357.5	397.3	119.8	118.0	367.5	388.4	206.3	311.8	219.9	314.8	424.5	387.5	288.6
Apr	325.3	315.0	358.5	400.7	121.1	118.9	367.6	385.7	206.9	304.0	221.2	279.5	427.2	365.2	289.1
May	326.3	316.4	358.2	401.0	121.2	119.1	367.1	382.3	206.5	304.9	223.0	286.4	429.8	366.2	289.4
June	327.9	316.7	360.1	401.8	121.7	119.1	366.6	388.9	205.8	307.4	224.4	295.0	432.8	374.8	290.4

¹ Includes items not shown separately.
² Fuel oil, coal, and bottled gas; gas (piped) and electricity; and motor fuel. Motor oil, coolant, etc. also included through 1982.
³ Relative importance, December 1985.

NOTE.—Data beginning 1983 incorporate a rental equivalence measure for homeownership costs and therefore are not strictly comparable with figures for earlier periods.

Source: Department of Labor, Bureau of Labor Statistics.

Source: Economic Indicators, Council of Economic Advisers.

CONSUMER PRICE INDEX—U.S. CITY AVERAGE AND AVAILABLE LOCAL AREA DATA: ALL ITEMS

(1967=100, unless otherwise indicated)

Area[1]	Pricing schedule[2]	Other index base	All Urban Consumers							Urban Wage Earners						
			1985		1986					1985		1986				
			May	June	Jan.	Feb.	Mar.	Apr.	May	May	June	Jan.	Feb.	Mar.	Apr.	May
U.S. city average			321.3	322.3	328.4	327.5	326.0	325.3	326.3	317.8	318.7	324.3	323.2	321.4	320.4	321.4
Chicago, Ill.-Northwestern Ind.	M		319.8	324.1	326.3	326.4	323.9	323.7	324.2	306.9	310.9	312.9	312.8	309.7	309.1	309.6
Detroit, Mich.	M		316.1	317.0	323.1	322.9	320.0	318.8	321.7	306.6	307.4	313.4	312.3	309.3	308.1	311.0
Los Angeles-Long Beach, Anaheim, Calif.	M		319.1	319.3	326.8	326.6	328.2	326.8	329.4	314.1	314.1	320.9	320.4	321.6	320.2	322.7
New York, N.Y.-Northeastern N.J.	M		312.6	313.2	323.1	322.3	322.4	321.4	320.6	305.8	306.3	315.8	314.7	314.5	313.2	312.3
Philadelphia, Pa.-N.J.	M		314.2	314.2	320.3	320.1	319.1	317.8	318.9	317.2	317.2	323.0	322.8	321.4	319.7	320.8
Anchorage, Alaska (10/67 = 100)	1	10/67	278.8	—	287.1	—	291.2	—	288.9	271.9	—	280.2	—	284.4	—	281.8
Baltimore, Md.	1		323.1	—	332.0	—	331.1	—	329.1	322.3	—	331.1	—	329.5	—	326.8
Boston, Mass.	1		315.2	—	327.1	—	324.9	—	332.6	313.2	—	324.5	—	322.3	—	319.3
Cincinnati, Ohio-Ky.-Ind.	1		330.4	—	333.2	—	329.4	—	332.0	324.0	—	326.0	—	321.8	—	324.8
Denver-Boulder, Colo.	1		356.3	—	364.4	—	355.7	—	356.3	351.9	—	359.1	—	350.1	—	350.3
Miami, Fla. (11/77 = 100)	1	11/77	171.0	—	174.6	—	174.5	—	173.0	172.2	—	175.7	—	175.1	—	173.4
Milwaukee, Wis.	1		330.9	—	333.9	—	329.1	—	332.0	350.2	—	353.0	—	347.2	—	350.6
Northeast, Pa.	1		306.0	—	311.6	—	309.3	—	309.2	305.2	—	310.6	—	308.3	—	308.1
Portland, Oreg.-Wash.	1		310.4	—	321.3	—	315.0	—	314.6	301.2	—	311.0	—	304.3	—	303.2
St. Louis, Mo.-Ill.	1		315.9	—	322.4	—	319.2	—	318.6	313.0	—	319.1	—	315.0	—	314.2
San Diego, Calif.	1		372.1	—	381.9	—	379.2	—	382.8	336.5	—	344.7	—	341.9	—	345.2
Seattle-Everett, Wash.	1		321.0	—	327.0	—	325.0	—	323.5	308.4	—	313.5	—	311.4	—	309.4
Washington, D.C.-Md.-Va.	1		319.8	—	331.1	—	325.0	—	329.6	323.0	—	332.6	—	330.5	—	330.2

Area	Base period						
Atlanta, Ga.		328.0	336.9	334.9	326.0	334.3	331.7
Buffalo, N.Y.		307.3	310.1	308.0	293.7	295.8	292.7
Cleveland, Ohio		346.4	350.2	346.9	325.3	328.3	324.4
Dallas-Ft. Worth, Tex.		339.6	347.0	341.4	333.5	340.4	334.1
Honolulu, Hawaii		293.5	301.2	299.0	300.4	308.5	306.0
Houston, Tex.		337.6	337.2	330.0	335.0	334.3	327.7
Kansas City, Mo.-Kansas		320.1	321.1	320.7	310.5	310.1	308.9
Minneapolis-St. Paul, Minn.-Wis.		336.7	339.9	338.4	332.3	334.9	332.3
Pittsburgh, Pa.		325.9	330.1	328.1	308.3	311.4	307.8
San Francisco-Oakland, Calif.		333.2	341.1	339.3	328.7	336.0	333.2
Region[3]							
Northeast	12/77	170.4	174.5	173.7	168.4	172.3	171.1
North Central	12/77	174.2	175.4	173.9	171.0	171.8	170.0
South	12/77	173.8	176.6	175.1	173.7	176.1	174.1
West	12/77	174.6	177.5	176.8	172.8	175.4	174.5
Population size class[3]							
A-1	12/77	170.9	174.7	173.9	167.2	170.5	169.3
A-2	12/77	176.0	178.7	177.4	173.2	175.5	173.8
B	12/77	174.7	176.9	175.6	172.3	174.2	172.7
C	12/77	172.3	174.7	173.4	172.9	175.0	173.4
D	12/77	171.9	174.0	172.7	173.5	175.2	173.6
Region/population size class cross classification[3]							
Class A:							
Northeast	12/77	167.5	171.8	171.0	164.2	168.1	166.9
North Central	12/77	177.6	179.2	177.8	172.8	174.0	172.1
South	12/77	174.1	177.3	175.5	174.2	177.0	174.9
West	11/77	176.1	179.8	179.6	172.2	175.5	174.9
Class B:							
Northeast	12/77	173.5	176.4	174.7	170.5	173.4	171.7
North Central	12/77	172.6	173.7	172.1	169.0	169.7	167.7
South	12/77	175.3	178.2	177.0	172.2	174.6	173.2
West	12/77	176.2	177.6	176.7	176.8	178.2	177.1

(continued)

CONSUMER PRICE INDEX—U.S. CITY AVERAGE AND AVAILABLE LOCAL AREA DATA: ALL ITEMS (concluded)

(1967=100, unless otherwise indicated)

Area[1]	Pricing sche-dule[2]	Other index base	All Urban Consumers 1985 May	June	1986 Jan.	Feb.	Mar.	Apr.	May	Urban Wage Earners 1985 May	June	1986 Jan.	Feb.	Mar.	Apr.	May
Class C:																
Northeast	2	12/77	—	179.0	—	183.1	—	183.0	—	—	183.7	—	187.8	—	187.4	—
North Central	2	12/77	—	169.6	—	170.4	—	168.5	—	—	166.7	—	167.1	—	165.1	—
South	2	12/77	—	172.8	—	175.3	—	173.6	—	—	174.5	—	176.6	—	174.3	—
West	2	12/77	—	168.4	—	171.1	—	170.5	—	—	167.2	—	169.6	—	168.9	—
Class D:																
Northeast	2	12/77	—	173.7	—	178.9	—	177.9	—	—	173.8	—	178.6	—	177.2	—
North Central	2	12/77	—	170.4	—	170.7	—	170.0	—	—	172.5	—	172.4	—	171.4	—
South	2	12/77	—	172.2	—	174.7	—	173.2	—	—	174.0	—	176.0	—	174.0	—
West	2	12/77	—	172.5	—	174.8	—	172.6	—	—	174.2	—	176.3	—	173.9	—

[1] Area is generally the Standard Metropolitan Statistical Area (SMSA), exclusive of farms. L.A.-Long Beach, Anaheim, Calif. is a combination of two SMSA's, and N.Y., N.Y.-Northeastern N.J. and Chicago, Ill.-Northwestern Ind. are the more extensive Standard Consolidated Areas. Area definitions are those established by the Office of Management and Budget in 1973, except for Denver-Boulder, Colo. which does not include Douglas County. Definitions do not include revisions made since 1973.

[2] Foods, fuels, and several other items priced every month in all areas; most other goods and services priced as indicated:

M - Every month.

1 - January, March, May, July, September, and November.

2 - February, April, June, August, October, and December.

[3] Regions are defined as the four Census regions.

The population size classes are aggregations of areas which have urban population as defined:

A-1 - More than 4,000,000.

A-2 - 1,250,000 to 4,000,000.

B - 385,000 to 1,250,000.

C - 75,000 to 385,000.

D - Less than 75,000.

Population size class A is the aggregation of population size classes A-1 and A-2.

– Data not available.

NOTE: Local area CPI indexes are byproducts of the national CPI program. Because each local index is a small subset of the national index, it has a smaller sample size and is, therefore, subject to substantially more sampling and other measurement error than the national index. As a result, local area indexes show greater volatility than the national index, although their long-term trends are quite similar. Therefore, the Bureau of Labor Statistics strongly urges users to consider adopting the national average CPI for use in escalator clauses.

Source: Monthly Labor Review, U.S. Department of Labor, Bureau of Labor Statistics.

Federal Budget: Procedure and Timetable

Congressional Budget Timetable

CONGRESSIONAL BUDGET ACT OF 1974: THE NEW BUDGET PROCESS IN TEN STEPS

1. To give Congress an earlier and better start in reviewing and reshaping the budget, the Executive Branch must submit a "current services budget" by November 10th for the new fiscal year that starts the following October 1st. The current services budget should project the spending required to maintain ongoing programs throughout the following fiscal year at existing commitment levels, or at commitment levels specified by existing legislation based on current economic assumptions. The Joint Economic Committee should review and assess the current services budget and report to Congress by December 31st.

2. The President will continue to submit his new budget to Congress in late January or early February. In addition to the traditional budget totals and breakdowns, the budget document must include a list of existing "tax expenditures"—i.e., estimates of revenues lost to the Treasury through preferential tax treatment—as well as any proposed changes in tax expenditures. The budget must also contain estimates of expenditures for programs for which funds are appropriated one year in advance and five-year budget projections of all federal spending under existing programs.

3. Reports of all standing committees to the House and Senate Budget Committees of the spending plans of those committees on all matters under their jurisdiction, including spending under new legislation, are required by March 15th for the upcoming fiscal year.

4. An annual report of the Congressional Budget Office to the Budget Committees on alternative budget levels and national budget priorities is required on or before April 1st.

5. By April 15th, the Budget Committees must report concurrent resolutions to the House and Senate floors, and Congress will have to clear the initial budget resolution by May 15th. This initial budget resolution sets target totals for appropriations, outlays, taxes, the budget surplus or deficit, and the federal debt. Within these overall targets, the resolution will break down appropriations and outlays by the functional categories used in the President's budget document, as well as by classifications used by the appropriations subcommittees for the 13 appropriations bills. The resolution will include any recommended changes in tax revenues and in the level of the federal debt ceiling.

6. Committees report bills or resolutions authorizing new budget authority by May 15th.

7. The basic appropriations process proceeds within the Appropriations Committees, but is subject to targets of the budget resolution.

8. Scorekeeping reports will be issued periodically by the Congressional Budget Office on the status of budget authority, revenue, outlays and debt legislation, comparing the amounts and changes in such legislation with the First Congressional Budget Resolution.

9. Subject to prior authorization, all appropriations bills have to be cleared by the middle of September—no later than the seventh day after Labor Day. By September 15th, after finishing action on all appropriations and other spending bills, Congress must adopt a second, and final, budget resolution that may either affirm or revise the budget targets set by the initial resolution. This resolution must provide for a final budget reconciliation by changing either one or more of the following: (1) appropriations (both for the upcoming fiscal year or carried over from previous fiscal years) and/or entitlements; (2) revenues; and (3) the public debt. The final resolution will direct the committees that have jurisdiction over these matters to report the necessary legislative changes. The Budget Committees will then combine these changes and report them to the floor in the form of a reconciliation bill.

If Congress has withheld all appropriations and entitlement bills from the President until passage of the final reconciliation bill, then this bill becomes the final budget legislation, subject to Presidential signature (or veto). If, on the other hand, each individual appropriations bill has been signed by the President upon passage by the Congress, the final reconciliation bill—upon signature by the President—supersedes all the previously passed individual bills.

10. The new fiscal year begins on October 1st.

FEDERAL BUDGET: PROCEDURE AND TIMETABLE

Congressional Budget Timetable

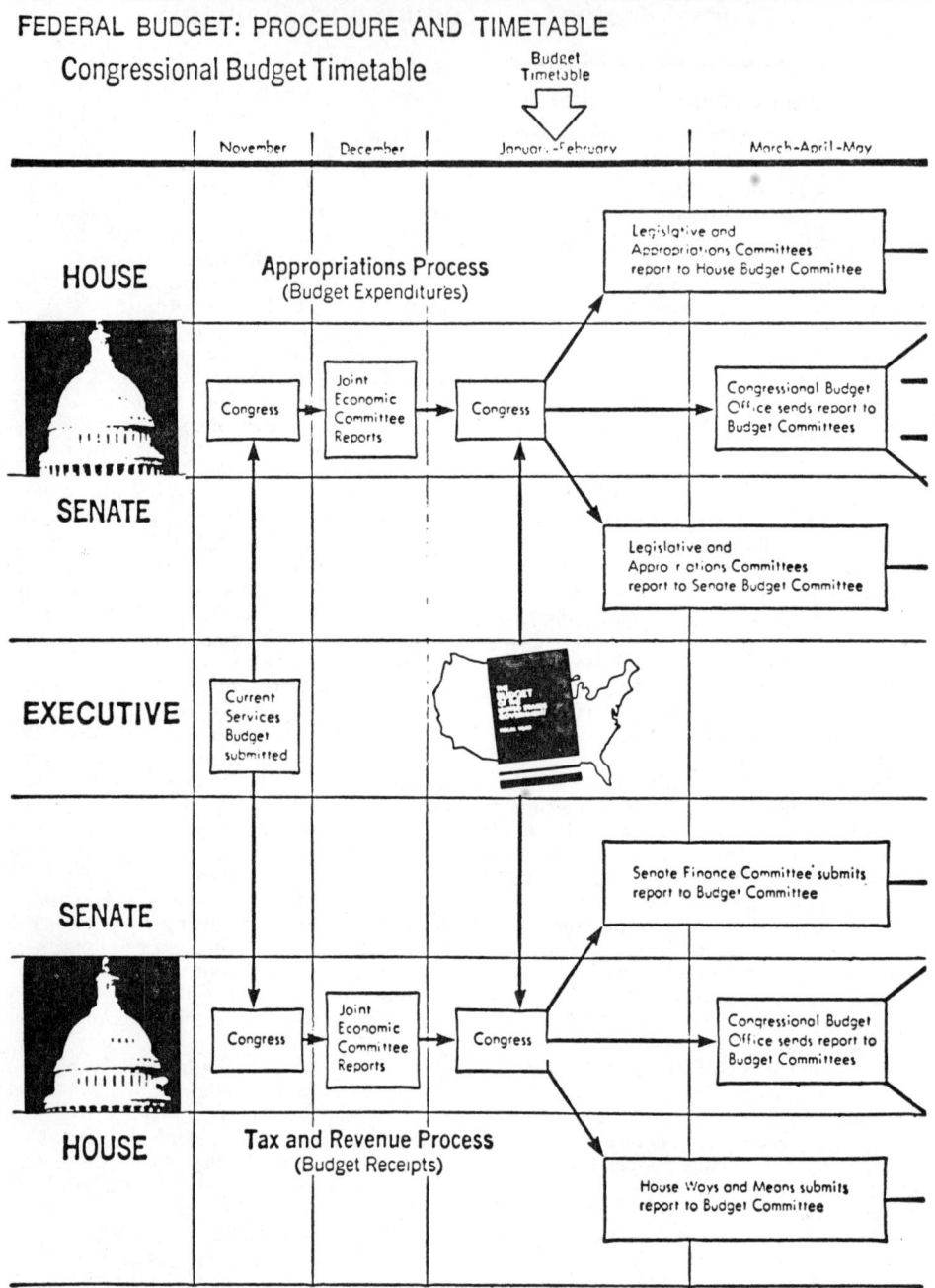

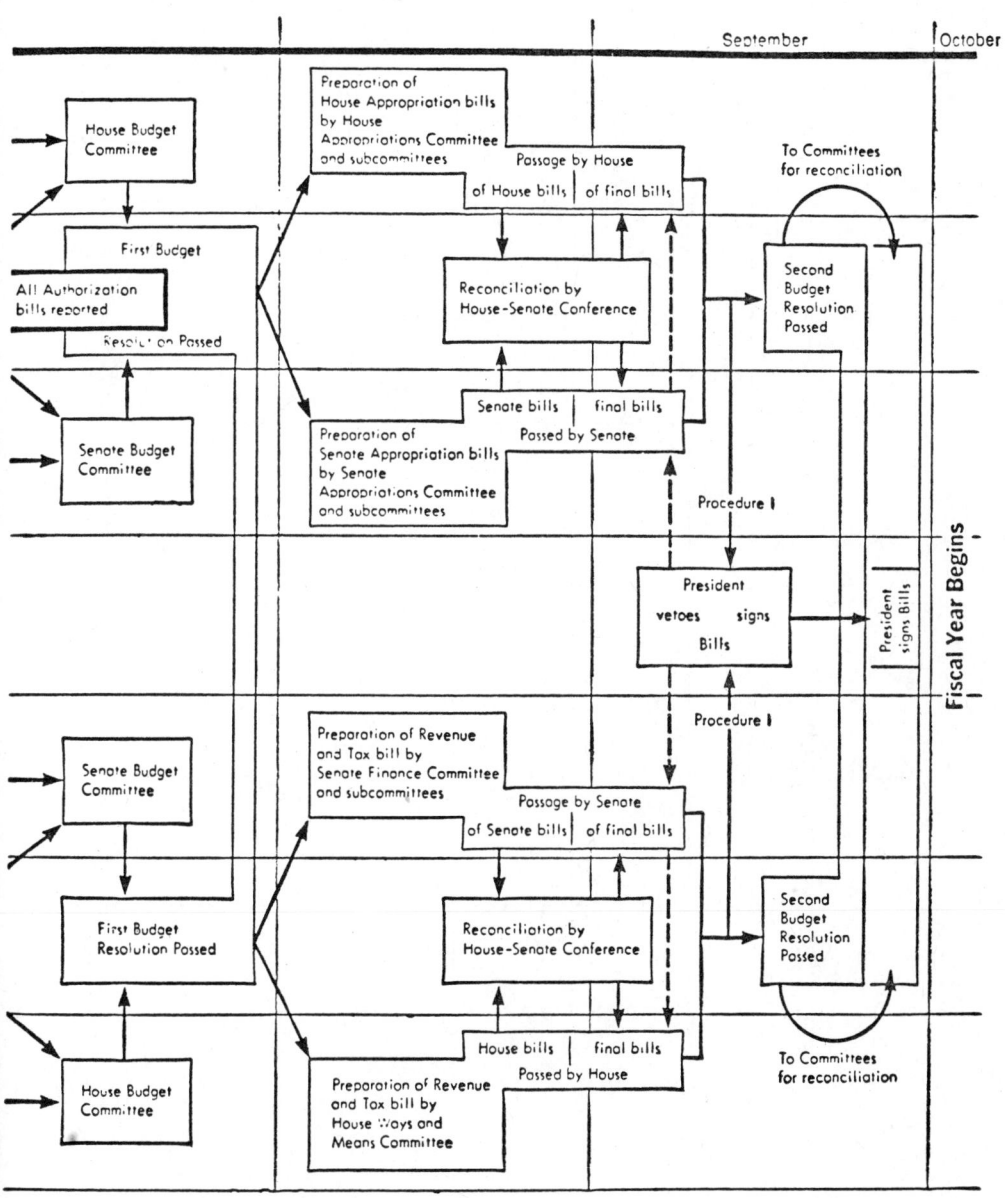

September | October

House Budget Committee

Preparation of House Appropriation bills by House Appropriations Committee and subcommittees

Passage by House
of House bills | of final bills

To Committees for reconciliation

First Budget

All Authorization bills reported

Resolution Passed

Reconciliation by House-Senate Conference

Second Budget Resolution Passed

Senate Budget Committee

Preparation of Senate Appropriation bills by Senate Appropriations Committee and subcommittees

Senate bills | final bills
Passed by Senate

Procedure I

President
vetoes   signs
Bills

President signs Bills

Fiscal Year Begins

Senate Budget Committee

Preparation of Revenue and Tax bill by Senate Finance Committee and subcommittees

Passage by Senate
of Senate bills | of final bills

Procedure I

First Budget Resolution Passed

Reconciliation by House-Senate Conference

Second Budget Resolution Passed

House Budget Committee

Preparation of Revenue and Tax bill by House Ways and Means Committee

House bills | final bills
Passed by House

To Committees for reconciliation

Source: The Conference Board, "The Federal Budget: Its Impact on the Economy," Michael E. Levy, assisted by Delos R. Smith.

SELECTED UNEMPLOYMENT RATES

PERCENT* (SEASONALLY ADJUSTED)

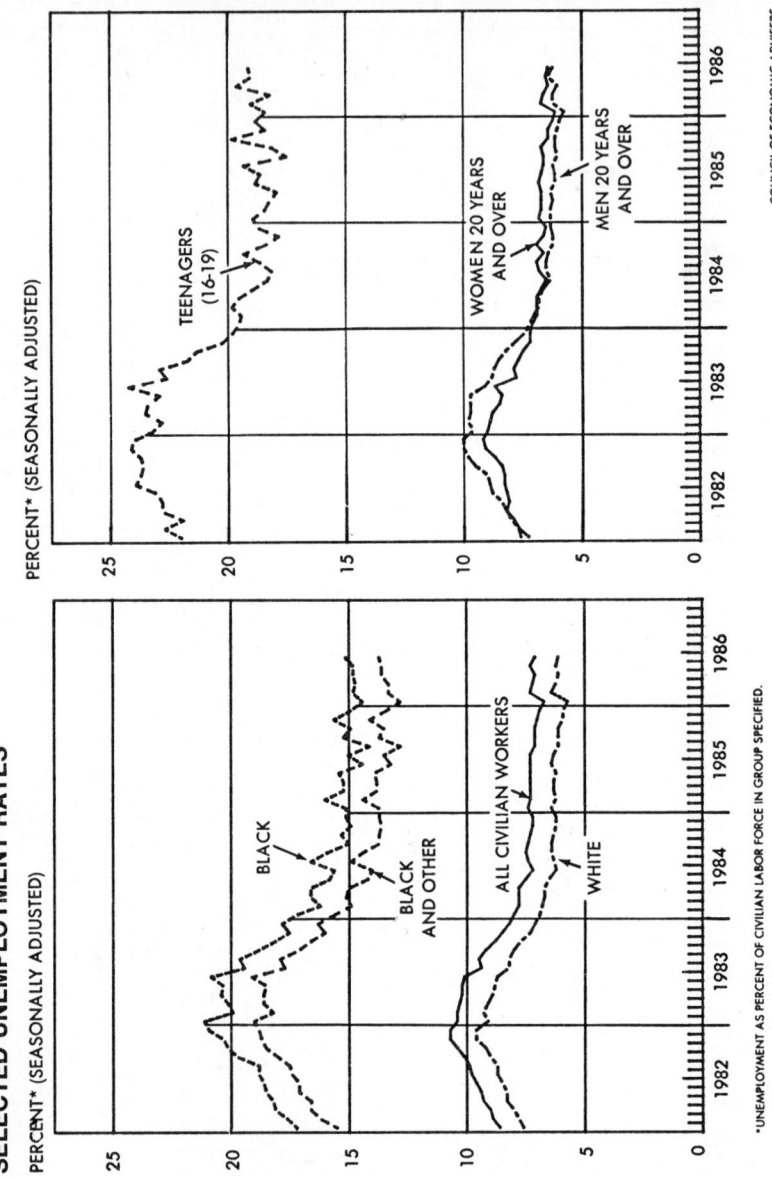

*UNEMPLOYMENT AS PERCENT OF CIVILIAN LABOR FORCE IN GROUP SPECIFIED.

SOURCE: DEPARTMENT OF LABOR

COUNCIL OF ECONOMIC ADVISERS

[Monthly data seasonally adjusted]

Period	Unemployment rate, all workers [1]	All civilian workers	By sex and age			By race			By selected groups						Labor force time lost (percent) [2]
			Men 20 years and over	Women 20 years and over	Both sexes 16–19 years	White	Black and other	Black	Experienced wage and salary workers	Married men, spouse present	Women who maintain families	Full-time workers	Part-time workers		
1979	5.8	5.8	4.2	5.7	16.1	5.1	11.3	12.3	5.5	2.8	8.3	5.3	8.8	6.3
1980	7.0	7.1	5.9	6.4	17.8	6.3	13.1	14.3	6.9	4.2	9.2	6.9	8.8	7.9
1981	7.5	7.6	6.3	6.8	19.6	6.7	14.2	15.6	7.3	4.3	10.4	7.3	9.4	8.5
1982	9.5	9.7	8.8	8.3	23.2	8.6	17.3	18.9	9.3	6.5	11.7	9.6	10.5	11.0
1983	9.5	9.6	8.9	8.1	22.4	8.4	17.8	19.5	9.2	6.5	12.2	9.5	10.4	10.9
1984	7.4	7.5	6.6	6.8	18.9	6.5	14.4	15.9	7.1	4.6	10.3	7.2	9.3	8.6
1985	7.1	7.2	6.2	6.6	18.6	6.2	13.7	15.1	6.8	4.3	10.4	6.8	9.3	8.1
1985: June	7.2	7.3	6.4	6.7	18.6	6.4	13.2	14.4	6.9	4.6	9.9	6.9	9.5	8.2
July	7.2	7.3	6.2	6.6	19.3	6.3	13.5	15.0	6.9	4.4	10.3	7.0	9.4	8.2
Aug	6.9	7.1	6.0	6.6	17.5	6.1	12.8	14.1	6.7	4.1	10.8	6.8	9.0	8.1
Sept	7.0	7.1	6.1	6.7	18.1	6.1	13.7	15.2	6.8	4.3	11.3	6.8	9.3	8.1
Oct	7.0	7.1	6.1	6.4	19.8	6.1	13.5	14.9	6.7	4.2	10.4	6.8	9.6	7.9
Nov	6.9	7.0	6.0	6.4	18.4	5.9	14.1	15.6	6.6	4.3	10.0	6.7	8.8	7.9
Dec	6.8	6.9	5.9	6.2	18.8	5.9	13.4	14.9	6.5	4.3	9.4	6.6	9.0	7.8
1986: Jan	6.6	6.7	5.7	6.1	18.4	5.7	12.8	14.4	6.3	4.3	9.9	6.4	8.4	7.6
Feb	7.2	7.3	6.2	6.7	19.0	6.4	13.3	14.8	6.8	4.5	9.9	6.9	9.4	8.1
Mar	7.1	7.2	6.2	6.6	18.2	6.2	13.3	14.7	6.7	4.5	10.1	6.9	9.1	8.1
Apr	7.0	7.1	6.0	6.4	19.6	6.1	13.6	14.8	6.7	4.2	9.4	6.7	9.6	8.1
May	7.2	7.3	6.4	6.5	19.0	6.2	13.6	14.8	6.9	4.5	10.2	7.0	9.2	8.3
June	7.0	7.1	6.2	6.4	19.1	6.1	13.7	15.1	6.7	4.5	10.1	6.7	9.1	8.1

Unemployment rate (percent of civilian labor force in group)

Source: Department of Labor, Bureau of Labor Statistics.

[1] Unemployed as percent of total labor force including resident Armed Forces.
[2] Aggregate hours lost by the unemployed and persons on part time for economic reasons as percent of potentially available labor force hours.

Source: *Economic Indicators*, Council of Economic Advisers.

MONEY STOCK, LIQUID ASSETS, AND DEBT MEASURES

BILLIONS OF DOLLARS*(RATIO SCALE)

BILLIONS OF DOLLARS*(RATIO SCALE)

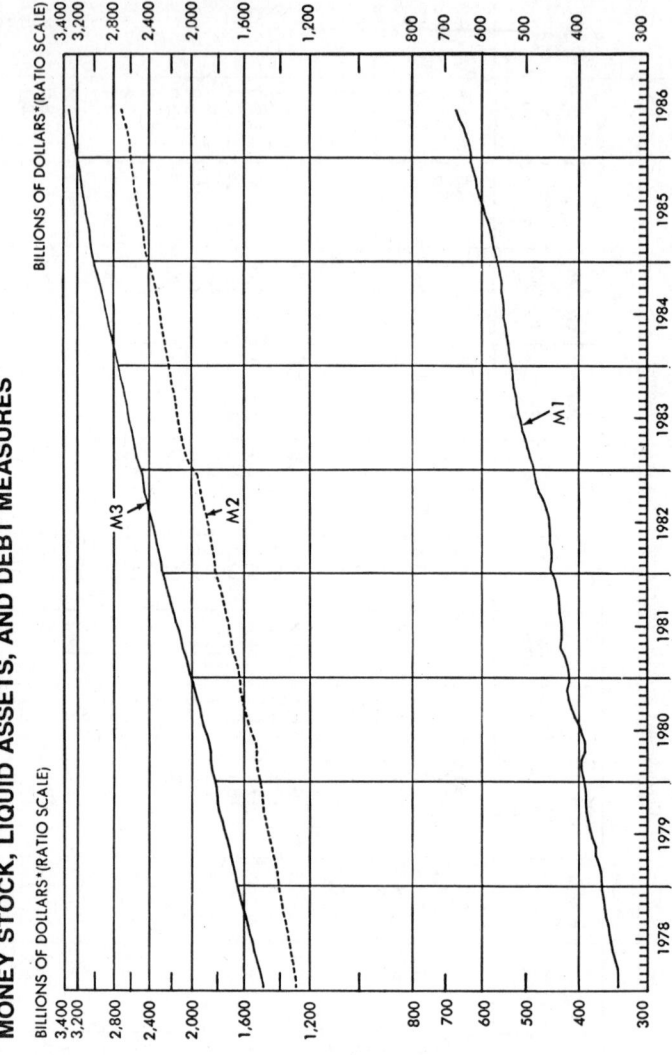

* AVERAGES OF DAILY FIGURES, SEASONALLY ADJUSTED
SOURCE: BOARD OF GOVERNORS OF THE FEDERAL RESERVE SYSTEM

COUNCIL OF ECONOMIC ADVISERS

[Averages of daily figures, except as noted; billions of dollars, seasonally adjusted]

Period	M1 — Sum of currency, demand deposits, travelers' checks, and other checkable deposits (OCDs)	M2 — M1 plus overnight RPs and Eurodollars, MMMF balances (general purpose and broker/dealer), MMDAs, and savings and small time deposits	M3 — M2 plus large time deposits, term RPs, term Eurodollars, and institution-only MMMF balances	L — M3 plus other liquid assets	Debt — Debt of domestic nonfinancial sectors (monthly average)[1]	Percent change from year or 6 months earlier[2] M1	M2	M3	Debt
1978: Dec.	363.0	1,388.9	1,646.4	1,909.0	3,169.4	8.3	8.0	11.8	13.3
1979: Dec.	388.7	1,497.5	1,803.2	2,114.8	3,554.9	7.1	7.8	9.5	12.2
1980: Dec.	414.2	1,630.3	1,987.4	2,323.3	3,894.5	6.6	8.9	10.2	9.6
1981: Dec.	441.1	1,792.8	2,233.6	2,593.7	4,269.7	6.5	10.0	12.4	9.6
1982: Dec.	479.9	1,952.6	2,443.5	2,850.1	4,661.3	8.8	8.9	9.4	9.2
1983: Dec.	527.1	2,186.0	2,697.3	3,163.5	5,192.0	9.8	12.0	10.4	11.4
1984: Dec.	558.5	2,373.8	2,986.5	3,532.3	5,952.0	6.0	8.6	10.7	14.6
1985: Dec.	626.6	2,565.8	3,199.9	3,837.0	6,809.8	12.2	8.1	7.1	14.4
1985: June	590.9	2,479.0	3,097.0	3,665.7	6,320.2	11.9	9.1	7.5	12.8
July	596.2	2,496.1	3,112.1	3,683.2	6,389.8	12.2	8.2	6.7	12.7
Aug.	604.8	2,515.4	3,130.1	3,711.2	6,460.3	12.9	7.9	6.4	13.1
Sept.	611.5	2,529.5	3,150.2	3,739.2	6,525.3	14.2	8.4	6.9	13.3
Oct.	614.2	2,538.4	3,164.9	3,760.7	6,592.0	13.8	8.7	7.5	13.3
Nov.	620.1	2,550.8	3,180.2	3,798.2	6,680.3	13.3	8.2	7.4	14.0
Dec.	626.6	2,565.8	3,199.9	3,837.0	6,809.8	12.4	7.1	6.8	16.1
1986: Jan	627.2	2,569.0	3,222.9	3,859.0	6,913.8	10.7	5.9	7.2	17.1
Feb	631.0	2,576.6	3,239.6	3,877.2	6,963.9	8.9	4.9	7.1	16.2
Mar	638.4	2,591.1	3,260.2	3,890.5	7,012.3	9.0	4.9	7.1	15.5
Apr	646.1	2,620.9	3,289.1	3,913.2	7,069.4	10.7	6.6	8.0	15.0
May	658.7	2,647.9	3,304.5	3,944.5	7,129.5	12.8	7.8	8.0	13.9
June	666.7	2,668.9	3,322.5	....	....	13.2	8.2	7.8	....

[1] Consists of outstanding credit market debt of the U.S. Government, State and local governments, and private nonfinancial sectors; data from flow of funds accounts.
[2] Annual changes are from December to December and monthly changes are from 6 months earlier at a seasonally adjusted annual rate.

Source: Board of Governors of the Federal Reserve System.

Source: *Economic Indicators*, Council of Economic Advisers.

Bank Failures and Corporate Bankruptcies

NUMBER AND DEPOSITS OF BANKS CLOSED BECAUSE OF FINANCIAL DIFFICULTIES, 1934–1985

Year	Number Total	Number Non-Insured[1]	Number Insured Total	Number Insured Without disbursements by FDIC[2]	Number Insured With disbursements by FDIC[3]	Deposits Total	Deposits Non-Insured[1]	Deposits Insured Total	Deposits Insured Without disbursements by FDIC[2]	Deposits Insured With disbursements by FDIC[3]	Assets[4] (in Thousands Dollars)
Total	**1,011**	**136**	**875**	**8**	**867**	**36,527,425**	**143,501**	**36,383,924**	**41,147**	**36,342,777**	**45,008,028**
1934	61	52	9	……	9	37,333	35,365	1,968	……	1,968	2,661
1935	32	6	26	1	25	13,988	583	13,405	85	13,320	17,242
1936	72	3	69	……	69	28,100	592	27,508	……	27,508	31,941
1937	84	7	77	2	75	34,205	528	33,677	328	33,349	40,370
1938	81	7	74	……	74	60,722	1,038	59,684	……	59,684	69,513
1939	72	12	60	……	60	160,211	2,439	157,772	……	157,772	181,514
1940	48	5	43	……	43	142,788	358	142,430	……	142,430	161,898
1941	17	2	15	……	15	29,796	79	29,717	……	29,717	34,804
1942	23	3	20	……	20	19,540	355	19,185	……	19,185	22,254
1943	5	……	5	……	5	12,525	……	12,525	……	12,525	14,058
1944	2	……	2	……	2	1,915	……	1,915	……	1,915	2,098
1945	1	……	1	……	1	5,695	……	5,695	……	5,695	6,392
1946	2	1	1	……	1	494	147	347	……	347	351
1947	6	1	5	……	5	7,207	167	7,040	……	7,040	6,798
1948	3	……	3	……	3	10,674	……	10,674	……	10,674	10,360
1949	9	4	5	1	4	9,217	2,552	6,665	1,190	5,475	4,886
1950	5	1	4	……	4	5,555	42	5,513	……	5,513	4,005
1951	5	3	2	……	2	6,464	3,056	3,408	……	3,408	3,050
1952	4	1	3	……	3	3,313	143	3,170	……	3,170	2,388
1953	5	1	4	2	2	45,101	390	44,711	26,449	18,262	18,811
1954	4	2	2	……	2	2,948	1,950	998	……	998	1,138
1955	5	……	5	……	5	11,953	……	11,953	……	11,953	11,985
1956	3	1	2	……	2	11,690	360	11,330	……	11,330	12,914
1957	3	1	2	1	1	12,502	1,255	11,247	10,084	1,163	1,253
1958	9	5	4	……	4	10,413	2,173	8,240	……	8,240	8,905
1959	3	……	3	……	3	2,593	……	2,593	……	2,593	2,858
1960	2	1	1	……	1	7,965	1,035	6,930	……	6,930	7,506

Year	Number of banks (Total)	Number (a)	Number (b)	Deposits (Total)	Deposits (a)	Deposits (b)	Deposits	Deposits	Adjusted Deposits
1961	9	4	5	10,611	1,675	8,936		8,936	9,820[5]
1962	3	2	1	4,231	1,220	3,011	3,011	...	...
1963	2	...	2	23,444	...	23,444		23,444	26,179
1964	8	1	7	23,867	429	23,438		23,438	25,849
1965	9	4	5	45,256	1,395	43,861		43,861	58,750
1966	8	1	7	106,171	2,648	103,523		103,523	120,647
1967	4	...	4	10,878	...	10,878		10,878	11,993
1968	3	...	3	22,524	...	22,524		22,524	25,154
1969	9	...	9	40,134	...	40,134		40,134	43,572
1970	8	1	7	55,229	423	54,806		54,806	62,147
1971	6	...	6	132,058	...	132,058		132,058	196,520
1972	3	2	1	99,784	79,304	20,480		20,480	22,054
1973	6	...	6	971,296	...	971,296		971,296	1,309,675
1974	4	...	4	1,575,832	...	1,575,832		1,575,832	3,822,596
1975	14	1	13	340,574	1,000	339,574		339,574	419,950
1976	17	1	16	865,659	800	864,859		864,859	1,039,293
1977	6	...	6	205,208	...	205,208		205,208	232,612
1978	7	...	7	854,154	...	854,154		854,154	994,035
1979	10	...	10	110,696	...	110,696		110,696	132,988
1980	10	...	10	216,300	...	216,300		216,300	236,164
1981	10	...	10	3,826,022	...	3,826,022		3,826,022	4,859,060
1982	42	...	42	9,908,379	...	9,908,379		9,908,379	11,632,415
1983	48	...	48	5,441,608	...	5,441,608		5,441,608	7,026,923
1984	79	...	79	2,883,162	...	2,883,162		2,883,162	3,276,411
1985[6]	120	...	120	8,059,441	...	8,059,441		8,059,441	8,741,268

[1] For information regarding each of these banks, see table 22 in the 1963 *Annual Report* (1963 and prior years), and explanatory notes to tables regarding banks closed because of financial difficulties in subsequent annual reports. One noninsured bank placed in receivership in 1934, with no deposits at time of closing, is omitted (see table 22 note 9). Deposits are unavailable for seven banks.

[2] For information regarding these cases, see table 23 of the *Annual Report* for 1963.

[3] For information regarding each bank, see the *Annual Report* for 1958, pp. 48-83 and pp. 98-127, and tables regarding deposit insurance disbursements in subsequent annual reports. Deposits are adjusted as of December 31, 1982.

[4] Insured banks only.

[5] Not available.

[6] Includes data for one bank granted financial assistance although no disbursement was required until January, 1986.

Source: Federal Deposit Insurance Corporation *1985 Annual Report*

Corporate Reorganizations

REORGANIZATION PROCEEDINGS UNDER CHAPTER 11 OF THE BANKRUPTCY CODE IN WHICH COMMISSION ENTERED APPEARANCE

Debtor	District	Fiscal Year Filed	Fiscal Year Closed
A.H. Robins Co., Inc.	E.D. VA	1985	
AIA Industries, Inc.	E.D. PA	1984	
AIC Photo	E.D. NY	1985	
Air Florida System, Inc.	S.D. FL	1984	
Air One Inc.	E.D. MO	1985	
Airlift International, Inc.	S.D. FL	1981	
Altec Corp.	C.D. CA	1985	
AM International[2]	N.D. IL	1982	1985
Amarex Inc.	W.D. OK	1983	
Anglo Energy, Ltd.	S.D. NY	1984	
ATI, Inc.	D. NJ	1985	
Baldwin United Corp.	S.D. OH	1984	
Bear Lake West Inc.[1]	D. ID	1982	
Beehive International	D. UT	1985	
Berry Industries Corp.	C.D. CA	1985	
The Bishop's Glen Fndtn., Inc.[1]	N.D. FL	1985	
Branch Industries, Inc.	S.D. NY	1985	
Briggs Transportation[3]	D. MN	1983	1985
Capitol Air Inc.	S.D. NY	1985	
Chalet Gourmet Corp.	C.D. CA	1985	
Charter Co.	M.D. FL	1984	
Citel, Inc.	N.D. CA	1985	
Citywide Securities Corp.[1]	S.D. NY	1985	
Colohial Discount Corp.[2]	S.D. IN	1982	1985
Columbia Data Products, Inc.	D. MD	1985	
Commodore Corporation	N.D. IN	1985	
Commonwealth Oil Refining Co., Inc.	W.D. TX	1984	
Computer Communications, Inc.[2]	C.D. CA	1981	1985
Computer Devices, Inc.	D. MA	1984	
Computer Usage Co.	N.D. CA	1985	
Consolidated Packaging Corp.	D. CO	1984	
Continental Airlines Corp.	S.D. TX	1984	
Cook United, Inc.	N.D. OH	1985	
Crompton Co., Inc.	S.D. NY	1985	
The Diet Institute, Inc.	D. NJ	1985	
Dreco Energy Service Ltd.	S.D. TX	1982	
Emons Industries, Inc.	S.D. N.Y.	1984	
Empire Oil & Gas Co.	D. CO	1982	
Energetics Inc.[2]	D. CO	1985	1985
Energy Exchange Corp.	W.D. OK	1985	
Enterprise Technologies, Inc.	S.D. TX	1984	
ESM Securities, Inc.[3]	S.D. FL	1985	1985
EVANS Products Co.	S.D. FL	1985	
Equestrian Ctrs. of America, Inc.	C.D. CA	1985	
Fidelity American Financial Corp.[1]	E.D. PA	1981	
Flight Transportation Co.[3]	D. MN	1983	1985
General Resources Corp.	N.D. GA	1980	
Grove Finance Company[1][2]	D. UT	1981	1985
Hardwick Cos., Inc.[1]	S.D. NY	1984	1985
Haven Properties, Inc.[1]	D. OR	1981	
ICX, Inc.	D. CO	1984	

REORGANIZATION PROCEEDINGS UNDER CHAPTER 11 *(continued)*

Debtor	District	Fiscal Year Filed	Fiscal Year Closed
Information Displays, Inc.[3]	S.D. NY	1984	1985
International Waste Water[1]	M.D. PA	1985	
Internat'l Inst. of App. Tech. Inc.	D. DC	1983	
Interstate Motor Freight Systems[3]	W.D. MI	1984	1985
K-Tel International, Inc.	D. MN	1985	
Kelly-Johnson Enterprises, Inc.	W.D. OK	1985	
Koss Corp.	D. WI	1985	
Robert C. LaBine/Pro. Assoc.[1]	E.D. MI	1983	
The Lionel Corp.[2]	S.D. NY	1982	1985
Magic Circle Energy Corp.	W.D. OK	1985	
Manoa Finance Co., Inc.[1]	D. HA	1983	
Mansfield Tire & Rubber Co.	N.D. OH	1980	
Manville Corp.	S.D. NY	1982	
Marion Corp.	S.D. AL	1983	
Midwestern Companies Inc.	W.D. MO	1984	
Mobile Home Industries, Inc.	N.D. FL	1985	
ND Resource, Inc.	D. AZ	1985	
New Brothers, Inc.	S.D. GA	1985	
North Atlantic Airlines, Inc.[1]	D. VT	1984	
Nucorp Energy Inc.	S.D. CA	1982	
OmniDentex Systems Corp.[2]	D. MA	1985	1985
Pacific Express Holding, Inc.	E.D. CA	1984	
Paiute Oil & Mining Corp.	D. UT	1985	
Peoples Restaurants, Inc.	M.D. FL	1985	
Pizza Time Theatre, Inc.[2]	N.D. CA	1984	1985
Provincetown-Boston Airline	M.D. FL	1985	
Quickprint of America, Inc.[2]	C.D. CA	1984	1985
Revere Copper & Brass Inc.[2]	S.D. NY	1983	1985
Roblin Industries, Inc.	W.D. NY	1985	
Ronco Teleproducts, Inc.	N.D. IL	1984	
SPW Corporation	N.D. TX	1985	
Sambo's Restaurants, Inc.[2]	C.D. CA	1982	1985
Salant Corp.	S.D. NY	1985	
Satelco, Inc.	N.D. TX	1985	
Saxon Industries, Inc.[2]	S.D. NY	1982	1985
Seatrain Lines, Inc.	S.D. NY	1981	
Seneca Oil Co.	W.D. OK	1985	
Shelter Resources Corp.[2]	N.D. OH	1982	1985
South Atlantic Financial Corp.[2]	S.D. FL	1983	1985
Southern Industrial Banking Corp.[1][2]	E.D. TN	1983	1985
Standard Metals Corp.	D. CO	1984	
State Capital Corp.	M.D. FL	1985	
Stewart Energy Systems[1][2]	D. ID	1982	1985
Storage Technology, Inc.	D. CO	1985	
Swanton Corp.	S.D. NY	1985	
Taco Eds, Inc.[1]	N.D. OH	1984	
Taurus Oil Co.[2]	D. CO	1984	1985
Texas General Resources, Inc.[2]	S.D. TX	1983	1985
Tomlinson Oil Co., Inc.[2]	S.D. NY	1984	1985
Towner Petro	W.D. OK	1985	
Trans Western Exploration	N.D. OK	1985	
Transcontinental Energy Corp.	N.D. TX	1985	

REORGANIZATION PROCEEDINGS UNDER CHAPTER 11 *(concluded)*

Debtor	District	Fiscal Year Filed	Fiscal Year Closed
Unioil[2]	D. CO	1985	1985
Victor Technologies, Inc.[2]	N.D. CA	1984	1985
Videostation, Inc.	C.D. CA	1985	
Visa Energy Corp.[3]	D. CO	1984	1985
Wheatland Investment Co.[1]	E.D. WA	1985	
Wheeling-Pitts. Steel Corp.	W.D. PA	1985	
Wickes Companies[2]	C.D. CA	1982	1985
Woods Communication Corp.[4]	E.D. MI	1984	1985
Wright Air Lines, Inc.	N.D. OH	1985	
Xonics, Inc.[2]	N.D. IL	1984	1985
Total Cases Opened (FY 1985)		53	
Total Cases Closed (FY 1985)			31

[1]Debtor's securities not registered under Section 12(g) of the Exchange Act.
[2]Plan of reorganization confirmed.
[3]Debtor liquidated under Chapter 7.
[4]Chapter 11 case dismissed.

Source: U.S. Securities and Exchange Commission *Fifty First Annual Report 1985.*

Government Budget, Receipts, and Deficits: Historical Data

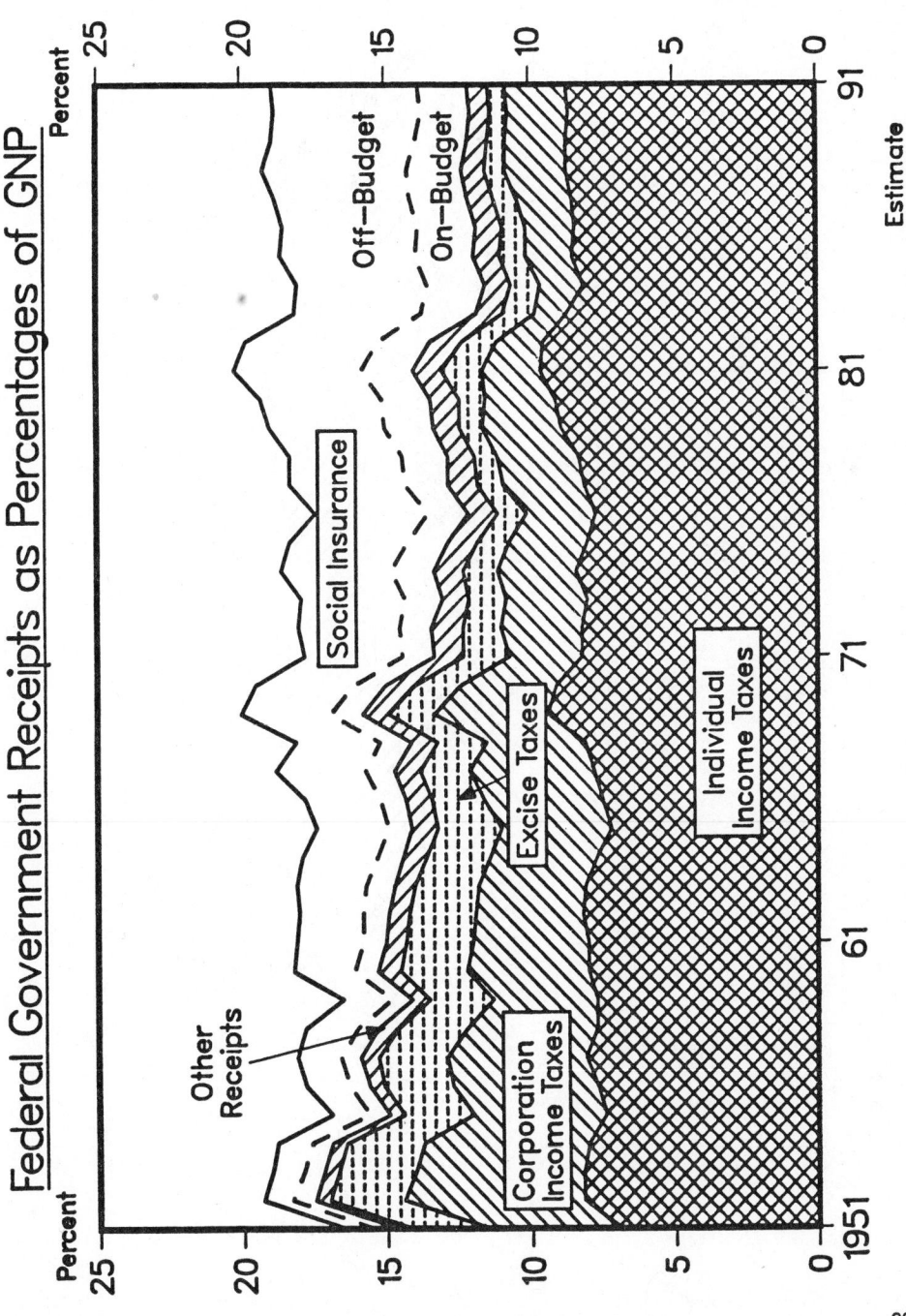

Federal Government Receipts as Percentages of GNP

Other Receipts

Social Insurance

Off—Budget

On—Budget

Excise Taxes

Corporation Income Taxes

Individual Income Taxes

Estimate

Source: *Historical Tables*, Budget of the United States Government, Fiscal 1987, Executive Office of the President, Office of Management and Budget.

Federal Government Outlays as Percentages of GNP

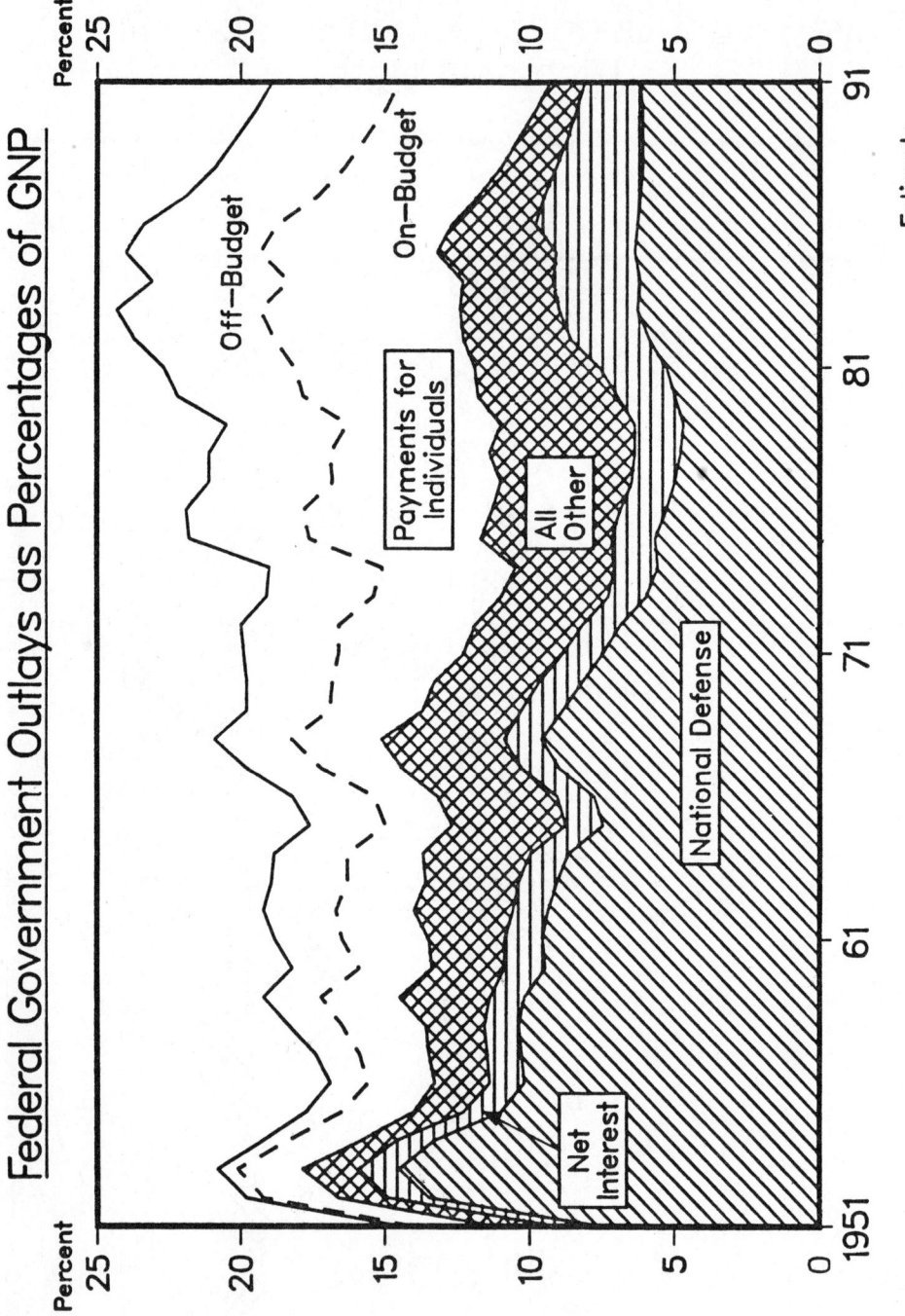

Source: *Historical Tables*, Budget of the United States Government, Fiscal 1987, Executive Office of the President, Office of Management and Budget.

Percentage Composition of Federal Government Receipts

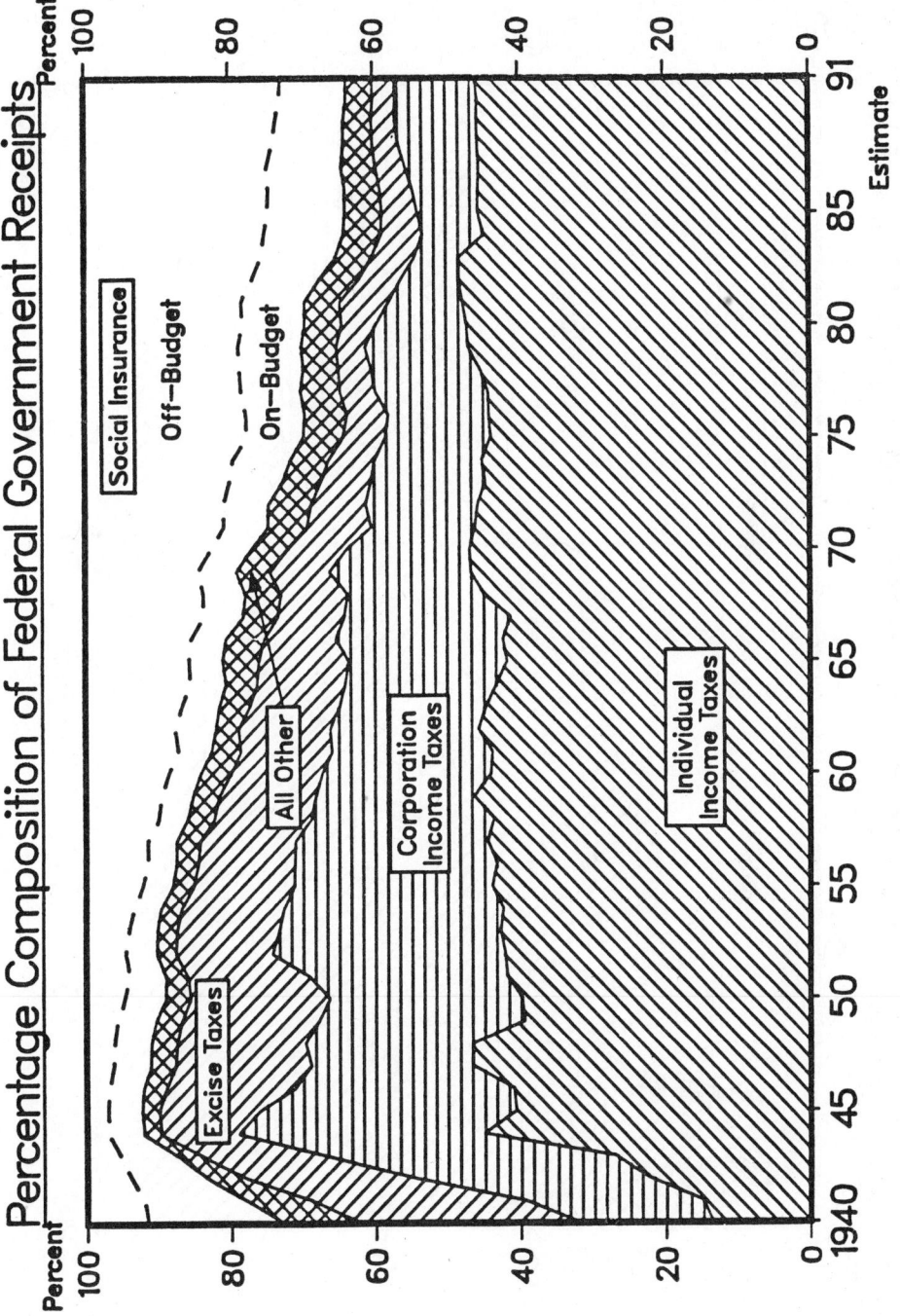

Social Insurance

Off–Budget

On–Budget

Excise Taxes

All Other

Corporation Income Taxes

Individual Income Taxes

Estimate

Source: Historical Tables, Budget of the United States Government, Fiscal 1987, Executive Office of the President, Office of Management and Budget.

Percentage Composition of Federal Government Outlays

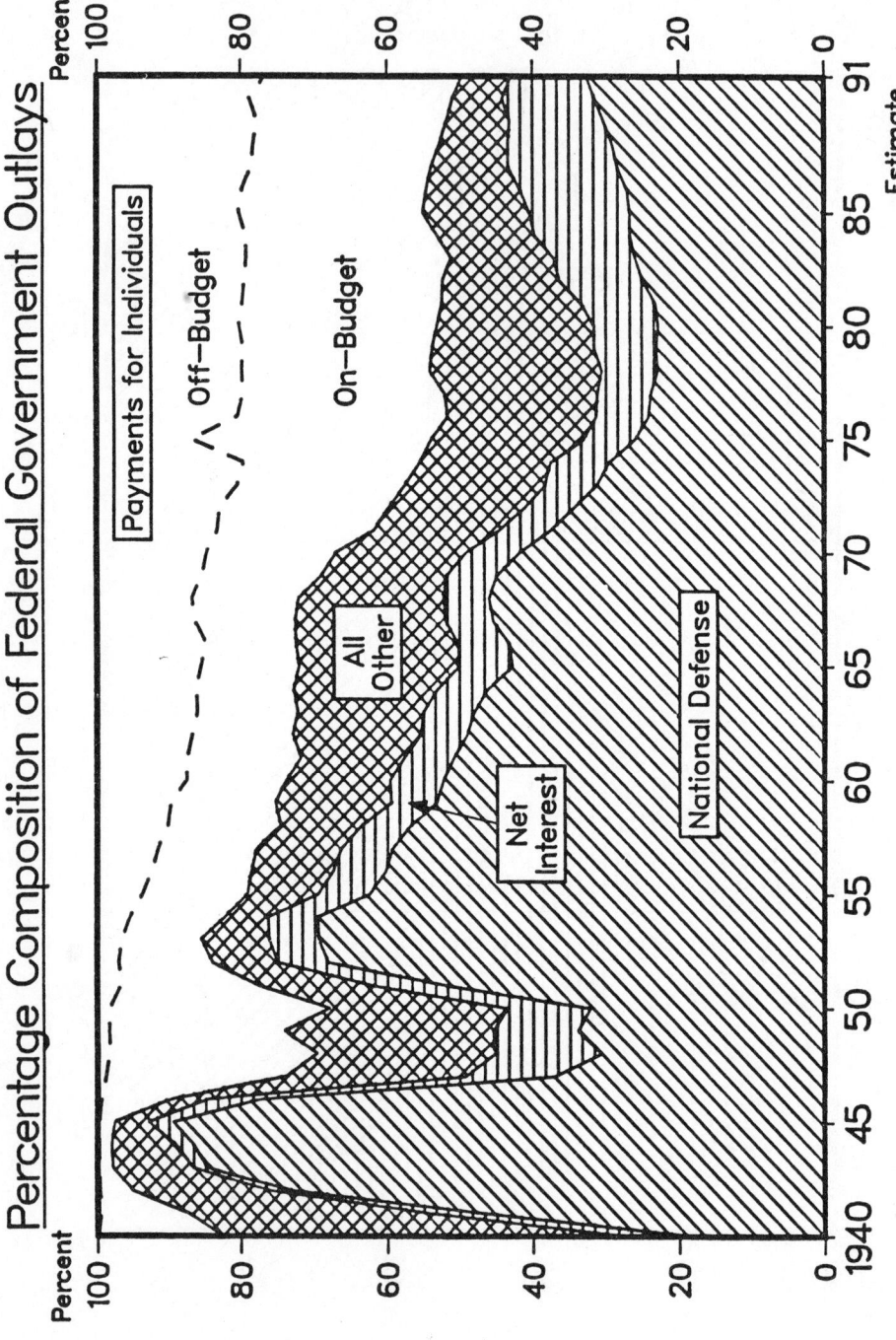

Payments for Individuals

Off–Budget

On–Budget

All Other

Net Interest

National Defense

Percent

100 · 80 · 60 · 40 · 20 · 0

1940 45 50 55 60 65 70 75 80 85 91

Estimate

Source: *Historical Tables,* Budget of the United States Government, Fiscal 1987, Executive Office of the President, Office of Management and Budget.

TOTAL GOVERNMENT EXPENDITURES AS PERCENTAGES OF GNP: 1947-1985
(percent)

	Federal outlays		Total Federal	Addendum: Federal Grants-in-Aid NIPA Basis	State and Local Government Expenditures From Own Sources Net of Nontax Receipts (NIPA Basis)	Total Government Expenditures
	On-budget	Off-Budget				
1947	15.2%	0.1%	15.3%	(0.7)%	4.6%	19.9%
1948	11.8	0.1	12.0	(0.7)	5.3	17.3
1949	14.5	0.2	14.7	(0.8)	5.8	20.5
1950	15.7	0.2	15.9	(0.9)	6.7	22.6
1951	14.1	0.4	14.5	(0.8)	6.1	20.6
1952	19.2	0.5	19.8	(0.7)	6.0	25.8
1953	20.2	0.6	20.8	(0.8)	5.9	26.8
1954	18.4	0.8	19.2	(0.8)	5.4	25.6
1955	16.6	1.0	17.7	(0.8)	6.9	24.5
1956	15.7	1.2	16.9	(0.8)	6.9	23.8
1957	16.0	1.4	17.4	(0.8)	7.1	24.5
1958	16.7	1.7	18.3	(1.0)	7.6	26.0
1959	17.3	1.9	19.2	(1.3)	7.7	26.9
1960	16.0	2.1	18.2	(1.4)	7.6	25.7
1961	16.6	2.2	18.8	(1.3)	8.1	26.9
1962	16.8	2.4	19.2	(1.4)	8.1	27.3
1963	16.4	2.5	18.9	(1.4)	8.2	27.1
1964	16.3	2.5	18.8	(1.6)	8.2	27.1
1965	15.1	2.5	17.6	(1.6)	8.3	25.8
1966	15.5	2.7	18.2	(1.7)	8.3	26.5
1967	17.3	2.6	19.8	(1.9)	8.6	28.5
1968	18.3	2.6	20.9	(2.1)	8.9	29.8
1969	17.0	2.7	19.8	(2.1)	9.2	29.0
1970	17.0	2.8	19.8	(2.3)	9.4	29.2
1971	16.8	3.1	19.9	(2.5)	10.0	29.8
1972	16.8	3.2	20.0	(2.8)	9.8	29.8
1973	15.6	3.5	19.1	(3.1)	9.2	28.4
1974	15.3	3.7	19.0	(2.9)	9.5	28.5
1975	17.8	4.0	21.8	(3.2)	10.0	31.8
1976	17.8	4.1	21.9	(3.4)	9.9	31.8
TQ	17.1	4.3	21.4	(3.4)	9.9	31.3
1977	17.0	4.2	21.1	(3.4)	9.1	30.3
1978	17.0	4.1	21.1	(3.4)	8.8	29.9
1979	16.5	4.1	20.5	(3.2)	8.5	29.0
1980	17.9	4.3	22.2	(3.2)	8.6	30.7
1981	18.2	4.5	22.7	(3.0)	8.3	31.0
1982	18.9	4.8	23.7	(2.7)	8.6	32.4
1983	19.9	4.4	24.3	(2.6)	8.6	33.0
1984	18.6	4.5	23.1	(2.5)	8.3	31.4
1985	19.5	4.5	24.0	(2.5)	8.5	32.5

* 0.05 percent or less.

See page 211 for explanatory notes.

Government Budget, Receipts, and Deficits

TOTAL GOVERNMENT EXPENDITURES BY MAJOR CATEGORY OF EXPENDITURE AS PERCENTAGES OF GNP: 1947-1985
(In billions of dollars)

	Defense and International	Net Interest	Social Security and Medicare	Other Federal Payments for Individuals	Other Federal (Except Net Interest)	State and Local From Own Sources (Except Net Interest)	Total Government
1947	8.3%	1.9%	0.2%	3.8%	1.2%	4.5%	19.9%
1948	5.5	1.8	0.2	3.4	1.1	5.3	17.3
1949	7.3	1.7	0.2	3.6	1.9	5.8	20.5
1950	6.9	1.8	0.3	4.8	2.1	6.7	22.6
1951	8.6	1.5	0.5	2.8	1.0	6.1	20.6
1952	14.2	1.4	0.6	2.6	1.0	6.0	25.8
1953	15.0	1.4	0.7	2.3	1.4	5.9	26.8
1954	13.8	1.3	0.9	2.5	0.7	6.4	25.6
1955	11.6	1.3	1.1	2.6	1.1	6.8	24.5
1956	10.8	1.2	1.3	2.4	1.3	6.8	23.8
1957	11.0	1.2	1.5	2.4	1.2	7.1	24.5
1958	11.2	1.3	1.8	2.9	1.3	7.6	26.0
1959	10.9	1.2	2.0	2.8	2.3	7.7	26.9
1960	10.1	1.4	2.3	2.5	1.9	7.5	25.7
1961	10.2	1.3	2.4	3.0	2.0	8.1	26.9
1962	10.4	1.3	2.6	2.7	2.2	8.1	27.3
1963	10.0	1.3	2.7	2.7	2.3	8.1	27.1
1964	9.5	1.3	2.6	2.6	2.8	8.2	27.1
1965	8.3	1.2	2.6	2.4	3.0	8.3	25.8
1966	8.6	1.2	2.8	2.3	3.2	8.4	26.5
1967	9.7	1.2	3.1	2.4	3.3	8.7	28.5
1968	10.2	1.2	3.3	2.5	3.5	9.0	29.8
1969	9.4	1.3	3.5	2.6	2.8	9.4	29.0
1970	8.7	1.3	3.7	2.9	3.0	9.6	29.2
1971	7.9	1.3	4.0	3.6	3.0	10.1	29.8
1972	7.3	1.2	4.1	4.0	3.3	9.9	29.8
1973	6.3	1.2	4.6	3.7	3.3	9.4	28.4
1974	6.0	1.3	4.6	3.9	2.9	9.8	28.5
1975	6.1	1.2	5.1	5.1	4.0	10.2	31.8
1976	5.7	1.3	5.3	5.4	3.9	10.1	31.8
TQ	5.5	1.4	5.4	4.9	4.1	10.1	31.3
1977	5.4	1.4	5.4	4.9	4.0	9.3	30.3
1978	5.2	1.4	5.4	4.4	4.5	9.0	29.9
1979	5.0	1.3	5.3	4.4	4.2	8.9	29.0
1980	5.5	1.4	5.6	4.8	4.2	9.2	30.7
1981	5.7	1.6	6.0	4.9	3.8	9.0	31.0
1982	6.3	2.0	6.4	5.0	3.3	9.4	32.4
1983	6.7	1.9	6.7	5.3	3.0	9.0	33.0
1984	6.6	2.3	6.4	4.5	2.6	9.0	31.4
1985	6.8	2.6	6.5	4.3	3.1	9.2	32.5

See page 211 for explanatory notes.

TOTAL GOVERNMENT EXPENDITURES BY MAJOR CATEGORY OF EXPENDITURE: 1947-1985
(in billions of dollars)

Year	Defense and International	Net Interest	Social Security and Medicare	Other Federal Payments for Individuals	Other Federal (Except Net Interest)	State and Local From Own Sources (Except Net Interest)	Total Government
1947	18.6	4.3	0.5	8.6	2.6	10.2	44.9
1948	13.7	4.4	0.6	8.5	2.7	13.1	43.0
1949	19.2	4.6	0.7	9.5	5.6	15.3	54.3
1950	18.4	4.9	0.8	12.9	5.6	17.8	60.5
1951	27.2	4.7	1.6	8.8	3.3	19.1	64.7
1952	48.8	4.7	2.1	8.9	3.3	20.6	88.4
1953	54.9	5.2	2.7	8.3	5.0	21.7	97.8
1954	50.9	4.8	3.4	9.3	2.5	23.6	94.5
1955	45.0	4.9	4.4	10.0	4.2	26.5	95.1
1956	44.9	5.2	5.5	9.9	5.3	26.6	99.4
1957	48.6	5.7	6.7	10.5	5.5	31.4	108.0
1958	50.2	5.7	8.2	12.9	5.5	34.3	116.8
1959	52.2	5.9	9.7	13.3	11.2	36.9	129.2
1960	51.1	7.1	11.6	12.8	9.7	38.2	130.5
1961	52.8	6.8	12.5	15.6	10.2	42.0	139.9
1962	58.0	7.0	14.4	15.2	12.4	45.0	151.9
1963	58.7	7.9	15.8	15.7	13.4	47.9	159.3
1964	59.7	8.2	16.6	16.2	17.8	51.8	170.4
1965	55.9	8.4	17.5	16.3	20.0	55.9	173.9
1966	63.7	9.0	20.8	17.1	23.6	62.2	196.3
1967	77.0	9.5	24.7	19.0	26.5	69.3	226.0
1968	87.2	10.1	28.3	21.7	29.8	76.9	254.1
1969	87.1	11.7	33.0	24.5	26.3	86.9	269.5
1970	86.0	12.8	36.5	28.7	30.1	94.8	288.9
1971	83.0	13.2	42.5	38.4	31.4	106.9	315.5
1972	84.0	14.2	47.6	45.8	37.8	113.9	343.2
1973	80.8	15.3	57.1	48.1	42.3	120.8	364.5
1974	85.1	17.9	65.5	55.5	41.8	138.2	403.9
1975	93.6	18.9	77.5	77.3	60.6	155.9	483.9
1976	96.1	22.8	89.7	92.3	67.0	172.4	540.3
TQ	24.7	6.1	24.0	21.8	18.5	45.4	140.6
1977	103.6	26.2	104.4	93.9	77.4	180.3	585.8
1978	112.0	29.5	116.6	96.5	98.2	196.4	649.2
1979	123.8	32.0	130.6	104.5	102.0	218.6	711.4
1980	146.7	36.9	150.6	129.1	111.9	244.9	820.2
1981	170.6	49.0	178.7	147.3	112.8	268.7	927.2
1982	197.6	61.9	202.6	156.9	103.7	294.0	1,016.5
1983	221.8	63.7	223.3	174.9	98.6	312.7	1,094.9
1984	243.3	84.2	235.8	166.4	95.2	333.7	1,158.6
1985	268.9	102.9	254.4	169.5	124.0	360.5	1,280.4

See page 211 for explanatory notes.

TOTAL GOVERNMENT SURPLUSES OR DEFICITS (-) IN ABSOLUTE AMOUNTS AND AS PERCENTAGES OF GNP: 1947-1985

(dollar amounts in billions)

	Federal Government			State and Local (NIPA Basis)	Total Government	As Percentages of GNP		
	On-Budget	Off-Budget	Total Federal			Total Federal	State and Local Government	Total Government
1947	2.9	1.2	4.0	1.6	5.6	1.8%	0.7%	2.5%
1948	10.5	1.2	11.8	0.6	12.4	4.7	0.2	5.0
1949	-.7	1.3	0.6	-.2	0.4	0.2	-.1	0.2
1950	-4.7	1.6	-3.1	-1.3	-4.4	-1.2	-.5	-1.7
1951	4.3	1.8	6.1	-.5	5.6	1.9	-.2	1.8
1952	-3.4	1.9	-1.5	-.4	-2.0	-.4	-.1	-.6
1953	-8.3	1.8	-6.5	0.3	-6.2	-1.8	0.1	-1.7
1954	-2.8	1.7	-1.2	0.3	-1.4	-.3	0.1	-.4
1955	-4.1	1.1	-3.0	-1.6	-4.6	-.8	-.4	-1.2
1956	2.5	1.5	3.9	-.8	3.2	0.9	-.2	0.8
1957	2.6	0.8	3.4	-.9	2.5	0.8	-.2	0.6
1958	-3.3	0.5	-2.8	-2.0	-4.8	-.6	-.4	-1.1
1959	-12.1	-.7	-12.8	-1.8	-14.6	-2.7	-.4	-3.0
1960	0.5	-.2	0.3	0.4	0.7	0.1	0.1	0.1
1961	-3.8	0.4	-3.3	-.3	-3.7	-.6	-.1	-.7
1962	-5.9	-1.3	-7.1	*	-7.1	-1.3	*	-1.3
1963	-4.0	-.8	-4.8	0.3	-4.4	-.8	0.1	-.8
1964	-6.5	0.6	-5.9	0.8	-5.3	-.9	0.1	-.8
1965	-1.6	0.2	-1.4	0.8	-1.7	-.2	0.1	-.1
1966	-3.1	-.6	-3.7	0.6	-3.1	-.5	0.1	-.4
1967	-12.6	4.0	-8.6	-1.5	-10.1	-1.1	-.2	-1.3
1968	-27.7	2.6	-25.2	-.4	-24.7	-3.0	0.*	-2.9
1969	-.5	3.7	3.2	0.4	2.9	0.3	*	0.3
1970	-8.7	5.9	-2.8	3.7	0.8	-.3	0.4	0.1
1971	-26.1	3.0	-23.0	-.5	-23.5	-2.2	0.*	-2.2
1972	-26.4	3.1	-23.4	8.2	-15.2	-2.0	0.7	-1.3
1973	-15.4	0.5	-14.9	14.9	*	-1.2	1.2	*
1974	-8.0	1.8	-6.1	10.6	4.5	-.4	0.8	0.3
1975	-55.3	2.0	-53.2	5.9	-47.4	-3.5	0.4	-3.1
1976	-70.5	-3.2	-73.7	6.8	-66.9	-4.3	0.4	-3.9
TQ	-13.3	-1.4	-14.7	-1.4	-16.2	-3.3	-.3	-3.6
1977	-49.7	-3.9	-53.6	24.4	-29.3	-2.8	1.3	-1.5
1978	-54.9	-4.3	-59.2	31.4	-27.8	-2.7	1.4	-1.3
1979	-38.2	-2.0	-40.2	26.5	-13.7	-1.6	1.1	-.6
1980	-72.7	-1.1	-73.8	25.7	-48.1	-2.8	1.0	-1.8
1981	-73.9	-5.0	-78.9	32.5	-46.5	-2.6	1.1	-1.6
1982	-120.0	-7.9	-127.9	34.8	-93.1	-4.1	1.1	-3.0
1983	-208.0	0.2	-207.8	43.4	-164.4	-6.3	1.3	-4.9
1984	-185.6	0.3	-185.3	63.1	-122.2	-5.0	1.7	-3.3
1985	-221.6	9.4	-212.3	60.8	-151.5	-5.4	1.5	-3.8

NOTES TO HISTORICAL TABLES AND CHARTS

Because of the numerous changes in the way budget data have been presented over time, there are inevitable difficulties in trying to produce comparable data to cover so many years. The general rule underlying all of these tables is to provide data in as meaningful and comparable a fashion as is possible. The data are always presented on a basis consistent with current budget concepts. Insofar as is possible such changes are made for all years. For example, one major function in the 1986 Budget was entitled "Social Security and Medicare," with separate subfunctions for Social Security and for Medicare. In the 1987 Budget, Social Security and Medicare are shown as separate major functions. The data have been reconstructed to show these as separate functions from the origin of the programs.

NOTE ON THE FISCAL YEAR

The Federal fiscal year begins on October 1 and ends on the subsequent September 30. It is designated by the year in which it ends; for example, fiscal year 1986 began October 1, 1985 and ended on September 30, 1986. Prior to fiscal year 1977 the Federal fiscal years began on July 1 and ended on June 30. In calendar year 1976 the July–September period was a separate accounting period (known as the transition quarter or TQ) to bridge the period required to shift to the new fiscal years.

BUDGET SUMMARY

(In billions of dollars)

	1985	1986	1987	1988	1989	1990	1991
Receipts	734.1	777.1	850.4	933.2	996.1	1,058.1	1,124.0
Outlays	946.3	979.9	994.0	1,026.8	1,063.6	1,093.8	1,122.7
Surplus or deficit (−)	− 212.3	− 202.8	− 143.6	− 93.6	− 67.5	− 35.8	1.3
Gramm-Rudman-Hollings deficit targets		− 171.9	− 144.0	− 108.0	− 72.0	− 36.0	0.0
Difference		30.9	− 0.4	− 14.4	− 4.5	− 0.2	− 1.3

Note.—Totals include social security, which is off-budget.

Source: *The United States Budget in Brief,* Fiscal Year 1987, Executive Office of the President, Office of Management and Budget.

Note: The Balanced Budget and Emergency Deficit Control Act is commonly referred to as Gramm-Rudman-Hollings for its principal architects. The proposed budget has as its major objective, a balanced budget by 1991 to meet the deficit reduction targets set out in the Act.

Federal Deficit Projections Under Current Policy and Gramm-Rudman-Hollings

Fiscal Years 1986-1991
($bils)

	1986	1987	1988	1989	1990	1991
(A) Current Services Budget as of August 30, 1985 ..	242.6	253.1	255.9	243.8	237.9	
(B) Mid-Session Review of Fiscal '86 Budget	177.8	139.3	99.8	53.6	17.7	
(C) "Realistic" Current Policy Budget, January 1, 1986 (average of A + B)...............	210	196	178	149	128	100
(D) G-R-H Deficit Targets ..	172	144	108	72	36	0
(E) Potential Mandated Budget Cuts[1].........	12[2]	52	70	77	92	100

[1]For fiscal 1987-1990, the deficit targets must be missed by more than $10 billion for sequestration to be ordered.
[2]Limited by formula to $11.7 billion in fiscal 1986 only.
Sources: Office of Management and Budget, Tax Foundation computations.

Source: Tax Foundation, Incorporated, One Thomas Circle, NW, Washington, DC 20005.

OWNERSHIP OF U.S. GOVERNMENT SECURITIES

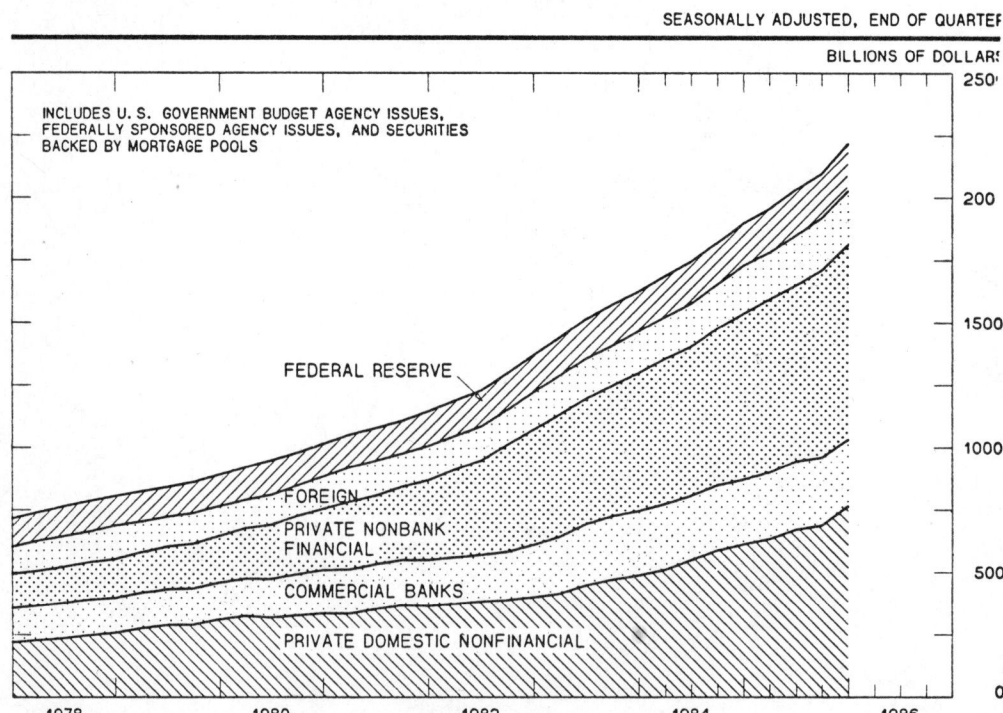

Source: *Federal Reserve Chartbook*, Board of Governors of the Federal Reserve System.

INDUSTRIAL PRODUCTION AND CAPACITY UTILIZATION

SEASONALLY ADJUSTED, MONTHLY

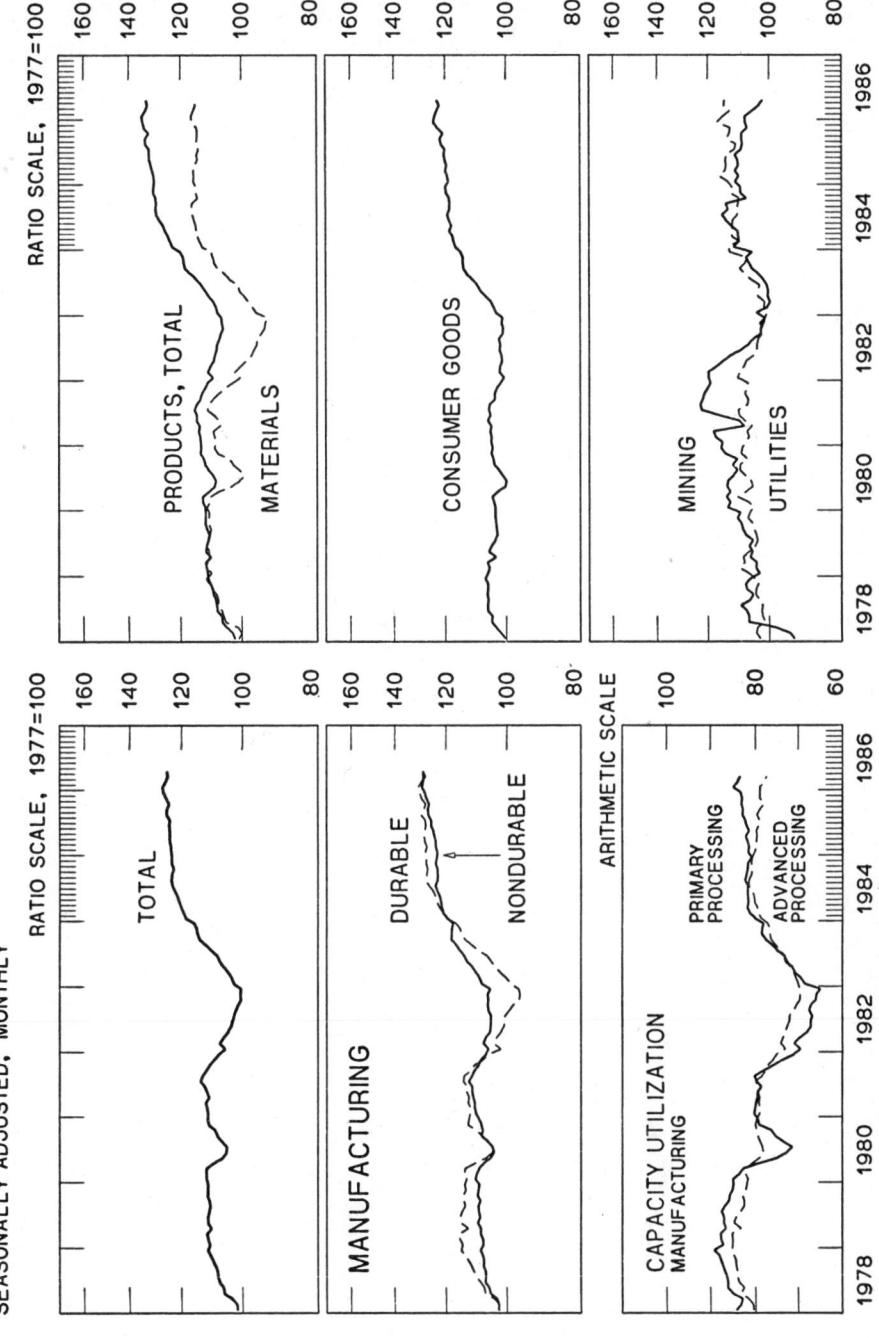

Source: Federal Reserve Chart Book, Board of Governors of the Federal Reserve System.

U.S. BUDGET RECEIPTS AND OUTLAYS (millions of dollars)

Source or type	Fiscal year 1984	Fiscal year 1985	Calendar year 1984 H1	1984 H2	1985 H1	1985 H2	1986 Feb.	1986 Mar.	1986 Apr.
RECEIPTS									
1 All sources	**666,457**	**733,996**	**341,808**	**341,392**	**380,618**	**364,790**	**53,370**	**49,557**	**91,438**
2 Individual income taxes, net	295,960	330,918	144,691	157,229	166,783	169,987	25,370	12,572	45,120
3 Withheld	279,350	298,941	140,657	145,210	149,288	155,725	27,295	25,141	21,905
4 Presidential Election Campaign Fund	35	35	29	5	29	6	2	8	10
5 Nonwithheld	81,346	97,685	61,463	19,403	76,155	22,295	1,253	3,482	42,555
6 Refunds	64,770	65,743	57,458	7,387	58,684	8,038	3,181	16,060	19,350
Corporation income taxes									
7 Gross receipts	74,179	77,413	40,328	35,190	42,193	36,528	1,941	10,714	11,192
8 Refunds	17,286	16,082	10,045	6,847	8,370	7,751	1,321	2,601	2,476
9 Social insurance taxes and contributions, net	241,902	268,805	131,372	118,690	144,598	128,017	22,046	22,785	31,756
10 Employment taxes and contributions[1]	212,180	238,288	114,102	105,624	126,038	116,276	19,207	22,229	28,391
11 Self-employment taxes and contributions[2]	8,709	10,468	7,667	1,086	9,482	985	641	643	6,510
12 Unemployment insurance	25,138	25,758	14,942	10,706	16,213	9,281	2,467	190	2,999
13 Other net receipts[3]	4,580	4,759	2,329	2,360	2,350	2,458	372	366	366
14 Excise taxes	37,361	35,865	18,304	18,961	17,259	18,470	2,265	2,531	2,512
15 Customs deposits	11,370	12,079	5,576	6,329	5,807	6,354	948	1,036	1,087
16 Estate and gift taxes	6,010	6,422	3,102	3,029	3,204	3,323	487	533	680
17 Miscellaneous receipts[4]	16,965	18,576	8,481	8,812	9,144	9,861	1,635	1,989	1,568

Outlays

	851,781	946,323	420,700	446,943	463,842	488,739	78,290	79,700	81,510
18 All types	851,781	946,323	420,700	446,943	463,842	488,739	78,290	79,700	81,510
19 National defense	227,413	252,748	114,639	118,286	124,186	134,675	21,268	24,002	22,842
20 International affairs	15,876	16,176	5,426	8,550	6,675	8,367	-208	1,676	732
21 General science, space, and technology	8,317	8,627	3,981	4,473	4,230	4,727	840	549	761
22 Energy	7,086	5,685	1,080	1,423	680	3,305	179	967	358
23 Natural resources and environment	12,593	13,357	5,463	7,370	5,892	7,553	838	838	1,130
24 Agriculture	13,613	25,565	7,129	8,524	11,705	15,412	2,103	1,207	3,489
25 Commerce and housing credit	6,917	4,229	2,572	2,663	-260	644	-725	-319	604
26 Transportation	23,669	25,838	10,616	13,673	11,440	15,360	1,723	1,963	2,271
27 Community and regional development	7,673	7,680	3,154	4,836	3,408	3,901	519	615	638
28 Education, training, employment, social services	27,579	29,342	13,445	13,737	14,149	14,481	2,727	2,377	2,440
29 Health	30,417	33,542	15,551	15,692	16,945	17,237	2,885	2,385	3,205
30 Social security and medicare	235,764	254,446	119,420	119,613	128,351	129,037	21,641	22,009	22,234
31 Income security	112,668	128,200	58,684	61,558	65,246	59,457	10,683	10,409	11,113
32 Veterans benefits and services	25,614	26,352	12,849	13,317	11,956	14,527	2,327	1,080	2,340
33 Administration of justice	5,660	6,277	2,807	2,992	3,016	3,212	567	511	546
34 General government	5,053	5,228	2,462	2,552	2,857	3,634	375	1,165	-48
35 General-purpose fiscal assistance	6,768	6,353	2,943	3,458	2,659	3,391	172	61	885
36 Net interest[3]	111,058	129,436	54,748	61,293	65,143	67,448	12,958	10,668	10,359
37 Undistributed offsetting receipts[6]	-31,957	-32,759	-16,270	-17,061	-14,436	-17,953	-2,583	-2,464	-4,387

1. Old-age, disability, and hospital insurance, and railroad retirement accounts.
2. Old-age, disability, and hospital insurance.
3. Federal employee retirement contributions and civil service retirement and disability fund.
4. Deposits of earnings by Federal Reserve Banks and other miscellaneous receipts.
5. Net interest function includes interest received by trust funds.
6. Consists of rents and royalties on the outer continental shelf and U.S. government contributions for employee retirement.

SOURCE. "Monthly Treasury Statement of Receipts and Outlays of the U.S. Government," and the *Budget of the U.S. Government, Fiscal Year 1987.*

Source: *Federal Reserve Bulletin*, Board of Governors of the Federal Reserve System.

Largest Companies

The 100 Largest U.S. Industrial Corporations (ranked by sales)

Rank '85	Rank '84	Company	Sales ($000)	Assets ($000)	Assets Rank	Net Income ($000)	Net Income Rank	Stockholders' Equity ($000)	Stockholders' Equity Rank
1	2	General Motors (Detroit)	96,371,700	63,832,800	2	3,999,000	3	29,524,700	2
2	1	Exxon (New York)	86,673,000*	69,160,000	1	4,870,000	2	29,096,000	3
3	3	Mobil (New York)	55,960,000*	41,752,000	4	1,040,000	14	14,089,000	8
4	4	Ford Motor (Dearborn, Mich.)	52,774,400	31,603,600	8	2,515,400	4	12,268,600	12
5	6	International Business Machines (Armonk, N.Y.)[1]	50,056,000	52,634,000	3	6,555,000	1	31,990,000	1
6	5	Texaco (White Plains, N.Y.)	46,297,000	37,703,000	7	1,233,000	12	13,628,000	10
7	11	Chevron (San Francisco)	41,741,905*	38,899,492	6	1,547,360	10	15,554,525	5
8	8	American Tel. & Tel. (New York)	34,909,500	40,462,500	5	1,556,800	9	14,633,300	6
9	7	E. I. du Pont de Nemours (Wilmington, Del.)	29,483,000	25,140,000	12	1,118,000	13	12,659,000	11
10	9	General Electric (Fairfield, Conn.)	28,285,000	26,432,000	10	2,336,000	5	13,904,000	9
11	10	Amoco (Chicago)[2]	27,215,000*	25,198,000	11	1,953,000	6	11,588,000	13
12	12	Atlantic Richfield (Los Angeles)	22,357,000	20,279,000	14	(202,000)	464	5,506,000	20
13	14	Chrysler (Highland Park, Mich.)[3]	21,255,500	12,605,300	23	1,635,200	8	4,215,300	30
14	13	Shell Oil (Houston)[4]	20,309,000*	26,528,000	9	1,650,000	7	4,129,000	7
15	15	U.S. Steel (Pittsburgh)	18,429,000	18,446,000	15	409,000**	43	6,305,000	17
16	16	United Technologies (Hartford)	15,748,674	10,528,105	29	312,724	54	4,373,344	28
17	17	Phillips Petroleum (Bartlesville, Okla.)	15,676,000	14,045,000	20	418,000	41	1,644,000	82
18	19	Tenneco (Houston)	15,400,000	20,437,000	13	172,000	91	5,903,000	19
19	18	Occidental Petroleum (Los Angeles)	14,534,400	11,585,900	26	696,000**	18	3,281,000	39
20	20	Sun (Radnor, Pa.)	13,769,000	12,923,000	22	527,000	30	5,289,000	21
21	29	Boeing (Seattle)	13,636,000	9,246,000	34	566,000	25	4,364,000	29
22	22	Procter & Gamble (Cincinnati)[5]	13,552,000	9,683,000	32	635,000	20	5,272,000	22
23	23	R.J. Reynolds Industries (Winston-Salem, N.C.)[6]	13,533,000*	16,930,000	18	1,001,000	15	4,796,000	23
24	24	Standard Oil (Cleveland)	13,002,000*	18,330,000	16	308,000	55	8,018,000	14
25	21	ITT (New York)[7]	12,714,276	14,272,499	19	293,501	58	6,469,792	16
26	36	Beatrice (Chicago)[8,9]	12,595,000	10,379,000	30	479,000	34	2,357,000	58
27	32	Philip Morris (New York)	12,149,000*	17,429,000	17	1,255,000	11	4,737,000	25
28	25	Dow Chemical (Midland, Mich.)	11,537,000	11,830,000	25	58,000	214	4,792,000	24
29	34	McDonnell Douglas (St. Louis)	11,477,700	7,268,400	38	345,700	48	26,334,600	4
30	37	Rockwell International (Pittsburgh)[10]	11,337,600	7,332,800	37	595,300	23	2,948,300	47
31	27	Unocal (Los Angeles)	10,738,000*	10,797,000	27	325,000	50	1,630,000	85
32	30	Westinghouse Electric (Pittsburgh)	10,700,200	9,681,600	33	605,300	22	3,234,700	40
33	28	Eastman Kodak (Rochester, N.Y.)	10,631,000	12,142,000	24	332,000	49	6,562,000	15
34	33	Dart & Kraft (Northbrook, Ill.)	9,942,300	5,501,800	54	466,100	36	2,880,200	49
35	31	Goodyear Tire & Rubber (Akron, Ohio)	9,896,700	6,953,500	39	412,400	42	3,507,400	34
36	43	Lockheed (Burbank, Calif.)	9,535,000	4,184,000	74	401,000	45	1,511,000	88
37	26	Allied-Signal (Morris Township, N.J.)[12,13]	9,115,000	13,271,000	21	(279,000)	467	6,130,000	18
38	39	General Foods (Rye Brook, N.Y.)[14]	9,022,418	4,553,725	69	324,907	51	1,940,244	68

Employees Number	Rank	Net Income as Percent of Sales %	Rank	Net Income as Percent of Stockholders' Equity %	Rank	Earnings per Share '85/$	'84/$	'75/$	Growth Rate 1975–85 %	Rank	Total Return to Investors 1985 %	Rank	1975–85 Average %	Rank	Industry Code
811,000†	1	4.2	227	13.5	186	12.28	14.22	4.32	11.01	157	(6.58)	411	7.86	347	40
146,000†	12	5.6	144	16.7	111	6.46	6.77	2.80	8.73	196	24.13	231	12.42	272	29
163,600	8	1.9	346	7.4	321	2.55	3.11	1.99	2.52	267	13.08	321	13.24	254	29
369,300†	3	4.8	187	20.5	56	13.63	15.79	1.85	22.14	30	30.15	193	13.57	246	40
405,535	2	13.1	19	20.5	58	10.67	10.77	3.34	12.32	127	27.15	210	13.14	257	44
54,481	59	2.7	307	9.1	285	5.11	1.03‡	3.06	5.26	236	(7.67)	413	8.74	333	29
60,845	51	3.7	252	10.0	272	4.52	4.48	2.27	7.11	214	24.96	223	14.10	237	29
337,600	4	4.5	201	9.9§	275	1.37	1.25	5.13	(12.37)	334	31.20	188	2.14	404	36
146,017	11	3.8	248	8.8	288	4.61	5.93	1.81	9.80	173	38.99	144	7.72	352	28
304,000†	5	8.3	58	16.8	109	5.13	5.03	1.58	12.46	124	30.15	194	15.93	207	36
49,545	64	7.2	87	16.9	104	7.42	7.70	2.68	10.72	161	20.19	266	14.89	224	29
31,300	118	—	—			(0.97)	2.21	1.54	—		46.52	112	12.72	267	29
107,850†	21	7.7	71	38.8	5	9.38	5.94	(2.16)	—		49.18	102	18.82	159	40
35,167	103	8.1	62	11.7	233	N.A.	5.73	1.90	—		—		—		29
79,649†	38	2.2	329	6.1§	345	2.56**	3.52**	6.87	(9.40)	327	3.92	370	(1.48)	420	29
184,800	7	2.0	337	7.2	325	2.12	4.90	1.94	0.87	280	21.51	255	16.46	199	41
25,300	144	2.7	306	24.7§	32	1.44	1.75	0.75	6.74	222	(13.97)	428	5.76	376	29
111,000	20	1.1	375	2.1§	384	0.75	4.01	4.15	(15.72)	338	9.65	338	9.67	324	29
42,353	79	4.8	185	15.6§	145	4.53**	3.08	2.64	5.55	232	16.20	299	14.66	229	10
37,818	96	3.8	245	10.0	269	4.72	4.67	2.10	8.44	198	14.15	311	18.04	174	29
104,000	22	4.2	226	13.0	200	3.75	5.39	0.53	21.54	33	38.83	145	32.46	32	41
62,200	47	4.7	191	12.0	224	3.80	5.35	2.02	6.50	224	24.46	229	7.76	350	43
147,513	10	7.4	80	19.0§	78	3.60	4.11	1.48	9.31	184	10.18	336	13.69	240	21
42,100	80	2.4	322	3.8	369	1.31	6.14	0.85	4.36	246	20.32	265	12.79	263	10
232,000	6	2.3	325	4.5	362	1.89	2.97	3.20	(5.13)	309	31.75	184	11.08	302	36
100,000	25	3.8	247	20.3	59	5.06	4.23	1.71	11.46	147	70.44	42	11.72	287	20
114,000	19	10.3	33	26.5	26	10.47	7.24	1.81	19.19	50	11.74	329	15.17	220	21
53,200	61	0.5	392	1.2	392	0.31	3.02	3.32	(21.12)	345	52.39	87	1.17	410	28
97,067	26	3.0	287	1.3	390	8.60	8.10	2.27	14.25	101	4.82	364	19.96	140	41
123,266	17	5.3	156	20.2	60	4.00	3.25	0.74	18.38	59	18.32	285	23.74	87	41
20,214	174	3.0	285	19.9	61	2.36	4.03	1.70	3.32	255	(26.62)	447	12.22	279	29
125,571	16	5.7	142	18.7	81	3.52	3.04	0.94	14.05	104	72.12	38	25.75	63	36
128,950	15	3.1	281	5.1	355	1.46	3.81	2.53	(5.36)	312	9.24	342	0.28	416	38
73,318	43	4.7	190	16.2	128	3.22	3.01	1.67[11]	6.79	219	55.99	84	17.01	192	20
134,115†	14	4.2	224	11.8	229	3.84	3.87	2.24	5.54	233	24.46	228	9.10	329	30
87,800	34	4.2	218	26.5	25	6.10	5.28	1.16	18.02	63	12.20	324	34.59	26	41
143,800	13	—	—			(3.28)	5.03	2.78	—		37.55	151	11.98	284	41
56,000	56	3.6	257	16.8	110	6.61	6.10	2.43	10.52	164	—		—		20

The 100 Largest U.S. Industrial Corporations (ranked by sales)

Rank '85	Rank '84	Company	Sales ($000)	Assets ($000)	Assets Rank	Net Income ($000)	Net Income Rank	Stockholders' Equity ($000)	Equity Rank
39	35	Union Carbide (Danbury, Conn.)	9,003,000	10,581,000	28	(581,000)	475	4,019,000	31
40	38	Xerox (Stamford, Conn.)	8,947,600	9,816,700	31	475,300	35	4,386,200	27
41	40	PepsiCo (Purchase, N.Y.)	8,478,902	5,861,160	51	543,690	27	1,837,682	71
42	44	General Dynamics (St. Louis)[15]	8,410,600	4,448,100	71	383,300	46	1,335,800	100
43	48	LTV (Dallas)	8,198,800	6,306,700	45	(723,900)	478	652,200	205
44	46	Coca-Cola (Atlanta)	8,138,904	6,897,706	40	722,299	16	2,979,057	45
45	49	Sara Lee (Chicago)[5,16]	8,117,206	3,215,794	100	206,312	75	1,066,045	125
46	42	Ashland Oil (Russell, Ky.)[10]	7,891,223	3,927,633	78	146,722	106	929,411	151
47	45	Minnesota Mining & Manufacturing (St. Paul)	7,846,000	6,593,000	42	664,000	19	4,008,000	32
48	41	Amerada Hess (New York)	7,653,439	6,219,453	46	(260,409)	465	2,260,590	63
49	50	W.R. Grace (New York)	7,260,100	5,420,900	56	146,900	105	2,404,500	56
50	55	Coastal (Houston)	7,254,300	8,294,300	36	142,400	108	772,000	180
51	53	Anheuser-Busch (St. Louis)	7,000,300*	5,121,400	57	443,700	39	2,173,000	66
52	52	Caterpillar Tractor (Peoria, Ill.)	6,769,000	6,016,000	49	198,000	80	3,068,000	42
53	51	Monsanto (St. Louis)[17]	6,747,000	8,877,000	35	(98,000)**	448	3,407,000	35
54	47	Georgia-Pacific (Atlanta)	6,716,000	4,866,000	63	187,000	87	2,147,000	67
55	65	Digital Equipment (Maynard, Mass.)[5]	6,686,316	6,368,857	43	446,682	38	4,554,599	26
56	56	Honeywell (Minneapolis)	6,624,600	5,033,700	60	281,600	60	2,566,900	52
57	59	TRW (Cleveland)	6,615,343¶	3,735,418	80	(7,088)	414	1,014,915	132
58	60	Hewlett-Packard (Palo Alto, Calif.)[18]	6,505,000	5,680,000	53	489,000	33	3,982,000	33
59	57	Johnson & Johnson (New Brunswick, N.J.)	6,421,300	5,095,100	58	613,700	21	3,350,900	36
60	58	Raytheon (Lexington, Mass.)	6,408,537	3,441,015	90	375,905	47	1,928,982	69
61	72	Ralston Purina (St. Louis)[10]	5,863,900	2,637,300	125	256,400	65	924,500	154
62	70	Champion International (Stamford, Conn.)	5,769,759	6,098,129	47	163,139	95	2,599,088	51
63	69	Sperry (New York)[14]	5,687,200	5,773,400	52	286,700	59	3,001,100	44
64	64	General Mills (Minneapolis)[19]	5,654,100¶	2,662,600	120	(72,900)	443	1,023,300	130
65	121	ConAgra (Omaha)[19]	5,498,157	1,547,138	198	91,728	154	458,253	267
66	67	Motorola (Schaumburg, Ill.)	5,443,000	4,370,000	72	72,000	192	2,284,000	61
67	90	IC Industries (Chicago)	5,292,100¶	4,818,400	64	162,800	96	1,638,600	83
68	66	Weyerhaeuser (Tacoma, Wash.)	5,205,579	6,005,279	50	200,116	78	3,324,051	37
69	62	Aluminum Co. of America (Pittsburgh)	5,162,700	6,353,600	44	(16,600)	422	3,307,900	38
70	68	Bethlehem Steel (Bethlehem, Pa.)	5,117,700	4,742,600	65	(196,000)	462	1,011,300	136
71	106	Northrop (Los Angeles)	5,056,600	2,332,700	143	214,400	74	899,000	162
72	76	Burroughs (Detroit)	5,037,700	4,556,400	68	248,200	69	2,492,400	53
73	73	Colgate-Palmolive (New York)	5,019,698	2,814,005	112	109,442	137	907,048	158
74	122	Textron (Providence)	4,990,500¶	4,337,400	73	251,800	67	1,633,300	84
75	63	Texas Instruments (Dallas)	4,924,500	3,076,100	102	(118,700)	451	1,427,700	93
76	74	Archer Daniels Midland (Decatur, Ill.)[5]	4,738,767	2,967,117	107	163,908	94	1,803,394	73
77	81	Borden (New York)	4,716,172	2,932,246	108	193,804	84	1,407,795	95
78	84	American Brands (New York)	4,692,367*	4,926,053	61	420,870	40	2,425,409	55
79	78	American Home Products (New York)	4,684,742	3,395,211	92	717,140	17	2,291,758	60
80	94	Pillsbury (Minneapolis)[19]	4,670,600	2,778,500	115	191,800	86	1,165,400	114
81	93	Emerson Electric (St. Louis)[10]	4,649,200	3,256,800	98	401,100	44	2,222,200	65
82	75	Litton Industries (Beverly Hills, Calif.)[20]	4,590,649	4,646,273	66	299,471	57	939,362	146
83	80	International Paper (New York)	4,502,000	6,039,000	48	133,000	121	3,195,000	41
84	92	Bristol-Myers (New York)	4,444,000	3,721,200	82	531,400	29	2,451,000	54
85	85	Martin Marietta (Bethesda, Md.)	4,410,064¶	2,258,069	149	249,392	68	707,957	192

Employees Number	Rank	Net Income as Percent of Sales %	Rank	Net Income as Percent of Stockholders' Equity %	Rank	EPS '85/$	EPS '84/$	EPS '75/$	Growth Rate 1975–85 %	Rank	Total Return 1985 %	Rank	1975–85 Average %	Rank	Industry Code
91,459	31	—	—	—	—	(2.78)	1.53	2.08	—		101.66	10	6.58	363	28
102,396	24	5.3	152	9.7§	279	4.44	2.53	3.07	3.76	252	64.86	60	5.98	373	38
150,000	9	6.4	109	29.6	16	5.83	2.25	1.47	14.77	93	70.80	41	13.60	244	49
103,300	23	4.6	197	28.7	19	9.05	8.08	1.59	19.01	54	(0.82)	391	25.35	67	41
56,800	54	—	—			(8.94)	(5.84)	1.02	—		(31.65)	449	(3.11)	425	33
38,520	92	8.9	49	24.3	34	5.51	4.76	2.00	10.67	162	37.65	150	10.09	314	49
92,800	30	2.5	315	19.4	69	3.61	3.25	0.13	38.90	7	62.18	67	22.32	110	20
32,800	110	1.9	345	12.7§	208	4.12	(7.40)	2.95	3.41	254	59.15	75	15.58	213	29
85,466	36	8.5	54	16.6	113	5.77	6.27	2.29	9.68	176	17.73	292	8.74	336	38
8,290†	322	—	—			(3.08)	2.01	1.51	—		13.49	319	16.07	203	29
116,900	18	2.0	336	6.1	342	2.82	4.02	5.31	(6.13)	315	25.45	221	12.29	276	28
16,237	210	2.0	338	12.6§	209	3.61	3.00	1.73**	7.65	207	109.19	9	28.02	44	29
39,769	87	6.3	111	19.2§	70	2.84	2.47	0.63	16.31	73	76.98	30	17.14	190	49
53,616	60	2.9	290	6.5	335	2.02	(4.47)	4.65	(7.99)	324	36.58	156	1.11	411	45
56,103	55	—	—			(1.27)**	5.42	4.31	—		10.51	334	6.35	366	28
38,000	95	2.8	299	8.2§	297	1.64	0.97	1.54	0.64	285	7.84	356	2.17	403	26
89,000	33	6.7	97	9.8	277	7.42	5.73	1.28	19.18	51	19.64	272	11.25	295	44
94,022	27	4.3	213	11.0	249	6.16	5.10	1.98	12.02	138	18.58	281	19.32	149	44
93,186	28	—	—			(0.27)	7.14	3.08	—		24.74	227	16.67	198	36
84,000	37	7.5	74	12.3	218	1.91	2.59	0.38	17.60	68	8.58	347	12.33	275	44
74,900	42	9.6	41	18.3	85	3.36	2.75	1.06	12.23	130	46.88	111	7.39	356	42
73,000	44	5.9	130	19.5	66	4.60	2.88	1.17	14.70	96	34.66	168	18.05	173	36
70,400	45	4.4	209	27.7	22	3.15	2.68	0.95	12.73	119	32.37	182	13.12	259	20
43,000	78	2.8	294	6.3	339	1.59	(0.36)	1.82	(1.34)	295	13.39	320	6.92	359	26
77,716	40	5.0	170	9.6	281	5.15	4.17	3.81	3.06	260	34.70	167	6.80	362	44
63,162	46	—	—			(1.63)	4.98	3.19	—		35.29	162	12.07	283	20
30,410	126	1.7	357	19.5§	65	2.65	1.97**	0.24	27.08	15	55.92	85	40.33	12	20
90,200	32	1.3	370	3.2	374	0.61	3.27	0.49	2.28	272	15.80	303	12.89	261	36
43,050	77	3.1	283	9.9	273	3.04	2.89	1.32	8.66	197	35.32	161	22.34	109	20
35,079	104	3.8	243	6.0§	347	1.32	1.52	1.51	(1.34)	294	9.15	344	1.22	409	26
40,100†	85	—	—			(0.23)	3.13	0.92	—		5.43	360	10.11	313	33
44,500†	75	—	—			(4.37)	(2.91)**	5.54	—		(9.61)	417	(3.37)	427	33
46,900	68	4.2	216	23.9	36	4.63	3.63	0.72	20.46	42	25.64	218	29.96	38	41
60,519	52	4.9	177	10.0	270	5.46	5.40	4.14	2.81	263	15.24	305	0.53	413	44
40,600†	83	2.2	331	12.1	223	1.39	0.86	1.73	(2.16)	303	35.89	159	5.95	375	43
56,000	57	5.1	168	15.4	152	6.75	3.11	2.58	10.10	170	48.50	105	14.49	233	41
77,872	39	—	—			(4.76)	13.05	2.71	—		(10.22)	420	2.77	400	36
9,446	299	3.5	263	9.1	284	1.62	1.19	0.86	6.54	223	43.19	132	9.72	323	20
32,700†	111	4.1	228	13.8	180	3.75	3.56	1.50	9.56	180	63.27	65	19.71	145	20
76,546	41	9.0	48	16.8§	105	7.34	7.20	2.81	10.06	171	4.58	366	18.20	170	21
47,237	66	15.3	8	31.3	14	4.70	4.43	1.58	11.52	145	28.63	202	10.93	305	42
92,900	29	4.1	229	16.5	119	4.42	3.91	1.38	12.39	125	39.45	143	15.86	208	20
61,900	49	8.6	52	18.1	87	5.43	5.10	1.74	12.05	135	20.05	268	12.49	271	36
58,200	53	6.5	105	31.9	13	7.27	7.32	0.71	26.12	17	31.11	189	32.51	31	36
31,900	115	3.0	289	3.4§	373	2.16	1.88	4.93	(7.92)	323	(2.64)	400	2.71	401	26
35,700	102	12.0	20	21.7	47	3.86	3.45	1.11	13.27	113	27.35	209	16.19	201	42
50,000	63	5.7	143	35.2	7	4.36	(3.88)	0.70	20.13	44	20.40	263	26.31	58	41

The 100 Largest U.S. Industrial Corporations (ranked by sales) *(concluded)*

Rank			Sales	Assets		Net Income		Stockholders' Equity	
'85	'84	Company	($000)	($000)	Rank	($000)	Rank	($000)	Rank
86	88	North American Philips (New York)	4,395,213	2,643,040	124	81,543	169	1,050,600	127
87	•	Farmland Industries (Kansas City, Mo.)[22]	4,371,028¶	1,284,177	228	N.A.[21]		462,481	263
88	89	PPG Industries (Pittsburgh)	4,345,500	4,083,800	75	302,700	56	1,705,300	78
89	97	NCR (Dayton, Ohio)	4,317,166	3,939,840	77	315,216	52	2,318,360	59
90	87	CPC International (Englewood Cliffs, N.J.)	4,209,900	3,016,600	105	142,000	110	1,371,900	99
91	104	Dresser Industries (Dallas)[18]	4,111,200	3,224,500	99	(196,400)	463	1,646,200	80
92	82	Armco (Morristown, N.J.)	4,106,700	3,293,300	95	55,000	221	1,093,500	123
93	83	Diamond Shamrock (Dallas)	4,101,800	4,618,000	67	(604,700)	476	1,733,000	76
94	108	Kimberly-Clark (Dallas)	4,072,900	3,503,800	88	267,100	63	1,743,900	75
95	96	Agway (DeWitt, N.Y.)[5]	4,067,208	1,359,719	219	N.A.[21]		306,041	320
96	86	Deere (Moline, Ill.)[18]	4,060,648	5,462,227	55	30,505	295	2,258,616	64
97	98	H.J. Heinz (Pittsburgh)[23]	4,047,945	2,473,774	129	265,978	64	1,230,454	107
98	91	American Motors (Southfield, Mich.)	4,039,901	2,000,944	163	(125,263)	453	149,215	427
99	101	Pfizer (New York)	4,024,500	4,462,900	70	579,700	24	2,927,300	48
100	107	Campbell Soup (Camden, N.J.)[20]	3,988,705	2,437,525	132	197,824	82	1,382,487	98

The definitions and concepts underlying the figures in this directory are explained on page 221.

N.A. Not available.

* Does not include excise taxes; see the explanation of "sales" on page 221.

** Reflects an extraordinary credit of at least 10%; see the explanation of "net income" and "earnings per share" on page 221.

† Average for the year; see the reference to "employees" on page 222.

‡ Reflects an extraordinary charge of at least 10%; see the explanation of "net income" and "earnings per share" on page 221.

§ Dividends paid by company on its mandatory redeemable preferred stock were subtracted from net income in calculating this figure.

[1] Figures include ROLM (1984 rank: 397), acquired November 21, 1984.

[2] Name changed from Standard Oil (Indiana) April 23, 1985.

[3] Figures include Gulfstream Aerospace (1984 rank: 406), acquired August 16, 1985.

[4] Wholly owned by Royal Dutch/Shell Group (1984 International 500 rank: 1).

[5] Figures are for fiscal year ended June 30, 1985.

[6] Figures include Nabisco Brands (1984 rank: 54), acquired September 10, 1985.

[7] Financial subsidiaries would add 25% or more to sales if consolidated.

[8] Name changed from Beatrice Foods June 5, 1984.

[9] Figures are for fiscal year ended February 28, 1985.

[10] Figures are for fiscal year ended September 30, 1985.

| Employees | | Net Income as Percent of | | | | Earnings per Share | | | Growth Rate 1975–85 | | Total Return to Investors | | | | Indus-try Code |
| | | Sales | | Stock-holders' Equity | | | | | | | 1985 | | 1975–85 Average | | |
Num-ber	Rank	%	Rank	%	Rank	'85/$	'84/$	'75/$	%	Rank	%	Rank	%	Rank	
51,755	62	1.9	347	7.8	309	2.82	4.53	1.40	7.22	213	(2.28)	398	18.37	168	36
7,600	343	—		—		N.A.	N.A.	N.A.	—		—		—		29
37,500†	97	7.0	90	17.8	91	4.54	4.33	1.43	12.27	128	56.65	80	19.15	153	32
62,000	48	7.3	82	13.6	184	3.15	3.30	0.75	15.47	82	52.03	89	23.73	88	44
39,000	89	3.4	268	10.4	262	2.92	3.98	2.31	2.37	270	29.84	197	13.06	260	20
46,200	69	—		—		(2.58)	1.24	2.07	—		0.26	388	2.38	402	45
30,800	123	1.3	368	5.0	356	0.69	(4.55)‡	2.47	(11.99)	332	(3.85)	406	(3.32)	426	33
11,696	262	—		—		(5.09)	1.78	3.41	—		(18.14)	434	(3.46)	428	29
36,648	100	6.6	104	15.3	156	5.84	4.94	2.20	10.23	167	42.70	133	18.61	163	26
18,311†	192	—		—		N.A.	N.A.	N.A.	—		—		—		29
40,509	84	0.8	383	1.4	388	0.45	1.55	3.01	(17.32)	340	(1.95)	397	3.24	395	45
45,931	72	6.6	102	21.6	50	3.86	3.40	0.98	14.72	95	51.47	94	21.89	117	20
22,552	157	—		—		(1.24)	0.04**	(0.92)	—		(21.43)	438	(6.16)	432	40
39,200	88	14.4	12	19.8	63	3.44	3.06	1.05	12.60	122	21.29	258	16.85	196	42
44,716	74	5.0	174	14.3	173	3.06	2.96	1.30	8.90	191	45.22	121	15.93	206	20

[11] Figure is for Kraftco.
[12] Name changed from Allied September 19, 1985.
[13] Figures include Signal Companies (1984 rank: 61), acquired September 19, 1985.
[14] Figures are for fiscal year ended March 31, 1985.
[15] Figures include Cessna Aircraft (1984 rank: 380), acquired March 3, 1985.
[16] Name changed from Consolidated Foods April 2, 1985.
• Indicates that a corporation was not among the 500 in 1984.
¶ Includes sales from discontinued operations of at least 10%; see the explanation of "sales" on page 221.
N.A. Not available.
[17] Figures include G.D. Searle (1984 rank: 266), acquired October 1, 1985.
[18] Figures are for fiscal year ended October 31, 1985.
[19] Figures are for fiscal year ended May 31, 1985.
[20] Figures are for fiscal year ended July 31, 1985.
[21] Cooperatives provide only "net margin" figures, which are not comparable with the net income figures in these listings.
[22] Figures are for fiscal year ended August 31, 1985.
[23] Figures are for fiscal year ended April 30, 1985.

NOTES TO THE FORTUNE DIRECTORY

Sales All companies on the list must have derived more than 50% of their sales from manufacturing and/or mining. Sales include rental and other revenues but exclude dividends, interest, and other non-operating revenues. Sales of subsidiaries are included if they are consolidated. Sales from discontinued operations are included when these figures are published. When the sales are at least 10% higher for this reason, there is a symbol (¶) next to the sales figure. All figures are for the year ending December 31, 1985, unless otherwise noted. Sales figures do not include excise taxes collected by the manufacturer, and so the figures for some corporations—most of which sell gasoline, liquor, or tobacco—may be lower than those published by the corporations themselves. If they are at least 5% lower for this reason, there is an asterisk (*) next to the sales figures.

Assets are those shown at the company's fiscal year-end.

Net Income is shown after taxes and after extraordinary credits or charges if any are shown on the income statement. A double asterisk (**) signifies an extraordinary credit reflecting at least 10 percent of the net income shown, a double dagger (‡) an extraordinary charge of at least 10 percent. Figures in parentheses indicate a loss.

Stockholders' Equity is the sum of capital stock, surplus, and retained earnings at the company's year-end. Redeemable preferred stock is excluded when its redemption is either mandatory or outside the control of the company, except in the case of cooperatives. For purposes of calculating "net income as percent of stockholders' equity," any dividends paid on redeemable preferred stock, if that stock's redemption is either mandatory or outside the control of the company, have been subtracted from the net income figure.

Employees The figure shown is a year-end total except when it is followed by a dagger (†), in which case it is an average for the year.

Earnings per Share For all companies, the figures shown are the 'primary' earnings per share that appear on the company's income statement. These figures are based on a weighted average of the number of common shares and common-stock equivalents outstanding during the year. Per-share earnings for 1984 and 1985 are adjusted for stock splits and stock dividends. They are not restated for mergers, acquisitions, or accounting changes made after 1975. A double asterisk (**) signifies an extraordinary credit reflecting at least 10 percent of the net income shown, a double dagger (‡) an extraordinary charge of at least 10 percent. Results are listed as not available (N.A.) where the companies are cooperatives, joint ventures, or wholly owned subsidiaries of other companies, or if the figures were not published in 1975. The growth rate is the average annual growth, compounded. No growth rate is given if the company had a loss in either 1975 or 1985.

Total Return to Investors includes both price appreciation and dividend yield, to an investor in the company's stock. The figures shown assume sales at the end of 1985 of stock owned at the end of 1975 or 1984. It has been assumed that any proceeds from cash dividends, the sale of rights and warrant offerings, and stock received in spin-offs were reinvested at the end of the year in which they were received. Returns are adjusted for stock splits, stock dividends, recapitalizations, and corporate reorganizations as they occur; however, no effort has been made to reflect the cost of brokerage commissions or of taxes. Results are listed as not available (N.A.) if shares are not publicly traded or traded on only a limited basis. If companies have more than one class of shares outstanding, only the more widely held and actively traded has been considered.

Total-return percentages shown are the returns received by the hypothetical investor described above. The ten-year figures are annual averages, compounded. If corporations were substantially reorganized—e.g., because of mergers—the predecessor companies used in calculating total return are the same as those cited in the footnotes to the earnings-per-share figures.

Industry Code numbers used in the directory indicate which industry represents the greatest volume of industrial sales for each company. The numbers refer to the industry groups below, which are based on categories established by the U.S. Office of Management and Budget and issued by the Federal Statistical Policy and Standards Office. The median figures in the tables refer only to results of companies among the 500; no attempt has been made to calculate medians in groups with fewer than four companies.

Code No.	Industry
10	Mining, crude-oil production
20	Food
21	Tobacco
22	Textiles
23	Apparel
25	Furniture
26	Forest products
27	Publishing, printing
28	Chemicals
29	Petroleum refining
30	Rubber products
31	Leather
32	Building materials
33	Metals
34	Metal products
36	Electronics
37	Transportation equipment
38	Scientific and photographic equipment
40	Motor vehicles and parts
41	Aerospace
42	Pharmaceuticals
43	Soaps, cosmetics
44	Computers (includes office equipment)
45	Industrial and farm equipment
46	Jewelry, silverware
47	Toys, sporting goods
49	Beverages

The 100 Largest International Industrial Corporations (ranked by sales)

Rank '85	Rank '84	Company	Country	Sales ($000)	Assets ($000)	Net Income ($000)	Stock-Holders' Equity ($000)	Employees	Total Return to Investors % In Local Currency 5/31/85–5/31/86	In Local Currency 5-Year Avg.	In U.S. Dollars 5/31/85–5/31/86	In U.S. Dollars 5-Year Avg.	Industry Code
1	1	Royal Dutch/Shell Group	Neth./Britain	81,743,514	74,920,360	3,928,208	33,863,575	142,000	9.09	26.84	44.83	26.62	29
2	2	British Petroleum	Britain	53,100,765	43,589,870	866,745	14,317,060	127,940	15.60	15.59	33.57	7.97	29
3	5	IRI[1]	Italy	26,758,000	N.A.	(664,000)	N.A.	483,714	—	—	—	—	33
4	4	Toyota Motor[2]	Japan	26,040,288	17,227,126	1,624,184	10,621,800	79,901	29.58	20.91	86.95	27.06	40
5	3	ENI[1]	Italy	24,460,958	26,842,566	427,180	4,828,717	129,268	—	—	—	—	29
6	6	Unilever	Neth./Britain	21,627,167	13,474,625	668,521	4,888,435	304,000	47.30	29.90	70.21	21.32	20
7	8	Matsushita Electric Industrial[3]	Japan	20,749,190	21,451,841	1,012,044	10,130,401	133,963	7.42	5.97	54.86	11.40	36
8	10	Hitachi[4]	Japan	20,525,413	20,214,653	860,448	6,523,092	164,951	23.12	6.02	77.81	11.49	36
9	9	Pemex (Petróleos Mexicanos)[1]	Mexico	20,380,539[5]	36,633,436[5]	6,178[5]	18,880,864[5]	183,179[5]	—	—	—	—	29
10	7	Elf-Aquitaine[1]	France	20,105,843[6]	22,382,551[6]	708,069[6]	5,918,615[6]	73,000[6]	—	—	—	—	29
11	11	Française des Pétroles[1]	France	19,267,668[6]	12,318,881[6]	163,940[6]	2,977,955[6]	44,557[6]	—	—	—	—	29
12	13	Nissan Motor[4]	Japan	18,226,032	14,501,737	332,240	5,352,371	108,500	(7.17)	1.69	33.96	6.83	40
13	12	Philips' Gloeilampenfabrieken	Netherlands	18,079,488	19,202,251	276,710	5,864,561	345,600	4.78	31.77	39.10	31.54	36
14	15	Siemens[7]	W. Germany	17,833,563	19,462,811	490,555	4,697,100	348,000	12.73	27.62	49.40	27.66	36
15	16	Volkswagen	W. Germany	17,831,490	14,251,964	225,930	2,857,036	259,047	133.40	31.74	209.33	31.78	40
16	17	Daimler-Benz	W. Germany	17,799,929	14,622,167	589,130	3,775,171	231,077	70.09	49.00	125.42	49.05	40
17	28	Nestlé	Switzerland	17,158,824[6]	12,227,184[6]	711,141[6]	5,214,078[6]	154,769[6]	38.56	24.73	86.02	26.49	20
18	14	Petrobrás (Petróleo Brasileiro)[1]	Brazil	16,046,448	12,858,595	1,790,566	5,576,909	61,421	—	—	—	—	29
19	18	Bayer	W. Germany	15,598,199	12,404,526[6]	427,662[6]	4,089,806[6]	176,080[6]	38.64	26.08	83.75	26.13	28
20	22	BASF	W. Germany	15,071,964[6]	11,584,983[6]	338,793[6]	4,336,085[6]	130,173[6]	37.06	23.21	81.66	23.25	28
21	21	Hoechst	W. Germany	14,509,874[6]	11,184,839[6]	407,529[6]	3,126,972[6]	180,561[6]	31.69	26.50	74.52	26.54	28
22	25	Fiat	Italy	14,193,244	18,958,633	694,423	4,379,496	226,222	336.08	134.61	439.64	119.94	40
23	38	Samsung	South Korea	14,193,095	8,221,531	113,258	998,875	129,039	—	—	—	—	36
24	23	Mitsubishi Heavy Industries[4]	Japan	14,111,863	14,378,590	164,628	1,540,052	90,300	33.15	7.43	91.87	13.02	40
25	39	Hyundai	South Korea	14,024,594	8,493,891	79,601	1,162,416	156,000	—	—	—	—	37
26	29	General Motors of Canada	Canada	13,905,168[6]	3,114,234	521,975	1,594,584	48,106	16.37	15.40	16.20	12.25	40
27	27	Imperial Chemical Industries	Britain	13,895,128	12,018,065	663,338	5,050,275	118,600	21.20	32.30	40.12	23.46	28
28	19	Kuwait Petroleum[1,2]	Kuwait	13,640,512	18,883,540	693,200	12,853,554	15,044	—	—	—	—	29
29	130	VÖEST-Alpine	Austria	13,632,904	6,693,486	(189,247)	283,282	69,917	—	—	—	—	33
30	30	Renault[1]	France	13,593,545[6]	14,034,898[6]	(1,215,915)[6]	(981,019)[6]	196,414[6]	—	—	—	—	40
31	35	Toshiba[4]	Japan	13,502,659	12,405,968	352,588	2,182,940	114,000	16.82	5.99	68.86	11.45	36
32	20	Nippon Oil[4]	Japan	13,477,574	6,338,588	50,772	1,293,845	10,300	—	—	—	—	29
33	31	Nippon Steel[4]	Japan	12,534,517	15,410,287	207,080	2,696,291	72,081	16.42	(1.57)	66.67	3.46	33
34	24	Petróleos de Venezuela[1]	Venezuela	11,846,756	18,132,045	1,478,281	15,402,221	43,131	—	—	—	—	29
•		Pertamina[1]	Indonesia	11,579,413	N.A.	616,788	N.A.	N.A.	—	—	—	—	29
36	26	BAT Industries	Britain	11,397,244	12,773,800	829,173	5,306,040	197,960	26.42	95.33	46.11	82.50	21
37	32	Thyssen[7]	W. Germany	11,357,871	7,119,221	146,699	1,154,873	128,372	59.73	29.57	111.67	20.60	33

(continued)

The 100 Largest International Industrial Corporations (concluded)

Rank '85	Rank '84	Company	Country	Sales ($000)	Assets ($000)	Net Income ($000)	Stock-Holders' Equity ($000)	Employees	In Local Currency 5/31/85–5/31/86	In Local Currency 5-Year Avg.	In U.S. Dollars 5/31/85–5/31/86	In U.S. Dollars 5-Year Avg.	Industry Code
38	37	Peugeot	France	11,162,493	9,376,623	604,341	890,043	176,800	161.37	48.80	231.52	40.49	40
39	117	George Weston Holdings[4]	Britain	11,149,184	3,233,870	126,687	1,025,880	56,000	—	—	—	—	20
40	34	Canadian Pacific	Canada	11,011,127	15,334,949	180,626	4,405,923	123,400	(11.49)	4.03	(11.61)	1.19	33
41	41	Honda Motor[9]	Japan	10,752,813	5,973,667	532,060	2,806,101	50,609	(11.11)	6.14	28.29	11.58	40
42	36	Volvo	Sweden	10,014,445	8,479,604	320,264	2,350,363	67,857	102.23	108.81	144.23	86.16	40
43	43	Lucky-Goldstar	South Korea	9,859,920	5,958,868	78,501	1,090,084	62,500	—	—	—	—	29
44	45	Petrofina	Belgium	9,834,332	7,198,541	287,478	1,667,138	22,700	31.18	—	71.41	—	29
45	42	Ford Motor of Canada	Canada	9,775,557	2,125,635	145,690	768,395	29,700	9.06	28.53	8.90	25.03	40
46	40	Idemitsu Kosan[4]	Japan	9,439,451[5]	6,859,045[5]	20,730[5]	157,507[5]	5,921[5]	—	—	—	—	29
47	50	NEC[4]	Japan	9,246,225	10,801,598	274,872	1,901,494	90,102	58.58	25.89	128.99	32.34	36
48	46	CGE (Cie. Générale d'Électricité)[1]	France	8,741,903	13,990,916	84,752	981,299	153,800	—	—	—	—	36
49	48	Daewoo	South Korea	8,698,021	8,985,506	53,587	842,915	92,745	—	—	—	—	45
50	33	Esso UK	Britain	8,645,944[8]	6,261,329	820,752	1,343,994	5,803	—	—	—	—	33
51	44	Indian Oil[1,4]	India	8,279,652	2,462,375	70,615	679,212	31,081	—	—	—	—	29
52	53	Mitsubishi Electric[4]	Japan	8,200,629	7,234,498	192,570	1,538,339	68,745	(5.03)	2.56	37.20	7.88	36
53	49	Ruhrkohle	W. Germany	7,646,883	6,950,534	38,765	411,902	133,157	—	—	—	—	10
54	58	Saint-Gobain[1]	France	7,555,704[6]	10,149,051[6]	81,803[6]	1,278,188[6]	148,922[6]	—	—	—	—	32
55	51	Ciba-Geigy	Switzerland	7,404,403	10,954,854	598,171	6,785,437	81,012	36.53	31.36	83.29	33.21	28
56	56	Montedison	Italy	7,400,890	8,725,420	59,178	958,034	69,653	135.59	—	193.24	—	28
57	57	DSM[1]	Netherlands	7,265,333[6]	4,856,655[6]	121,094[6]	1,030,434[6]	26,615[6]	—	—	—	—	28
58	64	Robert Bosch	W. Germany	7,207,950	6,177,692	124,862	1,686,327	142,923	—	—	—	—	40
59	47	Rio Tinto-Zinc	Britain	6,880,582	10,207,480	271,036	2,538,576	75,197	15.85	9.75	33.94	2.49	10
60	121	Showa Shell Sekiyu[10]	Japan	6,819,821[5]	4,760,524[5]	10,937[5]	227,561[5]	3,157[5]	—	—	—	—	29
61	61	Thomson[1]	France	6,682,916[6]	9,964,569[6]	14,023[6]	672,794[6]	107,900[6]	—	—	—	—	36
62	67	Mazda Motor[11]	Japan	6,680,968	4,432,569	160,151	1,422,969	29,148	—	—	—	—	40
63	116	Türkiye Petrolleri[1]	Turkey	6,643,699	6,046,181	456,145	1,252,817	16,670	—	—	—	—	29
64	54	General Electric	Britian	6,556,571	5,990,892	520,809	2,953,298	165,593	14.77	56.82	32.68	46.45	36
65	55	Veba Oel	W. Germany	6,475,507[6]	3,040,985[6]	(20,302)[6]	521,093[6]	15,975[6]	51.62	23.96	100.94	24.00	29
66	68	Esso (Germany)	W. Germany	6,439,953[8]	1,880,064	64,509	532,693	3,670	—	—	—	—	29
67	62	Sunkyong	South Korea	6,436,703	2,480,751	55,057	425,305	19,454	—	—	—	—	29
68	84	Fujitsu[4]	Japan	6,396,195	6,855,159	364,498	2,424,171	74,187	7.57	26.05	55.07	32.52	44
69	63	Imperial Oil	Canada	6,345,188	6,579,907	464,157	3,608,867	14,674	(17.14)	6.05	(17.27)	3.17	29
70	72	Nippon Kokan[4]	Japan	6,285,820	10,308,247	77,896	1,099,215	36,851	8.60	(3.51)	.56.45	1.29	33
71	66	Fried. Krupp	W. Germany	6,276,035	4,404,635	28,707	674,002	67,402	—	—	—	—	33
72	74	Rhône-Poulenc[1]	France	6,243,962[6]	6,032,368[6]	257,318[6]	1,710,689[6]	78,000[6]	—	—	—	—	28
73	70	Sanyo Electric[12]	Japan	6,227,998	6,233,127	149,342	2,083,785	25,429	2.72	(2.47)	47.76	2.46	36

		Company	Country										
74	75	Mannesmann	W. Germany	6,171,069	4,808,384	77,700	1,080,194	107,804	38.22	14.12	83.20	14.16	45
75	71	Schlumberger	Neth. Antilles	6,119,447	11,282,232	351,036	6,877,209	72,810	(38.20)	(3.24)	(21.62)	(8.65)	38
76	69	Grand Metropolitan[7]	Britain	6,036,606	6,078,663	338,158	2,767,702	137,200	59.09	34.15	83.76	25.26	49
77	65	Maruzen Oil[4]	Japan	6,014,768	2,676,195	102,048	(111,837)	1,992	—	—	—	—	29
78	106	Statoil	Norway	5,979,417	6,082,190	253,968	659,103	7,005	—	—	—	—	29
79	52	Barlow Rand[7]	South Africa	5,861,085	3,647,252	(21,569)	692,127	151,514	52.45	(6.95)	(22.96)	(2.20)	20
80	81	Sony[11,13]	Japan	5,776,507	6,841,224	297,409	2,832,252	44,908	(12.64)	6.73	26.05	3.82	36
81	77	Alcan Aluminum	Canada	5,718,000	6,861,000	(180,000)	2,746,000	70,000	36.01	—	35.81	—	33
82	80	Neste[1]	Finland	5,684,359	4,019,925	20,221	195,278	8,496	—	7.25	—	—	29
83	89	Brown Boveri	Switzerland	5,638,741	9,599,029	37,386	2,539,806	97,800	51.90	63.28	101.32	7.29	36
84	91	Broken Hill Proprietary[14]	Australia	5,631,217	8,033,384	527,606	3,925,987	58,000	110.50	—	127.72	48.72	33
85	73	Chinese Petroleum[1]	Taiwan	5,520,716	4,397,197	437,655	2,851,960	22,077	—	—	—	—	29
86	83	Akzo Group	Netherlands	5,422,732	4,268,446	253,826	1,503,849	65,000	68.90	58.03	124.25	57.73	28
87	110	Sacilor[1]	France	5,406,709[6]	7,702,740[6]	(585,129)[6]	(2,812,369)[6]	69,504[6]	(12.62)	9.37	10.96	3.26	33
88	76	Kobe Steel[4]	Japan	5,314,869	7,746,303	42,555	606,542	32,524	18.19	(0.77)	69.44	4.27	33
89	90	Sumitomo Metal Industries[4]	Japan	5,313,817	9,039,637	103,260	1,284,880	34,010	1.75	(8.65)	46.38	(4.02)	33
90	87	Ford Motor	Britain	5,240,633[8]	5,294,480	148,992	1,830,815	51,200	—	—	—	—	40
91	86	Michelin	France	5,190,997	3,041,444	110,052	968,055	N.A.	240.00	31.35	331.20	24.01	30
92	92	Chrysler Canada	Canada	5,154,632	1,129,958	101,079	358,362	12,356	2.41	48.94	2.26	44.89	40
93	93	Mitsubishi Chemical Industries[15]	Japan	5,112,348	4,512,822	97,657	416,882	16,474	35.17	24.24	94.49	30.57	28
94	78	Nippon Mining[4]	Japan	5,044,411	3,785,721	16,221	348,554	8,083	4.83	25.25	51.52	31.60	29
95	98	BTR	Britain	5,027,639	4,460,859	293,450	1,467,397	85,800	(166.28)	81.80	207.82	69.80	45
96	101	Adam Opel	W. Germany	5,024,802[8]	2,912,276	(45,936)	624,352	57,273	82 55.	—	—	—	40
97	97	BMW (Bayerische Motoren Werke)	W. Germany	5,006,668	3,017,392	102,187	793,277	47,777	18.08	—	—	—	33
98	99	Kawasaki Steel[4]	Japan	5,000,796[5]	7,765,223[5]	83,071[5]	1,335,554[5]	27,863[5]	—	(2.03)	71.21	3.10	29
99	111	ENPETROL[1]	Spain	4,930,725	2,018,463	14,804	649,498	5,946	—	—	—	—	
100	102	Ford-Werke	W. Germany	4,905,511[8]	2,468,041	(85,274)	438,414	45,991	3.47	(0.72)	37.13	(0.69)	40

The definitions and concepts underlying the figures in this directory are explained on page 226.

• Not on last year's list.

N.A. Not available.

1 Government-owned.
2 Figures are for fiscal year ended June 30, 1985.
3 Figures are for fiscal year ended November 20, 1985.
4 Figures are for fiscal year ended March 31, 1985.
5 Parent only.
6 Also includes certain subsidiaries owned 50% or less, either fully or on a prorated basis.
7 Figures are for fiscal year ended September 30, 1985.
8 Revenues include certain sales to foreign affiliates of the U.S. parent company.
9 Figures are for fiscal year ended February 28, 1985.
10 Name changed from Showa Oil on January 1, 1985.
11 Figures are for fiscal year ended October 31, 1985.
12 Figures are for fiscal year ended November 30, 1985.
13 Includes only wholly owned subsidiaries.
14 Figures are for fiscal year ended May 31, 1985.
15 Figures are for fiscal year ended January 31, 1985.

NOTES TO THE INTERNATIONAL 100*

Sales All companies on the list must have derived more than 50% of their sales from manufacturing and/or mining. Sales do not include excise taxes or customs duties levied according to either volume or value sales, and so the figures for some companies—most of which sell gasoline, liquor, or tobacco—may be lower than those published by the companies themselves. Unless otherwise noted, figures exclude intracompany transactions and include consolidated subsidiaries more than 50% owned, either fully or on a prorated basis. Figures have been converted to dollars using an exchange rate that consists of the official average rate during each company's fiscal year (ended December 31, 1985, unless otherwise noted).

Assets Totals shown at each company's year-end. Figures have been converted to dollars at the official exchange rate at each company's year-end.

Net Income is shown after taxes, minority interests, and extraordinary items. Figures have been converted to dollars using an exchange rate that consists of the official average rate during each company's fiscal year (ended December 31, 1985, unless otherwise noted).

Stockholders' Equity is shown at each company's year-end. Minority interest is not included. Figures have been converted to dollars at the official exchange rate at each company's year-end.

Employees The figure shown is either a year-end or yearly average number as published.

* Selected from the Fortune 500.

Total Return to Investors includes both price appreciation and dividend yield to an investor in the company's stock. The figures shown assume sales at the end of May 1986 of stock owned at the end of May 1981 or 1985. Any proceeds from cash dividends, the sale of rights and warrant offerings, and stock received in spin-offs are assumed to have been reinvested on the date they were received. Returns are adjusted for stock splits, stock dividends, recapitalizations, and corporate reorganizations as they occur; however, no effort has been made to reflect the cost of brokerage commissions or of taxes. For all companies, share prices used are those quoted on local exchanges. Results are not listed if shares are not publicly traded or are traded on only a limited basis. If a company has more than one class of shares outstanding, only the more widely held and actively traded have been considered.

Total return percentages shown are the returns received by a hypothetical investor as described above. The five-year figures are annual averages, compounded.

Industry Code Numbers used in the directory indicate which industry represents the greatest volume of industrial sales for each company. The numbers refer to the industry groups listed on page 222, which are based on categories established by the U.S. Office of Management and Budget and issued by the Federal Statistical Policy and Standards Office. The median figures in the tables refer only to results of companies in the 500. No attempt has been made to calculate medians in groups or countries with fewer than four companies.

The 25 Largest Industrial Companies in the World (ranked by sales)

Rank '85	Rank '84	Company	Headquarters	Industry	Sales ($000)	Net Income ($000)
1	3	General Motors	Detroit	Motor vehicles and parts	96,371,700	3,999,000
2	1	Exxon	New York	Petroleum refining	86,673,000	4,870,000
3	2	Royal Dutch/Shell Group	The Hague/London	Petroleum refining	81,743,514	3,928,208
4	4	Mobil	New York	Petroleum refining	55,960,000	1,040,000
5	6	British Petroleum	London	Petroleum refining	53,100,765	866,745
6	5	Ford Motor	Dearborn, Mich.	Motor vehicles and parts	52,774,400	2,515,400
7	8	International Business Machines	Armonk, N.Y.	Computers, office equip.	50,056,000	6,555,000
8	7	Texaco	Harrison, N.Y.	Petroleum refining	46,297,000	1,233,000
9	13	Chevron	San Francisco	Petroleum refining	41,741,905	1,547,360
10	10	American Tel. & Tel.	New York	Electronics	34,909,500	1,556,800
11	9	E.I. du Pont de Nemours	Wilmington, Del.	Chemicals	29,483,000	1,118,000
12	11	General Electric	Fairfield, Conn.	Electronics	28,285,000	2,336,000
13	12	Standard Oil (Ind.)	Chicago	Petroleum refining	27,215,000	1,953,000
14	17	IRI	Rome	Metals	26,758,000	(664,000)
15	16	Toyota Motor	Toyota City (Japan)	Motor vehicles and parts	26,040,288	1,624,184
16	14	ENI	Rome	Petroleum refining	24,460,958	427,180
17	15	Atlantic Richfield	Los Angeles	Petroleum refining	22,357,000	(202,000)
18	18	Unilever	Rotterdam/London	Food	21,627,167	668,521
19	22	Chrysler	Highland Park, Mich.	Motor vehicles and parts	21,255,500	1,635,200
20	21	Matsushita Electric Industrial	Osaka (Japan)	Electronics	20,749,191	1,021,044
21	24	Hitachi	Tokyo	Electronics	20,525,413	860,448
22	23	Pemex (Petróleos Mexicanos)	Mexico City	Petroleum refining	20,380,539	6,178
23	19	Shell Oil	Houston	Petroleum refining	20,309,000	1,650,000
24	20	Elf-Aquitaine	Paris	Petroleum refining	20,105,843	708,069
25	26	Française des Pétroles	Paris	Petroleum refining	19,267,668	163,940

• Not on last year's list.

U.S. companies   Non-U.S. companies

The 25 Largest Diversified Service Companies (ranked by sales)

Rank '85	'84	Company	Sales[1] ($000)	Assets ($000)	Assets Rank	Net Income ($000)	Net Income Rank	Stockholders' Equity ($000)	Equity Rank
1	1	Phibro-Salomon (New York)	27,896,000	88,601,000	1	557,000	1	2,954,000	2
2	3	InterNorth (Omaha)	10,727,253	9,892,727	3	(14,055)‡	76	1,650,345	8
3	2	RCA (New York)	9,991,700	6,705,000	4	369,100	4	2,549,800	4
4	3	Union Pacific (New York)[2]	7,797,894	10,709,838	2	501,207	2	4,356,151	1
5	5	Fleming Companies (Oklahoma City)	7,094,991	1,164,876	39	60,082	28	446,894	36
6	4	Super Value Stores (Eden Prairie, Minn.)[3]	6,587,527	1,173,803	38	107,212	21	469,170	34
7	10	McKesson (San Francisco)[4]	4,999,592	1,545,409	31	64,954	27	558,622	26
8	8	CBS (New York)	4,785,500	3,508,700	9	27,400	44	481,300	33
9	6	Halliburton (Dallas)	4,778,695	4,661,963	6	(339,276)‡	87	2,857,854	3
10	9	Fluor (Irvine, Calif.)[5]	4,168,444	2,796,364	16	(633,324)	88	1,033,904	14
11	13	Hospital Corp. of America (Nashville)	4,151,715	6,259,060	5	338,613**	5	2,092,133	5
12	•	Gulf & Western Industries (New York)[5]	3,844,100	4,064,100	7	247,800	7	1,737,700	7
13	16	Alco Standard (Valley Forge, Pa.)[6]	3,823,053	1,287,756	35	51,362	30	441,953	38
14	15	ARA Holding (Philadelphia)[6,7]	3,535,933	1,693,565	29	N.A.		106,207	78
15	77	Electronic Data Systems (Dallas)[8]	3,406,400	1,595,200	30	189,800	10	530,600	29
16	•	ENSERCH (Dallas)	3,391,035	3,357,844	11	(38,508)	82	1,028,002	15
17	11	American Broadcasting (New York)[9]	3,298,500	N.A.		N.A.		N.A.	
18	18	Wetterau (Hazelwood, Mo.)[4]	3,081,101	556,322	62	26,556	45	171,963	62
19	21	Ryder System (Miami)	2,905,287	3,740,632	8	125,316	18	973,335	17
20	22	Dun & Bradstreet (New York)	2,771,669	2,672,993	18	294,708	6	1,355,714	10
21	24	Sysco (Houston)[10]	2,627,750	681,121	58	50,325	31	339,051	45
22	•	Charter (Jacksonville, Fla.)	2,571,916	647,234	59	1,274**	71	(147,160)	100
23	27	Greyhound (Phoenix)	2,561,663	2,931,491	13	120,088	19	1,160,258	12
24	28	National Medical Enterprises (Los Angeles)[11]	2,530,100	2,841,900	15	149,000	16	937,100	18
25	19	Associated Milk Producers (San Antonio)	2,464,583	374,771	73	N.A.[12]		115,107	75

The definitions and concepts underlying the figures in this directory are explained on page 221.
* Not on last year's list.
N.A. Not available.
* Average for the year; see the reference to "employees" on page 222.
** Reflects an extraordinary credit of at least 10%; see the explanations of "net income" and "earnings per share" on page 221.
† Reflects an extraordinary charge of at least 10%; see the explanations of "net income" and "earnings per share" on page 221.
§ Dividends paid by company on its mandatory redeemable preferred stock were subtracted from net income in calculating this figure.
[1] Net sales include all operating revenues and revenues from discontinued operations when they are published. All figures are for the fiscal year ending December 31, 1985, unless otherwise noted. Sales of subsidiaries are included when they are consolidated. All companies on the list must have derived more than 50% of their revenues from non-manufacturing and/or non-mining businesses. Excluded (but eligible for the lists that follow) are companies deriving more than 50% of their revenues solely from banking, life insurance, finance, retailing, transportation, or utilities.

Employees		Net Income as Percent of				Earnings per Share			Growth Rate 1975–85		Total Return to Investors			
		Sales		Stock-holders' Equity							1985		1975–85 Average	
Number	Rank	%	Rank	%	Rank	'85($)	'84($)	'75($)	%	Rank	%	Rank	%	Rank
6,300	53	2.0	43	18.9	16	3.78	1.48	0.92	15.18	28	38.01	39	29.36	16
11,911	41	—		—		(1.42)§	5.61	1.45	—		12.59	66	17.05	57
87,000	4	3.7	31	13.7§	42	4.04	3.30	1.40	11.18	36	69.52	15	17.67	54
44,419*	9	6.4	16	10.8§	50	4.18	4.01	1.60	10.04	41	37.02	41	14.85	61
15,600	30	0.9	61	13.4	43	2.87	2.70	0.95	11.69	35	16.79	60	24.13	34
24,626	19	1.6	49	22.9	10	2.90	2.08	0.36	23.20	16	44.33	32	33.67	12
13,200	35	1.3	52	11.6	47	3.60	3.78	2.70	2.92	54	44.66	31	21.41	42
25,841	18	0.6	66	4.6§	65	0.81	7.15	4.30	(15.37)	63	64.68	20	14.49	63
64,955	6	—		—		(3.12)‡	2.87	1.92	—		2.97	73	4.61	77
26,958	17	—		—		(8.01)	0.01	0.96	—		7.64	70	5.40	76
89,500	3	8.2	12	16.2	25	3.75**	3.35	0.45	23.62	14	(3.93)	81	25.69	28
18,500	27	6.5	15	14.2§	37	3.31	3.57	2.61	2.40	56	79.94	12	19.32	51
18,400	28	1.3	50	11.4§	48	2.32	2.85	1.39	5.22	49	29.80	50	23.56	37
112,000*	1	—		—		N.A.	5.19	3.25	—		—		—	
40,000	11	5.6	20	35.8	3	N.A.	1.35	0.30	—		—		—	
20,000	23	—		—		(1.12)	1.67	1.35	—		13.05	65	14.55	62
N.A.		—		—		N.A.	6.71	0.66	—		94.72	5	29.10	18
10,525	43	0.9	60	15.4	28	2.51	2.05	1.29	6.89	44	61.34	23	18.28	53
27,459	16	4.3	27	12.9	45	2.60	2.86	0.34	22.58	18	41.03	36	28.23	21
58,352	7	10.6	4	21.7	13	3.88	6.86**	0.79	17.25	25	31.21	48	23.76	35
9,100	45	1.9	46	14.8	33	2.35	2.14	0.55	15.61	27	34.01	46	29.38	15
2,700	84	0.1	72	—		(0.72)	(45.67)	0.19‡	—		137.50	2	(0.22)	79
36,942*	12	4.7	25	10.3§	53	2.48	2.56	1.87	2.86	55	39.63	37	17.19	56
68,800	5	5.9	18	15.9	26	1.98	1.74	0.20	25.85	10	(2.30)	80	43.03	7
3,516	74	—		—		N.A.	N.A.	N.A.	—		—		—	

[2] Company was No. 3 among last year's Largest Transportation Companies.
[3] Figures are for fiscal year ended February 28, 1985.
[4] Figures are for fiscal year ended March 31, 1985.
[5] Figures are for fiscal year ended October 31, 1985.
[6] Figures are for fiscal year ended September 30,1985.
[7] Name changed from ARA Services December 28, 1984, when company was acquired by management.
[8] Wholly owned by General Motors (No. 1 on the FORTUNE 500).
[9] Company was acquired by Capital Cities Communications (No. 306 on the FORTUNE 500) January 3, 1986.
[10] Figures are for fiscal year ended June 30, 1985.
[11] Figures are for fiscal year ended May 31, 1985.
[12] Cooperatives provide only net margin figures, which are not comparable with the net income figures in these listings.

The 25 Largest Life Insurance Companies (ranked by assets)

Rank 1985	Rank 1984	Company	Assets[1] ($000)	Premium and Annuity Income[2] ($000)	Rank	Net Investment Income ($000)	Rank
1	1	Prudential (Newark)*	91,139,140	14,331,883	1	5,574,956	2
2	2	Metropolitan (New York)*	76,494,165	7,316,008	2	6,320,569	1
3	3	Equitable Life Assurance (New York)*	47,989,964	2,594,629	9	2,744,543	4
4	4	Aetna Life (Hartford)[7]	37,889,119	3,594,092	6	3,021,503	3
5	5	New York Life (New York)*	27,977,512	3,830,010	5	2,236,879	7
6	6	John Hancock Mutual (Boston)*	26,256,393	2,351,141	12	1,443,128	8
7	7	Travelers (Hartford)[8]	25,571,766	4,270,704	3	2,311,455	6
8	9	Teachers Insurance & Annuity (New York)	23,159,057	2,240,201	14	2,328,272	5
9	8	Connecticut General Life (Bloomfield)[9]	22,245,808	3,922,072	4	1,420,243	9
10	10	Northwestern Mutual (Milwaukee)*	17,897,884	2,417,095	11	1,321,031	10
11	11	Massachusetts Mutual (Springfield)*	15,578,620	2,420,736	10	1,253,008	12
12	12	Bankers Life (Des Moines)*	14,926,963	3,031,677	7	1,255,354	11
13	14	New England Mutual (Boston)*	10,907,567	2,300,488	13	897,301	13
14	13	Mutual of New York (New York)*	10,138,178	1,654,149	16	703,136	15
15	15	Mutual Benefit (Newark)*	9,444,085	1,422,616	20	826,573	14
16	16	Connecticut Mutual (Hartford)*	7,922,994	1,391,561	22	585,903	16
17	17	State Farm Life (Bloomington, Ill.)	6,588,267	1,156,082	28	576,470	17
18	24	IDS Life (Minneapolis)[10]	5,869,833	1,438,520	19	482,623	19
19	23	Executive Life (Los Angeles)	5,597,532	1,365,688	24	574,244	18
20	20	Nationwide Life (Columbus, Ohio)	5,377,375	827,969	34	320,531	24
21	22	Variable Annuity Life (Houston)	5,254,035	695,247	37	477,389	20
22	19	Lincoln National Life (Fort Wayne, Ind.)[11]	5,073,674	1,550,655	17	321,849	23
23	18	Southwestern Life (Philadelphia)[12]	4,893,560	1,349,264	25	172,343	49
24	21	Continental Assurance (Chicago)[13]	4,882,649	1,374,859	23	162,648	50
25	28	Pacific Mutual (Newport Beach, Calif.)*	4,617,346	1,296,282	26	365,044	22

Data for all companies are on the statutory accounting basis required by state insurance regulatory authorities.

• Not on last year's list.

* Indicates a mutual company.

[1] As of December 31, 1985.

[2] Includes premium income from life, accident, and health policies, annuities, and from contributions to deposit administration funds.

[3] After dividends to policyholders and federal income taxes, excluding capital gains and losses. Figures in parentheses indicate a loss.

[4] Face value of all life policies, including variable life insurance, as of December 31, 1985.

[5] Change between December 31, 1984, and December 31, 1985.

Net Gain from Operations[3]			Life Insurance in Force[4]		Increase in Life Insurance in Force[5]				Employees[6]	
	Rank									
($000)	Mutual	Stock	($000)	Rank	($000)	Rank	Percent	Rank	Number	Rank
152,192	4•		560,966,167	1	27,975,946	2	5.3	26	60,706	1
169,662	2		482,799,703	2	18,037,757	3	3.9	30	38,000	3
(229,857)	23		287,822,648	3	39,611,336	1	16.0	11	30,200	4
333,419		1	207,880,770	4	3,244,450	22	1.6	35	16,100	9
187,131	1		178,884,038	5	(300,948)	44	—		19,079	5
155,926	3		158,973,210	6	312,618	36	0.2	37	19,037	7
317,158		3	144,145	47	6,938	40	—		45,937	2
118,008		6	15,272,355	41	1,612,612	29	11.8	18	2,548	35
327,343		2	113,941,139	10	3,913,799	20	3.6	31	12,104	11
14,318	12		121,042,513	9	13,478,023	8	12.5	16	7,635	17
79,881	6		68,635,562	12	3,218,955	23	4.9	29	8,000	16
108,190	5		65,780,844	13	6,359,449	15	10.7	21	8,820	15
(11,810)	21		52,185,874	21	6,206,645	18	13.5	14	9,036	13
(1,492)	19		51,418,008	22	55,201	39	0.1	38	8,960	14
44,247	7		50,761,019	24	(2,474,870)	47	—		4,197	26
28,470	9		44,868,281	26	991,302	32	2.3	34	6,323	20
63,166		12	92,806,767	11	9,946,938	11	12.0	17	18,141	8
23,351		18	16,604,561	40	2,875,252	25	20.9	7	5,611	22
3,255		21	34,971,210	28	7,066,264	14	25.3	5	600	44
58,131		13	16,810,494	39	463,799	34	2.8	33	7,008	18
(10,122)		25	3,664	48	(309)	42	—		1,129	42
196,355		4	129,942,632	8	15,717,525	4	13.8	13	2,626	34
32,618		15	62,252,981	15	(6,004,765)	48	—		1,977	39
71,993		10	60,213,247	18	13,487,923	7	28.9	4	N.A.	
14,597	11		26,953,579	31	3,925	41	17.0	9	2,525	36

[6] Includes home office, field force, and full-time agents.
[7] Wholly owned by Aetna Life & Casualty (No. 3 on Diversified Financial list).
[8] Wholly owned by Travelers Corp. (No. 7 on Diversified Financial list).
[9] Wholly owned by CIGNA (No. 6 on Diversified Financial list).
[10] Wholly owned by American Express (No. 2 on Diversified Financial list).
[11] Wholly owned by Lincoln National (No. 15 on Diversified Financial list).
[12] Wholly owned by Tenneco (No. 18 on the FORTUNE 500).
[13] Wholly owned by Loews (No. 10 on Diversified Financial list).

The 25 Largest Commercial Banking Companies (ranked by assets)

Rank '85	Rank '84	Company	Assets[1] ($000)	Deposits ($000)	Deposits Rank	Loans[2] ($000)	Loans Rank	Employees Number	Employees Rank
1	1	Citicorp (New York)	173,597,000	104,959,000	1	115,264,000	1	81,300	2
2	2	BankAmerica Corp. (San Francisco)	118,541,125	94,210,950	2	82,742,252	2	83,299	1
3	3	Chase Manhattan Corp. (New York)	87,685,442	61,353,049	3	61,022,855	3	46,450	3
4	4	Manufacturers Hanover Corp. (New York)	76,525,769	46,261,146	4	57,652,292	4	32,218	5
5	5	J. P. Morgan & Co. (New York)	69,375,000	39,845,000	5	36,278,000	7	13,506	15
6	6	Chemical New York Corp.	56,990,174	34,505,315	7	38,528,208	5	19,691	8
7	7	Security Pacific Corp. (Los Angeles)	53,503,239	32,873,391	8	36,510,012	6	30,358*	6
8	9	Bankers Trust New York Corp.	50,581,041	28,723,505	9	24,793,354	9	10,543	22
9	8	First Interstate Bancorp (Los Angeles)	48,991,038	35,554,486	6	32,283,751	8	34,303*	4
10	10	First Chicago Corp.	38,892,506	27,147,535	10	23,758,725	11	14,276	12
11	11	Mellon Bank Corp. (Pittsburgh)	33,406,195	18,582,625	13	21,957,190	12	15,807*	10
12	12	Continental Illinois Corp. (Chicago)	30,528,000	17,759,000	14	20,054,000	13	9,334	27
13	13	Wells Fargo & Co. (San Francisco)	29,429,394	19,501,300	11	24,196,653	10	14,000	14
14	16	Bank of Boston Corp.	28,296,340	19,214,058	12	19,307,661	14	20,000	7
15	14	First Bank System (Minneapolis)	25,484,355	16,039,194	18	14,254,800	19	9,575*	26
16	17	Marine Midland Bank (Buffalo)[3]	23,385,612	16,593,427	17	15,159,385	15	11,867*	19
17	19	RepublicBank Corp. (Dallas)	23,205,593	15,764,377	19	14,941,137	17	8,686	32
18	22	MCorp (Dallas)	22,586,271	17,583,421	15	15,079,738	16	11,694	21
19	18	InterFirst Corp. (Dallas)	22,071,000	17,504,000	16	14,826,000	18	9,287	28
20	23	Irving Bank Corp. (New York)	21,650,661	14,026,275	25	12,564,803	22	9,700	25
21	20	Norwest Corp. (Minneapolis)	21,418,600	14,336,800	23	13,143,700	20	15,300	11
22	21	Texas Commerce Bancshares (Houston)	20,076,000	14,612,000	22	13,087,000	21	8,266*	37
23	25	NCNB Corp. (Charlotte, N.C.)	19,754,317	13,950,398	26	11,948,106	25	9,981	24
24	37	SunTrust Banks (Atlanta)[4]	19,405,563	14,728,105	21	10,986,141	28	15,873	9
25	15	Crocker National Corp. (San Francisco)[5]	19,208,000	14,981,000	20	11,956,000	24	12,000	17

N.A. Not available.

* Average for the year; see the reference to "employees" on page 222.

** Reflects an extraordinary credit of at least 10%; see the explanations of "net income" and "earnings per share" on page 221.

§ Dividends paid by company on its mandatory redeemable preferred stock were subtracted from net income in calculating this figure.

[1] As of December 31, 1985.

Net Income ($000)	Rank	Stockholders' Equity ($000)	Rank	Net Income as Percent of Equity %	Rank	Earnings per Share '85($)	'84($)	'75($)	Growth Rate: 1975–85 %	Rank	Total Return to Investors 1985 %	Rank	1975–85 Average %	Rank
998,000	1	7,765,000	1	12.8§	53	7.12	6.45	2.83	9.67	51	33.97	66	10.91	82
(337,215)	100	4,547,057	2	—		(2.68)	1.77	2.19	—		(8.10)	91	2.72	87
564,818	3	4,397,136	3	12.7§	54	6.39	4.50	2.71	8.96	60	62.61	19	18.17	64
407,475	4	3,547,389	5	11.5	69	8.38	7.12	4.80	5.73	75	39.79	59	13.05	79
705,400	2	4,392,000	4	16.1	15	7.81	6.07	2.38	12.62	30	71.10	11	14.81	75
390,187	5	2,819,982	6	13.8	38	7.33	6.48	2.95	9.52	52	40.47	55	21.91	47
322,847	7	2,434,333	9	13.3	48	4.35	3.96	1.10	14.77	19	28.83	75	25.53	27
371,248	6	2,495,363	8	14.9	26	5.39	4.76	1.45	13.99	21	39.98	58	25.66	25
313,058	8	2,514,112	7	12.5	56	6.84	6.16	2.13	12.36	31	29.16	74	22.58	42
168,999	16	2,090,044	10	8.1	89	2.84	1.19	2.72	0.43	86	46.64	40	11.48	81
201,695	9	1,637,182	12	11.7§	65	7.44	5.64	3.13	9.06	57	17.49	82	13.93	77
151,000**	20	1,872,000	11	8.1	90	0.53**	(26.99)	3.24	(16.57)	91	71.74	10	(0.48)	89
190,034	11	1,457,960	14	13.0	51	8.30	6.85	2.83	11.36	38	40.27	57	21.80	49
173,797	14	1,474,587	13	11.8	63	8.46	8.35	2.40	13.43	26	65.16	17	22.91	40
166,781	18	1,239,678	16	13.5	42	5.68	4.15	2.09	10.51	43	65,31	16	13.34	78
125,119	27	1,193,394	19	10.5	75	6.06	5.01	1.19	17.68	13	39.10	62	19.80	56
140,179	21	1,220,328	17	11.5	68	4.61	4.66	2.23	7.54	71	26.79	78	12.54	80
132,374	22	1,279,998	15	10.3	76	3.02	3.56	1.24	9.35	53	4.36	87	14.12	76
61,100	50	1,181,000	20	5.2	95	0.91	1.76	1.40	(4.22)	88	7.19	86	0.75	88
115,979	32	955,926	30	12.1	61	6.14	5.11	2.57	9.10	56	44.89	46	23.51	36
107,600	34	1,219,300	18	8.8	84	3.20	1.90	2.42	2.81	81	45.50	45	9.63	83
53,000	59	1,180,000	21	4.5	97	1.62	5.64	1.54	0.48	85	(24.76)	93	8.56	85
164,489	19	1,039,116	26	15.8	17	4.60	4.07	1.09	15.49	15	30.57	72	22.22	44
166,831	17	1,077,618	24	15.5	21	3.34	2.68	0.53	20.27	8	43.35	50	24.02	34
38,000**	78	1,163,000	23	3.3	99	N.A.	(15.93)	3.63	—		—		—	

[2] Net of unearned discount and loan loss reserve. Figure includes lease financing.
[3] Company is 51% owned by the Hongkong & Shanghai Banking Corp. (No 22 among last year's Largest Commercial Banking Companies Outside the U.S.).
[4] Company was formed by the merger of Sun Banks (1984 rank: 37) and Trust Co. of Georgia (1984 rank: 62) July 1, 1985.
[5] Wholly owned by Midland Bank (No. 18 among last year's Largest Commercial Banking Companies Outside the U.S.).

The 50 Largest International Banks*

The top 50** bank holding companies in the world are listed according to the size of their assets. Also shown are each bank's total deposits and its respective ranking (in parentheses) as well as the total capital and pretax earnings, along with its ranking (again in parentheses) in those categories. For any bank to be ranked in deposits, capital or earnings, the bank must first be among the top 50 in assets. Those cases where bank figures were not available or could not be confirmed for accuracy are indicated by dashes.

Rank 1984	Rank 1985	Name of Bank	Assets (US $ millions) 1985	Assets (US $ millions) 1984	Deposits	Capital	Pretax Earnings
1	1	Citicorp / United States	$167,201	$142,732	$104,959(4)	$7,765(1)	$1,716(1)
2	2	Dai-Ichi Kangyo Bank[1] / Japan	157,614	118,721	124,134(1)	3,126(18)	642(11)[2]
3	3	Fuji Bank[1,3] / Japan	142,088	144,768	109,285(2)	3,206(17)	693(10)
5	4	Sumitomo Bank[1] / Japan	135,349	112,380	108,085(3)	3,326(14)	758(9)[2]
6	5	Mitsubishi Bank[1] / Japan	132,901	110,365	102,391(5)	3,253(16)	611(12)[2]
7	6	Sanwa Bank[1] / Japan	122,973	98,940	9,643(7)	2,731(22)	607(13)[2]
8	7	Banque Nationale de Paris / France	120,859	98,939	100,136(6)	2,396(32)	491(23)
9	8	Caisse Nationale de Credit Agricole / France	120,672	92,381	83,178(14)	5,136(2)	— —
4	9	BankAmerica Corp. / United States	114,751	113,710	94,211(8)	4,547(4)	−427(187)
10	10	Credit Lyonnais / France	109,445	90,445	93,490(10)	1,274(67)	428(30)
13	11	Norinchukin Bank[1,3,4] / Japan	106,724	82,842	94,200(9)	506(156)	— —
12	12	National Westminster Bank / United Kingdom	103,498	83,445	88,531(12)	4,263(8)	1,148(4)
15	13	Industrial Bank of Japan[1,5] / Japan	102,741	80,074	89,372(11)	2,146(35)	386(35)
11	14	Societe Generale / France	95,864	87,086	80,788(15)	1,944(37)	367(40)
18	15	Deutsche Bank[3] / West Germany	93,855	73,697	85,849(13)	3,740(9)	1,017(5)
16	16	Barclays / United Kingdom	93,108	78,265	78,732(16)	4,724(3)	1,219(3)

Rank	Bank	Country						Prior
17	Tokai Bank[1]	Japan	90,397	75,858	73,665(17)	1,843(40)	365(41)	17
18	Mitsui Bank[1]	Japan	88,476	73,383	71,168(19)	1,653(47)	326(44)	19
19	Chase Manhattan Corp.	United States	84,865	81,632	61,353(27)	4,459(6)	898(7)	14
20	Midland Bank	United Kingdom	82,941	71,873	72,925(18)	2,637(24)	501(19)	21
21	Mitsubishi Trust and Banking Corp.[1]	Japan	80,546	61,484	70,780(20)	1,663(46)	283(56)	25
22	Sumitomo Trust and Banking Co.[1,3,4]	Japan	79,180	57,860	70,044(22)	1,705(43)	295(51)	29
23	Long-Term Credit Bank of Japan[1,3,4]	Japan	78,859	65,245	67,879(23)	1,618(51)	289(54)	23
24	Bank of Tokyo[1,3,4]	Japan	78,172	65,600	62,182(24)	1,632(49)	401(33)	22
25	Dresdner Bank	West Germany	74,890	55,490	70,662(21)	2,197(34)	379(38)	31
26	Taiyo Kobe Bank[1,3,4]	Japan	74,477	58,516	58,309(29)	1,349(62)	219(69)	28
27	Manufacturers Hanover Corp.	United States	74,334	73,055	46,261(41)	3,547(11)	597(14)	20
28	Mitsui Trust & Banking Co.[1,3]	Japan	72,901	54,572	62,005(25)	1,455(59)	— —	33
29	Cie. Financiere de Paribas	France	71,586	56,163	52,438(36)	3,389(13)	523(16)	30
30	Hongkong and Shanghai Banking Corp.	Hongkong	68,833	59,627	61,606(26)	2,802(21)	— —	27
31	J. P. Morgan & Co.	United States	67,611	61,214	39,845(50)	4,392(7)	916(6)	26
32	Royal Bank of Canada[6]	Canada	67,227	64,417	61,127(28)	2,975(19)	504(17)	24
33	Daiwa Bank[1,3,4]	Japan	66,826	51,749	57,709(30)	1,005(94)	182(85)	34
34	Union Bank of Switzerland[3,4]	Switzerland	66,088	50,659	56,588(31)	3,704(10)	496(21)	36
35	Yasuda Trust and Banking Co.[1,3,4]	Japan	62,660	46,104	53,362(33)	1,179(77)	152(97)	40
36	Lloyds Bank	United Kingdom	62,566	51,446	56,034(32)	3,310(15)	801(8)	35
37	Swiss Bank Corp.[3]	Switzerland	60,589	46,018	53,007(34)	3,498(12)	419(31)	42
38	Banco do Brasil[3,4]	Brazil	58,241	48,778	22,801(83)	4,506(5)	1,557(2)	39
39	Bank of Montreal[6]	Canada	57,212	55,446	52,233(37)	2,525(26)	315(46)	32
40	Westdeutsche Landesbank	West Germany	56,514	45,079	52,594(35)	1,619(50)	64(151)	43

The 50 Largest International Banks (concluded)

Rank 1984	Rank 1985	Name of Bank	Assets (US $ millions) 1985	Assets (US $ millions) 1984	Deposits	Capital	Pretax Earnings
41	41	Banca Nazionale del Lavoro[3,4] Italy	56,129	46,068	46,123(42)	1,700(44)	282(57)
37	42	Chemical New York Corp. United States	54,381	49,808	34,505(58)	2,820(20)	526(15)
53	43	Commerzbank West Germany	54,000	38,616	52,062(38)	1,516(55)	262(58)
51	44	Bayerische Vereinsbank West Germany	52,679	39,560	49,414(39)	1,170(79)	213(71)
38	45	Canadian Imperial Bank of Commerce[6] Canada	52,421	49,477	47,624(40)	2,452(30)	394(34)
44	46	Security Pacific Corp. United States	52,285	44,835	32,873(62)	2,439(31)	495(22)
48	47	Algemene Bank Nederland Netherlands	50,277	41,490	42,948(47)	1,461(57)	258(59)
49	48	Nippon Credit Bank[1,3,4] Japan	49,832	40,594	43,247(45)	1,011(93)	199(75)
47	49	Bankers Trust New York Corp. United States	48,074	42,645	28,724(71)	2,495(28)	488(24)
45	50	First Interstate Bancorp United States	47,996	44,095	35,554(55)	2,514(27)	380(37)

* In order to compile the global banking rankings, *Institutional Investor* first asked more than 500 of the world's leading bank holding companies to provide us with their assets, deposits, capital and pretax earnings in local currencies as of year-end (unless otherwise noted) 1984 and 1985. For the sake of comparability, we then converted the local currencies into U.S. dollars at year-end rates for all those on calendar years. For those not on calendar years, all of which are noted in the tables, the conversion rates used are those prevailing at the end of each bank's fiscal year. The conversion figures were provided by the money desk of a major U.S. bank.

It should be noted that the banks were asked to report consolidated figures for all other banks in which they have an interest of 50 percent or more. Those that chose not to provide consolidated figures are noted. The banks were also asked if their figures included recent mergers and acquisitions; those that said they did not are also noted. Figures reflect consolidated bank holding company interests only; industrial and other nonbank holdings are not included.

Banks were asked to report their figures published in these tables using the following definitions:

Total assets: Exclude contra accounts where contra accounts are defined as acceptances, bonds or other securities held for customers, letters of credit, guarantees, etc.

Total deposits: Do not include treasury operations.

Capital: Include funds supplied by shareholders, including permanent preferred stock, share capital, retained earnings or undistributed profits and contingent type reserves. Exclude reserves for possible loan losses, subordinated debt and redeemable preferred stock.

Pretax earnings: Include earnings before taxes and extraordinary items.

** The table reproduced here includes only the top 50 of the top 200 banks in assets listed in the *Institutional Investor*.

[1] September 30, 1985, 1984.

[2] Earnings not consolidated.

[3] Figures do not include all subsidiaries owned 50 percent or more.

[4] Not adjusted for all mergers and acquisitions.

[5] Subsidiaries' figures calculated on a March 31, 1985, 1984 basis.

[6] October 31, 1985, 1984.

· Source: *Institutional Investor*, June 1986.

The 100 Largest Brokerage Houses*

Rank 1986	Name of Firm	Total Capital	Equity Capital	Subordinated Debt	"Excess" Net Capital	Number of Employees	Number of Offices	Number of Registered Representatives
1	Salomon Brothers	$2,315,287,716	$1,647,065,716	$ 668,222,000	$474,878,396	4,290	8	926
2	Shearson Lehman Brothers	2,251,000,000	1,237,000,000	1,014,000,000	239,776,000	21,018	357	5,618
3	Merrill Lynch, Pierce, Fenner & Smith	2,169,521,000	1,619,521,000	550,000,000	400,321,000	32,500	525	10,500
4	Prudential-Bache Securities	1,259,260,000	1,016,318,000	242,942,000	314,035,000	13,147	328	5,330
5	Goldman, Sachs & Co.	1,201,000,000[1]	868,000,000	333,000,000	699,674,500	4,516	16	1,040
6	First Boston Corp.	1,042,200,000	703,800,000	338,400,000[2]	303,600,000	3,418	20	1,081
7	Drexel Burnham Lambert	958,250,000	728,458,000	229,792,000	135,448,000	7,679	60	2,088[3]
8	Dean Witter Reynolds	884,030,000	609,030,000	275,000,000	51,497,000	16,314	684	7,033
9	Bear, Stearns & Co.	800,000,000	581,500,000	218,500,000	153,276,000	4,700	12	1,300
10	E.F. Hutton & Co.	755,998,000	586,353,000	169,645,000	38,886,000	16,665	469	7,246
11	Paine Webber	532,188,322	359,866,022	172,322,300	67,439,741	11,721	275	3,917
12	Donaldson, Lufkin & Jenrette	479,000,000	213,000,000	266,000,000	33,377,000	2,882	14	500
13	Morgan Stanley & Co.	454,609,000	369,609,000	85,000,000	64,717,000	3,947	6	1,158
14	Stephens	376,669,499	376,669,499	—	90,391,207	239	1	132
15	Kidder, Peabody, & Co.	363,210,000[4]	245,308,000	117,902,000	72,618,000	6,047	74	2,098
16	Shelby Cullom Davis & Co.	281,437,541	281,437,541	—	208,424,027	22	2	4
17	Smith Barney, Harris Upham & Co.	275,836,000	195,908,000	79,928,000	73,071,000	5,500	97	2,000
18	Allen & Co.	250,387,387	250,387,387	—	—	NA	1	NA
19	Thomson McKinnon Securities	250,210,000	200,210,000	50,000,000	33,736,000	4,855	179	2,403
20	Spear, Leeds & Kellogg	213,000,000	153,000,000	60,000,000	29,287,000	1,250	14	140
21	A. G. Edwards & Sons	195,752,000	195,752,000	—	62,958,000	4,906	274	2,513
22	Van Kampen Merritt	184,352,031	184,352,031	—	24,684,312	321	10	16
23	L. F. Rothschild, Unterberg, Towbin	157,020,000	133,995,000	23,025,000	24,889,000	1,700	10	584
24	John Nuveen & Co.	153,521,000	153,521,000	—	49,083,000	525	15	188
25	Oppenheimer & Co.	144,079,433	79,494,808	64,584,625	25,274,621	1,787	9	544
26	Neuberger & Berman	127,041,087	127,041,087	—	65,712,449	398	1	72
27	UBS Securities	110,518,110	60,518,110	50,000,000	68,065,875	112	1	40
28	Jefferies Group	100,126,000	70,126,000	30,000,000	57,485,000	411	7	156
29	Cowen & Co.	97,489,468	88,529,468	8,960,000	40,887,300	954	16	452
30	Charles Schwab & Co.	93,560,840	43,385,840	50,175,000	21,024,464	1,538	90	675
31	Advest Group	91,864,000	64,228,000	27,636,000	17,714,000	1,726	78	728
32	Dillon, Read & Co.	91,427,000	88,927,000	2,500,000	19,465,000	525	4	218
33	Nomura Securities International	80,347,851	80,347,851	—	29,440,565	220	5	69
34	Prescott, Ball & Turben	79,026,992	69,026,992	10,000,000	14,223,762	1,123	48	356
35	M. A. Schapiro & Co.	77,930,000	77,930,000	—	71,830,000	25	1	5
36	Wertheim & Co. Inc.	77,342,415	70,421,415	6,921,000	26,256,107	583	7	177

The 100 Largest Brokerage Houses (concluded)

Rank 1986	Name of Firm	Total Capital	Equity Capital	Subordinated Debt	Excess Net Capital	Number of Employees	Number of Offices	Number of Registered Representatives
37	Allen & Co. Inc.	75,820,000*	72,320,000	3,500,000	5,455,000	183	2	70
38	Janney Montgomery Scott	74,251,296	74,251,296	—	20,375,784	954	35	477
39	Glickenhaus & Co.	70,361,000	70,361,000	—	8,173,680	108	4	54
40	Stern Brothers & Co.	70,352,000	70,352,000	—	39,549,000	86	7	28
41	Brown Brothers Harriman & Co.	70,300,478	70,300,478	—	—	1,172	9	255
42	Lazard Freres & Co.	70,000,000	70,000,000	—	42,900,000	463	1	86
43	Daiwa Securities America	66,537,000	66,537,000	—	42,841,000	120	3	75
44	Gruss Partners	64,816,854	64,816,854	—	22,735,673	11	1	8
45	Alex. Brown & Sons	64,164,902	50,164,902	14,000,000	26,999,649	1,192	19	320
46	Nikko Securities Co.	63,215,016	63,215,016	—	28,896,924	120	4	45
47	Fidelity Brokerage Services	63,138,000	63,138,000	—	23,107,000	564	28	187
48	Bateman Eichler, Hill Richards	58,318,077	37,058,260	21,259,817	2,514,942	841	33	416
49	Quick & Reilly Group	54,873,038	54,288,038	585,000	23,153,158	469	48	119
50	Legg Mason	54,560,000	52,591,000	1,969,000	7,294,500	1,000	38	410
51	Kaufmann, Alsberg & Co.	53,721,783	53,721,783	—	28,794,259	30	1	3
52	Mabon, Nugent & Co.	53,317,559	53,317,559	—	10,335,862	500	4	237
53	Ziegler Co.	50,306,000	50,306,000	—	16,673,000	350	32	55
54	Piper, Jaffray & Hopwood	50,081,873	47,748,540	2,333,333	4,447,665	1,539	523	616
55	S. D. Securities	49,060,000	49,060,000	—	38,620,000	12	1	4
56	Gruntal & Co. (Consolidated)	48,338,000	39,138,000	9,200,000	12,541,000	1,341	34	625
57	Moseley, Hallgarten, Estabrook & Weeden	47,592,000	29,742,000	17,850,000	11,318,000	902	32	330
58	Interstate Securities Corp.	46,660,204	43,660,204	3,000,000	7,800,988	940	32	556
59	Blunt Ellis & Loewi	44,827,248	24,327,248	20,500,000	3,523,932	1,120	74	500
60	J.C. Bradford & Co.	44,788,355	42,788,355	2,000,000	7,563,740	928	48	430
61	Edward D. Jones & Co.	43,700,000	31,220,000	12,480,000	20,271,000	3,131	914	968
62	McMahan & Co.	42,867,000	40,643,000	2,224,000	11,300,000	35	1	NA
63	Dain Bosworth	42,748,529	41,411,029	1,337,500	1,255,498	1,243	41	516
64	Keefe, Bruyette & Woods	42,079,795	38,742,277	3,337,518	25,284,535	136	4	64
65	Ohio Co.	40,668,474	40,668,474	—	10,434,823	555	48	189
66	Boettcher & Co.	39,555,357	39,555,357	—	9,592,256	919	24	550
67	Deutsche Bank Capital Corp.	39,086,166	39,086,166	—	15,993,658	111	1	38
68	Carl Marks & Co.	38,942,701	38,942,701	—	5,672,594	140	1	39

Rank	Firm							
69	Arnold & S. Bleichroeder	38,136,796	35,136,796	3,000,000	18,693,817	170	1	32
70	Ryan, Beck & Co.	35,081,892	35,081,892	—	18,989,997	165	2	63
71	William Blair & Co.	35,000,000	35,000,000	—	11,306,000	366	2	201
72	Hambrecht & Quist	33,928,472[5]	33,928,472	—	10,961,000	235	6	59
73	Tucker, Anthony & R. L. Day	33,767,875	30,987,875	2,780,000	6,528,730	1,222	40	709
74	Easton & Co.	33,550,000	30,850,000	2,700,000	18,640,000	17	2	5
75	Robert W. Baird & Co.	32,756,000	32,756,000	—	15,880,000	630	32	256
76	Eppler, Guerin & Turner	31,892,557	31,892,557	—	22,012,123	468	30	246
77	McDonald & Co. Securities	31,601,879	31,601,879	—	8,068,388	465	22	137
78	Wedbush, Noble, Cooke	31,362,000	30,895,000	467,000	12,940,000	600	21	250
79	Clayton Brown & Associates	31,331,000	31,331,000	—	NA	164	5	73
80	Rothschild Inc.	30,945,517	16,945,517	14,000,000	12,815,226	142	1	34
81	Morgan, Keegan & Co.	30,538,901	30,538,901	—	14,101,960	508	15	208
82	Crowell, Weedon & Co.	29,366,795	29,366,795	—	6,333,511	358	10	167
83	Montgomery Securities	28,665,287	28,665,287	—	14,399,651	308	1	125
84	Furman Selz Mager Dietz & Birney	28,384,000	28,384,000	—	13,916,000	170	2	99
85	Bernard L. Madoff	26,034,884	26,034,884	—	14,584,067	55	1	10
86	Rauscher Pierce Refsnes	25,671,177	21,377,177	4,294,000	1,954,946	894	26	337
87	MKI Securities Corp.	24,617,776	13,017,776	11,600,000	8,225,736	338	1	119
88	Yamaichi International (America)	23,853,000	23,853,000	—	1,058,000	97	3	18
89	Sanford C. Bernstein & Co.	23,633,395	19,188,856	4,444,539	11,268,655	261	1	31
90	Wheat, First Securities	23,454,853	20,954,853	2,500,000	6,159,604	1,084	56	592
91	Herzog, Heine, Geduld	22,108,935	18,494,032	3,614,903	4,801,248	340	3	58
92	Butcher & Singer	21,564,759	15,599,259	5,965,500	6,020,369	808	33	353
93	Raymond, James & Associates	21,471,236	21,471,236	—	5,745,451	786	36	379
94	Ernst & Co.	20,996,000	20,996,000	—	5,257,924	196	4	44
95	Franklin Distributors	20,832,602	20,832,602	—	10,098,142	300	11	145
96	J. J. B. Hilliard, W. L. Lyons	20,575,693	17,853,292	2,722,401	7,520,900	598	42	280
97	Eberstadt Fleming	20,328,000	20,328,000	—	8,065,000	202	4	16
98	First Manhattan Co.	19,000,000	19,000,000	—	11,200,000	210	2	67
99	Miller Tabak Hirsch & Co.	18,943,000	17,615,000	1,328,000	10,227,000	50	1	26
100	Stifel, Nicolaus & Co.	18,771,722	18,771,722	—	5,094,682	725	36	296[3]

* Based on broker-dealer capital
[1] As of 11/29/85
[2] Long-term debt
[3] Income-producing only
[4] As of 11/30/85
[5] As of 9/30/85

Source: Ranking America's Biggest Brokers, *Institutional Investor*, April 1986.

America's Most and Least Admired Corporations*

The most admired

IBM remains the most admired large U.S. corporation, though its score for eight attributes is down from last year's 8.44. Coca-Cola's score, 8.34 last year, dropped sharply.

RANK	COMPANY	INDUSTRY GROUP	SCORE
1	IBM	Office equipment, computers	8.31
2	3M	Precision instruments	8.12
3	Dow Jones	Publishing, printing	8.07
4	Coca-Cola	Beverages	7.98
5	Merck	Pharmaceuticals	7.91
6	Boeing	Aerospace	7.90
7	Rubbermaid	Rubber, plastic products	7.80
8	Procter & Gamble	Soaps, cosmetics	7.79
9	Exxon	Petroleum refining	7.72
10	J.P. Morgan	Commercial banking	7.71

The least admired

Financial Corp. of America is the least admired of 292 companies. New to the least admired list are LTV, Control Data, Amax, BankAmerica, and Bethlehem Steel.

RANK	COMPANY	INDUSTRY GROUP	SCORE
292	Financial Corp. of America	Diversified financial	3.23
291	LTV	Metal manufacturing	3.66
290	Pan Am	Transportation	3.71
289	American Motors	Motor vehicles and parts	3.75
288	Manville .	Glass, building materials	3.79
287	Control Data	Office equipment, computers	3.89
286	Amax	Mining, crude-oil production	3.90
285	BankAmerica	Commercial banking	4.09
284	Crown Zellerbach	Forest products	4.23
283	Bethlehem Steel	Metal manufacturing	4.25

*To rank corporate reputations, FORTUNE polled 8,000 executives, outside directors, and financial analysts. The response was good: about 50%. Those surveyed were asked to rate the ten largest companies in their own industry (or, for analysts, the industry they follow) on eight key attributes of reputation: quality of management; quality of products or services; innovativeness; long-term investment value; financial soundness; ability to attract, develop, and keep talented people; community and environmental responsibility; and use of corporate assets. Ratings are on a scale of 0 (poor) to 10 (excellent).

INDUSTRIAL PRODUCTION—MAJOR MARKET GROUPS AND SELECTED MANUFACTURES

[1977=100; monthly data seasonally adjusted]

	Products										Materials	
	Final products							Intermediate products				
Period	Total	Consumer goods			Equipment			Total	Con-struction supplies	Busi-ness sup-plies	Total	Energy
		Total	Durable goods	Nondura-ble goods	Total ¹	Business	Defense and space equip-ment					
1977 proportion	*44.77*	*25.52*	*6.89*	*18.63*	*19.25*	*14.34*	*3.67*	*12.94*	*5.95*	*6.99*	*42.28*	*11.69*
1978	106.9	104.3	103.7	104.5	110.3	112.2	101.2	106.9	106.9	106.9	105.9	101.1
1979	111.0	103.9	99.9	105.4	120.4	124.7	105.6	110.8	108.7	112.7	110.3	104.1
1980	112.2	102.7	88.4	108.1	124.7	125.1	115.4	106.9	100.6	112.3	105.3	105.5
1981	115.2	104.1	89.7	109.3	129.9	127.6	119.8	107.3	98.6	114.7	107.7	104.7
1982	109.5	101.4	82.9	108.3	120.2	113.6	133.0	101.7	88.3	113.1	96.7	101.2
1983	114.7	109.3	98.5	113.3	121.7	115.4	143.1	111.2	100.6	120.3	102.8	98.4
1984	127.8	118.2	112.6	120.2	140.5	134.9	157.9	124.9	114.0	134.2	114.6	104.0
1985	132.0	120.7	112.9	123.6	147.0	141.2	173.6	130.6	118.9	140.5	114.7	104.4
1985: June	131.6	120.4	112.0	123.5	146.6	140.7	173.4	131.4	119.2	141.7	114.3	105.1
July	131.8	120.1	111.3	123.4	147.3	141.3	173.9	130.7	119.4	140.3	113.8	103.5
Aug	133.3	121.5	114.0	124.2	149.0	143.0	175.5	132.0	121.5	140.9	114.5	102.7
Sept	133.3	121.8	112.9	125.1	148.6	142.2	177.5	132.3	121.3	141.7	114.2	103.4
Oct	131.9	120.8	111.4	124.3	146.6	139.6	178.7	131.5	120.0	141.2	114.2	104.2
Nov	133.7	122.7	115.5	125.4	148.3	141.7	180.7	132.7	120.9	142.7	114.3	102.5
Dec	134.4	124.2	116.8	127.0	147.9	141.4	180.7	132.9	120.7	143.3	115.9	105.8
1986: Jan	134.4	123.9	116.6	126.5	148.4	142.9	179.3	134.4	124.0	143.2	116.2	104.1
Feb	132.8	123.2	116.3	125.7	145.5	141.1	176.7	134.1	123.5	143.1	115.4	103.9
Mar ʳ	131.5	122.5	113.0	126.0	143.4	139.1	178.5	134.1	123.5	143.0	114.0	102.7
Apr ʳ	132.6	124.4	116.2	127.5	143.5	140.3	178.8	135.0	124.2	144.1	114.4	102.9
May ʳ	131.9	123.9	113.4	127.8	142.6	139.6	179.5	134.9	124.3	143.9	113.9	102.6
June ᵖ	131.2	123.7	113.5	127.5	141.1	138.0	179.7	134.0	123.0	......	113.4	102.0

¹ Includes rigs and prefabs, not shown separately.

[1977=100; monthly data seasonally adjusted]

| | Durable manufactures | | | | | | | | Nondurable manufactures | | | |
| Period | Primary metals | | Fabri-cated metal products | Non-electrical machin-ery | Electrical machin-ery | Transportation equipment | | Lumber and products | Appar-el prod-ucts | Print-ing and pub-lishing | Chemi-cals and prod-ucts | Foods |
	Total	Iron and steel				Total	Motor vehicles and parts					
1977 proportion	*5.33*	*3.49*	*6.46*	*9.54*	*7.15*	*9.13*	*5.25*	*2.30*	*2.79*	*4.54*	*8.05*	*7.96*
1978	107.0	107.5	105.7	111.7	112.9	106.3	104.6	102.4	103.1	107.8	106.8	104.3
1979	108.5	108.0	109.4	122.6	125.7	108.3	95.9	102.0	98.3	112.7	111.4	106.7
1980	90.4	86.3	101.8	123.3	130.3	96.9	71.1	92.9	97.3	115.1	106.4	111.4
1981	95.0	92.5	101.6	129.8	134.1	95.1	71.6	90.1	96.1	118.6	112.6	113.7
1982	65.8	57.5	86.6	115.6	128.4	87.6	66.8	82.8	87.3	120.2	103.8	114.9
1983	73.0	66.1	89.1	118.3	143.8	99.2	85.8	100.2	95.3	129.8	114.0	120.4
1984	82.4	73.5	102.8	142.0	172.4	113.6	105.6	109.1	102.8	147.9	121.7	127.1
1985	80.6	70.6	107.9	146.4	169.3	123.2	112.8	112.9	101.8	155.2	127.1	131.0
1985: June	78.3	67.6	107.4	145.6	169.5	121.8	110.5	113.5	99.2	156.7	126.4	131.8
July	79.0	68.7	107.3	147.5	165.7	123.7	112.8	113.0	100.6	154.3	126.4	132.2
Aug	82.0	71.6	107.8	149.2	166.1	126.8	116.8	114.8	100.4	156.3	128.2	132.6
Sept	80.3	69.7	107.5	146.5	165.1	126.2	115.3	115.9	101.8	156.2	129.0	132.5
Oct	83.1	74.4	108.4	143.0	165.1	124.5	111.7	116.5	102.6	157.0	127.9	130.7
Nov	83.6	75.3	107.9	145.6	168.9	126.5	114.5	115.6	103.9	159.0	128.0	131.4
Dec	81.7	72.0	108.8	146.0	171.9	126.8	115.4	116.5	105.0	158.4	128.5	132.6
1986: Jan	84.9	75.5	109.3	146.2	167.9	128.9	117.8	119.9	105.8	158.9	130.5	133.2
Feb	80.7	69.9	109.4	144.6	165.5	128.1	117.8	118.2	103.6	155.4	130.9	133.8
Mar ʳ	77.4	64.9	108.5	143.2	165.6	124.3	110.4	118.5	104.0	158.1	131.1	133.0
Apr ʳ	78.1	65.6	108.6	141.6	167.1	127.9	114.8	119.0	104.3	160.0	132.0	134.0
May ʳ	76.9	63.4	107.8	142.5	164.4	125.6	110.8	......	103.6	161.1	132.0	135.2
June ᵖ	72.2	......	107.2	141.5	163.6	126.8	112.8	......	......	160.5	......	......

Source: Board of Governors of the Federal Reserve System.

Source: *Economic Indicators*, Council of Economic Advisers.

America's Top 100 Growth Companies (above $25 million sales)

Rank	Company	Stk. Exch.	5-Year EPS Growth Rate %	Latest 12-Month EPS	Year to Date Price Chg. %
1	Digital Commun.	M	146	1.66	-34.5
2	Rhodes	M	128	1.61	51.9
3	Cannon Group	N	127	3.29	19.1
4	Environdyne Industries	M	123	0.80	124.6
5	Fleetwood Enterprises	N	123	1.69	-5.6
6	United Presidential	M	106	1.35	46.3
7	A.L. Labs	A	104	0.92	46.9
8	National Health	M	102	1.31	4.1
9	Dual Lite	M	100*	0.73	42.1
10	VMX	M	99*	-0.14	-22.0
11	Intertrans	M	97	0.67	50.0
12	Brunswick	N	95	2.37	63.9
13	Virginia Beach Fed. S&L	M	95	0.92	21.7
14	CasaBlanca Industries	A	93*	-0.21	161.9
15	Price	M	93	1.20	40.7
16	Clothes Time	M	92	0.73	93.8
17	RB&W	A	92*	0.84	14.1
18	Royal Int'l Optical	N	92	0.85	-45.3
19	Centuri	M	91*	0.06	43.5
20	Empire of Carolina	A	89*	1.36	63.6
21	Maxco	O	88*	0.61	9.1
22	King World Productions	M	86	1.60	34.1
23	Leucadia National	N	86	2.73	7.5
24	American Integrity	M	85	1.41	-4.4
25	Biomet	M	85	0.47	53.1
26	Atlantic Southeast Air	M	84	0.94	23.3
27	Fedders	N	84*	0.45	117.1
28	Genentech	M	84	0.20	146.7
29	Cipher Data Products	M	83	0.38	-3.6
30	American Continental	M	81	2.86	8.3
31	Kuhlman	N	81	1.06	5.6
32	Siliconix	MN	81	0.71	12.1
33	Syntrex	M	81*	0.12	5.6
34	General Shale Products	M	80	2.50	19.0
35	Stratus Computer	MO	80	0.53	-7.4
36	Tyson Foods	M	80	0.96	105.5
37	Mylan Labs	N	79	0.86	33.3
38	Zenith Labs	N	79	1.52	31.3
39	Waxman Industries	M	78	0.81	13.3
40	InteCom	M	77*	-0.41	7.5
41	Lam Research	M	77*	0.42	-9.9
42	Winn Enterprises	A	77*	-0.43	-15.6
43	Seton	A	76	0.90	37.8
44	Slattery Group	N	76*	-0.02	-18.6
45	Western S&L	N	75*	2.63	112.0
46	Equatorial Commun.	M	74*	0.15	0.0
47	Fortune Fin'l	M	74*	4.69	42.7
48	Hofmann Industries	A	74*	-0.21	-10.0
49	Transcon	N	74*	0.35	28.6
50	United Fin'l Grp. Del.	M	74*	-0.72	-34.6
51	Fuqua Industries	N	71	4.01	31.0
52	Home Depot	N	71	0.46	67.0

America's Top 100 Growth Companies (above $25 million sales) *(concluded)*

Rank	Company	Stk. Exch.	5-Year EPS Growth Rate %	Latest 12-Month EPS	Year to Date Price Chg. %
53	Hunt (J.B.) Transport	M	71	1.53	81.8
54	Safeguard Scientific	N	71*	0.75	12.5
55	Casey's General Stores	M	70	0.99	43.8
56	NWA	N	70	2.39	8.7
57	Toro	N	70*	1.92	35.7
58	Douglas & Lomason	M	68	3.51	35.3
59	Total Petroleum	A	68*	2.89	21.6
60	Levitt	A	67*	0.42	54.3
61	Triangle	A	67*	0.76	18.2
62	Ultimate	A	65	0.74	42.7
63	Etz Lavud	A	65	0.74	42.7
64	Pauley Petroleum	A	65*	1.78	36.8
65	Circuit City Stores	N	64	1.98	83.9
66	Green Tree Acceptance	N	64	5.14	63.8
67	Mentor Minn.	M	64	0.57	-14.3
68	Pasquale Food Cl. B	MA	64	0.46	41.7
69	Republic Gypsum	N	64	0.90	21.2
70	Valid Logic Systems	M	64*	0.01	-32.4
71	Redlaw Industries	A	63*	0.27	16.7
72	Southmark	N	63	2.04	18.1
73	Alza Cl. A	A	62*	0.42	55.3
74	Chrysler	N	62*	8.95	13.8
75	Gibraltar Fin'l	N	62*	2.13	8.2
76	KLM Royal Dutch Air	N	62	3.13	2.7
77	Uniforce Temp.	M	62	0.74	55.1
78	American Software	M	61	0.84	4.0
79	Arundel	A	61*	1.53	12.3
80	Kellwood	N	60	3.03	47.7
81	Sandgate	A	60	3.04	12.0
82	Newbery	A	59*	0.37	41.4
83	Sceptre Resources	A	59*	0.33	-36.0
84	Amcast Industrial	M	58*	-1.22	9.1
85	National-Standard	N	58*	0.49	2.8
86	Federal Screw Works	M	57*	1.04	4.2
87	Turner Broadcasting	A	57*	0.50	83.2
88	APL	N	56*	2.53	3.5
89	First Southern S&L	M	56*	1.84	20.5
90	United First Fed. S&L	M	55*	2.65	80.0
91	Limited (The)	N	54	1.28	55.6
92	Computer Horizons	M	53	0.86	25.8
93	Decision Industries	N	53	0.64	5.7
94	Hines, Edward Lumber	O	53*	1.46	-82.2
95	Kit Manufacturing	A	53*	0.81	87.2
96	Minstar	M	53 0.96	45.6	
97	Nu-Med	M	53*	0.54	-1.6
98	American Biltrite	A	52*	1.05	29.1
99	Bally's Park Place	N	52	1.00	35.8
100	Comair	M	52	0.47	-5.7

* Other than a quarterly multiple because of fiscal-year change. A—American Stock Exchange. M—Nasdaq National Market Over the Counter. N—New York Stock Exchange. O—Nasdaq Over the Counter.

Source: Reprinted by permission *Financial World*, 1986 published by Financial World Partners.

Largest Certified Public Accounting (CPA) Firms*

Alexander Grant & Company
605 Third Avenue
New York, NY 10016
212-599-0100

Arthur Andersen & Company[1]
69 West Washington Street
Chicago, IL 60602
312-346-6262

Arthur Young & Company[1]
277 Park Avenue
New York, NY 10017
212-922-2000

Cherry, Bekaert & Holland
1 NCNB Plaza
Charlotte, NC 28280
704-377-3741

Clifton, Gunderson & Co.
808 Commercial National Bank Building
Peoria, IL 61602
309-671-4511

Coopers & Lybrand[1]
1251 Avenue of the Americas
New York, NY 10020
212-536-2000

Deloitte Haskins & Sells[1]
1114 Avenue of the Americas
New York, NY 10036
219-790-0500

Fox and Company
1660 Lincoln Street
Denver, CO 80264
303-861-5555

Ernst & Whinney[1]
2000 National City Center
Cleveland, OH 44114
216-861-5000

Kenneth Leventhal & Company
2049 Century Park East
Los Angeles, CA 90067
213-277-0880

Laventhol & Horwath
1845 Walnut Street
Philadelphia, PA 19103
215-299-1700

KMG Main Hurdman
55 East 52nd Street
New York, NY 10055
212-909-5000

McGladrey Hendrickson & Pullen
640 Capital Square
4th & Locust
Des Moines, IA 50309
515-284-8660

Moss Adams & Co.
2830 Bank of California Center
Seattle, WA 98164
206-223-1820

Oppenheim, Appel, Dixon & Co.
One New York Plaza
New York, NY 10004
212-422-1000

Pannell, Kerr, Forster & Co.
420 Lexington Avenue
New York, NY 10017
212-867-8000

Peat, Marwick, Mitchell & Co.[1]
345 Park Avenue
New York, NY 10022
212-758-9700

Price Waterhouse & Co.[1]
1251 Avenue of the Americas
New York, NY 10020
212-489-8900

Seidman & Seidman
110 Union Bank Building
Grand Rapids, MI 49503
616-744-2111

Touche Ross & Company[1]
1633 Broadway
New York, NY 10019
212-489-1600

* Firms with the largest number of American Institute of Certified Public Accountants (AICPA) members.

[1] One of the "Big 8" accounting firms.

Source: American Institute of Certified Public Accountants.

Capital Sources for Startup Companies and Small Businesses

Sources of Venture Capital

INTRODUCTION

What Is An SBIC?

Although individual investors have been providing venture capital for new and small business in the United States for many years, no institutional sources of such financing existed until 1958 when Congress passed the Small Business Investment Act.

Small business investment companies (SBICs) and minority enterprise small business investment companies (MESBICs) are financial institutions created to make equity capital and long-term credit (with maturities of at least 5 years) available to small, independent businesses. SBICs are licensed by the Federal Government's Small Business Administration, but they are privately-organized and privately-managed firms which set their own policies and make their own investment decisions. In return for pledging to finance only small businesses, SBICs may qualify for long-term loans from SBA. Although all SBICs will consider applications for funds from socially and economically disadvantaged entrepreneurs. MESBICs normally make all their investments in this area.

What Have SBICs Done?

To date, SBICs have disbursed over $6-billion by making over 70,000 loans and investments. The concerns they have financed have far out-performed all national averages as measured by increases in assets, sales, profits, and new employment.

Need Money? Which SBIC Should You See?

This Directory of members of the National Association of Small Business Investment Companies (NASBIC) lists over 400 SBICs and MESBICs. They represent approximately 90% of the industry's resources and are located in all parts of the country.

In using this Directory, you should consider the following factors:

A. *Geography:* Generally speaking, SBICs are more likely to make loans and investments near their offices, even though many of them operate regionally or even nationally. Therefore, it would probably be wise to contact first those SBICs closest to your business.

B. *Investment Policy:* Even though most SBICs have both equity investments and straight loans in their portfolios, each of them has a policy on which type of financing it prefers. This Directory utilizes a code symbol which indicates that policy; you should match your requirements with that information.

C. *Industry Preferences:* Here again, SBICs differ widely. Because of the expertise of its officers and directors, an SBIC often specializes in making loans and investments in certain industries. This Directory indicates such specialization.

D. *Size of Financing:* Because they differ in size and investment policies, SBICs establish different dollar limits on the financings they make. This Directory has a symbol showing the preferred maximum size of loan or investment for each SBIC.

It should be emphasized that the information given in the Directory should be considered only as a general guide. Every SBIC departs from its usual policies in special cases. Furthermore, SBICs often work together in making loans or investments in greater amounts than any of them could make separately. No SBIC should be ruled out as a possible source of financing, since this Directory is designed to give you an idea about which ones are *most likely* to be interested in your application.

Is Your Firm Eligible for SBIC Financing?

Probably so, since the overwhelming majority of all business firms qualify as small. As a general rule, companies are eligible if they have net worth under $6-million and average after-tax earnings of less than $2-million during the past two years. *In addition,* your firm may qualify as small either under an employment standard or amount of annual sales. Both these standards vary from industry to industry.

Source: *Venture Capital, Where to Find It,* published by the National Association of Small Business Investment Companies, 618 Washington Building, Washington, D.C. 20005. Copies available at $1.00 each.

A phone call or a note to any NASBIC member—or to our Washington office—will clear up the eligibility question quickly.

How Do You Present Your Case To An SBIC?

There is nothing mysterious about asking an SBIC for money. You should prepare a report on your operations, financial condition, and requirements. Specifically, the report should include detailed information on key personnel, products, proposed new product lines, patent positions, market data and competitive position, distribution and sales methods, and other pertinent materials.

How Long Will It Take?

There are no hard and fast rules about the length of time it will take an SBIC to investigate and close a transaction. Ordinarily, an initial response, either positive or negative, is made quickly. On the other hand, the thorough study an SBIC must make before it can make a final decision could take several weeks.

Naturally, a well-documented presentation on your part will reduce the amount of time the SBIC will require.

How Are SBIC Financings Structured?

Every single SBIC financing is tailored individually to meet your needs and to make the best use of the SBIC's funds. You and the SBIC will negotiate the terms. The SBIC might buy shares of your stock or it might make a straight loan.

Usually, SBICs are interested in generating capital gains, so they will purchase stock in your company or advance funds through a note, or debenture, with conversion privileges or rights to buy stock at a predetermined later date.

How Can SBIC Money Provide Additional Credit Lines?

If the SBIC money is provided to you in a subordinated position, it will often do double or triple duty. Industry averages show that for every SBIC dollar placed with a small business concern, two additional senior dollars become available from commercial banks or other sources.

Are There Unique Advantages To SBIC Financing?

Yes, indeed! Before it receives its license, an SBIC must prove that its management and directors are experienced individuals with a broad range of business and professional talents.

This expertise will be applied to assist your business, supplementing the skills of your own management team. Here again, the actual pattern of management and financial counseling will be cut to fit each specific situation.

SBICs can make only long-term loans or equity investments; therefore, their interests

and yours will coincide—both of you will want your firm to grow and prosper.

Will I Be Treated Fairly?

As mentioned above, SBICs are licensed by the Federal Government only after their officers and directors have been carefully screened. Furthermore, all the SBICs listed in this Directory are NASBIC members and all have voluntarily subscribed to the Association's Code of Ethics and Trade Practice Rules.

The Code provides, in part, that "the constant goal of each SBIC shall be to improve the welfare of the small business concerns which it serves. Each SBIC shall promote and maintain ethical standards of conduct and deal fairly and honestly with all small business concerns seeking its assistance."

What Is NASBIC?

It is the national trade association which represents the overwhelming majority of all active SBICs and MESBICs. It was formed in 1958, soon after the passage of the Small Business Investment Act, and has worked on behalf of small business generally and the SBIC industry in particular for 28 years.

In addition to providing educational and informational services for its members, NASBIC presses for a rational legal and regulatory framework for the industry. It also cooperates closely with other independent business associations in advancing the interests of small business on the Federal level.

Need More Information?

Contact any SBIC in this Directory. Write the National Association of Small Business Investment Companies (NASBIC), 1156 15 Street, N.W., Suite 1101, Washington, D.C. 20005.

EXPLANATION OF CODES

Preferred Limit for Loans or Investments

A—up to $100,000
B—up to $250,000
C—up to $500,000
D—up to $1-million
E—Above $1-million

Investment Policy

*   —Will consider either loans or investments
** —Prefers to make long-term loans
***—Prefers financings with the right to acquire stock interest.

Industry Preferences

1. Communications
2. Construction & Real Estate Development
3. Natural Resources

4. Hotels, Motels & Restaurants
5. Manufacturing & Processing
6. Medical & Health Services
7. Recreation & Amusements
8. Research & Technology
9. Retailing, Wholesaling & Distribution
10. Service Trades
11. Transportation
12. Diversified

MESBIC—a specialized SBIC which invests in socially or economically disadvantaged small businesses.

Non-SBIC Members

This Directory also lists a number of Associate Members of NASBIC. Some of these firms are non-SBIC venture capitalists who also invest in small businesses. Others are firms which provide professional services to SBICs and to small business concerns.

ALABAMA
First SBIC of Alabama
Mr. David C. DeLaney, Pres.
16 Midtown Park East
Mobile, AL 36606
(205) 476-0700
C ** 12

Hickory Venture Capital Corp.
J. Thomas Noojin, Pres/Chmn.
Jeffrey C. Atkinson, VP
699 Gallatin St., Ste. A-2
Huntsville, AL 35801
(205) 539-1931
E *** 12

Remington Fund, Inc., (The)
Ms. Lana Sellers, Pres.
P.O. Box 10686
Birmingham, AL 35202
(205) 326-3509

Tuskegee Capital Corp.
Mr. A.G. Bartholomew
VP/Gen. Mgr.
4453 Richardson Rd.
Montgomery, AL 36108
(205) 281-8059
MESBIC A ** 12

ALASKA
Alaska Business Investment Corp.
Mr. James L. Cloud, VP
PO Box 600
Anchorage, AK 99510
(907) 278-2071
B * 12

Calista Business Investment Corp.
Mr. Nelson N. Angapak, Pres.
Mr. Matthew Nicolai, VP/Gen. Mgr.
516 Denali St.
Anchorage, AK 99501
(907) 277-0425
MESBIC B * 12

ARIZONA
FBS Venture Capital Co.
Mr. William McKee
Pres.
Mr. Stephen W. Buchanan
Inv. Ofcr.
6900 E. Camelback Rd., Ste. 452
Scottsdale, AZ 85251
(602) 941-2160
C *** 1,5,6,8

Branch Office
Norwest Growth Fund, Inc.
Mr. Robert F. Zicarelli, Chmn.
Mr. Stephen J. Schewe, Assoc.
8777 East Via de Ventura, Ste 335
Scottsdale, AZ 85258
(602) 483-8940
E *** 1,6,8,12
(Main Office in MN)

Rocky Mountain Equity Corp.
Mr. Anthony J. Nicoli, Pres.
4530 N. Central Ave., Ste. 3
Phoenix, AZ 85012
(602) 274-7558
A ** 4,7,8,10

Sun Belt Capital Corp.
Mr. Bruce Vinci, Pres.
Mr. Joseph Henske, VP
Mr. Craig C. Lindsay, Mgr.
320 N. Central Ave., Ste. 700
Phoenix, AZ 85004
(602) 253-7600
A *** 2,4,8

VNB Capital Corp.
Mr. James G. Gardner, Pres.
Mr. John Holliman, VP/Gen Mgr.
15 E. Monroe, Suite 1200
Phoenix, AZ 85004
(602) 261-1577
D *** 1,5,6,8,11,12

ARKANSAS
Capital Management Services, Inc.
Mr. David L. Hale, Pres.
1910 N. Grant, Ste. 200
Little Rock, AR 72207
(501) 664-8613
MESBIC A * 12

First SBIC of Arkansas, Inc.
Mr. Fred C. Burns, Pres.
Worthen Bank Bldg.
200 W. Capitol Ave., Ste. 700
Little Rock, AR 72201
(501) 378-1876
A *** 12

Independence Financial
  Services, Inc.
Mr. John Freeman, Pres.
PO Box 3878
Batesville, AR 72503
(501) 793-4533
B * 6,9,12

Kar-Mal Venture Capital, Inc.
Ms. Amelia S. Karam, Pres.
2821 Kavanaugh Blvd.
Little Rock, AR 72205
(501) 661-0010
MESBIC B *** 9

Power Ventures, Inc.
Mr. Dorsey D. Glover, Pres.
Hwy. 270 N./PO Box 518
Malvern, AR 72104
(501) 332-3695
MESBIC A * 12

Worthern Finance & Inv. Inc.
Mr. Ricor de Silveira, Pres.
PO Box 1681
Little Rock, AR 72203
(501) 378-1082
MESBIC C ** 4,5,6,9,10,11

CALIFORNIA
Branch Office
Atalanta Investment Co., Inc.
Mr. Alan W. Livingston, Pres.
141 El Camino Dr.
Los Angeles, CA 90212
(213) 273-1730
D *** 1,2,5,6,7,8
(Main Office in NY)

Bancorp Venture Capital, Inc.
Mr. Paul R. Blair, Pres.
Mr. Ron Miracle
2082 Michelson Dr., Suite 302
Irvine, CA 92715
(714) 752-7220
E *** 12

BankAmerica Ventures, Inc.
Mr. Robert W. Gibson, Pres.
Mr. Patrick J. Topolski, VP
555 California St., #3908
42nd Floor
San Francisco, CA 94104
(415) 622-2230
D * 12

Bay Venture Group
Mr. William R. Chandler
Gen. Ptnr.
One Embarcadero Ctr., Ste. 3303
San Francisco, CA 94111
(415) 989-7680
B *** 1,5,6,8

Brentwood Associates
Mrs. Leslie R. Shaw
VP Fin. & Admin.
11661 San Vicente Blvd., Ste. 707
Los Angeles, CA 90049
(213) 826-6581
E *** 1,12

Business Equity & Dev. Corp.
Mr. Ricardo J. Olivarez, Pres.
1411 W. Olympic Blvd., Ste. 200
Los Angeles, CA 90015
(213) 385-0351
MESBIC B * 1,5,12

CFB Venture Capital Corp.
Mr. Richard J. Roncaglia, VP
530 B St., 2nd Fl.
San Diego, CA 92101
(619) 230-3304
B *** 1,5,6,8

CIN Investment Co.
Mr. Robert C. Weeks, Pres.
444 Market St., 25th Flr.
San Francisco, CA 94111
(415) 398-7677
D *** 1,8

California Capital Investors, Ltd
Mr. Arthur Bernstein, Gen. Ptnr.
Ms. Lynda Gibson, Off. Admin.
11812 San Vicente Blvd.
Los Angeles, CA 90049
(213) 820-7222
C *** 1,5,6,10,11,12

California Partners
Mr. Tim Draper, VP/CFO
3000 Sand Hill Rd.
Bldg. 4, Ste. 210
Menlo Park, CA   94025
(415) 854-7472
C *** 1,5,6,8

Camden Investments, Inc.
Mr. Edward G. Victor, Pres.
Mr. Craig M. Cogut, Counsel
Ms. Carolyn Zwirn, Asst. Sec.
9560 Wilshire Blvd., #310
Beverly Hills, CA 90212
(213) 859-9738
C *** 12

Charterway Investment Corp.
Mr. Harold Chuang, Pres.
222 S. Hill St., Ste. 800
Los Angeles, CA 90012
(213) 687-8534
MESBIC B *** 2,4,5,7,9

Branch Office
Citicorp Venture Capital, Ltd.
Mr. J. Matthew Mackowski, VP
One Sansome St., Ste. 2410
San Francisco, CA 94104
(415) 627-6472
E *** 1,5,6,8,11
(Main Office in NY)

Branch Office
Citicorp Venture Capital, Ltd.
Mr. David A. Wegmann, VP
2200 Geng Rd., Ste. 203
Palo Alto, CA   94303
(415) 424-8000
E *** 1,5,6,8,11
(Main Office in NY)

Cogeneration Capital Fund
Mr. Howard Cann, Mng. Gen. Ptnr.
Jonathan S. Saiger, Gen. Ptnr.
300 Tamal Plaza, Ste. 190
Corte Madera, CA 94925
(415) 924-3525
D * 8

Continental Investors, Inc.
Mr. Lac Thantrong, Pres.
8781 Seaspray Dr.
Huntington Beach, CA 92646
(714) 964-5207
MESBIC B ** 4,6,9,10,12

Crocker Ventures, Inc.
Mr. Ray McDonough
One Montgomery St.
San Francisco, CA 94104
(415) 983-3636
A * 12

Crosspoint Investment Corp.
Mr. Max S. Simpson, Pres.
1951 Landings Dr.
Mountain View, CA 94043
(415) 964-3545
B *** 1,5,8

Dime Investment Corp.
Mr. Chun Y. Lee, Pres.
2772 W. 8th St.
Los Angeles, CA 90005
(213) 739-1847
MESBIC A * 5,8,9,12

Enterprise Venture Cap. Corp.
Mr. Ernest de la Ossa, Pres.
Mr. Douglas S. Milroy, Op. Mgr.
1922 The Alameda, Ste. 306
San Jose, CA 95126
(408) 249-3507
B * 1,5,8

First American Cap. Funding, Inc.
Dr. Luu Trankiem, Pres.
9872 Chapman Ave., #216
Garden Grove, CA 92641
(714) 638-7171
MESBIC B * 12

First SBIC of California
Mr. Timothy Hay, Pres.
Mr. John Geer, Mng. Ptnr.
Mr. Brian Jones, Mng. Ptnr.
Mr. James McGoodwin, Mng. Ptnr.
Mr. Everett Cox, Mng. Ptnr.
Mr. Dmitry Bosky, Mng. Ptnr.
650 Town Center Drive, 17th Fl.
Costa Mesa, CA 92626
(714) 556-1964
E *** 12

Branch Office
First SBIC of California
Mr. John D. Padgett, Mng. Ptnr.
Mr. Tony Stevens, Mng. Ptnr.
155 N. Lake Ave., Suite 1010
Pasadena, CA 91109
(818) 304-3451
E *** 12

Branch Office
First SBIC of California
Mr. James B. McElwee, Mng. Ptnr.
5 Palo Alto Square, Suite 938
Palo Alto, CA 94304
(415) 424-8011
E *** 12

Hamco Capital Corp.
Mr. William R. Hambrecht, Pres.
Ms. Colleen E. Curry, VP/Sec.
One Post St., 4th Fl.
San Francisco, CA 94104
(415) 393-9813
C * 1,5,6,8

Branch Office
(Bohlen Capital Corp.)
Harvest Ventures, Inc.
Mr. Harvey J. Wertheim, Pres.
Bldg. SW3, 10080 N. Wolfe Rd.
Suite 365
Cupertino, CA 95014
D * 1,3,5,6,8
(Main Office in NY)

InterVen Partners
Mr. David B. Jones, Pres.
Mr. Jonathan E. Funk, VP
Mr. Kenneth M. Deemer, VP
Mr. Keith R. Larson, VP
445 S. Figueroa, Ste. 2940
Los Angeles, CA 90071
(213) 622-1922
E *** 1,6,8,12

Ivanhoe Venture Capital, Ltd.
Mr. Alan Toffler, Mng. Gen. Ptnr.
Mr. P. F. Wulff, Gen. Ptnr.
Mr. William Wright, Gen. Ptnr.
737 Pearl St., Ste. 201
La Jolla, CA 92037
(619) 454-8882
B *** 1,5,6,12

JeanJoo Finance, Inc.
Mr. Frank R. Remski, Gen. Mngr.
Mr. Chul-Ho Kim, Attorney
700 So. Flower St., Suite 3305
Los Angeles, CA 90017
(213) 627-6660
MESBIC B * 12

Lasung Investment & Finance Co.
Mr. Jung Su Lee, Pres.
3600 Wilshire Blvd., Ste. 1410
Los Angeles, CA 90010
(213) 384-7548
MESBIC B ** 9,12

Latigo Capital Partners
Mr. Donald A. Peterson
Gen. Ptnr.
23410 Civic Ctr. Way, Ste. E-2
Malibu, CA 90265
(213) 456-7024
C * 1,4,5,6,7,8,9

Los Angeles Capital Corp.
Mr. Kuytae Hwang, Pres.
606 N. Larchmont Blvd., Ste. 309
Los Angeles, CA 90004
(213) 460-4646
MESBIC B * 2,4,5,12

Branch Office
MBW Management, Inc.
Doan Resources
Mr. James R. Weersing, Mng. Dir.
350 Second St., Suite 7
Los Altos, CA 94022
(415) 941-2392
D *** 1,5,6,8
(Main Office in MI)

MCA New Ventures, Inc.
Mr. W. Roderick Hamilton, Pres.
100 Universal City Plaza
Universal City, CA 91608
(818) 777-2937
MESBIC B *** 1,5,7

Merrill, Pickard, Anderson
 & Eyre I
Mr. Steven L. Merrill, Mng. Ptnr.
Two Palo Alto Sq., Ste. 425
Palo Alto, CA 94306
(415) 856-8880
E *** 1,6,8

Myriad Capital, Inc.
Mr. Chuang-I Lin, Pres.
2225 W. Commonwealth Ave., #111
Alhambra, CA 91801
(818) 289-5689
MESBIC B * 1,2,5,8,9,10,11

Branch Office
Nelson Capital Corp.
Mr. Norman Tulchin, Chmn.
10000 Santa Monica Blvd.
Los Angeles, CA 90067
(213) 556-1944
E * 12
(Main Office in NY)

New Kukje Investment Co.
Mr. C.K. Noh, Pres.
958 S. Vermont Ave., #C
Los Angeles, CA 90006
(213) 389-8679
MESBIC B * 12

New West Ventures
Mr. Tim Haidinger, Pres.
4350 Executive Dr., #206
San Diego, CA 92121
(619) 457-0722
E *** 1,4,5,6,9,10,11

Branch Office
New West Ventures
4600 Campus Dr., #103
Newport Beach, CA 92660
E *** 1,5,6,9,10,11,12

Branch Office
Orange Nassau Capital Corp.
Mr. John W. Blackburn, VP
Westerly Place
1500 Quail St., Ste. 540
Newport Beach, CA 92660
(714) 752-7811
C ** 12
(Main Office in MA)

Opportunity Capital Corp.
Mr. J. Peter Thompson, Pres.
50 California St., Ste. 2505
San Francisco, CA 94111
(415) 421-5935
MESBIC B *** 1,5,11,12

PBC Venture Capital, Inc.
Mr. Henry Wheeler
Pres./Gen. Mgr.
PO Box 6008
Bakersfield, CA 93386
(805) 395-3206
A *** 2,5,6,8,9,12

PCF Venture Capital Corp.
Mr. Eduardo B. Cu-Unjieg, Pres.
Ms. Gina M. Guerrero, Inv. Off.
575 Mariner's Island Blvd., #103
San Mateo, CA 94404
(415) 574-4747
B * 12

San Joaquin Capital Corp.
Mr. Chester W. Troudy, Pres.
1675 Chester Ave., Ste. 330
PO Box 2538
Bakersfield, CA   93303
(805) 323-7581
D *** 2,5,7,12

San Jose SBIC, Inc.
Mr. Robert T. Murphy, Pres.
100 Park Ctr. Pl., Ste. 427
San Jose, CA   95113
(408) 293-8052
C * 1,6,12

Seaport Ventures, Inc.
Mr. Michael Stolper, Pres.
Ms. Carole Rhoades, VP
525 B St., Ste. 630
San Diego, CA   92101
(619) 232-4069
B *** 12

Union Venture Corp.
Mr. Brent T. Rider, Pres.
Mr. Christopher L. Rafferty, VP
Mr. Jeffrey Watts, Sr., Inv. Off.
Mr. Thomas H. Peterson, Inv. Off.
225 S. Lake Ave., #601
Pasadena, CA   91101
(818) 304-1989
D *** 1,5,6,8

Branch Office
Union Venture Corp.
Mr. John W. Ulrich, VP
Mr. Lee R. McCracker, Inv. Ofcr.
18300 Von Karman
Irvine, CA   92713
(714) 553-7130
D *** 1,5,6,8

Unity Capital Corp.
Mr. Frank W. Owen, Pres.
4343 Morena Blvd., #3-A
San Diego, CA   92117
(619) 275-6030
MESBIC A ** 5,12

VK Capital Co.
Mr. Franklin Van Kasper
Gen. Ptnr.
50 California St., #2350
San Francisco, CA   94111
(415) 391-5600
A * 12

Westamco Investment Co.
Mr. Leonard G. Muskin, Pres.
Mr. Scott T. Van Every, VP
3929 Wilshire Blvd., Ste. 400
Beverly Hills, CA   90211
(213) 652-8288
C * 12

Wilshire Capital Inc.
Mr. Kyn Han Lee, Pres.
3932 Wilshire Blvd., Ste. 305
Los Angeles, CA   90010
(213) 388-1314
MESBIC A ** 12

Branch Office
Wood River Capital Corp.
Mr. Peter C. Wendell, VP
3000 Sand Hill Rd., Ste. 280
Menlo Park, CA   94025
(415) 854-1000
D *** 1,5,6,10,12
(Main Office in NY)

Branch Office
Worthen Finance & Inv. Inc.
Mr. Ellis Chane, Mgr.
3660 Wilshire Blvd.
Los Angeles, CA   90010
(213) 480-1908
MESBIC D ** 12
(Main Office in AR)

Yosemite Capital Investment
Mr. J. Horace Hampton, Pres.
448 Fresno St.
Fresno, CA   93706
(209) 485-2431
MESBIC A *** 12

COLORADO
Colorado Growth Capital, Inc.
Mr. Nicholas Davis, Chmn./Pres.
Ms. Debra Chauez, Inv. Analyst
1600 Broadway, Ste. 2125
Denver, CO   80202
(303) 831-0205
B * 5,12

Enterprise Fin. Cap. Dev. Corp.
Mr. Robert N. Hampton, Pres.
PO Box 5840
Snowmass Village, CO   81615
(303) 923-4144
E * 12

Branch Office
FBS Venture Capital Company
Mr. Brian P. Johnson, VP
3000 Pearl St., #206
Boulder, CO   80301
(303) 442-6885
C *** 1,5,6,8
(Main Office in AZ)

InterMountain Ventures, Ltd.
Mr. Norman M. Dean, VP
Mr. E. E. Kuhns, Chmn.
1100 10th St., P.O. Box 1406
Greeley, Colorado   80632
(303) 356-3229
B *** 12

Mile Hi SBIC
Mr. E. Preston Sumner, Inv. Adv.
2505 W. 16th Ave.
Denver, CO   80204
(303) 629-5339
MESBIC A *** 1,5,6,8,12

UBD Capital Inc.
Mr. Richard B. Wigton, Pres.
1700 Broadway
Denver, CO   80274
(303) 863-6329
B * 12

CONNECTICUT
Asset Capital & Management Corp.
Mr. Ralph Smith, Pres.
608 Ferry Blvd.
Stratford, CT   06497
(203) 375-0299
A ** 2

Capital Impact
Mr. Kevin S. Tierney, Pres.
Ms. Joann M. Haines, VP
Ms. Francis P. Murray, Inv. Ofcr.
Mr. John Cuticelli, Jr., Sr. VP
961 Main St.
Bridgeport, CT   06601
(203) 384-5670
C * 2,5,9,10,11,12

Capital Resource Co. of CT L.P.
Mr. I. M. Fierberg, Gen. Ptnr.
Ms. Janice Romanowski, Gen. Ptnr.
699 Bloomfield Ave.
Bloomfield, CT   06002
(203) 243-1114
B ** 12

First Connecticut SBIC (The)
Mr. David Engelson, Pres.
177 State St.
Bridgeport, CT   06604
(203) 366-4726
D * 12

Marcon Capital Corp.
Mr. Martin Cohen, Chmn.
49 Riverside Ave.
Westport, CT   06880
(203) 226-6893
C *** 1,2,9,10,12

Northeastern Capital Corp.
Mr. Louis Mingione
Pres./Exec. Dir.
61 High St.
East Haven, CT   06512
(203) 469-7901
A * 12

Regional Financial Enterprises
Mr. Robert M. Williams
Gen. Ptnr.
Mr. George E. Thomassy III
Gen. Ptnr.
Mr. Howard C. Landis
Gen. Ptnr.
36 Grove St.
New Canaan, CT   06840
(203) 966-2800
E *** 1,5,6,8,9,12

SBIC of Connecticut
Mr. Kenneth F. Zarrilli, Pres.
Mr. Emanuel Zimmer, Treas.
1115 Main St., #610
Bridgeport, CT   06604
(203) 367-3282
A * 2,9,12

DISTRICT OF COLUMBIA
Allied Capital Corp.
Mr. George C. Williams, Chmn.
Mr. David Gladstone, Pres.
1625 I St., NW, Ste. 603
Washington, DC   20006
(202) 331-1112
E *** 1,5,6,9,10,12

American Security Capital Corp.
Mr. Brian K. Mercer, VP
730 15th St., NW
Washington, DC   20013
(202) 624-4843
C *** 12

Broadcast Capital, Inc.
Mr. John Oxendine, Pres.
1771 N St., N.W., #404
Washington, D.C.   20036
(202) 429-5393
MESBIC A *** 1

Branch Office
Continental Investors, Inc.
Mr. Lac Thantrong, Pres.
2020 K St., NW, Ste. 350
Washington, DC   20006
(202) 466-3709
MESBIC B * 4,6,9,10,12
(Main Office in CA)

D.C. Bancorp Venture Capital Co.
Mr. Allan A. Weissburg, Pres.
1801 K St., NW
Washington, DC   20006
(202) 955-6970
C *** 5,6,9,10,12

Fulcrum Venture Capital Corp.
Mr. Divakar Kamath, Pres.
Ms. Renate K. Todd, VP
2021 K St., NW, Ste. 701
Washington, DC   20006
(202) 833-9590
MESBIC C *** 1,2,5,6,11,12

Syncom Capital Corp.
Mr. Herbert P. Wilkins, Pres.
1030 15th St., NW, Ste. 203
Washington, DC   20005
(202) 293-9428
MESBIC C **** 1

Washington Finance & Inv. Corp.
Mr. Chang H. Lie, Pres.
2600 Virginia Ave., NW, #515
Washington, DC   20037
(202) 338-2900
MESBIC A *** 2,4,10,12

Branch Office
Worthen Finance & Inv. Inc.
Mr. Vernon Weaver, Mgr.
2121 K St., NW, Ste. 830
Washington, DC   20037
(202) 659-9427
MESBIC C ** 4,5,6,9,10,11
(Main Office in AR)

FLORIDA
Caribank Capital Corp.
Mr. Michael E. Chaney, Pres.
Mr. Harold F. Messner, VP
Ms. Elaine E. Healy, Invst. Ofcr.
255 E. Dania Beach Blvd.
Dania, FL 33004
(305) 925-2211
B *** 1,3,6,7,8,11

FAIC Capital Corp.
Mr. Joseph N. Hardin, Jr., Pres.
2701 S. Bayshore Dr., Ste. 402
Coconut Grove, FL 33133
(305) 854-6840
B *** 12

First Tampa Capital Corp.
Mr. Thomas L. du Pont
Pres.
Mr. Larry S. Hyman
Fin. & Inv. Mgr.
501 E. Kennedy Blvd., Ste. 806
Tampa, FL 33602
(813) 221-2171
C * 12

Ideal Financial Corp.
Mr. Ectore Reynaldo, Gen. Mgr.
780 NW 42nd Ave., Ste. 304
Miami, FL 33126
(305) 442-4653
MESBIC A ** 12

J & D Capital Corp.
Mr. Jack Carmel, Pres.
12747 Biscayne Blvd.
North Miami, FL 33160
(305) 893 0303
D * 2,5,9,12

Market Capital Corp.
Mr. Ernest E. Eads, Pres.
Mr. Jay A. Musleh, VP
Mr. Billy M. Shaw, Sec/Tres.
PO Box 22667
Tampa, FL 33630
(813) 247-1357
B ** 9

Small Business Assistance Corp.
Mr. Charles S. Smith, Pres.
Mr. H. N. Tillman, Secretary
2612 W. 15th St.
Panama City, FL 32401
(904) 785-9577
B * 4

Southeast Venture Capital Ltd. I
Mr. Clement L. Hofmann, Pres.
One Southeast Financial Ctr.
Miami, FL 33131
(305) 375-6470
D *** 1,5,6,8,12

Universal Financial Services, Inc
Mr. Norman Zipkin, Pres.
3550 Biscayne Blvd., Ste. 702
Miami, FL 33137
(305) 538-5464
MESBIC B ** 12

Venture Opportunities Corp.
Mr. A. Fred March, Pres.
444 Brickell Ave., Ste. 650
Miami, FL 33131
(305) 358-0359
MESBIC A *** 1,5,6,9,11,12

Verde Capital Corp.
Mr. Jose Dearing, Pres.
255 Alhambra Circle, #720
Coral Gables, FL 33134
(305) 444-8938
MESBIC B * 12

GEORGIA
Mighty Capital Corp.
Mr. Gary E. Korynoski
VP/Gen. Mgr.
50 Technology Park
Atlanta, Ste. 100
Norcross, GA 30092
(404) 448-2232
A * 12

North Riverside Capital Corp.
Mr. Thomas R. Barry, Pres.
Ms. Elizabeth G. Anderson, VP
5775-D Peachtree Dunwoody Rd.
Suite #650
Atlanta, GA 30342
(404) 252-1076
D *** 12

HAWAII
Bancorp Hawaii SBIC, Inc.
Mr. Thomas T. Triggs, VP/Mgr.
P.O. Box 2900
Honolulu, HI 96846
(808) 521-6411
A *** 12

Pacific Venture Capital, Ltd.
Mr. Dexter J. Taniguchi, Pres.
1405 N. King St., Ste. 302
Honolulu, HI 96817
(808) 847-6502
MESBIC A * 12

IDAHO
First Idaho Venture Capital Corp.
Mr. Ron J. Twilegar, Pres.
Mr. Dennis J. Clark, VP
P.O. Box 1739
Boise, ID 83701
(208) 345-3460
B *** 6,12

ILLINOIS
Abbott Capital Corp.
Mr. Richard E. Lassar, Pres.
9933 Lawler Ave., Ste. 125
Skokie, IL 60077
(312) 982-0404
A *** 1,6,10

Alpha Capital Venture Partners
Mr. Andrew H. Kalnow, Mng. Ptnr.
Mr. Daniel O'Connell, Gen. Ptnr.
3 First National Pl., Ste. 1400
Chicago, IL 60602
(312) 372-1556
C * 12

Amoco Venture Capital Co.
Mr. Gordon E. Stone, Pres.
200 E. Randolph Dr.
Chicago, IL 60601
(312) 856-6523
MESBIC C *** 3,8

Business Ventures, Inc.
Mr. Milton Lefton, Pres.
20 N. Wacker Dr., Ste. 550
Chicago, IL 60606
(312) 346-1580
B *** 12

Chicago Community Ventures Inc.
Ms. Phyllis E. George, Pres.
104 S. Michigan, #215
Chicago, IL 60603
(312) 726-6084
MESBIC B *** 4,5,12

Combined Fund, Inc. (The)
Mr. E. Patric Jones, Pres.
Ms. Carolyn Sauage, Analyst
1525 E. 53rd St., #908
Chicago, IL 60615
(312) 363-0300
C * 1,12

Continental IL Venture Corp.
Mr. John L. Hines, Pres.
231 S. LaSalle St.
Chicago, IL 60697
(312) 828-8021
E *** 1,5,6,8,9,10

First Capital Corp. of Chicago
Mr. John A. Canning, Jr., Pres.
Three First National Pl.
Ste. 1330
Chicago, IL 60670-0501
(312) 732-5400
E *** 1,5,6,9

Frontenac Capital Corp.
Mr. David A.R. Dullum, Pres.
208 S. LaSalle St., #1900
Chicago, IL 60604
(312) 368-0044
E *** 12

Mesirow Venture Capital
Mr. James C. Tyree
Managing Director
Mr. William P. Sutter, Jr.
Vice President
350 N. Clark
Chicago, IL 60610
(312) 670-6000
E *** 1,2,3,4,5,6,7,8,9,10,11,12

Branch Office
Nelson Capital Corp.
Mr. Irwin B. Nelson, Pres.
2340 Des Plaines Ave.
Des Plaines, IL 60018
(312) 296-2280
E * 12
(Main Office in NY)

Northern Capital Corp.
Mr. Robert L. Underwood, Pres.
50 S. LaSalle St.
Chicago, IL 60675
(312) 444-5399
D *** 12

Tower Ventures, Inc.
Mr. Robert T. Smith, Pres.
Sears Tower, BSC 43-50
Chicago, IL 60684
(312) 875-0571
MESBIC B *** 12

Walnut Capital Corp.
Mr. Burton W. Kanter, Chmn.
Mr. David L. Bogetz, VP
Three First National Plaza
Chicago, IL 60602
(312) 269-1732
C * 1,5,6,8

INDIANA
Circle Ventures, Inc.
Mr. Samuel Sutphin II, VP
20 N. Meridian St., 3rd Flr.
Indianapolis, IN 46240
(317) 636-7242
A *** 12

Equity Resource Co., Inc.
Mr. Michael J. Hammes, VP/Sec.
202 S. Michigan St.
South Bend, IN 46601
(219) 237-5255
B *** 5,12

1st Source Capital Corp.
Mr. Christopher Murphy, III
Pres.
Mr. Eugene L. Cavanaugh, Jr.
VP
100 N. Michigan
South Bend, IN 46601
(219) 236-2180
B *** 1,3,5,6,7,8,9,11

White River Capital Corp.
Mr. David J. Blair, Pres.
Mr. Thomas D. Washburn, Vice-Chm
500 Washington St., PO Box 929
Columbus, IN 47202
(812) 376-1759
B *** 1,5,9,10,12

IOWA
MorAmerica Capital Corp.
Mr. Donald E. Flynn, Exec. VP
Mr. David R. Schroder, VP
300 American Bldg.
Cedar Rapids, IA 52401
(319) 363-8249
D *** 12

KANSAS
Kansas Venture Capital, Inc.
Mr. Larry High, VP
One Townsite Plaza
1030 First Nat'l Bank Towers
Topeka, KS 66603
(913) 233-1368
A * 5

KENTUCKY
Equal Opportunity Finance, Inc.
Mr. Frank Justice, Pres.
Mr. David Sattich, Mgr.
Mr. Donald L. Davis, Asst. Mgr.
420 Hurstbourne Ln., Ste. 201
Louisville, KY 40222
(502) 423-1943
MESBIC B * 12

Financial Opportunities, Inc.
Mr. Gary F. Duerr, Gen. Mgr.
833 Starks Bldg.
Louisville, KY 40202
(502) 584-8259
A * 9

Mountain Ventures, Inc.
Mr. L. Raymond Moncrief, Pres.
911 N. Main St.
PO Box 628
London, KY 40741
(606) 864-5175
C * 1,5,6,10

LOUISIANA
Commercial Capital, Inc.
Mr. Milton Coxe, Acting Pres.
Mr. Michael D. Whitney, Treas.
Mr. Lou Braddock, Sec.
PO Box 1776
Covington, LA 70434-1776
(504) 345-8820
A * 12

Dixie Business Inv. Co., Inc.
Mr. L. Wayne Baker, Pres.
Ms. Evelyn S. Bolding, Asst. Mgr.
PO Box 588
Lake Providence, LA 71254
(318) 559-1558
A ** 9,10,12

First Southern Capital Corp.
Mr. Charest Thibaut, Chmn./CEO
Ms. Carol S. Perrin, Inv. Ofcr.
PO Box 14418
Baton Rouge, LA 70898
(504) 769-3004
D *** 12

Louisiana Equity Capital Corp.
Mr. Melvin L. Rambin, Pres.
Mr. Jack McDonald, Inv. Ofcr.
Mr. Tom J. Adomek, Inv. Analyst
Louisiana Nat'l Bank-PO Box 1511
Baton Rouge, LA 70821
(504) 389-4421
C *** 1,5,6,12

Walnut Street Capital Co.
Mr. William D. Humphries
Mng. Gen. Ptnr.
231 Carondelet St., #702
New Orleans, LA 70130
(504) 525-2112
B *** 12

MAINE
Maine Capital Corp.
Mr. David M. Coit, Pres.
70 Center St.
Portland, ME 04101
(207) 772-1001
A *** 12

MARYLAND
First Maryland Capital, Inc.
Mr. Joseph Kenary, Pres.
107 W. Jefferson St.
Rockville, MD 20850
(301) 251-6630
A *** 12

Greater Washington Investors, Inc
Mr. Don A. Christensen, Pres.
Mr. Martin S. Pinson, Sr. VP
Mr. Jeffrey T. Griffin, VP
Mr. Cyril W. Draffin, Jr., VP
5454 Wisconsin Ave., Ste. 1315
Chevy Chase, MD 20815
(301) 656-0626
D *** 8,12

Suburban Capital Corp.
Mr. Henry P. Linsert, Jr., Pres.
Mr. Steve Dubin, VP
6610 Rockledge Dr.
Bethesda, MD 20817
(301) 493-7025
D *** 5,6,8,12

MASSACHUSETTS
Atlantic Energy Capital Corp.
Mr. Joost E. Tjaden, Pres.
260 Franklin St., Ste. 1501
Boston, MA 02110
(617) 451-6220
C * 1,3,5,6,8,9,10,11,12

BancBoston Ventures, Inc.
Mr. Paul F. Hogan, Pres.
Mr. Jeffrey W. Wilson, VP/Treas.
Ms. Diana H. Frazier, VP
100 Federal St.
Boston, MA 02110
(617) 434-5700
E * 1,5,6,8

Branch Office
Boston Hambro Capital Co.
Mr. Robert Sherman, VP
One Boston Pl., Ste. 723
Boston, MA 02106
(617) 722-7055
C *** 1,5,6
(Main Office in NY)

Branch Office
Churchill International
Mr. Roy G. Helsing, VP
Ms. Julie Dunbar, Mgr.
9 Riverside Rd.
Weston, MA 02193
(617) 893-6555
D *** 1,8
(Main Office in CA)

Branch Office
First SBIC of California
Mr. Michael Cronin, Mng. Ptnr.
50 Milk St., 15th Fl.
Boston, MA 02109
(617) 542-7601
E *** 12
(Main Office in CA)

Branch Office
Fleet Venture Resources, Inc.
Mr. James A. Saalfield, VP
60 State St.
Boston, MA 02100
(617) 367-6700
E *** 1,5,6,8,9,10,11,12

Branch Office
Narragansett Capital Corp.
265 Franklin St., 11th Floor
Boston, MA 02110
(Main Office RI)

New England Capital Corp.
Mr. Z. David Patterson, Exec. VP
Mr. Thomas C. Tremblay, VP
Mr. Stuart D. Pompian, VP
One Washington Mall, 7th Flr.
Boston, MA 02108
(617) 722-6400
D *** 1,5,6,8,12

New England MESBIC, Inc.
Dr. Etang Chen, Pres.
50 Kearney Rd., Ste. 3
Needham, MA 02194
(617) 449-2066
MESBIC A * 1,4,5,6,8,9,12

Orange Nassau Capital Corp.
Mr. Joost E. Tjaden, Pres.
260 Franklin St., Ste. 1501
Boston, MA 02110
(617) 451-6220
C * 1,6,9,10,11,12

TA Associates
  Advent III Capital Co.
  Advent IV Capital Co.
  Advent V Capital Co.
  Advent Atlantic Capital Co.
  Advent Industrial Capital Co.
  Chestnut Capital Corp.
  Chestnut Capital Int'l II
  Devonshire Capital Corp.
Mr. David D. Croll, Mng. Ptnr.
Mr. Richard Churchill, Gen. Ptnr.
Mr. Stephen Gormley, Gen. Ptnr.
Mr. William Collatos, Gen. Ptnr.
Mr. James F. Wade, Assoc.
45 Milk St.
Boston, MA 02109
(617) 338-0800
E *** 1

Branch Office
Transportation Capital Corp.
Mr. Jon Hirch, Asst. VP
566 Commonwealth Ave., Ste. 810
Boston, MA 02215
(617) 262-9701
B ** 11
(Main Office in NY)

UST Capital Corp.
Mr. Arthur F.F. Snyder, Chmn.
Mr. C. Walter Dick, VP
30 Court St.
Boston, MA 02108
(617) 726-7138
B * 1,5,6,8,9,12

Vadus Capital Corp.
Mr. Joost E. Tjaden, Pres.
260 Franklin St., Ste. 1501
Boston, MA 02110
(617) 451-6220
C * 1,6,9,10,11,12

Worcester Capital Corp.
Mr. Kenneth Kidd, VP/Mgr.
446 Main St.
Worcester, MA 01608
(617) 793-4508
A *** 1,6,8

MICHIGAN
Comerica Capital Corp.
Mr. John D. Berkaw, Pres.
30150 Telegraph Rd., Ste. 245
Birmingham, MI 48010
(313) 258-5800
D * 1,5,6,8,12

Doan Resources L.P.
Mr. Ian R.N. Bund, Gen. Ptnr.
2000 Hogback Rd., Suite 2
Ann Arbor, MI 48105
(313) 971-3100
D *** 1,5,6,8

Metro-Detroit Investment Co.
Mr. William J. Fowler, Pres.
Mr. George Caracostas, VP
30777 Northwestern Hwy., Ste. 300
Farmington Hills, MI 48018
(313) 851-6300
MESBIC B * 5,6,9

Michigan Cap. & Service, Inc.
Ms. Mary L. Campbell, VP
500 First Nat'l Bldg.
201 S. Main St.
Ann Arbor, MI 48104
(313) 663-0702
D * 1,5,6,12

Michigan Tech Capital Corp.
Mr. Edward J. Koepel, Pres.
Technology Park, 1700 Duncan Ave.
PO Box 529
Hubbell, MI 49934
(906) 487-2643
B *** 3,5,8

Motor Enterprises, Inc.
Mr. James Kobus, Mgr.
3044 W. Grand Blvd., Rm. 13-152
Detroit, MI 48202
(313) 556-4273
MESBIC A ** 5

Mutual Investment Co., Inc.
Mr. Timothy J. Taylor, Treas.
21415 Civic Center Dr., Ste. 217
Southfield, MI 48076
(313) 559-5210
MESBIC B ** 9

Branch Office
Regional Financial Enterprises
Mr. Barry P. Walsh, Sr. Assoc.
Mr. James A. Parsons, Ptnr.
315 E. Eisenhower Pkwy., Ste.300
Ann Arbor, MI 48104
(313) 769-0941
E *** 1,5,6,8,9,12
(Main Office in CT)

MINNESOTA
Control Data Capital Corp.
Mr. Doug C. Curtis, Jr., Pres.
Mr. D. R. Pickerell, Sec.
3601 W. 77th St.
Minneapolis, MN 55435
(612) 921-4118
D * 1,5,6,8,

Control Data Community Ventures
Fund, Inc.
Mr. Thomas F. Hunt, Jr., Pres.
3601 W. 77th St.
Minneapolis, MN 55435
(612) 921-4352
MESBIC C * 1,5,6,8,12

DGC Capital Co.
Mr. Jerry H. Udesen, Chmn.
603 Alworth Bldg.
Duluth, MN 55802
(218) 722-0058
A * 3,5,6,7,9,10

Branch Office
FBS Venture Capital Company
Mr. W. Ray Allen, Exec. VP
Mr. John H. Bullion, VP
7515 Wayzata Blvd., Ste. 110
Minneapolis, MN 55426
(612) 544-2754
C *** 1,5,6,8
(Main Office in AZ)

Northland Capital Corp.
Mr. George G. Barnum, Jr.
Pres.
Ms. Elizabeth Barnum
Asst. Sec./Treas.
613 Missabe Bldg., 277 W. 1st St.
Duluth, MN 55802
(218) 722-0545
B *** 12

North Star Ventures, Inc.
Mr. Terrence W. Glarner, Pres.
100 S. Fifth St., #2200
Minneapolis, MN 55402
(612) 333-1133
D *** 1,5,6,8,12

North Star Ventures II
Mr. Terrence W. Glarner, Pres.
100 S. Fifth St., #2200
Minneapolis, MN 55402
(612) 333-1133
D *** 1,5,6,8,12

Northwest Venture Partners
Mr. Robert F. Zicarelli, Chmn.
222 S. Ninth St., #2800
Minneapolis, MN 55402
(612) 372-8770
E *** 12

Norwest Growth Fund, Inc.
Mr. Daniel J. Haggerty, Pres.
Mr. Douglas E. Johnson, VP
Mr. Leonard J. Brandt, VP

Mr. Timothy A. Stepanek, VP
222 S. Ninth St., #2800
Minneapolis, MN 55402
(612) 372-8770
E *** 1,5,6,8,12

Retailers Growth Fund, Inc.
Mr. Cornell L. Moore, Pres.
Mr. Rick Olson, Treas.
2318 Park Ave.
Minneapolis, MN 55404
(612) 872-4929
A ** 4,9,11

Shared Ventures, Inc.
Mr. Howard Weiner, Pres.
6550 York Ave. S., Ste. 419
Minneapolis, MN 55435
(612) 925-3411
B *** 1,4,5,6,9,11

Threshold Ventures, Inc.
Mr. John L. Shannon, VP
430 Oak Grove St., Ste. 303
Minneapolis, MN 55403
(612) 874-7199
B *** 1,5,6,9,12

MISSISSIPPI
Columbia Ventures, Inc.
Mr. Maurice Reed, Chmn.
Mr. Richard P. Whitney, Pres.
P.O. Box 1066
Jackson, MS 39215
(Fully Invested)

Invesat Capital Corp.
Mr. John Bise, Pres.
PO Box 3288
Jackson, MS 39207
(601) 969-3242
D * 12

Vicksburg SBIC
Mr. David L. May, Pres.
PO Box 852
Vicksburg, MS 39180
(601) 636-4762
A * 12

MISSOURI
Bankers Capital Corp.
Mr. Raymond E. Glasnapp, Pres.
Mr. Lee Glasnapp, VP
3100 Gillham Rd.
Kansas City, MO 64109
(816) 531-1600
A * 12

Capital For Business, Inc.
Mr. James B. Hebenstreit, Pres.
Mr. William O. Cannon, VP
Mr. Bart Bergman, VP
11 S. Meramec, #800
St. Louis, MO 63105
(314) 854-7427
C *** 1,5,6,8,9,10,12

Branch Office
Capital For Business, Inc.
Mr. Bart Bergman, VP
720 Main St., Suite 700
Kansas City, MO 64105
(816) 234-2357
C *** 1,5,6,8,9,10,12

Intercapco, Inc.
Mr. Thomas E. Phelps, Pres.
Mr. Mark J. Lincoln, VP
7800 Bonhomme Ave.
Clayton, MO 63100
(314) 863-0600
C *** 12

Intercapco West, Inc.
Mr. Thomas E. Phelps, Chmn.
Mr. Mark J. Lincoln, Pres.
7800 Bonhomme Ave.
Clayton, MO 63105
(314) 863-0600
C *** 12

Branch Office
MorAmerica Capital Corp.
Mr. Kevin F. Mullane, VP
Ste. 2724 - Commerce Tower Bldg.
911 Main St.
Kansas City, MO 64105
(816) 842-0114
D *** 12
(Main Office in Iowa)

United Missouri Capital Corp.
Mr. Joseph Kessinger
Exec. VP/Mgr.
928 Grand Ave., 1st Flr.
Kansas City, MO 64106
(816) 556-7115
B * 5,6,8,10

NEW HAMPSHIRE
Granite State Capital, Inc.
Mr. Albert Hall, III, Mng. Dir.
10 Fort Eddy Rd.
Concord, NH 03301
(603) 228-9090
A * 1,5,6,10,12

Lotus Capital Corp.
Mr. Richard J. Ash, Pres.
875 Elm St.
Manchester, NH 03101
(603) 668-8617
B *** 1,6,8,12

NEW JERSEY
Capital Circulation Corp.
Ms. Judy M. Kao, Dir/Sec.
208 Main St.
Ft. Lee, NJ 07024
(201) 947-8637
MESBIC B * 12

ESLO Capital Corp.
Mr. Leo Katz, Pres.
2401 Morris Ave., Ste. 220EW
Union, NJ 07083
(201) 687-4920
B * 12

First Princeton Capital Corp.
Mr. S. Lawrence Goldstein, Pres.
227 Hamburg Tpke.
Pompton Lakes, NJ 07442
(201) 831-0330
B *** 12

Monmouth Capital Corp.
Mr. Eugene W. Landy, Pres.
Mr. Ralph B. Patterson, Exec VP
PO Box 335 - 125 Wyckoff Rd.
Eatontown, NJ 07724
(201) 542-4927
C * 4,5,7,12

Branch Office
MBW Management, Inc.
Doan Resources
Philip E. McCarthy, Mng. Dir.
365 South St., 2nd Floor
Morristown, NJ 07960
(201) 285-5533
D *** 1,5,6,8
(Main Office in MI)

Rutgers Minority Investment Co.
Mr. Oscar Figueroa, Pres.
180 University Ave., 3rd Fl.
Newark, NJ 07102
(201) 648-5627
MESBIC B *** 12

Tappan Zee Capital Corp.
Mr. Jack Birnberg, Chmn.
201 Lower Notch Rd.
Little Falls, NJ 07424
(201) 256-8280
D * 12

Unicorn Ventures, Ltd.
Mr. Frank P. Diassi, Gen. Ptnr.
Mr. Arthur B. Baer, Gen. Ptnr.
6 Commerce Dr.
Cranford, NJ 07016
(201) 276-7880
D *** 12

Unicorn Ventures II, L.P.
Mr. Frank P. Diassi, Gen. Ptnr.
Mr. Arthur B. Baer, Gen. Ptnr.
6 Commerce Dr.
Cranford, NJ 07016
(201) 276-7880
D *** 12

NEW MEXICO
Albuquerque SBIC
Mr. Albert T. Ussery, Pres.
PO Box 487
Albuquerque, NM 87103
(505) 247-0145
A *** 12

Associated SW Investors, Inc.
Mr. John R. Rice, Pres.
2400 Louisiana, N.E., #4
Albuquerque, NM 87110
(505) 881-0066
MESBIC B * 1,5,6,8

Equity Capital Corp.
Mr. Jerry A. Henson, Pres.
231 Washington Ave., Ste. 2
Santa Fe, NM 87501
(505) 988-4273
B *** 5,9,12

Fluid Capital Corp.
Mr. George T. Slaughter, Pres.
8421 B Montgomery Blvd., NE
Albuquerque, NM 87111
(505) 292-4747
C *** 1,2,4,5,6,12

Southwest Capital Inv. Inc.
Mr. Martin J. Roe, Pres.
3500-E Commanche Rd., NE
Albuquerque, NM 87107
(505) 884-7161
C * 12

NEW YORK
American Commercial Capital Corp.
Mr. Gerald J. Grossman, Pres.
310 Madison Ave., Ste. 1304
New York, NY 10017
(212) 986-3305
B * 2,4,5,11,12

AMEV Capital Corp.
Mr. Martin S. Orland, Pres.
One World Trade Ctr., Ste. 5001
New York, NY 10048
(201) 775-9100
D *** 1,4,5,6,9,10,11,12

Atalanta Investment Co., Inc.
Mr. L. Mark Newman, Chmn.
450 Park Ave., Ste. 2102
New York, NY 10022
(212) 832-1104
D *** 1,2,5,6,7,8

Atlantic Capital Corp.
Mr. Harald Paumgarten, Pres.
40 Wall St.
New York, NY 10005
(212) 612-0616
E *** 12

Boston Hambro Capital Co.
Mr. Edwin A. Goodman, Pres.
17 E. 71st St.
New York, NY 10021
(212) 288-7778
C *** 1,5,6

BT Capital Corp.
Mr. James G. Hellmuth, Chmn.
Mr. Noel Urben, Pres.
Mr. Keith Fox, VP
Ms. Martha Cassidy, Asst. VP
280 Park Ave.
New York, NY 10017
(212) 850-1916
E *** 5,10

The Central New York SBIC, Inc.
Mr. Albert Wertheimer, Pres.
351 S. Warren St., Ste. 600

Syracuse, NY 13202
(315) 478-5026
A *** 1,7

Chase Manhattan Capital Corp.
Mr. Gustav H. Koven, Pres.
1 Chase Manhattan Plaza
23rd. Fl.
New York, NY 10081
(212) 552-6275
E *** 1,3,5,6,7,8,10,11,12

Chemical Venuture Capital Corp.
Mr. Steven J. Gilbert, Pres./CEO
Mr. Jeffrey C. Walker, VP
Mr. Michael J. Feldman, VP
277 Park Ave., 10th Fl.
New York, NY 10172
(212) 310-4949
E *** 1,4,5,6,7,8,9,10,11,12

Citicorp Venture Capital Ltd.
Mr. Peter G. Gerry, Pres.
Ms. Diane Rivas, Asst Mgr.
153 East 53rd St., 28th Fl.
New York, NY 10043
(212) 559-1127
E *** 12

Clinton Capital Corp.
Mr. Mark Scharfman, Pres.
Mr. Alan Leavitt, VP
419 Park Ave. S.
New York, NY 10016
(212) 696-4334
E ** 12

CMNY Capital Co., Inc.
Mr. Robert Davidoff, VP
77 Water St.
New York, NY 10005
(212) 437-7078
C *** 1,5,9,10,12

College Venture Equity Corp.
Mr. Francis M. Williams, Pres.
Mr. Joseph M. Williams, VP
256 Third St., PO Box 135
Niagara Falls, NY 14303
(813) 248-3878
A ** 2,5,6,11,12

Croyden Capital Corp.
Mr. Victor L. Hecht, Pres.
45 Rockefeller Pl., Ste. 2165
New York, NY 10111
(212) 974-0184
B *** 12

Edwards Capital Co.
Mr. Edward Teitlebaum, Mng. Ptnr.
215 Lexington Ave., #805
New York, NY 10016
(212) 686-2568
A ** 11

Elk Associates Funding Corp.
Mr. Gary C. Granoff, Pres.
600 Third Ave., #3810
New York, NY 10016
(212) 972-8550
MESBIC B ** 11, 12

Equico Capital Corp.
Mr. Duane E. Hill, Pres.
1290 Ave. of the Amer., Ste. 3400
New York, NY 10019
(212) 397-8660
MESBIC C *** 12

Everlast Capital Corp.
Mr. Frank J. Segreto, VP/CEO
350 Fifth Ave., Ste. 2805
New York, NY 10118
(212) 695-3910
MESBIC B * 2,9,10

Fairfield Equity Corp.
Mr. Matthew A. Berdon, Pres.
Mr. Samuel L. Highleyman, VP
200 E. 42nd St.
New York, NY 10017-5893
(212) 867-0150
B * 1,5,7,9

Ferranti High Technology, Inc.
Mr. Sanford R. Simon, Pres.
Mr. Michael R. Simon, VP
Mr. Keith C. Laugworthy, VP Sec.
515 Madison Ave., #1125
New York, NY 10022
(212) 688-9828
D * 1,5,8,12

Fifty-Third Street Ventures, L.P.
Ms. Patricia Cloherty, Gen. Ptnr.
Mr. Daniel Tessler, Gen. Ptnr.
420 Madison Ave., #1101
New York, NY 10017
(212) 752-8010
D *** 1,5,6,8

J.H. Foster & Co., Ltd.
Mr. John H. Foster, Ptnr.
Mr. Michael J. Connelly, Exec. VP
437 Madison Ave.
New York, NY 10024
(212) 753-4810
E *** 6,10,11,12

Franklin Corp. (The)
Mr. Allen Farkas, Pres.
1185 Ave. of the Americas
27th Flr.
New York, NY 10036
(212) 719-4844
E *** 5,6,8,9,11

Fundex Capital Corp.
Mr. Howard Sommer, Pres.
Mr. Martin Albert, VP
525 Northern Blvd.
Great Neck, NY 11021
(516) 466-8550
D * 12

GHW Capital Corp.
Mr. Jack Graff, Pres.
489 Fifth Ave., 2nd Fl.
New York, NY 10017
(212) 687-1708
B * 12

The Hanover Capital Corp.
Mr. John A. Selzer, VP
Mr. Stephen E. Levenson, VP
150 E. 58th St., Ste. 2710
New York, NY 10155
(212) 980-9670
B * 12

Harvest Ventures
   Asea-Harvest Partners I
   Bohlen Capital Corp.
   European Dev. Cap. Ltd.
Ptnrshp.
   Noro Capital Ltd.
   767 Ltd. Ptnrshp.
   WFG-Harvest Ptnrs., Ltd.
Mr. Harvey Wertheim, Gen. Ptnr.
767 Third Ave.
New York, NY 10017
(212) 838-7776
D * 1,3,5,6,8

Ibero-American Investors Corp.
Mr. Emilio L. Serrano, Pres./CEO
Chamber of Commerce Bldg.
55 St. Paul St.
Rochester, NY 14604
(716) 262-3440
MESBIC B * 5,9,12

Intergroup Venture Capital Corp.
Mr. Ben Hauben, Pres.
230 Park Ave., Ste. 206
New York, NY 10169
(212) 661-5428
A * 12

Irving Capital Corp.
Mr. J. Andrew McWethy, Exec. VP
Mr. Barry Solomon, VP
Mr. Steve Tuttle, VP
1290 Ave. of Americas, 3rd Fl.
New York, NY 10104
(212) 408-4800
E *** 12

Key Venture Capital Corp.
Mr. John M. Lang, Pres.
Mr. Mark R. Hursty, Exec. VP/Mng.
Mr. Richard C. VanAuken, Asst. VP
60 State St.
Albany, NY 12207
(518) 447-3227
B *** 12

Kwiat Capital Corp.
Mr. Sheldon Kwiat, Pres.
Mr. Lowell Kwiat, VP/Sec.
576 Fifth Ave.
New York, NY 10036
(212) 391-2461
A ** 1,5,6,7,8,12

M & T Capital Corp.
Mr. Joseph V. Parlato, Pres.
Ms. Norma E. Gracia, Treas.
One M & T Pl., 5th Fl.
Buffalo, NY 14240
(716) 842-5881
D * 1,5,6,8,9,11,12

Medallion Funding Corp.
Mr. Alvin Murstein, Pres.
205 E. 42nd St., Ste. 2020
New York, NY 10017
(212) 682-3300
MESBIC B ** 11

Minority Equity Capital Co., Inc.
Mr. Donald Greene
Pres.
Mr. Clarence Arrington
Inv. Ofcr.
275 Madison Ave., Ste. 1901
New York, NY 10016
(212) 686-9710
MESBIC C *** 1,5,6,9,11,12

Multi-Purpose Capital Corp.
Mr. Eli B. Fine, Pres.
31 S. Broadway
Yonkers, NY 10701
(914) 963-2733
A *** 12

NatWest USA Capital Corp.
Mr. Orville G. Aarons, Sr. VP
175 Water St.
New York, NY 10038
(212) 602-1200
D * 1,3,5,6,11

Nelson Capital Corp.
Mr. Irwin B. Nelson, Pres.
591 Stewart Ave.
Garden City, NY 11530
(516) 222-2555
E * 12

Norstar Bancorp
Mr. Raymond A. Lancaster, Pres.
Mr. Joseph L. Reinhart, Analyst
Mr. Stephen Puricelli, Analyst
1450 Western Ave.
Albany, NY 12203
(518) 447-4492
D * 12

North American Funding Corp.
Mr. Franklin Wong, VP/Gen. Mgr.
177 Canal St.
New York, NY 10013
(212) 226-0080
MESBIC B * 12

North Street Capital Corp.
Mr. Ralph L. McNeal, Sr., Pres.
250 North St., RA-6S
White Plains, NY 10625
(914) 335-7901
MESBIC B *** 12

NYBDC Capital Corp.
Mr. Marshall R. Lustig, Pres.
41 State St.
Albany, NY 12207
(518) 463-2268
A * 12

Pan Pac Capital Corp.
Dr. Ing-Ping J. Lee, Pres.
19 Rector St., 35th Fl.
New York, NY 10006
(212) 344-6680
MESBIC A ** 12

Questech Capital Corp.
Dr. Earl W. Brian, Chmn.
Mr. John E. Koonce, Pres.
Ms. Barbara J. Hann, VP
600 Madison Ave.
New York, NY 10022
(212) 758-8522
D * 1,5,6,8

R & R Financial Corp.
Mr. Martin Eisenstadt, VP
1451 Broadway
New York, NY 10036
(212) 790-1400
A ** 12

Rand SBIC, Inc.
Mr. Donald A. Ross, Pres.
Mr. Thomas J. Bernard, VP
Mr. Keith B. Wiley, VP
1300 Rand Bldg.
Buffalo, NY 14203
(716) 853-0802
C *** 1,5,6,7,8,9,10,12

Peter J. Schmitt Co., Inc.
Mr. Mark A. Flint, Mgr.
PO Box 2
Buffalo, NY 14240
(716) 821-1400
A *** 9

Small Bus. Electronics Inv. Co.
Mr. Stanley Meisels, Pres.
1220 Peninsula Blvd.
Hewlett, NY 11557
(516) 374-0743
A * 12

Southern Tier Capital Corp.
Mr. Milton Brizel, Pres.
Mr. Harold Gold, Sec.
55 S. Main St.
Liberty, NY 12754
(914) 292-3030
A * 12

Branch Office
Tappan Zee Capital Corp.
120 N. Main St.
New City, NY 10956
(914) 634-8890
D * 12
(Main Office in NJ)

TLC Funding Corp.
Mr. Philip G. Kass, Pres.
141 S. Central Ave.
Hartsdale, NY 10530
(914) 683-1144
B ** 4,9,12

Transportation Capital Corp.
Mr. Melvin L. Hirsch, Pres.
Mr. Robert Silver, VP
Mr. Jon Hirsch, Asst. VP
Ms. Margaret Shiroky, Asst. Sec.
60 E. 42nd St., Ste. 3126
New York, NY 10165
(212) 697-4885
MESBIC B ** 11

Transworld Ventures, Ltd.
Mr. Jack H. Berger, Pres.
331 W. End Ave., Ste. 1A
New York, NY 10023
(212) 496-1010
A *** 5,10,12

Triad Capital Corp. of NY
Mr. L. Jim Barrera, Pres.
960 Southern Blvd.
Bronx, NY 10459
(212) 589-6541
MESBIC A * 1,3,6,8,9,10

Vega Capital Corp.
Mr. Victor Harz, Pres.
Mr. Ronald A. Linden, VP
720 White Plains Rd.
Scarsdale, NY 10583
(914) 472-8550
D * 12

Venture SBIC, Inc.
Mr. Arnold Feldman, Pres.
249-12 Jericho Tpke.
Floral Park, NY 11001
(516) 352-0068
A ** 2,9,12

Branch Office
Walnut Capital Corp.
Mr. Julius Goldfinger, Pres.
110 E. 59th St., 37th Floor
New York, NY 10016
(212) 750-1000
C * 1,5,6,8
(Main Office in IL)

Winfield Capital Corp.
Mr. Stanley Pechman, Pres.
237 Mamaroneck Ave.
White Plains, NY 10605
(914) 949-2600
D * 12

Wood River Capital Corp.
Ms. Elizabeth W. Smith, Pres.
645 Madison Ave.
New York, NY 10022
(212) 750-9420
D *** 1,5,6,10,12

Branch Office
Worthen Finance & Inv. Inc.
Mr. Guy Meeker, Mgr.
535 Madison Ave., 17th Fl.
New York, NY 10022
(212) 750-9100
MESBIC D ** 12
(Main Office in AR)

NORTH CAROLINA
Branch Office
Carolina Venture Capital Corp.
Mr. Thomas H. Harvey, III, Pres.
P.O. Box 646
Chapel Hill, NC 27514
B *** 1,2,4,7,11,12
(Main Office in SC)

Delta Capital, Inc.
Mr. Alex B. Wilkins, Jr., Pres.
Mr. Martha C. Kirker, Sec.
227 N. Tryon St., Ste 201
Charlotte, NC 28202
(704) 372-1410
B * 2,4,5,8,9,10

Falcon Capital Corp.
Dr. P.S. Prasad, Pres.
400 W. Fifth St.
Greenville, NC 27834
(919) 752-5918
A *** 2,4,6,9,10

Heritage Capital Corp.
Mr. Herman B. McManaway, Pres.
Mr. William R. Starnes, VP
Mr. G. Kinsey Roper, VP
2290 First Union Plaza
Charlotte, NC 28282
(704) 334-2867
C *** 12

Kitty Hawk Capital, Ltd.
Mr. Walter H. Wilkinson Jr.
Gen. Ptnr.
One Tryon Ctr., Ste. 2030
Charlotte, NC 28284
(704) 333-3777
C *** 1,5,6,8,12

NCNB SBIC Corp.
Mr. Troy McCrory, Pres.
One NCNB Plaza, T05-2
Charlotte, NC 28255
(704) 374-5000
C * 12

NCNB Venture Corp.
Mr. Mike Elliott, Pres.
One NCNB Plaza, T39
Charlotte, NC 28255
(704) 374-0435
D *** 1,5,6,8,12

OHIO
A.T. Capital Corp.
Mr. Shailesh J. Mehta, Pres.
Mr. Robert C. Salipante, VP
900 Euclid Ave., T-18
Cleveland, OH 44101
(216) 687-4970
C * 1,6,8

Capital Funds Corp.
Mr. Carl G. Nelson, VP/Mgr.
Mr. David B. Chilcote, Asst. VP
127 Public Sq.
Cleveland, OH 44114
(216) 622-8628
C * 1,5,6,9,12

Clarion Capital Corp.
Mr. Morton Cohen
Chmn/Pres.
Mr. Michael Boeckman
VP/Chief Fin. Ofcr.
Mr. Roger W. Eaglen
VP
3555 Curtis Blvd.
Eastlake, OH 44114
(216) 953-0555
C *** 1,3,5,6,8,10,12

First Ohio Capital Corp.
Mr. Michael J. Aust, VP
606 Madison Ave.
Toledo, OH 43604
(419) 259-7146
B *** 12

Gries Investment Co.
Mr. Robert D. Gries, Pres.
Mr. Richard Brezic, VP
720 Statler Office Tower
Cleveland, OH 44115
(216) 861-1146
B *** 12

National City Capital Corp.
Mr. Michael Sherwin, Pres.
623 Euclid Ave.
Cleveland, OH 44114
(216) 575-2491
C *** 12

Branch Office
River Capital Corp.
Mr. Peter D. Van Oosterhout,
Pres.
796 Huntington Bldg.
Cleveland, OH 44115
(216) 781-3655
D *** 12
(Main Office in RI)

SeaGate SBIC
Mr. Charles Brown, VP
245 Summit St., #1403
Toledo, OH 43603
(419) 259-8397
A *** 5,6,12

OKLAHOMA
Alliance Business Investment Co.
Mr. Barry M. Davis, Pres.
Mr. Mark R. Blankenship, VP
One Williams Ctr., Ste. 2000
Tulsa, OK 74172
(918) 584-3581
C *** 1,3,5,6,7,9,11,12

First OK Investment Capital Corp.
Mr. David H. Pendley, Pres.
Mr. Arthur J. Miller, VP
120 N. Robinson, Ste. 880C
Oklahoma City, OK 73102
(405) 272-4693
D *** 1,5,6,9,10,11,12

Southwest Venture Capital, Inc.
Mr. Donald J. Rubottom, Pres.
2700 E. 51st St., Ste. 340
Tulsa, OK 74105
(918) 742-3177
A *** 5,6,9,10

Western Venture Capital Corp.
Mr. William B. Baker, Pres./CEO
4900 S. Lewis
Tulsa, OK 74105
(918) 749-7981
D ** 12

OREGON
Branch Office
InterVen Partners
Mr. Wayne B. Kingsley, Chmn.
Mr. Keith L. Larson, VP
227 SW Pine St., Ste. 200
Portland, OR 97204
(503) 223-4334
E *** 1,6,8,12
(Main Office in CA)

Northern Pacific Capital Corp.
Mr. John J. Tennant, Jr., Pres.
Mr. Joseph P. Tennant, Sec.
1201 SW 12th Ave.
Portland, OR 97205
(503) 241-1255
B *** 5,9,11

Branch Office
Norwest Growth Fund, Inc.
Mr. Anthony Miadich, VP
Mr. Dale J. Vogel, VP
1300 SW Fifth Ave., Ste. 3018
Portland, OR 97201
(503) 223-6622
E *** 1,6,8,12
(Main Office in MN)

Trendwest Capital Corp.
Mr. Mark E. Nicol, Pres.
PO Box 5106
Klamath Falls, OR 97601
(503) 882-8059
B *** 12

PENNSYLVANIA
Alliance Enterprise Corp.
(The Sun Company)
Mr. Terrence Hicks, VP
1801 Market St., 3rd Fl.
Philadelphia, PA 19103
(215) 977-3925
MESBIC B * 1,5

Enterprise Vent. Cap. Corp of PA
Mr. Donald W. Cowie, VP
227 Franklin St., #215
Johnstown, PA 15901
(814) 535-7597
A * 12

Branch Office
First SBIC of California
Mr. Daniel A. Dye, Mng. Ptnr.
PO Box 512
Washington, PA 15301
(412) 223-0707
E *** 12
(Main Office in CA)

First Valley Capital Corp.
Mr. Matthew W. Thomas, Pres.
One Center Sq., Ste. 201
Allentown, PA 18101
(215) 776-6760
B * 12

Gtr. Phil. Ven. Cap. Corp., Inc.
Mr. Martin M. Newman, Gen. Mgr.
225 S. 15th St., Ste. 920
Philadelphia, PA 19102
(215) 732-1666
MESBIC B *** 4,5,6

Meridian Capital Corp.
Mr. Knute C. Albrecht, Pres/CEO
Mr. Jay M. Ackerman, VP
Blue Bell West, Ste. 122
Blue Bell, PA 19422
(215) 278-8907
B *** 12

PNC Capital Corp.
Mr. David M. Hillman, Exec. VP
Mr. Jeffrey H. Schutz, VP
Mr. Peter Del Presto, Inv.
Analyst
5th Ave. & Wood St., 19th Fl.
Pittsburgh, PA 15222
(412) 355-2245
C *** 1,5,6,8,9,10

PUERTO RICO
First Puerto Rico Capital, Inc.
Mr. Eliseo E. Font, Pres.
PO Box 816
Mayaguez, PR 00709
(809) 832-9171
MESBIC A * 12

North America Investment Corp.
Mr. S. Ruiz-Betancourt, Pres.
Banco Popular Ctr., Ste. 1710
Hato Rey, PR 00919
(809) 754-6177
MESBIC B ** 5,6,9,12

RHODE ISLAND
Domestic Capital Corp.
Mr. Nathaniel B. Baker, Pres.
815 Reservoir Ave.
Cranston, RI 02910
(401) 946-3310
B * 4,5,11,12

Fleet Venture Resources, Inc.
Mr. Robert M. Van Degna, Pres.
111 Westminster St.
Providence, RI 02920
(401) 278-6770
E *** 1,5,6,8,9,10,11,12

Narragansett Capital Corp.
Mr. Arthur D. Little, Chmn.
Mr. Gregory P. Barber, VP
Mr. Roger A. Vandenberg, VP
40 Westminster St.
Providence, RI 02903
(401) 751-1000
E * 1,5,7,8,9,12

Old Stone Capital Corp.
Mr. Arthur Barton, VP
One Old Stone Sq., 11th Fl.
Providence, RI 02901
(401) 278-2559
D *** 1

River Capital Corp.
Mr. Peter D. Van Oosterhout
Pres.
Mr. Robert A. Comey, VP
Mr. Peter C. Canepa, VP
One Hospital Trust Plaza
Providence, RI 02903
(401) 278-8819
D *** 12

SOUTH CAROLINA
Carolina Venture Capital Corp.
Mr. Thomas H. Harvey III, Pres.
14 Archer Rd.
Hilton Head Island, SC 29928
(803) 842-3101
B *** 1,2,4,7,11,12

Reedy River Ventures
Mr. John M. Sterling, Gen. Ptnr.
Mr. Tee C. Hooper, Gen. Ptnr.
PO Box 17526
Greenville, SC 29606
(803) 297-9198
B *** 1,5,9,12

TENNESSEE
Chickasaw Capital Corp.
Mr. Thomas L. Moore, Pres.
P.O. Box 387
Memphis, TN 38147
(901) 523-6470
MESBIC D *** 2,5,6,9,10,12

Financial Resources, Inc.
Mr. Milton C. Picard, Chmn.
2800 Sterick Bldg.
Memphis, TN 38103
(901) 527-9411
B *** 1,5,6,8,10,12

Leader Capital Corp.
Mr. Edward Pruitt, Pres.
P.O. Box 708, 158 Madison Ave.
Memphis, TN 38101-0708
(901) 578-2405

Suwannee Capital Corp.
Mr. Peter R. Pettit, Pres.
Mr. Melvin Hill, VP
3030 Poplar Ave.
Memphis, TN 38111
(901) 345-4200
C ** 9

Tennessee Equity Capital Corp.
Mr. Walter S. Cohen, Pres./CEO
1102 Stonewall Jackson
Nashville, TN 37220
(615) 373-4502
MESBIC C *** 1,2,4,5,7,9,10,12

Valley Capital Corp.
Mr. Lamar J. Partridge
Pres.
Ms. Faye Munger
Exec. Sec./Admin. Assist.
100 W. Martin L. King Blvd., #806
Chattanooga, TN 37402
(615) 265-1557
MESBIC B *** 1,5,6,9,11,12

West Tennessee Venture Cap. Corp.
Mr. Osbie Howard, VP
Mr. Bennie L. Marshall, Mgr.
PO Box 300, 152 Beale St.
Memphis, TN 38101
(901) 527-6091
MESBIC B * 1,5,6,7,10,11,12

TEXAS
Branch Office
Alliance Business Investment Co.
3990 One Shell Pl.
Houston, TX 77002
(713) 224-8224
C *** 1,3,5,6,8,11,12
(Main Office in OK)

Allied Bancshares Capital Corp.
Mr. Philip A. Tuttle, Pres.
Ms. Mary Bass, Inv. Ofcr.
P.O. Box 3326
Houston, TX 77253
(713) 226-1625
D *** 1,6,8,9,11,12

Americap Corp.
Mr. James L. Hurn, Pres.
Mr. Ben Andrews, VP
7575 San Felipe, #160
Houston, TX 77063
(713) 780-8084
C *** 1,5,6,8,12

Brittany Capital Co.
Mr. Steven S. Peden, Gen. Ptnr.
2424 LTV Tower, 1525 Elm St.
Dallas, TX 75201
(214) 954-1515
B *** 12

Business Cap. Corp. of Arlington
Mr. Keith Martin, Pres.
1112 Copeland Rd., Ste. 420
Arlington, TX 76011-4994
(817) 261-4936
A *** 12

Capital Marketing Corp.
Mr. John King Myrick, Pres.
Mr. Morris Whetstone, Gen. Mgr.
PO Box 1000
Keller, TX 76248
(817) 656-7380
E ** 2,9

Capital Southwest Venture Corp.
Mr. William R. Thomas, Pres.
Mr. J. Bruce Duty, VP
Mr. Patrick Hamner, Inv. Assoc.
12900 Preston Rd., Ste. 700
Dallas, TX 75230
(214) 233-8242
D *** 1,3,5,6,8,9,11,12

Central Texas SBIC
Mr. David G. Horner, Pres.
Mr. Ross Miller, Sec.
Mr. David Senior, Dir.
514 Austin Ave., P.O. Box 2600
Waco, TX 76702-2600
(817) 753-6461
A ** 5,9,12

Charter Venture Group, Inc.
Mr. Jerry Finger, Pres.
2600 Citadel Plaza Dr., 6th Fl.
Houston, TX 77008
(713) 863-0704
B *** 12

Branch Office
Citicorp Venture Capital, Ltd.
Mr. Thomas F. McWilliams, VP
Diamond Shamrock Twr., #2920-LB87
717 Harwood
Dallas, TX 75221
(214) 880-9670
E *** 12
(Main Office in NY)

Energy Capital Corp.
Mr. Herbert F. Poyner, Jr., Pres.
953 Esperson Bldg.
Houston, TX 77002
(713) 236-0006
D *** 3

Enterprise Capital Corp.
Mr. Fred S. Zeidman
Pres.
Mr. Fiore Jalarieo, Jr.
CFO/Treas.
Ms. Eta G. Paransky
Consultant/ Inv. Advisor
3501 Allen Pkwy.
Houston, TX 77019
(713) 521-4401
D *** 1,5,6,7,8,12

FCA Investment Co.
Mr. R. S. Baker, Jr., Chmn.
Ms. Peggy Kliesing, Asst. Treas.
3000 Post Oak Blvd., #1790
Houston, TX 77056
(713) 965-0077
D *** 5,6,8,9,12

The Grocers SBI Corp.
Mr. Milton Levit, Pres.
3131 E. Holcombe Blvd., #101
Houston, TX 77021
(713) 747-7913
B ** 9

Branch Office
Hickory Venture Capital Corp.
3811 Turtle Creek Blvd.
#1000, LB33
Dallas, TX 75219
(214) 522-1892
E *** 12
(Main Office in AL)

InterFirst Venture Corp.
Mr. J.A. O'Donnell, Pres.
901 Main St., 10th Floor
Dallas, TX 75283
(214) 977-3164
E *** 12

Livingston Capital Ltd.
Mr. J. Livingston Kosberg, Ptnr.
Mr. Mark J. Brookner, Gen. Ptnr.
Ms. Glory S. Green, Sec.
PO Box 2507
Houston, TX 77252
(713) 872-3213
B *** 12

Lone Star Capital, Ltd.
Mr. Stuart Schube, Pres.
Mr. Martin D. O'Malley, Assoc.
2401 Fountainview, Ste. 950
Houston, TX 77057
(713) 266-6616
E * 1,5,6,9,12

Mapleleaf Capital Corp.
Mr. Edward M. Fink, Pres.
55 Waugh Dr., #710
Houston, TX 77007
(713) 880-4494
E *** 12

MESBIC Financial Corp. of Dallas
Mr. Thomas Gerron, VP/Controller
Mr. Don Lawhorne, Pres.
Mr. Norman Campbell, VP
12655 North Central Expwy., #814
Dallas, TX 75243
(214) 637-1597
MESBIC C *** 12

MESBIC Financial Corp. of Houston
Mr. Richard Rothfeld, Pres.
1801 Main St., Ste. 320
Houston, TX 77002
(713) 228-8321
MESBIC B * 5,8,9,10,12

Mid-State Capital Corp.
Mr. Smith E. Thomasson, Pres.
PO Box 7554
Waco, TX 76714
(817) 776-9500
B *** 12

MVenture Corp.
Mr. Joseph B. Longino, Jr., Pres.
Mr. J. Wayne Gaylord, Exec. VP
PO Box 662090
Dallas, TX 75266-2090
(214) 741-1469
D *** 1,5,6,10,11,12

Omega Capital Corp.
Mr. Ted E. Moor, Jr., Pres.
755 S. 11th St., #250
Beaumont, TX 77701
(409) 832-0221
A *** 5,12

Branch Office
Orange Nassau Capital Corp.
Mr. Richard D. Tadler, VP
One Galleria Tower
13355 Noel Rd., Ste. 635
Dallas, TX 75240
(214) 385-9685
C ** 12
(Main Office in MA)

Red River Ventures, Inc.
Mr. D.W. Morton, Pres.
777 E. 15th St.
Plano, TX 75074
(214) 422-4999
B * 12

Republic Venture Group, Inc.
Mr. Robert H. Wellborn, Pres.
Mr. William W. Richey, VP/Treas.
Mr. Bart A. McLean, Inv. Ofcr.
Ms. Sherry Richardson
Inv. Ofcr.
PO Box 225961
Dallas, TX 75265
(214) 922-5078
D *** 1,3,5,6,12

Retzloff Capital Corp.
Mr. James K. Hines, Pres.
Mr. Steve Retzloff, Exec. VP
Ms. Diane S. Langdon, Sec.

P.O. Box 41250
Houston, TX 77240
(713) 466-4633
C *** 5,6,9,12

San Antonio Venture Group, Inc.
Mr. Tom Woodley, Inv. Advisor
Mr. Mike Parish, Inv. Advisor
2300 W. Commerce
San Antonio, TX 78207
(512) 223-3633
B *** 4,5,6,9,10

SBI Capital Corp.
Mr. William E. Wright, Pres.
PO Box 771668
Houston, TX 77215-1668
(713) 975-1188
C *** 1,5,6,8

Southern Orient Capital Corp.
Dr. Cheng Ming Lee, Chmn.
2419 Fannin, Ste. 200
Houston, TX 77002
(713) 225-3369
MESBIC A * 4,9,10,12

Southwestern Ven. Cap. of TX,Inc.
Mr. James A. Bettersworth, Pres.
PO Box 1719
Seguin, TX 78155
(512) 379-0380
B * 12

Branch Office
Southwestern Ven. Cap. of TX,Inc.
N. Frost Ctr., Ste. 700
1250 NE Loop 410
San Antonio, TX 78209
B * 12

Sunwestern Capital Corp.
Mr. Thomas W. Wright, Pres.
Mr. James F. Leary, Exec. VP
12221 Merit Dr., #1680
Dallas, TX 75251
(214) 239-5650
C *** 1,3,5,6,8,12

Texas Capital Corp.
Mr. David Franklin, VP
Mr. Tom Beecroft, Asst. VP
1341 W. Mockingbird, #1250E
Dallas, TX 75247
(214) 638-0638
C *** 12

United Mercantile Capital Corp.
Mr. L. Joe Justice, Chmn.
PO Box 66
El Paso, TX 79940
(915) 533-6375
A *** 5,11

United Oriental Cap. Co.
Mr. Don J. Wang, Pres.
908 Town & Country Blvd., #310
Houston, TX 77024
(713) 461-3909
MESBIC B * 12

Wesbanc Ventures, Ltd.
Mr. Stuart Schube, Gen. Ptnr.
2401 Fountainview, #950
Houston, TX 77057
(713) 977-7421
E * 1,5,6,9,12

VIRGINIA
East West United Investment Co.
Mr. Doug Bui, Pres.
6723 Whittier Ave., Ste. 206B
McLean, VA 22101
(703) 821-6616
MESBIC A ** 4,9,12

Hillcrest Group
James River Capital Associates
UV Capital Corp.
Mr. A. Hugh Ewing, III
Gen. Ptnr.
Mr. James B. Farinholt, Jr.
Gen. Ptnr.

Mr. John P. Funkhouser
Gen. Ptnr.
9 S. 12th St., P.O. Box 1776
Richmond, VA 23219
(804) 643-7358
C *** 12

Metropolitan Capital Corp.
Mr. S. W. Austin, VP
2550 Huntington Ave.
Alexandria, VA 22303
(703) 960-4698
B *** 5,8

Branch Office
River Capital Corp.
1033 N. Fairfax St.
Alexandria, VA 22314
(703) 739-2100
D *** 12
(Main Office in RI)

Sovran Funding Corp.
Mr. David A. King, Jr., Pres.
Sovran Ctr., 6th Fl.
One Commercial Pl.
Norfolk, VA 23510
(804) 441-4041
C *** 12

WASHINGTON
Peoples Capital Corp.
Mr. R. W. Maider, Pres.
2411 Fourth Ave., Ste. 400
Seattle, WA 98121
(206) 344-8105
B * 1,6,9

Seafirst Capital Corp.
Mr. R. Bruce Harrod, Pres.
Columbia Seafirst Center
14th Floor
P.O. Box C-34103
Seattle, WA 98124-1103
(206) 442-3501
C * 2

WISCONSIN
Bando-McGlocklin Inv. Co., Inc.
Mr. George Schonath, CEO
Mr. Sal Bando, Pres.
Mr. Jon McGlocklin, Exec. VP
13555 Bishops Ct., Ste. 205
Brookfield, WI 53005
(414) 784-9010
C ** 5,6,9,10,11

Capital Investments, Inc.
Mr. Robert L. Banner, VP
744 N. 4th St.
Milwaukee, WI 53203
(414) 273-6560
C * 1,5,9,12

M & I Ventures Corp.
Mr. Daniel P. Howell, VP
770 N. Water St.
Milwaukee, WI 53202
(414) 765-7910
C *** 5,6,8,12

Madison Capital Corp.
Mr. Roger H. Ganser, Pres.
102 State St.
Madison, WI 53703
(608) 256-8185
B * 6,8,12

Marine Venture Capital, Inc.
Mr. H. Wayne Foreman, Pres.
Mr. Reed R. Prior, VP
111 E. Wisconsin Ave.
Milwaukee, WI 53202
(414) 765-2274
C *** 12

Branch Office
MorAmerica Capital Corp.
Mr. Steven J. Massey, VP
600 E. Mason St.
Milwaukee, WI 53202

(414) 276-3839
D *** 12
(Main Office in Iowa)

Super Market Investors, Inc.
Mr. John W. Andorfer, Pres.
Mr. David Maass, VP
PO Box 473
Milwaukee, WI 53201
(414) 547-7999
A ** 9

Twin Ports Capital Co.
Mr. Paul Leonidas, Pres.
R. F. Joki, Sec./Treas.
1230 Poplar Ave.
PO Box 849
Superior, WI 54880
(715) 392-5525
A * 12

Wisconsin Community Capital Inc.
Mr. Louis Fortis, Pres.
Ms. Nancy Bornstein, VP
14 W. Mifflin St., #314
Madison, WI 53703
(608) 256-3441
A * 3,5,10

Wisconsin MESBIC, Inc. (The)
Mr. Charles A. McKinney, Chmn.
Mr. William P. Beckett, Pres.
622 N. Water St., Ste. 500
Milwaukee, WI 53202
(414) 278-0377
MESBIC B *** 12

WYOMING
Capital Corp. of Wyoming, Inc.
Mr. Larry J. McDonald, Pres.
Mr. Scott Weaver, VP
Ms. Luella Brown, VP
Ms. Jean Hughley, Asst. VP
PO Box 3599
Casper, WY 82602
(307) 234-5438
B * 3,5,9,10,11,12

NON-SBIC MEMBERS

Mr. Robert B. Leisy
Consultant
14408 E. Whittier Blvd., B-5
P.O. Box 4405
Whittier, CA 90605
(213) 698-4862

Accel Partners
Mr. James R. Swartz, Mng. Ptnr.
Mr. Dixon R. Doll, Mg. Ptnr.
Mr. Arthur Patterson, Mng. Ptnr.
One Palmer Sq.
Princeton, NJ 08542
(609) 683-4500
E * 1,5,6,8,9,10,12

Alimansky Venture Group, Inc.
Mr. Burt Alimansky, Mng. Dir.
790 Madison Ave., Ste. 705
New York, NY 10021
(212) 472-0502
E *** 1,3,5,6,7,8,9,10,11,12

R.W. Allsop & Associates
Mr. Robert W. Allsop, Gen. Ptnr.
Mr. Gregory B. Bultman, Gen Ptnr.
Mr. Robert L. Kuk, Gen. Ptnr.
Mr. Larry C. Maddox, Gen. Ptnr.
Mr. Paul D. Rhines, Gen. Ptnr.
2750 First Ave., NE, Ste. 210
Cedar Rapids, IA 52402
(319) 363-8971
D *** 1,5,6,9,12

Allstate Insurance Co. -
Venture Capital Division
Mr. Leonard A. Batterson
Sr. Inv. Mgr.
Allstate Plaza E-2
Northbrook, IL 60062
(312) 291-5681
E *** 1,4,5,6,8,10,11,12

Arete Ventures, Inc.
Mr. Robert W. Shaw, Jr., Pres.
990 Hammond Dr., Ste. 620
Atlanta, GA 30328
(404) 396-2480

Arthur Andersen & Co.
Mr. John Cherin, Mng. Ptnr.
8251 Greensboro Dr., #400
McLean, VA 22102
(703) 734-7300

Arthur Andersen & Co.
Mr. Brian P. Murphy, Ptnr.
111 SW Columbia, #1400
Portland, OR 97201
(503) 220-6068

Arthur Andersen & Co.
Mr. Robert W. Philip, Ptnr.
P.O. Box 650026
Dallas, TX 75265
(214) 741-8300

Arthur Andersen & Co.
Mr. Richard J. Strotman, Ptnr.
33 W. Monroe St.
Chicago, IL 60603
(312) 580-0033

Atlantic Venture Partners
Mr. Robert H. Pratt, Gen. Ptnr.
PO Box 1493
Richmond, VA 23212
(804) 644-5496
D *** 12

The Babcock Group
Mr. Warner King Babock, Pres.
Mr. Piers Curry, Baystreet Ptnrs.
P.O.Box 1022
49 Locust Ave.
New Cannan, CT 06840
(203) 972-3579

Bain Capital
Mr. Geoffrey S. Rehnert
Sr. Associate
Two Copley Pl.
Boston, MA 02116
(617) 572-3000
C *** 12

Baker & Kirk, P.C.
Mr. Michael A. Baker, Pres.
1020 Holcombe, Suite 1444
Houston, TX 77030
(713) 790-9316

Battery Ventures
Mr. Richard D. Frisbie
Gen. Ptnr.
Mr. Robert G. Barrett
Gen. Ptnr.
Mr. Oliver D. Curme
Assoc.
Mr. Sheryl E. Cuker
Research Assoc.
60 Batterymarch St., #1400
Boston, MA 02110
(617) 542-0100
D *** 1

Beacon Partners
Mr. Leonard Vignola, Jr.
Mng. Ptnr.
71 Strawberry Hill Ave., #614
Stamford, CT 06902
(203) 348-8858
D *** 1,4,5,6,7,9,11

Berry Cash Southwest Ptnrshp.
Mr. Harvey B Cash, Gen. Ptnr.
Mr. Glenn A. Norem, Gen. Ptnr.
Ms. Nancy J. Schuele, Assoc.

1 Galleria Tower, Ste. 1375
13355 Noel Rd.
Dallas, TX 75240
(214) 392-7279
D *** 1,8

William Blair Venture Partners
Mr. Samuel B. Guren, Gen. Ptnr.
135 S. LaSalle St., 29th Floor
Chicago, IL 60603
(312) 236-1600
E *** 12

Brownstein, Zeidman & Schomer
Mr. Thomas C. Evans, Ptnr.
1401 New York Ave., N.W., #900
Washington, DC 20036
(202) 879-5760

Burton & Co., Inc.
Mr. Reginald C. Burton, Pres.
P.O. Box 7319
Philadelphia, PA 19101-7319
(312) 263-6663

Camperdown Ventures
Mr. S. Cary Beckwith, III
Gen Ptnr.
115 E. Camperdown Way
Greenville, SC 29601
(803) 233-7770

Capital Services & Resources, Inc
Mr. Charles Y. Bancroft, Treas.
5159 Wheelis Dr., Ste. 104
Memphis, TN 38117
(901) 761-2156
E * 1,4,5,6,8,9

Cardinal Development Cap. Fund I
Mr. Richard F. Bannon, Ptnr.
155 E. Broad St.
Columbus, OH 43215
(614) 464-5550
E *** 1,5,6,8,9,10,11,12

Centennial Fund, The
Mr. G. Jackson Tankersley
Gen. Ptnr.
Mr. Steven C. Halstedt
Gen. Ptnr.
Mr. Charles T. Closson
Gen. Ptnr.
Mr. Mark Dubovoy
VP/Gen. Ptnr.
1999 Broadway, Suite 2100
P.O. Box 13977
Denver, CO 80202
(303) 298-9066
D *** 1,6,8

Cherry Tree Ventures
Mr. Gordon Stofer, Gen. Ptnr.
Mr. Tony Christianson, Gen. Ptnr.
Mr. Thomas Jackson, Inv. Ofcr.
Mr. John Bergstrom, Inv. Analyst
640 Northland Executive Ctr.
3600 W. 80th St.
Minneapolis, MN 55431
(612) 893-9012
D *** 1,5,6,10

Mr. Roger B. Collins
R & C Investments
PO Box 52586
Tulsa, OK 74152
(918) 744-5604
B * 1,3,4,5,9,10,11,12

Columbine Venture Mgmt., Inc.
Mr. Mark Kimmel, Pres.
5613 DTC Pkwy., #510
Englewood, CO 80111
(303) 694-3222

CooleyGodwardCastroHuddles&Tatum
Mr. James C. Gaither, Gen. Ptnr.
One Maritime Plaza, 20th Floor
San Francisco, CA 94111
(415) 981-5252

Coopers & Lybrand
Mr. Robert H. Stavers
One Almaden Blvd., #500
San Jose, CA 95113
(408) 295-1020
1,2,3,5,6,8,9

Corp. For Innovation Development
Mr. Marion C. Dietrich, Pres/CEO
Mr. Donald K. Taylor, VP
Mr. M. Archie Leslie, VP
One N. Capitol Ave., Ste. 520
Indianapolis, IN 46204
(317) 635-7325
C *** 1,5,6,8,9

Criterion Venture Partners
Mr. David Wicks, Jr., Sr. Ptnr.
Mr. M. Scott Albert, Ptnr.
Mr. C. W. Brown, Assoc.
333 Clay St., Ste. 4300
Houston, TX 77002
(713) 751-2400
D *** 1,6,8,9,10,11,12

Dana Venture Capital Corp.
Mr. Gene C. Swartz, Pres.
P.O. Box 1000
Toledo, OH 43697
(419) 535-4780
E * 12

Deloitte Haskins & Sells
Mr. Sanford Antignas
Sr. Consultant
1114 Ave. of Americas
New York, NY 10036
(212) 790-0539

DeSoto Capital Corp.
Mr. William Rudner, Chmn.
Mr. Rudolph H. Holmes, III, Pres.
Mr. James A. Baker, Exec. VP
60 N. Third St.
Memphis, TN 38103
(901) 523-6894
A *** 5,12

Development Corp. of Montana
Mr. Richard L. Bourke, Pres.
350 N. Last Chance Gulch
PO Box 916
Helena, MT 59624
(406) 442-3850
B *** 12

Development Finance Corp.
of New Zealand
Mr. Chris C. Ellison, Mgr.
Mr. Andrew Stedman
Technology & Invest. Consultant
100 Spear St., Ste. 1430
San Francisco, CA 94105
(415) 777-2847

DnC Capital Corp.
Mr. Jack A. Prizzi, VP
600 Fifth Ave.
New York, NY 10020
(212) 765-4800
C *** 1,5,6,8,12

Early Stages Co. (The)
Mr. Frank W. Kuehn, Ptnr.
Mr. William Lanphear, IV, Ptnr
Mr. Micheline L. Chau, Assoc.
244 California St., Ste. 300
San Francisco, CA 94111
(415) 986-5700
C *** 6,7,9,10

El Dorado Ventures
Mr. Brent Rider, Ptnr.
Mr. Gary Kalbach, Ptnr.
Mr. Greg S. Anderson, Gen. Mgr.
2 N. Lake Ave., Ste. 480
Pasadena, CA 91101
(818) 793-1936
D * 12

Elf Technologies, Inc.
Mr. John H. Mahar, Exec. VP
Ms. Christine Civiale, Asst. VP
High Ridge Park, P.O. Box 10037
Stamford, CT 06904
(203) 358-5120
E *** 3,5,8

Ernst & Whinney
Mr. Larry Gray, Ptnr.
5941 Variel
Woodland Hills, CA 91367
(818) 888-0707

Fine & Ambrogne
Mr. Arnold M. Zaff, Ptnr.
Exchange Place
Boston, MA 02109
(617) 367-0100

First Chicago Investment Advisors
Mr. Patrick A. McGivney, VP
Mr. T. Bondurant French, VP
Mr. Michael I Gallie, VP
Mr. David S. Timson, VP
Three First National Plaza
Ste. 0140, 9th Fl.
Chicago, IL 60670
(312) 732-4919
D *** 1,5,6,8,9

Fostin Capital Corp.
Mr. William E. Woods, Pres.
Mr. Thomas M. Levine, Exec. VP
P.O. Box 67
Pittsburgh, PA 15230
(412) 928-8900
C *** 1,6,8

Gatti Tomerlin & Martin Corp.
Mr. John Gatti, Chmn.
Mr. Monte Tomerlin, Pres.
Mr. Harlon Martin, Jr., Exec. VP
405 N. St. Mary's, Suite 222
San Antonio, TX 78205
(512) 229-9028
E *** 1,3,5,6,9,10,12

General Electric Ven. Cap. Corp.
Mr. Harry T. Rein
Pres.
Mr. Stephen L. Waechter
VP/Treas.
3135 Easton Tnpk.
Fairfield, CT 06431
(203) 373-3356
D *** 1,5,6,8,10,12

Golder, Thoma & Cressey
Mr. Stanley C. Golder, Gen. Ptnr.
Mr. Carl D. Thoma, Gen. Ptnr.
Mr. Bryan C. Cressey, Gen. Ptnr.
Mr. Bruce V. Rauner, Gen. Ptnr.
120 S. LaSalle St., Ste. 630
Chicago, IL 60603
(312) 853-3322
E *** 1,4,5,6,8,10,11

Grayrock Capital, Ltd.
Mr. W. J. Gluck, Pres.
2 International Blvd.
Rexdale, Ont. M9W 1A2, Canada
(416) 675-4808
D *** 1,6,7,9,10

Great American Investment Corp.
Mr. James A. Arias, Pres.
Mr. Tim Scanlon, VP
4209 San Mateo NE
Albuquerque, NM 87110
(505) 883-6273
C *** 12

HLPM, Inc.
Mr. Robert W. Fletcher, Pres.
Mr. Albert L. Earley, VP
545 S. Third St.
Louisville, KY 40202
(502) 588-8459

Heizer Corp.
Mr. E.F. Heizer, Jr., Chmn./Pres.
261 S. Bluffs Edge Dr.
Lake Forest, IL 60045
(312) 641-2200

Heller Financial Inc.
Mr. Robert Spitalnic, Sr. VP
101 Park Ave.
New York, NY 10178
(212) 880-7062
E *** 5,9,10,12

Helms, Mulliss & Johnston
B. Bernard Burns, Jr., Esq.
227 N. Tryon St., PO Box 31247
Charlotte, NC 28231
(704) 372-9510

Houston Venture Partners
Mr. Howard Hill, Jr., Gen. Ptnr.
Mr. Thomas Fatjo, Jr., Gen. Ptnr.
Mr. Roger Ramsey, Gen. Ptnr.
Mr. Kent Smith, Gen. Ptnr.
401 S. Louisiana
Houston, TX 77002
(713) 222-8600
E * 12

Hunton & Williams
C. Porter Vaughan, III, Esq.
P.O. Box 1535
Richmond, VA 23212
(804) 788-8200

Hutton Venture Investment Ptnrs.
Mr. James E. McGrath, Pres.
1 Battery Park Plaza, #1801
New York, NY 10004
(212) 742-6486
D *** 1,5,6,8

IEG Venture Mgmt., Inc.
Mr. Francis I. Blair
Pres.
Mrs. Marian M. Zamlynski
Op. Mgr./VP
401 N. Michigan Ave., #2020
Chicago, IL 60611
(312) 644-0890
C *** 1,3,6,8

Indiana Capital Corp.
Mr. Samuel Rea, Pres.
5612 Jefferson Blvd., W.
Ft. Wayne, IN 46804
(219) 432-8622

Inst. of Private Enterprise
Dr. Rollie Tillman, Dir.
312 Carroll Hall, #012-A
Chapel Hill, NC 27514
(919) 962-8201

Interstate Capital Corp.
Mr. William C. McConnell Jr.
Pres.
701 E. Camino Real, #9A
Boca Raton, FL 33432
(305) 395-8466
B *** 3,5,6,8

Investors in Industry
(See 3i under T)

Japan Associate Finance Co., Ltd.
Mr. Teiji Imahara, Chmn.
Toshiba Bldg., 10th Fl.
1-1-1 Shibaura Minato-KU
Tokyo, Japan
(03) 456-5101
E *** 1,5,9,10

Jenkens, Huchison & Gilchrist
Mr. John R. Holzgraefe, Ptnr.
Mr. Mark Wigder, Ptnr.
Mr. W. Alan Kailer, Ptnr.
1455 Ross Ave., 29th Flr.
Dallas, TX 75202
(214) 855-4500

Kirkland & Ellis
Mr. Edward T. Swan
200 E. Randolph Dr.
Chicago, IL 60601
(312) 861-2465

Kleinwort, Benson (NA) Corp.
Mr. Alan L. J. Bowen, Sr., VP
Mr. Christopher Wright, VP
Ms. Michele Hurtubise
Office Mgr.
333 S. Grand, #2900
Los Angeles, CA 90071
(213) 680-2297
E * 3,5,6,9,11,12

Knight & Irish Associates, Inc.
Dr. Joan S. Irish, Pres.
Ms. Faith I. Bliga, VP
420 Lexington Ave., Ste. 2358
New York, NY 10170
(212) 490-0135

Lord, Bissell & Brook
Mr. John K. O'Connor, Ptnr.
115 S. LaSalle St., #3500
Chicago, IL 60603
(312) 443-0615

Lubrizol Enterprises, Inc.
Mr. Donald L. Murfin, Pres.
Mr. Bruce H. Grasser, VP
Mr. James R. Glynn, VP-Fin./Tres.
Mr. David R. Anderson, VP
29400 Lakeland Blvd.
Wickliffe, OH 44092
(216) 943-4200
E *** 8

MRI Ventures
Mr. Charles Moll, VP
Ms. Carol Radosevich, Ven. Mgr.
1650 University Blvd., NE, #500
Albuquerque, NM 87102
(505) 768-6200
D *** 1,5,6,8,12

Madison Venture Capital Corp.
Mr. Norman C. Schultz, Pres.
26515 Carmel Rancho Blvd., #201
Carmel, CA 93923
(408) 625-9650

Manuf. Hanover Vent. Cap. Corp.
Mr. Thomas J. Sandleitner, Pres.
Mr. Edward L. Koch, III, VP
140 E. 45th St., 30th Fl.
New York, NY 10017
(212) 350-6701
E *** 1,4,5,6,7,9,10,11,12

Mayer, Brown, & Platt
Herbert B. Max, Esq.
520 Madison Ave.
New York, NY 10022
(212) 437-7132

Med-Wick Associates, Inc.
Mr. A.A.T. Wickersham, Chmn/Pres.
1902 Fleet National Bank Bldg.
Providence, RI 02903
(401) 751-5270

Menlo Ventures
Mr. Ken E. Joy, Gen. Ptnr.
3000 Sand Hill Rd.
Menlo Park, CA 94025
(415) 854-8540
E *** 12

Michigan Inv. Div., Treas. Dept.
Mr. Michael J. Finn, Admin.
P.O. Box 15128
Lansing, MI 48901
(517) 373-4330
D * 12

Miller Venture Partners
Mr. William I. Miller
Gen. Ptnr.
Mr. Ira G. Peppercorn
Sr. Inv. Mgr.
P.O. Box 808
Columbus, IN 47202
(812) 376-3331
B *** 3,5,6,8,11

Moore BersonLifflander&Mewhinney
Mr. Joel L. Berson
595 Madison Ave.
New York, NY 10022

Morgan Holland Ventures Corp.
Mr. James F. Morgan, Mng. Ptnr.
Mr. Daniel J. Holland, Mng. Ptnr.
Mr. John A. Delahanty, Gen. Ptnr.
Mr. Robert Rosbe, Jr., Gen. Ptnr.
Mr. Edwin M. Kania, Jr., Assoc.
1 Liberty Sq.
Boston, MA 02109
(617) 423-1765
E *** 1,5,6,8

Morgenthaler Ventures
Mr. David T. Morgenthaler
Mng. Ptnr.
Mr. Robert D. Pavey
Gen. Ptnr.
Mr. Paul S. Brentlinger
Gen. Ptnr.
Mr. Robert C. Bellas, Jr.
Gen. Ptnr.
700 National City Bank Bldg.
Cleveland, OH 44114
(216) 621-3070
E *** 1,5,6,8,10

Morrison & Foerster
Tino Kamarck, Esq.
Marco Adelfrio, Esq.
2000 Pennsylvania Ave., NW
Washington, DC 20006
(202) 887-1500

NEPA Venture Fund, L.P.
Mr. Frederick J. Beste, III
Pres.
Ben Franklin Adv. Tech. Ctr.
Lehigh Univ.
Bethlehem, PA 18015
(215) 865-6550
E *** 12

New Enterprise Associates
Mr. Charles Newhall III,
Gen. Ptnr.
300 Cathedral St., Ste. 110
Baltimore, MD 21201
(301) 244-0115
E * 1,6

Nippon Investment & Finance Co.
Ltd.
Mr. Yasutoshi Sasada, Pres.
Mr. Motoki Sugiyama, Gen. Mgr.
39F, Nishi-Shinjuku 1-25-1,
Shinjuku-ku
Tokyo 163 JAPAN
(03) 349-0961
E *** 12

NBM Participatie Beheer B.V.
Mr. Michiel A. de Haan, Gen. Mgr.
Postbus 1800
1000 BV AMSTERDAM
The Netherlands, NL
(020) 543-3346
E * 1,5,6,8,10,11

Noro-Moseley Partners
Mr. Charles Moseley, Gen. Ptnr.
100 Galleria Pkwy., #1240
Atlanta, GA 30339
(404) 955-0020

North American Capital Corp.
Mr. Stanley P. Roth, Chmn.
510 Broad Hollow Rd., #205
Melville, NY 11747
(516) 752-9696
E * 12

North American Cap. Group, Ltd.
Mr. Gregory I. Kravitt, Pres.
Ms. Mindy Warshawsky, Assoc.
7250 N. Cicero
Lincolnwood, IL 60646
(312) 982-1010
D *** 2,4,5,6,9,10

Olwine, Connelly, Chase, et al
Mr. Roger Mulvihill
299 Park Ave.
New York, NY 10017
(212) 207-1831

Onondaga Vent. Capital Fund, Inc.
Mr. Irving W. Schwartz, Exec. VP
327 State Tower Bldg.
Syracuse, NY 13202
(315) 478-0157
B *** 12

Oxford Partners
Mr. Kenneth Rind, Gen. Ptnr.
1266 Main St.
Stamford, CT 06902
(203) 964-0592
E *** 1,6,8

Ozanam Capital Co.-I, LP
Ms. Janis L. Mullin, Gen. Ptnr.
Mr. Adam Robins, Gen. Ptnr.
Mr. Robert Berliner, Gen. Ptnr.
4711 Golf Rd., #706
Skokie, IL 60076
(312) 674-2297
B *** 5,9

Pathfinder Venture Cap. Fund
Mr. A.J. Greenshields, Gen. Ptnr.
7300 Metro Blvd., Ste. 585
Minneapolis, MN 55435
(612) 835-1121
D *** 1,5,6,8

Peat, Marwick, Mitchell & Co.
Mr. Terence D. Dibble, Ptnr.
725 South Figueroa St.
Los Angeles, CA 90017
(213) 972-4000

Peat, Marwick, Mitchell & Co.
Mr. Ronald R. Booth, Ptnr.
1700 IDS Center
Minneapolis, MN 55402
(612) 341-2222

Peat, Marwick, Mitchell & Co.
Mr. Michael E. Lavin, Ptnr.
303 E. Wacker Dr.
Chicago, IL 60601
(312) 938-5043

Peat, Marwick, Mitchell & Co.
Mr. Edgar R. Wood, Jr., Ptnr.
1800 First Union Pl.
Charlotte, NC 28282
(704) 335-5300

Pepper, Hamilton & Scheetz
Mr. Michael B. Staebler, Ptnr.
Mr. Hugh D. Camitta, Esq.
100 Renaissance Ctr., Ste. 3600
Detroit, MI 48243
(313) 259-7110

Peregrine Associates
Mr. Gene I. Miller, Ptnr.
Mr. Frank LaHaye, Ptnr.
606 Wilshire Blvd., Ste. 602
Santa Monica, CA 90401
(213) 458-1441
E *** 1,5,6,8,9,10,12

Pioneer Capital Corp.
Mr. Christopher W. Lynch, Ptnr.
Mr. Frank M. Polestra, Ptnr.
60 State St.
Boston, MA 02109
(617) 742-7825
D * 12

Piper, Jaffray & Hopwood, Inc.
Mr. Frank Bennett,
Mr. R. Hunt Greene, 1st VP
Piper Jaffray Tower
222 So. 9th St.
P.O Box 28
Minneapolis, MN 55402
(612) 342-6000
D *** 1,5,6,8,9,10

Branch Office
Piper, Jaffray & Hopwood
Mr. Gary L. Takacs, VP
1600 IBM Building
Seattle, WA 98101
D *** 1,5,6,8,9,10

Primus Capital Fund
Mr. Loyal Wilson, Mng. Ptnr.
Mr. David A. DeVore, Ptnr.
Mr. William C. Mulligan, Ptnr.
One Cleveland Ctr., #2140
Cleveland, OH 44114
(216) 621-2185
E *** 1,5,6,8,9,12

RBK Management Co.
Mr. Robert B. Kaplan, Pres.
140 S. Dearborn St., #420
Chicago, IL 60603
(312) 263-6058

Reprise Capital Corp.
Mr. Stanley Tulchin, Chmn.
Mr. Irwin B. Nelson, Pres.
591 Stewart Ave.
Garden City, NY 11530
(516) 222-1028
E *** 12

Riordan & McKinzie
Michael P. Ridley, Esq.
300 South Grand Ave., Ste. 2900
Los Angeles, CA 90017
(213) 629-4824

Rothschild Ventures, Inc.
Mr. Jess L. Belser, Pres.
One Rockefeller Pl.
New York, NY 10020
(212) 757-6000
E *** 1,5,6,8,12

Rust Capital Ltd.
Mr. Jeffery C. Garvey, Pres.
Mr. Kenneth P. DeAngelis, Exec VP
Mr. Joseph C. Aragona, VP
Mr. William P. Wood, VP
114 W. 7th St., 1300 Norwood Twr.
Austin, TX 78701
(512) 479-0055
D **** 1,4,5,6,12

Salomon Brothers, Inc.
Mr. Melvin W. Ellis, VP
One New York Plaza
New York, NY 10004
(212) 747-6293
E * 1,6,8

Santa Fe Private Equity Fund
Mr. A. David Silver, Gen. Ptnr.
Ms. Kay Tsunemori, Assoc.
Mr. Kyle A. Legkoff, Assoc.
Ms. Angela H. Peck, Assoc.
524 Camino Del Monte Sol
Santa Fe, NM 87501
(505) 983-1769
D *** 6

SB Capital Corp., Ltd.
Mr. Mitch Kostuch, Exec. VP
Mr. Peter Standeven, VP
Mr. David McCart, Inv. Ofcr.
85 Bloor St. E., #506
Toronto, Ontario M4W 1A9
(416) 967-5439
D *** 1,5,6,8,12

Scientific Advances, Inc.
Mr. Charles G. James, Pres.
Mr. Paul F. Purcell, VP
Mr. Thomas W. Harvey, VP
Mr. Daniel J. Shea, VP
601 W. Fifth Ave.
Columbus, OH 43201
(614) 294-5541
D *** 8

Security Pacific Bus. Credit, Inc
Mr. Nicholas Battaglino, VP
Mr. David J. Freidman, VP
228 E. 45th St.
New York, NY 10017
(212) 309-9302
E ** 5,9,12

South Atlantic Venture Fund
Mr. Donald Burton, Gen. Ptnr.
Mr. Richard Brandewie, Gen. Ptnr.
Ms. Sandra Barber, Admin. Ptnr.
220 East Madison, Suite 530
Tampa, FL 33602-4825
(813) 229-7400
D *** 1,5,6,8,10,12

Spensley, Horn, Jubas & Lubitz
Mr. Bruce W. McRoy, Esq., Ptnr.
1880 Century Park E., #500
Los Angeles, CA 90067
(213) 553-5050

Stephenson Merchant Banking
Mr. A. Emmet Stephenson, Jr.
Sr. Ptnr.
Mr. Thomas Kent Mitchell
Dirctor
100 Garfield St.
Denver, CO 80206
(303) 355-6000
E *** 1,5,6,9,10,11,12

S.W.S. Ltd.
Mr. Steven B. Schaffel, Pres.
Mr. Ira B. Raymond, Exec. VP
Mr. Wendell H. Jones, VP
122 E. 42nd St.
New York, NY 10168
(212) 682-9550
E ** 4,11,12

3i Capital Corp.
Mr. David R. Shaw, Pres.
Ms. Dorothy Langer
99 High St., Ste. 1530
Boston, MA 02110
(617) 542-8560

Taylor International
Mr. Don Snow
1801 Quincy St., N.W.
Washington, D.C. 20011
(202) 955-1330

Taylor & Turner
Mr. Marshall Turner, Gen. Ptnr.
Mr. William Taylor, Gen. Ptnr.
220 Montgomery St., Penthouse 10
San Francisco, CA 94104
(415) 398-6821
D * 1,5,6,8

Tektronix Development Co.
Mr. M. H. Chaffin, Jr.
VP/Gen. Mgr.
P.O. Box 4600-M/S 94-383
Beaverton, OR 97075
(503) 629-1121

Texas Infinity Corp.
Mr. C. Charles Bahr, CEO

P.O. Box 2678
Richardson, TX 75083
(214) 231-7070

Tulsa Industrial Authority
Mr. Rick L. Weddle, Gen. Mgr.
616 S. Boston
Tulsa, OK 74119
(918) 585-1201
E *** 5,6

UNC Ventures
Mr. Edward Dugger, III, Pres.
Mr. James W. Norton, Jr., VP
195 State St., #700
Boston, MA 02109
(617) 723-8300
D *** 1,5,6,8,11

Venad Management, Inc.
Ms. Joy London, Ptnr.
375 Park Ave., #3303
New York, NY 10152
(212) 759-2800

Venco SBIC
Bill McAleir, Chmn.
Phil Bardos, Pres.
One Financial Square
Oxnard, CA 93030
(805) 656-4621
B * 5,6,12

The Venture Capital Fund
of New England
Mr. Richard Farrell, Gen. Ptnr.
100 Franklin St.
Boston, MA 02110
(617) 451-2575
C *** 1,5,8

Venture Economics, Inc.
Mr. Stanley Pratt, Chmn.
Ms. Jane K. Morris, VP
16 Laurel Ave., P.O. Box 348
Wellesley Hills, MA 02181
(617) 431-8100

Venture Founders Corp.
Mr. Alexander Dingee, Jr., Pres
Mr. Grogory Hulecki, Inv. Mgr.
Mr. Ross Yeiter, Treas.
One Cranberry Hill
Lexington, MA 02173
(617) 863-0900
D *** 1,5,6,8

Whitehead Associates, Inc.
Mr. Joseph A. Orlando, Pres.
Mr. William E. Engbers, VP
15 Valley Dr.
Greenwich, CT 06830
(203) 629-4633
D *** 1,5,6,8,10,12

William Blair Venture Partners
Mr. Samuel B. Guren
Gen. Ptnr.
Mr. Scott F. Meadow
Gen. Ptnr.
Mr. James Crawford, III
Gen. Ptnr.
Mr. Gregg S. Newmark
Assoc.
135 S. LaSalle St., 29th Fl.
Chicago, IL 60603
(312) 236-1600
E *** 12

Arthur Young
  Entrepreneurial Services
Mr. Jerome S. Engel, Ptnr.
Mr. Marc Berger, Ptnr.
1 Sansome St., Suite 3300
San Francisco, CA 94104
(415) 393-2733

Arthur Young & Co.
Mr. Robert J. Brennan, Dir.
1111 Summer St.
Stamford, CT 06905
(203) 356-1800

Arthur Young & Co.
Mr. John J. Huntz, Jr., Ptnr.
235 Peachtree St., NE
2100 Gas Light Tower
Atlanta, GA 30043
(404) 581-1130

Arthur Young & Co.
Mr. Al Boos, Ptnr.
6501 Americas Parkway NE, Ste 400
Albuquerque, NM 87110
(505) 881-6363

Arthur Young & Co.
Mr. Dennis Serlen, Gen. Ptnr.
277 Park Ave.
New York, NY 10172
(212) 407-1611

Arthur Young & Co,
Mr. Paul E. Gricus
1100 Fleet Center
Providence, RI 02903
(401) 274-1800

Arthur Young & Co.
Mr. Edward B. Beanland, Ptnr.
2121 San Jacinto, Ste. 700
Dallas, TX 75201
(214) 969-8666

Small Business Administration (SBA) Field Offices

Alabama
908 South 20th Street
Birmingham, Alabama 35256
205/254-1344

Alaska
Federal Building
701 C Street, Box 67
Anchorage, Alaska 99513
907/271-4022

Box 14
101 12th Avenue
Fairbanks, Alaska 99701
907/456-0211

Arizona
3030 North Central Avenue
Phoenix, Arizona 85012
602/241-2200

301 West Congress Street
Federal Bldg., Box 33
Tucson, Arizona 85701
602/792-6715

Arkansas
320 W. Capitol Avenue
Little Rock, Arkansas 72201
501/378-5871

California
2202 Monterey Street
Fresno, California 93721
209/487-5189

660 J Street, Suite 215
Sacramento, California
95814
916/440-4461

880 Front Street
San Diego, California 92188
619/293-5440

*450 Golden Gate Avenue
P.O. Box 36044
San Francisco, California
94102
415/556-7487

211 Main Street
San Francisco, California
94105
415/974-0642

350 South Figueroa Street
Los Angeles, California 90071
213/688-2956

Fidelity Federal Bldg.
2700 North Main Street
Santa Ana, California 92701
714/836-2494

111 West St. John Street
San Jose, California 95113
408/275-7584

Colorado
*Executive Tower Building
1405 Curtis Street
Denver, Colorado 80202
303/844-5441

721 19th Street
Denver, Colorado 80202
303/844-2607

Connecticut
One Hartford Square W.
Hartford, Connecticut 06106
203/244-4041

Delaware
844 King Street
Wilmington, Delaware 19801
302/573-6294

District of Columbia
1111 18th St., N.W.
Washington, D.C. 20036
202/634-4950

Florida
400 West Bay Street
Jacksonville, Florida 32202
904/791-3782

2222 Ponce De Leon Blvd.
Coral Gables, Florida 33134
305/350-5521

700 Twiggs Street
Tampa, Florida 33602
813/228-2594

3500 45th Street
West Palm Beach, Florida
33407
305/689-2223

Georgia
*1375 Peachtree Street, N.E.
Atlanta, Georgia 30367
404/881-4999

1720 Peachtree Road, N.W.
Atlanta, Georgia 30309
404/881-4749

52 North Main Street
Statesboro, Georgia 30458
912/489-8719

Guam
Pacific News Bldg.
238 O'Hara Street
Agana, Guam 96910
671/472-7277

Hawaii
300 Ala Moana
P.O. Box 2213
Honolulu, Hawaii 96850
808/546-8950

Idaho
1005 Main Street
Boise, Idaho 83702
208/334-1096

Illinois
*219 South Dearborn Street
Chicago, Illinois 60604
312/353-0359

219 South Dearborn Street
Chicago, Illinois 60604
312/353-4528

Washington Building
Four North Old State
Capitol Plaza
Springfield, Illinois 62701
217/492-4416

Indiana
501 East Monroe Street
South Bend, Indiana 46601
219/236-8361

New Federal Bldg.
575 North Pennsylvania Street
Indianapolis, Indiana 46209
317/269-7272

Iowa
210 Walnut Street
Des Moines, Iowa 50309
515/284-4422

373 Collins Road, N.E.
Cedar Rapids, Iowa 52402
319/399-2571

Kansas
Main Place Bldg.
110 East Waterman Street
Wichita, Kansas 67202
316/269-6271

Kentucky
600 Federal Place
Louisville, Kentucky 40201
502/582-5971

Louisiana
1661 Canal Street
New Orleans, Louisiana
70112
504/589-6685

500 Fannin Street
Federal Bldg. & Courthouse
Shreveport, Louisiana 71101
318/226-5196

Maine
40 Western Avenue
Augusta, Maine 04330
207/622-8378

Maryland
8600 LaSalle Road
Towson, Maryland 21204
301/962-4392

Massachusetts
*60 Batterymarch Street
Boston, Massachusetts
02110
617/223-3204

150 Causeway Street
Boston, Massachusetts 02114
617/223-2100

302 High Street
Holyoke, Massachusetts
01040
413/536-8770

1550 Main Street
Springfield, Massachusetts
01103
413/785-0268

Michigan
477 Michigan Avenue
McNamara Bldg.
Detroit, Michigan 48226
313/226-6075

220 West Washington Street
Marquette, Michigan 49885
906/225-1108

* Regional Office

Minnesota
100 North 6th Street
Minneapolis, Minnesota
55403
612/349-3550

Mississippi
Gulf National Life
Insurance Bldg.
111 Fred Haise Blvd.
Biloxi, Mississippi 39530
601/435-3676

100 West Capitol Street
New Federal Bldg.
Jackson, Mississippi 39269
601/960-4378

Missouri
*911 Walnut Street
Kansas City, Missouri 64106
816/374-5288

818 Grande Avenue
Kansas City, Missouri 64106
816/374-3419

815 Olive Street
St. Louis, Missouri 63101
314/425-6600

Federal Court House Bldg.
339 Broadway
Cape Girardeau, Missouri
63701
314/335-6039

309 North Jefferson
Springfield, Missouri 65803
417/864-7670

Montana
2601 First Avenue North
Billings, Montana 59101
406/657-6047

301 South Park Avenue
Helena, Montana 59626
406/449-5381

Nebraska
South 19th Street
Omaha, Nebraska 68102
402/221-4691

Nevada
301 East Stewart Street
Las Vegas, Nevada 89125
702/385-6611

50 South Virginia Street
Reno, Nevada 89505
702/784-5268

New Hampshire
55 Pleasant Street
Concord, New Hampshire
03301
603/224-4724

New Jersey
1800 East Davis Street
Camden, New Jersey 08104
609/757-5183

60 Park Place
Newark, New Jersey 07102
201/645-2434

New Mexico
Patio Plaza Building
5000 Marble Ave., N.E.
Albuquerque, N.M. 87110
505/766-3430

New York
*26 Federal Plaza
New York, New York 10278
212/264-7772

445 Broadway
Albany, New York 12207
518/472-6300

111 West Huron Street
Buffalo, New York 14202
716/846-4301

333 East Water Street
Elmira, New York 14901
607/733-4686

35 Pinelaw Road
Melville, New York 11747
516/454-0750

26 Federal Plaza
New York, New York 10278
212/264-4355

100 State Street
Rochester, New York 14614
716/263-6700

100 South Clinton St.
Federal Bldg.
Syracuse, New York 13260
315/423-5383

North Carolina
230 South Tryon Street
Charlotte, North Carolina
28202
704/371-6563

---

* Regional Office

215 South Evans Street
Greenville, North Carolina
27834
919/752-3798

North Dakota
657 2nd Avenue
Fargo, North Dakota 58102
701/237-5771

Ohio
1240 East 9th St.
AJC Federal Bldg.
Cleveland, Ohio 44199
216/522-4180

85 Marconi Boulevard
Columbus, Ohio 43215
614/469-6860

550 Main Street
Cincinnati, Ohio 45202
513/684-2814

Oklahoma
200 N.W. 5th Street
Oklahoma City, Oklahoma
73102
405/231-4301

333 W. Fourth Street
Tulsa, Oklahoma 74103
918/581-7495

Oregon
1220 S.W. Third Avenue
Federal Building
Portland, Oregon 97204
503/423-5221

Pennsylvania
*One Bala Cynwyd Plaza
231 St. Asaphs Road
Bala Cynwyd, Pennsylvania
19004
215/596-5889

100 Chestnut Street
Harrisburg, Pennsylvania
17101
717/782-3840

960 Penn Avenue
Convention Tower
Pittsburgh, Pennsylvania
15222
412/644-2780

Penn Place
20 North Pennsylvania Avenue
Wilkes-Barre, Pennsylvania
18701
717/826-6497

Puerto Rico
Federal Building
Carlos Chardon Avenue
Hato Rey, Puerto Rico 00919
809/773-3480

Rhode Island
380 Westminster Mall
Providence, Rhode Island
02903
401/351-7500

South Carolina
1835 Assembly Street
Columbia, South Carolina
29201
803/765-5376

South Dakota
101 South Main Avenue
Sioux Falls, South Dakota
57102
605/336-2980

Tennessee
404 James Robertson
Parkway
Nashville, Tennessee 37219
615/251-5881

Texas
Federal Building
300 East 8th Street
Austin, Texas 78701
512/482-5288

400 Mann Street
Corpus Christi, Texas 78408
512/888-3331

*8625 King George Drive
Bldg. C
Dallas, Texas 75235
214/767-7643

1100 Commerce Street
Dallas, Texas 75242
214/767-0605

4100 Rio Bravo Street
Pershing W. Bldg.
El Paso, Texas 79902
915/543-7586

221 West Lancaster Avenue
Ft. Worth Texas 76102
817/334-5463

222 East Van Buren Street
Harlingen, Texas 78550
512/423-8934

* Regional Office

2525 Murthworth
Houston, Texas 77054
713/660-4401

1611 10th Street
Lubbock, Texas 79401
806/743-7466

100 South Washington Street
Marshall, Texas 75670
214/935-5257

727 East Durango Street
Federal Bldg.
San Antonio, Texas 78206
512/229-6250

Utah
125 South State Street
Salt Lake City, Utah 84138
801/524-5800

Vermont
87 State Street
Montpelier, Vermont 05602
802/229-0538

Virginia
400 North 8th Street
Richmond, Virginia 23240
804/771-2617

Virgin Islands
Veterans Drive
St. Thomas, Virgin Islands
00801
809/774-8530

P.O. Box 4010
Christiansted, Virgin Islands
00820
809/773-3480

Washington
2615 4th Avenue
Seattle, Washington 98121
206/442-5676

915 Second Avenue
Seattle, Washington 98174
206/442-5534

920 Riverside Avenue
Spokane, Washington 99210
509/456-3786

West Virginia
109 North 3rd Street
Clarksburg, West Virginia
26301
304/623-5631

628 Charleston National Plaza
Charleston, West Virginia
25301
304/347-5220

Wisconsin
500 South Barstow Street
Eau Claire, Wisconsin 54701
715/834-9012

212 East Washington Avenue
Madison, Wisconsin 53703
608/264-5261

310 West Wisconsin Avenue
Milwaukee, Wisconsin 53203
414/291-3941

Wyoming
100 East B Street
Casper, Wyoming 82602
307/261-5761

Returns on Various Types of Investments*

R. S. Salomon, Jr.
Mallory J. Lennox

Cashing in collectibles and commodities—literally—at the start of the decade would have been a smart move. Since 1980, cash has provided a compound annual rate of return that is more than twice the rate of inflation and more than twice the return available from the best-performing tangible asset. The ascendancy of financial assets in the 1980s has been dramatic and unassailable (see Figures 1 and 2). During this time, stocks and bonds have provided returns of 17.4% and 15.2%, respectively, against an inflation rate of 5%. In contrast, none of the tangible assets has provided real returns, and half have provided negative nominal returns.

Of the tangible group, commodities have fared the worst. The combination of record carrying costs and only modest inflation rates has been especially unattractive for commodity investors. Collectibles, which are rarely financed by borrowing, fared better than commodity-related assets, but they also failed to protect investors' purchasing power. Housing provided the best return of the tangible group—4.8%—which nearly matched inflation. Earlier in the decade, the advent of variable-rate mortgages muted the effect of rising rates on home prices, and more recently, lower mortgage rates have prompted a recovery in the housing sector.

Salomon Brothers is forecasting an economic environment that is ideally suited to the continued superior performance of financial assets over the next 12–18 months. We expect continued growth in the economy but at a moderate pace—2%-4%—so that an overheating economy is not likely to contribute to pricing pressures. Costs are expected to remain low. Raw material prices, especially oil, are not likely to spiral upward. Labor union disputes center around job security, not wage increases, these

days: contracts settled in the first quarter of this year had an average annual pay increase of just 1.6%. In sum, we expect continued low inflation rates this year—2%—and next—3.5%—a pace that is not likely, in our view, to spur investment interest in tangible assets as inflation hedges.

The political climate also appears to favor financial assets. The proposed tax reform measures would have several benefits. Rising tax rates enhance the appeal of some forms of tangible assets, since it is easier to avoid tax consequences when disposing of them. Falling tax rates reduce this appeal. Furthermore, the proposals are likely to stimulate savings and investment and to discourage consumption—especially purchases financed with debt. Lower marginal tax rates give individuals a greater stake in their financial future and, at the same time, raise the after-tax cost of borrowing. The proposal would further reduce the attractiveness of debt-financed consumption by limiting the deductibility of interest payments. Finally, lower tax rates suggest that more investment decisions will be motivated by economics rather than by tax considerations.

Against this economic and political backdrop, we feel confident that financial assets will occupy the top ranks again in next year's survey (this year's rankings appear in Figure 3). Foreign exchange is not likely to maintain the top spot, but should provide a real return over the next 12 months based on our forecast of an additional 10%–12% decline in the U.S. dollar. Interest rates are likely to drift lower for the balance of the year before stabilizing as economic growth reaccelerates.

In this context, we believe that long-dated financial assets will continue to outperform cash equivalents over the next 12 months. Equities are expected to provide the best returns, which we estimate at 15% over the next 12 months. Lower interest rates, continued high-quality earnings, and overfunded pension plans should bias price/earnings multiples upward to an estimated 14 times earnings from 12 times currently. At the same time, continued economic growth is expected to boost reported earnings by 10% this year and by 12% in 1987.

Because prices have risen by only 1.5% over the past 12 months, it was not too difficult to preserve purchasing power, and all but three assets—farmland, silver and oil—provided investors with positive real and nominal returns.

* Although the information in this report has been obtained from sources which Salomon Brothers Inc. believes to be reliable, we do not guarantee its accuracy and such information may be incomplete or condensed. All opinions and estimates included in this report constitute our judgment as of this date and are subject to change without notice. This report is for information purposes only and is not intended as an offer or solicitation with respect to the purchase or sale of any security.

Editor's Note: Stock returns are for the S&P 500 and include appreciation plus dividends. Bond returns are for Salomon Brothers Index and include appreciation plus interest.

Source: What a Difference a Decade Makes, by R. S. Salomon, Jr. and Mallory J. Lennox © Salomon Brothers Inc., June 9, 1986.

Figure 1. The 1980s — A Decade for Financial Assets
(Compound Annual Rate of Return, 1980-86)

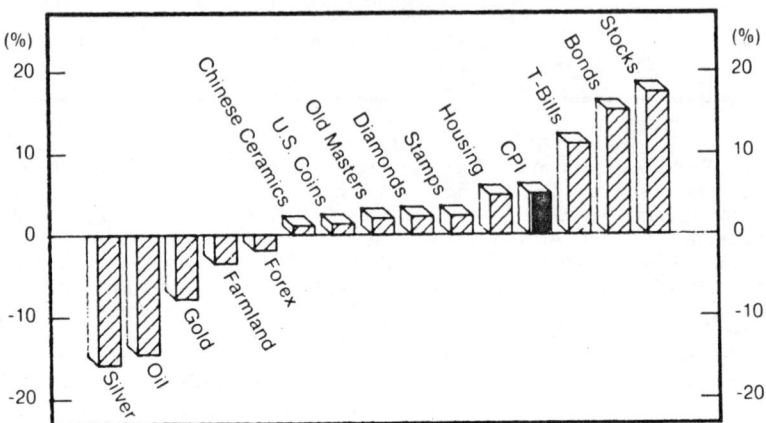

The volatility of returns has not abated, and getting it right in the short run is still key to good longer-term performance. In the case of oil, for example, two years of declines have nearly wiped out the investment return for the past ten years. In the 1984 survey, oil ranked first on a ten-year basis, with an average return of 10.1%; this year it's dead last with a ten-year return of 1%. Stamps rose by 14.5% this past year, providing the best return among the tangible assets and the fourth-best return overall. This significant improvement from the price declines of the past five years reflects the absence of speculators in this market and the return of the true collector. Also, the International Stamp

Exhibition, which takes place once every ten years, was held in Chicago, Illinois, last week. The last International Exhibit was held in 1976, and prices rose by 21% that year, compared with an average of 13% during the preceding five years.

Gold ranked fifth, somewhat surprisingly. With oil prices—everyone's favorite inflation proxy—cut in half, one would expect gold—everyone's favorite inflation hedge—to have also performed poorly. However, the price of the metal rose by 9.2%, on fears of supply disruptions as hostilities in South Africa escalated. Diamonds ranked sixth with a return of 7.5%, a dramatic improvement over the 1.2% average

Figure 2. The 1970s — A Decade for Collectibles and Commodities
(Compound Annual Rate of Return, 1970-80)

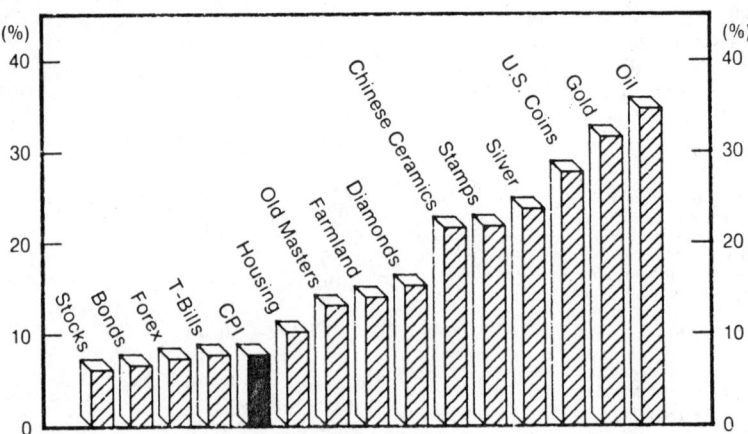

Figure 3. One-Year Rankings, 1986 vs. 1985

	Period Ended 1 Jun 1986		Period Ended 1 Jun 1985	
	Return	Rank	Return	Rank
Foreign Exchange	35.0%	1	(11.3)%	13
Stocks	34.8	2	28.7	2
Bonds	26.0	3	42.9	1
Stamps	14.5	4	(9.6)	11
Gold	9.2	5	(20.3)	14
Diamonds	7.5	6	0.0	9
U.S. Coins	7.2	7	11.5	4
Housing	7.2	8	2.5	8
Treasury Bills	7.1	9	9.5	5
Old Masters[a]	4.8	10	13.6	3
CPI	**1.5**	**11**	**3.7**	**7**
Chinese Ceramics[a]	1.5	12	5.9	6
U.S. Farmland	(12.2)	13	(10.0)	12
Silver	(15.5)	14	(34.3)	15
Oil	(48.8)	15	(4.5)	10
Range	35.0%-(48.8)%		42.9%-(34.3)%	

[a] Source: Sotheby's.

return for 1980–85. Since diamonds are a dollar-based commodity, the weakness in the U.S. dollar has translated a 7.5% price hike into a significant cut in price for the rest of the world, particularly for the Japanese, who have reportedly been especially active in the diamond markets recently.

On a longer-term basis, the spectacular returns of the past two years have helped stocks and bonds climb up out of the basement (see Figure 4). On a ten-year basis, stocks now rank second and bonds rank fourth. As recently as 1983, the ten-year rankings were 12th and 13th, respectively, out of 15. On a 15-year basis, all ten tangible assets provided real returns. However, for shorter intervals, that number drops dramatically to seven on a ten-year basis, and to two on a five-year basis. Stocks, bonds and cash have provided real returns over all three time periods.

Figure 4. Compound Annual Rates of Return

	15 Years	Rank	10 Years	Rank	5 Years	Rank	1 Year	Rank
U.S. Coins	18.2%	1	15.1%	1	2.2%	8	7.2%	7
Gold	15.2	2	10.5	7	(6.6)	13	9.2	5
Stamps	14.3	3	13.9	2	(2.0)	11	14.5	4
Oil	13.0	4	1.0	15	(15.4)	15	(48.8)	15
Diamonds	10.5	5	9.7	9	2.7	7	7.5	6
Chinese Ceramics[a]	10.4	6	12.0	4	1.5	10	1.5	12
Bonds	9.3	7	10.6	5	20.9	1	26.0	3
Treasury Bills	9.2	8	10.2	8	9.0	3	7.1	9
Old Masters[a]	8.5	9	10.6	6	7.7	4	4.8	10
Silver	8.5	10	1.9	14	(13.5)	14	(15.5)	14
Housing	8.2	11	7.8	10	4.1	5	7.2	8
Stocks	8.2	12	12.0	3	16.5	2	34.8	2
U.S. Farmland	7.4	13	4.1	12	(6.2)	12	(12.2)	13
CPI	**6.9**	**14**	**6.8**	**11**	**4.0**	**6**	**1.5**	**11**
Foreign Exchange	4.2	15	2.4	13	1.8	9	35.0	1

Inflation Scorecard (Number of Assets That Outperformed Inflation)

Tangibles	10 out of 10	7 out of 10	2 out of 10	6 out of 10
• Collectibles	4 out of 4	4 out of 4	1 out of 4	3 out of 4
• Commodities	4 out of 4	2 out of 4	0 out of 4	2 out of 4
• Real Estate	2 out of 2	1 out of 2	1 out of 2	1 out of 2
Financials	3 out of 4	3 out of 4	3 out of 4	4 out of 4

[a] Source: Sotheby's.
Note: All returns are for the period ended June 1, 1986, based on latest available data.

Stock Market: U.S. and Foreign

Stock Exchanges

Common Stocks (shares of ownership in a corporation) are traded on several exchanges. The best known are the New York Stock Exchange and the American Stock Exchange, both located in Manhattan's financial district. Generally, the stocks of the largest companies are traded on the New York Stock Exchange, while somewhat smaller companies are traded on the American Exchange. There are also a number of regional exchanges such as the Midwest Exchange in Chicago and the Pacific Exchange in San Francisco. These exchanges trade stocks of local corporations as well as stocks listed on the New York and American Exchanges.

In addition, there is the Over-The Counter-Market (OTC) which, unlike the exchanges previously mentioned, does not have a specific location but consists of a network of brokers and dealers linked by telephone and private wires. Smaller or relatively new companies are traded on the OTC. Trading information for many (but far from all) stocks on the OTC market is collected and displayed on a computerized system, the National Association of Security Dealers Automatic Quote System (NASDAQ).

Large institutional traders (mutual and pension funds, insurance companies, etc.) often trade blocks of stocks directly with one another. This information is collected and displayed on the Instinet System.

Major Stock Exchanges: U.S. and Canada

UNITED STATES

AMERICAN STOCK EXCHANGE, INC.
86 Trinity Place
New York, New York 10006

BOSTON STOCK EXCHANGE, INC.
53 State Street
Boston, Massachusetts 02109

THE CINCINNATI STOCK EXCHANGE, INC.
205 Dixie Terminal Building
Cincinnati, Ohio 45202

INTERMOUNTAIN STOCK EXCHANGE, INC.
39 Exchange Place
Salt Lake City, Utah 84111

MIDWEST STOCK EXCHANGE, INC.
120 South LaSalle Street
Chicago, Illinois 60603

NEW YORK STOCK EXCHANGE, INC.
11 Wall Street
New York, New York 10005

PACIFIC STOCK EXCHANGE, INC.
301 Pine Street
San Francisco, California 94104
and

618 South Spring Street
Los Angeles, California 90014

PHILADELPHIA STOCK EXCHANGE, INC.
17th Street & Stock Exchange Place
Philadelphia, Pennsylvania 19103

SPOKANE STOCK EXCHANGE, INC.
225 Peyton Building
Spokane, Washington 99201

CANADA

ALBERTA STOCK EXCHANGE
300–5th Avenue S.W.
Calgary, Alberta T2P 3C4

MONTREAL STOCK EXCHANGE
The Stock Exchange Tower
800 Victoria Square
Montreal, Quebec H4Z 1A9

TORONTO STOCK EXCHANGE
2 First Canadian Place
Toronto, Ontario M5X 1J2

VANCOUVER STOCK EXCHANGE
536 Howe Street
Vancouver, B.C. V6C QE1

WINNIPEG STOCK EXCHANGE
303–167 Lombard Avenue
Winnipeg, Manitoba R3B OT6

Investment Returns on Stocks, Bonds, and Bills

Roger G. Ibbotson* and Laurence B. Siegel**

Our look at history consists of examining the returns of five capital market sectors. We measure total returns (capital gains plus income) on common stocks, long-term corporate bonds, long-term government bonds, U.S. Treasury bills, and rates of inflation on consumer goods. Comparing the returns from the various sectors gives us insights into the returns available from taking risk and the relationships between capital market returns and inflation.

THE RISKS AND REWARDS

We display graphically the rewards and risks available from the U.S. capital markets over the past 60 years. Exhibit 1 shows the growth of an investment in common stocks, long-term government bonds, and Treasury bills as well as the increase in the inflation index over the 60-year period. Each of the series is initiated at $1 at year-end 1925. The vertical scale is logarithmic so that equal distances represent equal percentage changes anywhere along the axis. The graph vividly portrays that common stocks were the big winner over the entire period. If $1 were invested in stocks at year-end 1925 and all dividends reinvested, the dollar investment would have grown to $279.12 by year-end 1985. This phenomenal growth was not without substantial risk, especially during the earlier portion of the period. In contrast, long-term government bonds (with a constant 20-year maturity) exhibited much less risk, but grew to only $11.03.

A virtually riskless strategy (for those with short-term time horizons) has been to buy U.S. Treasury bills. However, Treasury bills have had a marked tendency to track inflation, with the result that their real (inflation adjusted) return is near zero for the entire 1926–1984 period. Note that the tracking is only prevalent over the latter portion of the period. During periods of deflation (such as the late 1920s and early 1930s) the Treasury bill returns were near zero, but not negative, since no one intentionally buys securities with negative yields. Beginning in the early 1940s, the yields (returns) on Treasury bills were pegged by the government at low rates while high inflation was experienced. The government pegging ended with the U.S. Treasury-Federal Reserve Accord in March 1951.

We summarize the investment returns in Exhibit 2 by presenting the average annual returns over the 1926–1985 period. Common stocks returned a compounded (geometric mean) total return of 9.8 percent per year. The annual compound return from capital appreciation alone was 4.8 percent. After adjusting for inflation, annual compounded total returns were 6.6 percent per year.*

The average total return over any single year (arithmetic mean) for stocks was 12.0 percent, with positive returns recorded in two-thirds of the years (40 out of 60 years). The risk or degree of return fluctuation is measured by standard deviation as 21.2 percent. The frequency .distribution (histogram) counts the number of years the returns fell in each 5 percent return increment. Note the wide variations in common stock returns relative to the other capital market sectors. Annual stock returns ranged from 54.0 percent in 1933 to −43.3 percent in 1931.

A simple example illustrates the difference between geometric and arithmetic means. Suppose $1 were invested in a common stock portfolio that experiences successive annual returns of +50 percent and −50 percent. At the end of the first year, the portfolio is worth $1.50. At the end of the second year, the portfolio is worth $0.75. The annual arithmetic mean is 0 percent, whereas the annual geometric mean (compounded return) is −13.4 percent. Naturally, it is the geometric mean that more directly measures the change in wealth over more than one period. On the other hand, the arithmetic mean is a better representation of typical performance over any single annual period.

The other capital market sectors also had returns commensurate with their risks. Long-term corporate bonds outperformed the default-free, long-term government bonds, which in turn outperformed the essentially riskless U.S. Treasury bills. Over the entire period the riskless U.S. Treasury bills had a return almost identical with the inflation rate. Thus, we again note that the real rate of interest (the inflation-adjusted riskless rate) has been on average very near 0 percent historically.

---

* Professor, Yale School of Management, New Haven, Connecticut.

** Managing Partner, Ibbotson Associates, Inc., Chicago, Illinois.

* Editor's note: While common stock total returns over the current decade have exceeded inflation by a substantial amount, the combined effect of inflation and taxes has made these returns quite meager in real terms. Other asset returns, adjusted for inflation and taxes, have been negative. Thus for common stocks, total returns over 1976–1985 were 14.3 percent as compared with 9.8 percent for long-term corporate bonds and 9.0 percent for U.S. Treasury bills. All figures neglect taxes. The inflation rate over the period was 7.3 percent. After taxes, it is evident that only common stocks earned a positive real return over the period. Assuming a 40 percent tax rate and future 6 percent inflation, and investment must earn 10 percent before taxes to break even.

EXHIBIT 1: WEALTH INDEXES OF INVESTMENTS IN THE U.S. CAPITAL MARKETS,
1926–1985 (assumed initial investment of $1.00 at year-end 1925, includes reinvest-
ment income)

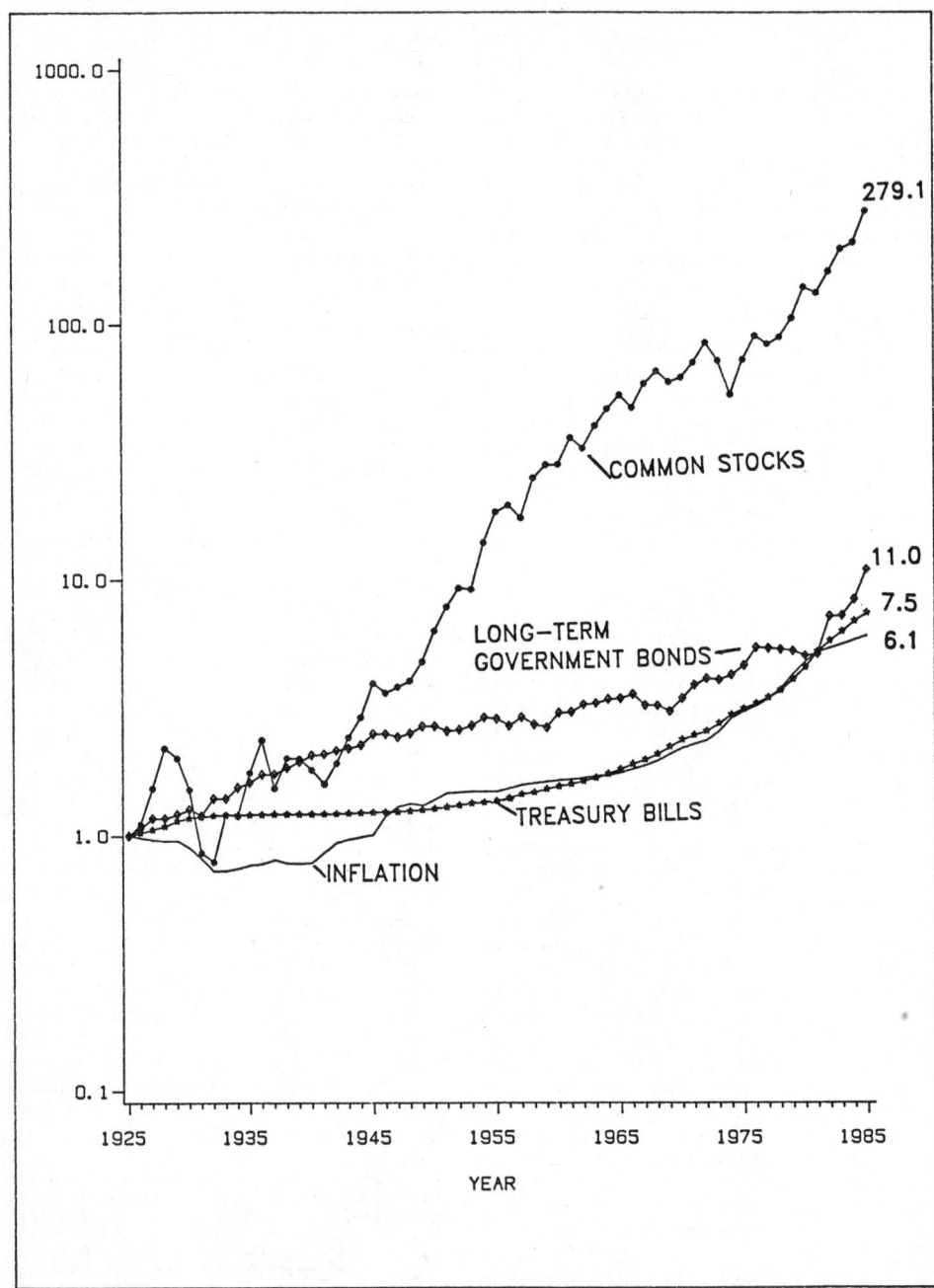

Source: Roger G. Ibbotson and Rex A. Sinquefield, *Stocks, Bonds, Bills, and Inflation: The Past and The Future* (1982 Edition), Financial Analysts Research Foundation (Charlottesville, Va.: 1982); for 1926–1981; *Stocks, Bonds, Bills, and Inflation: 1986 Yearbook*, published by Ibbotson Associates [8 S. Michigan Avenue, Suite 707, Chicago, IL. 60603, phone 312-263-3434], 1986, for updates.

EXHIBIT 2: BASIC SERIES: TOTAL ANNUAL RETURNS, 1926–1985

SERIES	GEOMETRIC MEAN	ARITHMETIC MEAN	STANDARD DEVIATION	DISTRIBUTION
COMMON STOCKS	9.8%	12.0%	21.2%	
LONG TERM CORPORATE BONDS	4.8	5.1	8.3	
LONG TERM GOVERNMENT BONDS	4.1	4.4	8.2	
U.S. TREASURY BILLS	3.4	3.5	3.4	
INFLATION	3.1	3.2	4.9	

Ibbotson Associates • Chicago

                                                                        -90×   0×   +90×

Source: *Stocks, Bonds, Bills and Inflation: 1986 Yearbook*, Ibbotson Associates, Inc., Chicago, 1986.

MEASUREMENT OF THE FIVE SERIES

The returns were computed by compounding monthly returns, with no adjustments made for transactions costs or taxes. We describe each of the five total return series which are listed annually in Exhibit 3. The index numbers in Exhibit 3 are dollar values of a $1 investment made on December 31, 1925. They can be converted to yearly returns by taking the ratio of a given year-end index value to the previous year-end value, then subtracting one (1). For example, the return for common stocks for 1985 equals (279.115 ÷ 211.198) − 1 = 0.322, or 32.2 percent.

Common Stocks

The total return index is based upon Standard & Poor's (S&P) Composite Index with dividends reinvested monthly. To the extent that the 500 stocks currently included in the S&P Composite Index (prior to March 1957, there were 90 stocks) are representative of all stocks in the United States, the market value weighting scheme allows the returns of the index to correspond to the aggregate stock market returns in the U.S. economy.

Long-Term Corporate Bonds

We measure the total returns of a corporate bond index with approximately 20 years to maturity. We use Salomon Brothers' High-Grade Long-Term Corporate Bond Index from its beginning in 1969 through 1985. For the period 1946–68 we backdate Salomon Brothers' index using Salomon Brothers' monthly yield data and similar methodology. For the period 1926–45

we compute returns using Standard & Poor's monthly high-grade corporate composite bond yield data, assuming a 4 percent coupon and a 20-year maturity.

Long-Term Government Bonds

To measure the total returns of long-term U.S. government bonds, we use the bond data obtained from the U.S. Government Bond File (constructed by Lawrence Fisher) at the Center for Research in Security Prices (CRSP) at the University of Chicago. We attempt to maintain a 20-year bond portfolio whose returns do not reflect the potential tax benefits, impaired negotiability, or the special redemption or call privileges frequently characterizing government bond prices and yields.

U.S. Treasury Bills

For the U.S. Treasury bill index, we again use the data in the CRSP U.S. Government Bond File. We measure one-month holding period returns for the shortest-term bills not less than one month in maturity. Since U.S. Treasury bills were not initiated until 1929, we use short-term coupon bonds whenever bill quotes are unavailable.

Consumer Price Index

We utilize the Consumer Price Index for All Urban Consumers (CPI-U), not seasonally adjusted, to measure inflation. The CPI-U, and its predecessor, the CPI (which we use prior to January 1978) is constructed by the Bureau of Labor Statistics, U.S. Department of Labor, Washington, D.C.

EXHIBIT 3: BASIC SERIES, INDEXES OF YEAR-END CUMULATIVE WEALTH, 1925–1985 (year-end 1925 = 1.000)

Year	Common Stocks		Long-Term Government Bonds		Long-Term Corporate Bonds	U.S. Treasury Bills	Consumer Price Index
	Total Returns	Capital Appreciation Only	Total Returns	Capital Appreciation Only	Total Returns	Total Returns	Rates of Inflation
1925	1.000	1.000	1.000	1.000	1.000	1.000	1.000
1926	1.116	1.057	1.078	1.039	1.074	1.033	0.985
1927	1.535	1.384	1.174	1.095	1.154	1.065	0.965
1928	2.204	1.908	1.175	1.061	1.186	1.099	0.955
1929	2.018	1.681	1.215	1.059	1.225	1.152	0.957
1930	1.516	1.202	1.272	1.072	1.323	1.179	0.899
1931	0.859	0.636	1.204	0.981	1.299	1.192	0.814
1932	0.789	0.540	1.407	1.108	1.439	1.204	0.730
1933	1.214	0.792	1.406	1.073	1.588	1.207	0.734
1934	1.197	0.745	1.547	1.146	1.808	1.209	0.749
1935	1.767	1.053	1.624	1.170	1.982	1.211	0.771
1936	2.367	1.346	1.746	1.225	2.116	1.213	0.780
1937	1.538	0.827	1.750	1.194	2.174	1.217	0.804
1938	2.016	1.035	1.847	1.228	2.307	1.217	0.782
1939	2.008	0.979	1.957	1.271	2.399	1.217	0.778
1940	1.812	0.829	2.076	1.319	2.480	1.217	0.786
1941	1.602	0.681	2.095	1.305	2.548	1.218	0.862
1942	1.927	0.766	2.162	1.315	2.614	1.221	0.942
1943	2.427	0.915	2.207	1.310	2.688	1.225	0.972
1944	2.906	1.041	2.270	1.314	2.815	1.229	0.993
1945	3.965	1.361	2.513	1.423	2.930	1.233	1.015
1946	3.645	1.199	2.511	1.392	2.980	1.238	1.199
1947	3.853	1.199	2.445	1.327	2.911	1.244	1.307
1948	4.065	1.191	2.528	1.340	3.031	1.254	1.343
1949	4.829	1.313	2.691	1.395	3.132	1.268	1.318
1950	6.360	1.600	2.692	1.366	3.198	1.283	1.395
1951	7.888	1.863	2.586	1.281	3.112	1.302	1.477
1952	9.336	2.082	2.616	1.262	3.221	1.324	1.490
1953	9.244	1.944	2.711	1.270	3.331	1.348	1.499
1954	14.108	2.820	2.906	1.325	3.511	1.360	1.492
1955	18.561	3.564	2.868	1.271	3.527	1.381	1.497
1956	19.778	3.658	2.708	1.164	3.287	1.415	1.540
1957	17.648	3.134	2.910	1.208	3.573	1.459	1.587
1958	25.298	4.327	2.733	1.097	3.494	1.482	1.615
1959	28.322	4.694	2.671	1.029	3.460	1.526	1.639
1960	28.455	4.554	3.039	1.124	3.774	1.566	1.663
1961	36.106	5.607	3.068	1.092	3.956	1.600	1.674
1962	32.955	4.945	3.280	1.122	4.270	1.643	1.695
1963	40.469	5.879	3.319	1.092	4.364	1.695	1.723
1964	47.139	6.642	3.436	1.084	4.572	1.754	1.743
1965	53.008	7.244	3.460	1.047	4.552	1.823	1.777
1966	47.674	6.295	3.586	1.036	4.560	1.910	1.836
1967	59.104	7.560	3.257	0.895	4.335	1.991	1.892
1968	65.642	8.139	3.248	0.846	4.446	2.094	1.981
1969	60.059	7.210	3.083	0.754	4.086	2.232	2.102
1970	62.465	7.222	3.457	0.791	4.837	2.378	2.218
1971	71.406	8.001	3.914	0.843	5.370	2.482	2.292
1972	84.956	9.252	4.136	0.840	5.760	2.577	2.371
1973	72.500	7.645	4.090	0.775	5.825	2.756	2.579
1974	53.311	5.373	4.268	0.748	5.647	2.976	2.894
1975	73.144	7.068	4.661	0.754	6.474	3.149	3.097
1976	90.584	8.422	5.441	0.815	7.681	3.309	3.246
1977	84.076	7.453	5.405	0.750	7.813	3.479	3.466
1978	89.592	7.532	5.342	0.682	7.807	3.728	3.778
1979	106.112	8.459	5.277	0.615	7.481	4.115	4.281
1980	140.513	10.639	5.069	0.530	7.285	4.578	4.812
1981	133.615	9.605	5.162	0.475	7.215	5.251	5.242
1982	162.221	11.023	7.245	0.589	10.374	5.805	5.445
1983	198.744	12.926	7.294	0.530	10.862	6.315	5.652
1984	211.198	13.106	8.420	0.542	12.642	6.937	5.875
1985	279.115	16.558	11.027	0.639	16.549	7.473	6.097

Source: Ibbotson and Sinquefield, *Stocks, Bonds, Bills, and Inflation.*

PORTFOLIOS WITHOUT MANAGEMENT

Cumulative Without Dividends — Annual Compound Growth Rate

	1976-1985			1977-1985			1978-1985			1979-1985			1980-1985			1981-1985			1982-1985			1983-1985			1984-1985			First Quarter 1986 Percent Change		
	1800 Cos.	1000 Cos.	500 Cos.	1800	1000	500	1800	1000	500	1800	1000	500	1800	1000	500	1800	1000	500	1800	1000	500	1800	1000	500	1800	1000	500	1800	1000	500
Top 5%	20.7	18.2	15.3	18.7	16.5	13.7	20.5	18.7	16.4	22.1	20.4	18.2	20.8	19.3	17.1	19.9	18.6	16.0	24.0	22.9	20.8	22.6	21.6	19.6	17.3	18.1	17.6	20.6	20.7	20.1
Top 10%	19.9	17.5	14.7	18.0	15.8	13.1	19.6	18.0	15.7	21.1	19.6	17.4	19.8	18.4	16.3	18.9	17.6	15.2	22.8	21.8	19.8	21.3	20.5	18.6	15.8	16.9	16.4	19.4	19.6	19.2
Top 15%	19.0	16.8	14.0	17.5	15.3	12.7	19.0	17.5	15.2	20.4	19.0	16.9	19.1	17.9	15.8	18.1	17.0	14.7	22.0	21.1	19.2	20.3	19.8	18.0	14.9	16.1	15.7	18.6	18.9	18.4
Top 20%	18.7	16.5	13.7	17.0	14.9	12.3	18.6	17.1	14.9	19.9	18.6	16.5	18.6	17.4	15.4	17.5	16.6	14.3	21.3	20.6	18.6	19.7	19.3	17.5	13.5	15.4	14.6	17.9	18.3	17.9
Top 25%	18.3	16.2	13.4	16.6	14.6	11.9	18.2	16.7	14.6	19.5	18.2	16.2	18.1	17.0	15.0	17.0	16.2	13.9	20.8	20.1	18.2	19.1	18.8	17.1	12.9	14.3	14.1	17.3	17.8	17.4
Top 30%	18.0	16.0	13.2	16.3	14.4	11.6	17.9	16.4	14.3	19.1	17.9	15.9	17.7	16.7	14.7	16.6	15.9	13.5	20.3	19.7	17.8	18.5	18.4	16.7	12.3	13.9	13.8	16.9	17.1	17.0
Top 35%	17.8	15.7	13.0	16.0	14.1	11.4	17.6	16.1	14.0	18.7	17.6	15.6	17.3	16.4	14.4	16.2	15.5	13.2	19.8	19.3	17.4	18.1	18.1	16.3	11.8	13.4	13.3	16.4	16.9	16.7
Top 40%	17.5	15.5	12.8	15.7	13.9	11.6	17.2	15.6	13.8	18.4	17.3	15.3	17.0	16.1	14.1	15.8	15.2	12.9	19.4	18.9	17.1	17.7	17.6	15.9	11.4	13.0	13.0	15.9	16.5	16.3
Top 45%	17.2	15.3	12.6	15.4	13.6	11.0	16.9	15.6	13.6	18.1	17.0	15.1	16.6	15.8	13.9	15.5	14.9	12.7	19.0	18.5	16.8	17.3	17.2	15.7	10.9	12.6	12.6	15.5	16.2	16.0
Top 50%	17.0	15.1	12.4	15.2	13.4	11.0	16.6	15.4	13.4	17.7	16.7	14.8	16.3	15.5	13.6	15.2	14.5	12.4	18.6	18.2	16.5	16.8	16.9	15.4	10.4	12.2	12.2	15.1	15.8	15.7
Top 55%	16.7	14.8	12.0	14.9	13.2	10.8	16.3	15.1	13.1	17.4	16.5	14.6	16.0	15.2	13.4	14.8	14.2	12.2	18.2	17.9	16.1	16.4	16.5	15.1	9.9	11.8	11.8	14.7	15.4	15.4
Top 60%	16.5	14.6	12.0	14.6	12.9	10.6	16.1	14.9	12.9	17.1	16.1	14.3	15.7	14.9	13.2	14.5	13.9	11.9	17.8	17.5	15.8	16.0	16.1	14.6	9.4	11.4	11.4	14.2	15.1	15.0
Top 65%	16.2	14.4	11.6	14.4	12.7	10.4	15.7	14.6	12.7	16.8	15.9	14.0	15.3	14.6	12.9	14.1	13.6	11.6	17.4	17.1	15.5	15.6	15.8	14.5	8.9	10.9	11.1	13.7	14.7	14.7
Top 70%	15.9	14.1	11.6	14.1	12.5	10.1	15.4	14.3	12.4	16.5	15.7	13.8	15.0	14.3	12.6	13.7	13.3	11.3	16.9	16.7	15.1	15.1	15.4	14.1	8.3	10.4	10.6	13.3	14.3	14.3
Top 75%	15.6	14.1	11.0	13.8	12.2	9.6	15.1	14.0	12.1	16.1	15.3	13.5	14.6	14.0	12.3	13.3	12.9	11.0	16.5	16.3	14.8	14.6	15.0	13.8	7.7	9.9	10.2	12.8	13.9	13.9
Top 80%	15.3	13.5	11.0	13.5	11.9	9.6	14.7	13.7	11.8	15.7	14.9	13.0	14.2	13.6	11.8	12.8	12.6	10.7	15.9	15.8	14.4	14.1	14.5	13.4	7.0	9.3	9.6	12.3	13.4	13.4
Top 85%	14.8	13.0	10.6	13.0	11.6	9.3	14.3	13.3	11.5	15.2	14.4	12.8	13.7	13.2	11.6	12.3	12.0	10.2	15.3	15.3	13.9	13.4	14.0	12.9	6.1	8.4	9.0	11.7	12.9	12.9
Top 90%	14.3	12.6	10.1	12.6	11.1	8.9	13.8	12.9	11.1	14.6	14.0	12.3	13.1	12.6	11.1	11.7	11.5	9.7	14.6	14.7	13.3	12.6	13.3	12.4	4.6	7.3	8.0	10.9	12.1	12.3
Top 95%	14.1	12.5	10.1	11.8	10.5	8.4	13.0	12.1	10.5	13.8	13.2	11.7	12.1	11.9	10.4	10.7	10.5	9.0	13.4	14.1	12.5	11.5	12.4	11.5				9.7	11.0	11.3
S&P 500 Index	8.9			7.8			10.5			11.9			11.8			9.2			14.6			14.5			13.2			13.1		
Dow Ind. Avg.	6.1			4.9			8.1			9.8			10.7			9.9			15.3			13.9			10.9			17.6		

Cumulative With Dividends — Annual Compound Growth Rate

	1976-1985			1977-1985			1978-1985			1979-1985			1980-1985			1981-1985			1982-1985			1983-1985			1984-1985			First Quarter 1986 Percent Change		
	1800 Cos.	1000 Cos.	500 Cos.	1800	1000	500	1800	1000	500	1800	1000	500	1800	1000	500	1800	1000	500	1800	1000	500	1800	1000	500	1800	1000	500	1800	1000	500
Top 5%	25.0	23.0	20.3	23.1	21.3	18.7	24.9	23.6	21.6	26.5	25.3	23.3	25.0	24.0	22.1	24.0	23.2	20.9	27.8	27.4	25.6	26.2	25.8	24.2	20.9	22.2	22.1	21.3	21.5	20.9
Top 10%	24.1	22.3	19.7	22.3	20.6	18.1	24.1	22.9	20.9	25.4	24.5	22.6	24.0	23.2	21.3	22.9	22.3	20.1	26.7	26.5	24.6	24.9	24.8	23.4	19.4	21.0	20.9	20.1	20.4	20.0
Top 15%	23.7	21.9	19.3	21.7	20.1	17.7	23.4	22.4	20.4	24.8	23.9	22.1	23.3	22.6	20.8	22.2	21.6	19.6	25.9	25.5	23.9	24.0	24.1	22.6	18.4	20.2	20.1	19.2	19.7	19.3
Top 20%	23.3	21.6	19.0	21.3	19.7	17.4	23.0	21.9	20.1	24.2	23.1	21.3	22.7	22.1	20.0	21.6	21.2	19.2	25.2	25.0	23.4	23.2	23.5	22.1	17.6	19.5	19.5	18.6	19.1	18.7
Top 25%	23.0	21.2	18.7	20.9	19.4	17.1	22.6	21.6	19.7	23.8	23.1	21.3	22.3	21.7	20.0	21.0	20.4	18.8	24.6	24.5	23.0	22.7	23.0	21.7	18.0	19.0	19.0	18.0	18.6	18.3
Top 30%	22.7	20.7	18.4	20.6	19.1	16.9	22.3	21.3	19.5	23.4	22.8	21.0	21.9	21.4	19.7	20.6	20.1	18.4	24.1	24.1	22.6	22.2	22.6	21.3	17.0	18.4	18.6	17.5	18.4	18.3
Top 35%	22.4	20.7	18.2	20.3	18.9	16.6	22.0	21.0	19.2	23.0	22.2	20.8	21.5	21.1	19.5	20.1	19.8	18.1	23.6	23.7	22.2	21.7	22.2	20.9	16.3	18.0	18.2	17.0	17.7	17.5
Top 40%	22.1	20.5	18.0	20.0	18.6	16.4	21.6	20.8	19.0	22.7	22.2	20.5	21.1	20.8	19.2	19.8	19.5	17.8	23.2	23.3	21.9	21.3	21.8	20.6	15.8	17.5	17.8	16.6	17.3	17.2
Top 45%	21.8	20.3	17.8	19.8	18.4	16.2	21.3	20.5	18.8	22.4	21.9	20.2	20.8	20.5	18.9	19.5	19.1	17.6	22.8	23.0	21.5	20.9	21.5	20.2	15.3	17.0	17.8	16.1	17.0	16.9
Top 50%	21.6	20.1	17.6	19.5	18.2	16.0	21.0	20.3	18.5	22.1	21.6	20.0	20.5	20.2	18.7	19.1	19.1	17.3	22.4	22.6	21.2	20.4	21.1	20.0	14.8	16.7	17.0	15.8	16.6	16.6
Top 55%	21.3	19.8	17.4	19.2	17.9	15.8	20.7	20.0	18.3	21.8	21.4	19.7	20.1	19.9	18.4	18.8	18.5	17.0	22.0	22.2	20.9	20.0	20.7	19.3	14.3	16.2	16.6	15.3	16.2	16.2
Top 60%	21.1	19.6	17.2	18.9	17.7	15.6	20.4	19.8	18.1	21.4	21.1	19.4	19.8	19.7	18.2	18.5	18.5	16.7	21.6	21.9	20.6	19.6	20.0	19.0	13.8	15.8	16.2	14.9	15.9	15.9
Top 65%	20.8	19.4	17.0	18.7	17.5	15.1	20.1	19.5	17.8	21.1	20.7	19.2	19.5	19.4	19.2	18.1	17.9	16.2	21.2	21.5	20.2	19.1	20.0	18.7	13.3	15.4	15.4	14.4	15.5	15.5
Top 70%	20.5	19.2	16.8	18.4	17.2	15.1	19.8	19.2	17.6	20.8	20.4	18.9	19.1	19.0	17.6	17.7	17.5	15.9	20.7	21.1	19.9	18.7	19.6	18.7	12.8	14.9	15.4	14.0	15.1	15.2
Top 75%	20.3	18.9	16.5	18.1	17.0	14.6	19.5	18.9	17.3	20.4	20.1	18.6	18.8	18.7	17.3	17.3	17.1	15.5	20.2	20.7	19.5	18.2	19.1	18.3	12.2	14.4	15.0	13.5	14.7	14.8
Top 80%	19.9	18.6	16.3	17.8	16.7	14.6	19.1	18.6	16.9	20.0	19.8	18.3	18.3	18.3	17.0	16.8	17.1	15.1	19.7	20.2	19.1	17.6	18.7	17.9	11.6	13.8	14.5	13.0	14.2	14.3
Top 85%	19.6	18.3	16.0	17.4	16.4	14.3	18.7	18.2	16.6	19.5	19.3	17.9	17.8	17.9	16.6	16.3	16.6	15.1	19.1	19.7	18.7	17.0	18.2	17.4	11.0	13.2	14.0	12.4	13.7	13.8
Top 90%	19.1	17.9	15.6	16.9	15.9	13.9	18.1	17.8	16.2	18.9	18.7	17.4	17.2	17.3	16.1	15.6	16.0	14.6	18.3	19.0	18.0	16.2	17.4	16.9	10.3	12.4	13.2	11.6	12.9	13.2
Top 95%	18.4	17.3	15.1	16.1	15.2	13.4	17.4	17.1	15.6	18.1	18.1	16.8	16.2	16.5	15.3	14.6	15.1	13.8	17.1	18.1	17.2	14.9	16.5	16.0	7.9	11.3	12.2	10.4	11.8	12.2
S&P 500 Index	14.3			13.3			16.1			17.6			17.4			14.6			20.2			19.8			18.4			14.1		
Dow Ind. Avg.	12.1			10.9			14.3			16.1			17.0			15.9			21.4			19.6			16.4			18.8		

(continued)

275

RETURNS ON PORTFOLIOS WITHOUT MANAGEMENT (concluded)

Annual Without Dividends — Percent Change

	1976 1800	1976 1000	1976 500	1977 1800	1977 1000	1977 500	1978 1800	1978 1000	1978 500	1979 1800	1979 1000	1979 500	1980 1800	1980 1000	1980 500	1981 1800	1981 1000	1981 500	1982 1800	1982 1000	1982 500	1983 1800	1983 1000	1983 500	1984 1800	1984 1000	1984 500	1985 1800	1985 1000	1985 500
Top 5%	50.7	44.7	38.4	12.6	5.3	-1.1	18.2	14.4	10.6	41.3	37.7	35.8	35.0	31.5	29.8	11.6	9.1	4.3	38.5	35.5	32.6	41.4	35.5	28.8	4.2	5.1	3.8	38.7	37.8	37.6
Top 10%	47.2	42.1	36.1	10.7	3.9	-2.3	16.0	12.3	8.9	37.5	34.4	31.6	34.1	28.9	27.6	9.4	7.4	2.8	35.1	32.3	29.4	38.6	33.2	27.2	2.4	3.7	2.5	35.8	35.7	35.7
Top 15%	45.2	40.3	34.4	9.4	3.0	-3.1	14.6	11.1	7.8	35.0	33.0	29.1	32.0	27.2	27.2	8.1	6.0	1.8	32.8	30.3	27.5	36.5	30.7	26.0	1.4	2.7	1.1	34.2	34.3	34.4
Top 20%	43.4	39.0	33.3	8.4	2.3	-3.8	13.5	10.1	7.0	33.4	30.5	27.4	28.5	25.9	25.0	7.0	5.1	1.1	31.2	28.6	25.9	35.5	29.8	25.2	0.5	1.9	1.1	32.9	33.3	33.3
Top 25%	42.1	37.8	32.3	7.5	1.6	-4.8	12.6	9.3	6.2	32.1	29.1	26.1	27.2	24.8	23.9	6.1	4.3	0.4	30.0	27.2	25.3	33.3	28.8	24.4	-0.1	0.6	0.0	31.7	32.4	32.5
Top 30%	41.0	36.8	31.4	6.7	1.0	-4.8	11.8	8.6	5.6	30.9	28.0	24.9	26.2	23.8	23.0	5.2	3.6	-0.3	27.1	25.9	23.4	32.0	28.0	23.7	-1.1	0.1	-0.5	30.7	31.6	31.7
Top 35%	40.1	35.9	30.6	6.1	0.4	-5.2	10.9	7.9	5.0	29.7	26.9	23.9	25.2	22.9	22.2	4.5	2.9	-0.8	26.0	23.9	22.3	31.0	27.3	23.0	-2.3	-0.5	-0.9	29.8	30.2	30.3
Top 40%	39.2	35.1	29.9	5.4	-0.2	-5.6	10.1	7.3	4.4	28.5	25.9	23.0	24.2	22.0	21.4	3.8	2.2	-1.4	25.0	23.0	21.3	30.5	26.6	22.4	-3.6	-1.0	-1.4	29.0	29.5	30.3
Top 45%	38.3	34.3	29.2	4.9	-0.7	-6.0	9.3	6.7	3.9	27.4	25.0	22.2	23.3	21.1	20.7	3.1	1.6	-1.9	23.9	23.1	20.4	29.7	25.9	21.9	-4.2	-1.5	-2.2	27.4	28.9	29.1
Top 50%	37.5	33.6	28.6	4.2	-1.3	-6.5	8.7	6.1	3.4	26.4	24.2	21.4	22.4	20.3	20.0	2.4	1.0	-2.4	23.3	22.1	19.5	28.9	25.2	21.3	-4.8	-2.0	-2.2	26.6	28.2	28.5
Top 55%	36.7	32.8	28.0	3.6	-1.7	-6.8	7.5	5.6	3.0	25.4	23.3	20.6	21.6	19.5	19.3	1.7	0.4	-2.9	22.9	21.2	18.7	28.1	23.8	20.7	-5.4	-2.5	-3.1	25.8	27.5	27.9
Top 60%	35.9	32.1	27.2	3.0	-2.2	-7.2	6.9	5.0	2.5	24.4	22.4	19.9	20.6	18.6	18.6	1.0	-0.2	-3.4	21.8	20.3	17.8	27.3	23.1	20.1	-6.0	-3.6	-3.1	25.0	26.8	27.3
Top 65%	34.9	31.3	26.5	2.5	-2.7	-7.6	6.4	4.4	2.0	23.5	21.5	19.1	19.8	17.9	17.9	0.2	-0.8	-3.9	20.8	19.3	16.9	26.4	22.3	19.5	-6.7	-4.2	-4.1	25.0	26.0	26.7
Top 70%	34.0	30.5	25.7	1.8	-3.3	-8.0	5.5	3.8	1.5	22.5	20.7	18.3	18.8	17.1	17.1	-0.5	-1.4	-4.5	19.7	18.4	16.0	25.4	21.4	18.9	-7.5	-4.9	-4.1	24.2	25.2	26.0
Top 75%	33.1	29.7	24.9	1.1	-3.9	-8.5	4.7	3.1	0.9	21.4	19.7	17.5	17.7	16.1	16.2	-1.3	-2.1	-5.1	18.6	17.3	15.0	24.3	20.4	18.3	-8.4	-5.7	-5.4	23.3	24.4	25.3
Top 80%	32.1	28.7	24.1	0.4	-4.5	-9.0	3.8	2.4	0.3	20.2	18.6	16.5	16.7	15.3	15.3	-2.1	-2.9	-5.9	17.3	16.2	13.9	23.1	19.3	17.6	-9.6	-6.7	-6.3	22.4	24.4	24.4
Top 85%	30.8	27.7	23.1	-0.5	-5.1	-9.6	2.5	1.6	-0.5	18.9	17.4	15.4	15.3	14.1	14.4	-3.1	-3.8	-6.6	16.0	14.8	12.7	22.1	17.3	16.7	-11.2	-8.2	-7.5	21.3	23.4	24.4
Top 90%	29.4	26.4	21.8	-1.7	-5.9	-10.3	1.0	0.5	-1.3	17.2	15.9	14.1	13.7	12.7	13.0	-4.4	-5.0	-7.6	14.0	13.1	11.1	21.5	20.4	15.7				19.9	22.1	23.3
Top 95%	27.1	24.6	19.7	-3.1	-7.1	-11.4	-1.0	-1.0	-2.5	14.9	13.9	12.2	11.4	10.7	11.2	-6.1	-6.7	-9.0	11.4	10.8	8.9	19.3	17.3	14.1				17.8	20.5	21.7
S&P 500 Index	19.1			-11.5			1.1			12.3			25.8			-9.7			14.8			17.3			1.4			26.3		
Dow Ind. Avg.	17.9			-17.3			-3.1			4.2			14.9			-9.2			19.6			20.3			-3.7			27.7		

Annual With Dividends — Percent Change

	1976 1800	1976 1000	1976 500	1977 1800	1977 1000	1977 500	1978 1800	1978 1000	1978 500	1979 1800	1979 1000	1979 500	1980 1800	1980 1000	1980 500	1981 1800	1981 1000	1981 500	1982 1800	1982 1000	1982 500	1983 1800	1983 1000	1983 500	1984 1800	1984 1000	1984 500	1985 1800	1985 1000	1985 500
Top 5%	55.2	49.2	43.1	16.5	9.4	3.1	22.9	19.3	15.8	46.5	43.5	41.8	39.8	36.8	35.3	16.6	14.4	9.9	43.0	40.6	38.0	45.4	40.0	33.7	7.9	9.4	8.5	42.1	41.8	42.0
Top 10%	51.7	46.7	40.8	14.5	7.8	1.9	20.7	17.4	14.2	42.8	40.2	37.6	37.0	34.2	33.1	14.3	12.7	8.3	39.6	37.4	34.7	42.5	37.7	32.0	5.8	7.9	7.1	39.3	39.7	40.0
Top 15%	49.6	45.0	39.1	13.2	6.9	1.1	19.3	16.1	13.1	40.7	37.8	35.1	34.9	32.6	31.6	13.0	11.4	7.3	37.3	35.4	32.8	40.8	36.2	31.0	5.0	6.9	6.3	37.6	38.5	38.7
Top 20%	48.0	43.6	37.9	12.3	6.3	0.4	18.3	15.2	12.2	38.8	36.3	34.1	33.3	31.0	30.5	11.8	10.4	6.5	35.7	33.7	31.3	39.4	35.2	30.1	4.0	6.0	5.5	36.3	37.4	37.7
Top 25%	46.7	42.4	37.0	11.4	5.6	-0.2	17.4	14.4	11.4	37.4	34.8	32.1	32.1	30.1	29.5	10.9	9.5	5.8	34.2	32.3	29.9	38.4	34.2	29.3	3.2	5.3	5.0	35.2	36.5	36.8
Top 30%	45.6	41.4	36.1	10.5	5.0	-0.7	16.6	13.6	10.8	36.0	33.8	31.0	31.0	29.1	28.6	10.0	8.8	5.2	32.9	31.1	28.8	37.2	33.4	28.6	2.4	4.7	4.5	34.2	35.7	36.1
Top 35%	44.6	40.5	35.3	9.9	4.2	-1.6	15.8	13.0	10.3	35.0	32.0	29.9	30.1	27.4	27.9	9.2	8.1	4.6	31.1	30.0	27.7	36.3	32.5	28.0	1.8	4.1	4.0	33.3	35.0	35.4
Top 40%	43.8	39.7	34.6	9.3	3.8	-2.4	15.0	12.4	9.7	33.9	31.8	29.0	29.2	27.4	27.1	8.5	7.4	4.0	30.6	29.0	26.7	34.5	31.8	27.4	1.1	3.6	3.5	32.4	34.3	34.7
Top 45%	42.8	38.9	33.9	8.7	3.3	-2.1	14.0	11.8	9.2	32.8	31.0	28.2	28.2	26.3	26.3	7.8	6.8	3.5	29.5	28.1	25.8	33.7	31.1	26.8	0.1	3.0	3.0	31.6	33.6	34.1
Top 50%	42.0	38.2	33.2	8.1	2.7	-2.4	13.4	11.2	8.7	31.7	30.0	27.4	27.3	25.7	25.6	7.1	6.2	2.9	28.4	27.2	24.9	32.8	30.4	26.2	-0.2	2.5	2.1	30.8	32.9	33.5
Top 55%	41.2	37.4	32.6	7.5	2.3	-3.2	12.9	10.6	8.3	30.7	29.0	26.6	26.5	25.0	25.0	6.4	5.5	2.4	27.4	26.3	24.1	32.1	29.0	25.6	-0.8	1.9	1.7	30.1	32.3	32.9
Top 60%	40.4	36.7	31.9	6.9	1.3	-3.2	12.3	10.0	7.8	29.8	28.2	25.9	25.6	24.1	24.2	5.7	4.9	1.9	26.3	25.4	23.1	32.1	28.7	25.0	-1.4	1.4	1.2	29.2	31.6	32.3
Top 65%	39.5	35.9	31.0	6.3	1.3	-4.0	11.6	9.5	7.3	28.9	27.2	25.1	24.7	23.2	23.5	4.9	4.3	1.3	25.4	24.4	22.2	31.2	27.7	24.4	-2.1	0.9	0.6	28.4	30.8	31.6
Top 70%	38.6	35.1	30.2	5.7	0.8	-4.0	11.1	8.9	6.8	27.8	26.5	24.3	23.7	22.4	22.7	4.1	3.6	0.7	24.2	23.4	21.3	30.4	26.0	23.8	-2.8	0.3	1.2	27.6	30.1	31.0
Top 75%	37.6	34.2	29.4	5.0	0.2	-4.5	10.2	8.2	6.2	26.6	25.6	23.5	22.7	21.5	21.9	3.2	2.1	0.1	23.0	22.3	20.3	30.4	25.0	23.2	-3.5	-0.4	-0.6	26.7	29.3	30.3
Top 80%	36.6	33.2	28.6	4.2	-0.5	-5.1	9.1	7.5	5.6	25.6	24.5	22.5	21.6	20.6	21.0	2.5	1.1	-0.7	21.8	21.3	19.3	29.4	23.6	22.4	-4.3	-1.1	-0.6	26.8	28.5	29.7
Top 85%	35.4	32.2	27.6	3.4	-1.2	-5.6	8.5	6.7	4.9	24.3	23.2	21.4	20.3	19.4	20.0	1.5	0.1	-1.5	19.8	19.8	18.0	28.2	25.0	20.5	-5.3	-1.9	-2.2	24.6	27.5	28.8
Top 90%	33.8	30.9	26.3	2.2	-2.0	-6.4	7.0	5.6	4.1	22.6	21.7	20.1	18.7	18.2	18.7	1.0	-0.1	-2.5	18.5	18.1	16.4	27.0	23.6	20.5	-6.5	-3.0	-3.6	23.2	26.1	27.6
Top 95%	31.5	29.0	24.2	0.7	-3.2	-7.4	5.6	4.2	2.8	20.3	19.7	18.2	16.4	16.2	16.9	1.8	-1.7	-4.0	15.7	15.9	14.2	25.5	21.8	18.9	-8.1	-4.5	-3.6	21.1	24.5	26.1
S&P 500 Index	24.0			-7.2			6.4			18.7			32.4			-5.3			21.5			22.6			6.3			31.8		
Dow Ind. Avg.	23.0			-12.9			2.8			10.7			22.2			-3.7			27.2			26.1			1.4			33.7		

The data on this page represent an analytical device that enables the user to measure relative fund performance on a scientific grading system.

The tables were developed with three precepts in mind.

• While it is often done, comparing fund performance with stock market indexes can be highly misleading.

• Comparison with what other funds have done can be equally misleading.

• The only true way to measure the performance of managed funds is to compare the performance of those funds with the results achieved by other funds totally without management.

The problem with using index comparison is vividly illustrated by looking at the 1981 section of the tables, excluding dividends (lower right).

Here we see that the Standard & Poor's 500 stock index declined 9.7 percent, without inclusion of dividends. The Dow Jones industrial average was off 9.2 percent.

The performance of both was substantially worse than the median performance of our random portfolios, off only 2.4 at the 500 company level, but up 1.0 percent at the 1,000 company level and up 2.4 percent at the 1,800 company level.

Stated quite simply, while few investors could duplicate the S&P 500 or the Dow average in a portfolio, an investor could have thrown darts at a stock page and performed better than the two popular measures of stock performance, the S&P 500 or the Dow, for 1981.

To obtain the results of unmanaged funds for our comparison, it is necessary to duplicate the investment process and then measure the results.

This we have done in Portfolios Without Management by generating 30,000 random portfolios each year from 1974 on, with 35 stocks in each portfolio selected at random at the beginning of each year.

Scientific random sampling methods have been used at all times to eliminate any bias in our results. We chose to generate a very large number of portfolios each year to reduce sampling error to a small fraction of a percentage point.

We have applied this process to 10,000 portfolios in each of three separate company-size groups: the largest 1,800 companies, the largest 1,000 companies, and the largest 500 companies, based on annual revenue.

Performance results have been measured and are reported separately for each group and time period, with and without dividends, and these results are presented in these tables so the user can select the group deemed most appropriate for his analytical purpose.

These tables are remarkably easy to use. For any fund performance in any specific period, you need only look at the table for that period and simply read the relative score for this particular performance result.

With no more effort than that, you have a scientific rating of the fund's relative performance in the specified period.

You can use the ratings to analyze the performance of a given fund over a period of years, with or without dividends, both on an annual and cumulative basis.

The ratings also enable you to quickly compare the relative performance of one fund against others in any time period.

And you may also find it instructive to rate the equity component of a fund for comparison with the performance of the fund as a whole.

To illustrate how easy it is to use this report, let's take a simple example.

In 1981, let's say that you have a fund with an 8.3 percent gain, including dividends.

You simply look at the appropriate year in the bottom table, and note that the portfolio ranks between the 45 and 40 percent group.

This tells you immediately that your fund out-performed approximately 60 percent of the portfolios without management, and but did not achieve the performance of the top 40 percent.

You also can see at a glance that median performance at the top 50 percent level was 7.1 percent in the 1,800 company group, 6.2 percent in the 1,000 company group and 2.9 percent in the 500 company group, so your fund was well above the median in all three groups.

Source: The Media General Financial Weekly, Media General Financial Services, 301 East Grace Street, Richmond, VA 23219, May 12, 1986.

The Constant Dollar Dow

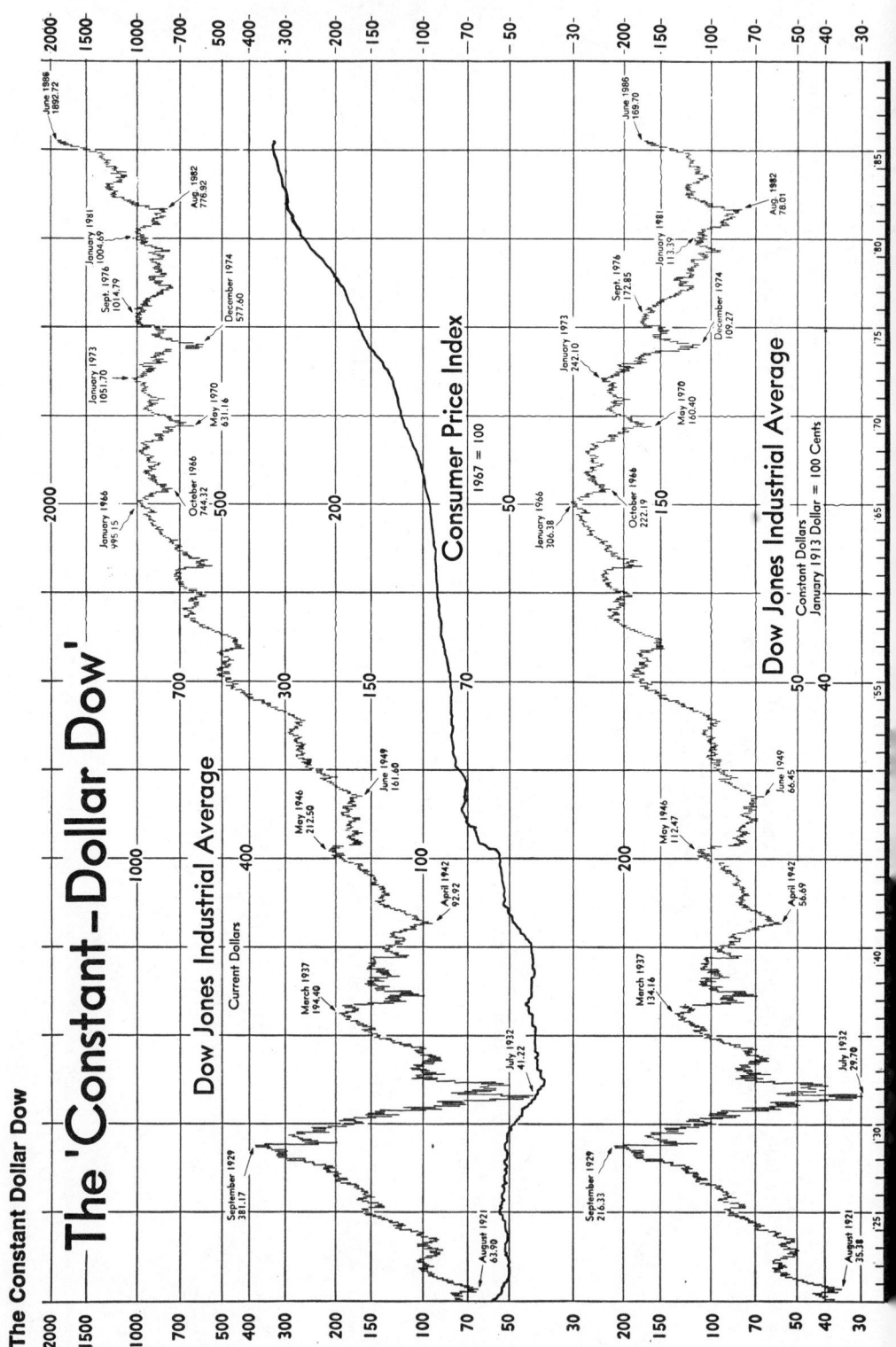

The 'Constant-Dollar Dow'

Dow Jones Industrial Average
Current Dollars

September 1929
381.17

August 1921
63.90

July 1932
41.22

March 1937
194.40

April 1942
92.92

May 1946
212.50

June 1949
161.60

October 1946
744.32

January 1966
995.15

January 1973
1051.70

May 1970
631.16

Sept. 1976
1014.79

January 1981
1004.69

December 1974
577.60

Aug. 1982
776.92

June 1986
1892.72

Consumer Price Index
1967 = 100

Dow Jones Industrial Average
Constant Dollars
January 1913 Dollar = 100 Cents

September 1929
216.33

August 1921
35.38

July 1932
29.70

March 1937
134.16

April 1942
56.69

May 1946
112.47

June 1949
66.45

October 1946
222.19

January 1966
306.38

January 1973
242.10

May 1970
160.40

Sept. 1976
172.85

January 1981
113.39

December 1974
109.27

Aug. 1982
78.01

June 1986
169.70

Cash Dividends on NYSE Listed Common Stocks

	Common stocks		
	Number of issues listed at year end	Number paying cash dividends during year	Estimated aggregate cash payments (millions)
1929	842	554	$ 2,711
1930	848	576	2,667
1935	776	387	1,336
1940	829	577	2,099
1941	834	627	2,281
1942	834	648	1,997
1943	845	687	2,063
1944	864	717	2,223
1945	881	746	2,275
1946	933	798	2,669
1947	964	851	3,255
1948	986	883	3,806
1949	1,017	887	4,235
1950	1,039	930	5,404
1951	1,054	961	5,467
1952	1,067	975	5,595
1953	1,069	964	5,874
1954	1,076	968	6,439
1955	1,076	982	7,488
1956	1,077	975	8,341
1957	1,098	991	8,807
1958	1,086	961	8,711
1959	1,092	953	9,337
1960	1,126	981	9,872
1961	1,145	981	10,430
1962	1,168	994	11,203
1963	1,194	1,032	12,096
1964	1,227	1,066	13,555
1965	1,254	1,111	15,302
1966	1,267	1,127	16,151
1967	1,255	1,116	16,866
1968	1,253	1,104	18,124
1969	1,290	1,121	19,404
1970	1,330	1,120	19,781
1971	1,399	1,132	20,256
1972	1,478	1,195	21,490
1973	1,536	1,276	23,627
1974	1,543	1,308	25,662
1975	1,531	1,273	26,901
1976	1,550	1,304	30,608
1977	1,549	1,360	36,270
1978	1,552	1,373	41,151
1979	1,536	1,359	46,937
1980	1,540	1,361	53,072
1981	1,534	1,337	60,628
1982	1,499	1,287	62,224
1983	1,518	1,259	67,102
1984	1,511	1,243	68,215
1985	1,503	1,206	74,237

Source: New York Stock Exchange *1986 Fact Book.*

THE MAJOR MARKET AVERAGES

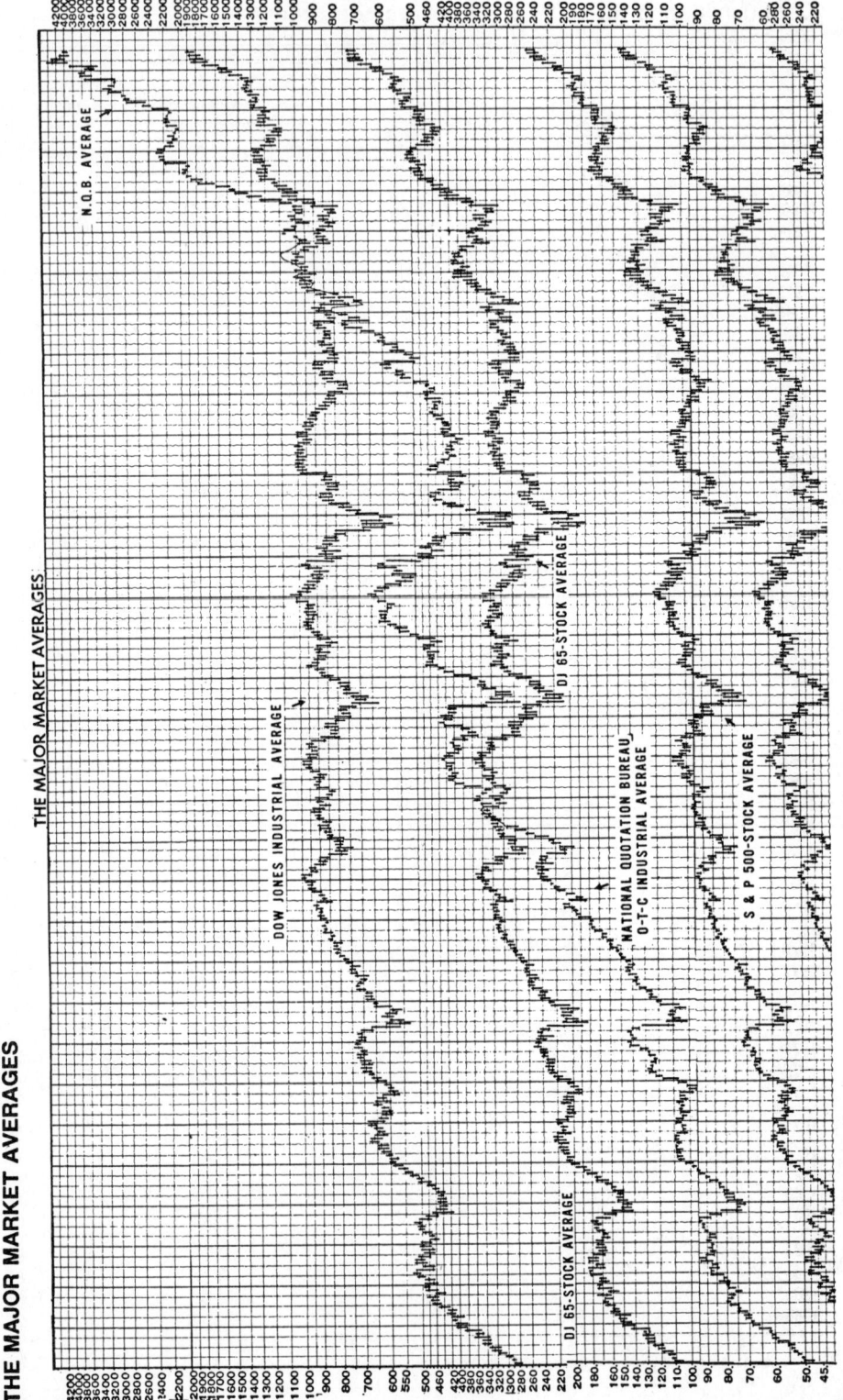

THE MAJOR MARKET AVERAGES

M.O.B. AVERAGE

DOW JONES INDUSTRIAL AVERAGE

DJ 65-STOCK AVERAGE

NATIONAL QUOTATION BUREAU O-T-C INDUSTRIAL AVERAGE

S & P 500-STOCK AVERAGE

DJ 65-STOCK AVERAGE

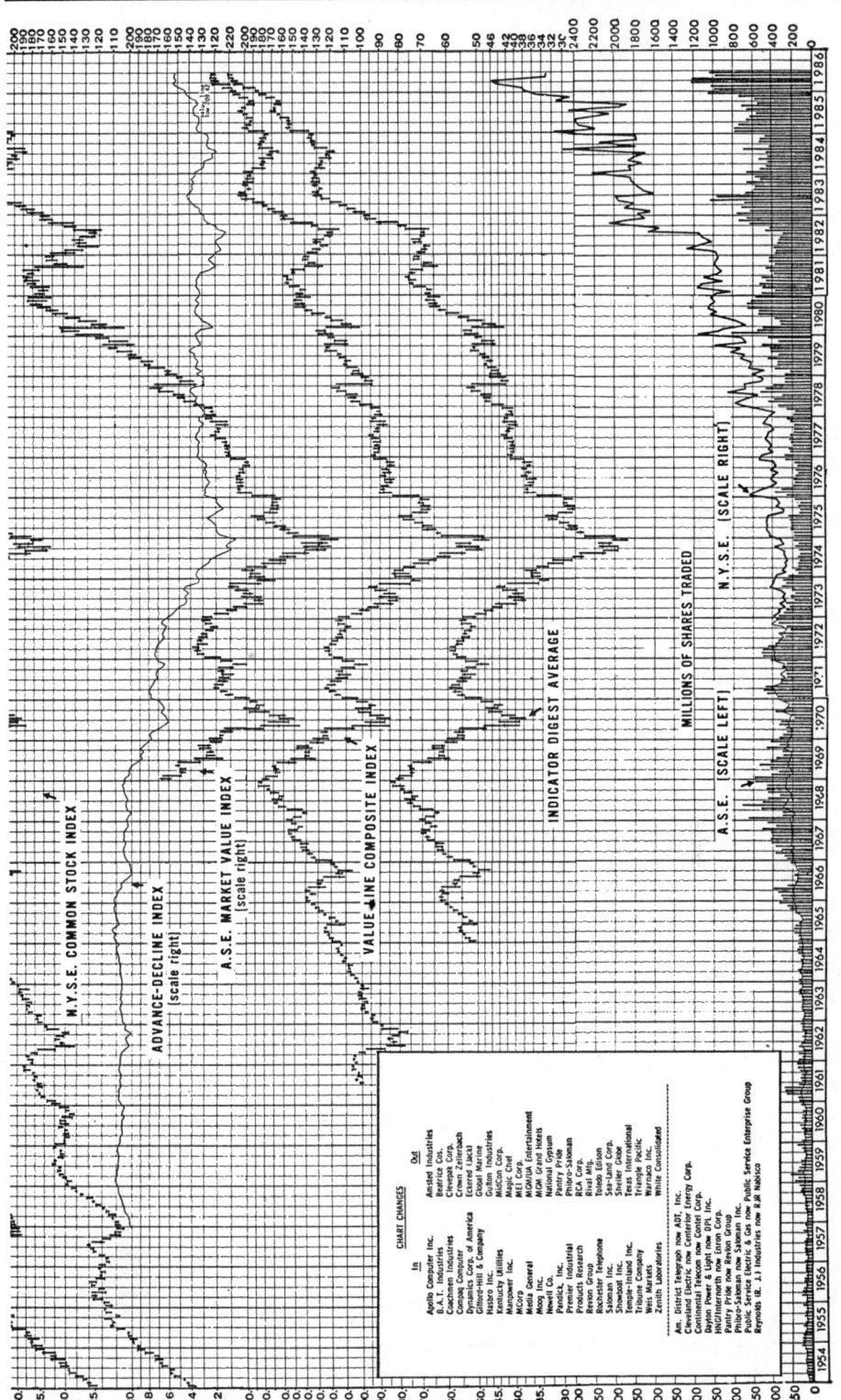

N.Y.S.E. COMMON STOCK INDEX

ADVANCE-DECLINE INDEX
[scale right]

A.S.E. MARKET VALUE INDEX
[scale right]

VALUE LINE COMPOSITE INDEX

INDICATOR DIGEST AVERAGE

MILLIONS OF SHARES TRADED

N.Y.S.E. (SCALE RIGHT)

A.S.E. (SCALE LEFT)

CHART CHANGES

In	Out
Apollo Computer Inc.	Ansted Industries
B.A.T. Industries	Beatrice Cos.
Coachmen Industries	Cleveland Corp.
Compaq Computer	Crown Zellerbach
Dynamics Corp. of America	Eckerd (Jack)
Gifford-Hill & Company	Global Marine
Hasbro Inc.	Gulton Industries
Kentucky Utilities	MidCon Corp.
Manpower Inc.	MEI Corp.
MCorp	Magic Chef
Media General	MGM/UA Entertainment
Moog Inc.	MGM Grand Hotels
Newell Co.	National Gypsum
Pandick, Inc.	Pentry Pride
Premier Industrial	Philoro-Salomon
Products Research	RCA Corp.
Revlon Group	Shal Mfg.
Rochester Telephone	Toledo Edison
Salomon Inc.	Sea-Land Corp.
Showboat Inc.	Shelter Globe
Temple-Inland Inc.	Texas International
Tribune Company	Triangle Pacific
Weis Markets	Warnaco Inc.
Zenith Laboratories	White Consolidated

Am. District Telegraph now ADT, Inc.
Cleveland Electric now Centerior Energy Corp.
Continental Telecom now Contel Corp.
Dayton Power & Light now DPL Inc.
MGIC/Internorth now Enron Corp.
Pantry Pride now Revlon Group
Philoro-Salomon now Salomon Inc.
Public Service Electric & Gas now Public Service Enterprise Group
Reynolds (R. J.) Industries now RJR Nabisco

Source: *5-Trend CYCLI-GRAPHS.* The charts are courtesy of Securities Research Company, a division of United Business Service, 208 Newbury Street, Boston, MA 02116, July quarterly edition, 1986.

Quarterly Dow Jones Industrial Stock Average

The table below lists the earnings (losses) of the Dow Jones Industrial Average based on generally accepted accounting principles. The price-earnings ratio for the DJI correctly reflects deficit/negative earnings for the 1982 September and December quarters. The 1985 December quarter and year-end dividend reflects $2.00 GM dividend distribution value of one share of class H common for each 20 shares of common held. The 1984 December quarter and year-end dividend reflects $1.87½ GM dividend distribution value of one share of class E common for each 20 shares of common held. N.A.-Not available. d-Indicates deficit/negative earnings for the quarter.

Year	Quarter Ended	Clos. Avg.	Qtrly Chg.	% Chg.	Qtrly Earns	12-Mth Earns	P/E Ratio	Qtrly Divs	12-Mth Divs	Divs Yield	Payout Ratio
1986	June 30	1892.72	+ 74.11	+ 4.08	N.A.	N.A.	N.A.	16.94	65.37	3.45	N.A.
	Mar. 31	1818.61	+ 271.94	+ 17.58	24.73	96.43	18.9	16.22	63.38	3.49	.6573
1985	Dec. 31	1546.67	+ 218.04	+ 16.41	24.69	96.11	16.1	17.19	62.03	4.01	.6454
	Sept. 30	1328.63	− 6.83	− 0.51	17.60	90.78	14.6	15.02	61.83	4.65	.6811
	June 28	1335.46	+ 68.68	+ 5.14	29.41	102.26	13.1	14.95	61.53	4.61	.6017
	Mar. 29	1266.78	+ 55.21	+ 4.56	24.41	107.87	11.7	14.87	61.56	4.86	.5707
1984	Dec. 31	1211.57	+ 4.86	+ 0.40	19.36	113.58	10.7	16.99	60.63	5.00	.5338
	Sept. 28	1206.71	+ 74.31	+ 6.56	29.08	108.11	11.2	14.72	58.41	4.84	.5403
	June 29	1132.40	− 32.49	− 2.79	35.02	102.07	11.1	14.98	57.67	5.09	.5650
	Mar. 30	1164.89	− 93.75	− 7.45	30.12	87.38	13.3	13.94	56.39	4.84	.6453
1983	Dec. 30	1258.64	+ 25.51	+ 2.07	13.89	72.45	17.4	14.77	56.33	4.47	.7775
	Sept. 30	1233.13	+ 11.17	+ 0.91	23.04	56.12	22.0	13.98	54.59	4.43	.9727
	June 30	1221.96	+ 91.93	+ 8.13	20.33	11.59	105.4	13.70	54.05	4.42	4.6635
	Mar. 31	1130.03	+ 83.49	+ 7.98	15.19	9.52	118.7	13.88	54.10	4.79	5.6828
1982	Dec. 31	1046.54	+ 150.29	+ 16.77	d2.44	9.15	114.3	13.03	54.14	5.17	5.9169
	Sept. 30	896.25	+ 84.32	+ 10.38	d21.49	35.15	25.5	13.44	55.55	6.20	1.5804
	June 30	811.93	− 10.84	− 1.32	18.26	79.90	10.2	13.75	55.84	6.88	.6989
	Mar. 31	822.77	− 52.23	− 5.97	14.82	97.13	8.5	13.92	56.28	6.84	.5794
1981	Dec. 31	875.00	+ 25.02	+ 2.94	23.56	113.71	7.7	14.44	56.22	6.42	.4944
	Sept. 30	849.98	− 126.90	− 12.99	23.26	123.32	6.9	13.73	56.18	6.61	.4539
	June 30	976.88	− 26.99	− 2.69	35.49	128.91	7.6	14.19	55.98	5.73	.4266
	Mar. 31	1003.87	+ 39.88	+ 4.14	31.40	123.60	8.1	13.86	54.99	5.48	.4449
1980	Dec. 31	963.99	+ 31.57	+ 3.39	33.17	121.86	7.9	14.40	54.36	5.64	.4461
	Sept. 30	932.42	+ 64.50	+ 7.43	28.85	111.58	8.4	13.53	53.83	5.77	.4824
	June 30	867.92	+ 82.17	+ 10.46	30.18	116.40	7.5	13.20	52.81	6.08	.4537
	Mar. 31	785.75	− 52.99	− 6.32	29.66	120.77	6.5	13.23	52.10	6.63	.4314
1979	Dec. 31	838.74	− 39.93	− 4.54	22.89	124.46	6.7	13.87	50.98	6.08	.4096
	Sept. 28	878.67	+ 36.69	+ 4.36	33.67	136.26	6.4	12.51	51.45	5.85	.3776
	June 29	841.98	− 20.20	− 2.34	34.55	128.99	6.5	12.49	50.35	5.98	.3903
	Mar. 30	862.18	+ 57.17	+ 7.10	33.35	124.10	6.9	12.11	49.48	5.74	.3987
1978	Dec. 29	805.01	− 60.81	− 7.02	34.69	112.79	7.1	14.34	48.52	6.03	.4302
	Sept. 30	865.82	+ 46.87	+ 5.72	26.40	101.59	8.5	11.41	47.42	5.48	.4668
	June 30	818.95	+ 61.59	+ 8.13	29.66	91.37	9.0	11.62	46.74	5.71	.5115
	Mar. 31	757.36	− 73.81	− 8.88	22.04	89.23	8.5	11.15	46.53	6.14	.5215
1977	Dec. 30	831.17	− 15.94	− 1.88	23.49	89.10	9.3	13.24	45.84	5.51	.5145
	Sept. 30	847.11	− 69.19	− 7.55	16.18	89.86	9.4	10.73	44.73	5.28	.4978
	June 30	916.30	− 2.83	− 0.31	27.52	97.18	9.4	11.41	43.85	4.79	.4512
	Mar. 31	919.13	− 85.52	− 8.51	21.91	95.51	9.6	10.46	42.63	4.64	.4463
1976	Dec. 31	1004.65	+ 14.46	+ 1.46	24.25	96.72	10.4	12.13	41.40	4.12	.4280
	Sept. 30	990.19	− 12.59	− 1.27	23.50	95.81	10.3	9.85	38.90	3.93	.4060
	June 30	1002.78	+ 3.33	+ 0.33	25.85	90.68	11.1	10.19	38.10	3.80	.4202
	Mar. 31	999.45	+ 147.04	+ 17.25	23.12	81.87	12.2	9.23	36.88	3.69	.4505
1975	Dec. 31	852.41	+ 58.53	+ 7.37	23.34	75.66	11.3	9.63	37.46	4.39	.4951
	Sept. 30	793.88	− 85.11	− 10.72	18.37	75.47	10.5	9.05	38.28	4.82	.5072
	June 30	878.99	+ 110.84	+ 12.61	17.04	83.83	10.5	8.97	38.66	4.40	.4612
	Mar. 31	768.15	+ 151.91	+ 24.65	16.91	93.47	8.2	9.81	38.56	5.02	.4125
1974	Dec. 31	616.24	+ 8.37	+ 1.38	23.15	99.04	6.2	10.45	37.72	6.12	.3809
	Sept. 30	607.87	− 194.54	− 24.24	26.73	99.73	6.1	9.43	37.89	6.23	.3799
	June 28	802.41	− 44.27	− 5.23	26.68	93.26	8.6	8.87	36.82	4.59	.3948
	Mar. 29	846.68	− 4.18	− 0.49	22.48	89.46	9.5	8.97	36.22	4.28	.4049
1973	Dec. 31	850.86	− 96.24	− 11.31	23.84	86.17	9.9	10.62	35.33	4.15	.4100
	Sept. 28	947.10	+ 55.39	+ 6.21	20.26	82.09	11.5	8.36	33.70	3.56	.4105
	June 29	891.71	− 59.30	− 6.23	22.88	77.56	11.5	8.27	33.10	3.71	.4268
	Mar. 30	951.01	− 69.01	− 6.76	19.19	71.98	13.2	8.08	32.70	3.44	.4543
1972	Dec. 29	1020.02	+ 66.75	+ 7.00	19.76	67.11	15.2	8.99	32.27	3.16	.4808
	Sept. 29	953.27	+ 24.24	+ 2.61	15.73	62.15	15.3	7.76	31.13	3.27	.5009
	June 30	929.03	− 11.67	− 1.24	17.30	58.87	15.8	7.87	30.88	3.32	.5245
	Mar. 30	940.70	+ 50.50	+ 5.67	14.32	56.76	16.6	7.65	30.81	3.27	.5428
1971	Dec. 31	890.20	+ 3.01	+ 0.00	14.80	55.09	16.2	7.85	30.86	3.47	.5602
	Sept. 30	887.19	− 3.95	− 0.00	12.45	53.43	16.6	7.51	31.26	3.52	.5851
	June 30	891.14	− 13.23	− 1.46	15.19	53.45	16.7	7.80	31.55	3.54	.5903
	Mar. 31	904.37	+ 65.45	+ 7.80	12.65	52.36	17.3	7.70	32.21	3.56	.6152

Source: Reprinted by courtesy of *Barron's National Business and Financial Weekly*, August 11, 1986.

Stock Market Averages by Industry Group

These definitions apply to the following charts.

Price scale: The price ranges are always read from the scale at the right-hand side of each chart. This scale is equal to 15 times the earnings and dividend scale at the left, so when the price range bars and the earnings line coincide, it shows the price is at 15 times earnings. When the price is above the earnings line, the ratio of price to earnings is greater than 15 times earnings; when below, it is less.

Monthly price ranges represented by the solid vertical bars show the highest and lowest point of each month's transactions. Cross-bars indicate the month's closing price.

Monthly ratio-cator: The plottings for this line are obtained by dividing the closing price of the stock by the closing price of the Dow Jones Industrial Average on the say day. The resulting percentage is multiplied by a factor of 4.5 to bring the line closer to the price bars and is read from the right-hand scale. The plotting indicates whether the stock has kept pace, outperformed, or lagged behind the general market as represented by the DJIA.

Volume: The number of shares traded each month is shown by vertical bars at the bottom of each chart on an arithmetical scale.

Source: *5-Trend CYCLI-GRAPHS.* The charts are courtesy of Securities Research Company, a division of United Business Service, 208 Newbury Street, Boston, MA 02116, July quarterly edition, 1986.

STOCK MARKET AVERAGES BY INDUSTRY GROUP

PRICES & EARNS. SOURCE: S&P

RATIO-CATOR FACTOR: 7 (700)

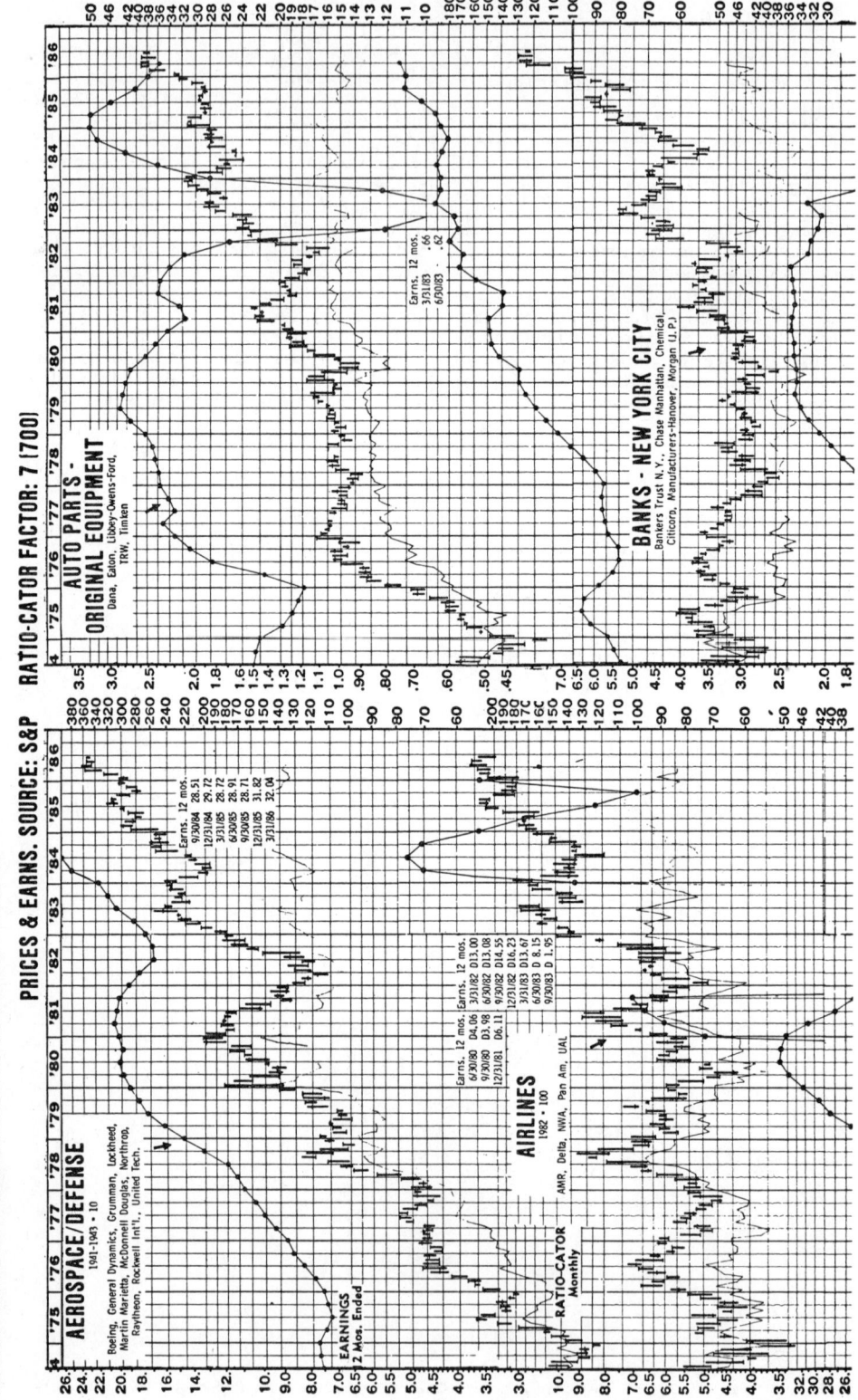

AEROSPACE/DEFENSE
1941-1943 = 10

Boeing, General Dynamics, Grumman, Lockheed, Martin Marietta, McDonnell Douglas, Northrop, Raytheon, Rockwell Int'l., United Tech.

EARNINGS
2 Mos. Ended

Earns., 12 mos.
9/30/84   28.51
12/31/84 29.72
3/31/85   28.72
6/30/85   28.91
9/30/85   28.71
12/31/85 31.82
3/31/86   32.04

AIRLINES
1982 = 100

AMR, Delta, NWA, Pan Am, UAL

RATIO-CATOR
Monthly

Earns., 12 mos.
6/30/80   D4.06
9/30/80   D3.98
12/31/81 D6.11

Earns., 12 mos.
3/31/82   D3.00
9/30/82   D4.55
12/31/82 D6.23
3/31/83   D13.67
6/30/83   D 8.15
9/30/83   D 1.95

AUTO PARTS - ORIGINAL EQUIPMENT
Dana, Eaton, Libbey-Owens-Ford, TRW, Timken

Earns, 12 mos.
3/31/83   .66
6/30/83   .62

BANKS - NEW YORK CITY
Bankers Trust N.Y., Chase Manhattan, Chemical, Citicorp, Manufacturers-Hanover, Morgan (J.P.)

284

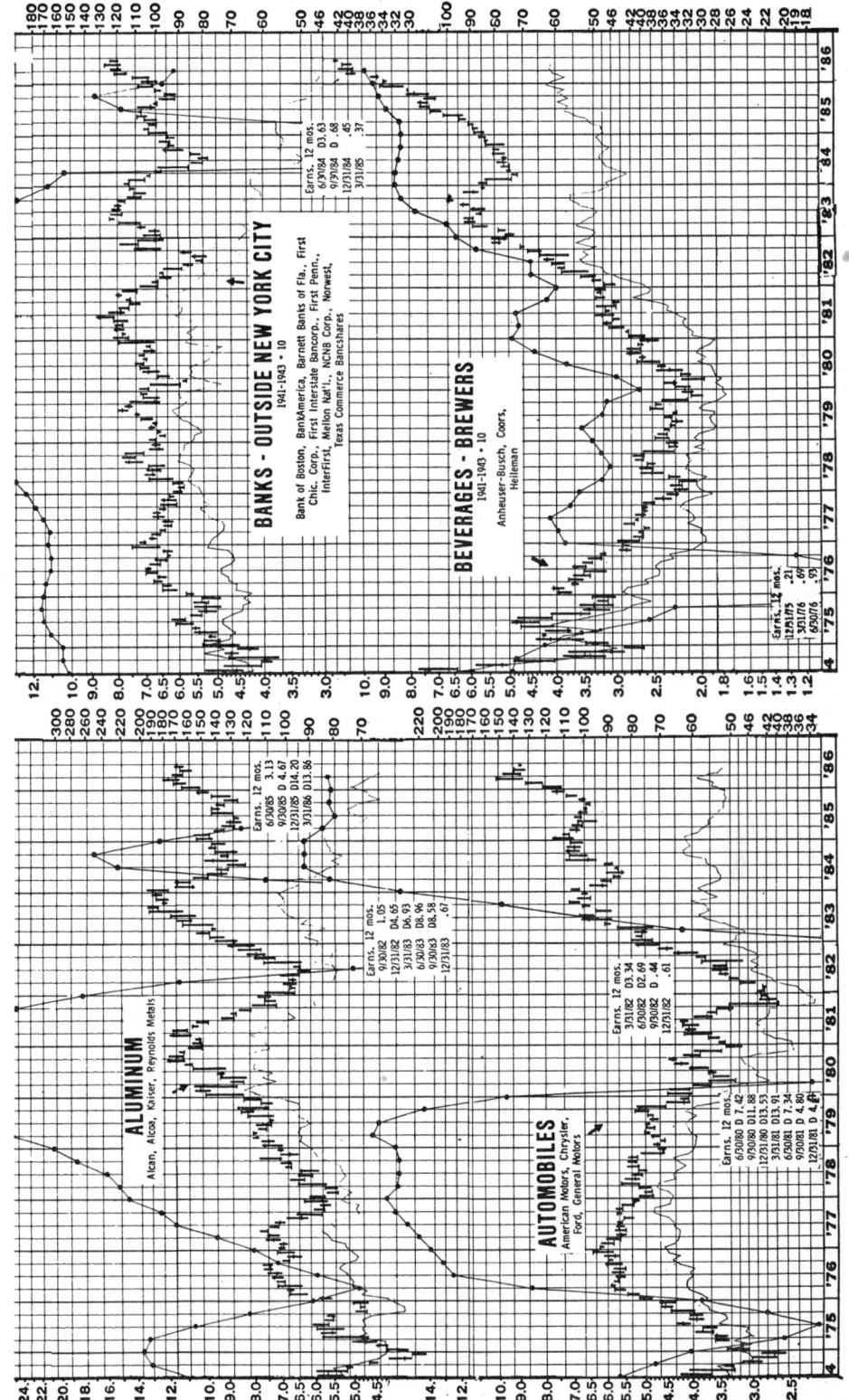

BANKS - OUTSIDE NEW YORK CITY
1941-1943 = 10

Bank of Boston, BankAmerica, Barnett Banks of Fla., First
Chic. Corp., First Interstate Bancorp., First Penn.,
InterFirst, Mellon Nat'l., NCNB Corp., Norwest,
Texas Commerce Bancshares

Earns. 12 mos.
6/30/84 D3.63
9/30/84 D .68
12/31/84   .45
3/31/85   .37

BEVERAGES - BREWERS
1941-1943 = 10

Anheuser-Busch, Coors,
Heileman

Earns. 12 mos.
12/31/75   .21
3/31/76   .69
6/30/76   .93

ALUMINUM
Alcan, Alcoa, Kaiser, Reynolds Metals

Earns. 12 mos.
6/30/85   3.13
9/30/85   D 4.67
12/31/85 D14.20
3/31/86   D13.86

Earns. 12 mos.
9/30/82   1.05
12/31/82 D4.65
3/31/83   D6.93
6/30/83   D8.96
9/30/83   D8.58
12/31/83   .67

AUTOMOBILES
American Motors, Chrysler,
Ford, General Motors

Earns. 12 mos.
3/31/82   D3.34
6/30/82   D2.69
9/30/82   D .44
12/31/82   .61

Earns. 12 mos.
6/30/80 D 7.42
9/30/80 D11.88
12/31/80 D13.53
3/31/81 D13.91
6/30/81 D 7.34
9/30/81 D 4.80
12/31/81 D 4.6

285

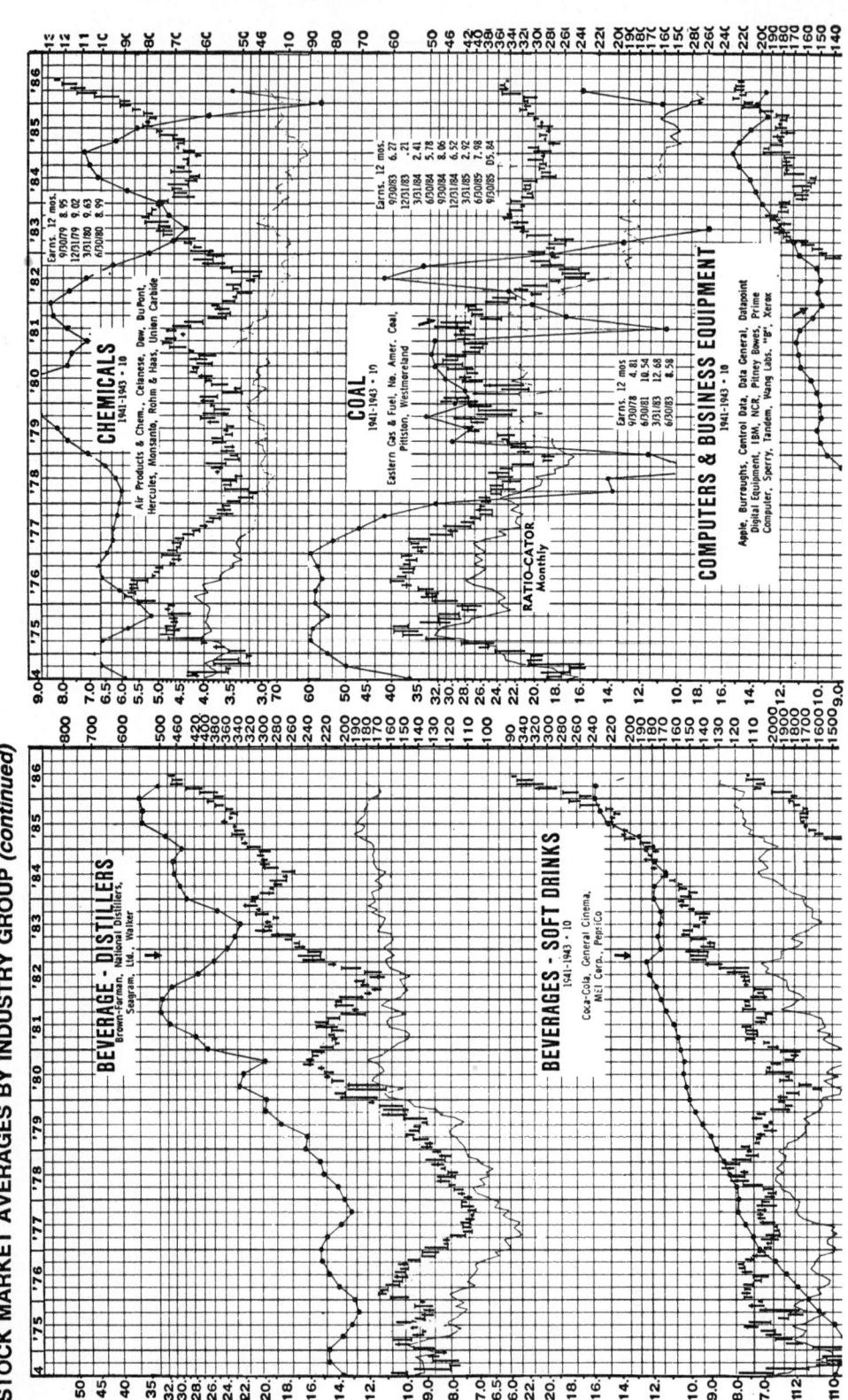

CHEMICALS
1941-1943 - 10

Air Products & Chem., Celanese, Dow, DuPont,
Hercules, Monsanto, Rohm & Haas, Union Carbide

Earns. 12 mos.	
9/30/79	8.95
12/31/79	9.02
3/31/80	9.63
6/30/80	8.99

COAL
1941-1943 - 10

Eastern Gas & Fuel, No. Amer. Coal,
Pittston, Westmoreland

Earns. 12 mos	
9/30/78	4.81
6/30/81	10.54
3/31/83	12.68
6/30/83	8.58

RATIO-CATOR
Monthly

COMPUTERS & BUSINESS EQUIPMENT
1941-1943 - 10

Apple, Burroughs, Control Data, Data General, Datapoint
Digital Equipment, IBM, NCR, Pitney Bowes, Prime
Computer, Sperry, Tandem, Wang Labs, "B", Xerox

Earns. 12 mos	
9/30/83	6.27
12/31/83	6.21
3/31/84	2.41
6/30/84	5.78
9/30/84	8.06
12/31/84	6.52
3/31/85	2.92
6/30/85	7.98
9/30/85	05.84

BEVERAGE - DISTILLERS

Brown-Forman, National Distillers,
Seagram, Ltd., Walker

BEVERAGES - SOFT DRINKS
1941-1943 - 10

Coca-Cola, General Cinema,
MEI Corp., PepsiCo

286

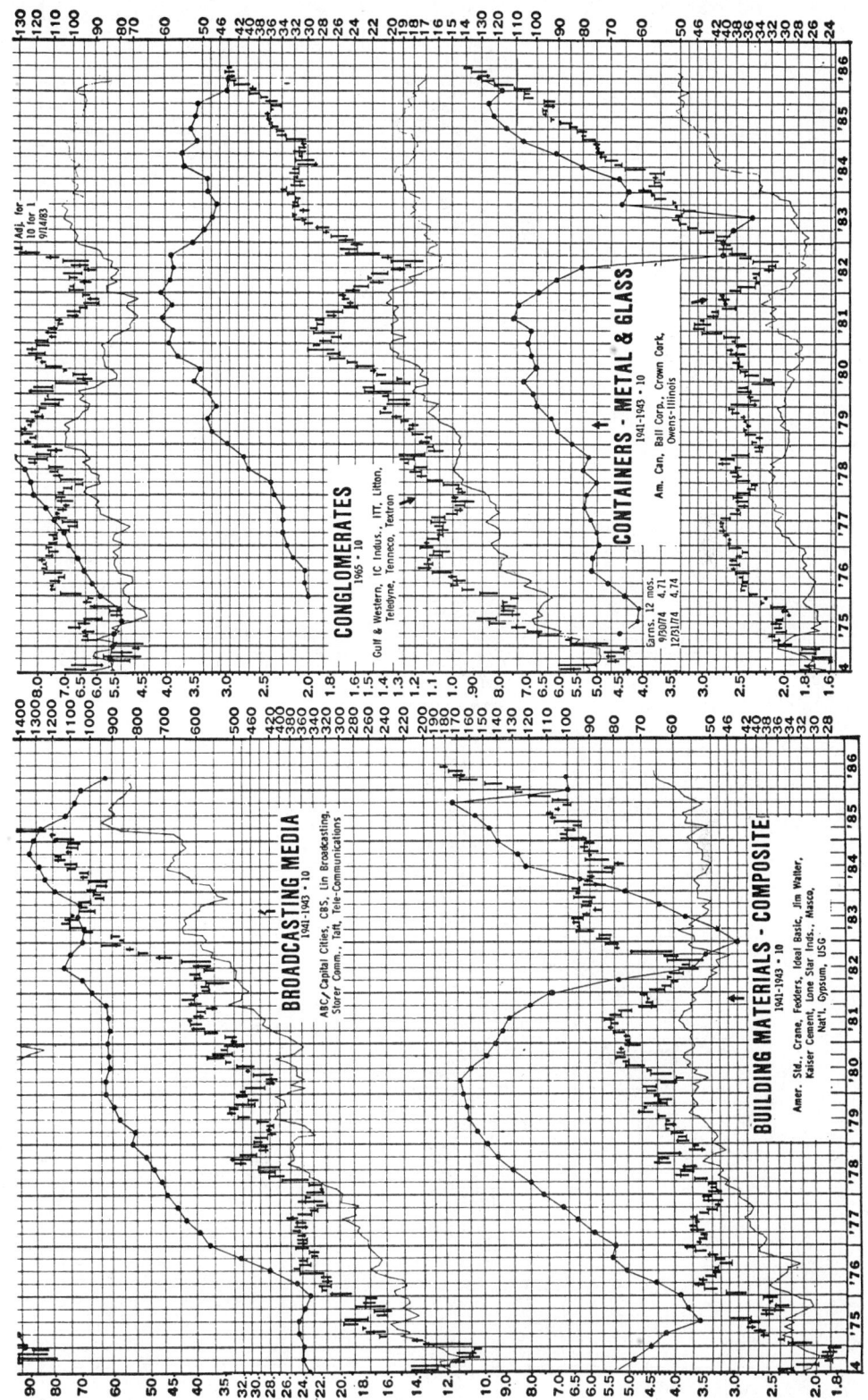

CONGLOMERATES
1965 · 10

Gulf & Western, IC Indus., ITT, Litton,
Teledyne, Tenneco, Textron

CONTAINERS - METAL & GLASS
1941-1943 · 10

Am. Can, Ball Corp., Crown Cork,
Owens-Illinois

Earns. 12 mos.
9/30/74   4.71
12/31/74 4.74

Adj. for
10 for 1
9/14/83

BROADCASTING MEDIA
1941-1943 · 10

ABC/ Capital Cities, CBS, Lin Broadcasting,
Storer Comm., Taft, Tele-Communications

BUILDING MATERIALS - COMPOSITE
1941-1943 · 10

Amer. Std., Crane, Fedders, Ideal Basic, Jim Walter,
Kaiser Cement, Lone Star Inds., Masco,
Nat'l. Gypsum, USG

STOCK MARKET AVERAGES BY INDUSTRY GROUP (continued)

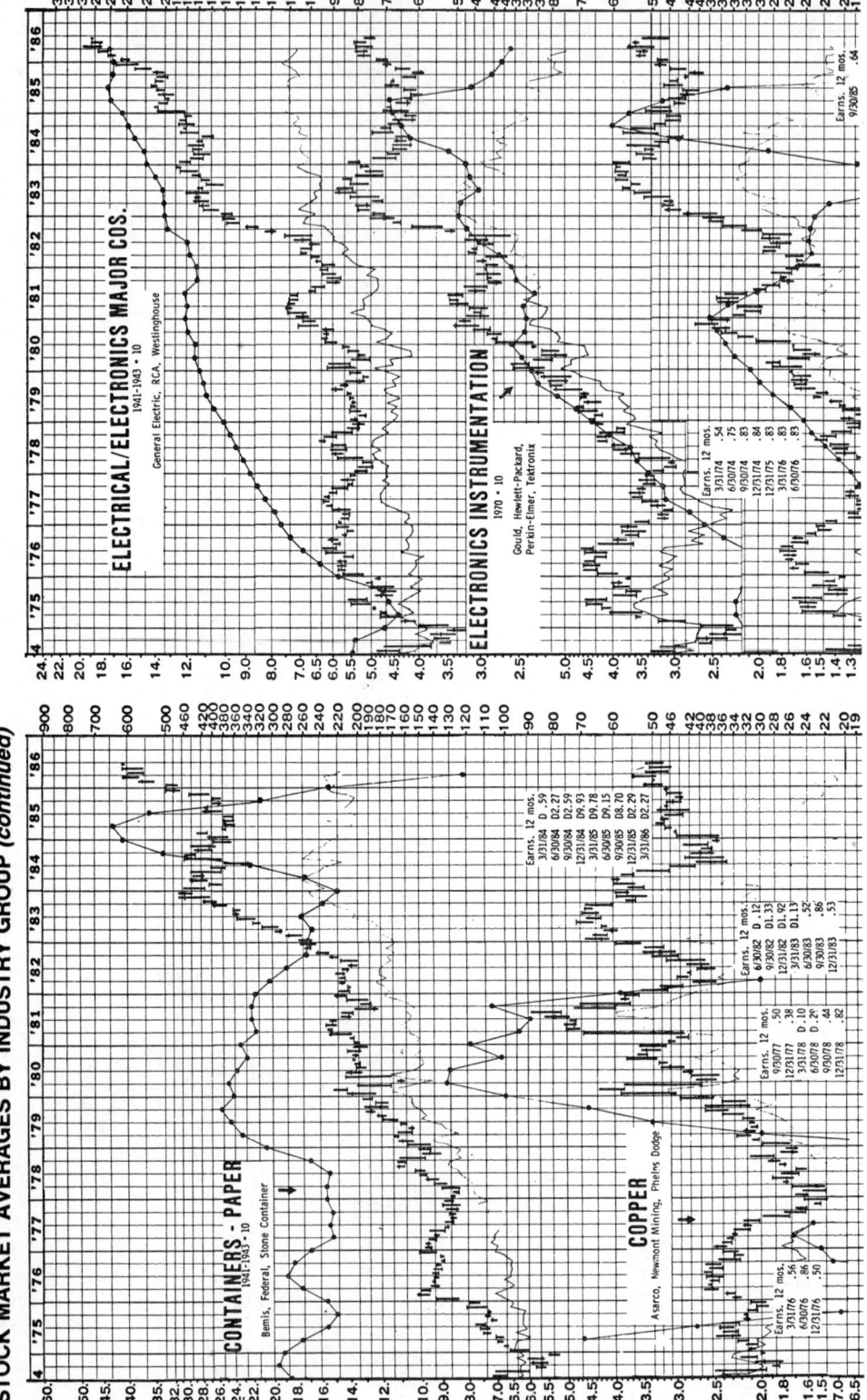

ELECTRICAL/ELECTRONICS MAJOR COS.
1941-1943 = 10

General Electric, RCA, Westinghouse

ELECTRONICS INSTRUMENTATION
1970 = 10

Gould, Hewlett-Packard,
Perkin-Elmer, Tektronix

Earns. 12 mos.	
3/31/74	.54
6/30/74	.75
9/30/74	.83
12/31/74	.84
12/31/75	.83
3/31/76	.83
6/30/76	.83

Earns. 12 mos. .64
9/30/85

CONTAINERS - PAPER
1941-1943 = 10

Bemis, Federal, Stone Container

Earns. 12 mos.	
3/31/84	D .59
6/30/84	D2.27
9/30/84	D2.59
12/31/84	D9.93
3/31/85	D9.78
6/30/85	D9.15
9/30/85	D8.70
12/31/85	D2.29
3/31/86	D2.27

COPPER

Asarco, Newmont Mining, Phelps Dodge

Earns. 12 mos.	
6/30/82	D .12
9/30/82	.50
12/31/82	D1.33
3/31/83	D1.92
6/30/83	D .10
9/30/83	.52
12/31/83	.86
12/31/83	.53

Earns. 12 mos.	
9/30/77	.50
12/31/77	.38
3/31/78	D .10
6/30/78	D .20
9/30/78	.44
12/31/78	.82

Earns. 12 mos.	
3/31/76	.56
6/30/76	.86
12/31/76	.50

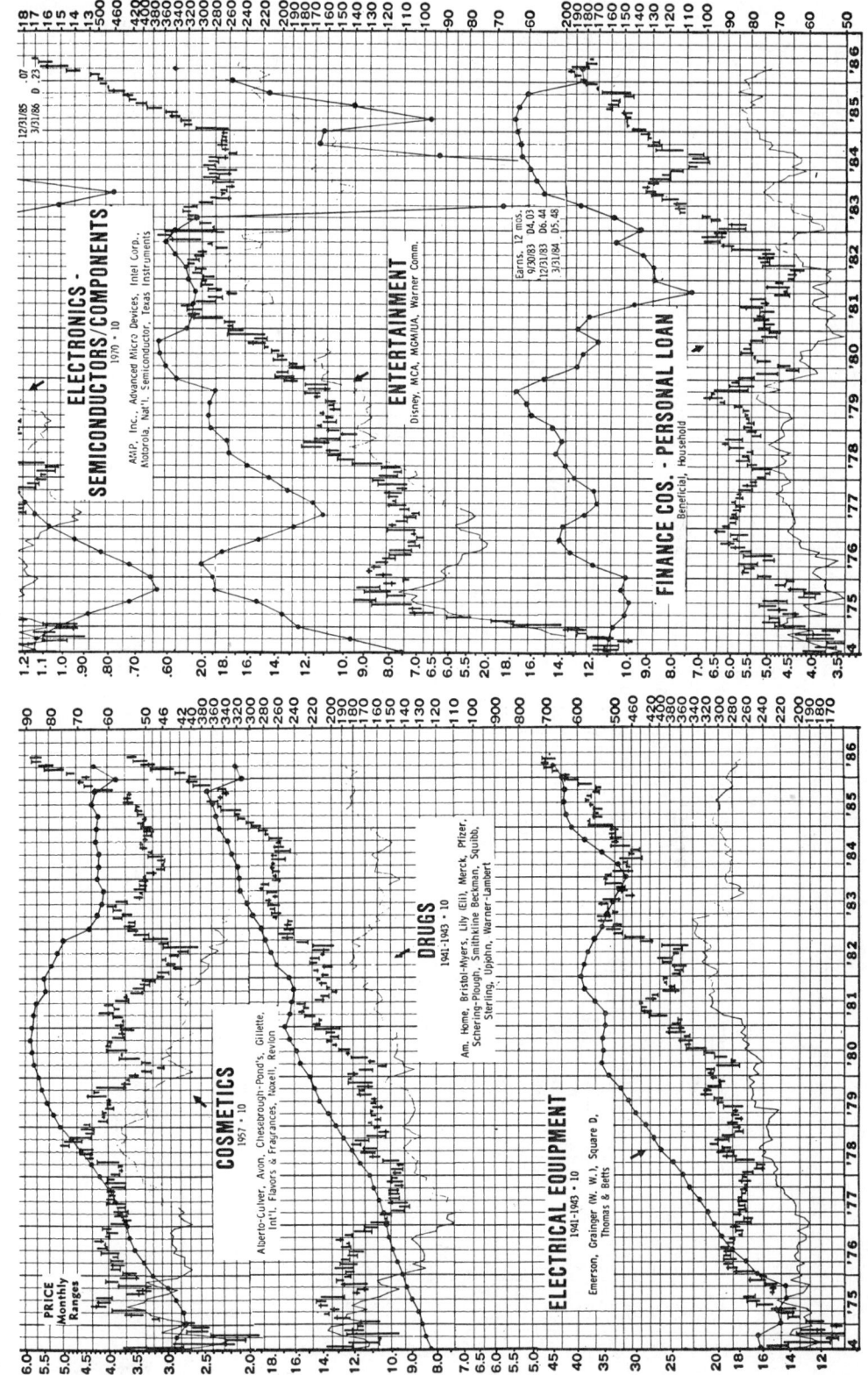

ELECTRONICS -
SEMICONDUCTORS/COMPONENTS
1970 = 10

AMP, Inc., Advanced Micro Devices, Intel Corp.,
Motorola, Nat'l. Semiconductor, Texas Instruments

12/31/85 .07
3/31/86 D .23

ENTERTAINMENT
Disney, MCA, MGM/UA, Warner Comm.

Earns. 12 mos.
9/30/83   D4.03
12/31/83 D6.44
3/31/84   D5.48

FINANCE COS. - PERSONAL LOAN
Beneficial, Household

PRICE
Monthly
Ranges

COSMETICS
1957 = 10

Alberto-Culver, Avon, Chesebrough-Pond's, Gillette,
Int'l. Flavors & Fragrances, Noxell, Revlon

DRUGS
1941-1943 = 10

Am. Home, Bristol-Myers, Lily (Eli), Merck, Pfizer,
Schering-Plough, Smithkline Beckman, Squibb,
Sterling, Upjohn, Warner-Lambert

ELECTRICAL EQUIPMENT
1941-1943 = 10

Emerson, Grainger (W. W.), Square D,
Thomas & Betts

289

STOCK MARKET AVERAGES BY INDUSTRY GROUP *(continued)*

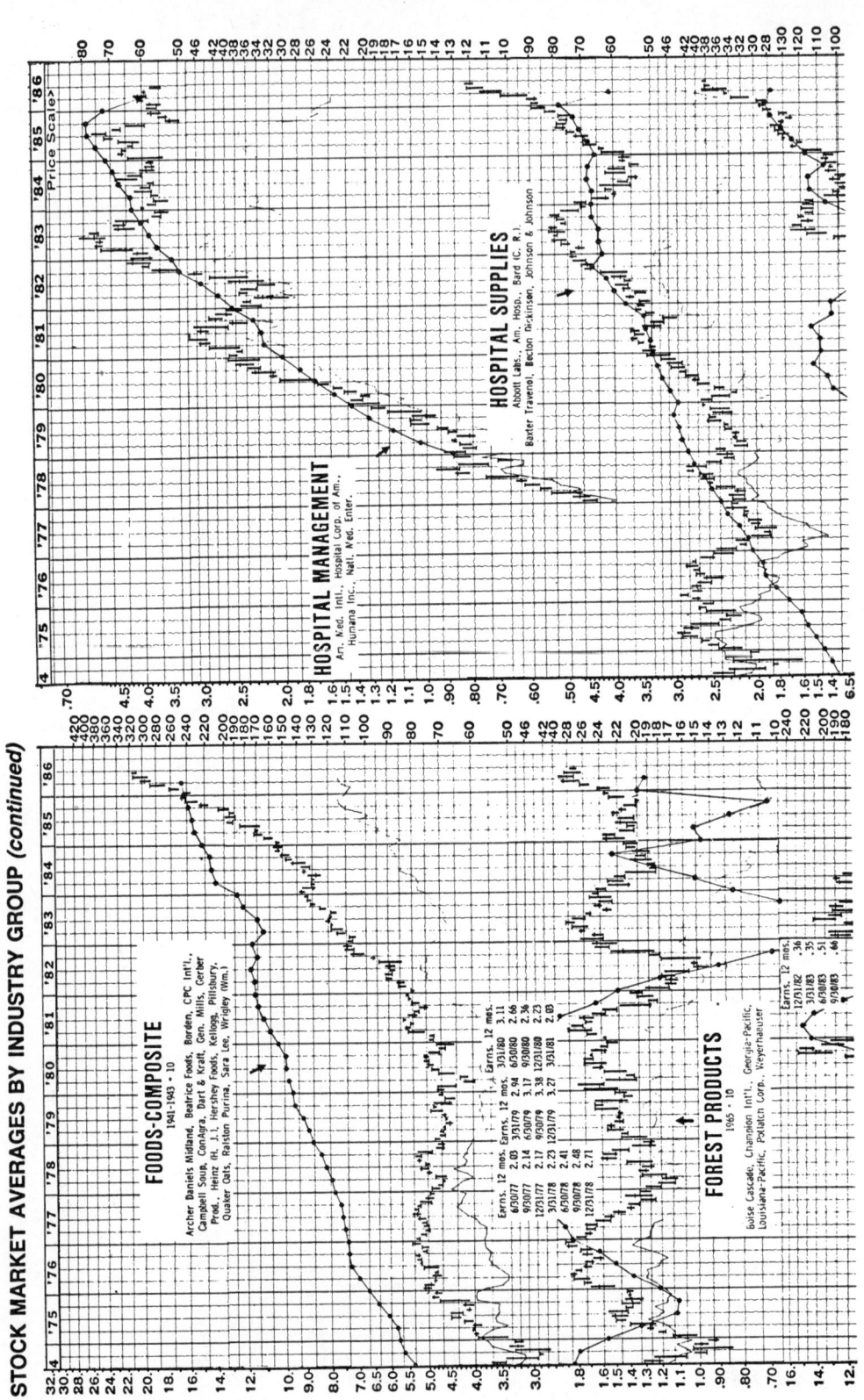

FOODS-COMPOSITE
1941-1943 = 10

Archer Daniels Midland, Beatrice Foods, Borden, CPC Int'l.,
Campbell Soup, ConAgra, Dart & Kraft, Gen. Mills, Gerber
Prod., Heinz (H. J.), Hershey Foods, Kellogg, Pillsbury,
Quaker Oats, Ralston Purina, Sara Lee, Wrigley (Wm.)

	Earns. 12 mos.		Earns. 12 mos.
6/30/77	2.05	3/31/79	2.94
9/30/77	2.14	6/30/79	3.17
12/31/77	2.17	9/30/79	3.38
3/31/78	2.23	12/31/79	3.27
6/30/78	2.41		
9/30/78	2.48		
12/31/78	2.71		

	Earns. 12 mos.
3/31/80	3.11
6/30/80	2.66
9/30/80	2.36
12/31/80	2.23
3/31/81	2.05

HOSPITAL MANAGEMENT

Am. Med. Intl., Hospital Corp. of Am.,
Humana Inc., Natl. Med. Enter.

HOSPITAL SUPPLIES

Abbott Labs., Am. Hosp., Bard (C. R.)
Baxter Travenol, Becton Dickinson, Johnson & Johnson

FOREST PRODUCTS
1965 = 10

Boise Cascade, Champion Int'l., Georgia-Pacific,
Louisiana-Pacific, Potlatch Corp., Weyerhaeuser

	Earns. 12 mos.
12/31/82	.36
3/31/83	.35
6/30/83	.51
9/30/83	.66

290

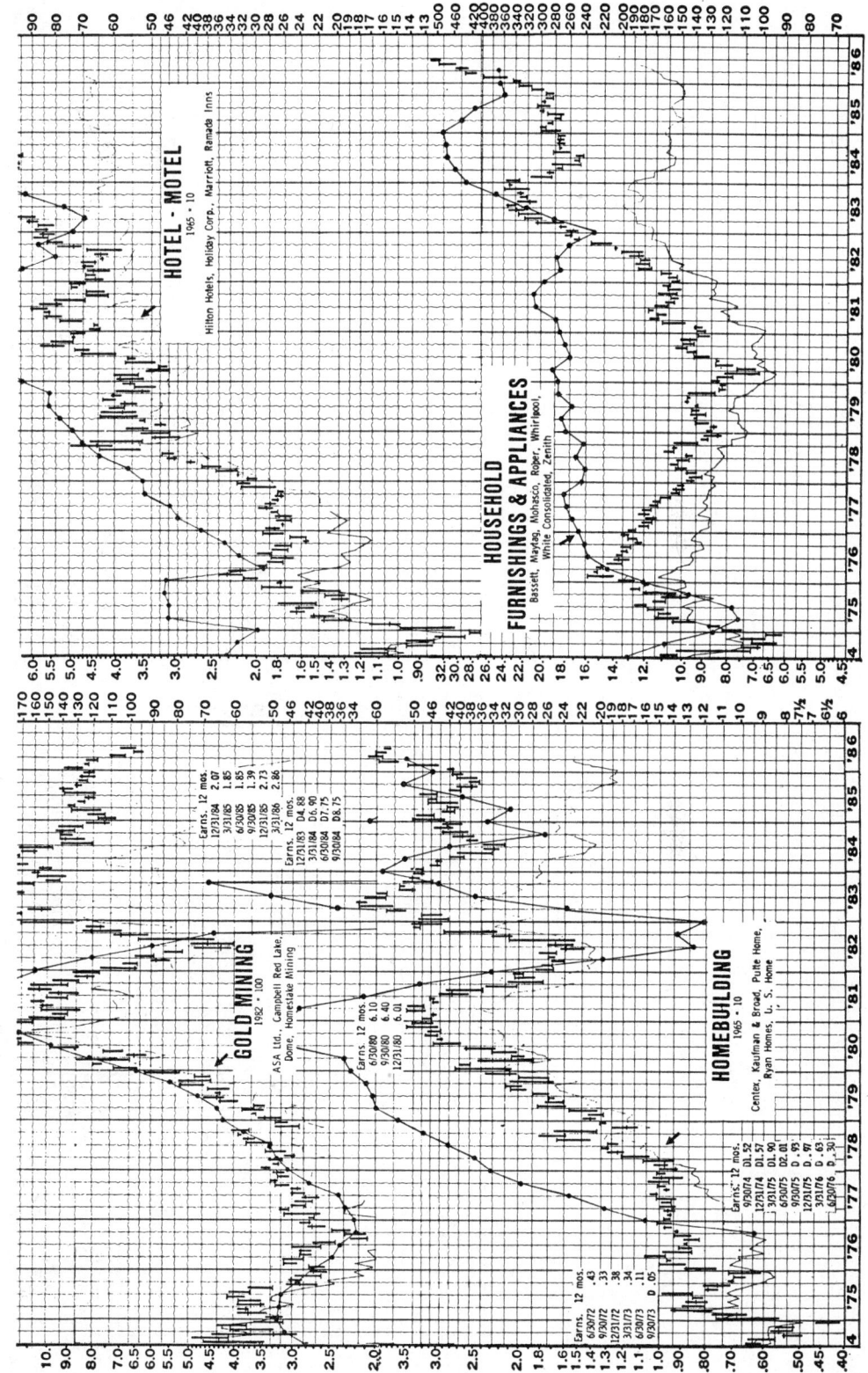

HOTEL - MOTEL
1965 = 10

Hilton Hotels, Holiday Corp., Marriott, Ramada Inns

HOUSEHOLD FURNISHINGS & APPLIANCES

Bassett, Maytag, Mohasco, Roper, Whirlpool, White Consolidated, Zenith

GOLD MINING
1982 = 100

ASA Ltd., Campbell Red Lake, Dome, Homestake Mining

Earns. 12 mos.
12/31/83 04.88
3/31/84 06.90
6/30/84 07.75
9/30/84 08.75

Earns. 12 mos.
12/31/84 2.07
3/31/85 1.85
6/30/85 1.39
12/31/85 2.73
3/31/86 2.86

Earns. 12 mos.
6/30/80 6.10
9/30/80 6.40
12/31/80 6.01

Earns. 12 mos.
6/30/72 .43
9/30/72 .33
12/31/72 .38
3/31/73 .34
6/30/73 .11
9/30/73 D .05

HOMEBUILDING
1965 = 10

Centex, Kaufman & Broad, Pulte Home, Ryan Homes, U. S. Home

Earns. 12 mos.
9/30/74 D1.52
12/31/74 D1.57
3/31/75 D1.90
6/30/75 D2.01
12/31/75 D .93
3/31/76 D .97
12/31/76 D .63
6/30/76 D .30

STOCK MARKET AVERAGES BY INDUSTRY GROUP *(continued)*

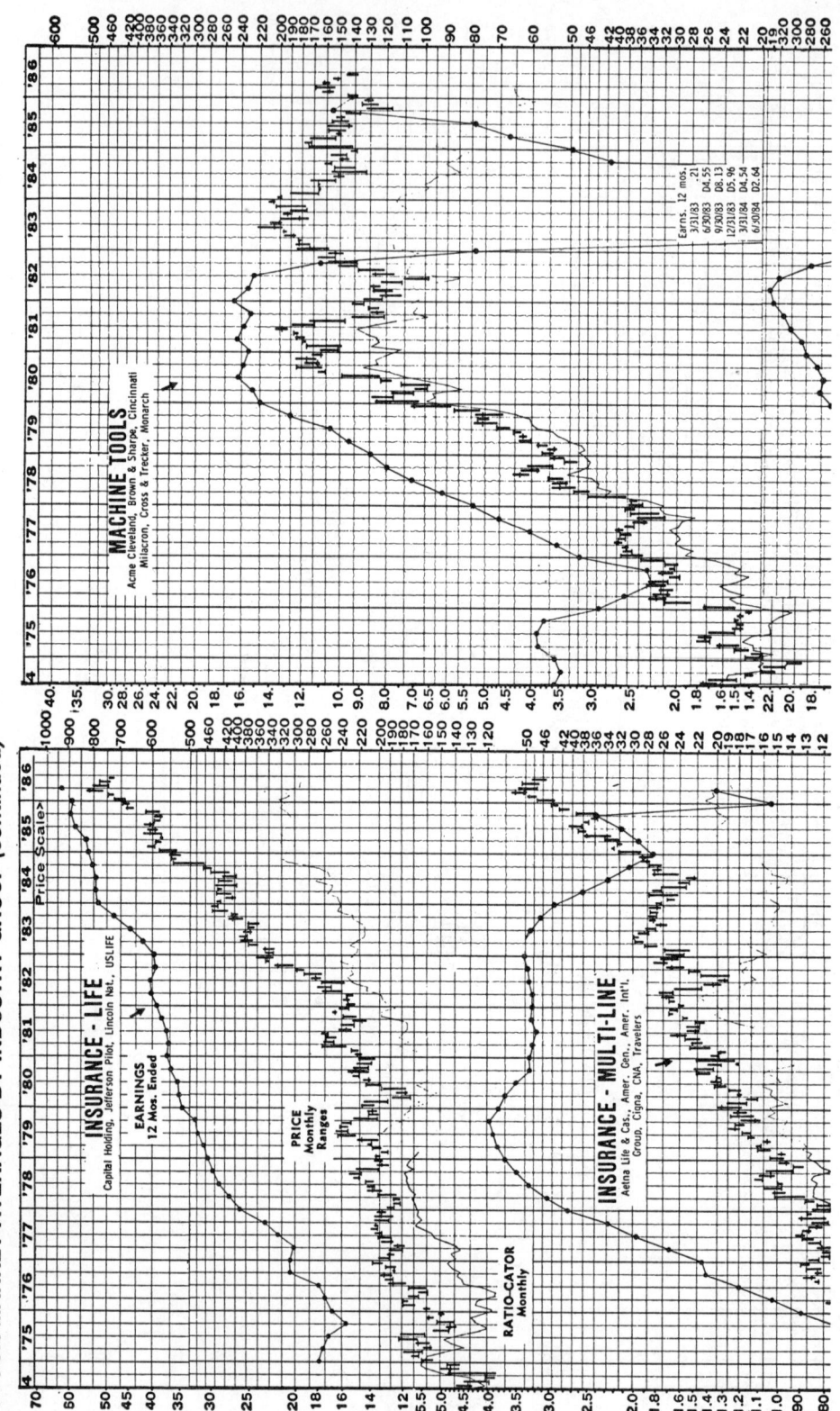

INSURANCE - LIFE
Capital Holding, Jefferson Pilot, Lincoln Nat., USLIFE

EARNINGS
12 Mos. Ended

PRICE
Monthly
Ranges

RATIO-CATOR
Monthly

Price Scale>

INSURANCE - MULTI-LINE
Aetna Life & Cas., Amer. Gen., Amer. Int'l,
Group, Cigna, CNA, Travelers

MACHINE TOOLS
Acme Cleveland, Brown & Sharpe, Cincinnati
Milacron, Cross & Trecker, Monarch

Earns. 12 mos.
3/31/83   .21
6/30/83   04.55
9/30/83   08.13
12/31/83 05.96
3/31/84   04.54
6/30/84   02.64

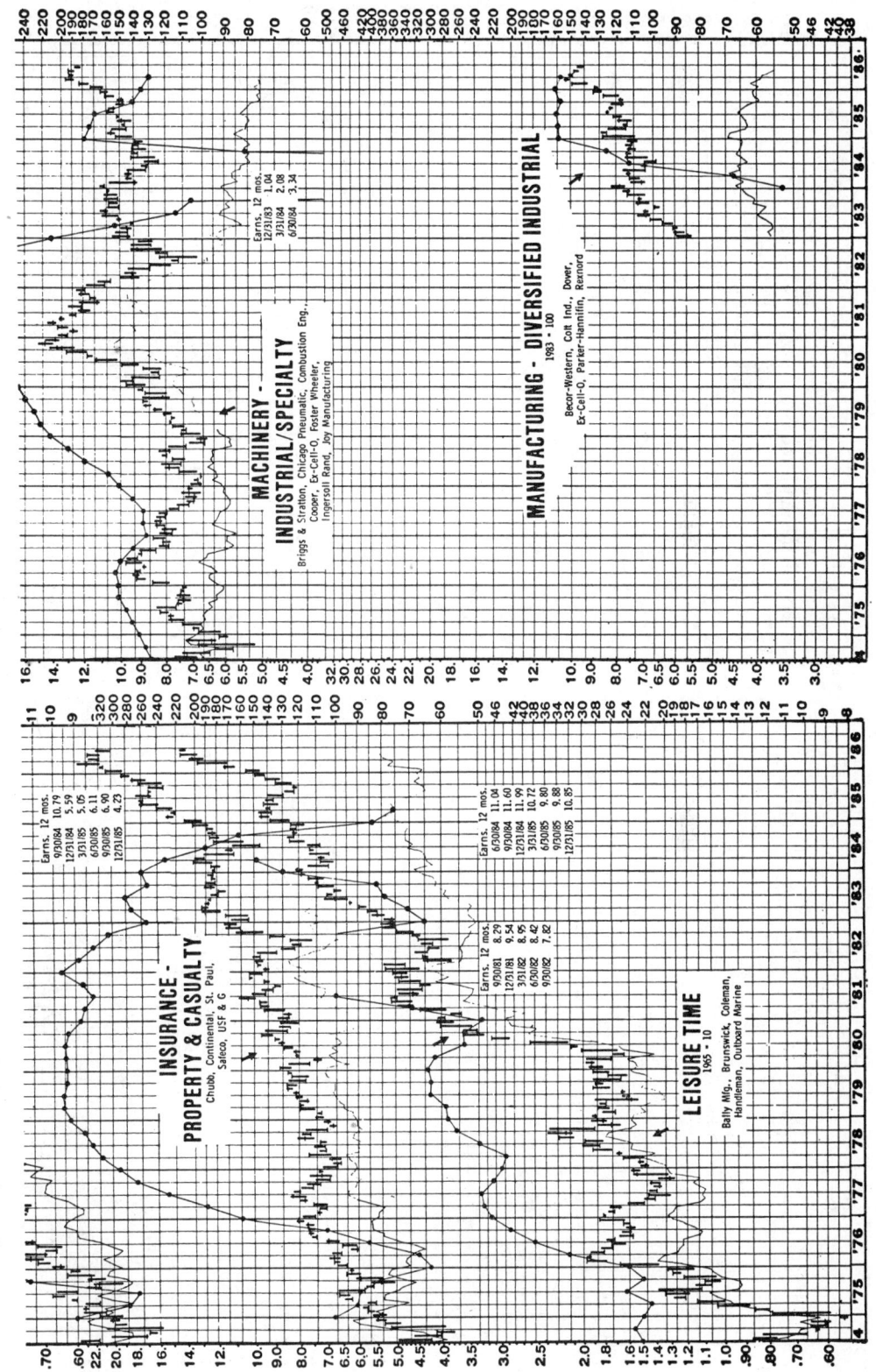

MACHINERY -
INDUSTRIAL/SPECIALTY

Briggs & Stratton, Chicago Pneumatic, Combustion Eng.,
Cooper, Ex-Cell-O, Foster Wheeler,
Ingersoll Rand, Joy Manufacturing

Earns. 12 mos.
12/31/83   1.04
3/31/84   2.08
6/30/84   3.34

MANUFACTURING - DIVERSIFIED INDUSTRIAL
1983 = 100

Bacor-Western, Colt Ind., Dover,
Ex-Cell-O, Parker-Hannifin, Rexnord

INSURANCE -
PROPERTY & CASUALTY

Chubb, Continental, St. Paul,
Safeco, USF & G

Earns. 12 mos.
9/30/84   10.79
12/31/84   5.59
3/31/85   5.05
6/30/85   6.11
9/30/85   6.90
12/31/85   4.23

LEISURE TIME
1965 = 10

Bally Mfg., Brunswick, Coleman,
Handleman, Outboard Marine

Earns. 12 mos.
6/30/84   11.04
9/30/84   9.54
12/31/84 11.60
3/31/85   11.99
6/30/85   10.72
9/30/85   9.80
12/31/85 10.85

Earns. 12 mos.
9/30/81   8.29
12/31/81 9.54
3/31/82   8.95
6/30/82   8.42
9/30/82   7.82

293

STOCK MARKET AVERAGES BY INDUSTRY GROUP (continued)

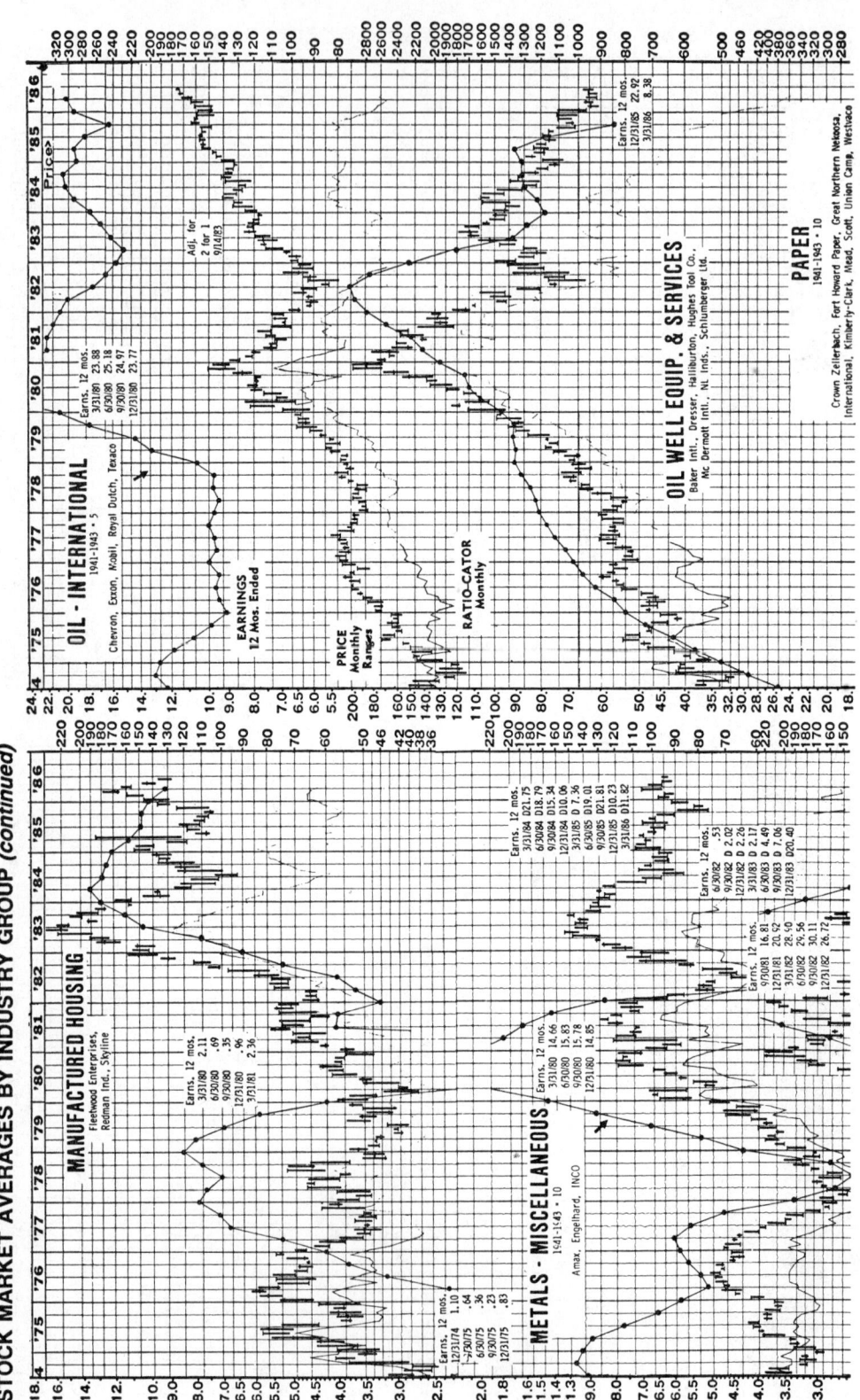

OIL - INTERNATIONAL
1941-1943 · 5

Chevron, Exxon, Mobil, Royal Dutch, Texaco

Adj. for
2 for 1
9/14/83

Earns. 12 mos.
3/31/87 23.88
6/30/80 25.18
9/30/80 24.97
12/31/80 23.77

EARNINGS
12 Mos. Ended

PRICE
Monthly
Ranges

RATIO-CATOR
Monthly

OIL WELL EQUIP. & SERVICES

Baker Intl., Dresser, Halliburton, Hughes Tool Co.,
Mc Dermott Intl., NL Inds., Schlumberger Ltd.

Earns. 12 mos.
12/31/85 22.92
3/31/86   8.38

PAPER
1941-1943 · 10

Crown Zellerbach, Fort Howard Paper, Great Northern Nekoosa,
International, Kimberly-Clark, Mead, Scott, Union Camp, Westvaco

MANUFACTURED HOUSING

Fleetwood Enterprises,
Redman Inds., Skyline

Earns. 12 mos.
3/31/80 1.10
6/30/80 2.11
9/30/80   .69
12/31/80 .35
3/31/81   .96
        2.36

Earns. 12 mos.
12/31/74 1.10
6/30/75   .64
9/30/75   .36
12/31/75 .23
         .83

METALS - MISCELLANEOUS
1941-1943 · 10

Amax, Engelhard, INCO

Earns. 12 mos.
3/31/80 14.66
6/30/80 15.83
9/30/80 15.78
12/31/80 14.85

Earns. 12 mos.
3/31/84 D21.75
6/30/84 D18.79
9/30/84 D15.34
12/31/84 D10.06
3/31/85 D 7.36
6/30/85 D19.01
9/30/85 D21.81
12/31/85 D10.23
3/31/86 D11.82

Earns. 12 mos.
6/30/82   .53
9/30/82 D 2.02
12/31/82 D 2.26
3/31/83 D 2.17
6/30/83 D 4.49
9/30/83 D 7.06
12/31/83 D20.40

Earns. 12 mos.
9/30/81 16.81
12/31/81 20.52
3/31/82 28.40
9/30/82 29.56
         30.11
12/31/82 26.72

294

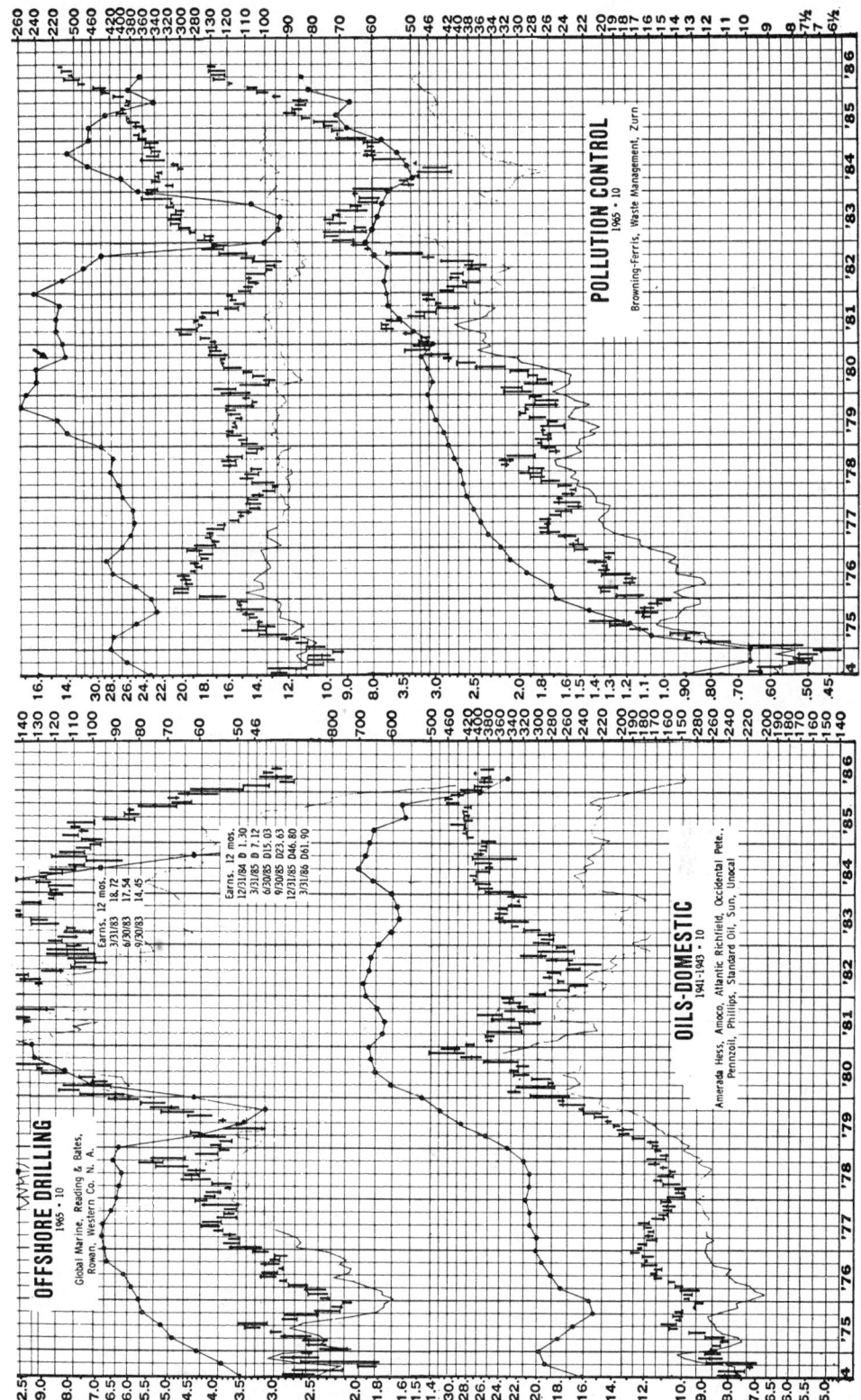

OFFSHORE DRILLING
1965 · 10

Global Marine, Reading & Bates,
Rowan, Western Co. N. A.

Earns. 12 mos.
3/31/83   18.72
6/30/83   17.54
9/30/83   14.45

Earns. 12 mos.
12/31/84 Ⓓ 1.30
3/31/85   Ⓓ 7.12
6/30/85   D15.03
9/30/85   D23.63
12/31/85 D46.80
3/31/86   D61.90

POLLUTION CONTROL
1965 · 10

Browning-Ferris, Waste Management, Zurn

OILS–DOMESTIC
1941-1943 · 10

Amerada Hess, Amoco, Atlantic Richfield, Occidental Pete.,
Pennzoil, Phillips, Standard Oil, Sun, Unocal

STOCK MARKET AVERAGES BY INDUSTRY GROUP *(continued)*

RESTAURANTS
1965 - 10
Church's Fried Chicken, Luby's Cafeterias,
McDonald's, Wendy's

PUBLISHING
1941-1943 - 10
Dun & Bradstreet, Harcourt Brace, Macmillan,
McGraw-Hill, Meredith, Time

PUBLISHING - NEWSPAPERS
1970 - 10
Dow Jones, Gannett Co., Knight Ridder,
N. Y. Times, Times Mirror

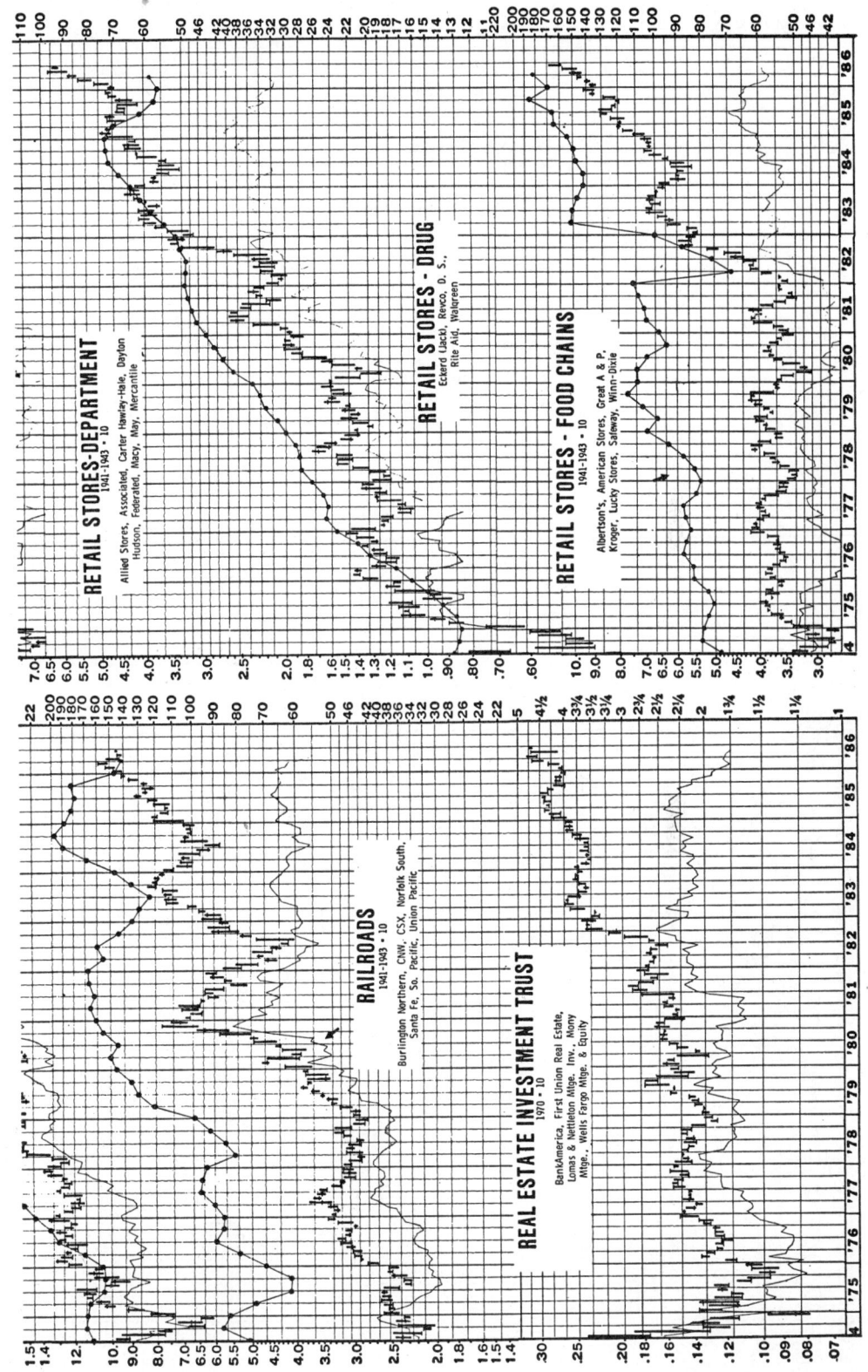

RETAIL STORES-DEPARTMENT
1941-1943 = 10

Allied Stores, Associated, Carter Hawley-Hale, Dayton
Hudson, Federated, Macy, May, Mercantile

RETAIL STORES - DRUG

Eckerd (Jack), Revco, D. S.,
Rite Aid, Walgreen

RETAIL STORES - FOOD CHAINS
1941-1943 = 10

Albertson's, American Stores, Great A & P,
Kroger, Lucky Stores, Safeway, Winn-Dixie

RAILROADS
1941-1943 = 10

Burlington Northern, CNW, CSX, Norfolk South,
Santa Fe, So. Pacific, Union Pacific

REAL ESTATE INVESTMENT TRUST
1970 = 10

BankAmerica, First Union Real Estate,
Lomas & Nettleton Mtge. Inv., Mony
Mtge., Wells Fargo Mtge. & Equity

STOCK MARKET AVERAGES BY INDUSTRY GROUP (continued)

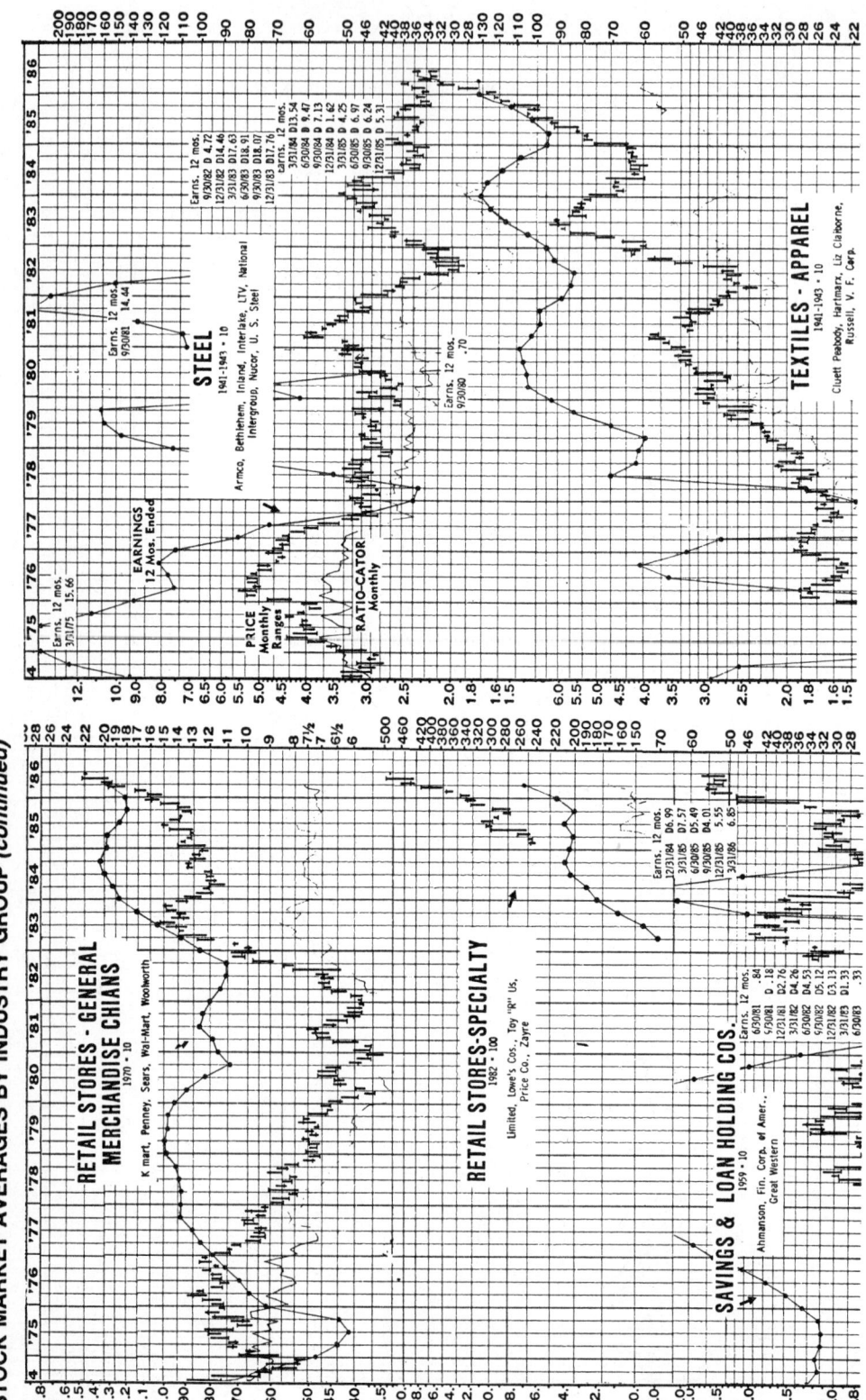

RETAIL STORES - GENERAL MERCHANDISE CHIANS
1970 = 10

K mart, Penney, Sears, Wal-Mart, Woolworth

RETAIL STORES-SPECIALTY
1982 = 100

Limited, Lowe's Cos., Toy "R" US, Price Co., Zayre

Earns. 12 mos.	
12/31/84	D6.99
3/31/85	D7.57
6/30/85	D5.49
9/30/85	D4.01
12/31/86	6.85

SAVINGS & LOAN HOLDING COS.
1959 = 10

Ahmanson, Fin. Corp. of Amer., Great Western

Earns. 12 mos.	
6/30/81	.84
9/30/81	D .18
12/31/81	D2.76
3/31/82	D4.26
6/30/82	D4.53
9/30/82	D5.12
12/31/82	D3.13
3/31/83	D1.33
6/30/83	.33

STEEL
1941-1943 = 10

Armco, Bethlehem, Inland, Interlake, LTV, National Intergroup, Nucor, U. S. Steel

Earns. 12 mos.	
9/30/81	14.44

PRICE Monthly Ranges

EARNINGS 12 Mos. Ended

Earns. 12 mos.	
3/31/75	15.66

RATIO-CATOR Monthly

Earns. 12 mos.	
9/30/80	.70

Earns. 12 mos.	
9/30/82	D 4.72
12/31/82	D14.46
3/31/83	D17.63
6/30/83	D18.91
12/31/83	D17.76

Earns. 12 mos.	
3/31/84	D13.54
6/30/84	D 9.47
9/30/84	D 7.13
12/31/84	D 1.62
3/31/85	D 4.25
6/30/85	D 6.97
9/30/85	D 6.24
12/31/85	D 5.31

TEXTILES - APPAREL
1941-1943 = 10

Cluett Peabody, Hartmarx, Liz Claiborne, Russell, V. F. Corp.

298

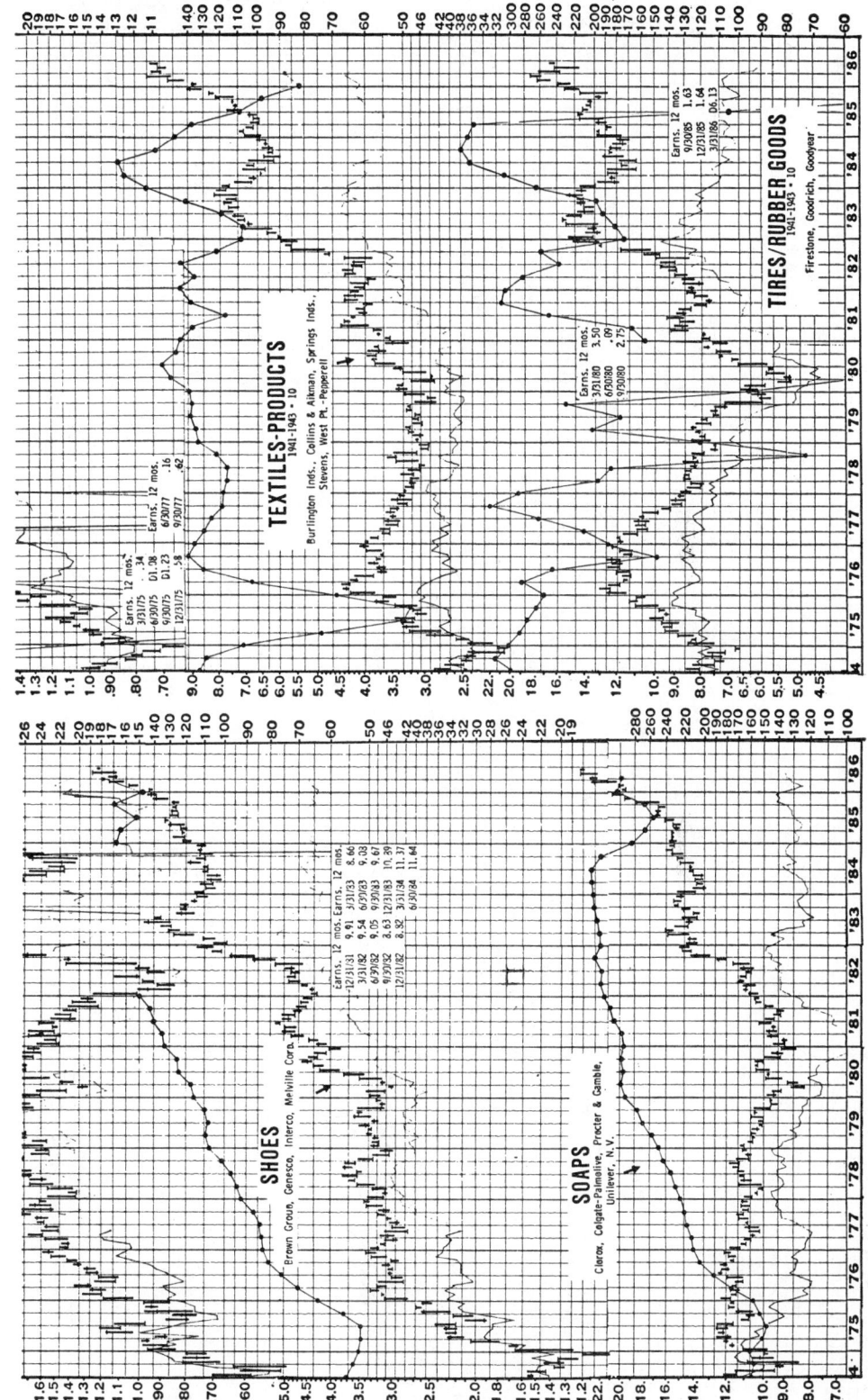

TEXTILES-PRODUCTS 1941-1943 = 10

Burlington Inds., Collins & Aikman, Springs Inds., Stevens, West Pt.-Pepperell

Earns. 12 mos.
3/31/75   .34
6/30/75   D1.08
9/30/75   D1.23
12/31/75   .58

Earns. 12 mos.
6/30/77   .16
9/30/77   .62

TIRES/RUBBER GOODS 1941-1943 = 10

Firestone, Goodrich, Goodyear

Earns. 12 mos.
3/31/80   3.50
6/30/80   .09
9/30/80   2.75

Earns. 12 mos.
9/30/85   1.63
12/31/85   1.64
3/31/86   D6.13

SHOES

Brown Group, Genesco, Interco, Melville Corp.

Earns. 12 mos.
12/31/81   9.91
3/31/82   9.54
6/30/82   9.67
9/30/82   3.63
12/31/82   8.32

Earns. 12 mos.
3/31/83   8.66
6/30/83   9.08
9/30/83   9.67
12/31/83   10.89
3/31/84   11.37
6/30/84   11.64

SOAPS

Clorox, Colgate-Palmolive, Procter & Gamble, Unilever, N. V.

STOCK MARKET AVERAGES BY INDUSTRY GROUP *(concluded)*

TOBACCO

Am. Brands, Phillip Morris, Reynolds

EARNINGS
12 Mos. Ended

PRICE
Monthly
Ranges

RATIO-CATOR
Monthly

TOYS
1965 = 10

Coleco, Hasbro Bradley, Mattel, Tonka

UTILITIES - ELECTRIC COS.
1941-1943 = 10

Am El Pwr, Balt G&E, Central & SW, Comm Ed, Con Ed, Detroit Ed,
Dominion Resources, Duke, Fla P&L, Middle So Utils, Niagra Mohawk,
No States Pwr, Ohio Ed, Pac G&E, Phil El, Pub Service E&G,
Pub Serv Ind, So Cal Ed, So Co, Texas Utils

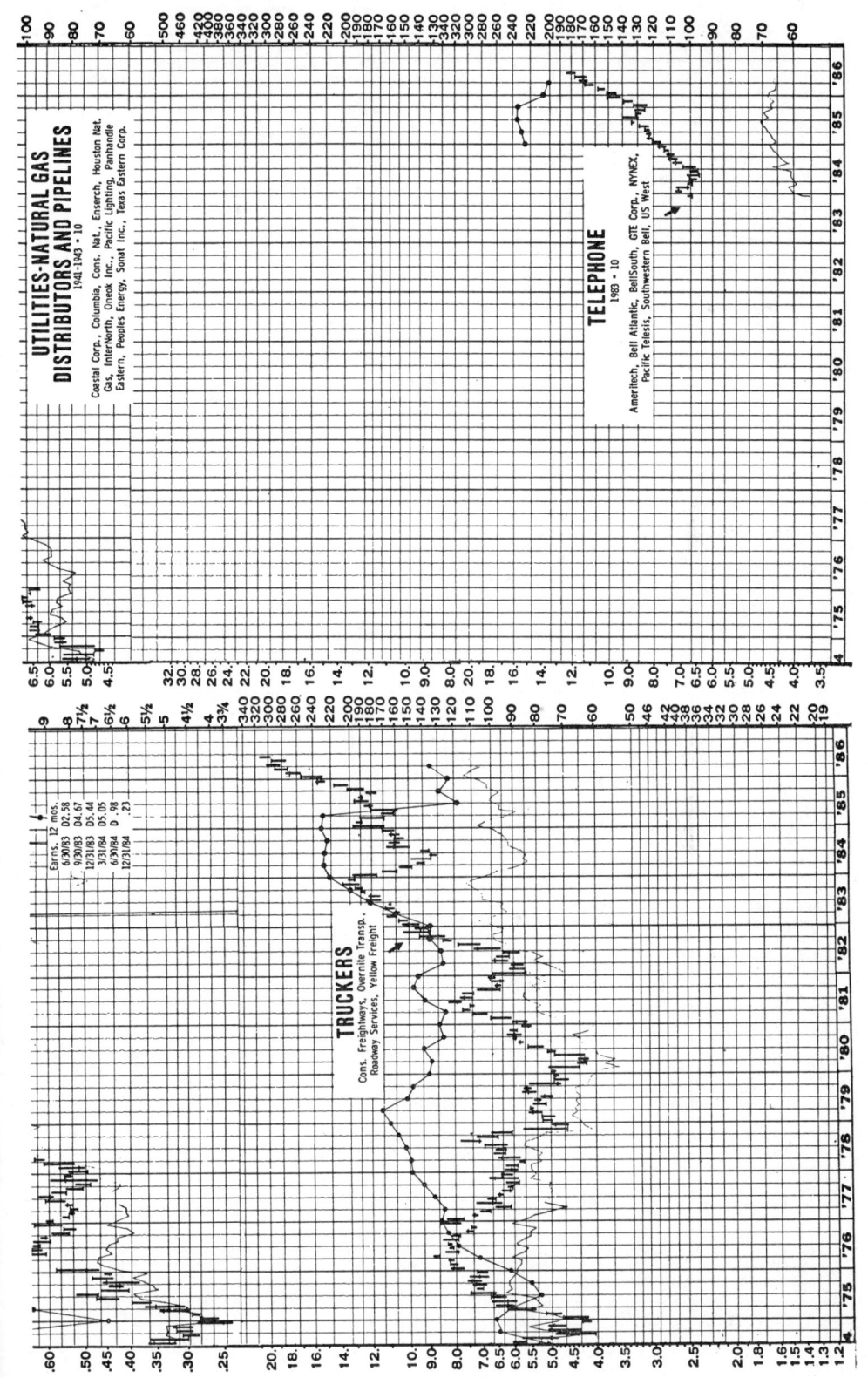

UTILITIES-NATURAL GAS
DISTRIBUTORS AND PIPELINES
1941-1943 • 10

Coastal Corp., Columbia, Cons. Nat., Enserch, Houston Nat.
Gas, InterNorth, Oneok Inc., Pacific Lighting, Panhandle
Eastern, Peoples Energy, Sonat Inc., Texas Eastern Corp.

TELEPHONE
1983 • 10

Ameritech, Bell Atlantic, BellSouth, GTE Corp., NYNEX,
Pacific Telesis, Southwestern Bell, US West

TRUCKERS

Cons. Freightways, Overnite Transp.,
Roadway Services, Yellow Freight

	Earns. 12 mos.	
	6/30/83	02.58
	9/30/83	04.67
	12/31/83	05.44
	3/31/84	05.05
	6/30/84	D .98
	12/31/84	.23

Dow Jones 65 Components

Dow Jones 65 Components

Thirty stocks used in Dow Jones Industrial Average are:

Allied-Signal	General Electric	Owens-Illinois
Aluminum Co	General Motors	Philip Morris
Amer Can	Goodyear	Procter & Gamb
Amer Express	Inco	Sears Roebuck
Amer T&T	IBM	Texaco
Bethlehem Steel	Inter Paper	Union Carbide
Chevron	McDonalds	United Technologies
DuPont	Merck	USX Corp
Eastman Kodak	Minnesota M&M	Westinghouse El
Exxon	Navistar Inter	Woolworth

Twenty Transportation Stocks used are:

AMR Corp	Delta Air Lines	Pan Am Corp
Amer President	Eastern Air Lines	Santa Fe So Pacific
Burlington North	Federal Express	TWA
Canadian Pacific	Leaseway Transp	UAL Inc.
Carolina Freight	Norfolk Southern	Union Pac Corp
Consolid Freight	NWA Inc	USAir Group
CSX Corp	Overnite Transp	

Fifteen Utility Stocks used are:

Am Elec Power	Consol Nat Gas	Panhandle Eastern
Centerior Energy	Detroit Edison	Peoples Energy
Colum-Gas Sys	Houston Indust	Phila Elec
Comwlth Edison	Niag Mohawk P	Pub Serv Enterp
Consol Edison	Pacific Gas & El	Sou Cal Edison

Source: Reprinted by permission of *The Wall Street Journal*, © Dow Jones & Company, Inc. 1986. All rights reserved.

FINANCIAL DATA ON DOW JONES INDUSTRIALS

	History				Earnings			P/E Ratio			Dvds	
	52-Week		5-Year		Last	%	5-Yr.		5-Year Avg		Indic.	
	High	Low	High	Low	12Mos	Ch	Growth	Today	High	Low	Amt	Yield
	$	$	$	$	$	%	%	-	-	-	$	%
Dow Jones Ind. ...	1909.03	1297.94	1909.03	776.92	114.79	10.05	6	15.4	47.1	11.4	67.14	3.8
AlliedSignal	49.06	36.75	NC	NC	-4.29	NC	NC	NE	NC	NC	1.80	4.5
Alum Co Am	46.38	31.50	48.63	21.88	-.16	-100.00	NC	NE	16.1	10.0	1.20	3.6
Am Can ....;	85.00	50.75	85.00	25.75	6.16	24.95	9	13.2	16.2	11.3	2.90	3.6
Am Express Co ...	70.13	40.38	70.13	17.63	5.26	82.01	8	11.2	14.1	8.5	1.36	2.3
Am Tel & T	26.00	19.88	NC	NC	1.49	11.19	NC	15.9	NC	NC	1.20	5.1
Bethlehem Stl ...... •	22.00	6.38	32.00	6.38	-4.79	NE	NC	NE	6.6	4.1	.00	.0
Chevron Cp ....•	41.50	33.63	51.75	23.50	4.53	2.72	-8	8.1	9.0	6.1	2.40	6.6
DuPont	87.38	54.88	87.38	30.00	6.24	38.98	2	12.1	11.7	7.8	3.00	4.0
Eastman Kodak ...	64.38	42.25	65.44	40.19	1.18	-67.93	-21	47.6	20.4	14.9	2.52	4.5
Exxon ....•	61.63	48.38	61.63	24.88	7.66	25.99	5	7.9	7.2	5.5	3.60	6.0
Gen Electric	82.63	56.25	82.63	25.56	5.25	2.94	9	13.7	12.3	8.9	2.32	3.2
Gen Motors	88.63	64.25	88.63	33.88	11.42	5.74	NC	5.9	18.9	11.4	5.00	7.4
Goodyear Tire ..... •	36.75	25.13	36.88	15.88	2.60	-23.75	2	11.7	9.1	6.2	1.60	5.2
Inco Ltd	16.88	10.38	23.63	7.88	.15	NE	NC	74.2	54.9	37.1	.20	1.8
Intl Bus Mach	161.88	122.25	161.88	48.38	10.53	4.67	13	12.5	13.3	9.2	4.40	3.3
Intl Paper	68.50	44.25	68.50	32.75	2.57	198.84	-16	24.5	20.3	15.0	2.40	3.8
McDonald's Cp	76.75	41.53	76.75	14.38	3.52	13.92	14	18.0	13.3	8.8	.66	1.0
Merck & Co	108.38	51.75	108.38	32.00	4.26	21.71	8	25.3	17.0	12.5	2.20	2.0
Minn Mng Mfg	115.00	74.25	115.00	48.00	6.19	3.00	2	17.8	14.3	10.8	3.60	3.3
Navistar Intl .... □	11.63	6.50	26.13	2.75	.69	NE	NC	10.0	NC	NC	.00	.0
Owens-Illinois	40.63	22.75	40.63	10.44	2.93	21.58	8	12.5	12.8	8.9	.95	2.6
Philip Morris	76.88	36.00	76.88	21.00	5.74	38.65	17	12.3	10.4	7.6	2.30	3.3
Proct & Gambl	82.50	55.00	82.50	32.56	4.15	-1.43	0	18.6	13.1	9.6	2.70	3.5
Sears, Roebuck ...	50.38	31.75	50.38	14.88	3.45	-13.97	15	12.5	11.4	7.4	1.76	4.1
Texaco	40.88	26.00	49.13	26.00	4.69	318.75	-17	6.2	15.2	10.2	3.00	10.3
Union Carbide	33.13	16.09	33.13	10.91	-2.82	-100.00	NC	NE	14.3	9.2	1.50	6.8
Utd Technol	56.25	36.25	56.25	15.63	2.13	-46.35	-11	18.9	9.6	6.6	1.40	3.5
US Steel	33.00	15.25	35.25	15.25	1.81	-25.82	NC	8.6	7.8	5.4	1.20	7.7
Westinghouse ....•	57.75	32.00	57.75	10.94	3.90	21.50	10	13.9	10.0	6.1	1.40	2.6
Woolworth FW	49.00	21.94	49.00	7.94	5.61	147.14	NC	7.6	8.9	5.6	1.12	2.6
Unweighted Avg. .	61.36	38.48	65.04	22.04	3.40	23.27	2	16.9	14.3	9.8	1.99	3.9

Source: *The Media General Financial Weekly*, Media General Financial Services, 301 East Grace Street, Richmond, VA 23219, July 28, 1986.

DOW JONES INDUSTRIAL, TRANSPORTATION AND UTILITY AVERAGES

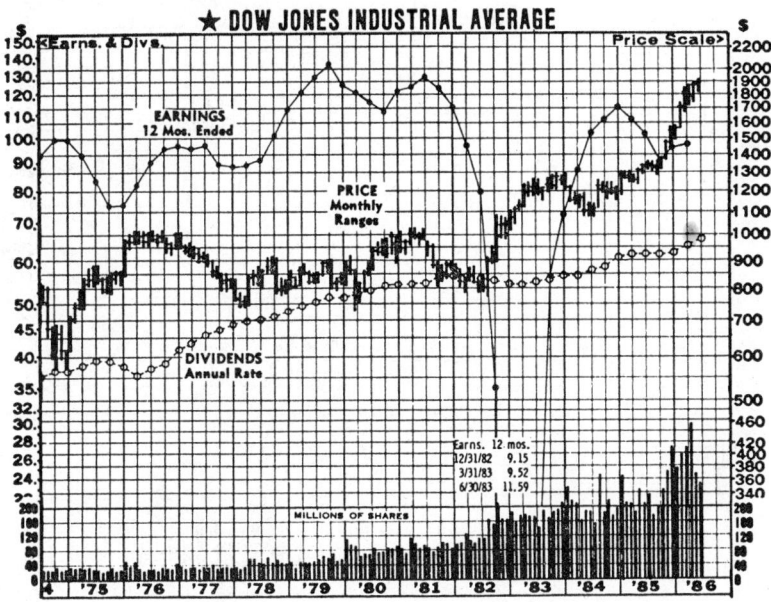

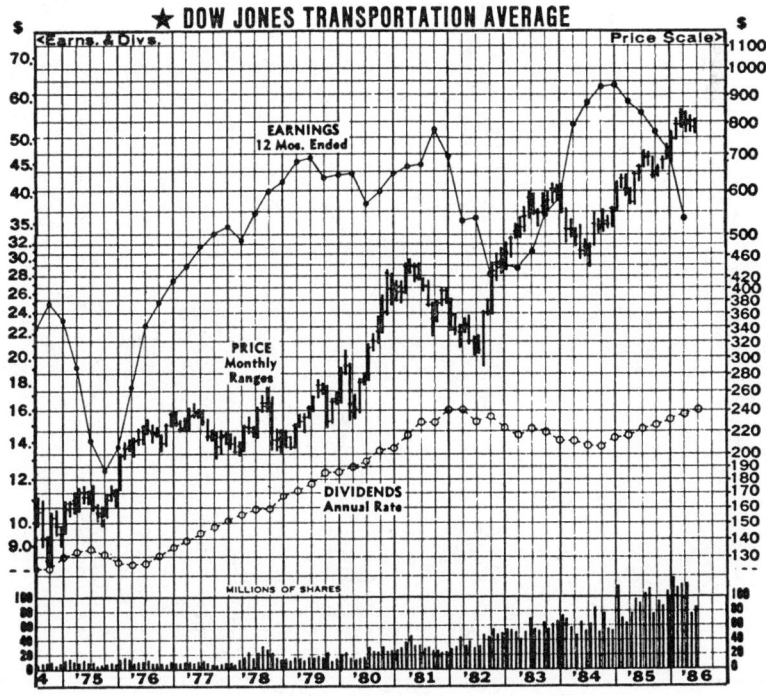

DOW JONES INDUSTRIAL, TRANSPORTATION AND UTILITY AVERAGES *(concluded)*

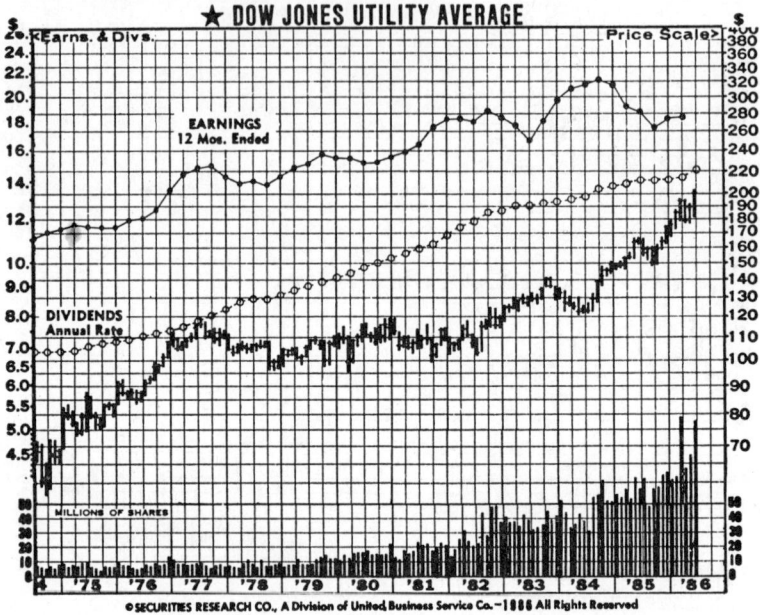

Source: *5-Trend CYCLI-GRAPHS.* The charts are courtesy of Securities Research Company, a division of United Business Service, 208 Newbury Street, Boston, MA 02116, July quarterly edition, 1986.

Shares Sold on Registered Exchanges

	Number of shares (millions)			Percent of total		
	NYSE	ASE	Other exchanges	NYSE	ASE	Other exchanges
1935	513.6	84.7	63.6	77.6%	12.8%	9.6%
1940	282.7	47.9	41.4	76.0	12.9	11.1
1945	496.0	152.4	96.1	66.6	20.5	12.9
1950	655.3	114.9	86.9	76.5	13.4	10.1
1955	820.5	243.9	148.0	67.7	20.1	12.2
1960	958.3	300.6	129.6	69.0	21.6	9.3
1965	1,809.4	582.2	195.3	69.9	22.5	7.5
1970	3,213.1	878.5	444.1	70.8	19.4	9.8
1971	4,265.3	1,049.3	601.1	72.1	17.7	10.2
1972	4,496.2	1,103.2	699.8	71.4	17.5	11.1
1973	4,336.6	740.4	653.2	75.7	12.9	11.4
1974	3,821.9	475.3	541.9	79.0	9.8	11.2
1975	5,056.5	540.9	637.6	81.1	8.7	10.2
1976	5,649.2	637.0	749.5	80.3	9.1	10.7
1977	5,613.3	651.9	758.2	79.9	9.3	10.8
1978	7,618.0	992.2	872.6	80.3	10.5	9.2
1979	8,675.3	1,161.3	1,026.2	79.9	10.7	9.4
1980	12,389.9	1,658.8	1,437.0	80.0	10.7	9.3
1981	12,843.1	1,472.3	1,594.9	80.7	9.3	10.0
1982	18,210.8	1,582.6	2,662.1	81.1	7.0	11.9
1983	24,253.5	2,209.4	3,683.8	80.5	7.3	12.2
1984	25,150.2	1,584.0	3,722.3	82.6	5.2	12.2
1985	30,221.8	2,114.7	4,709.1	81.6	5.7	12.7

Source: New York Stock Exchange *1986 Fact Book.*

Market Value of Shares Sold on Registered Exchanges

	Market value (millions)			Percent of total		
	NYSE	ASE	Other exchanges	NYSE	ASE	Other exchanges
1935	$ 13,335	$ 1,205	$ 736	87.3%	7.9%	4.8%
1940	7,166	643	595	85.3	7.7	7.0
1945	13,462	1,728	1,036	83.0	10.6	6.4
1950	18,725	1,481	1,571	86.0	6.8	7.2
1955	32,745	2,593	2,530	86.5	6.8	6.7
1960	37,960	4,176	3,083	83.9	9.2	6.8
1965	73,200	8,612	7,402	82.0	9.7	8.3
1970	103,063	14,266	13,579	78.7	10.9	10.4
1971	147,098	17,664	20,169	79.5	9.6	10.9
1972	159,700	20,453	23,873	78.3	10.0	11.7
1973	146,451	10,430	21,156	82.3	5.9	11.9
1974	99,178	5,048	14,023	83.9	4.3	11.9
1975	133,819	5,678	17,595	85.2	3.6	11.2
1976	164,545	7,468	22,956	84.4	3.8	11.8
1977	157,250	8,532	21,421	84.0	4.6	11.4
1978	210,426	15,204	23,625	84.4	6.1	9.5
1979	251,098	20,596	28,279	83.7	6.9	9.4
1980	397,670	34,696	43,485	83.6	7.3	9.1
1981	415,913	26,385	48,390	84.8	5.4	9.9
1982	514,263	20,731	69,054	85.1	3.4	11.4
1983	815,113	31,501	110,505	85.2	3.3	11.5
1984	815,655	21,349	115,143	85.7	2.2	12.1
1985	1,023,202	26,332	150,252	85.3	2.2	12.5

Source: NYSE member firm reports to the Securities & Exchange Commission.

Source: New York Stock Exchange *1986 Fact Book.*

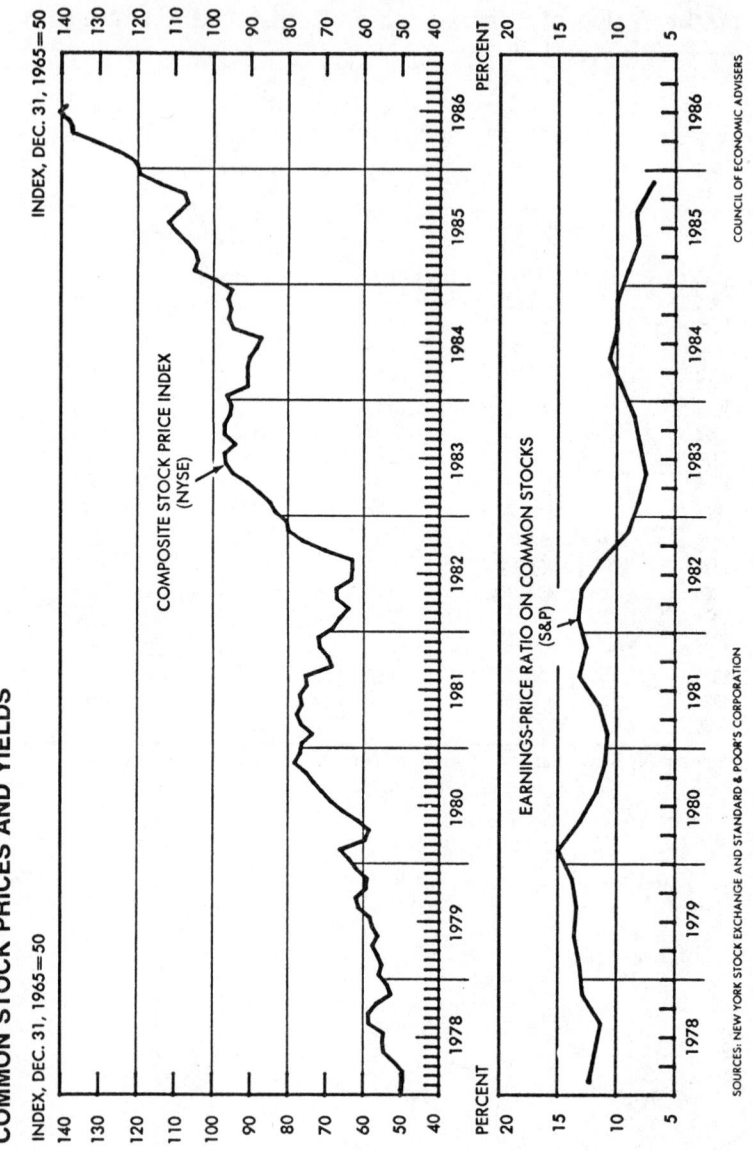

COMMON STOCK PRICES AND YIELDS

INDEX, DEC. 31, 1965=50

INDEX, DEC. 31, 1965=50

COMPOSITE STOCK PRICE INDEX
(NYSE)

PERCENT

EARNINGS-PRICE RATIO ON COMMON STOCKS
(S&P)

PERCENT

SOURCES: NEW YORK STOCK EXCHANGE AND STANDARD & POOR'S CORPORATION

COUNCIL OF ECONOMIC ADVISERS

Period	Common stock prices [1]							Common stock yields (percent) [5]	
	New York Stock Exchange indexes (Dec. 31, 1965=50) [2]					Dow-Jones industrial average [3]	Standard & Poor's composite index (1941-43=10) [4]	Dividend-price ratio	Earnings-price ratio
	Composite	Industrial	Transportation	Utility	Finance				
1980	68.10	78.70	60.61	37.35	64.25	891.41	118.78	5.26	12.66
1981	74.02	85.44	72.61	38.91	73.52	932.92	128.05	5.20	11.96
1982	68.93	78.18	60.41	39.75	71.99	884.36	119.71	5.81	11.60
1983	92.63	107.45	89.36	47.00	95.34	1,190.34	160.41	4.40	8.03
1984	92.46	108.01	85.63	46.44	89.28	1,178.48	160.46	4.64	10.02
1985	108.09	123.79	104.11	56.75	114.21	1,328.23	186.84	4.25	8.12
1985: July	111.64	126.94	111.67	59.68	119.85	1,343.17	192.54	4.14	
Aug	109.09	124.92	109.92	56.99	114.68	1,326.18	188.31	4.23	
Sept	106.62	122.35	104.96	55.93	110.21	1,317.95	184.06	4.32	8.35
Oct	107.57	123.65	103.72	55.84	112.36	1,351.58	186.18	4.28	
Nov	113.93	130.53	108.61	59.07	122.83	1,432.88	197.45	4.06	
Dec	119.33	136.77	113.52	61.69	128.86	1,517.02	207.26	3.88	6.92
1986: Jan	120.16	137.13	115.72	62.46	132.36	1,534.86	208.19	3.90	
Feb	126.43	144.03	124.18	65.18	142.13	1,652.73	219.37	3.72	
Mar	133.97	152.75	128.66	68.06	153.94	1,757.35	232.33	3.50	
Apr	137.27	157.30	126.17	69.46	155.07	1,807.05	237.97	3.43	
May	137.37	158.59	122.21	68.65	151.28	1,801.80	238.46	3.42	
June r	140.82	163.15	120.65	70.69	151.73	1,867.70	245.30	3.36	
July p	138.32	158.06	112.03	74.20	150.23	1,809.92	240.18	3.43	
Week ended:									
1986: June 21	140.80	163.12	120.27	70.93	151.11	1,868.38	245.42	3.35	
28	142.20	164.39	119.39	72.41	153.09	1,878.06	247.91	3.33	
July 5	144.62	167.00	119.98	73.84	156.63	1,901.54	251.84	3.27	
12	139.58	160.34	115.83	72.91	151.48	1,827.81	242.74	3.40	
19	136.07	154.96	110.60	73.82	148.50	1,779.22	235.84	3.52	
26	137.39	156.30	108.82	75.34	149.47	1,794.85	238.25	3.45	
Aug 2 p	135.82	154.38	107.12	75.11	146.80	1,773.87	235.82	3.49	

[1] Average of daily closing prices.
[2] Includes all the stocks (more than 1,500) listed on the NYSE.
[3] Includes 30 stocks.
[4] Includes 500 stocks.
[5] Standard & Poor's series. Dividend-price ratios based on Wednesday closing prices. Earnings-price ratios based on prices at end of quarter.

NOTE.—All data relate to stocks listed on the New York Stock Exchange (NYSE).

Sources: New York Stock Exchange, Dow-Jones & Company, Inc., and Standard & Poor's Corporation.

Source: *Economic Indicators*, Council of Economic Indicators.

NEW SECURITY ISSUES OF CORPORATIONS
Millions of dollars

Type of issue or issuer, or use	1983	1984	1985	1985 Aug.	Sept.	Oct.	Nov.	Dec.	1986 Jan.	Feb.	Mar. p
1 All issues[1]	120,299r	132,531	201,751	14,861	11,304	11,595	13,568	19,429	17,479	24,001r	29,967
2 Bonds[2]	68,718r	109,903	166,236	11,465	8,833	9,271	10,913	14,440	14,079	19,539r	25,022
Type of offering											
3 Public	47,594r	73,579	120,039	11,465	8,833	9,271	10,913	14,440	14,079	19,539r	25,022
4 Private placement	21,126	36,326	46,195	n.a.	n.a.	n.a.	n.a.	n.a.	n.a.	n.a.	n.a.
Industry group											
5 Manufacturing	17,001r	24,607	52,278	2,352	2,079	1,953	4,072	2,704	4,694	3,950	8,825
6 Commercial and miscellaneous	7,540	13,726	15,215	921	186	898	933	735	624	1,216	784
7 Transportation	3,833	4,694	5,743	459	177	348	125	187	633	373	340
8 Public utility	9,125	10,679	12,957	857	1,042	863	1,114	1,090	820	2,540	2,133
9 Communication	3,642	2,997	10,456	1,295	367	690	100	2,318	0	1,200	1,907
10 Real estate and financial	27,577	53,199	69,587	5,581	4,982	4,519	4,569	7,407	7,308	10,230	11,033
11 Stocks[3]	51,579	22,628	35,515	3,396	2,471	2,324	2,655	4,989	3,400	4,462r	4,945
Type											
12 Preferred	7,213	4,118	6,505	754	653	406	782	908	570	975	1,035
13 Common	44,366	18,510	29,010	2,642	1,818	1,918	1,873	4,081	2,830	3,487r	3,910
Industry group											
14 Manufacturing	14,135	4,054	5,700	235	820	279	746	1,045	827	1,269r	723
15 Commercial and miscellaneous	13,112	6,277	9,149	1,293	507	403	596	1,220	683	434	643
16 Transportation	2,729	589	1,544	127	107	113	21	200	78	302	308
17 Public utility	5,001	1,624	1,966	73	47	408	12	201	176	153	357
18 Communication	1,822	419	978	18	7	41	5	146	231	282	0
19 Real estate and financial	14,780	9,665	16,178	1,650	983	1,080	1,275	2,177	1,405	2,022r	2,914

1. Figures, which represent gross proceeds of issues maturing in more than one year, sold for cash in the United States, are principal amount or number of units multiplied by offering price. Excludes offerings of less than $100,000, secondary offerings, undefined or exempted issues as defined in the Securities Act of 1933, employee stock plans, investment companies other than closed-end, intracorporate transactions, and sales to foreigners.

2. Monthly data include only public offerings.

3. Beginning in August 1981, gross stock offerings include new equity volume from swaps of debt for equity.

SOURCE. Securities and Exchange Commission and the Board of Governors of the Federal Reserve System.

Source: *Federal Reserve Bulletin*, Board of Governors of the Federal Reserve System.

How to Understand and Analyze Financial Statements*

Fred B. Renwick†

Analyzing financial statements in corporate annual reports can be easy, fun, and rewarding, if you know what to look for. This short essay explains in a nutshell what to look for and how to analyze financial statements.

Only four statements are important to understand and analyze, namely:

- The *balance sheet*, which states the financial condition of the corporation as of one particular date: the date posted at the top of the statement.
- The *income statement*, which shows the amount of earnings for the year currently ending, and conveys information regarding the efficiency and profitability of the business.
- The *statement of retained earnings*, which gives further information regarding one of the lines on the balance sheet, and also shows the division of net income for the year between dividend payout to stockholders and earnings retained and reinvested in the business.
- The *statement of sources and uses of funds*, which gives further information regarding total current assets and total current liabilities as stated on the balance sheet; and shows the net changes during the year in working capital.

Additionally, corporate annual reports usually contain supplementary information which expands upon items in the four basic statements, and includes: (1) a letter or report of independent accountants and auditors addressed to stockholders and directors of the company certifying and validating the figures in the four statements, (2) notes which report material information regarding line items in each statement, (3) segment information which summarizes selected information by industry and geographic segments, (4) restatement pursuant to Financial Accounting Standards Board (FASB) *Statement of Financial Accounting Standards No. 33* to account for effects of inflation and changing prices on items in the four primary statements, and (5) a long-term (5 or 10-year) summary of selected items from the four primary statements.

The following section explains each statement in detail, Section II explains how to analyze the statements, Section III explains notes and supplementary information.

1. FOUR FINANCIAL STATEMENTS: WHAT TO LOOK FOR

BALANCE SHEETS

Exhibit 1 shows a balance sheet for Universal Manufacturing Corporation (UMC), a hypothetical company which produces and distributes goods and services in the health industry. Universal's single line of business is divided into two industry segments: human and animal health products, and environmental health products and services.

Observe the format of Universal's balance sheet, the *report form*, where total assets, $26 million, are itemized first and total financing (total liabilities and stockholders' equity), $26 million, are itemized below the asset section. Some corporations prefer to use the *account form*, where assets are listed on the left side of the form and liabilities and owners' equity sections are listed to the right of the asset section. UMC is using the *report form*.

The balance sheet shows the ownership of total corporate assets as of the date of the statement. For example, the following calculation implies that if UMC's tangible assets were liquidated as of the date posted at the top of the balance sheet, $17.8 million would be available for distribution among the preferred and common stockholders.

Total assets owned by UMC	$26,000,000
Less: Intangibles	200,000
Total tangible assets owned by UMC	$25,800,000
Amount required to pay total liabilities	8,000,000
Amount remaining for the stockholders	$17,800,000

Further, the above example illustrates a critical point: the difference between *current market value* (the amount UMC's assets would really bring if sold) versus the *accounting book value* (the $17.8 million). Relationships exist between market and book values, but accounting statements (except for FASB *No. 33*) are factual reports of *book*, not *market*, values of corporate assets.

The following paragraphs explain each line entry on balance sheets.

Starting at the top of the balance sheet, after the name of the corporation, title, and date of the statement, total assets are itemized, with current assets (total, $13.6 million) always first.

* See also the definition of financial terms, page 369.

† Fred B. Renwick is Professor of Finance at the Graduate School of Business Administration, New York University, New York, N.Y.

EXHIBIT 1

UNIVERSAL MANUFACTURING CORPORATION
Balance Sheet
December 31, 1983

Assets	1983	1982
Current assets		
Cash	$ 350,000	$ 250,000
Marketable securities at cost		
(market value: 1983, $2,980,000; 1982, $1,900,000)	2,850,000	1,830,000
Accounts receivable		
Less: Allowance for bad debt: 1983, $24,000; 1982, $21,000	4,800,000	4,370,000
Inventories	5,600,000	4,950,000
Total current assets	$13,600,000	$11,400,000
Fixed assets (property, plant, and equipment)		
Land	$ 734,000	$ 661,000
Building	5,762,000	5,258,000
Machinery	11,435,000	10,011,000
Office equipment	614,000	561,000
	18,545,000	16,491,000
Less: Accumulated depreciation	6,435,000	5,671,000
Net fixed assets	12,110,000	10,820,000
Prepayments and deferred charges	90,000	61,600
Intangibles (goodwill, patent, trademarks)	200,000	200,000
Total assets	$26,000,000	$22,481,600

Liabilities	1983	1982
Current liabilities		
Accounts payable	$ 2,910,000	$ 2,300,000
Notes payable	1,420,000	730,000
Accrued expenses payable	430,000	350,000
Federal income taxes payable	1,240,000	1,320,000
Total current liabilities	$ 6,000,000	$ 4,700,000
Long-term liabilities		
First mortgage bonds, 8% interest, due 2003	$ 2,000,000	$ 2,000,000
Total liabilities	$ 8,000,000	$ 6,700,000

Stockholders' Equity

	1983	1982
Capital stock		
Preferred stock, 6% cumulative, $100 par value each;		
authorized, issued, and outstanding 13,600 shares	1,360,000	1,360,000
Common stock, 30 cents par value each; authorized, issued,		
and outstanding 760,000 shares	228,000	228,000
Capital surplus	1,112,000	1,112,000
Accumulated retained earnings	15,300,000	13,081,600
Total stockholders' equity	$18,000,000	$15,781,600
Total liabilities and stockholders' equity	$26,000,000	$22,481,600

Current assets consist of:

1. *Cash*, $350,000, which is what you would expect, namely pocket-book currency and coins in the treasurer's office, plus demand deposits at a commercial bank. Cash is synonymous with liquidity,

2. *Marketable securities*, $2.85 million, which usually are cash equivalents or highly liquid securities such as Treasury Bills of the federal government or negotiable certificates of deposit (CDs), or demand notes issued by large corporations,

3. *Accounts receivable*, $4.8 million, which consist of payments due from customers who purchased UMC's goods and services on credit and have not paid yet but are scheduled to pay within the next few

months. Since a small fraction of customers might never pay (because of death, financial disaster, flood, or other catastrophe), an allowance is made, $24,000, pursuant to good accounting practices for bad debts,

4. *Inventories*, $5.6 million, which consist of (a) finished goods in stock and ready for sale or shipment, (b) work and merchandise in process, and (c) supplies and raw materials inventories; and are priced on the balance sheet at the lower of cost or market on either a first-in-first-out (Fifo) or last-in-first-out (Lifo) basis. Pricing policy is usually stated in a note.

Total current assets, $13.6 million, are the sum of the four aforecited figures and usually are earmarked for use within the coming 12 months. In other words, *current* means within the next 12 months.

Fixed assets (property, plant and equipment) are the permanent tangible capital owned by the business, and are listed *at cost* (original purchase price) next on the balance sheet; and consists of:

1. *Land*, $734,000, or ground upon which buildings or other assets such as forests, air or water rights, and the like are built,
2. *Building*, $5.762 million, which are structures such as offices, warehouses, and the like where business is conducted,
3. *Machinery*, $11.435 million, which are mechanical apparatuses for increasing productivity and economic efficiency,
4. *Office equipment*, $614,000, which is what you would expect, namely desks, typewriters, copiers, and the like.

Accumulated depreciation, $6.435 million, is the total depreciation (deterioration of property, plant, and equipment due to physical wear and tear) accumulated to date for accounting purposes against UMC's assets. It is important to know about three concepts of depreciation, namely: (1) depreciation calculated for tax purposes which is figured pursuant to the Tax Code to benefit from allowable accelerated rates of depreciation, (2) accounting depreciation, which can be either straight-line or accelerated and is usually explained in a note, (3) economic depreciation, which comes from technological obsolescence and deterioration in ability to continue generating future income at current rates due to changes in demand and markets for the goods and services produced by UMC. The balance sheet states only number two, accounting depreciation.

Net fixed assets, $12,110,000, are the sum of the four above figures, minus accounting depreciation; and are used by the business to generate future (beyond the coming 12 months) income.

Prepayments and deferred charges, $90,000, state total amounts paid in advance for assets not yet obtained (such as paid-up premiums on a fire insurance policy covering the next five years, or rental paid on computers for the next three years); and for benefits to be received in future years for expenditures already made (such as for research and development, moving the business to a new location, or expenses incurred in bringing a new product to market).

Intangibles, $200,000, are assets such as goodwill, trademarks, franchises, patents, copyrights, and the like which have no physical existence; yet are valuable in producing business income.

Total assets, $26 million, are current, plus fixed, plus prepayments and deferred charges, plus intangibles; and state the size of the business and are the total property owned by the business.

Look next at the lower part of the balance sheet, which concerns the financing of the business. Financing must come from either borrowing (liabilities) or ownership equity.

Underneath the asset section of the balance sheet (or on the right side if the company uses the account form), total current liabilities, $6 million, always are itemized next, then long-term liabilities, $2 million, then finally stockholders' equity of $18 million.

Total current liabilities consist of bills due and payable by UMC within the next 12 months, all of which fall into one of four categories:

1. *Accounts payable*, $2.91 million, which are bills currently owed and due to creditors,
2. *Notes payable*, $1.42 million, which are current obligations owed to a bank or other short-term lender,
3. *Accrued expenses payable*, $430,000, include wages due employees, fees to attorneys, current pension or retirement obligations, and the like.
4. *Federal income taxes payable*, $1.24 million, is the current tax payable to the Internal Revenue Service, and is sufficiently important to merit a line of its own on the corporate balance sheet.

Long-term liabilities, $2 million for UMC, can include straight debt (like UMC's which pays 8 percent interest and matures in 2003), convertible bonds (bonds which pay interest like straight bonds but are convertible upon demand of the bond owner into a stated number of shares of common stock), or "other" long-term debt (like pollution control and industrial revenue bonds or sinking-fund debentures). UMC has only straight debt outstanding.

Total liabilities, $8 million, are the sum of current and long-term liabilities and constitute the total financing obtained from borrowings.

Stockholders' equity, $18 million consists of:

1. *Capital stock*, $1.588 million, which includes both preferred stock and common stock but no convertible preferred stock and no warrants or rights to purchase either bonds or common stock,
2. *Capital surplus*, $1.112 million, which is the amount paid in by shareholders over the par or legal value of 30 cents for each common share,
3. *Accumulated retained earnings*, $15.3 million, which are earnings not paid out in dividends but have been retained and reinvested in the business. Further information regarding accumulated retained earnings since inception of the business is set forth below in the *statement of retained earnings*.

Capital stock represents proprietary interest in the company, is represented by stock certificates authorized and issued by the company, and can belong to either of several classes, including:

1. *Preferred stock,* which has preference or takes priority over other shares regarding dividend payout (6 percent in UMC's case), and which can be cumulative, which means that if the company fails to pay dividends for whatever reason for any year, then the 6 percent of $100 or $6 per preferred share accumulates on the books and must be paid before common stockholders can receive future dividends. Total preferred stock authorized and issued by UMC is $100 per share times 13,600 shares or $1.36 million.
2. *Common stock,* which represents the remaining ownership of the company and is entitled to receive a dividend along with fluctuations in value of the stock. Par value is the legal stated value of each common share; so the par value (30 cents per share times 760,000 shares or $228,000) plus the additional amount or capital surplus ($1.112 million) together state the amount UMC received upon issuing 760,000 shares, namely $1.34 million divided by 760,000 or $1.76 per share.

The bottom line, *total liabilities and stockholders equity,* states the financing of the corporation, and shows where UMC obtained the $26 million to buy the total assets itemized at the top of the balance sheet.

We turn next to income statements.

INCOME STATEMENTS

Exhibit 2 shows UMC's income statement, where the important items to look for, after the name of the company, the title, and date of the statement at the heading, are:

1. *Net sales,* which is where most of the business revenue comes from for most businesses, except rental and leasing companies, $23,850,000.
2. *Net Operating Income* (NOI) or profit before interest and taxes, which states profit from business operations, without regard to financing, $5,878,000.
3. *Total Income* before interest and taxes, which states the return on total capital available to the business during the year, $6,220,000.
4. *Less:* provision for federal income tax, $2,240,000.
5. *Total Income,* after tax but before interest deduction, which states the after-tax profitability of the corporation and is widely used in computing cost of capital for a business enterprise, $3,980,000.

EXHIBIT 2

UNIVERSAL MANUFACTURING CORPORATION
Consolidated Income Statement
December 31, 1983 and 1982

	1983	1982
Net sales	$23,850,000	$19,810,000
Cost of sales and operating expenses		
Cost of goods sold	8,940,000	7,209,000
Depreciation	800,000	750,000
Selling and administrating expenses	8,232,000	6,814,000
Operating profit	$ 5,878,000	$ 5,037,000
Other income		
Dividends and interest	342,000	183,000
Total income	$ 6,220,000	$ 5,220,000
Less: Interest on bonds	160,000	160,000
Income before provision for federal income tax	$ 6,060,000	$ 5,060,000
Provision for federal income tax	2,240,000	1,980,000
Net profit for year	$ 3,820,000	$ 3,080,000
Common shares outstanding	760,000	760,000
Net earnings per share	$ 4.92	$ 3.95

Statement of Accumulated Retained Earnings

	1983	1982
Balance January 1	$13,081,600	$11,413,200
Net profit for year	3,820,000	3,080,000
Total	$16,901,600	$14,493,200
Less: Dividends paid on		
Preferred stock	81,600	81,600
Common stock	1,520,000	1,330,000
Balance December 31	$15,300,000	$13,081,600

6. *Net income* (NI) or profit for the year, which states earnings after taxes and after all fixed charges. The net profit for the year is available for (a) dividend payout to preferred stockholders, (b) dividend payout to common stockholders, and (c) retention and reinvestment in the business, $3,820,000.

7. *Net earnings per share* (EPS), which equals total earnings available for distribution to common stockholders ($3.82 million minus 6% dividend owed on 13,600 shares of $100 par value preferred stock, or $3,738,400), divided by 760,000 common shares outstanding, $4.92.

$3,820,000 − 0.06(13,600)($100) =
$3,738,400
$3,738,400/760,000 =
$4.92 per share

Cost of sales and operating expenses falls into one of three categories:

1. *Cost of goods sold,* which states the amount of labor, material, and other expenses in producing the items sold, $8,940,000.
2. *Depreciation expense,* which states the amount of capital (producer's durables) consumed in producing the goods and services sold and which must be replaced or restored to its original capacity, $800,000.
3. *Selling and administrating expenses,* which includes office expenses, executives salaries, salespersons salaries, advertising and promotion expenses and the like, $8,232,000.

Operating profit, also called net operating income, $5.878 million, is the income from business operations, and is an important indicator of how efficiently the fixed assets were employed during the year.

Other income, $342,000, is from UMC's marketable securities of $1.83 million at cost as of one year ago.

Total income, $6.22 million, is the sum of operating profit from the business and income from other sources.

Interest on bonds, $160,000, (8 percent of 2 million) is itemized next on the income statement, followed by:

Income after interest, before tax	$6,060,000
Provision for federal income tax	2,240,000
Net profit for the year	3,820,000
Net earnings per share	$4.92

We turn next to statements of accumulated retained earnings.

STATEMENTS OF ACCUMULATED RETAINED EARNINGS

The bottom part of Exhibit 2 contains the accumulated retained earnings statement for UMC, and shows at the beginning of the bal-

ance, since the starting date of the business to January 1 of the current year, $13,081,600—to which is added the net profit for the year, $3,820,000, to get total accumulated retained earnings of $16,901,600.

Dividends paid to stockholders are itemized next:

Preferred stock dividend: 6 percent of $1,360,000	$ 81,600
Common stock dividend: $2.00 per share declared times 760,000 shares	1,520,000
Total dividends paid	$1,601,600

Balance, December 31 (15.3 million) equals the difference between the total available ($16,901,600) and total dividends paid. Retained earnings are an important source of finance of corporate capital assets.

We turn next to statements of sources and uses of funds.

STATEMENT OF SOURCE AND APPLICATION OF FUNDS

Exhibit 3 is a statement of source and application or use of funds for UMC. Ordinarily, *funds* imply cash; but in a broader sense, *funds* include cash equivalents and substitutes for cash, such as short-term credit, notes, and account payable and accrued liabilities to meet the short-term financing needs of the business. So *funds* in the broader sense imply net *working capital,* which is the difference between current assets and current liabilities.

Sources of funds in general include transactions which increase the amount of working capital, such as:

1. Net profit from operations.
2. Sale or consumption of noncurrent assets.
3. Long-term borrowing.
4. Issuing additional shares of capital stock.
5. Annual depreciation.

Uses of funds in general include transactions which decrease working capital, such as:

1. Declaring cash dividends.
2. Repaying long-term debt.
3. Buying noncurrent assets.
4. Repurchasing outstanding capital stock.

In the case of UMC and Exhibit 3, funds were provided by net income, $3.82 million, and current depreciation expense, $800,000. Some analysts worry that depreciation is not cash, depreciation is a bookkeeping entry. But the capital was consumed in the process of producing the goods and services sold; so the business pays the cash to itself to ultimately replace the consumed capital. Depreciation expense is a source of funds.

Total funds provided for UMC are $4,-620,000.

EXHIBIT 3

UNIVERSAL MANUFACTURING CORPORATION
Statement of Source and Application of Funds
December 31, 1983

	1983	
Funds were provided by		
Net income	$3,820,000	
Depreciation	800,000	
Total		$4,620,000
Funds were used for		
Dividends on preferred stock	$ 81,600	
Dividends on common stock	1,520,000	
Plant and equipment	1,720,300	
Sundry assets	398,100	
Total		$3,720,000
Increase in Working Capital		$ 900,000
Analysis of changes in working capital—1983		
Changes in current assets		
Cash	$ 100,000	
Marketable securities	1,020,000	
Accounts receivable	430,000	
Inventories	650,000	
Total		$2,200,000
Changes in current liabilities		
Accounts payable	$ 610,000	
Notes payable	690,000	
Accrued expenses payable	80,000	
Federal income tax payable	(80,000)	
Total		$1,300,000

Uses of funds are itemized next, where all uses fall into one of four categories:

Dividends on preferred stock	$ 81,600
Dividends on common stock	1,520,000
Plant and equipment	1,720,300
Sundry assets	398,100
Total uses or application of funds	$3,720,000

Increase in working capital, $900,000, is the difference between the total funds provided, $4.62 million, and the total funds used, $3.72 million.

An *analysis of changes in working capital* for the year is included in the statement of source and application of funds, and gives further information regarding the $900,000 increase in working capital, which is explained by analyzing changes in current assets together with changes in current liabilities.

Changes in current assets total $2.2 million, itemized as follows:

1. *Cash* increased from $250,000 to $350,000, giving a net change of $100,000,
2. *Marketable securities* increased from $1.83 million to $2.85 million, giving a net change of $1.02 million,
3. *Accounts receivable* increased from $4.37 million to $4.8 million, giving a net change of $430,000,
4. *Inventories* increased from $4.95 million to $5.6 million, giving a net change of $650,000.

Changes in current liabilities total $1.3 million, itemized as follows:

1. *Accounts payable* increased from $2.3 million to $2.91 million, giving a net change of $610,000,
2. *Notes payable* increased from $730,000 to $1.42 million, giving a net change of $690,000,
3. *Accrued expenses payable* increased from $350,000 to $430,000, giving a net change of $80,000,
4. *Federal income taxes payable* decreased from $1.32 million to $1.24 million, giving a net change of ($80,000).

The difference between the changes in current assets ($2.2 million) and changes in current liabilities ($1.3 million) equals the $900,000 increase in working capital.

We turn next to understanding more regarding how to analyze financial statements.

II. ANALYZING FINANCIAL STATEMENTS

The analysis of all four statements consists primarily of calculating ratios; but other methods including the time trend of the ratio, information theory, and flow-of-funds analysis are sometimes used. We shall limit our analysis to using ratios.[1]

In general, financial analysts, investors, creditors, and others look for two kinds of information regarding business enterprises:

1. *Risk*, including financial, business, market, and country or political risks,
2. *Return*, including productivity, efficiency, and profitability of corporate capital investments.

A third factor, *growth rate*, is important too, primarily because high steady growth is usually worth more than low or no growth.

BALANCE SHEET RATIOS

Balance sheet ratios belong to one of the three following categories:

1. *Liquidity and turnover ratios*, which indicate the ability of the corporation to pay current liabilities,
2. *Capitalization*, also called *leverage*, or *debt ratios*, which is the amount of borrowing relative to other factors such as total capitalization, total assets, or total equity,
3. *Net asset ratios*, which indicate the amount of assets backing each class of outstanding securities.

Liquidity ratios are calculated to judge whether the corporation owns sufficient cash and cash-equivalents or substitutes to comfortably pay short-term obligations, and include:

1. *Current liquidity*, the ability to pay current liabilities from current assets:

Current ratio:

$$\frac{\text{Current assets}}{\text{Current liabilities}} = \frac{\$13,600,000}{\$\ 6,000,000} = 2.3 \text{ to } 1$$

In total dollar amounts, the numerator in the current ratio, minus the denominator, states *net working capital*, where

Total current assets	$13,600,000
Less: Total current liabilities	6,000,000
Working capital	$ 7,600,000

2. *Quick asset* (sometimes called *acid test*) *ratio:*

$$\frac{\text{Quick assets}}{\text{Current liabilities}} = \frac{\$8,000,000}{\$6,000,000} = 1.33$$

Where quick assets are total current assets minus inventories, because inventories usually are less liquid than either cash, marketable securities, or accounts receivable:

Total current assets	$13,600,000	
Less: Inventories	5,600,000	
Quick assets		$8,000,000
Less: Total current liabilities		6,000,000
Net quick assets		$2,000,000

3. The *cash plus marketable securities ratio* indicates the firm's ability to pay current liabilities without relying on either inventories or accounts receivable:

$$\frac{\text{Cash plus marketable securities}}{\text{Total current liabilities}} = \frac{\$3,200,000}{\$6,000,000}$$
$$= 0.53$$

Liquidity and turnover of inventories ratios indicate how close inventories approximate true liquidity through total sales, and are the three following figures:

1. *Inventory as a percent of total current assets:*

$$\frac{\text{Inventory}}{\text{Total current assets}} = \frac{\$5,600,000}{\$13,600,000}$$
$$= 41.18 \text{ percent}$$

2. *Cost of goods sold*, including depreciation and capital consumption, *to average inventory ratio:*

$$\frac{\text{Cost of goods sold plus depreciation}}{\text{Inventory}} = \frac{\$9,740,000}{\$5,600,000} = 1.74$$

3. *Inventory turnover ratio:*

$$\frac{\text{Net sales}}{\text{Inventory}} = \frac{\$23,850,000}{\$5,600,000} = 4.26 \text{ times}$$

Liquidity of receivables ratios indicate how close accounts receivable approximate true liquidity through total sales, and are the two following figures:

1. *Average collection period ratio*, which indicates the number of day's sales in accounts receivables:

$$\frac{\text{Receivables} \times \text{Days in year}}{\text{Annual sales}} =$$
$$\frac{\$4,800,000 \times 360}{\$23,850,000} = 72.45$$

2. *Accounts receivable turnover ratio:*

$$\frac{\text{Annual sales}}{\text{Accounts receivable}} = \frac{\$23,850,000}{\$4,800,000} = 4.97$$

Liquidity and turnover of tangible and fixed asset ratios indicate relationships between total sales and total assets, and are given by the following two figures:

1. Fixed asset turnover ratio:

$$\frac{\text{Sales}}{\text{Net fixed assets}} = \frac{\$23,850,000}{\$12,110,000} = 1.97$$

2. Total asset turnover ratio:

$$\frac{\text{Net sales}}{\text{Average total tangible assets}} = \frac{\$23,850,000}{\$25,800,000}$$
$$= 0.9244$$

Capitalization ratios include:

1. Debt ratio:

$$\frac{\text{Total liabilities}}{\text{Total assets}} = \frac{\$8,000,000}{\$26,000,000} = 30.77 \text{ percent}$$

2. Current liabilities as a percent of total liabilities:

$$\frac{\text{Current liabilities}}{\text{Total liabilities}} = \frac{\$6,000,000}{\$8,000,000} = 75 \text{ percent}$$

3. Debt-to-net-worth ratio:

$$\frac{\text{Total liabilities}}{\text{Net Worth}} = \frac{\$8,000,000}{\$18,000,000} = 0.4444$$

4. Long-term debt capitalization ratio:

$$\frac{\text{Long-term debt}}{\text{Total capitalization}} = \frac{\$2,000,000}{\$19,800,000}$$
$$= 10.10 \text{ percent}$$

5. Preferred stock ratio:

$$\frac{\text{Preferred stock}}{\text{Total capitalization}} = \frac{\$1,360,000}{\$19,800,000}$$
$$= 6.87 \text{ percent}$$

6. Common stock ratio:

$$\frac{\text{Common stock plus accumulated earnings}}{\text{Total capitalization}} = \frac{\$16,440,000}{\$19,800,000}$$
$$= 83.03 \text{ percent}$$

7. Summary:

Total assets	$26,000,000	
Less: Intangibles	$ 200,000	
Less: Total current liabilities	$ 6,000,000	
Total capitalization	$19,800,000	100.00%
Bonds (long-term debt)	2,000,000	10.10
Preferred stock	1,360,000	6.87
Common stock (including capital surplus and retained earnings)	16,440,000	83.03

8. Long-term debt as a percent of total liabilities:

$$\frac{\text{Long-term debt}}{\text{Total liabilities}} = \frac{\$2,000,000}{\$8,000,000} = 25.00 \text{ percent}$$

Net asset value ratios include:

1. Net asset value per $1,000 bond; $9,900 per bond.

$$\frac{\begin{array}{c}\text{Net tangible assets}\\ \text{available to meet}\\ \text{bondholders' claims}\end{array}}{\begin{array}{c}\text{Number of \$1,000}\\ \text{bonds outstanding}\end{array}} = \frac{\$19,800,000}{2,000,000}$$

where the numerator is calculated as follows:

Total assets	$26,000,000
Less: Intangibles	200,000
Total tangible assets	$25,800,000
Less: Current liabilities	6,000,000
Net tangible assets available to meet bondholders' claims	$19,800,000

2. Net asset value per share of preferred stock: $1,308.82

$$\frac{\begin{array}{c}\text{Net assets backing}\\ \text{the preferred stock}\\ \text{Number of shares}\\ \text{of preferred stock}\\ \text{outstanding}\end{array}}{} = \frac{\$17,800,000}{13,600}$$

where the numerator is calculated as follows:

Total assets	$26,000,000
Less: Intangibles	200,000
Total tangible assets	$25,800,000
Less: Current liabilities	6,000,000
Less: Long-term liabilities	2,000,000
Net assets backing the preferred stock	$17,800,000

3. Net book value per share of common stock: $21.63

$$\frac{\begin{array}{c}\text{Net assets available}\\ \text{for the common stock}\\ \text{Total number of}\\ \text{shares outstanding}\end{array}}{} = \frac{\$16,440,000}{760,000} = \$21.63$$

where the numerator is calculated as follows:

Total assets	$26,000,000
Less: Intangibles	200,000
Total tangible assets	$25,800,000
Less: Current liabilities	6,000,000
Less: Long-term liabilities	2,000,000
Less preferred stock	1,360,000
Net assets available for the common stock	$16,440,000

Finally, estimate the youngest average plant age by dividing the current (1983) depreciation expense accrual ($800,000 from the Statement of Source and Application of Funds) into accumulated depreciation ($6,435,000 from the Balance Sheet) to get 8.04 years. Because some plants and pieces of equipment may have been fully written off over time, we can say that UMC's Fixed Assets, on average, are over 8 years old.

INCOME STATEMENT RATIOS

Income statement ratios belong to one of the two following categories:

1. *Coverage*, which analyzes financial risk by relating the financial charges of a corporation to its ability to service them.
2. *Productivity* or *capital efficiency ratios*, which relate income to total sales and to investment.

Coverage ratios include:

1. Interest coverage ratio: 38.875

$$\frac{\text{Net operating income before interest and taxes}}{\text{Interest charges on bonds}} = \frac{\$6,220,000}{\$160,000} = 38.875$$

2. Cash flow coverage ratio, which indicates the firm's ability to service debt, which is related to both interest and principal payments and is not met out of earnings per se, but out of cash: 19.5 times.

$$\frac{\text{Annual cash flow before interest and taxes}}{\text{Interest on bonds plus principal repayments}/(1-T)} = \frac{\$7,020,000}{\$\ 360,000} = 19.5$$

where:

Net operating income before interest and taxes	$6,220,000
Plus annual depreciation expense	800,000
Annual cash flow before interest and taxes	$7,020,000
Face value 20-year 8% bonds due 2003	$2,000,000
Annual Repayment rate after taxes $2,000,000 divided by 20 years	100,000
Before tax annual bond repayment rate $100,000 divided by 1 minus the effective tax rate, say 50 %	$200,000
Plus: 8% interest on $2,000,000	160,000
Interest plus principal repayments	$360,000

Since interest payments are made before taxes, the adjustment is necessary to convert principal repayments which are made after taxes to before-tax equivalents.

3. Preferred dividend coverage ratio: 46.81

$$\frac{\text{Income available for paying preferred dividends}}{\text{Total dividends to preferred shareholders}} = \frac{\$3,820,000}{\$81,600} = 46.81$$

4. Earnings per common share: $4.92

$$\frac{\text{Earnings available for distribution to common shareholders}}{\text{Total number of common shares outstanding}} = \frac{\$3,738,400}{760,000} = \$4.92$$

where:

Net profit for the year	$3,820,000
Less: Dividend requirements on preferred stock	81,600
Earnings available for common stock	$3,738,400

5. Primary earnings for the year: $4.94

$$\frac{\text{Earnings for the year}}{\text{Common stock plus stock equivalents}} = \frac{\$3,820,000}{773,500} = \$4.94$$

Assuming the 13,600 preferred shares had been convertible and converted, on a share-for-share basis, into common stock.

$$13,600 + 760,000 = 773,600 \text{ common shares after conversion}$$

6. Fully diluted earnings per share: $4.79

$$\frac{\text{Adjusted earnings}}{\text{Adjusted shares outstanding}} = \frac{\$3,900,000}{813,600}$$
$$= \$4.79$$

where:

Earnings for the year	$3,820,000
Plus: interest on convertible bonds	$ 160,000
Less: income tax applicable to interest deduction	80,000
Adjusted earnings for the year..........	$3,900,000
Common shares outstanding	760,000
Preferred convertible stock equivalent common shares	13,600
Twenty common shares per $1,000 convertible bond (2,000) outstanding ..	40,000
Adjusted shares outstanding	813,600

7. Summary:

Earnings per share	$4.92
Primary earnings..........	4.94
Fully diluted earnings......	4.79

8. Price-earnings ratio: Approximately 15 times

$$\frac{\text{Market price of stock}}{\text{Earnings per share}} = \frac{\$72.25}{\$4.92} = 14.69$$

Productivity or capital efficiency ratios include:

1. Operating margin of profit: 24.65%.

$$\frac{\text{Operating profit}}{\text{Sales}} = \frac{\$5,878,000}{\$23,850,000} = 24.65\%$$

Previous year:

$$= \frac{\$5,037,000}{\$19,810,000} = 25.43\%$$

2. Operating cost ratio: 75.35%.

	Amount	Ratio
Net sales	$23,850,000	100.00%
Operating costs............	17,972,000	75.35
Operating profit	$ 5,878,000	24.65%

3. Net profit ratio: 16.02%.

$$\frac{\text{Net profit for the year}}{\text{Net sales}} = \frac{\$3,820,000}{\$23,850,000} = 16.02\%$$

Previous year: 15.55%

$$= \frac{\$3,080,000}{\$19,810,000} = 15.55\%$$

RATIOS FROM STATEMENTS OF ACCUMULATED RETAINED EARNINGS

Retained earnings statements ratios belong to one of the two following categories:

1. Dividend payout ratio.
2. Earnings retention ratio.

The dividend payout ratio for UMC is: 40.66%.

$$\frac{\text{Dividends paid to common stockholders}}{\text{Income available for common stockholders}} = \frac{\$1,520,000}{\$3,738,400} = 40.66\%$$

where:

Net profit for the year $3,820,000
Dividends on preferred stock 81,600
Earnings available for common $3,738,400

The earnings retention ratio for UMC is: 59.34%.

$$\frac{\text{Earnings retained}}{\text{Earnings available for payout}} = \frac{\$2,218,400}{\$3,738,400} = 59.34\%$$

where:

Net profit for the year $3,820,000
  Less: Dividends paid on
  preferred stock .... $ 81,600
  Less: Dividends paid on
  common stock 1,520,000
Earnings retained $2,218,400

Summary:

Dividend payout ratio......	40.66%
Earnings retention ratio....	59.34
Earnings available	100.00%

Dividends per share: $2.00.

$$\frac{\text{Total dividends paid to common shareholders}}{\text{Number of common shares outstanding}} = \frac{\$1,520,000}{760,000} = \$2.00$$

Balance December 31, $15,300,000.

RATIOS FROM STATEMENTS OF SOURCE AND APPLICATION OF FUNDS

Since an analysis was stated directly on the statement of source and use of funds in Exhibit 3, that part of the analysis is completed; however we still need to calculate profitability ratios which belong to one of the two following categories:

1. Return on assets.
2. Return on equity.

Return on assets ratios include:
  Return on total assets: 27.67%.

$$\frac{\text{Total income}}{\text{Last year's total assets}} = \frac{\$6,220,000}{\$22,481,600}$$
$$= 27.67\%$$

After tax return on total assets: 17.70%.

$$\frac{\begin{array}{c}\text{Total income after tax}\\ \text{but before interest}\end{array}}{\text{Last year's total assets}} = \frac{\$3,980,000}{\$22,481,600}$$
$$= 17.70\%$$

where:

Total income $6,220,000
  Less: Provision for total taxes 2,240,000
After tax total income $3,980,000

Return on equity ratio: 25.92%.

$$\frac{\begin{array}{c}\text{Income available for}\\ \text{distribution to common}\\ \text{stockholders}\end{array}}{\begin{array}{c}\text{Last year's total}\\ \text{equity of common}\\ \text{stockholders}\end{array}} = \frac{\$3,738,400}{\$14,421,600}$$
$$= 25.92\%$$

where:

Last year's total stockholder
  equity $15,781,600
  Less: Preferred stock value 1,360,000
Last year's common stock
  equity $14,421,600

We turn next to further discussion of notes and supplemental information.

III. NOTES AND SUPPLEMENTAL INFORMATION

As explained in the introduction, financial statements in corporate annual reports usually are accompanied by:

- A *report of independent accountants and auditors* certifying the statements conform to generally accepted accounting principles and that generally accepted auditing standards and procedures were used.
- *Notes* which further explain details and disclose relevant information regarding line items on all four statements.
- *Segment information,* which summarizes selected items by business, industry, and geographic segment.
- A *restatement* of almost everything in current (in contrast with the traditional historical original purchase) prices, and to account for the effects of inflation on items reported in the standard statements.
- *Long-term record* summarizing selected items over a five- or ten-year time span.

EXHIBIT 4
SEGMENT REPORTING AND FOREIGN OPERATIONS

Industry Segments

	Segment No. 1	Segment No. 2	Consolidated
1983			
Sales, unaffiliated customers	$20,044,000	$3,806,000	$23,850,000
Sales, intersegment			
Total sales	$20,044,000	$3,806,000	$23,850,000
Pretax operating income	5,435,000	443,000	5,878,000
Identifiable assets at December 31	21,700,000	4,300,000	26,000,000
Depreciation expense	666,000	134,000	800,000
Capital spending	1,884,300	234,100	2,118,400
1982			
Sales, unaffiliated customers	$16,629,000	$3,181,000	$19,810,000
Sales, intersegment			
Total sales	$16,629,000	$3,181,000	$19,810,000
Pretax operating income	4,627,000	410,000	5,037,000
Identifiable assets at December 31	19,027,000	3,473,000	22,500,000
Depreciation expense	611,000	127,000	738,000
Capital spending	1,751,000	190,000	
1981			
Sales, unaffiliated customers	$14,461,000	$2,779,000	$17,240,000
Sales, intersegment			
Total sales	$14,461,000	$2,779,000	$17,240,000
Pretax operating income	4,163,000	378,000	4,541,000
Identifiable assets at December 31	16,614,000	3,341,000	19,955,000
Depreciation expense	551,000	102,000	653,000
Capital spending	1,969,000	238,000	2,207,000

Geographic Segments

	Domestic	Foreign		Eliminations	Consolidated
		OECD	Other		
1983					
Sales, unaffiliated customers	$12,647,000	$9,029,000	$2,175,000		$23,850,000
Sales, intersegment	2,171,000	346,000	21,000	($2,539,000)	
Total sales	$14,818,000	$9,375,000	$2,196,000	($2,539,000)	$23,850,000
Pretax operating income	3,690,000	1,820,000	211,000	157,000	5,878,000
Identifiable assets at December 31	16,549,000	10,168,000	2,353,000	(3,070,000)	26,000,000
1982					
Sales, unaffiliated customers	$10,519,000	$7,511,000	$1,780,000		$19,810,000
Sales, intersegment	2,614,000	246,000	14,000	($2,878,000)	
Total sales	$13,133,000	$7,757,000	$1,794,000	($2,878,000)	$19,810,000
Pretax operating income	3,512,000	1,449,000	126,000	50,000	5,037,000
Identifiable assets at December 31	14,728,000	8,660,000	2,005,000	(2,893,000)	22,500,000
1981					
Sales, unaffiliated customers	$ 9,504,000	$ 6,152,000	$1,584,000		$17,240,000
Sales, intersegment	2,677,000	155,000	3,000	($2,835,000)	
Total sales	$12,181,000	$ 6,307,000	$1,587,000	($2,835,000)	$17,240,000
Pretax operating income	3,552,000	1,234,000	119,000	(364,000)	4,541,000
Identifiable assets at December 31	13,627,000	7,818,000	1,590,000	(3,179,000)	19,955,000

REPORT OF INDEPENDENT ACCOUNTANTS

A typical report of independent accountants is addressed to the stockholders and board of directors of the corporation and will read as follows:

"In our opinion, the accompanying consolidated financial statements, appearing on pages — through —, present fairly the financial position of Universal Manufacturing Corporation and its subsidiary companies at December 31, 1983 and 1982, and the results of their operations and changes in financial position for the years then ended,

in conformity with generally accepted accounting principles consistently applied. Also, in our opinion, the five-year comparative consolidated summary of operations presents fairly the financial information included therein. Our examinations of these statements were made in accordance with generally accepted auditing standards and accordingly included such tests of the accounting records and such other auditing procedures as we considered necessary in the circumstances."

The report will be signed with the name and address of the accounting firm and dated.

EXHIBIT 5

UNIVERSAL MANUFACTURING CORPORATION
SCHEDULE OF INCOME FROM CONTINUING OPERATIONS
AND OTHER CHANGES IN SHAREHOLDERS' EQUITY
ADJUSTED FOR EFFECTS OF CHANGING PRICES
For the Year Ended December 31, 1983

	As Reported (historical cost)	General Inflation (constant 1983 $)	Specific (current) Costs
		Adjusted for	
Income from continuing operations			
Net sales	$23,850,000		
Other income	342,000		
Total revenue from continuing operations	$24,192,000	$24,192,000	$24,192,000
Costs and other deductions			
Depreciation expenses	800,000	1,076,000	1,115,000
Other costs and expenses	17,172,000	17,699,000	17,273,000
Interest expense	160,000	160,000	160,000
Federal and foreign income taxes	2,240,000	2,240,000	2,240,000
Total costs and other deductions	$20,372,000	$21,175,000	$20,788,000
Net income from continuing operations	$ 3,820,000	$ 3,017,000	$ 3,404,000
Purchasing power gain on net monetary liabilities (Net amounts owed)		1,000	1,000
Increase in current cost of inventories and property, plant and equipment during 1983			1,911,000
Less: effect of increase in general price level during 1983			2,788,000
Excess of increase in specific prices over increase in the general price level...........................			($ 877,000)
Net income	$ 3,820,000		
Adjusted net income		$ 3,018,000	
Net change in shareholders' equity from above	$ 3,820,000	$ 3,018,000	$ 2,528,000

Summarized Balance Sheet
Adjusted for Changing Prices
At December 31, 1983

	As reported	General Inflation (constant 1983 $)	Specific (current) Costs
		Adjusted for	
Assets			
Inventories	$ 5,600,000	$ 6,175,000	$ 5,670,000
Property, plant and equipment	12,110,000	13,354,000	16,327,000
All other assets	8,290,000	9,141,000	7,506,000
Total assets	$26,000,000	$28,670,000	$29,503,000
Total liabilities	8,000,000	7,600,000	7,600,000
Shareholders' equity...........................	$18,000,000	$21,070,000	$21,903,000

EXHIBIT 5 *(concluded)*

Supplementary financial data
Five-Year Comparison of Selected Data
Adjusted for Changing Prices

	Years Ended December 31				
	1979	1980	1981	1982	1983
Sales					
As reported	$14,020,000	$15,610,000	$17,240,000	$19,810,000	$23,850,000
1983 constant dollars	19,543,000	20,211,000	20,063,000	20,970,000	23,850,000
Net income					
As reported					$ 3,820,000
1983 constant dollars					3,017,000
Current costs					3,404,000
Earnings per share					
As reported					$4.92
1983 constant dollars					3.86
Current costs					4.37
Common stock dividends					
declared per share					
As reported	$1.40	$1.43	$1.55	$1.75	$2.00
1983 constant dollars	1.95	1.85	1.80	1.85	2.00
Net assets at year-end					
As reported					$18,000,000
1983 constant dollars					21,070,000
Current costs					21,903,000
Purchasing power gain on					
net monetary liabilities					1,000
Market price per common share					
at year-end					
Actual	$69.25	$68.13	$55.50	$67.63	$72.25
1983 constant dollars	90.50	84.95	64.80	72.45	68.50
Average consumer price index*	181.5	195.4	217.4	239.0	253.0

* Hypothetical, for illustrative purposes only.

NOTES TO FINANCIAL STATEMENTS

Notes disclose additional information regarding entries in all four primary statements, and usually are considered an integral part of the statements, included in and covered by the auditor's certification. Some corporations include the next three items to be discussed, segment information, effects of inflation, and long-term comparative summary of operations, in the notes. If included in some place other than the notes, then look for whether the statement was excluded from the auditor's audit.

SEGMENT INFORMATION

Notes disclosing geographic area and industry segment information usually summarize selected items such as net sales, operating income, total assets, depreciation and amortization, and capital expenditures for industry segments (business segments or product groups) and foreign operations.

Exhibit 4 shows the segment information for UMC's two segments.

As you can see from Exhibit 4, industry segment number one, Human and Animal Health Products, accounts for 84 percent ($20,044,000 divided by $23,850,000) of total sales, and 92 percent ($5,435,000 divided by $5,878,000) of UMC's operating income; all supported by 83.46 percent ($21,700,000 divided by

$26,000,000) of total assets. Eleven percent ($234,100 divided by $2,118,400) of total capital expenditures were made in industry segment number two, Environmental Health Products and Services for the treatment of water and air pollution.

Exhibit 4 also shows, based on the following ratios, that UMC's business is roughly 60 percent domestic United States; 40 percent non-domestic:

Net Sales:

$$\frac{\text{United States}}{\text{Total company}} = \frac{\$14,818,000}{\$23,850,000} = 62.13\%$$

Operating income:

$$\frac{\text{United States}}{\text{Total company}} = \frac{\$3,690,000}{\$5,037,000} = 62.78\%$$

Total assets:

$$\frac{\text{United States}}{\text{Total company}} = \frac{\$16,549,000}{\$26,000,000} = 63.65\%$$

SUPPLEMENTAL INFORMATION ON INFLATION ACCOUNTING

Pursuant to Financial Accounting Standards Board (FASB) *Statement of Financial Accounting Standards No. 33*, public enterprises that have either (1) inventories and property, plant, and equipment (before deducting accumulated

EXHIBIT 6

TEN-YEAR FINANCIAL SUMMARY
UNIVERSAL MANUFACTURING CORPORATION

	1983	1982	1981	1980	1979	1978	1977	1976	1975	1974
Net sales	$23,850,000	$19,810,000	$17,240,000	$15,610,000	$14,020,000	$12,604,000	$11,040,000	$9,426,000	$8,324,000	$7,611,000
Total income before tax	6,060,000	5,060,000	4,535,000	4,164,000	3,783,000	3,619,000	3,195,000	2,747,000	2,521,000	2,286,000
Net profit for the year	3,820,000	3,080,000	2,775,000	2,555,000	2,288,000	2,105,000	1,827,000	1,512,000	1,314,000	1,179,000
Earnings per share	4.92	3.95	3.56	3.28	2.94	2.71	2.36	1.95	1.70	1.53
Dividends per share	2.00	1.75	1.55	1.43	1.40	1.40	1.24	1.12	1.10	1.03
Net working capital	7,600,000	6,700,000	6,300,000	5,500,000	5,023,000	3,596,000	3,424,000	2,964,000	2,604,000	2,261,000
Total assets	26,000,000	22,481,600	19,934,000	17,594,000	15,390,000	12,433,000	9,890,000	8,348,000	7,365,000	6,643,000
Net plant and equipment	12,110,000	10,820,000	9,918,000	8,747,000	6,743,000	4,740,000	3,635,000	3,150,000	2,830,000	2,479,000
Long term debt	2,000,000	2,000,000	2,000,000	2,000,000	2,000,000	2,000,000	2,000,000	1,000,000	1,000,000	1,000,000
Preferred stock	1,360,000	1,360,000	1,360,000	1,360,000	1,360,000	1,360,000	1,360,000	1,360,000	1,360,000	1,360,000
Common stock and surplus	1,340,000	1,340,000	1,340,000	1,340,000	1,340,000	1,340,000	1,340,000	1,340,000	1,340,000	1,340,000
Book value per share	21.63									

depreciation) amounting to more than $125 million or (2) total assets amounting to more than $1 billion (after deducting accumulated depreciation) are required to report supplementary information in addition to the primary financial statements. FASB *Standards No. 33* are:

For fiscal years ended on or after December 25, 1979, enterprises are required to report:

a. Income from continuing operations adjusted for the effects of general inflation.
b. The purchasing power gain or loss on net monetary items.

For fiscal years ended on or after December 25, 1979, enterprises are also required to report:

a. Income from continuing operations on a current cost basis.
b. The current cost amounts of inventory and property, plant, and equipment at the end of the fiscal year.
c. Increases or decreases in current cost amounts of inventory and property, plant, and equipment, net of inflation.

Enterprises are required to present a five-year summary of selected financial data, including information on income, sales and other operating revenues, net assets, dividends per common share, and market price per share. In the computation of net assets, only inventory and property, plant, and

equipment need be adjusted for the effects of changing prices.

UMC, because of its "small company" asset size, would be exempt from FASB *No. 33*'s reporting requirement. However, Exhibit 5 restates UMC's statement of income from continuing operations, restated for changing prices, for the year ending December 31, 1983; and UMC's five-year comparison of selected data adjusted for changing prices.

A final note on Notes: Feel free to speak with your friendly auditor, or sleuth on your own, regarding additional information which might remain undisclosed and could pertain to:

a. Liabilities arising out of company pension plans (e.g., ERISA).
b. Contractual obligations (e.g., the capitalized value of lease payments).
c. Legal judgments currently enforceable.
d. Contingent liabilities (e.g., pending lawsuits or possible income tax assessment).

TEN-YEAR FINANCIAL SUMMARY

Long-term performance of UMC is summarized and reported on the ten-year financial summary statement, Exhibit 6.

The long-term view is used for detecting trends and changes in trends in important factors such as net sales, total assets, net operating income, earnings per share, and dividends per share. On balance, the trends for UMC look pretty good: upward.

A Guide to SEC Corporate Filings

A basic purpose of the Federal securities laws is to provide disclosure of material financial and other information on companies seeking to raise capital through the public offering of their securities, as well as companies whose securities are already publicly held. This aims at enabling investors to evaluate the securities of these companies on an informed and realistic basis.

The Securities Act of 1933 is a *disclosure* statute. It generally requires that, before securities may be offered to the public, a registration statement must be filed with the Commission disclosing prescribed categories of information. Before the sale of securities can begin, the registration statement must become "effective," and investors must be furnished a prospectus containing the most significant information in the registration statement.

The Securities Exchange Act of 1934 deals in large part with securities already outstanding and requires the registration of securities listed on a national securities exchange, as well as "Over-the-Counter" securities in which there is a substantial public interest. Issuers of registered securities must file annual and other periodic reports designed to provide a public file of current material information. The Exchange Act also requires disclosure of material information to holders of registered securities in solicitations of proxies for the election of directors or approval of corporate action at a stockholder's meeting, or in attempts to acquire control of a company through a tender offer or other planned stock acquisition. It provides that insiders of companies whose equity securities are registered must report their holdings and transactions in all equity securities of their companies.

Effective December 15, 1980, the Securities and Exchange Commission adopted and proposed major changes in its disclosure systems under the Securities Act of 1933 and the Securities Exchange Act of 1934. These changes were intended to reinforce the concept of an integrated disclosure system.

The changes that were adopted include amendments to Form 10-K, amendments to the Proxy rules, expansion of amendments to Regulation S-K (which governs non-financial statement disclosure rules), uniform financial statement instructions, a general revision of Regulation S-X (which governs the form, content and requirements of financial statements), as well as a new simplified optional form for the registration of securities issued in certain business combinations.

The integrated disclosure system is based on the belief that investors expect to be furnished the same basic information package, both to support current information requirements of an active trading market and to provide information in connection with the sale of newly issued securities under the Securities Act.

The program is intended to:

Improve disclosure to investors and other users of financial information

Achieve a single disclosure system at reduced cost

Reduce current impediments to combining shareholder communications with official SEC filings

Form 10-K
Items Reported
Part I (must be filed 90 days after close of fiscal year)

1. **Business.** Identifies principal products and services of the company, principal markets and methods of distribution and, if "material," competitive factors, backlog and expectation of fulfillment, availability of raw materials, importance of patents, licenses, and franchises, estimated cost of research, number of employees, and effects of compliance with ecological laws.

   If there is more than one line of business, for each of the last three fiscal years a statement of total sales and net income for each line which, during either of the last two fiscal years, accounted for 10 percent or more of total sales or pretax income.

2. **Properties.** Location and character of principal plants, mines, and other important properties and if held in fee or leased.

3. **Legal Proceedings.** Brief description of material legal proceedings pending; when civil rights or ecological statutes are involved, proceedings must be disclosed.

4. **Principal Security Holders and Security Holdings of Management.** Identification of owners of 10 percent or more of any class of securities and of securities held by directors and officers according to amount and percent of each class.

Form 10-K
Part II

5. **Market for the Registrants' Common Stock and Related Security Holder Matters.** In-

Source: *A Guide to SEC Corporate Filings*, Disclosure, Inc., 5161 River Road, Bethesda, MD 20816. Provided by Disclosure. To order copies of any SEC filings, call 800–638–8241.

cludes principal market in which voting securities are traded with high and low sales prices (in the absence thereof, the range of bid and asked quotations for each quarterly period during the past two years) and the dividends paid during the past two years. In addition to the frequency and amount of dividends paid, this item contains a discussion concerning future dividends.

6. **Selected Financial Data.** These are five-year selected data including net sales and operating revenue; income or loss from continuing operations, both total and per common share; total assets; long-term obligations including redeemable preferred stock; cash dividends declared per common share. Also, additional items that could enhance understanding and trends in financial condition and results of operations. Further, the effects of inflation and changing prices should be reflected in the five-year summary.

7. **Management's Discussion and Analysis of Financial Condition and Results of Operations.** Under broad guidelines, this includes: liquidity, capital resources and results of operations; trends that are favorable or unfavorable as well as significant events or uncertainties; causes of any material changes in the financial statements as a whole; limited data concerning subsidiaries; discussion of effects of inflation and changing prices. Projections or other forward-looking information may or may not be included.

8. **Financial Statements and Supplementary Data.** Two-year audited balance sheets as well as three-year audited statements of income and changes in financial condition.

Form 10-K
Part III

9. **Directors and Executive Officers of the Registrant.** Name, office, term of office and specific background data on each.
10. **Remuneration of Directors and Officers.** List of each director and 3 highest paid officers with aggregate annual remuneration exceeding $40,000 and total paid all officers and directors.

Form 10-K
Part IV

11. **Exhibits, Financial Statement Schedules and Reports on Form 8-K.** Complete, audited annual financial information and a list of exhibits filed. Also, any unscheduled material events or corporate changes filed in an 8-K during the year.

Form 10-K
Schedules

I. Marketable securities. Other security investments
II. Amounts due from directors, officers, and principal holders of equity securities other than affiliates
III. Investments in securities of affiliates
IV. Indebtedness of affiliates (not current)
V. Property, plant and equipment
VI. Reserves for depreciation, depletion, and amortization of property, plant and equipment
VII. Intangible assets
VIII. Reserves for depreciation and amortization of intangible assets
IX. Bonds, mortgages, and similar debt
X. Indebtedness to affiliates (not current)
XI. Guarantees of securities of other issuers
XII. Reserves
XIII. Capital shares
XIV. Warrants or rights
XV. Other securities
XVI. Supplementary profit and loss information
XVII. Income from dividends (equity in net profit and loss of affiliates)

18-K (must be filed 9 months after close of fiscal year)

Annual report for foreign governments and political subdivisions thereof.

20-F (must be filed 6 months after close of fiscal year)

Annual report filed by certain foreign issuers of securities trading in the United States.

Item 1. Business
Item 2 Management Discussion & Analysis of the Statements of Income
Item 3 Property
Item 4 Control of Registrant
Item 5 Directors and Officers of Registrant
Item 6 Remuneration of Directors and Officers
Item 7 Options to Purchase Securities from Registrant or Subsidiaries
Item 8 Pending Legal Proceedings
Item 9 Nature of Trading Market

Item 10   Capital Stock to be Registered
Item 11   Debt Securities to be Registered
Item 12   Other Securities to be Registered
Item 13   Exchange Controls and other Limitations Affecting Security Holders
Item 14   Taxation
Item 15   Changes in Securities and Changes in Security for Registered Securities
Item 16   Defaults upon Senior Securities
Item 17   Interest of Management in Certain Transactions
Item 18   Financial Statements and Exhibits

10-Q (must be filed 45 days after close of fiscal quarter)

This is the quarterly financial report filed by most companies, which, although unaudited, provides a continuing view of a company's financial position during the year. It must be filed within 45 days of the close of a fiscal quarter.

Form 10-Q
Items Reported
Part I

FINANCIAL STATEMENTS

1. Income Statement
2. Balance Sheet
3. Statement of source and application of funds
4. A narrative analysis of material changes in the amount of revenue and expense items in relation to previous quarters, including the effect of any changes in accounting principals.

Form 10-Q
Part II

1. **Legal Proceedings.** Brief description of material legal proceedings pending; when civil rights or ecological statutes are involved, proceedings must be disclosed.
2. **Changes in Securities.** Material changes in the rights of holders of any class of registered security.
3. **Changes in Security for Registered Securities.** Material withdrawal or substitution of assets securing any class of registered securities of the registrant.
4. **Defaults upon Senior Securities.** Material defaults in the payment if principal, interest, sinking fund or purchase fund installment,

dividend, or other material default not cured within 30 days.
5. **Increase in Amount Outstanding of Securities or Indebtedness.** Amounts of new issues, continuing issues or reissues of any class of security or indebtedness with a reasonable statement of the purposes for which the proceeds will be used.
6. **Decreases in amount Outstanding of Securities or Indebtedness.** Amounts of decreases, through one or more transactions, in any class of outstanding securities or indebtedness.
7. **Submission of Matters to a Vote of Security Holders.** Information relating to the convening of a meeting of shareholders, whether annual or special, and the matters voted upon, with particular emphasis on the election of directors.
8. **Other Materially Important Events.** Information on any other item of interest to shareholders not already provided for in this form.

8-K (coprorate changes 1–6 must be filed 15 days after the event. 7 has no mandatory filing time.)

This is a report of unscheduled material events or corporate changes deemed of importance to the shareholders or to the SEC.
1. Changes in Control of Registrant.
2. Acquisition or Disposition of Assets.
3. Bankruptcy or Receivership.
4. Changes in Registrant's Certifying Accountant.
5. Other Materially Important Events.
6. Resignations of Registrant's Directors.
7. Other Materially Important Events.

10-C (must be filed 10 days after change)

"Over-the-counter" companies use this form to report changes in name and amount of NASDAQ-listed securities. It is similar in purpose to the 8-K.

13-F (must be filed 45 days after close of fiscal quarter)

A quarterly report of equity holdings required of all institutions with equity assets of $100 million or more. This includes banks, insurance companies, investment companies, investment advisors and large internally managed endowments, foundations and pension funds.

Proxy Statement

A proxy statement provides official notification to designated classes of stockholders of matters to be brought to a vote at a shareholders' meeting. Proxy votes may be solicited for changing the company name, transferring large blocks of stock, electing new officers, or many other matters. Disclosures normally made via a proxy statement may in some cases be made using Form 10-K (Part III).

Registration Statements

Registration statements are of two principal types: (1) "offering" registrations filed under the 1933 Securities Act, and (2) "trading" registrations filed under the 1934 Securities Exchange Act.

"Offering" registrations are used to register securities before they may be offered to investors. Part I of the registration, a preliminary prospectus or "red herring," is promotional in tone; it carries all the sales features that will be contained in the final prospectus. Part II of the registration contains detailed information about marketing agreements, expenses of issuance and distribution, relationship of the company with experts named in the registration, sales to special parties, recent sales of unregistered securities, subsidiaries of registrant, franchises and concessions, indemnification of directors and officers, treatment of proceeds from stock being registered, and financial statements and exhibits.

"Offering" registration statements vary in purpose and content according to the type of organization issuing stock:

S-1   Companies reporting under the '34 Act for less than 3 years. Permits no incorporation by reference and requires complete disclosure in the prospectus.

S-2   Companies reporting under the '34 Act for 3 years or more but do not meet the minimum voting stock requirement. Reference of '34 Act reports permits incorporation and presentation of financial information in the prospectus or in an annual report to shareholders delivered with the prospectus.

S-3   Companies reporting under the '34 Act for 3 or more years and having at least $150 million of voting stock held by non-affiliates, or as an alternative test, $100 million of voting stock coupled with an annual trading volume of 3 million shares. Requires minimal disclosure in the prospectus and allows maximum incorporation by reference of '34 Act reports.

S-4   Registration used in certain business combinations or registrations. Replaces S-14, S-15, 7/85.

N-1A   Used by open end Management Investment Companies other than separate accounts of insurance companies.

N-2   (Formerly S-4) Used by closed-end investment companies.

N-5   Registration of small business investment companies.

NSAR   Replaces form N-1R, N-30A-2, N-30A-3, N-5R, 2-MD.

S-6   Used by unit investment trusts registered under the Investment Act of 1940 on Form N-8B-2.

S-8   Used to register securities to be offered to employees under stock option and various other benefit plans.

S-11   Used by real estate companies, primarily limited partnerships and investment trusts.

S-18   Short form registration up to $7.5 million.

SE   Non-electronic exhibits of registrants filing with the EDGAR PILOT PROJECT.

F-1   Registration of securities by foreign private issuers eligible to use form 20-F, for which no other form is prescribed.

F-2   Registration of securities of foreign private issuers meeting certain 34 act filing requirements.

F-3   Registration of securities of foreign issuers offered pursuant to certain types of transactions.

F-6   Registration of depository shares evidenced by American depository receipts.

"Trading" registrations are filed to permit trading among investors on a securities exchange or in the over-the-counter market. Registration statements which serve to register securities for trading fall into three categories:

(1) **Form 10** is used by companies during the first two years they are subject to the 1934 Act filing requirements. It is a combination registration statement and annual report with information content similar to that of SEC-required annual reports.

(2) **Form 8-A** is used by 1934 Act registrants wishing to register *additional* securities for trading.

(3) **Form 8-B** is used by "successor issuers" (usually companies which have changed their name or state of incorporation) as notification that previously registered securities are to be traded under a new corporate identification.

QUICK REFERENCE CHART TO CONTENTS OF SEC FILINGS

REPORT CONTENTS	10-K	19-K / 20-F	10-Q	8-K	10-C	6-K	Proxy Statement	Prospectus	'34 Act F-10 8-A 8-B	'33 Act "S" Type	ARS	Listing Application	N-SAR
Auditor													
☐ Name	A	A	■				■	A	A		A	■	A
☐ Opinion	A	A	■						A		A		A
☐ Changes				A		■							
Compensation Plans													
☐ Equity	■		■				F	F	A		F	■	
☐ Monetary	■		■				F	A			F		
Company Information													
☐ Nature of Business	A	A				F		A	A		A	■	
☐ History	F	A							A		A	■	
☐ Organization and Change	F	F	A	■	F			A		F	A		
Debt Structure	A					F		A	A		A	A	A
Depreciation & Other Schedules	A	A				F		A	A		A		
Dilution Factors	A	A	F			F		A	A		A	A	
Directors, Officers, Insiders													
☐ Identification	F	A				F	A	A	A	■	A	F	
☐ Background	■	A				F	F	A	■		A		
☐ Holdings	■	A		■			A	A	A		A		
☐ Compensation	■	A					A	A	A		A		
Earnings Per Share	A	A	A			F			A			A	A
Financial Information													
☐ Annual Audited	A	A							A			A	A
☐ Interim Audited	■	A					■				■		
☐ Interim Unaudited	■		A			F		F			F	F	
Foreign Operations	A					■		A	A		A		F
Labor Contracts				■					F		F		
Legal Agreements	F			■					F		F		
Legal Counsel								A			A	■	
Loan Agreements	F		F				■		F		F		■
Plants and Properties	A	F		■				F	A		F		
Portfolio Operations													
☐ Content (Listing of Securities)													A
☐ Management													A
Product-Line Breakout	A							A			A		
Securities Structure	A	A			■			A	A		A		
Subsidiaries	A	A						A	A		A		
Underwriting				■				A	A		A		
Unregistered Securities	■							F			F		
Block Movements	■		F						A			■	

Legend A – always included · included · if occured or significant · F – frequently included · ■ special circumstances only

TENDER OFFER/ACQUISITION REPORTS	13D	13 G	14D-1	14D-9	13E-3	13E-4
Name of Issuer (Subject Company)	A	A	A	A	A	A
Filing Person (or Company)	A	A	A	A	A	A
Amount of Shares Owned	A	A				
Percent of Class Outstanding	A	A				
Financial Statements of Bidders			F		F	F
Purpose of Tender Offer			A	A	A	A
Source and Amount of Funds	A		A		A	
Identity and Background Information			A	A	A	
Persons Retained, Employed or to be Compensated			A	A	A	A
Exhibits	F		F	F	F	F

Prospectus

When the sale of securities as proposed in an "offering" registration statement is approved by the SEC, any changes required by the SEC are incorporated into the prospectus. This document must be made available to investors before the sale of the security is initiated. It also contains the actual offering price, which may have been changed after the registration statement was approved.

Annual Report to Shareholders

The Annual Report is the principal document used by most major companies to communicate directly with shareholders. Since it is not a required, official SEC filing, companies have considerable discretion in determining what types of information this report will contain and how it is to be presented.

Recent changes (effective December 15, 1980) required by the SEC were made to standardize the presentation of disclosure items in annual reports to make them consistent with similar requirements in SEC filings. For example, selected financial data relating to a registrant's financial condition and results of continuing operations will be presented in the Annual Report in the same manner as in the 10-K.

In addition to financial information, the Annual Report to Shareholders often provides nonfinancial details of the business which are not reported elsewhere. These may include marketing plans and forecasts of future programs and plans.

Form 8 (Amendment)

Form 8 is used to amend or supplement filings previously submitted. 1933 Act registration statements are amended by filing an amended registration statement (pre-effective amendment) or by the prospectus itself, as previously noted.

Listing Application

Like the ARS, a listing application is not an official SEC filing. It is filed by the company with the NYSE, AMEX or other stock exchange to document proposed new listings. Usually a Form 8-A registration is filed with the SEC at about the same time.

N-SAR

This report is the equivalent of the 10-K for registered management-investment firms. In addition to annual financial statements, this report shows diversification of assets, portfolio turnover activity, and capital gains experience.

Tender Offers/Acquisition Reports

13-G (must be filed 45 days after end of each calendar year)

An annual report (short form of 13D) which must be filed by all reporting persons (primarily institutions) meeting the 5% equity ownership rule within 45 days after the end of each calendar year.
1. Name of issuer
2. Name of person filing
3. 13D-1 or 13D-2 applicability
4. Amount of shares beneficially owned:
   Percent of class outstanding
   Sole or shared power to vote
   Sole or shared power to dispose
5. Ownership of 5% or less of a class of stock
6. Ownership of more than 5% on behalf of another person
7. Identification of subsidiary which acquired the security being reported on by the parent holding company (if applicable)
8. Identification and classification of members of the group (if applicable)
9. Notice of dissolution of the group (if applicable)

13-D (must be filed within 10 days of the acquisition date)

Similar information of 5% equity ownership in connection with a tender offer filed within ten days of the acquisition date:
1. Security and issuer
2. Identity and background of person filing the statement
3. Source and amount of funds or other consideration
4. Purpose of the transaction
5. Interest in securities of the issuer
6. Contracts, arrangements or relationships with respect to securities of the issuer
7. Material to be filed as exhibits which may include but are not limited to:
   a. Letter agreements between the parties
   b. Formal offer to purchase

14D-1

Tender offer filing made with the SEC at time offer is made to holders of equity securities of target company, if acceptance of offer would give the offerer over 5% ownership of the subject securities:

1. Security and subject company
2. Identity and background information
3. Past contacts, transactions or negotiations with subject company
4. Source and amount of funds or other consideration
5. Purpose of the tender offer and plans or proposals of the bidder
6. Interest in securities of the subject company
7. Contracts, arrangements or relationships with respect to the subject company's securities
8. Persons retained, employed or to be compensated
9. Financial statements of certain bidders
10. Additional information
11. Material to be filed as exhibits which may include but are not limited to:
    a. The actual offer to purchase
    b. The letter to shareholders
    c. The letter of transmittal with notice of guaranteed delivery
    d. The press release
    e. The summary publication in business newspapers or magazines
    f. The summary advertisement to appear in business newspapers or magazines.

14D-9 (must be filed 10 days after making the tender offer)

A solicitation/recommendation statement that must be submitted to equity holders and filed at the SEC by the management of a firm subject to a tender offer within ten days of the making of the tender offer:

1. Security and subject company
2. Tender offer of the bidder
3. Identify and background
4. The solicitation or recommendation
5. Persons retained, employed or to be compensated
6. Recent transactions and intent with respect to securities

7. Certain negotiations and transactions by the subject company
8. Additional information
9. Material to be filed as exhibits

13E-4

Issuer tender offer statement pursuant to the Securities Exchange Act of 1934:

1. Security and issuer
2. Source and amount of funds
3. Purpose of the tender offer and plans or proposals of the issuer or affiliates
4. Interest in securities of the issuer
5. Contracts, arrangements or relationships with respect to the issuer's securities
6. Person retained, employed or to be compensated
7. Financial information
8. Additional information
9. Material to be filed as exhibits which may include but are not limited to:
   The offer to purchase which is being sent to the shareholders to whom the tender offer is being made.

13E-3

Transaction statement pursuant to the Securities Exchange Act of 1934 with respect to a public company or affiliate going private-

1. Issuer and class of security subject to the transaction
2. Identity and background of the individuals
3. Past contacts, transactions or negotiations
4. Terms of the transaction
5. Plans or proposals of the issuer or affiliate
6. Source and amount of funds or other considerations
7. Purpose, alternatives, reasons and effects
8. Fairness of the transaction
9. Reports, opinions, appraisals and certain negotiations
10. Interest in securities of the issuer
11. Contracts, arrangements or relationships with respect to the issuer's securities
12. Present intention and recommendation of certain persons with regard to the transaction
13. Other provisions of the transaction
14. Financial information
15. Persons and assets employed, retained or utilized
16. Additional information
17. Material to be filed as exhibits

How to Read the New York Stock Exchange and American Stock Exchange Quotations

(1)	(2)	(3)	(4)	(5)	(6)	(7)	(8)	(9)	(10)	(11)
52 Weeks				Yld	P-E	Sales				Net
High	Low	Stock	Div.	%	Ratio	100s	High	Low	Close	Chg.
					A A A					
14¾	9⅛	AAR	.44	4.3	7	26	10½	10¼	10¼	¼
52¼	32¼	ACF	2.76	6.0	10	51	46	45½	46	
27	12⅞	AMF	1.24	5.1	12	1453	24¼	23¾	24⅛ +	¼
24¾	10⅞	AM Intl				51	13⅞	13¾	13¾	
11⅜	6⅜	APL				51	6⅜ d	6¼	6¼	⅛

The composite quotations take into account prices paid for a stock on the New York or American Exchanges, plus those prices paid on regional exchanges, Over-the-Counter (OTC) and elsewhere, as shown in the example from the Wall Street Journal.

The stock market quotations are explained below:

(1) The highest price per share paid in the past 52 weeks in terms of ⅛ of a dollar, i.e., 10⅛ means $10.125.

(2) The lowest price paid per share in the last 52 weeks.

(3) The name of the company in abbreviated form.

(4) The regular annual dividend paid. Special or extra dividends are specified by letters given in the footnotes in the Explanatory Notes shown below.

(5) The yield, that is, the annual dividend divided by the current price of the stock expressed in percent. For example, a stock that sells for $20.00 per share and pays a dividend of $2.00 per share has a yield of 10 percent (2/20).

(6) The P/E ratio is the current price of the stock divided by the company's last reported annual earnings per share. The P/E ratio is generally high for companies which are thought to have a relatively large and persistent earning's growth rate. The average P/E ratio for the Dow Jones stocks varied from 7.7 to 10.2 during the last five years.

(7) The number of shares sold on the day reported in 100s of shares.

(8) The highest price paid per share on the day reported.

(9) The lowest price paid per share on the day reported.

(10) The last price paid per share on the day reported.

(11) The change in the closing price from the previous day's closing price.

EXPLANATORY NOTES
(For New York and American Exchange listed issues)

Sales figures are unofficial.

The 52-Week High and Low columns show the highest and the lowest price of the stock in consolidated trading during the preceding 52 weeks plus the current week, but not the current trading day.

u—Indicates a new 52-week high. d—Indicates a new 52-week low.

s—Split or stock dividend of 25 percent or more in the past 52 weeks. The high-low range is adjusted from the old stock. Dividend begins with the date of split or stock dividend.

n—New issue in the past 52 weeks. The high-low range begins with the start of trading in the new issue and does not cover the entire 52-week period.

g—Dividend or earnings in Canadian money. Stock trades in U.S. dollars. No yield or PE shown unless stated in U.S. money.

Unless otherwise noted, rates of dividends in the foregoing table are annual disbursements based on the last quarterly or semi-annual declaration. Special or extra dividends or payments not designated as regular are identified in the following footnotes.

a—Also extra or extras. b—Annual rate plus stock dividend. c—Liquidating dividend. e—Declared or paid in preceding 12 months. i—Declared or paid after stock dividend or split up. j—Paid this year, dividend omitted, deferred or no action taken at last dividend meeting. k—Declared or paid this year, an accumulative issue with dividends in arrears. r—Declared or paid in preceding 12 months plus stock dividend. t—Paid in stock in preceding 12 months, estimated cash value on ex-dividend or ex-distribution date.

x—Ex-dividend or ex-rights. v—Ex-dividend and sales in full. z—Sales in full.

wd—When distributed. wi—When issued. ww—With warrants. xw—Without warrants.

vi—In bankruptcy or receivership or being reorganized under the Bankruptcy Act, or securities assumed by such companies.

How to Read Over-the-Counter NASDAQ Listings

(1)　(2)	(3)	(4)	(5)	(6)
	Sales			Net
Stock & Div.	100s	Bid	Asked	Chg.
CentVtPS 1.92	8	13⅝	13¾ +	⅛
Centrn CP 2.56	4	23¼	23½	. . .
Centura Enrg	135	10½	10¾ −	½
CenturyBK .48	573	13	13⅛ −	⅛
CenturyOil Gs	49	7⅜	7⅝	. . .
Cetus Corptn	231	17⅛	17⅜ +	⅛
CFS Cont .40	18	13⅝	13⅞ +	⅛
CGA Assc Inc	155	10½	11 −	¼
Chalco Ind Inc	2	6	6½ −	¼

The over-the-counter quotations are explained below.

(1) The company's name, usually abbreviated.

(2) Annual regular dividend per share, unless accompanied by a notation which is explained in the OTC Explanatory Notes (below).

(3) Number of shares sold that day in hundreds, i.e., 2 means 200 shares.

(4) Bid price per share at closing time, i.e., the price at which broker-dealer will buy the stock from the investor. Prices do not include mark-up or commission.

(5) Ask price per share at closing time, i.e., the price at which the broker-dealer will sell the stock.*

(6) The change in the closing bid price from the previous day.

---

* Bid and ask prices are usually quoted in ⅛ (12.5 cents) of a dollar, i.e., 12⅛ means $12.125, 12½ means $12.50, etc. Very inexpensive stocks are quoted at ¹⁄₁₆ (6.25 cents) and ¹⁄₃₂ (3.125 cents) of a dollar.

OTC EXPLANATORY NOTES

z—Sales in full.

a—Annual rate plus cash extra. b—Paid so far in 1981, no regular rate. c—Payment of accumulated dividends. d—Paid in 1980. e—Cash plus stock paid in 1980. f—Cash plus stock paid in 1981. g—Annual rate plus stock dividend. h—Paid in 1981, latest dividend omitted. i—Percent paid in stock in 1980. j—Percent in stock paid in 1981, latest dividend omitted. k—Percent in stock paid in 1981. n—Asked price not applicable. p—Granted temporary exception from Nasdaq qualifications. q—In bankruptcy proceedings. ut—Units. wt—Warrants. x—Ex-dividend, ex-rights or ex-distribution. (z) No representative quote.

The Ex-dividend Explained

The ex-dividend status of a stock is indicated by an *x* in the newspaper quotation or *xd* on the ticker tape. This is an abbreviation for *without dividend*.

A stock that is purchased during the ex-dividend period will not pay a previously declared dividend to its new owner. The ex-dividend period spans four business days before the so-called record date—the date a dividend issuing corporation uses to tally its shareowners. An ex-dividend stock buyer is not entitled to a dividend because his name is not recorded with the dividend issuing corporation until after the record date.

The New York Stock Exchange requires that the buyer in every transaction be recorded with the issuing corporation on the fifth business day following a trade. A stock buyer, therefore, must purchase his shares at least five business days before the record date in order for the corporation to record his name in time for him to receive his dividend. A purchase one day later disqualifies a buyer from a dividend because the transfer of ownership cannot be completed by the record date. Therefore, on the fourth business day prior to the record date, a stock is sold ex-dividend.

In our example below, the corporation's Board has decided to pay a 50¢ dividend to shareholders of record on Monday, the 10th. A person buying shares up to the close of business on Monday, the 3rd, would be eligible for the dividend because normal settlement (5 business days) will be made on Monday the 10th. On Tuesday, the 4th, however, the stock would begin selling ex-dividend because a stock purchaser as of that date could not settle till after the record date.

On the ex-dividend date, the Exchange specialist will reduce all open buy orders and open sell stop orders by the amount of the dividend. This is done to more equitably reflect the stock's value since purchasers of stock on or after the ex-dividend date are ineligible for a dividend.

EX-DIVIDEND EXPLANATION

Any Month Date	Calendar Day	Status
3	Monday	With/Dividend
4	Tuesday	Ex-Dividend (Without Dividend)
5	Wednesday......	" "
6	Thursday	" "
7	Friday...........	" "
8	Saturday	Not a trading day
9	Sunday	Not a trading day
10	Monday	Record Date/Business Day
11	Tuesday	Business Day

Source: *Taking The Mystery Out of Ex-Dividend*, The New York Stock Exchange, Inc.

Margin Accounts Explained

Stocks may be purchased by paying the purchase price in full (plus commissions and taxes) or on a margin account. With the margin account, the investors put up part of the purchase price in cash or securities, and the broker lends the remainder. The margin investor must pay the usual commissions as well as interest on the broker's loan. The stocks purchased on margin are held by the broker as collateral on the loan. Dividends are applied to the margin account and help offset the interest payments.

Margin (M) is defined as the market value (V) of the securities less the broker's loan (L), divided by the market value of the securities. The ratio is expressed as a percentage:

$$M = \frac{V - L}{V} \times 100$$

Example: You buy 100 shares of a stock at $20 per share at a total cost (V) of $2,000. You put up $1,200 in cash and borrow (L) $800 from the broker. The margin at the time of purchase is

$$M = \frac{\$2,000 - \$800}{\$2,000} \times 100 = 60\%$$

The margin at the time of purchase is called *initial margin*. The smallest allowed value of initial margin (set by the Federal Reserve) is currently 50%. Thus, with the above stock, if you buy 100 shares at $20 per share on 50% initial margin, you put up $1,000 (.5 × $2,000), and the broker's loan is $1,000.

After the purchase there is a *maintenance margin* (set by the Exchange) below which the margin is not permitted to decrease. The maintenance margin on the New York Stock Exchange is 25%. Some brokers, however, require a higher maintenance margin of about 30%. Thus, if the 100 shares of stocks discussed above decrease in price from $20 to $13 per share then the margin is

$$M = \left(\frac{\$1,300 - \$1,000}{\$1,300} \right) \times 100 = 23\%$$

The margin of 23% is now below the maintenance margin of 25% set by the Exchange. The securities are said to be *under margined*, and a call for additional cash (or securities) is issued by the broker in order to bring up the margin to 25%. If the investor does not meet the call for additional cash (margin call) within a specified time, the stocks in the margin account are immediately sold.

MARGIN REQUIREMENTS (percent of market value and effective date)

	Mar. 11, 1968	June 8, 1968	May 6, 1970	Dec. 6, 1971	Nov. 24, 1972	Jan. 3, 1974
Margin stocks	70	80	65	55	65	50
Convertible bonds	50	60	50	50	50	50
Short sales	70	80	65	55	65	50

Note: Regulations G, T, and U of the Federal Reserve Board of Governors, prescribed in accordance with the Securities Exchange Act of 1934, limit the amount of credit to purchase and carry margin stocks that may be extended on securities as collateral by prescribing a maximum loan value, which is a specified percentage of the market value of the collateral at the time the credit is extended. Margin requirements are the difference between the market value (100 percent) and the maximum loan value. The term "margin stocks" is defined in the corresponding regulation.

Source: *Federal Reserve Bulletin*.

Short Selling Explained

Short selling provides an opportunity to profit from a decline in the price of a stock. If you believe that a stock is due for a substantial decline, you arrange to have your broker borrow the stock from another investor who owns the shares. The borrowed stock is then sold. This cash is held as collateral against the borrowed shares. When (and if) the stock price declines, you purchase the stock at the market price and use it to replace the borrowed shares. The broker arranges the return of your cash collateral less the cost of the repurchased stock. Your profit per share is the price received on the sale of the stock less the purchase price.

There are certain cash outlays and costs associated with the short sale. Generally there is no charge for borrowing the stock, although occasionally stock lenders may charge a premium over the market price. You must deposit $2,000 or the required initial margin, whichever is the greater, at the time the stock is borrowed. Thus, if you borrow 100 shares of a stock priced at $50 per share and the margin required is 50%,

you must put up $2,500 (.5 × $50 × 100) in cash or securities. The margin deposit is returned when you close out the short sale. You pay commission when the stock is sold and when it is repurchased. In addition, you must pay the stock lender any dividends which are declared during the period you are short the stock. It is well to remember that if cash is used for the deposit, there is a loss of the interest which you would have obtained if the cash had been invested.

The dividend payments and interest loss can be reduced or eliminated if you short stocks which pay little or no dividends and use interest-bearing securities (such as T-bills or negotiable certificates of deposit) as the margin deposit.

An increase in the price of the stock can result in substantial losses since you may be forced to repurchase at a higher price than you sold. If there are many short sellers seeking to purchase the stock in order to close out their position, prices may be driven to very high levels.

The short sale cannot be executed while the stock price is declining on the exchange. According to the rules of the SEC, the stock must undergo an increase in price prior to the execution of a short sale.

How to Read Mutual Fund Quotations

The following is an example of typical fund quotations as reported in the Wall Street Journal. The mutual fund quotations are explained in the adjacent column.

(1)	(2) NAV	(3) Offer Price	(4) NAV Chg.
Able Assoc	24.33	N.L.+	.80
Acorn Fnd	28.28	N.L.+	.03
ADV Fund	15.38	N.L.+	.02
Afuture Fd	15.59	N.L.+	.10
AIM funds			
Conv Yld	15.42	16.49+	.09
Edsn Gld	14.59	15.60+	.09
HiYld Sc	8.98	9.60+	.02
Alpha Fnd	17.82	N.L.+	.01
Am Birthrt	12.29	13.43−	.03
American Funds Group			
Am Bal	8.73	9.54	. . .
Amcap F	6.21	6.79+	.01
Am Mutl	12.46	13.62−	.01

(1) Name of fund in abbreviated form.
(2) NAV means "net asset value" per share of the stock. It is the price at which the fund will buy shares from investors.
The NAV is obtained from

$$NAV = \frac{M + C - L}{N}$$

M = market value of all stock in the fund's portfolio at the end of the trading day
C = fund's cash or cash equivalent position
L = fund's liabilities
N = number of shares issued by fund

(3) Offer price is the price per share at which the fund will sell shares to investors. With no load (NL, no sales charge) funds, the offer price and the NAV are the same. With load funds, a sales charge (load) is added to the NAV to arrive at the sales price.
(4) The NAV change is the change in net asset value (at the close of the stock market) from that of the previous day.

Top 50 Performing Mutual Funds for 5 Years

What $10,000 Grew to In 5 Years (1981–1985)**

1	*Vanguard Qual. Dividend I (c)	$ 35,878
2	+Fidelity Magellan Fund	34,889
3	*Sequoia (c)	30,763
4	*Loomis-Sayles Capital Dev.	28,846
5	*Lindner Fund (c)	28,821
6	*Windsor (c)	28,292
7	Phoenix Stock Fund Series	28,241
8	Phoenix Growth Fund Series	27,576
9	Fidelity Destiny	27,466
10	*Mutual Qualified Income	27,395
11	Franklin Utilities	26,837
12	*Century Shares Trust	26,627
13	*Lehman Opportunity Fund	26,524
14	*Evergreen Total Return	26,477
15	+Fidelity Equity Income	26,299
16	Washington Mutual Inv.	26,202
17	*Nicholas	26,053
18	Income Fund of America	26,047
19	NEL Growth	25,864
20	*Northeast Investors Trust	25,679
21	*Ivy Growth Fund	25,631
22	Guardian Park Avenue	25,536
23	*Fidelity Puritan Fund	25,415
24	United Income	25,171
25	United Continental Income	25,068
26	BLC Capital Accumulation	24,969
27	*Mutual Shares Corp.	24,966
28	Pilgrim MagnaCap Fund	24,881
29	Oppenheimer Equity Income	24,789
30	*Pennsylvania Mutual	24,637
31	*American Leaders	24,626
32	Sigma Capital Shares	24,589
33	*Lehman Capital Fund	24,524
34	Lutheran Brotherhood Fund	24,308
35	*Tudor Fund	24,308
36	*SAFECO Income	24,293
37	*Stratton Dividend Fund	24,271
38	Delaware	24,230
39	A-C Pace	24,180
40	American Mutual	24,172
41	Sentinel Common Stock	24,136
42	*Elfun Tax-Exempt Income	24,057
43	Nationwide Growth Fund	23,945
44	Kemper High Yield	23,897
45	*Fidelity High Income	23,876
46	Provident Fund for Income	23,783
47	Sentinel Balanced	23,766
48	United International Growth	23,678
49	*Wellesley Income	23,611
50	*Partners Fund	23,515

Top 50 Performing Mutual Funds for 10 Years

What $10,000 Grew To In 10 Years (1976–1985)**

1	+Fidelity Magellan Fund	$ 186,700
2	*Twentieth Century Growth	124,377
3	*Lindner Fund (c)	120,505
4	*Evergreen Fund	114,461
5	*Twentieth Century Select	111,024
6	A-C Pace	103,431
7	*Sequoia (c)	99,551
8	*Pennsylvania Mutual	89,780
9	O-T-C Securities	86,546
10	*Value Line Leveraged Growth	86,432
11	*Nicholas	85,930
12	Pioneer II	84,274
13	*Acorn	83,964
14	Fidelity Destiny	83,022
15	AMEV Growth Fund	82,505
16	*Weingarten Equity	82,299
17	*Mutual Shares Corp.	81,533
18	Security Ultra	78,303
19	*Loomis-Sayles Capital Dev.	77,923
20	A-C Venture	77,068
21	Fidelity Equity Income	75,919
22	A-C Comstock	74,305
23	Phoenix Stock Fund Series	73,725
24	Sigma Venture Shares	73,526
25	NEL Growth	73,350
26	*Partners Fund	73,335
27	Mass Capital Development	73,258
28	Oppenheimer Special	72,345
29	AMCAP	71,601
30	*Leverage Fund of Boston	71,258
31	Guardian Park Avenue	70,676
32	*Tudor Fund	70,174
33	Stein Roe Special	69,995
34	Growth Fund of America	69,334
35	*Windsor (c)	68,368
36	New York Venture	67,781
37	Kemper Summit	67,303
38	*SAFECO Growth	66,905
39	United Vanguard	66,568
40	Oppenheimer Time	66,188
41	*Janus	64,584
42	Templeton Growth Fund	64,490
43	Sigma Capital Shares	64,464
44	IDS Growth	64,458
45	*Explorer	64,130
46	*Plitrend	64,129
47	*Charter	62,954
48	Seligman Capital Fund	61,801
49	*AMEV Special Fund	60,054
50	*Scudder Development	59,687

* No-Load Fund, + Low-Load Fund, (No-Symbol) Load Fund.
** Does not take into account loads or income taxes that would have to be paid. Includes reinvestment of all capital gains.
(c) Fund Closed.

Source: Reprinted from *Donoghue's Mutual Funds' Almanac*, 17 Annual Edition 1986–1987. With permission of William E. Donoghue. *Donoghue's Mutual Funds Almanac* is a yearly publication. For information call (800) 343-5413; in Massachusetts call (617) 429-5930.

PERFORMANCE OF MUTUAL FUNDS

BARRON'S / LIPPER GAUGE

FUND NAME	OBJ.	LOAD	TOTAL NET ASTS (MIL) 6/30/86	NAV 6/30/86	PERFORMANCE (RETURN ON INITIAL $10,000 INVESTMENT) 12/31/85-6/30/86	6/30/85-6/30/86	6/30/81-6/30/86	YIELD % 6/30/86	PER SHARE LATEST 12 MONTHS CAP GAINS	INC DIVS	LATEST AVAILABLE PRICE/EARNINGS	ANNUAL % TURNOVER
ABT EMERGING GROWTH	CA	SC	38.7	$10.27	$13,251.60	$15,318.50	$	0.0	$0.18	$0.00	29.8	101
ABT GROWTH & INCOME TR	GI	SC	122.5	13.92	11,431.90	12,781.20	20,008.30	5.0	3.52	0.78	12.8	130
ABT SECURITY INCOME	OI	SC	18.8	10.92	10,542.20	11,289.00	☆	3.1	1.10	0.36	N/A	166
ABT UTILITY INCOME FD	UT	SC	109.2	14.96	11,385.10	11,917.30	19,585.30	7.6	1.15	1.18	11.5	47
ACORN FUND	SG	NO	424.4	42.77	12,073.20	13,204.40	22,034.60	1.1	1.97	0.50	28.3	32
ADAM INVESTORS	CA	NO	14.1	16.48	11,673.10	12,863.90	☆	3.6	0.74	0.62	N/A	169
ADTEK FUND	CA	NO	30.1	11.73	11,834.20	12,011.00	☆	3.3	0.72	0.40	N/A	179
ADVEST ADVANTAGE GOVT (R)	FI	NO	129.9	9.96	10,256.30	☆	☆	0.0	0.09	0.19	N/A	N/A
ADVEST ADVANTAGE GRO (R)	G	NO	13.6	11.11	11,110.00	☆	☆	0.0	0.00	0.00	N/A	N/A
ADVEST ADVANTAGE INC (R)	_	NO	25.7	10.55	10,550.00	☆	☆	0.0	0.00	0.00	N/A	N/A
ADVEST ADVANTAGE SPEC (R)	CA	NO	4.6	10.12	10,120.00	☆	☆	0.0	0.00	0.00	N/A	N/A
AETNA INCOME SHARES	FI	NO	191.7	13.33	10,779.20	11,848.20	22,616.10	7.5	0.00	0.99	17.2	58
AFFILIATED FUND	GI	SC	3,124.6	11.63	12,048.00	13,272.70	24,322.60	4.7	0.81	0.56	14.8	49
AFUTURE FUND	G	NO	24.9	15.77	11,884.20	12,609.90	15,292.90	0.7	0.00	0.10	N/A	193
AGE HIGH INCOME	FI	LO	782.2	3.83	11,051.60	11,796.20	22,140.60	12.8	0.00	0.49	N/A	26
ALLEGRO GROWTH	G	NO	1.5	11.75	11,508.30	☆	☆	0.0	0.00	0.00	N/A	N/A
ALLIANCE BOND-HIGH YLD	FI	SC	240.3	10.30	10,933.20	12,127.50	☆	13.6	0.00	1.39	N/A	N/A
ALLIANCE BOND-US GOVT	FI	SC	128.9	9.23	10,392.90	☆	☆	0.0	0.00	0.62	N/A	N/A
ALLIANCE CONVERTIBLE	FI	SC	48.9	9.90	10,764.30	☆	☆	0.0	0.04	0.25	N/A	N/A
ALLIANCE COUNTERPOINT	GL	NO	37.9	15.29	12,624.90	14,165.20	☆	1.6	0.04	0.24	N/A	6
ALLIANCE GLOBAL	GL	SC	3.3	10.43	11,411.40	☆	☆	0.0	0.00	0.00	N/A	N/A
ALLIANCE INTERNATIONAL	IF	SC	139.3	21.97	13,124.30	19,042.70	25,155.00	0.1	0.41	0.03	N/A	40
ALLIANCE MORTGAGE INC	FI	SC	726.0	9.57	10,363.10	11,101.70	☆	12.0	0.20	1.15	N/A	164
ALLIANCE TECHNOLOGY	TK	SC	153.2	24.41	11,832.80	14,060.40	☆	0.0	0.00	0.01	39.9	259
ALPHA FUND	G	SC	28.2	8.39	12,489.20	14,354.70	24,898.10	2.7	0.30	0.22	19.7	60
AARP CAPITAL GROWTH	G	NO	57.4	23.41	12,186.40	13,249.60	☆	0.4	0.18	0.08	N/A	42
AARP GENERAL BOND	FI	NO	74.5	15.97	10,578.10	11,423.80	☆	9.0	0.05	1.44	N/A	54
AARP GNMA	FI	NO	1,341.6	15.82	10,415.10	11,300.00	☆	10.0	0.03	1.58	N/A	67
AARP GROWTH AND INCOME	GI	NO	89.5	22.34	11,862.30	13,347.80	☆	2.8	0.08	0.63	N/A	13
AMANA MUTUAL-INCOME	_	NO	0.1	10.00	$			1.8	0.00	0.00	N/A	N/A
AMCAP FUND	G	NO	1,506.4	10.34	11,687.40	12,971.00	21,975.90	1.8	0.65	0.19	24.7	27
AMERICAN BALANCED FUND	B	SC	165.6	11.86	11,521.40	12,898.80	24,101.00	5.2	1.10	0.64	19.7	63
AMER CAPITAL COMSTOCK	CA	SC	1,001.4	16.01	11,430.50	12,041.60	22,011.10	2.3	0.48	0.38	23.7	64
AMER CAPITAL CORP BOND	FI	SC	110.6	7.51	10,843.00	11,940.60	22,148.70	11.1	0.00	0.83	N/A	62
AMER CAPITAL ENTERPRISE	G	SC	718.0	15.36	12,272.50	13,379.60	19,669.00	1.6	1.63	0.26	37.9	114
AMER CAPITAL GOVT	FI	SC	7,161.2	11.86	10,527.80	11,402.60	☆	9.2	0.59	1.11	N/A	N/A
AMER CAPITAL GROWTH	G	NO	29.9	27.27	12,250.20	13,106.10	17,032.30	0.3	5.78	0.09	28.4	117
AMER CAPITAL HARBOR	GI	SC	262.4	15.41	11,876.30	12,829.80	23,620.80	5.3	0.63	0.84	18.2	89
AMER CAPITAL HIGH YIELD	FI	SC	543.4	10.82	10,988.40	12,149.70	23,134.40	11.9	0.00	1.29	0.0	82
AMER CAPITAL LIFE STOCK	G	SC	1.8	10.03	$9,950.40	☆	☆	0.0	0.00	0.00	N/A	N/A
AMER CAPITAL LIFE GOVT	FI	NO	4.0	10.24	10,344.40	☆	☆	0.0	0.00	0.00	N/A	N/A
AMER CAPITAL OTC	SG	SC	129.4	11.95	11,761.80	12,185.60	☆	0.3	0.44	0.03	28.0	90
AMER CAPITAL PACE	CA	SC	2,229.3	24.38	11,250.60	12,379.20	24,419.30	3.2	0.40	0.79	24.6	40
AMER CAPITAL VENTURE	CA	SC	415.0	17.31	12,004.20	11,790.90	21,198.10	0.9	0.51	0.15	28.1	101
AMERICAN GROWTH	G	SC	71.3	9.34	11,351.80	11,484.60	18,527.30	4.2	0.00	0.39	20.2	58
AMERICAN HERITAGE	CA	SC	0.4	2.05	8,649.80	8,134.90	6,346.70	0.0	0.00	0.00	N/A	N/A
AMERICAN INVESTORS	G	NO	81.7	8.13	11,338.90	12,260.50	7,776.90	2.3	0.44	0.19	29.8	204

Fund	Obj	Load	Net Assets	NAV	Value 1	Value 2	Value 3	Yld	Col	Col	%	Rank
AMERICAN INV INCOME	FI	NO	23.3	9.24	10,522.00	11,460.20	15,683.20	12.1	0.00	1.12	N/A	117
AMERICAN LEADERS	GI	NO	115.9	13.16	11,299.40	12,324.80	26,472.60	3.8	0.61	0.52	14.6	32
AMA MEMB RETR PLAN EQUITY	G	NO	171.3	48.54	12,074.60	13,192.70	23,302.90	0.0	0.00	0.00	N/A	N/A
AMERICAN MUTUAL	GI	SC	1,962.2	19.41	11,740.50	11,405.90	26,274.70	3.6	0.86	0.72	17.8	24
AMERICAN NATIONAL BOND	FI	SC	7.7	15.27	10,578.60	13,384.40	20,991.20	9.2	0.00	1.40	N/A	13
AMERICAN NATIONAL GROWTH	G	SC	102.5	5.38	11,807.90	12,344.70	20,377.40	1.6	1.01	0.08	23.6	42
AMERICAN NATIONAL INCOME	EI	SC	62.0	22.19	11,202.60	13,599.80	22,575.50	3.5	0.71	0.76	16.6	24
API TRUST (R)	CA	NO	6.3	12.21	11,698.90	13,981.90	☆	4.8	9.88	0.61	N/A	N/A
AMER TELECOMMUN-GROWTH	TK	NO	45.1	96.23	11,981.90	13,924.80	☆	2.2	1.06	2.27	19.5	108
AMER TELECOMMUN-INCOME	S	NO	103.8	103.13	12,654.60	14,777.60	28,048.60	5.2	1.06	5.37	11.4	21
AMEV CAPITAL FD	CA	SC	105.6	15.13	12,465.40	15,719.60	26,873.70	1.3	2.10	0.20	26.9	134
AMEV FIDUCIARY FD	CA	LO	15.8	21.30	13,353.90	15,057.60	25,977.30	0.8	0.59	0.17	N/A	127
AMEV GROWTH FD	CA	SC	162.6	18.34	13,573.60	15,210.80	20,354.00	0.8	1.23	0.15	28.1	136
AMEV SPECIAL FD	FI	NO	27.5	27.55	13,423.00	11,709.40	15,497.20	0.5	0.00	0.14	N/A	132
AMEV US GOVT FD	FI	SC	45.0	10.23	13,375.50	11,566.90	18,007.60	10.3	0.69	1.05	N/A	240
ANALYTIC OPTIONED EQU	OI	NO	84.3	15.12	10,846.80	11,780.30	☆	3.1	0.00	0.48	N/A	54
ARMSTRONG ASSOCIATES	G	NO	11.7	8.72	11,237.10	13,849.70	23,265.30	2.7	0.10	0.23	N/A	53
ASSOCIATED PLANNERS STK	CA	SC	5.0	15.03	12,825.10	12,541.60	23,575.10	0.5	0.70	0.07	21.2	N/A
AXE-HOUGHTON FUND B	B	NO	191.2	13.31	12,131.70	13,517.30	20,205.10	4.8	0.00	0.66	N/A	97
AXE-HOUGHTON INCOME	FI	NO	45.6	5.56	10,997.50	11,836.50	21,771.90	8.9	0.06	0.49	22.4	90
AXE-HOUGHTON STOCK	G	NO	107.8	10.80	10,750.90	12,384.10	☆	0.4	0.00	0.04	N/A	191
BABSON BOND TRUST	FI	NO	62.4	1.67	11,822.10	13,508.70	20,138.00	9.8	0.26	0.16	19.5	39
BABSON ENTERPRISE	SG	NO	61.6	14.50	11,839.30	12,962.60	☆	1.7	2.98	0.24	20.3	38
DAVID L BABSON GROWTH	GI	NO	253.9	13.62	11,960.90	16,565.40	☆	5.1	0.01	0.76	N/A	35
BABSON VALUE	GI	NO	5.4	15.02	14,343.40	☆	☆	2.3	1.86	0.34	N/A	13
BAIRD CAP DEVELOPMENT	GI	NO	0.3	18.46	10,570.90	☆	☆	0.9	0.00	0.17	N/A	65
BANKERS GRANIT FIX INC (R)	FI	NO	0.9	10.34	10,589.00	☆	☆	0.0	0.00	0.71	N/A	N/A
BANKERS GRANIT GOVT (R)	FI	NO	1.6	10.35	13,700.50	☆	☆	0.0	0.02	0.67	N/A	N/A
BANKERS GRANIT GR STK (R)	GI	NO	1.3	14.84	11,231.00	☆	☆	0.0	0.00	0.18	N/A	N/A
BANKERS GRANIT STOCK (R)	GI	NO	65.2	11.93	11,740.30	13,218.40	24,774.20	5.9	0.43	0.23	N/A	36
BARTLETT BASIC VALUE	EI	NO	25.0	13.52	10,601.90	11,075.20	21,666.30	8.3	0.00	0.81	N/A	66
BARTLETT CORPORATE CASH	I	NO	14.0	1.07	#10,150.70	12,914.10	☆	0.0	0.00	0.08	N/A	N/A
BARTLETT FIXED INCOME	GI	NO	6.7	9.99	11,535.70	13,510.60	☆	3.6	1.81	0.15	N/A	83
BASCOM HILL INVESTORS	G	NO	3.9	18.34	11,797.10	12,242.70	☆	0.0	0.00	0.67	N/A	N/A
BEACON HILL MUTUAL	FI	NO	215.4	27.44	10,353.00	13,940.70	☆	0.0	0.00	0.00	N/A	N/A
BENHAM GNMA	FI	NO	5.0	10.16	10,974.70	15,106.60	☆	2.9	0.00	0.76	N/A	46
BENHAM TARGET 1990	FI	NO	4.2	14.80	11,907.50	17,051.10	26,114.60	2.5	0.00	2.18	N/A	N/A
BENHAM TARGET 1995	FI	NO	4.4	51.19	12,443.10	18,566.60	19,606.20	2.9	0.48	1.26	N/A	34
BENHAM TARGET 2000	FI	NO	2.3	33.31	13,373.60	12,238.30	☆	3.2	0.00	0.97	N/A	37
BENHAM TARGET 2005	FI	NO	4.2	22.32	14,506.00	13,730.90	23,742.20	1.9	0.00	0.72	N/A	18
BENHAM TARGET 2010	GI	NO	5.5	16.58	11,306.30	14,262.10	22,689.10	0.7	0.11	0.32	N/A	N/A
BERWYN FUND	GI	NO	0.2	12.24	#10,025.00	12,809.40	22,488.20	0.0	0.00	0.09	N/A	N/A
BLANCHARD STRATEGIC GRO	CA	NO	55.8	8.02	11,967.70	12,263.80	☆	3.5	0.95	0.00	19.8	27
BLC CAPITAL ACCUMULATION	FI	SC	43.9	20.48	10,298.10	12,076.20	20,681.10	11.6	0.00	0.71	N/A	N/A
BLC GOVT SEC INCOME	FI	SC	26.5	20.83	12,044.70	13,863.30	☆	1.7	1.46	1.18	19.1	41
BLC GROWTH FUND	CA	SC	2.4	21.84	12,438.90	☆	20,017.50	0.0	0.00	0.37	N/A	83
BMI EQUITY FUND	FI	SC	530.2	38.71	10,996.30	12,091.10	☆	9.8	1.44	0.00	N/A	142
BOND FUND OF AMERICA	FI	SC	22.8	14.66	10,844.70	13,907.40	29,681.40	9.3	86.00	1.44	N/A	112
BOND PORT FOR ENDOWMENTS	G	NO	474.2	922.95	12,194.40	12,214.90	17,393.60	1.3	3.04	0.47	17.3	59
BOSTON CO CAPITAL APPREC	FI	NO	8.0	35.34	#10,227.30	9,685.40	20,461.70	0.0	0.00	0.38	N/A	N/A
BOSTON CO GNMA	FI	NO	29.1	12.31	11,056.90	16,526.20	☆	11.1	0.14	1.34	N/A	173
BOSTON CO MANAGED INCO	G	NO	67.5	12.02	12,566.50	12,964.30	☆	1.3	1.46	0.31	25.7	258
BOSTON CO SPECIAL GROWTH	G	NO	6.8	24.15	11,111.20	13,095.30	☆	1.4	0.79	0.17	N/A	70
BOSTON MUTUAL FUND	G	NO	3.8	11.44	10,380.20		☆	0.4	0.00	0.01	N/A	9
BOWSER GROWTH	G	NO	2.9	2.45	13,770.80		☆	8.7	36.95	10.20	N/A	85
BRUCE FUND	G	NO	90.3	117.52	12,013.10		☆	1.1	1.69	0.20	21.9	79
BULL&BEAR CAPITAL GROWTH	GI	NO	8.3	16.88	11,854.50		☆	4.8	1.27	0.60	N/A	95
BULL&BEAR EQUITY-INCOME	EI	NO		11.90								

PERFORMANCE OF MUTUAL FUNDS (continued)

FUND NAME	OBJ.	LOAD	TOTAL NET ASTS (MIL) 6/30/86	NAV 6/30/86	PERFORMANCE (RETURN ON INITIAL $10,000 INVESTMENT) 12/31/85-6/30/86	6/30/85-6/30/86	6/30/81-6/30/86	PER SHARE LATEST 12 MONTHS CAP GAINS	INC DIVS	YIELD % 6/30/86	LATEST AVAILABLE PRICE/EARNINGS	ANNUAL % TURNOVER
BULL&BEAR HIGH YIELD	F	NO	113.6	14.93	10,922.10	11,774.40	☆	0.00	1.89	12.7	N/A	127
BULL&BEAR SPECIAL EQU (R)	CA	NO	1.5	19.15	$12,766.70	☆	☆	0.00	0.00	0.0	N/A	N/A
BULL&BEAR US GOVT SEC	FI	NO	8.8	14.84	$10,208.00	☆	☆	0.00	0.47	0.0	N/A	N/A
BULLOCK AGGRESSIVE GRO	G	SC	6.5	10.08	13,315.70	13,566.60	☆	0.30	0.00	0.0	N/A	151
BULLOCK BALANCED SHARES	B	SC	72.8	15.83	11,953.10	13,682.90	26,255.80	0.35	0.72	4.5	14.0	20
BULLOCK DIVIDEND SHARES	GI	SC	374.3	4.09	12,416.40	14,000.00	26,244.70	0.62	0.13	3.0	17.6	15
BULLOCK GROWTH FUND	G	SC	180.3	11.61	12,706.60	14,011.30	21,818.90	0.00	0.16	1.3	22.5	66
BULLOCK HIGH INCO SHS	FI	SC	188.1	10.79	10,621.90	11,492.00	19,880.70	0.00	1.45	13.5	N/A	61
BULLOCK MONTHLY INCOME	FI	SC	44.2	12.43	10,726.50	11,773.80	23,678.90	0.00	1.26	10.1	N/A	142
BULLOCK US GOVT INC	FI	SC	67.0	12.23	10,305.80	10,890.60	☆	0.00	1.32	10.9	N/A	90
CALDWELL FUND	G	NO	0.5	13.57	11,955.90	☆	☆	0.03	0.37	N/A	N/A	N/A
CALVERT EQUITY	GI	NO	8.7	23.42	11,852.20	13,211.50	☆	0.00	0.34	1.5	N/A	38
CALVERT INCOME	FI	NO	21.0	17.58	10,894.20	12,193.20	☆	0.00	1.59	9.0	N/A	11
CALVERT SOCIAL INV GRO	GI	NO	74.9	25.19	12,404.20	13,291.20	☆	0.16	0.77	3.0	N/A	54
CANADIAN FUND	IF	SC	24.9	8.37	10,209.50	10,515.90	14,369.90	0.45	0.20	2.3	N/A	28
CAPITAL PRES T NOTE TR	FI	NO	28.5	11.29	11,011.30	11,941.50	19,769.40	0.23	1.01	8.9	N/A	53
CAP SUPERVISORS HELIOS	G	NO	23.0	3,641.44	12,884.80	14,081.50	☆	0.84	4.32	1.2	N/A	70
CARDINAL FUND	GI	SC	81.4	16.50	12,383.20	13,724.10	27,188.70	0.00	0.34	2.0	19.7	13
CARDINAL GOVT GUARTD	FI	SC	82.1	9.34	10,229.50	☆	☆	0.00	0.40	0.0	N/A	N/A
CARNEGIE CAPPIELLO GROW	G	SC	50.5	15.65	11,828.60	12,896.00	☆	0.46	0.24	1.5	N/A	50
CARNEGIE HI YLD GOVT	FI	LO	22.1	10.62	10,554.50	11,714.50	☆	0.00	0.82	7.8	N/A	N/A
CARNEGIE TOTAL RETURN	GI	LO	43.0	10.80	11,352.30	☆	☆	0.00	0.15	0.0	N/A	N/A
CENTURY SHARES TRUST	S	NO	163.3	20.98	12,125.10	13,592.40	26,897.50	0.71	0.54	2.5	23.5	6
CHARTER FUND	CA	NO	89.6	8.49	12,354.80	13,558.30	19,798.10	0.51	0.17	1.9	23.5	68
CHEAPSIDE DOLLAR	G	NO	57.9	13.57	12,132.50	13,097.80	15,892.70	0.73	0.24	1.8	20.1	59
CHEMICAL FUND	TK	NO	775.2	9.67	12,200.70	14,063.80	19,458.80	3.13	0.14	1.2	21.4	62
CIGNA AGGRESSIVE GROWTH	SG	SC	20.1	13.74	11,179.60	12,364.60	☆	0.27	0.11	0.8	22.0	66
CIGNA GROWTH	G	SC	235.2	16.41	11,962.30	13,215.40	20,346.20	1.06	0.40	2.4	N/A	39
CIGNA HIGH YIELD	FI	SC	203.7	10.79	11,225.60	12,278.30	24,229.50	0.00	1.27	11.8	N/A	79
CIGNA INCOME	FI	SC	246.3	8.08	11,209.40	12,438.50	23,360.20	0.00	0.71	8.9	N/A	38
CIGNA VALUE	GI	SC	44.0	13.67	11,042.60	11,958.30	☆	0.30	0.40	2.9	N/A	46
CLAREMONT—BOND	FI	NO	2.9	10.76	10,227.10	10,931.30	☆	0.00	0.19	1.8	N/A	487
CLAREMONT—COMBINED	GI	NO	6.0	12.85	11,618.40	12,748.00	☆	0.00	0.00	0.0	N/A	48
CLAREMONT—STOCK	G	NO	3.0	11.92	10,806.90	11,663.40	☆	0.00	0.00	0.0	N/A	44
CLIPPER FUND	GI	NO	64.0	42.34	11,705.80	12,818.70	☆	0.38	0.84	2.0	11.6	15
COLONIAL ADV STR GOLD	AU	SC	19.5	14.33	9,998.50	10,634.50	☆	0.00	0.05	0.3	N/A	N/A
COLONIAL CORP CASH I	EI	LO	379.9	49.59	10,533.10	10,977.30	☆	0.63	4.57	9.2	18.9	288
COLONIAL CORP CASH II	EI	LO	281.8	48.23	10,275.90	10,517.60	☆	0.20	4.12	8.5	15.7	106
COLONIAL EQUITY INCOME	EI	SC	10.8	17.51	11,679.40	13,002.30	☆	1.80	0.00	0.0	15.0	156
COLONIAL FUND	GI	SC	154.7	19.13	11,937.30	13,401.70	23,229.80	0.45	0.90	4.6	15.0	69
COLONIAL GOVT SEC PLUS	FI	SC	2,422.2	12.79	10,921.00	11,950.50	23,968.40	0.41	1.06	8.2	N/A	249
COLONIAL GOVT MORTGAGE	FI	SC	18.1	14.52	10,421.40	11,151.30	☆	0.26	1.31	9.0	N/A	565
COLONIAL GROWTH SHARES	G	SC	85.7	13.67	12,286.90	13,177.70	20,774.30	0.53	0.12	0.8	19.4	49
COLONIAL HIGH YIELD	FI	SC	295.2	7.79	10,979.50	12,001.60	22,549.60	0.00	0.96	12.3	N/A	63
COLONIAL INCOME FUND	FI	SC	151.6	7.29	10,723.40	11,750.30	22,192.50	0.00	0.83	11.4	N/A	51
COLONIAL OPTION INC I	OI	SC	1,263.9	8.23	10,603.40	11,636.10	17,930.80	0.94	0.21	2.4	26.0	121
COLONIAL OPTION INC II	OI	SC	214.4	11.32	10,772.40	11,463.00	☆	1.30	0.28	2.3	21.2	210
COLUMBIA FIXED INCOME	FI	NO	102.0	12.99	10,451.90	11,498.30	☆	0.00	1.32	10.2	N/A	94
COLUMBIA GROWTH	G	NO	292.3	29.90	11,933.40	12,875.40	24,914.20	2.56	0.40	1.3	21.8	93
COLUMBIA SPECIAL (R)	CA	NO	25.3	33.30	13,898.20	☆	☆	0.00	0.00	0.0	N/A	112
COMMERCE INCOME SHARES	I	SC	70.2	11.25	11,296.00	11,957.10	22,080.30	0.78	0.36	3.1	26.2	168
COMMONWEALTH A&B	GI	SC	10.7	1.71	11,621.20	12,465.60	22,062.90	0.09	0.09	5.1	N/A	55
COMMONWEALTH C	GI	SC	43.1	2.32	11,471.50	12,376.10	20,810.40	0.12	0.10	4.4	N/A	59
COMPANION FUND	GI	NO	86.0	14.40	12,053.20	12,914.30	20,914.30	1.25	0.43	2.9	16.9	43
COMPOSITE BOND & STOCK	B	NO	74.1	10.84	11,262.50	12,047.40	21,390.70	0.64	0.70	6.3	14.2	125

Fund	Obj	Load	Net Assets	NAV	Value 1	Value 2	Value 3	Col A	Col B	Col C	Col D	Rank
COMPOSITE GROWTH FD	GI	NO	69.3	12.77	11,920.60	12,734.00	22,172.60	3.4	0.72	0.45	14.7	117
COMPOSITE INCOME FUND	FI	NO	50.6	9.45	10,471.60	11,150.20	22,119.50	12.6	0.00	1.19	N/A	90
COMPOSITE US GOVT SEC	FI	LO	90.1	1.06	10,432.70	11,235.20		10.8	0.00	0.11	N/A	N/A
CONCORD FUND	G	NO	1.7	28.38	10,350.10	10,731.10	16,048.10	3.9	0.00	1.12	23.6	N/A
CONSTELLATION GROWTH	CA	NO	151.3	30.04	13,786.10	14,960.20	18,611.60	0.0	0.00	0.00	N/A	N/A
CONTINENTAL EQUITY + (R)	G	LO	2.2	10.18	$10,387.80	☆	☆	0.0	0.00	0.00	N/A	N/A
CONTINENTAL OPTION INC +	OI	SC	12.8	8.73	9,620.10	☆	☆	0.0	0.00	0.38	N/A	N/A
CONTINENTAL OP INC + II (R)	OI	LO	0.1	9.82	10,020.40	☆	☆	0.0	0.00	0.00	N/A	N/A
CONTINENTAL US GOVT + (R)	FI	LO	2.1	9.86	$10,061.20			0.0	0.53	0.00	N/A	N/A
CONVERTIBLE YIELD SEC	FI	SC	21.8	13.71	11,745.80	12,403.60	17,660.10	5.2	0.00	0.72	N/A	103
COPLEY TAX-MANAGED	GI	NO	27.6	10.77	11,481.90	12,350.90	24,421.80	0.0	0.00	0.00	N/A	19
CORPORATE CASH MGT	FI	NO	302.3	46.21	10,143.50	10,462.70		8.9	0.00	4.10	N/A	129
CORPORATE LEADERS TR-B (X)	GI	SC	76.1	14.69	12,074.30	13,574.50	23,949.00	7.9	1.40	1.21	N/A	N/A
CORPORATE PREFERRED FD	FI	LO	48.0	48.03	10,107.50	10,524.40		9.7	0.00	4.63	N/A	N/A
COUNTRY CAPITAL GROWTH	G	SC	75.1	20.64	11,530.70	12,889.40	21,073.10	3.1	0.95	0.64	21.3	60
COUNTRY CAPITAL INCOME	FI	SC	4.7	11.32	11,185.70	12,201.80	21,589.70	7.2	0.00	0.81	N/A	88
CRITERION BD INV QUAL	FI	LO	108.6	10.39	11,060.30	11,918.90	23,185.40	10.4	0.52	1.14	N/A	93
CRITERION BD USG HI YLD	FI	SC	2,105.9	9.85	10,423.70	11,058.00	☆	8.8	0.46	0.88	N/A	N/A
CRITERION TECHNOLOGY	TK	SC	0.2	15.83	12,074.80	13,529.90	☆	0.0	0.00	0.00	N/A	N/A
CRITERION US GOVT INSTL	FI	LO	164.9	9.89	10,426.40			0.0	0.19	0.33	N/A	N/A
CUMBERLAND GROWTH	CA	NO	2.1	34.97	11,625.70	12,334.10	18,100.90	1.7	0.00	0.59	N/A	N/A
DEAN WITTER CONVERT (R)	FI	NO	1,342.3	12.04	11,929.30	☆	☆	0.4	0.00	0.55	21.5	51
DEAN WITTER DEV GRO (R)	SG	SC	188.1	9.94	11,295.50	11,970.70	☆	0.4	0.14	0.04	18.4	6
DEAN WITTER DIVID GRO (R)	GI	SC	1,084.4	18.98	11,876.50	13,356.50	25,696.00	2.7	0.00	0.52	N/A	126
DEAN WITTER HIGH YIELD	FI	SC	1,049.8	14.33	11,134.10	12,077.10	23,206.80	12.6	0.00	1.80	19.2	61
DEAN WITTER IND VAL (R)	G	NO	76.3	15.21	12,150.00	13,819.60	18,670.30	2.2	0.00	0.33	22.4	78
DEAN WITTER NTRL RES (R)	NR	NO	38.4	7.31	10,221.20	10,550.40	10,023.40	3.0	1.10	0.21	17.4	170
DEAN WITTER OPT INC (R)	OI	NO	591.2	10.19	10,784.90	11,495.80	☆	2.2	0.00	0.23	N/A	8
DEAN WITTER TX-ADVAN	FI	NO	303.9	10.32	10,320.70	10,765.40		7.9	0.00	0.81	N/A	98
DEAN WITTER US GOVT (R)	FI	NO	9,697.3	10.28	10,244.40	10,901.40		11.0	0.00	1.12	N/A	64
DEAN WITTER WORLD WIDE (R)	GL	SC	325.8	16.13	12,570.70	15,937.20	25,025.90	0.6	0.49	0.09	19.8	75
DECATUR INCOME	EI	NO	1,071.4	18.57	10,764.50	12,740.30		4.7	1.56	0.91	15.9	312
DECISION FUNDS-GOVT INC	FI	SC	3.7	11.08	10,724.50	11,733.00		9.3	0.12	1.03	N/A	32
DECISION FUNDS-GRO	G	SC	1.7	14.89	12,115.50	13,816.60		0.0	0.18	0.12	N/A	51
DECISION FUNDS-GRO & INC	GI	NO	2.7	14.75	12,384.00	13,858.20	25,649.40	0.4	0.16	0.05	16.1	132
DELAWARE FUND	GI	SC	426.9	24.38	10,450.00	13,163.50	☆	2.8	2.00	0.70	N/A	N/A
DELAWARE GNMA SR (R)	FI	SC	34.8	9.27	10,417.60	☆	☆	0.0	0.00	0.84	N/A	N/A
DELAWARE US GOVT SR (R)	FI	SC	35.6	9.25	$17,607.60		☆	0.0	0.00	0.82	N/A	N/A
DELCAP FUND I	CA	SC	6.3	16.78		12,145.80		0.0	0.00	0.00	N/A	104
DELCHESTER BOND FUND	FI	SC	126.8	8.17	11,116.70	14,137.00	23,925.60	14.7	1.19	1.19	30.2	85
DELTA TREND FUND	CA	NO	110.1	8.91	13,064.50	15,256.10	22,450.10	1.4	0.00	0.12	N/A	55
DIT AGGRESSIVE GROWTH	CA	NO	46.0	29.60	13,436.20	13,140.40	☆	0.0	0.34	0.00	N/A	68
DIT CAPITAL GROWTH	G	NO	12.6	16.47	12,065.90	11,867.70		0.0	0.00	0.07	N/A	152
DIT CURRENT INCOME	_	NO	4.9	10.57	11,023.80	12,972.80	17,133.50	10.7	0.02	1.13	20.0	55
DE VEGH MUTUAL	G	NO	60.3	15.89	11,796.40	10,983.50		1.6	1.29	0.27	N/A	257
DFA-FIXED INCOME PORT	FI	NO	315.4	102.32	10,487.20	13,043.30		8.4	0.43	8.60	23.0	10
DFA SMALL COMPANY	SG	NO	1,047.4	209.71	11,869.50	11,610.50	19,116.60	1.2	6.49	2.45	N/A	27
DIV/GROWTH DIVIDEND SR	EI	NO	4.7	26.30	11,610.50	11,380.90		4.1	1.68	1.10	N/A	47
DIV/GRO LASER & ADV TECH	TK	NO	0.3	11.83	11,380.90	9,916.20		0.0	0.00	0.00	23.6	26
DODGE & COX BALANCED	B	NO	27.5	34.28	11,630.70	13,274.30	23,300.00	4.8	1.79	1.68	24.7	22
DODGE & COX STOCK	GI	NO	46.0	33.02	11,760.90	13,773.40	25,533.50	2.9	2.60	1.01	18.6	114
DREXEL BURNHAM FUND	GI	LO	137.5	23.84	12,216.40	13,758.70	22,747.10	3.5	2.05	0.86	N/A	57
DREXEL SR-BOND-DEB (R)	FI	NO	14.2	11.81	10,768.40	11,820.40	☆	8.3	0.13	0.99	N/A	N/A
DREXEL SR-CONVERTIBLE (R)	FI	NO	36.3	10.77	$10,770.00		☆	0.0	0.00	0.00	N/A	49
DREXEL SR-EMERGING GRO (R)	SG	NO	45.1	17.44	13,192.60	15,347.40		0.0	0.17	0.00	N/A	407
DREXEL SR-GOVT (R)	FI	NO	283.4	10.76	10,417.80	10,968.50		7.8	0.31	0.85	N/A	42
DREXEL SR-GROWTH (R)	G	NO	22.6	12.70	11,312.80	12,453.10		2.2	0.42	0.29	N/A	

PERFORMANCE OF MUTUAL FUNDS (continued)

FUND NAME	OBJ.	LOAD	TOTAL NET ASTS (MIL) 6/30/86	NAV 6/30/86	PERFORMANCE (RETURN ON INITIAL $10,000 INVESTMENT) 12/31/85-6/30/86	6/30/85-6/30/86	6/30/81-6/30/86	YIELD % 6/30/86	CAP GAINS	INC DIVS	PRICE/ EARNINGS	ANNUAL % TURNOVER
DREXEL SR-OPTION INC (R)	OI	NO	36.2	10.94	11,009.80	11,624.30	☆	2.8	0.70	0.32	N/A	84
DREYFUS A BONDS PLUS	FI	NO	223.3	15.02	10,769.30	11,940.30	21,635.60	9.3	0.00	1.40	N/A	21
DREYFUS CAPITAL VALUE	CA	NO	10.9	22.13	13,211.90			0.0	0.00	0.57	N/A	N/A
DREYFUS CONVERTIBLE SEC	—	NO	157.8	9.14	12,199.80	13,768.50	22,980.00	5.8	0.65	0.00	25.6	32
DREYFUS CORP CASH	EI	NO	0.2	0.00	N/A			0.0	0.00	0.59	N/A	N/A
DREYFUS FUND	GI	SC	2,670.5	13.75	11,732.00	12,741.20	19,933.10	4.0	1.75	1.56	19.9	83
DREYFUS GNMA	FI	NO	1,800.1	15.43	10,314.00	11,210.90	☆	10.1	1.09	0.20	N/A	N/A
DREYFUS GRO OPPORTUNITY	G	SC	505.8	12.07	11,595.40	13,643.80	15,899.20	1.6	1.94	0.78	28.3	56
DREYFUS LEVERAGE FUND	CA	SC	529.9	21.39	11,837.30	13,321.80	23,457.10	3.5	0.00	0.00	21.5	82
DREYFUS NEW LEADERS	SG	NO	79.5	24.03	13,261.60	15,977.40	☆	0.0	0.51	0.20	24.4	81
DREYFUS THIRD CENTURY	G	NO	175.5	8.04	10,720.00	11,834.60	15,723.50	2.5	0.23	0.13	N/A	45
EAGLE GROWTH SHARES	G	SC	4.2	7.77	10,210.20	10,932.10	15,147.40	1.6	1.49	0.59	24.4	246
EATON & HOWARD STOCK	GI	NO	86.0	15.05	11,672.50	13,004.20	23,631.40	3.7	0.30	1.20	15.5	70
EATON VANCE GOVT OBLIG	FI	SC	336.4	12.40	10,735.90	11,514.80	☆	9.6	0.63	0.14	N/A	82
EATON VANCE GROWTH	G	SC	85.3	8.24	11,746.80	13,388.10	21,593.80	1.7	0.00	0.60	22.0	59
EATON VANCE HIGH YIELD	—	SC	30.7	5.31	10,774.10	11,878.30	23,035.30	11.3	0.00	1.03	N/A	51
EATON VANCE INC OF BOSTON	—	SC	42.9	10.22	10,916.10	12,032.60	22,151.20	10.1	0.96	0.52	10.7	57
EATON VANCE INVESTORS	B	SC	237.6	8.58	11,192.50	12,250.70	22,461.80	5.7	1.27	0.05	17.4	64
EATON VANCE SPL EQUITIES	G	SC	50.1	21.73	11,902.50	12,509.40	20,056.00	0.2	2.07	1.13	24.5	45
EATON VANCE TX-MGD (X)	UT	SC	568.9	23.09	12,635.90	14,829.60	☆	4.7	2.07	1.13	12.4	85
88 FUND	G	SC	0.2	10.41	10,889.10	10,600.80	☆	0.0	1.64	0.99	N/A	N/A
ELFUN TRUSTS	G	NO	525.7	31.26	11,940.10	13,483.40	24,937.40	3.1	155.00	80.00	22.5	20
ENDOWMENTS INC	GI	NO	38.3	20.39	11,544.00	12,736.10	24,872.50	3.9	0.93	0.92	17.3	18
ENERGY FUND	NR	NO	384.9	13.45	10,653.10	11,493.60	16,386.70	4.5	0.00	0.00	17.5	82
EQUITEC SIEBEL AGGRES (R)	CA	NO	5.8	9.88	\$13,450.00		☆	0.0	0.00	0.11	N/A	N/A
EQUITEC SIEBEL HI YLD (R)	FI	NO	4.5	13.99	\$9,989.90		☆	1.8	0.01	0.25	N/A	N/A
EQUITEC SIEBEL TOTL RETN	GI	SC	59.5	9.93	11,776.30	13,451.70	☆	0.0	0.00	0.11	N/A	77
EQUITEC SIEBEL US GOVT (R)	FI	NO	14.4	9.93	\$10,039.90		☆	0.7	0.53	0.17	N/A	5
EUROPACIFIC GROWTH	IF	SC	131.2	22.75	12,574.00	15,700.60	☆	0.9	0.65	0.14	17.9	59
EVERGREEN FUND	G	NO	713.6	14.91	12,536.10	14,206.80	24,937.80	0.9	0.75	1.01	14.0	82
EVERGREEN TOTAL RETURN	EI	NO	568.4	19.96	11,946.40	13,241.00	29,227.90	4.9	1.29	0.33	26.9	19
EXPLORER FUND (X)	TK	NO	359.4	36.35	10,776.80	11,734.70	15,792.90	0.3	0.00	0.08	28.3	3
EXPLORER II	SG	NO	42.0	23.25	11,529.90	11,677.20	☆	0.9	0.06	0.06	25.5	149
FAIRFIELD FUND	SG	NO	57.3	12.36	12,210.50	13,342.50	17,929.10	0.5	23.98	2.19	N/A	129
FAIRMONT FUND	CA	NO	76.2	237.09	11,437.20	13,456.60	17,479.80	0.9	0.85	0.40	18.3	22
FARM BUREAU GROWTH FUND	GI	NO	47.3	9.89	10,319.20	12,402.20	☆	2.3	0.00	0.43	N/A	N/A
FEDERATED BOND (R)	FI	NO	1.4	10.80	10,148.40	10,615.70	☆	8.0	0.00	0.86	N/A	38
FEDERATED CORP CASH	FI	NO	144.5	11.23	10,391.00	11,389.50	☆	10.5	0.02	1.17	N/A	141
FEDERATED GNMA TRUST	GI	NO	1,046.4	16.61	10,976.40	14,248.30	☆	1.8	0.07	0.29	15.1	46
FEDERATED GROWTH TRUST	FI	SC	53.7	12.74	11,461.20	11,840.80	22,585.00	12.2	0.00	1.55	N/A	26
FEDERATED HIGH INCOME	G	NO	334.2	11.17	11,071.30		☆	0.0	0.03	0.29	N/A	N/A
FEDERATED HI QUAL STK (R)	FI	NO	2.1	11.04	10,347.30	11,913.90	☆	12.2	0.07	1.35	N/A	31
FEDERATED HIGH YIELD TR	FI	NO	83.1	10.61	10,527.80	11,033.80	☆	10.6	0.06	1.13	N/A	235
FEDERATED INCOME TRUST	FI	NO	452.6	10.14	10,641.40	11,327.60	☆	9.5	0.98	0.97	N/A	126
FEDERATED INTMDT GOVT	FI	NO	1,249.1	10.45	11,070.70	11,096.30	☆	9.5	0.71	0.98	N/A	138
FEDERATED SH-INTMDT GOVT	B	NO	2,915.9	15.67	11,697.90	12,046.80	24,420.70	5.6	0.68	0.90	15.3	42
FEDERATED STOCK & BOND	GI	NO	63.6	22.59	10,290.20	12,970.10	☆	2.9	0.00	0.65	14.9	35
FEDERATED STOCK TRUST	GI	NO	449.6	9.87	\$11,162.30		☆	0.0	0.00	0.42	N/A	N/A
FEDERATED US GOVT (R)	FI	NO	4.1	11.14	10,197.50	10,719.30	18,068.20	8.6	0.00	0.00	N/A	20
FENIMORE INTL (R)	IF	NO	55.2	12.30	11,594.70	13,061.60	☆	1.9	0.88	0.37	18.1	135
FIDELITY ADJUSTABLE RATE	FI	NO	273.4	12.90	12,414.90	14,308.60	29,328.00	2.9	0.95	0.46	16.3	86
FIDELITY CONTRAFUND	G	NO	92.7	16.04					1.14			
FIDELITY DESTINY I	G	SC	1,165.7									

340

Fund	Obj	Ld	Net Assets	NAV	$10,000	5-Yr	10-Yr					Rank
FIDELITY DESTINY II	G	SC	4.6	16.53	16,334.00	☆	22,616.70	0.0	0.00	0.00	N/A	N/A
FIDELITY DISCOVERER	CA	NO	136.8	26.35	12,109.40	13,117.50	27,745.60	1.6	0.00	0.42	21.4	246
FIDELITY EQUITY-INCOME	EI	LO	3,090.9	29.33	11,611.30	12,686.20	21,362.80	5.6	1.78	1.70	16.4	118
FIDELITY FLEXIBLE BOND	FI	NO	249.9	7.38	10,877.40	11,972.90	☆	9.9	0.98	0.73	N/A	164
FIDELITY FREEDOM FUND	CA	NO	942.8	17.39	12,169.50	13,965.50	24,896.90	2.0	1.98	0.35	24.0	100
FIDELITY FUND	FI	NO	873.7	19.39	12,151.80	13,575.10	20,393.00	3.6	0.00	0.72	21.4	215
FIDELITY GNMA	FI	NO	600.3	10.50	10,517.10	☆	☆	9.4	0.00	0.64	N/A	137
FIDELITY GOVT SECURITIES	GI	NO	406.6	10.18	10,898.10	11,835.90	☆	11.1	0.13	0.95	N/A	N/A
FIDELITY GROWTH & INC	FI	NO	267.2	13.86	13,860.00	☆	25,581.30	0.8	3.99	0.00	21.1	157
FIDELITY HIGH INCOME	FI	NO	1,333.2	10.00	11,275.50	12,406.20	37,547.10	9.2	1.75	1.12	18.8	126
FIDELITY MAGELLAN FUND	G	LO	7,412.0	54.12	13,002.80	15,241.20	☆	10.3	0.13	0.46	23.0	129
FIDELITY MERCURY	GI	LO	224.0	18.94	12,624.60	14,483.40	☆		1.75	0.07	N/A	72
FIDELITY MORTGAGE	FI	NO	617.5	10.42	10,450.50	11,303.70	☆		0.13	1.07	N/A	63
FIDELITY OVERSEAS	IF	LO	1,826.3	27.20	14,904.10	20,937.50	☆		0.45	0.00	20.0	122
FIDELITY OTC	SG	LO	946.5	20.30	12,743.30	14,838.00	☆		0.01	0.01	15.0	133
FIDELITY PURITAN	EI	NO	2,189.5	13.98	11,512.20	12,631.40	26,564.20	6.9	1.16	0.97	12.0	36
FIDELITY QUALIFIED DVD	EI	LO	206.1	15.63	11,662.40	12,405.10	☆	7.5	1.22	1.21	N/A	N/A
FIDELITY SEL AIR TRANS (R)	EI	LO	0.9	10.13	10,663.20	☆	☆	0.0	0.00	0.00	N/A	N/A
FIDELITY SEL AMER GOLD (R)	AU	LO	7.6	10.18	10,159.70	☆	☆	0.0	0.00	0.00	N/A	N/A
FIDELITY SEL BIO TECH (R)	S	LO	57.2	14.14	14,140.00	☆	☆	0.0	0.00	0.00	N/A	271
FIDELITY SEL BROKERAGE (R)	S	LO	25.5	13.61	12,272.30	☆	☆	0.0	0.00	0.00	N/A	N/A
FIDELITY SEL CHEMICAL (R)	TK	LO	42.5	16.05	12,954.00	☆	☆	0.0	0.00	0.00	15.2	163
FIDELITY SEL COMPUTER (R)	TK	LO	10.8	12.90	11,355.60	☆	☆	0.0	0.00	0.00	N/A	N/A
FIDELITY SEL DEFENSE (R)	S	LO	10.6	16.60	11,600.30	☆	☆	0.0	0.00	0.00	13.4	170
FIDELITY SEL ELECTRONIC (R)	TK	LO	2.9	10.10	9,090.90	12,528.30	☆	0.0	0.00	0.00	N/A	N/A
FIDELITY SEL ENERGY (R)	NR	LO	44.3	10.41	9,524.20	☆	☆	0.0	0.00	0.00	33.5	159
FIDELITY SEL ENERGY SER (R)	NR	LO	1.0	9.16	9,015.70	☆	☆	0.0	0.00	0.00	20.9	243
FIDELITY SEL FINANCIAL (R)	S	LO	208.6	36.82	13,216.10	10,019.20	11,195.20	0.0	0.00	0.00	N/A	N/A
FIDELITY SEL FOOD (R)	S	LO	37.7	15.41	13,388.40	☆	☆	0.0	0.00	0.00	21.5	46
FIDELITY SEL HEALTH (R)	H	LO	408.1	38.04	14,011.00	14,900.80	38,560.50	0.0	0.00	0.00	N/A	N/A
FIDELITY SEL LEISURE (R)	S	LO	348.1	24.57	13,834.50	☆	☆	0.0	0.00	0.00	N/A	N/A
FIDELITY SEL LIFE INS (R)	S	LO	2.4	11.74	11,943.00	15,203.80	☆	0.0	0.00	0.00	N/A	N/A
FIDELITY SEL PREC-MTLS (R)	AU	LO	102.8	8.50	10,011.80	15,739.90	8,962.20	0.0	0.00	0.00	23.9	126
FIDELITY SEL PROP&CAS (R)	S	LO	7.4	12.62	12,384.70	☆	☆	0.0	0.00	0.00	N/A	N/A
FIDELITY SEL RETAIL (R)	S	LO	38.3	13.38	13,653.10	8,284.60	☆	0.0	0.00	0.00	10.0	52
FIDELITY SEL S&L (R)	TK	LO	50.5	14.57	14,425.70	☆	☆	0.0	0.00	0.00	N/A	214
FIDELITY SEL SOFTWARE (R)	TK	LO	17.8	13.55	12,196.20	☆	☆	0.0	0.00	0.00	N/A	68
FIDELITY SEL TECH (R)	TK	LO	239.7	22.66	10,304.70	☆	23,619.60	0.0	0.00	0.00	21.6	62
FIDELITY SEL TELECOM (R)	TK	LO	6.2	13.11	11,918.20	11,485.00	☆	0.0	0.00	0.00	N/A	108
FIDELITY SEL UTILITIES (R)	UT	LO	112.2	27.39	12,282.50	☆	☆	0.0	0.00	0.00	N/A	110
FIDELITY SPL SITUATIONS	CA	LO	38.2	17.30	12,824.30	13,426.50	21,595.20	1.3	1.16	0.24	18.9	88
FIDELITY THRIFT TRUST	FI	NO	292.9	11.24	10,797.40	14,961.10	21,488.20	7.5	3.21	0.84	N/A	38
FIDELITY TREND	G	NO	834.6	51.42	12,238.00	11,736.90	☆	1.5	0.33	0.79	26.1	N/A
FTP-EQUITY PRT GROWTH	CA	NO	74.7	14.44	12,813.80	13,576.30	☆	0.1	0.34	0.02	N/A	152
FTP-EQUITY PRT INCOME	EI	NO	497.1	13.50	11,620.70	14,859.90	☆	5.9	0.80	0.80	17.6	96
FTP-FIXED INCOME PORT	FI	NO	345.1	11.16	10,892.10	12,714.90	☆	9.4	1.04	1.04	N/A	133
FIDUCIARY CAPITAL GROWTH	GI	NO	65.5	26.38	12,315.60	13,385.30	☆	0.7	0.02	0.19	N/A	54
FIDUCIARY VALQUEST	CA	NO	1.8	10.82	10,566.40	13,284.70	☆	0.0	0.03	0.00	18.9	235
FINANCIAL DYNAMICS	G	NO	87.9	9.02	12,136.20	13,284.70	19,447.30	0.6	1.24	0.06	26.1	N/A
FINANCIAL HIGH YIELD BND	FI	NO	36.3	8.77	11,109.80	12,264.10	21,813.30	2.5	0.45	1.05	N/A	96
FINANCIAL INDUST FUND	GI	NO	417.0	5.27	11,439.90	12,859.40	21,813.30	0.0	0.45	0.13	17.6	133
FINANCIAL INDUST INCOME	EI	NO	341.8	9.10	11,995.10	13,719.10	27,618.30	4.4	1.89	0.48	17.1	54
FINANCIAL PORT-ENERGY	NR	NO	1.1	8.16	9,807.70	10,390.60	☆	1.9	0.15	0.15	N/A	235
FINANCIAL PORT-EUROPEAN	IF	NO	0.2	8.04	$10,050.00	☆	☆	0.0	0.00	0.00	N/A	N/A
FINANCIAL PORT-FINANCIAL	S	NO	0.2	8.13	$10,162.50	☆	☆	0.0	0.00	0.00	N/A	N/A
FINANCIAL PORT-GOLD	AU	NO	2.2	4.07	10,024.60	8,702.30	☆	2.6	0.00	0.10	N/A	46

PERFORMANCE OF MUTUAL FUNDS (continued)

Performance columns show RETURN ON INITIAL $10,000 INVESTMENT. Per-share figures are for the LATEST 12 MONTHS. Price/Earnings and Annual % Turnover are LATEST AVAILABLE. (☆ = data not available for that period.)

FUND NAME	OBJ.	LOAD	TOTAL NET ASTS (MIL) 6/30/86	NAV 6/30/86	Perf 12/31/85-6/30/86	Perf 6/30/85-6/30/86	Perf 6/30/81-6/30/86	YIELD % 6/30/86	CAP GAINS	INC DIVS	PRICE/ EARNINGS	ANNUAL % TURNOVER
FINANCIAL PORT-HEALTH	H	NO	6.2	15.20	14,218.90	15,035.10	☆	0.1	0.00	0.01	N/A	203
FINANCIAL PORT-LEISURE	S	NO	7.0	15.61	13,962.40	15,290.00	☆	0.3	0.00	0.04	N/A	160
FINANCIAL PORT-PACIFIC	IF	NO	4.8	11.79	13,838.00	15,764.40	☆	0.3	0.00	0.03	N/A	161
FINANCIAL PORT-TECH	TK	NO	2.8	10.24	11,570.60	13,281.50	☆	0.0	0.00	0.00	N/A	175
FINANCIAL PORT-UTILITIES	UT	NO	0.2	8.29	$10,362.50	☆	☆	0.0	0.00	0.00	N/A	N/A
FINANCIAL SELECT INCOME	FI	NO	19.4	7.32	11,200.70	12,470.80	20,579.70	9.8	0.00	0.72	N/A	146
FINANCIAL US GOVT	FI	NO	3.5	7.63	$10,432.90	☆	☆	0.0	0.00	0.32	N/A	N/A
FIRST INV ADJ RATE PRF	FI	NO	37.9	0.92	10,160.60	10,494.70	☆	8.4	0.24	0.07	N/A	105
FIRST INV BOND APPREC	FI	SC	188.7	13.88	11,428.70	12,210.10	19,123.30	9.1	0.80	1.28	39.3	150
FIRST INV DISCOVERY	SG	SC	42.7	10.99	10,406.90	10,658.90	13,978.90	1.1	0.00	0.12	28.9	27
FIRST INV FD FOR GROWTH	G	SC	65.4	6.58	10,974.30	10,922.80	12,188.70	0.0	0.41	0.00	11.1	41
FIRST INV FD FOR INCOME	FI	SC	1,645.9	11.98	10,951.50	11,714.80	18,114.40	12.9	0.00	0.79	N/A	96
FIRST INV GOVT	FI	SC	132.4	13.76	10,437.80	11,124.10	☆	10.8	0.08	1.30	N/A	107
FIRST INV INTERNATIONAL	GL	SC	29.0	12.64	12,085.70	12,104.80	☆	0.2	1.44	0.03	N/A	61
FIRST INV NTRL RESOURCES	NR	SC	8.5	3.18	7,459.70	6,632.50	5,090.40	6.6	0.00	0.21	N/A	37
FIRST INV 90/10	OG	SC	12.2	5.05	10,322.90	10,443.40	☆	6.6	0.51	0.84	23.0	250
FIRST INV OPTION FD	OI	SC	206.6	14.64	11,370.20	11,257.60	15,583.10	2.6	0.48	0.14	N/A	155
FIRST INV SPECIAL BOND	FI	SC	10.1	14.79	13,396.70	12,408.60	☆	11.2	0.00	1.67	N/A	153
FIRST INV US GOVT PLUS-I	I	SC	2.7	12.24	10,692.00	☆	☆	0.0	0.00	0.00	N/A	N/A
FPA CAPITAL	G	SC	52.5	9.49	10,588.60	13,343.80	18,708.00	2.8	1.02	0.37	21.5	76
FPA NEW INCOME	FI	SC	6.1	13.18	10,400.80	11,551.20	20,356.10	8.9	0.00	0.84	N/A	132
FPA PARAMOUNT (X)	GI	SC	127.9	19.45	10,963.20	10,842.70	25,421.70	5.6	1.54	0.78	12.2	158
FPA PERENNIAL FUND	GI	SC	56.8	10.37	$10,141.10	11,850.10	☆	2.6	0.60	0.51	14.4	59
FIRST TRUST US GOVT	FI	LO	129.5	18.35	12,457.60	☆	☆	0.0	0.00	0.33	N/A	N/A
FLAG INV TELEPHONE INC	I	NO	103.2	21.24	11,809.10	13,726.10	☆	5.8	0.86	1.08	N/A	26
FLEX FUND-BOND	FI	NO	5.5	23.89	10,728.40	11,396.70	☆	8.9	0.00	1.88	N/A	239
FLEX FUND-CORP INCOME	EI	NO	4.8	13.06	12,527.00	☆	☆	0.0	0.00	0.27	N/A	4
FLEX FUND-CAPITAL GAINS	CA	NO	9.1	13.63	12,357.20	13,351.30	☆	2.1	0.00	0.21	N/A	244
FLEX FUND-RETIRMNT GRO	CA	NO	62.9	4.21	11,409.20	13,102.30	☆	3.1	0.00	0.42	16.5	163
44 WALL STREET	CA	LO	34.4	6.42	13,048.80	10,794.90	3,292.80	0.0	0.00	0.00	20.8	112
44 WALL STREET EQUITY	LO	LO	12.9	10.62	13,046.70	14,657.50	10,155.80	0.0	0.00	0.00	N/A	186
FOUNDERS GROWTH	G	NO	69.4	15.84	10,979.70	14,054.30	22,054.50	1.6	0.00	0.16	20.7	126
FOUNDERS EQUITY INCOME	EI	NO	12.0	11.97	12,451.40	11,521.10	18,395.10	4.8	0.31	0.77	N/A	18
FOUNDERS MUTUAL	GI	NO	201.7	34.25	12,837.30	14,401.30	24,012.00	2.7	1.84	0.34	17.8	192
FOUNDERS SPECIAL	CA	NO	96.5	9.05	10,097.80	13,036.40	18,187.20	0.8	0.00	0.27	31.1	22
FRANKLIN CORP CASH	EI	LO	74.1	11.63	11,015.60	10,477.60	☆	8.6	0.00	0.77	N/A	36
FRANKLIN DYNATECH	TK	LO	43.1	7.19	12,458.30	11,594.80	19,810.10	2.1	0.00	0.25	27.6	53
FRANKLIN EQUITY FUND	G	LO	161.3	6.82	9,702.20	14,124.90	25,331.90	1.6	0.23	0.11	14.9	1
FRANKLIN GOLD FUND	AU	LO	93.1	15.97	11,443.40	8,176.80	10,979.50	4.5	0.00	0.31	28.2	24
FRANKLIN GROWTH	G	LO	44.1	2.19	11,026.30	12,833.70	22,064.90	1.6	0.18	0.26	22.5	156
FRANKLIN INCOME	I	LO	183.3	6.51	11,053.30	11,319.50	23,869.10	9.9	0.05	0.22	7.9	9
FRANKLIN OPTION	OI	LO	19.3	7.34	10,355.70	11,958.50	19,499.00	0.0	1.03	0.12	N/A	7
FRANKLIN US GOVERNMENT	FI	LO	3,031.5	8.08	11,816.40	11,312.30	21,425.30	12.1	0.00	0.89	N/A	93
FRANKLIN UTILITIES	UT	LO	187.6	15.53	10,823.80	12,203.60	28,889.90	6.7	0.52	0.54	9.7	N/A
FREEDOM GOLD & GOVT	AU	SC	41.6			11,649.60	☆	7.5	1.20		42.0	
FREEDOM GOVT PLUS (R)	FI	NO	24.5	10.15	$10,150.00	☆	☆	0.0	0.00	0.00	N/A	N/A
FREEDOM REGIONAL BANK	S	NO	63.1	13.46	13,465.60	☆	☆	0.0	0.48	0.17	10.9	N/A
FT INTERNATIONAL	IF	LO	89.6	20.58	13,665.00	19,646.60	☆	0.4	0.34	0.08	N/A	61
FUND FOR US GOVT SEC	FI	LO	902.4	8.56	10,301.60	10,975.70	21,537.10	11.3	0.00	0.96	N/A	N/A
FUND OF AMERICA	FI	SC	161.6	12.20	10,991.60	12,123.00	23,509.20	3.5	0.12	0.43	26.7	35
FUNDAMENTAL INVESTORS	GI	NO	531.1	15.59	12,198.70	14,029.30	26,432.50	2.4	1.51	0.40	23.9	20
FUNDTRUST AGGRESSIVE GR	GI	NO	21.9	14.17	11,664.40	13,013.80	☆	1.8	0.09	0.25	N/A	N/A
FUNDTRUST EQUITY	CA	NO	1.0	11.22	11,220.00	☆	☆	0.0	0.00	0.00	N/A	N/A
FUNDTRUST GROWTH FUND	G	NO	20.2	13.35	11,338.40	12,434.80	☆	2.9	0.07	0.39	N/A	16

Fund	Obj	Load	Net Assets	NAV									
FUNDTRUST GROWTH & INC	GI	NO	23.0	13.28	11,408.80	12,421.70			3.0	0.15	0.40	N/A	47
FUNDTRUST HIGH YIELD	FI	NO	2.3	10.37	10,940.00	★			0.0	0.00	0.56	N/A	N/A
FUNDTRUST INCOME FUND	I	NO	18.4	10.89	10,601.90	11,298.90			11.0	0.01	1.20	N/A	120
FUNDTRUST INTERNATIONAL	IF	NO	6.5	13.27	13,125.60	★			0.0	1.90	0.00	N/A	N/A
GPM FUND	GI	NO	6.4	23.12	11,921.70	13,053.20		25,172.90	3.0	0.00	0.69	N/A	N/A
GABELLI ASSET	G	NO	24.7	11.21	$11,210.00	★		★	0.0	1.40	0.00	N/A	N/A
GATEWAY GROWTH PLUS	G	NO	2.7	10.81	$10,810.00	★		★	2.5	0.03	0.00	18.6	103
GATEWAY OPTION INCOME	OI	NO	37.6	15.21	11,009.00	11,524.60		16,747.60	8.2	13.14	0.40	12.1	122
GEICO ADJ RATE PREFERRED	FI	NO	79.1	25.32	10,173.40	10,631.40			6.2	0.00	2.07	N/A	N/A
GEMINI FUND (X)	G	NO	101.6	78.31	11,831.30	12,744.40		26,472.30	0.0	0.16	5.30	N/A	198
GENERAL AGGRESSIVE GRO	CA	NO	26.5	22.72	13,341.20	16,345.30		25,185.40	9.4	2.96	0.00	23.6	N/A
GENL ELEC LT INTEREST	FI	NO	606.4	12.36	11,149.30	12,351.30		22,068.50	0.0	2.96	1.17	23.6	N/A
GENL ELEC S&S PROGRAM	G	NO	877.4	43.39	11,956.80	11,374.90		22,068.50	3.5	0.84	1.57		N/A
GENL ELEC S&S PROGRAM	G	NO	877.4	43.39	11,956.80	11,374.90		21,089.80	3.5	0.00	1.57		1
GENL ELEC S&S PROGRAM	G	NO	17.2	14.01	11,061.80	12,981.20			4.9	0.00	0.71		N/A
GENERAL SECURITIES	GI	NO	0.8	14.37	11,692.40	12,570.70			2.9	1.35	0.42	31.7	N/A
GIBRALTAR FUND	CA	NO	21.0	11.86	11,860.00	★			0.0	3.09	0.00	34.5	100
GINTEL CAPITAL APPREC	GI	NO	88.1	44.56	12,040.90	13,948.80			2.7	0.00	1.20	N/A	25
GINTEL ERISA	GI	NO	132.2	94.72	11,903.60	13,081.90		26,650.20	1.7	1.68	1.68	N/A	N/A
GINTEL FUND	G	NO	9.8	102.51	$10,251.00	★		★	0.0	0.00	0.04	N/A	N/A
GAM GLOBAL	GL	NO	23.5	194.12	13,121.50	18,454.00		8,103.60	0.0	12.36	0.04		30
GAM INTERNATIONAL	IF	NO	20.6	9.98	10,450.30	9,812.30		★	0.4	0.14	0.76		17
GOLCONDA INVESTORS LTD	AU	NO	1.6	13.55	11,966.20	12,867.50		★	5.6	1.02	1.02		94
GIT EQUITY INCOME	EI	NO	7.8	11.29	12,047.30	12,047.30		★	9.1	0.00	1.15		70
GIT A RATED INCOME	FI	NO	15.3	9.99	11,006.70	11,934.90		★	11.5	0.36	0.30		48
GIT MAX INCOME	FI	NO	2.9	15.17	12,287.20	14,101.90		★	0.6	0.25	0.11		30
GIT SELECT GROWTH	SG	NO	18.6	18.08	12,983.10	14,959.40		★	0.2	0.35	0.02		99
GIT SPECIAL GROWTH	SG	NO	17.3	13.97	13,041.00	14,616.10		★	2.0	0.53	0.31		71
GRADISON EMERGING GROWTH	G	NO	32.9	15.25	11,621.20	12,814.40		★	5.3	0.25	0.76		57
GRADISON ESTABLISHED GRO	GI	NO	1.0	14.22	11,431.30	11,884.10		19,283.00	9.7	0.23	1.32		350
GREENFIELD FUND	GI	NO	14.1	13.50	10,951.60	11,877.80			0.5	0.62	0.05	35.8	162
GREENSPRING FUND	GI	NO	20.3	11.15	11,708.90	12,998.60		16,655.10	1.2	0.87	0.22	N/A	24
GREENWAY FUND	CA	NO	829.2	17.78	12,253.60	13,410.30		23,073.10	0.0	0.00	0.07	21.2	14
GROWTH FUND OF AMERICA	G	SC	54.7	12.81	12,635.30	★		★	1.9	1.99	0.24	N/A	43
GROWTH FD OF WASHINGTON	G	SC	83.5	11.89	12,203.30	12,886.80		20,530.40	0.0	0.00	0.00	N/A	N/A
GROWTH INDUSTRY SHARES	G	NO	6.4	15.93	11,678.90	★		★	0.0	0.61	0.00	N/A	N/A
GT EUROPE GROWTH	IF	NO	4.2	16.16	13,517.30	★		★	0.0	0.16	0.02	N/A	N/A
GT INTERNATIONAL GRO	IF	NO	3.3	17.81	14,535.60	15,896.30		17,050.60	0.0	0.00	0.01	19.1	81
GT JAPAN GROWTH	IF	NO	48.5	25.39	14,400.40	11,872.90		★	6.2	0.00	0.76	17.4	48
GT PACIFIC GROWTH FD	IF	NO	45.5	12.26	10,823.40	12,822.80		24,834.40	3.6	6.44	1.76	17.3	57
GUARDIAN BOND FUND	FI	NO	558.1	45.72	11,775.80	14,390.60		30,618.90	1.3	2.34	0.32	N/A	80
GUARDIAN MUTUAL	G	NO	132.5	24.42	12,823.00	14,155.40			1.0	0.65	0.19	N/A	61
GUARDIAN PARK AVENUE	G	SC	44.8	18.64	12,601.90	11,319.70			5.7	0.05	0.08	31.1	42
GUARDIAN STOCK FUND	G	SC	1.5	1.51	10,769.40	13,665.80		19,551.50	2.8	0.20	0.23	N/A	144
GUIDANCE INVESTMENTS	I	NO	257.4	8.07	12,036.40	11,898.80		22,652.20	9.4	0.00	1.53	N/A	100
HAMILTON FUNDS	GI	SC	1,085.2	16.24	10,745.90	14,999.30			0.2	0.02	0.02	27.6	9
J HANCOCK BOND	FI	SC	32.9	14.94	12,830.90	14,663.70		21,975.40	1.1	0.77	0.20	N/A	67
J HANCOCK GLOBAL	GL	SC	98.9	17.91	13,147.20	13,917.30			0.4	0.00	0.02	N/A	15
J HANCOCK GROWTH	G	SC	14.0	7.21	11,985.00	11,892.80		19,136.00	8.7	0.00	0.84	N/A	9
J HANCOCK SPEC EQUITY	SG	SC	165.4	9.61	10,875.40	11,340.40		★	10.0	0.00	1.07	N/A	14
J HANCOCK US GOVT SEC	FI	SC	322.6	10.68	10,442.80	★		★	0.0	0.00	0.14	N/A	N/A
J HANCOCK US GUAR MORT	FI	SC	71.2	9.96	$10,099.90	★		★	0.0	0.00	0.24	N/A	N/A
J HANCOCK VAR SR AGG GRO	CA	NO	115.7	9.89	$10,134.30	★		★	0.0	0.00	0.10	N/A	N/A
J HANCOCK VAR SR BOND	FI	NO	6.1	9.99	$10,215.70	★		★	0.0	0.00	0.18	N/A	N/A
J HANCOCK VAR SR STOCK	CA	NO	11.1	10.03	12,326.10	13,023.00		17,241.30	0.0	1.06	0.23	N/A	93
J HANCOCK VAR SR TOT RTN	B	NO	45.7	12.77	13,146.20	14,970.60		14,289.40	0.0	0.00	0.02	43.2	107
HARTWELL GROWTH FUND	CA	NO	26.2	17.80	12,035.50	13,752.00			0.5	0.22	0.20	N/A	64
HARTWELL LEVERAGE FUND	CA	NO	36.4	15.85	12,022.60				0.0	0.00	0.08	N/A	N/A
HEARTLAND VALUE	CA	LO		11.71							0.00		
HERITAGE CAPITAL APPREC	CA	LO											

●Copyright Lipper Analytical Services, Inc.

343

PERFORMANCE OF MUTUAL FUNDS (continued)

FUND NAME	OBJ.	LOAD	TOTAL NET ASTS (MIL) 6/30/86	NAV 6/30/86	PERFORMANCE (RETURN ON INITIAL $10,000 INVESTMENT) 12/31/85-6/30/86	6/30/85-6/30/86	6/30/81-6/30/86	YIELD % 6/30/86	PER SHARE LATEST 12 MONTHS CAP GAINS	INC DIVS	PRICE/EARNINGS	ANNUAL % TURNOVER
HIGH YIELD SECURITIES	FI	SC	$89.3	$10.06	10,700.40	$11,576.60	$21,040.70	12.3	$0.00	$1.24	N/A	65
HOME INV GUAR INCOME (R)	FI	NO	166.9	10.49	10,345.80	11,152.70	☆	11.1	0.09	1.17	N/A	19
HUTTON INV SR-BASIC VAL	G	NO	299.5	13.06	11,698.20	12,821.80	☆	2.6	0.13	0.34	N/A	16
HUTTON INV SR-BOND (R)	FI	NO	316.2	12.90	11,212.70	12,761.50	☆	8.8	0.00	1.13	N/A	717
HUTTON INV SR-GOVT	FI	NO	4,353.3	10.51	10,819.70	11,721.60	☆	10.5	0.00	1.10	N/A	457
HUTTON INV SR-GROWTH (R)	G	NO	1,215.9	16.87	12,199.20	13,423.00	☆	1.6	1.55	0.28	N/A	603
HUTTON INV SR-OPTION	OI	NO	86.3	9.05	10,439.50	10,777.00	☆	7.0	0.37	0.65	N/A	206
HUTTON INV SR-PREC METAL	AU	NO	25.9	9.23	10,048.80	9,109.20	☆	0.3	0.00	0.02	N/A	65
HUTTON INV SPECIAL EQU (R)	SG	NO	265.6	15.75	12,022.20	13,240.50	☆	0.3	0.00	0.04	N/A	146
IDEX FUND	CA	SC	60.0	12.96	12,101.60	12,988.70	24,723.50	1.4	0.02	0.18	N/A	N/A
IDS BOND FUND	FI	LO	1,772.8	5.43	11,347.40	12,516.40	☆	9.7	0.00	0.52	N/A	164
IDS DISCOVERY FUND	SG	SC	328.7	8.89	11,774.80	13,551.00	☆	1.2	0.11	0.10	28.3	52
IDS EQUITY +	GI	SC	403.3	11.34	12,356.80	14,023.20	20,510.60	3.3	0.18	0.37	20.4	110
IDS EXTRA INCOME	FI	SC	809.7	5.38	11,215.00	12,173.10	☆	10.8	0.04	0.58	N/A	89
IDS FEDERAL INCOME	G	SC	201.6	5.10	10,517.00	☆	☆	0.5	0.01	0.41	N/A	N/A
IDS GROWTH FUND	G	SC	870.7	25.93	13,414.40	14,622.80	21,534.90	0.1	0.04	0.11	29.3	40
IDS INTERNATIONAL	IF	NO	183.8	9.40	13,165.30	17,558.30	☆	0.0	0.00	0.01	N/A	38
IDS LIFE CAPITAL RES	G	NO	295.6	17.79	11,059.20	☆	☆	0.0	0.00	0.31	N/A	N/A
IDS LIFE EQUITY	G	NO	0.3	10.38	$10,380.00	☆	☆	0.0	0.00	0.00	N/A	N/A
IDS LIFE GOVT	FI	NO	0.5	10.03	$10,521.90	☆	☆	0.0	0.00	0.48	N/A	N/A
IDS LIFE INCOME	—	NO	0.5	10.03	$10,548.60	☆	☆	0.0	0.00	0.51	N/A	N/A
IDS LIFE MANAGED	B	NO	1.6	10.48	$10,480.00	☆	☆	0.0	0.00	0.00	N/A	N/A
IDS LIFE SPEC INCOME	FI	NO	282.8	12.50	11,156.00	14,311.70	☆	2.3	0.02	1.05	N/A	89
IDS MANAGED RETIREMENT	B	SC	268.8	7.46	12,790.20	12,857.20	☆	6.8	0.54	0.17	17.7	83
IDS MUTUAL	B	SC	1,305.2	13.31	11,706.40	14,416.60	24,805.90	1.4	0.64	0.90	31.2	105
IDS NEW DIMENSIONS	G	SC	597.8	12.11	13,134.50	9,418.20	25,980.40	1.9	0.00	0.16	N/A	N/A
IDS PRECIOUS METALS	AU	SC	11.4	4.22	10,373.70	☆	☆	2.8	0.00	0.08	N/A	78
IDS PROGRESSIVE	CA	SC	197.6	8.13	11,370.60	12,957.40	25,178.10	2.8	0.50	0.22	25.8	176
IDS SELECTIVE	FI	SC	1,089.4	8.92	11,108.40	12,301.20	25,050.00	9.7	0.00	0.86	N/A	122
IDS STOCK	GI	SC	1,520.4	22.54	12,387.20	13,835.70	21,966.80	2.9	0.64	0.64	20.9	N/A
IDS STRATEGY AGGR EQ (R)	CA	NO	148.8	10.64	13,559.10	15,809.00	☆	0.0	0.10	0.00	26.2	26
IDS STRATEGY EQUITY (R)	G	NO	71.2	7.58	11,372.50	12,543.10	☆	2.8	0.09	0.21	N/A	36
IDS STRATEGY INCOME (R)	FI	NO	94.2	6.12	11,099.30	12,201.30	☆	8.4	0.09	0.51	N/A	80
INCOME FUND OF AMERICA	EI	SC	557.4	12.80	11,230.80	12,150.10	25,992.00	6.7	0.80	0.88	13.9	51
INDUSTRIAL-AMERICAN	G	SC	6.3	9.14	9,896.90	☆	☆	0.0	0.00	0.08	22.9	N/A
INDUSTRIAL-BOND	FI	SC	0.2	9.35	10,237.40	☆	☆	0.0	0.00	0.34	N/A	N/A
INDUSTRIAL-GOVERNMENT	FI	SC	23.0	9.18	10,126.20	☆	☆	0.0	0.00	0.64	N/A	N/A
INDUSTRIAL-OPTION INC	OI	SC	35.0	9.08	10,706.70	☆	☆	0.0	0.00	0.76	N/A	N/A
INDUSTRY FUND OF AMERICA	CA	NO	0.5	5.58	9,425.70	8,678.10	7,072.20	0.0	0.00	0.00	N/A	N/A
INSIDER REPORTS	G	LO	4.7	13.42	10,770.50	10,840.10	☆	0.0	0.03	0.17	N/A	32
INTEGRATED CAP APPREC (R)	G	NO	113.9	14.65	12,502.20	14,023.60	☆	1.2	0.00	2.23	N/A	36
INTEGRATED CORP INVESTOR	FI	NO	17.2	23.40	9,899.20	10,299.40	☆	9.6	0.00	0.00	N/A	N/A
INTL CASH-EUROCASH	IF	LO	0.1	0.00	N/A	☆	☆	0.0	0.00	0.00	N/A	5
INTERNATIONAL INVESTORS	AU	SC	692.8	9.49	10,205.90	9,163.60	13,330.60	5.1	0.00	0.48	28.6	577
INTERSTATE CAP GROWTH	CA	NO	3.8	6.72	10,162.80	11,107.40	6,553.00	0.0	0.00	0.44	18.9	18
INVESTMENT CO OF AMERICA	GI	SC	3,664.4	14.29	12,060.60	13,846.50	26,382.80	2.9	1.48	0.44	19.4	112
INVEST PORT-EQUITY (R)	G	NO	223.6	11.64	10,629.20	12,124.70	☆	0.3	0.17	0.04	N/A	426
INVEST PORT-GOVT PLUS (R)	FI	NO	3,762.7	8.53	11,270.70	11,270.70	☆	9.3	0.21	0.80	N/A	138
INVEST PORT-HIGH YLD (R)	FI	NO	129.1	9.73	11,125.90	11,917.00	☆	9.9	0.10	0.97	N/A	149
INVEST PORT-OP INC (X,R)	OI	NO	331.6	8.19	10,375.10	10,855.70	20,029.90	2.3	1.06	0.20	21.5	26
INVESTMENT TRUST BOSTON	GI	NO	73.3	12.82	11,830.10	13,162.60	☆	2.5	1.05	0.34	16.3	43
ITB HIGH INCOME PLUS	FI	SC	22.7	14.99	10,831.20	11,686.20	☆	10.3	0.20	1.56	N/A	N/A

INVESTORS RESEARCH	CA	SC	74.5	7.71	15,328.00	15,467.30	30,376.40	1.4	0.31	0.11	27.3	65
IRI STOCK FUND	G	LO	15.5	10.74	12,444.30	14,329.20		2.2	0.87	0.25	N/A	37
ISI GROWTH FUND	G	SC	14.6	7.89	11,333.20	12,411.00	18,421.60	2.5	0.00	0.20	N/A	163
ISI INCOME FUND	_	SC	6.9	3.78	10,323.50	10,629.80	18,155.60	5.6	0.00	0.21	N/A	N/A
ISI TRUST FUND	GI	SC	109.9	11.15	10,777.00	11,551.60	16,065.70	4.9	0.02	0.55	27.7	97
IVY GROWTH	G	SC	166.4	16.05	11,355.20	12,696.80	27,411.60	2.8	1.34	0.46	20.0	132
IVY INSTITUTIONAL (X)	G	NO	145.4	149.02	11,762.40	13,673.60		3.9	14.58	6.15	21.1	79
IVY INTERNATIONAL	IF	NO	4.8	11.15	#10,045.00	☆	☆	0.0	0.73	0.00	N/A	N/A
JANUS FUND	CA	NO	542.1	15.79	11,971.20	13,103.90	23,221.70	3.3	0.54	0.44	31.1	163
JANUS VALUE	CA	NO	10.8	14.70	12,088.80	13,146.90		3.0	0.09	0.68	N/A	68
JANUS VENTURE	SG	NO	31.2	32.55	13,082.80	14,393.90		2.1	0.70	0.50	N/A	293
JP GROWTH FUND	G	SC	25.8	16.78	11,976.00	13,011.50	24,520.40	2.8	1.64	0.84	N/A	94
JP INCOME FUND	FI	SC	19.7	9.89	11,069.20	12,463.30	23,950.50	8.5	0.00	0.30	21.4	6
KEMPER GROWTH FUND	G	SC	301.3	13.83	11,409.30	12,643.10	21,185.70	2.1	1.44	1.28	N/A	97
KEMPER HIGH YIELD	FI	SC	304.3	11.46	11,196.30	12,129.60	25,641.90	11.2	0.00	0.99	N/A	87
KEMPER INCOME & CAP PRES	FI	SC	179.6	9.15	10,982.10	11,884.00	23,292.20	10.8	0.82	0.16	N/A	243
KEMPER INTERNATIONAL FD	IF	SC	141.2	22.50	12,398.70	17,958.40	☆	0.7	1.40	0.27	23.2	135
KEMPER OPTION INCOME (X)	OI	SC	707.0	10.50	10,379.50	10,798.60	16,946.80	2.4	0.13	0.11	21.5	181
KEMPER SUMMIT FUND	G	SC	342.8	6.44	11,965.80	13,047.40	22,241.90	1.7	0.42	0.78	22.4	60
KEMPER TOTAL RETURN	B	LO	578.6	17.83	12,012.60	13,280.50	22,089.80	4.3	0.05	1.02	N/A	176
KEMPER US GOVT SEC	FI	LO	1,942.1	9.86	10,995.80	11,901.10	22,215.70	10.3	0.00	1.68	N/A	556
KEYSTONE B-1 (R)	FI	NO	192.4	17.49	10,836.70	12,072.20	22,499.40	9.6	0.00	2.00	N/A	48
KEYSTONE B-2 (R)	FI	NO	424.9	19.99	10,949.50	12,035.80	22,035.10	10.0	0.46	1.00	N/A	103
KEYSTONE B-4 (X,R)	FI	NO	1,556.7	8.28	10,937.60	11,917.70	21,510.90	12.1	0.34	0.13	11.9	43
KEYSTONE INTERNATIONAL	IF	NO	67.3	7.06	12,429.60	15,597.20	18,590.80	1.8	0.44	0.56	16.9	73
KEYSTONE INTERNATIONAL (R)	_	NO	418.5	10.50	11,672.40	12,779.40	23,276.10	5.3	0.08	0.11	19.6	109
KEYSTONE K-1 (R)	FI	NO	297.4	9.23	12,065.40	14,013.60	22,316.10	1.2	0.44	0.36	22.3	109
KEYSTONE K-2 (R)	FI	NO	55.0	10.65	10,073.80	8,387.90	9,356.90	3.4	0.08	0.94	30.3	42
KEYSTONE PREC METALS (R)	AU	NO	117.8	25.81	12,338.00	13,450.50	21,395.50	1.9	0.94	0.50	21.8	106
KEYSTONE S-1 (R)	GI	NO	273.5	10.63	12,260.70	13,232.20	20,290.80	1.9	0.36	0.01	25.3	137
KEYSTONE S-3 (R)	G	NO	709.7	6.71	11,893.40	12,991.30	15,343.60	0.1	0.88	0.21	25.6	60
KEYSTONE S-4 (R)	G	NO	29.9	17.74	11,647.60	☆	☆	0.0	0.00	0.70	N/A	N/A
KIDDER PEABODY EQU INC (R)	EI	NO	125.0	14.70	10,083.40	☆	☆	1.0	0.26	0.16	N/A	N/A
KIDDER PEABODY GOV INC (R)	FI	NO	39.5	16.10	11,961.40	11,776.70	☆	1.2	0.04	0.07	17.8	203
KIDDER PEABODY SPL GR (R)	G	NO	49.9	10.86	11,776.70	13,165.80	☆	0.0	1.18	0.38	N/A	N/A
LEGG MASON TOTAL RETURN	G	NO	668.0	30.02	12,070.00			1.1	0.00	0.00	38	38
LEGG MASON VALUE TRUST	G	SG	52.4	12.07	12,502.90	13,391.10	28,191.80	2.4	2.53	0.25	N/A	162
LEGG MASON SPECIAL INV	SG	NO	126.3	21.24	11,960.70	13,448.60	23,621.50	1.7	2.05	0.53	24.1	46
LEHMAN CAPITAL FUND	GI	NO	449.2	21.00	11,354.50	12,660.60	26,833.40	4.9	1.39	0.47	19.9	24
LEHMAN INVESTORS	CA	NO	109.7	27.58	11,140.30	12,639.10	14,486.70	0.0	0.51	0.75	23.8	28
LEHMAN OPPORTUNITY	GI	NO	28.1	15.06	11,025.30	11,793.40	17,620.20	9.9	0.68	0.00	16.3	78
LEPERCQ-ISTEL FUND	CA	NO	30.5	9.00	10,354.50	11,271.10	19,674.00	0.5	0.00	0.78	30.0	168
LEVERAGE FUND OF BOSTON	AU	NO	115.4	7.95	10,340.00	10,309.70	11,653.30	1.6	0.00	0.01	N/A	30
LEXINGTON GNMA INCOME	FI	NO	15.5	3.50	12,663.70	13,844.00	14,601.50	4.0	0.20	0.20	19.3	151
LEXINGTON GOLDFUND	G	NO	35.2	19.70	12,201.90	13,413.90	21,056.40	0.1	0.83	0.83	15.4	86
LEXINGTON GROWTH	G	NO	133.0	14.67	12,688.20	14,020.50		10.9	2.16	0.02	N/A	51
LEXINGTON RESEARCH	G	SC	13.3	10.54	10,294.00	11,228.80		7.1	0.74	1.15	N/A	N/A
LG FUND FOR GROWTH	FI	LO	44.5	4.50	10,769.70	11,521.40	19,464.20		0.10	0.32	110	110
LG US GOVT SECURITIES	FI	NO	9.7	11.38	10,766.20				0.05	0.44	N/A	N/A
LIBERTY FUND	FI	NO	2.4	14.69	12,149.20	13,337.60	13,337.60	5.6	0.63	0.83	N/A	N/A
LIFE OF VIRGINIA-BOND	G	NO	1.5	12.30	11,680.30	11,788.30	30,108.60	5.6	0.55	0.40	N/A	9
LIFE OF VIRGINIA-COM STK	GI	NO	1.4	24.85	11,159.70	11,742.00	25,042.80	8.6	0.59	2.15	9.8	46
LIFE OF VIRGINIA-TOT RTN	EI	NO	63.3	21.16	11,043.80	12,178.10		0.5	0.86	0.11	N/A	25
LINDNER DIVIDEND (X)	G	NO	391.4	29.20	11,295.90	15,209.70	34,795.20	2.6	0.77	0.55	10.9	209
LINDNER FUND (X)	G	NO	83.9	26.09	13,580.50	14,669.40	27,310.20	0.6	5.86	0.16	16.2	186
LMH FUND	G	NO	232.2	25.11	12,695.60	20,760.30		3.7	1.25	0.94	36.0	82
LOOMIS-SAYLES CAPITAL (X)	B	NO	173.1	10.87	11,043.10	11,805.80	20,760.30	11.0	0.14	1.20	27.1	14
LOOMIS-SAYLES MUTUAL	FI	SC	536.7	8.95	11,419.50	12,240.50	15,467.00	0.0	0.39	0.00	24.2	
LORD ABBETT BOND-DEB	SG	SC	318.0									

©Copyright Lipper Analytical Services, Inc.

PERFORMANCE OF MUTUAL FUNDS (continued)

FUND NAME	OBJ.	LOAD	TOTAL NET ASTS (MIL) 6/30/86	NAV 6/30/86	PERFORMANCE (RETURN ON INITIAL $10,000 INVESTMENT) 12/31/85-6/30/86	6/30/85-6/30/86	6/30/81-6/30/86	YIELD % 6/30/86	PER SHARE LATEST 12 MONTHS CAP GAINS	PER SHARE LATEST 12 MONTHS INC DIVS	LATEST AVAILABLE PRICE/EARNINGS	LATEST AVAILABLE ANNUAL % TURNOVER
LORD ABBETT US GOVT	FI	SC	213.8	3.24	10,677.50	11,575.20	21,943.00	10.6	0.07	0.34	N/A	363
LORD ABBETT VALUE APPREC	G	SC	336.8	13.60	12,442.80	14,421.60		1.6	0.86	0.23	20.3	21
LOWRY MARKET TIMING	CA	SC	93.4	10.47	10,705.50	10,625.20		0.8	0.26	0.09	N/A	61
LUTHERAN BRO FUND	GI	SC	175.5	17.42	11,118.20	12,046.50	25,368.90	3.6	0.90	0.65	14.8	40
LUTHERAN BRO INCOME	FI	SC	433.4	8.89	10,422.70	11,102.20	21,510.80	11.0	0.00	0.97	N/A	39
MANHATTAN FUND	CA	NO	288.1	9.97	12,162.20	13,692.10	28,397.20	0.8	0.59	0.08	22.2	155
HORACE MANN BALANCED	B	NO	3.5	15.07	11,374.70	12,426.10		1.8	0.18	0.28	N/A	30
HORACE MANN GROWTH	G	NO	83.8	26.86	11,706.10	12,682.40	20,617.30	2.4	2.20	0.68	21.0	28
HORACE MANN INCOME	I	NO	0.7	14.00	11,307.10	12,527.20		4.6	0.01	0.65	N/A	9
MARINER EQUITY	CA	NO	5.5	9.99	*9,990.00	☆	☆	0.0	0.00	0.00	N/A	N/A
MARINER INTERM BOND	G	NO	14.1	10.05	*10,132.60	☆	☆	0.0	0.00	0.08	N/A	N/A
MASS CAPITAL DEVELOPMENT	G	SC	1,035.1	13.77	11,840.50	12,703.30	22,062.30	1.5	0.88	0.22	23.1	101
MASS FINL BOND	FI	SC	309.0	14.87	10,919.40	12,179.10	23,733.50	9.7	0.00	1.44	N/A	262
MASS FINL DEVELOPMENT	GI	SC	287.7	14.79	12,437.30	13,650.50	21,406.70	1.8	0.98	0.26	23.5	75
MASS FINL EMERGING GRO	SG	SC	300.6	21.51	13,164.00	14,235.60		0.0	0.00	0.00	28.4	68
MASS FINL HIGH INCOME	FI	SC	843.3	7.21	10,810.10	12,043.90	25,192.40	12.9	0.09	0.93	N/A	49
MASS FINL INTL TR-BOND	GL	SC	118.0	12.21	11,786.60	13,782.10	21,855.70	6.2	0.65	0.77	N/A	307
MASS FINL SPECIAL	CA	SC	129.4	9.91	12,878.40	13,538.90		1.0	0.55	0.10	24.2	125
MASS FINL TOTAL RETURN	B	SC	310.1	11.34	11,901.60	13,268.00	25,220.20	5.3	0.56	0.60	18.7	71
MASS INVESTORS GROWTH	G	SC	1,035.4	13.42	12,136.40	13,393.90	20,168.20	1.7	1.45	0.23	24.8	66
MASS INVESTORS TRUST	GI	SC	1,326.4	14.41	12,058.10	13,598.70	20,917.50	2.9	1.08	0.43	19.8	33
MATHERS FUND	G	NO	162.5	19.51	11,513.10	12,665.00	17,242.70	3.7	5.01	0.81	26.0	278
MAXIM BOND	FI	NO	9.4	1.24	10,922.40	12,086.20		5.6	0.00	0.06	N/A	N/A
MAXIM GROWTH	G	NO	34.2	1.31	10,929.80	12,177.50		2.9	0.00	0.03	N/A	N/A
MBL GROWTH FUND	G	NO	30.3	14.60	12,237.90	13,664.90		2.7	0.61	0.40	N/A	33
MEDICAL RESEARCH INV	H	NO	1.4	14.77	12,787.90			0.0	0.00	0.00	N/A	N/A
MEDICAL TECHNOLOGY FUND	H	NO	97.6	15.87	13,494.90			0.1	0.06	0.01	33.8	21
MEESCHAERT CAPITAL	G	NO	32.6	30.54	12,177.00	13,217.90	19,967.50	3.0	0.25	0.92	N/A	102
MERIDIAN FUND	G	NO	18.4	17.02	13,082.20	14,521.60	17,867.40	0.6	0.00	0.10	N/A	156
MERRILL LYN BASIC VALUE	GI	SC	823.7	18.07	11,650.00	12,859.40	25,603.30	3.3	1.02	0.59	16.7	29
MERRILL LYN CAPITAL	GI	SC	572.5	24.43	11,910.60	13,109.20	24,037.60	2.1	2.10	0.57	19.6	154
MERRILL LYN CORP DIV	EI	LO	237.2	10.67	10,565.30	11,201.60		8.9	0.00	0.94	N/A	131
MERRILL LYN EQUI-BOND (R)	B	LO	17.0	14.16	11,038.50	12,228.80	21,476.90	4.4	0.07	0.62	N/A	4
MERRILL LYN FEDERAL	FI	SC	6,405.6	10.05	10,654.40	11,542.80		9.3	0.35	0.94	N/A	284
MERRILL LYN FD TOMOROW (R)	G	NO	631.8	16.65	12,576.70	13,276.00		0.7	0.08	0.12	18.2	7
MERRILL LYN HIGH INCOME	FI	LO	529.9	8.58	10,966.90	11,809.60	21,455.30	11.7	0.00	1.00	N/A	82
MERRILL LYN HIGH QUALITY	FI	LO	193.7	11.73	10,740.10	11,783.50	22,215.40	9.7	0.00	1.14	N/A	141
MERRILL LYN INTL HLDGS	GL	SC	282.3	13.49	12,162.30	14,963.90		2.1	1.27	0.31	N/A	94
MERRILL LYN INTERMEDIATE	FI	LO	94.5	11.70	10,807.20	11,770.70	21,643.30	9.5	0.00	1.10	N/A	48
MERRILL LYN NATRL RES (R)	NR	NO	190.0	10.70	10,785.90	14,967.70	29,489.60	0.4	0.19	0.07	27.8	N/A
MERRILL LYN PACIFIC	IF	SC	333.2	28.75	14,967.70	11,526.60		5.0	0.98	0.11	N/A	31
MERRILL LYN PHOENIX	G	SC	121.1	13.51	12,053.50	13,122.70	18,364.10	0.5	0.62	0.70	15.7	36
MERRILL LYN SPEC VALUE	SG	SC	114.7	16.55	12,204.10	13,309.10		0.0	0.00	0.08	20.7	36
METRO PORTFOLIO INV STK	CA	NO	5.6	14.95	10,404.50	13,628.10		0.0	0.11	0.00	N/A	27
MFS GOVT GUARANTEED SEC	FI	LO	381.3	10.19	*10,679.20	11,182.40		10.2	0.00	1.05	N/A	158
MFS GOVT SEC HIGH YIELD	FI	NO	229.1	9.80	*13,460.20	☆	☆	0.0	0.00	0.37	N/A	N/A
MFS-MANAGED SECTOR TR	S	NO	50.4	11.32	11,790.70	12,204.10	17,994.90	0.0	0.00	0.00	N/A	107
MIDAMERICA HIGH GROWTH	CA	SC	13.0	5.86	10,976.80	12,473.20		1.4	0.24	0.08	N/A	13
MIDAMERICA HIGH YIELD FD	FI	SC	3.4	11.14	11,278.60	12,211.20	21,344.20	9.1	0.00	1.02	N/A	42
MIDAMERICA MUTUAL	GI	SC	34.5	7.56	*9,114.30	☆	☆	3.1	0.53	0.24	20.2	N/A
MIDAS GOLD SHS & BULLION	AU	SO	2.7	6.38	10,627.10	11,348.20		0.0	0.00	0.00	N/A	N/A
MIDWEST INCOME TR/INTMDT	FI	NO	56.9	10.67	10,627.10	11,348.20	18,027.80	8.8	0.00	0.93	N/A	N/A

MAS EQUITY	G	NO	110.7	39.32	12,868.90	14,692.90	★	3.5	0.47	1.37	N/A	N/A
MAS FIXED INCOME	FI	NO	82.3	29.68	10,818.80	12,138.10	★	8.5	0.35	2.54	N/A	N/A
MAS VALUE	GI	NO	664.8	37.47	12,575.80	13,863.60	☆	3.8	0.99	1.44	N/A	N/A
MIMLIC INVESTORS I	GI	SC	6.5	11.03	10,729.60	11,404.00	☆	1.3	0.24	0.14	N/A	N/A
MIMLIC MORTGAGE	FI	SC	11.2	10.40	10,324.20	11,264.00	☆	10.2	0.00	1.06	N/A	N/A
MONEY MARKET/OPTIONS	OG	NO	10.2	21.47	12,443.00	13,672.90	19,334.20	7.3	0.00	1.57	N/A	N/A
MONITREND FUND	CA	LO	22.7	20.34	11,262.90	12,048.50	☆	0.6	0.07	0.12	N/A	53
WL MORGAN GROWTH	TK	NO	768.8	14.28	11,482.80	13,257.50	21,659.70	1.5	1.13	0.23	22.4	39
MUTUAL BEACON FUND (X)	GI	NO	63.4	19.73	11,444.30	13,037.10	18,678.30	1.3	0.00	0.25	13.9	72
MUTUAL BENEFIT FUND	GI	SC	15.6	15.01	12,384.80	14,003.40	27,271.40	2.2	0.61	0.33	19.4	32
MUTUAL OMAHA AMERICA	FI	NO	33.4	10.58	10,606.00	11,442.10	18,555.90	8.6	0.00	0.91	N/A	N/A
MUTUAL OMAHA GROWTH	G	SC	32.0	8.15	12,423.80	13,417.10	20,264.80	1.3	0.30	0.11	22.4	110
MUTUAL OMAHA INCOME	I	SC	99.5	9.69	11,023.40	12,079.30	20,950.10	8.3	0.20	0.81	22.4	136
MUTUAL QUALIFIED INCOME (X)	GI	NO	544.6	21.78	11,543.20	12,987.30	26,958.00	4.0	1.10	0.90	17.5	96
MUTUAL SHARES CORP (X)	GI	NO	1,347.5	65.81	11,613.70	12,980.70	26,201.30	3.0	3.95	2.05	18.0	91
NAESS & THOMAS SPECIAL	SG	NO	42.3	49.84	12,251.70	12,905.20	16,518.80	0.0	0.00	0.00	33.5	103
NATL AVIATION & TECH	TK	SC	88.8	11.76	11,650.40	11,780.20	16,037.00	2.1	0.41	0.25	20.5	5
NATIONAL BALANCED	B	SC	2.3	15.56	11,685.60	13,047.70	25,368.60	5.1	1.61	0.88	N/A	25
NATIONAL BOND	FI	SC	472.6	3.45	10,732.80	11,845.00	21,378.90	13.3	0.00	0.45	N/A	140
NATIONAL FEDERAL SEC TR	FI	SC	1,012.6	11.41	10,458.20	11,167.80	☆	10.4	0.36	1.20	N/A	165
NATIONAL GROWTH	G	SC	78.2	11.88	12,333.50	13,954.70	16,371.10	1.3	0.00	0.16	19.0	54
NATIONAL INDUSTRIES (R)	GI	NO	31.9	14.45	12,127.90	12,783.80	14,630.00	1.7	0.50	0.25	19.1	70
NATIONAL PREFERRED	FI	SC	4.3	8.74	11,631.10	12,597.50	24,610.30	8.4	0.33	0.76	19.0	61
NATIONAL PREMIUM INC	OI	SC	1.1	13.01	11,868.40	☆	☆	0.0	0.00	0.58	N/A	N/A
NATIONAL REAL ESTATE	S	SC	11.6	10.55	12,314.50	13,322.10	☆	2.3	0.31	0.25	N/A	62
NATIONAL STOCK	GI	SC	281.7	11.18	11,953.30	13,338.00	21,689.30	3.8	0.43	0.44	N/A	41
NATL TELECOM & TECH	TK	SC	71.9	14.85	11,032.40	12,260.50	☆	1.5	0.00	0.22	29.6	12
NATIONAL TOTAL INCOME	EI	SC	78.1	8.39	12,507.50	13,878.70	26,656.40	6.0	0.21	0.52	16.4	38
NATIONAL TOTAL RETURN	EI	SC	260.0	7.70	12,053.00	13,111.50	23,980.50	4.9	0.08	0.38	16.4	14
NATIONAL VALUE	CA	SC	0.7	12.00	#12,000.00	☆	☆	0.0	0.00	0.00	N/A	N/A
NATIONWIDE BOND	FI	SC	17.0	10.20	10,759.20	11,694.80	21,013.40	9.4	0.02	0.96	N/A	5
NATIONWIDE FUND	GI	SC	369.4	14.86	12,083.00	13,953.40	23,870.90	2.8	0.59	0.43	14.8	28
NATIONWIDE GROWTH	G	SC	167.1	10.33	12,124.40	13,556.00	28,928.60	2.5	1.34	0.27	26.3	85
NAUTILUS FUND	TK	SC	20.5	13.03	9,782.30	10,243.70	13,089.10	0.0	0.00	0.00	N/A	41
NEL EQUITY FUND	GI	SC	31.4	24.95	12,627.80	13,707.90	23,412.00	3.3	1.77	0.84	N/A	99
NEL GOVT SEC TRUST	FI	SC	160.1	13.37	10,717.00	☆	☆	0.0	0.03	0.89	N/A	N/A
NEL GROWTH FUND	G	SC	314.0	30.34	12,664.90	13,866.00	28,912.60	0.7	2.17	0.22	33.4	203
NEL INCOME FUND	FI	SC	46.2	11.45	10,838.90	11,643.80	20,681.80	10.1	0.00	1.16	N/A	217
NEL RETIREMENT EQUITY	GI	SC	101.7	27.21	12,902.50	14,572.60	26,239.20	1.5	2.73	0.42	29.0	173
NEUWIRTH FUND	G	NO	29.0	18.20	12,984.20	14,389.70	21,462.10	0.2	1.20	0.04	N/A	86
NEW ALTERNATIVES FUND	NR	SC	1.2	41.84	12,243.70	13,537.70	☆	1.3	0.77	0.54	N/A	23
"NEW BEGINNING" GROWTH	SG	NO	40.7	32.76	12,413.80	14,255.90	☆	0.0	0.00	0.00	N/A	130
"NEW BEGINNING" INC & GR	GI	NO	5.0	19.43	12,417.90	13,591.80	☆	2.2	0.00	0.42	N/A	158
"NEW BEGINNING" INV RESV	FI	NO	3.4	9.94	10,344.60	10,705.40	☆	6.8	0.00	0.67	N/A	N/A
"NEW BEGINNING" YIELD	FI	NO	5.5	10.78	10,491.10	10,905.00	☆	5.3	0.00	0.57	N/A	1
NEW ECONOMY FUND	G	SC	766.0	11.69	11,775.40	13,686.40	☆	0.9	1.13	0.20	32.9	22
NEW PERSPECTIVE FUND	GL	SC	865.7	10.33	11,453.60	14,031.50	23,005.00	2.0	0.68	0.21	31.5	27
NEW YORK VENTURE	G	SC	166.7	10.75	12,010.50	13,697.90	26,390.30	1.7	0.72	0.18	24.6	75
NEWPORT FAR EAST (R)	IF	NO	2.4	16.53	14,250.00	16,480.60	☆	0.0	0.00	0.00	N/A	N/A
NEWTON GROWTH FUND	G	NO	35.1	25.17	10,917.50	12,109.50	20,276.80	2.5	7.46	0.71	22.6	143
NEWTON INCOME FUND	FI	NO	10.9	8.49	10,516.40	11,079.90	19,535.50	9.4	0.00	0.79	N/A	480
NICHOLAS FUND	G	NO	1,084.2	35.97	11,520.60	12,219.30	25,904.80	2.4	0.18	0.88	19.6	14
NICHOLAS INCOME	FI	NO	47.8	4.01	10,639.60	11,569.00	22,127.80	9.9	0.00	0.39	N/A	12
NICHOLAS II (X)	SG	NO	339.4	18.48	11,891.90	12,853.30	☆	0.9	0.06	0.16	18.0	10
NICHOLSON GROWTH (R)	CA	NO	0.2	16.36	11,586.40	11,213.20	☆	0.0	0.00	0.00	N/A	79
NODDINGS CALAMOS GROWTH	GI	NO	6.9	11.39	11,252.10	11,871.00	★	3.6	0.05	0.41	N/A	N/A
NODDINGS CALAMOS INCOME	EI	NO	12.9	12.09	11,773.00	12,602.70	★	2.8	0.13	0.34	N/A	N/A

PERFORMANCE OF MUTUAL FUNDS (continued)

FUND NAME	OBJ.	LOAD	TOTAL NET ASTS (MIL) 6/30/86	NAV 6/30/86	PERFORMANCE (RETURN ON INITIAL $10,000 INVESTMENT) 12/31/85-6/30/86	6/30/85-6/30/86	6/30/81-6/30/86	YIELD % 6/30/86	PER SHARE LATEST 12 MONTHS CAP GAINS	INC DIVS	LATEST AVAILABLE PRICE/EARNINGS	ANNUAL % TURNOVER
NOMURA PACIFIC BASIC	IF	NO	44.9	17.80	14,684.20	☆	☆	0.0	0.06	0.30	N/A	N/A
NORTH STAR APOLLO	CA	NO	24.3	10.96	10,917.70	11,852.60		1.8	0.33	0.20	N/A	36
NORTH STAR BOND FUND	FI	NO	35.4	10.34	10,697.50	11,650.50	22,134.50	8.9	0.27	0.94	N/A	22
NORTH STAR REGIONAL FUND	G	NO	89.4	22.07	13,348.90	15,195.40	27,513.00	1.6	4.44	0.41	17.8	80
NORTH STAR RESERVE	FI	NO	32.5	10.18	#10,246.90	☆	☆	0.0	0.00	0.06	N/A	N/A
NORTH STAR STOCK FUND	CA	NO	71.9	15.92	11,677.00	12,967.20	22,463.50	2.5	0.80	0.41	17.4	62
NORTHEAST INV GROWTH	G	NO	16.4	19.89	13,340.20	15,263.10	23,186.60	0.7	0.20	0.13	N/A	37
NORTHEAST INV TRUST	FI	NO	302.4	13.58	11,312.10	12,467.40	24,627.10	10.8	0.00	1.46	N/A	22
NOVA FUND	TK	NO	26.5	16.78	11,032.80	11,683.30	17,812.50	0.2	0.28	0.04	30.7	89
OHIO NATIONAL-BOND	FI	NO	1.8	10.67	10,696.10	14,106.40	☆	7.8	0.00	0.82	N/A	N/A
OHIO NATIONAL-EQUITY	G	NO	14.9	19.06	12,708.10	12,332.40		2.6	0.00	0.50	N/A	N/A
OHIO NATIONAL-OMNI (R)	G	SC	8.4	12.88	11,955.60			4.6	0.00	0.59	N/A	N/A
OLYMPIC TR-B SERIES (R)	CA	SC	4.4	18.14	12,579.80			0.0	0.00	0.00	N/A	N/A
OLYMPIC TR-TOTL RETN (R)	GI	NO	0.7	14.83	10,991.10	☆	☆	1.7	0.00	0.41	N/A	N/A
OMEGA FUND	CA	NO	36.5	15.90	11,785.60	12,990.90	14,775.40	0.0	0.39	0.28	28.2	188
ONE HUNDRED FUND	G	NO	12.6	23.72	13,663.60	14,552.10	16,681.60	0.0	0.00	0.00	N/A	130
ONE HUNDRED & ONE FUND	GI	NO	2.2	19.30	12,173.30	13,377.70	23,490.80	2.8	0.29	0.55	N/A	166
OPPENHEIMER A I M	GI	SC	379.2	28.66	13,515.40	18,850.10	20,776.10	0.3	0.06	0.10	31.2	29
OPPENHEIMER CHALLENGER	CA	LO	15.7	15.85	12,277.30	15,130.90		0.5	0.64	0.00	N/A	113
OPPENHEIMER DIRECTORS	CA	SC	284.8	23.72	11,306.90	12,403.00	16,332.90	3.8	0.00	0.91	20.1	63
OPPENHEIMER EQUITY	EI	SC	381.1	9.26	11,462.00	12,842.30	26,673.00	4.9	0.15	0.45	28.5	123
OPPENHEIMER FUND	G	SC	284.6	12.48	11,666.90	13,125.10	15,155.30	1.4	0.02	0.18	35.8	86
OPPENHEIMER GLD & SP MIN	AU	SC	29.1	6.43	10,190.20	9,377.30		0.4	0.00	0.02	20.8	12
OPPENHEIMER HIGH YIELD	FI	SC	627.3	17.54	10,793.40	11,725.80	20,085.70	13.5	0.00	2.36	N/A	113
OPPENHEIMER PREMIUM INC	OI	SC	418.1	19.35	10,005.40	10,969.20	16,940.70	2.5	2.56	0.52	22.2	149
OPPENHEIMER REGENCY	G	SC	170.9	16.73	11,550.30	12,670.20	☆	1.2	0.12	0.20	30.1	171
OPPENHEIMER RET BLUE CHP	CA	SC	8.9	12.83	11,884.30	13,131.30	☆	2.1	0.64	0.28	N/A	N/A
OPPENHEIMER RET US GOVT	FI	SC	11.1	10.51	10,390.70	11,172.00	☆	10.1	0.46	1.08	N/A	N/A
OPPENHEIMER SPECIAL	G	SC	772.6	23.82	11,305.20	12,284.40	17,087.20	2.6	0.48	0.61	26.6	17
OPPENHEIMER TARGET	CA	SC	145.3	24.35	12,865.90	14,745.30	32,568.60	1.6	0.10	0.38	17.4	119
OPPENHEIMER TIME	CA	SC	299.6	20.17	13,114.40	14,658.40	25,727.10	1.5	0.10	0.31	29.6	176
OPPENHEIMER US GOVT TR	FI	SC	158.4	10.17	10,641.30	11,421.70	☆	9.4	0.21	0.97	N/A	N/A
OVER-THE-COUNTER SEC	SG	SC	263.2	21.24	12,078.40	13,551.10	24,493.30	0.3	1.10	0.06	20.6	30
OTC 100 FUND	G	NO	37.0	13.92	12,559.20	13,162.30	☆	0.2	0.02	0.03	N/A	23
P-C CAPITAL FUND	CA	NO	6.0	13.36	12,025.20	12,678.50	18,573.90	4.2	0.00	0.56	32.4	N/A
PACIFIC HORIZON AGG GRO	CA	NO	101.8	30.49	14,370.70	15,708.00	☆	0.0	0.00	0.05	N/A	233
PACIFIC HORIZON HI YLD	FI	NO	22.8	16.46	10,931.90	12,021.30	☆	11.6	0.00	1.91	N/A	167
PAINEWEBBER AMERICA	GI	SC	95.2	17.20	11,726.90	12,846.90	☆	4.5	0.19	0.78	11.6	34
PAINEWEBBER ATLAS	GL	SC	218.0	18.02	12,964.90	17,389.30	☆	0.6	0.78	0.11	34.2	129
PAINEWEBBER GNMA	FI	LO	2,712.3	10.08	10,358.90	11,399.00	☆	12.2	0.00	1.23	N/A	3
PAINEWEBBER HIGH YIELD	FI	LO	438.8	10.76	11,077.90	12,000.40	☆	13.1	0.02	1.41	N/A	1
PAINEWEBBER INV GRADE	FI	LO	260.6	10.72	10,781.10	12,075.30	☆	11.8	0.01	1.26	N/A	1
PAINEWEBBER MSTR GRO (R)	G	NO	274.9	0.00	N/A	☆	☆	0.2	0.00	0.00	N/A	N/A
PAINEWEBBER MSTR INC (R)	I	NO	125.9	9.84	#9,930.60		☆	0.0	0.00	0.14	N/A	N/A
PAINEWEBBER OLYMPUS	G	SC	3.7	13.16	12,473.90	13,894.60	☆	0.0	0.00	0.12	27.4	25
PARIBAS MCI 450 (R)	GI	NO	4.9	10.57	#10,570.00	☆	☆	0.0	0.00	0.00	N/A	N/A
PARIBAS QUANTUS EQ (R)	G	LO	2.4	10.42	#10,420.00	☆	☆	0.1	0.00	0.00	N/A	N/A
PARNASSUS FUND	G	LO	430.6	19.59	11,109.00	12,895.20	☆	0.1	0.11	0.02	N/A	12
PARTNERS FUND	G	NO	49.0	20.63	12,022.10	13,302.10	25,985.50	3.2	1.27	0.65	15.1	146
PAX WORLD FUND	B	NO	7.9	14.18	11,462.50	12,521.70	22,813.20	3.6	0.71	0.52	16.7	48
PDC&J PERFORMANCE	CA	NO	5.8	15.26	12,829.70	13,549.60	☆	5.5	0.00	0.84	N/A	66
PDC&J PRESERVATIONS	FI	NO		10.96	10,563.90	11,256.10	☆	5.0	0.00	0.54	N/A	N/A

PENN SQUARE MUTUAL	GI	NO	213.1	10.27	11,533.20	12,966.70	21,453.30	3.5	0.63	0.37	24.0	16
PENNSYLVANIA MUTUAL (X)	SG	NO	399.7	8.09	11,686.80	12,960.10	24,712.70	1.6	0.39	0.13	20.2	15
PERMANENT PORTFOLIO	S	NO	71.3	12.64	10,896.60	11,736.30	☆	0.0	0.00	0.00	25.8	17
PHILADELPHIA FUND	B	SC	119.0	9.69	11,480.70	12,515.10	17,962.50	2.0	0.82	0.20	21.8	60
PHOENIX BALANCED	_	SC	139.5	14.48	12,015.90	13,571.50	29,749.60	4.8	0.68	0.71	13.2	154
PHOENIX CONVERTIBLE	G	SC	96.7	19.18	11,505.80	12,612.10	24,682.50	5.0	0.66	0.98	18.6	170
PHOENIX GROWTH	_	SC	219.7	19.74	12,014.60	13,523.10	32,654.30	3.1	0.32	0.61	16.5	151
PHOENIX HIGH QUAL BOND	G	NO	16.2	10.23	11,022.50	12,113.10	☆	8.2	0.00	0.83	N/A	233
PHOENIX HIGH YIELD	FI	SC	91.6	9.88	11,168.10	12,043.40	22,294.80	11.8	0.00	1.16	N/A	75
PHOENIX STOCK	CA	SC	93.4	16.96	12,071.20	13,348.10	30,858.50	2.7	0.09	0.45	19.7	196
PIERPONT CAP APPREC	G	NO	24.7	14.36	12,689.70	14,573.20	☆	0.4	0.16	0.05	N/A	N/A
PIERPONT EQUITY	GI	NO	13.8	12.89	12,258.10	13,466.10	☆	2.3	0.22	0.30	N/A	57
PILGRIM ADJUSTABLE RATE	FI	LO	882.6	22.26	10,138.10	10,549.80	☆	8.5	0.00	1.89	N/A	N/A
PILGRIM CORP CASH	FI	NO	14.1	10.00	10,043.20	☆	☆	0.5	0.00	0.00	N/A	3
PILGRIM GNMA	_	LO	222.1	15.15	10,604.60	11,577.00	21,265.60	11.4	0.00	1.72	N/A	133
PILGRIM HIGH YIELD	FI	LO	13.8	8.25	10,871.40	11,771.30	25,962.60	12.5	0.00	1.03	16.0	36
PILGRIM MAGNACAP	G	SC	187.8	10.66	12,273.50	13,771.30	☆	1.1	0.16	0.12	N/A	N/A
PILGRIM PREFERRED	_	LO	55.1	25.63	$10,544.30	☆	☆	0.0	0.00	0.72	N/A	255
PILOT FUND	CA	SC	74.1	10.99	11,605.10	11,754.00	19,634.90	0.0	1.96	0.00	26.9	65
PINE STREET FUND	GI	NO	65.9	14.38	11,890.90	12,967.20	22,765.40	3.3	0.54	0.54	21.1	37
PINNACLE FUND	CA	NO	1.9	29.74	12,937.90	13,641.00	☆	0.4	0.00	0.11	N/A	26
PIONEER BOND FUND	FI	LO	29.9	9.62	10,610.30	11,533.30	21,420.70	10.2	0.00	0.98	N/A	18
PIONEER FUND	GI	SC	1,461.9	23.81	11,186.40	12,426.00	18,925.90	3.0	1.51	0.74	23.8	18
PIONEER II	GI	SC	2,892.3	19.51	11,275.50	12,650.10	22,281.50	2.6	1.15	0.52	26.2	11
PIONEER THREE	GI	SC	572.3	17.63	11,832.80	13,043.30	☆	2.0	0.36	0.36	20.1	N/A
PORT WASHINGTON FUND	CA	NO	0.1	10.44	12,460.90	☆	☆	0.0	0.01	0.00	N/A	37
T ROWE PRICE EQUITY INC	EI	NO	66.3	12.89	12,055.60	☆	☆	0.0	0.00	0.32	N/A	N/A
T ROWE PRICE CAP APPREC	CA	NO	0.1	0.00	N/A	☆	☆	0.0	0.00	0.00	N/A	N/A
T ROWE PRICE GNMA	FI	NO	209.2	9.96	10,344.60	12,240.10	19,396.40	3.9	0.69	0.57	20.8	121
T ROWE PRICE GROWTH & INC	GI	NO	399.8	14.68	11,158.30	14,051.50	☆	1.9	1.18	0.59	23.3	69
T ROWE PRICE GROWTH STK	G	NO	1,365.5	19.95	12,188.40	12,270.10	23,054.90	11.8	0.13	0.38	N/A	164
T ROWE PRICE HIGH YIELD	FI	NO	707.9	11.25	11,224.80	17,704.70	☆	0.9	0.25	1.33	N/A	62
T ROWE PRICE INTL FUND	IF	NO	625.1	23.43	13,307.90	☆	17,051.90	0.0	0.00	0.22	23.5	49
T ROWE PRICE NEW AMER GR	G	NO	97.5	14.96	12,734.40	12,592.80	17,433.30	0.0	0.85	0.10	27.1	37
T ROWE PRICE NEW ERA	NR	NO	531.5	19.73	11,371.90	12,671.00	20,631.00	2.5	0.42	0.50	26.9	31
T ROWE PRICE NEW HORIZON	SG	NO	1,517.0	16.98	11,615.80	11,812.20	☆	0.5	0.00	0.09	N/A	185
T ROWE PRICE NEW INCOME	FI	NO	932.8	9.06	10,851.50	11,125.50	☆	9.2	0.00	0.83	N/A	21
T ROWE PRICE SH-TERM BD	FI	NO	125.8	5.19	10,493.60	13,848.40	☆	8.7	0.10	0.44	24.2	10
PRIMECAP	G	NO	101.7	41.95	11,912.90	12,199.20	☆	0.6	0.24	0.24	N/A	38
PRINCIPAL EQUITY	GI	SC	1.3	7.52	11,930.70	☆	☆	0.9	0.00	0.06	N/A	N/A
PRINCIPAL PRES GOVT	FI	LO	24.3	9.89	11,062.20	☆	18,323.50	0.0	0.00	0.46	N/A	56
PRINCIPAL PRES S&P 100	GI	SC	8.2	10.67	11,522.60	13,920.90	20,638.40	0.1	0.42	0.18	19.9	158
PRINCIPAL WORLD	GL	SC	4.9	8.70	12,520.40	13,199.90	23,314.60	3.1	0.00	0.27	N/A	147
PRO FUND	G	NO	33.5	13.65	12,223.00	11,783.50	☆	1.7	0.40	0.24	N/A	30
PRO INCOME FUND	_	NO	20.0	9.34	10,793.30	12,160.30	☆	8.2	0.07	0.77	26.0	110
PROVIDENT FD FOR INCOME	FI	SC	108.5	4.97	10,921.90	10,805.60	19,605.70	6.0	0.64	0.30	N/A	106
PRU-BACHE ADJ RATE PRF	FI	NO	295.8	23.74	10,284.40	13,157.40	☆	9.1	0.04	2.16	N/A	123
PRU-BACHE EQUITY (R)	G	NO	282.3	10.05	11,926.70	17,145.50	☆	0.6	0.00	0.06	N/A	222
PRU-BACHE GLOBAL (R)	GL	NO	300.7	10.25	13,694.10	11,181.60	21,942.30	0.0	0.19	0.00	24.0	110
PRU-BACHE GNMA (H)	FI	NO	269.1	15.63	10,333.20	13,504.10	☆	9.0	1.66	1.42	N/A	59
PRU-BACHE GROWTH OPP (R)	G	NO	102.2	15.48	12,018.60	12,018.60	☆	0.2	0.16	0.03	N/A	245
PRU-BACHE GOVT INTMDT	FI	LO	623.5	10.80	10,729.60	11,561.10	☆	9.4	0.32	1.02	N/A	59
PRU-BACHE GOVT PLUS (R)	FI	NO	3,913.1	10.55	10,609.10	11,470.40	☆	7.7	0.00	0.82	N/A	N/A
PRU-BACHE HIGH YIELD (R)	FI	NO	1,310.9	10.80	11,043.50	11,890.30	☆	11.5	0.00	1.23	N/A	N/A
PRU-BACHE INCOMVRTIBLE (R)	S	NO	264.3	11.31	11,467.50	☆	☆	0.0	0.00	0.30	N/A	N/A

PERFORMANCE OF MUTUAL FUNDS (continued)

FUND NAME	OBJ.	LOAD	TOTAL NET ASTS (MIL) 6/30/86	NAV 6/30/86	PERFORMANCE (RETURN ON INITIAL $10,000 INVESTMENT) 12/31/85-6/30/86	6/30/85-6/30/86	6/30/81-6/30/86	YIELD % 6/30/86	PER SHARE LATEST 12 MONTHS CAP GAINS	INC DIVS	LATEST AVAILABLE PRICE/EARNINGS	ANNUAL % TURNOVER
PRU-BACHE OPTION GRO (R)	OG	NO	$74.3	$9.06	$11,335.00	$12,439.20	$★	1.6	$1.05	$0.16	N/A	107
PRU-BACHE RESEARCH (R)	G	NO	191.0	13.54	13,147.00	14,780.10	★	1.4	0.00	0.19	N/A	216
PRU-BACHE UTILITY (R)	UT	NO	833.6	15.07	12,498.40	13,719.90		5.2	0.50	0.80	N/A	39
PUTNAM CAPITAL (X)	SG	NO	14.1	8.85	12,667.40	14,186.80		0.5	1.03	0.05	N/A	99
PUTNAM CONV INC-GRO TR	FI	SC	643.2	17.01	11,787.90	12,856.60	24,300.50	5.5	0.44	0.94	12.5	120
PUTNAM CORP CASH ARP	FI	LO	585.5	47.00	10,295.70	10,741.50	23,583.00	9.4	0.00	4.41	N/A	70
PUTNAM CORP CASH DSP	EI	LO	349.0	49.36	10,839.60	11,380.30	★	11.7	0.00	5.77	N/A	287
PUTNAM ENERGY RESOURCES	NR	SC	31.9	11.06	9,441.50	10,126.70	8,791.50	2.4	0.00	0.27	27.3	130
GEORGE PUTNAM FD BOSTON	B	SC	369.2	14.87	11,737.80	13,175.60	23,466.20	5.9	0.11	0.88	15.7	187
PUTNAM GROWTH & INCOME	GI	SC	1,133.6	13.73	12,004.20	13,547.00	24,198.20	4.2	1.13	0.59	16.7	243
PUTNAM HEALTH SCIENCE	H	SC	301.2	23.67	13,418.40	14,717.40	★	0.9	2.65	0.22	33.0	43
PUTNAM HIGH INCOME GOVT	FI	SC	3,770.8	12.56	10,802.00	11,826.80	★	8.8	0.48	1.12	N/A	171
PUTNAM HIGH YIELD TRUST	FI	SC	2,429.8	16.01	10,912.70	11,953.70	23,076.30	13.9	0.00	2.22	N/A	161
PUTNAM INCOME	FI	SC	188.8	7.42	10,679.30	11,588.40	23,672.90	10.7	0.00	0.79	N/A	312
PUTNAM INFO SCIENCE	TK	SC	146.0	14.68	11,513.70	12,582.90	★	0.5	0.00	0.07	31.5	89
PUTNAM INTL EQUITIES	GL	SC	322.1	28.65	12,977.30	17,701.90	28,257.80	0.4	1.53	0.13	26.7	167
PUTNAM INVESTORS	G	SC	1,159.7	12.52	12,366.10	13,527.70	22,077.70	1.5	1.77	0.20	20.3	79
PUTNAM OPTION INCOME (X)	OI	SC	1,201.5	11.24	10,989.20	11,927.20	18,719.80	2.5	1.48	0.29	19.1	183
PUTNAM OPTION INCOME II	OI	SC	947.6	11.78	10,938.60	11,540.50	★	3.2	1.45	0.40	21.6	23
PUTNAM US GOVERNMENT	FI	SC	938.9	14.43	10,367.40	11,079.00	★	11.6	0.01	1.66	N/A	136
PUTNAM VISTA	CA	SC	211.0	21.34	12,214.10	13,189.90	23,268.10	2.8	0.57	0.60	25.6	200
PUTNAM VOYAGER	CA	SC	424.1	24.63	13,038.60	14,601.30	23,972.00	0.6	0.96	0.14	25.6	60
QUANTUM FUND	CA	SC	0.6	12.27	11,274.90	11,568.60	★	0.0	0.60	0.00	N/A	N/A
QUASAR ASSOCIATES(X)	G	NO	204.5	77.93	13,181.70	15,432.20	25,689.70	0.1	2.89	0.08	29.3	78
QUEST FOR VALUE FUND	CA	NO	74.1	27.31	11,885.30	13,224.90	32,154.00	0.7	1.82	0.20	19.1	42
RAINBOW FUND	G	SC	2.0	5.59	11,970.00	12,939.80	14,223.90	0.0	0.00	0.00	N/A	164
REA-GRAHAM FUND	B	SC	38.7	14.32	10,446.50	12,254.50	★	2.9	1.83	0.47	N/A	196
REICH & TANG EQUITY	FI	NO	104.1	15.89	11,997.20	13,526.10	★	2.5	0.00	0.40	N/A	20
REICH & TANG GNMA INC	GI	NO	2.9	10.11	$10,299.70		★	0.0	0.00	0.18	N/A	N/A
RESERVE EQUITY CONTRARIAN	GI	NO	21.7	16.78	11,606.10	13,385.60	★	2.9	0.01	0.48	N/A	6
RESERVE EQUITY GROWTH	G	NO	2.1	15.11	11,706.70	13,288.30	★	1.9	0.00	0.28	N/A	3
RETIREMENT PLAN AM-BOND	FI	NO	47.2	7.86	10,418.90	11,329.60	18,599.90	11.2	0.02	0.88	N/A	15
RETIREMENT PLAN AM-EQU	EI	NO	12.5	20.97	11,703.70	13,286.60	21,757.70	0.9	1.20	0.20	N/A	67
RIGHTIME FUND	S	NO	125.7	34.89	12,221.00	★	★	0.0	0.19	0.05	N/A	N/A
ROCHESTER CONVERT GRO	EI	LO	0.6	10.16	$10,160.00	★	★	0.0	0.00	0.00	N/A	N/A
ROCHESTER CONVERT INC	FI	LO	1.4	9.98	#9,980.00	★	★	0.0	0.00	0.00	N/A	N/A
ROCHESTER GROWTH FUND	G	SC	3.7	12.58	13,440.20	16,358.90	16,358.90	0.0	0.00	0.00	N/A	275
ROCHESTER TAX-MGD	G	SC	32.9	11.54	11,106.80	11,621.30	17,883.20	0.0	0.00	0.00	N/A	109
RNC INCOME	_	SC	0.4	9.95	#9,969.90	★	★	0.0	0.00	0.02	N/A	N/A
RNC REGENCY GROWTH	G	NO	1.9	13.22	12,240.70	★	★	0.0	0.00	0.00	N/A	N/A
ROYCE EQUITY INC (R)	EI	NO	4.8	5.70	11,484.00	★	★	0.0	0.00	0.04	N/A	N/A
ROYCE HIGH YIELD (R)	FI	NO	10.0	10.18	10,764.10	★	★	0.0	0.00	0.56	N/A	N/A
ROYCE VALUE	SG	NO	161.0	9.67	11,556.50	12,630.70	★	0.4	0.30	0.04	21.2	16
RUSHMORE GNMA	FI	NO	7.3	9.83	10,256.40	★	★	0.0	0.00	0.44	N/A	N/A
RUSHMORE OTC	G	NO	0.8	12.16	12,280.30	★	★	0.0	0.00	0.11	N/A	N/A
RUSHMORE STK MKT	G	NO	1.1	11.89	12,053.00	★	★	0.0	0.00	0.16	N/A	N/A
RUSHMORE US GOVT	FI	NO	0.3	10.33	10,674.10	★	★	0.0	0.00	0.33	N/A	N/A
ST CLAIR CORPORATE DIV	FI	NO	9.8	10.01	10,009.10	10,309.30	★	7.3	0.00	0.72	N/A	5
SAFECO EQUITY FUND	GI	NO	53.0	12.62	12,188.20	13,717.60	20,383.00	2.7	1.21	0.36	18.8	56
SAFECO GROWTH FUND	G	NO	79.7	17.33	11,257.00	12,055.60	18,446.10	2.2	2.97	0.41	23.2	29
SAFECO INCOME FUND	EI	NO	93.4	16.23	11,864.90	13,167.60	26,263.20	4.4	0.55	0.72	18.8	29
SALEM FUNDS	G	NO	10.9	12.79	11,815.20	12,834.30	★	1.4	0.09	0.18	N/A	N/A

Fund	Obj	Ld	Net Assets	NAV	Value 1	Value 2	Value 3	% 1	% 2	% 3	% 4	Col A	Col B
SANTA BARBARA FUND	CA	NO	0.1	10.07	$10,070.00	☆	☆	0.0	0.00	0.00	N/A	N/A	N/A
SBSF FUND	G	NO	92.7	14.80	11,321.30	12,778.90	☆	5.7	0.00	0.85	N/A	N/A	80
SCHIELD AGGRESSIVE GRO	CA	LO	2.3	12.78	10,685.60	☆	☆	0.0	0.00	0.00	N/A	N/A	N/A
SCHIELD VALUE PORT	TK	SC	2.4	12.98	10,289.70	☆	☆	0.0	0.53	0.11	32.5	106	
SCI/TECH HOLDINGS	G	NO	307.3	12.14	11,932.20	14,144.00	23,685.00	0.9	1.88	0.23	26.2	58	
SCUDDER CAPITAL GROWTH	SG	NO	498.3	19.06	12,186.70	13,570.70	17,082.90	1.1	2.75	0.51	25.8	26	
SCUDDER DEVELOPMENT	G	NO	358.9	75.34	12,292.40	12,992.10	☆	0.7	0.07	1.47	N/A	N/A	
SCUDDER GOVT MORT	FI	NO	182.2	15.08	10,360.60	☆	☆	3.9	1.42	0.68	15.0	73	
SCUDDER GROWTH & INCOME	GI	NO	393.8	16.60	12,138.20	13,450.30	20,830.50	9.7	0.00	1.28	11.7	30	
SCUDDER INCOME	FI	NO	197.4	13.19	10,789.10	11,744.00	22,247.10	1.3	1.68	0.49	N/A	20	
SCUDDER INTERNATIONAL	IF	NO	639.6	37.42	12,759.40	16,862.20	24,723.80	5.2	0.47	0.54	N/A	71	
SCUDDER TARGET GENL 1986	FI	NO	1.3	10.10	10,329.60	10,728.80	☆	6.2	0.12	0.65	N/A	43	
SCUDDER TARGET GENL 1987	FI	NO	5.6	10.61	10,366.80	10,918.70	☆	7.4	0.11	0.78	N/A	49	
SCUDDER TARGET GENL 1990	FI	NO	15.7	10.60	10,701.40	11,383.00	☆	7.8	0.05	0.90	N/A	58	
SCUDDER TARGET GENL 1994	FI	NO	6.2	11.68	10,737.30	11,639.30	☆	5.1	0.52	0.52	N/A	114	
SCUDDER TARGET USGT 1986	FI	NO	0.7	9.89	10,329.70	10,680.00	☆	6.2	0.65	0.63	N/A	42	
SCUDDER TARGET USGT 1987	FI	NO	1.5	10.01	10,374.80	10,907.80	☆	6.7	0.47	0.70	N/A	64	
SCUDDER TARGET USGT 1990	FI	NO	5.8	10.46	10,758.30	11,335.70	☆	0.0	0.30	0.00	N/A	N/A	
SCUDDER ZERO TARGT 1990	FI	NO	1.0	10.94	$10,767.70	☆	☆	0.0	0.70	0.00	N/A	N/A	
SCUDDER ZERO TARGT 1995	FI	NO	1.0	11.36	$11,115.50	☆	☆	0.0	0.00	0.00	N/A	N/A	
SCUDDER ZERO TARGT 2000	FI	NO	1.0	11.93	$11,340.30	☆	☆	0.0	0.00	0.00	N/A	90	
SECURITY ACTION FUND	CA	SC	75.8	10.49	12,291.40	13,328.10	☆	2.4	0.00	0.25	N/A	91	
SECURITY EQUITY FUND	G	SC	267.2	5.97	12,073.40	13,412.20	20,630.20	16.0	0.27	0.40	17.1	79	
SECURITY INC-CORP BOND	FI	SC	43.2	8.42	10,683.20	11,769.80	21,589.90	11.8	0.40	0.99	N/A	3	
SECURITY INC-US GOV (R)	FI	SC	2.1	5.32	10,413.70	☆	☆	0.0	0.99	0.33	13.2	25	
SECURITY INVESTMENT FUND	GI	SC	107.7	9.86	11,440.40	12,064.10	17,313.40	5.6	0.33	0.56	N/A	N/A	
SECURITY OMNI	CA	SC	26.8	5.26	$10,541.10	☆	☆	0.0	0.16	0.00	25.3	104	
SECURITY ULTRA FUND	CA	SC	118.7	9.94	11,777.30	12,853.60	19,702.40	4.5	0.00	0.46	21.2	33	
SELECTED AMERICAN SHARES	GI	NO	154.8	14.37	12,088.50	13,690.10	28,051.00	3.2	0.65	0.48	23.2	73	
SELECTED SPECIAL SHARES	G	NO	38.0	20.57	11,289.00	12,412.40	18,779.70	3.0	1.11	0.64	21.1	93	
SELIGMAN CAPITAL	CA	SC	221.8	16.63	13,044.50	13,797.90	25,977.00	0.0	1.70	0.00	24.2	57	
SELIGMAN COMM & INFORMTN	TK	SC	52.3	12.76	12,683.90	14,272.90	☆	3.0	0.07	0.49	20.2	57	
SELIGMAN COMMON STOCK	GI	SC	578.8	15.70	12,559.70	14,170.90	26,041.70	1.3	0.00	0.10	24.3	80	
SELIGMAN GROWTH	G	SC	742.8	7.15	12,990.20	14,087.50	20,886.40	12.4	1.34	0.98	N/A	N/A	
SELIGMAN HIGH YIELD	FI	SC	52.8	7.95	11,121.60	12,138.80	☆	8.1	0.56	1.16	10.1	84	
SELIGMAN INCOME	I	SC	131.5	14.12	11,322.90	12,472.60	23,060.20	10.4	0.00	0.77	N/A	N/A	
SELIGMAN SECURED MORT	FI	SC	48.7	7.34	10,199.50	11,291.10	☆	8.8	0.26	0.76	N/A	71	
SELIGMAN U.S. GOVT	FI	SC	53.3	8.48	11,368.60	12,762.50	☆	5.2	0.22	0.67	13.7	92	
SENTINEL BALANCED FUND	B	SC	35.6	12.88	11,710.90	12,808.00	26,785.10	9.1	0.32	0.62	N/A	15	
SENTINEL BOND FUND	FI	SC	19.8	6.81	10,904.70	11,725.10	21,939.20	3.3	0.21	0.85	13.5	102	
SENTINEL COMMON STOCK	GI	SC	512.6	23.55	12,595.40	14,002.30	28,413.80	1.7	0.06	0.32	33.9	26	
SENTINEL GROWTH FUND	G	SC	59.6	17.84	12,023.10	13,801.20	24,319.80	2.2	0.40	0.35	16.3	44	
SENTRY FUND	G	SC	45.6	15.42	12,608.80	14,245.90	18,843.90	3.2	1.50	1.52	15.1	33	
SEQUOIA FUND (X)	G	NO	710.0	46.20	11,677.40	12,435.40	30,900.20	0.0	0.60	0.00	42.5	62	
SHEARSON AGGRESSIVE GRO	CA	SC	129.9	17.25	13,658.00	14,718.40	☆	0.0	3.69	0.55	21.1	64	
SHEARSON APPRECIATION	G	SC	278.3	28.11	12,375.20	14,000.40	25,404.00	2.5	0.00	0.33	18.5	86	
SHEARSON FUNDAMENTAL VAL	G	SC	119.0	7.45	10,612.50	11,231.20	☆	0.0	0.55	0.19	14.5	31	
SHEARSON GLOBAL	GL	SC	295.1	34.53	12,341.00	16,364.90	☆	11.7	0.33	0.00	N/A	N/A	
SHEARSON HIGH YIELD	FI	SC	481.1	19.66	10,967.30	11,859.00	22,720.50	0.0	0.00	2.30	N/A	N/A	
SHEARSON LEHMAN INTL (R)	IF	NO	165.6	18.42	$10,233.30	☆	☆	0.0	0.00	0.00	N/A	N/A	
SHEARSON LEHMAN INTMDT (R)	FI	NO	35.2	11.67	10,600.20	☆	☆	0.0	0.07	0.39	N/A	N/A	
SHEARSON LEHMAN LG GVT (R)	FI	NO	1,273.7	9.20	10,507.00	☆	☆	0.0	0.14	0.41	N/A	N/A	
SHEARSON LEHMAN SP GRO (R)	GI	NO	122.6	14.22	10,157.10	☆	☆	0.0	0.00	0.00	N/A	N/A	
SHEARSON LEHMAN OPT (R)	OI	NO	468.7	14.70	11,343.30	11,135.40	☆	9.8	0.76	0.39	N/A	83	
SHERMAN, DEAN FUND	CA	NO	1,447.4	13.21	10,379.30	7,871.30	5,299.30	0.7	0.00	1.30	N/A	N/A	
			2.0	4.72	8,597.40					0.03			

PERFORMANCE OF MUTUAL FUNDS (continued)

FUND NAME	OBJ.	LOAD	TOTAL NET ASTS (MIL) 6/30/86	NAV 6/30/86	PERFORMANCE (RETURN ON INITIAL $10,000 INVESTMENT) 12/31/85- 6/30/86	6/30/85- 6/30/86	6/30/81- 6/30/86	YIELD % 6/30/86	PER SHARE LATEST 12 MONTHS — CAP GAINS	INC DIVS	PRICE/ EARNINGS	ANNUAL % TURNOVER
SIEBEL CAPITAL PARTNERS	CA	NO	37.2	14.58	11,934.50	13,201.30	☆	6.9	0.79	1.03	N/A	136
SIGMA CAPITAL SHARES	CA	SC	101.9	10.09	12,098.30	13,777.30	27,319.80	1.4	0.30	0.14	21.3	9
SIGMA INCOME SHARES	FI	SC	28.3	8.86	10,707.40	12,003.00	23,341.30	10.5	0.00	0.92	N/A	20
SIGMA INVESTMENT SHARES	GI	SC	83.9	10.89	12,676.40	13,912.50	24,611.20	2.8	0.43	0.30	18.4	18
SIGMA SPECIAL FUND	GI	SC	21.1	10.33	12,113.70	13,716.50	20,110.80	1.3	0.06	0.13	N/A	4
SIGMA TRUST SHARES	B	SC	38.9	14.25	11,522.90	12,690.10	23,345.50	5.2	0.49	0.76	16.5	19
SIGMA VENTURE SHARES	SG	SC	92.7	14.17	12,354.00	13,263.30	23,384.00	1.0	0.22	0.13	26.2	12
SIGMA WORLD	IF	SC	7.0	14.51	12,750.40	15,823.30	☆	0.0	0.00	0.00	N/A	21
SMITH, BARNEY EQUITY	G	NO	79.9	17.04	11,994.90	12,560.00	21,164.90	2.3	1.83	0.42	17.0	21
SMITH, BARNEY INC & GR	GI	SC	262.2	11.21	11,385.40	11,281.90	22,941.90	5.9	0.13	0.67	12.2	73
SMITH, BARNEY US GOVT	FI	SC	413.1	13.66	10,365.50	13,944.40		11.3	0.04	1.55	N/A	25
SOGEN INTERNATIONAL	G	LO	60.1	17.21	12,155.00	13,428.10	28,091.60	3.1	2.22	0.60	21.1	67
SOUND SHORE	G	NO	20.4	13.57	11,870.20	13,762.50	☆	1.0	0.00	0.14	N/A	58
SOUTHEASTERN GROWTH (R)	GI	NO	86.8	14.18	12,705.70	14,085.20		0.0	0.21	0.00	N/A	N/A
SOVEREIGN INVESTORS	GI	SC	32.2	28.11	12,681.60	14,021.10	26,191.50	3.8	0.87	1.08	17.2	31
STATE BOND COMMON STOCK	GI	SC	34.6	7.47	12,344.60	13,507.50	18,103.10	1.5	0.20	0.11	19.9	26
STATE BOND DIVERSIFIED	GI	SC	15.6	8.16	12,102.00	14,406.40	22,385.00	3.2	0.29	0.27	N/A	26
STATE BOND PROGRESS	B	NO	9.1	12.00	12,863.50	13,336.70	18,609.40	1.2	0.18	0.14	N/A	31
STATE FARM BALANCED	B	NO	44.1	18.45	11,532.70	13,549.60	22,333.50	3.9	0.36	0.73	18.2	18
STATE FARM GROWTH	G	NO	259.0	13.43	11,605.50	11,349.20	19,526.90	2.5	0.22	0.33	19.2	13
STATE FARM INTERIM	FI	NO	12.1	10.32	10,635.00	12,820.20	20,077.20	8.5	0.00	0.88	N/A	N/A
STATE STREET INVESTMENT (R)	GI	LO	590.2	86.85	11,522.30	11,362.00	17,991.30	2.5	4.00	2.25	22.8	19
STEADMAN AMER INDUSTRY	G	NO	8.1	3.17	10,968.90	13,876.70	9,721.80	0.0	0.00	0.00	N/A	249
STEADMAN ASSOCIATED FUND	EI	NO	26.1	1.12	12,397.80	10,247.50	17,704.40	5.4	0.00	0.06	N/A	211
STEADMAN INVESTMENT	G	NO	9.3	1.65	11,379.30	11,616.50	11,646.30	0.0	0.00	0.01	N/A	406
STEADMAN OCEANOGRAPHIC	G	NO	5.6	6.18	12,237.60	14,191.60	9,097.00	0.6	0.20	0.00	30.1	90
STEINROE CAPITAL OPP	G	NO	219.2	31.53	13,351.20	13,524.80	18,610.00	0.3	0.00	0.04	36.5	101
STEINROE DISCOVERY	SG	NO	133.5	13.77	12,272.70	☆	☆	0.0	0.00	0.20	N/A	N/A
STEINROE GOVT PLUS	FI	NO	12.0	10.10	$10,306.80	☆	☆	0.0	0.00	0.30	N/A	N/A
STEINROE HIGH YLD BOND	FI	NO	32.0	9.91	$10,243.40	☆	☆	8.5	0.00	0.84	N/A	286
STEINROE MANAGED BONDS	FI	NO	183.4	9.94	11,047.80	12,191.30	21,921.40	1.6	0.58	0.34	21.9	96
STEINROE SPECIAL FUND	CA	NO	347.9	21.10	12,044.00	13,213.90	24,654.60	1.3	0.21	0.28	22.9	114
STEINROE STOCK	G	NO	255.8	21.33	12,470.30	13,176.50	19,267.50	4.9	1.07	1.37	16.7	100
STEINROE TOTAL RETURN	B	NO	149.2	27.42	11,737.50	12,738.30	20,171.60	1.1	0.00	0.27	26.0	179
STEINROE UNIVERSE FUND	CA	NO	114.7	24.34	13,100.10	13,689.90	19,893.90	0.0	0.00	0.30	N/A	127
STRATEGIC CAPITAL GAINS	EI	SC	8.3	7.87	9,459.10	11,590.60	☆	9.0	0.00	0.00	N/A	5
STRATEGIC INVESTMENTS	AU	SC	65.6	3.46	9,115.60	6,161.70	8,321.00	0.1	0.00	0.31	N/A	26
STRATEGIC SILVER	S	SC	16.3	3.71	8,477.60	7,203.70	☆	2.0	0.00	0.00	N/A	35
STRATTON GROWTH FUND	GI	NO	19.3	22.34	11,968.40	12,925.70	23,726.30	7.3	2.03	0.48	14.6	14
STRATTON MONTHLY DIV	UT	NO	33.6	30.45	11,387.60	12,788.90	26,180.30	0.0	0.00	2.22	N/A	N/A
STRONG INCOME	B	NO	44.9	12.69	12,492.00	13,082.90	☆	4.2	0.00	0.95	N/A	173
STRONG INVESTMENT	-	LO	315.0	22.48	11,925.50	14,068.40	☆	0.0	0.42	0.70	N/A	N/A
STRONG OPPORTUNITY	CA	LO	17.1	17.95	11,950.00	13,318.40	☆	3.1	1.04	0.05	N/A	305
STRONG TOTAL RETURN	CA	LO	446.5	22.41	12,442.90	12,118.20	☆	0.6	0.28	0.13	20.9	93
SUMMIT INVESTORS FD	G	SC	62.3	7.60	12,292.30	14,569.10	☆	0.7	1.21	0.10	N/A	100
SUNBELT GROWTH FUND	G	SC	93.3	19.04	11,769.00	12,999.80	☆	0.5	0.61	0.25	25.3	72
SURVEYOR FUND	G	SC	106.9	18.06	12,927.70	13,945.10	18,358.20	1.7	0.04	0.35	23.4	48
TECHNOLOGY FUND	TK	SC	631.8	14.07	11,637.70	13,285.00	19,024.60	2.2	0.61	0.25	N/A	4
TEMPLETON FOREIGN	IF	SC	179.1	15.83	12,038.00	12,930.50	☆	1.8	0.04	0.35	15.9	6
TEMPLETON GLOBAL I(X)	GL	SC	327.1	44.67	12,011.30	12,930.50	29,631.70	1.8	2.80	0.85	19.3	15
TEMPLETON GLOBAL II	GL	SC	521.6	14.31	11,710.30	12,930.50	☆	1.7	0.37	0.25	19.3	15
TEMPLETON GROWTH	GL	SC	1,783.7	12.49	11,595.30	12,939.40	20,994.60	1.6	0.48	0.21	19.2	20

Fund	Type	Load										
TEMPLETON WORLD	GL	SC	3,207.8	16.23	11,642.80	13,085.60	24,460.20	2.6	0.53	0.43	19.8	16
TENNECO-FD OF SOUTHWEST	CA	SC	16.7	12.96	11,493.20	12,135.40	15,074.10	1.1	0.00	0.14	N/A	53
TENNECO-INVESTORS INCOME	FI	SC	17.9	5.25	10,869.00	11,620.90	21,394.20	9.1	0.00	0.48	N/A	237
TENNECO-US TREND FD	G	SC	88.6	15.46	11,607.30	12,563.40	18,024.10	1.5	0.52	0.23	N/A	45
THE BOND ACCUMULATION	FI	SC	12.6	10.87	10,605.10	11,335.00		7.4	0.06	0.81	N/A	155
THE STOCK ACCUMULATION	CA	SC	6.3	14.25	11,853.50	13,737.50	☆	1.6	0.23	0.23	N/A	25
THOMSON MCKINNON GOVT (R)	FI	NO	242.4	10.48	10,613.60	13,737.00		0.0	0.00	0.70	N/A	198
THOMSON MCKINNON GRO (R)	G	NO	189.7	15.30	12,268.40	13,737.00		2.9	0.88	0.45	N/A	198
THOMSON MCKINNON INC (R)	_	NO	311.5	10.38	10,656.50	11,423.70		11.0	0.00	1.14	N/A	114
THOMSON MCKINNON OPPTY (R)	CA	NO	65.6	16.08	12,237.40	13,376.00		0.0	0.80	0.00	N/A	66
TRANSATLANTIC FUND	G	NO	84.7	23.52	13,369.40	19,193.90	16,694.20	0.0	0.38	0.00	N/A	73
TRUSTEES COMMINGLED INTL	IF	NO	650.4	39.52	12,920.20	15,966.20	20,398.70	2.5	2.54	1.03	N/A	29
TRUSTEES COMMINGLED US	IF	NO	197.8	34.82	11,350.40	12,211.30	27,695.20	3.6	4.10	1.32	19.6	23
TUDOR FUND	GI	NO	190.6	25.24	12,295.80	13,759.30		0.4	2.48	0.11	29.0	123
TWENTIETH CENTURY GIFT	G	LO	7.1	19.11	14,659.70	16,176.20		0.9	0.17	0.00	N/A	134
TWENTIETH CENTURY GROWTH	CA	NO	1,050.5	21.01	13,112.00	14,853.00	20,334.60	0.9	0.00	0.18	31.6	116
TWENTIETH CENTURY SELECT	G	NO	1,986.8	37.78	13,014.70	14,414.20	27,206.60	1.4	0.00	0.51	22.2	119
TWENTIETH CENTRY ULTRA (R)	CA	LO	410.9	10.12	12,509.80	13,367.90	☆	0.1	0.00	0.01	36.4	100
TWENTIETH CENTURY US GOV	FI	NO	181.1	100.66	10,524.50	11,109.10		9.2	0.56	9.29	N/A	573
TWENTIETH CENTURY VISTA	CA	LO	168.8	7.74	14,827.60	15,828.20		0.0	0.00	0.00	39.7	174
UNIFIED GROWTH FUND	G	NO	27.6	25.47	12,142.00	13,036.40	21,195.70	1.4	0.00	0.35	N/A	37
UNIFIED INCOME FUND	_	NO	12.6	13.04	10,953.50	11,429.30	20,376.40	8.0	0.00	1.04	N/A	5
UNIFIED MUTUAL SHARES	GI	NO	19.9	18.45	11,734.40	12,871.10	22,238.30	3.1	0.00	0.57	21.9	297
UNITED ACCUMULATIVE	GI	SC	734.6	9.55	12,490.50	13,307.00	26,947.80	3.4	0.99	0.34	27.1	271
UNITED CONTL INCOME	FI	SC	342.7	6.36	10,945.60	12,301.10	24,531.80	9.3	0.00	0.59	15.7	157
UNITED BOND FUND	B	SC	215.1	20.53	12,399.60	13,949.50	29,885.00	3.9	1.52	0.87	23.8	22
UNITED GOLD & GOVT	AU	LO	5.5	5.57	11,223.50			0.0	0.00	0.12	N/A	58
UNITED GOVERNMENT	FI	SC	134.0	5.53	10,981.80	11,984.80	23,176.90	8.6	0.08	0.51	N/A	58
UNITED HIGH INCOME	FI	SC	1,187.7	14.23	11,019.50	14,207.70	29,422.30	12.3	0.71	1.75	22.3	38
UNITED INCOME	EI	NO	844.1	19.13	12,440.80	15,282.00	26,146.50	2.8	0.18	0.54	20.8	132
UNITED INTL GROWTH	GL	NO	188.9	8.26	12,036.80	11,422.70	☆	1.8	0.04	0.15	N/A	N/A
UNITED MISSOURI BK BOND	FI	NO	20.3	10.85	10,726.10	12,661.30	☆	12.2	0.83	1.32	N/A	65
UNITED MISSOURI BK STOCK	GI	NO	31.7	13.52	11,532.80	14,899.60	☆	7.0	0.26	0.98	N/A	223
UNITED NEW CONCEPTS	SG	NO	60.1	6.88	12,900.50			1.0		0.07	27.5	
UNITED RETIREMENT SHARES	GI	SC	99.4	7.42	11,860.80	12,974.50	24,036.40	4.6	0.01	0.34	19.3	69
UNITED SCIENCE & ENERGY	TK	SC	195.6	11.43	11,977.70	13,542.40	20,594.50	2.8	0.29	0.32	23.8	146
UNITED VANGUARD FUND	G	SC	525.1	7.42	11,966.30	13,180.00	24,982.40	2.7	0.00	0.20	26.6	160
US BOSTON-BOSTON I (R)	GI	NO	18.6	13.31	11,950.40	13,299.20	☆	0.9	0.00	0.11	N/A	N/A
US BOSTON-INTL (R)	IF	NO	2.8	11.51	11,294.20	11,736.00	☆	1.2	0.05	0.13	N/A	N/A
US GOLD SHARES	AU	NO	214.8	3.32	9,518.90	6,617.40	9,552.40	7.8	0.00	0.26	5.8	10
US GOOD & BAD TIMES	GI	NO	32.6	18.37	11,990.90	12,771.40	19,566.90	0.9	0.29	0.17	15.2	99
US GOVT GUARANTEED SEC	FI	NO	137.5	14.67	10,469.10			0.0	0.03	0.96	N/A	163
US GROWTH FUND	G	NO	11.9	9.88	12,396.50	13,094.70	☆	0.4	0.00	0.06	N/A	163
US INCOME FUND	_	NO	2.9	11.20	10,372.70	11,137.60	☆	3.4	0.00	0.38	N/A	271
US LOCAP FUND (R)	SG	NO	3.2	8.43	11,500.70	11,078.80	☆	0.2	0.00	0.02	N/A	6
US PROSPECTOR FUND (X,R)	AU	NO	61.0	0.53	9,636.40	9,814.80	☆	0.0	0.00	0.00	35.8	20
US NEW PROSPECTOR (R)	AU	NO	27.3	0.96	10,000.00		☆	0.0	0.00	0.00	36.2	N/A
USAA CORNERSTONE	S	NO	21.9	12.93	11,786.70	12,192.80	☆	2.4	0.05	0.31	N/A	15
USAA GOLD	AU	NO	17.5	6.14	10,233.30	7,908.60		2.0	0.00	0.12	N/A	N/A
USAA GROWTH FUND	G	NO	202.2	18.50	12,308.70	12,906.00	18,298.80	1.5	0.30	0.28	29.6	128
USAA INCOME FUND	FI	NO	199.9	11.96	10,542.10	11,228.20	21,339.90	9.6	0.01	1.15	10.4	79
USAA SUNBELT ERA	SG	NO	156.5	20.95	12,643.30	13,020.70	☆	0.5	0.00	0.10	26.2	74
VALLEY FORGE FUND	G	NO	9.7	10.36	10,247.30	10,707.80	19,241.00	4.3	0.59	0.46	N/A	24
VALUE LINE AGGRES INC	FI	NO	19.3	10.31	$10,453.60	14,083.60	☆	0.0	0.00	0.41	N/A	N/A
VALUE LINE FUND	GI	NO	271.7	18.33	12,929.40	13,755.80	17,948.10	1.1	0.00	0.21	24.6	129
VALUE LINE CENTURION	G	NO	146.2	13.81	13,005.50	13,089.30	☆	0.8	0.29	0.11	N/A	N/A
VALUE LINE CONVERTIBLE	FI	NO	58.4	13.03	12,120.70			2.7	0.00	0.35	N/A	N/A

PERFORMANCE OF MUTUAL FUNDS (concluded)

FUND NAME	OBJ.	LOAD	TOTAL NET ASTS (MIL) 6/30/86	NAV 6/30/86	PERFORMANCE (RETURN ON INITIAL $10,000 INVESTMENT) 12/31/85-6/30/86	6/30/85-6/30/86	6/30/81-6/30/86	YIELD % 6/30/86	PER SHARE LATEST 12 MONTHS CAP GAINS	INC DIVS	LATEST AVAILABLE PRICE/EARNINGS	ANNUAL % TURNOVER
VALUE LINE INCOME	EI	NO	159.1	7.73	11,988.20	12,981.10	21,601.50	6.0	0.43	0.48	21.0	148
VALUE LINE LVGE GROWTH	CA	NO	303.4	27.27	13,244.90	13,903.50	21,448.30	1.2	0.00	0.34	22.7	121
VALUE LINE SPECIAL SIT	G	NO	266.0	17.11	12,352.00	13,355.80	15,012.50	0.2	0.00	0.03	31.5	88
VALUE LINE US GOVT SEC	FI	NO	94.9	12.90	10,442.70	11,407.30	☆	10.1	0.14	1.31	N/A	64
VANCE, SANDERS SPECIAL	G	SC	107.8	13.47	10,924.50	11,471.20	14,588.40	0.4	0.00	0.05	30.4	83
VAN ECK GOLD/RESOURCES	AU	SC	8.6	8.54	☆	$9,232.40	☆	0.0	0.00	0.00	N/A	N/A
VANGUARD CONVERTIBLE	FI	NO	0.2	10.02	$10,020.00	☆	☆	0.0	0.00	0.00	N/A	N/A
VANGUARD FI GNMA PORT	FI	NO	1,605.2	9.79	10,377.10	11,372.00	22,088.80	10.5	0.00	1.03	N/A	50
VANGUARD FI HIGH YIELD	FI	NO	1,018.9	9.24	11,085.20	12,082.40	22,446.30	12.2	0.00	1.13	N/A	100
VANGUARD FI INC SHT TERM	FI	NO	269.9	10.74	10,637.40	11,292.60	☆	8.9	0.00	0.95	N/A	50
VANGUARD FI INV GRADE	FI	NO	426.0	8.56	10,685.10	11,730.70	21,785.40	10.7	0.00	0.92	N/A	50
VANGUARD FI US TREASURY	FI	NO	3.3	10.22	☆	☆	☆	0.0	0.00	0.08	N/A	N/A
VANGUARD INDEX TRUST	GI	NO	492.2	27.34	12,053.60	13,522.00	23,649.70	3.2	1.61	0.91	18.2	35
VANGUARD QUAL DVD I (X)	EI	NO	179.5	19.80	11,325.30	12,700.90	35,135.80	6.6	1.95	1.37	17.5	60
VANGUARD QUAL DVD II	FI	NO	121.1	9.02	11,270.00	12,196.20	23,578.20	9.9	0.00	0.89	N/A	34
VANGUARD QUAL DVD III	FI	NO	134.1	22.61	10,128.50	10,389.80	☆	8.1	0.00	1.83	N/A	90
VANGUARD SPECIAL-ENERGY	NR	NO	8.5	9.83	9,908.70	9,066.40	☆	4.5	0.05	0.44	15.0	156
VANGUARD SPECIAL-GOLD	AU	NO	26.3	6.52	10,598.90	14,327.40	☆	3.2	0.00	0.21	23.5	40
VANGUARD SPECIAL-HEALTH	H	NO	50.8	19.17	12,699.10	13,807.80	☆	0.7	0.10	0.13	23.5	59
VANGUARD SPECIAL-SERVICE	S	NO	83.4	20.59	12,777.50	12,187.50	☆	0.8	0.00	0.16	22.7	54
VANGUARD SPECIAL-TECH	TK	NO	16.7	12.91	11,161.40	12,241.70	☆	0.6	0.00	0.08	N/A	85
VANGUARD STAR	GI	NO	389.1	11.87	11,236.40	☆	☆	5.5	0.27	0.66	N/A	N/A
VANGUARD WORLD-INTL GRO	IF	NO	353.5	10.58	11,581.50	☆	☆	0.0	0.00	0.00	N/A	N/A
VANGUARD WORLD-US GRO	G	NO	185.2	13.66	11,685.20	☆	☆	0.0	0.02	0.00	21.6	61
VAN KAMPEN MERRITT-GOVT	FI	SC	2,861.8	16.23	10,590.60	11,769.20	19,853.00	11.8	0.00	1.91	N/A	172
VARIABLE STOCK FUND	G	SC	8.7	10.91	11,441.00	12,618.70	22,787.70	2.3	1.09	0.27	N/A	86
VENTURE INCOME (+) PLUS	FI	SC	62.6	39.71	10,378.90	11,795.00	16,023.70	14.5	11.15	1.58	N/A	165
WADE FUND	G	SC	0.6	9.50	10,975.70	12,042.40	18,116.50	1.2	1.26	0.06	N/A	6
WALL STREET FUND	G	NO	10.8	20.16	12,056.60	13,277.00	☆	0.6	0.00	0.02	14.8	76
WASHINGTON AREA GRO (R)	G	NO	16.5	12.63	12,291.70	13,492.40	☆	0.1	0.45	0.02	N/A	N/A
WASHINGTON MUTUAL INV	GI	SC	1,476.8	13.88	12,115.00	13,632.50	28,467.00	3.7	0.35	0.49	21.9	26
WAYNE HUMMER GROWTH FUND	G	NO	12.2	23.42	11,729.20	13,062.80	☆	1.7	1.03	0.24	N/A	26
WEINGARTEN EQUITY	CA	NO	224.4	16.60	13,708.50	14,676.80	27,397.80	0.7	0.10	0.17	11.3	97
WELLESLEY INCOME	I	NO	338.2	16.47	11,214.50	12,409.90	25,086.20	8.3	0.10	1.38	16.3	19
WELLINGTON FUND	B	NO	1,027.4	12.90	11,619.90	12,914.40	25,582.60	5.9	0.30	0.98	N/A	27
WESTERGAARD FUND	CA	SC	21.2	16.83	12,011.20	11,882.00	☆	1.6	0.21	0.21	12.3	85
WINDSOR FUND (X)	GI	NO	4,834.9	13.15	11,822.30	12,979.10	28,291.90	4.6	0.74	0.79	15.5	23
WINDSOR II	GI	NO	667.4	9.89	12,157.30	13,309.30	☆	2.4	0.00	0.31	N/A	N/A
WORLD OF TECHNOLOGY	TK	SC	9.7	12.04	12,472.20	14,028.40	☆	0.0	0.00	0.00	34.0	121
WORLD TRENDS	CA	NO	43.7	26.55	12,106.60	☆	☆	0.0	0.00	0.05	26.4	104
WPG FUND	GL	NO	49.5	27.42	13,454.50	☆	23,477.50	3.1	2.27	0.85	N/A	N/A
YES FUND	FI	LO	188.8	7.75	10,308.90	10,548.00	☆	12.5	0.00	0.97	N/A	224
ZENITH FD-BOND INCOME	FI	NO	15.2	115.47	10,836.60	11,671.20	☆	9.5	1.67	11.09	N/A	N/A
ZENITH FD-CAPITAL GROWTH	CA	NO	5.8	248.69	18,355.20	26,645.00	☆	0.3	45.74	0.90	N/A	N/A

How to read the *Barron's*/Lipper gauge. These tables show the return on a $10,000 investment over three periods: six months, one year, and five years.

FUND NAME-Mutual fund name, occasionally shortened, appearing in alphabetical order. The majority of open-end funds registered with the Securities and Exchange Commission are included with the exception of the money market and municipal bond funds.

OBJ.-Investment objective of the fund as determined by both the language in the prospectus and a review of the funds' investment characteristics, such as yield, turnover, etc.

TOTAL NET ASSETS-Fund assets minus liabilities, fund expenses, advisory fees and commissions. NAV (Net Asset Value)-Total net assets divided by the number of shares outstanding. PERFORMANCE-The theoretical ending value of a $10,000 investment for the period analyzed. For complete comparability and regardless of a fund's stated policy, calculations include all capital gains distributions and income dividends, reinvested on the ex-dividend date at ex-date net asset value. Any fund charges not reflected in net asset value or gross income and any tax consequences incurred by the shareholder aren't taken into consideration.

YIELD-The latest 12 months' worth of income dividends divided by the adjusted ending net asset value. The ending net asset value is adjusted periodically for the impact of capital gains paid during the previous 12 months.

PER SHARE-LATEST 12 MONTHS CAP GAINS-Total amount of capital gains per share paid during the last 12 months.

PER SHARE-LATEST 12 MONTHS INC DIVS-Total amount of income dividends per share paid during the last 12 months.

LATEST AVAILABLE-PRICE/EARNINGS-The weighted, average reported price/earnings per share ratio of the underlying equities in the portfolio, based on latest 12 months earnings reported in the latest issue of the "Lipper-Equity Analysis Report on the Weighted Average Holdings of Large Investment Companies."

LATEST AVAILABLE—ANNUAL TURNOVER-The ratio of the smaller of purchases and sales divided by average total net assets expressed as a percentage. The turnover shown is for the latest reported fiscal year.

☆-Fund not in existence for full time period covered.

‡-Fund's first public offering occurred during the present calendar year.

N/A-Not available due either to size or availability of data.

(W)-Fund writes options; (PW)-Purchase/Write options; and (P)-Purchases options; (R)-Fund charges ½ of 1% each on sales and redemption. (X)-Fund closed to new accounts.

AMA MEMBERS RETIREMENT PLAN EQUITY-Available to certain members of the American Medical Association. The first public offering was Dec. 31, 1963. Data is only available from Dec. 31, 1979.

BOND PORTFOLIO FOR ENDOWMENTS, INC. and ENDOWMENTS, INC. FUNDS.-Shares are available only to institutions exempt from federal taxation under Section 501 (c) (1) of the Internal Revenue Code.

EATON VANCE TAX MANAGED-The performance reflects the impact of a reversal of a tax reserve of $2.14 per share on Dec. 31, 1985 when the fund became a regulated investment company under Sub Chapter M of the IRS code.

ELFUN TRUSTS-Available to certain employees of the General Electric Co., regular and senior members of the Elfun Society.

GENERAL ELECTRIC S-5 PROGRAM: GENERAL ELECTRIC LONG TERM INTEREST-Available to General Electric employees.

HARTWELL GROWTH FUND:-On Feb. 6, 1984, the net asset value for Hartwell Growth Fund was increased by $0.79 per share to reflect the receipt of payment in settlement of a class action lawsuit against Viatron Computer Systems.

IVY GROWTH-A new investment adviser was appointed to the fund on April 1, 1985.

PRUDENTIAL BACHE UTILITY-For periods which include Aug. 24, 1984, the dividend, and therefore the performance: includes a reversal of a reserve for taxes of $2.95 per share when the company became a regulated investment company under Sub Chapter M under the IRS code. On that date the net asset value was $20.35.

SCUDDER GROWTH & INCOME FUND-On Nov. 13, 1984 this Fund adopted its present name and objective. Prior performance is attributed to Scudder Common Stock Fund which had an objective of long-term capital growth.

SECTOR INVESTMENT FUND-Does not accrue an advisory fee. The shareholders pay to the adviser a quarterly fee of 1.00% per annum on their accounts on the average daily value. The fund is not permitted to purchase unregistered securities options, or borrow money.

●Copyright Lipper Analytical Services, Inc.

INVESTMENT OBJECTIVE DEFINITIONS:

AU-GOLD ORIENTED FUND-A fund which has at least 65% of its assets in shares of gold mines, gold-oriented mining finance houses, gold coins or bullion.

B-BALANCED FUND-A fund whose primary objective is stability of net asset value, achieved by maintaining a balanced portfolio of both stocks and bonds. Typically, the stock/bond ratio ranges around 60%/40%.

CA-CAPITAL APPRECIATION FUND-Any fund which meets at least two of the following criteria: (1) The investment objective shown in the prospectus is capital appreciation or similar wording. (2) A turnover rate of 100% or more is either expected or realized. (3) The fund is permitted to borrow more than 10% of the value of its portfolio. (4) The prospectus permits short selling, the purchase of options, or investing in common stocks or unregistered securities.

EI-EQUITY INCOME FUND-A fund which normally has 60% or more of its assets in equities and has an above average yield.

FI-FIXED INCOME FUND-A fund which typically has more than 75% of its assets in fixed income issues, such as money market instruments, bonds and preferred stocks.

G-GROWTH FUND-A fund which normally invests in companies whose long-term earnings are expected to grow significantly faster than the earnings of the stocks represented in the major unmanaged stock averages.

GI-GROWTH & INCOME FUND-A fund which combines a growth of earnings objective and an income requirement for level and/or rising dividends.

GL-GLOBAL FUND-A fund which normally invests at least 25% of its portfolio in securities traded outside of the United States and may own U.S. securities as well.

H-HEALTH FUND-A fund which invests 65% of its equity portfolio in health and medical company shares.

I-INCOME FUND-A fund which normally invests less than 75% in fixed income issues and less than 50% in equities, and whose principal aim is the generation of income.

IF-INTERNATIONAL FUND-A fund which invests more than 50% of its assets in securities whose primary trading markets are outside of the United States.

OG-OPTION GROWTH FUND-A fund which attempts to increase its net asset value by investing at least 5% of its portfolio in options.

OI-OPTION INCOME FUND-A fund which writes covered options on at least 50% of its portfolio.

NR-NATURAL RESOURCE FUND-A fund which typically invests more than 65% of its equity commitment in natural resource stocks.

S-SPECIALTY FUND-A fund which, by prospectus, limits its investments to a well-defined specialty, such as banks and utilities.

SG-SMALL COMPANY GROWTH FUND-A fund whose prospectus language and portfolio practice limits its investment to companies on the basis of the size of the company. (Those funds that use smaller companies some of the time or in conjunction with larger companies will not be considered a Small Company Growth Fund.)

TK-SCIENCE & TECHNOLOGY FUND-A fund which invests 65% of its equity portfolio in science and technology stocks.

UT-UTILITY FUND-A fund which invests 65% of its equity portfolio in utility shares.

LOAD-This tells whether a fund has a sales charge known as a load. Load definitions are:

SC-Sales charge-The fund is a load fund up to a maximum 8½% load.

LO-Low-load fund. A fund which charges a load up to 4½%.

NO-No-load fund. A fund which has no sales charge.

Source: Publisher; Lipper Analytical Services, Inc. Reprinted by courtesy of *Barron's National Business and Financial Weekly*, August 11, 1986.

Largest Money Market Funds Invested in Government Securities

Fund	Telephone In State	Out-of-State
Capital Preservation	(800) 982-6150 (CA)	(800) 227-8380
CMA Government Securities (Merrill Lynch)	(212) 637-4467	(800) 225-7455
Dreyfus Money Market Instruments Government	(718) 895-1206	(800) 645-6561
First Variable Rate Fund	(301) 951-4820	(800) 368-2748
Fund for Government Investors	(301) 657-1500	(301) 657-1500
Hutton Government Fund	(212) 742-6003	(212) 742-6003
Liberty U.S. Government Money Market Trust[1]	(412) 288-1900	(800) 245-5000
Pacific Horizon Funds/Government Money Market	(800) 645-3515	(800) 645-3515
Merrill Lynch Government	(617) 357-1460	(800) 225-1576
Shearson Government & Agencies	(215) 542-8025	(215) 542-8025 (collect)

[1] Previously called AARP U.S. Government Trust

Mutual Funds Which Invest Abroad

Foreign investments provide a possible opportunity for increased returns and portfolio diversification. Since most investors lack the time, background and information, the only practical way for them to participate is through the purchase of U.S. based mutual funds which invest abroad. A number of these funds are listed below. In general, these mutual funds are divided into three categories: **global funds** which invest in both U.S. and foreign stocks, **international funds** which invest in foreign stocks, and **regional funds** which invest in the equities of a specific country or region. Here we have combined the first two categories.

Global/International Funds	Telephone in State	Out-of-State
Alliance International	(800) 522-2322 (NY)	(800) 221-5672
Fidelity Overseas	(617) 523-1919	(800) 544-6666
First Investors International	(201) 855-2500	(800) 423-4026
Kemper International Fund	(312) 332-6472	(800) 537-3863
Keystone International	(617) 338-3395	(800) 225-2618
Merrill/Lynch Sci/Tech	(609) 282-2042	(212) 282-2042
Prudential Bache Global	(212) 214-2271	(212) 214-2271
Putnam International Equities	(617) 292-1000	(800) 225-1581
Scudder International[1]	(800) 225-2470	(800) 453-3305
Templeton Foreign/Global/World Funds	(813) 823-8712	(800) 237-0738
T. Rowe Price International[1]	(301) 542-2308	(800) 638-5660
United International Growth	(800) 892-5811 (MO)	(800) 821-5664

[1] no-load

Regional Funds	Telephone in State	Out-of-State
Calvin Bullock Canadian	(212) 513-4200	(800) 221-5757
GT Pacific[1]	(800) 824-8361	(800) 824-1580
Merrill Lynch Pacific	(212) 692-2049	(212) 692-2049
Japan Fund	(Closed end, NYSE)	
Korean Fund	(Closed end, NYSE)	
Mexico Fund	(Closed end, NYSE)	

[1] no-load

Mutual Funds Investing in Gold and Precious Metals

Fidelity Select Portfolio-Precious Metals
82 Devonshire Street
Boston, MA 02109
Telephone: (800) 225-6666
(617) 523-1919
Golconda Investors
11 Hanover Square
New York, NY 10005
Telephone: (800) 431-6060
(212) 847-4200
Goldfund
155 Bovet Road
San Mateo, CA 94402
Telephone: (800) 632-2180
(415) 570-3000

International Investors
122 E. 42 Street
New York, NY 10168
Telephone: (800) 221-2220
(212) 687-5200
Lexington Goldfund
P.O. Box 1515
Saddlebrook, NJ 07662
Telephone: (800) 526-0056
Strategic Investments
2030 Royal Lane
Dallas, TX 75229
Telephone: (800) 527-5027
(214) 484-1326
United Services Gold Shares
P.O. Box 29467
San Antonio, TX 78229
Telephone: (800) 531-5777
(512) 696-1234

Selected No Load/Low Load Mutual Fund Families with Switching Privileges

No load funds do not charge an initial sales fee while low load funds apply an initial sales fee of 1% to 3%. In comparison load funds charge a sales fee of about 8½%. With no load funds all of your investment is put to work immediately. The performance of no load funds is comparable to that of load funds.

The funds listed below permit switching (exchanges) between other members of the fund family (including money market funds) unless otherwise indicated. Thus, investors who expect a marked decline have the option of switching into a money market fund while investors who expect a bull market may choose to switch into a growth oriented fund. Switching may be done by mail or by phone, generally with no additional charge. For income tax purposes any exchange of shares is treated both as a new purchase and a new sale.

Since the performance of funds is quite variable, it is probably best for investors to diversify among three or four fund families.

Investors should study the fund prospectus carefully prior to investing, paying particular attention to average rates of return over the last five and ten year periods, and to risk level (fluctuations in the net asset value). Investors should also familiarize themselves with the switching procedures and restrictions, if any. The information can be obtained by phoning the fund.

Fund objectives vary and it is important to select the fund with objectives similar to yours. A detailed listing of funds by objective, performance record, and much more is given in Donoghues's *Mutual Fund Almanac* (Box 540, Holliston, MA 01746).

We employ the following classifications:

M = Money market fund
B = Bond funds with income as the primary objective
I = Income funds provide income through investments in a mixture of high dividend stocks and bonds with limited capital gains opportunity
GI = Growth income funds invest in common stock and attempt to achieve both capital gains and income through dividend payments and interest. Similar to so called balanced funds. Suited for many conservative investors seeking capital gains.
G = These funds primarily seek capital gains though equity investment in companies with high growth potential. For the more aggressive investor willing to assume greater risks to obtain greater gains.

Babson Group of Funds
3 Crown Center
2440 Pershing Road
Kansas City, MO 64108
(800) 821-5591
(816) 471-5200
Babson Growth Fund (G)
Babson Income (B)
Babson MMF Federal Portfolio (M)
Babson MMF Prime Portfolio (M)
Babson Tax Free Income Fund MMP (M)

Babson Tax Free Inc Long Term (I)
Babson Tax Free Inc Short Term (I)
UMB M.M.F. Federal Portfolio (M)
UMB M.M.F. Prime Portfolio (M)

Bull & Bear Management Corporation
  11 Hanover Square
  New York, NY 10005
  (800) 431-6060
  (212) 785-0900
Bull & Bear Capital Growth (G)
Bull & Bear Dollar Reserves (M)
Bull & Bear Equity Income (I)
Golconda Investors (Goldfund) (GI)

Columbia Management Company
  P.O. Box 1350
  Portland, OR 97207
  (800) 547-1037
  (503) 222-3600
Columbia Daily Income(I)
Columbia Fixed Income Securities (I)
Columbia Growth (G)

Dreyfus Corporation
  767 Fifth Avenue
  New York, NY 10022
  (212) 715-6000
  (718) 895-1206 (general information)
  (800) 645-6561
Dreyfus A Bonds Plus (I)
Dreyfus CA Tax Exempt Bond Fund (B)
[1] Dreyfus Fund (G)
Dreyfus Growth Opportunity (G)
[1] Dreyful Leverage (G)
Dreyfus Liquid Assets (M)
Dreyfus Money Market Instruments Government Series (M)
Dreyfus Money Market Instruments MM Series (M)
Dreyfus NY Tax Exempt Bond Fund (B)
Dreyfus Tax Exempt MMF, Inc. (M)
Dreyfus Special Income (I)
Dreyfus Tax Exempt Bond (B)
Dreyfus Third Century (G)
General Government Securities, MMF (M)
General Money Market Fund (M)
General Tax Exempt Money Market (M)
Fidelity Investments Corporation
  82 Devonshire Street
  Boston, MA 02109
  (800) 225-6190
  (617) 523-1919
Fidelity Cash Reserves (M)
Contrafund (G)
Financial Reserves Fund (M)
Fidelity Corp. Bond (B)
Fidelity Daily Income (M)
[1] Fidelity Destiny (G)
Fidelity Discoverer (G)
Fidelity Equity Income (I)

Fidelity Freedom Fund (GI)
Fidelity Fund (GI)
Fidelity Gov't Securities (I)
Fidelity High Income (B)
Fidelity High Yield Muni (I)
Fidelity Limited Term Municipals (B)
Fidelity Mass Tax-Free Money Market Portfolio (M)
[2] Fidelity Mercury (G)
Fidelity MMT/Domestic (M)
Fidelity MMT/Government (M)
Fidelity MMT/U.S. Treasury (M)
Fidelity Muni Bond (B)
Fidelity Thrift Trust (B)
Fidelity Trend (G)
[2] Fidelity Select-American Gold (G)
[2] Fidelity Select-Bio-Technology (G)
[2] Fidelity Select-Energy (G)
[2] Fidelity Select-Energy Services (G)
[2] Fidelity Select-Financial Services (G)
[2] Fidelity Select-Health CR (G)
[2] Fidelity Select-Precious Metals (G)
[2] Fidelity Select-Technology (G)
[2] Fidelity Select-Utilities (G)
Fidelity Tax Exempt MM Trust (M)
Fidelity U.S. Gov't Reserves (M)
Freedom Fund (GI)
[2] Magellan Fund (G)
Puritan (I)
Rodney Square Fund Money Market (M)
Rodney Square Fund U.S. Government (M)

Financial Programs Inc.
  P.O. Box 2040
  Denver, CO 80201
  (800) 525-9831
  (303) 779-1233 (Denver)
  (800) 332-9145 (Colorado)
Financial Bond Shares/Select Income (I)
Financial Daily Income Shares (M)
Financial Dynamics (G)
Financial Industrial Fund (GI)
Financial Industrial Inc. (I)
Financial Tax Free Income Shares (I)
Financial Tax Free Money Fund (M)

Twentieth Century Investors, Inc.
  P.O. Box 200
  Kansas City, MO 64112
  (816) 531-5575
Twentieth Century Reserves (M)
Twentieth Century Growth (G)
Twentieth Century Select (GI)
Twentieth Century US Government (I)
[2] Twentieth Century Ultra (G)
Twentieth Century Vista Investors (G)

Lehman Management Co.
  55 Water Street
  New York, NY 10041
  (800) 221-5350
  (212) 668-4308
Lehman Capital Fund (G)
Lehman Cash Management (M)

---

[1] Load fund (8.5% sales charge).
[2] Low load fund (2%–3% sales charge); 20th Century Utra (1% sales charge).

Lehman Government Fund (M)
Lehman Tax Free MMF, Inc. (M)
Lehman Investors Fund (GI)
Lehman Opportunity Fund (GI)

Lexington Management Corp.
  Park 80 W Plaza Two
  Saddle Brook, NJ 07662
  (800) 526-0056/7
Lexington GNMA Income (I)
Lexington Goldfund Inc. (G)
Lexington Growth (G)
Lexington Government Secs. MMF (M)
Lexington Money Market Trust (M)
Lexington Research (G)
Lexington Tax Exempt Bond Fund (B)
Lexington Tax Free Money Fund (M)

Neuberger & Berman Management Inc.
  342 Madison Avenue
  New York, NY 10036
  (800) 367-0776
  (212) 850-8300
Energy (G)
Guardian Mutual (GI)
Liberty (I)
Manhattan (G)
Neuberger & Berman Government MF (M)
Neuberger & Berman Tax Free Money Fund
  (M)
Partners Fund (G)

Scudder Fund Distributors, Inc.
  155 Federal Street
  Boston, MA 02110
  (800) 225-2470
  (617) 426-8300
Scudder Capital Growth (G)
Scudder Cash Investment Trust (M)
Scudder Common Stock (GI)
Scudder Development (G)
Scudder Gov't Money Fund (M)
Scudder Income (GI)
Scudder International (G)
Scudder Managed Muni Bond (B)
Scudder NY Tax Free Bond (B)
Scudder Tax Free Money Fund (M)

Stein Roe & Farnham
  150 South Wacker Drive
  Chicago, IL 60606
  (800) 621-0320
  (312) 368-7800
Stein Roe Discovery (G)
Stein Roe Tax Exempt Bond Fund (B)
Stein Roe Universe (G)
Stein Roe Cash Reserves (M)
Stein Roe Gov't Reserves (M)
Stein Roe Tax Exempt MF (M)
Stein Roe Total Return (G)
Stein Roe & Farnham Capital Opportunity (G)
Stein Roe & Farnham Stock (G)
Stein Roe Bond (I)
Stein Roe Special Fund (G)

T. Rowe Price Investor Services, Inc.
  100 E. Pratt Street
  Baltimore, MD 21202
  (800) 638-5660
  (301) 547-2008
Price Growth & Income Fund (GI)
Price Growth Stock (G)
Price International Fund (G)
Price New Era (G)
Price New Horizons (G)
Price New Income (I)
Price Tax Free Income (I)
T. Rowe Price Prime Reserve (B)
T. Rowe Price Tax Exempt MF (M)
T. Rowe Price Tax Free Income Fund (I)
T. Rowe Price U.S. Treasury MF (M)

Value Line Securities, Inc.
  711 Third Avenue
  New York, NY 10017
  (800) 223-0818
  (212) 687-3965
The Value Line Cash Fund, Inc. (M)
Value Line Bond (I)
Value Line Fund (G)
Value Line Income (I)
Value Line Leveraged Growth (G)
Value Line Special Situations (G)
Value Line Tax Exempt Fund (I)
Value Line Tax Exempt High Yield Portfolio
  (B)

Vanguard Group
  Drummers Lane
  Valley Forge, PA 19482
  (800) 523-7025
  (800) 362-0530 (Pennsylvania)
Energy (G)
Explorer (G)
Gold & Precious Metals (G)
Health Care (G)
Ivest (G)
Morgan Growth (G)
Qualified Dividend Port II (I)
Qualified Dividend Port I (GI)
Service Economy (G)
Technology (G)
Trustees' Commingled Fund-U.S. Portfolio (GI)
Vanguard Fixed Income GNMA (B)
Vanguard MMT Federal Fund (M)
Vanguard MMT Insured Portfolio (M)
Vanguard MMT Prime (M)
Vanguard Muni. Bond Fund Long Term M.M.
  (M)
Vanguard Fixed Income High Yield (B)
Vanguard Fixed Income Investment Grade (B)
Vanguard Index Trust (G)
Vanguard Muni High Yield (B)
Vanguard Muni Intermediate Term (B)
Vanguard Muni Long Term (B)
Vanguard Muni Short Term (B)
Wellesley Income (I)
Wellington (GI)
Windsor (G)

Foreign Securities Investments

This section provides data on the performance of major foreign securities markets and also listings of foreign stocks traded on the New York and American Exchanges. Over 200 foreign stocks and ADRs are also traded on the Over-The-Counter (OTC) market. A complete listing of foreign OTC stocks is available from the National Association of Securities Dealers, 1735 K Street, Washington, DC 20006.

Foreign securities not traded on the above exchanges may generally be purchased through stock brokers or major foreign banks in the country of interest. Most of these banks, which have U.S. branches in New York and other major cities, provide details concerning opening a foreign brokerage account.

A difficulty associated with foreign stock selection is that of obtaining timely information. The following general information sources may be helpful in this regard.

The Wall Street Journal
The Asian Wall Street Journal
Dow Jones & Company
22 Cortlandt Street
New York, NY 10007
The Asian Wall Street Journal, a weekly, is particularly helpful for the Asian region, including stock market coverage.

Barron's
20 Burnett Road
Chicopee, MA 01021
The weekly *International Trader* section is of special interest.

Capital International Perspectives
3 Place Des Bergues
1201 Geneva, Switzerland
Capital International Perspectives is a leading monthly publication dealing with international investments.

The Financial Times
Bracken House
10 Cannon Street
London EC4P 4BY, England
The Financial Times provides comprehensive coverage of European businesses and securities markets and is published daily.

Moody's Investor Services, International Manual
99 Church Street
New York, NY 10007
The International Manual provides financial information on about 3,000 major foreign corporations.

Worldwide Investment Research, Ltd.
7730 Carondelet
St. Louis, MO 63105
This publication provides annual and other financial reports on thousands of foreign firms and also publishes *Worldwide Investment Notes.*

Disclosure
5161 River Road
Bethesda, MD 20816
This service also provides annual reports and filings on foreign firms.

A listing of mutual funds investing in foreign securities is given on page 356.

RETURN ON WORLD STOCK MARKETS

	Market Value	Ⓐ Return in each Currency %			Ⓑ Currency Valuation %			Ⓒ Return in U.S. Dollar %		
	Billion Dollar	3 m	1 y	5 y	3 m	1 y	5 y	3 m	1 y	5 y
New York	2205.3	13.1	32.2	11.9	0.0	0.0	0.0	13.1	32.2	11.9
Tokyo	1250.6	20.6	26.7	19.0	12.7	41.1	3.6	36.0	78.9	23.3
London	397.2	22.9	44.1	21.4	1.4	17.6	-8.1	24.6	69.5	11.6
Toronto	208.1	5.1	16.6	5.5	0.3	-2.3	-3.2	5.4	13.9	2.1
Frankfurt	212.5	6.9	76.6	24.9	4.1	30.5	-2.1	11.3	130.5	22.3
Sydney	63.9	13.2	37.0	9.9	4.8	2.0	-9.3	18.7	39.7	-0.3
Paris	118.1	28.3	50.4	20.1	3.6	29.6	-7.1	32.9	94.9	11.6
Zurich	97.0	0.6	42.0	14.7	5.1	32.2	-0.3	5.7	87.7	14.4
Hong Kong	35.5	-7.2	17.6	3.5	-0.2	-0.2	-7.5	-7.4	17.4	-4.3
Milano	108.0	55.9	162.5	23.7	4.4	22.6	-8.0	62.8	221.8	13.8
Amsterdam	58.7	3.4	52.4	29.9	3.9	30.5	-2.5	7.5	98.8	26.7
Singapore	24.7	-4.4	-27.7	-6.4	-3.1	1.1	-0.8	-7.4	-26.9	-7.1
Total	**4779.5**							20.2	53.8	15.5

Source: *Tokyo Stock Market Quarterly Review*, 1986 Vol. 2. March 31, 1986. A publication of Daiwa Securities Co. Ltd. Available through Daiwa Securities America, Inc. One Liberty Plaza, New York, NY 10038.

NOTES

Market Value Estimate for the end of March, 1986.

Return in each currency Return derived solely based upon each market's Stock Price Index (dividends are not included) for the periods ending on the last trading date of the latest quarter. Five-years data are shown in the annual compound rate. Stock price indices referred to are; S & P500, Tokyo Stock Price Index, FT industrial, Toronto composite, Commerzbank general index, Sydney Stock Exchange all ordinaries, CAC industrial, Swiss Bank Corporation general, index, Hang Seng Bank index, Banca Commerciale Italiana index, ANP-CBS industrial, and Straits Times industrial.

Currency valuation Rate of change of each currency's value in U.S. dollar terms (NY market) for the corresponding periods. Five-years data are shown in the annual compound rate.

Return in U.S. Dollar Return of each market in U.S. $ terms. Five-years data are shown in the annual compound rate.

PERFORMANCES OF FOREIGN SECURITIES MARKETS

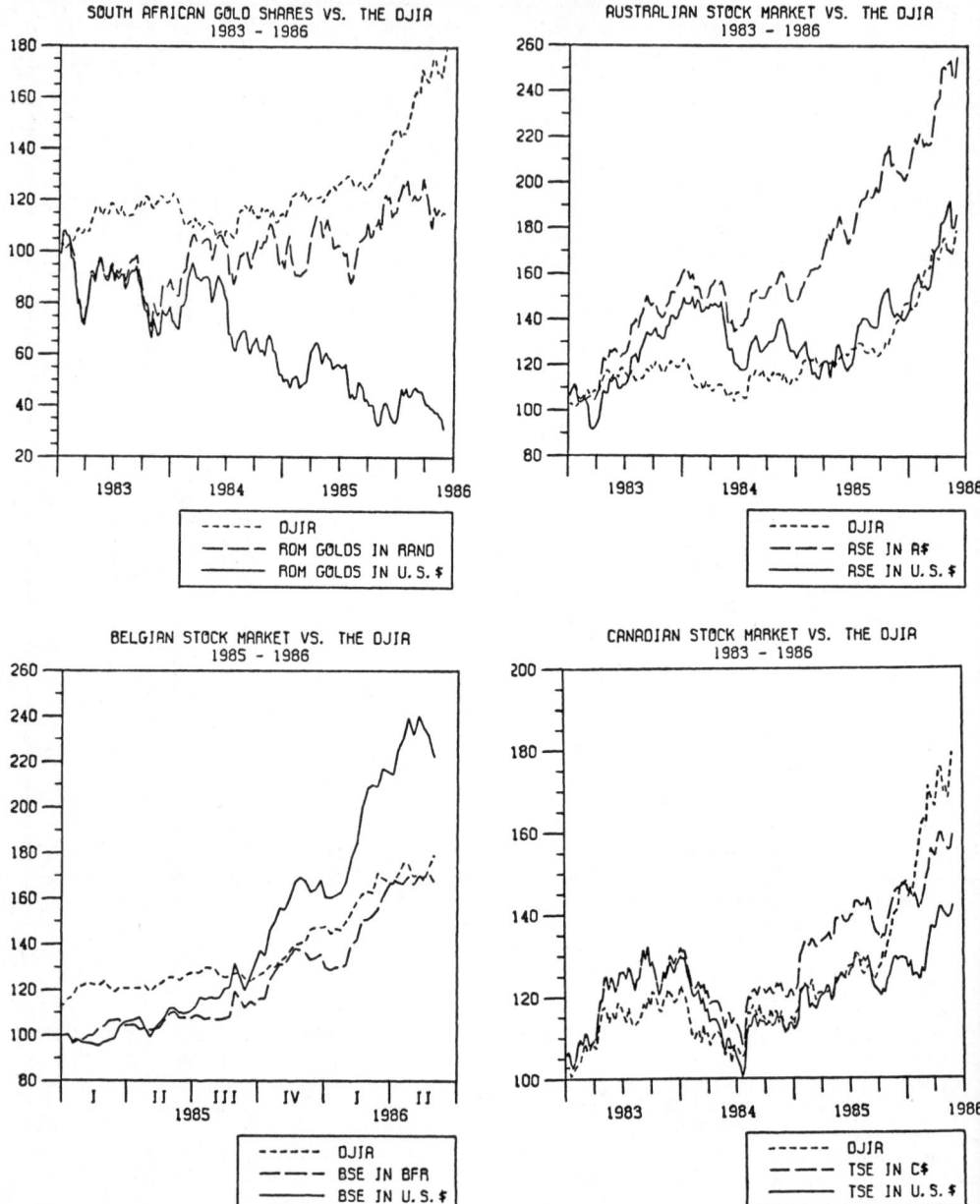

PERFORMANCES OF FOREIGN SECURITIES MARKETS *(continued)*

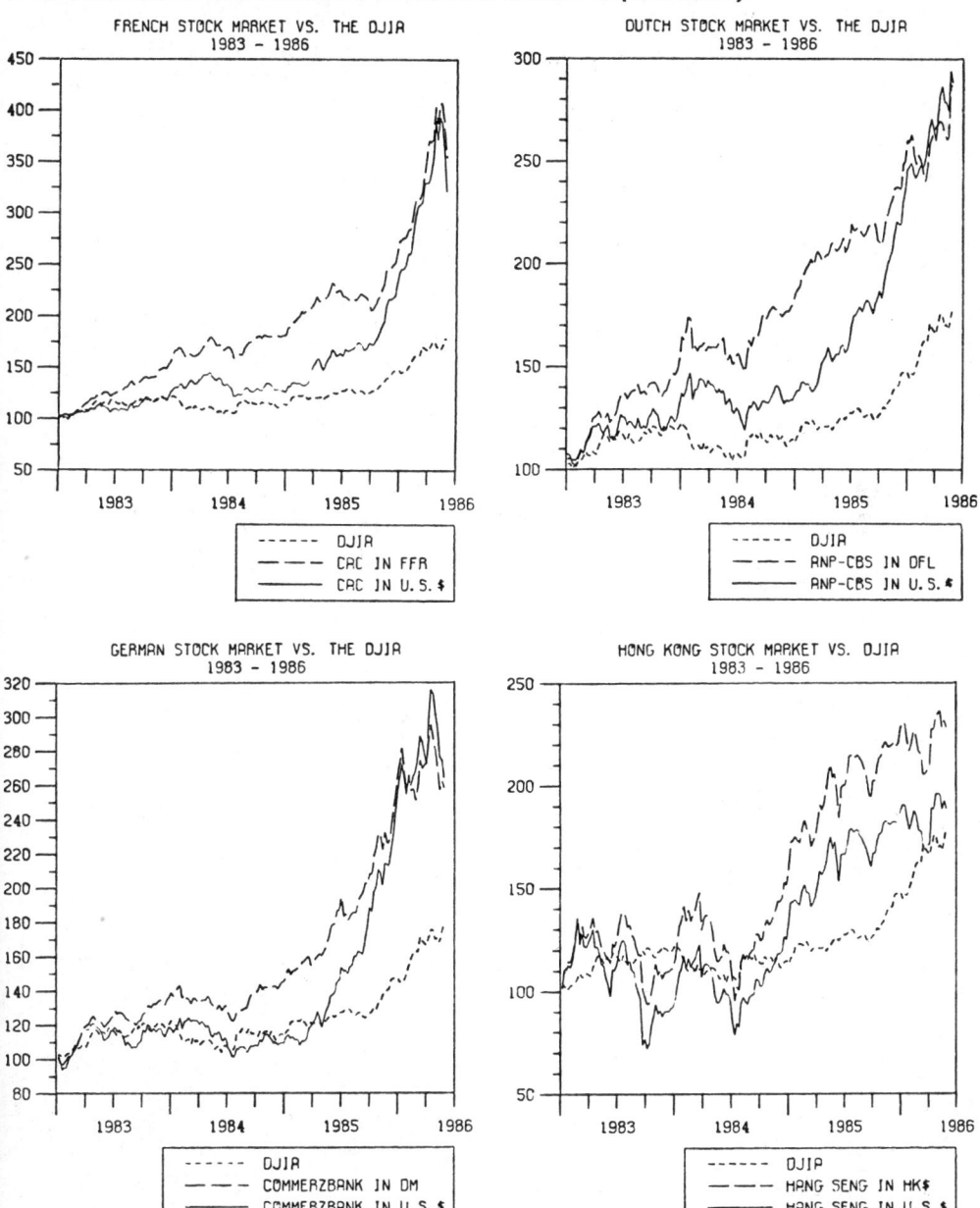

PERFORMANCES OF FOREIGN SECURITIES MARKETS
(concluded)

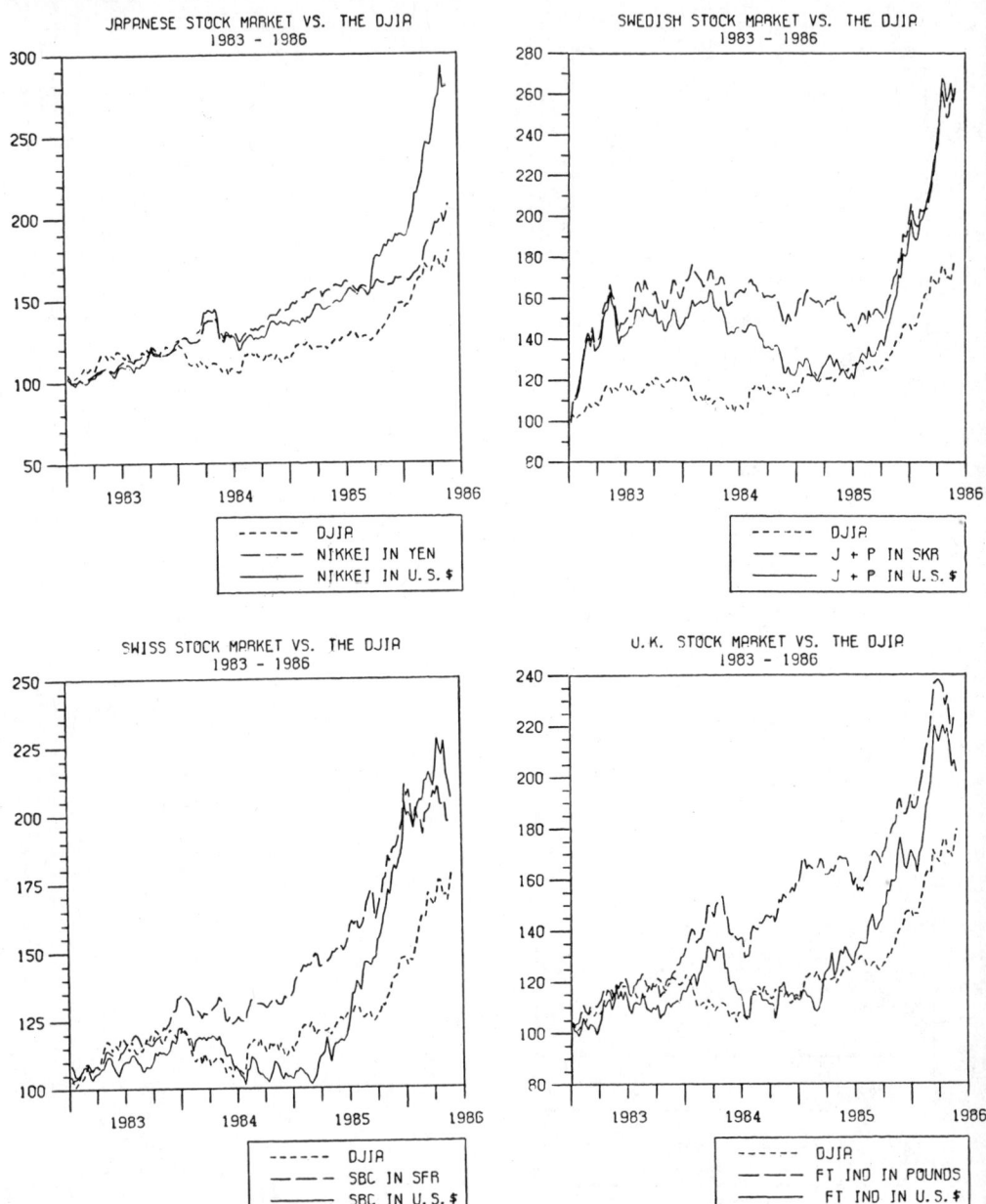

Source: *International Investment Monthly*, June 1986. Drexel Burnham Lambert Incorporated.

FOREIGN STOCKS LISTED ON THE NEW YORK STOCK EXCHANGE

Listed foreign stocks, December 31, 1985

Country	Company	Industry
Bahamas	Commodore International Ltd.	Integrated microcomputer manufacturer
Bermuda	Sea Containers Ltd. (4 issues)	Cargo container lessor
British W.I.	Club Med, Inc.	Hotel, resort operator
Canada	Alcan Aluminium Ltd.	Aluminum producer
	AMCA International Limited	Industrial prods.; construct. services
	Bell Canada Enterprises Inc.	Telecommunications serv. & equip. supplier
	Campbell Red Lake Mines Ltd.	Gold producer
	Campbell Resources Inc.	Diversified natural resources
	Canadian Pacific Limited	Transportation; telecom.; oil; mining
	Carling O'Keefe Limited	Beer, wine producer
	Dome Mines Limited	Gold producer
	Genstar Corp. (2 issues)	Construction, building mat'l producer
	Hiram Walker Resources Ltd.	Distiller; gas utility
	Inco Ltd.	Nickel, copper producer
	Inspiration Resources Corporation	Metals; chemical producer
	LAC Minerals, Ltd.	Gold mining
	MacMillan Bloedel Ltd.	Lumber, newsprint, pulp producer
	Massey-Ferguson Ltd.	Farm equipment producer
	McIntyre Mines Ltd.	Coal producer
	Mitel Corporation	Telecommunications equip. manufacturer
	Moore Corporation Ltd.	Business forms manufacturer
	Northern Telecom Ltd.	Telecommunications equip. manufacturer
	Northgate Exploration Limited	Holding co.- metal producer
	Ranger Oil Limited	Oil & gas explorer, producer
	Seagram Co. Ltd.	Distilled spirits producer
	TransCanada PipeLines Ltd.	Natural gas transmission
	Westcoast Transmission Co., Ltd.	Natural gas distributor
Denmark	Novo Industri A/S	Industrial enzymes; pharmaceuticals
Great Britain	British Petroleum Company Ltd.	Holding co. - integrated int'l oil co.
	British Telecommunications PLC	Telecommunications serv., equip. supplier
	Imperial Chemical Industries PLC	Diversified chemical producer
	Plessey Company Ltd.	Telecommun., electronic equip. mfr.
	"Shell" Transport and Trading Public Ltd. Co.	Holding co., - integrated int'l oil co.
	Tricentrol PLC	Oil, gas producer
	Unilever PLC	Brand name consumer goods
Israel	Elscint Ltd.	Medical imaging equip. manufacturer
Japan	Hitachi, Ltd.	Electronic, electrical manufacturer
	Honda Motor Co., Ltd.	Motor vehicle manufacturer
	Kubota, Ltd.	Agricultural mach.; pipe manufacturer
	Kyocera Corp.	Ceramic manufacturer
	Matsushita Electric Industrial Co., Ltd.	Consumer electronic manufacturer
	Pioneer Electronic Corporation	Consumer electronic manufacturer
	Sony Corporation	Consumer electronic manufacturer
	TDK Corporation	Electronic comp.; magnetic tape producer
Netherlands	KLM Royal Dutch Airlines	Air transportation
	Royal Dutch Petroleum Co.	Holding company - integrated int'l oil co.
Netherlands Antilles	Erbamont N.V.	Pharmaceuticals
	Schlumberger, Ltd.	Oilfield services; electronics
	Unilever, N.V.	Brand name consumer goods
Panama	Norlin Corporation	Financial, corporate printers
	Syntex Corporation	Pharmaceuticals
Philippines	Benguet Corporation	Construction; gold producer
South Africa	ASA Limited	Closed-end inv. co. - gold mining
Spain	Banco Central, S.A.	International banking

Source: New York Stock Exchange *1986 Fact Book.*

Securities Markets: Notable Dates

1792 Original brokers' agreement subscribed to by 24 brokers (May 17).

1817 Constitution and the name "New York Stock Exchange Board" adopted (March 8).

1830 Dullest day in history of exchange—31 shares traded (March 16).

1840s Outdoor trading in unlisted securities begins at Wall and Hanover Streets, moves to Wall and Broad, then shifts south along Broad Street.*

1863 Name changed to "New York Stock Exchange" (NYSE) (January 29).

1867 Stock tickers first introduced (November 15).

1868 Membership made salable (October 23).

1869 Gold speculation resulted in "Black Friday" (September 24).

1871 Continuous markets in stocks established.

1873 NYSE closed September 18–29.
      Failure of Jay Cooke & Co. and others (September 18).
      Trading hours set at 10 A.M. to 3 P.M.; Saturdays, 10 A.M. to noon (December 1).

1878 First telephones introduced in the exchange (November 13).

1881 Annunciator board installed for paging members (January 29).

1885 Unlisted Securities Department established (March 25).

1886 First million-share day—1,200,000 shares traded (December 15).

1908 E. S. Mendels forms New York Curb Agency in first departure from informal trading.*

1910 Unlisted Securities Department abolished (March 31).

1911 Trading rules established with formation of New York Curb Market Association.*

1914 Exchange closed from July 31 through December 11—World War I.

1915 Stock prices quoted in dollars as against percent of par value (October 13).

1919 Separate ticker system installed for bonds (January 2).

1920 Stock Clearing Corporation established (April 26).

1921 New York Curb Market association

moves indoors at 86 Trinity Place; name shortened to New York Curb Market and ticker service initiated (June 21).*

1927 Start of ten-share unit of trading for inactive stocks (January 3).

1929 Stock market crash; 16,410,000 shares traded (October 29).
      New York Curb Market modifies its name to New York Curb Exchange.*

1930 Faster ticker—500 characters per minute—installed (September 2).

1931 Exchange building expanded; Telephone Quotation Department formed to send stock quotes to member firm offices.*

1933 New York Stock Exchange closed for bank holiday, March 4–14.

1934 Enactment of Securities Exchange Act of 1934 (June 6).

1938 First salaried president elected—Wm. McC. Martin, Jr. (June 30).

1946 Listed stocks outnumber unlisted stocks for first time since the 1934 act imposed restrictions on unlisted trading.*

1952 Trading hours changed: weekdays, 10 A.M. to 3:30 P.M. Closed Saturdays (September 29).*

1953 Name of New York Curb Exchange changed to American Stock Exchange.*

1958 First member corporation—Woodcock, Hess & Co. (June 4).
      Mary C. Roebling becomes first woman governor.*

1962 Committee system of administration replaced by expanded paid staff reporting to president. Specialist system strengthened, surveillance of trading increased, listing and delisting standards introduced, and board restructured to give greater representation to commission and out-of-town brokers.*

1964 New member classification—Registered Trader (August 3).
      New ticker—900 characters per minute—put into service (December 1).†
      Am-Quote computerized telephone-quotation service was completed as first step in major automation program.*

1965 Fully automated quotation service introduced (March 8).
      Electronic Systems Center created (October 15).
      First women, Phyllis S. Peterson and Julia Montgomery Walsh, elected to regular membership.*

1966 New NYSE Stock Price Index inaugurated (July 14).
      AMEX Price Change Index System introduced; computer complex installed

* Refers to American Exchange (AMEX) (formerly Curb Exchange).

† Applies to both the New York Stock Exchange and the American Exchange. Other entries refer to the New York Stock Exchange.

Sources: New York Stock Exchange 1985 Fact Book and American Stock Exchange Data Book and The Wall Street Journal.

for ticker, surveillance, and compared-clearance operations.*

1967 First woman member admitted—Muriel F. Siebert (December 28).

1968 Ticker speed increased to maximum 900 characters per minute; transmission begun to six European countries. Trading floor modernized; line capacity for communications doubled. Visitors gallery expanded.*

1969 Central Certificate Service fully activated (February 26).

1970 Public ownership of member firms approved (March 26).

Securities Investor Protection Corporation Act signed (December 30).

1971 First negotiated commission rates effective (April 5).

First member organization listed—Merrill Lynch (July 27).

AMEX incorporates and marks 50th anniversary of move indoors; Listed Company Advisory Committee formed, composed of nine chief executives of AMEX-listed companies.*

1972 NYSE reorganization, based on Martin Report, approved (January 20).

Board of Directors, with ten public members, replaced Board of Governors (July 13).

Securities Industry Automation Corporation established with AMEX to consolidate facilities of both exchanges (July 17).*

First salaried chairman took office—James J. Needham (August 28).

Board of Governors reorganized to include ten public and ten industry representatives plus full-time salaried chairman as chief executive officer.*

1973 Depository Trust Company succeeded Central Certificate Service (May 11).

Chicago Board of Options Exchange opened with trading in 16 classes of call options (April 26).

AMEX formally adopts affirmative action employment plan; Market Value Index System introduced to replace Price Change Index.*

1974 Trading hours extended to 4 P.M. (October 1).

Consolidated tape begun; 15 stocks reported (October 18).

1975 Fixed commission system abolished (April 30).

Full consolidated tape begun (June 16).

AMEX trades call options.*

Trading begins in call options and odd lots of U.S. government instruments.*

1976 New data line installed, handling 36,000 characters per minute (January 19).

Specialists began handling odd lots in their stocks (May 24).

Varo, Inc.—first stock traded on both NYSE and AMEX (August 23).

Competition between specialists begun (October 11).

1977 Independent audit committee on listed companies' boards required (January 6).

Competitive Trader category for members approved (January 19).

National Securities Clearing Corporation (NSCC) began merging the clearing operations of the Stock Clearing Corporation of NYSE with American Stock Exchange Clearing Corporation and National Clearing Corporation of the NASD (January 20).

Foreign broker/dealers permitted to obtain membership (February 3).

Full Automated Bond System in effect (July 27).

1978 First 60 million share day in history (63,493,000 shares) (April 17).

Intermarket Trading System (ITS) began.

Registered Competitive Market-Maker category for members approved (May 2).

First 65 million share day in history (66,370,000 shares) (August 3).

Trading in Ginnie Maes inaugurated on the AMEX Commodities Exchange (ACE)* (September 12).

AMEX reached an index high of 176.87 (September 13).

1979 Trading began at pilot post on the exchange floor. First stage in a $12-million upgrading of exchange facilities (January 29).

Board of Directors of NYSE approved plan for the creation of the New York Futures Exchange, a wholly owned subsidiary of NYSE. Futures contracts in seven financial instruments will be traded on the NYSE (March 1).

New York Commodities Exchange and NYSE terminated merger talks (March 15).

81,619,000 shares were traded on the NYSE, making it the heaviest trade day in exchange history (October 10).

1980 American Stock Exchange reached an all-time daily stock volume record of 14,980,680 shares sold (January 15).*

NYSE volume of 67,752,000 shares traded was second largest volume on record to date (January 16).

NYSE Futures Exchange opened (August 7).

Option seat on the American Stock Exchange sold at an all-time high of $160,000 (December 24).*

NYSE index reached an all time high of 81.02 (November 28).

1981 First 90 million share day in the history of the Exchange, 92,881,000 (January 7).

The New York Stock Exchange subsidiary, the New York Futures Exchange, started trading futures in Domestic Bank Certificates of Deposit.

1982 A new AMEX subsidiary The American Gold Coin Exchange (AGCE) began trading in the Canadian Maple Leaf (January 21).*

Trading in NYSE Common Stock Index Futures began on the New York Futures Exchange (May 6).*

Trading started through experimental linkage between ITS operated by NYSE and six other exchanges and Computer Assisted Execution Service (CAES) operated by NASD, in 30 stocks exempted from exchange off-board trading rules under SEC Rule 19c-3. (May 17)

Record advance of 38.81 points reached in NYSE trading as measured by Dow Jones Industrial Average (August 17).

First 100 million share day (132,681,120 shares. (August 18).

Trading in Interest Rate Options on U.S. Treasury Bills & Notes started in May on the AMEX.*

Trading soared to an all time high of 147,081,070 shares on the NYSE (October 7).

All time options high of 340,550 contracts were traded on the AMEX (October 7).*

Dow Jones Industrial Average plunged 36.33 points, the largest one-day loss since the record plunge of 38.33 points on October 28, 1929 (October 25).

1983 Trading in options on NYSE Common Stock Index Futures started on New York Futures Exchange (January 28).

NYSE started trading options on the NYSE Common Stock Index (September 23).

Dow Jones Industrial Average reached an all time high of 1260.77 (September 26).

New shares of common stocks of seven regional telephone companies and shares of the "new" AT&T began trading on a "when issued" basis. Divestiture of AT&T effective January 1, 1984 (November 21).

AMEX stock trading went over the two billion share mark for the first time.

The AMEX list of stock options increased by four index options, two on specific industry groups, one on the AMEX Market Value Index.*

1984 Largest NYSE trading day of 159,-999,031 shares traded (January 5).

CBOT (Chicago Board of Trade) began trading a futures contract on the Major Market Index (July 23).*

Trading began in NYSE Double Index Options (July 23).

NYSE volume soared to a record 236,565,110 shares traded (August 3).

Super DOT 250 (electronic order-routing system) launched on NYSE (November 16).

1985 For the first time the NYSE index went over 100, closing at 101.12 (January 21).

19,091,950 shares were traded on the AMEX, the highest single day volume ever. (February 6).*

Ronald Reagan visited the NYSE, the first President to do so while in office (March 28).

Trading in options on gold bullion started on AMEX (April 26).*

50 billionth share listed in NYSE (May 30).

NYSE began trading options in three over-the-counter stocks (June 3).

NYSE reached an all time index high of 113.49 (July 17).

Amex and Toronto Stock Exchange linked together as part of the first two-way electronic hookup between primary equity markets in different countries (September 24).

Instinet Corporation and the AMEX reached an agreement enabling European institutional investors to have access to the AMEX options market via Reuter's electronic terminals.

The opening trading time on both the NYSE and AMEX went from 10:00 A.M. to 9:30 A.M. (September 30).

The Dow Jones Industrial Average reached an all-time high of 1368.50 (October 16).

Options traded on two listed stocks on the NYSE (October 16).

Tokyo Stock Exchange admitted its first foreign member firms (December 1).

A daily record of 119,969 contracts traded on the AMEX Major Markets Index Option (December 13).*

1986 The Dow Jones Industrial Average for the first time closed above 1600 at 1600.69 (February 6).

The Dow Jones Industrial Average for the first time closed above 1700 at 1713.99. (February 27).

The Dow Jones Industrial Average for the first time closed above 1800 at 1804.24 (March 20).

The Dow Jones Industrial Average for the first time closed above 1900 at 1903.54 (July 1).

The Directors of the NYSE voted to

abandon the one-share-one-vote rule which gives common shareholders equal voting rights (July 3).

The Dow Jones Industrials tumbled 61.87 points to close at 1839 (July 7).

The Dow Jones Industrials nose-dived a record 86.61 points on a record volume of 237,600,000 shares traded (September 11).

Investment and Financial Terms

Abandonment value   The amount that can be realized by liquidating a project before its economic life has ended.*

Accelerated depreciation   Depreciation methods that write off the cost of an asset at a faster rate than the write-off under the straight-line method. The three principal methods of accelerated depreciation are: (1) sum-of-the-years'-digits, (2) double-declining balance, and (3) units-of-production.*

Accountant's Opinion   (See: *Auditor's Report.*)

Accruals   Accruals   Continuing   recurring short-term liabilities. Examples are accrued wages, accrued taxes, and accrued interest.*

Accrued interest   Interest accrued on a bond since the last interest payment was made. The buyer of the bond pays the market price plus accrued interest. Exceptions include bonds that are in default and income bonds. (See: *Flat income bond.*)†

Acquisition   The acquiring of control of one corporation by another. In "unfriendly" takeover attempts, the potential buying company may offer a price well above current market values, new securities and other inducements to stockholders. The management of the subject company might ask for a better price or try to join up with a third company. (See: *Merger, Proxy*)††

* Entries from *Managerial Finance*, 6th edition, by J. Fred Weston and Eugene F. Brigham.

† Entries from *The Language of Investing Glossary.*

** Entries from *Tax-Exempt Securities & the Investor.*

†† Entries from the *Glossary.*

¶ Entries from the Federal Reserve *Glossary.*

Sources: From *Managerial Finance*, 6th ed., by J. Fred Weston and Eugene F. Brigham. Copyright © 1978 by The Dryden Press, Copyright © 1962, 1966, 1969, 1972, 1975 by Holt, Rinehart and Winston. Reprinted by permission of Holt, Rinehart and Winston, CBS College Publishing.

The *Language of Investing Glossary* published by the New York Stock Exchange, Inc.

The *Glossary* published by the New York Stock Exchange.

Tax-Exempt Securities & the Investor published by the Securities Industry Association.

The *Glossary* published by the Board of Governors of the Federal Reserve System.

Ad valorem tax   A tax based on the value (or assessed value) of property.**

Aging schedule   A report showing how long accounts receivable have been outstanding. It gives the percent of receivables not past due and the percent past due by, for example, one month, two months, or other periods.*

American Depository Receipt (ADR)   Issued by American banks, an ADR is a certificate which serves as a proxy for a foreign stock deposited in a foreign bank. For all practical purposes, trading an ADR is equivalent to trading the foreign stock. Hundreds of ADRs are traded on U.S. stock exchange.

Amortization   Accounting   for   expenses   or charges as applicable rather than as paid. Includes such practices as depreciation, depletion, write-off of intangibles, prepaid expenses, and deferred charges.†

Amortize   To liquidate on an installment basis; an amortized loan is one in which the principal amount of the loan is repaid in installments during the life of the loan.*

Annual report   The formal financial statement issued yearly by a corporation. The annual report shows assets, liabilities, earnings—how the company stood at the close of the business year, how it fared profit-wise during the year and other information of interest to shareowners.†

Annuity   A series of payments of a fixed amount for a specified number of years.*

Arbitrage   A technique employed to take advantage of differences in price. If, for example, ABC stock can be bought in New York for $10 a share and sold in London at $10.50, an arbitrageur may simultaneously purchase ABC stock here and sell the same amount in London, making a profit of 50 cents a share, less expenses. Arbitrage may also involve the purchase of rights to subscribe to a security, or the purchase of a convertible security—and the sale at or about the same time of the security obtainable through exercise of the rights or of the security obtainable through conversion. (See: *Convertible, Rights*)††

Arrearage   Overdue   payment;   frequently omitted dividend on preferred stock.

Assessed valuation   The valuation placed on property for purposes of taxation.**

Assets   Everything a corporation owns or due to it: Cash, investments, money due it, materials and inventories, which are called current assets; buildings and machinery, which are known as fixed assets; and patents and good will, called intangible assets. (See: *Liabilities.*)†

Assignment   A relatively inexpensive way of liquidating a failing firm that does not involve going through the courts.*

Assignment   Notice to an option writer that an

option holder has exercised the option and that the writer will now be required to deliver (receive) under the terms of the contract.††

Ask (See: *Bid and asked*.)†

Auction market The system of trading securities through brokers or agents on an exchange such as the New York Stock Exchange. Buyers compete with other buyers while sellers compete with other sellers for the most advantageous price.††

Auditor's report Often called the accountant's opinion, it is the statement of the accounting firm's work and its opinion of the corporation's financial statements, especially if they conform to the normal and generally accepted practices of accountancy.††

Averages Various ways of measuring the trend of securities prices, one of the most popular of which is the Dow-Jones average of 30 industrial stocks listed on the New York Stock Exchange. The prices of the 30 stocks are totaled and then divided by a divisor which is intended to compensate for past stock splits and stock dividends and which is changed from time to time. As a result point changes in the average have only the vaguest relationship to dollar price changes in stocks included in the average. (See: *NYSE composite index*.)††

Balance sheet A condensed financial statement showing the nature and amount of a company's assets, liabilities and capital on a given date. In dollar amounts the balance sheet shows what the company owned, what it owed, and the ownership interest in the company of its stockholders. (See: *Assets, Earnings report*.)†

Balloon payment When a debt is not fully amortized, the final payment is larger than the preceding payments and is called a *balloon* payment.*

Bankers acceptance Bankers acceptances are negotiable time drafts, or bills of exchange, that have been accepted by a bank which, by accepting, assumes the obligation to pay the holder of the draft the face amount of the instrument on the maturity date specified. They are used primarily to finance the export, import, shipment, or storage of goods.¶

Bankruptcy A legal procedure for formally liquidating a business, carried out under the jurisdiction of courts of law.*

Basis book A book of mathematical tables used to convert yields to equivalent dollar prices.**

Basis point One gradation on a 100-point scale representing one percent; used especially in expressing variations in the yields of bonds. Fixed income yields vary often and slightly within one percent and the basis point scale easily expresses these changes in hundredths of one percent. For example, the difference between 12.83% and 12.88% is 5 basis points.††

Basis price The price expressed in yield or percentage of return on the investment.**

Bear market A declining market. (See: *Bull market*.)†

Bearer bond A bond which does not have the owner's name registered on the books of the issuer and which is payable to the holder. (See: *Coupon bond, Registered bond*.)†

Bearer security A security that has no identification as to owner. It is presumed to be owned, therefore, by the bearer or the person who holds it. Bearer securities are freely and easily negotiable since ownership can be quickly transferred from seller to buyer.**

Beta coefficient Measures the extent to which the returns on a given stock move with "the stock market."*

Bid and asked Often referred to as a quotation or quote. The bid is the highest price anyone has declared that he wants to pay for a security at a given time, the asked is the lowest price anyone will take at the same time. (See: *Quote*.)†

Block A large holding or transaction of stock—popularly considered to be 10,000 shares or more.†

Blue chip A company known nationally for the quality and wide acceptance of its products or services, and for its ability to make money and pay dividends.†

Blue-sky laws A popular name for laws various states have enacted to protect the public against securities frauds. The term is believed to have originated when a judge ruled that a particular stock had about the same value as a patch of blue sky.†

Board room A room for registered representatives and customers in a broker's office where opening, high, low, and last prices of leading stocks used to be posted on a board throughout the market day. Today such price displays are normally electronically controlled although most board rooms have replaced the board with the ticker and/or individual quotation machines.†

Bond Basically an IOU or promissory note of a corporation, usually issued in multiples of $1,000 or $5,000, although $100 and $500 denominations are not unknown. A bond is evidence of a debt on which the issuing company usually promises to pay the bondholders a specified amount of interest for a specified length of time, and to repay the loan on the expiration date. In every case a bond represents debt—its holder is a creditor of the corporation and not a part owner as is the shareholder. (See: *Collateral, Convertible, Debenture, General Mortgage Bond, Income Bond*.)††

Bond funds Registered investment companies whose assets are invested in diversified portfolios of bonds.*

Book A notebook the specialist in a stock uses to keep a record of the buy and sell orders at specified prices, in sequence of receipt, which are left with him by other brokers. (See *Specialist*.)†

Book value The accounting value of an asset. The book value of a share of common stock is equal to the net worth (common stock plus retained earnings) of the corporation divided by the number of shares of stock outstanding.*

Break-even analysis An analytical technique for studying the relation between fixed cost, variable cost, and profits. A break-even *chart* graphically depicts the nature of break-even analysis. The break-even *point* represents the volume of sales at which total costs equal total revenues (that is, profits equal zero).*

Broker An agent, who handles the public's orders to buy and sell securities, commodities, or other property. For this service a commission is charged. (See: *Commission broker, dealer*.)†

Brokers' loans Money borrowed by brokers from banks or other brokers for a variety of uses. It may be used by specialists and to help finance inventories of stock they deal in; by brokerage firms to finance the underwriting of new issues of corporate and municipal securities; to help finance a firm's own investments; and to help finance the purchase of securities for customers who prefer to use the broker's credit when they buy securities. (See: *Margin*.)†

Bull market An advancing market. (See: *Bear market*.)†

Business risk The basic risk inherent in a firm's operations. Business risk plus financial risk resulting from the use of debt equals total corporate risk.*

Call (1) An option to buy (or "call") a share of stock at a specified price within a specified period. (2) The process of redeeming a bond or preferred stock issue before its normal maturity. (See: *Options*.)*

Call premium The amount in excess of par value that a company must pay when it calls a security.*

Call price The price that must be paid when a security is called. The call price is equal to the par value plus the call premium.*

Call privilege A provision incorporated into a bond or a share of preferred stock that gives the issuer the right to redeem (call) the security at a specified price.*

Callable A bond issue, all or part of which may be redeemed by the issuing corporation under definite conditions before maturity. The term also applies to preferred shares which may be redeemed by the issuing corporation.†

Capital asset An asset with a life of more than one year that is not bought and sold in the ordinary course of business.*

Capital budgeting The process of planning expenditures on assets whose returns are expected to extend beyond one year.*

Capital gain or capital loss Profit or loss from the sale of a capital asset. A capital gain, under current federal income tax laws, may be either short-term (12 months or less) or long-term (more than 12 months). A short-term capital gain is taxed at the reporting individual's full income tax rate. A long-term capital gain is subject to a lower tax. The capital gains provisions of the tax law are complicated. You should consult your tax advisor for specific information.†

Capital market line A graphical representation of the relationship between risk and the required rate of return on an efficient portfolio.*

Capital markets Financial transactions involving instruments with maturities greater than one year.*

Capital rationing A situation where a constraint is placed on the total size of the capital investment during a particular period.*

Capital stock All shares representing ownership of a business, including preferred and common. (See: *Common stock, Preferred stock*.)†

Capital structure The permanent long-term financing of the firm represented by long-term debt, preferred stock, and net worth (net worth consists of capital, capital surplus, and retained earnings). Capital structure is distinguished from *financial structure*, which includes short-term debt plus all reserve accounts.*

Capitalization Total amount of the various securities issued by a corporation. Capitalization may include bonds, debentures, preferred and common stock, and surplus. Bonds and debentures are usually carried on the books of the issuing company in terms of their par or face value. Preferred and common shares may be carried in terms of par or stated value. Stated value may be an arbitrary figure decided upon by the directors or may represent the amount received by the company from the sale of the securities at the time of issuance. (See: *Par*.)†

Capitalization rate A discount rate used to find the present value of a series of future cash receipts; sometimes called *discount rate*.*

Carry-back; carry forward For income tax purposes, losses that can be carried backward or forward to reduce federal income taxes.*

Cash budget A schedule showing cash flows (receipts, disbursements, and net cash) for a firm over a specified period.*

Cash cycle The length of time between the purchase of raw materials and the collection of accounts receivable generated in the sale of the final product.*

Cash flow Reported net income of a corporation *plus* amounts charged off for depreciation, depletion, amortization, extraordinary charges to reserves, which are bookkeeping deductions and not paid out in actual dollars and cents. (See: *Amortization, Depreciation*.)††

Cash sale A transaction on the floor of the Stock Exchange which calls for delivery of the securities the same day. In "regular way" trades, the seller is to deliver on the fifth business day except for bonds, which is the next day. (See: *Regular way delivery*.)†

Certainty equivalents The amount of cash (or rate of return) that someone would require *with certainty* to make him indifferent between this certain sum (or *rate of return*) and a particular uncertain, risky sum (or rate of return).*

Certificate The actual piece of paper which is evidence of ownership of stock in a corporation. Watermarked paper is finely engraved with delicate etchings to discourage forgery.††

Certificate of Deposit (CD) A money market instrument issued by banks. The time CD is characterized by its set date of maturity and interest rate and its wide acceptance among investors, companies and institutions as a highly negotiable short-term investment vehicle.††

CFTC The Commodity Futures Trading Commission, created by Congress in 1974 to regulate exchange trading in futures.††

Characteristic line A linear least-squares regression line that shows the relationship between an individual security's return and returns on "the market." The slope of the characteristic line is the beta coefficient.*

Chattel mortgage A mortgage on personal property (not real estate). A mortgage on equipment would be a chattel mortgage.*

Closed-end investment company (See: *Investment company*.)

Coefficient of variation Standard deviation divided by the mean: CV.*

Collateral Assets that are used to secure a loan.*

Collateral trust bond A bond secured by collateral deposited with a trustee. The collateral is often the stocks or bonds of companies controlled by the issuing company but may be other securities.†

Commercial paper Unsecured, short-term promissory notes of large firms, usually issued in denominations of $1 million or more. The rate of interest on commercial paper is typically somewhat below the prime rate of interest.*

Commission The broker's basic fee for purchasing or selling securities or property as an agent.†

Commission broker An agent who executes the public's orders for the purchase or sale of securities or commodities.†

Commitment fee The fee paid to a lender for a formal line of credit.*

Commodities (See: *Futures*.)

Common stock Securities which represent an ownership interest in a corporation. If the company has also issued preferred stock, both common and preferred have ownership rights. Common stockholders assume the greater risk, but generally exercise the greater control and may gain the greater reward in the form of dividends and capital appreciation. The terms of common stock and capital stock are often used interchangeably when the company has no preferred stock.†

Compensating balance A required minimum checking account balance that a firm must maintain with a commercial bank. The required balance is generally equal to 15 to 20 percent of the amount of loans outstanding. Compensating balances can raise the effective rate of interest on bank loans.*

Competitive trader A member of the Exchange who trades in stocks on the Floor for an account in which he has an interest. Also known as a Registered Trader.†

Composite cost of capital A weighted average of the component costs of debt, preferred stock, and common equity. Also called the *weighted-average cost of capital*, but it reflects the cost of each additional dollar raised, not the average cost of all capital the firm has raised throughout its history.*

Composition An informal method of reorganization that voluntarily reduces creditors' claims on the debtor firm.*

Compound interest An interest rate that is applicable when interest in succeeding periods is earned not only on the initial principal but also on the accumulated interest of prior periods. Compound interest is contrasted to *simple interest*, in which returns are not earned on interest received.*

Compounding The arithmetic process of determining the final value of a payment or series of payments when compound interest is applied.*

Conditional sales contract A method of financing new equipment by paying it off in installments over a one-to-five-year period. The seller retains title to the equipment until payment has been completed.*

Conglomerate A corporation that has diversified its operations, usually by acquiring enterprises in widely varied industries.†

Consolidated balance sheet A balance sheet showing the financial condition of a corporation and its subsidiaries. (See: *Balance sheet*.)†

Consolidated tape The ticket tape reporting transactions in NYSE listed securities that take place on the NYSE or any of the participating regional stock exchanges and other markets. Similarly, transactions in AMEX-listed securities, and certain other securities listed on regional stock exchanges, are reported and identified on a separate tape.††

Consolidated tax return An income tax return that combines the income statement of several affiliated firms.*

Continuous compounding (discounting) As opposed to discrete compounding, interest is added continuously rather than at discrete points in time.*

Conversion price The effective price paid for common stock when the stock is obtained by converting either convertible preferred stocks or convertible bonds. For example, if a $1,000 bond is convertible into 20 shares of stock, the conversion price is $50 ($1,000/20).*

Conversion ratio or conversion rate The number of shares of common stock that may be obtained by converting a convertible bond or share of convertible preferred stock.*

Convertibles Securities (generally bonds or preferred stocks) that are exchangeable at the option of the holder for common stock of the issuing firm.*

Correlation coefficient Measures the degree of relationship between two variables.*

Correspondent A securities firm, bank, or other financial organization which regularly performs services for another in a place or market to which the other does not have direct access. Securities firms may have correspondents in foreign countries or on exchanges of which they are not members. Correspondents are frequently linked by private wires. Member organizations of the N.Y.S.E. with offices in New York City may also act as correspondents for out-of-town member organizations which do not maintain New York City offices.†

Cost of capital The discount rate that should be used in the capital budgeting process.*

Coupon bond Bond with interest coupons attached. The coupons are clipped as they come due and are presented by the holder for payment of interest. (See: *Bearer bond, Registered bond*.)†

Coupon rate The stated rate of interest on a bond.*

Covariance The correlation between two variables multiplied by the standard deviation of each variable:

$$\text{Cov} = r_{xy}\sigma_x\sigma_y.*$$

Covenant Detailed clauses contained in loan agreements. Covenants are designed to protect the lender and include such items as limits on total indebtedness, restrictions on dividends, minimum current ratio, and similar provisions.*

Coverage A term usually connected with revenue bonds. It is a ratio of net revenues pledged to principal and interest payments to debt service requirements. It is one of the factors used in evaluating the quality of an issue.**

Covered option An option position that is offset by an equal and opposite position in the underlying security.††

Covering Buying a security previously sold short. (See: *Short sale, Short covering*.)†

Cumulative dividends A protective feature on preferred stock that requires all past preferred dividends to be paid before any common dividends are paid.*

Cumulative preferred A stock having a provision that if one or more dividends are omitted, the omitted dividends must be paid before dividends may be paid on the company's common stock.†

Cumulative voting A method of voting for corporate directors which enables the shareholder to multiply the number of his shares by the number of directorships being voted on and cast the total for one director or a selected group of directors. A 10-share holder normally casts 10 votes for each of, say 12 nominees to the board of directors. He thus has 120 votes. Under the cumulative voting principle he may do that or he may cast 120 (10 × 12) votes for only one nominee, 60 for two, 40 for three, or any other distribution he chooses. Cumulative voting is required under the corporate laws of some states, is permitted in most others.†

Current assets Those assets of a company which are reasonably expected to be realized in cash, or sold, or consumed during the normal operating cycle of the business. These include cash, U.S. government bonds, receivables and money due usually within one year, and inventories.†

Current liabilities Money owed and payable by a company, usually within one year.†

Current return (See: *Yield*.)

Current yield A relation stated as a percent of the annual interest to the actual market price of the bond.**

Cut-off point In the capital budgeting process, the minimum rate of return on acceptable investment opportunities.*

Day order An order to buy or sell which, if not executed expires at the end of the trading day on which it was entered.†

Dealer An individual or firm in the securities business who buys and sells stocks and bonds as a principal rather than as an agent. The dealer's profit or loss is the difference between the price paid and the price received for the same security. The dealer's confirmation must disclose to the customer that the principal has been acted upon. The same individual or firm may function, at different times, either as broker or dealer. (See: *NASD, Specialist.*)††

Debenture A long-term debt instrument that is not secured by a mortgage on specific property.*

Debit balance In a customer's margin account that portion of purchase price of stock, bonds, or commodities covered by credit extended by the broker to the margin customer.†

Debt limit The statutory or constitutional maximum debt that a municipality can legally incur.**

Debt ratio Total debt divided by total assets.*

Debt service Refers to the payments required for interest and retirement of the principal amount of a debt.**

Default The failure to fulfill a contract. Generally, default refers to the failure to pay interest or principal on debt obligations.*

Degree of leverage The percentage increase in profits resulting from a given percentage increase in sales. The degree of leverage may be calculated for financial leverage, operating leverage, or both combined.*

Denomination The face amount or par value of a security which the issuer promises to pay on the maturity date. Most municipal bonds are issued with a minimum denomination of $5,000, although a few older issues are available in $1,000 denominations.**

Depletion accounting Natural resources, such as metals, oil and gas, and timber, which conceivably can be reduced to zero over the years, present a special problem in capital management. Depletion is an accounting practice consisting of charges against earnings based upon the amount of the asset taken out of the total reserves in the period for which accounting is made. A bookkeeping entry, it does not represent any cash outlay nor are any funds earmarked for the purpose.†

Depository trust company (DTC). A central securities certificate depository through which members effect security deliveries between each other via computerized bookkeeping entries thereby reducing the physical movement of stock certificates.†

Depreciation Normally, charges against earnings to write off the cost, less salvage value, of an asset over its estimated useful life. It is a bookkeeping entry and does not represent any cash outlay nor are any funds earmarked for the purpose.†

Devaluation The process of reducing the value of a country's currency stated in terms of other currencies; for example, the British pound might be devalued from $2.30 for one pound to $2.00 for one pound.*

Director Person elected by shareholders to establish company policies. The directors appoint the president, vice presidents, and all other operating officers. Directors decide, among other matters, if and when dividends shall be paid. (See: *Management, Proxy.*)†

Discount The amount by which a preferred stock or bond may sell below its par value. Also used as a verb to mean "takes into account" as the price of the stock has discounted the expected dividend cut. (See: *Premium.*)†

Discount rate The interest rate used in the discounting process; sometimes called *capitalization rate.**

Discounted cash flow techniques Methods of ranking investment proposals. Included are (1) internal rate of return method, (2) net present value method, and (3) profitability index or benefit/cost ratio.*

Discounting The process of finding the present value of a series of future cash flows. Discounting is the reverse of compounding.*

Discounting of accounts receivable Short-term financing where accounts receivable are used to secure the loan. The lender does not *buy* the accounts receivable but simply uses them as collateral for the loan. Also called *assigning accounts receivable.**

Discount rate The interest rate at which eligible depository institutions may borrow funds, usually for short periods, directly from the Federal Reserve Banks. The law requires the board of directors of each Reserve Bank to establish the discount rate every 14 days subject to the approval of the Board of Governors.¶

Discretionary account An account in which the customer gives the broker or someone else discretion, which may be complete or within specific limits, either to the purchases, or sale of securities or commodities including selection, timing, amount, and price to be paid or received.†

Diversification Spreading investments among different companies in different fields. Another type of diversification is also offered by the securities of many individual companies because of the wide range of their activities. (See: *Investment trust.*)†

Dividend The payment designed by the board of directors to be distributed pro rata among the shares outstanding. On preferred shares, it is generally a fixed amount. On common shares, the dividend varies with the fortunes of the company and the amount of cash on hand, and may be omitted if business is poor or the directors determine to withhold earnings to invest in plant and equipment. Sometimes a company will pay a dividend out of past earnings even if it is not currently operating at a profit.†

Dividend yield The ratio of the current dividend to the current price of a share of stock.*

Dollar bond A bond that is quoted and traded in dollars rather than in terms of yield.**

Dollar cost averaging A system of buying securities at regular intervals with a fixed dollar amount. Under this system the investor buys by the dollars' worth rather than by the number of shares. If each investment is of the same number of dollars, payments buy more when the price is low and fewer when it rises. Thus temporary downswings in price benefit the investor if he continues periodic purchases in both good times and bad and the price at which the shares are sold is more than their average cost. (See: *Formula investing.*)†

Double-barrelled bond A bond secured by the pledge of two or more sources of repayment, e.g., secured by taxes as well as revenues.**

Double exemption Refers to securities that are exempt from state as well as Federal income taxes.**

Double taxation Short for *double taxation of dividends.* The federal government taxes corporate profits once as corporate income; any part of the remaining profits distributed as dividends to stockholders may be taxed again as income to the recipient stockholder.†

Dow theory A theory of market analysis based upon the performance of the Dow-Jones industrial and transportation stock price averages. The theory says that the market is in a basic upward trend if one of these averages advances above a previous important high, accompanied or followed by a similar advance in the other. When the averages both dip below previous important lows, this is regarded as confirmation of a basic downward trend. The theory does not attempt to predict how long either trend will continue, although it is widely misinterpreted as a method of forecasting future action.†

Down tick (See: *Up tick.*)

Dow theory A theory of market analysis based upon the performance of the Dow Jones industrial and transportation stock price averages. The Theory says that the market is in a basic upward trend if one of these averages advances above a previous important high, accompanied or followed by a similar advance in the other. When the averages both dip below previous important lows, this is regarded as confirmation of a downward trend. The Dow Jones is one type of market index. (See: *NYSE Composite Index.*)††

Earnings report A statement—also called an *income statement*—issued by a company showing its earnings or losses over a given period. The earnings report lists the income earned,

expenses, and the net result. (See: *Balance sheet.*)†

EBIT Acronym for *earnings before interest and taxes.**

Economical ordering quantity (EOQ) The optimum (least cost) quantity of merchandise which should be ordered.*

EPS Acronym for *earnings per share.**

Equipment trust certificate A type of security, generally issued by a railroad, to pay for new equipment. Title to the equipment, such as a locomotive, is held by a trustee until the notes are paid off. An equipment trust certificate is usually secured by a first claim on the equipment.†

Equity The net worth of a business, consisting of capital stock, capital (or paid-in) surplus, earned surplus (or retained earnings), and occasionally, certain net worth reserves. *Common equity* is that part of the total net worth belonging to the common stockholders. *Total equity* would include preferred stockholders. The terms *common stock, net worth,* and *common equity* are frequently used interchangeably.†

Exchange acquisition A method of filling an order to buy a large block of stock on the floor of the exchange. Under certain circumstances, a member-broker can facilitate the purpose of a block by soliciting orders to sell. All orders to sell the security are lumped together and crossed with the buy order in the regular action market. The price to the buyer may be on a net basis or on a commission basis.†

Exchange distribution A method of selling large blocks of stock on the floor of the exchange. Under certain circumstances, a member-broker can facilitate the sale of a block of stock by soliciting and getting other member-brokers to solicit orders to buy. Individual buy orders are lumped together and crossed with the sell order in the regular auction market. A special commission is usually paid by the seller; ordinarily the buyer pays no commission.†

Exchange rate The rate at which one currency can be exchanged for another; for example, $2.30 can be exchanged for one British pound.*

Excise tax A tax on the manufacture, sale, or consumption of specified commodities.*

Ex-dividend A synonym for "without dividend." The buyer of a stock selling ex-dividend does not receive the recently declared dividend. Every dividend is payable on a fixed date to all shareholders recorded on the books of the company as of a previous date of record. For example, a dividend may be declared as payable to holders of record on the books of the company on a given Friday. Since five business days are allowed for delivery of stock in a "regular way" transaction on the New York

Stock Exchange, the Exchange would declare the stock "ex-dividend" as of the opening of the market on the preceding Monday. That means anyone who bought it on and after Monday would not be entitled to that dividend. When stocks go ex-dividend, the stock tables include the symbol "x" following the name. (See: *Cash sale, Net change, Transfer.*)†

Ex-dividend date   The date on which the right to the current dividend no longer accompanies a stock. (For listed stock, the ex-dividend date is four working days prior to the date of record.)*

Exercise   Action taken by an option holder that requires the writer to perform the terms of the contract.††

Exercise price   The price that must be paid for a share of common stock when it is bought by exercising a warrant.*

Expected return   The rate of return a firm expects to realize from an investment. The expected return is the mean value of the probability distribution of possible returns.*

Expiration date   The date the option contract expires.††

Ex-rights   the date on which stock purchase rights are no longer transferred to the purchaser of the stock.*

Extension   An informal method of reorganization in which the creditors voluntarily postpone the date of required payment on past-due obligations.*

External funds   Funds acquired through borrowing or by selling new common or preferred stock.

Extra   The short form of *extra dividend.* A dividend in the form of stock or cash in addition to the regular or usual dividend the company has been paying.†

Face value   The value of a bond that appears on the face of the bond, unless the value is otherwise specified by the issuing company. Face value is ordinarily the amount the issuing company promises to pay at maturity. Face value is not an indication of market value. Sometimes referred to as par value. (See: *Par.*)†

Factoring   A method of financing accounts receivable under which a firm sells its accounts receivable (generally without recourse) to a financial institution (the *factor*).*

Federal funds   Reserve balances that depository institutions lend each other, usually on an overnight basis. In addition, Federal funds include certain other kinds of borrowings by depository institutions from each other and from federal agencies.¶

Field warehousing   A method of financing inventories in which a "warehouse" is established at the place of business of the borrowing firm.*

Financial accounting standards board (FASB)   A private (nongovernment) agency which functions as an accounting standards-setting body.*

Financial intermediation   Financial transactions which bring savings surplus units together with savings deficit units so that savings can be redistributed into their most productive uses.*

Financial lease   A lease that does not provide for maintenance services, is not cancellable, and is fully amortized over the life of the lease.*

Financial leverage   The ratio of total debt to total assets. There are other measures of financial leverage, especially ones that relate cash inflows to required cash outflows.*

Financial markets   Transactions in which the creation and transfer of financial assets and financial liabilities take place.*

Financial risk   That portion of total corporate risk, over and above basic business risk, that results from using debt.*

Fiscal year   A corporation's accounting year. Due to the nature of their particular business, some companies do not use the calendar year for their bookkeeping. A typical example is the department store which finds December 31 too early a date to close its books after the Christmas rush. For that reason many stores wind up their accounting year January 31. Their fiscal year, therefore, runs from February 1 of one year through January 31 of the next. The fiscal year of other companies may run from July 1 through the following June 30. Most companies, though, operate on a calendar year basis.†

Fixed charges   Costs that do not vary with the level of output, especially fixed financial costs such as interest, lease payments, and sinking fund payments.*

Flat income bond   This term means that the price at which a bond is traded includes consideration for all unpaid accruals of interest. Bonds which are in default of interest or principal are traded flat. Income bonds, which pay interest only to the extent earned are usually traded flat. All other bonds are usually dealt in "and interest," which means that the buyer pays to the seller the market price plus interest accrued since the last payment date.†

Float   The amount of funds tied up in checks that have been written but are still in process and have not yet been collected.*

Floating exchange rates   Exchange rates may be fixed by government policy *(pegged)* or allowed to *float* up or down in accordance with supply and demand. When market forces are allowed to function, exchange rates are said to be floating.*

Floor   The huge trading area—about two-thirds the size of a football field—where stocks and bonds are bought and sold on the New York Stock Exchange.†

Floor broker A member of the Stock Exchange who executes orders on the floor of the exchange to buy or sell any listed securities. (See: *Commission broker, Two-dollar broker.*)†

Flotation cost The cost of issuing new stocks or bonds.*

Formula investing An investment technique. One formula calls for the shifting of funds from common shares to preferred shares or bonds as the market, on average, rises above a certain predetermined point—and the return of funds to common share investments as the market average declines. (See: *Dollar cost averaging.*)†

Free and open market A market in which supply and demand are freely expressed in terms of price. Contrasts with a controlled market in which supply, demand, and price may all be regulated.†

Fundamental research Analysis of industries and companies based on factors such as sales, assets, earnings, products or services, markets, and management. As supplied to the economy, fundamental research includes consideration of gross national product, interest rates, unemployment, inventories, savings, and so on. (See: *Technical research.*)†

Funded debt Usually long-term, interest-bearing bonds or debentures of a company. Could include long-term bank loans. Does *not* include short-term loans, preferred, or common stock.†

Funding The process of replacing short-term debt with long-term securities (stocks or bonds).*

General mortgage bond A bond which is secured by a blanket mortgage on the company's property, but which may be outranked by one or more other mortgages.†

General obligation bond A bond secured by the pledge of the issuer's full faith, credit and taxing power.**

General purchasing power reporting A proposal by the FASB that the current values of nonmonetary items in financial statements be adjusted by a general price index.*

Gilt-edged High-grade bond issued by a company which has demonstrated its ability to earn a comfortable profit over a period of years and pay its bondholders their interest without interruption.†

Give up A term with many different meanings. For one, a member of the exchange on the floor may act for a second member by executing an order for him with a third member. The first member tells the third member that he is acting on behalf of the second member and "gives up" the second member's name rather than his own.††

Gold fix The setting of the price of gold by dealers (especially in an twice-daily London meeting at the central bank); the fix is the fundamental worldwide price for setting prices of gold bullion and gold-related contracts and products.††

Good delivery Certain basic qualifications must be met before a security sold on the exchange may be delivered. The security must be in proper form to comply with the contract of sale and to transfer title to the purchaser.†

Good 'til cancelled order (GTC) or open order An order to buy or sell which remains in effect until it is either executed or cancelled.†

Goodwill Intangible assets of a firm established by the excess of the price paid for the going concern over its book value.*

Government bonds Obligations of the U.S. government, regarded as the highest grade issues in existence.†

Growth stock Stock of a company with a record of growth in earnings at a relatively rapid rate.†

Guaranteed bond A bond which has interest or principal, or both, guaranteed by a company other than the issuer. Usually found in the railroad industry when large roads, leasing sections of trackage owned by small railroads, may guarantee the bonds of the smaller road.†

Guaranteed stock Usually preferred stock on which dividends are guaranteed by another company; under much the same circumstances as a bond is guaranteed.†

Hedge (See: *Arbitrage, Options, Short sale.*)

Hedging The purchase or sale of a derivative security (such as options or futures) in order to reduce or neutralize all or some portion of the risk of holding another security.††

Holding company A corporation which owns the securities of another, in most cases with voting control.†

Hurdle rate In capital budgeting, the minimum acceptable rate of return on a project. If the expected rate of return is below the hurdle rate, the project is not accepted. The hurdle rate should be the marginal cost of capital.*

Hypothecation The pledging of securities as collateral—for example, to secure the debit balance in a margin account.†

Improper accumulation Earnings retained by a business for the purpose of enabling stockholders to avoid personal income taxes.*

Inactive stock An issue traded on an exchange or in the over-the-counter market in which there is a relatively low volume of transactions. Volume may be no more than a few hundred shares a week or even less. On the New York

Stock Exchange many inactive stocks are traded in 10-share units rather than the customary 100. (See: *Round lot.*)†

In-and-out Purchase and sale of the same security within a short period—a day, a week, even a month. An in-and-out trader is generally more interested in day-to-day price fluctuations than dividends or long-term growth.†

Income bond Generally income bonds promise to repay principal but to pay interest only when earned. In some cases unpaid interest on an income bond may accumulate as a claim against the corporation when the bond becomes due. An income bond may also be issued in lieu of preferred stock.†

Incremental cash flow Net cash flow attributable to an investment project.*

Incremental cost of capital The average cost of the increment of capital raised during a given year.*

Indenture A written agreement under which bonds and debentures are issued, setting forth maturity date, interest rate, and other terms.†

Independent broker Members on the floor of the NYSE who execute orders for other brokers having more business at that time than they can handle themselves, or for firms who do not have their Exchange member on the floor. Formerly known as *two-dollar brokers* from the time when these independent brokers received $2 per hundred shares for executing such orders. Their fees are paid by the commission brokers. (See: *Commission broker.*)†

Index A statistical yardstick expressed in terms of percentages of a base year or years. For instance, the Federal Reserve Board's index of industrial production is based on 1967 as 100. An index is not an average. (See: *Averages, NYSE common stock index.*)†

Industrial revenue bond A security backed by private enterprises that have been financed by a municipal issue.**

Insolvency The inability to meet maturing debt obligations.*

Institutional Investor An organization whose primary purpose is to invest its own assets or those held in trust by it for others. Includes pension funds, investment companies, insurance companies, universities, and banks.†

Interest Payments a borrower pays a lender for the use of his money. A corporation pays interest on its bonds to its bondholders. (See: *Bond, dividend.*)†

Intermarket Trading System (ITS) An electronic communications network now linking the trading floor of seven registered exchanges to foster competition among them in stocks listed on either the NYSE or AMEX and one or more regional exchanges. Through ITS, any broker or market-maker on the floor of any participating market can reach out to other participants for an execution whenever the nationwide quote shows a better price is available.††

Internal financing Funds made available for capital budgeting and working-capital expansion through the normal operations of the firm; internal financing is approximately equal to retained earnings plus depreciation.*

Internal rate of return (IRR) The rate of return on an asset investment. The internal rate of return is calculated by finding the discount rate that equates the present value of future cash flows to the cost of the investment.*

Intrinsic value ¹That value which, in the mind of the analyst, is justified by the facts. It is often used to distinguish between the *true value* of an asset (the intrinsic value) and the asset's current market price.*

²The dollar amount of the difference between the exercise price of an option and the current cash value of the underlying security. Intrinsic value and time value are the two components of an option premium, or price.††

Investment The use of money for the purpose of making more money, to gain income or increase capital, or both.††

Investment banker Also known as an *underwriter*. The middleman between the corporation issuing new securities and the public. The usual practice is for one or more investment bankers to buy outright from a corporation a new issue of stocks or bonds. The group forms a syndicate to sell the securities to individuals and institutions. Investment bankers also distribute very large blocks of stocks or bonds—perhaps held by an estate. (See: *Primary Distribution, Syndicate.*)††

Investment company A company or trust which uses its capital to invest in other companies. There are two principal types: the closed-end and the open-end, or mutual fund. Shares in closed-end investment companies, some of which are listed on the New York Stock Exchange, are readily transferable in the open market and are bought and sold like other shares. Capitalization of these companies remains the same unless action is taken to change, which is seldom. Open-end funds sell their own new shares to investors, stand ready to buy back their old shares, and are not listed. Open-end funds are so called because their capitalization is not fixed; they issue more shares as people want them.†

Investment counsel One whose principal business consists of acting as investment adviser and a substantial part of his business consists of rendering investment supervisory services.†

Investment tax credit Business firms can deduct as a credit against their income taxes a specified percentage of the dollar amount of new investments in each of certain categories of assets.*

IRA Individual Retirement Account. A pension plan with major tax advantages. Any worker can begin an IRA and obtain a tax deduction for cash contributions up to $2,000 annually. IRA permits investment through intermediaries like mutual funds, insurance companies and banks or directly in stocks and bonds through stockbrokers. (See: *Keogh Plan*.)††

Issue Any of a company's securities, or the act of distributing such securities.†

Issuer A municipal unit that borrows money through the sale of bonds or notes.**

Keogh Plan Tax advantaged personal retirement program that can be established by a self-employed individual. Currently, annual contributions to a plan can be up to $15,000. Such contributions and reinvestments are not taxed as they accumulate but will be when withdrawn (presumably at retirement when taxable income may be less). (See: *IRA*.)††

Legal list A list of investments selected by various states in which certain institutions and fiduciaries, such as insurance companies and banks, may invest. Legal lists are often restricted to high quality securities meeting certain specifications. (See: *Prudent Man Rule*.)††

Legal opinion An opinion concerning the legality of a bond issue usually written by a recognized law firm specializing in public borrowings.**

Leverage The effect on a company when the company has bonds, preferred stock, or both outstanding. Example: If the earnings of a company with 1,000,000 common shares increases from $1,000,000 to $1,500,000—earnings per share would go from $1 to $1.50, or an increase of 50 percent. But if earnings of a company that had to pay $500,000 in bond interest increased that much—earnings per common share would jump from 50 cents to $1 a share, or 100 percent.††

Leverage factor The ratio of debt to total assets.*

Liabilities All the claims against a corporation. Liabilities include accounts and wages and salaries payable, dividends declared payable, accrued taxes payable, fixed or long-term liabilities such as mortgage bonds, debentures, and bank loans. (See: *Assets, balance sheet*.)†

Lien A lender's claim on assets that are pledged for a loan.*

Limit, limited order, or limited price order An order to buy or sell a stated amount of a security at a specified price, or at a better price, if obtain-

able after the order is represented in the Trading Crowd.†

Limited tax bond A bond secured by a pledge of a tax or group of taxes limited as to rate or amount.**

Line of credit An arrangement whereby a financial institution (bank or insurance company) commits itself to lend up to a specified maximum amount of funds during a specified period. Sometimes the interest rate on the loan is specified, at other times, it is not. Sometimes a commitment fee is imposed for obtaining the line of credit.*

Liquidation The process of converting securities or other property into cash. The dissolution of a company, with cash remaining after sale of its assets and payment of all indebtedness being distributed to the shareholders.†

Liquidity [1]Refers to a firm's cash position and its ability to meet maturing obligations.*

[2]The ability of the market in a particular security to absorb a reasonable amount of buying or selling at reasonable price changes. Liquidity is one of the most important characteristics of a good market.†

Listed stock The stock of a company which is traded on a securities exchange. The various stock exchanges have different standards for listing. Some of the guides used by the New York Stock Exchange for an original listing are national interest in the company, a minimum of 1.1-million shares publicly held among not less than 2,000 round-lot stockholders. The publicly held common shares should have a minimum aggregate market value of $18 million. The company should have net income in the latest year of over $2.5-million before federal income tax and $2-million in each of the preceding two years.††

Load The portion of the offering price of shares of open-end investment companies in excess of the value of the underlying assets which cover sales commissions and all other costs of distribution. The load is usually incurred only on purchase, there being, in most cases, no charge when the shares are sold (redeemed).†

Lock-box plan A procedure used to speed up collections and to reduce float.*

Locked in An investor is said to be locked in when he had a profit on a security he owns but does not sell because his profit would immediately become subject to the capital gains tax. (See: *Capital gain*.)†

Long Signifies ownership of securities: "I am long 100 U.S. Steel" means the speaker owns 100 shares. (See: *Short position, short sale*.)†

Management The board of directors, elected by the stockholders, and the officers of the corporation, appointed by the board of directors.†

Manipulation An illegal operation. Buying or selling a security for the purpose of creating a false or misleading appearance of active trading or for the purpose of raising or depressing the price to induce purchase or sale by others.†

Margin The amount paid by the customer when using a broker's credit to buy or sell a security. Under Federal Reserve regulations, the initial margin required since 1945 has ranged from the current rate 50 percent of the purchase price up to 100 percent. (See: *Brokers' loans, Equity, Margin call.*)††

Margin call A demand upon a customer to put up money or securities with the broker. The call is made when a purchase is made; also if a customer's equity in a margin account declines below a minimum standard set by the exchange or by the firm. (See: *Margin.*)†

Margin—profit on sales The *profit margin* is the percentage of profit after tax to sales.*

Marginal cost The cost of an additional unit. The marginal cost of capital is the cost of an additional dollar of new funds.*

Marginal efficiency of capital A schedule showing the internal rate of return on investment opportunities.*

Marginal revenue The additional gross revenue produced by selling one additional unit of output.*

Marketability The measure of the ease with which a security can be sold in the secondary market.**

Market order An order to buy or sell a stated amount of a security at the most advantageous price obtainable after the order is represented in the trading crowd. (See: *Good 'til cancelled order, Limit order, Stop order.*)††

Market price In the case of a security, market price is usually considered the last reported price at which the stock or bond sold.†

Maturity The date on which a loan or a bond or debenture comes due and is to be paid off.†

Member corporation A securities brokerage firm, organized as a corporation, with at least one member of the New York Stock Exchange, who is an officer or an employee of the corporation.††

Member firm A securities brokerage firm organized as a partnership and having at least one general partner who is a member of the New York Stock Exchange, Inc. (See: *Member corporation.*)†

Member organization This term includes New York Stock Exchange Member Firm *and* Member Corporation. (See: *Member corporation, Member firm.*)†

Merger Any combination that forms one company from two or more previously existing companies.*

Money market Financial markets in which funds are borrowed or lent for short periods (i.e., less than one year). (The money market is distinguished from the capital market, which is the market for long-term funds.)*

Mortgage A pledge of designated property as security for a loan.*

Mortgage bond A bond secured by a mortgage on a property. The value of the property may or may not equal the value of the bonds issued against it. (See: *Bond, Debenture.*)††

Municipal bond A bond issued by a state or a political subdivision, such as county, city, town, or village. The term also designates bonds issued by state agencies and authorities. In general, interest paid on municipal bonds is exempt from federal income taxes and state and local income taxes within the state of issue.†

Mutual fund (See: *Investment company.*)

Naked option An option position that is *not* offset by an equal and opposite position in the underlying security.††

NASD The National Association of Securities Dealers, Inc. An association of brokers and dealers in the over-the-counter securities business.††

NASDAQ An automated information network which provides brokers and dealers with price quotations on securities traded over-the-counter. NASDAQ is an acronym for National Association of Securities Dealers Automated Quotations.†

Negotiable Refers to a security, title to which is transferable by delivery. (See: *Good delivery.*)†

Negotiable Order of Withdrawal account An interest earning account on which checks may be drawn. Withdrawals from NOW accounts may be subject to a 14-day or more notice requirement although such is rarely imposed. NOW accounts may be offered by commercial banks, mutual savings banks, and savings and loan associations and may be owned only by individuals and certain nonprofit organizations and governmental units.¶

Net asset value Usually used in connection with investment companies to mean net asset value per share. An investment company computes its assets daily, or even twice daily, by totaling the market value of all securities owned. All liabilities are deducted, and the balance divided by the number of shares outstanding. The resulting figure is the net asset value per share. (See: *Assets, Investment Company.*)††

Net change The change in the price of a security from the closing price on one day and the closing price on the following day on which the stock is traded. The net change is ordinarily the last figure on the stock price list. The mark + 1⅛ means up $1.125 a share from the last sale on the previous day the stock traded.†

Net debt   Gross debt less sinking fund accumulations and all self-supporting debt.**

Net present value (NPV) method   A method of ranking investment proposals. The NPV is equal to the present value of future returns, discounted at the marginal cost of capital, minus the present value of the cost of the investment.*

Net worth   The capital and surplus of a firm—capital stock, capital surplus (paid-in capital), earned surplus (retained earnings), and, occasionally, certain reserves. For some purposes, preferred stock is included; generally, net worth refers only to the common stockholders' position.*

New housing authority bonds   A bond issued by a local public housing authority to finance public housing. It is backed by Federal funds and the solemn pledge of the U.S. Government that payment will be made in full.**

New issue   A stock or bond sold by a corporation for the first time. Proceeds may be issued to retire outstanding securities of the company, for new plant or equipment, or for additional working capital, or to acquire a public ownership interest in the company for private owners.††

New York Futures Exchange (NYFE)   A subsidiary of the New York Stock Exchange devoted to the trading of futures products.††

New York Stock Exchange (NYSE)   The largest organized securities market in the United States, founded in 1792. The Exchange itself does not buy, sell, own, or set the prices of securities traded there. The prices are determined by public supply and demand. The Exchange is a not-for-profit corporation of 1,366 individual members, governed by a Board of Directors consisting of 10 public representatives, 10 Exchange members or allied members and a full-time chairman, executive vice chairman and president.††

New issue market   Market for new issues of municipal bonds and notes.**

Nominal interest rate   The contracted or stated interest rate, undeflated for price-level changes.*

Noncumulative   A type of preferred stock on which unpaid dividends do not accrue. Omitted dividends are, as a rule, gone forever. (See: *Cumulative preferred*.)††

Normal probability distribution   A symmetrical, bell-shaped probability function.*

Notes   Short-term unsecured promises to pay specified amounts of money. For municipal notes maturities generally range from six to twelve months.**

NYSE composite index   A composite index covering price movements of all common stocks listed on the "Big Board." It is based on the close of the market December 31, 1965 as 50.00 and is weighted according to the number of shares listed for each issue. The index is computed continuously and printed on the ticker tape each half hour. Point changes in the index are converted to dollars and cents so as to provide a meaningful measure of changes in the average price of listed stocks. The composite index is supplemented by separate indexes for four industry groups: industries, transportation, utilities, and finances. (See: *Averages*.)††

Odd lot   An amount of stock less than the established 100-share unit. (See: *Round lot*.)††

Off-board   This term may refer to transactions over-the-counter in unlisted securities, or to a transaction involving listed shares that is not executed on a national securities exchange.††

Offer   The price at which a person is ready to sell. Opposed to bid, the price at which one is ready to buy. (See: *Bid and asked*.)†

Official statement   Document prepared by or for the issuer that gives in detail the security and financial information about the issue.**

Open interest   In options and futures trading, the number of outstanding option contracts, at a given point in time, which have not been exercised and have not yet reached expiration.††

Open order   (See: *Good 'til cancelled order*.)

Open-end investment company   (See: *Investment company*.)

Operating leverage   The extent to which fixed costs are used in a firm's operation. Break-even analysis is used to measure the extent to which operating leverage is employed.*

Opportunity cost   The rate of return on the best *alternative* investment that is available. It is the highest return that will *not* be earned if the funds are invested in a particular project. For example, the opportunity cost of *not* investing in bond A yielding 8 percent might be 7.99 percent, which could be earned on bond B.*

Option   A right to buy (call) or sell (put) a fixed amount of a given stock at a specified price within a limited period of time. The purchaser hopes that the stock's price will go up (a call) or down (a put) by an amount sufficient to provide a profit when the stock is sold. If the stock price holds steady or moves in the opposite direction, the price paid for the option is lost entirely. There are several other types of options available to the public but these are basically combinations of puts and calls. Individuals may write (sell) as well as purchase options. Options are also traded on stock indexes, futures, and debt instruments.††

Orders good until a specified time   A market

or limited price order which is to be represented in the Trading Crowd until a specified time, after which such order or the portion thereof not executed is to be treated as cancelled.†

Ordinary income Income from the normal operations of a firm. Operating income specifically excludes income from the sale of capital assets.*

Organized security exchanges Formal organizations having tangible, physical locations. Organized exchanges conduct an auction market in designated ("listed") investment securities. For example, the New York Stock Exchange is an organized exchange.*

Overbought An opinion as to price levels. May refer to a security which has had a sharp rise or to the market as a whole after a period of vigorous buying, which it may be argued, has left prices "too high."†

Overdraft system A system where a depositor may write checks in excess of his balance, with his bank automatically extending a loan to cover the shortage.*

Oversold The reverse of overbought. A single security or a market which, it is believed, has declined to an unreasonable level.††

Over-the-counter A market for securities made up of securities dealers who may or may not be members of a securities exchange. The over-the-counter market is conducted over the telephone and deals mainly with stocks of companies without sufficient shares, stockholders, or earnings to warrant listing on an exchange. Over-the-counter dealers may act either as principals or as brokers for customers. The over-the-counter market is the principal market for bonds of all types. (See: *NASD, NASDAQ.*)††

Paper profit (LOSS) An unrealized profit or loss on a security still held. Paper profits and losses become realized profits only when the security is sold. (See: *Profit taking.*)††

Par In the case of a common share, par means a dollar amount assigned to the share by the company's charter. Par value may also be used to compute the dollar amount of the common shares on the balance sheet. Par value has little relationship to the market value of common stock. Many companies issue no-par stock but give a stated per share value on the balance sheet. In the case of preferred stocks, it signifies the dollar value upon which dividends are figured. With bonds, par value is the face amount, usually $1,000.††

Par value The nominal or face value of stock or bond.*

Participating preferred A preferred stock which is entitled to its stated dividend and, also, to additional dividends on a specified basis upon payment of dividends on the common stock.†

Passed dividend Omission of a regular or scheduled dividend.†

Payback period The length of time required for the net revenues of an investment to return the cost of the investment.*

Paying agent Place where principal and interest is payable. Usually a designated bank or the treasurer's office of the issuer.**

Payout ratio The percentage of earnings paid out in the form of dividends.*

Pegging A market stabilization action taken by the manager of an underwriting group during the offering of new securities. He does this by continually placing order to buy at a specified price in the market.*

Penny stocks Low-priced issues often highly speculative, selling at less than $1 a share. Frequently used as a term of disparagement, although a few penny stocks have developed into investment-caliber issues.†

Perpetuity A stream of equal future payments expected to continue forever.*

Pledging of accounts receivable Short-term borrowing from financial institutions where the loan is secured by accounts receivable. The lender may physically take the accounts receivable but typically has recourse to the borrower; also called *discounting of accounts receivable.**

Point In the case of shares of stock, a point means $1. If ABC shares rises 3 points, each share has risen $3. In the case of bonds a point means $10, since a bond is quoted as a percentage of $1,000. A bond which rises 3 points gains 3 percent of $1,000, or $30 in value. An advance from 87 to 90 would mean an advance in dollar value from $870 to $900. In the case of market averages, the word point means merely that and no more. If, for example, the NYSE Composite Index rises from 90.25 to 91.25, it has risen a point. A point in this average, however, is not equivalent to $1. (See: *Indexes.*)††

Pooling of interest An accounting method for combining the financial statements of firms that merge. Under the pooling-of-interest procedure, the assets of the merged firms are simply added to form the balance sheet of the surviving corporation. This method is different from the "purchase" method, where goodwill is put on the balance sheet to reflect a premium (or discount) paid in excess of book value.*

Portfolio Holdings of securities by an individual or institution. A portfolio may contain bonds, preferred stocks, common stocks and other securities.††

Portfolio effect The extent to which the variation in returns on a combination of assets (a "portfolio") is less than the sum of the variations of the individual assets.*

Portfolio theory Deals with the selection of

optimal portfolios; that is, portfolios that provide the highest possible return for any specified degree of risk.*

Preemptive right A provision contained in the corporate charter and by laws that gives holders of common stock the right to purchase on a pro rata basis new issues of common stock (or securities convertible into common stock.)*

Preferred stock A class of stock with a claim on the company's earnings before payment may be made on the common stock and usually entitled to priority ove⁻ common stock if the company liquidates. Usually entitled to dividends at a specified rate—when declared by the board of directors and before payment of a dividend on the common stock—depending upon the terms of the issue. (See: *Cumulative preferred, Participating preferred.*)†

Premium The amount by which a bond or preferred stock, may sell above its par value. For options, the price that the buyer pays the writer for an option contract ("option premium") is synonymous with "the price of an option." (See: *Discount.*)††

Present value (PV) The value today of a future payment, or stream of payments, discounted at the appropriate discount rate.*

Price-earnings ratio A popular way to compare stocks selling at various price levels. The PE ratio is the price of a share of stock divided by earnings per share for a twelve-month period. For example, a stock selling for $50 a share and earning $5 a share is said to be selling at a price-earnings ratio of 10.††

Primary distribution Also called primary offering. The original sale of a company's securities. (See: *Investment banker.*)††

Primary market Market for new issues of securities.

Prime rate The lowest interest rate charged by commercial banks to their most credit-worthy and largest corporate customers; other interest rates, such as personal, automobile, commercial and financing loans are often pegged to the prime.††

Principal The person for whom a broker executes an order, or dealers buying or selling for their own accounts. The term *principal* may also refer to a person's capital or to the face amount of a bond.††

Productivity The amount of physical output for each unit of productive input.¶

Pro forma A projection. A *pro forma* financial statement is one that shows how the actual statement will look if certain specified assumptions are realized. *Pro forma* statements may be either future or past projections. An example of a backward *pro forma* statement occurs when two firms are planning to merge and shows

what their consolidated financial statements would have looked like if they had been merged in preceding years.*

Profit center A unit of a large, decentralized firm that has its own investments and for which a rate of return on investment can be calculated.*

Profit margin The ratio of profits after taxes to sales.*

Profitability index (PI) The present value of future returns divided by the present value of the investment outlay.*

Profit-taking Selling stock which has appreciated in value since purchase, in order to realize the profit. The term is often used to explain a downturn in the market following a period of rising prices. (See: *Paper profit.*)††

Progressive tax A tax that requires a higher percentage payment on higher incomes. The personal income tax in the United States, which is at a rate of 14 percent on the lowest increments of income to 70 percent on the highest increments, is progressive.*

Prospectus The official selling circular that must be given to purchasers of new securities registered with the Securities and Exchange Commission. It highlights the much longer Registration Statement filed with the commission.††

Proxy Written authorization given by a shareholder to someone else to represent him and vote his shares at a shareholders' meeting.††

Proxy statement Information given to stockholders in conjunction with the solicitation of proxies.††

Prudent man rule An investment standard. In some states, the law requires that a fiduciary, such as a trustee, may invest the fund's money only in a list of securities designated by the state—the so-called legal list. In other states, the trustee may invest in a security if it is one that would be bought by a prudent man of discretion and intelligence, who is seeking a reasonable income and preservation of capital.††

Public Offering (See: *Primary Distribution.*)

Pure (or primitive) security A security that pays off $1 if one particular state of the world occurs and pays off nothing if any other state of the world occurs.*

Put An option to sell a specific security at a specified price within a designated period.*

Puts and calls (See: *Option.*)

Quote The highest bid to buy and the lowest offer to sell a security in a given market at a given time. If you ask your broker for a "quote" on a stock, he may come back with something like "45¼ to 45½." This means that $45.25 is the highest price any buyer wanted to pay at the time the quote was given on the floor of the exchange and that $45.50 was the lowest price which any seller would take at the same time. (See: *Bid and asked.*)††

Rally A brisk rise following a decline in the general price level of the market, or in an individual stock.†

Rate of return The internal rate of return on an investment.*

Ratings Designations used by investors' services to give relative indications of quality.**

Record date The date on which you must be registered as a shareholder of a company in order to receive a declared dividend or, among other things, to vote on company affairs. (See: *Ex dividend, Transfer.*)††

Recourse arrangement A term used in connection with accounts-receivable financing. If a firm sells its accounts receivable to a financial institution under a recourse agreement, then, if the accounts receivable cannot be collected, the selling firm must repurchase the account from the financial institution.*

Redemption price The price at which a bond may be redeemed before maturity, at the option of the issuing company. Redemption value also applies to the price of the company must pay to call in certain types of preferred stock. (See: *Callable.*)†

Red Herring (See: *Prospectus.*)

Rediscount rate The rate of interest at which a bank may borrow from a Federal Reserve Bank.*

Refinancing Same as refunding. New securities are sold by a company and the money is used to retire existing securities. Object may be to save interest costs, extend the maturity of the loan, or both.*

Refunding Sale of new debt securities to replace an old debt issue.*

Registered bond A bond which is registered on the books of the issuing company in the name of the owner. It can be transferred only when endorsed by the registered owner. (See: *Bearer bond, Coupon bond.*)†

Registered representative The man or woman who serves the investor customers of a broker /dealer. In a New York Stock Exchange Member Organization, a Registered Representative must meet the requirements of the exchange as to background and knowledge of the securities business. Also known as an Account Executive or Customer's broker.††

Registrar Usually a trust company or bank charged with the responsibility of keeping a record of the owners of corporation's securities and preventing the issuance of more than the authorized amount. (See: *Transfer.*)††

Registration Before a public offering may be made of new securities by a company, or of outstanding securities by controlling stockholders—through the mails or in interstate commerce—the securities must be registered under the Securities Act of 1933. A statement is filed with the SEC by the issuer. It must disclose pertinent information relating to the company's operations, securities, management and purpose of the public offering.

Before a security may be admitted to dealings on a national securities exchange, it must be registered under the Securities Exchange Act of 1934. The application for registration must be filed with the exchange and the SEC by the company issuing the securities.††

Regression analysis A statistical procedure for predicting the value of one variable (dependent variable) on the basis of knowledge about one or more other variables (independent variables).*

Regulation T The federal regulation governing the amount of credit which may be advanced by brokers and dealers to customers for the purchase of securities. (See: *Margin.*)†

Regulation U The federal regulation governing the amount of credit which may be advanced by a bank to its customers for the purchase of listed stocks. (See: *Margin.*)†

Reinvestment rate The rate of return at which cash flows from an investment are reinvested. The reinvestment rate may or may not be constant from year to year.*

REIT Real Estate Investment Trust, an organization similar to an investment company in some respects but concentrating its holdings in real estate investments. The yield is generally liberal since REIT's are required to distribute as much as 90 percent of their income. (See: *Investment company.*)†

Reorganization When a financially troubled firm goes through reorganization, its assets are restated to reflect their current market value, and its financial structure is restated to reflect any changes on the asset side of the statement. Under a reorganizations the firm continues in existence; this is contrasted to bankruptcy, where the firm is liquidated and ceases to exist.*

Replacement-cost accounting A requirement under SEC release no. 190 (1976) that large companies disclose the replacement costs of inventory items and depreciable plant.*

Repurchase agreements When the Federal Reserve makes a repurchase agreement with a government securities dealer, it buys a security for immediate delivery with an agreement to sell the security back at the same price by a specific date (usually within 15 days) and receives interest at a specific rate. This arrangement allows the Federal Reserve to inject reserves into the banking system on a temporary basis to meet a temporary need and to withdraw these reserves as soon as that need has passed.¶

Required rate of return The rate of return that stockholders expect to receive on common stock investments.*

Residual value The value of leased property at the end of the lease term.*

Retained earnings That portion of earnings not paid out in dividends. The figure that appears on the balance sheet is the sum of the retained earnings for each year throughout the company's history.*

Return (See: *Yield.*)

Revenue bond A bond payable from revenues derived from tolls, charges, or rents paid by users of the facility constructed from the proceeds of the bond issue.**

Rights When a company wants to raise more funds by issuing additional securities, it may give its stockholders the opportunity, ahead of others, to buy the new securities in proportion to the number of shares each owns. The piece of paper evidencing this privilege is called a right. Because the additional stock is usually offered to stockholders below the current market price, rights ordinarily have a market value of their own and are actively traded. In most cases they must be exercised within a relatively short period. Failure to exercise or sell rights may result in actual loss to the holder. (See: *Warrant.*)†

Rights offering A securities flotation offered to existing stockholders.*

Risk The probability that actual future returns will be below expected returns. It is measured by standard deviation or coefficient of variation of expected returns.*

Risk-adjusted discount rates The discount rate applicable for a particular risky (uncertain) stream of income: the riskless rate of interest plus a risk premium appropriate to the level of risk attached to the particular income stream.*

Risk premium The difference between the required rate of return on a particular risky asset and the rate of return on a riskless asset with the same expected life.*

Risk-return trade-off function (See *Security market line.*)

Round lot A unit of trading or a multiple thereof. On the NYSE the unit of trading is generally 100 shares in stocks and $1,000 or $5,000 par value in the case of bonds. In some inactive stocks, the unit of trading is ten shares. (See: *Odd Lot.*)††

Sale and leaseback An operation whereby a firm sells land, buildings, or equipment to a financial institution and simultaneously executes an agreement to lease the property back for a specified period under specific terms.*

Salvage value The value of a capital asset at the end of a specified period. It is the current market price of an asset being considered for replacement in a capital budgeting problem.*

Scale order An order to buy (or sell) a security which specifies the total amount to be bought (or sold) and the amount to be bought (or sold) at specified price variations.†

Seat A traditional figure-of-speech for a membership on an exchange.††

SEC The Securities and Exchange Commission, established by Congress to help protect investors. The SEC administers the Securities Act of 1933, the Securities Exchange Act of 1934, the Securities Act Amendments of 1975, the Trust Indenture Act, the Investment Company Act, the Investment Advisers Act, and the Public Utility Holding Company Act.†

Secondary distribution Also known as a secondary offering. The redistribution of a block of stock, sometimes after it has been sold by the issuing company. The sale is handled off the NYSE by a securities firm or group of firms and the shares are usually offered at a fixed price related to the current market price of the stock. Usually the block is a large one, such as might be involved in the settlement of an estate. The security may be listed or unlisted. (See: *Investment banker, Primary distribution.*)††

Secondary market Market for issues previously offered or sold.**

Securities and Exchange Commission (See *SEC.*)

Securities, junior Securities that have lower priority in claims on assets and income than other securities (*senior securities*). For example, preferred stock is junior to debentures, but debentures are junior to mortgage bonds. Common stock is the most junior of all corporate securities.*

Securities, senior Securities having claims on income and assets that rank higher than certain other securities (*junior securities*). For example, mortgage bonds are senior debentures, but debentures are senior to common stock.*

Security market line A graphic representation of the relation between the required return on a security and the product of its risk times a normalized market measure of risk. Risk-return relationships for individual securities or investments.*

Self-supporting debt Debt incurred for a project or enterprise requiring no tax support other than the specific tax or revenue earmarked for that purpose.*

Seller's option A special transaction on the NYSE which gives the seller the right to deliver the stock or bond at any time within a specified period, ranging from not less than 6 business days to not more than 60 days.††

Selling group A group of stock brokerage firms formed for the purpose of distributing a new issue of securities; part of the investment banking process.*

Sensitivity analysis Simulation analysis in which key variables are changed and the resulting change in the rate of return is observed. Typically, the rate of return will be more sensitive to changes in some variables than it will in others.*

Serial bond An issue which matures in part at periodic stated intervals.†

Service lease A lease under which the lessor maintains and services the asset.*

Settlement Conclusion of a securities transaction when a customer pays a broker/dealer for securities purchased or delivers securities sold and receives from the broker the proceeds of a sale. (See: *Regular Way Delivery, Cash Sale.*)††

Short covering Buying stock to return stock previously borrowed to make delivery on a short sale.†

Short position Stocks, options, or futures sold short and not covered as of a particular date. On the NYSE, a tabulation is issued once a month listing all issues on the Exchange in which there was a short position of 5,000 or more shares and issues in which the short position had changed by 2,000 or more shares in the preceding month. Short position also means the total amount of stock an individual has sold short and has not covered, as of a particular date.††

Short sale A transaction by a person who believes a security will decline and sells it, though the person does not own any. For instance: You instruct your broker to sell short 100 shares of XYZ. Your broker borrows the stock so delivery of the 100 shares can be made to the buyer. The money value of the shares borrowed is deposited by your broker with the lender. Sooner or later you must cover your short sale by buying the same amount of stock you borrowed for return to the lender. If you are able to buy XYZ at a lower price than you sold it for, your profit is the difference between the two prices— not counting commissions and taxes. But if you have to pay more for the stock than the price you received, that is the amount of your loss. Stock exchange and federal regulations govern and limit the conditions under which a short sale may be made on a national securities exchange. Sometimes people will sell short a stock they already owns in order to protect a paper profit. This is known as selling short against the box.††

Sinking fund Money regularly set aside by a company to redeem its bonds, debentures or preferred stock from time to time as specified in the indenture or charter.††

SIPC Securities Investor Protection Corporation, which provides funds for use, if necessary, to protect customers' cash and securities which may be on deposit with a SIPC member firm in the event the firm fails and is liquidated under the provisions of the SIPC Act. SIPC is not a government agency. It is a nonprofit membership corporation created, however, by an act of Congress.†

Special bid A method of filling an order to buy a large block of stock on the floor of the New York Stock Exchange. In a special bid, the bidder for the block of stock—a pension fund, for instance, will pay a special commission to the broker who represents him in making the purchase. The seller does not pay a commission. The special bid is made on the floor of the exchange at a fixed price which may not be below the last sale of the security or the current bid in the regular market, whichever is higher. Member firms may sell this stock for customers directly to the buyer's broker during trading hours.†

Special offering Opposite of special bid. A notice is printed on the ticker tape announcing the stock sale at a fixed price usually based on the last transaction in the regular auction market. If there are more buyers than stock, allotments are made. Only the seller pays the commission. (See: *Secondary distribution.*)†

Special tax bond A bond secured by a special tax, such as a gasoline tax.**

Specialist A member of the New York Stock Exchange, Inc., who has two functions: First, to maintain an orderly market in the securities registered to the specialist. In order to maintain an orderly market, the Exchange expects specialists to buy or sell for the own account, to a reasonable degree, when there is a temporary disparity between supply and demand. Second, the specialist acts as a broker's broker. When a commission broker on the Exchange floor receives a limit order, say, to buy at $50 a stock then selling at $60—he cannot wait at the post where the stock is traded to see if the price reaches the specified level. So he leaves the order with the specialist, who will try to execute it in the market if and when the stock declines to the specified price. At all times the specialist must put his customers' interests above his own. There are about 400 specialists on the NYSE. (See: *Limited Order.*)††

Speculation The employment of funds by a speculator. Safety of principal is a secondary factor. (See: *Investment.*)†

Speculator One who is willing to assume a relatively large risk in the hope of gain.††

Spin off The separation of a subsidiary or division of a corporation from its parent by issuing shares in a new corporate entity. Shareowners in the parent receive shares in the new company in proportion to their original holding and the total value remains approximately the same.††

Split The division of the outstanding shares of a corporation into a larger number of shares. A 3-for-1 split by a company with 1 million shares outstanding results in 3 million shares outstanding. Each holder of 100 shares before the 3-for-1 split would have 300 shares, although his proportionate equity in the company would remain the same; 100 parts of 1 million are the equivalent of 300 parts of 3 million. Ordinarily splits must be voted by directors and approved by shareholders. (See: *Stock dividends.*)

Standard deviation A statistical term that measures the variability of a set of observations from the mean of the distribution (σ.)*

State-preference model A framework in which decisions are based on probabilities of payoffs under alternative states of the world.*

Stock ahead Sometimes an investor who has entered an order to buy or sell a stock at a certain price will see transactions at that price reported on the ticker tape while his own order has not been executed. The reason is that other buy and sell orders at the same price came in to the specialist ahead of his and had priority. (See: *Book, Specialist.*)†

Stock dividend A dividend paid in securities rather than cash. The dividend may be additional shares of the issuing company, or shares of another company (usually a subsidiary) held by the company.††

Stock split An accounting action to increase the number of shares outstanding; for example, in a 3-for-1 split, shares outstanding would be tripled and each stockholder would be tripled and each stockholder would receive three new shares for each one formerly held. Stock splits involve no transfer from surplus to the capital account.*

Stockholder of record A stockholder whose name is registered on the books of the issuing corporation.†

Stock Index Futures Futures contracts based on market indexes, e.g., NYSE Composite Index Futures Contracts.††

Stop limit order A stop order which becomes a limit order after the specified stop price has been reached. (See: *Limit order, Stop order.*)†

Stop order An order to buy at a price above or sell at a price below the current market. Stop buy orders are generally used to limit loss or protect unrealized profits on a short sale. Stop sell orders are generally used to protect unrealized profits or limit loss on a holding. A stop order becomes a market order when the stock sells at or beyond the specified price and, thus, may not necessarily be executed at that price.†

Stopped stock A service performed—in most cases by the specialist—for an order given him by a commission broker. Let's say XYZ just sold at $50 a share. Broker A comes along with an order to buy 100 shares at the market. The lowest offer is $50.50. Broker A believes he can do better for his client than $50.50, perhaps might get the stock at $50.25. But he doesn't want to take a chance that he'll miss the market—that is, the next sale might be $50.50 and the following one even higher. So he asks the specialist if he will stop 100 at ½ ($50.50). The specialist agrees. The specialist guarantees Broker A he will get 100 shares at 50½ if the stock sells at that price. In the meantime, if the specialist or broker A succeeds in executing the order at $50.25, the stop is called off. (See: *Specialist.*)†

Street name Securities held in the name of a broker instead of his customer's name are said to be carried in a *street name.* This occurs when the securities have been bought on margin or when the customer wishes the security to be held by the broker.†

Subdivision Any legal and authorized political entity under a state's jurisdiction (county, city, water district, school district, etc.).**

Subjective probability distributions Probability distributions determined through subjective procedures without the use of statistics.*

Subordinated debenture A bond having a claim on assets only after the senior debt has been paid off in the event of liquidation.*

Subscription price The price at which a security may be purchased in a rights offering.*

Switch order or contingent order An order for the purchase (sale) of one stock and the sale (purchase) of another stock at a stipulated price difference.†

Swapping Selling one security and buying a similar one almost at the same time to take a loss, usually for tax purposes.††

Switching Selling one security and buying another.†

Syndicate A group of investment bankers who together underwrite and distribute a new issue of securities or a large block of an outstanding issue.†

Synergy A situation where "the whole is greater than the sum of its parts"; in a synergistic merger, the postmerger earnings exceed the sum of the separate companies' premerger earnings.*

Systematic risk That part of a security's risk that cannot be eliminated by diversification.*

Take-over The acquiring of one corporation by another—usually in a friendly merger but sometimes marked by a "proxy fight." In "unfriendly" take-over attempts, the potential buying company may offer a price well above current market values, new securities, and other inducements to stockholders. The management of the subject company might ask for a better price or fight the take-over or merger with another company. (See: *Proxy*.)†

Tangible assets Physical assets as opposed to intangible assets such as goodwill and the stated value of patents.*

Tax base The total resources available for taxation.**

Tax-exempt bond Another name for a municipal bond. The interest on a municipal bond is presently exempt from Federal income tax.**

Tax shelter A medium or process intended to reduce or eliminate the tax burden of an individual. They range from such conventional ones as tax-exempt municipal securities and interest or dividend exclusion to sophisticated limited partnerships in real estate, cattle raising, equipment leasing, oil drilling, research and development activities and motion picture production.††

Technical research Analysis of the market and stocks based on supply and demand. The technician studies price movements, volume, and trends and patterns which are revealed by charting these factors, and attempts to assess the possible effect of current market action on future supply and demand for securities and individual issues. (See: *Fundamental research*.)†

Tender offer A public offer to buy shares from existing stockholders of one public corporation by another company or other organization under specified terms good for a certain time period. Stockholders are asked to "tender" (surrender) their holdings for stated value, usually at a premium above current market price, subject to the tendering of a minimum and maximum number of shares.††

Term issue An issue that has a single maturity.**

Term loan A loan generally obtained from a bank or an insurance company with a maturity greater than one year. Term loans are generally amortized.*

Thin market A market in which there are comparatively few bids to buy or offers to sell, or both. The phrase may apply to a single security or to the entire stock market. In a thin market, price fluctuations between transactions are usually larger than when the market is liquid. A thin market in a particular stock may reflect lack of interest in that issue or a limited supply of or demand for stock in the market. (See: *Bid and asked, Liquidity, Offer*.)†

Third market Trading of stock exchange listed securities in the over-the-counter market by non-exchange-member brokers.††

Time order An order which becomes a market or limited price order at a specified time.†

Time value The part of an option premium that is in excess of the intrinsic value.††

Tips Supposedly "inside" information on corporation affairs.†

Trader Individuals who buy and sell for their own accounts for short-term profit. Also, an employee of a broker/dealer or financial institution who specializes in handling purchases and sales of securities for the firm and/or its clients. (See: *Investor, Speculator*.)††

Trading floor (See: *Floor*.)

Trading market The secondary market for outstanding securities.**

Trading post One of 23 trading locations on the floor of the New York Stock Exchange at which stocks assigned to that location are bought and sold. About 75 stocks are traded at each post.†

Transfer This term may refer to two different operations. For one, the delivery of a stock certificate from the seller's broker to the buyer's broker and legal change of ownership, normally accomplished within a few days. For another, to record the change of ownership on the books of the corporation by the transfer agent. When the purchaser's name is recorded, dividends, notices of meetings, proxies, financial reports, and all pertinent literature sent by the issuer to its securities holders are mailed direct to the new owner. (See: *Registrar, Street name*.)††

Transfer agent A transfer agent keeps a record of the name of each registered shareowner, his or her address, the number of shares owned, and sees that certificates presented for transfer are properly cancelled and new certificates issued in the name of the new owner. (See: *Registrar*.)††

Treasury bills Short-term U.S. Treasury securities issued in minimum denominations of $10,000 and usually having original maturities of 3, 6, or 12 months. Investors purchase bills at prices lower than the face value of the bills; the return to the investors is the difference between the price paid for the bills and the amount received when the bills are sold or when they mature. Treasury bills are the type of security used most frequently in open market operations.¶

Treasury bonds Long-term U.S. Treasury securities usually having initial maturities of more than 10 years and issued in denominations of $1,000 or more, depending on the specific issue.

Bonds pay interest semiannually, with principal payable at maturity.¶

Treasury notes Intermediate-term coupon-bearing U.S. Treasury securities having initial maturities from 1 to 10 years and issued in denominations of $1,000 or more, depending on the maturity of the issue. Notes pay interest semiannually, and the principal is payable at maturity.¶

Treasury stock Stock issued by a company, but later reacquired. It may be held in the company's treasury indefinitely, reissued to the public, or retired. Treasury stock receives no dividends, and has no vote while held by the company.††

Trust receipt An instrument acknowledging that the borrower holds certain goods in trust for the lender. Trust receipt financing is used in connection with the financing of inventories for automobile dealers, construction equipment dealers, appliance dealers, and other dealers in expensive durable goods.*

Trustee The representative of bondholders who acts in their interest and facilitates communication between them and the issuer. Typically these duties are handled by a department of a commercial bank.*

Turnover rate The volume of shares traded in a year as a percentage of total shares listed on an exchange, outstanding for an individual issue, or held in an institutional portfolio.††

Underwriter (See: *Investment banker.*)

Underwriting (1) The entire process of issuing new corporate securities. (2) The insurance function of bearing the risk of adverse price fluctuations during the period in which a new issue of stock or bonds is being distributed.*

Underwriting syndicate A syndicate of investment firms formed to spread the risk associated with the purchase and distribution of a new issue of securities. The larger the issue, the more firms typically are involved in the syndicate.*

Unlimited tax bond A bond secured by pledge of taxes that are not limited by rate or amount.**

Unlisted A security not listed on a stock exchange. (See: *Over-the-counter.*)†

Unsystematic risk That part of a security's risk associated with random events; unsystematic risk can be eliminated by proper diversification.*

Up tick A term used to designate a transaction made at a price higher than the preceding transaction. Also called a *plus-tick*. A *zero-plus* tick is a term used for a transaction at the same price as the preceding trade but higher than the preceding different price.

Conversely, a *down tick*, or *minus* tick, is a term used to designate a transaction made at a price lower than the preceding trade.

A plus sign, or a minus sign, is displayed throughout the day next to the last price of each company's stock traded at each trading post on the floor of the New York Stock Exchange. (See: *Short sale.*)†

Utility theory A body of theory dealing with the relationships among money income, utility (or "happiness"), and the willingness to accept risk.*

Value additivity principle Neither fragmenting cash flows or recombining them will affect the resulting values of the cash flows.*

Variable annuity A life insurance policy where the annuity premium (a set amount of dollars) is immediately turned into units of a portfolio of stocks. Upon retirement, the policyholder is paid according to accumulated units, the dollar value of which varies according to the performance of the stock portfolio. Its objective is to preserve, through stock investment, the purchasing value of the annuity which otherwise is subject to erosion through inflation.††

Volume The number of shares traded in a security or an entire market during a given period. Volume is usually considered on a daily basis and a daily average is computed for longer periods.†

Voting right The common stockholder's right to vote their stock in the affairs of a company. Preferred stock usually has the right to vote when preferred dividends are in default for a specified period. The right to vote may be delegated by the stockholder to another person. (See: *Cumulative voting, Proxy.*)††

Warrant A certificate giving the holder the right to purchase securities at a stipulated price within a specified time limit or perpetually. Sometimes a warrant is offered with securities as an inducement to buy. (See: *Rights.*)††

Weighted cost of capital A weighted average of the component costs of debt, preferred stock, and common equity. Also called the *composite cost of capital.*

When issued A short form of "when, as, and if issued." The term indicates a conditional transaction in a security authorized for issuance but not as yet actually issued. All "when issued" transactions are on an "if" basis, to be settled if and when the actual security is issued and the exchange or National Association of Securities Dealers rules the transactions are to be settled.†

Wire house A member firm of an exchange maintaining a communications network linking either its own branch offices, offices of correspondent firms, or a combination of such offices.†

Working capital Refers to a firm's investment in short-term assets—cash, short-term securities, accounts receivable, and inventories. *Gross working capital* is defined as a firm's total current assets. *Net working capital* is defined as current assets minus current liabilities. If the term *working capital* is used without further qualification, it generally refers to gross working capital.*

Working control Theoretically, ownership of 51 percent of a company's voting stock is necessary to exercise control. In practice—and this is particularly true in the case of a large corporation—effective control sometimes can be exerted through ownership, individually or by a group acting in concert, of less than 50 percent.†

Yield Also known as return. The dividends or interest paid by a company expressed as a percentage of the current price. A stock with a current market value of $3.20 is said to return 8 percent ($3.20 ÷ $40.00). The current yield on a bond is figured the same way.††

Yield to maturity The yield of a bond to maturity takes into account the price discount from or premium over the face amount. It is greater than the current yield when the bond is selling at a discount and less than the current yield when the bond is selling at a premium.†

Zero coupon bonds Bonds which do not convey a coupon (i.e., do not pay interest) but which are offered at a substantial discount from par value and appreciate to their full value (usually $1,000) at maturity. However, under U.S. tax law, the imputed interest is taxed as it accrues. The appeal of Zero coupon bonds is primarily for IRA and other tax sheltered retirement accounts.

Acquisition Takeover Glossary

Asset Play A firm whose underlying assets are worth substantially more (after paying off the firm's liabilities) than the market value of its stock.

Breakup value The sum of the values of the firm's assets if sold off separately.

Crown jewel option The strategem of selling off or spinning off the asset that makes the firm an attractive takeover candidate.

Four-nine position A holding of approximately 4.9% of the outstanding shares of a company. At 5%, the holder must file a form [13d] with the SEC, revealing his position. Thus, a four-nine position is about the largest position that one can quietly hold.

Source: From the *AAII Journal*, American Association of *Individual Investors*, 612 North Michigan Avenue, Chicago, IL 60611. Excerpted from Ben Branch "White Knight Rescues Investors From Terminology."

Black knight A potential acquirer that management opposes and would prefer to find an alternative to (i.e. a *white knight*).

Going private The process of buying back the publicly held stock so that what was heretofore a public firm becomes private.

Golden handcuffs Employment agreement that makes the departure of upper level managers very costly to them. For instance, such managers may lose very attractive stock option rights by leaving prior to their normal retirement age.

Golden handshake A provision in a preliminary agreement to be acquired in which the target firm gives the acquiring firm an option to purchase its shares or assets at attractive prices or to receive a substantial bonus if the proposed takeover does not occur.

Golden parachute Extremely generous separation payments for upper level executives that are required to be fulfilled if the firm's control shifts.

Greenmail Incentive payments to dissuade the interest of outsiders who may otherwise seek control of a firm. The payment frequently takes the form of a premium price for the outsiders' shares, coupled with an agreement from them to avoid buying more stock for a set period of time.

The firm bears the cost of the payment. The stock price generally falls after the payment and the removal of the outside threat.

In play The status of being a recognized takeover candidate.

Junk bonds High-risk, high-yield bonds that are often used to finance takeovers.

LBO A leveraged buyout. A purchase of a company financed largely by debt that is backed by the firm's own assets.

Loaded laggard A stock of a company whose assets, particularly its liquid assets, have high values relative to the stock's price.

Lockup agreement An agreement between an acquirer and target that makes the target very unattractive to any other acquirer; similar to a *golden handshake*.

PacMan defense The tactic of seeking to acquire the firm that has targeted your own firm as a takeover prospect.

Poison pill A provision in the corporate bylaws or other governance documents providing for a very disadvantageous result for a potential acquirer should its ownership position be allowed to exceed some preassigned threshold. For example, if anyone acquires more than 20% of Company A's stock, the acquirer might then have to sell $100 worth of its own stock to other shareholders at $50.

Raider A hostile outside party that seeks to take over other companies.

Scorched earth defense A tactic in which the defending company's management engages in practices that reduce their company's value to such a degree that it is no longer attractive to the potential acquirer. This approach is more often threatened than actually employed.

Shark repellant Anti-takeover provisions such as the poison pill.

Short swing profit A gain made by an insider (including anyone with more than 10% of the stock) who holds stock for less than six months. Such gains must be paid back to the company whose shares were sold.

Standstill agreement A reciprocal understanding between a company's management and an outside party that usually owns a significant minority position. Each party gives up certain rights in exchange for corresponding concessions by the other party. For example, the outside group may agree to limit its stock purchases to keep its ownership percentage below some level (for instance, 20%). In exchange, management may agree to a minority board representation by the outsider.

13d A form that must be filed with the SEC when a single investor or an associated group owns 5% or more of a company's stock. The form reveals the size of the holding and the investor's intentions.

Two-tier offer A takeover device in which a relatively high per share price is paid for controlling interest in a target and a lesser per share price is paid for the remainder.

White knight defense Finding an alternative and presumably more friendly acquirer than the present takeover threat.

White squire defense Finding an important ally to purchase a strong minority position (for example, 25%) of the potential acquisition's stock. Presumably this ally (the "white squire") will oppose and hopefully block the efforts of any hostile firm seeking to acquire the vulnerable firm.

Securities and Exchange Commission

JUDICIARY PLAZA
450 FIFTH STREET, NW
WASHINGTON, DC 20549
INFORMATION: 202-272-2650
FREEDOM OF INFORMATION ACT:
202-272-7450
FILINGS BY REGISTERED COMPANIES:
202-272-2624

FULL AND FAIR DISCLOSURE

The Securities Act of 1933 requires issuers of securities making public offerings of securities in interstate commerce or through the mails, directly or by others on their behalf, to file registration statements containing financial and other pertinent data about the issuer and the securities being offered. A similar requirement applies to such offerings on behalf of a controlling person of the issuer. Unless a registration statement is in effect with respect to such securities, it is unlawful to sell the securities in interstate commerce or through the mails. (There are certain limited exemptions, such as government securities, nonpublic offerings, and intrastate offerings, as well as offerings not exceeding $1,500,000 in amount, which comply with the commission's Regulation A.)

Source: This material was abstracted from the United States Government Manual.

The effectiveness of a registration statement may be refused or suspended after a public hearing, if the statement contains material misstatements or omissions, thus barring sale of the securities until it is appropriately amended. Registration of securities does not imply approval of the issue by the commission or that the commission has found the registration disclosures to be accurate. It does not insure investors against loss in their purchase but serves rather to provide information upon which investors may make an informed and realistic evaluation of the worth of the securities.

Persons responsible for filing false information with the commission subject themselves to the risk of fine or imprisonment or both; and persons connected with the public offering may be liable in damages to purchasers of the securities if the disclosures in the registration statement and prospectus are materially defective. Also, the above act contains antifraud provisions which apply generally to the sale of securities, whether or not registered (48 Stat. 74; 15 U.S.C. 77a et seq.).

REGULATION OF SECURITIES MARKETS AND PERSONS CONDUCTING A SECURITIES BUSINESS

The Securities Exchange Act of 1934 assigns to the commission board regulatory responsibilities over the securities markets, the self-regulatory organizations within the securities industry, and persons conducting a business in securities. The commission is directed to facilitate the establishment of a national market system for securities and a national system for the clearance and settlement of securities transactions. Securities exchanges and certain clearing agencies are required to register with the commission, and associations of brokers or dealers are permitted to register with the commission. The securities Exchange Act also provides for the establishment of the Municipal Securities Rulemaking Board to formulate rules for the municipal securities industry. The commission oversees the self-regulatory activities of the national securities exchanges and associations, registered clearing agencies, and the Municipal Securities Rulemaking Board. In addition, the commission regulates industry professionals, such as securities brokers and dealers, certain municipal securities professionals, and transfer agents.

The Securities Exchange Act authorizes national securities exchanges, national securities associations, clearing agencies, and the Municipal Securities Rulemaking Board to adopt rules that are designed, among other things to promote just and equitable principles of trade and to protect investors. The commission is required to approve or disapprove most proposed rules of these self-regulatory organizations and has the power to abrogate or amend existing rules of the national securities exchanges, national securities associations, and the Municipal Securities Rulemaking Board.

In addition, the commission has broad rulemaking authority over the activities of brokers, dealers, municipal securities dealers, securities information processors, and transfer agents. The commission may regulate such securities trading practices as short sales and stabilizing transactions. It may regulate the trading of options on national securities exchanges and the activities of members of exchanges who trade on the trading floors and may adopt rules governing broker-dealer sales practices in dealing with investors. The commission also is authorized to adopt rules concerning the financial responsibility of brokers and dealers and reports to be made by brokers and dealers. The Securities Exchange Act also empowers the Board of Governors of the Federal Reserve System to prescribe rules relating to the extension of credit by brokers and dealers for securities transactions. Such rules include the establishment of minimum margin requirements with respect to securities registered on national securities exchanges and certain securities traded over-the-counter (48 Stat. 881; U.S.C. 78a et seq.).

The Securities Exchange Act also requires the filing of registration applications and annual and other reports with national securities exchanges and the commission by companies whose securities are listed upon the exchanges, by companies that have assets of $3 million or more and 500 or more shareholders of record, and by companies that distributed securities pursuant to a registration statement declared effective by the commission under the Securities Act of 1933. Such applications and reports must contain financial and other data prescribed by the commission as necessary or appropriate for the protection of investors and to issue fair dealing. In addition, the solicitation of proxies, authorizations, or consents from holders of such registered securities must be made in accordance with rules and regulations prescribed by the commission. These rules provide for disclosures to securities holders of information relevant to the subject matter of the solicitation.

Disclosure of the holdings and transactions by officers, directors, and large (10 percent) holders of equity securities of companies is also required, and any and all persons who acquire more than 5 percent of certain equity securities are required to file detailed information with the commission and any exchange upon which such securities may be traded. Moreover, any person making a tender offer for certain classes of equity securities is required to file reports with the commission, if as a result of the tender offer such person would own more than 5 percent of the outstanding shares of the particular class of equity involved. The commission also is authorized to promulgate rules governing the repurchase by a corporate issuer of its own securities.

REGULATION OF MUTUAL FUNDS AND OTHER INVESTMENT COMPANIES

The Investment Company Act of 1940 provides for the registration with the commission of investment companies and subjects their activities to regulation to protect investors. The regulation covers sales and management fees, composition of boards of directors, and capital structure. Also, various transactions of investment companies, including transactions with affiliated interests, are prohibited unless the commission first determines that such transactions are fair. Under the act, the commission may institute court action to enjoin the consummation of mergers and other plans for reorganization of investment companies if such plans are unfair to security holders. It also may impose sanctions by administrative proceedings against investment company managements for violations of the act and other federal securities laws, and file court actions to enjoin acts and practices of management officials involving breaches of fiduciary duty involving personal misconduct and to disqualify such officials from office (54 Stat. 789; 15 U.S.C. 80a–1—80a–52).

REGULATION OF COMPANIES CONTROLLING ELECTRIC OR GAS UTILITIES

The Public Utility Holding Company Act of 1935 provides for regulation by the commission of the purchase and sale of securities and assets by companies in electric and gas utility holding company systems, their intra-system transactions and service and management arrangements. It limits holding companies to a single coordinated utility system and requires simplification of complex corporate and capital structures and elimination of unfair distribution of voting power among holders of system securities.

The issuance and sale of securities by holding companies and their subsidiaries, unless exempt (subject to conditions and terms which the commission is empowered to impose) as an issue expressly authorized by the state commission in the state in which the issuer is incorporated, must be found by the commission to meet statutory standards, namely: that the new security is reasonably adapted to the security structure and earning power of the issuer; that the proposed financing is necessary and appropriate to the economical and efficient operation of the company's business; that the consideration received, and fees, commissions, and other remuneration paid, are fair; and that the terms and conditions of the sale are not detrimental to investors, consumers, or the public.

The purchase and sale of utility properties and other assets may not be made in contravention of rules, regulations, or orders of the commission regarding the consideration to be received, maintenance of competitive conditions, fees and commissions, accounts, disclosure of interest, and similar matters. In passing upon proposals for reorganization, merger, or consolidation, the commission must be satisfied that the objectives of the act generally are complied with and that the terms of the proposal are fair and equitable to all classes of security holders affected (49 Stat. 803; 15 U.S.C 79–92z–6).

REGULATION OF INVESTMENT COUNSELORS AND ADVISERS

The Investment Advisers Act of 1940 provides that persons who, for compensation, engage in the business of advising others with respect to their security transactions must register with the commission. The act prohibits certain types of fee arrangements, makes unlawful practices of investment advisers involving fraud or deceit, and requires, among other things, disclosure of any adverse interests the advisers may have in transactions executed for clients. The act authorizes the commission to issue rules proscribing acts and practices that may operate as a fraud or deceit upon investors (54 Stat. 847; 15 U.S.C. 80b–1—80b–21).

REHABILITATION OF FAILING CORPORATIONS

Chapter 11, section 1109(a), of the Bankruptcy Code (92 Stat. 2629; 11 U.S.C. 1109) provides for Commission participation as a statutory party in corporate reorganization proceedings administered in Federal courts. The principal functions of the Commission are to protect the interests of public investors involved in such cases through efforts to ensure their adequate representation and to participate on legal and policy issues which are of concern to public investors generally.

INDEPENDENT REPRESENTATION OF THE INTERESTS OF HOLDERS OF DEBT SECURITIES

The interests of purchasers of publicly offered debt securities issued pursuant to trust indentures are safeguarded under the provisions of the Trust Indenture Act of 1939. This act, among other things, requires the exclusion from such indentures of certain types of exculpatory clauses and the inclusion of certain protective provisions. The independence of the indenture trustee, who is a representative of the debt holder, is assured by proscribing certain relationships that might conflict with the proper exercise of his duties (53 Stat. 1149; 15 U.S.C. 77aaa–77bbbb).

ENFORCEMENT ACTIVITIES

The commission's enforcement activities are designed to secure compliance with the federal securities laws administered by the commission and the rules and regulations adopted thereunder. These activities include measures to compel obedience to the disclosure requirements of the registration and other provisions of the acts; to prevent fraud and deception in the purchase and sale of securities; to obtain court orders enjoining acts and practices that operate as a fraud upon investors or otherwise violate the laws; to revoke the registrations of brokers, dealers, and investment advisers who willfully engage in such acts and practices; to suspend or expel from national securities exchanges or the National Association of Securities Dealers, Inc., any member or officer who has violated any provision of the federal securities laws; and to prosecute persons who have engaged in fraudulent activities, or other willful violations of those laws. In addition, attorneys or accountants who violate the securities laws face possible loss of their privilege to practice before the commission. To this end, private investigations are conducted into complaints or other evidences of securities violations. Evidence thus established of law violations in the purchase and sale of securities is used in appropriate administrative proceedings to revoke registration or in actions instituted in federal courts to restrain or enjoin such activities. Where the evidence tends to establish fraud or other willful violation of the securities laws, the facts are referred to the Attorney General for criminal prosecution of the offenders. The commission may assist in such prosecutions.

INVESTOR INFORMATION AND PROTECTION

Complaints and inquiries may be directed to the home office or to any regional office. Registration statements and other public documents filed with the commission are available for public inspection in the public reference room at the home office. Much of the information also is available in its New York, Chicago, and Los Angeles regional offices, and to a lesser extent in the other regional offices of the commission. Reproduction of the public material may be purchased from the commission as prescribed rates.

Small Business Activities Information on security laws which pertain to small businesses in relation to securities offerings may be obtained from the Commission. Phone, 202-272-2644.

Consumer Activities Publications detailing the Commission's activities, which include material of assistance to the potential investor, are available from the Publications Unit. In addition, the Office of Consumer Affairs and Information Services answers questions from investors, assists investors with specific problems regarding their relations with broker-dealers and companies, and advises the Commission and other offices and divisions regarding problems frequently encountered by investors and possible regulatory solutions to such problems. Phone, 202-272-7440.

Reading Rooms The Commission maintains a public reference room (phone, 202-272-7450) and also a library (phone, 202-272-2618) where additional information may be obtained.

Contracts Contact the Office of Administrative Services. Phone, 202-272-7000.

REGIONAL OFFICES (Securities and Exchange Commission)

Region	Address
1. New York, New Jersey	26 Federal Plaza, New York, NY 10078 Phone: 212-264-1636
2. Maine, Vermont, New Hampshire, Massachusetts, Connecticut, Rhode Island	150 Causeway Street, Boston, MA 02114 Phone: 617-223-2721
3. Tennessee, North Carolina, South Carolina, Mississippi, Alabama, Georgia, Florida, Louisiana (southeastern portion only)	1375 Peachtree Street NE, Atlanta, GA 30367 Phone: 404-881-4768
4. Minnesota, Wisconsin, Michigan, Iowa, Missouri, Illinois, Indiana, Ohio, Kentucky	219 S. Dearborn Street, Chicago, IL 60604 Phone: 312-353-7390
5. Kansas, Oklahoma, Texas, Arkansas, Louisiana (except southeastern portion)	411 W. 7th Street, Fort Worth, TX 76102 Phone: 817-334-3821
6. North Dakota, South Dakota, Colorado, Kansas, Utah, Wyoming, New Mexico	410 17th Street, Denver, CO 80202 Phone: 303-837-2071
7. California, Nevada, Arizona, Hawaii	5757 Wilshire Boulevard, Los Angeles, CA 90036 Phone: 213-468-3167
8. Washington, Oregon	915 Second Avenue, Seattle, WA 98174 Phone: 206-442-7990
9. Pennsylvania, West Virginia, Virginia, Maryland, Delaware	4015 Wilson Boulevard, Arlington, VA 22203 Phone: 703-235-3700

POST-WORLD WAR II BULL MARKETS

No.	Previous Bear Market Bottom		Rise to Bull Market Peak			Bull Market Peak		Decline to Next Bear Market Bottom		
	Date	DJIA	Dow Points	Percent	No. of Months	Date	DJIA	Dow Points	Percent	No. of Months
1	06/13/49	161.60	132.19	81.8%	42.6	01/05/53	293.79	38.30	13.0%	8.3
2	09/14/53	255.49	265.56	103.9	30.5	04/06/56	521.05	101.26	19.4	18.5
3	10/22/57	419.79	265.68	63.3	26.4	01/05/60	685.47	119.42	17.4	9.7
4	10/25/60	566.05	168.86	29.8	13.6	12/13/61	734.91	199.15	27.1	6.4
5	06/26/62	535.76	459.39	85.7	43.4	02/09/66	995.15	250.83	25.2	7.9
6	10/07/66	744.32	240.89	32.4	25.9	12/03/68	985.21	354.05	35.9	17.7
7	05/26/70	631.16	420.54	66.6	31.5	01/11/73	1,051.70	474.10	45.1	22.8
8	12/06/74	577.60	437.19	75.7	21.5	09/21/76	1,014.79	272.67	26.9	17.2
9	02/28/78	742.12	165.62	22.3	6.3	09/08/78	907.74	122.48	13.5	2.2
10	11/14/78	785.26	118.58	15.1	15.0	02/13/80	903.84	144.71	16.0	2.3
11	04/21/80	759.13	264.92	34.9	12.2	04/27/81	1,024.05	247.13	24.1	15.5
12	08/12/82	776.92	510.28	65.7	15.6	11/29/83	1,287.20	200.63	15.6	7.8
13	07/24/84	1,086.57	479.14	44.1	17.3	01/31/86	1,570.98			
Averages				52.2	23.4				23.3	11.4

Source: Reprinted by permission, *Financial World 1986*, published by Financial World Partners.

Hulbert Performance Rating of Investment Advisory Letters

FIVE-YEAR PERFORMANCE RATING.

NEWSLETTER (Composition of Portfolio)	6/86 Gain	1986 Gain	1985 Gain	1984 Gain	1983 Gain	1982 Gain	1981 Gain	7/1 to 12/31/80 Gain	Risk Rating Note 1	See Note #2
Addison Report (Portfolios fully invested in "monitored" lists)										
a. Conservative stocks (Fully invested)	+2.6%	+22.9%	+15.3%	+4.4%	+28.9%	n/a	n/a	n/a	4.09	37-C
b. Speculative Stocks (Fully invested)	-2.5%	+17.7%	+17.6%	-13.6%	+89.6%	n/a	n/a	n/a	6.02	34-C
Astute Investor (Portfolio fully invested in stocks rated "buy")	+1.2%	+29.9%	+44.3%	-5.9%	n/a	n/a	n/a	n/a	5.46	16-C
(Astute Investor—Timing Only)	+1.3%	+18.4%	+26.2%	+0.5%	n/a	n/a	n/a	n/a	n/a	n/a
BI Research (Portfolio fully invested in stocks rated "Buy")	+33.5%	+41.3%	+65.9%	+14.3%	n/a	n/a	n/a	n/a	12.10	2-C
Cabot Market Letter (Model Portfolio: Stocks and, at times, T-Bills)	+4.1%	+21.3%	+37.4%	-22.7%	+7.3%	+32.8%	+2.5%	n/a	6.63	12-A
(Cabot Market Letter—Timing Only)	+1.3%	+18.3%	+26.3%	+0.7%	+16.4%	+13.9%	-3.7%	n/a	n/a	n/a
Calif. Technology Stock Letter (Model Portfolio: Stocks & T-Bills)	-0.0%	+8.9%	-5.9%	-47.9%	+1.7%	n/a	n/a	n/a	9.37	7-A
(Calif. Technology Stock Letter—Timing Only)	+0.3%	+12.3%	+25.5%	+1.2%	+15.4%	n/a	n/a	n/a	n/a	n/a
Canadian Business Service Investment Report										
a. Very Conservative Stocks (Fully invested)	-2.2%	+4.0%	+20.7%	-4.9%	n/a	n/a	n/a	n/a	3.94	25-C
b. Conservative stocks (fully invested)	-1.7%	+18.3%	+17.2%	+0.3%	n/a	n/a	n/a	n/a	4.15	26-C
c. Average risk stocks (fully invested)	+5.1%	+44.5%	+39.7%	-6.4%	n/a	n/a	n/a	n/a	5.54	11-C
d. Higher risk stocks (fully invested)	-3.7%	+9.5%	+21.4%	-10.7%	n/a	n/a	n/a	n/a	5.28	9-C
e. Speculative stocks (fully invested)	-2.8%	+22.7%	+13.8%	-10.8%	n/a	n/a	n/a	n/a	7.19	3-C
The Chartist										
a. Actual Cash Account (Stocks and, at times, T-Bills)	+2.0%	+20.2%	+23.3%	+1.0%	+25.1%	+32.7%	-9.7%	+23.4%	3.73	7-A
(Actual Cash Account—Timing Only)	+0.9%	+10.3%	+20.6%	+5.0%	+16.2%	+12.1%	n/a	n/a	n/a	n/a
b. Traders' Stocks (fully invested)	+4.0%	+41.2%	+52.2%	+6.4%	+30.5%	n/a	n/a	n/a	5.74	29-C
Dessauer's Journal (International Portfolio: Stocks,Bonds,Currencies)	-3.4%	+19.3%	+41.8%	-0.0%	+21.0%	+20.1%	n/a	n/a	3.53	50-B

The Dines Letter (Supervised Lists of Stocks, Bonds, Options, T-Bills):										
#1. Good-Grade for Moderate Gains	-0.4%	+39.2%	+12.5%	-41.1%	+43.5%	+15.1%	-20.4%	+10.2%	7.35	9-A
#2. Speculative	+14.8%	+70.4%	+18.1%	+37.0%	+8.6%	+9.1%	+15.5%	+5.8%	7.83	9-A
#3. Growth	-6.8%	+51.7%	+23.3%	+71.9%	+7.0%	+25.1%	+14.2%	+5.8%	8.57	10-A
#4. Short-Term Trading	-5.2%	+107.3%	-2.6%	+27.4%	+90.1%	-4.3%	-13.2%	+19.3%	17.63	9-A
(Short-Term Trading Portfolio–Timing Only)	+1.3%	+18.5%	+18.0%	+1.9%	+15.2%	+18.1%	+16.5%	+11.3%	n/a	n/a
Income (Discontinued early 1984)	n/a	n/a	n/a	n/a	+13.2%	+20.1%	+14.2%	+5.8%	n/a	n/a
Gold (Discontinued early 1984)	n/a	n/a	n/a	n/a	+9.1%	-8.4%	-39.4%	+28.9%	n/a	n/a
Dow Theory Forecasts (Portfolios fully invested in each list's stocks)										
a. Income Stocks (Invested in those "especially recommended")	+6.8%	+30.6%	+35.1%	+12.9%	+20.5%	+20.2%	-8.2%	+14.9%	3.14	16-C
b. Investment Stocks (Invested in those "especially recommended")	+3.2%	+29.9%	+35.3%	+2.3%	+15.6%	+28.4%	-4.2%	+21.8%	3.64	22-C
c. Growth Stocks (Invested in those "especially recommended")	-1.9%	+16.1%	+28.8%	-6.8%	+11.7%	+14.9%	+5.2%	+22.5%	4.77	21-C
d. Speculative Stocks (Invested in those "especially recommended")	-0.6%	+16.1%	+35.3%	-4.7%	+11.7%	+13.4%	-5.9%	+27.5%	4.51	31-C
e. Low-Priced Stocks (Invested in those "especially recommended")	-2.5%	+9.8%	n/a	n/a	n/a	n/a	n/a	n/a	n/a	38-C
f. Special Situations Stocks (Merged into Low-Priced Portfolio)										
Dow Theory Letters (Recommendations in "Investment Position" Box)	+0.8%	+6.4%	-5.9%	+1.8%	-6.8%	+19.2%	+10.2%	n/a	2.88	7-D
Emerging & Special Situations (Fully invested in stocks rated "buy")	+6.8%	+16.4%	+44.2%	-4.6%	+6.6%	n/a	n/a	n/a	7.47	18-C
Financial World (Fully invested in A+-rated stocks)	+3.0%	+32.3%	+19.3%	n/a	n/a	n/a	n/a	n/a	4.46	123-C
Fund Exchange Report (Mutual Funds)										
a. Balanced Model Portfolio	+1.6%	+18.1%	+20.2%	n/a	n/a	n/a	n/a	n/a	3.30	7-A
b. Conservative Growth Model Portfolio	+1.0%	+17.7%	+28.6%	n/a	n/a	n/a	n/a	n/a	3.31	5-A
c. Conservative Growth Margined Portfolio	+3.8%	+40.6%	+45.5%	n/a	n/a	n/a	n/a	n/a	5.40	5-A
d. Aggressive Growth Model Portfolio	+0.5%	+22.6%	+29.7%	n/a	n/a	n/a	n/a	n/a	4.24	5-A
e. Aggressive Growth Margined Portfolio	+2.8%	+44.3%	+40.1%	n/a	n/a	n/a	n/a	n/a	6.86	5-A
f. Taxable Bond Model Portfolio	+0.6%	+7.8%	+18.9%	n/a	n/a	n/a	n/a	n/a	1.68	5-A
g. Gold Model Portfolio	+0.5%	+2.4%	-9.9%	n/a	n/a	n/a	n/a	n/a	4.46	0-A
Fundline ("Fund-A-Month Accumulation Portfolio"–Mutual Funds)	+1.7%	+12.2%	n/a	n/a	n/a	n/a	n/a	n/a	n/a	2-A
(Fundline–Timing Only)	+0.5%	+14.4%	n/a	n/a	n/a	n/a	n/a	n/a	n/a	n/a
Garside Forecast (Fully invested in recommended stocks)	-0.1%	+5.9%	+17.8%	+1.6%	n/a	n/a	n/a	n/a	3.58	18-C
Granville Market Letter (*Not* including phone service)										
a. Open Stock Positions (was "Aggressive Traders' Portfolio)	+1.6%	-6.4%	-22.7%	+2.9%	-25.2%	-29.7%	-3.3%	+10.6%	3.94	41-C
b. Option Portfolio (Fully invested when in options))	-21.4%	-71.9%	-97.8%	n/a	n/a	n/a	n/a	n/a	33.79	43-C

FIVE-YEAR PERFORMANCE RATING (continued)

NEWSLETTER (Composition of Portfolio)	6/86 Gain	1986 Gain	1985 Gain	1984 Gain	1983 Gain	1982 Gain	1981 Gain	7/1 to 12/31/80 Gain	Risk Rating Note 1	See Note #2
Growth Fund Guide										
a. Aggressive Growth Funds (Fully invested in funds most highly rated)	+1.2%	+30.7%	+33.8%	-18.3%	+22.4%	n/a	n/a	n/a	4.81	3-C
b. Growth Funds (Fully invested in funds most highly rated)	+2.8%	+27.0%	+31.2%	+0.8%	+24.2%	n/a	n/a	n/a	3.78	3-C
c. Quality Growth Funds (Fully invested in funds most highly rated)	+2.5%	+16.5%	+26.4%	+5.5%	+22.4%	n/a	n/a	n/a	2.48	3-C
d. Special Situations Funds (Fully invested in funds most highly rated)	+3.5%	+32.3%	+20.9%	-3.6%	+30.3%	n/a	n/a	n/a	4.35	1-C
Growth Stock Outlook (Supervised Portfolio: Stocks, T-Bills)	+1.3%	+11.5%	+24.7%	+3.5%	+33.1%	+24.0%	+11.8%	+34.0%	3.06	41-A
(Growth Stock Outlook—Timing Only)	+0.9%	+10.2%	+19.5%	+5.4%	+17.6%	+18.5%	-0.6%	+14.9%	n/a	n/a
Harry Browne's Special Reports (Variable [Speculative] Portfolio)	+0.5%	+13.2%	+14.8%	+4.1%	+8.1%	+17.2%	-6.9%	n/a	1.97	6-A
Heim Investment Letter (Usually stocks and/or T-Bills)	+0.5%	+3.5%	+4.8%	+1.6%	+2.6%	-8.4%	+10.5%	+2.6%	0.80	0-A
High Technology Growth Stocks										
a. Model Portfolio: Stocks, T-Bills	-1.5%	+15.1%	-4.8%	-36.3%	n/a	n/a	n/a	n/a	8.98	32-A
High Technology Growth Stocks Model Portfolio—Timing Only)	+1.3%	+18.0%	+25.5%	+1.5%	n/a	n/a	n/a	n/a	n/a	n/a
b. Timeliness Portfolio (Stocks, T-Bills)	-1.2%	+27.6%	n/a	n/a	n/a	n/a	n/a	n/a	n/a	29-A
High Technology Investments										
a. Long-Term Portfolio I (Stocks and, at times, T-Bills)	-1.9%	-3.5%	+50.0%	-23.3%	+3.5%	n/a	n/a	n/a	9.53	2-A
a. Long-Term Portfolio II (Stocks and, at times, T-Bills)	+3.8%	+3.5%	+103.3%	-2.6%	-19.2%	n/a	n/a	n/a	10.55	2-A
(Long-Term Portfolio II—Timing Only)	+0.5%	+0.7%	+15.8%	+8.6%	+12.0%	n/a	n/a	n/a	n/a	n/a
Howard Ruff's Financial Success Report										
a. "Phantom Investor" (Stocks, commodities, coins, T-Bills)	n/a	n/a	+2.3%	-13.2%	-14.9%	+43.8%	-2.4%	-6.8%	n/a	n/a
b. "Optimum Switch Hitter" (Mutual Funds)	n/a	n/a	+12.6%	n/a	n/a	n/a	n/a	n/a	n/a	n/a
Holt Investment Advisory										
a. Aggressive Portfolio (At times, stocks, bonds, options, T-Bills)	+1.9%	-6.1%	-17.4%	-0.4%	-8.2%	-11.8%	+7.9%	-6.1%	3.98	11-B
(Holt Investment Advisory Aggressive Portfolio—Timing Only)	-0.2%	-3.9%	-5.4%	-1.2%	-6.6%	+4.0%	+11.4%	-6.7%	n/a	n/a
b. Investors' Portfolio	-1.9%	+2.3%	n/a	n/a	n/a	n/a	n/a	n/a	n/a	3-B
Indicator Digest										
a. Growth Portfolio: Stocks, T-Bills	+1.6%	+15.3%	+6.9%	-10.3%	+11.8%	n/a	n/a	n/a	3.50	15-B
(Indicator Digest Growth Portfolio—Timing Only)	+1.4%	+13.3%	+18.7%	+1.1%	+17.0%	n/a	n/a	n/a	n/a	n/a
b. Total Return Portfolio (Stocks, Funds, T-Bills)	+2.5%	+16.0%	n/a	n/a	n/a	n/a	n/a	n/a	n/a	4-B
Insider Indicator (Portfolio fully invested in past year's 'buys')	+0.7%	+17.3%	+25.6%	n/a	n/a	n/a	n/a	n/a	4.07	143-C
Insiders (Insiders' Portfolio)	-2.0%	+13.6%	+20.2%	n/a	n/a	n/a	n/a	n/a	4.21	36-C
International Harry Schultz Letter										
a. US Stocks in the "List" (formerly "Investment Table")	-0.7%r	+12.4%	+8.7%	+7.4%	+2.1%	-5.5%	-17.5%	+41.2%	2.90	26-B
b. Non-U.S. Stocks in the "List" (Fully invested)	+1.7%	+27.1%	n/a	n/a	n/a	n/a	n/a	n/a	n/a	48-C
c. Portfolio constructed out of gold/silver trading advice (non-margined)	+0.5%	-2.3%	-2.8%	+20.3%	n/a	n/a	n/a	n/a	2.39	0-C

Investech										
a. Long-Term (Model) Portfolio: Stocks, Options, T-Bills	-4.1%	+6.1%	+32.7%	-16.7%	n/a	n/a	n/a	n/a	7.10	7-B
(Investech Model Portfolio–Timing Only)	*+0.9%*	*+13.2%*	*+15.8%*	*+1.8%*	*n/a*	*n/a*	*n/a*	*n/a*	*n/a*	*n/a*
b. Mutual Fund Portfolio	+0.8%	+27.3%	n/a	n/a	n/a	n/a	n/a	n/a	n/a	1-A
Investment Quality Trends (Fully invested in 'undervalued' stocks)	+1.7%	+11.5%	n/a	n/a	n/a	n/a	n/a	n/a	n/a	68-C
Investment Values (Fully invested in stocks rated 'Buy')	+2.6%	+16.2%	+18.6%	n/a	n/a	n/a	n/a	n/a	5.48	31-C
Kenneth Gerbino Investment Letter (Fully invested in "buys")	+11.3%	+73.1%	+0.4%	n/a	n/a	n/a	n/a	n/a	8.23	17-C
Kinsman's Low-Risk Growth Letter										
a. Conservative Model Portfolio (Stocks, Bonds, Funds)	+0.5%	+9.0%	+10.3%	+7.3%	+9.0%	+18.2%	+7.2%	+6.0%	1.48	12-A
b. Aggressive Model Portfolio (Stocks, Bonds, Funds)	+0.6%	+13.8%	n/a	n/a	n/a	n/a	n/a	n/a	n/a	15-C
LaLoggia's Special Situations Report										
a. Master List of Takeover Candidates (Fully Invested in "Buys")	+1.9%	+17.2%	+31.3%	-6.3%	n/a	n/a	n/a	n/a	3.66	24-C
b. Breakout Stocks for Traders (Fully Invested in "Buys")	+0.6%	+27.1%	n/a	n/a	n/a	n/a	n/a	n/a	n/a	17-C
Lynn Elgert Report (Model Portfolio: Stocks and, at times, T-Bills)	-2.2%	+12.1%	+41.7%	n/a	n/a	n/a	n/a	n/a	6.46	14-A
(Lynn Elgert Report–Timing Only)	*+1.0%*	*+14.5%*	*+22.5%*	*n/a*	*n/a*	*n/a*	*n/a*	*n/a*	*n/a*	*n/a*
Margo's Market Monitor										
a. Model Portfolio: Stocks and, at times, T-Bills	+5.2%	+36.6%	+22.2%	-5.8%	n/a	n/a	n/a	n/a	4.32	15-A
(Margo's Market Monitor Model Portfolio–Timing Only)	*+1.3%*	*+18.6%*	*+22.9%*	*+4.0%*	*n/a*	*n/a*	*n/a*	*n/a*	*n/a*	*n/a*
b. Model Sector Fund Portfolio (Mutual Funds)	+3.5%	+27.1%	n/a	n/a	n/a	n/a	n/a	n/a	n/a	1-A
Market Logic										
a. Master Portfolio (Stocks and at times T-Bills)	-1.3%	+23.6%	+37.3	-13.7%	+28.0%	+41.0%	+8.6%	+18.9%	5.78	36-B
(Market Logic–Timing Only)	*+1.3%*	*+18.4%*	*+26.2%*	*+1.3%*	*+17.5%*	*+17.9%*	*+2.2%*	*+12.5%*	*n/a*	*n/a*
b. Actual Options Portfolio (Options, T-Bills)	-0.0%	+8.3%	+22.2%	+5.8%	+13.5%	+25.9%	+14.2%	+5.8%	2.27	4-A
Market Mania ('Under Observation Portfolio: Stocks, Options, T-Bills)	+4.7%	+39.0%	+1.8%	+6.4%	n/a	n/a	n/a	n/a	7.83	39-A
(Market Mania–Timing Only)	*+1.3%*	*+18.4%*	*+24.5%*	*+3.5%*	*n/a*	*n/a*	*n/a*	*n/a*	*n/a*	*n/a*
McKeever Strategy Letter ($50,000 Model Portfolio: Commodities, T-Bills)	-19.4%	+63.7%	+99.3%	-13.3%	n/a	n/a	n/a	n/a	23.48	4-A
Medical Technology Stock Letter (Model Portfolio: Stocks, T-Bills)	+3.2%	+38.4%	+83.3%	n/a	n/a	n/a	n/a	n/a	7.60	11-A
(Medical Technology Stock Letter–Timing Only)	*+1.3%*	*+18.4%*	*+26.2%*	*n/a*	*n/a*	*n/a*	*n/a*	*n/a*	*n/a*	*n/a*
Merrill Lynch Stockfinder Research Service										
a. Stocks Rated "Buy" for Intermediate Term (Fully Invested)	-0.1%	+26.0%	n/a	n/a	n/a	n/a	n/a	n/a	n/a	74-C
b. Convertible Preferred and Bond Portfolio (Fully Invested)	+1.9%	+18.7%	n/a	n/a	n/a	n/a	n/a	n/a	n/a	28-C
MJF Growth Stock Advisory (Fully Invested in "Open Recommendations")	+6.8%	+49.2%	n/a	n/a	n/a	n/a	n/a	n/a	n/a	16-C
Mutual Fund Forecaster (Traders' portfolio of mutual funds)	+1.3%	+22.0%	n/a	n/a	n/a	n/a	n/a	n/a	n/a	12-B
Mutual Fund Investing										
a. Portfolio I ("Moderate Risk")	+1.6%	+19.3%	n/a	n/a	n/a	n/a	n/a	n/a	n/a	6-A
(Mutual Fund Investing Port 1–Timing only)	*+1.1%*	*+13.7%*	*n/a*	*n/a*	*n/a*	*n/a*	*n/a*	*n/a*	*n/a*	*n/a*
b. Portfolio II ("Safe & Secure")	+1.1%	+9.6%	n/a	n/a	n/a	n/a	n/a	n/a	n/a	3-A
Mutual Fund Letter										
a. Highly Aggressive Portfolio	+0.8%	+19.1%	n/a	n/a	n/a	n/a	n/a	n/a	n/a	4-A
b. Moderately Aggressive Portfolio	+1.2%r	+16.0%	n/a	n/a	n/a	n/a	n/a	n/a	n/a	3-A
c. Growth & Income Portfolio	+1.4%	+12.4%	n/a	n/a	n/a	n/a	n/a	n/a	n/a	3-A
d. Income Portfolio	+1.8%	+10.2%	n/a	n/a	n/a	n/a	n/a	n/a	n/a	3-A

FIVE-YEAR PERFORMANCE RATING (continued)

NEWSLETTER (Composition of Portfolio)	6/86 Gain	1986 Gain	1985 Gain	1984 Gain	1983 Gain	1982 Gain	1981 Gain	7/1 to 12/31/80 Gain	Risk Rating Note 1	See Note #2
Mutual Fund Monitor										
a. Investment Portfolio	+1.7%	+12.1%	n/a	n/a	n/a	n/a	n/a	n/a	n/a	4-A
b. IRA/Keogh Portfolio	+1.7%	+15.0%	n/a	n/a	n/a	n/a	n/a	n/a	n/a	3-A
c. International Portfolio	+6.4%	+32.7%	n/a	n/a	n/a	n/a	n/a	n/a	n/a	4-A
d. Trader Portfolio	+2.3%	+17.5%	n/a	n/a	n/a	n/a	n/a	n/a	n/a	7-A
(Mutual Fund Monitor Traders' Portfolio–Timing Only)	*+1.3%*	*+18.1%*	*n/a*	*n/a*	*n/a*	*n/a*	*n/a*	*n/a*	*n/a*	*n/a*
Mutual Fund Strategist										
a. Compuvest Portfolio (was "Buy-and-Hold" Portfolio)	+1.4%	+20.6%	+23.9%	n/a	n/a	n/a	n/a	n/a	1.95	4-C
b. Cycle/Reversal Portfolio (was "Compuvest Timing" Portfolio)	+0.5%	+19.2%	+30.9%	n/a	n/a	n/a	n/a	n/a	4.21	3-A
New Issues (Fully invested in all open recommendations)	-3.5%	+12.6%	+18.1%	-30.7%	+11.6%	n/a	n/a	n/a	6.61	167-C
Nicholson Report (Model Portfolio: Stocks and T-Bills)	-1.5%	-0.9%	+21.4%	-7.2%	-11.4%	n/a	n/a	n/a	5.43	27-C
No Load Fund-X ("Follow the Stars Strategy")										
a. Class 1 Funds (Most Speculative Growth Funds)	+1.3%	+27.2%	+22.7%	n/a	n/a	n/a	n/a	n/a	3.67	5-C
b. Class 2 Funds (Speculative Growth Funds)	+4.0%	+25.5%	+25.2%	n/a	n/a	n/a	n/a	n/a	3.43	5-C
c. Class 3 Funds (Higher Quality Growth Funds)	+5.2%	+30.4%	+38.1%	n/a	n/a	n/a	n/a	n/a	2.87	5-C
No-Load Fund Investor										
a. Funds for aggressive investors	+2.1%	+28.3%	n/a	n/a	n/a	n/a	n/a	n/a	n/a	5-C
b. Funds that may hold sizeable cash positions	+3.4%	+22.7%	n/a	n/a	n/a	n/a	n/a	n/a	n/a	3-C
c. Funds for conservative, long-term investors	+2.2%	+21.3%	n/a	n/a	n/a	n/a	n/a	n/a	n/a	5-C
d. International funds	+2.5%	+27.9%	n/a	n/a	n/a	n/a	n/a	n/a	n/a	0-C
Nourse Investor Report										
a. Portfolio started 12/7/84 (Stocks, T-Bills)	+0.5%	+24.7%	+22.1%	n/a	n/a	n/a	n/a	n/a	3.46	14-B
(Nourse Investor Report's 12/7/84 Portfolio–Timing Only)	*+1.3%*	*+18.7%*	*+11.9%*	*n/a*	*n/a*	*n/a*	*n/a*	*n/a*	*n/a*	*n/a*
b. Portfolio started 8/30/85 (Stocks, T-Bills)	+4.3%	+15.3%	n/a	n/a	n/a	n/a	n/a	n/a	n/a	8-A
Option Advisor										
a. Conservative Portfolio (Options and T-Bills)	-4.4%	+86.0%	+0.6%	+153.3%	-83.5%	n/a	n/a	n/a	12.19	5-A
b. Aggressive Portfolio (Options and T-Bills)	-5.1%r	-13.0%	-43.2%	+27.6%	-83.1%	n/a	n/a	n/a	21.48	14-A
OTC Insight (Model Portfolios: Stocks, T-Bills)										
a. $10,000 Conservative	+6.9%	+31.1%	+52.6%	n/a	n/a	n/a	n/a	n/a	4.57	8-A
b. $10,000 Moderately Aggressive	+8.6%	+40.7%	+70.0%	n/a	n/a	n/a	n/a	n/a	6.48	9-A

c. $10,000 Aggressive	+9.5%	+45.0%	+59.4%	n/a	n/a	n/a	n/a	n/a	7.99	7-A
d. $25,000 Conservative	+4.3%	+30.9%	+66.7%	n/a	n/a	n/a	n/a	n/a	3.75	9-A
e. $25,000 Moderately Aggressive	+2.3%	+33.4%	+66.0%	n/a	n/a	n/a	n/a	n/a	6.00	9-A
f. $25,000 Aggressive	+5.8%	+42.0%	+77.8%	n/a	n/a	n/a	n/a	n/a	7.81	8-A
g. $50,000 Conservative	+6.1%	+38.8%	+60.5%	n/a	n/a	n/a	n/a	n/a	3.88	12-A
h. $50,000 Moderately Aggressive	+5.9%	+50.4%	+77.5%	n/a	n/a	n/a	n/a	n/a	6.81	11-A
i. $50,000 Aggressive	+8.4%	+56.1%	+59.0%	n/a	n/a	n/a	n/a	n/a	7.89	10-A
Outlook (Standard & Poor's)										
a. Foundation Stocks (Those best situated for purchase)	+1.7%	+17.4%	+19.6%	-14.5%	+12.3%	+19.9%	+8.8%	+18.1%	4.49	3-C
b. Growth Stocks (Those best situated for purchase)	+8.1%	+21.9%	+5.4%	+1.0%	+10.5%	+11.0%	+19.6%	+17.6%	6.02	5-C
c. Speculative Stocks (Those best situated for purchase)	-5.3%	-3.2%	+50.7%	+1.0%	+21.4%	+31.0%	-1.6%	+19.6%	5.13	8-C
d. Income Stocks (Those best situated for purchase)	+6.9%	+28.5%	+29.0%	+12.8%	+28.0%	+10.6%	+10.8%	+17.9%	3.67	6-C
Patient Investor (Fully invested in stocks rated "Buy")	+3.7%	+27.9%	+25.1%	n/a	n/a	n/a	n/a	n/a	3.99	9-C
Personal Finance										
a. Income Portfolio (Fully invested in those recommended as "buys")	+4.4%r	+12.2%	+63.7%	+5.8%	n/a	n/a	n/a	n/a	5.58	17-C
b. Growth Portfolio (Fully invested in those recommended as "buys")	-3.9%	+5.9%	+34.8%	-26.8%	n/a	n/a	n/a	n/a	6.65	20-C
Peter Dag Investment Letter (Model Portfolio: Mutual Funds)	+1.2%	+6.9%	+14.5%	+5.5%	+6.0%	n/a	n/a	n/a	1.16	4-A
(Peter Dag Investment Letter–Timing Only)	+1.1%	+13.6%	+16.2%	+7.7%	+15.9%	n/a	n/a	n/a	n/a	n/a
Plain Talk Investor										
a. Personal Portfolio (Stocks and T-Bills)	+2.3%	+24.2%	+35.5%	n/a	n/a	n/a	n/a	n/a	4.05	20-A
b. High Risk Portfolio	+0.2%	+13.1%	+1.4%	n/a	n/a	n/a	n/a	n/a	2.96	8-A
(Plain Talk Investor High Risk–Timing Only)	+1.2%	+10.8%	+12.4%	n/a	n/a	n/a	n/a	n/a	n/a	n/a
Professional Investor										
a. NYSE Scan (Fully invested)	-1.0%	+20.2%	+20.4%	-22.1%	+14.1%	+34.5%	-6.1%	+14.4%	3.63	39-C
b. AMEX Scan (Fully invested)	+1.8%	+28.9%	+21.0%	-9.8%	+48.2%	+39.1%	-6.9%	+34.0%	3.09	55-C
c. OTC Scan (Fully invested)	+3.1%	+26.4%	+31.4%	-1.7%	+29.3%	+21.6%	-4.4%	+30.8%	2.48	49-C
d. Investment Grade Scan (Fully invested)	+8.7%	+43.5%	+50.2%	-10.5%	-18.5%	+23.7%	+3.0%	+12.5%	5.20	2-C
Professional Tape Reader										
a. Model Portfolio: Stocks and, at times, T-Bills	-2.0%	+1.8%	+6.4%	-23.6%	-9.8%	+30.0%	-6.7%	+22.9%	4.51	27-A
(Professional Tape Reader Model Portfolio–Timing only)	-0.3%	+7.8%	+16.7%	-3.1%	+8.6%	+20.8%	+2.4%	+13.5%	n/a	n/a
b. Mutual Fund Switching Portfolio	+0.7%	+6.0%	n/a	n/a	n/a	n/a	n/a	n/a	n/a	1-A
Professional Timing Service										
a. Open Stock Positions (Fully Invested)	-6.0%r	-17.9%	+27.6%	-19.0%	+22.4%	-2.5%	n/a	n/a	6.86	3-C
b. Gold futures trading (non-margined)	+0.3%	+2.6%	+11.4%	n/a	n/a	n/a	n/a	n/a	3.51	0-C
c. Stock index futures trading (non-margined)	+1.0%	+0.8%	+3.6%	n/a	n/a	n/a	n/a	n/a	1.23	0-C

FIVE-YEAR PERFORMANCE RATING (concluded)

NEWSLETTER (Composition of Portfolio)	6/86 Gain	1986 Gain	1985 Gain	1984 Gain	1983 Gain	1982 Gain	1981 Gain	7/1 to 12/31/80 Gain	Risk Rating Note 1	See Note #2
Prudent Speculator (Actual TPS Portfolio*: Stocks and at times T-Bills)	-5.5%r	+65.6%	+62.2%	-13.1%	+72.9%	+49.0%	+2.9%	+26.5%	10.02	144-A
PSR Prophetwatch										
a. Micro-Cap Model Portfolio	-1.2%	+21.6%	+17.4%	n/a	n/a	n/a	n/a	n/a	5.74	35-A
b. Mini Cap Model Portfolio	-0.5%	+5.8%	n/a	n/a	n/a	n/a	n/a	n/a	n/a	16-A
RHM Survey of Warrants, Options & Low-Priced Stocks (Invested in "Buys")	-3.3%	+13.2%	+6.6%	-42.2%	+8.6%	+23.2%	-50.1%	n/a	6.17	26-C
Speculator										
a. Selected Stocks (Fully invested in those best situated for purchase)	+0.1%	+23.8%	+21.9%	-38.6%	+8.8%	+45.3%	-10.8%	n/a	4.68	64-C
b. Trading Portfolio (Stocks and T-Bills)	+3.1%	+47.5%	-3.2%	+5.1%	n/a	n/a	n/a	n/a	5.21	8-A
(Speculator Trading Portfolio—Timing Only)	+0.8%	+18.4%	+19.4	+0.0%	n/a	n/a	n/a	n/a	n/a	n/a
Stockmarket Cycles										
a. Model Portfolio (Stocks, T-Bills)	-0.2%	+6.6%	+23.6%	n/a	n/a	n/a	n/a	n/a	6.05	3-A
(Stock Market Cycles Model Portfolio—Timing Only)	+0.1%	+14.8%	+25.1%	n/a	n/a	n/a	n/a	n/a	n/a	n/a
b. Mutual Fund Portfolio	+2.3%	+16.1%	+11.4%	n/a	n/a	n/a	n/a	n/a	5.80	0-A
Switch Fund Advisory (Model Portfolio: Mutual Funds)	+2.0%	+16.1%	+20.8%	+1.8%	+16.4%	n/a	n/a	n/a	1.74	8-A
(Switch Fund Advisory Model Portfolio—Timing Only)	+0.8%	+13.3%	+18.5%	+2.5%	+14.6%	n/a	n/a	n/a	n/a	n/a
Systems & Forecasts (Stocks, Bonds, Options, Mutual Funds)	+2.5%	+9.9%	+22.0%	+22.2%	-6.9%	n/a	n/a	n/a	2.08	5-B
(Systems & Forecasts—Timing Only)	+1.7%	+13.6%	+20.1%	+4.1%	+8.2%	n/a	n/a	n/a	n/a	n/a
Telephone Switch Newsletter										
a. Equity/Cash Switch Plan	+1.5%	+25.8%	+8.5%	-12.1%	+19.0%	+39.2%	+6.0%	+31.7%	4.77	5-A
(Telephone Switch Newsletter—Equity Timing Only)	+1.3%	+18.4%	+23.6%	+4.7%	+17.5%	+30.3%	+0.7%	+19.2%	n/a	n/a
b. Gold/Cash Switch Plan	+0.5%	-4.9%	-1.1%	-5.9%	-7.8%	n/a	n/a	n/a	3.64	0-A
c. International Funds/Cash Switch Plan	+6.4%	+34.4%	+37.4%	-1.5%	n/a	n/a	n/a	n/a	4.16	4-A
Tony Henfrey's Gold Letter (Gold Share Portfolio for U.S.-dollar investors)	n/a	n/a	-28.3%	-28.1%	+6.9%	+93.3%	n/a	n/a	n/a	n/a
United Business & Investment Reports										
a. Growth Stocks (Fully invested in those best situated for purchase)	+0.7%	+22.2%	+21.6%	-5.5%	+1.7%	+6.7%	-14.1%	+15.8%	4.27	28-C
b. Cyclical Stocks (Fully invested in those best situated for purchase)	-1.6%	+4.4%	+15.2%	-16.9%	+7.0%	+15.6%	-12.9%	+28.2%	5.19	20-C
c. Income Stocks (Fully invested in those best situated for purchase)	+7.2%	+21.2%	+20.3%	+4.2%	+14.7%	+13.8%	-3.8%	+4.6%	3.68	8-C
United Mutual Fund Selector (Fully invested in those best situated for current purchase)										
a. Aggressive Growth Funds (No-load and low-loads only)	+3.8%	+30.5%	n/a	n/a	n/a	n/a	n/a	n/a	n/a	1-C
b. Growth Funds (No-load and low-loads only)	+1.4%	+21.3%	n/a	n/a	n/a	n/a	n/a	n/a	n/a	1-C
c. Growth & Income Funds (No-load and low-loads only)	+1.5%	+15.4%	n/a	n/a	n/a	n/a	n/a	n/a	n/a	1-C
d. Income Funds (No-load and low-loads only)	+0.7%	+8.2%	n/a	n/a	n/a	n/a	n/a	n/a	n/a	2-C

								Risk ratio [1]	No.-Rating [2]
Value Line Convertibles (Fully Invested in "Recommended Issues")	-0.8%	+35.4%	n/a	n/a	n/a	n/a	n/a	n/a	n/a	20-C
Value Line Inv. Survey (Fully invested in "Group I" Timeliness Stocks)	+3.0%	+31.6%	+35.1%	-8.6%	+34.8%	n/a	n/a	n/a	4.80	100-C
Value Line New Issues Service (Fully invested in stocks rated "Buy")	-7.1%	+12.7%	+47.4%	-29.8%	n/a	n/a	n/a	n/a	9.14	14-C
Value Line OTC Spec'l Sit. Survey (Fully invested in "esp.-recc." stocks	+0.4%	+24.7%	+23.7%	-24.0%	+24.1%	+50.2%	-17.6%	+72.3%	6.33	17-C
Wall Street Digest (Fully invested in stocks rated "buy")	+3.3%	+29.7%	+13.1%	n/a	n/a	n/a	n/a	n/a	6.08	22-C
Weber's Fund Advisor (Real World Portfolio: Mutual Funds)	+2.3%	+21.7%	+22.1%	n/a	n/a	n/a	n/a	n/a	3.58	2-A
Wellington's Worry-Free Investing										
a. Model Mutual Fund Portfolio	+3.5%	+25.2%	+29.5%	n/a	n/a	n/a	n/a	n/a	2.44	6-A
b. Leveraged Mutual Fund Portfolio	+5.1%	+34.4%	n/a	n/a	n/a	n/a	n/a	n/a	n/a	7-A
Zweig Forecast (Model Portfolio: Stocks, T-Bills)	+5.5%	+25.3%	+41.8%	+2.7%	+1.5%	+24.6%	+24.0%	+23.2%	3.71	16-A
(Zweig Forecast—Timing Only)	+0.7%	+12.8%	+24.3%	+0.5%	+14.3%	+13.5%	+4.5%	+13.6%	n/a	n/a
Zweig Performance Ratings Report (Fully invested in 'buys' and 'shorts')	+3.8%	+32.8%	+29.8%	+5.9%	+17.5%	n/a	n/a	n/a	3.82	53-C
The Riskless rate of return: a T-Bill only portfolio	+0.5%	+3.3%	+7.6%	+9.8%	+9.0%	+10.9%	+14.2%	+5.8%	0.07	
STOCK AVERAGES										
a. DJIA (including dividends, reinvested monthly)	+1.2%	+24.9%	+33.6%	+1.0%	+25.9%	+27.2%	-3.7%	+14.3%	3.34	
b. Standard & Poor's 500 (including dividends, reinvested monthly)	+1.7%	+20.8%	+31.7%	+6.2%	+22.5%	+21.6%	-4.9%	+21.7%	3.36	
c. Wilshire 5000 Value-Weighted Index (dividends reinvested monthly)	+1.4%	+21.0%	+32.6%	+3.0%	+23.5%	+18.7%	-3.7%	+23.2%	3.42	
d. AMEX Market Value Index (without dividends)	+0.6%	+15.5%	+20.5%	-8.4%	+31.0%	+6.2%	-8.0%	+17.3%	3.40	
e. NASDAQ OTC Composite (without dividends)	+1.3%	+24.8%	+31.4%	-11.2%	+19.9%	+18.7%	-3.2%	+27.2%	3.96	

In general when constructing these model portfolios, the HFD adheres to each newsletter's actual recommendations, resorting to the following procedures only when the newsletter is silent or vague about what to do. If a newsletter says nothing to the contrary, the portfolio the HFD constructs will be fully invested (with no margin) in those recommendations most highly recommended at a given time, with each position carrying equal weight. With each transaction, furthermore, the portfolio is rebalanced to keep this equal weighting. Cash positions earn the T-Bill rate, dividends are credited, and a 2% round-trip commission is deducted (0.05% for commodities). Transactions are made at the closing price on the day the newsletter is received (or at the average of the high and low in trading after hotline recommendations); initial public offerings are purchased at the average of their high and low aftermarket prices (therefore the gains and losses for new issues newsletters exclude first day premiums). A more complete description is available upon request.

The Timing Portfolios (those in italics following some letters' listings) were constructed exactly as were their corresponding portfolios, except that the stock portions were replaced by the NYSE Composite Index. For example, if a newsletter recommends that 60% be in stocks and 40% in T-Bills, its corresponding Timing Portfolio will have 60% "invested" in the NYSE Composite and 40% earning the T-Bill rate. You thus can see whether a newsletter's stock picks did better or worse than the market as a whole.

(r) May gains calculated from a revised figure for portfolio's 5/30/86 value.

(1) The risk ratio is the standard deviation of each newsletter's monthly performance since 1/1/85; the larger the number, the greater the risk.

(2) The figure to the left in this column is the number of securities in the portfolio at the end of the month (cash equivalents don't count). The figure to the right signifies how clear and complete are each newsletter's recommendations, with: an 'A' rating signifies that the letter recommends a model portfolio; a 'B' rating signifies that the letter gives overall portfolio allocations but not advice on what to buy or sell to get in line with that advice; a 'C' rating is for letters with just lists of recommended stocks. A 'D' rating is reserved for those letters for which advice sometimes is missing from issue to issue and for which recommendations sometimes come in the form of categories of investments rather than specific securities.

* The Prudent Speculator's actual portfolio utilizes margin. As an on-going portfolio, its margin level need only be kept above the maintenance level of 30%; a new subscriber, however, would be unable to use anything less than 50% margin. The HFD's calculations assume that each year the portfolio starts out with 50% margin.

Source: Hulbert Financial Digest, Inc., 643 South Carolina Avenue, S.E., Washington, D.C. 20003.

Bonds and Money Market Instruments

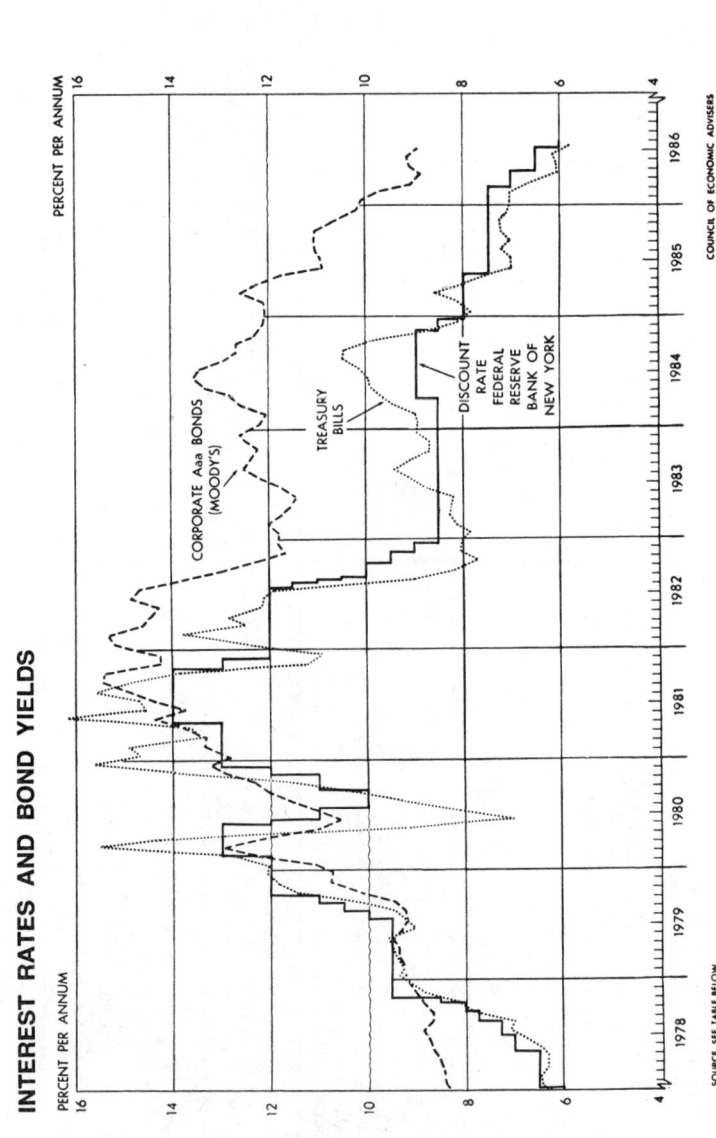

INTEREST RATES AND BOND YIELDS

PERCENT PER ANNUM

PERCENT PER ANNUM

CORPORATE Aaa BONDS (MOODY'S)

TREASURY BILLS

DISCOUNT RATE FEDERAL RESERVE BANK OF NEW YORK

1978 1979 1980 1981 1982 1983 1984 1985 1986

SOURCE: SEE TABLE BELOW

COUNCIL OF ECONOMIC ADVISERS

[Percent per annum]

| Period | U.S. Treasury security yields | | | High-grade municipal bonds (Standard & Poor's) [3] | Corporate Aaa bonds (Moody's) [4] | Prime commercial paper, 6 months [1] | Discount rate (N.Y. F.R. Bank) [5] | Prime rate charged by banks [5] | New-home mortgage yields (FHLBB) [6] |
| | 3-month bills (new issues) [1] | Constant maturities [2] | | | | | | | |
		3-year	10-year						
1980	11.506	11.55	11.46	8.51	11.94	12.29	11.77	15.27	12.66
1981	14.029	14.44	13.91	11.23	14.17	14.76	13.41	18.87	14.70
1982	10.686	12.92	13.00	11.57	13.79	11.89	11.02	14.86	15.14
1983	8.63	10.45	11.10	9.47	12.04	8.89	8.50	10.79	12.57
1984	9.58	11.89	12.44	10.15	12.71	10.16	8.80	12.04	12.38
1985	7.48	9.64	10.62	8.18	11.37	8.01	7.69	9.93	11.55
1985: July	7.05	9.18	10.31	8.90	10.97	7.57	7.50–7.50	9.50–9.50	11.34
Aug	7.18	9.31	10.33	9.18	11.05	7.74	7.50–7.50	9.50–9.50	11.24
Sept	7.08	9.37	10.37	9.37	11.07	7.86	7.50–7.50	9.50–9.50	11.17
Oct	7.17	9.25	10.24	9.24	11.02	7.79	7.50–7.50	9.50–9.50	11.09
Nov	7.20	8.88	9.78	8.64	10.55	7.69	7.50–7.50	9.50–9.50	11.01
Dec	7.07	8.40	9.26	8.51	10.16	7.62	7.50–7.50	9.50–9.50	10.94
1986: Jan	7.04	8.41	9.19	8.06	10.05	7.62	7.50–7.50	9.50–9.50	10.89
Feb	7.03	8.10	8.70	7.44	9.67	7.54	7.50–7.50	9.50–9.50	10.68
Mar	6.59	7.30	7.78	7.07	9.00	7.08	7.50–7.00	9.50–9.00	10.50
Apr	6.06	6.86	7.30	7.32	8.79	6.47	7.00–6.50	9.00–8.50	10.27
May	6.12	7.27	7.71	7.67	9.09	6.53	6.50–6.50	8.50–8.50	r 10.22
June r	6.21	7.41	7.80	7.98	9.13	6.63	6.50–6.50	8.50–8.50	10.14
July p	5.84	6.86	7.30	7.62	8.88	6.24	6.50–6.00	8.50–8.00	
Week ended:									
1986: June 28	6.09	7.14	7.45	7.69	9.02	6.51	6.50–6.50	8.50–8.50	
July 5	5.99	6.99	7.35	7.63	8.93	6.41	6.50–6.50	8.50–8.50	
12	5.85	6.92	7.33	7.58	8.89	6.32	6.50–6.00	8.50–8.00	
19	5.78	6.73	7.19	7.55	8.84	6.19	6.00–6.00	8.00–8.00	
26	5.72	6.82	7.26	7.70	8.86	6.17	6.00–6.00	8.00–8.00	
Aug 2 p	5.86	6.91	7.43	7.65		6.17	6.00–	8.00–	

[1] Bank-discount basis.
[2] Yields on the more actively traded issues adjusted to constant maturities by the Treasury Department.
[3] Weekly data are Wednesday figures.
[4] Series excludes public utility issues for January 17, 1984 through October 11, 1984 due to lack of appropriate issues.

[5] Average effective rate for year; opening and closing rate for month and week.
[6] Effective rate (in the primary market) on conventional mortgages, reflecting fees and charges as well as contract rate and assumed, on the average, repayment at end of 10 years.

Sources: Department of the Treasury, Board of Governors of the Federal Reserve System, Federal Home Loan Bank Board, Moody's Investors Service, and Standard & Poor's Corporation.

Source: Economic Indicators, Council of Economic Advisers.

SHORT-TERM INTEREST RATES

MONTHLY AVERAGES, EXCEPT FOR DISCOUNT AND PRIME RATES, WHICH ARE EFFECTIVE DATES OF CHANGE

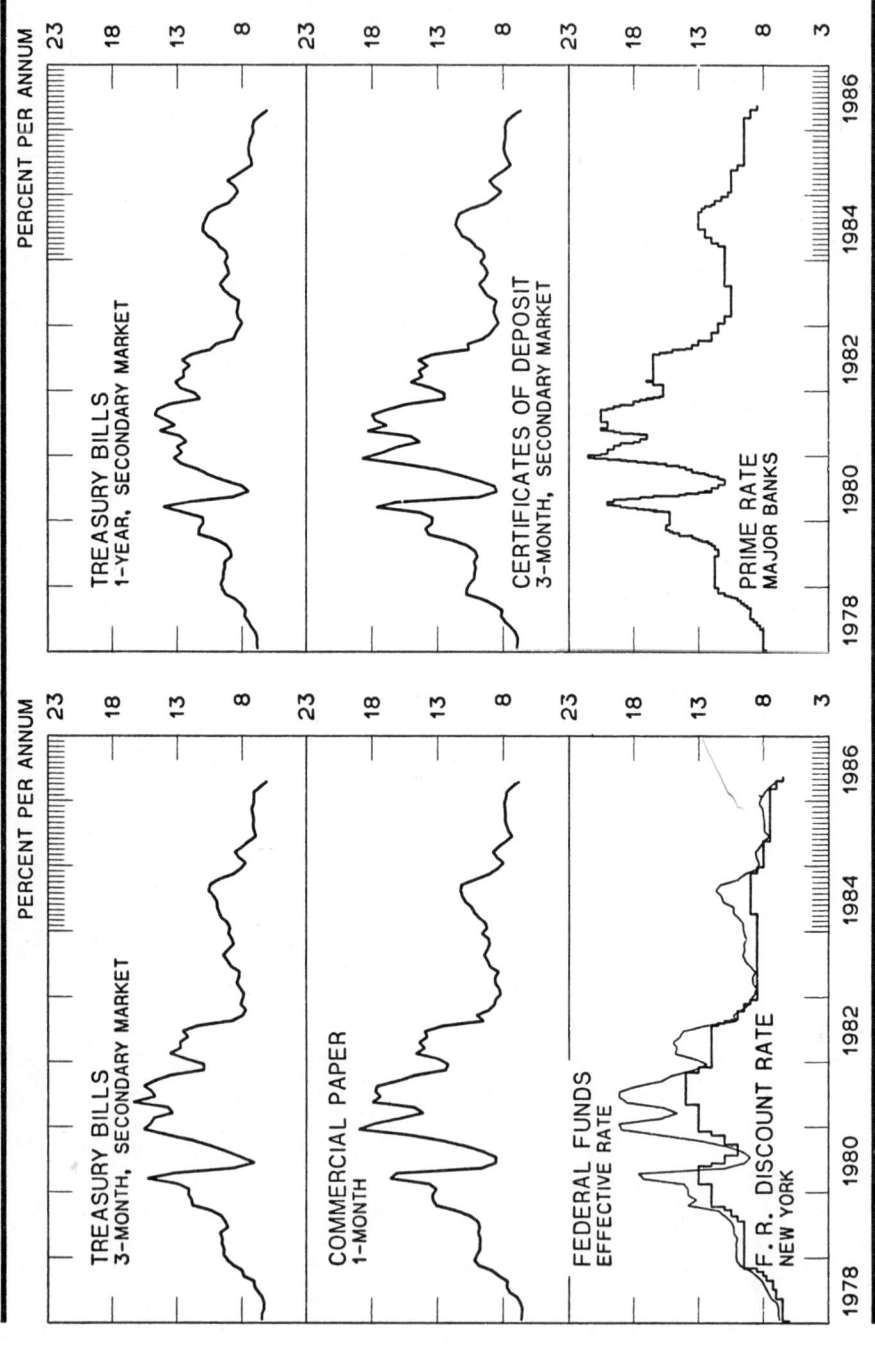

Source: *Federal Reserve Chart Book*, Board of Governors of the Federal Reserve System.

LONG-TERM INTEREST RATES

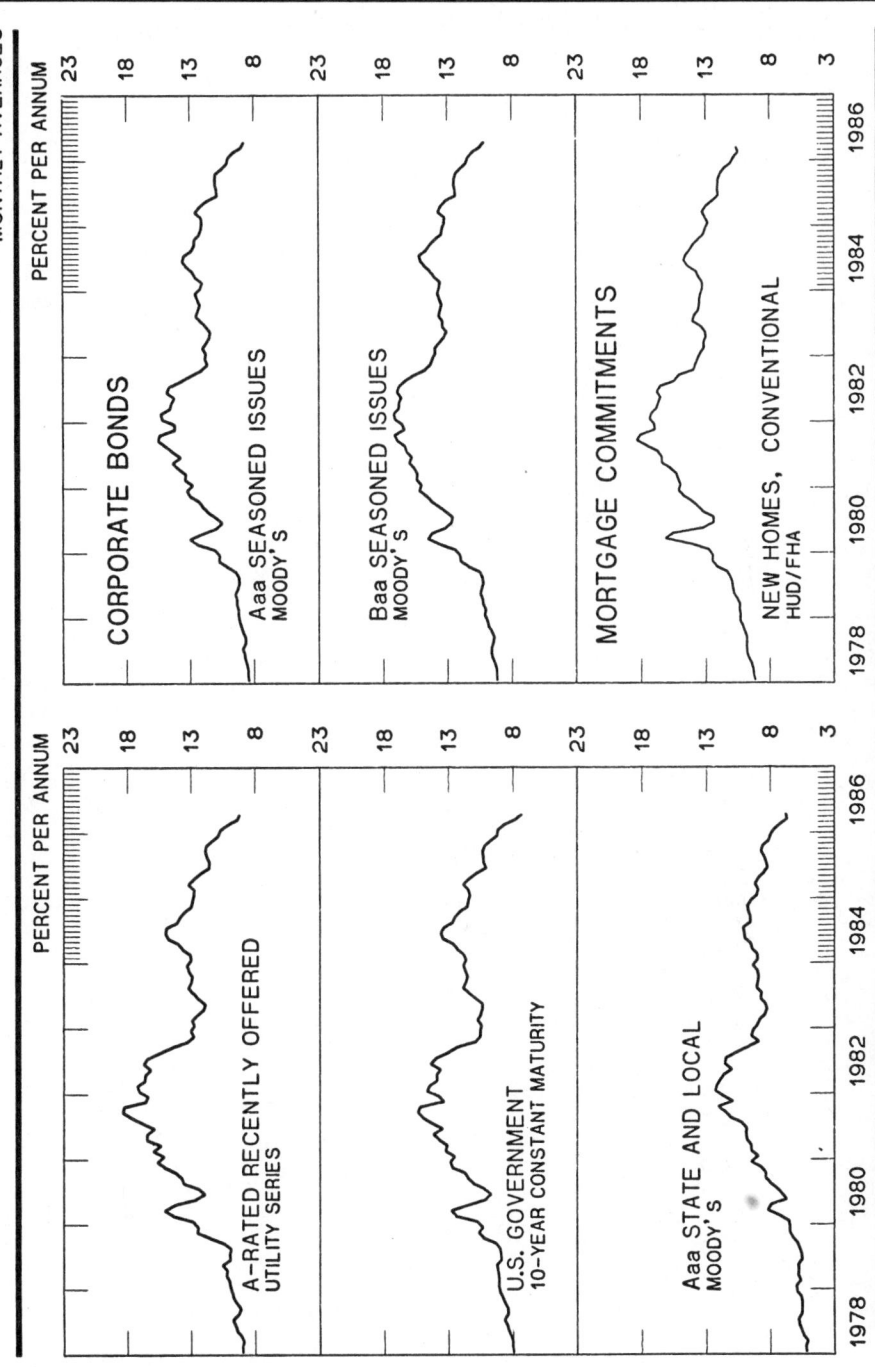

MONTHLY AVERAGES

PERCENT PER ANNUM

CORPORATE BONDS

Aaa SEASONED ISSUES
MOODY'S

Baa SEASONED ISSUES
MOODY'S

MORTGAGE COMMITMENTS

NEW HOMES, CONVENTIONAL
HUD/FHA

PERCENT PER ANNUM

A-RATED RECENTLY OFFERED
UTILITY SERIES

U.S. GOVERNMENT
10-YEAR CONSTANT MATURITY

Aaa STATE AND LOCAL
MOODY'S

Source: *Federal Reserve Chart Book*, Board of Governors of the Federal Reserve System.

Credit Ratings of Fixed Income and Money Market Securities

KEY TO STANDARD & POOR'S CORPORATE AND MUNICIPAL BOND RATING DEFINITIONS

A Standard & Poor's corporate or municipal debt rating is a current assessment of the creditworthiness of an obligor with respect to a specific debt obligation. This assessment may take into consideration obligors such as guarantors, insurers, or lessees.

The debt rating is not a recommendation to purchase, sell or hold a security, inasmuch as it does not comment as to market price or suitability for a particular investor.

The ratings are based on current information furnished by the issuer or obtained by Standard & Poor's from other sources it considers reliable. Standard & Poor's does not perform an audit in connection with any rating and may, on occasion, rely on unaudited financial information. The ratings may be changed, suspended or withdrawn as a result of changes in, or unavailability of, such information, or for other circumstances.

The ratings are based, in varying degrees, on the following considerations:

I. Likelihood of default—capacity and willingness of the obligor as to the timely payment of interest and repayment of principal in accordance with the terms of the obligation;
II. Nature of and provisions of the obligation;
III. Protection afforded by, and relative position of, the obligation in the event of bankruptcy, reorganization or other arrangement under the laws of bankruptcy and other laws affecting creditor's rights.

AAA

Debt rated **AAA** have the highest rating assigned by Standard & Poor's to a debt obligation. Capacity to pay interest and repay principal is extremely strong.

AA

Debt rated **AA** have a very strong capacity to pay interest and repay principal and differ from the highest rated issues only in a small degree.

A

Debt rated **A** have a strong capacity to pay interest and repay principal although they are somewhat more susceptible to the adverse effects of changes in circumstances and economic conditions than debts in higher rated categories.

BBB

Debt rated **BBB** are regarded as having an adequate capacity to pay interest and repay principal. Whereas they normally exhibit adequate protection parameters, adverse economic conditions or changing circumstances are more likely to lead to a weakened capacity to pay interest and repay principal for debts in this category than for debts in higher rated categories.

BB, B, CCC, CC

Debt rated **BB, B, CCC,** and **CC** are regarded, on balance, as predominantly speculative with respect to capacity to pay interest and repay principal in accordance with the terms of the obligation. **BB** indicates the lowest degree of speculation and **CC** the highest degree of speculation. While such debts will likely have some quality and protective characteristics, these are outweighed by large uncertainties or major risk exposures to adverse conditions.

C

The rating **C** is reserved for income bonds on which no interest is being paid.

D

Debt rated **D** are in default, and payment of interest and/or repayment of principal is in arrears.

Plus (+) or minus (−)

The ratings from **AA** to **B** may be modified by the addition of a plus or minus sign to show relative standing within the major rating categories.

Provisional ratings

The letter *p* indicates that the rating is provisional. A provisional rating assumes the successful completion of the project being financed by the debts being rated and indicates that payment of debt service requirements is largely or entirely dependent upon the successful and timely completion of the project. This rating, however, while addressing credit quality subsequent to completion of the project, makes no comment on the likelihood of, or the risk of default upon failure of, such completion. The investor should exercise his own judgment with respect to such likelihood and risk.

Source: From Standard & Poor's Debt Rating Division.

* Continuance of the rating is contingent upon S&P's receipt of an executed copy of the escrow agreement or closing documentation confirming investments and the cash flows.

L*

The letter "L" indicates that the rating pertains to the principal amount of those bonds where the underlying deposit collateral is fully insured by the Federal Savings & Loan Insurance Corp. or the Federal Deposit Insurance Corp.

NR

Indicates that no rating has been requested, that there is insufficient information on which to base a rating or that S&P does not rate a particular type of obligation as a matter of policy.

Debt Obligations

Debt Obligations of issuers outside the United States and its territories are rated on the same basis as domestic corporate and municipal issues. The ratings measure the creditworthiness of the obligor but do not take into account currency exchange and other uncertainties.

Bond Investment Quality Standards

Under present commercial bank regulations issued by the Comptroller of the Currency, bonds rated in the top four categories (AAA, AA, A, BBB, commonly known as "Investment Grade" ratings) are generally regarded as eligible for bank investment. In addition, the Legal Investment Laws of various states impose certain rating or other standards for obligations eligible for investment by savings banks, trust companies, insurance companies and fiduciaries generally.

KEY TO STANDARD & POOR'S PREFERRED STOCK RATING DEFINITIONS

A Standard & Poor's preferred stock rating is an assessment of the capacity and willingness of an issuer to pay preferred stock dividends and any applicable sinking fund obligations. A preferred stock rating differs from a bond rating inasmuch as it is assigned to an equity issue, which issue is intrinsically different from, and subordinated to, a debt issue. Therefore, to reflect this difference, the preferred stock rating symbol will normally not be higher than the bond rating symbol assigned to, or that would be assigned to, the senior debt of the same issuer.

The preferred stock ratings are based on the following considerations.

I. Likelihood of payment—capacity and willingness of the issuer to meet the timely payment of preferred stock dividends and any applicable sinking fund requirements in accordance with the terms of the obligation.
II. Nature of, and provisions of, the issue.
III. Relative position of the issue in the event of bankruptcy, reorganization, or other arrangements affecting creditors' rights.

AAA

This is the highest rating that may be assigned by Standard & Poor's to a preferred stock issue and indicates in extremely strong capacity to pay the preferred stock obligations.

AA

A preferred stock issue rated AA also qualifies as a high-quality fixed income security. The capacity to pay preferred stock obligations is very strong, although not as overwhelming as for issues rated AAA.

A

An issue rated A is backed by a sound capacity to pay the preferred stock obligations, although it is somewhat more susceptible to the adverse effects of changes in circumstances and economic conditions.

BBB

An issue rated BBB is regarded as backed by an adequate capacity to pay the preferred stock obligations. Whereas it normally exhibits adequate protection parameters, adverse economic conditions or changing circumstances are more likely to lead to a weakened capacity to make payments for a preferred stock in this category than for issues in the A category.

BB, B, CCC

Preferred stock rated BB, B, and CCC are regarded, on balance, as predominately speculative with respect to the issuer's capacity to pay preferred stock obligations. BB indicates the lowest degree of speculation and CCC the highest degree of speculation. While such issues will likely have some quality and protective characteristics, these are outweighed by large uncertainties or major risk exposures to adverse conditions.

CC

The rating CC is reserved for a preferred stock issue in arrears on dividends or sinking fund payments but that is currently paying.

C

A preferred stock rated C is a non-paying issue.

D

A preferred stock rated D is a non-paying issue with the issuer in default on debt instruments.

NR

NR indicates that no rating has been requested, that there is insufficient information on which to base a rating, or that S&P does not rate a particular type of obligation as a matter or policy.

Plus (+) or Minus (−) To provide more detailed indications of preferred stock quality, the ratings from **AA** to **B** may be modified by the addition of a plus or minus sign to show relative standing within the major rating categories.

The preferred stock rating is not a recommendation to purchase or sell a security, inasmuch as market price is not considered in arriving at the rating. Preferred stock *ratings* are wholly unrelated to Standard & Poor's earnings and dividend *rankings* for common stocks.

MUNICIPAL NOTES

A Standard & Poor's role rating reflects the liquidity concerns and market access risks unique to notes. Notes due in 3 years or less will likely receive a long-term debt rating. The following criteria will be used in making that assessment.

—Amortization schedule (the larger the final maturity relative to other maturities the more likely it will be treated as a note).
—Source of Payment (the more dependent the issue is on the market for its refinancing, the more likely it will be treated as a note).

Note rating symbols are as follows:

SP-1 Very strong or strong capacity to pay principal and interest. Those issues determined to possess overwhelming safety characteristics will be given a plus (+) designation.
SP-2 Satisfactory capacity to pay principal and interest.
SP-3 Speculative capacity to pay principal and interest.

TAX-EXEMPT DEMAND BONDS

Standard & Poor's assigns "dual" ratings to all long-term debt issues that have as part of their provisions a demand or double feature.

The first rating addresses the likelihood of repayment of principal and interest as due, and the second rating addresses only the demand feature. The long-term debt rating symbols are used for bonds to denote the long-term maturity and the commercial paper rating symbols are used to denote the put option (for example, "AAA/A-1+"). For the newer "demand notes," S&P's note rating symbols, combined with the commercial paper symbols, are used (for example, "SP-1+/A-1+").

KEY TO STANDARD & POOR'S COMMERCIAL PAPER RATING DEFINITIONS

A Standard & Poor's Commercial Paper Rating is a current assessment of the likelihood of timely payment of debt having an original maturity of no more than 365 days.

Ratings are graded into four categories, ranging from **A** for the highest quality obligations to **D** for the lowest. The four categories are as follows:

A

Issues assigned this highest rating are regarded as having the greatest capacity for timely payment. Issues in this category are further refined with the designations 1, 2, and 3 to indicate the relative degree of safety.

A-1 This designation indicates that the degree of safety regarding timely payment is very strong.
A-2 Capacity for timely payment on issues with this designation is strong. However, the relative degree of safety is not as overwhelming as for issues designated **A-1**.
A-3 Issues carrying this designation have a satisfactory capacity for timely payment. They are, however, somewhat more vulnerable to the adverse effects of changes in circumstances than obligations carrying the higher designations.

B

Issues rated **B** are regarded as having only an adequate capacity for timely payment. However, such capacity may be damaged by changing conditions for short-term adversities.

C

This rating is assigned to short-term obligations with a doubtful capacity for payment.

D

This rating indicates that the issue is either a default or is expected to be in default upon maturity.

The Commercial paper Rating is not a recommendation to purchase or sell a security. The ratings are based on current information furnished to Standard & Poor's by the issuer or obtained from other sources it considers reliable. The ratings may be changed, suspended, or withdrawn as a result of changes in, or unavailability of, such information.

KEY TO MOODY'S MUNICIPAL RATINGS*

Aaa

Bonds which are rated **Aaa** are judged to be of the best quality. They carry the smallest degree of investment risk and are generally referred to as "gilt edge." Interest payments are

---

* Note: Those bonds in the **Aa, A, Baa, Ba** and **B** groups which Moody's believes possess the strongest investment attributes are designated by the symbols **Aa 1, A 1, Baa 1, Ba 1** and **B 1**.

Source: Moody's Investors Service, Inc.

protected by a large or by an exceptionally stable margin and principal is secure. While the various protective elements are likely to change, such changes as can be visualized are most unlikely to impair the fundamentally strong position of such issues.

Aa

Bonds which are rated **Aa** are judged to be of high quality by all standards. Together with the **Aaa** group they comprise what are generally known as high grade bonds. They are rated lower than the best bonds because margins of protection may not be as large as in **Aaa** securities or fluctuation of protective elements may be of greater amplitude or there may be other elements present which make the long term risks appear somewhat larger than in **Aaa** securities.

A

Bonds which are rated **A** possess many favorable instrument attributes and are to be considered as upper medium grade obligations. Factors giving security to principal and interest are considered adequate, but elements may be present which suggest a susceptibility to impairment sometime in the future.

Baa

Bonds which are rated **Baa** are considered as medium grade obligations; i.e., they are neither highly protected nor poorly secured. Interest payments and principal security appear adequate for the present but certain protective elements may be lacking or may be characteristically unreliable over any great length of time. Such bonds lack outstanding investment characteristics and in fact have speculative characteristics as well.

Ba

Bonds which are rated **Ba** are judged to have speculative elements; their future cannot be considered as well assured. Often the protection of interest and principal payments may be very moderate, and thereby not well safeguarded during both good and bad times over the future. Uncertainty of position characterizes bonds in this case.

B

Bonds which are rated **B** generally lack characteristics of the desirable investment. Assurance of interest and principal payments or of maintenance of other terms of the contract over any long period of time may be small.

Caa

Bonds which are rated **Caa** are of poor standing. Such issues may be in default or there may be present elements of danger with respect to principal or interest.

Ca

Bonds which are rated **Ca** represent obligations which are speculative in a high degree. Such issues are often in default or have other marked shortcomings.

C

Bonds which are rated **C** are the lowest rated class of bonds, and issues so rated can be regarded as having extremely poor prospects of ever attaining any real investment standing.

Con.(—)

Bonds for which the security depends upon the completion of some act or the fulfillment of some condition are rated conditionally. These are bonds secured by (a) earnings of projects under construction, (b) earnings of projects unseasoned in operation experience, (c) rentals which begin when facilities are completed, or (d) payments to which some other limiting condition attaches. Parenthetical rating denotes probable credit stature upon completion of construction or elimination of basis of condition.

KEY TO MOODY'S CORPORATE RATINGS*

Aaa

Bonds which are rated **Aaa** are judged to be of the best quality. They carry the smallest degree of investment risk and are generally referred to as "gilt edge." Interest payments are protected by a large or by an exceptionally stable margin and principal is secure. While the various protective elements are likely to change, such changes as can be visualized are most unlikely to impair the fundamentally strong position of such issues.

Aa

Bonds which are rated **Aa** are judged to be of high quality by all standards. Together with the **Aaa** group they comprise what are generally known as high grade bonds. They are rated lower than the best bonds because margins of protection may not be as large as in **Aaa** securities or fluctuation of protective elements may be of greater amplitude or there may be other elements present which make the long term risks appear somewhat larger than in **Aaa** securities.

A

Bonds which are rated **A** possess many favorable investment attributes and are to be consid-

---

* *Note:* Moody's applies numerical modifiers, 1, 2 and 3 in each generic rating classification from **Aa** through **B** in its corporate bond rating system. The modifier 1 indicates that the security ranks in the higher end of its generic rating category; the modifier 2 indicates a mid-range ranking; and the modifier 3 indicates that the issue ranks in the lower end of its generic rating category.

ered as upper medium grade obligations. Factors giving security to principal and interest are considered adequate but elements may be present which suggest a susceptibility to impairment sometime in the future.

Baa

Bonds which are rated **Baa** are considered as medium grade obligations, i.e., they are neither highly protected nor poorly secured. Interest payments and principal security appear adequate for the present but certain protective elements may be lacking or may be characteristically unreliable over any great length of time. Such bonds lack outstanding investment characteristics and in fact have speculative characteristics as well.

Ba

Bonds which are rated **Ba** are judged to have speculative elements; their future cannot be considered as well assured. Often the protection of interest and principal payments may be very moderate and thereby not well safeguarded during both good and bad times over the future. Uncertainty of position characterizes bonds in this class.

B

Bonds which are rated **B** generally lack characteristics of the desirable investment. Assurance of interest and principal payments or of maintenance of other terms of the contract over any long period of time may be small.

Caa

Bonds which are rated **Caa** are of poor standing. Such issues may be in default or there may be present elements of danger with respect to principal or interest.

Ca

Bonds which are rated **Ca** represent obligations which are speculative in a high degree. Such issues are often in default or have other marked shortcomings.

C

Bonds which are rated **C** are the lowest rated class of bonds and issues so rated can be regarded as having extremely poor prospects of ever attaining any real investment standing.

KEY TO MOODY'S COMMERCIAL PAPER RATINGS

The term "Commercial Paper" as used by Moody's means promissory obligations not having an original maturity in excess of nine months. Moody's makes no representation as to whether such Commercial Paper is by any other definition "Commercial Paper" or is ex-

empt from registration under the Securities Act of 1933, as amended.

Moody's Commercial Paper ratings are opinions of the ability of issuers to repay punctually promissory obligations not having an original maturity in excess of nine months. Moody's makes no representation that such obligations are exempt from registration under the Securities Act of 1933, nor does it represent that any specific note is a valid obligation of a rated issuer or issued in conformity with any applicable law. Moody's employs the following three designations, all judged to be investment grade, to indicate the relative repayment capacity of rated issuers:

Issuers rated **Prime-1** (or related supporting institutions) have a superior capacity for repayment of short-term promissory obligations. Prime-1 repayment capacity will normally be evidenced by the following characteristics:

-Leading market positions in well established industries.
-High rates of return on funds employed.
-Conservative capitalization structures with moderate reliance on debt and ample asset protection.
-Broad margins in earnings coverage of fixed financial charges and high internal cash generation.
-Well established access to a range of financial markets and assured sources of alternate liquidity.

Issuers rated **Prime-2** (or related supporting institutions) have a strong capacity for short-term promissory obligations. This will normally be evidenced by many of the characteristics cited above but to a lesser degree. Earnings trends and coverage ratios, while sound, will be more subject to variation. Capitalization characteristics, while still appropriate, may be more affected by external conditions. Ample alternate liquidity is maintained.

Issuers rated **Prime-3** (or related supporting institutions) have an acceptable capacity for repayment of short-term promissory obligations. The effect of industry characteristics and market composition may be more pronounced. Variability in earnings and profitability may result in changes in the level of debt protection measurements and the requirement for relatively high financial leverage. Adequate liquidity is maintained.

Issuers rated **Not Prime** do not fall within any of the Prime rating categories.

If an issuer represents to Moody's that its Commercial Paper obligations are supported by the credit of another entity or entities, the name or names of such supporting entity or entities are listed within parenthesis beneath the name of the issuer. In assigning ratings to such issuers,

Moody's evaluates the financial strength of the indicated affiliated corporations, commercial banks, insurance companies, foreign governments or other entities, but only as one factor in the total rating assessment. Moody's makes no representation and gives no opinion on the legal validity or enforceability of any support arrangement. You are cautioned to review with your counsel any questions regarding particular support arrangements.

KEY TO MOODY'S PREFERRED STOCK RATINGS*

Moody's Rating Policy Review Board Extended its rating services to include quality designations on preferred stocks on October 1, 1973. The decision to rate preferred stocks, which Moody's had done prior to 1935, was prompted by evidence of investor interest. Moody's believes that its rating of preferred stocks is especially appropriate in view of the ever-increasing amount of these securities outstanding, and the fact that continuing inflation and its ramifications have resulted generally in the dilution of some of the protection afforded them as well as other fixed-income securities.

Because of the fundamental differences between preferred stocks and bonds, a variation of our familiar bond rating symbols is being used in the quality ranking of preferred stocks. The symbols, presented below, are designed to avoid comparison with bond quality in absolute terms. It should always be borne in mind that preferred stocks occupy a junior position to bonds within a particular capital structure.

Preferred stock rating symbols and their definitions are as follows:

aaa

An issue which is rated aaa is considered to be a top-quality preferred stock. This rating indicates good asset protection and the least risk of dividend impairment within the universe of preferred stocks.

aa

An issue which is rated aa is considered a high-grade preferred stock. This rating indicates that there is reasonable assurance that earnings and asset protection will remain relatively well maintained in the foreseeable future.

a

An issue which is rated a is considered to be an upper-medium grade preferred stock.

*Note: Moody's applies numerical modifiers 1, 2 and 3 in each rating classification from 1 indicates that the security ranks in the higher end of its generic rating category; the modifier 2 indicates a mid-range ranking; and the modifier 3 indicates that the issue ranks in the lower end of its generic rating category.

Source: Moody's Investors Service, Inc.

While risks are judged to be somewhat greater than in the "aaa" and "aa" classifications, earnings and asset protection are, nevertheless, expected to be maintained at adequate levels.

baa

An issue which is rated baa is considered to be medium grade, neither highly protected nor poorly secured. Earnings and asset protection appear adequate at present but may be questionable over any great length of time.

ba

An issue which is rated ba is considered to have speculative elements and its future cannot be considered well assured. Earnings and asset protection may be very moderate and not well safeguarded during adverse periods. Uncertainty of position characterized preferred stocks in this class.

b

An issue which is rated b generally lacks the characteristics of a desirable investment. Assurance of dividend payments and maintenance of other terms of the issue over any long period of time may be small.

caa

An issue which is rated caa is likely to be in arrears on dividend payments. This rating designation does not purport to indicate the future status of payments.

"ca"

An issue which is rated "ca" is speculative in a high degree and is likely to be in arrears on dividends with little likelihood of eventual payment.

"c"

This is the lowest rated class of preferred or preference stock. Issues so rated can be regarded as having extremely poor prospects of ever attaining any real investment standing.

KEY TO SHORT-TERM LOAN RATINGS

MIG 1/VMIG 1

This designation denotes best quality. There is present strong protection by established cash flows, superior liquidity support or demonstrated broadbased access to the market for refinancing.

MIG 2/VMIG 2

This designation denotes high quality. Margins of protection are ample although not so large as in the preceding group.

MIG 3/VMIG 3

This designation denotes favorable quality. All security elements are accounted for but there is lacking the undeniable strength of the preceding grades. Liquidity and cash flow protection may be narrow and market access for refinancing is likely to be less well established.

MIG 4/VMIG 4

This designation denotes adequate quality. Protection commonly regarded as required of an investment security is present and although not distinctly or predominantly speculative, there is specific risk.

Issues or the features associated with **MIG** or **VMIG** ratings are identified by date of issue, date of maturity or maturities or rating expiration date and description to distinguish each rating from other ratings. Each rating designation is unique with no implication as to any other similar issue of the same obligor. **MIG** ratings terminate at the retirement of the obligation while **VMIG** rating expiration will be a function of each issue's specific structural or credit features.

MAJOR MONEY MARKET AND FIXED INCOME SECURITIES

Type	Interest: When Paid	Marketability	Minimum Amount of Issue	Maturity
A. *Interest Fully Taxable*				
Corporate Bonds and Notes	S[1]	Very good to poor depending on quality	$1,000	1 to 50 years
Corporate Preferred Stock (Pays dividends as a fixed percentage of face value. Dividends not obligatory, but if declared must be paid before that of the common stock. Dividends fully taxable for individuals, but 85% exempt from federal tax for corporations)	Generally quarterly	Good to poor depending on quality	$100 or less	No maturity
Federal Home Loan Mortgage Corporate Bonds	S	Fair	$25,000	Up to 25 years
Federal Home Loan Mortgage Certificates	S	Fair	$100,000	Up to 3 years
Farmers' Home Administration Notes and Certificates	Annual	Fair	$25,000	1 to 25 years
Federal Housing Administration Debentures (Guaranteed by the U.S. Government)	S	Very good	$50	1 to 40 years
Federal National Mortgage Association Bonds	S	Fair	$25,000	2 to 25 years
Government National Mortgage Modified Pass through Certificates (interest plus some repayment of principal, guaranteed by U.S. Government)	Monthly	Good	$25,000	30 years; average life 12 years
Federal Home Loan Bank Bonds and Notes	S	Good	$10,000	1 to 20 years
Export-Import Bank Debentures and Certificates	S	Good	$5,000	3 to 7 years
International Bank for Reconstruction Development (World Bank), Inter-American Development Bank, Asia Development Bank	S	Fair to poor	$1,000	3 to 25 years
Foreign and Eurodollar Bonds and Notes	May be Annual or S	Poor	$1,000 (amounts vary in foreign currencies)	1 to 30 years
Bankers Acceptances (short-term debt obligations (resulting from international trade and guaranteed by a major bank)	Discounted[2] on a 360-day year basis	Fair	$5,000	1 to 270 days
Commercial Paper (short-term debt issued by a major corporation)	Discounted on a 360-day year basis	No secondary market	$100,000 (occasionally smaller)	1 to 270 days

MAJOR MONEY MARKET AND FIXED INCOME SECURITIES *(concluded)*

Type	Interest: When Paid	Marketability	Minimum Amount of Issue	Maturity
Negotiable Certificates of Deposit (short-term debt issued by banks and which can be sold on the open market)	Interest paid on maturity; 360-day year basis	Fair	$100,000 (occasionally smaller)	30 days to 1 year
Non-negotiable Certificate of Deposit (savings certificates)	Interest paid on maturity; 360-day year basis	Non-negotiable	$500 $10,000	30 months 6 months
Collateralized Mortgage Obligations (CMO)	S or monthly	Good	$1,000	typically 2 to 20 years
Repurchase Agreements (generally short term loans by large investors, secured by U.S. Government or other high quality issues)[3]	Interest paid on maturity; 360-day year basis	No secondary market	$100,000	1 to 30 days (sometimes more)
Zero Coupon Bonds (Bonds stripped of coupons)	Bonds issued at deep discount. Full yield realized at maturity	Good	$1,000 on maturity	1 to 30 years
B. Interest Exempt from State and Local Income Taxes				
U.S. Treasury Bonds and Notes	S	Very good	$1,000	1 to 20 years
U.S. Treasury Bills	Discounted on a 360-day basis	Very good	$10,000	90 days to 1 year
U.S. Series EE Savings Bonds[4]	Issued at discount, full interest, paid on maturity	No secondary market: available for resale	$50 minimum $15,000 maximum	11 years (can be redeemed before maturity at reduced yields
U.S. Series HH Savings Bonds	S	No secondary market	$500 $15,000 maximum	10 years
Federal Land Bank Bonds	S	Good	$1,000	1 to 10 years
Federal Financing Bank Notes and Bonds	S	Good	$1,000	1 to 20 years
Tennessee Valley Authority Notes and Bonds	S	Fair	$1,000	5 to 25 years
Banks for Cooperatives Bonds	Interest: 360-day year basis	Good	$5,000	180 days
Federal Intermediate Credit Bank Bonds	Interest: 360-day year basis	Good	$5,000.	270 days
Federal Home Loan Bank Notes and Bonds	Discounted: 360-day year basis	Good	$10,000.	30 to 360-day year basis (some more)
Farm Credit Bank Notes and Bonds	Interest: 360-day year basis	Good	$50,000.	270 days (some more)
C. Interest Exempt from Federal Income Tax				
State and Local Notes and Bonds (in-State issues, usually exempt from State and local income taxes)	S	Good to fair depending on rating	$5,000.	1 to 50 years
Housing Authority Bonds (in-State issues usually exempt from State and local income taxes)	S	Good to fair	$5,000.	1 to 40 years

[1] S means semiannually.
[2] A discount means interest paid in advance, thus a 10% discounted security maturing at $10,000 would cost $9,000 to purchase.
[3] Recently some banks have issued repurchase agreements for smaller amounts of money, i.e., several thousands of dollars.
[4] Since November 1982, U.S. Savings Bonds pay variable interest equal to 85% of the 5 year Treasury securities' rate adjusted semi-annually and have a minimum guaranteed rate of 7.5%.

U.S. Treasury Bonds, Notes, and Bills: Terms Defined*

U.S. Treasury bonds, notes and bills are interest paying securities representing a debt on the part of the U.S. Government. Treasury bonds have a maturity of over 5 years, while notes mature within 5 to 7 years. Bills are discussed below. Both Treasury bonds and notes are generally issued in minimum denominations of $1,000 and pay interest semiannually. The amount of semiannual interest paid is determined by the coupon rate specified on the bond and is calculated on a 365-day year basis. For a $1,000 face value† bond the interest is given by:

semiannual interest = 1/2 ($1,000
$$\times \text{ coupon rate})$$

Bonds may be priced higher (at a premium) or lower (at a discount) than the face value (par) depending on current interest rates. The *current yield* is the rate the investor receives based on the prices actually paid for a bond. The price is given by:

$$\text{current yield} = \frac{\$1,000 \times \text{coupon rate}}{\text{purchase price}}$$

Thus, a $1,000 face value bond with an 8% coupon rate purchased at $850 has a current yield by:

$$\text{current yield} = \frac{\$1,000 \times 8\%}{\$850} = 9.41\%$$

The *yield to maturity* (YTM) is the yield obtained on taking into account the years remaining to maturity, annual interest payments, and the capital gain (or loss) realized at maturity. It is obtained from special tables.

However, the yield to maturity (YTM) may be found approximately from the formula

$$\text{YTM} = \frac{I + A}{B}$$

I = annual interest rate

$$A = \frac{\$1,000 - M}{N}$$

$$B = \frac{\$1,000 + M}{2}$$

where M = current market price of the bond
N = years remaining to maturity

---

* The terms *current yield, yield to maturity,* etc. defined in this section are generally applicable to all fixed incomes.

† Face value is the amount of the bond or note payable upon maturity.

As an example, a bond ($1,000 face value) has a 10% coupon and is currently priced at $1,100 with 10 years remaining to maturity. What is the approximate YTM?

$$I = \$1,000 \times .1 = \$100 \text{ interest per year}$$

$$A = \frac{\$1,000 - \$1,100}{10} = \$-10$$

$$B = \frac{\$1,000 + \$1,100}{2} = \$1,050$$

$$\text{YTM} = \frac{\$100 - \$10}{\$1,050} = .0857 = 8.57\%$$

U.S. Treasury bills (T-bills) are U.S. Government debt obligations which mature within one year. They are offered by the Federal Reserve Bank with maturities of 90 days (3 month bills) and 182 days (six month bills). Nine-month bills and one-year bills are also available. Treasury bills are sold in a minimum denomination of $10,000. Interest is paid by the discount method based on a 360-day year. With the discount method, interest is, in effect, paid at the time the bill is purchased. Thus a 91-day $10,000 bill (face value) with an 8% discount interest rate would provide the buyer with $202.22 ($10,000 $\times .08 \times {}^{91}\!/_{360}$) interest at the time of purchase. This amount is deducted from the face value of the bill at the time of purchase so the buyer actually pays a net amount of $9,797.78 ($10,000 − $202.22). When the bill matures, the buyer receives $10,000 on redemption.

Since T-bills pay interest at the time of purchase (discount basis) on a 360-day year basis, while bonds (and notes) pay interest semiannually on a 365-day year basis, the two rates cannot be compared directly. To compare the two rates, the discount rate must be converted to the so-called *bond equivalent yield*, given by

$$\text{bond equivalent yield} = \frac{365 \times \text{discount rate}}{360 - (\text{discount rate} \times \text{days to maturity})}$$

As an example, a newly issued 91-day note with a discount rate of 12% has a

$$\text{bond equivalent yield} = \frac{365 \times (.12)}{360 - (.12 \times 91)}$$
$$= 12.55\%$$

Interest from U.S. Treasury bonds, notes, and bills are subject to federal income tax, but are exempt from state and local income taxes.

How to Read U.S. Government Bond and Note Quotations

TREASURY BONDS AND NOTES

(1) Rate	(2) Mat.	(3) Date	(4) Bid	(5) Asked	(6) Bid Chg.	(7) Yld.
6¾s,	1981	Jun n ...	99.3	99.7 +	.1	16.51
9⅛s,	1981	Jun n ...	99.12	99.16 +	.2	15.10
9⅜s,	1981	Jul n	98.21	98.25 +	.3	16.54
7s,	1981	Aug	97.26	98.10 +	.2	15.19
7⅝s,	1981	Aug n ...	97.30	98.2 +	.6	17.66
8⅜s,	1981	Aug n ...	98.2	98.6 +	.2	17.15
9⅝s,	1981	Aug n ...	98.5	98.9 +	.4	16.53
6¾s,	1981	Sep n ...	96.29	97.1 +	.5	16.10
10⅛s,	1981	Sep n ...	97.28	98 +	.4	16.28
12⅝s,	1981	Oct n ...	98.14	98.18 +	.4	16.18
7s,	1981	Nov n ...	96.4	96.8 +	.10	15.86
7¾s,	1981	Nov n ...	96.18	96.22 +	.13	15.55
12⅛s,	1981	Nov n ...	98.1	98.5 +	.3	16.14
7¼s,	1981	Dec n ...	95.12	95.16 +	.10	15.14

The above exhibit is an example of U.S. Government bond and note quotations as it appears in *The Wall Street Journal.*

(1) Indicates the coupon rate of interest which is designated by *s*. Rates are quoted to ⅛ of a percent. Thus 8⅜ means 8.375%. The semiannual interest payments are calculated, as described elsewhere, using this rate.

(2) Indicates the year of maturity.

(3) Indicates the month (of the above year) in which the bond or note matures. The letter *n* means the security is a note. Otherwise a bond is implied.

(4) The *bid price* per bond or note (the price at which the bond can be sold to the dealer), expressed as a percentage of the face value ($1,000) of the bond. Prices are quoted in terms of 1/32 of a percent. Thus 98.5 means 98⁵⁄₃₂. To find the dollar value of the price, convert 98⁵⁄₃₂ to a decimal (98⁵⁄₃₂ = .98156) and multiply by the face value of the bond to give $981.56 (.98156 × $1,000).

(5) The *ask price* per bond or note (the price at which the dealer will sell the bond). The dollar value is found as indicated above.

(6) The change in the bid price from the closing price of the previous day.

(7) The yield if the bond is held to maturity, based on the ask price.

Some U.S. Treasury bonds can be called back for redemption prior to maturity. These are shown with two dates (under item 2 for example)—*1993–98* indicating that the bonds mature in 1998, but may be called back and redeemed any time after 1993.

Some newspapers (such as *The New York Times*) use a slight modification of the above arrangement, though the various terms have the same meaning as defined above. Thus, a bond maturing in June of 1985 and bearing a 10⅜% coupon is indicated by *May ' 85 10⅜.*

How to Read U.S. Treasury Bill Quotations

(1) U.S. Treas. Mat. date	(2) Bills Bid	(3) Asked Discount	(4) Yield
-1981-			
6–18	17.62	17.44	17.69
6–25	17.15	17.03	17.33
7– 2	15.39	15.01	15.31
7– 9	15.18	15.04	15.39
7–16	15.02	14.78	15.17
7–23	14.83	14.67	15.10
7–30	14.72	14.42	14.88
8– 6	14.11	13.89	14.36
8–13	13.94	13.72	14.22
8–20	13.94	13.72	14.26
8–27	13.92	13.70	14.28
9– 3	13.97	13.63	14.24
9–10	13.72	13.64	14.29
9–17	13.52	13.34	14.00
9–24	13.63	13.43	14.14
10– 1	13.74	13.54	14.30

The above exhibit is an example of Treasury bill quotations as it appears in *The Wall Street Journal.*

(1) The date of maturity, i.e., 6–18 means June 18, 1981.

(2) The bid price at market close quoted as a *discount* rate in percent. This bid price is the price at which the dealer will buy the bill. To convert the discount rate to a dollar price use the formula

dollar price = $10,000 − (discount rate × days to maturity × .2778)

In the above, the discount must be expressed in percent. For example, if the dealer bids 16.18% discount for a bill which will mature in 110 days, the dollar price is given by

dollar price = $10,000 − (16.18 × 110 × .2778) = $9,505.57 per bill

(3) The asked price at market close expressed as a discount rate in percent. The asked price is the price at which the dealer will sell a bill to a buyer. To convert to a dollar price use the above formula.

(4) The bond equivalent yield expressed in percent. This is calculated (as explained elsewhere) from the asked price expressed as a dis-

count rate. This rate is used to compare T-bill yields to that of bonds, notes and certificates of deposit.

Some newspapers (e.g., *The New York Times*) use a somewhat different arrangement, though the meaning of the terms is the same as defined above. Thus, a bill maturing on June 4, 1981, is indicated as such. Also included in some newspapers is the change in bid price expressed as a discount rate.

How to Read Corporate Bond Quotations*

Corporate bonds are debt securities issued by private corporations. They generally have a face value (the amount due on maturity) of $1,000 and a specified interest rate (coupon rate) paid semiannually. Many corporate bonds have a *call* provision which permits the company to recall and redeem the bond after a specified date. Call privileges are usually exercised when interest rates fall sufficiently. Investors, therefore, cannot count on *locking in* high interest rates with corporate bonds. Bond quality designations used by Moody's and Standard & Poor's are given elsewhere in the Almanac (pp. 372–377).

The following is an example of price quotations for bonds traded on The New York Stock Exchange as they appear in *The Wall Street Journal*.

CORPORATION BONDS

VOLUME, $18,990,000

(1) Bonds	(2) Cur YID	(3) Vol	(4) High	(5) Low	(6) Close	(7) Net Chg
AlaP	9s2000 14.	6	63	62	63	2
AlaP	8½s01 15.	10	57½	57½	57½	...
AlaP	8⅞s03 15.	25	60	59½	60	+ ½
AlaP	10⅞05 15.	3	72	72	72	− 2¼
AlaP	10½05 15.	12	70½	70½	70½	− 1
AlaP	12⅝10 16.	7	81¼	81⅛	81⅛	− 1⅝
AlaP	15¼10 16.	111	94⅝	93⅝	94	...
AlaP	14¾491 15.	31	97	96½	96½	...
AlaP	17⅜11 17.	99	104	103½	103¾	− ¼
Alexn	5½96 cv	34	61¾	61⅝	61¾	+ ¾
Allgl	10¾499 15.	2	70½	70½	70½	...
AllstF	8⅛87 11.	2	76⅜	76⅜	76⅜	+ 1⅞
AllstF	9⅝86 12.	10	83⅛	83	83	+ 1⅞

(1) The name of the issue in abbreviated form, followed by the coupon rate of interest

in percent (designated by the letter *s*), and the year in which the bond matures. The coupon rate is stated in terms of ⅛ of a percent; 9⅜ means 9.375%.

(2) This is the current yield which is calculated as stated elsewhere. (See U.S. Treasury Bonds, Notes, and Bills, p. 380.)

(3) This item is the number of bonds sold that day.

(4) This is the highest price quoted for the bond sold on that day, expressed as a percentage of face value ($1,000). To convert to dollars, express the price as a decimal and multiply by the face value of the bond. As an example:

$$58\frac{1}{2} = (.5850 \times \$1,000.) = \$585$$

(5) This is the lowest price quoted that day. It is converted into dollars as described above.

(6) This is the price at the close of the market that day.

(7) This is the change in the closing price from that of the previous day. To convert to dollars, express as a decimal and multiply by $1,000. Thus, −1⅞ means a decrease per bond of $18.75 (.01875 × $1,000) from that of the previous day.

Tax-Exempt Bonds

Tax exempt (municipal) bonds are issued by state and local governments and are free from federal income tax on interest payments. The bonds are often issued in $5,000 denominations and pay interest semiannually. Capital gains are taxable. In addition, holders of out-of-state bonds may be subject to state and local income taxes of the state in which they reside. For example, a New York City resident holding Los Angeles municipal bonds would be subject to New York State and City income taxes on the interest.

The taxable equivalent yield of a tax exempt bond is obtained by means of the expression

$$\text{taxable equivalent yield} = \frac{\text{tax exempt yield}}{1 - (F + S + L)}$$

where

F is the federal tax bracket of the investor
S is the state tax bracket of the investor
L is the local tax bracket of the investor

Thus, an investor in the 50% federal bracket, 10% state bracket and 3% local bracket who holds a bond with a current yield of 6% which is exempt from all income taxes would enjoy a taxable equivalent yield (TEY) given by

$$\text{TEY} = \frac{6\%}{1 - (.5 + .1 + .03)} = 16.21\%$$

---

* Yield terms are the same as those defined in the section on U.S. Treasury Bonds, Notes and Bills, p. 416.

Section continues on p. 420.

TAX EXEMPT VERSUS TAXABLE YIELDS

To equal a tax-free yield of: a taxable investment has to earn:

tax bracket	5½%	6%	6½%	7%	7½%	8%	8½%	9%	9½%	10%	10½%	11%
28%	7.64%	8.33%	9.03%	9.72%	10.42%	11.11%	11.81%	12.50%	13.19%	13.89%	14.58%	15.28%
30	7.86	8.57	9.29	10.00	10.71	11.43	12.14	12.86	13.57	14.29	15.00	15.71
31	7.97	8.70	9.42	10.14	10.87	11.59	12.32	13.04	13.77	14.49	15.22	15.94
32	8.09	8.82	9.56	10.29	11.03	11.76	12.50	13.24	13.97	14.71	15.44	16.18
34	8.33	9.09	9.85	10.61	11.36	12.12	12.88	13.64	14.39	15.15	15.91	16.67
36	8.59	9.38	10.16	10.94	11.72	12.50	13.28	14.06	14.84	15.63	16.41	17.19
37	8.73	9.52	10.32	11.11	11.90	12.70	13.49	14.29	15.08	15.87	16.67	17.47
39	9.02	9.84	10.66	11.48	12.30	13.11	13.93	14.75	15.57	16.39	17.21	18.03
42	9.48	10.34	11.21	12.07	12.93	13.79	14.66	15.52	16.38	17.24	18.10	18.97
43	9.65	10.53	11.40	12.28	13.16	14.04	14.91	15.79	16.67	17.54	18.42	19.30
44	9.82	10.71	11.61	12.50	13.39	14.29	15.18	16.07	16.96	17.86	18.75	19.64
46	10.19	11.11	12.03	12.96	13.89	14.81	15.74	16.67	17.59	18.52	19.44	20.37
49	10.78	11.76	12.75	13.73	14.71	15.69	16.67	17.65	18.63	19.61	20.59	21.57
54	11.96	13.04	14.13	15.22	16.30	17.39	18.48	19.57	20.65	21.74	22.83	23.91
55	12.22	13.33	14.44	15.56	16.67	17.78	18.89	20.00	21.11	22.22	23.33	24.44
59	13.41	14.63	15.85	17.07	18.29	19.51	20.73	21.95	23.17	24.39	25.61	26.83
63	14.86	16.22	17.57	18.92	20.27	21.62	22.97	24.32	25.68	27.03	28.38	29.73
64	15.28	16.67	18.06	19.44	20.83	22.22	23.61	25.00	26.39	27.78	29.17	30.56
68	17.19	18.75	20.31	21.88	23.44	25.00	26.56	28.13	29.69	31.25	32.81	34.38
70	18.33	20.00	21.67	23.33	25.00	26.67	28.33	30.00	31.67	33.33	35.00	36.67

A taxable yield of 16.21% would be necessary to provide the same yield as the 6% current yield on the tax exempt security.

TYPES OF TAX EXEMPT BONDS AND NOTES

General Obligation bonds, also known as GO's, are backed by a pledge of a city's or state's full faith and credit for the prompt repayment of both principal and interest. Most city, county and school district bonds are secured by a pledge of unlimited property taxes. Since general obligation bonds depend on tax resources, they are normally analyzed in terms of the size of the resources being taxed.

Revenue bonds are payable from the earnings of a revenue-producing enterprise such as a sewer, water, gas or electric system, airport, toll bridge, college dormitory, lease payments from property rented to industrial companies, and other income-producing facilities. Revenue bonds are analyzed in terms of their earnings.

Limited and Special Tax bonds are payable from the pledge of the proceeds derived by the issuer from a specific tax such as a property tax levied at a fixed rate, a special assessment, or a tax on gasoline.

Municipal notes are short term obligations maturing from 30 days to a year and are issued in anticipation of revenues coming from the sales of bonds (BANS), taxes (TANS), or other revenues (RANS).

Project notes, issued by local housing and urban renewal agencies, are backed by a U.S. Government guarantee and are also tax exempt.

How to Understand Tax-Exempt Bond Quotations

Generally the prices of municipal bonds are quoted in terms of the yield to maturity (defined elsewhere) rather than in percentage of face value, as with other bonds. The yield to maturity can be converted to a dollar price if the years remaining to maturity and the rate of interest due are known. Certain tables used for this purpose are given in the *Basis Book* (published by the Financial Publishing Company, 82 Brookline Avenue, Boston, Massachusetts). The books list the dollar price (per $1,000 face value of the bond) corresponding to a given coupon rate, yield, and years to maturity.

Some municipal bonds, however, are quoted directly in terms of percentage of face value. Thus, a bid price (the price at which the dealer will buy the bonds from the investor) of 98⅝ for a $5,000 face value bond can be converted to a dollar price by first converting the bid to a decimal expression (.98625) and then multiplying by the face value of the bond. The result

in this case is $4,931.25 (.98625 × $5,000). The same calculation applies to the ask price (the price at which the dealer will sell the bond to the investor).

Prices of tax exempt bonds are not quoted in the daily press. They can be obtained by calling municipal bond dealers. Extensive quotations are given in some relatively expensive publications:

The Blue List
Standard & Poor's
25 Broadway
New York, New York 10004
(212) 208-8471

The Daily Bond Buyer
and
The Weekly Bond Buyer
The Bond Buyer
1 State Street Plaza
New York, New York 10004
(212) 943-8200

Bond Week (Formerly Money Manager)
Institutional Investor
488 Madison Avenue
New York, New York 10022
(212) 303-3300

Government National Mortgage Association (GNMA) Modified Pass Through Certificates

A GNMA Mortgage-Backed Security is a government-guaranteed security which is collateralized by a pool of federally-underwritten residential mortgages. The investor receives a monthly check for a proportionate share of the principal and interest on a pool of mortgages whether or not the payments have actually been collected from the borrowers.

The GNMA Mortgage-Backed Security offers the highest yield of any federally-guaranteed security. In addition, the GNMA security offers a very competitive return in comparison to private corporation debt issues. Moreover, the investor receives a monthly return on the GNMA guaranteed investment, rather than semi-annual payments as on most bonds. This monthly payment represents a cash flow available for reinvestment and has the effect of increasing the yield on GNMAs by 10 to 18 basis points (a basis point is 0.1%) when compared to the yield equivalent received on a bond investment with the same "coupon" rate but paying interest semi-annually.

On single-family securities (the most popular form) the maturity is typically 30 years. However, statistical studies have determined that the average life of a single-family security is approximately 12 years, due to prepayments of principal. Nevertheless, some of the mortgages in any pool are likely to remain outstanding for the full 30-year period.

The minimum size of original individual certificates is $25,000 with increments of $5,000 above that amount.

Due to the uncertainties in the maturity of the above mentioned pass-through certificates, collateralized mortgage obligations (CMOs)

have been introduced. CMOs are bonds backed by Ginnie Maes, Freddie Macs, and other mortgage instruments providing investors with a wide choice of maturities ranging from 2 to 20 years. Essentially, the monthly payments from the underlying mortgage instruments are initially allocated to the nearest maturity CMO and subsequently to CMO maturities of successively longer duration. CMO interest payments are made semiannually or monthly.

Tax-Exempt Mutual Funds: Selected No Loads

Funds listed below invest in municipal bonds. Interest is free of federal income tax. However, capital gains are subject to federal income tax and state income taxes generally apply.

	Telephone
Dreyfus Tax-Exempt Bond Fund	800-645-6561
Fidelity:	
High Yield Municipals	800-544-6666
Limited Term Municipals	800-544-6666
Municipal Bond Fund	800-544-6666
Nuveen Municipal Bond Fund	800-621-7210
Scudder Managed Municipal	
Bond Fund	800-453-3305
Steinroe Tax-Exempt Bond	
Fund	800-621-0320
Vanguard:	
Municipal Bond-High Yield	800-662-7447
Municipal Bond-Intermediate	800-662-7447
Municipal Bond-Long Term	800-662-7447

10 Largest Tax-Exempt Money Market Funds by Assets[1,2]

Fund	Assets (millions)
Merrill Lynch CMA	7,585.7
Federated Tax-Free Trust	4,095.6
Fidelity Tax-Exempt Money Market	3,937.9
Dreyfus Tax-Exempt Money Fund	2,612.7
Nuveen Tax-Exempt Money Market Trust	2,448.3
Municipal Cash Reserve Management	2,197.5
Provident Municipal Temporary Investments	2,025.5
Kemper	1,413.0
Daily Tax-Free	1,328.3
Federated Tax-Free Instruments	1,279.0

[1] As of June 9, 1986.
[2] Interest exempt from Federal Income Tax.

How to Understand Convertible Securities

The term "Convertible Securities" refers to securities that can be exchanged for another type of security, usually the common stock of the company issuing the convertible.

The two basic types of convertible securities are debentures (commonly known as bonds) and preferred stock. These securities have intrinsic value. Bonds represent a debt of the issuing company. Preferred stock represents an ownership interest. Intrinsic value may be enhanced by the convertible feature.

There are other certificates or contracts which are sometimes considered to be convertible securities but which have no intrinsic value based on ownership interest or debt. Their value is derived solely from their ability to be converted into another type of security. To do so requires a payment in addition to the surrender of the security. These are rights, warrants and options. To many investors these securities may offer certain advantages. However, our emphasis here will be on convertible securities—bonds and preferred stock—which have broader application as investment vehicles.

CONVERTIBLE BONDS

Convertible debt securities are almost always issued in the form of debentures. That is, there is no specific collateral pledged by the issuing corporation in the indenture which states the terms under which the security is issued. Rather, the promise to pay interest on stated dates and the principal amount at maturity is backed by the full faith and credit of the corporation. However, even the most sophisticated investors and those in the securities industry commonly refer to this type of security as a convertible bond.

Convertible bonds have been extolled as the ultimate investment medium offering the desir-

Source: Reprinted, with permission, from *Understanding Convertible Securities*, © New York Stock Exchange, Inc., 1982. Further reprinting is prohibited without express written approval of New York Stock Exchange, Inc.

able features of other securities without the normal risks. If this were so, it would not be for long. Demand for such a security would be so great that the price would be driven up to the point where the element of risk would be very evident. Convertible bonds like all other securities have both advantages and disadvantages and the informed investor can measure these against his own objectives.

Here are the three most important characteristics:

1. Convertible bonds pay interest—which, as a general rule yields more than the dividends on common stock of comparable quality and less than the interest on straight (non-convertible) bonds of equivalent quality and maturity.

    The issuing company's obligation to pay this interest comes before dividends on preferred and common stock.
2. Convertible bonds offer appreciable possibilities linked to the earnings and growth of the company. As the common stock rises in value to reflect this growth, the price of the convertible bond should also increase. Conversely, as the common stock declines in value, so should the convertible bond decline.
3. Convertible bonds enjoy some of the stability and relative safety associated with straight bonds and preferred stock. For each outstanding convertible bond, it is possible to estimate an investment value. This is the price below which the convertible bond is not expected to fall, if interest rates remain constant, even if the common stock price falls to such an extent as to render the convertible feature virtually valueless. Investment value is arrived at by estimating a price that would produce a yield comparable to straight bonds of equivalent quality. Investment value, it should be stressed, is only an estimate and subject to change from many influences such as fluctuating interest rates, economic and business conditions, ratings given by investment advisory services and the general well-being of the issuing company.

These characteristics can perhaps best be understood by examining how convertible bonds come into existence and how they behave in various circumstances.

XYZ COMPANY ISSUES CONVERTIBLE BONDS

Let's assume that the XYZ Company wants to raise more capital to expand its business. Interest rates are high and XYZ does not want to pay 12% or more to borrow money in the conventional bond market. XYZ is also reluc-

tant at this time to issue additional common stock as a means of raising additional capital. This could be due to a number of reasons, one of which might be unwillingness to dilute the equity interest of its present stockholders. For example, if there are presently ten million shares outstanding and an additional million are issued, earnings per share will normally be reduced by ten percent at the moment of issue, and the market price of the common stock probably would fall proportionately unless it could support the higher price earnings ratio. (The dilution problem is not quite the same when additional stock is issued to acquire an interest in or control of another company. The acquired company will presumably have its own earnings to contribute to earnings per share.) The XYZ Company is also mindful of the fact that dividends on stock are paid after federal income taxes, whereas interest on debt securities, like bonds, is a deduction before taxes.

Accordingly, the management of the XYZ Company decides to issue convertible bonds. In conjunction with the underwriting firm, the interest is set at 10% and the bonds are priced at par—an even $1,000 per $1,000 face amount bond. Bond prices are commonly stated as a percentage of par which, in this case, would be 100. It is further stipulated that each $1,000 bond can be converted into 25 shares of XYZ common stock. At the time that the bonds are marketed, the common stocks is trading at $32 per share.

DEFINITION OF TERMS

In any discussion of convertible bonds, various terms, related to the above figures, are widely used. Before proceeding, these should be defined.

Market Price Price at which a convertible bond can be bought or sold at a given point in time. Market price is stated as a percentage of par, usually $1,000. 100 means $1,000, 90 means $900, 110 means $1,100, etc.

Conversion Ratio Number of shares of common stock obtainable through conversion of one bond. In the case of XYZ, conversion ratio is 25.

Conversion Price The reciprocal of conversion ratio or the price of the stock when the number of shares obtainable through conversion of one $1,000 bond equals exactly $1,000. Conversion price is $40 when conversion ratio is 25.

Conversion Value Current value of total shares into which a bond can be converted. Conversion value of XYZ $1,000 bond with conversion ratio of 25 shares is $800 when XYZ common stock is trading at $32 per share.

Conversion Premium Percentage difference between conversion value and market value of bond. When conversion value is $800 and market value is $1,000, conversion premium is 25% since difference between conversion and market values ($1,000 − $800 = $200) is 25% of conversion value ($800). This figure represents the judgment of investors, as expressed in the marketplace, with respect to the worth of the three characteristics of convertible securities discussed above. These were yield, appreciation potential and relative safety. With some issues, supply and demand is also a factor in the premium.

Investment Value Estimated price, usually set by investment advisory services, at which bond would be selling if it had no convertible feature. Investment value is arrived at by estimating the price at which the convertible bond would have to sell to provide a percentage yield comparable to percentage yield on a non-convertible bond of equivalent quality and maturity. Investment value, like market price, is normally stated as a percentage of $1,000. For the XYZ Bonds, investment value will be assumed to be 75 providing a current yield of 13.33%.

Premium Over Investment Value Percentage difference between estimated investment value and market price of bond. When market price is 100 and investment value is estimated at 75, the difference is 25 which is 33% of 75. Thus, the premium over investment value is 33%. This figure can be considered a measurement of the worth of the conversion privilege as well as an indication of the proportion of the price that is subject to the risks associated with common stock.

To summarize, the position of XYZ Convertible Bonds, and the related stock at the time the bonds are marketed, is as follows:

Market Price of Bond.............100	($1,000)
Yield 10%	
Conversion Ratio.............................25	
Conversion Price...........$40	$\left(\dfrac{\$1,000}{25}\right)$
Market Price of Stock....................$32	
Conversion Value............$800	(25 × $32)
Conversion Premium ...25%	$\left(\dfrac{\$1,000 - \$800}{\$800}\right)$
Investment Value.........75	($750)
Premium Over Investment Value 33%	$\left(\dfrac{\$1,000 - \$750}{\$750}\right)$

Obviously, no owners of the bonds would convert them into the common stock at this time, since they would be exchanging $1,000 for $800. However, it is not necessary to convert a convertible bond into stock in order to enjoy its advantages. Bonds are frequently sold many times before they are finally converted into stock and many investors have actively participated in the convertible bond market without ever exercising the conversion privilege. Let's now explore what could happen to the XYZ Convertible Bonds under various circumstances.

IF THE STOCK GOES UP

If the XYZ Company prospers and is considered to have appreciation potential, the price of the common stock should go up. By the same token, the price of the XYZ Convertible Bond should also rise. Let's assume the stock goes up by 25% to $40 per share. Normally, the bond will also go up but not necessarily at the same rate as the stock. There is a good reason for this. As the bond price increases, it acts more like a stock and less like a bond. Investment value is left further behind. The risk increases. Yield diminishes too. Accordingly, even though the appreciation potential of the stock may not have changed, the other factors (greater risk and lower yield) will tend to hold back the price of the bond. Therefore, a rise in the XYZ stock of 25% from $32 to $40 might be reflected in a rise in the bond of 20% from 100 to 120. The most significant figures are now as follows:

Market Price of Bond.............120	($1,200)
Current Yield 8.33%	$\left(\dfrac{\$100}{\$1,200}\right)$
Market Price of Stock....................$40	
Conversion Value $1,000	(25 × $40)
Conversion Premium..20%	$\left(\dfrac{\$1,200 - \$1,000}{\$1,000}\right)$
Premium Over Investment Value 60%	$\left(\dfrac{\$1,200 - \$750}{\$750}\right)$

Conversion is still unrealistic. But bondholders who bought at the offering may want to take profits by selling their bonds to other investors who believe the stock will continue to go up but are not quite certain enough in their belief to buy the stock itself. Let's assume now that XYZ common stock goes up to $60 per share, an increase of 87½% since the bonds were issued. What is likely to happen to the XYZ bonds? The bond price may now rise to the level where virtually all of the bond-like characteristics are lost and, from the standpoint of risk, the bond is interchangeable with the stock. If we assume this is so, the bond's conversion value should be approximately the same as its market value and conversion premium will disappear. The picture would now look like this:

Market Price of Bond.............150	($1,500)	
Current Yield.........6.67%	$\left(\dfrac{\$100}{\$1,500}\right)$	
Market Price of Stock....................$60		
Conversion Value $1,500	(25 × $60)	
Conversion Premium 0	$\left(\dfrac{\$1,500 - \$1,500}{\$1,500}\right)$	
Premium Over Investment Value 100%		

Now the owner of the bond will think very seriously about converting. His decision may depend to some extent on the comparative yields of the bond and the stock. Interest on the bond is $100 per year. If the dividend on the stock is less than $4.00 per share, conversion would result in less income. If, on the other hand, the dividend is $4.20 (a yield of 7%) conversion would result in more current income.

In the meantime, while the stock has been rising from $32 to $60 per share, the company has presumably been using the money received from the sale of the convertible bonds to expand its business and improve its earnings. This should have put it in a better position to absorb the dilution that conversion into common stock entails.

When a convertible bond's conversion value and market price become the same, the stock and the bond should move up and down together within a limited range to maintain this relationship. It is virtually impossible for a convertible bond to sell with a negative conversion premium (below its conversion value) for any length of time. If this should happen, professional traders will quickly move in and employ a device known as arbitrage to make a small but rapid profit. They will buy the bonds and simultaneously sell the stock short. Converting the bonds enables them to replace the stock borrowed for the short sale. If, for example, XYZ convertibles are selling at $1,450 while the conversion value is $1,500, the trader can buy ten bonds for $14,500. By selling short 250 shares, he receives $15,000 for an immediate gross profit of $500. This activity will tend to drive the price of the bond back up to or above conversion value.

IF THE STOCK GOES DOWN

Let us now consider what might happen to the XYZ convertible bonds if the common stock took an opposite course and declined from the price of $32 per share which it was enjoying at the time that the convertible bonds were issued. As the price falls the convertible bond's price will also fall. However, the bond's downside potential is less than that of the stock, since the bond should not decline below its investment value which is the estimated value of the bond when we disregard the conversion feature. We have assumed this to be a price of 75 which is 25% below par. Therefore, while the stock is falling from $32 to an unknown level, the bond should only travel from 100 to 75. This factor serves as a brake on the bond and is the reason why convertible bonds are generally considered to be a more conservative investment than the stock of the same issuing company. In reality, conditions which would cause a stock to decline drastically would probably produce a re-adjustment in the investment value of the convertible bond. Investment value is also subject to adjustment when money rates change.

To see how the convertible bond might be affected by a decline in the common stock of the XYZ Company, let's assume that the market price of the stock sags from its original price of $32 all the way down to $16 per share. It has lost half its value. If we estimated correctly the investment value of the convertible bond, and if other factors are the same, it will be selling in the area of $750. Thus, a drop of 50% in the price of the stock produces a drop of 25% in the price of the bond. The table of values will now be as follows:

Market Price of Bond 75	($750)	
Current Yield...........13.33%	$\left(\dfrac{\$100}{\$750}\right)$	
Market Price of Stock....................$16		
Conversion Value $400	(25 × $16)	
Conversion Premium ...87½%	$\left(\dfrac{\$750 - \$400}{\$400}\right)$	
Premium Over Investment Value 0		

Thus, we have seen in this example that the price of a convertible bond is controlled primarily by the price of the stock into which it is convertible. However, when the stock goes up, the bond's rise should be held back somewhat as risk increases and yield decreases. Conversely, when the stock goes down, the bond's decline is cushioned as yield increases and investment value is approached. This is an oversimplification which disregards other influences but, hopefully, it provides a basic understanding of how convertible bonds behave. Prices, yields and ratios were chosen in order to illustrate the example and simplify the arithmetic. They are not intended to reflect actual market conditions at any time.

HEDGING

We have seen that convertible bonds offer an investor opportunities to participate in the stock market with somewhat less risk (and less profit potential) than is normally encountered with direct investment in common stocks. This opportunity can be pursued even further by employing hedges. Although extremely complex in practice, the basic principles of hedging are actually quite simple.

Typically, a hedge is established when an investor buys convertible bonds and, at the same time, sells short the stock into which the bond is convertible. If the stock goes up, there should be a profit in the bonds and a loss in the stock. If the stock goes down, there should be a profit in the stock and a loss in the bonds. Obviously, there is no advantage in a hedge unless the profit exceeds the loss and expenses. There is no way to assure a profit but the skillful and judicious use of hedges can greatly reduce the risk of loss and enhance the possibility of profit. An essential feature is the ability to sell stock short without margin when the corresponding convertible security is held.

Convertible hedges are a highly sophisticated investment technique and should not be attempted without a complete understanding of all of their ramifications.

CALLABILITY AND OTHER LIMITATIONS

An important factor to consider with convertible bonds is the call feature. This is the right of the issuing company to redeem the bonds before maturity at a stated price slightly above par. Usually the original purchasers of a bond are given some protection against this privilege of the company through an initial period during which the bond is non-callable. If a bond has been on the market for four years and commands a price of 130, this price may be short lived if the bond can be called at 105 after five years. When a convertible bond issue listed on the New York Stock Exchange is called for redemption some notice is always given in a newspaper of general circulation to permit the holders to exercise their conversion privilege or sell the bond to someone else who may convert it. Holders of record of registered bonds are notified directly. If, for some reason, the bond is not converted before expiration date

for conversion, which may be the same or a few days before the redemption date, it is then worth no more nor less than the call price. It is, therefore, most important for holders of convertible bonds to know what the call features are and to be sure that they will receive information about calls when and if they occur. Obviously, the best way to do this is to hold registered bonds.

Most convertible bonds are convertible into stock at a fixed rate during the entire life of the bond. However, this rate may change because of a stock split, stock dividend, merger or other circumstances. The conversion privilege may expire before the bond matures or it may not be effective until some time after the bond is issued. Sometimes the conversion rate declines at regular intervals. A bond that is convertible into 25 shares of common stock when first issued may become convertible into only 20 shares after five years, 15 shares after ten years, etc. Although the typical convertible bond is exchangeable for the common stock of the issuing company, this is also subject to variation. Conversion may be made into a combination of common and preferred stock. Or a bond of one company may be convertible into the stock of a parent company.

All of these possible limitations should be checked by investors when investigating convertible securities. A member firm of the New York Stock Exchange, Inc. can usually supply the essential information.

MARGIN AND COMMISSION

Two other features of convertible bonds have traditionally appealed to investors—margin requirements and commission rates. Although the current margin requirement for the purchase of common stock or convertible bonds is the same—50%, the convertible bond rate has usually been significantly less. In 1973, for instance, an investor with $6,500 available in cash could have bought $10,000 worth of common stock or $13,000 of convertible bonds. (Margin requirements are subject to change by the Federal Reserve Board).

The commission paid to a member firm broker for the purchase or sale of listed stocks is one of the lowest fees paid for the transfer of property of any kind. However, in most cases, the commission paid for the purchase or sale of bonds is even lower on a given dollar investment.

CONVERTIBLE PREFERRED STOCK

Convertible preferred stock possesses many of the basic characteristics of convertible bonds and will normally perform in approximately the same manner when subject to the same conditions and influences. However, there are also basic differences which should be pointed out.

Convertible preferred stock represents an equity interest and is, therefore, junior to all debt securities including convertible bonds and would not—all else being equal—have as high a degree of relative safety as convertible bonds. However, all else is rarely equal and the con-vertible preferred stock of Company A could have more relative safety than the convertible bonds of Company B. Convertible preferred stocks do not have maturity dates as do bonds but are usually subject to redemption.

Convertible preferreds, like common stock, require 50% margin currently, and are subject to the same commission structure.

FOREIGN SHORT-TERM AND LONG-TERM INTEREST RATES: SELECTED COUNTRIES

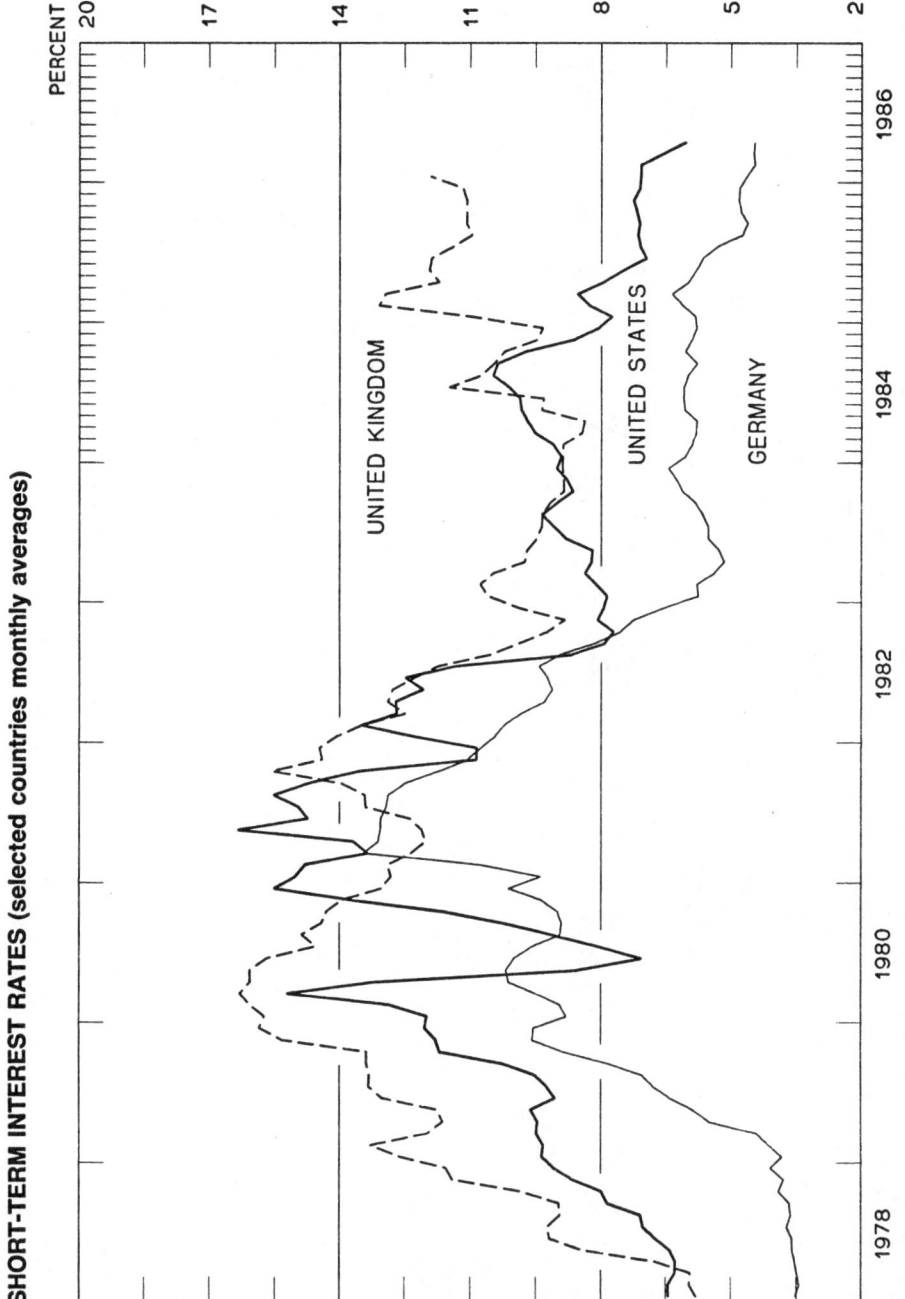

SHORT-TERM INTEREST RATES (selected countries monthly averages)

PERCENT

UNITED KINGDOM

UNITED STATES

GERMANY

1978   1980   1982   1984   1986

Source: *Federal Reserve Chart Book*, Board of Governors of the Federal Reserve System.

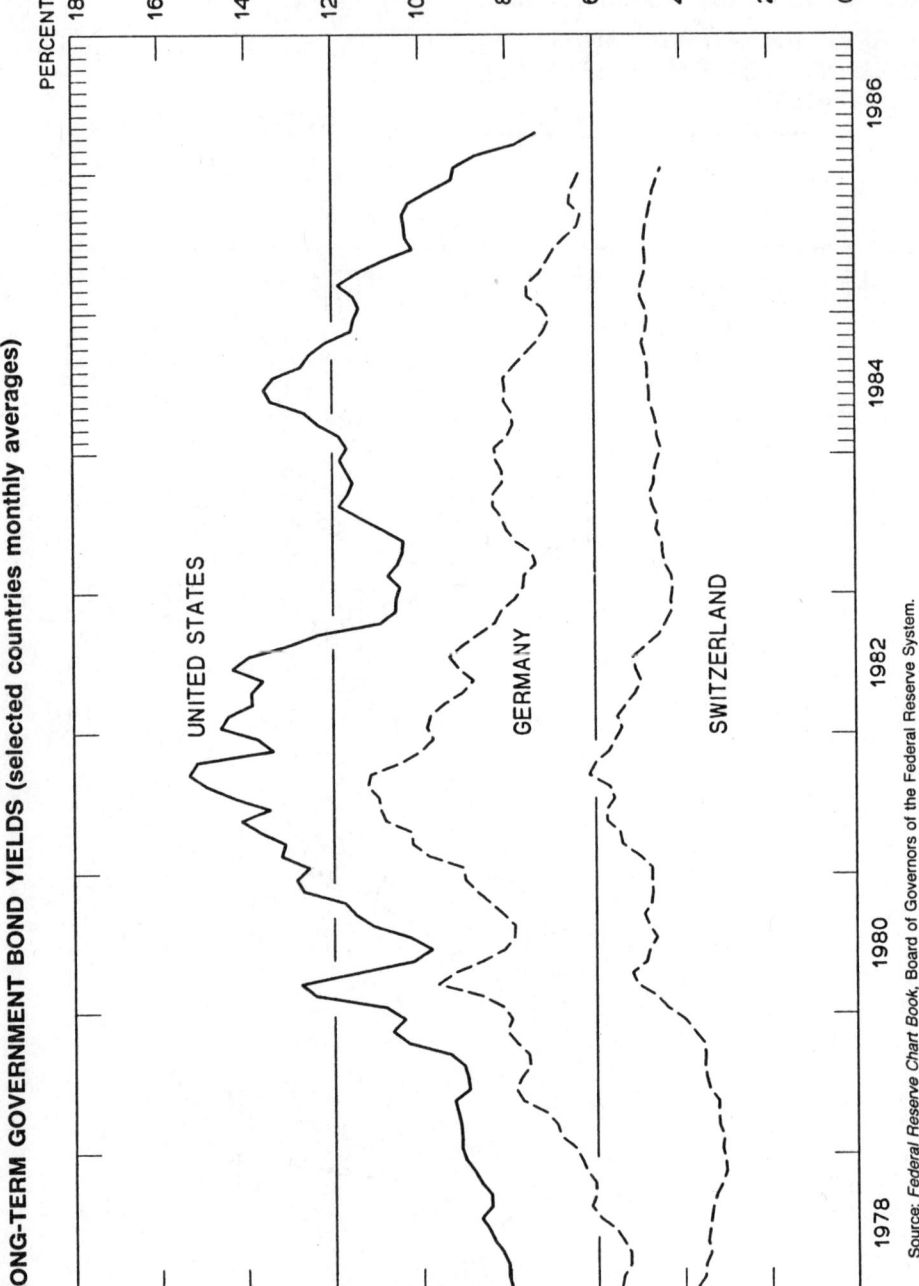

LONG-TERM GOVERNMENT BOND YIELDS (selected countries monthly averages)

PERCENT

UNITED STATES

GERMANY

SWITZERLAND

18 16 14 12 10 8 6 4 2 0

1978   1980   1982   1984   1986

Source: *Federal Reserve Chart Book*, Board of Governors of the Federal Reserve System.

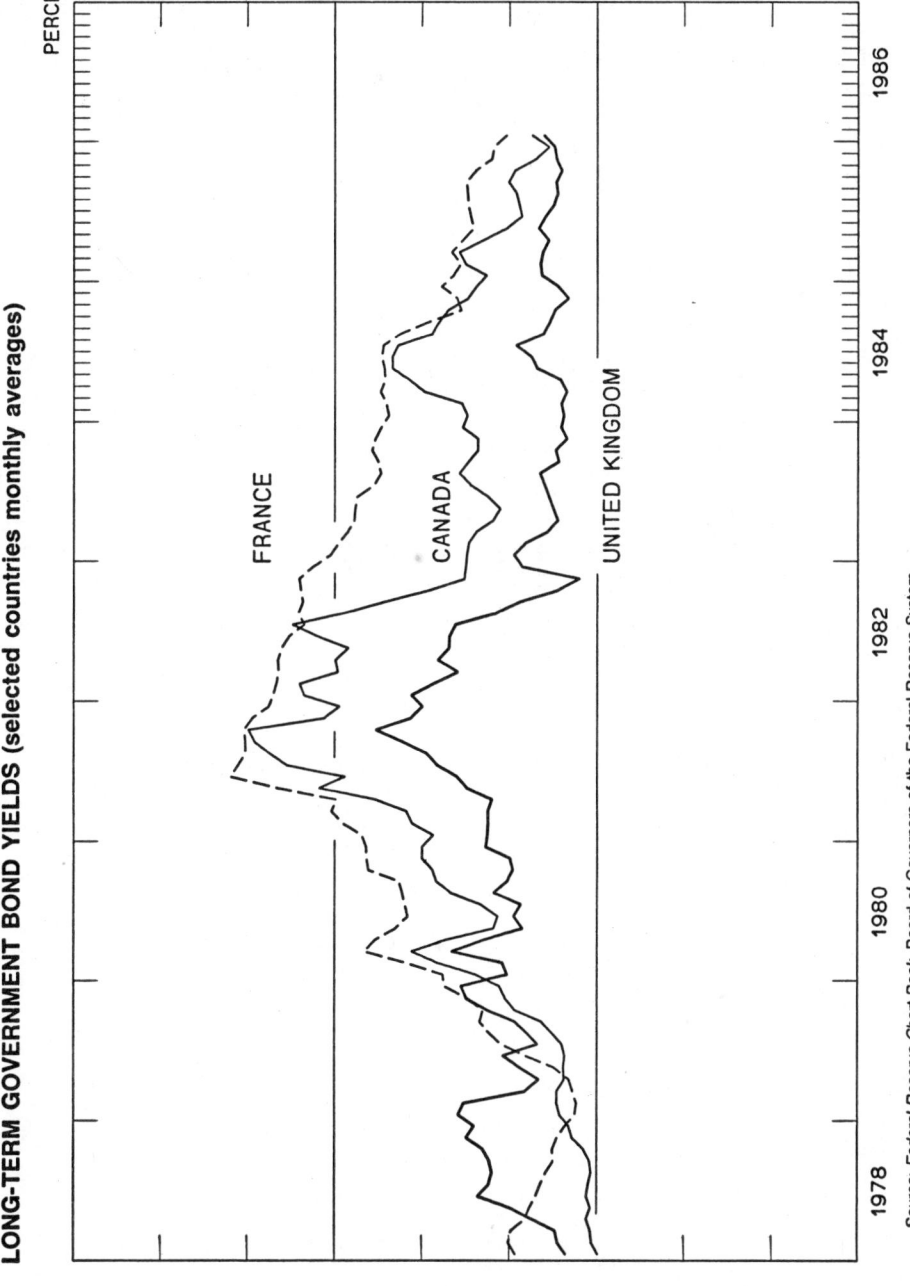

LONG-TERM GOVERNMENT BOND YIELDS (selected countries monthly averages)

PERCENT

FRANCE

CANADA

UNITED KINGDOM

Source: Federal Reserve Chart Book, Board of Governors of the Federal Reserve System.

FOREIGN TREASURY BILL RATES (bond-equivalent yields, at or near end of month)

	1982 Dec	1983 Dec	1984 Dec	1985 Nov	1985 Dec	1986 Jan	1986 Feb	1986 Mar	1986 Apr	1986 May	1986 Jun
United States	8.15	9.28	7.99	7.40	7.25	7.15	7.23	6.50	6.24	6.45	6.13
Canada	9.80	9.71	9.84	8.85	9.24	10.55	11.55	10.19	9.02	8.33	8.59
Belgium	12.42	11.00	10.90	8.72	9.89	9.89	9.89	9.89	8.38	7.71	7.45
Ireland	15.25	12.01	15.10	10.41	11.15	14.32	15.02	12.08	9.69	8.76	9.16
Italy	19.11	16.95	14.69	13.16	13.10	13.73	13.59	13.15	12.39	11.23	10.78
Netherlands	5.63	5.63	5.88	5.88	5.69	5.72	6.13	5.56	6.88	6.50	5.88
Spain	15.28	14.46	12.00	9.25	9.25	9.25	9.25	9.25	9.25	n.a.	n.a.
Sweden	12.90	11.75	11.83	13.28	12.49	11.70	11.14	10.63	10.19	9.90	9.85
United Kingdom	9.96	9.04	9.33	11.33	11.49	12.47	12.21	11.04	10.09	9.56	9.52
Australia	9.39	8.54	12.27	18.45	19.40	18.46	17.03	14.88	12.84	12.78	12.38
Japan	5.42	4.91	4.91	4.91	4.91	4.91	4.41	3.90	3.39	3.39	3.39
New Zealand	11.25	7.80	13.50	20.02	17.62	18.27	18.48	21.64	20.41	17.34	15.64
South Africa	14.62	18.43	21.94	12.90	12.99	12.02	11.96	11.97	11.58	11.02	10.75
Brazil	115.40	179.15	273.03	245.33	379.77	n.a.	n.a.	15.40	16.79	15.90	18.60
Mexico	57.44	53.78	48.67	70.70	72.98	74.89	77.75	78.78	80.84	80.74	88.50
Philippines	14.54	15.99	47.14	16.63	16.45	16.68	23.43	23.56	19.65	15.79	n.a.
Singapore	2.74	2.59	2.91	2.89	2.94	2.96	2.80	2.64	2.58	2.35	2.42

Source: World Financial Markets, a publication of Morgan Guaranty Trust Company of New York.

FOREIGN MONEY-MARKET RATES (bond-equivalent yields on major short-term (mostly 3–4-month) money-market instruments other than Treasury bills, at or near end of month)

	1982	1983	1984	1985		1986					
	Dec	Dec	Dec	Nov	Dec	Jan	Feb	Mar	Apr	May	Jun
United States	8.94	9.89	8.34	8.01	8.01	7.91	7.80	7.34	7.17	6.96	6.75
Canada	9.95	9.87	10.10	9.25	9.45	11.25	12.05	10.80	8.85	8.65	8.65
Belgium	12.52	11.15	10.85	8.72	9.89	9.89	9.89	8.52	8.11	7.71	7.40
France	12.75	12.19	10.69	8.87	9.12	8.93	8.57	8.37	7.50	7.24	7.24
Germany	6.20	6.30	5.75	4.80	4.80	4.60	4.35	4.65	4.60	4.60	4.55
Ireland	15.75	12.19	15.13	10.50	12.00	15.25	16.25	14.63	10.75	10.25	9.25
Italy	19.00	17.88	16.88	14.63	15.13	16.00	16.75	15.00	12.75	12.13	12.25
Netherlands	5.25	6.00	5.75	5.94	5.75	5.81	5.88	5.50	5.56	6.00	6.19
Portugal	15.05	24.11	24.57	22.49	20.71	18.28	18.55	18.75	17.76	17.07	n.a.
Spain	16.98	19.00	12.21	10.47	10.51	10.68	10.72	11.59	12.27	11.63	12.06
Switzerland	3.88	3.88	5.00	4.13	4.75	4.43	4.13	4.06	4.50	4.69	5.50
United Kingdom	10.50	9.31	9.88	11.50	12.75	12.75	12.25	11.06	10.13	9.69	9.75
Australia	9.85	9.05	12.90	18.65	19.75	18.75	18.00	16.20	16.10	14.85	14.84
Japan	6.96	6.45	6.33	7.55	7.03	6.12	5.92	5.16	4.53	4.66	4.64
New Zealand	16.50	11.75	15.00	20.20	20.00	23.50	23.50	22.30	21.30	16.10	n.a.
South Africa	15.26	19.12	22.78	13.20	n.a.	12.55	12.40	12.35	11.95	11.25	10.80
Chile	55.90	20.68	20.68	19.56	22.42	19.56	19.56	14.03	19.56	12.68	14.03
Hong Kong	9.25	14.88	8.25	6.50	6.50	6.63	6.81	7.25	7.81	6.02	6.75
Indonesia	18.50	19.50	19.00	14.50	15.00	14.50	14.50	20.25	16.50	16.00	15.00
Korea	8.00	8.00	8.00	8.00	8.00	8.00	8.00	8.00	8.00	8.00	8.00
Malaysia	8.50	9.80	10.30	8.25	8.20	8.30	8.70	8.75	15.00	9.80	10.00
Philippines	15.96	15.61	33.21	22.45	14.61	23.05	26.05	26.45	19.32	14.57	n.a.
Singapore	8.69	8.44	7.00	5.44	5.88	5.53	5.31	5.00	4.94	5.06	4.88
Taiwan	n.a.	8.07	7.85	4.51	4.10	3.17	3.10	3.37	3.99	3.58	3.68
Thailand	12.25	16.00	12.00	15.00	15.50	11.50	11.25	10.00	10.00	9.50	8.50

Source: *World Financial Markets*, a publication of Morgan Guaranty Trust Company of New York.

FOREIGN GOVERNMENT BOND YIELDS (long-term issues, at or near end of month)

	1982 Dec	1983 Dec	1984 Dec	1985 Nov	1985 Dec	1986 Jan	Feb	Mar	Apr	May	Jun
United States	10.61	12.00	11.61	10.06	9.49	9.45	8.31	7.50	7.70	8.37	7.79
Canada	11.69	12.02	11.66	10.34	10.04	10.49	9.96	9.54	9.32	9.52	9.42
Austria	8.81	8.02	8.04	7.55	7.61	7.62	7.68	7.63	9.00	7.14	7.19
Belgium	12.66	11.89	11.56	9.43	9.60	9.62	9.38	8.41	7.46	7.93	7.86
Denmark	20.14	12.96	14.60	10.50	9.67	10.12	9.27	9.26	8.63	10.17	10.17
Finland	10.64	11.16	10.73	10.50	10.58	9.74	9.96	8.77	8.89	8.27	8.27
France	15.40	13.96	12.70	11.22	11.33	10.79	10.00	9.19	8.53	8.58	8.65
Germany	7.90	8.38	7.17	6.79	6.57	6.64	6.32	6.21	5.78	6.31	6.17
Ireland	14.54	14.25	14.90	12.10	11.84	11.92	10.68	9.35	8.57	9.17	9.31
Italy	19.70	17.69	14.52	13.70	13.66	13.43	13.80	13.35	12.27	10.87	10.85
Netherlands	8.16	8.58	7.72	7.01	6.96	6.81	6.84	6.44	6.15	6.39	6.38
Norway	13.32	12.50	12.00	12.70	13.10	13.10	13.20	12.80	12.80	12.80	13.10
Portugal	16.63	22.11	22.23	n.a.	n.a.	n.a.	n.a.	n.a.	n.a.	n.a.	n.a.
Spain	15.46	17.25	13.93	12.12	12.30	12.35	12.36	12.22	12.06	11.44	10.98
Sweden	13.01	12.30	12.04	13.10	12.11	12.23	11.60	10.81	9.81	10.06	9.79
Switzerland	4.23	4.53	4.60	4.53	4.42	4.42	4.27	4.16	4.24	4.39	4.49
United Kingdom	10.62	9.94	10.25	10.17	10.35	10.56	9.83	8.75	8.73	9.11	9.32
Australia	13.00	13.65	13.50	15.05	14.85	14.10	13.70	12.60	12.25	12.65	12.85
Japan	7.96	7.45	6.47	6.36	5.92	5.57	5.33	4.67	4.79	5.57	n.a.
New Zealand	12.84	10.50	16.90	17.10	17.10	18.15	18.60	18.90	16.80	15.15	15.20
South Africa	11.31	13.64	16.55	17.50	n.a.	17.57	17.30	17.65	17.40	17.09	16.99
Philippines	13.64	14.47	18.54	n.a.	n.a.	n.a.	n.a.	n.a.	n.a.	n.a.	n.a.
Venezuela	15.00	13.50	14.00	12.00	12.00	12.25	12.00	12.00	12.00	12.00	12.00

Source: World Financial Markets, a publication of Morgan Guaranty Trust Company of New York.

FOREIGN CORPORATE BOND YIELDS (long-term issues, at or near end of month)

	1982	1983	1984	1985		1986					
	Dec	Dec	Dec	Nov	Dec	Jan	Feb	Mar	Apr	May	Jun
United States	11.75	12.63	12.25	10.75	10.15	10.38	9.00	8.63	9.00	9.20	9.00
Canada	12.74	12.89	12.42	10.98	10.74	12.08	12.95	12.46	12.24	10.35	10.10
France	15.86	14.35	12.94	11.68	11.76	11.38	10.81	10.13	9.82	9.44	9.85
Germany	8.20	8.30	7.20	7.00	6.90	6.80	6.80	6.70	6.60	6.40	6.50
Netherlands	7.80	8.51	7.51	n.a.	n.a.	n.a.	6.86	6.53	n.a.	n.a.	n.a.
Norway	14.13	13.25	12.75	13.50	14.00	14.00	14 82	14.00	14.00	14.00	14.25
Spain	17.10	20.07	18.32	15.80	14.92	14.87	12.73	14.40	13.91	13.99	13.71
Sweden	13.37	12.21	12.33	13.50	13.25	13.21	4.71	11.99	10.93	11.20	11.04
Switzerland	5.80	4.92	5.09	4.99	4.93	4.78	10.88	4.64	4.98	4.77	4.83
United Kingdom	12.34	11.57	11.64	11.18	11.47	11.59	10.88	9.96	9.80	10.05	10.32
Japan	7.55	7.09	6.21	7.56	6.90	6.70	5.96	5.40	5.14	5.20	5.14
Korea	16.00	14.20	15.00	13.60	13.60	13.00	12.60	12.40	12.40	12.80	12.80
Venezuela	18.00	18.00	18.00	17.00	17.00	17.50	17.00	17.00	17.00	17.00	17.00

Source: World Financial Markets, a publication of Morgan Guaranty Trust Company of New York.

Composition of Dow Jones 20 Bonds Averages

The Dow Jones Bond Averages are a simple arithmetic average compiled daily by using the New York Exchange closing bond prices. A list of the bonds on which these averages are based follows:

10 PUBLIC UTILITIES

Name	Coupon	Age
Alabama Pwr	9¾%	2004
Amer T&T	8.8%	2005
Comwlth Ed	8¾%	2005
Cons Ed	7.9%	2001
Cons Pwr	9¾%	2006
Detroit Edison	9%	1999
Mich Bell	7%	2012
Pac G&E	7¾%	2005
Phil Elec	7⅜%	2001
Pub Svc Ind	9.6%	2005

10 INDUSTRIALS

Name	Coupon	Age
BankAm	7⅞%	2003
Beth Steel	6⅞%	1999
Dow Chem	4.35%	1988
Exxon	6%	1997
Ford Mtr	8⅛%	1990
GM Accept	12%	2005
NCR	4⅜%	1987
Pfizer	9⅛%	2000
Socony	4⅛%	1993
Weyerhaeusr	5.20%	1991

Source: Reprinted by courtesy of Barron's *Business and Financial Weekly.*

Components Barron's Confidence Index

Barron's Confidence Index is the ratio of the average yield to maturity on best grade corporate bonds to the intermediate grade corporate bonds average yield to maturity. The ratio is high when investors are confidently buying bonds below top grade and low when investors take refuge in high grade bond issues. A list of the bonds on which the confidence index is based follows:

Best Grade Bonds

Name	Coupon	Age
AT&T	8¾%	2000
Balt G&E	8⅜%	2006
Exxon Pipeline	9%	2004
Gen. Elec.	8½%	2004
GMAC	8¼%	2006
IBM	9⅜%	2004
Ill. Bell T	7⅝%	2006
Pfizer	9¼%	2000
Proc. & G.	8¼%	2005
Sears Roe	7⅞%	2007

Intermediate Grade Bonds

Name	Coupon	Age
Ala Power	9¾%	2004
Beneficial Corp.	9%	2005
Cater Trac	8%	2001
Comwlth Ed	9⅛%	2008
Crown Zell	9¼%	2005
Firestone	9¼%	2004
GTE	9⅜%	1999
Union Carbide	8½%	2005
US Steel	7¾%	2001
Woolworth	9%%	1999

Monetary Aggregates Defined

Money supply data has been revised and expanded to reflect the Federal Reserve's redefinition of the monetary aggregates. The redefinition was prompted by the emergence in recent years of new monetary assets—for example, negotiable order of withdrawal (NOW) accounts and money-market mutual fund shares—and alterations in the basic character of established monetary assets—for example, the growing similarity of and substitution between the deposits of thrift institutions and those of commercial banks.

M1-A has been discontinued with M1-B now designated as "M-1." M-1 is currency in circulation plus all checking accounts including those which pay interest, such as NOW accounts. M-1 excludes deposits due to foreign commercial banks and official institutions.

M-2 as redefined adds to M1-B overnight repurchase agreements (RPs) issued by commercial banks and certain overnight Eurodollars (those issued by Carribbean branches of member banks) held by U.S. nonbank residents, money-market mutual fund shares, and savings and small-denomination time deposits (those issued in denominations of less than $100,000) at all depository institutions. Depository institutions are commercial banks (including U.S. agencies and branches of foreign banks, Edge Act Corporations, and foreign investment companies), mutual savings banks, savings and loan associations, and credit unions.

M-3 as redefined is equal to new M-2 plus large-denomination time deposits (those issued as in denominations of $100,000 or more) at all depository institutions (including negotiable CDs) plus term RPs issued by commercial banks and savings and loan associations.

L, the very broad measure of liquid assets, equals new M-3 plus other liquid assets consisting of other Eurodollar holdings of U.S. nonbank residents, bankers acceptances, commercial paper, savings bonds, and marketable liquid Treasury obligations.

Federal Reserve Banks

Federal Reserve Bank of

BOSTON	600 Atlantic Avenue, Boston, Massachusetts 02106—(617) 973-3462
NEW YORK	33 Liberty Street (Federal Reserve P.O. Station). New York, New York 10045—(212) 791-5823 (Telephone 24 hours a day, including Saturday & Sunday)
Buffalo Branch	160 Delaware Avenue (P.O. Box 961), Buffalo, New York 14240—(716) 849-5046
PHILADELPHIA	100 North Sixth Street (P.O. Box 90), Philadelphia, Pennsylvania 19105—(215) 574-6580
CLEVELAND	1455 East Sixth Street (P.O. Box 6387), Cleveland, Ohio 44101—(216) 241-2800
Cincinnati Branch	150 East Fourth Street (P.O. Box 999), Cincinnati, Ohio 45201—(513) 721-4787 ext 333
Pittsburgh Branch	717 Grant Street (P.O. Box 867), Pittsburgh, Pennsylvania 15230—(412) 261-7864
RICHMOND	701 East Byrd Street (P.O. Box 27622), Richmond, Virginia 23261— (804) 643-1250
Baltimore Branch	502 South Sharp Street, Baltimore, Maryland 21201 (P.O. Box 1378), Baltimore, Maryland 21203—(301) 576-3300
Charlotte Branch	401 South Tyron Street (P.O. Box 300), Charlotte, North Carolina 28230—(704) 373-0200
ATLANTA	104 Marietta Street, N.W., (P.O. Box 1731) Atlanta, Georgia 30301—(404) 586-8657
Birmingham Branch	1801 Fifth Avenue, North (P.O. Box 10447), Birmingham, Alabama 35202—(205) 252-3141 ext. 215
Jacksonville Branch	515 Julia Street, Jacksonville, Florida 32231—(904) 632-4245
Miami Branch	9100 N.W. Thirty-sixth Street Extension, Miami, Florida 33178 (P.O. Box 520847), Miami, Florida 33153—(305) 591-2065
Nashville Branch	301 Eighth Avenue, North, Nashville, Tennessee 37203—(615) 259-4006
New Orleans Branch	525 St. Charles Avenue (P.O. Box 61630), New Orleans, Louisiana 70161 (540) 586-1505 ext. 230, 240, 242
CHICAGO	230 South LaSalle Street (P.O. Box 834), Chicago, Illinois 60690—(312) 786-1110 (Telephone 24 hours a day, including Saturday & Sunday)
Detroit Branch	160 Fort Street, West (P.O. Box 1059), Detroit, Michigan 48231—(313) 961-6880 ext. 372, 373
ST. LOUIS	411 Locust Street (P.O. Box 442), St. Louis, Missouri 63166—(314) 444-8444
Little Rock Branch	325 West Capitol Avenue (P.O. Box 1261), Little Rock, Arkansas 72203—(501) 372-5451 ext. 270
Louisville Branch	410 South Fifth Street (P.O. Box 32710), Louisville, Kentucky 40232 (502) 587-7351 ext. 237, 301
Memphis Branch	200 North Main Street (P.O. Box 407), Memphis, Tennessee 38101—(800) 238-5293 ext. 225
MINNEAPOLIS	250 Marquette Avenue, Minneapolis, Minnesota 55480—(612) 340-2051
Helena Branch	400 North Park Avenue, Helena, Montana 59601—(406) 442-3860
KANSAS CITY	925 Grand Avenue (Federal Reserve Station), Kansas City, Missouri 64198—(816) 881-2783
Denver Branch	1020 16th Street (P.O. Box 5228, Terminal Annex), Denver, Colorado 80217 (303) 292-4020
Oklahoma City Branch	226 Northwest Third Street (P.O. Box 25129), Oklahoma City, Oklahoma 73125—(405) 235-1721 ext. 182
Omaha Branch	102 South Seventeenth Street, Omaha, Nebraska 68102—(402) 341-3610 ext. 242

DALLAS

400 South Akard Street (Station K), Dallas, Texas 75222—(214) 651-6177

El Paso Branch

301 East Main Street (P.O. Box 100), El Paso, Texas 79999—(915) 544-4730 ext. 57

Houston Branch

1701 San Jacinto Street (P.O. Box 2578), Houston, Texas 77001—(713) 659-4433 ext 19, 74, 75, 76

San Antonio Branch

126 East Nueva Street (P.O. Box 1417), San Antonio, Texas 78295—(512) 224-2141 ext 61, 66

SAN FRANCISCO

101 Market Street (P.O. Box 7702), San Francisco, California 94120—(415) 392-6639

Los Angeles Branch

409 West Olympic Boulevard (P.O. Box 2077, Terminal Annex), Los Angeles, California 90051 (213) 683-8563

Portland Branch

915 S.W. Stark Street (P.O. Box 3436), Portland, Oregon 97208—(503) 228-7584

Salt Lake City Branch

120 South State Street (P.O. Box 30780), Salt Lake City, Utah 84130—(801) 355-3131

Seattle Branch

1015 Second Avenue (P.O. Box 3567), Seattle, Washington 98124—(206) 442-1650

TREASURY

General information concerning Treasury Securities and requests for forms:
Bureau of the Public Debt, Dept. F
Washington, D.C. 20226
Telephone: (202) 287-4113

Specific questions concerning Bills:
Bureau of the Public Debt, Dept. X
Washington, D.C. 20226
Telephone: (202) 287-4113

Specific questions concerning registered Notes or Bonds:
Bureau of the Public Debt, Dept. A
Washington, D.C. 20226
Telephone: (202) 287-4113

Options and Futures

What Are Stock Options?

There are two types of stock options—call and put. A call option is the right to buy a specified number of shares of a stock at a given price before a specific date. A put option is the right to sell a specific number of shares of a stock at a given price before a specific date. Options, unlike a futures contract, are a right *not an obligation* to buy or sell stock. The price at which the stock may be bought or sold is referred to as the exercise (or striking) price. The date at which the option expires is the *expiration* date. The term "in-the-money" option refers to either a call option with an exercise price less than that of the market price of the stock, or a put option with an exercise price above the market price of the stock.

Expiration months are set at intervals of three months for the cycles: the January–April–July–October cycle, February–May–August–November cycle, and the March–June–September–December cycle. Options expire at 11:59 P.M. Eastern Standard Time on the Saturday immediately following the third Friday of the expiration month.

The exercise prices are set at 5 point (dollar) intervals for stocks trading below $50, 10 point intervals for stocks trading between $50 to $200, and 20 point intervals for securities trading above $200. Initial exercise prices are set above and below the price of the security. Thus, if a security is priced at 32½ on the New York Stock Exchange at the time new options are opened, the opening exercise prices would be set at 30 and 40. If the price of the security is close to a standard exercise price, three prices are set: at the standard price, as well as above and below the latter.

Standard option contracts are written for 100 shares of stock of the underlying security. The price at which the seller (writer) agrees to sell an option to the buyer is called the *premium*. The premium is quoted *per share* of the underlying stock so that the price per contract is 100 times the quote.

After the option is issued, the premium will fluctuate with the price of the stocks. With call options the premium will increase with an increase in the price of stock. With put options the premium will increase when the stock price declines. The reason should be clear from the following examples. Assume that in January a July call option is written at the exercise price of 50 ($50 per share) on the XYZ Corporation stock. We assume that the stock is selling at $51. The call option writer (seller) asks and receives a premium of $2 ($200 per option contract). After brokerage commission on the sale (say $25 per contract) the option writer nets a profit of $175 per contract. The call option buyer pays $200 for the contract plus the commission or $225. Assume that the stock increases to 60 per share. The option holder (buyer) can, in principle, purchase the stock at 50 (the Exercise price) and sell it at 60 netting a profit on transaction of $10 per share (neglecting commissions). Clearly the call option has acquired increased value which will be reflected in the premium (option price). Let us assume that the premium increases from 2 to 10 ($200 to $1,000 per contract). If the option holder now sells the option, he will make a profit (after commissions) of $750 on a $250 investment ($200 premium and $50 commission).

Alternatively, the option holder may elect to exercise the option and acquire the shares at 50 (the exercise price). The option writer must then deliver 100 shares of XYZ Corporation at $50 per share.

If the stock price drops below the exercise price and remains so until expiration of the option, the call option buyer can lose his entire investment. Sometimes the loss may be reduced if the option is sold before it matures. The holder then is said to have *closed out* his position.

Similar arguments apply to put options. In this case the option holder benefits if the price of the stock decreases below the exercise price. Assume that the above stock drops to 40. The put holder could, in principle, buy the stock at 40 and sell it at 50 (the exercise price) to the put writer. The put holder would make a profit of $10 per share (neglecting commissions). The put premium would reflect this situation and, as a result, increase.

Instead of selling the option and taking a profit, the put holder may elect to exercise the option and sell 100 shares to the put writer who must purchase these shares at the 50 exercise price.

If the market price of the stock is greater than the exercise price when the put option expires, the holder will lose his investment.

Options are traded on the Chicago Board of Options Exchange, the American Stock Exchange, the Pacific Stock Exchange and the Philadelphia Stock Exchange.

How to Read Option Quotations

(1) Option & NY Close	(2) Strike Price	(3) Calls—Last			(4) Puts—Last		
		Aug	Nov	Feb	Aug	Nov	Feb
Slb							
94¾	100	2½	7	9½	5⅞	7¾	a
94¾	110	⅝	3⅜	5½	a	16	a
94¾	120	⅛	1⅛	b	a	a	b
94¾	130	1/16	b	b	a	b	b
Skylin	15	3⅜	4	a	a	⅝	a
17⅝	20	⅝	1 11/16	2¼	a	a	a
Southn	10	a	2⅜	2 7/16	b	b	b

Source: Reprinted by permission of *The Wall Street Journal*
© Dow Jones and Company, Inc., 1981. All rights reserved.

(1) The name of the company in abbreviated form. Below the company name is the New York or American Exchange closing price of the stock in terms of ⅛ of a dollar.
(2) The striking (exercise) price of the option.
(3) The expiration month of the call option, beneath which is the option's premium (price) per share of stock. Contracts are for 100 shares of stock so that, for example, the price of a contract quoted as 2⅛ ($2.125 per share) is $212.50. Options expire on the Saturday following the third Friday of the expiration month. The premium does not include commissions.
(4) The same as item 3, but for a put option. The letter *a* means the option was not traded that day, and *b* means the option is not offered.

Stock Market Futures*

Standard & Poor's 500 Stock Index futures† combine the unique aspects of the futures market with the opportunities of stock ownership and stock options by helping many investors manage their inherent stock market risks, and at the same time allowing others to participate in broad market moves. S&P 500 Index futures can play an important role in an individual's or institution's overall market strategy.

Stock ownership is subject to several risks. Lower earnings reports or changes in industry fundamentals can cause severe declines in individual issues. Or, a promising industry or company might drop because the entire market is heading down. A myriad of decisions go into individual stock selection—but the first question is usually what is the state and direction of the entire market.

The introduction of the Standard & Poor's 500 Stock Index contract allows investors to hedge, and therefore, virtually eliminate their portfolio exposure in a declining market without disturbing their holdings. At the same time, others can purchase or sell the contract according to their expectations of future market activity. This simultaneous ability to hedge the risks of stock ownership and to take advantage of broad market moves creates opportunities for everyone with positions in or opinions about the stock market.

A NEW MARKET FOR TODAY'S INVESTOR

S&P 500 Index futures are traded on the Index and Option Market division of the Chicago Mercantile Exchange. One of the largest commodity exchanges in the world, the CME introduced financial futures trading in 1972 when it formed the International Monetary Market to trade contracts in foreign currencies. Later, the IMM added futures contracts in Gold, 90-Day Treasury Bills, Three-Month Domestic Certificates of Deposit, and Three-Month Eurodollar Time Deposits.

THE S&P 500 INDEX

The Standard & Poor's Stock Price Index has been the standard by which professional portfolio managers and individuals have measured their performance for 65 years. Begun in 1917 as an index based on 200 stocks, the list was expanded to 500 issues in 1957.

Currently, the Index is one of the U.S. Commerce Department's 12 leading economic indicators.

The S&P 500 Index is made up of 400 industrial, 40 public utilities, 20 transportation, and 40 financial companies and represents approximately 80% of the value of all issues traded on the New York Stock Exchange.

The S&P 500 Index is calculated by giving more "weight" to companies with more stock issued and outstanding in the market. Basically, each stock's price is multiplied by its number of shares outstanding. This assures that each

* Although every attempt has been made to ensure the accuracy of the information in this section, the Chicago Mercantile Exchange assumes no responsibility for any errors or omissions. All matters pertaining to rules and specifications herein are made subject to and are superseded by official Exchange rules.

† Editor's Note: Futures based on the Value Line (Kansas City Exchange) and the New York Stock Exchange (New York Futures Exchange) indices are also traded. The principles are the same as with the S&P 500 futures.

Source: *Opportunities in Stock Futures*, Index and Option Market, Chicago Mercantile Exchange, 444 West Jackson Street, Chicago, IL 60606.

stock influences the Index with the same importance that it carries in the actual stock market.

The Index is calculated by multiplying the shares outstanding of each of the 500 stocks by its market price. These amounts are then totaled and compared to a 1941–43 base period.

Calculations are performed continually while the market is open for each of the 500 stocks in the Index. The resulting Index is available minute-by-minute via quote machines throughout the world.

WHAT IS FUTURES TRADING?

The practice of buying or selling goods at prices agreed upon today, but with actual delivery made in the future, dates back to the 12th century. In the United States, organized futures exchanges were active as early as the 1840s. Today, the markets offer futures in grains, meats, lumber, metals, poultry products, currencies and interest-bearing securities.

The ability to contract today at a fixed price for future delivery performs two vital economic functions: risk transfer and price discovery.

For example, suppose a producer of cattle sees that someone is willing to buy his animals for delivery six months hence at a price that insures him an adequate profit. He decides to sell his production, with delivery after the animal matures, at the contracted price. In the process, he has locked in a price that is satisfactory to him and has insulated himself against the risk that the price may fall. In other words, he has transferred the risk of lower prices to someone else. Conversely, the purchaser of his animals has locked in his price and is assured that he will not have to pay a higher price in the future. This transaction could take place directly between the two men, or could be accomplished through futures trading at the CME—without the need for buyer and seller to actually meet. The open public trading system at the CME makes it easy to discover what the market currently considers to be a fair price for future delivery.

If the sale takes place on the Chicago Mercantile Exchange, the Exchange guarantees that both parties adhere to their agreement by placing itself and its resources between them. The Exchange thus becomes the buyer and the seller of the contract. This assures both parties that the contract will be carried out because the Exchange stands behind both parts of the agreement.

When delivery day arrives, the product is delivered to designated delivery points and is inspected to make sure it is of the quality stipulated by the contract. The seller receives payment at the agreed price and buyer receives the produce.

Since full payment does not occur until the delivery day, the performance of both parties to the contract requires a good faith deposit or performance bond—known as the margin—when the contract is entered. Margins usually amount to a small percentage of the contract's total face value.

This payment differs from margin for stock purchases in that it is not a partial payment. It serves as a guarantee for both buyer and seller that there are sufficient funds on either side to cover adverse price movements that might otherwise bring the ability to meet contract terms into question.

At the close of business each day, each futures position is revalued at the contract's current closing price. This price is compared to the previous day's close (or if an initial position, the purchase or sale price) and the net gain or loss is calculated. Gains and losses are taken or made from the margin account each day in cash. There are no paper gains or losses in futures trading. If a margin account falls below a specified level, futures traders are required to deposit more money to maintain their positions.

All futures market participants should understand the operation of futures markets and consult with a Registered Commodity Representative before opening a futures trading account.

The S&P 500 Index futures contract is quoted in terms of the actual Index, but carries a face value of 500 times the Index. The contract does not move point-for-point with the actual Index, but it says close enough to act as an effective proxy for the Index, and by extension, for the stock market as a whole.

If, for example, the futures price is quoted at 108.75, then the face value of the contract would be $54,375 (500 × 108.75). Minimum futures price increments, or movements, are .05 of the Index or $25. So if the futures quote is at 108.75, trades can continue to take place at that level, or move to 108.80 or to 108.70, with each .05 move equal to $25.

Trading opens at 9:00 A.M. and closes at 3:15 P.M. (Chicago time) with contracts trading for settlement in March, June, September and December. The final settlement day is the third Thursday of the contract month. At the close of business on that day all open positions have one final mark-to-market calculation—only on this day the expiration of the contract is marked to the actual closing level of the S&P 500 Index itself. Unlike traditional commodities, there is no physical delivery of the underlying commodity or resulting payment for the commodity in S&P 500 futures.

It is this unique cash settlement feature of the S&P 500 futures contract that eliminates the prohibitively expensive costs of delivering 500 individual issues in varying amounts. Since there are little or no delivery costs, investors are assured that there will be no institutional factors to influence the futures contract's price. Thus, the price of the futures contract will reflect the current expectations about the direction of future stock prices. The International Monetary Market division of the CME pioneered this innovative concept in 1981, when its Eurodollar Time Deposit contract became the first cash settlement futures contract ever traded.

The S&P 500 futures contract should be viewed as a complement to equity ownership, not a substitute for it. Among the many benefits of S&P futures is the hedging ability that holders of stock can employ to provide an effective, cost efficient means of protecting security holdings against temporary market declines rather than selling and disturbing stock holdings. In addition, investors find the futures market equally as liquid for both buyers and sellers. Unlike the stock exchanges, short sellers do not require an up-tic before a trade can take place and there are no additional margin requirements.

SITUATIONS & STRATEGIES

Outright positions, either long or short, spreading and hedging are all uses for S&P futures. The contract also offers an unusually large number of hedging strategies when combined with equity portfolios and options. The following examples will show some of these uses in more detail.

LONG POSITION

Situation: An individual sees that interest rates are declining, the economy is firming and believes the entire market is undervalued. He notes that the S&P 500 futures contract for September delivery is at 108.85 and the actual S&P 500 Index is at 108.70.

It is apparent that most futures market participants also believe a move up is imminent. As supply and demand factors are balanced in an open marketplace, the intrinsic value of the September contract is established. The market is willing to pay a slight premium (.15) for the futures contract over the actual Index.

He calls his Registered Commodity Representative, enters an order to buy one September S&P 500 futures contract at the market and makes a good faith deposit to his account to guarantee his ability to meet his contractual commitment. For purposes of the following example, a margin account balance of $5,000 will be used. Margin requirements for actual positions vary. Individuals should contact their Registered Commodity Representatives for current information.

Day	Position	Cost	S&P Future Closing Price	Gain or (Loss) Points X $5 (.01 equals 1 point)		Account Balance	Cumulative Gain or (Loss)
1	Long one contract	108.85	108.90	.05	$ 25	$5,025	$ 25
2	same	108.85	108.60	(.30)	(150)	4,875	(125)
3	same	108.85	108.40	(.20)	(100)	4,775	(225)
4	same	108.85	107.00	(1.40)	(700)	4,075	(925)
5	same	108.85	108.00	1.00	500	4,575	(425)
6	same	108.85	108.70	.70	350	4,925	(75)
7	same	108.85	109.50	.80	400	5,325	325
Sub Total Period one		108 85	109 50	65	$325	$5,325	$325

Period one: Our investor was a little off on his timing and his margin account was debited each day that losses occurred. If his margin balance had fallen to the maintenance minimum ($2,000 per contract) in this example he would have been required to make an additional payment to bring his balance back to the initial margin level ($5,000). As it is, he ended the period with a credit of $325 in cash.

Period two: With minor backing and filling, the trend is up and the S&P futures price closes period two at a level of 115 65

	Position	Cost	S&P Future Closing Price	Gain or (Loss) Points X $5 (.01 equals 1 point)		Account Balance	Cumulative Gain or (Loss)
Sub Total Period Two	Long one contract	108.85	115.65	6.80	$3,400	$8,400	$3,400

Observations: During the first two weeks our investor's judgment of the market was correct and the S&P futures price advanced 680 index points or 6.25% This translated into a gain of $3,400 on his initial investment of $5,000, or a gain of 68%

At this point our investor believes that the market is due for a correction and decides to lock in his profit. He calls his RCR and instructs him to to "cover" his September long position. His broker will then enter a sell order. After the close of business, the Exchange Clearing House will match the investor's previous long position and his new short position for a net zero position. All margins will be returned with cash credited to the investor's account with his broker the next day. Brokerage commissions have not been included in this example, but they are usually extremely reasonable and generally are quoted to include *both* the purchase and sale of the contract

SHORT POSITION

If, instead of a rising market our investor believed that tight money would increase interest rates and the economy was weakening, he might have concluded that the S&P 500 Index

pany's own growth, the expectation is that the growth will be reflected in higher share prices. However carefully constructed and diversified a portfolio may be, it is still subject in varying degrees to the risk that the market will decline. In order to protect principal values in a declin-

Day	Position	Cost	S&P Future Closing Price	Gain or (Loss) Points X $5 (.01 equals 1 point)		Account Balance	Cumulative Gain or (Loss)
	Short one						
1	contract	108.85	110.05	(1.20)	$ 600	$4.400	($ 600)
2	same	108.85	112.50	(2.45)	(1.225)	3.175	(1,825)
3	same	108.85	112.00	(.50)	(250)	3.425	(1,575)
4	same	108.85	109.50	(2.50)	(1.250)	4.675	(325)
5	same	108.85	108.75	.75	375	5.050	50
6	same	108.85	107.40	1.35	675	5.725	725
7	same	108.85	107.05	.35	175	5.900	900
Sub Total		108.85	107.05	1.80	$ 900	$5.900	$ 900

In our hypothetical example. the short position eventually worked. If the price had gone to a closing level of 114.85. the investor's account balance would have dropped to the maintenance margin level of $2.000 and he would have been required to add additional funds to bring his balance back to $5.000.

futures price of 108.85 was an overvaluation and that the price was vulnerable to a decline.

He decides to call his Registered Commodity Representative and enter a sell order for one September S&P 500 Stock Index future. Selling is just as easy as buying in an open outcry market. All bids to buy and offers to sell must be made publicly in the trading arena and are subject to immediate acceptance by any member. This differs greatly from stock exchanges where specialists or market makers require an up-tic from the previous sale to transact a short sale.

Let's again assume the initial margin required is $5,000. The above table shows the status of the short position over the course of seven trading days.

Our investor decides at this point that he wants to cover his short position and lock in his profit. The next morning before the opening of trading, he enters an order to buy one September S&P Index contract to cover his short at the opening.

The opening is down on news that industrial production was weak and his position is covered at 106.55. His gain on his short then amounts to 2.30 at $25 per .05 or $1,150. The money is credited to his account the following day.

REDUCING THE VOLATILITY OF A STOCK PORTFOLIO

One reason for equity ownership is to take advantage of the long-term growth prospects of the company in which stock is purchased. Over time, higher earnings per share might be translated into a higher dividend payout. In the case of a company with a high return on investment and profits that are reinvested in the com-

ing market, investors have traditionally sold stock to raise cash or shifted to more defensive issues with less volatility. These tactics very often are short-run solutions that disturb carefully tailored long-run objectives. S&P 500 Index futures can be used to add protection against a market downturn and allow an investor to maintain his equity holdings based on the prospects of the companies rather than the direction of the market.

SHORT HEDGE AGAINST A DIVERSIFIED PORTFOLIO

Situation: An investor owns a well-diversified portfolio with a current market value of $110,000. The S&P 500 futures contract is at 108.85. The market appears weak and the investor believes that there is substantial downside risk during the next three months. He decides to short S&P 500 futures to protect his portfolio.

Action: The S&P 500 futures contract at 108.85 represents a contract value of $54,425 (500 × 108.85). In order to protect his portfolio, he sells two contracts ($110,000 divided by $54,425 equals 2.02).

This hypothetical example assumed that the volatility of the portfolio very closely matched that of the market as measured by the S&P 500 futures contract prices. In reality, portfolios may be more or less sensitive to market moves. Statistical regression analysis for individual issues and entire portfolios can be calculated to measure past price volatility relative to the market. Expressed as "beta," it is a statistical measure of past movements which may change in the future. However, it is useful when hedging market risk in portfolios that are more volatile than the market.

Day	Position Short 2 Contracts	Closing Price S&P Contract	Gain or (Loss) Contract Points X $5 X 2 Contracts (.01 equals 1 point)		Value of Stock Portfolio	Portfolio Gain or (Loss)
1	108.85	110.05	(1.20)	($1.200)	$111.213	$1.213
18	108.85	109.50	(.65)	(650)	110.657	657
36	108.85	107.40	1.45	1.450	108.535	(1.465)
54	108.85	106.05	2.80	2.800	107.171	(2.829)
72	108.85	103.10	5.75	5.750	104.190	(5.810)
90	108.85	100.65	8.20	8.200	101.714	(8.286)
Position Closed	108.85	100.65	8.20	$8.200	$101.714	($8.286)

Observations: The market dropped and our investor hedged the cash decline in his portfolio with an offsetting gain in his futures position. Of course if he were wrong about the direction of the market and it went up, he would have had losses in his futures positions but his stocks may have participated in the advance. The investor throughout this period, did not have to disturb his holdings and continued to receive his dividend payments.

Let us assume that the S&P 500 has a beta of 1.00, (that is, a given percentage move in the market gives rise to the same percentage move in the S&P 500) and our hypothetical portfolio has a beta of 1.50. Our portfolio's past market action relative to moves in the market was 50% greater than a given move in the general market. To compensate for this greater volatility, our hedger would require more S&P contracts to offset a greater decline in the value of his portfolio. Known as a hedge ratio, the dollar value of the portfolio is divided by the dollar value of the S&P 500 futures contract, the resulting figure is multiplied by the beta of the portfolio. Using our investor's portfolio and having calculated a beta of 1.5, we arrive at three contracts instead of two when the beta was 1.00:

$$\frac{\$110,000}{54,425} \times 1.5 = 3.03 \text{ contracts}$$

Thus, our investor would have sold three contracts to offset the portfolio's greater volatility to the market.

The concept of volatility and hedge ratios also may be applied to industry groupings and individual stocks. However, as the number of individual stock holdings that are being hedged decreases, then the greater is the chance that factors affecting that smaller group will make their prices react differently relative to the market than they have in the past.

ADDITIONAL USES OF THE S&P 500 FUTURES CONTRACT

Spreads: The simultaneous purchase and sale of different contract months to take advantage of perceived price discrepancies is called "spreading." The technique is considered by many to be less volatile than an outright long or short position, and as such, spreads generally carry lower margin requirements.

A characteristic of the futures market is that the closest contract date behaves more like the cash market. (In the S&P 500 futures contract, the cash market is the actual S&P 500 Index.) More distant months or back months have a greater component of their price determined by the expectations of what the price will be in the future.

These changing expectations of price levels of the S&P 500 contract into the future creates spreading opportunities. Options strategists will use the S&P 500 futures contract to reduce market risk when writing uncovered puts and calls. Block traders, investment bankers, stock specialists, options principals and anyone with the risk of stock market volatility, now have a vehicle and a well-capitalized liquid market to buy and sell market risk—the Standard & Poor's 500 Stock Index futures contract.

CONTRACT TERMS SUMMARY

Size	500 times the value of the S&P 500 Index
Delivery	Mark-to-market at closing value of the actual S&P 500 Index on Settlement Date
Hours	9:00 am to 3:15 pm Central Time
Months Traded	March, June, September, December
Clearing House Symbol	SP
Ticker Symbol	SP
Prices	Contract quoted in terms of S&P 500 Index
Minimum Fluctuation in Price	.05 ($25)
Limit Move	3.00 ($1.500)
Last Day of Trading	3rd Thursday of Contract Month
Settlement Date	Last Day of Trading

Understanding the Commodities Market

COMMODITY EXCHANGES

A Commodity Exchange is an organized market of buyers and sellers of various types of commodities. It is public to the extent that anyone can trade through member firms. It provides a trading place for commodities, regulates the trading practices of the members, gathers and transmits price information, inspects and governs commodities traded on the Exchange, supervises warehouses that store the commodity, and provides means for settling disputes between members. All transactions must be conducted in a pit on the Exchange floor within certain hours.

FUTURES CONTRACT

A futures contract is a contract between two parties where the buyer agrees to accept delivery at a specified price from the seller of a particular commodity, in a designated month in the future, if it is not liquidated before the contract reaches maturity. A futures contract is not an option; nothing in it is conditional. Each contract calls for a specified amount, and grade of product. For example: *A person buying a February Pork Belly contract at 52.40 in effect is making a legal obligation, now, to accept delivery of 38,000 pounds of frozen Pork Bellies, to be delivered during the month of February, for which the buyer will pay 52.40 per pound.*

The average trader does not take delivery of a futures contract, since he normally will close out his position before the futures contract matures. As a matter of fact, a survey conducted by a leading exchange has estimated that less than 3% of the contracts traded are settled by actual delivery.

Editor's Note: The scope of the commodities market has been broadened in recent years to include contracts on financial (debt) instruments (T-bills, bonds, etc.) and composite stock market indices such as Value Line, S&P 500, and the New York Stock Exchange. With the stock market index futures, settlement is made in cash in amount based on the underlying index. Cash, not the securities, is used to offset the long and short positions. The cash value of the contract is defined as the index quotation × 500.

THE HEDGER AND SPECULATOR

A hedger buys or sells a futures contract in order to reduce the risk of loss through price

Source: Commodity Educational Services, Division of Commodity Cassettes, Inc., 778 Frontage Road, Northfield, IL 60093.

variation. A short hedger sells a futures contract to protect the possible decline in the actual commodity owned by him. A long hedger purchases a futures contract to protect the possible advance in the value of an actual commodity needed to be purchased in the future.

The speculator is an important factor in the volume of future trading today. He, in effect, voluntarily assumes the risk, which the hedger tries to avoid, with the expectations of making a profit. He is somewhat of an insurance underwriter. The largest number of traders on any commodity exchange is the speculator. In order for the hedger to participate, he must have continuous trading interests and activity in the market. This trading activity stems from the role of the speculator, because he involves himself in buying or selling of futures contracts with the idea of making a profit on the advance or decline of prices. The speculator tries to forecast prices in advance of delivery and is willing to buy or sell on this basis. A speculator involves himself in an inescapable risk.

CAN YOU BE A SPECULATOR?

Now, can you be a speculator? Before considering entering into the futures market as a speculator, there are several facts which you should understand about the market and also about yourself. In order to enter into the futures market, you must understand that you are dealing with a margin account. Margins are as low as 5 to 10% of the total value of the futures contract, so you are obtaining a greater leverage on your capital.

Fluctuations in price are rapid, volatile, and wide. It is possible to make a very large profit in a short period of time, but also, it is possible to take a substantial loss. In fact, surveys taken by the Agricultural Department have shown that up to 75% of the individuals speculating in commodity markets have lost money. This does not mean that some of their trades were not profitable, but after a period of time with a given sum of money they ended up being a loser.

Now taking you as an individual, let us see whether you have the characteristics to become a commodity trader. Number one and the most important is that you do not take money that you have set aside for your future, or money you need daily to support your family or yourself. Number two, and almost equally important, is that you must be willing to assume losses and be willing to assume these losses with such a temperament that it is not going to affect your everyday life. Money used in the futures market should be money that has been set aside for strictly risk purposes, and if this money is not risk capital, your methods of trading could be seriously affected, because you cannot afford to be a loser.

Another very important factor is that you must not feel that you are going to take a thousand, two thousand, five or ten thousand dollars and place this with a brokerage firm and not follow the daily happenings of the market. Price fluctuations are fast, and as stated before, wide, so you must not only be in contact with your Account Executive daily, but know and study the technical facts that may be affecting the particular market in which you are speculating.

The individual who makes his first trade by buying a contract on Monday and selling this contract on the following Wednesday, making six hundred dollars on a $1,000 investment, in a period of two days, suddenly says to himself, *"Where has this market been all my life? Why am I working? Why not just concentrate on this market, if every two days or so I can make six hundred dollars?"* This is a fallacy, since this is an individual that is going to destroy himself and most likely his family. The next trade he will feel confident that because of his first profitable trade the market will always go his way even though he is now showing a loss in his position. He still feels that the market will turn around in his direction. If you become married to a particular commodity futures contract and constantly feel that the losses you are taking at the present time will reverse into profits, you are really fighting the market and in most cases fighting a losing battle. This could lead to disaster. There is a saying that you let your profits ride, but liquidate your losses fast.

In any way that you are uneasy with a position that you are holding, it is better to liquidate it. If, prior to the time of buying or selling a contract, you are not sure that this is the right step to take, do not take it. To protect yourself against this hazard you should pre-decide on every trade and exactly how much you intend to lose.

Another important point is not to involve yourself in too many markets. It is difficult to know all the technical facts and be able to follow numerous markets. In addition, if you are in a winning position, be conservative as to how you add additional contracts or pyramid your position. Being conservative will sometimes cause you to miss certain moves in certain markets and you may feel this to be wrong, but over a long period of time, this conservatism will be profitable to you.

If at this point you feel that you are ready, both financially and mentally to trade commodities, the next step is to begin the actual mechanics of trading a futures contract.

OPENING AN ACCOUNT

The first important factor is to decide which brokerage firm will afford you the best service. To accomplish this, you should do a little research by checking with the various exchanges

about different brokerage firms. You should study their advertising, market letters, and other information. These should all be presented in a business-like manner and have no unwarranted claims, such as a guarantee of profit without indicating the possibility of loss.

The brokerage firm must be able to handle orders on all commodity exchanges. Do not pick just any Account Executive in a firm, but one you feel confident to help you make market decisions. Become acquainted with the Account Executive through phone or personal conversations. His knowledge of the factors entering into the market and the understanding of current market trends are important in your final choice.

After making a decision on the brokerage firm and the Account Executive that would be best for you, contact him and have him send you the literature concerning different contracts, and also, any additional information as to his organization. He will then send you the necessary signature cards required by the firm to open an account, and ask you for a deposit of margin money.

You will be trading in regulated commodities, and margin money will be deposited in a segregated fund at the brokerage firm's bank. A segregated account means that the money will only be used for margin and not for expenses of the brokerage firm.

Now you decide to enter into your first trade. Your Account Executive and you decide to enter into a December Live Cattle contract on the Chicago Mercantile Exchange. Your order will be executed as follows: Your Account Executive will place this order with his order desk who will then transmit the order to the floor of the Chicago Mercantile Exchange. There your order will be executed on the trading floor, in the pit. All technical details connected with the transaction will be handled by the brokerage firm.

Upon filling of your order, the filled order will be transmitted back to your Account Executive, who will then contact you, advising you that you have purchased one December Live Cattle contract at a given price. You will also receive a written confirmation on this transaction. You will **now** show an open position in December Live Cattle on the books of the brokerage firm.

MECHANICS OF A TRADE

Let us go back one step to explain in detail just how your order to buy one December Cattle was handled on the floor of the exchange. All buying and selling in the pit is done by open out-cry, and every price change is reported on the exchange ticker system. Each firm has brokers in the different pits, a pit meaning a trading area for the purpose of buying and selling contracts.

When your order was received on the exchange floor, it was time stamped and then given to a runner. This is a person who takes the order from the desk on the exchange floor and gives it to one of the brokers in the December Cattle trading pit. He is then responsible to the brokerage firm to fill that order, if possible, at the stated price. After filling the order, he then has the runner return it to the desk where it is time stamped and transmitted back to the order desk at the brokerage house, and the filled order is reported to you.

MARGIN

Futures trading requires the trader to place margin with his brokerage firm. Initial margin is required and this amount varies with each commodity. The minimum margin is established by each commodity exchange. Additional funds are needed when the equity of your account falls below this level. This is known as a maintenance margin call.

All margin calls must be met immediately. Normally you will be given a reasonable amount of time to comply with this request. If you do not comply, the firm has the right to liquidate your trades or a sufficient number of trades to restore your account to margin requirements.

The brokerage firm has the right to raise margin requirements to the customer at any time. This is normally done if the price of the commodity is changing sharply or if it is the brokerage firm's opinion that due to the volatility of the market the margin requirement is not sufficient at that particular time.

Most commodity contracts have a minimum fluctuation and also a maximum fluctuation for any one particular day. For example, if you are trading frozen Pork Bellies on the Chicago Mercantile Exchange the fluctuation is considered in points. A point equals three dollars and eighty cents. This means that if you buy a contract at 52.40 and the next price tick is 52.45, you have made a paper profit of five points or nineteen dollars. The maximum fluctuation on a belly contract is 200 points, so your profit or loss cannot exceed in one day more than 200 points from the previous day's settlement. There are exceptions in some commodity contracts, where the spot month has no limit.

Let us assume that you had originally placed in the hands of your brokerage firm two thousand dollars margin money, and that you and your Account Executive decide to purchase a December Live Cattle contract whose initial margin is $1200 with maintenance of $900.00. After the purchase of the contract your account would show initial margin required $1200 dollars with excess funds of eight hundred dollars. At the end of each day the settlement price

of December Cattle would be applied to your purchase price and your account would be adjusted to either an increase due to profit or decrease due to loss in your contract.

Further, assume that in a period of two or three days there is a decline in the price of the December Cattle contract and your account now shows a loss of three hundred dollars. Since maintenance margin is only nine hundred dollars on this contract, you will still show an excess of eight hundred dollars over and above maintenance margin. But, in the next four days suppose there is an additional loss of nine hundred dollars. Your account will now need one hundred dollars to maintain the maintenance margin and four hundred dollars additional in order to bring your account up to initial margin. Your Account Executive, or a man from the margin department of the brokerage firm will then contact you, stating that you must place additional money with the firm in order to maintain the December Cattle contract.

At this point, you must decide whether you should continue with the contract, feeling that it may be profitable in the next few days, and thus sending the brokerage firm the required four hundred dollars to maintain your position, or whether to assume your loss and sell the contract.

Let us assume that you decide to sell your December contract at this point and that the selling price causes a loss of four hundred dollars. Added to this loss would be the commission of forty dollars, so your total loss on the transaction would be four hundred forty dollars. A confirmation and purchase and sales statement will be sent to you, showing the original price paid for the contract, the price for which it was sold, the gross loss of four hundred dollars plus the commission of forty dollars making the total loss four hundred forty dollars, and your new ledger balance on deposit with the firm as fifteen hundred sixty dollars.

As shown in our example, commission was charged only when the contract was closed out. A single commission is charged for each round-turn transaction consisting of the creation and liquidation of a single contract.

CONTROLLED, DISCRETIONARY, AND MANAGED ACCOUNTS

There are two methods of trading your account. The first is the professional approach where you and your Account Executive decide on each trade with no discretion being given directly to your Account Executive. This method was illustrated in the discussion about margins. The second method is called a controlled discretionary or managed account. Under this method, you are giving your Account Executive authorization to trade your account at his discretion at any time and as many times that he considers that a trade should be made. The Chicago Mercantile Exchange, and the Board of Trade have rules governing this type of relationship. The following is an excerpt from the C.M.E. rule regarding controlled, discretionary and managed accounts.

REQUIREMENTS

No clearing member shall accept or carry an account over which any individual or organization, other than the person in whose name the account is carried, exercises trading authority or control, hereinafter referred to as controlled accounts, unless:

The account is initiated with a minimum of $5000*, and maintained at a minimum equity of $3,750*, regardless of lesser applicable margin requirements. In determining equity the accounts or ledger balances and positions in all commodities traded at the clearing member shall be included. Whenever at the close of any business day the equity, calculated with all open positions figured to the settling price, in any such account is below the required minimum, the clearing member shall immediately notify the customer in person, by telephone or telegraph and by written confirmation of such notice mailed directly to the customer, not later than the close of the following business day. Such notice shall advise the customer that unless additional funds are promptly received to restore the customer's controlled account to no less than $5,000*, the clearing member shall liquidate all of the customer's open futures positions at the Exchange.

In the event the call for additional equity is not met within a reasonable time, the customer's entire open position shall be liquidated. No period of time in excess of five business days shall be considered reasonable unless such longer period is approved in writing by an officer or partner of the clearing member upon good cause shown.

REVIEWING YOUR CONFIRMATIONS AND STATEMENTS

An important factor in trading is that you must be sure that no errors occur in your account. For every trade made you should receive a confirmation, and for every close-out a profit and loss statement known as a Purchase-and-Sale, showing the financial results of each transaction closed out in your account. In addition, a monthly statement showing your ledger balance, your open position, the net profit or loss in all contracts liquidated since the date of your

last previous statement, and the net unrealized profit and loss on all open contracts figured to the market should be sent to you.

You should carefully review these statements. Upon receiving a confirmation of a trade you should immediately check its accuracy as far as type of commodity, month, trading price and quantity of contracts. If this does not agree with your original order, it should be immediately reported to the main office of your brokerage firm, and any differences should be explained and adjustments should be made.

If you do not receive a confirmation on a trade after it was orally reported to you by your Account Executive, be sure to contact him and the main office so that if an error was made it can be corrected immediately. You should receive written confirmation when you deposit money with your brokerage firm. If within a few days, you have not received this confirmation, report it immediately to the main office of your brokerage firm.

Never assume that an order has been filled until you receive an oral confirmation from your broker. A ticker or a board that you may be observing can be running several minutes behind and is not the determining factor as to whether your trade was executed or not. Until you receive this oral confirmation, never re-enter an order to buy or sell, against that position.

If you receive a confirmation in the mail showing a trade not belonging to you, immediately notify the main office of your brokerage firm and have them explain why this is on a confirmation with your account number. If it is an error, be sure that it is adjusted immediately and a written confirmation sent to you showing the adjustment of the error. If an error is made and it is profitable to you do not consider this any differently than if it was not profitable. Regardless of whether there is a profit or loss, all errors should be immediately reported to the brokerage firm.

Be sure that when you request funds to be mailed from your account that they are received within a few days from the time of your request. If not, contact the accounting department of the brokerage firm to see what is the cause of the delay.

Never make a check out to an individual. Always make your check out to the brokerage firm.

DAY TRADING

Day trading is where there is a buy and sell made during the trading hours on one particular day. Day trading is not considered to be a sound practice for the new speculator and inexperienced trader. Day trading is something that should be executed only by a sophisticated trader who is in frequent communication with the floor, and even then, on a limited basis.

---

* Minimums can be changed by each exchange, so consult your Account Executive for current regulations.

ORDERS

In order to trade effectively in the commodity market there are several basic types of orders. The most common order is a market order. A market order is one which you authorize your Account Executive to buy or sell at the existing price. This is definitely not a predetermined price, but is executed at a bid or offer at that particular moment.

Example: Buy 5 Feb Pork Bellies at the market.

LIMITED OR PRICE ORDERS AND "OB" DESIGNATION

This type of order to buy or sell commodities at a fixed or "limited" price and the ordinary "market" order are the most common types of orders.

Example: Buy Three Jan Silver 463.10. This limit order instructs the floor broker to buy three contracts of January Silver futures at 463.10. Even with this simple order, however, one presumption is necessary—that the market price prevailing when the order enters the pit is 463.10 or higher. If the price is below 463.10, the broker could challenge on the basis that the client may have meant *"Buy Three Jan Silver 463.10 stop."* Therefore, while it is always assumed that a "limit: order means 'or better,' " if possible, it saves confusion and challenges if the "OB" designation is added to the limit price. This is particularly true on orders near the market, or on pre-opening orders with the limit price based on the previous close, because no one knows whether the opening will be higher or lower than the close, *i.e., Buy Three Jan Silver 463.10 OB.*

STOP ORDERS *(Orders having the effect of market orders)*

Buy Stop Buy stop orders must be written at a price higher than the price prevailing at the time of entry. If the prevailing price for December Wheat is 456 per bushel, a buy stop order must designate a price above 456.

Example: "Buy 20 Dec Wht 456½ Day Stop." The effect of this order is that if December Wheat touches 456½ the order to buy 20 December Wheat becomes a market order. From that point, 456½ on, all the above discussion regarding market orders applies.

Sell Stop Sell stop orders must be written at a price lower than the price prevailing at the time of entry in the trading pit. If the prevailing price of December Wheat is 456 per bushel, a sell stop order must designate a price below 456.

Example: "Sell 20 Dec Wht 455 Day Stop." If this order enters the trading pit with the above price of 456 prevailing, the order to sell 20 December Wheat becomes a market order. From that point 455 on, all the above discussion regarding market orders applies.

Buy stop orders have several specific uses. If you are short a December Wheat at 456, and wish to limit your loss to ½ cent per bushel, the above buy stop order at 456½ would serve this purpose. However, it is important to realize that such *"stop loss"* orders do not actually limit the loss to exactly ½ cent when *"elected"* or *"touched off"* because they become market orders and must be executed at whatever price the market conditions dictate.

Another use is when you are without a position and believe that, because of chart analysis or for other reasons, a buy of December Wheat at 456½ would signal the beginning of an important uptrend in Wheat prices. Thus, the same order to *"Buy 20 Dec Wheat 456½ Day Stop"* would serve this purpose.

Sell stop orders have the same uses in reverse. That is, if you are long 20 December Wheat at 456 and wish to limit this loss to 1 cent per bushel, the above sell stop order at 455 would serve this purpose, within the limitations of the market order possibilities. Similarly, if you are without a position and believe that a sale of December Wheat at 455 would signal a downtrend in wheat prices, and you wish to be short the market, you could use the order to *"Sell 20 December Wheat 455 Day Stop"* for this purpose.

STOP LIMIT ORDERS *(Variations of stop orders)*

Stop limit orders should be used by you when you wish to give the floor broker a limit beyond which he cannot go in executing the order which results when a stop price is *"elected."*

Example: "Buy 20 Dec Wheat 456½ Day Stop Limit." This instructs the broker that when the price of 456½ is reached and *"elects"* this stop order, instead of making it a market order, it becomes a limited order to be executed at 456½ *(or lower)*, but no higher than 456½. Another possibility:

Example: "Buy One February Pork Belly 58.10 Day Stop Limit 58.25 (or any other price above 58.10)." This instructs the broker that when the price of 58.10 *"elects"* the stop order instead of making it a market order, it becomes a limited order to buy at 58.25 *(or lower)*, but no higher as with any limit order.

Stop limit orders are particularly useful to you when you have no position and wish to enter a market via the stop order, but want to put some reasonable limit as to what you will pay. On the other hand, stop limit orders are not useful to you when you have an open position and wish to prevent a loss beyond a certain point. The reason is that by limiting the broker to a certain price after a *"stop loss"* order is elected, **you also run the risk that the market may exceed the limit too fast for the broker to execute.** This would leave you with your original position because the broker would have to wait for the return to the limit before executing. With a straight stop *(no limit)* order, the broker must execute *"at the market."*

Example: "Buy One February Pork Belly 58.10 Day Stop Limit 58.25." Suppose the market moves to 58.10 but then only 20 February Pork Bellies are offered at that price. Your broker bids for one at 58.10 but another broker in the pit catches the seller's eye first and buys 20 and your broker misses the sale. Your broker then bids 58.20 but the best offer is 58.30. He bids 58.25, but the offer at 58.30 remains unchanged. Then another broker bids for and buys February Pork Bellies at 58.30 and the market moves on up. Your broker is left with no execution to your order unless the market later declines to your limit making a fill possible.

If you did not have a position you might be disappointed, but you would be unhurt financially. However, if you had a position and were trying to limit your loss you would have defeated your purpose with the stop limit order, if you truly wanted *"out"* after the stop was elected.

Stop limit orders on the sell side have exactly the same uses, advantages and disadvantages as discussed above, but in reverse:

Example: "Sell 20 December Wheat 455 Day Stop Limit." This means that when the market declines to 455 per bushel, the broker may sell at 455 *(or higher)*, but no lower.

Another Example: "Sell One February Pork Belly 58.25 Stop Limit 58.10." This instructs the broker to sell a belly after the stop price of 58.25 is reached and *"elects"* the stop order, but no lower than 58.10.

M.I.T. ORDERS *(Market-if-touched)*

By adding MIT *(Market-If-Touched)* to a limit order, the limit order will have the effect of a market order when the limit price is reached or touched. This type of order is useful to you, when you have an open position and if a certain limit price is reached.

Example: "Sell One September Sugar 950 MIT." The floor broker is told that if and when the price of September Sugar rises to 9½¢ per pound, he is to sell one contract

at the market. At this price of 9½¢ all prior discussion on market orders applies.

Under certain market conditions, not enough contracts are bid at 9½ cents to fill all offers to sell. Thus, you may see your straight limit price appear on the ticker, but your broker fails to make the sale.

But by adding MIT to the limit price, you will receive an execution, because the order becomes a market order, if the price is touched. However, the price will not necessarily be a good one in your eyes, since it became a market order when touched.

The same reasoning is true on the buy side of MIT orders but in reverse. Assume you are short one contract of September Sugar, with the prevailing price at 9½¢ per pound and you want to cover or liquidate your short at 9¢.

Example: "Buy One September Sugar 9¢ MIT." If and when the price of September sugar declines to 9¢ per pound, the floor broker must buy one contract at the market. Aside from the disadvantages of any market order, the MIT designation on the buy order prevents the disappointment which might arise if a straight limit buy at 9¢ were entered without the MIT added.

SPREAD ORDERS

As explained in the Glossary, a spread is a simultaneous long or short position in the same or related commodity. Thus a spread order would be to buy one month of a certain commodity and sell another month of the same commodity, or buy one month of one commodity and sell the same or another month of a related commodity.

Example: "Buy 5 July Beans Market and Sell 5 May Beans Market" or "Buy 10 Kansas City Dec Wheat Market and Sell 10 Chicago May Wheat Market."

Another Example: "Buy 5 May Corn Market and Sell 5 May Wheat Market."

In the example of the related commodity spread, normally the reason you would use such a spread, is that you expect to make a profit out of an expected tightness in the Corn Market, in the hope the corn contract will gain in value faster than wheat.

There may be a situation where you have a position either long or short in a commodity and want to change to a nearer or more distant option of the same commodity. For example you are long 5,000 bushels of May Soybeans on May 20 and want to avoid a delivery notice by moving your position forward into the July option. The basic spread order would be:

"Buy 5 July Beans Market and Sell 5 May Beans Market."

Sometimes you may prefer not to use market orders, in which case you use the difference spread.

Example: "Buy 5 July Beans and Sell 5 May Beans July 2¢ Over." Even though the prices of the two options are not specified, the broker is allowed to execute at any time he can do so with July selling at 2¢ or less above May. Over or under designations are a necessity for clarity to the floor broker. Omitting either is like omitting the price.

All orders, except market orders, can be cancelled, prior to execution. Naturally, a market order is executed immediately upon reaching the pit, so its cancellation is almost impossible.

There are other variations of orders, but for you the new speculator, the types mentioned are sufficient for your trading.

Options on Stock Market Indices, Bond Futures, and Gold Futures

STOCK MARKET INDEX OPTIONS

Stock market index related options are options whose prices are determined by the value of a stock market average such as the Standard and Poor (S&P) 500 Index or the New York Stock Exchange Composite Index, among others. Two types of such options are currently traded; index options and index futures options. The former are settled in cash while the latter are settled by delivery of the appropriate index futures contract.

Both types of options move in the same way in response to the underlying market index, thereby providing investors the opportunity to speculate on the market averages. The buyer of a call index option is betting that the underlying market index value will increase significantly above the strike price (before the option expires) so as to provide a profit when the option is sold. On the other hand, the buyer of a put option is speculating that the market index value will fall sufficiently below the strike price before the option expires so as to provide a profit when the put option is sold. Options writers (sellers), on the other hand, assume an opposite position.

While index futures (page 438) also permit speculation on the market averages, index option tend to be less risky since option *buyers* are not subject to margin calls and losses are limited to the price (premium) paid for the option. However, index option writers (sellers), in return for the premium received, are subject to margin calls and are exposed to losses of indeterminate magnitude. However, writers of call options on index *futures* can protect themselves by holding the underlying futures contract.

Index Options

A number of index options based on the broad market averages are now traded:

S&P 100 Index [Chicago Board of Options Exchange (CBOE)]

S&P 500 Index (Chicago Board of Options Exchange)

S&P 250 Over The Counter [OTC] (Chicago Board of Options Exchange)

Major Market Index [American Exchange (Amex)]

NASDAQ 100 Index [National Association of Security Dealers (NASD)]

Value Line Index (Philadelphia Exchange)

National OTC Index (Philadelphia Exchange)

NYSE Options Index (New York Stock Exchange)

NYSE Double Index (New York Stock Exchange)

A brief description of some of the more important indices follows.

The S&P 100 Index is a so-called weighted index obtained by multiplying the current price of each of the 100 stocks by the number of shares outstanding and then adding all of the products to obtain the weighted sum. The weighted sum is then multiplied by a scaling factor to provide an index of a convenient magnitude. The S&P 500 Index is calculated simularly except that all of the S&P 500 stocks are included.

The NYSE Index is based on the weighted sum of all of the stocks traded on the New York Exchange while the AMEX Index is based on the weighted sum of all of the issues traded on the American Exchange. Also traded is the NYSE Double Index Option, based on a value which is twice the NYSE index; thus, a one point move in the NYSE Index results in a two point move in the premium of the Double Index Option.

The Major Market Index differs from the above in that it is just the simple (unweighted) sum of 20 blue chip stocks multiplied by a factor of one tenth. This index behaves very similarly to the Dow Jones Index.

Generally index options expire on the Saturday following the third Friday of the expiration month. Hence the last trading day is on the third Friday of the expiration month. The price of an index option contract is $100 times the premium as quoted in the financial press.

Example: The July 120 (an option with a strike price of 120 expiring in July) Major Market Index call option is quoted (Exhibit 1, see page 450) at 3.00. The cost of an option contract is $300 ($100 × 3).

Option premiums consist of the sum of two

EXHIBIT 1   INDEX OPTIONS QUOTATIONS

CHICAGO BOARD

CBOE 100 INDEX

Strike	Calls—Last			Puts—Last		
Price	June	Sept	Dec	June	Sept	Dec
145	15¼	....	....	1/16	1	....
150	13¾	....	....	⅛	1¾	....
155	9⅛	10	....	7/16	3⅛	....
160	5⅛	9¼	....	17/16	4⅝	8¼
165	2⅛	6½	8⅝	3⅞	7¼	10½
170	11/16	3¾	6	7⅝	12	13½

Total call volume 20846.   Total call open int. 62006.
Total put volume 25167.   Total put open int. 103733.
The index closed at 163.55, +1.91.

AMERICAN EXCHANGE

MAJOR MARKET INDEX

Strike	Calls—Last			Puts—Last		
Price	Jul	Oct	Jan	Jul	Oct	Jan
115	5¾	8⅝	10	1⅞	3¾	5½
120	3	5¾	7	4	5⅞	7½
125	1⅛	3¼	....	7⅜	....	....
130	7/16	2¼	3⅝	....	....	

Total call volume 2351.   Total call open int. 14572.
Total put volume 5276.   Total put open int. 9593.
The index closed at 118.69, +1.00.

components; the intrinsic value and the time value. The intrinsic value of a *call* option is $100 times the difference obtained by subtracting the strike price from the current value of the index. The instrinsic value of a *put* option is $100 times the difference obtained by subtracting the current value of the index from the strike price. The time value is the money which an option buyer is willing to pay in the expectation that the option will become more valuable (*increase its intrinsic value*) before it expires. Obviously the time value decreases as the time to expiration decreases.

It should be noted that there is a distinction between exercising an index option and selling an index option to close out a position. Exercising an option gives the holder the right to a cash amount equal to the *intrinsic* value of the option. Hence, the time value of the option is lost. When an option is sold to close out a position, the option holder receives a cash amount equal to the *premium* which contains both the intrinsic value and the time value of the option. Thus, in most cases it is more profitable to sell the option. The profit realized (before commissions and taxes) on the *sale* of an option contract is equal to $100 times the difference obtained by subtracting the premium paid when the option was purchased from the premium received when the option was sold.

Example: On May 24 the CBOE 100 Index was 163.55. In anticipation of a market decline,

an investor buys a September 165-put option quoted at 7¼ for a total premium of $725 (7.25 × 100) per option. Assume that on August 10 the puts were selling at a total premium of $850 due to a decline in the CBOE 100 Index to 160.10. If the investor sells the put option he will realize a profit, before commissions and taxes, of $125 (850 − 725). If the market moves in a contrary direction he could lose his entire investment.

Index Futures Options

Index futures options (also called futures options) are the right to buy (call) or sell (put) the underlying index futures contracts (see page 438). Futures options are currently traded on the New York Futures Exchange and the Chicago Mercantile Exchange. The dollar value of the underlying contract for the New York Futures Exchange option is equal to the New York Stock Exchange Composite Index multiplied by 500 while that for the Chicago Mercantile Exchange option is equal to the S&P 500 Index multiplied by 500. Quotations for futures options as they appear in *The Wall Street Journal* are shown in Exhibit 2. The total futures option premium per option is equal to the quoted value multiplied by 500. Gains and losses are calculated in the same way as index options.

The expiration day of the S&P 500 futures option is on the third Thursday of the expiration month while that for the NYSE futures option is the business day prior to the last business day of the expiration month.

Example: On May 24, 1983, the New York Composite Index is 94.39. An investor expects the Index to increase during the next six months and buys a September 96 futures call option at a total premium of $1750 (3.50 × 500), as indicated in Exhibit 2. Assume that by August 10 the Index is at 100 and that the September call premium is quoted at 8.00 corresponding to a total premium per option of $4000 (8.00 × 500). By selling the option at the current value the investor can realize a profit of $2250 (4000 − 1750) before commissions and taxes.

Example: Assume that on May 24, 1983 when the S&P 500 Index is at 163.43, an investor expects a market decline within six months. He purchases a September 155 S&P put option at a total premium per option of $1150 (2.30 × 500), as indicated in the quotations shown in Exhibit 2. Assume that the Index declines to 150 on August 10 and that the quoted put premium is 6.50 corresponding to a total premium per option of $3250 (6.50 × 500). By selling the option at the current value the investor can realize a profit of $2100 (3250 − 1150), before commissions and taxes.

While a number of the same basic concepts apply to both index options and future options, there are differences between the two because the futures options have underlying index futures contracts which are traded on the open

EXHIBIT 2   FUTURES OPTIONS

CHICAGO MERCANTILE EXCHANGE

S&P 500 STOCK INDEX — Price = $500 times premium.

Strike Price	Calls—Settle			Puts—Settle		
	Jun	Sep	Dec	Jun	Sep	Dec
135	....	.....	....	.05	....	....
140	23.90	24.25	....	.05	.45	....
145	18.90	20.20	....	.05	.90	....
150	13.95	15.25	....	.10	1.25	....
155	9.20	11.50	....	.30	2.30	4.50
160	4.95	8.60	....	1.05	3.60	....
165	1.90	5.50	8.75	3.00	5.75	7.80
170	.45	3.50	....	6.50	9.50	....
175	.10	1.80	....	11.15	14.00	....

Estimated total vol. 1,440
Calls: Fri. vol. 766; open int. 6,216
Puts: Fri. vol 532; open int. 6,552

N.Y. FUTURES EXCHANGE

NYSE COMPOSITE INDEX — Price = $500 times premium.

Strike Price	Calls—Settle			Puts—Settle		
	Jun	Sep	Dec	Jun	Sep	Dec
84	10.90	11.70	....	.05	.40	.75
86	8.90	10.00	11.00	.05	.70	1.50
88	5.95	8.50	9.70	.05	1.00	1.75
90	5.15	7.00	8.30	.25	1.50	2.30
92	3.35	5.50	7.00	.50	2.00	2.95
94	1.95	4.50	6.00	1.15	3.00	3.75
96	.95	3.50	5.00	2.10	3.90	4.95
98	.40	2.75	3.95	3.50	5.25	6.05
100	.15	1.75	3.25	....	6.25	7.00

Estimated total vol. 1,405
Calls: Fri. vol. 844; open int. 4,836
Puts: Fri. vol. 549; open int. 4,801

S&P 500 Index 163.43
New York Composite Index = 94.39

Source: Reprinted by permission of *The Wall Street Journal*, Dow Jones & Co., Inc. All rights reserved.

market. This makes possible a number of trading strategies with futures options which are not available with index options; for example, simultaneously buying an index futures contract and writing a corresponding call option. Also, for the reason given above, there is a distinction between selling a futures option, the usual procedure, and exercising the option. When a futures option is exercised, the option is exchanged for a position in the index futures market which may result in a loss in the time value of the option.

Investors planning to trade options should read two free booklets available from any of the options exchanges:

Understanding the Risks and Uses of Options

Listed Options On Stock Indices

Subindex Options

Subindex options are based on an index made up of leading publicly traded companies within a specific industry. These options permit speculation on an industry without the necessity of selecting specific stocks within the industry. As with all stock index options they are settled in cash.

Subindex options currently traded are:

American Stock Exchange (AMEX)
    Computer Technology Index Option
    Oil and Gas Index Option
    Transportation Index Option

Pacific Stock Exchange
    Technology Index Option

Philadelphia Stock Exchange
    Gold/Silver Index Option

U.S. TREASURY BOND FUTURES OPTIONS

Options on U.S. Treasury Bonds (T-Bonds), traded on the Chicago Board of Trade, are the right to buy (call) or sell (put) a T-Bond futures contract. The T-Bond futures contract underlying the option is for $100,000 of Treasury Bonds, bearing an 8% or equivalent coupon, which do not mature (and are non-callable) for at least 15 years. When long term interest rates decline, the value of the futures contract and the call option increases while the value of a put option decreases. The reverse is true when long term rates increase.

Premiums for T-bond futures *options* are quoted in $1/64$ of 1% (point): Hence each $1/64$ of a point is equal to $15.63 ($100,000 × .01 × $1/64$) per option. Thus a premium quote of 2–16 means 2 $16/64$ or (2 × 64 + 16) × $15.63 or $2250.72 per option. It should be noted that prices of T-bond *futures* are quoted in $1/32$ (of a point) worth $31.25 per futures contract.

As with options trades in general, the profit (before taxes and commissions) is the premium received (per option) when the option is sold minus the premium paid when the option was purchased.

The last trading day for the options is the first Friday, preceded by at least five business days, in the month *prior* to the month in which the underlying futures contract expires. For example, in 1983 a December option stops trading on November 18, 1983.

GOLD FUTURES OPTIONS

The most widely traded gold futures option is on the New York Comex Exchange. The option is the right to buy (call) or sell (put) a gold futures contract for 100 Troy ounces of pure gold. Both the futures contract and the corresponding call option increase or decrease with the price of gold. Put option premiums move in the opposite direction to the price of gold.

Option premiums are in dollars per ounce of gold. Thus a quoted premium of 2.50 corresponds to total premium of $2500 (2.50 × 100) per option.

The profit (before commissions and taxes) to an option buyer is simply the premium received when the option is sold less the premium paid when the option was purchased.

The last trading day for gold futures options is the second Friday in the month *prior* to the expiration date of the underlying gold futures contract. Thus in 1983 a December option expires on Friday November 11, 1983. Example: In August an investor buys a December 400 (an option with a strike price of 400 on a December gold futures contract) Comex call option quoted at 25.00. The total price per option is $2500 (25.00 × 100).

On November 5, the price of gold has increased and the investor sells the option at a quoted premium of 50.00 or $5000.00 (50 × 100) per option. His profit is $2500 (5000 − 2500).

The Commodities Glossary

Acreage allotment The portion of a farmer's total acreage that he can harvest and still qualify for government price supports, low interest crop loans and other programs. It currently applies to specialty crops—tobacco, peanuts and extra long staple cotton—for which complex federal marketing orders have been written to control production closely. Before the 1977 farm bill was passed, the same term also applied more loosely to the portion of a farmer's wheat or feed grain acreage for which government payments would be made. A farmer could harvest 100 acres of wheat, for instance, but he'd receive price support payments only for 70 acres if that was his allotment. The allotment in this sense is called "program acreage" in the new farm bill.

Arbitrage The simultaneous buying and selling of futures contracts to profit from what the trader perceives as a discrepancy in prices. Usually this is done in futures in the same commodity traded on different exchanges, such as cocoa in New York and cocoa in London or silver in New York and silver in Chicago. Some arbitrage occurs between cash markets and futures markets.

Asking price The price offered by one wishing to sell a physical commodity or a futures contract. Sometimes a futures market will close with an asking price when no buyers are around.

Backwardation An expression peculiar to New York markets. It means "nearby" contracts are trading at a higher price, or "premium," to the deferreds. See also *Inverted market.*

Basis A couple of meanings: (1) The difference between the price of the physical commodity (the cash price) and the futures price of that commodity. (2) A geographic reference point for a cash price; for example, the price of a beef carcass is quoted "basis Midwest packing plants."

Bear A trader who thinks prices will decline. "Bearish" is often used to describe news or developments that have, or are expected to have, a downward influence on prices. A bear market is one in which the predominant price trend is down. Some think this term originated with an old axiom about "selling the skin before you've caught the bear."

Bid The price offered by one who wishes to purchase a physical commodity or a futures contract. Sometimes a futures market will close with a bid price when no sellers are around.

Broker An agent who buys and sells futures on behalf of a client for a fee. They work for brokerage firms, some of which have extensive research and analysis departments that occasionally issue trading advice. A few firms have so many customers who follow such advisories that recommendations to buy or sell can influence market prices materially.

Bull A trader who thinks prices will go up. "Bullish" describes developments that have, or are expected to have, an upward influence on prices. A bull market is one in which the predominant price trend is up. Some theorize this term originally related to a bull's habit of tossing its head upward.

Butterfly An unusual sort of spread involving three contract months rather than two. Often used to move profits or losses from one year to the next for tax purposes.

Cash The price at which dealings in the physical commodity take place. Used more sweepingly, it can mean simply the physical commodity itself (as in "cash corn" or "cash lumber"), or refer to a market. For example, the cash hog market is a terminal (or, collectively, all terminals) where live hogs are sold by farmers and bought by meat packers.

Chart A graph of futures prices (and sometimes other statistical trading information) plotted in such a way that the charter believes gives insight into future price movements. Several futures markets regularly are influenced by buying or selling based on traders' price-chart indications.

Clearing house The part of all futures exchanges (usually a separate corporation with its

Source: The *Dow Jones Commodities Handbook*, edited by Dan Ruck, Dow Jones Books, Dow Jones Company, Inc. 1979.

own members, fees, etc.) which clears all trades made on the exchange during the day. It matches the buy transactions with the equal number of sell transactions to provide orderly control over who owns what and who owes what to whom. Although futures traders theoretically trade contracts among themselves, the clearing house technically is in the middle of each transaction—being the buyer to every seller and the seller to every buyer. That's how it keeps track of what is going on.

Close The end of the trading session. On some exchanges, the "close" lasts for several minutes to accommodate customers who have entered buy or sell orders to be consummated "at the close." On those exchanges, the closing price may be a range encompassing the highest and lowest prices of trades consummated at the close. Other exchanges officially use settlement prices as the closing prices.

Cold storage Refrigerated warehouses where perishable commodities are stored. In effect. the warehouses are secondary sources of commodities that aren't immediately available from the producers. The Agriculture Department periodically reports the quantities of various commodities stored in warehouses. Futures traders watch these reports to see if the supplies are building or dwindling abnormally fast, which indicates how closely supply and demand are balanced.

Commission The fee charged by a broker for making a trade on behalf of customers.

Contract In the case of futures, an agreement between two parties to make and in turn accept delivery of a specified quantity and quality of a commodity (or whatever is being traded) at a certain place (the delivery point) by a specified time (indicated by the month and year of the contract).

Country Refers to a place relatively close to a farmer where he can sell or deliver his crop or animals. For instance, a country elevator typically is located in a small town and accepts grain from farmers in the immediate vicinity. A country shipping point is a place where farmers in an area combine their marketings for shipment. A country price is the one these elevators, shipping points or whatever pay for the farmers' goods; it's based on the terminal-market prices, less transportation and handling costs.

Covering Buying futures contracts to offset those previously sold. "Short covering" often causes prices to rise even though the overall market trend may be down.

Crop report Estimates issued periodically by the Department of Agriculture on estimated size and condition of major U.S. crops. Similar reports are made on livestock.

Crush The process of reducing the raw, unusable soybean into its two major components, oil and meal. A "crush spread" is a futures spreading position in which a trader attempts to profit from what he believes to be discrepancies in the price relationships between soybeans and the two products. The "crush margin" is the gross profit that a processor makes from selling oil and meal minus the cost of buying the soybeans.

Deferred contracts In futures, those delivery months that are due to expire sometime beyond the next two or three months.

Delivery The tendering of the physical commodity to fulfill a short position in futures. This takes place only during the delivery month and normally takes the form of a warehouse receipt (from an exchange-accredited warehouse, elevator or whatever) that shows where the cash commodity is.

Delivery point The place(s) at which the cash commodity may be delivered to fulfill an expiring futures contract.

Discretionary accounts A futures trading account in which the customer puts up the money but the trading decisions are made at the discretion of the broker or some other person, or maybe a computer. Also known as "managed accounts."

Evening up Liquidating a futures position in advance of a significant crop report or some other scheduled development so as not to be caught on the wrong side of a surprise. In concentrated doses, evening up can cause a bull market to retreat somewhat and a bear market to rebound somewhat.

First notice day The first day of a delivery period when holders of short futures positions can give notice of their intention to deliver the cash commodity to holders of long positions. The number of contracts circulated on first notice day and how they are accepted or not accepted by the longs is often interpreted as an indication of future supply-demand expectations and thus often influence prices of all futures being traded, not just the delivery-month price. This effect also sometimes occurs on subsequent notice days. Rules concerning notices to deliver vary from contract to contract.

F.O.B. Free on Board, meaning that the commodity will be placed aboard the shipping vehicle at no cost to the purchaser, but thereafter the purchaser must bear all shipping costs.

Forward Contract A commercial agreement for the merchandising of commodities in which actual delivery is contemplated but is deferred for purposes of commercial convenience or necessity. Such agreements normally specify the quality and quantity of goods to be delivered at the particular future date. The forward contract may specify the price at which the commodity will be exchanged, or the agreement may stipulate that the price will be determined at some time prior to delivery.

Fundamentalist A trader who bases his buy-sell decisions on supply and demand trends or developments rather than on technical or chart considerations.

Futures Contracts traded on an exchange that call for a cash commodity to be delivered and received at a specified future time, at a specified place and at a specified price. Similar arrangements made directly between buyer and seller are called "forward contracts." They aren't traded on an exchange.

Hedge Using the futures market to reduce the risks of unforeseen price changes that are inherent in buying and selling cash commodities. For example, as an elevator operator buys cash grain from farmer, he can "hedge" his purchases by selling futures contracts; when he sells the cash commodity, he purchases an offsetting number of futures contracts to liquidate his position. If prices rise while he owns the cash grain, he sells the cash grain at a profit and closes out his futures at a loss, which almost always is no greater than his profit in the cash transaction. If prices fall while he owns the cash grain, he sells the cash grain at a loss but recoups all or almost all of the loss by buying back futures contracts at a price correspondingly lower than at which he first sold them. Some users of commodities assure themselves of supplies of their raw materials at a set price by buying futures, which is another form of hedging. When the time comes to acquire inventories, they can either take delivery on their futures contracts or, more likely, simply buy their supplies in the cash market. Futures-contract prices tend to match cash prices at the time the futures expire, so if cash prices have risen the users' higher costs are offset by profits on their futures contracts.

Hedger The Commodity Futures Trading Commission says a hedger in a general sense is someone who uses futures trading as a temporary, risk-reducing substitute for a cash transaction planned later in his main line of business. All other futures traders are classified as speculators. There are more legally specific definitions of hedging and hedgers in such markets as grains, soybeans, potatoes and cotton, where limits are placed on the number of contracts speculators may trade or own. The Commission has broadened these limits to allow hedging in closely related, rather than exactly matching, commodities. A sorghum producer, for instance, can use corn futures as a hedging tool where he couldn't before this rule-broadening. The more general distinction between hedgers and speculators may be important to potential traders. Some may want to use a market like interest rate futures to offset some expected heavy borrowing. The government hasn't set any speculative trading limits in those markets, but lenders or company directors are more apt to back a plan to trade futures for hedging purposes rather than speculation.

Inverted market A futures market where prices for deferred contracts are lower than those for nearby-delivery contracts because of great near-term demand for the cash commodity. Normally, prices of deferred contracts are higher, in part reflecting storage costs.

Last trading day The day when trading in an expiring contract ceases, and traders must either liquidate their positions or prepare to make or accept delivery of the cash commodity. After that, there is no more futures trading for that particular contract month and year.

Life of contract The period of time during which futures trading in a particular contract month and year may take place. This is usually less than a year, but sometimes up to 18 months.

Limit move The maximum that a futures price can rise or fall from the previous session's settlement price. This limit, set by each exchange, varies from commodity to commodity. Some exchanges have variable limits, whereby the limit is expanded automatically if the market moves by the limit for a certain number of consecutive trading sessions. When prices fail to move the expanded limit, or after a specified period of time, the limits revert to normal.

Liquidation Closing out a previous position by taking an opposite position in the same contract. Thus, a previous buyer liquidates by selling, and a previous seller liquidates by buying.

Long A trader who has bought futures, speculating the prices will rise. He is "long" until he liquidates by selling or fulfills his contracts by making delivery.

Margin The amount of "good faith" money that commodity traders must put in order to trade futures. The margins, set by each exchange, usually amount to 5% to 10% of the total value of the commodity contract. The "initial margin" is the amount of money that must be put up to establish a position in a futures market. Exchanges establish this margin, too, but brokerage firms often require even larger amounts to protect their own financial interests. "Maintenance margin" is the money that traders must put up to retain their position in the futures markets.

Margin call A request by a brokerage firm that a customer put up more money. That means the market price has gone against the customer's position and the brokerage firm wants the customer to cover his paper loss, which would become a real loss if the position were liquidated.

Nearby contracts The futures that expire the soonest. Those that expire later are called deferred contracts.

New crop The supply of a commodity that will be available after harvest. The term also is sometimes used in connection with pigs and hogs because the major farrowing periods in the spring and fall are referred to as "crops." There sometimes are substantial price differences between futures contracts related to new-crop supplies and those related to old-crop supplies.

Nominal price An artificial price—usually the midpoint between a bid and an asked price—that gives an indication of the market price level even though no actual transactions may have taken place at that price.

Old crop The supply from previous harvests.

Open The period each session when futures trading commences. Sometimes the open lasts several minutes to accommodate customers who have placed orders to buy or sell contracts "on the open.". On these exchanges, opening prices often are reported by the exchange as a range, although these seldom are widely disseminated because of space restrictions in newspapers and periodicals; they are carried on tickers and display panels during that trading day, however.

Open interest Outstanding futures contracts that haven't been liquidated by purchase or sale of offsetting contracts, or by delivery or acceptance of the physical commodity.

Option The right to buy or sell a futures contract over a specified period of time at a set price.

Overbought A term used to express the opinion that prices have risen too high too fast and so will decline as traders liquidate their positions.

Oversold Like "overbought," except the opinion is that prices have fallen too far too fast and so probably will rebound.

Pit The areas on exchange floors where futures trading takes place. Pits usually have three or more levels and can accommodate a large number of traders. On several New York exchanges the trading areas are called rings and consist of open-center, circular tables around which traders sit or stand.

Position A trader's holdings, either long or short. A position limit is the maximum number of contracts a speculator can hold under law; it doesn't apply to bona-fide hedgers, although there really isn't any objective way of telling whether a person in position to hedge actually is hedging or is speculating instead.

Profit taking A trader holding a long position turns paper profits into real ones by selling his contracts. A trader holding a short position takes profits by buying back contracts.

Reaction A decline in prices following a substantial advance.

Recovery An increase in prices following a substantial decline.

Settlement price The single closing price, determined by each exchange's price committee of directors. It is used primarily by the exchange clearing house to determine the need for margin capital to be put up by brokerage-firm members to protect the net position of that firm's total accounts. It's also issued by some exchanges as the official closing price, and it is used to determine the price limits and net price changes on the following trading day. (See also: *Close.*)

Set-aside Acreage withdrawn from crop production for a season and used for soil conservation under a production-control program. Wheat farmers this year must set aside two acres of land for each 10 acres they plant to wheat in order to get any federal price support or disaster aid. The Agriculture Department has also said corn, sorghum and barley producers similarly may be required to set aside some of their acreage if it appears that surpluses will grow too much otherwise.

Short A trader who has sold futures, speculating that prices will decline. He is "short" until he liquidates by buying back contracts or fulfills his contracts by taking delivery.

Short squeeze A situation in which "short" futures traders are unable to buy the cash commodity to deliver against their positions and so are forced to buy offsetting futures at prices much higher than they'd ordinarily be willing to pay.

Speculation Buying or selling in hopes of making a profit. The word connotes a high degree of risk.

Spot The same as cash commodities. Literally, delivery "on the spot" rather than in the future.

Spreads and straddles Terms for the simultaneous buying of futures in one delivery month and selling of futures in another delivery month (or even the simultaneous buying of futures in one commodity and selling of futures in a different but related commodity). One purpose is to profit from perceived discrepancies in price relationships. Another purpose is to transfer current trading profits to some future time to avoid immediate tax liability.

Stop-loss order An open order given to a brokerage firm to liquidate a position when the market reaches a certain price so as to prevent losses from mounting or profits from eroding. Sometimes market price trends are accelerated when concentrations of stop-loss orders are touched off.

Support price A level below which the government tries to keep the agricultural-commodity prices that farmers receive from falling. They're set basically by Congress when farm legislation is passed and adjusted from time to time by the President or Agriculture Secretary. Subsidy payments, commodity purchases, production controls or commodity-secured loans are among the devices used to make up the difference when market prices dip below the support level. Futures and cash prices often tend to remain near the support level when there are large crop surpluses because lower prices keep commodities off the market and higher ones quickly draw willing sellers.

Switch A trading maneuver in which a trader liquidates his position in one futures delivery and takes the position in another delivery month in expectation that prices will change more rapidly in the second contract than in the first. Thus, a trader might switch out of a position in an October silver futures contract into a position in a December silver futures contract. Warning: Some people use the word "switch" when they mean "spread" or "straddle." Feel free to correct them.

Technical factors Futures prices often are affected by influences related to the market itself, rather than to supply-demand fundamentals of the commodity with which the market is concerned. For example, if a market moves up or down the limit several days in succession there frequently is a subsequent "technical reaction" caused in part by the liquidation of contracts held by traders on the wrong side of the price move.

Terminal Refers to an elevator or livestock market at key distribution points to which commodities are sent from a wide area.

Trading range The amount that futures prices can fluctuate during one trading session—essentially, the price "distance" between limit up and limit down. If, for instance, the soybean futures price can advance or fall by a maximum of 20 cents per bushel in one day, the trading range is double that, or 40 cents per bushel. In one market, cocoa, price movements are restricted to a daily range of six cents a pound.

Visible supply The amount of a commodity that can be accounted for and computed accurately, usually because it is being kept in major known storage places.

Warehouse or elevator receipt The negotiable slip of paper that a short can hand over to fulfill an expiring futures contract's delivery requirement. The receipt shows how much of the commodity is in storage.

Dow Jones Futures and Spot Commodity Indexes

The method for arriving at the Dow Jones Futures and Spot Commodity Indexes differs from some others in the order in which the computations are made. Instead of first weighting each price, then adding them up and finally calculating the percentage or index, this method first turns each price into an index or percentage of its base-year price, then weights each individual index, and finally adds them up. Stated mathematically, the more usual method calculates the percentage relation of one average to another, while the Dow Jones Commodity Index method calculates the average of a set of percentage changes. These two methods do not result in exactly the same figures. However, they are equally valid when used consistently, and the indexes they produce are of the same general magnitude.

The Dow Jones Commodity Index method has two advantages. One is that it saves computation, because the factors or multipliers perform two computations at once. They calculate the individual percentages and weight them at one stroke. The other advantage is that if you have yesterday's index, you can apply the multipliers to today's individual price changes. Then all you do is add the resulting figures to yesterday's index, or subtract them from it, depending on whether they're up or down. That gives today's index. No need to recalculate the whole thing each day.

As for the weights, they were obtained by the usual mathematical methods. Basically, the weight of each commodity is the percentage of its commercial production value to the total commercial production value of all commodities in the index, in this case for the years 1927–31. In calculating the weights, consideration also was given to the relation between volume of trading in each commodity and its commercial production.

A further refinement was necessary because price changes of the various commodities are quoted in different units. Grain prices change in eighths of a cent, wool prices change in tenths of a cent, and all the other staples in the Dow Jones index move in hundredths of a cent. This adjustment merely required appropriate treatment in each case of the multiplier, so that it would give the right figure for any price change. In the case of grains it meant an adjustment of 20%, since one-tenth is that much smaller than one-eighth. In other cases a mere adjustment of decimal points was sufficient.

The twelve commodities, with the weight of each and the multiplier applied to the price changes of each, are:

Source: The *Dow Jones Commodities Handbook*, edited by Dan Ruck, Dow Jones Books, Dow Jones & Company, Inc.

	Weight	Multiplier
Wheat	19.5	16
Corn	8	11
Oats	5	13
Rye	4	5
Wool Tops	5.5	4
Cotton	23	10
Cottonseed Oil	4.5	4
Coffee	7	3
Sugar	8.5	27
Cocoa	5	5
Rubber	6	3
Hides	4	3

These are the essentials for calculating the spot index. However, the futures index requires one more set of unusual steps. That's because several times a year an actual quoted "future" disappears. For instance, while early in the year it is possible to buy wheat to be delivered in December, when the month of December actually arrives that "delivery" expires and is no longer quoted.

The result is that futures prices are affected not only by market conditions but also by how close the delivery date looms. Interest charges and other such factors influence them. On July 1, the December delivery is just five months off, but a month later it is only four months away, and a five-month delivery should not, in a precise index, be compared with a four-month delivery.

This problem is overcome by the use of two futures quotations for each commodity. They are combined to produce on each market day the calculated price that would apply to a delivery exactly five months off.

On the first day of July, only the December delivery is used, since it is just five months away and thus no adjustment need be made. On the second day, the two quotations used are those for the same December delivery and the one for May of the following year. The quoted price for December is adjusted by one day's proportion of the difference between it and May's quoted price. Since there are 151 days between December and May (except in leap years) the figure for one day's proportion is 1/151 of the price difference between the two. The resulting fraction is added to December's price, or subtracted from it, depending on whether May is quoted above or below December.

The following day 2/151 of the difference are added or subtracted, the third day 3/151 and so on until December 1, on which day only the May contract's price is used. On December 2, the combination used is May and July, and so on around the year.

To facilitate the work of calculating the futures index every hour of each business day and the spot index once a day, tables have been prepared—resembling somewhat tables of logarithms or bond yields—which give the figures arrived at by multiplying the various quotational units of each commodity by its factor or multiplier. For instance, the tables show the proper multiples for one-eighth, one-quarter, three-eighths, etc., when each is multiplied by each grain's factor or multiplier.

The commodity futures index is published once an hour and as of the close of commodity markets each day on the Dow Jones News Service, where also the spot index is published once daily. Both are published likewise in *The Wall Street Journal.*

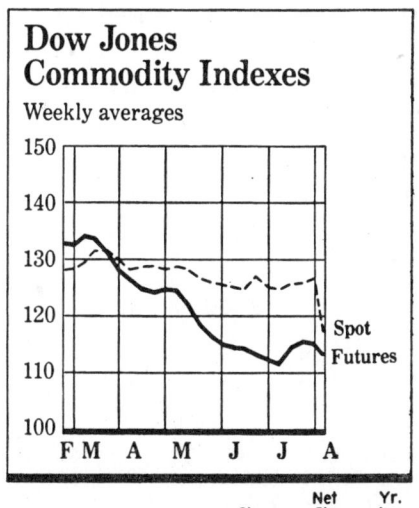

Dow Jones Commodity Indexes

Weekly averages

Spot
Futures

	Close	Net Chg.	Yr. Ago
Dow Jones Futures	114.84	+ 1.51	115.26
Dow Jones Spot	117.28	+ .89	114.66
Reuter United Kingdom	1455.1	− .5	1705.8
C R B Futures*	203.29	+ .4	219.20

*Division of Knight-Ridder.

Commodity Trading Facts and Figures

The following provides as complete a list of futures, options on futures and options on actuals contracts as we could put together.* It is possible we may have overlooked some contract because of the number of new contracts that have been introduced in the last year, or we may have listed a contract that has become inactive. The list includes some contracts that may be awaiting approval by exchange and/or government officials and are not trading yet.

Details of all contracts are current, to the best of our knowledge, but any one of the areas listed is subject to change. The daily limit figure given is the normal limit that prices can move up or down from the previous day's close. A number of exchanges have variable limit policies, which can alter these limits in a volatile market. In addition, there are no limits on spot month contracts in many cases. For more information on limit changes, current minimum margin requirements or other contract details, you should check with your broker.

---

* Only the U.S. and Canadian markets are included in the Dow Jones-Irwin *Business and Investment Almanac.*

U.S. Futures Contracts

Commodity	Trading months	Trading hours (local time)	Contract size	Minimum price fluctuation	Daily limit

Chicago Board of Trade

Commodity	Trading months	Trading hours (local time)	Contract size	Minimum price fluctuation	Daily limit
Corn	Mar/May/July Sept/Dec	9:30-1:15	5,000 bu.	1/4¢/bu. = $12.50	10¢/bu. = $500
Oats	Mar/May/July Sept/Dec	9:30-1:15	5,000 bu.	1/4¢/bu. = $12.50	6¢/bu. = $300
Soybeans	Jan/Mar/May/July Aug/Sept/Nov	9:30-1:15	5,000 bu.	1/4¢/bu. = $12.50	30¢/bu. = $1,500
Soybean Meal	Jan/Mar/May/July Aug/Sept/Oct/Nov	9:30-1:15	100 tons	10¢/ton = $10	$10/ton = $1,000
Soybean Oil	Jan/Mar/May/July Aug/Sept/Oct/Dec	9:30-1:15	60,000 lb.	1/100¢/lb. = $6	1¢/lb. = $600
Wheat (Soft winter)	Mar/May/July Sept/Dec	9:30-1:15	5,000 bu.	1/4¢/bu. = $12.50	20¢/bu. = $1,000
GNMA CDR	Mar/June Sept/Dec	8:00-2:00	$100,000 principal	1/32 pt. = $31.25	63/32 pt. = $2,000
GNMA (Cash-settled)	Mar/June Sept/Dec	8:00-2:00	$100,000 principal	1/32 pt. = $31.25	64/32 pt. = $2,000
U.S. Treasury Bonds	Mar/June Sept/Dec	8:00-2:00	$100,000 8% coupon	1/32 pt. = $31.25	64/32 pt. = $2,000
U.S. Treasury Notes (6½-10 yr.)	Mar/June Sept/Dec	8:00-2:00	$100,000 8% coupon	1/32 pt. = $31.25	64/32 pt. = $2,000

Source: Reproduced with permission of *Futures Magazine,* 219 Parkade, Cedar Falls, Iowa 50613.

Commodity	Trading months	Trading hours (local time)	Contract size	Mimimum price fluctuation	Daily limit
Municipal Bond Index	Mar/June Sept/Dec	8:00-2:00	$1,000 × Bond Buyer Index	1/32 pt. = $31.25	64/32 pt. = $2,000
Major Market Index-Maxi	March cycle plus next three consecutive months	8:15-3:15	$250 × AMEX Major Market Index	1/20 pt. = $12.50	None
NASDAQ-100 Index	March cycle plus next three consecutive months	8:15-3:15	$250 × NASDAQ-100 Index	1/20 pt. = $12.50	None
Gold	Feb/Apr Aug/Oct/Dec	8:00-1:30	1 kilogram = 32.15 oz.	10¢/oz. = $3.22	$50/oz. = $1,607.50
Silver	Feb/Mar/June Aug/Oct/Dec	8:05-1:25	1,000 troy oz.	1/10¢/oz. = $5	50¢/oz. = $500

Chicago Mercantile Exchange

Commodity	Trading months	Trading hours (local time)	Contract size	Mimimum price fluctuation	Daily limit
Cattle, Feeder	Jan/Mar/Apr/May Aug/Sept/Oct/Nov	9:05-1:00	44,000 lb.	2.5¢/cwt. = $11	1.5¢/lb. = $660
Cattle, Live	Feb/Apr/June Aug/Oct/Dec	9:05-1:00	40,000 lb.	2.5¢/cwt. = $10	1.5¢/lb. = $600
Eggs, Fresh White	All months except August	9:20-1:00	22,500 doz.	5/100¢/doz. = $11.25	2¢/doz. = $450
Hogs, Live	Feb/Apr/June/July Aug/Oct/Dec	9:10-1:00	30,000 lb.	2.5¢/cwt. = $7.50	1.5¢/lb. = $450
Pork Bellies	Feb/Mar/May July/Aug	9:10-1:00	40,000 lb.	2.5¢/cwt. = $9.50	2¢/lb. = $760

Chicago Mercantile Exchange
International Monetary Market Division

Commodity	Trading months	Trading hours (local time)	Contract size	Mimimum price fluctuation	Daily limit
Deutsche Mark	Jan/Mar/Apr/June July/Sept/Oct/Dec and spot month	7:20-1:20	125,000 DM	$0.0001/DM = $12.50	None
Canadian Dollar	"	7:20-1:26	100,000 CD	$0.0001/CD = $10	None
French Franc	"	7:20-1:28	250,000 FF	$0.00005/FF = $12.50	None
Swiss Franc	"	7:20-1:16	125,000 SF	$0.0001/SF = $12.50	None
British Pound	"	7:20-1:24	25,000 BP	$0.0005/BP = $12.50	None

Commodity	Trading months	Trading hours (local time)	Contract size	Minimum price fluctuation	Daily limit
Mexican Peso	"	7:20-1:18	1,000,000 MP	$0.00001/MP = $10	None
Japanese Yen	"	7:20-1:22	12,500,000 JY	$0.000001/JY = $12.50	None
European Currency Unit (ECU)	Mar/June Sept/Dec	7:10-1:30	125,000 ECU	$0.0001/ECU = $12.50	None
Treasury Bills (90-day)	Mar/June Sept/Dec	7:20-2:00	$1,000,000	1 pt. = $25	None
Domestic Certificates of Deposit (3-month)	Mar/June Sept/Dec	7:20-2:00	$1,000,000	1 pt. = $25	None
Eurodollar Time Deposit (3-month)	Mar/June/Sept/Dec and spot month	7:20-2:00	$1,000,000	1 pt. = $25	None

Chicago Mercantile Exchange
Index and Option Market Division

Commodity	Trading months	Trading hours (local time)	Contract size	Minimum price fluctuation	Daily limit
Standard & Poor's 500 Stock Index	Mar/June Sept/Dec	8:30-3:15	500 × S&P 500 Stock Index	5 pt. = $25	None
Standard & Poor's 100 Stock Index	Next four months and Mar/June Sept/Dec	8:30-3:15	500 × S&P 100 Stock Index	5 pt. = $25	None
Standard & Poor's Over-The-Counter Index (250 stocks)	Mar/June Sept/Dec	8:30-3:15	500 × S&P OTC Index	5 pt. = $25	None
Lumber (Random-length)	Jan/Mar/May July/Sept/Nov	9:00-1:05	130,000 bd. ft.	10¢/1,000 bd. ft. = $13	$5/1,000 bd. ft. = $650

Chicago Rice and Cotton Exchange

Commodity	Trading months	Trading hours (local time)	Contract size	Minimum price fluctuation	Daily limit
Rough Rice	Jan/Mar/May July/Sept/Nov	9:15-1:30	2,000 cwt. (200,000 lb.)	0.5¢/cwt. = $10	30¢/cwt. = $600
Cotton (Short-staple)	Mar/May/July Oct/Dec	9:30-2:00	100 bales (50,000 lb.)	0.01¢/lb. = $5	2¢/lb. = $1,000

Commodity	Trading months	Trading hours (local time)	Contract size	Minimum price fluctuation	Daily limit

Coffee, Sugar & Cocoa Exchange Inc.

Commodity	Trading months	Trading hours (local time)	Contract size	Minimum price fluctuation	Daily limit
Cocoa	Mar/May/July Sept/Dec	9:30-2:15	10 metric tons	$1/metric ton = $10	$88/metric ton = $880
Coffee "C"	Mar/May/July Sept/Dec	9:45-2:28 (2:30 closing call)	37,500 lb.	1/100¢/lb. = $3.75	4¢/lb. = $1,500
Sugar No. 11 (World)	Jan/Mar/May July/Sept/Oct	10:00-1:43 (1:45 closing call)	112,000 lb.	1/100¢/lb. = $11.20	1/2¢/lb. = $560
Sugar No. 14	Jan/Mar/May July/Sept/Nov	10:00-1:43 (1:45 closing call)	112,000 lb.	1/100¢/lb. = $11.20	1/2¢/lb. = $560
Consumer Price Index (CPI-W)	Jan/Apr July/Oct	9:30-2:30	1,000 × CPI-W	0.01 pt. = $10	3.00 pt. = $3,000

Commodity Exchange Inc. (COMEX)

Commodity	Trading months	Trading hours (local time)	Contract size	Minimum price fluctuation	Daily limit
Aluminum	Current calendar month, next two months and Jan/Mar/May July/Sept/Dec	9:30-2:15	40,000 lb.	5/100¢/lb. = $20	5¢/lb. = $2,000
Copper	"	8:50-2:15	25,000 lb.	5/100¢/lb. = $12.50	5¢/lb. = $1,250
Silver	"	9:05-2:25	5,000 troy oz.	10/100¢/oz. = $5	50¢/oz. = $2,500
Gold (Linked to Sydney Futures Exchange)	Current calendar month, next two months and Feb/Apr/June Aug/Oct/Dec	9:00-2:30	100 troy oz.	10¢/oz. = $10	$25/oz. = $2,500

Kansas City Board of Trade

Commodity	Trading months	Trading hours (local time)	Contract size	Minimum price fluctuation	Daily limit
Wheat (Hard red winter)	Mar/May/July Sept/Dec	9:30-1:15	5,000 bu.	1/4¢/bu. = $12.50	25¢/bu. = $1,250
Value Line Stock Index	Mar/June Sept/Dec	8:30-3:15	500 × the futures price	0.05 = $25	None
Mini Value Line Stock Index	Mar/June Sept/Dec	8:30-3:15	100 × the futures price	0.05 = $5	None

MidAmerica Commodity Exchange

Commodity	Trading months	Trading hours (local time)	Contract size	Minimum price fluctuation	Daily limit
Cattle, Live	All months	9:05-1:15	20,000 lb.	2.5/100¢/lb. = $5	1.5¢/lb. = $300

Commodity	Trading months	Trading hours (local time)	Contract size	Minimum price fluctuation	Daily limit
Hogs, Live	Feb/Apr/June July/Aug/Oct/Dec	9:10-1:15	15,000 lb.	2.5/100¢/lb. = $3.75	1.5¢/lb. = $225
Corn	Mar/May/July Sept/Dec	9:30-1:30	1,000 bu.	1/8¢/bu. = $1.25	10¢/bu. = $100
Oats	Mar/May/July Sept/Dec	9:30-1:30	1,000 bu.	1/8¢/bu. = $1.25	10¢/bu. = $100
Soybeans	Jan/Mar/May July/Aug/Sept/Nov	9:30-1:30	1,000 bu.	1/8¢/bu. = $1.25	30¢/bu. = $300
Soybean Meal	Jan/Mar/May/July Aug/Sept/Oct/Dec	9:30-1:30	20 tons	10¢/ton = $2	$10/ton = $200
Wheat (Soft winter)	Mar/May/July Sept/Dec	9:30-1:30	1,000 bu.	1/8¢/bu. = $1.25	20¢/bu. = $200
New York Gold	All months	8:00-1:40	33.2 fine troy oz.	10¢/oz. = $3.32	$25/oz. = $830
New York Silver	All months	8:05-1:40	1,000 troy oz.	10/100¢/oz. = $1	50¢/oz. = $500
Copper (High grade)	Next three months and Jan/Mar/May July/Sept/Dec	7:50-1:30	55,000 lb.	0.05¢/lb. = $27.50	5¢/lb. = $2,750
Platinum	Current month and Jan/Apr July/Oct	8:00-1:40	25 fine troy oz.	10¢/oz. = $2.50	$25/oz. = $625
U.S. Treasury Bonds	Feb/Mar/May June/Aug/Sept Nov/Dec	8:00-2:15	$50,000 face value	1/32 pt. = $15.62	64/32 pt. = $1,000
U.S. Treasury Bills (90-day)	Mar/June Sept/Dec	7:30-2:15	$500,000 face value	1 pt. = $12.50	None
British Pound	Mar/June Sept/Dec	7:20-1:34	12,500 BP	$0.0005/BP = $6.25	None
Canadian Dollar	Mar/June Sept/Dec	7:20-1:36	50,000 CD	$0.0001/CD = $5	None
Deutsche Mark	Mar/June Sept/Dec	7:20-1:30	62,500 DM	$0.0001/DM = $6.25	None
Japanese Yen	Mar/June Sept/Dec	7:20-1:32	6,250,000 JY	$0.000001/ JY = $6.25	None
Swiss Franc	Mar/June Sept/Dec	7:20-1:26	62,500 SF	$0.0001/SF = $6.25	None

Minneapolis Grain Exchange

Commodity	Trading months	Trading hours (local time)	Contract size	Minimum price fluctuation	Daily limit
Wheat (Hard red spring)	Mar/May/July Sept/Dec	9:30-1:15	5,000 bu.	1/8¢/bu. = $6.25	20¢/bu. = $1,000

Commodity	Trading months	Trading hours (local time)	Contract size	Minimum price fluctuation	Daily limit
Wheat (White)	Mar/May/July Sept/Dec	9:30-1:15	5,000 bu.	1/8¢/bu. = $6.25	20¢/bu. = $1,000

New York Cotton Exchange

Commodity	Trading months	Trading hours (local time)	Contract size	Minimum price fluctuation	Daily limit
Cotton No. 2	Mar/May/July Oct/Dec	10:30-3:00	50,000 lb. (approx. 100 bales)	1/100¢/lb. = $5	2¢/lb. = $1,000
Orange Juice	Jan/Mar/May July/Sept/Nov	10:15-2:45	15,000 lb.	5/100¢/lb. = $7.50	5¢/lb. = $750
Propane Gas (Liquefied)	All months	9:30-3:15	1,000 barrels (42,000 gal.)	1/100¢/gal. = $4.20	2¢/gal. = $840
U.S. Dollar Index	Mar/June Sept/Dec	8:20-2:40	$500 × U.S. Dollar Index	0.01 (1 basis pt.) = $5	None
European Currency Unit (ECU)	Mar/June Sept/Dec	8:20-2:40	100,000 ECU	0.01¢/ECU = $10	None
Five-Year U.S. Treasury Index	Mar/June Sept/Dec	8:25-3:10	$5,000 × U.S. Treasury Index	0.005 = $25	None

New York Futures Exchange

Commodity	Trading months	Trading hours (local time)	Contract size	Minimum price fluctuation	Daily limit
NYSE Composite Stock Index	Mar/June Sept/Dec	9:30-4:15	$500 × NYSE Index	0.05 pt. = $25	None
CRB Futures Price Index	Mar/May/July Sept/Dec	9:00-3:30	$500 × CRB Index	0.05 pt. = $25	None
NYSE Beta Index	Mar/June Sept/Dec	9:30-4:15	$250 × Beta Index	0.05 pt. = $12.50	None

New York Mercantile Exchange

Commodity	Trading months	Trading hours (local time)	Contract size	Minimum price fluctuation	Daily limit
Palladium	Mar/June Sept/Dec	8:50-2:20	100 troy oz.	5¢/oz. = $5	$6/oz. = $600
Platinum	Jan/Apr July/Oct	9:00-2:30	50 troy oz.	10¢/oz. = $5	$25/oz. = $1,250
Potatoes* (Cash-settled)	Mar/Apr May/Nov	9:45-2:00	50,000 lb.	1¢/50 lb. = $10	40¢/50 lb. = $400
No. 2 Heating Oil (New York)	All months	9:50-3:05	42,000 gal.	1/100¢/gal. = $4.20	2¢/gal. = $840

*Potato futures will no longer be traded after May 1987.

Commodity	Trading months	Trading hours (local time)	Contract size	Minimum price fluctuation	Daily limit
Unleaded Gasoline	All months	9:50-3:05	42,000 gal.	1/100¢/gal. = $4.20	2¢/gal. = $840
Crude Oil (Light sweet)	All months	9:45-3:10	1,000 barrels (42,000 gal.)	1¢/barrel = $10	$1/barrel = $1,000

Philadelphia Board of Trade

Commodity	Trading months	Trading hours (local time)	Contract size	Minimum price fluctuation	Daily limit
National Over-The-Counter Index	Mar/June Sept/Dec plus two near months	9:30-4:15	$500 × index	0.05 pt. = $25	None
British Pound	"	8:00-2:30	25,000 BP	$0.0005/BP = $12.50	None
Canadian Dollar	"	8:00-2:30	100,000 CD	$0.0001/CD = $10	None
Deutsche Mark	"	8:00-2:30	125,000 DM	$0.0001/DM = $12.50	None
Swiss Franc	"	8:00-2:30	125,000 SF	$0.0001/SF = $12.50	None
French Franc	"	8:00-2:30	250,000 FF	$0.00005/FF = $12.50	None
Japanese Yen	"	8:00-2:30	12,500,000 JY	$0.000001/JY = $12.50	None
European Currency Unit (ECU)	"	8:00-2:30	125,000 ECU	$0.0001/ECU = $12.50	None

Canadian Futures Contracts

Toronto Futures Exchange

Commodity	Trading months	Trading hours (local time)	Contract size	Minimum price fluctuation	Daily limit
Canadian Bonds (15-year)	Mar/June Sept/Dec	9:00-3:15	100,000 CD	1/32 pt. = $31.25	2 pt. = $2,000
Canadian T-Bills (13-week)	Mar/June Sept/Dec	9:00-3:15	1,000,000 CD	0.01 pt. = $24	0.60 pt. = $1,440
Toronto Stock Exchange (TSE) 300 Index	Next three months	10:00-4:15	$10 × index	1 pt. = $10	150 pt. = $1,500
TSE 300 Spot Contract	Daily	9:20-4:10	$10 × index	1 pt. = $10	None
TSE Oil and Gas Index	Next three months	10:00-4:15	$10 × index	1 pt. = $10	200 pt. = $2,500

Commodity	Trading months	Trading hours (local time)	Contract size	Minimum price fluctuation	Daily limit
U.S. Dollar	Next three months	8:30-4:00	U.S. $100,000	0.01¢ = $10	1¢ = $1,000

The Winnipeg Commodity Exchange

Commodity	Trading months	Trading hours (local time)	Contract size	Minimum price fluctuation	Daily limit
Domestic Feed Barley	Mar/May/July Oct/Dec	9:30-1:15	100 metric tons	10¢/ton = $10	$5/ton = $500
Alberta Domestic Feed Barley	Feb/Apr/June Sept/Nov	9:30-1:15	20 metric tons	10¢/ton = $2	$5/ton = $100
Flaxseed	Mar/May/July Oct/Dec	9:30-1:15	100 metric tons	10¢/ton = $10	$10/ton = $1,000
Domestic Feed Oats	Mar/May/July Oct/Dec	9:30-1:15	100 metric tons	10¢/ton = $10	$5/ton = $500
Rapeseed	Jan/Mar/June Sept/Nov	9:30-1:15	100 metric tons	10¢/ton = $10	$10/ton = $1,000
Rye	Mar/May/July Oct/Dec	9:30-1:15	100 metric tons	10¢/ton = $10	$5/ton = $500
Domestic Feed Wheat	Mar/May/July Oct/Dec	9:30-1:15	100 metric tons	10¢/ton = $10	$5/ton = $500
Gold	Mar/June Sept/Dec	10:00-1:25	20 oz.	10¢/oz. = $2	$25/oz. = $500
Silver	Jan/Apr July/Oct	10:00-1:25	200 oz.	1¢/oz. = $2	50¢/oz. = $100

Options on Futures

Options on futures have the same contract months, trading hours, limits, etc., as their underlying futures contracts.

Underlying futures contract	Contract size	Strike price increments	Minimum price fluctuation	Last trading day

Chicago Board of Trade

Underlying futures contract	Contract size	Strike price increments	Minimum price fluctuation	Last trading day
U.S. Treasury Bonds	$100,000	2 pt.	1/64 pt. = $15.62	Noon on Friday at least five business days before first notice day for underlying futures

Source: Reproduced with permission of *Futures Magazine*, 219 Parkade, Cedar Falls, Iowa 50613.

Underlying futures contract	Contract size	Strike price increments	Minimum price fluctuation	Last trading day
U.S. Treasury Notes	$100,000	2 pt.	1/64 pt. = $15.625 (1.0 = $1,000)	"
Soybeans	5,000 bu.	25¢ under $8; 50¢ above $8	1/8¢/bu. = $6.25 (1.0 = $50)	1 p.m. on Friday at least 10 business days prior to first notice day for underlying futures
Corn	5,000 bu.	10¢	1/8¢/bu. = $6.25 (1.0 = $50)	Noon on Friday at least 10 business days before first notice day for underlying futures
Silver	1,000 oz.	25¢ below $8/oz.; 50¢ between $8-$20; $1 above $20	10/100¢/oz. = $1 (1.0 = $10)	Last Friday at least five business days before first notice day for underlying futures

Chicago Mercantile Exchange Index and Option Market

Underlying futures contract	Contract size	Strike price increments	Minimum price fluctuation	Last trading day
S&P 500 Stock Index	500 × S&P Index	5 pt.	0.05 pt. = $25 (1.0 = $500)	Third Friday of contract month
Deutsche Mark	125,000 DM	1¢	0.01¢/DM = $12.50 (1.0 = $1,250)	Second London bank business day before third Wednesday of underlying futures contract month
Eurodollar Time Deposit (3-month)	$1,000,000	0.50 on IMM Index	0.01 (1 basis pt.) = $25 (1.0 = $2,500)	"
Swiss Franc	125,000 SF	1¢	0.01¢/SF = $12.50 (1.0 = $1,250)	"
British Pound	25,000 BP	2½¢	0.05¢/BP = $12.50 (1.0 = $250)	"
Japanese Yen	12,500,000 JY	0.01¢	$0.000001/ JY = $12.50	Two Fridays before third Wednesday of contract month
Canadian Dollar	100,000 CD	U.S. 1¢	$0.0001/CD = $10	"

Underlying futures contract	Contract size	Strike price increments	Minimum price fluctuation	Last trading day
U.S. Treasury Bills	$1,000,000	25 pt. intervals above 91; 50 below 91	1 pt. = $25	Business day prior to issue date
Cattle, Live	40,000 lb.	2¢	0.025¢/cwt. = $10 (1.0 = $400)	Last Friday more than three business days before first business day of delivery month of underlying futures
Hogs, Live	30,000 lb.	2¢	0.025¢/cwt. = $7.50 (1.0 = $300)	"
Pork Bellies	40,000 lb.	4¢	2.5¢/cwt.	Last business day prior to last five trading days of contract month

Coffee, Sugar and Cocoa Exchange

Cocoa	10 metric tons	$100 below $3,600; $200 above $3,600 for all months	$1/metric ton = $10	First Friday of month before futures expire
Sugar No. 11	112,000 lb. (50 long tons)	Varies*	1/100¢/lb. = $11.20 (1.0 = $1,120)	Second Friday of month before futures expire

* 1¢/lb. when futures price is below 15¢/lb. When futures price is 15¢-40¢ per lb., the increment will be 1¢ for two nearby months and 2¢ for deferred months. When futures price is above 40¢, the increment will be 2¢ for two nearby months and 4¢ for deferred months.

Commodity Exchange Inc. (COMEX)

Copper	25,000 lb.	1¢/lb. below 40¢; 2¢/lb. 40¢-80¢; 5¢/lb. above 80¢	5/100¢/lb. = $12.50	Second Friday of month prior to futures month
Gold	100 troy oz.	$10/oz. below $400; $20/oz. $400-$600; $30/oz. $600-$900; $40/oz. above $900	10¢/oz. = $10 (1.0 = $100)	Second Friday of month before futures expire
Silver	5,000 troy oz.	25¢/oz. below $8; 50¢/oz. $8-$15; $1/oz. above $15	1/10¢/oz. = $5 (1.0 = $100)	Second Friday of month prior to futures month

Underlying futures contract	Contract size	Strike price increments	Minimum price fluctuation	Last trading day

Kansas City Board of Trade

Wheat (Hard red winter)	5,000 bu.	10¢	1/8¢/bu. = $6.25 (1.0 = $50)	1 p.m. on Friday at least 10 business days before first notice day for underlying futures

MidAmerica Commodity Exchange

Gold	33.2 troy oz.	$10/oz.	10¢/oz. = $3.32 (1 = $33.20)	Second Friday of month prior to futures delivery
Wheat (Soft winter)	Five 1,000-bu. contracts	10¢	1/8¢/bu. = $6.25 (1.0 = $50)	1 p.m. on Friday at least 10 business days before first notice day for underlying futures
Soybeans	1,000 bu.	25¢	1/8¢/bu. = $1.25 (1.0 = $10)	12:15 p.m. on Friday at least 10 business days before first notice day for underlying futures

Minneapolis Grain Exchange

Wheat (Hard red spring)	5,000 bu.	10¢	1/8¢/bu. = $6.25 (1.0 = $50)	1 p.m. on Friday at least 10 business days before first notice day for underlying futures

New York Cotton Exchange

Cotton No. 2	1 NYCE cotton No. 2 futures contract	Nearest three delivery months: 1¢ up to 74¢/lb.; 2¢ at 75¢/lb. and above	1/100¢/lb. = $5 (1.0 = $500)	3 p.m. on first Friday in month preceding delivery month
Orange Juice	15,000 lb.	2.5¢	5/100¢/lb. = $7.50	First Friday of month preceding futures delivery month
European Currency Unit (ECU)	100,000 ECU	2¢/ECU	0.01¢/ECU = $10	Two Fridays before third Thursday of contract month
U.S. Dollar Index	$500 × U.S. Dollar Index	2 pt.	0.01 pt. = $5	Two Fridays before third Wednesday of contract month

Underlying futures contract	Contract size	Strike price increments	Minimum price fluctuation	Last trading day

New York Futures Exchange

Underlying futures contract	Contract size	Strike price increments	Minimum price fluctuation	Last trading day
NYSE Composite Stock Index	$500 × NYSE Index	2 pt.	0.05 pt. = $25 (1.0 = $500)	Last trading day of underlying futures

New York Mercantile Exchange

Underlying futures contract	Contract size	Strike price increments	Minimum price fluctuation	Last trading day
Crude Oil (Light sweet)	1,000 barrels (42,000 gal.)	$1/barrel	1¢/barrel = $10	3:10 p.m. on first Friday in month preceding delivery month

Winnipeg Commodity Exchange

Underlying futures contract	Contract size	Strike price increments	Minimum price fluctuation	Last trading day
Gold (Calls only)	20 oz.	$20/oz.	10¢/oz. = $2	Six business days before delivery month

Options on Actuals

This section includes exchange-traded options on physical commodities, such as metals or currencies, or on actual indexes or interest rate instruments. It does not include options on individual stocks or options offered by leverage transactions firms.

Underlying instrument	Contract months	Trading hours (local time)	Contract size	Strike price increments	Minimum price fluctuation

American Stock Exchange (AMEX)

Underlying instrument	Contract months	Trading hours (local time)	Contract size	Strike price increments	Minimum price fluctuation
Major Market Index (20 stocks)	Three consecutive near-term expiration months plus nearest month in March cycle	9:30-4:15	100 × index value	5 pt.	Premium 1/16 up to $3; 1/8 above $3 (1.0 = $100)
Institutional Index (European-style)	Three consecutive near-term expiration months plus two months from March cycle	9:30-4:15	100 × index	5 pt.	"
Computer Technology Index	Three consecutive near-term expiration months plus next two nearest months in January cycle	9:30-4:10	100 × index value	5 pt.	"

Source: Reproduced with permission of *Futures Magazine*, 219 Parkade, Cedar Falls, Iowa 50613.

Underlying instrument	Contract months	Trading hours (local time)	Contract size	Strike price increments	Minimum price fluctuation
Oil Index	"	9:30-4:10	100 × index value	5 pt.	"
Airline Index	"	9:30-4:10	100 × index value	5 pt.	"
U.S. Treasury Bills (90-day) (European-style)	Mar/June Sept/Dec	9:00-3:00	$1 million principal	1/5 pt. = 0.2%	0.01 pt. = $25 (1.0 = $2,500)
U.S. Treasury Notes (10-year)	Feb/May Aug/Nov	9:00-3:00	$100,000	2 pt.	1/32 pt. = $31.25 (1.0 = $1,000)

AMEX Commodities Corp. (ACC)

Underlying instrument	Contract months	Trading hours (local time)	Contract size	Strike price increments	Minimum price fluctuation
Gold Bullion	Feb/Apr/June Aug/Oct/Dec (4 mo. traded at one time)	9:00-2:30	100 oz.	$10 below $500/oz.; $20 above $500/oz.	10¢/oz. = $10 (1.0 = $100)

Chicago Board Options Exchange (CBOE)

Underlying instrument	Contract months	Trading hours (local time)	Contract size	Strike price increments	Minimum price fluctuation
S&P 100 Stock index	Four sequential months	8:30-3:15	100 × index	5 pt.	Premium 1/16 up to $3; 1/8 above $3 (1.0 = $100)
S&P 500 Stock Index	Mar/June Sept/Oct/Dec	8:30-3:15	100 × index	5 pt.	"
U.S. 30-Year Treasury Bonds (7¼%, 9¼%, 9⅞%)	Mar/June Sept/Dec	8:00-2:00	$100,000	2 pt.	1/32 pt. = $31.25 (1.0 = $1,000)
U.S. Five-Year Treasury Notes (7½%, 8⅛%, 9⅛%)	"	8:00-2:00	$100,000	1 pt.	"
British Pound	Next three months plus two on Mar/June Sept/Dec cycle	7:00-1:30	25,000 BP	5¢	0.05¢
Deutsche Mark	"	7:00-1:30	125,000 DM	1¢	0.01¢
Swiss Franc	"	7:00-1:30	125,000 SF	1¢	0.01¢
Japanese Yen	"	7:00-1:30	12,500,000 JY	0.01¢	0.0001¢
Canadian Dollar	"	7:00-1:30	100,000 CD	1¢	0.01¢

Underlying Instrument	Contract months	Trading hours (local time)	Contract size	Strike price increments	Minimum price fluctuation
French Franc	"	7:00-1:30	250,000 FF	0.5¢	0.005¢

New York Stock Exchange

Underlying Instrument	Contract months	Trading hours (local time)	Contract size	Strike price increments	Minimum price fluctuation
NYSE Index	Next three months	9:30-4:15	100 × index	5 pt.	1/16 pt. (1.0 = $100)
NYSE Beta Index	"	9:30-4:15	100 × index	5 pt.	1/16 pt. (1.0 = $100)

Pacific Stock Exchange

Underlying Instrument	Contract months	Trading hours (local time)	Contract size	Strike price increments	Minimum price fluctuation
PSE Technology Index	Four sequential months	6:30-1:15	100 × index	5 pt.	1/16 pt. (1.0 = $100)

Philadelphia Board of Trade

Underlying Instrument	Contract months	Trading hours (local time)	Contract size	Strike price increments	Minimum price fluctuation
Eurodollar	Mar/June Sept/Dec	8:30-3:00	$1 million	25 pt.	0.01 pt. = $25

Philadelphia Stock Exchange (PHLX)

Underlying Instrument	Contract months	Trading hours (local time)	Contract size	Strike price increments	Minimum price fluctuation
Deutsche Mark	Next two months and Mar/June Sept/Dec	8:00-2:30	62,500 DM	$0.01	$0.0001/DM = $6.25 (1.0 = $625)
European Currency Unit (ECU)	"	8:00-2:30	62,500 ECU	$0.02	$0.0001/ECU = $6.25 (1.0 = $625)
Swiss Franc	"	8:00-2:30	62,500 SF	$0.01	$0.0001/SF = $6.25 (1.0 = $625)
Canadian Dollar	"	8:00-2:30	50,000 CD	$0.01	$0.0001/CD = $5 (1.0 = $500)
British Pound	"	8:00-2:30	12,500 BP	$0.05	$0.0005/BP = $6.25 (1.0 = $125)
Japanese Yen	"	8:00-2:30	6,250,000 JY	$0.0001	$0.000001/ JY = $6.25 (1.0 = $625)
French Franc	"	8:00-2:30	125,000 FF	$0.005	$0.00005/FF = $6.25 (1.0 = $1,250)
Value Line Index	Next three months and March cycle	9:30-4:15	100 × index	5 pt.	1/16 pt. (1.0 = $100)

Underlying Instrument	Contract months	Trading hours (local time)	Contract size	Strike price increments	Minimum price fluctuation
Gold/Silver Stock Index	"	9:30-4:10	100 × index	5 pt.	1/16 pt. (1.0 = $100)
National Over-The-Counter Index	"	9:30-4:15	100 × index	5 pt.	1/16 pt. (1.0 = $100)

The Montreal Exchange

Canadian Bonds	Mar/Jun Sept/Dec	Montreal: 9:00-4:00	25,000 CD	2.50 CD	Premium 5¢ up to 2¢; 1/8 above $2
ME T-Bill Index	Next three months plus two on March cycle	8:35-4:00	$250,000 face value	50 basis pt.	1 pt. = $6

Toronto Futures Exchange

Silver	Mar/June Sept/Dec	9:05-4:00	100 oz.	25¢ below $5/oz.; 50¢ from $5-$15/oz.; $1 above $15/oz.	5¢ below $2; 12½¢ above $2
Canadian Bond (11 ¾% maturing Feb. 1, 2003)	Mar/June Sept/Dec	9:00-4:00	$25,000 face value at maturity	5¢ below $5; 12 ½¢ above $5	2.5 pt.

Toronto Stock Exchange

TSE 300 Index	Next three months	9:30-4:10	100 × index	$5	5¢ below $2; 1/8 above $2

Commodity Futures Trading Commission

Federal laws regulating commodity futures trading are enforced by the Commodity Futures Trading Commission. For information on commodity brokers call (202) 254-8630.

National Office
Commodity Futures Trading Commission
2033 K Street, NW
Washington, DC 20581
  Telephone: (202) 254-6387

Regional Offices
Eastern Region
1 World Trade Center
New York, NY 10048
  Telephone: (212) 466-2061

Central Region
233 S. Wacker Drive
Chicago, IL 60606
  Telephone: (312) 353-5990

Southwestern Region
4901 Main Street
Kansas City, MO 64112
  Telephone: (816) 374-2994

510 Grain Exchange Building
Minneapolis, MN 55415
  Telephone: (612) 349-3255

Western Region
10850 Wilshire Boulevard
Los Angeles, CA 90024
  Telephone: (213) 209-6783

The Commodity Futures Trading Commission (CFTC), the Federal regulatory agency for futures trading, was established by the Commodity Futures Trading Commission Act of 1974 (88 Stat. 1389; 7 U.S.C. 4a), approved October 23, 1974. The Commission began operation in April 1975, and its authority to regulate futures trading was renewed by Congress in 1978 and in 1982.

The CFTC consists of five Commissioners who are appointed by the President with the advice and consent of the Senate. One Commissioner is designated by the President to serve as Chairman. The Commissioners serve staggered 5-year terms, and by law no more than three Commissioners can belong to the same political party.

FUNCTIONS AND ACTIVITIES
The Commission consists of five major operating components: the divisions of enforcement, economics and education, trading and markets, and the offices of the executive director and the general counsel.

The Commission regulates trading on the 11 U.S. futures exchanges, which at the end of fiscal 1983 were offering 93 active futures contracts. It also regulates the activities of some 5,025 commodity exchange members, 461 public brokerage houses (futures Commission merchants), about 55,000 Commission-registered futures industry salespeople and associated persons, and 4,100 commodity trading advisers and commodity pool operators. Some off-exchange transactions involving instruments similar in nature to futures contracts also fall under CFTC jurisdiction.

The Commission's regulatory and enforcement efforts are designed to ensure that the futures trading process is fair and that it protects both the rights of customers and the financial integrity of the marketplace. The CFTC approves the rules under which an exchange proposes to operate and monitors exchange enforcement of those rules. It reviews the terms of proposed futures contracts, and registers companies and individuals who handle customer funds or give trading advice. The Commission also protects the public by enforcing rules that require that customer funds be kept in bank accounts separate from accounts maintained by firms for their own use, and that such customer accounts be marked to present market value at the close of trading each day.

Futures contracts for agricultural commodities were traded in the United States for more than 100 years before futures trading was diversified to include trading in contracts for precious metals, raw materials, foreign currencies, commercial interest rates, and U.S. Government and mortgage securities. Contract diversification has grown in exchange trading volume, a growth not limited to the newer commodities.

Futures and Options Exchanges: Addresses

UNITED STATES

American Stock Exchange (AMEX)
86 Trinity Place
New York, NY 10006
  (212) 306-1000

Source: U.S. Government Manual.

AMEX Commodity Corporation (ACC)
86 Trinity Place
New York, NY 10006
  (212) 306-1000

Chicago Board of Trade (CBT)
141 West Jackson Boulevard
Chicago, IL 60604
  (312) 435-3500

Chicago Board Options Exchange (CBOE)
400 South LaSalle
Chicago, IL 60605
  (312) 786-5600

Chicago Mercantile Exchange (CME) and International Monetary Market (IMM)
30 South Wacker Drive
Chicago, IL 60606
  (312) 930-8200

Chicago Rice & Cotton Exchange (CRCE)
444 W. Jackson Boulevard
Chicago, IL 60606
  (312) 341-3078

Coffee, Sugar & Cocoa Exchange (CSCE)
4 World Trade Center
New York, NY 10048
  (212) 938-2800

Commodity Exchange, Inc. (COMEX)
4 World Trade Center
New York, NY 10048
  (212) 938-2900

International Monetary Market [IMM] (see Chicago Merchantile Exchange [CME]

Kansas City Board of Trade (KCBT)
4800 Main Street
Kansas City, MO 64112
  (816) 753-7500

Midamerica Commodity Exchange (MCE)
444 West Jackson Boulevard
Chicago, IL 60606
  (312) 341-3000

Minneapolis Grain Exchange (MGE)
150 Grain Exchange Building
400 S. Fourth Street
Minneapolis, MN 55415
  (612) 338-6212

New York Cotton Exchange & Associates (NYCE)
4 World Trade Center
New York, NY 10048
  (212) 938-2650

New York Futures Exchange (NYFE)
20 Broad Street
New York, NY 10005
  (212) 623-4949
  (800) 221-7722

New York Mercantile Exchange (NYME)
4 World Trade Center
New York, NY 10048
  (212) 938-2222

New York Stock Exchange
11 Wall St.
New York, NY 10005
  (800) 656-8533

Pacific Stock Exchange
301 Pine St.
San Francisco, CA 94104
  (415) 393-4000

Philadelphia Board of Trade
1900 Market St.
Philadelphia, PA 19103
  (215) 496-5025

Philadelphia Stock Exchange
1900 Market St.
Philadelphia, PA 19103
  (215) 496-5000

CANADIAN

Montreal Stock Exchange
800 Victoria Square
Montreal, Quebec, Canada H4Z 1A9
  (514) 871-2424

Toronto Futures Exchange
2 First Canadian Place
Exchange Tower
Toronto, Ontario, Canada M5X 1J2
  (416) 947-4700

Toronto Stock Exchange
2 First Canadian Place
Exchange Tower
Toronto, Ontario, Canada M5X 1J2
  (416) 947-4700

Vancouver Stock Exchange
609 Granville
Vancouver, British Columbia
Canada V7Y 1H1
  (604) 689-3334

The Winnipeg Commodity Exchange
500 Commodity Exchange Tower
360 Main Street
Winnipeg, Manitoba
Canada R3C 3Z4
  (204) 949-0495

SELECTED FOREIGN EXCHANGES

London Commodity Exchange Co. Ltd.
Cereal House, 58 Mark Lane
London, England EC3R 7NE
01-481-2080

The London International Financial Futures Exchange Ltd. (LIFFE)
Royal Exchange
London, England EC3
01-623-0444

The Hong Kong Futures Exchange Ltd.
Hutchison House, Second Floor
Harcourt Road
Hong Kong
5-251005

European Options Exchange (EOE)
DAM 21
1012 JS Amsterdam
The Netherlands
20-26 27 21

Paris Commodity Exchange
Bourse de Commerce
2, rue de Viarmes B.P. 53/01
75040 Paris, Cedex 01 France
1-508-82-50
(212) 751-9050-New York

The Singapore International Monetary Exchange Ltd.
24 Raffles Place
29-04 Clifford Centre
Singapore 0104

Sydney Futures Exchange Ltd.
13-15 O'Connell St.
Sydney, NSW, Australia 2000
02-233-7633

Futures and Securities Organizations

Futures Industry Association, Inc. (FIA)
1825 I Street, NW
Washington, DC 20006
(202) 466-5460

National Association of Futures Trading Advisors (NAFTA)
111 East Wacker Drive
Chicago, IL 60601
(312) 644-6610

National Association of Securities Dealers (NASD)
1735 K Street, NW
Washington, DC 20006
(202) 728-8000

National Futures Association (NFA)
200 West Madison
Chicago, IL 60606
(312) 781-1300

North American Securities Administrators Association, Inc. (NASAA)
425 13th Street, NW
Washington, DC 20004
(202) 783-2303

Commodity Charts

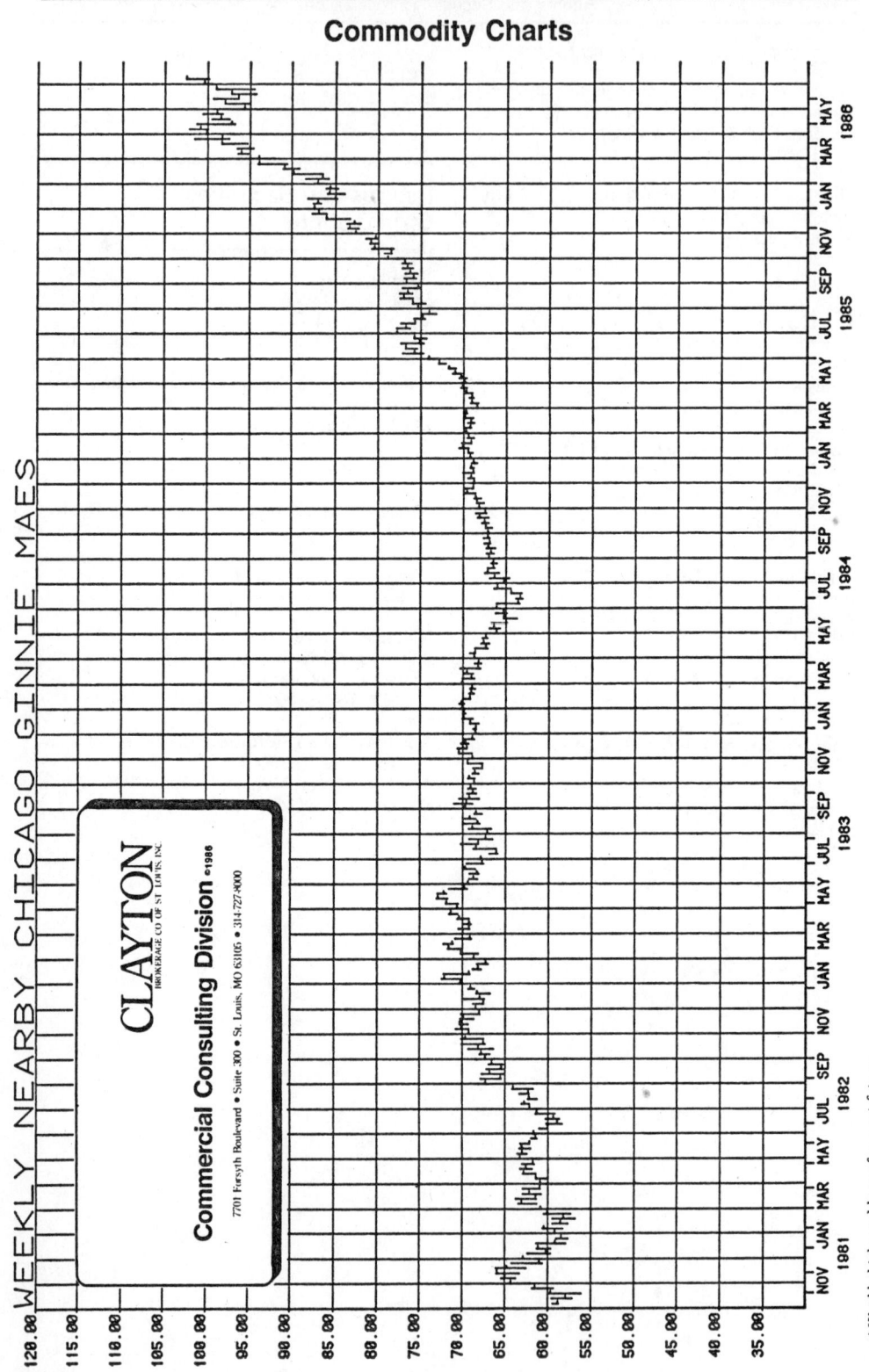

WEEKLY NEARBY CHICAGO GINNIE MAES

CLAYTON
BROKERAGE CO. OF ST. LOUIS, INC.

Commercial Consulting Division ©1986

7701 Forsyth Boulevard • Suite 300 • St. Louis, MO 63105 • 314-727-9000

* Weekly highs and lows of nearest futures.
Source: Clayton Brokerage Co. of St. Louis, Inc., 7701 Forsyth Boulevard, St. Louis, Missouri 63105.

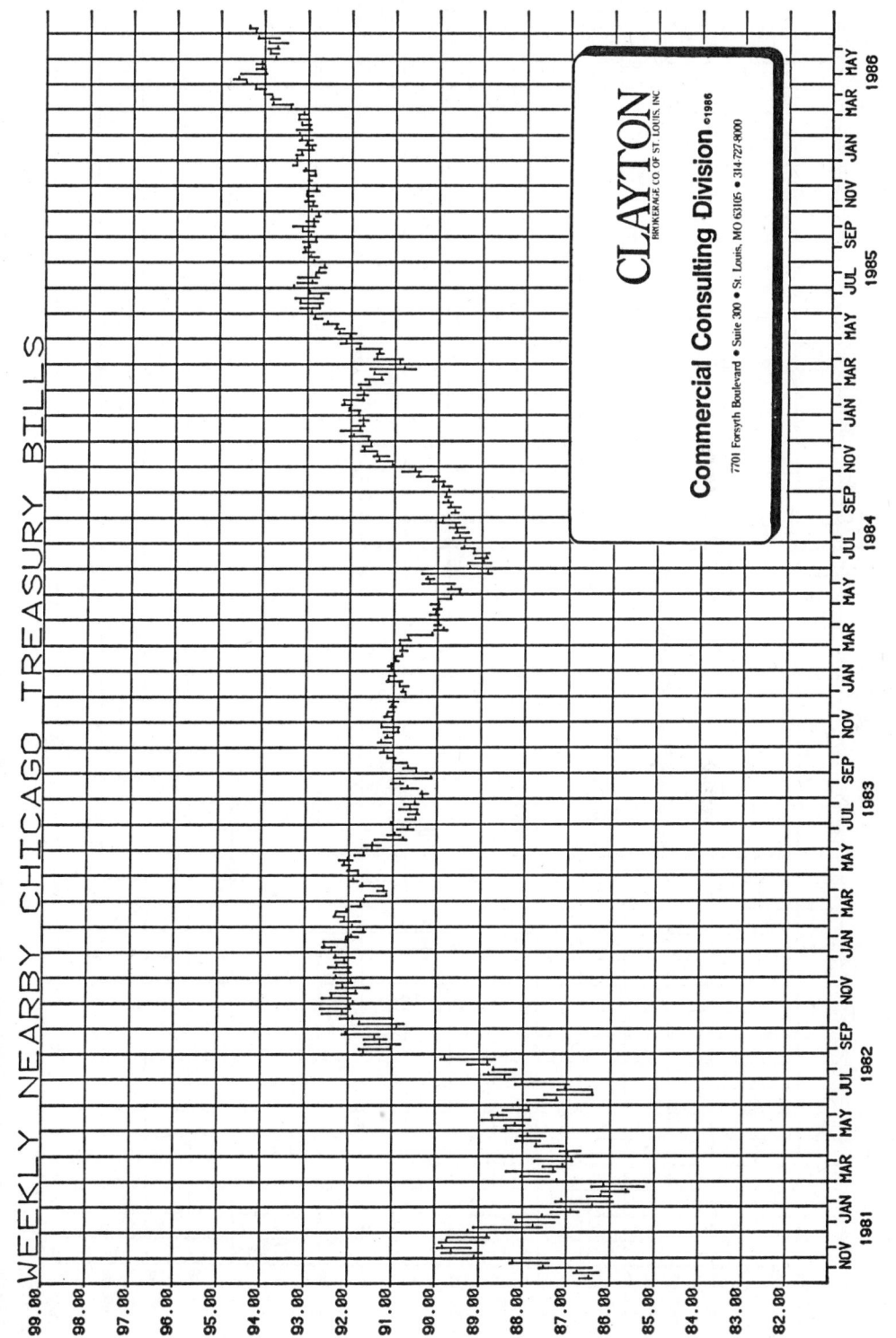

WEEKLY NEARBY CHICAGO TREASURY BILLS

CLAYTON
BROKERAGE CO OF ST. LOUIS, INC

Commercial Consulting Division ©1986

7701 Forsyth Boulevard • Suite 300 • St. Louis, MO 63105 • 314-727-8000

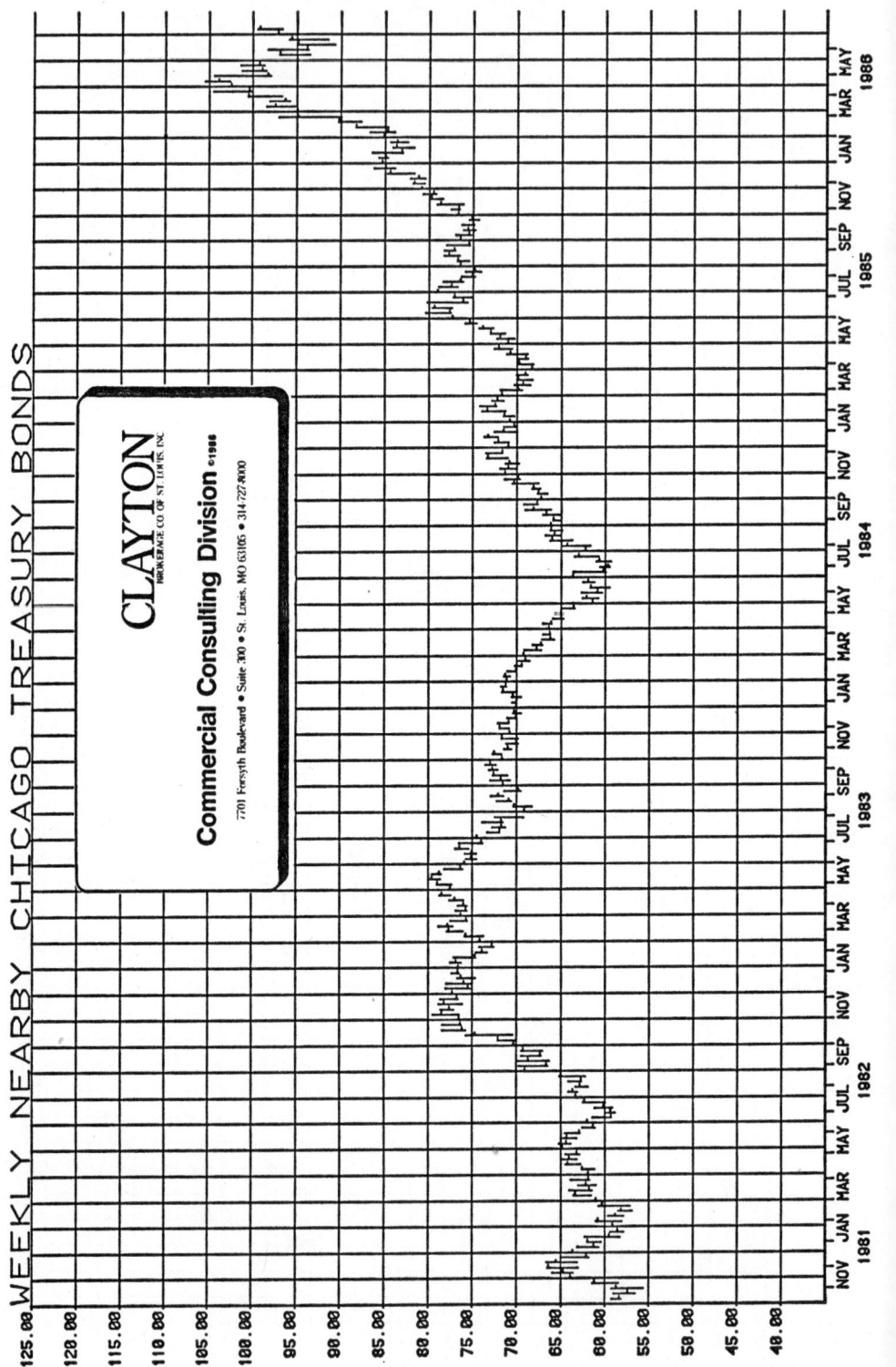

WEEKLY NEARBY CHICAGO TREASURY BONDS

CLAYTON
BROKERAGE CO OF ST. LOUIS, INC.

Commercial Consulting Division ©1986

7701 Forsyth Boulevard • Suite 300 • St. Louis, MO 63105 • 314-727-8000

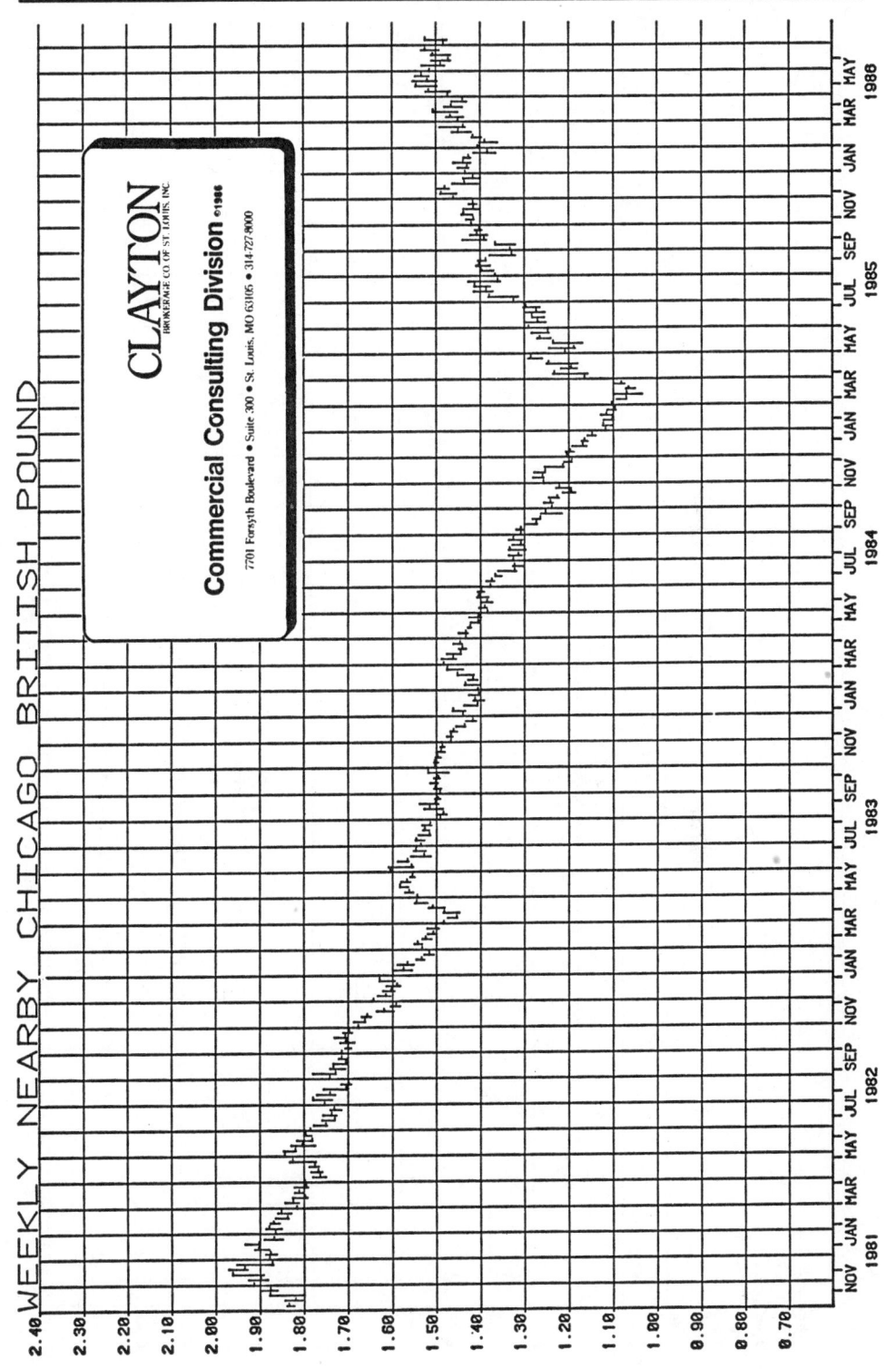

WEEKLY NEARBY CHICAGO BRITISH POUND

CLAYTON
BROKERAGE CO. OF ST. LOUIS, INC.

Commercial Consulting Division ©1986

7701 Forsyth Boulevard • Suite 300 • St. Louis, MO 63105 • 314-727-8900

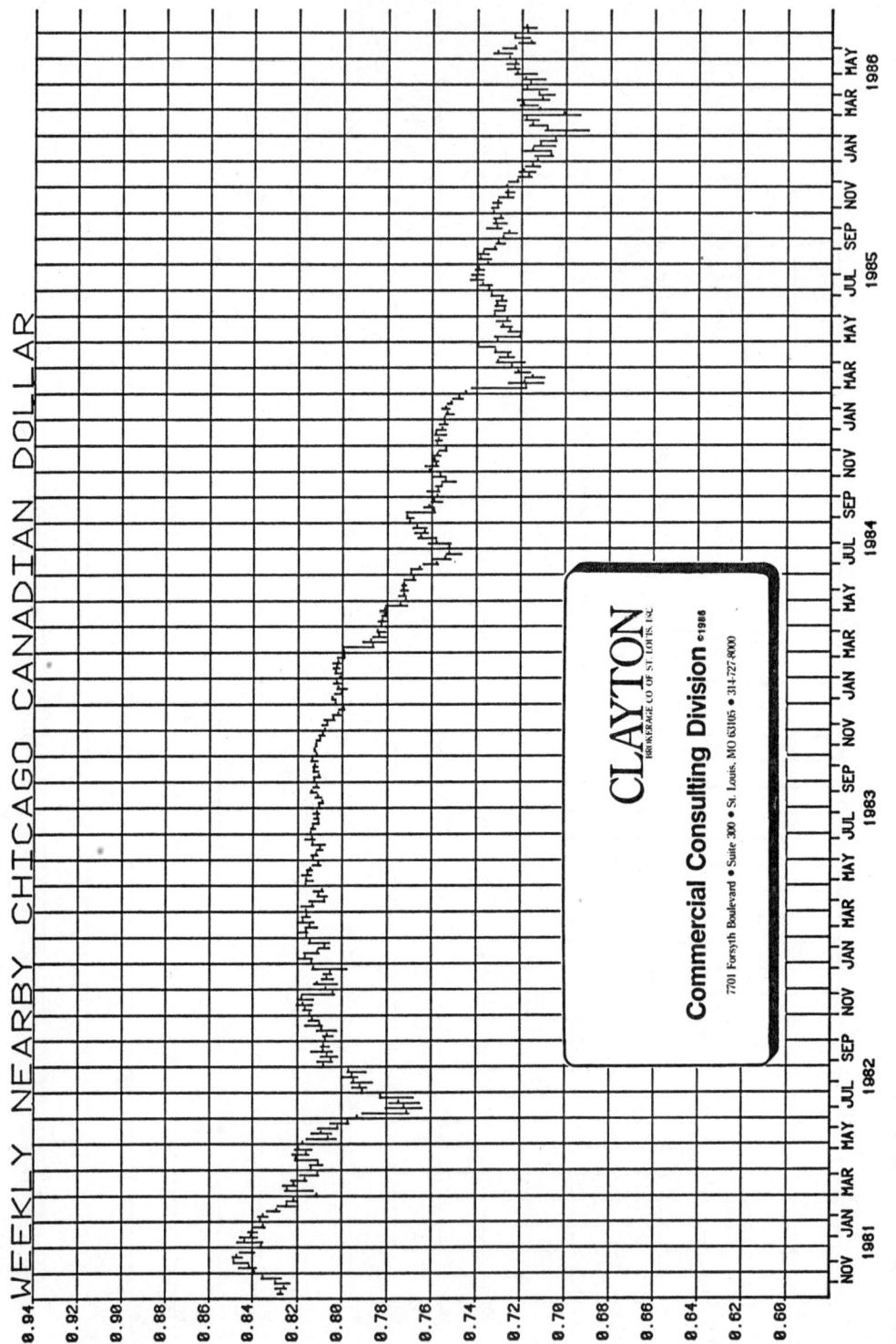

WEEKLY NEARBY CHICAGO CANADIAN DOLLAR

CLAYTON
BROKERAGE CO OF ST. LOUIS, INC.

Commercial Consulting Division ©1986

7701 Forsyth Boulevard ● Suite 300 ● St. Louis, MO 63105 ● 314-727-8000

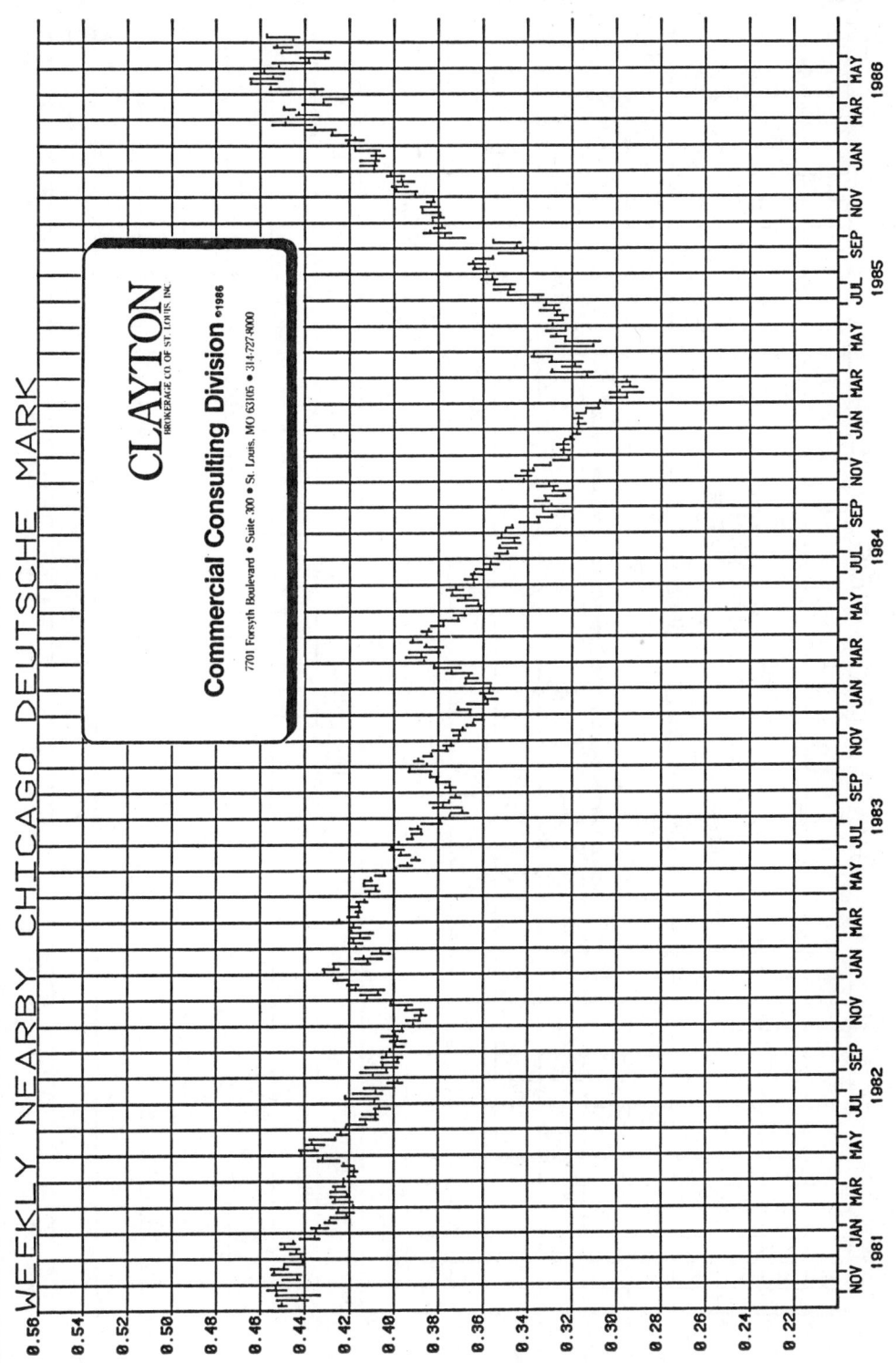

WEEKLY NEARBY CHICAGO DEUTSCHE MARK

CLAYTON
BROKERAGE CO. OF ST. LOUIS, INC.

Commercial Consulting Division ©1986

7701 Forsyth Boulevard • Suite 300 • St. Louis, MO 63105 • 314-727-9000

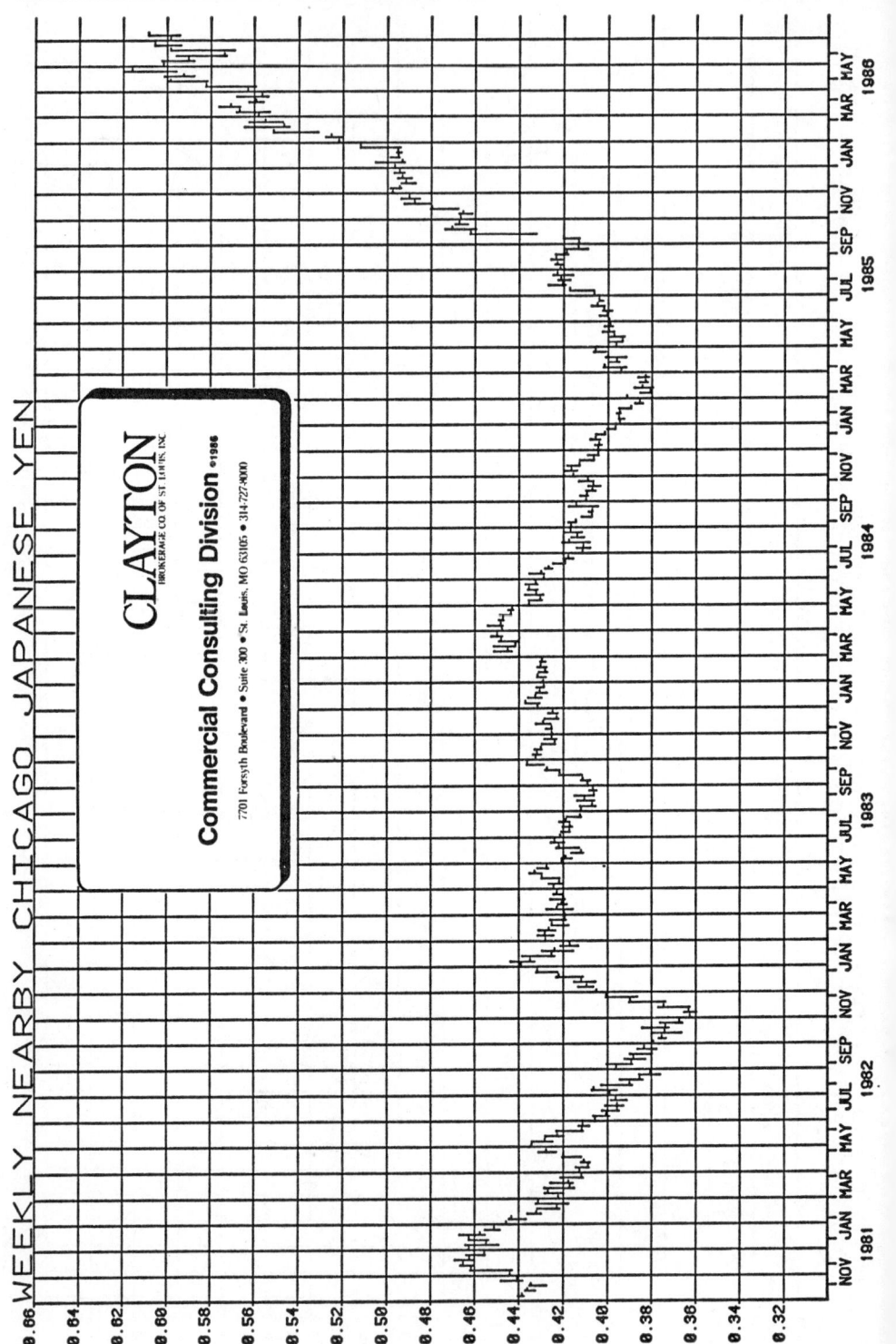

WEEKLY NEARBY CHICAGO JAPANESE YEN

CLAYTON
BROKERAGE CO. OF ST. LOUIS, INC.

Commercial Consulting Division ©1986

7701 Forsyth Boulevard • Suite 300 • St. Louis, MO 63105 • 314-727-9000

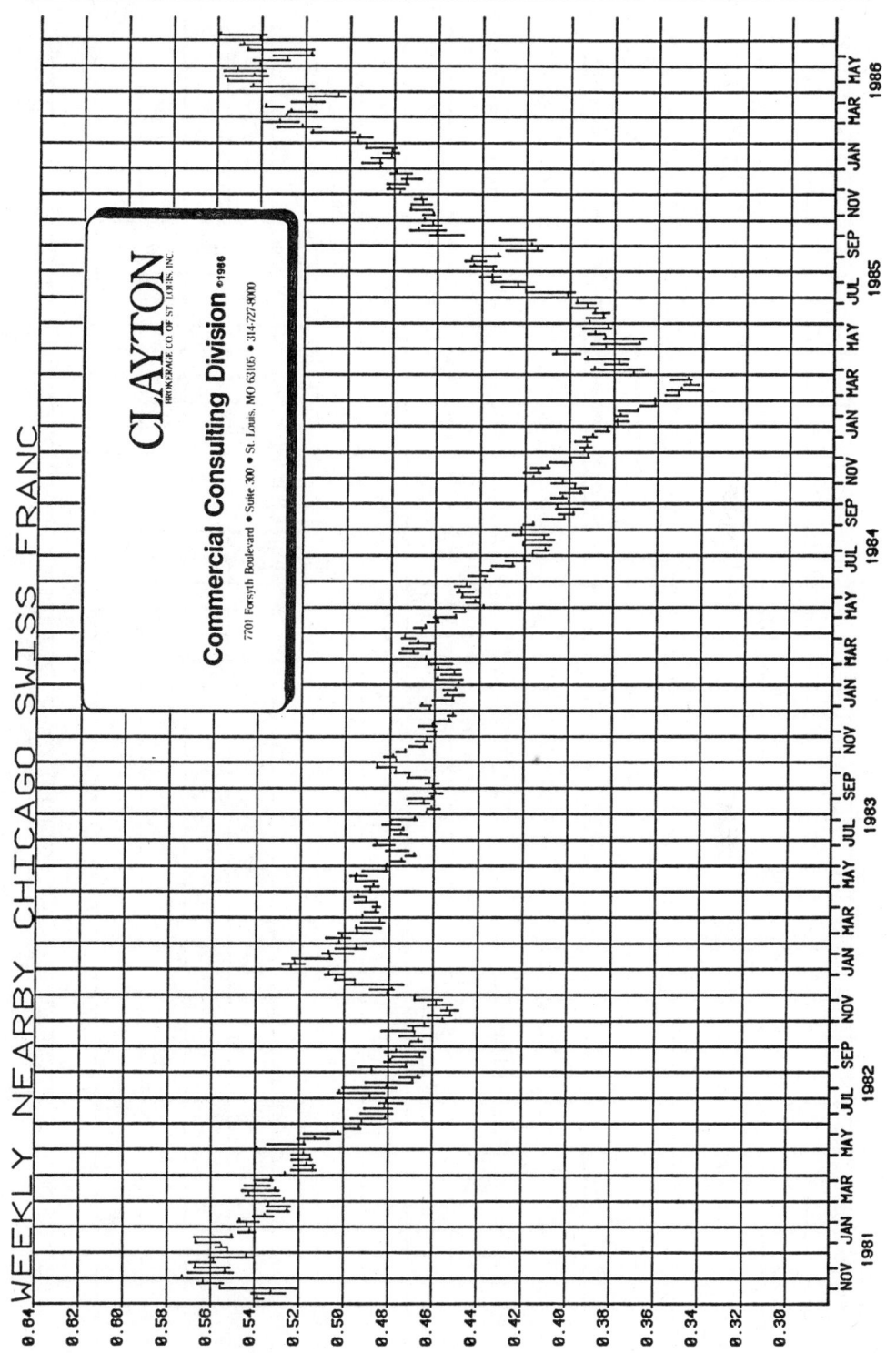

WEEKLY NEARBY CHICAGO SWISS FRANC

CLAYTON
BROKERAGE CO OF ST LOUIS, INC
Commercial Consulting Division ©1986
7701 Forsyth Boulevard • Suite 300 • St. Louis, MO 63105 • 314-727-8000

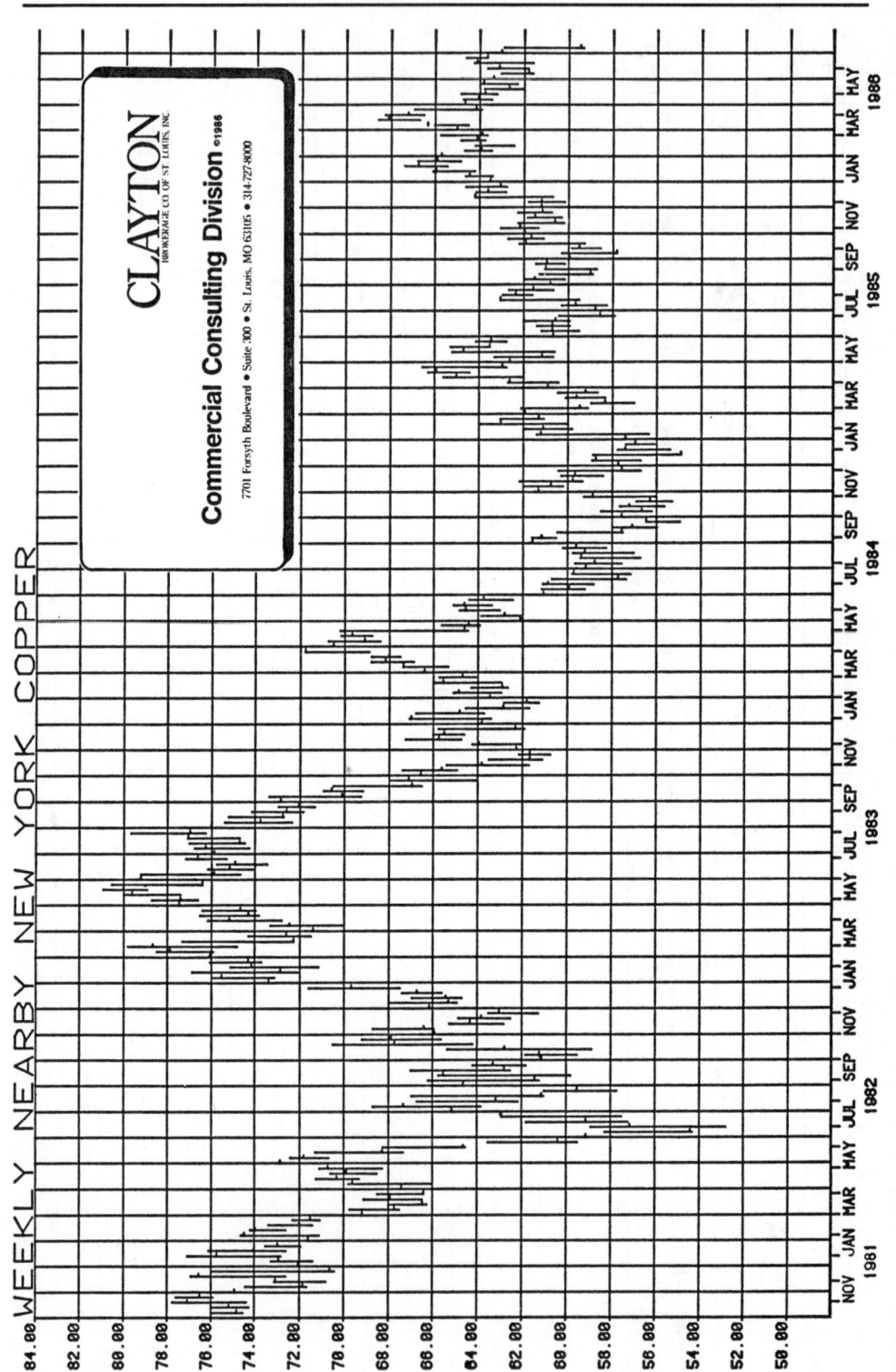

WEEKLY NEARBY NEW YORK COPPER

CLAYTON
BROKERAGE CO OF ST LOUIS, INC.

Commercial Consulting Division ©1986

7701 Forsyth Boulevard • Suite 300 • St. Louis, MO 63105 • 314-727-8000

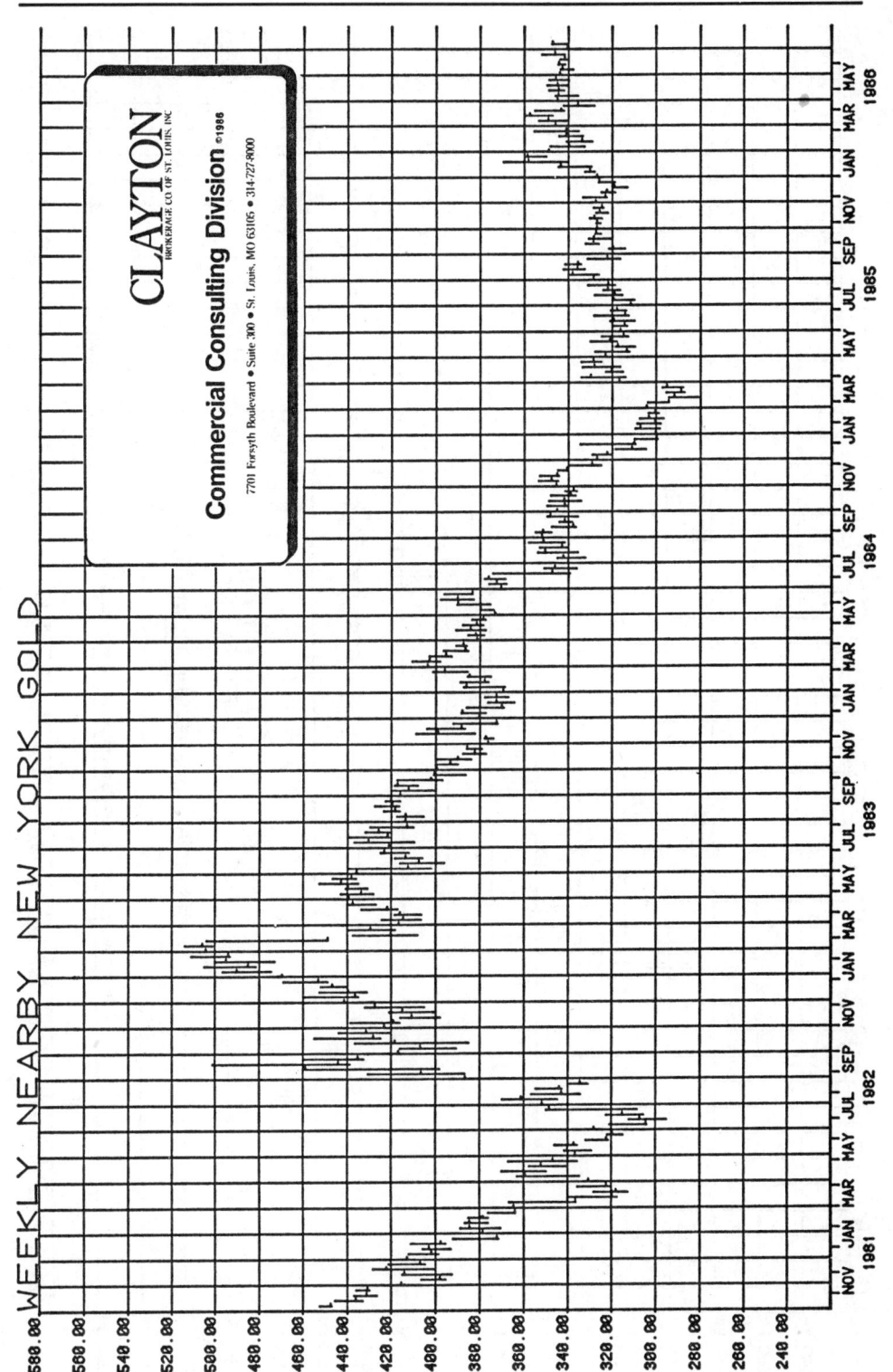

WEEKLY NEARBY NEW YORK GOLD

CLAYTON
BROKERAGE CO OF ST. LOUIS, INC

Commercial Consulting Division ©1986

7701 Forsyth Boulevard • Suite 300 • St. Louis, MO 63105 • 314-727-9000

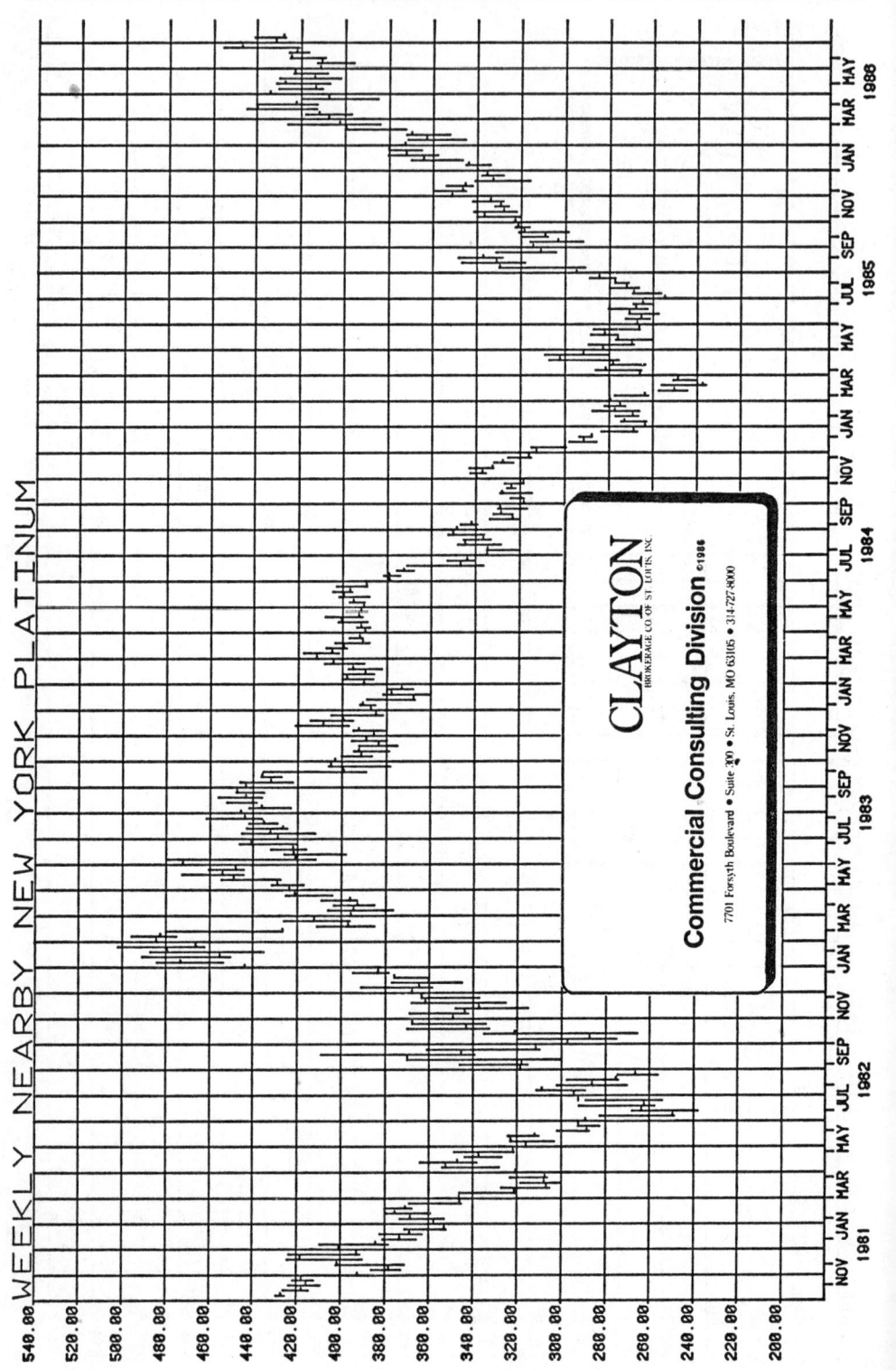

WEEKLY NEARBY NEW YORK PLATINUM

CLAYTON
BROKERAGE CO. OF ST. LOUIS, INC.

Commercial Consulting Division ©1986

7701 Forsyth Boulevard • Suite 300 • St. Louis, MO 63105 • 314/727-8000

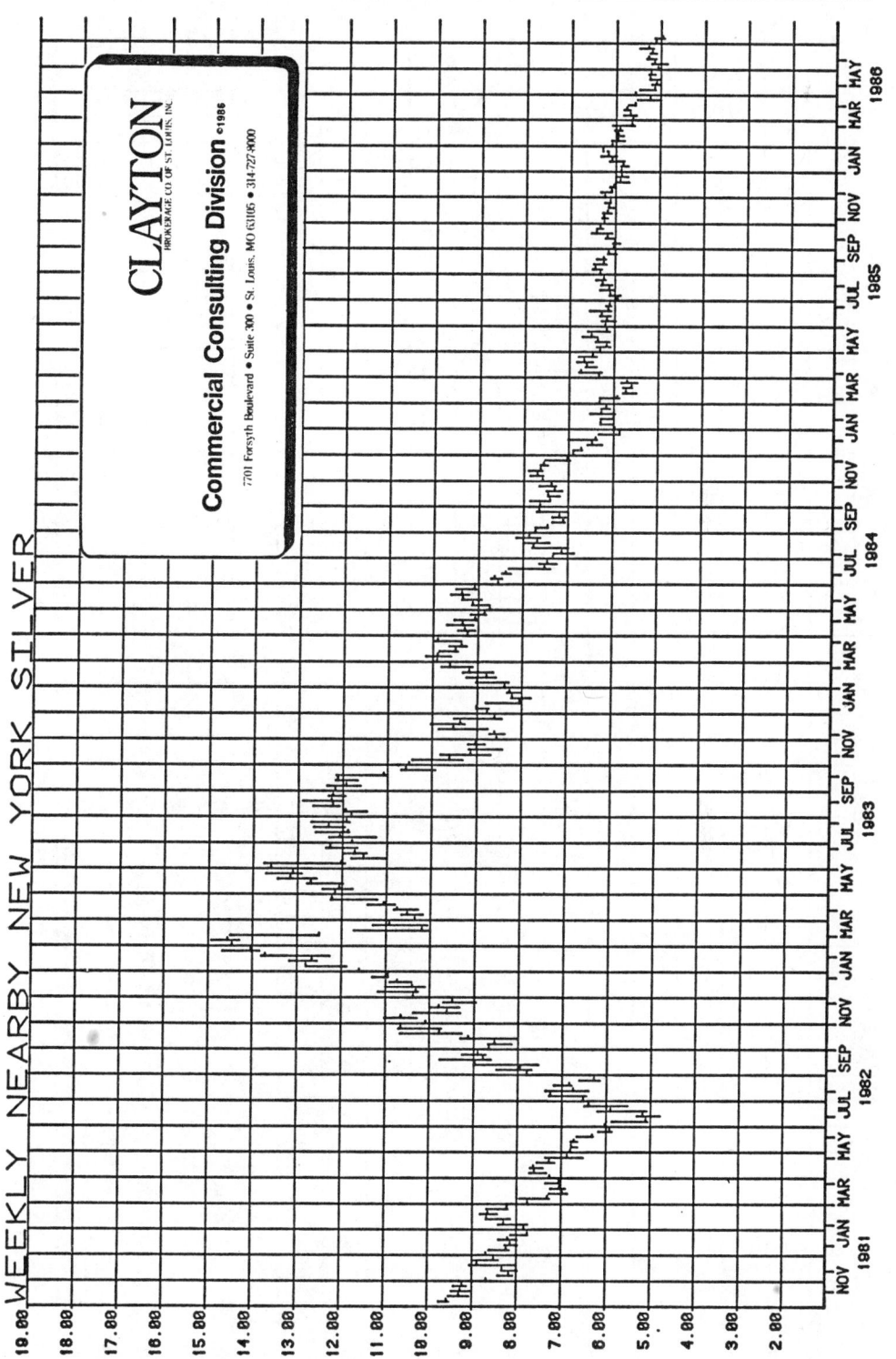

WEEKLY NEARBY NEW YORK SILVER

CLAYTON
BROKERAGE CO. OF ST. LOUIS, INC.

Commercial Consulting Division ©1986

7701 Forsyth Boulevard • Suite 300 • St. Louis, MO 63105 • 314-727-9000

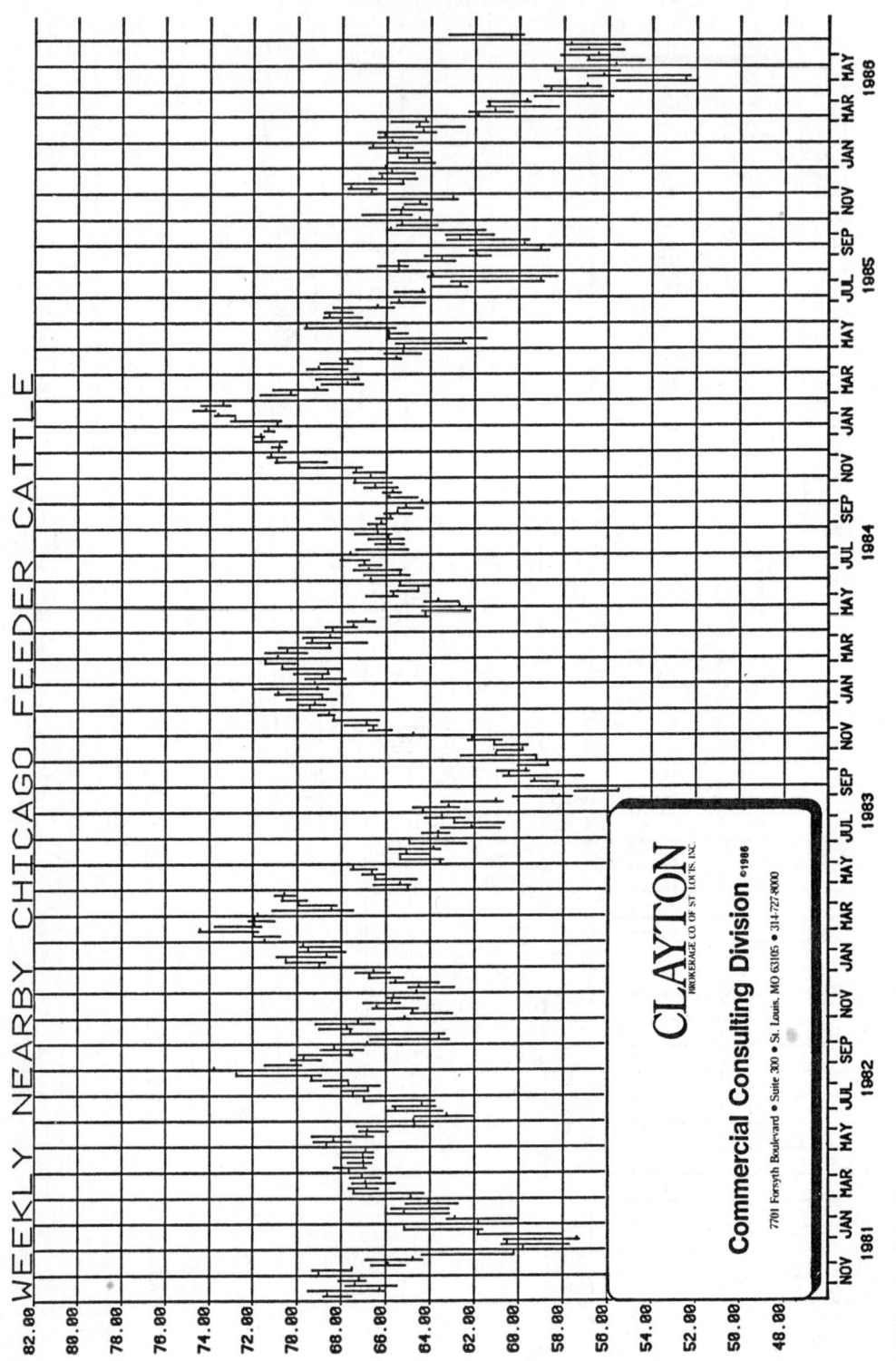

WEEKLY NEARBY CHICAGO FEEDER CATTLE

CLAYTON
BROKERAGE CO. OF ST. LOUIS, INC.
Commercial Consulting Division ©1986
7701 Forsyth Boulevard • Suite 300 • St. Louis, MO 63105 • 314-727-8000

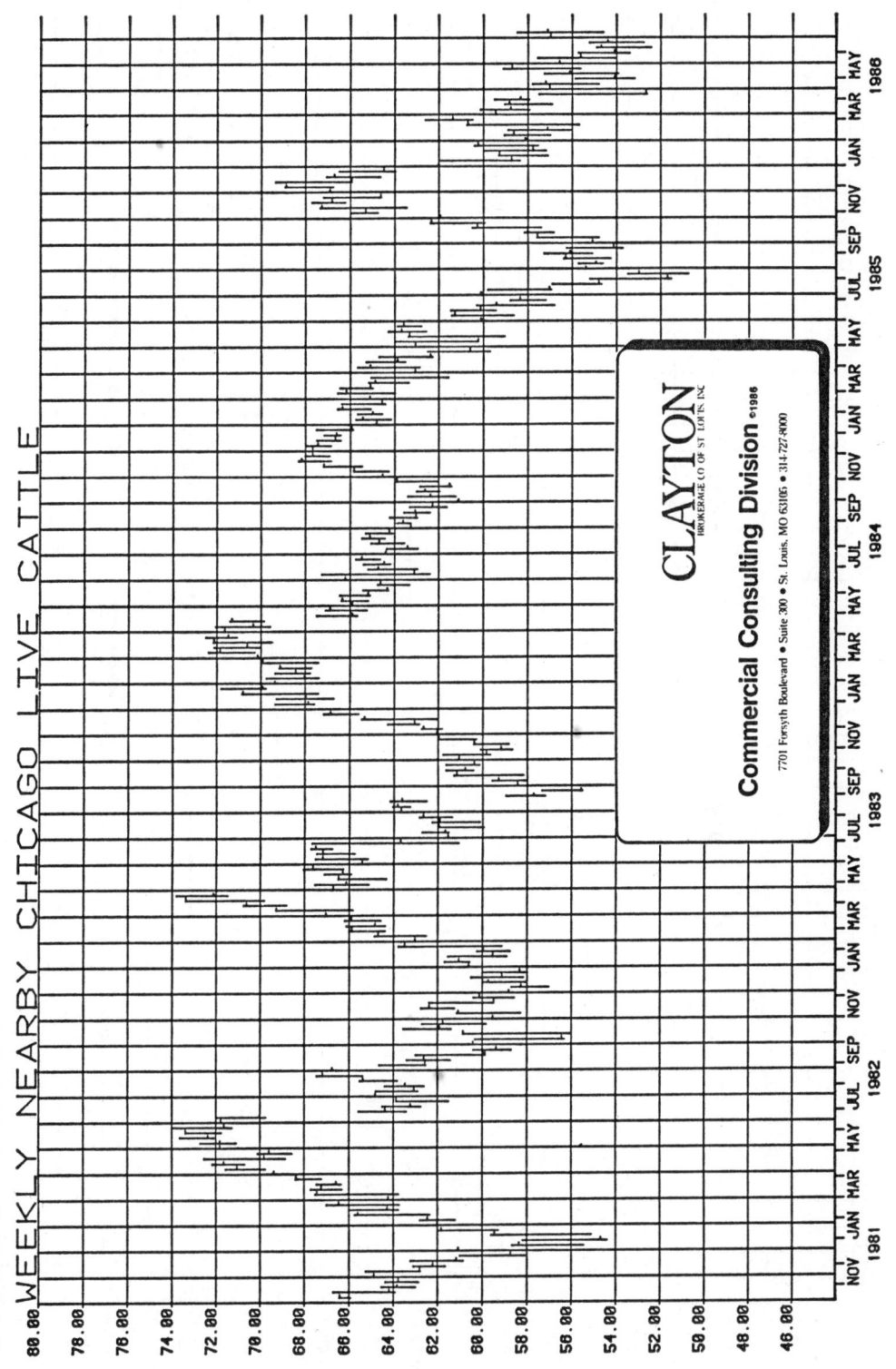

WEEKLY NEARBY CHICAGO LIVE CATTLE

CLAYTON
BROKERAGE CO OF ST LOUIS INC

Commercial Consulting Division ©1986

7701 Forsyth Boulevard • Suite 300 • St. Louis, MO 63105 • 314/727-8000

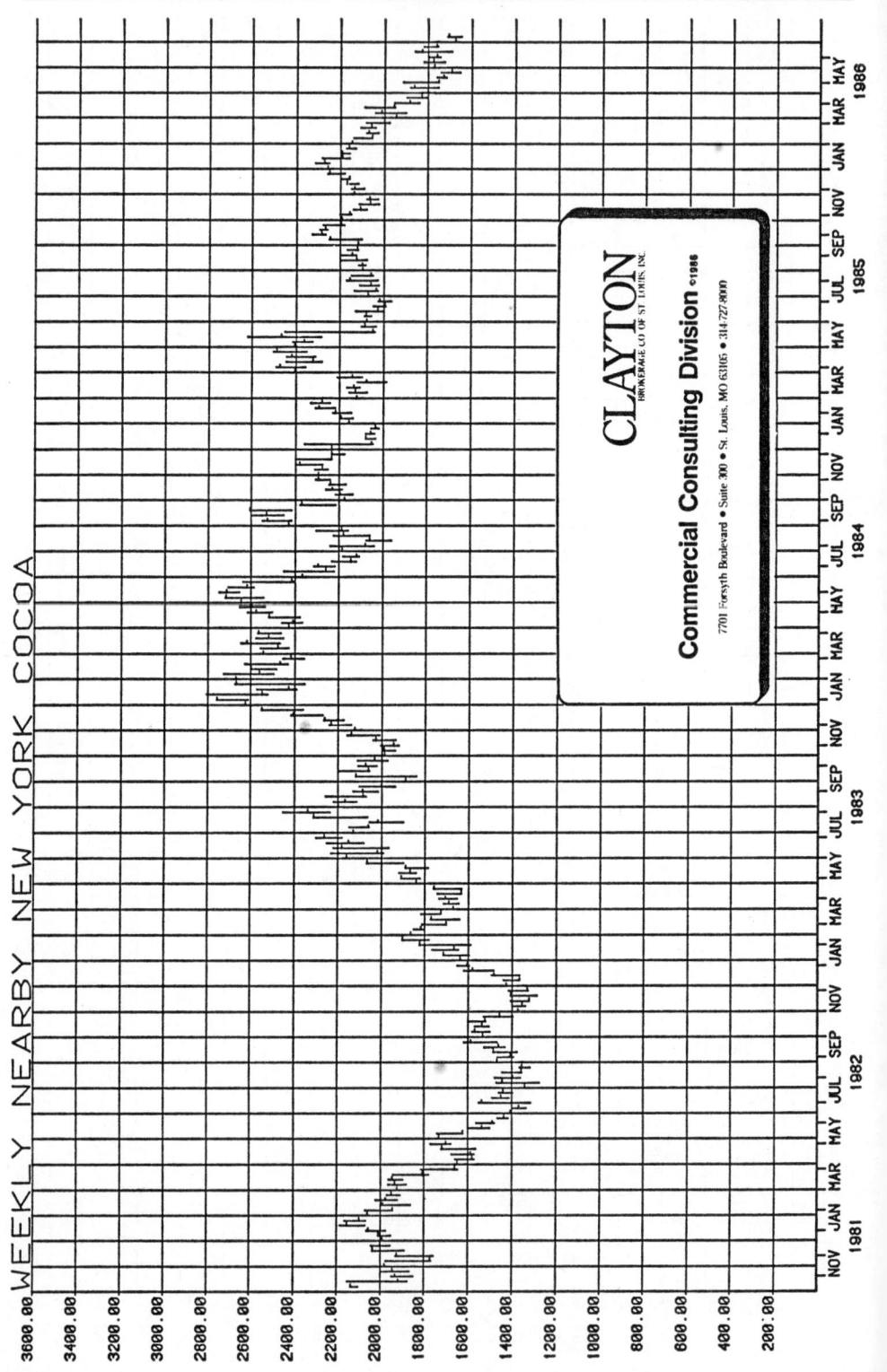

WEEKLY NEARBY NEW YORK COCOA

CLAYTON
BROKERAGE CO. OF ST. LOUIS, INC.

Commercial Consulting Division ©1986

7701 Forsyth Boulevard • Suite 300 • St. Louis, MO 63105 • 314-727-9000

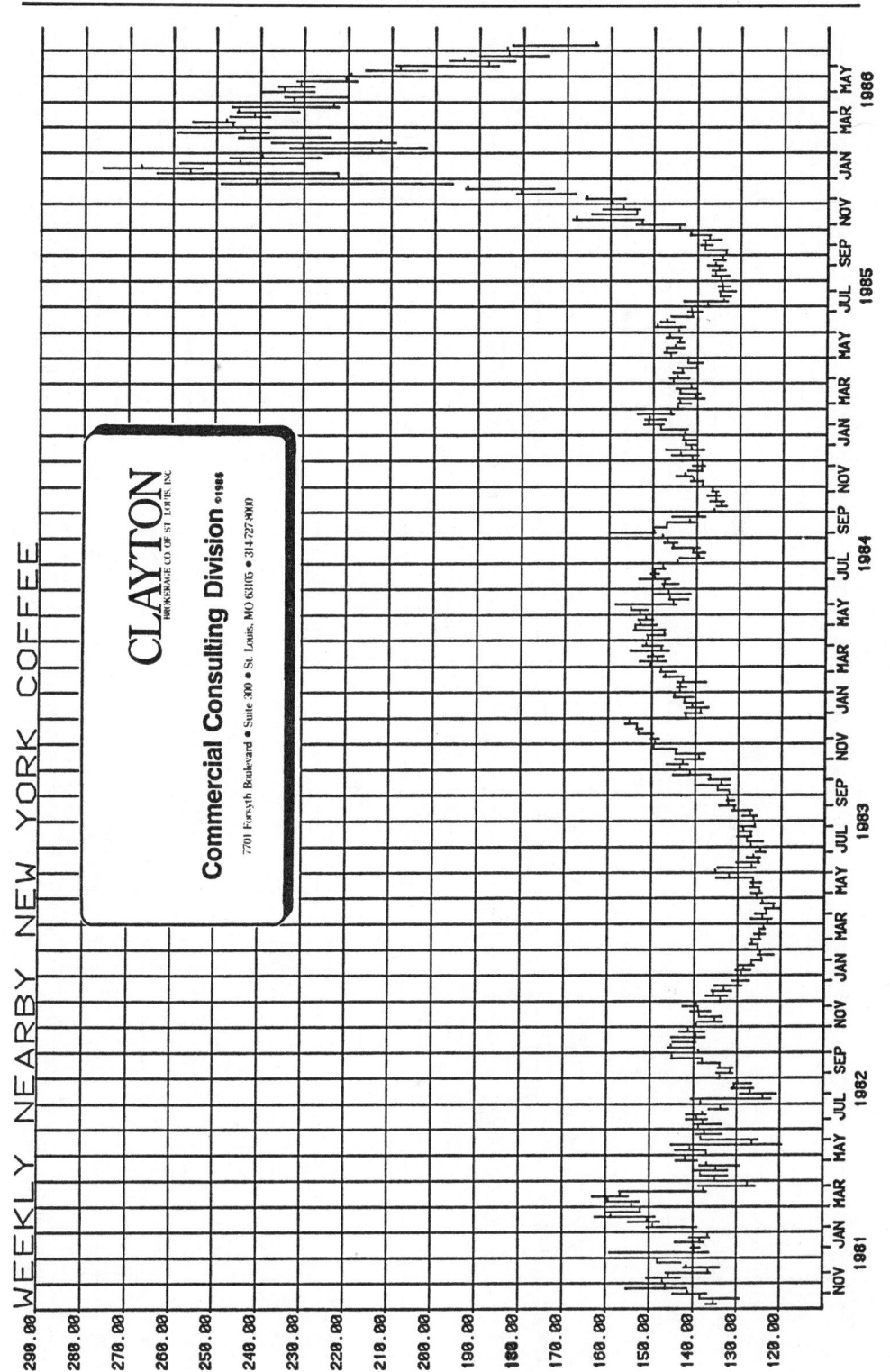

WEEKLY NEARBY NEW YORK COFFEE

CLAYTON
BROKERAGE CO OF ST. LOUIS INC.

Commercial Consulting Division ©1986

7701 Forsyth Boulevard • Suite 300 • St. Louis, MO 63105 • 314-727-9000

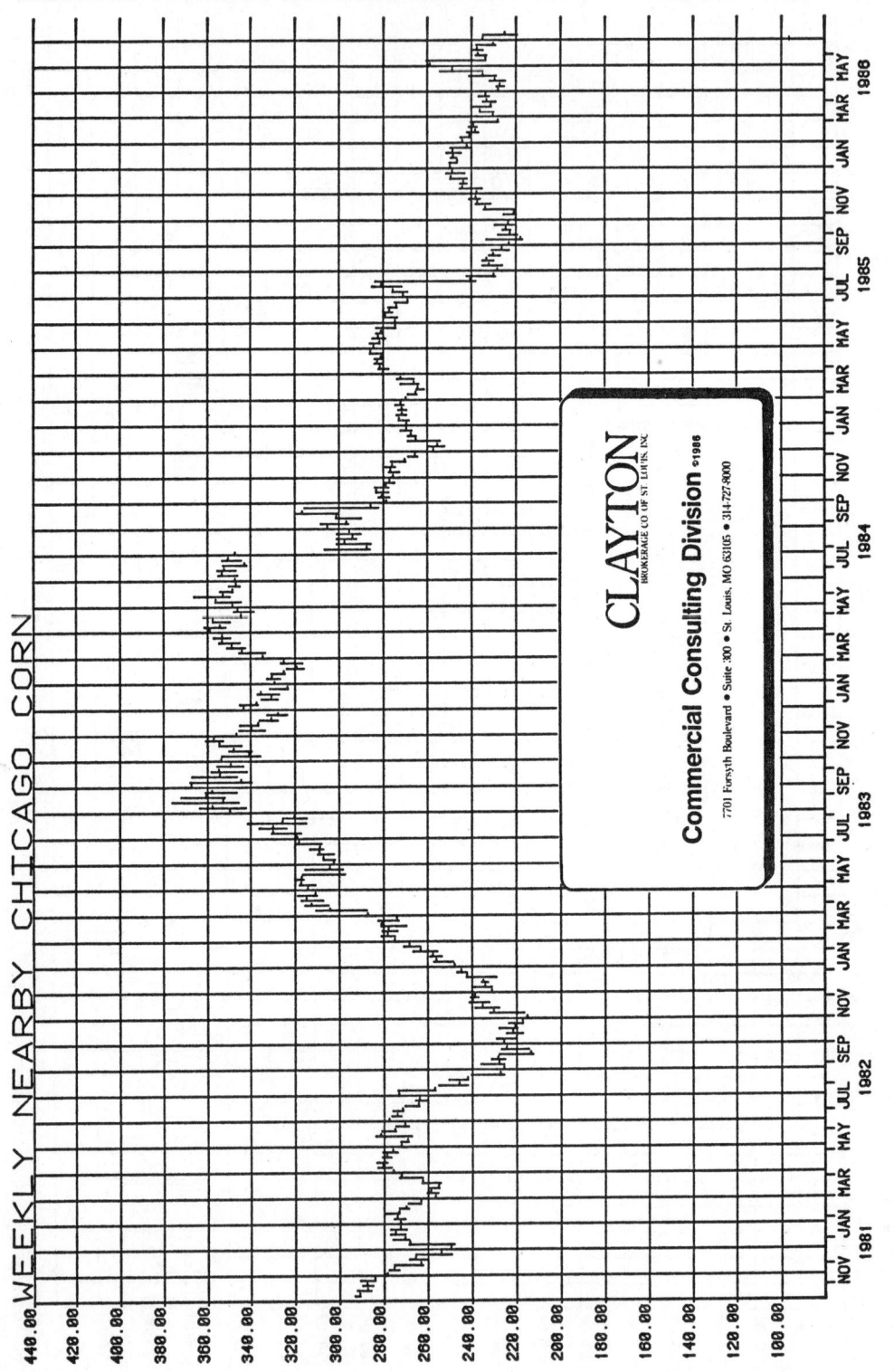

WEEKLY NEARBY CHICAGO CORN

CLAYTON
BROKERAGE CO. OF ST. LOUIS, INC.

Commercial Consulting Division ©1986

7701 Forsyth Boulevard • Suite 300 • St. Louis, MO 63105 • 314-727-8000

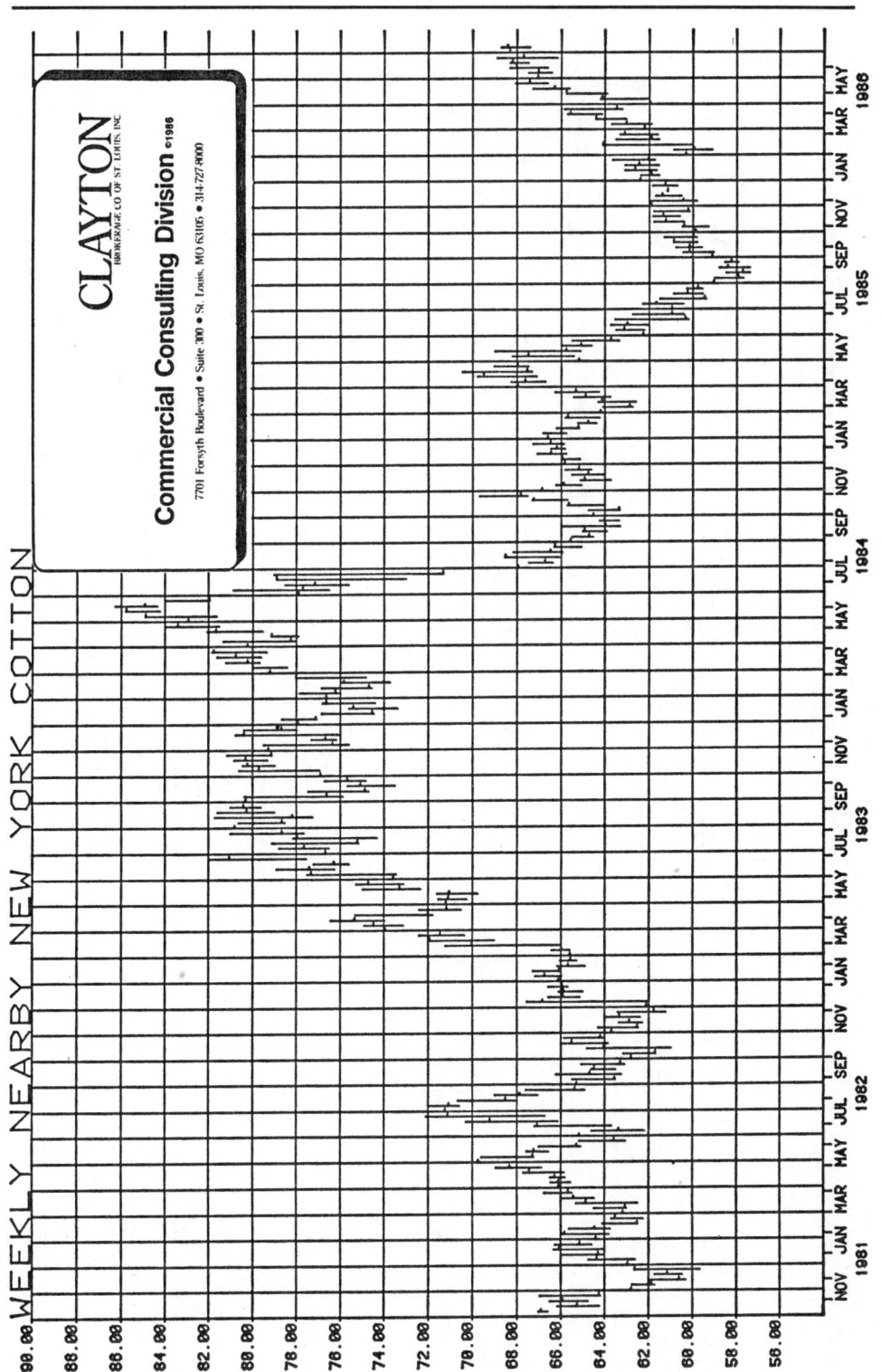

WEEKLY NEARBY NEW YORK COTTON

CLAYTON
BROKERAGE CO. OF ST. LOUIS, INC.

Commercial Consulting Division ©1986

7701 Forsyth Boulevard • Suite 300 • St. Louis, MO 63105 • 314-727-8000

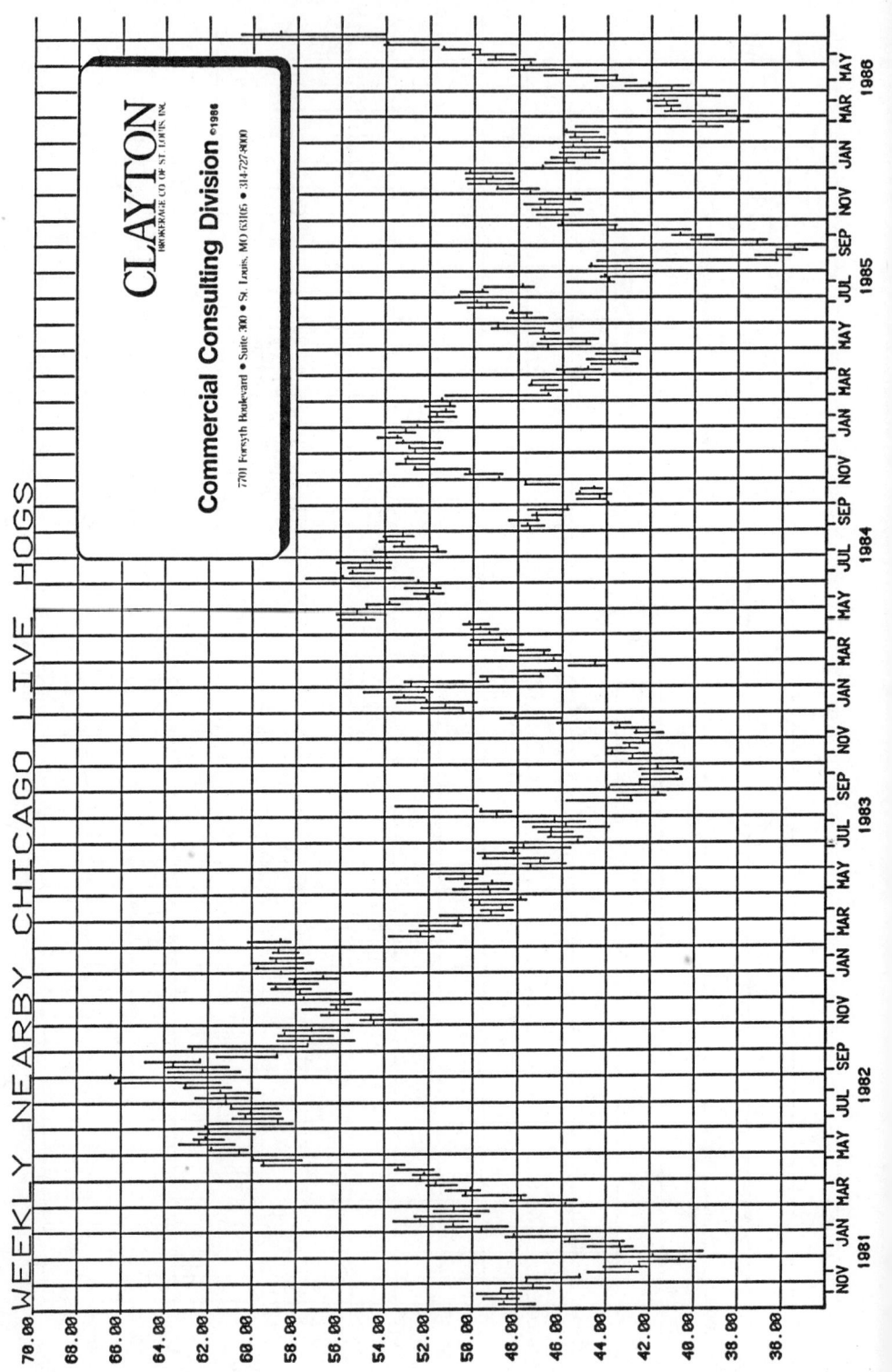

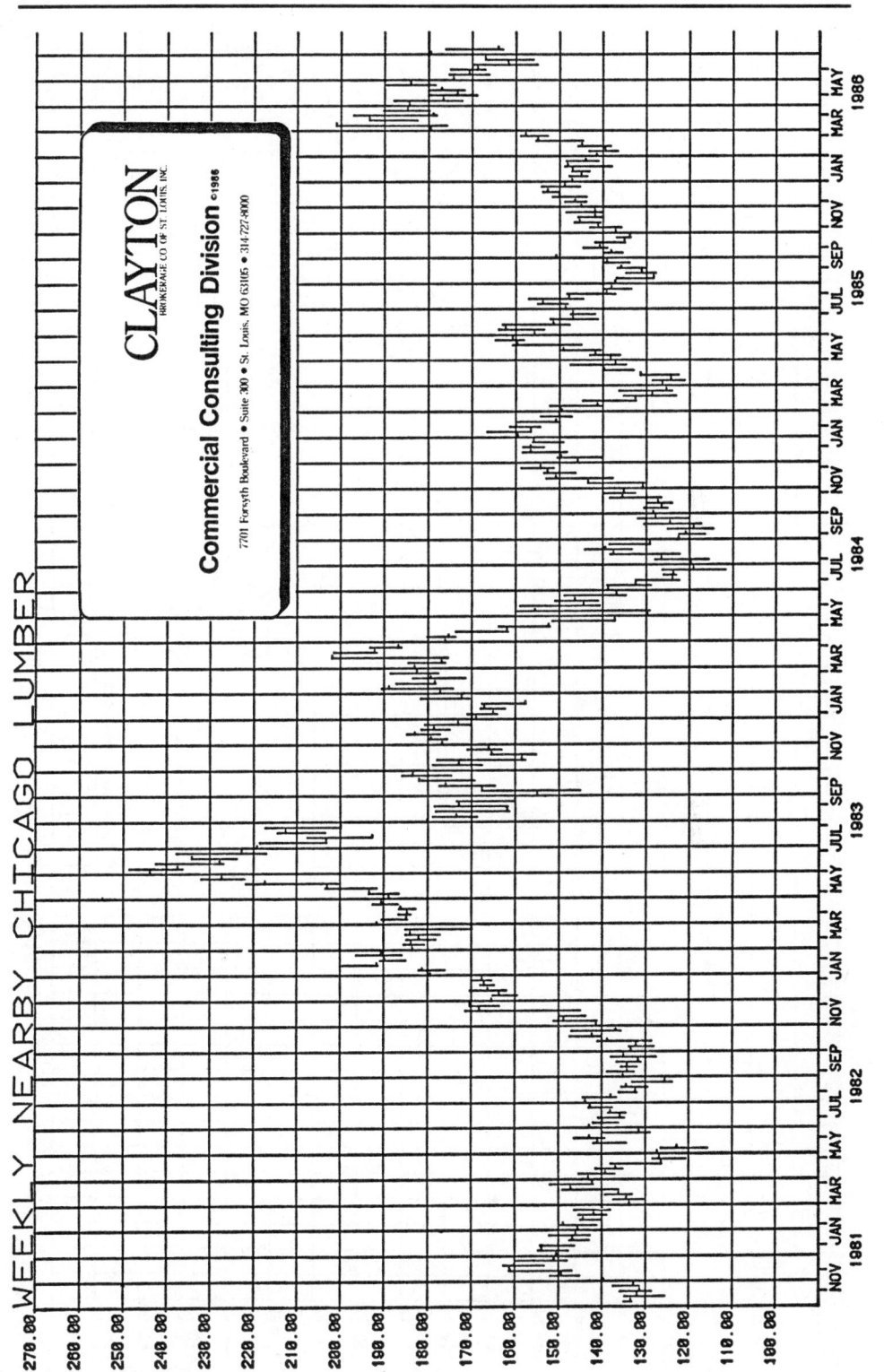

WEEKLY NEARBY CHICAGO LUMBER

CLAYTON
BROKERAGE CO OF ST LOUIS, INC.

Commercial Consulting Division ©1986

7701 Forsyth Boulevard • Suite 300 • St. Louis, MO 63105 • 314-727-8000

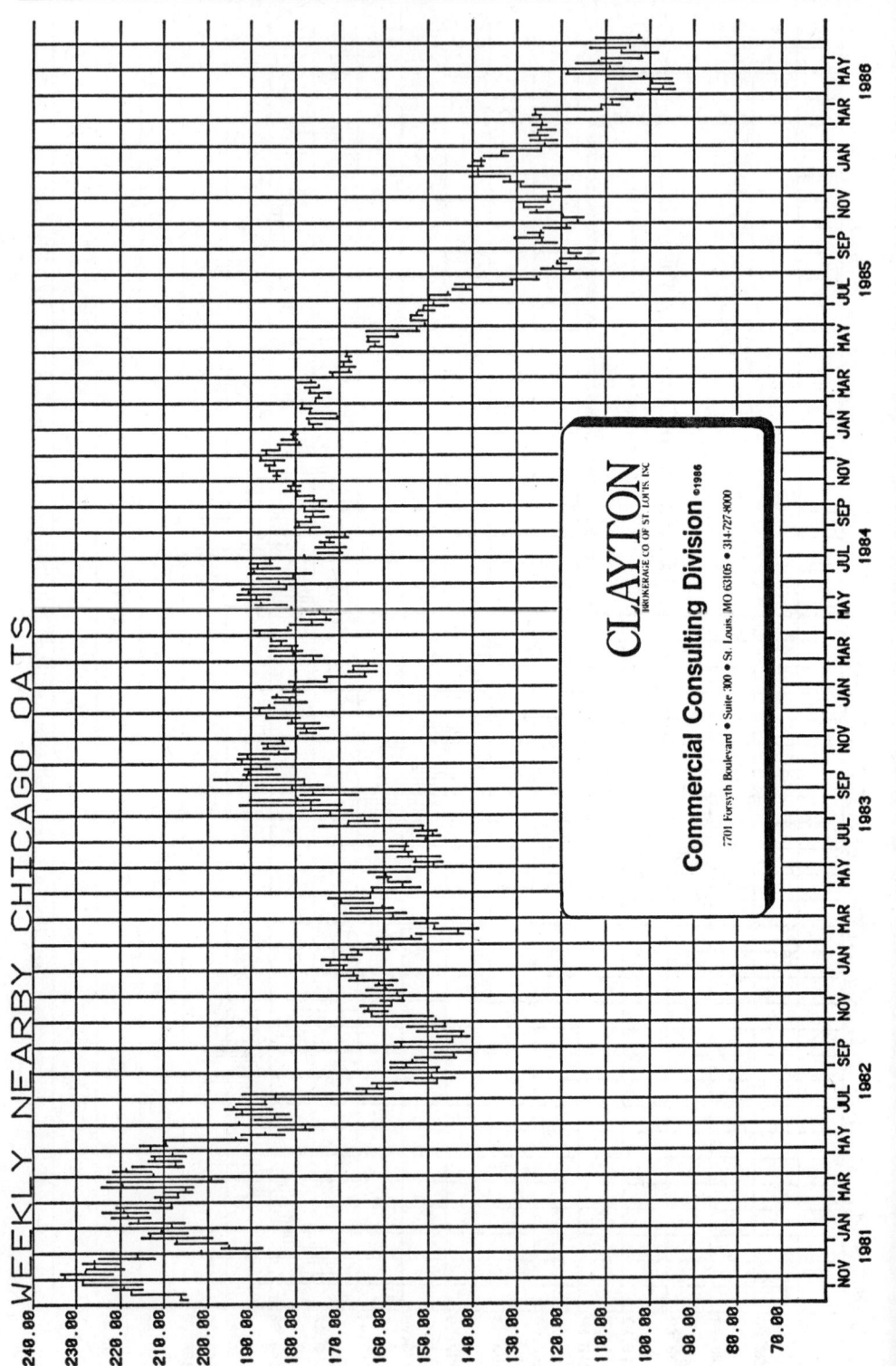

WEEKLY NEARBY CHICAGO OATS

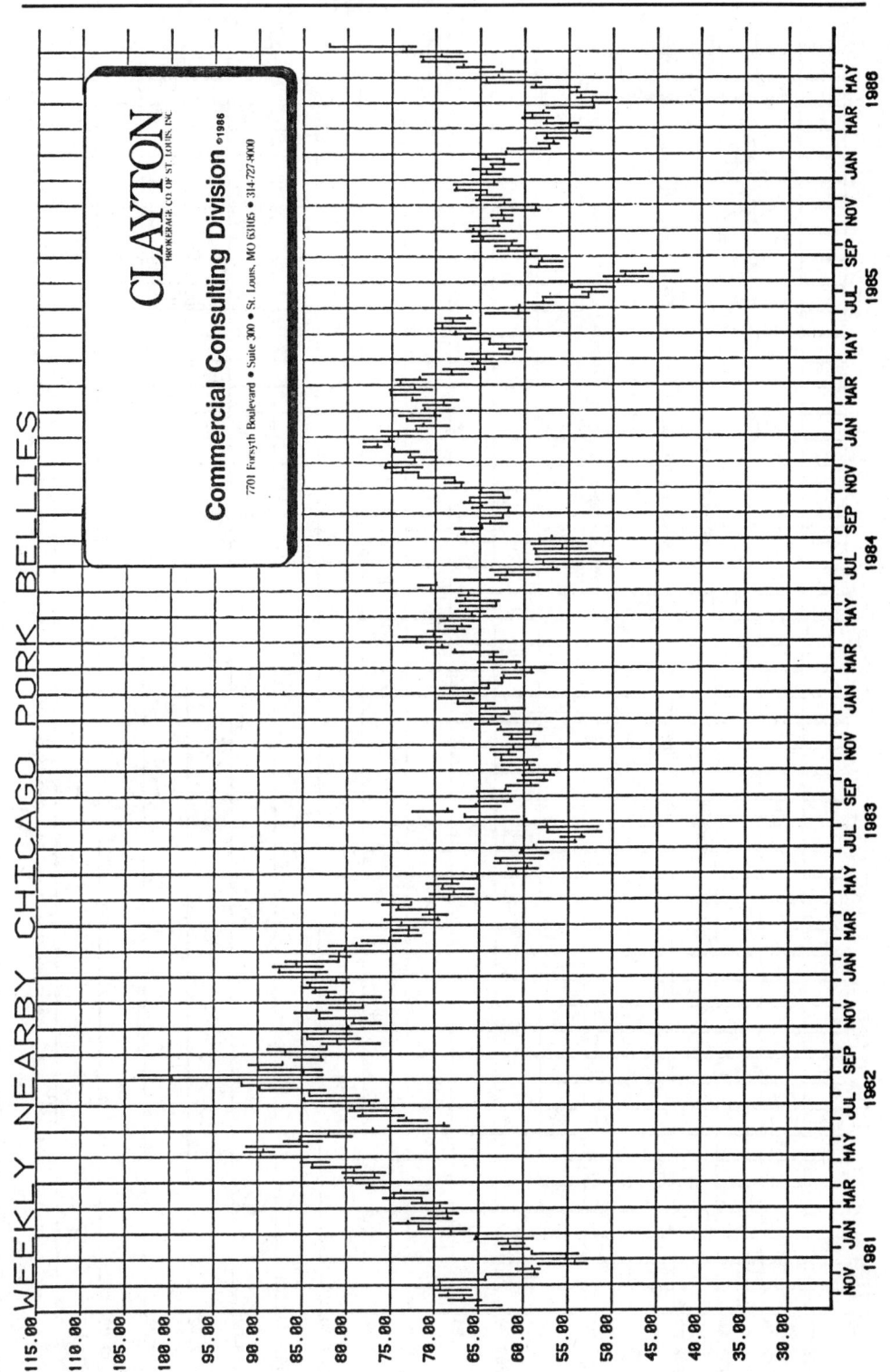

WEEKLY NEARBY CHICAGO PORK BELLIES

CLAYTON
BROKERAGE CO. OF ST. LOUIS, INC.

Commercial Consulting Division ©1986

7701 Forsyth Boulevard • Suite 300 • St. Louis, MO 63105 • 314-727-9000

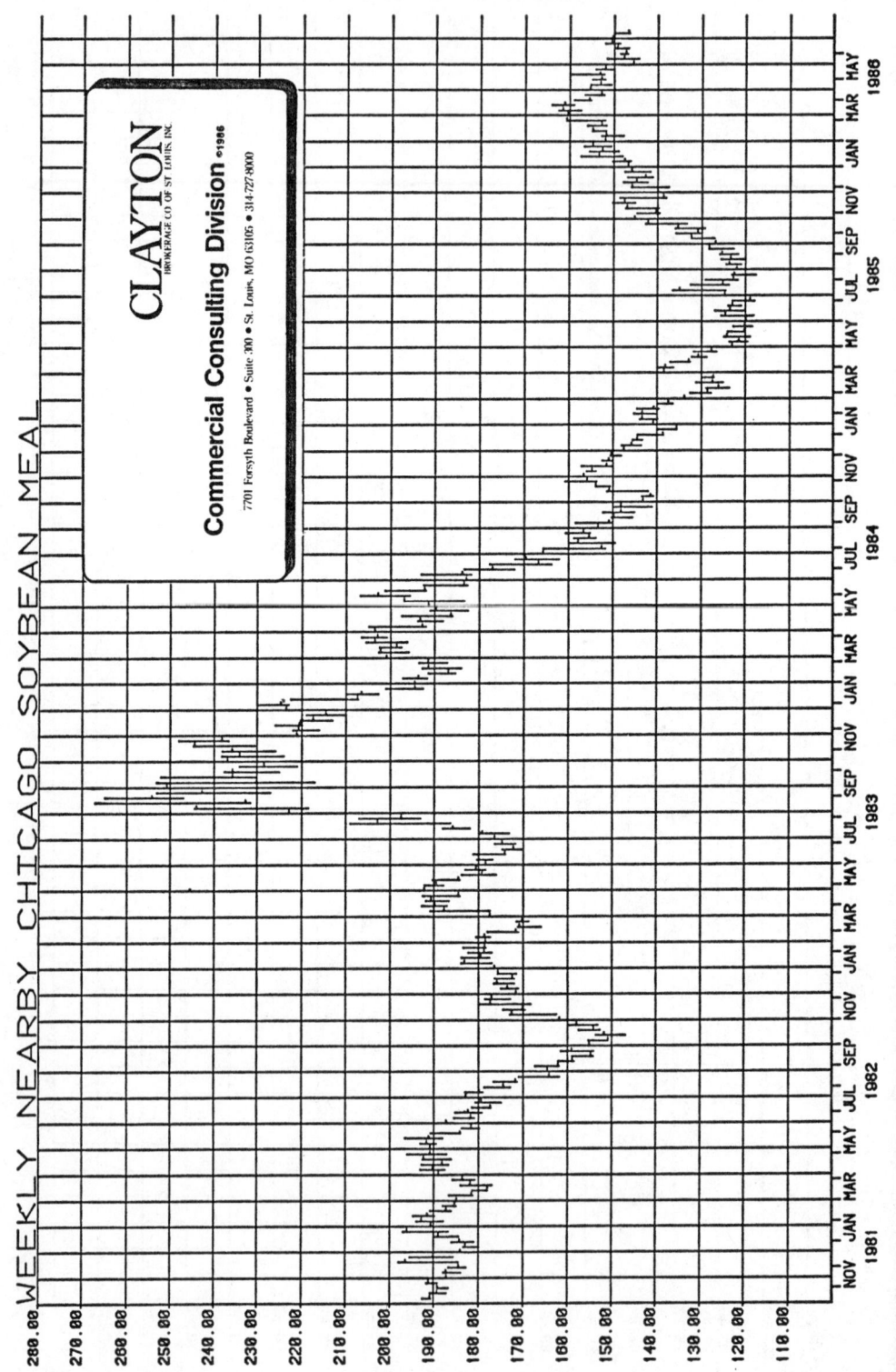

WEEKLY NEARBY CHICAGO SOYBEAN MEAL

CLAYTON
BROKERAGE CO OF ST LOUIS, INC.

Commercial Consulting Division ©1986

7701 Forsyth Boulevard • Suite 300 • St. Louis, MO 63105 • 314-727-8000

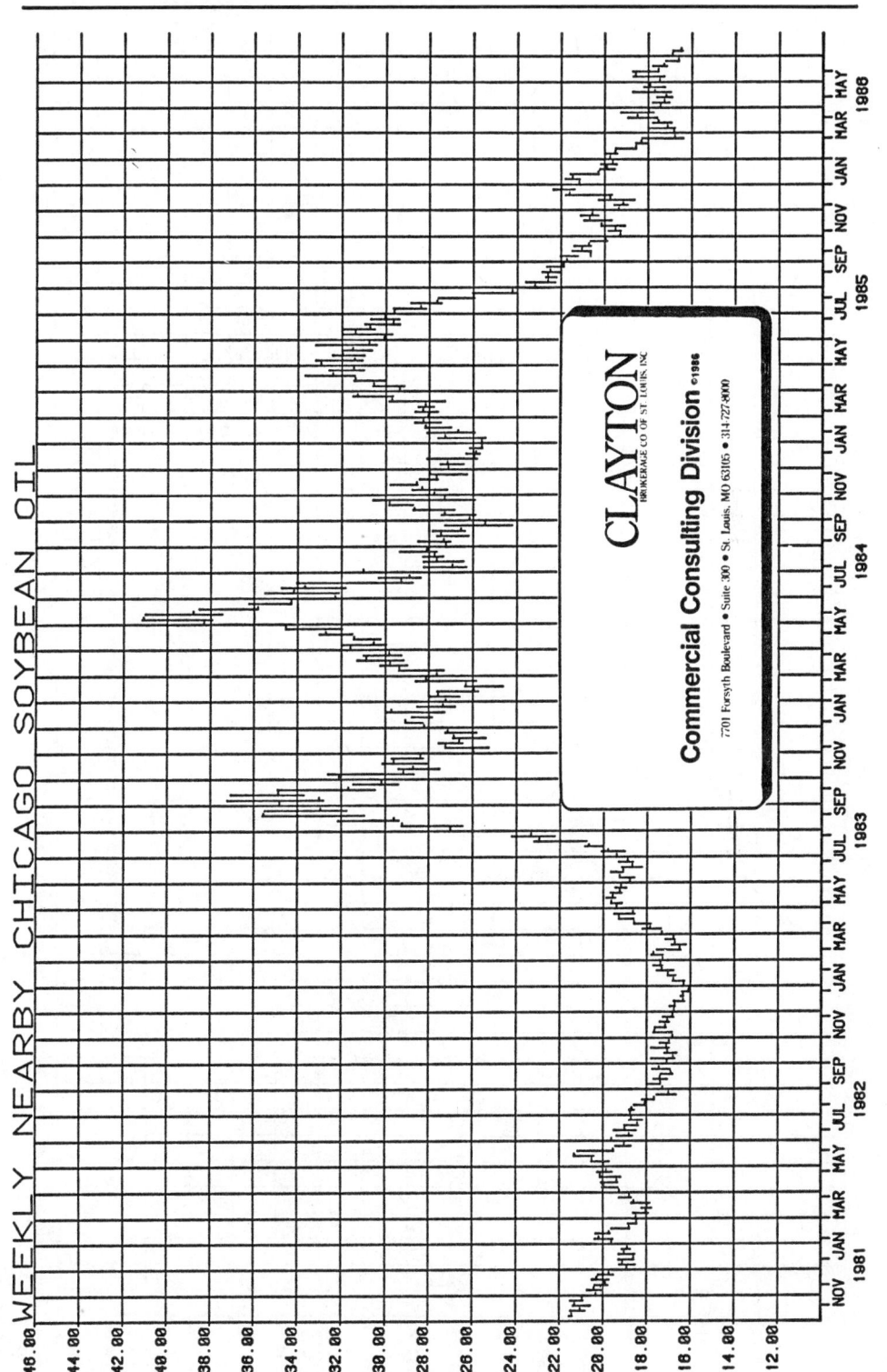

WEEKLY NEARBY CHICAGO SOYBEAN OIL

CLAYTON
BROKERAGE CO OF ST. LOUIS, INC.

Commercial Consulting Division ©1986

7701 Forsyth Boulevard • Suite 300 • St. Louis, MO 63105 • 314-727-9000

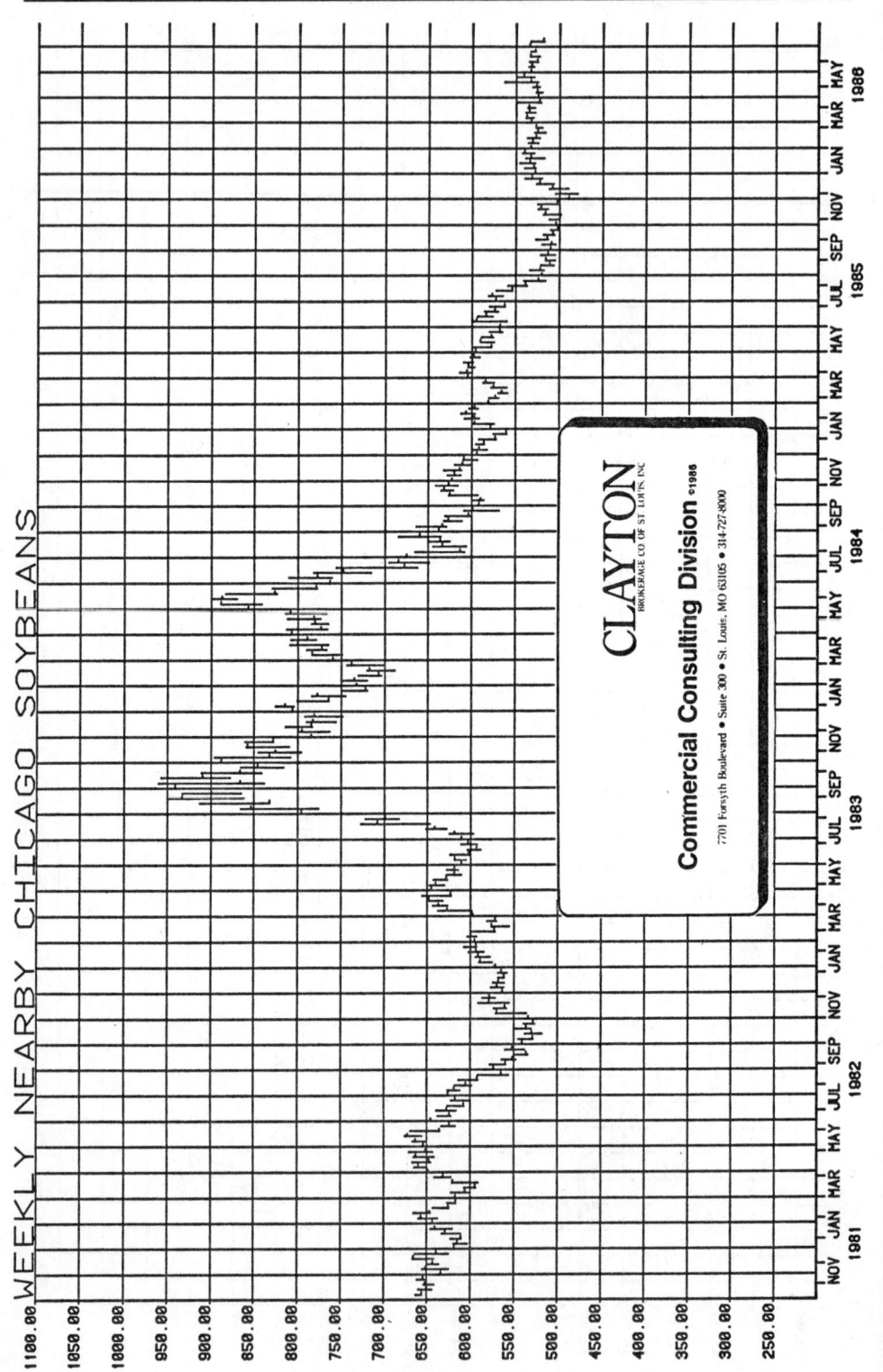

WEEKLY NEARBY CHICAGO SOYBEANS

CLAYTON
BROKERAGE CO OF ST LOUIS, INC

Commercial Consulting Division ©1986

7701 Forsyth Boulevard • Suite 300 • St. Louis, MO 63105 • 314-727-8000

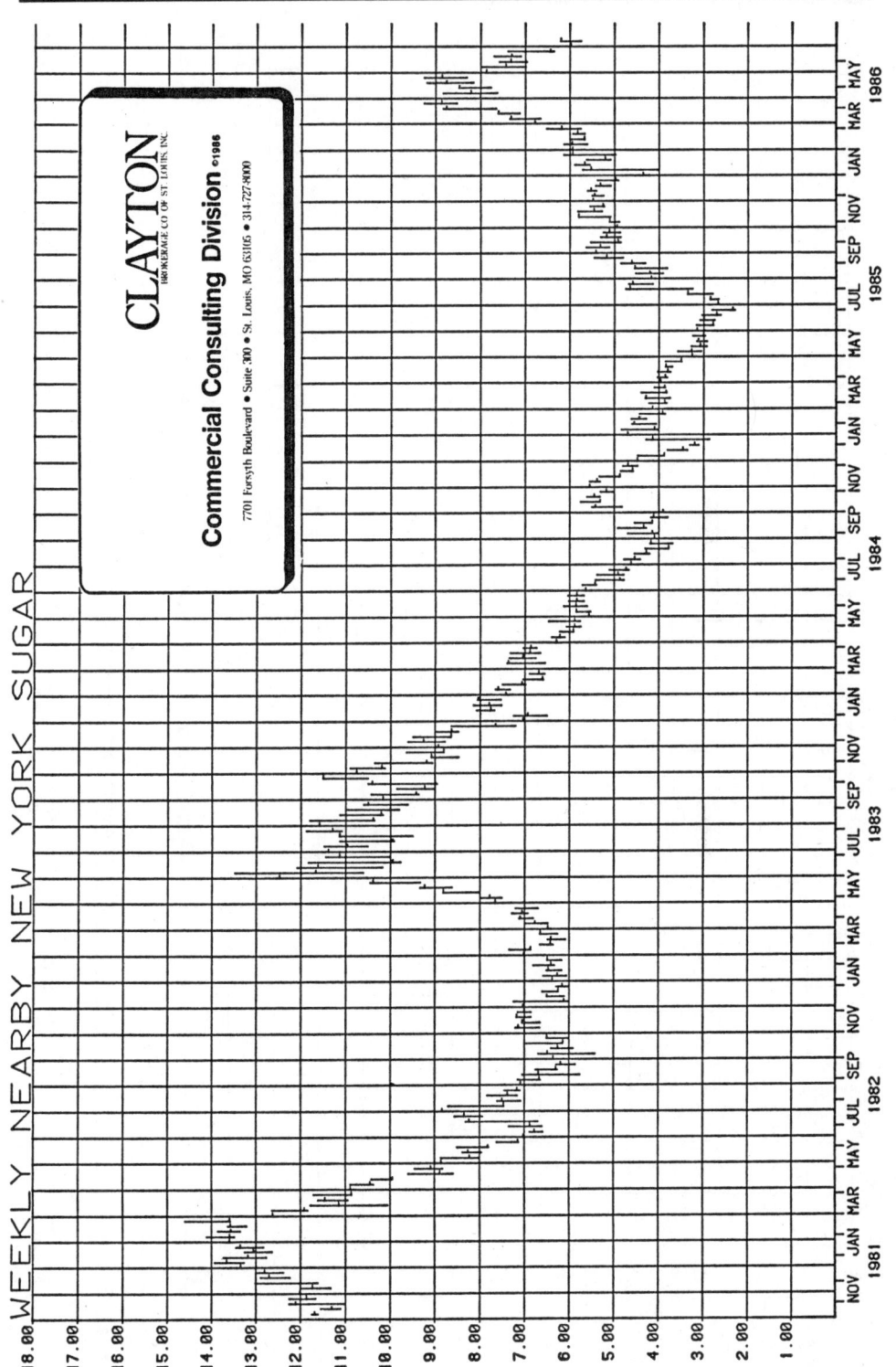

WEEKLY NEARBY NEW YORK SUGAR

CLAYTON
BROKERAGE CO OF ST LOUIS, INC

Commercial Consulting Division ©1986

7701 Forsyth Boulevard • Suite 300 • St. Louis, MO 63105 • 314-727-9000

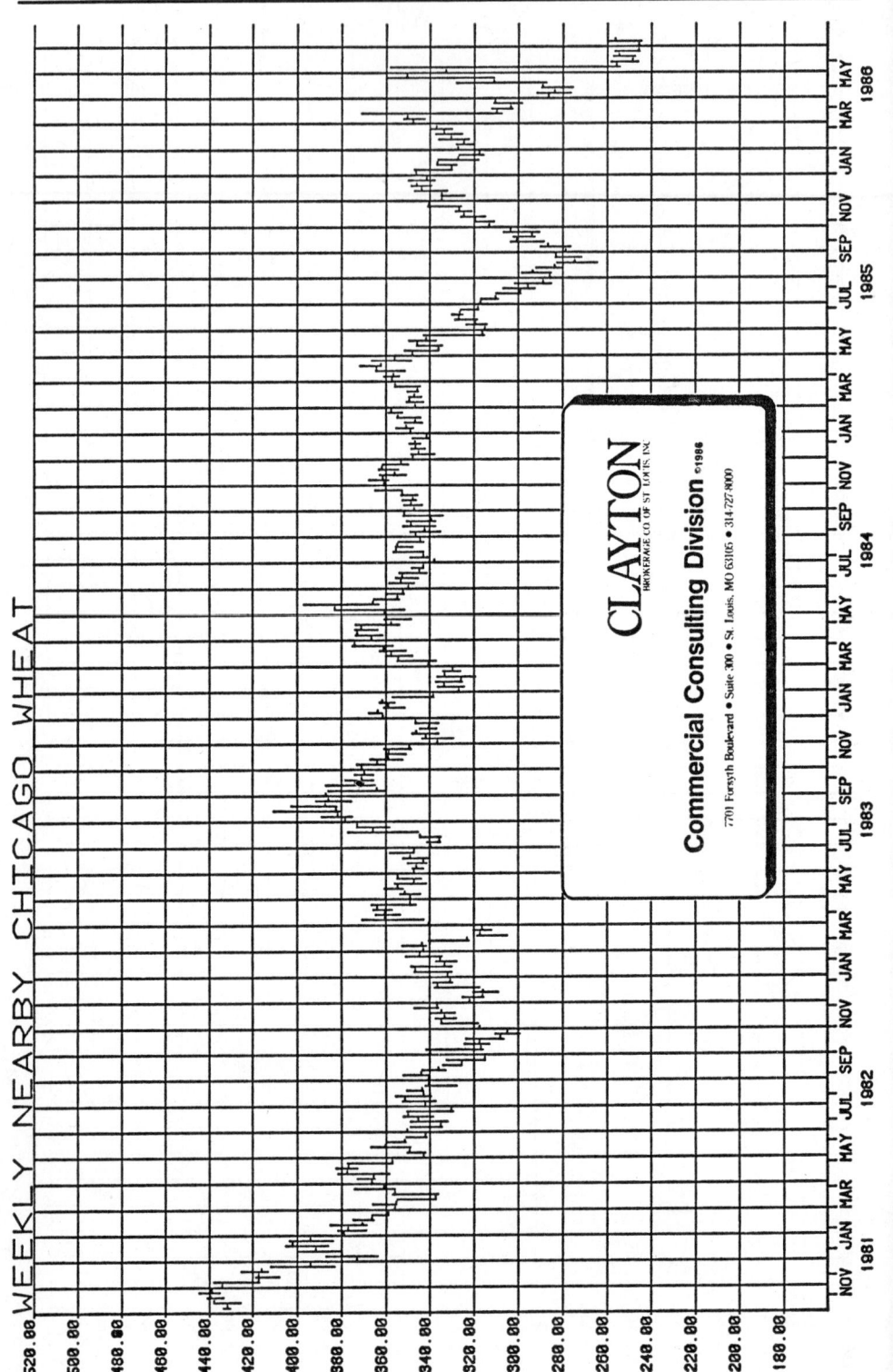

WEEKLY NEARBY CHICAGO WHEAT

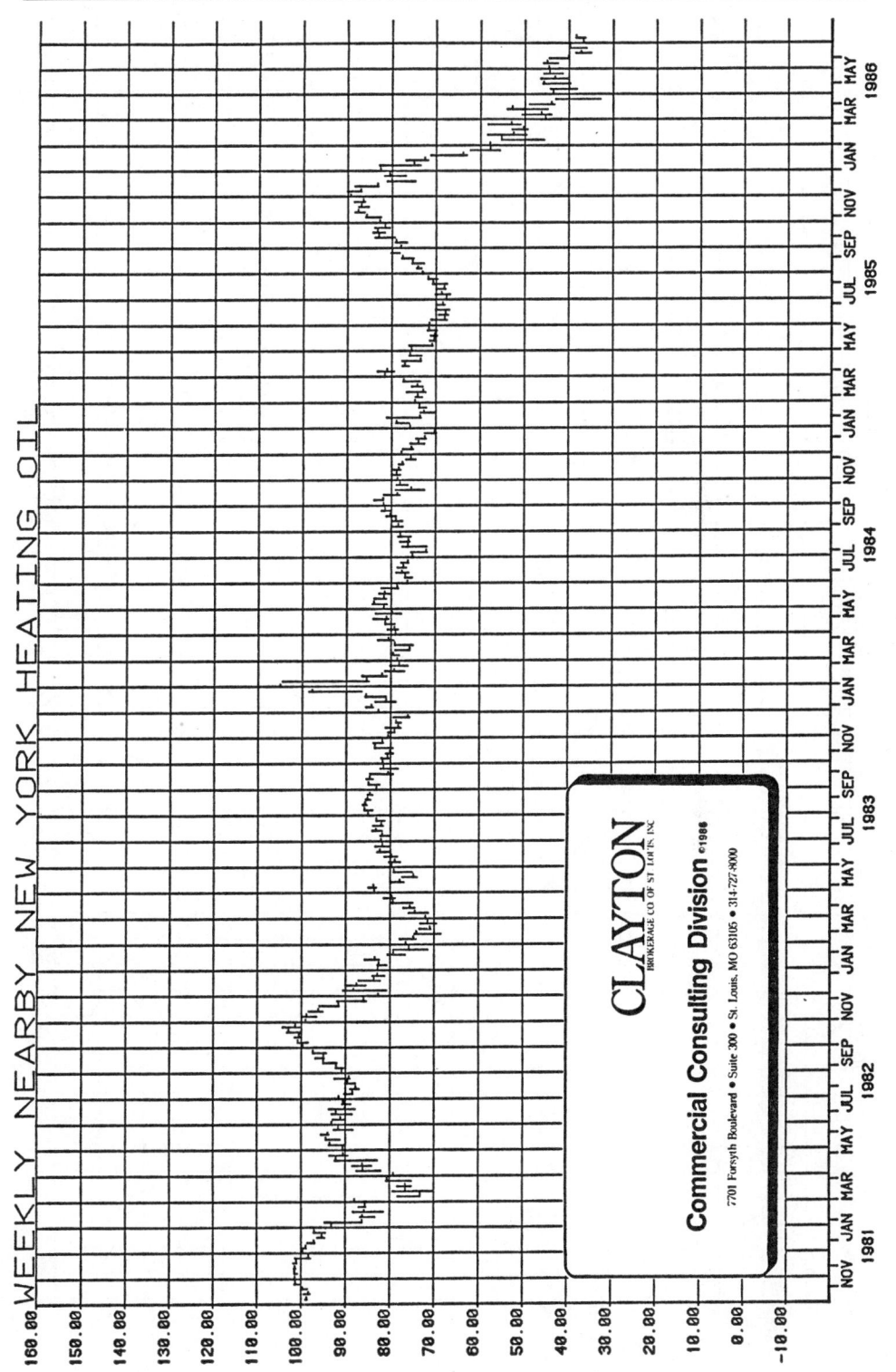

WEEKLY NEARBY NEW YORK HEATING OIL

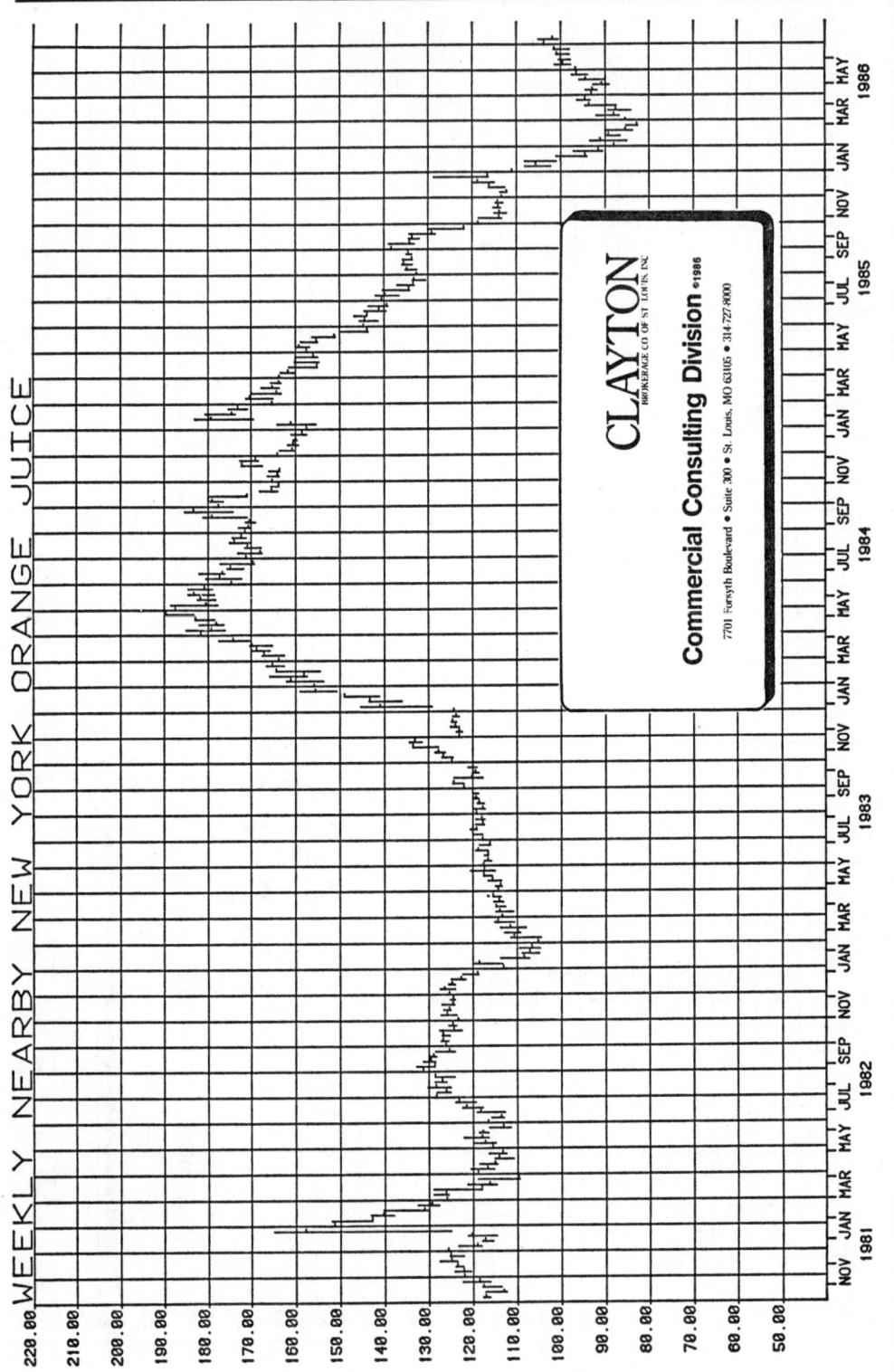

WEEKLY NEARBY NEW YORK ORANGE JUICE

CLAYTON
BROKERAGE CO OF ST LOUIS, INC.

Commercial Consulting Division ©1986

7701 Forsyth Boulevard • Suite 300 • St. Louis, MO 63105 • 314-727-8000

Taxes

The exhibits on pages 505–507 summarize some of the main features of the 1986 Tax Act as reported out of the Joint House and Senate Conference Committee. The Tax Bill was signed by the President on October 22, 1986.

Provisions Affecting Businesses

	CONFERENCE BILL	CURRENT LAW
Corporate tax rate	34% top rate; 2 lower rates on income up to $75,000	46% top rate; 4 lower rates on income up to $100,000
Investment tax credit	Repealed	6% to 10%
Depreciation	Less generous than current law for equipment; much less generous for real estate	Accelerated
Autos	5 years, 200% front-loaded	3 years, 150% front-loaded
Manufacturing equipment	7 years, 200% front-loaded	5 years, 150% front-loaded
Commercial real estate	31.5 years, straight line	19 years, 175% front-loaded
Business meals and entertainment	80% deductible; no deduction for stadium skyboxes	Fully deductible
Oil and gas	One-year write-off for most intangible drilling costs	One-year write off for intangible drilling costs
Bank bad debt reserves	Deductible only for banks with less than $500 million in assets	Deductible
Timber	Retains most timber write-offs	One-year write-off of most costs of growing trees
Research and development	Extend credit for 3 years	25% credit on incremental R&D; expired Dec. 31, 1985

Provisions Affecting Individuals

	CONFERENCE BILL	CURRENT LAW
Individual tax rates	2 rates: 15, 28%	14 rates: 11% to 50%
For joint filers[1]	15% up to $29,750 28% over $29,750	
Personal exemption	$2,000 ($1,950 in 1988); phased out for incomes above $149,250[2]	$1,080
Standard deduction[3]	Joint filer: $5,000; Head of household: $4,400; Singles: $3,000	Joint filer: $3,670; Head of household: $2,480; Singles: $2,480
Mortgage interest	Principal and second residence fully deductible; home equity loans deductible if used for home purchase, home improvement, medical or educational expenses	All mortgages, including home equity loans, fully deductible
Other interest deductions	Consumer interest not deductible; investment interest deductible up to amount equal to investment income[4]	$10,000 plus amount equal to investment income
Charitable contributions	Deductible only for itemizers	Fully deductible for itemizers and non-itemizers
State and local taxes	Deductible except for sales taxes	Fully deductible
Long-term capital gains	28% top rate	20% top rate
Short-term capital gains	28% top rate	50% top rate
Individual retirement account contributions	$2,000 deductible for low and middle income workers; phased out for upper-middle and high-income workers with pension plans	$2,000; $250 for nonworking spouse
401(K) Tax-deferred Savings Plans	Limited to $7,000 a year	Allows up to $30,000 a year
Medical deduction	Deductible in excess of 7.5% of AGI[5]	Deductible in excess of 5% of AGI
Two-earner deduction	No	Yes
Miscellaneous deductions	Deductible in excess of 2% of AGI	Fully deductible
Income averaging	Not allowed	Allowed
Tax shelters	Frohibits use of losses from "passive" investments to offset other income[4]	No limits on using losses from "passive" investments to offset other income

[1]In the Conference bill, no 0% bracket is included. Nonitemizing taxpayers would reduce taxable income by the amount of the standard deduction before calculating taxes. Under current law, this deduction is built into the tax rates and shows up as a 0% bracket.

[2]For joint filers.

[3]Called zero bracket amount under current law. Numbers under current law are for 1986; conference numbers are for 1988.

[4]Provision is phased in over a number of years.

[5]Adjusted Gross Income.

Effective Dates Of Proposed Tax-Law Changes

General effective date	**Jan. 1, 1987**
Individual rate cuts[1]	**Mar. 15, 1987**
Corporate rate cuts[1]	**July 1, 1987**
Capital gains rate rise[2]	**Jan. 1, 1987**
Increase standard deduction	**Jan. 1, 1988**
Increase personal exemption	**3-year phase-in**
Repeal investment tax credit	**Jan. 1, 1986**
Change depreciation	**Jan. 1, 1987**
Passive loss limits	**5-year phase-in**
Interest deduction limits	**5-year phase-in**

[1]A "blended" rate schedule, partway between the old rates and new rates, will apply for 1987.
[2]Top rate will be 28% for 1987

Businesses' Share Of U.S. Taxes

Corporate taxes as a percentage of federal revenue

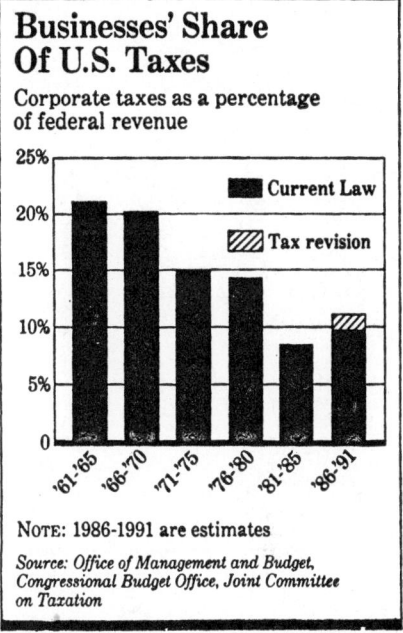

NOTE: 1986-1991 are estimates

Source: Office of Management and Budget, Congressional Budget Office, Joint Committee on Taxation

Rate Structure Beginning in 1987

For taxable years beginning in 1987, five-bracket rate schedules are provided, as shown in the table below.

For married individuals filing separate returns, the taxable income bracket amounts for 1987 begin at one-half the amounts for joint returns.

| Tax rate | Taxable income brackets | | |
	Married, filing joint returns	Heads of household	Singles
11%	0–$3,000	0–$2,500	0–$1,800
15%	3,000–28,000	2,500–23,000	1,800–16,800
28%	28,000–45,000	23,000–38,000	16,800–27,000
35%	45,000–90,000	38,000–80,000	27,000–54,000
38.5%	Above 90,000	Above 80,000	Above 54,000

MAJOR TAXES AND RATES USED BY STATES AS OF JANUARY 1, 1986

State	Income taxes Corporation	Income taxes Individual	General sales and use tax	Gasoline tax (per gallon)	Cigarette tax (per pack of 20)	Property tax
Alabama	5% (F)	2 to 5% (F)	4%[a]	11¢	16.5¢	X
Arizona	2.5 to 10.5 (F)	2 to 8 (F)	5[a]	16	15	X
Arkansas	1 to 6	1 to 7	4[a]	13.5	21	X
California	9.6	1 to 11	4.75[a]	9	10	X
Colorado	5[b]	3 to 8 (F)	3[a]	12	15	X
Connecticut	11.5[c]	1 to 13[d]	7.5	15[e]	26	X
Georgia	6	1 to 6	3[a]	7.5 + 3% of retail	12	X
Hawaii	5.85 to 6.435	2.25 to 11	4	15 to 18.5	40% wholesale	
Idaho	7.7	2 to 7.5	4	14.5	9.1	X
Illinois	4	2.5	5[a]	12	20	X
Indiana	3[f]	3	5	14.1	10.5	X
Iowa	6 to 12 (F)	.5 to 13 (F)	4	15	26	
Kansas	4.5[g]	2 to 9 (F[h])	3[a]	11	24	X
Kentucky	3 to 7.25	2 to 6 (F[h])	5	10[i]	3.001	X
Louisiana	4 to 8 (F)	2 to 6 (F)	4[a]	16	16	
Maine	3.5 to 8.93	1 to 10	5	14	28	X
Maryland	7	2 to 5	5	13[i]	13	X
Massachusetts	8.33[j]	5[k]	5	11	26	X
Michigan	2.35	5.1[b]	4	15	21	X
Minnesota	6 to 12	1.5 to 14 (F)	6[a]	17	23	X
Mississippi	3 to 5	3 to 5	6	9	18	X
Missouri	5 (F)	1.5 to 6 (F)	4.225[a]	7	13	X
Nebraska	4.75 to 6.65	19% of Federal income tax	3.5[a,e]	17.2	18[e]	X
New Jersey	9[l]	2 to 3.5	6	8	25	X
New Mexico	4.8 to 7.2	.7 to 7.8[m]	3.75[a]	11	12	X
New York	10[c]	2 to 13.5[b]	4[a]	8	21	
North Carolina	6	3 to 7	3[a]	12	2	X
North Dakota	3 to 10.5 (F)	2 to 9[n] (F)	4	13	18	X
Ohio	5.1 to 9.2[c]	.855 to 8.55[b]	5[a]	12	14	X
Oklahoma	5	.5 to 6[m] (F)	3.25[a]	10	18	
Pennsylvania	9.5	2.2	6	12	23.4	X
Rhode Island	8[c]	22.21% of Federal income tax	6	13[i]	23	X
South Carolina	6	2 to 7 (F)	5	13	7	X
Tennessee	6	6[d]	5.5[a]	12	13	
Utah	5	2.25 to 7.75 (F)	4.625[a,b]	14	12	X
Vermont	6 to 9[b]	26.5% of Federal income tax	4[b]	13	17	X
Virginia	6	2 to 5.75	3[a]	11	2.5	X
West Virginia	6 to 7[e]	2.1 to 13	5	10.5	17	X
Wisconsin	7.9	5 to 7.9	5	16	25	X
Florida	5.5		5[a]	4	21	X
Nevada			5.75[a]	11.25	15	X
South Dakota	These 5 states have no corporate income tax	These 7 states have no individual income tax	4[a]	13	23	
Texas			4.125[a]	10	20.5	
Washington			6.5[a]	18	23	X
Wyoming			3[a]	8	8	X
Alaska	1 to 9.4		These 5 states have no general sales tax	8	16	X
Delaware	8.7	1.2 to 9.7 (F)		11	14	
Montana	6.75[m]	2 to 11 (F)		15	16	X
New Hampshire	8.25	5[d]		14	17	X
Oregon	7.5	4 to 10 (F)		11	27	X

(X) Indicates state levies a property tax.
(F) Allows Federal income tax as a deduction.

[a] Local taxes are additional.
[b] Future reduction scheduled under current law.
[c] Alternative methods of calculation may be required.
[d] In Connecticut, New Hampshire, and Tennessee, tax applies to income from intangibles only, at various rates according to type.
[e] Future increases scheduled under current law.
[f] Tax is 3% of adjusted gross income. A supplemental net income tax is imposed at 4%.
[g] A 2-¼% surtax is imposed on taxable income in excess of $25,000.
[h] Deductions limited.
[i] Tax imposed at percent of wholesale value.
[j] Additional 14% surtax is imposed.
[k] Tax of 10% on income derived from intangibles, and 5% on all other income, and an additional 3.75% tax for 1986.
[l] Additional tax on net worth is part of the corporate franchise tax.
[m] Qualified taxpayers may elect to pay alternative taxes at varying rates.
[n] Optional tax of 10.5% of taxpayer's adjusted Federal income tax liability.
Source: Compiled by Tax Foundation from data reported by Commerce Clearing House.

Source: Reprinted by permission of Tax Foundation, Incorporated. One Thomas Circle, N.W., Washington, D.C. 20005–5802.

FEDERAL INCOME TAXES PAID BY HIGH- AND LOW-INCOME TAXPAYERS 1979 AND 1984[a]

Adjusted gross income class	Income level 1979	Income level 1984	Percent of tax paid 1979	Percent of tax paid 1984	Average tax 1979	Average tax 1984
Highest 5 percent	$39,901 or more	$59,460 or more	37.6	38.2	$17,407	$23,313
Highest 10 percent	32,711 or more	44,656 or more	49.5	51.0	11,456	15,549
Highest 25 percent	21,759 or more	29,316 or more	73.1	74.0	6,769	9,035
Highest 50 percent	11,870 or more	15,837 or more	93.2	92.9	4,315	5,669
Lowest 50 percent	11,869 or less	15,836 or less	6.8	7.1	313	434
Lowest 25 percent	5,565 or less	7,337 or less	.5	.8	46	92
Lowest 10 percent	2,212 or less	2,939 or less	(b)	.1	9	31

[a]Data for 1984 are preliminary.
[b]Less than .05 percent.
Source: Tax Foundation computations based on Treasury Department data.

HOW FEDERAL, STATE, AND LOCAL GOVERNMENTS SPEND EACH DOLLAR OF PUBLIC FUNDS SELECTED FISCAL YEARS 1960–1984

Function	Cents per dollar of total spending 1960	1970	1980	1984
Major social welfare programs, total ...	20.6	25.8	33.6	32.9
Social security (OASDHI)	7.1	10.8	15.6	16.4
Social services and income maintenance[a]	8.5	10.7	13.0	11.8
Government employee retirement ...	1.4	1.9	3.0	3.1
Veterans (not elsewhere classified)...	2.5	1.6	1.3	1.2
Railroad retirement	.6	.5	.5	.4
National defense and international relations.....................	32.3	25.3	15.6	17.4
Education	12.8	16.7	15.0	13.2
Interest on general debt.............	6.2	5.5	7.9	9.7
Environment and housing	5.4	4.4	4.9	5.8
Utilities and liquor stores	3.4	2.8	3.8	3.9
Transportation.....................	7.6	6.2	4.4	3.5
Public Safety......................	1.8	2.0	2.3	2.3
Government administration	1.8	1.9	2.2	2.1
Postal service (Federal)	2.5	2.3	1.9	1.9
Sanitation	1.1	1.0	1.4	1.1
All other.........................	4.5	6.1	7.0	6.2
Exhibit (billions): Total spending...................	$151.3	$333.0	$958.7	$1,428.0

[a] Includes public welfare, hospitals, health, and unemployment insurance benefits.
Source: Department of Commerce, Bureau of the Census; and Tax Foundation computations.

FEDERAL, STATE, AND LOCAL GOVERNMENT EXPENDITURES[a] SELECTED FISCAL YEARS 1950–1986

	Amount (billions)			Total expenditures	
Fiscal year	All governments	Federal	State and local	Per household	Per capita
1950.........	$ 70.3	$ 44.8	$ 25.5	$ 1,614	$ 466
1960.........	151.3	97.3	54.0	2,866	847
1965.........	205.7	130.1	75.6	3,581	1,067
1970.........	333.0	208.2	124.8	5,252	1,643
1975.........	560.1	340.5	219.6	7,875	2,612
1980.........	958.6	615.4	343.2	11,867	4,243
1981.........	1,109.8	717.4	392.4	13,474	4,857
1982.........	1,233.5	794.7	438.8	14,768	5,345
1983.........	1,351.0	872.5	478.5	16,099	5,798
1984.........	1,428.0	926.5	501.6	16,720	6,056
1985[b].......	1,590.3	1,021.1	569.2	18,324	6,682
1986[b].......	1,685.7	1,057.3	628.4	19,145	7,017

[a]Grants-in-aid are counted as expenditures of the first disbursing unit.
[b]Estimated by Tax Foundation.
Source: Basic data from U.S. Department of Commerce, Bureau of the Census; computations by Tax Foundation.

Source: Reprinted by permission of Tax Foundation, Incorporated.

Investing in Gold, Diamonds and Collectibles

Investing in Gold

Gold has been one of the more widely promoted investment vehicles over the last several years. Prices have moved from about $140 per ounce in early 1977 to over $800 in early 1980. However, by August 1985 prices declined to $291 an ounce. Because of such large fluctuations, the metal has stimulated a great deal of speculative interest among many investors.

Investment in gold can be made in a variety of ways:

Gold bullion (bars and wafers) This can be purchased through many stock brokers, bullion currency dealers, and some investment (mutual fund) companies. The purity of gold is indicated by the fineness. Pure gold has a fineness of 1.000 and corresponds to 24 karats.* Each bar is stamped with the fineness as determined by an assay, the refiner's number, a bar identification number and the weight. A bar fineness of .995 or better is acceptable.

Individuals who accept delivery of gold bars and who subsequently wish to resell must have the bar reassayed prior to sale because of the possibility of adulteration with cheaper metals. Because of the latter possibility, individuals should always buy from reputable dealers, and the bar should bear the stamp of well recognized refiners or assayers. Individuals taking physical possession of the metal also have sales taxes, storage, and insurance costs.

The purchaser may arrange to have the dealer (or agent) retain physical possession of the bullion. In this case, evidence of ownership is provided by a *gold deposit certificate* (receipt) issued by the dealer. Since gold certificates are generally nonnegotiable or assignable, there is no loss if it is stolen. The gold deposit certificate method of buying bullion eliminates sales taxes, storage risks (though the dealer will charge a modest storage fee) and the need for assay on resale. It is probably the most convenient way of purchasing gold.

Gold bullion coins Bullion coins are issued in large number by several governments which guarantee their gold content. They have no numismatic value. The best known gold bullion coins are the U.S. Gold One Ounce, South African Krugerrand, Canadian Maple Leaf, Austrian 100 Corona and the Gold Mexican 50 peso. The first three coins have a pure gold content of one ounce. The Austrian Corona has a gold content of .9802 ounce and the Mexican peso 1.2057 ounces. The premium (cost above the gold value) varies from dealer to dealer. For those who do not want to take physical possession, deposit certificates are available for the coins.

One of the largest bullion dealers is Deak International (212-757-0100) headquartered in New York City. Gold coins can also be purchased at banks where there is generally a very low premium over the gold content value.

Gold stocks The stocks of a number of Canadian and U.S. gold mining companies are traded on the New York (N), American (A) and Over-The-Counter (O) exchanges. Of course, with stocks, the investor is not just buying into gold, but also into the many special problems associated with running a company—production costs, quality of the ore, lifetime of the deposit, etc. However, many gold stocks pay dividends, whereas other gold investments do not pay any return during the holding period.

Some listed stocks are given below:

Agnico-Eagle Mines (O)
Campbell Red Lake Mines (N)
Dome Mines (N)
Sunshine Mining (N)
Homestake Mining Company (N)

A publicly-held New York Stock Exchange closed-end gold fund is ASA Limited. Several mutual funds which invest in gold are given in the mutual fund section of the Almanac (page 357).

South African gold mines are traded on the Over-The-Counter Market by means of ADR (American Depository Receipt). ADR is a claim on foreign stocks (South African gold shares, in this case) held by the foreign branches of large U.S. banks. Holders of ADRs are entitled to dividends which, in the case of South African gold shares, may be substantial. The ADRs of these companies are listed in *The Wall Street Journal* under the Foreign Securities section, which follows the OTC quotations.

Some major South African gold mining companies are:

---

* This "karats" is not to be confused with the "carats" that apply to diamonds.

511

Blyvooruitzicht
Buffelsfontein
East Driefontein
Kloof
President Brand
President Steyn
Randfontein
West Dreifontein
Western Deep Levels
Western Holdings

Mutual funds specializing in gold and precious metals A number of mutual funds (see page 357) specialize in gold and precious metals stocks. These funds provide diversification among a number of issues thereby reducing risk associated with any particular stock.

Options on gold stocks Put and call options are available on Homestake Mining (Chicago Options Exchange) and on ASA Limited (American Options Exchange). These options may be used for leveraged speculation or for hedging existing gold holdings. Holders of call options gain if the gold shares increase, while holders of put options benefit if prices decline.

The Philadelphia Stock Exchange trades a gold/silver option based on an index of seven different stocks in the industry.

Options on gold bullion Put and call options on gold bullion are traded on the International Options Market (IOM) of the Montreal Stock Exchange. IOM options are on 10 ounces of gold. Contract months are Feb/May/Aug/Nov.

Monex (Newport Beach, CA) provides put and call options on 32.15 ounces of gold. The Monex options are not tradeable but can be exercized during the option period. Expiration periods are 30, 60, 90, and 185 days. Mocatta Metals (New York) also offers futures contracts.

Since options are paid in full, they are not subject to margin calls or forced liquidation as is the case with futures contracts. At this time, quotations on bullion options are not available in the daily press.

Gold futures contract Gold futures contracts are obligations to buy or sell 100 ounces of gold on or before a specified date at a specified price. Futures contracts must be exercised if held to maturity, while options contracts need not be exercised if held to maturity. Futures contracts are purchased on margin, and hence, are subject to margin call and possible forced liquidation. They are widely quoted in the financial press, and the market is highly organized.

As with options, futures contracts may be used for leveraged speculation or for hedging. Speculators will buy contracts if they anticipate a price increase or sell contracts in anticipation of a price decrease.

Gold futures are traded on the N.Y. Commodity Exchange, the International Monetary Market of the Chicago Mercantile Exchange, and other markets.

Options on Gold Futures Contracts Options on Gold Futures contracts (the right to buy and sell a gold futures contract rather than the metal) are actively traded on the New York Comex. The futures contract underlying the options is for 100 ounces of gold. Contract months are April/Aug./Dec. Gold futures options premiums are reported daily in the *Wall Street Journal*.

Investing in Diamonds

Diamonds have appreciated on the average of about 12.6% over the ten-year period 1969–1979 (compared to a consumer price index of 6.1% during the same period of time). There have been periods (the recession of 1973—1974 and in 1981) when the price of investment quality diamonds slipped as much as 40%. A major factor stabilizing the market is DeBeers, a South African diamond company which handles as much as 80% of the world's diamonds. While the appreciation of diamonds has been impressive, potential buyers should be aware that prices are not quoted in the daily newspapers; therefore, selling the stones at a profit may be difficult. Quotes are available in the *Rappaport Diamond Report*, 15 West 47 Street, New York, NY 10036 and the *Marcum Reports*, P.O. Box 30150, Chicago, IL 60630-0150.

To locate reputable gem dealers check with:

American Gem Society
5901 West 3rd Street
Los Angeles, CA 90036-2898
(213) 936-4367

Accredited Gemologists Association
99 Pratt Street
Hartford, CT 06103
(203) 278-1800

Buyers should only deal with reputable firms, and the stones should be certified by an independent laboratory such as the Gemological Institute of America and International Gemological Institute with offices in New York City.

Diamonds are ranked in terms of the 4 C's—carat (one carat equals 1/142 'ounces weight), color, clarity, and cut.

Carat For investment purposes the diamond should be more than .5 carat. However, diamonds of more than 2 carats may be difficult to sell.

Color There are six main categories, each with subdivisions:

D,E,F—Colorless
G,H,I,J—Near colorless
K,L,M—Faint yellow
N,O,P,Q,R—Very light yellow
S,T,U,V,W,X,Y,Z—Light yellow
Fancy yellow stone

Color should be in the range from to D to H. However, Fancy Yellow Stones often command very high prices because of their scarcity.

Clarity Although bubbles, lines, and specks (inclusions) are natural to diamonds, they may interfere with the passage of light through the diamond. With a 10X magnification, a professional appraiser can grade the diamond according to the ten clarity grades:

FL—Flawless
IF—Internally flawless
VVS-1, VVS-2—Very, very slight inclusions
VS-1, VS-2—Very slight inclusions
SI-1, SI-2—Slight inclusions
I-1, I-2, I-3—Imperfect

Investment grade stones should be in the range FL to VS-2.

Cut There are several types of cuts—oval, marquise, pear shaped, round brilliant and emerald. Round brilliant stones are preferred for investment purposes. Proportions are important, and the preferred values are:

Depth % (total depth divided by girdle diameter): 57% to 63%.
Table (table diameter divided by girdle diameter): 57% to 66%.
Girdle thickness should be neither very thick nor very thin.

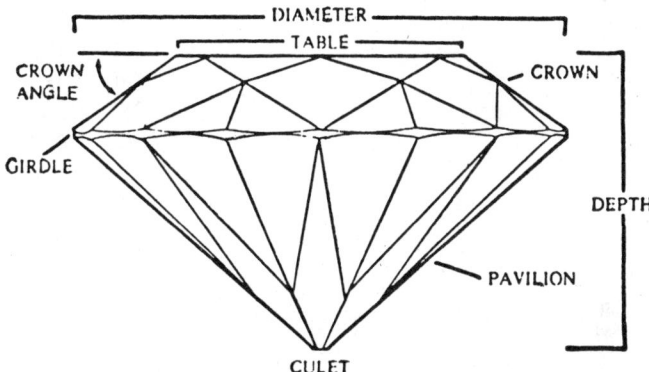

THE ROUND BRILLIANT DIAMOND

Investing in Collectibles

SOTHEBY'S ART INDEX ®

Category	Weight	Aug. 11	Aug. 4	Aug. 1985	Aug. 1984
Old Master Paintings	17	303	303	289	251
19th Century European Paintings	12	250	250	249	220
Impressionist & Post-Impressionist Paintings	18	432	432	371	317
Modern Paintings (1900-1950)	10	429	429	342	301
American Paintings (1800-pre-WW II)	3	687	687	635	589
Continental Ceramics	3	290	290	284	284
Chinese Ceramics	10	486	486	486	482
English Silver	5	338	338	298	237
Continental Silver	5	192	192	178	161
American Furniture	3	380	380	324	241
French & Continental Furniture	7	285	285	273	270
English Furniture	7	447	447	382	360
Weighted Aggregate	....	369	369	336	302

Sept. 1975=100.

©1986 Sotheby's

The data reflected in the Sotheby's Art Index are based on results of auction sales by affiliated companies of Sotheby's and other information deemed relevant by Sotheby's. Sotheby's does not warrant the accuracy of the data reflected therein. Nothing in any commentary furnished by Sotheby's nor any of the Sotheby's Indices is intended or should be relied upon as investment advice or as a prediction, warranty or guaranty as to future performance or otherwise. All individual prices quoted in this review are aggregate prices, inclusive of the buyer's premium.

Source: Reprinted by courtesy of *Barron's National Business and Financial Weekly*, August 11, 1986 and Sotheby's.

Investing in Real Estate

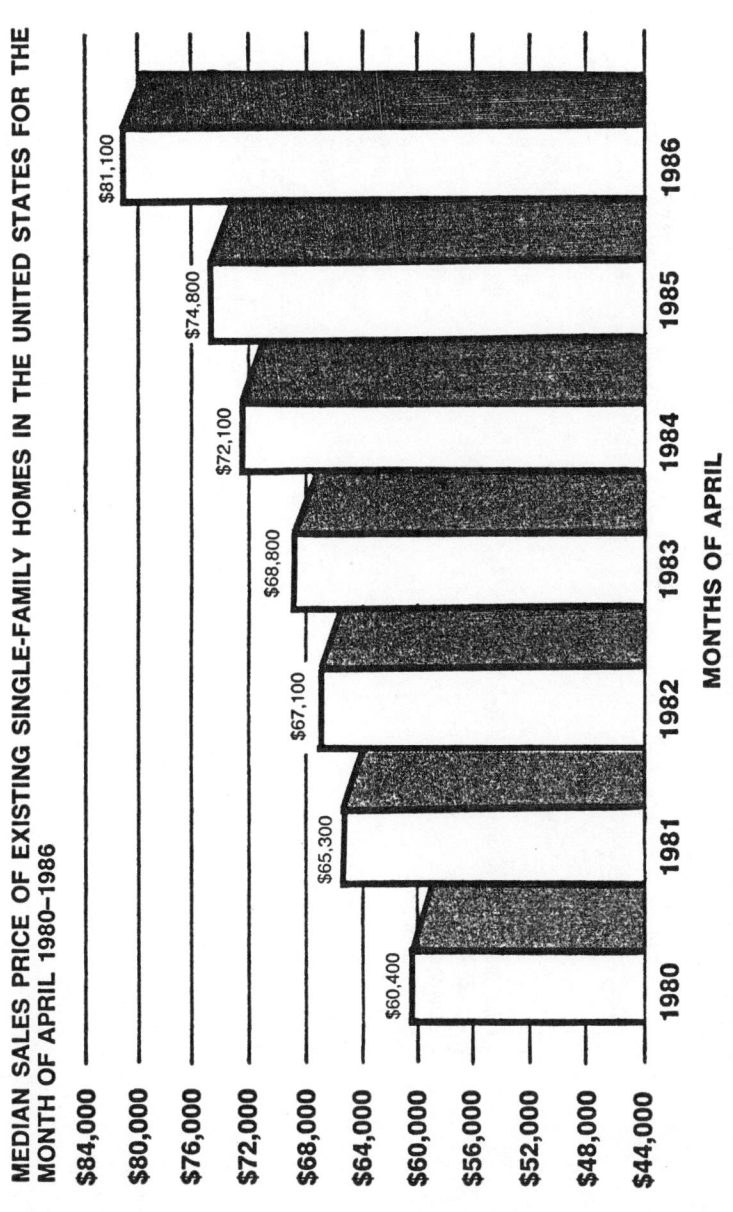

MEDIAN SALES PRICE OF EXISTING SINGLE-FAMILY HOMES IN THE UNITED STATES FOR THE MONTH OF APRIL 1980–1986

MONTHS OF APRIL

$84,000
$80,000
$76,000
$72,000
$68,000
$64,000
$60,000
$56,000
$52,000
$48,000
$44,000

1980 — $60,400
1981 — $65,300
1982 — $67,100
1983 — $68,800
1984 — $72,100
1985 — $74,800
1986 — $81,100

Source: National Association of Realtors®, Economics and Research Division, 777 14th Street, N.W., Washington, D.C. 20005.

MEDIAN SALES PRICE OF EXISTING SINGLE-FAMILY HOMES FOR METROPOLITAN AREAS* (not seasonally adjusted in thousands of dollars)

Metropolitan Area	Years			Quarters				
	1983	1984	1985	1985 I	1985 II	1985 III	1985 IV	1986 Iʳ
Albany/Schenectady/Troy	$49.4	$52.9	$60.3	$56.0	$61.5	$61.0	$61.5	$67.5
Akron	n/a	50.4	52.7	50.9	52.2	55.4	51.6	51.1
Orange County (Anaheim/Santa Ana MSA**)	134.9	133.7	136.2	132.1	135.2	137.8	139.6	138.0
Atlanta	63.0	66.2	n/a	73.5	72.0	72.0	n/a	n/a
Baltimore	n/a	66.1	72.6	67.6	71.9	77.4	72.8	71.6
Birmingham	62.8	65.1	64.5	62.0	65.0	65.4	64.6	67.1
Boston	82.6	100.0	134.2	108.6	131.0	138.8	144.8	145.6
Buffalo/Niagara Falls	n/a	44.8	46.7	46.9	47.0	46.3	46.7	49.7
Chicago	76.4	79.5	81.1	78.8	81.8	82.3	81.5	82.0
Cincinnati	57.2	58.9	60.2	59.6	61.1	61.8	58.5	62.1
Cleveland	n/a	62.7	64.4	61.9	66.4	67.0	62.2	62.1
Columbus	59.4	59.9	62.2	59.0	61.4	64.4	62.7	62.6
Dallas/Ft. Worth	76.0	82.2	87.7	86.6	87.1	89.8	87.2	93.4
Denver	78.3	82.7	84.3	82.4	83.7	85.9	84.5	84.6
Detroit	47.5	48.5	51.7	51.3	51.0	52.6	51.7	54.0
Ft. Lauderdale/Hollywood/Pompano Beach	73.9	73.1	74.6	71.0	73.3	76.8	75.5	72.6
Hartford	n/a	87.4	99.6	90.2	97.2	102.0	103.9	106.4
Houston	79.9	77.6	78.6	78.6	76.2	83.7	76.7	70.4
Indianapolis	52.8	53.1	55.0	52.5	55.4	55.3	55.1	55.7
Jacksonville	n/a	55.7	58.4	55.3	58.8	59.8	58.6	58.9
Kansas City	58.8	59.1	61.4	62.9	63.0	61.0	59.1	65.7
Los Angeles Area**	112.7	115.3	n/a	114.3	116.9	n/a	119.9	120.4
Louisville	47.4	48.9	50.6	50.4	51.0	51.4	49.2	48.1

Memphis	61.6	64.1	64.6	64.5	63.8	67.2	62.5	66.3
Miami/Hialeah	n/a	79.5	80.5	73.4	84.0	86.1	79.2	78.5
Milwaukee	68.0	68.2	67.5	66.6	68.7	66.7	68.1	67.6
Minneapolis/St. Paul	73.6	74.0	75.2	74.2	75.2	75.9	75.4	76.3
Nashville	61.0	62.9	66.1	64.7	66.0	66.6	66.6	68.4
New York/Northern New Jersey/Long Island	88.9	105.3	134.0	125.0	130.4	138.2	139.6	147.2
Oklahoma City	61.6	63.9	64.7	63.2	65.5	65.5	63.5	62.8
Orlando	n/a	70.1	70.3	67.3	71.9	72.4	69.0	70.3
Philadelphia	64.5	65.2	70.8	70.2	72.1	71.7	69.3	72.2
Phoenix	n/a	74.7	74.7	74.1	73.9	73.4	75.7	76.2
Portland	n/a	62.9	61.5	61.9	60.6	63.2	59.5	59.9
Providence	54.7	59.6	67.5	63.0	65.5	69.8	70.2	71.9
Rochester	54.8	59.7	64.2	60.3	64.0	65.8	63.7	66.3
St. Louis	58.9	61.8	65.7	60.8	65.7	68.8	65.9	67.5
Salt Lake City/Ogden	64.3	65.8	66.7	63.9	67.1	67.6	67.5	66.4
San Antonio	62.6	67.5	67.7	66.1	68.1	71.0	65.0	67.0
San Diego**	98.9	100.2	106.4	101.2	104.3	109.3	110.6	110.0
San Francisco Bay Area**	129.5	129.9	n/a	n/a	134.5	143.8	n/a	n/a
Santa Clara County (San Jose/Palo Alto MSA**)	127.6	123.1	n/a	n/a	128.0	138.7	n/a	n/a
Syracuse	n/a	50.7	58.8	53.7	56.8	60.7	61.2	59.6
Tampa/St. Petersburg/Clearwater	55.5	58.4	58.4	53.1	58.3	60.3	58.9	56.8
Tulsa	n/a	67.3	66.7	69.8	68.0	66.3	63.6	66.4
Washington, D.C.	89.4	93.0	97.1	94.9	97.5	98.3	97.3	101.1

n/a Not Available   r Revised

*All areas are metropolitan statistical areas (MSA) as defined by the U.S. Office of Management and Budget. They include the named central city and surrounding suburban areas. ** Provided by the California Association of REALTORS®

Source: National Association of Realtors®, Economics and Research Division, 777 14th Street, N.W., Washington, D.C. 20005.

HOUSING AFFORDABILITY

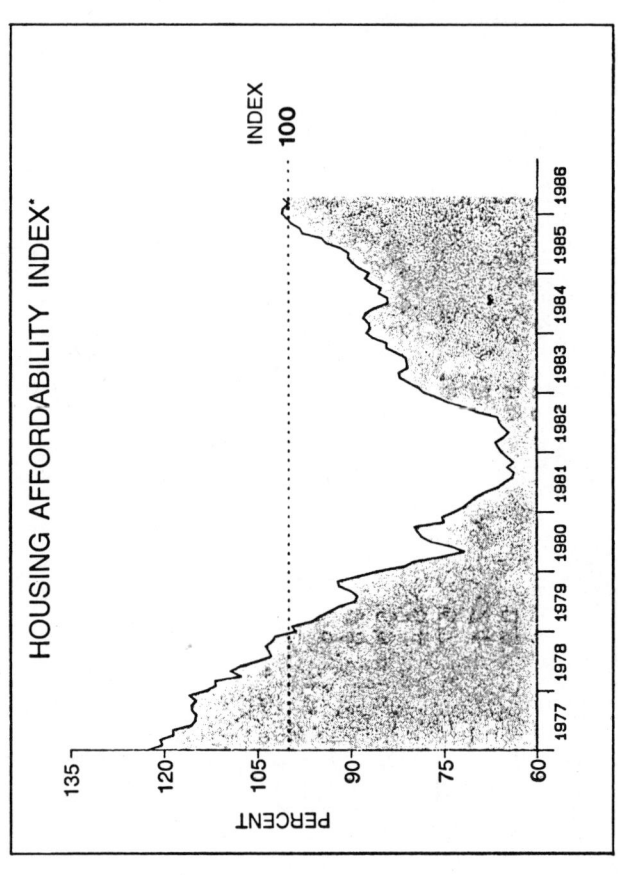

Year	Median-Priced Existing Single-Family Home	Mortgage Rate**	Monthly P & I Payment	Payment as % Income	Median Family Income	Qualifying Income***	Affordability Indexes		
							Composite	Fixed	ARM
1980	$62,200	12.95%	$549	31.3%	$21,023	$26,328	79.9	79.9	79.9
1981	66,400	15.12	677	36.3	22,388	32,485	68.9	68.9	68.9
1982	67,800	15.38	702	35.9	23,433	33,713	69.5	69.4	69.7
1983	70,300	12.85	616	30.1	24,580	29,546	83.2	81.7	85.2
1984	72,400	12.49	618	28.2	26,433	29,650	89.1	84.6	92.1
1985	75,500	11.74	609	26.2	27,940	29,243	95.5	90.3	101.3
1985									
Apr	$74,800	12.11%	$621	27.6%	$26,935	$29,788	90.4	85.5	96.0
May	75,200	12.11	624	27.7	27,061	29,448	90.4	85.0	96.0
Jun	76,500	11.76	618	27.3	27,186	29,675	91.6	85.6	96.3
Jul	76,700	11.47	606	26.6	27,312	29,099	93.9	88.0	99.1
Aug	77,200	11.33	604	26.4	27,438	28,973	94.7	89.1	101.1
Sep	75,900	11.20	587	25.6	27,563	28,197	97.8	91.8	104.7
Oct	75,200	11.32	588	25.5	27,689	28,201	98.2	92.2	105.4
Nov	74,900	11.26	582	25.1	27,814	27,957	99.5	93.7	106.7
Dec	75,500	11.12	581	24.9	27,940	27,873	100.2	94.5	107.5
1986									
Jan	$77,100	10.81%	$579	24.7%	$28,054	$27,771	101.0	96.6	106.4
Feb	77,400	10.83	582	24.8	28,168	27,923	100.9	97.7	106.4
Mar^r	79,800	10.62	590	25.1	28,283	28,306	99.9	97.8	105.0
Apr^p	81,100	10.37	587	24.8	28,397	28,185	100.8	99.1	104.9

r   Revised

p   Preliminary

*   Index equals 100 when median family income equals qualifying income.

**   Effective rate on loans closed on existing homes—Federal Home Loan Bank Board.

***   Based on current lending requirements of the Federal National Mortgage Association using a 20 percent downpayment.

Source: National Association of Realtors®, Economics and Research Division, 777 14th Street, N.W., Washington, D.C. 20005.

FARM REAL ESTATE VALUES: INDEXES OF THE AVERAGE VALUE PER ACRE OF LAND AND BUILDINGS, BY STATE, GROUPED BY FARM PRODUCTION REGION, FEB. 1, 1979–81; AND APRIL 1, 1982–85; AND FEB. 1, 1986[1]

State	1979	1980	1981	1982	1983	1984	1985	1986	Percent change 1985–86
				1977 = 100					
Northeast									
Maine [2]	126	135	143	149	152	162	185	215	16
New Hampshire [2]	126	135	143	149	152	162	185	215	16
Vermont [2]	126	135	143	149	152	162	185	215	16
Massachusetts [2]	126	135	143	149	152	162	185	215	16
Rhode Island [2]	126	135	143	149	152	162	185	215	16
Connecticut [2]	126	135	143	149	152	162	185	215	16
New York	113	119	126	132	129	133	128	131	2
New Jersey	111	120	123	128	125	129	141	157	11
Pennsylvania	127	140	144	133	128	138	127	122	- 4
Delaware	129	151	158	143	143	146	128	137	7
Maryland	133	166	188	178	160	165	158	142	−10
Lake States									
Michigan	124	138	157	152	141	141	121	108	−11
Wisconsin	139	159	179	174	165	155	126	106	−16
Minnesota	131	154	179	174	155	144	109	81	−26
Corn Belt									
Ohio	138	156	160	137	121	116	90	81	−10
Indiana	130	150	161	140	122	121	96	81	−16
Illinois	125	135	144	131	117	115	84	73	−13
Iowa	119	139	150	139	121	108	77	61	−21
Missouri	127	154	165	153	133	133	102	94	- 8
Northern Plains									
North Dakota	119	136	145	149	142	142	116	102	−12
South Dakota	132	141	150	150	140	136	101	87	−14
Nebraska	120	137	151	143	129	114	82	67	−18
Kansas	117	134	137	136	126	122	98	81	−17
Appalachian									
Virginia	128	139	149	143	144	143	140	147	5
West Virginia	126	150	160	177	177	172	143	139	- 3
North Carolina	122	141	155	149	150	158	142	129	- 9
Kentucky	133	147	153	154	149	143	129	124	- 4
Tennessee	122	136	146	138	131	135	127	128	1

State	1979	1980	1981	1982	1983	1984	1985	1986	Percent change 1985–86
				1977 = 100					
Southeast									
South Carolina	114	130	137	136	128	125	121	117	− 3
Georgia	118	132	139	128	124	122	116	110	− 5
Florida[3]	120	141	157	149	152	155	147	138	− 6
Alabama	120	149	176	174	165	162	154	152	− 1
Delta States									
Mississippi	129	156	198	189	174	183	163	147	−10
Arkansas	137	163	188	196	174	167	152	126	−17
Louisiana	132	169	200	199	195	195	181	145	−20
Southern Plains									
Oklahoma	121	143	156	164	156	156	126	107	−15
Texas	124	144	158	185	191	208	229	190	−17
Mountain States									
Montana	121	142	148	157	146	149	125	115	− 8
Idaho	117	134	144	151	140	140	129	111	−14
Wyoming[5]	118	126	135	140	133	136	122	106	−13
Colorado	126	147	161	164	161	166	154	126	−18
New Mexico[4,5]	126	166	178	185	176	180	162	133	−18
Arizona[4,5]	126	167	179	186	177	181	163	142	−13
Utah[4,5]	127	169	181	188	179	183	165	153	− 7
Nevada[4,5]	134	178	190	198	188	192	173	151	−13
Pacific States									
Washington	118	124	146	152	152	157	151	133	−12
Oregon	120	132	144	145	138	137	114	103	−10
California	138	166	201	221	223	223	201	183	− 9
48 States	125	145	158	157	148	146	128	112	−12

[1] These indexes are based on USDA surveys.

[2] Indexes for 1979–85 were estimated by combining survey data to obtain an average rate of change for these 6 New England States.

[3] Indexes for 1979–82 were estimated using the average of the percentage changes in the Georgia and Alabama indexes.

[4] Indexes for 1979–80 were estimated by combining survey data to obtain an average rate of change for these 4 Mountain States.

[5] Indexes for 1981–1985 were estimated using the average of the percentage changes in the Montana, Idaho, and Colorado indexes. 1986 indexes for Arizona and Nevada, based on the average of the percentage change in Montana, Idaho, and Colorado.

Source: *Agriculture Land Values*, Economics Research Service, U.S. Department of Agriculture.

Industrial Real Estate Market: Selected Cities

ATLANTA

METROPOLITAN INDUSTRIAL REAL ESTATE MARKET DATA

ATLANTA

INDUSTRIAL MARKET CHARACTERISTICS

	Central City	Suburbs
Total Space	23,000,000-24,000,000 sq. ft.	100,000,000-115,000,000 sq. ft.
Total Vacant	750,000-1,000,000 sq. ft.	7,500,000-9,000,000 sq. ft.
Vacancy Rate	3.5-4.3%	6.9-7.8%

DOLLAR VOLUME OF SALES AND LEASES COMPARED TO A YEAR AGO

Manufacturing		Warehousing Distribution		High Technology	
Sales	Leases	Sales	Leases	Sales	Leases
Same	Same	Same-Up 20%	Same-Up 25%	Same-Up 20%	Same-Up 30%

GROSS SALES AND LEASE PRICES OF PRIME INDUSTRIAL BUILDINGS AND SITES

	Central City		Suburbs	
	Per Square Foot	Change From a Year Ago	Per Square Foot	Change From a Year Ago
Building Sales Prices				
Less than 5,000 sq. ft.	$35.00-45.00	Up 5-10%	$40.00-50.00	Up 5-10%
5,000-20,000 sq. ft.	$25.00-35.00	Up 5-10%	$25.00-35.00	Same-Up 10%
20,000-40,000 sq. ft.	$20.00-30.00	Up 5-10%	$23.00-30.00	Up 5-10%
40,000-60,000 sq. ft.	$20.00-25.00	Up 5-12%	$20.00-25.00	Up 5-10%
60,000-100,000 sq. ft.	$16.00-23.00	Up 5-10%	$16.00-23.00	Up 5-10%
100,000 or more sq. ft.	$14.00-19.00	Up 5-10%	$14.00-21.00	Up 5-10%
Prime High Technology	$40.00-80.00	Up 8-10%	$40.00-85.00	Up 7-10%
Site Sales Prices				
Improved				
Less than 2 acres	$2.00-2.75	Up 5-12%	$2.50-4.00	Up 5-20%
2-5 acres	$1.75-2.50	Same-Up 14%	$2.50-3.50	Same-Up 20%
5-10 acres	$1.50-2.25	Same-Up 16%	$2.00-3.00	Same-Up 20%
10 or more acres	$1.00-2.00	Same-Up 10%	$1.50-2.75	Same-Up 20%
Unimproved				
Less than 10 acres	$1.00-2.00	Same-Up 12%	$2.00-3.50	Same-Up 20%
10-100 acres	$0.75-1.75	Same-Up 12%	$1.50-3.00	Same-Up 20%
100 or more acres	$0.50-1.00	Same-Up 10%	$1.25-5.50	Same-Up 20%
Lease Prices				
Less than 5,000 sq. ft.	$3.50-5.00	Same-Up 15%	$3.75-5.00	Same-Up 15%
5,000-20,000 sq. ft.	$2.75-3.75	Same-Up 15%	$3.25-4.25	Same-Up 15%
20,000-40,000 sq. ft.	$2.50-3.25	Same-Up 15%	$3.00-3.75	Same-Up 15%
40,000-60,000 sq. ft.	$2.25-2.75	Same-Up 15%	$2.75-3.50	Same-Up 15%
60,000-100,000 sq. ft.	$2.00-2.50	Same-Up 15%	$2.30-3.25	Same-Up 15%
100,000 or more sq. ft.	$1.75-2.30	Same-Up 15%	$2.45-3.00	Same-Up 15%
Prime High Technology	$8.00-12.00	Same-Up 15%	$8.00-11.00	Same-Up 15%

CHICAGO

METROPOLITAN INDUSTRIAL REAL ESTATE MARKET DATA

CHICAGO

INDUSTRIAL MARKET CHARACTERISTICS

	Central City	Suburbs
Total Space	170,000,000 sq. ft.	460,000,000 sq. ft.
Total Vacant	15,000,000 sq. ft.	27,000,000 sq. ft.
Vacancy Rate	8.8%	5.8%

DOLLAR VOLUME OF SALES AND LEASES COMPARED TO A YEAR AGO

Manufacturing		Warehousing Distribution		High Technology	
Sales	Leases	Sales	Leases	Sales	Leases
Same	Same	Up 10%	Up 10%	Same	Same

GROSS SALES AND LEASE PRICES OF PRIME INDUSTRIAL BUILDINGS AND SITES

	Central City		Suburbs	
	Per Square Foot	Change From a Year Ago	Per Square Foot	Change From a Year Ago
Building Sales Prices				
Less than 5,000 sq. ft.	$30.00	Same	$40.00	Same
5,000-20,000 sq. ft.	$24.00	Down 8%	$31.00	Same
20,000-40,000 sq. ft.	$20.00	Same	$29.00	Same
40,000-60,000 sq. ft.	$18.00	Down 8%	$25.00	Same
60,000-100,000 sq. ft.	$13.00	Same	$22.00	Up 5%
100,000 or more sq. ft.	$12.00	Same	$20.00	Up 5%
Prime High Technology	NA	NA	$50.00	Same
Site Sales Prices				
Improved				
Less than 2 acres	$1.50-5.00	Same	$2.00-5.00	Up 20%
2-5 acres	$1.25-5.00	Same	$2.00-4.00	Up 13%
5-10 acres	$1.25-2.00	Same	$2.00-3.00	Same
10 or more acres	$1.00-4.50	Same	$1.50-2.75	Same
Unimproved				
Less than 10 acres	NA	NA	$1.00	Same
10-100 acres	NA	NA	$0.75	Same
100 or more acres	NA	NA	$0.50	Same
Lease Prices				
Less than 5,000 sq. ft.	$4.25	Up 13%	$5.00	Same
5,000-20,000 sq. ft.	$3.50	Up 8%	$4.50	Same
20,000-40,000 sq. ft.	$3.25	Up 8%	$4.00	Same
40,000-60,000 sq. ft.	$3.00	Up 11%	$3.75	Same
60,000-100,000 sq. ft.	$2.50	Same	$3.50	Same
100,000 or more sq. ft.	$2.25	Same	$3.00	Same
Prime High Technology	NA	NA	$11.00	Same

HOUSTON

METROPOLITAN INDUSTRIAL REAL ESTATE MARKET DATA

HOUSTON

INDUSTRIAL MARKET CHARACTERISTICS

	Central City	Suburbs
Total Space	80,000,000 sq. ft.	120,000,000 sq. ft.
Total Vacant	9,000,000 sq. ft.	27,000,000 sq. ft.
Vacancy Rate	11.0%	22.5%

DOLLAR VOLUME OF SALES AND LEASES COMPARED TO A YEAR AGO

Manufacturing		Warehousing Distribution		High Technology	
Sales	Leases	Sales	Leases	Sales	Leases
Down 10%	Down 10%	Same	Up 10%	Same	Up 10%

GROSS SALES AND LEASE PRICES OF PRIME INDUSTRIAL BUILDINGS AND SITES

	Central City		Suburbs	
	Per Square Foot	Change From a Year Ago	Per Square Foot	Change From a Year Ago
Building Sales Prices				
Less than 5,000 sq. ft.	$30.00-45.00	Down 10%	$15.00-60.00	Down 10%
5,000-20,000 sq. ft.	$30.00-40.00	Down 10%	$30.00-50.00	Down 10%
20,000-40,000 sq. ft.	$20.00-35.00	Down 10%	$20.00-45.00	Down 10%
40,000-60,000 sq. ft.	$15.00-30.00	Down 10%	$15.00-35.00	Down 10%
60,000-100,000 sq. ft.	$10.00-25.00	Down 10%	$15.00-30.00	Down 10%
100,000 or more sq. ft.	$10.00-15.00	Down 10%	$12.00-20.00	Down 10%
Prime High Technology	$25.00-10.00	Down 10%	$30.00-60.00	Down 10%
Site Sales Prices				
Improved				
Less than 2 acres	$3.50-8.00	Same	$2.00-6.00	Down 10%
2-5 acres	$3.50-8.00	Same	$2.00-6.00	Down 10%
5-10 acres	$35.00-7.00	Same	$1.50-5.00	Down 10%
10 or more acres	$3.00-6.00	Same	$1.25-5.00	Down 10%
Unimproved				
Less than 10 acres	$2.50-8.00	Down 15%	$0.50-2.50	Down 10%
10-100 acres	NA	NA	$0.30-2.00	Down 10%
100 or more acres	NA	NA	$0.10-1.00	Down 10%
Lease Prices				
Less than 5,000 sq. ft.	$2.50-4.50	Same	$2.50-4.50	Same
5,000-20,000 sq. ft.	$2.50-4.00	Same	$2.50-4.00	Same
20,000-40,000 sq. ft.	$2.00-3.50	Same	$2.00-3.50	Same
40,000-60,000 sq. ft.	$1.50-3.00	Same	$1.50-3.00	Same
60,000-100,000 sq. ft.	$1.25-2.50	Down 10%	$1.50-2.50	Down 10%
100,000 or more sq. ft.	$1.15-2.00	Down 10%	$1.25-2.00	Down 10%
Prime High Technology	$3.50-8.00	Same	$4.00-8.00	Same

LOS ANGELES—CENTRAL

METROPOLITAN INDUSTRIAL REAL ESTATE MARKET DATA

LOS ANGELES--CENTRAL

INDUSTRIAL MARKET CHARACTERISTICS

	Central City	Suburbs
Total Space	NA	NA
Total Vacant	NA	NA
Vacancy Rate	NA	NA

DOLLAR VOLUME OF SALES AND LEASES COMPARED TO A YEAR AGO

Manufacturing		Warehousing Distribution		High Technology	
Sales	Leases	Sales	Leases	Sales	Leases
Up 5%	Up 5%	Up 10%	Up 10%	NA	NA

GROSS SALES AND LEASE PRICES OF PRIME INDUSTRIAL BUILDINGS AND SITES

	Central City		Suburbs	
	Per Square Foot	Change From a Year Ago	Per Square Foot	Change From a Year Ago
Building Sales Prices				
Less than 5,000 sq. ft.	$50.00	Up 10%	NA	NA
5,000-20,000 sq. ft.	$45.00	NA	NA	NA
20,000-40,000 sq. ft.	$40.00	NA	NA	NA
40,000-60,000 sq. ft.	$38.00	NA	NA	NA
60,000-100,000 sq. ft.	$35.00	NA	NA	NA
100,000 or more sq. ft.	$32.00	NA	NA	NA
Prime High Technology	NA	NA	NA	NA
Site Sales Prices				
Improved				
Less than 2 acres	$15.00	Up 10%	NA	NA
2-5 acres	$12.00	NA	NA	NA
5-10 acres	$10.00	NA	NA	NA
10 or more acres	NA	NA	NA	NA
Unimproved				
Less than 10 acres	NA	NA	NA	NA
10-100 acres	NA	NA	NA	NA
100 or more acres	NA	NA	NA	NA
Lease Prices				
Less than 5,000 sq. ft.	$5.40	NA	NA	NA
5,000-20,000 sq. ft.	$4.56	NA	NA	NA
20,000-40,000 sq. ft.	$4.20	NA	NA	NA
40,000-60,000 sq. ft.	$3.84	NA	NA	NA
60,000-100,000 sq. ft.	$3.60	NA	NA	NA
100,000 or more sq. ft.	$3.36	NA	NA	NA
Prime High Technology	NA	NA	NA	NA

NEW YORK—NEW YORK CITY

METROPOLITAN INDUSTRIAL REAL ESTATE MARKET DATA

NEW YORK--NEW YORK CITY

INDUSTRIAL MARKET CHARACTERISTICS

	Central City	Suburbs
Total Space	NA	NA
Total Vacant	NA	NA
Vacancy Rate	NA	NA

DOLLAR VOLUME OF SALES AND LEASES COMPARED TO A YEAR AGO

Manufacturing		Warehousing Distribution		High Technology	
Sales	Leases	Sales	Leases	Sales	Leases
Up 20%	Same	Up 20%	Up 20%	NA	NA

GROSS SALES AND LEASE PRICES OF PRIME INDUSTRIAL BUILDINGS AND SITES

	Central City		Suburbs	
	Per Square Foot	Change From a Year Ago	Per Square Foot	Change From a Year Ago
Building Sales Prices				
Less than 5,000 sq. ft.	$40.00-100.00	Up 25%	NA	NA
5,000-20,000 sq. ft.	$35.00-75.00	Up 20%	NA	NA
20,000-40,000 sq. ft.	$35.00-65.00	Up 20%	NA	NA
40,000-60,000 sq. ft.	$32.00-60.00	Up 20%	NA	NA
60,000-100,000 sq. ft.	$30.00-60.00	Up 20%	NA	NA
100,000 or more sq. ft.	$30.00-50.00	Up 15%	NA	NA
Prime High Technology	NA	NA	NA	NA
Site Sales Prices				
Improved				
Less than 2 acres	$10.00-100.00	Up 50%	NA	NA
2-5 acres	$8.00-25.00	Up 50%	NA	NA
5-10 acres	$7.00-10.00	Up 50%	NA	NA
10 or more acres	NA	NA	NA	NA
Unimproved				
Less than 10 acres	$5.00-10.00	Up 50%	NA	NA
10-100 acres	NA	NA	NA	NA
100 or more acres	NA	NA	NA	NA
Lease Prices				
Less than 5,000 sq. ft.	$6.00-10.00	Up 25%	NA	NA
5,000-20,000 sq. ft.	$4.00-9.00	Up 20%	NA	NA
20,000-40,000 sq. ft.	$4.00-8.00	Up 15%	NA	NA
40,000-60,000 sq. ft.	$4.00-6.00	Up 15%	NA	NA
60,000-100,000 sq. ft.	$3.75-7.00	Up 15%	NA	NA
100,000 or more sq. ft.	$3.75-6.50	Up 15%	NA	NA
Prime High Technology	NA	NA	NA	NA

Source: *Industrial Real Estate Market Survey*, Spring/Summer 1986, Society of Industrial Realtors® & the Economics and Research Division of the National Association of Realtors, 777 14th Street, NW, Washington, DC 20005.

CONVENTIONAL LOANS ON NEW HOMES

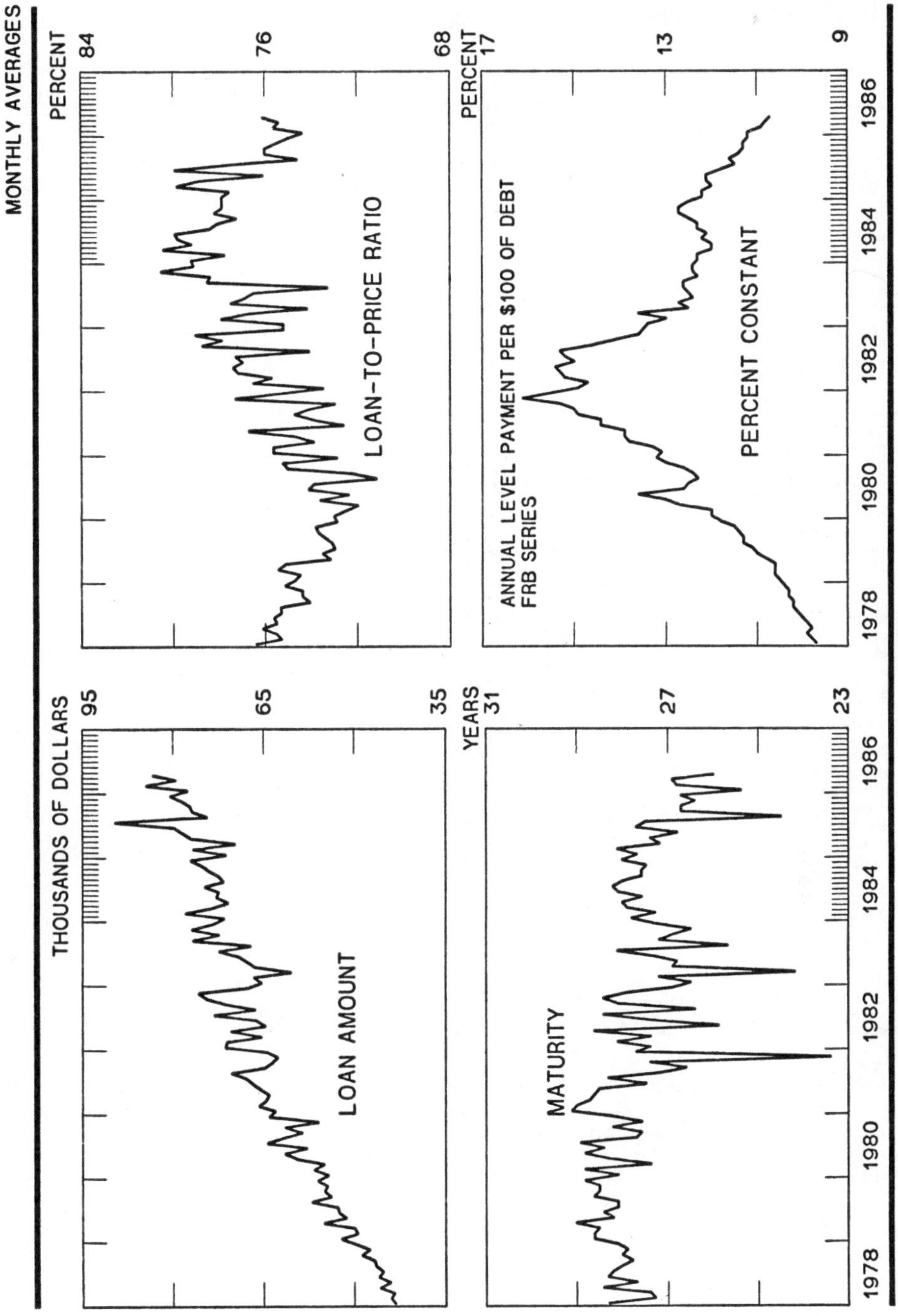
MONTHLY AVERAGES
THOUSANDS OF DOLLARS
95
65
35
LOAN AMOUNT
PERCENT
84
76
68
LOAN-TO-PRICE RATIO
YEARS
31
27
23
MATURITY
PERCENT
17
13
9
ANNUAL LEVEL PAYMENT PER $100 OF DEBT
FRB SERIES
PERCENT CONSTANT
1978
1980
1982
1984
1986
1978
1980
1982
1984
1986

Source: *Federal Reserve Chart Book*, Board of Governors of the Federal Reserve System.

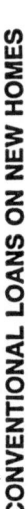

Industrial Property Sales Prices*

INDUSTRIAL PROPERTY SALES PRICES

	Central City Properties			Suburban Properties		
Metropolitan Area	Average Price Per Square Foot	Percent Change Average Price Per Sq. Ft.	Index (All Met Average = 100)	Average Price Per Square Foot	Percent Change - Average Price Per Sq. Ft.	Index (All Met Average = 100)
Akron	$24.37	0.16%	95	$18.33	2.29%	66
Albany	$15.50	0.00%	60	$20.16	-3.22%	73
Albuquerque	$33.57	0.00%	130	$33.57	0.00%	121
Atlanta	$32.33	19.74%	126	$32.98	8.56%	119
Austin	$50.00	-1.69%	194	—	—	—
Baltimore	$19.10	12.35%	74	$25.50	-1.92%	92
Birmingham	$18.17	—	71	$26.00	—	94
Boston	$30.21	0.00%	117	$45.64	0.00%	164
Bridgeport	$42.50	—	165	$41.67	—	150
Buffalo	$16.36	43.26%	64	$21.21	21.27%	76
Charlotte	$26.36	0.00%	102	$26.07	0.00%	94
Chicago	$19.50	-4.08%	76	$30.86	-2.25%	111
Cincinnati	$19.67	0.00%	76	$20.00	0.00%	72
Cleveland	$15.25	1.26%	59	$23.87	-2.09%	86
Columbia	$18.83	0.00%	73	$23.71	0.00%	85
Columbus	$18.00	0.45%	70	$22.21	-0.36%	80
Dallas	—	—	—	$40.36	1.18%	145
Denver	$31.57	-5.76%	123	$32.43	-6.22%	117
Des Moines	$19.86	19.14%	77	$19.86	18.00%	71
Detroit	$13.29	2.23%	52	$34.21	-0.64%	123
El Paso	$23.33	8.11%	91	—	—	—
Evansville	$14.20	0.00%	55	$15.83	-3.59%	57
Fort Lauderdale	$30.29	-0.46%	118	$31.86	-0.53%	115
Fort Smith	$15.42	0.00%	60	$16.71	-1.71%	60
Fort Wayne	$16.90	—	66	$16.90	—	61
Fresno	$20.07	-10.12%	78	—	—	—
Grand Rapids	$23.38	—	91	$22.64	—	81
Greensboro	$18.07	0.00%	70	$18.07	0.00%	65
Greenville, SC	$17.60	1.56%	68	$21.36	0.71%	77
Houston	$24.29	-9.23%	94	$31.21	-1.58%	112
Indianapolis	$15.62	-1.76%	61	$18.96	1.77%	68
Jackson, MI	$10.84	0.09%	42	$10.83	0.00%	39
Jackson, MS	$17.34	4.21%	67	—	—	—
Jacksonville	—	—	—	$16.05	2.88%	58
Kansas City — MSA	$14.88	-4.00%	58	$26.83	-9.97%	97
Lakeland	$19.57	1.45%	76	$19.29	1.53%	69
Los Angeles — Central	$40.00	-22.81%	155	—	—	—
Los Angeles — East	$51.14	5.90%	199	$37.92	1.12%	136
Los Angeles — Orange County	—	—	—	$53.79	1.76%	193
Los Angeles — South Bay	—	—	—	$51.58	-0.12%	186
Los Angeles — West	$66.58	—	259	—	—	—
Memphis	$15.00	23.25%	58	$19.50	6.15%	70
Miami	$17.75	14.37%	69	$29.54	-0.97%	106
Milwaukee	$20.71	42.04%	80	$20.71	9.23%	74
Minneapolis	$35.29	—	137	$34.14	—	123
Mobile	$19.29	0.00%	75	$19.29	0.00%	69
Montreal, Canada	—	—	—	$29.64	26.13%	107
Nashua, NH	$44.00	13.78%	171	$40.42	17.16%	145
New Jersey — Central	$11.33	—	44	$35.14	—	126
New Jersey — Northern	$19.00	20.03%	74	$47.00	11.53%	169

* The properties covered are "prime" (top 25 percent of overall desirability of existing inventory) of all sizes located in central city and suburban areas of 85 metropolitan areas in the US, Canada and Europe.

INDUSTRIAL PROPERTY SALES PRICES *(concluded)*

INDUSTRIAL PROPERTY SALES PRICES

Metropolitan Area	Central City Properties			Suburban Properties		
	Average Price Per Square Foot	Percent Change Average Price Per Sq. Ft.	Index (All Met Average = 100)	Average Price Per Square Foot	Percent Change Average Price Per Sq. Ft.	Index (All Met Average = 100)
New Orleans	$25.42	0.99%	99	$30.00	0.00%	108
New York City	$52.78	—	205	—	—	—
New York — New York Suburbs	—	—	—	$61.72	24.51%	222
Norfolk-Chesapeake-Virginia Beach	$24.57	0.08%	95	—	—	—
Oakland	$36.00	0.00%	140	$45.57	-0.93%	164
Oklahoma City	$18.63	0.00%	72	$23.43	0.95%	84
Omaha	$18.90	0.80%	73	$25.00	5.26%	90
Orlando	—	—	—	$16.90	—	91
Phoenix	$39.07	1.30%	152	—	—	—
Pittsburgh	$16.50	-34.21%	64	$26.80	-5.96%	96
Portland	$25.43	-1.09%	99	$27.14	-5.01%	98
Quad Cities IA/IL	$17.35	15.44%	67	—	—	—
Reno	$28.08	1.19%	109	$24.00	1.78%	86
Richmond	$17.33	0.00%	67	$23.29	0.04%	84
Sacramento	$35.43	5.32%	138	—	—	—
San Antonio	—	—	—	$33.43	0.00%	120
San Diego	$53.28	1.08%	207	$41.00	-4.65%	147
San Francisco	$62.00	0.00%	241	$55.83	0.00%	201
Sarasota	—	—	—	$26.76	0.04%	96
Seattle	$34.20	—	133	$35.86	—	129
Sioux City, IA	$14.00	1.45%	54	$14.50	-0.68%	52
South Bend	$12.21	-7.85%	47	$12.50	-3.85%	45
Springfield	$20.00	0.00%	78	$27.80	17.55%	100
St. Louis	$16.11	1.07%	63	$29.00	5.69%	104
Stamford	$63.30	19.82%	246	—	—	—
Stockton	$24.43	0.00%	95	$16.17	-4.88%	58
Syracuse	$17.33	8.31%	67	$23.00	5.94%	83
Tampa Bay Area	—	—	—	$28.57	13.55%	103
Terre Haute	$21.50	0.00%	84	$21.50	0.00%	77
Toledo	—	—	—	$13.33	-4.79%	48
Toronto, Canada	$32.67	—	127	$33.20	-6.11%	119
Tulsa	—	—	—	$25.71	5.24%	92
Washington, DC	$23.17	0.00%	90	$46.43	11.42%	167
Wichita	$17.00	0.00%	66	$17.00	0.00%	61
U.S. Average	$25.74	1.95%	100	$27.80	1.58%	100

Source: *Real Estate Quarterly,* Economics and Research Division, National Association of Realtors®, 777 14th Street, N.W, Washington, DC 20005

Glossary of Real Estate and REIT Terms

This glossary of terminology used in conjunction with discussions of real estate investment trusts has been prepared by the Research Department of the National Association of Real Estate Investment Trusts. Credit should be given to Realty Income Trust, a NAREIT member, which produced a glossary of terms upon which NAREIT drew heavily.

Acceleration clause A condition in a loan contract or mortgage note which permits the lender to demand immediate repayment of the entire balance if the contract is breached or conditions for repayment occur, such as sale or demolition.

Accrued interest or rent An amount of interest or rent which has been earned but which may not have been received in the same period as earned. On many short-term first mortgages, accrued interest is not received in cash until permanent financing is obtained.

Acquisition loan See C&D loan.

Advisor A REIT's investment advisor (usually pursuant to a renewable one-year contract) provides analysis of proposed investments, servicing of the portfolio, and other advisory services. Fee limits for advisory services are prescribed by many state securities regulators. Also spelled "adviser."

Amortization The process of retiring debt or recovering a capital investment through scheduled, systematic repayments of principal; that portion of fixed mortgage payment applied to reduction of the principal amount owed.

Anchor Tenant An important tenant, usually with an excellent credit rating (also known as a triple-A tenant), which takes a large amount of space in a shopping center or office building and is usually one of the first tenants to commit to lease. The anchor tenant usually is given lower rent because of the desirability of having that tenant at the property, both because of its credit rating and its ability to generate traffic.

Appraisal An opinion by an expert of the value of a property as of a specified date, supported by the presentation and analysis of relevant data. The appraisal may be arrived at by any or all of three methods: the cost approach (cost to reproduce), the market approach (comparison with other similar properties), or the income approach (capitalization of actual or projected income figures).

Assessed value The value of a property which is assigned to it by a taxing authority for pur-

Source: National Association of Real Estate Trusts, 1101 Seventeenth Street, N.W., Washington, D.C. 20036.

poses of assessing property taxes; often assessed value bears a fixed relationship by local statute to market value.

Asset swaps See swap program.

Assets Anything of value owned by the company. Assets are either financial, as cash or bonds; or physical, as real or personal property. For REIT tax purposes, more than 75% of the trust's assets must be property owned or securities backed by real estate.

Assumption of mortgage When the responsibility for repaying existing indebtedness secured by property is "assumed" by the second purchaser. In most jurisdictions, this relieves the first owner of the original obligations, at least to the extent that can be satisfied by sale of this asset after foreclosure.

Attribution More than 50% of a REIT's shares cannot be held by fewer than six people (otherwise it becomes a personal holding company for tax purposes). When someone has indirect control over someone else's shares (such as a trustee over shares held for the benefit of another) then "control" for personal holding company purposes may be "attributed." This complicated legal topic of "attribution" arises, however, only when the REIT's shares are held by a few.

Audit An examination of the financial status and operations of an enterprise, based mostly on the books of account, and undertaken to assure conformity to generally accepted accounting principles and to secure information for, or to check the accuracy of, the enterprise's balance sheet, income statement, and/or cash flow statement.

Balloon mortgage A mortgage loan which provides for periodic payments, which may include both interest and principal, but which leaves the loan less than fully ammortized at maturity, requiring a final large payment which is the "balloon." Usually the term does not apply to an "interest only" loan whose full principal is due upon maturity or upon call during its life.

Bankrupt When liabilities exceed assets, Federal laws enable the entity to dissolve in an orderly fashion (Chapter VII), or permit a court officer to restructure the company into a survivor "going business" (Chapter X), or permit existing management to do the same under court supervision (Chapter XI), or to do so despite the preferred position of secured creditors if real property is the only asset of the business (Chapter XII).

Beneficial owner The person who ultimately benefits from ownership of shares or other securities—in contrast to "nominees" (often pseudonyms for control of investment professionals so as to facilitate security transactions without having to track down beneficial owners to participate in each step of the procedures).

Blue sky laws State laws regulating conditions of sale of securities of companies, (particularly those just starting out of the "clear blue sky") for the protection of the investing public. National stock exchange rules usually supercede state laws pursuant to a "blue chip" exemption contained in such state laws. The federal securities laws dovetail with state laws and pertain to publicly held companies, primarily as to accounting and disclosure practices.

Bond A debt certificate which (a) represents a loan to a trust, (b) bears interest, and (c) matures on a stated future date. Short term bonds (generally with a maturity of five years or less from the date of issuance) are often called notes. See debentures.

Book value per share Shareholder equity as adjusted to tangible net worth (assets minus liabilities plus paid-in capital) per share outstanding.

Borrower A person or entity who received something of value, ordinarily money, and is obligated to pay it back, as the debtor to the creditor, usually pursuant to a note or "IOU" containing terms and conditions.

Broker A person who is paid to act as an intermediary in connection with a transaction, in contrast to a dealer or principal who buys or sells for his own account. In the REIT world, the term "broker" usually refers to a real estate salesman, although the term is also used for "stockbrokers" too.

Building lien An encumbrance upon the property by the contractor or subcontractors. Also known as a "mechanic's" or "materialman's" lien.

Building permit Written permission by the local municipality (usually through the building inspector or other agent) allowing construction work on a piece of property in accordance with plans which were submitted and conforming to local building codes and regulations.

Business trust An unincorporated business in which assets are given to trustees for management to hold or to sell, as investments. The business trust form was first fully developed in Massachusetts, under common law, and the term "Massachusetts business trust" is sometimes used to describe entities formed in other states. It is a form of business through a trustee or trustees who hold legal title to the property of the business. Capital contributions are made to the trustees by the beneficaries whose equitable title and interest in the property of the trust are evidenced by trust certificates, usually called shares of beneficial interest. The earnings of the trust are paid to them, as dividends are paid to stockholders. The beneficiaries generally enjoy limited liability, as the control and management of the trust rests solely with the trustees, but the trust form or organization can

be distinguished from a corporation. Early REIT tax laws relied on this distinction to define eligible real estate operations.

Capital gain The amount by which the net proceeds from resale of a capital item exceed the adjusted cost (or "book value") of the asset. If a capital asset is held for more than twelve months before disposition it is taxed on a more favorable basis than a gain after a shorter period of time.

Capitalization rate The rate of return utilized to value a given cash flow, the sum of a Discount Rate and a Capital Recapture Rate. It is applied to any income stream with a finite term over which the invested principal is to be returned to the investor or lender.

Cash flow The revenue remaining after all cash expenses are paid, i.e., non-cash charges such as depreciation are not included in the calculation.

Cash flow per share. Cash flow divided by the common shares outstanding. Shareholders must make this computation themselves since the SEC has prohibited companies from stating this calculation.

Net cash flow. Generally determined by net income plus depreciation less principal payments on long-term mortgages.

Cash on cash return The "cash flow" from a property expressed as a percentage of the cash "equity" invested in a property.

Chapter X See bankrupt.

Collateral An item of value, such as real estate or securities, which a borrower pledges as security. A mortgage gives the creditor the right to seize the real estate collateral after non-performance of the debtor.

Commitment A promise to make an investment at some time in the future if certain specified conditions are met. A REIT may charge a fee to the borrower at the time of making the commitment. A REIT's level of commitments minus expected repayments can be regarded as an indication of future funding requirements.

"Take-out" commitment is one provided by the anticipated long-term lender, usually with complicated terms and conditions that must be met before the "take out" becomes effective.

"Gap" commitment is an anticipated short-term loan to cover part of the final "take-out" that the long-term lender refuses to advance until certain conditions are met (like 90% rent-up of an apartment after construction is completed). The amount above the "floor" or basic part of the loan is the "gap," and the gap commitment is issued to enable the construction lender to make a construction loan commitment for the full amount of the takeout loan instead of only for the "floor" amount.

"Standby" commitment is one that the lender and borrower doubt will be used. It exists as reassurance to a short-term construction lender that if, after completion of a building, the borrower cannot find adequate long-term "take-out" financing, the construction lender will be repaid.

Compensating balances Money which is sometimes required by banks to be held in checking accounts by borrowers, as part of their loan agreement.

Condominium A form of fee ownership of whole units or separate portions of multi-unit buildings which facilitates the formal filing, recording and financing of a divided interest in real property. The condominium concept may be used for apartments, offices and other professional uses. See cooperatives.

Conduit tax treatment So long as most (if not all) earnings are passed along by an entity, then federal taxation is avoided at the entity's level. REITs, mutual funds, and certain kinds of holding companies are elibible for "conduit tax treatment" under certain conditions.

Constant The agreed-upon periodic (usually monthly) payment to pay the face interest rate, with any residual amount going to amortize the loan.

Construction and development loan (C&D) A short-term loan for the purpose of constructing a building, shopping center, or other improvement upon real estate, or developing a site in preparation for construction. A C&D loan is normally disbursed in increments (called *draws* or *draw-downs*) as building proceeds, rather than in a single disbursement, and is conditioned upon compliance with a variety of factors. It is usually repaid with the proceeds of the permanent loan. A land loan or purchase and development loan is sometimes made for the purpose of acquiring unimproved vacant land, usually as a future building site and for financing improvements to such land (street, sewers, etc.) as a prerequisite to construction of a building upon the site.

Contingent Interest Interest on a loan that is payable only if certain conditions occur, in contrast to interest that becomes an accrued liability (whether or not paid) at a specific time.

Cooperative A form of ownership whereby a structure is owned by a corporation or trust with each individual owner holding stock in the corporation representative of the value of his apartment. Title to the apartment is evidenced by a proprietary lease which often does not qualify as adequate collateral for some lenders.

Cost-to-carry The concept specified by the accounting profession to be used by REITs in computing anticipated interest cost on debt needed to "carry" non-earning or partially-earning assets until they're restored to earning status or sold.

Current Liabilities Money owed and due to be paid within one year.

Dealer Someone who buys property with the purpose of selling it at a profit rather than holding it as an investment. A dealer's profits are taxed at the ordinary income rate rather than the capital gains rate regardless of how long the property is held for resale (in contrast to the investor who sells a property after a year and pays at the capital gains rate). A REIT is not permitted to be a dealer unless it is willing to pay a 100% tax on gains from such sales in the year in which it is deemed to be a dealer; sales of foreclosed property do not fall within this definition. See principal.

Debenture An obligation which is secured only by the general credit of the issuing trust, as opposed to being secured by a direct lien on its assets, real estate or otherwise. A debenture is a form of a bond.

Declaration of Trust Similar to articles of incorporation for a corporation, this document contains rules for operation of the trust, selection of its governing trustees, etc., and is the keystone of a REIT.

Deed A legal instrument which conveys title from one to another. It must be (a) made between competent parties (b) have legally sound subject matter (c) correctly state what is being conveyed (d) contain good and valuable consideration (e) be properly executed by the parties involved and (f) be delivered to be valid.

Deed in lieu of foreclosure The device by which title to property is conveyed from the mortgagor (borrower) to the mortgagee (lender) as an alternative to foreclosure. While this procedure can transfer effective control more quickly, many lenders eschew it because undiscovered prior liens (from a workman who was never paid but hadn't gotten around to filing his valid, but late, claim for example) remain enforceable in contrast to the more formal foreclosure procedures which wipe out prior claims after due notice.

Deferred maintenance the amount of repairs that should have been made to keep a property in good running condition, but which have been put off. The term contemplates the desirability of immediate expenditures, although it does not necessarily denote inadequate maintenance in the past.

Deficiency dividend The process of paying an "extra" dividend after the close of the fiscal year so as to comply with REIT tax requirements to pay out more than 90% of income. See dividend.

Depreciation The loss in value of a capital asset, due to wear and tear which cannot be compensated for by ordinary repairs, or an allowance made to allow for the fact that the asset may become obsolete before it wears out. The purpose of a depreciation charge is to write off the original cost of an asset by equitably distributing charges against its operation over its useful life, matching "cost" to the period in which it was used to generate earnings. Depreciation is an optional noncash expense recognizable for tax purposes. If the REIT pays out more than its taxable earnings, then it is distributing a "return of capital" or—as is commonly stated in the industry—"paying out depreciation."

Development loans See Construction and development loan.

Dilution The situation which results when an increase occurs in a company's outstanding securities without a corresponding increase in the company's assets and/or income.

Discount rate An interest rate used to convert a future stream of payments into a single present value. See capitalization rate.

Dividend or distribution The distribution of cash or stock to shareholders of a company which is made periodically as a means of distributing all or a portion of net income or cash flow. Technically, a dividend can be paid only from net taxable income, so many REITs distribute cash and later characterize their distributions as capital gains or a tax-free return of capital if net taxable income is less than the cash paid out.

Dividend or distribution yield The annual dividend or distribution rate for a security expressed as a percent of its market price. For most REITs, the "annualized" rate is the previous quarter's distribution times four, regardless of how the distribution is characterized.

Draw A request from a borrower to obtain partial payment from the lender pursuant to a loan commitment. The lender reassures himself that the borrower has completed the required steps (such as putting in the concrete properly) before advancing money. Often, the borrower submits bills from subcontractors, which are then "paid" by the lender after inspecting the subcontractor's work. In such cases, the check is usually made out to the subcontractor but must be signed by the borrower, too, so that the lender ends up only with one borrower. See construction and development loan.

Effective Borrowing Costs The cost of borrowing after adjustment for compensating balances or fees in lieu of compensating balances, and selling expenses in the case of publicly sold debt.

Encumbrance A legal right or interest in real estate which diminishes its value. Encumbrances can take a number of forms, such as easements, zoning restrictions, mortgages, etc.

Entrepreneur An individual who is responsible for a commercial or real estate activity who takes a certain risk of loss in a transaction for the right to enjoy any profit which may result.

Equity The interest of the shareholders in a company as measured by their paid-in capital and undistributed income. The term is also used to describe (i) the difference between the current market value of a property and the liens or mortgages which encumber it or (ii) the cash which makes up the difference between the mortgage(s) and the construction or sale price.

Equity leveraging The process by which shares are sold at a premium above book value (in anticipation of greater earnings).

Equity participation Usually, the right of an investor to participate to some extent in the increased value of a project by receiving a percentage of the increased income from the project. If a REIT were to participate in a percentage of the net income of a venture (such as the shopping center's owner/lessor), then it could be deemed to be a partner in an active business. Thus, most REIT leases spell out the "equity participation" as a percentage of gross receipts or sales (which is a more stable measure of sales activity, anyway, and one readily identifiable from the lessor's federal income tax statement).

Escrow A deposit of "good faith" money which is entrusted to a third party (often a bank) until fulfillment of certain conditions and agreements, when the escrow may be released or applied as payment for the purchase of property or for services rendered.

Estoppel certificate An instrument used when a mortgage or lease is assigned to another. The certificate sets forth the exact remaining balance of the lease or mortgage as of a certain date and verifies any promises to tenants that may have been made by the first owner for which the second owner may be held accountable.

Exculpatory clause A clause which relieves one of liability for injuries or damages to another. Exculpatory clauses are placed in REIT documents with the intention of eliminating personal liability of its trustees, shareholders and officers.

Expenses The costs which are charges against current operations or earnings of a building, company or other reporting entity. They may have been "paid out" in cash, or accrued to be paid later, or charged as a bookkeeping procedure to reflect the "using up" of assets (as in depreciation) utilized in the production of income during the period of current operations.

Face value The value which is shown on the face of an instrument such as a bond, debenture or stock certificate. The "face rate" of a debt instrument is often known as its "coupon rate."

Fair market value See Market value.

Fee or fee simple Title to a property which is absolute, good and marketable; ownership without condition.

Fiduciary A relationship of trust and confidence between a person charged with the duty of acting for the benefit of another and the person to whom such duty is owed, as in the case of guardian and ward, trustee and beneficiary, executor and heir.

First mortgage That mortgage which has a prior claim over all other liens against real estate. In some jurisdictions, real estate taxes, mechanics liens, court costs, and other involuntary liens may take priority over such a contractual lien: title companies "clear" properties so as to reassure first mortgage lenders (and owners) of their uncontested position and to guarantee them of that position under certain conditions.

Fiscal year The 12-month period selected as a basis for computing and accounting for a business. A fiscal year need not coincide with the calendar year, except for all REITs initially qualifying for special tax treatment after 1976.

Fixed assets Assets, such as land, buildings and machinery, which cannot be quickly converted into cash. For REITs, most "fixed assets" are real property although some (like furniture in an apartment lobby) may be personal property.

Fixed charges Those interest charges, insurance costs, taxes and other expenses which remain relatively constant regardless of revenue. See net lease.

Floating rate A variable interest rate charged for the use of borrowed money. It is determined by charging a specific percentage above a fluctuating base rate, usually the prime rate as announced by a major commercial bank.

Floor loan A portion or portions of a mortgage loan commitment which is less than the full amount of the commitment and which may be funded upon conditions less stringent than those required for funding the full amount, or the "ceiling" of the loan. For example, the floor loan, equal to perhaps 80% of the full amount of the loan, may be funded upon completion of construction without any occupancy requirements, but substantial occupancy of the building may be required for funding the full amount of the loan, which is referred to as the "ceiling." See commitment, gap.

Foreclosure The legal process of enforcing payment of a debt by taking the properties which secure the debt, once the terms of the obligation are not followed. Upon foreclosure, the entire debt might not be fully discharged by transfer and disposition of the property (as determined by the courts). If so, a "deficiency judgment" may be obtained, at which point the lender is like any other creditor in attempting to get the debtor to pay the deficiency. Collection of the deficiency judgment in major real estate transactions is rare, but it becomes a major factor in negotiations if the borrower decides to return to the real estate business in the future.

Fully diluted earnings The hypothetical earnings per share of a company, computed after giving effect to the number of shares which would be outstanding if all convertible debt and warrants were exercised, and also to any reduction in interest payments resulting from such exercise.

Gap commitment See commitment, gap. Also see floor loan.

General lien A lien against the property of an individual or other entity generally, rather than against specific items of realty or personal property.

Ground lease See sale-leaseback.

Holding company A corporation that owns or controls the operations of various other companies. Many REITs were sponsored by bank or insurance holding companies whose subsidiary companies advise and manage REITs, pursuant to contracts with the REIT's trustees.

Independent contractor A firm hired to actively manage property investments. A tax-qualified REIT must hire an independent contractor to manage and operate its property, so as to distinguish itself as an investor rather than an active manager.

Income property Developed real estate, such as office buildings, shopping centers, apartments, hotels and motels, warehouses and some kinds of agricultural or industrial property, which produce a flow of income—in contrast to non-income generating real estate like raw land which would be bought and held for a speculative profit upon resale or development.

Indenture The legal document prepared in connection with, for example, a bond issue, setting forth the terms of the issue, its specific security, remedies in case of default, etc. It may also be called the "deed of trust."

Indentured trustee A trustee, generally the trust department of a major bank, which represents the interest of bondholders under a publicly offered issue.

Insider A person close to a trust who has intimate knowledge of financial developments before they become public knowledge.

Interest rate The percentage rate which an individual pays for the use of borrowed money for a given period of time.

Intermediate-term loan A loan for a term of three to ten years which is usually not fully amortized at maturity. Often, developers will seek interim loans by which to pay off construction financing, in anticipation of obtaining long-term financing at a later date on more favorable terms, either because long-term rates decline generally or because the project can show an established, stable earnings history.

Interim loan A type of loan which is to be repaid out of the proceeds of another loan. Ordinarily, not self-liquidating (amortized), the lender evaluates the risk of obtaining refinancing as much as the period risk. See C&D loans.

Investment advisor See advisor.

Joint venture The entity which is created when two or more persons or corporate entities join together to carry out a specific business transaction of real estate development. A joint venture is usually of limited duration and usually for a specific property; it can be treated as a partnership for tax purposes. The parties have reciprocal and paralleling rights and obligations.

Junior mortgage loan Any mortgage loan in which the lien and the right of repayment is subordinate to that of another mortgage loan or loans. A "second mortgage" is a junior mortgage. "Third, fourth," etc. mortgages are always deemed to be secondary.

Land loan See Construction and development loan.

Land-purchase leaseback See sale-leaseback.

Late charge The charge which is levied against a borrower for a payment which was not made in a timely manner.

Lease A contract between the owner of property (lessor) and a tenant (lessee) setting forth the terms, conditions and consideration for the use of the property for a specified period of time at a specified rental. See sale-leaseback and net lease.

Leasehold improvements The cost of improvements or betterments to property leased for a period of years, often paid for by the tenant. Such improvements ordinarily become the property of the lessor (owner) on expiration of the lease; consequently their cost is normally amortized over the life of the lease if the lessor pays for them.

Leverage The process of borrowing upon one's capital base with the expectation of generating a profit above the cost of borrowing.

Liability management The aspect of the management of a company concerned with the planning and procurement of funds for investment through the sale of equity, public debt and bank borrowings. In the REIT industry, the phrase contrasts to "asset management" or the real estate side of the business.

Line of credit Usually, an agreement between a commercial bank and a borrower under which the bank agrees to provide unsecured credit to the borrower upon certain terms and conditions. Normally, the borrower may draw on all or any part of the credit from time to time.

Limited partnership A partnership which limits certain of the partners' (the limited partners) liability to the amount of their investment. At least one partner (the "general partner") is fully liable for the obligations of the partnership and

its operations, usually with the limited partners participating as investors only.

Loan loss reserve A reserve set up to offset asset values in anticipation of losses that are reasonably expected. Initially, REITs had insufficient operating experience to anticipate losses in any one class of investments or for a portfolio as a whole, so tax authorities would not permit substantial contributions toward a reserve as an allowable period expense. When difficulties arose, the conversion of short-term loans to longer-term property holdings required some form of recognition of likely losses in the financial statements. A novel procedure for REITs was devised by requiring, for book purposes, computation of additions to the reserve based in part on the probable cost of sustaining the troubled assets over the longer period of time necessary to "cure" the problem. Also known as "allowance for losses."

Loan run-off The rate at which an existing mortgage portfolio will reduce (or "run-off") to zero if no new loans are added to the portfolio.

Loan swaps See asset swaps.

Long-term mortgage Any financing, whether in the form of a first or junior mortgage, the term of which is ten years or more. It is generally fully amortized.

Loss carry forwards The net operating loss (NOL) incurred in prior years, which may be applied for tax purposes against future earnings, thereby reducing taxable income. For REITs (which must pay out most of their taxable income), NOLs can be carried forward eight years; for non-REIT-taxed companies, NOL can be carried forward for only seven years.

Market value The highest price in terms of money which a property will bring in a competitive and open market under all conditions requisite to a fair sale—the buyer and the seller each acting prudently, knowledgeably, and at arm's length. See appraisal.

Moratorium A period in which payments of debts or other performance of a legal obligation is suspended temporarily, usually because of unforeseen circumstances which make timely payment or performance difficult or impossible. This forebearance can be whole or partial.

Mortgage A publicly recorded lien by which the property is pledged as security for the payment of a debt valid even beyond death ("mort" is death in French). In some states a mortgage is an actual conveyance of the property to the creditor until the terms of the mortgage are satisfied. While there is always a "note" secured by a mortgage document, both the note and mortgage instrument are commonly called "the mortgage." For types, see: first, junior, short-term, long-term, wrap-around and construction and development mortgage definitions.

Mortgage banker A non-depository lender who makes loans secured by real estate and then usually packages and sells those loans in large groups to institutional investors, pursuant to a "long-term commitment" he has negotiated with the life insurance company or other institutional investor. Mortgage bankers frequently arrange to service these mortgages for the out-of-town institutions, collecting regular payments, keeping the lender up to date on the progress of the loan, escrowing payments for taxes and insurance premiums, and, if necessary, administering foreclosure proceedings. Many REITs were sponsored by mortgage bankers.

Mortgage constant The total annual payments of principal and interest (annual debt service) on a mortgage with level-payment amortization schedule, expressed as a percentage of the initial principal amount of the loan.

Mortgagee in possession A lender or one who holds a mortgage who has taken possession of a property in order to protect an interest in the property. Usually, this is done with commercial properties as to which rents, management fees and other disbursements continue even if the mortgage is in default. The possession must be taken with the consent of the mortgagor (or a court, in cases of foreclosure) and the mortgagee must be careful to do only those things to the property that the mortgagor (or court) will agree to accept, should it resume its role as a credit-worthy owner.

Net Income The dollar amount that remains after all expenses, including taxes, are deducted from gross income. For regular companies, it is also called after-tax profit, the "bottom line" figure of how a company has performed with its investors' money. For REITs, it is net taxable income which, if fully distributed, is not taxed.

Net lease A lease, sometimes called a net-net (insurance and taxes) or even a net-net-net lease (insurance, taxes, and maintenance) in which the tenant pays all costs, including insurance, taxes, repairs, upkeep and other expenses, and the rental payments are "net" of all these expenses. See lease and fixed charges.

Net worth The remaining asset value of a property company or other entity after deduction of all liabilities against it.

Non-accrual loans See non-earning investments.

Non-earning investments The category of loans or investments which are not earning the originally anticipated rate of return. Some may be characterized as "partially earning." When interest is recorded as earned rather than as received (accrued interest), "non-accrual investments" are those which management expects not to receive interest as originally contemplated. In the vernacular, nonearning investments are "problem loans" or "troubled properties."

Non-qualified REIT A REIT that was formerly qualified, or conducts its affairs as if it is qualified, but that has elected for the tax year in question to be treated like a normal business corporation for tax purposes. Thus, some restraints (primarily against active management and holding property for sale) are lifted, while REIT conduit tax treatment is lost.

Occupancy rate The amount of space or number of apartments or offices or hotel rooms which are rented as compared with the total amount or number available. The rate is usually expressed as a percentage.

Operating expenses Expenses arising out of or relating to business activity such as interest expense, professional fees, salaries, etc.

Operating income Income received directly from business activity in the normal course, as contrasted with capital gains income, or other extraordinary income.

Option A right to buy or lease property at a certain specified price for specified terms. Consideration is typically given for the option, which is exercisable over a limited time span. If the option is not exercised, the consideration is forfeited. A loan to a developer secured by his option to obtain real estate is considered a "qualified" REIT asset.

Origination The process by which a loan is created, including the search for (or receipt of) the initial plans, the analysis and structuring of the proposed financing, and the review and acceptance procedures by which the commitment to make the investment is finally issued.

Overage income Rental income above a guaranteed minimum depending on a particular level of profit or retail sales volume by the tenant, payable under the terms of a lease.

Participations A lender often "participates out" or sells a portion of his loan to another lender while retaining a portion and managing the investment. REITs buy real estate secured participations as well as originating them.

Par Value The face value assigned to a security when it is issued. The stated par value of a security generally has nothing to do with its market or book value.

Passivity The state of owning investments but not actively managing them (as a property management firm does for the investor) or engaging in trading the securities (like a broker or dealer). This "passivity" test is implicit behind several of the REIT tax requirements.

Pension funds Money which is accumulated in trust to fund pensions for companies or unions and which is frequently invested in part in real estate. A co-mingled real estate pension fund account is managed, usually under contract to a financial institution, much like a REIT except that its shares are not publicly traded but instead sold to other pension funds.

Permanent financing See long-term loan.

Point An amount which represents 1% of the maximum principal amount of an investment. Used in connection with a discount from, or a share of, a principal amount deducted at the time funds are advanced, it represents additional compensation to the lender.

Portfolio The investments of a company, including investments in mortgages and/or ownership of real property. REIT portfolios usually consist of equity in property, short-term mortgages, long-term mortgages and/or subordinated land sale-lease-backs.

Portfolio turnover The average length of time from the funding of investments until they are paid off or sold.

Preferred shares Stocks which have prior claim on distributions (and/or assets in the event of dissolution) up to a certain definite amount before the shares of beneficial interest are entitled to anything. As a form of ownership, preferred shares stand behind senior subordinated and secured debtholders in dissolution, as well as other creditors.

Prepayment penalty The penalty which is imposed on the borrower for payment of the mortgage before it is due. Often a mortgage contains a clause specifying that there is to be no prepayment penalty, or limits the prepayment penalty to only the first few years of the mortgage term.

Price earning ratio A ratio which consists of the market price divided by current annualized earnings per share. Such a computation is now found in most daily stock listings. For REITs, annualization of quarterly earnings is computed by multiplying the most recent distribution by four, regardless of the distribution's later characterization as a dividend, return-of-capital, or capital gains.

Prime lending rate The rate at which commercial banks will lend money from time to time to their most credit-worthy customers, used as a base for most loans to financial intermediaries such as REITs.

Principal The buyer or seller in a real estate transaction as distinguished from an agent.

Principal The sum of money loaned. The amount of money to be repaid on a loan excluding interest charges.

Prior lien A lien or mortgage ranking ahead of some other lien. A prior lien need not itself be a first mortgage.

Pro forma Projected or hypothetical as opposed to actual as related, for example, to a balance sheet or income statement.

Problem investments See nonearning investments.

Prospectus A document describing an investment opportunity; the detailed description of new securities which must be supplied to prospective interstate purchasers under the Securities Act of 1933.

Provision for loan losses Periodic allocation of funds to loan loss reserves in recognition of a decline in the value of a loan or loans in a trust's portfolio due to a default on the part of the borrowers.

Proxy An authorization given by a registered security holder to vote stock at the annual meeting or at a special meeting of security holders.

Purchase and leaseback See sale-leaseback.

Pyramiding In stock market transactions, this term refers to the practice of borrowing against unrealized "paper" profits in securities to make additional purchases. In corporate finance, it refers to the practice of creating a speculative capital structure by a series of holding companies, whereby a relatively small amount of voting stock in the parent company controls a large corporate system. In real estate, it refers to the practice of financing 100% or more of the value of the property.

Qualified assets Assets which meet tax requirements for special REIT tax treatment, i.e. real property. In any tax year, 75% of a REIT's assets must be invested in real property, either through ownership or by securities secured by real estate. A "partially qualified" asset is one that qualifies under the 90% test of being a passive investment in a security, but not under the 75% real estate test.

Qualified income That portion of income which is classified as interest, rents, or other gain from real property, as spelled out in the REIT tax laws.

Raw land Land which has not been developed or improved.

RCA See revolving credit agreement.

Real estate investment trust (REIT, pronounced "reet") A trust established for the benefit of a group of investors which is managed by one or more trustees who hold title to the assets for the trust and control its acquisitions and investments, at least 75% of which are real estate related. A major advantage of a REIT is that no federal income tax need be paid by the trust if certain qualifications are met. Congress enacted these special tax provisions to encourage an assembly method, which is essentially designed to provide for investment in real estate what the mutual provided for investment in securities. The REIT provides the small investor with a means of combining his funds with those of others, and protects him from the double taxation that would be levied against an ordinary corporation or trust.

Revolving credit agreement (or "revolver") A formal credit agreement between a group of banks and a REIT, the terms of which are reviewed periodically when it is "rolled over" or "revolved" or refinanced by a similar agreement. For many trusts, "revolvers" have replaced informal lines of credit extended by individual banks to REITs, thereby providing a uniform (and usually restrictive) approach by all creditors, reassuring each bank that others in the RCA would not be paid off preferentially.

Registration statement The forms filed by a company with the Securities and Exchange Commission in connection with an offering of new securities or the listing of outstanding securities on a national exchange.

Reserves for loss See loan loss reserve.

Return of capital A distribution to shareholders in excess of the trust's earnings and profits, usually consisting of either depreciation or repayment of principal from properties or mortgages held by the trust. Each shareholder receiving such a distribution is required to reduce the tax basis of his shares by the amount of such distribution. For financial accounting purposes, what constitutes a return of capital may differ from that determined under Federal income tax requirements.

Return on equity A figure which consists of net income for the period divided by equity and which is normally expressed as a percentage.

Right of first refusal The right or option granted by a seller to a buyer, to have the first opportunity of acquiring a property.

Rights offering The privilege extended to a shareholder of subscribing to additional stock of the same or another class or to bonds, usually at a price below the market and in an amount proportional to the number of shares already held. Rights must be exercised within a time limit and often may be sold if the holder does not wish to purchase additional shares.

Sale-leaseback A common real estate transaction whereby the investor buys property from and simultaneously leases it back to, the seller. This enables the previous owner (often a developer) to "cash out" on an older property while retaining control.

Land sale-leaseback—this procedure, made common by several REITs that specialize in the transaction, affects only the land under income—producing improvements (such as shopping centers, etc.)—leaving the depreciable improvements in the hands of those who might benefit from the tax consequences. Since the improvements were probably financed with the proceeds of a first mortgage which remains in effect, the rights of the new investor are made second, or junior, to those of the first mortgage holder. Hence the common phrase "subordinated land sale-leaseback." In return for accepting a less secure position, the new investor usually obtains an "overage" clause whereby additional rent is paid anytime gross income of the shopping center (or whatever) exceeds a pre-determined floor.

Seasoned issues Securities of large, established companies which have been known to the investment public for a period of years, covering good times and bad.

Second mortgages See junior mortgage loan.

Secured debt For REITs, senior mortgage debt secured by specific properties. In case of default on "nonrecourse" debt, the lender may assume property ownership but may not pursue other assets of the lender.

Senior mortgage A mortgage which has first priority.

Senior unsecured debt Funds borrowed under open lines without security. Most bank lines to REITs were unsecured.

Shares of beneficial interest Tradable shares in a REIT. Analogous to common stock in a corporation.

Shareholders' equity Primarily money invested by shareholders through purchase of shares, plus the accumulation of that portion of net income that has been reinvested in the business since the commencement of operations.

Short-term mortgage A loan upon real estate for a term of three years or less, bearing interest payable periodically, with principal usually payable in full at maturity.

Sinking fund An arrangement under which a portion of a bond or preferred stock issue is retired periodically, in advance of its fixed maturity. The company may either purchase a stipulated quantity of the issue itself, or supply funds to a trustee or agent for that purpose. Retirement may be made by call at a fixed price, or by inviting tenders, or by purchase in the open market.

Sponsor The entity which initiated the formation of a REIT and usually acts (often via a subsidiary) as investment advisor to the trust thereafter. The sponsor puts the reputation of its institution on the line for the REIT and usually arranges lines of credit, provides support services and, occasionally, compensating balances.

Spread Difference between percentage return on an investment and cost of funds to support the investment.

Standby commitment See commitment, standby.

Standing loan Usually not amortized, the loan is secured by completed property that has not yet been refinanced with a "permanent" long-term mortgage.

Subordinated debt Debt which is junior to secured and unsecured senior debt, it may be convertible into shares of beneficial interest for

REITs. Senior subordinated debt is senior to other subordinated debt.

Subordinated ground lease See sale-leaseback.

Swap Program A procedure for reducing debt (by a troubled REIT) by trading an asset to the creditor in return for cancellation of part of a loan to the REIT. Often a cash premium payment is made in addition to reduction of the debt. The premium may then be distributed to the other creditors pro rata. The amount of the cash premium, or the ratio of cash-to-debt reduction to be applied against the value of the asset, is sometimes determined by a sealed-bid "auction" process as set forth in the "revolving credit agreement" between the creditors and the REIT. See RCA.

Syndicate A group of investors who transact business for a limited period of time and sometimes with a single purpose. It is a short-term partnership.

Take-out commitment See commitment.

Tax shelter The various aspects of an investment which offer relief from income taxes or opportunities to claim deductions from taxable income. Although tax shelters are an important facet of real estate investment, they do not have a direct influence on REIT investment choices because qualified trusts are exempt from income taxes.

Usury The charging of interest rates for the use of money higher than what's allowed by local law.

Warrants Stock purchase warrants or options give the holder rights to purchase shares of stock, generally running for a longer period of time than ordinary subscription rights given shareholders. Warrants are often attached to other securities, but they may be issued separately or detached after issuance.

Working capital Determined by subtracting current liabilities from current assets. It represents the amount available to carry on the day-to-day operation of the business.

Work-out When a borrower has problems, the process undertaken by the lender to help the borrower "work out" of the problems becomes known itself as a "work out." The presumption during a "work out" is that the borrower will eventually resume a more normal debtor's position once problems are solved within (presumably) a reasonably short time.

Wrap-around mortgage A type of junior mortgage used to refinance properties on which there is an existing first mortgage loan. The face amount of the wrap-around loan is equivalent to the unpaid balance on the existing mortgage plus cash advanced to the property owner upon funding. Such loans carry a higher interest rate than the existing mortgage. The wrap-around lender assumes the obligation to maintain payments of principal and interest on the existing mortgage so as to enhance his right to make claim from his secondary position.

Yield In the stock market, the rate of annual distribution or dividend expressed as a percentage of price. Current yield is found by dividing the market price into the distribution rate in dollars. In real estate, the term refers to the effective annual amount of income which is being accrued on an investment expressed as a percentage of its value.

Employee Benefits in Medium and Large Firms*

Retirement Coverage Widespread in Medium and Large Firms, 1985

More than 9 in 10 full-time employees in medium and large firms were covered by one or more private retirement plans in 1985, according to a survey of employee benefits by the U.S. Department of Labor's Bureau of Labor Statistics (BLS). Nearly 3 in 10 employees were covered by plans that allow participants to reduce their taxable income by channeling part of their salary to retirement funds, under section 401(k) of the Internal Revenue Code.

Retirement coverage was provided to employees through a variety of means. Defined benefit (or conventional) pension plans, which have formulas for determining an employee's annuity, covered 8 in 10 employees. Four in 10 workers participated in defined contribution plans also designed to provide retirement income. These plans, which usually predetermine the employer's contribution but not the employee's benefit, include savings and thrift, profit sharing, money purchase pension, and employee stock ownership plans. In addition, 2 in 10 workers with retirement coverage participated in capital accumulation plans (defined contribution plans that allow participants to withdraw the employer's contributions at their discretion). Defined contribution plans typically supplemented defined benefit pension plans.

For the first time, the survey developed information on salary reduction or 401(k) plans. Nearly 40 percent of the white-collar workers (those in professional-administrative or technical-clerical occupations) were in salary reduction plans, while only 16 percent of the blue-collar (or production) workers participated in these tax-deferred plans. Three-fifths of all participants (white- and blue-collar combined) could elect to make their 401(k) contributions to an existing savings and thrift plan where the employer matched at least part of the employee's contribution, another fifth of the participants were in a free standing 401(k) plan (no employer contribution), and the remainder could contribute to profit-sharing (15 percent) or money purchase pension plans (3 percent).

---

* Detailed information of the benefit provisions studied are available in a bulletin "Employee Benefits in Medium and Large Firms, 1985 published by the Bureau of Labor Statistics.
Source: "Retirement Coverage Widespread in Medium and Large Firms, 1985," in *News*, April 1985, U.S. Department of Labor, Bureau of Labor Statistics, Washington, DC 20212. For further historical and technical data call 202-523-9444.

This seventh annual survey of employee benefits provides representative data for 20.1 million full-time employees in a cross section of the Nation's private industries in 1985. The survey's scope generally was limited to establishments employing at least 100 or 250 workers, depending upon the industry.

The study provides information on paid leave, insurance, and private pension plans, as well as many other benefits that are paid, at least in part, by the employer. It covers both the extent of these benefits and the detailed characteristics of the benefit plans. Information also is provided on several benefits, such as salary reduction plans under section 401(k) and post-retirement health and life insurance, even if not financed by employers. Data are provided for all employees and for three employee groups—professional-administrative, technical-clerical, and production workers.

Paid Time Off

Time off with pay is available to employees in several different forms and amounts—from daily rest breaks of a few minutes to annual vacations of several weeks. In 1985, paid lunch time (available to a tenth of the workers) averaged 27 minutes a day, while paid rest periods (covering nearly three-fourths of the workers) averaged 26 minutes per day. The number of paid holidays averaged 10.1 days; the amount of vacation, which typically varied by length of service, averaged 8.6 days after 1 year of service, 15.9 days after 10 years, and 20.7 days after 20 years of service. Where personal leave (multipurpose paid leave) plans were in effect, the average number of days available was 3.7 per year. For three other paid leave benefits, each available to a majority of the employees, funeral leave averaged 3.2 days per occurrence and military leave averaged 11.5 days a year; time off for paid jury duty leave was usually provided as needed.

Disability Income Benefits

Workers may be protected against loss of income during temporary absences from work due to illness or accident through paid sick leave or sickness and accident insurance and, during extended periods of disability, through long-term disability insurance or disability pensions.

FULL-TIME EMPLOYEES PARTICIPATING IN SELECTED EMPLOYEE BENEFIT PROGRAMS, MEDIUM AND LARGE PRIVATE INDUSTRY ESTABLISHMENTS, UNITED STATES,[1] 1985. [In percent]

Employee Benefit Program	All Employees	Professional and Administrative Employees	Technical and Clerical Employees	Production Employees
Paid:				
Holidays	98	99	100	96
Vacations	99	99	100	99
Personal leave	26	33	37	18
Lunch period	10	3	3	17
Rest time	72	58	70	81
Funeral leave	88	87	89	87
Military leave	70	77	75	63
Jury duty leave	92	94	96	89
Sick leave	67	93	92	41
Sickness and accident insurance	52	30	38	70
Long-term disability insurance	48	64	61	32
Health insurance	96	97	96	96
Life insurance	96	97	96	96
Retirement	91	93	93	89
Defined benefit pension	80	81	82	78
Defined contribution plan[2]	41	49	49	32
Capital accumulation[3]	20	28	25	13

[1] The survey excludes data for executives and employees in constant travel status, such as airline pilots, as well as data for Alaska and Hawaii.

[2] Includes money purchase pension, profit sharing, savings and thrift, stock bonus, and employee stock ownership plans in which employer contributions must remain in the participant's account until retirement age, death, disability, separation from service, age 59½, or hardship.

[3] Includes plans in which employer contributions may be withdrawn from the participant's account without regard to the conditions listed in footnote 2.

In 1985, short-term disability protection was provided to 93 percent of workers by sick leave, sickness and accident insurance, or both. Long-term disability insurance was available to 48 percent of the workers, but 41 percent (some with long-term disability insurance) were eligible for immediate disability benefits under their pension plans.

Paid sick leave plans vary greatly in the number of days off available. For example, after 1 year of service, plans specifying a maximum annual benefit allowed an average of 15.9 days off per year with full pay; when days off were specified for each disability, the average was 59.9 days. The number of paid sick leave days also varied depending on whether the plan was coordinated with sickness and accident insurance and whether it allowed carryover of unused sick leave days from year to year. Sickness and accident insurance pays a portion of an employee's regular earnings, usually for a maximum of 26 weeks.

Long-term disability insurance typically pays 50 or 60 percent of regular earnings when an employee is disabled for a prolonged period. Long-term disability payments usually begin after sick leave and sickness and accident insurance are exhausted and continue as long as the person is disabled or until retirement age. Career-ending disabilities may entitle an employee to an immediate pension, but the pension may be deferred until other forms of income, such as long-term disability insurance, have ceased.

Health and Life Insurance

Health insurance plans continued to add provisions designed to counter rising health care costs. As in 1984, benefits became more common for less expensive alternatives to hospital stays: Coverage for treatment in extended care facilities was available to 67 percent of plan participants in 1985, up from 62 percent in 1984; coverage for home health care rose from 46 percent to 56 percent; and hospice care coverage increased from 11 percent to 23 percent. In addition, the percentage of participants whose health plans paid for a second surgical opinion increased from 38 percent in 1984 to 50 percent in 1985. A variety of other cost control features were surveyed for the first time in 1985, including pre-hospitalization testing (46 percent of health plan participants); treatment in ambulatory surgical centers (39 percent); and improved benefits for certain types of surgery performed on an outpatient basis (25 percent).

Thirty-five percent of the employees were in plans that required them to pay part of the premiums for their own coverage, the same as in 1984; and 53 percent were in plans requiring contributions for family coverage—the first time this proportion had not increased since first studied in 1980. However, 29 percent of the employees having major medical coverage were under plans requiring them to pay the first $150 or more of expenses before reimbursement by the insurance plan. This was up from 21 percent in 1984 and 12 percent in 1983.

Broadened coverage in other areas was not directly related to cost control. The percentage of health plan participants covered for alcoholism treatment increased from 61 to 68 percent between 1984 and 1985 and, for drug abuse treatment, from 52 to 61 percent. Participation in vision care plans also grew, to 35 percent, up from 30 percent in 1984. Under major medical plans, the most common lifetime maximum benefit shifted to $1 million, from $250,000 in previous years.

Group health insurance coverage continued after retirement in plans covering 70 percent of the employees. Nearly all of these employees were in plans that extended benefits to retirees up to age 65. Sixty-four percent of the employees were in plans that covered retirees 65 and over; 38 percent were in plans where retiree premiums were fully paid by the employer, 16 percent were in plans where the cost was financed by both employer and retiree, and 7 percent were in retiree paid plans. Retirees' benefits were usually the same as those for active workers, though payments were coordinated with Medicare.

Life insurance for 66 percent of the workers covered was based on their earnings, while most of the remainder were provided flat dollar amounts. Earnings-based formulas, typically paying one or two times annual earnings, applied to over four-fifths of the professional-administrative and technical-clerical workers. Flat amounts were common among production workers, where they applied to half of the plan participants and provided an average benefit of $10,000. Thirteen percent of all 1985 participants were in plans which also provided monthly income to surviving family members for a limited period, typically 24 months.

Defined Benefit Pension Plans

Eighty percent of the workers were covered by defined benefit pension plans in 1985, with the employer usually paying the full cost. Seventy percent of the participants had plans relating benefits to prior earnings; such plans, largely recorded for white-collar workers, frequently coordinate benefits with those from Social Security. Most of the remaining participants—particularly blue-collar workers—received specified dollar amounts of benefits for each year of service, which were rarely coordinated with Social Security benefits.

Sixty-seven percent of pension plan participants could retire with full benefits before age 65—up from 63 percent in 1983 and 1984. The two most common pre-age 65 requirements reported for full retirement benefits were any age, with 30 years service, and age 62, with 10 years' service. A reduced pension was available at age 55 to two-thirds of participants, with service requirements ranging from none to 25 years.

Employees are vested when they secure rights to all or a portion of pension benefits earned. Nearly 90 percent of the participants were in plans with cliff vesting provisions, which granted vested status upon satisfaction of a specified service requirement—almost always 10 years. Partial vesting occurred sooner in plans with graduated vesting provisions, covering one-eighth of the participants. Under graduated vesting, participants accrue gradually increasing benefit rights, reaching full vesting after 10 to 15 years.

Defined Contribution and Stock Plans

Forty-one percent of employees participated in one or more defined contribution plans designed for retirement, asset accumulation, or both. Two-thirds of the participants in defined contribution retirement plans, and one-seventh in capital accumulation plans, had their benefits wholly financed by the employer. Among the various plans available, 27 percent of the employees were in savings and thrift plans, 24 percent in employee stock ownership plans, 18 percent in profit sharing plans, 4 percent in money purchase pension plans, and 1 percent in stock bonus plans. Another 3 percent of the employees were eligible to purchase company stock currently at less than market price (stock purchase plans) or in the future at a designated price (stock option plans).

Other Benefits

In addition to the major benefits described above, BLS collected information on the incidence of 17 other benefit plans including nonproduction bonuses; employee discounts; recreation facilities; educational assistance; and child care. Benefits new to the survey in 1985 are subsidized commuting, travel accident insurance, financial counseling, prepaid legal services, and employer-financed flexible spending accounts. Data are available on the percent of full-time employees eligible for these benefits, although they do not indicate the proportion of employees actually using or receiving the benefits.

Computer Data Bases and Software

Selected On-Line Business/Financial Data Bases

On-line data bases are collections of computer stored data which are retrievable by remote terminals. The data bases are collected and organized by a so-called *producer*. The latter provides the data base to a *vendor* who distributes the data by means of a telecommunication network to the user. Often a vendor will offer a large number of different data bases. In some instances the producer and vendor are the same.

Using an on-line data base requires: (1) a *terminal* (a typewriter-like device usually equipped with a video display) to receive data and send commands to the vendor's computers, and (2) a *modem* for coupling the terminal to a telephone line. Printouts (hard copy) of the desired information can be obtained with the aid of electronic printers located at the user's terminal or, alternatively, ordered from the vendor.

The user accesses the data base by dialing a telephone number and then typing (on the terminal keyboard) a password provided by the vendor. Searching the data base is done with special commands and procedures peculiar to each base.

The contents of data bases vary. Some provide statistical data only—usually in the form of time series. Other bases provide bibliographic references and, in some instances, abstracts or the full text of articles.

Specifics concerning data base contents, instructions, and prices are available from vendors. Listed below are some major business data bases and vendors. More complete information concerning data bases is available from the sources given below.

ABI Inform
Provides references on all areas of business management with emphasis on "how-to" information.
Producer: Data Courier Inc. (Louisville, KY)
Vendors: BRS, DIALOG, SDC

Accountants Index
Contains reference information on accounting, auditing taxation, management and securities.
Producer: American Institute of Certified Public Accountants (New York, NY)
Vendors: SDC

Advertising and Marketing Intelligence
Covers consumer trends, new products, media planning, sale promotion.
Producer: New York Times Information Service and J. Walter Thompson Co. (Parsippany, NJ)
Vendors: N.Y. Times Information Service

American Profile
Provides statistical information on U.S. households including population, income, dependents, and also data on types of businesses in an area.
Producer: Donnelley Marketing (Stamford, CT)
Vendors: Business Information Service

BI Data
Maintains international statistical data including national accounts, labor, foreign trade, consumption, prices, production.
Producer: Business International Corp. (New York, NY)
Vendors: General Electric Information Service, I. P. Sharpe, DIALOG

Business Credit Service
Provides business credit and financial information.
Producer: TRW, Inc. (Orange, CA)
Vendors: TRW

Canadian Business Periodicals Index
Provides references to a wide variety of topics from Canadian business publications.
Producer: Micromedia Limited (Toronto, Canada)
Vendor: SDC

CIS Index
Contains references and abstracts from nearly every publication resulting from Senate and House Committee meetings since 1970.
Producer: Congressional Information Services, Inc. (Washington, DC)
Vendors: Dialog, SDC

Commodities Market Data Bank
Provides statistical data on all traded commodities.
Producer: Data Resources Inc. (Lexington, MA)
Vendors: Data Resources, Inc.

CompuServe, Inc.
Provides reference, statistical and full text retrieval of information of personal interest including health, recipes, gardening, financial and investment data including the Compustat and Value Line data bases.
Producer: CompuServe, Inc. (Columbus, OH)
Vendor: CompuServe

Compustat
Provides very extensive financial data on companies.
Producer: Standard And Poor's Compustat Service, Inc. (Englewood, CO)
Vendors: ADP, Business Information Services, CompuServe, Data Resources, Chase Econometrics/Interactive Data Corp.

Computerized Engineering Index
Provides a broad coverage of the international literature on engineering and technology.
Producer: Engineering Index (New York, NY)
Vendors: BRS, DIALOG, SDC

Disclosure II
Provides extracts of 10K and other reports filed with the Securities and Exchange Commission.
Producer: Disclosure Inc. (Bethesda, Maryland)
Vendors: Business Information Services (Control Data). Dialog, Dow Jones, New York Times Information Services, Mead Data Central.

Dow Jones News/Retrieval Service and Stock Quote Reporters
Contains text of articles appearing in major financial publications including the *Wall Street Journal* and *Barrons*. Quote Service provides quotes on stocks, bonds, mutual funds.
Producer: Dow Jones & Company (New York, NY)
Vendors: BRS, Dow Jones & Company

DRI Capsule/EEI Capsule
Provides over 3700 U.S. social and economic statistical time series such as population, income, money supply data, etc.
Producers: Data Resources, Inc. (Lexington, MA) and Evans Economics Inc. (Washington, DC)
Vendors: Business Information Services, United Telecom Group, I. P. Sharp

EIS Industrial Plants
Offers statistical data pertaining to industrial establishments with annual sales of more than $500,000 and with more than 20 employees. Data includes location of each plant, shipment values, market share.
Producer: Economic Information Systems (New York, NY)
Vendors: Business Information Services (Control Data), DIALOG

Federal Register Abstracts
Provides coverage of federal regulatory agencies as published in the Federal Register.
Producer: Capitol Services (Washington, DC)
Vendors: DIALOG, SDC

GTE Financial System One Quotation Service
Provides current U.S. and Canadian quotations and statistical data on stocks, bonds, options, commodities and other market data.
Producer: GTE Information Systems (Mount Laurel, NJ)
Vendor: GTE Information Systems, Inc.

The Information Bank
Provides an extensive current affairs data source consisting of abstracts from numerous English language publications.
Producer: The New York Times Information Service
Vendor: The New York Times Information Service

LEXIS
Contains full text references to a wide range of legal information including court decisions, regulations, government statutes.
Producer: Mead Data Central (New York, NY)
Vendor: Mead Data Central

NEXIS
Provides full text business and general news including management, technology, finance, science, politics, religion.
Producer: Mead Data Central (New York, NY)
Vendor: Mead Data Central

Quick Quote
    Provides current quotations, volume, high-low data for securities of U.S. public corporations.
    Producer: CompuServe Inc.
    Vendor: CompuServe

Quotron 800
    Provides up to the minute quotation and statistics on a broad range of securities such as stocks, bonds, options, commodities.
    Producer: Quotron Systems Inc. (Los Angeles, CA)
    Vendor: Quotron Systems Inc.

The Source
    Covers a broad variety of consumer services business and financial information including travel information, reservations, restaurant reviews etc.
    Producer: Source Telecomputing (McLean, VA)
    Vendor: Source Telecomputing Corp.

Value Line II
    Provides extensive financial data from the Value Line Investment Survey covering over 1600 major companies.
    Producer: Arnold Bernhard & Co. (New York, NY)
    Vendors: ADP Service, Chase Econometrics/Interactive Data Corp., CompuServe Data Resources, Inc.

For further information:

A. T. Kruzas and J. Schmittroth, *Encyclopedia of Information Systems*, Gale Research (Book Tower, Detroit, MI 48226) revised periodically.
The North American On Line Directory 1985, R. R. Bowker (New York, NY 10017) annual.
On Line Data Base Services Directory; Gale Research (address above) revised periodically.
The Federal Data Base Finder. A guide to more than 3,000 free and fee based data bases provided by the US Government. Available from Information USA, 1200 Beall Mt. Road, Potomac, MD 20854.
Guidance on Software Maintenance. Superintendent of Documents, Government Printing Office, Washington, DC 20402. Offers advice on maintaining software and suggestions on how to streamline your system.
Introduction to Software Packages. Superintendent of Documents (address given above). Sources of information on available software packages.
Databasics: Your Guide to On Line Business Information, Garland Publishing Co. (New York, NY 10016).

Directory On Line Data Bases, Cuadra Associates, 2001 Wilshire Boulevard, Santa Monica, CA 90403, A comprehensive standard reference.

Data Base Vendors

ADP Network Services, Inc.
175 Jackson Plaza
Ann Arbor, MI 48106
313-769-6800

BRS, Inc.
1200 Route 7
Latham, NY 12110
518-783-1161
800-833-4707

Business Information Services

Control Data Corporation
500 West Putnam Avenue
Greenwich, CT 06830
203-622-2000

Chaes Econometrics/Interactive Data Corporation
486 Totten Pond Road
Waltham, MA 02154
617-890-1234

CompuServe, Inc.
5000 Arlington Centre Boulevard
Columbus, OH 43220
614-457-8600

Data Resources, Inc. (DRI)
29 Hartwell Avenue
Lexington, MA 02173
617-861-0165

DIALOG Information Services, Inc.
3460 Hillview Avenue
Palo Alto, CA 94304
415-858-3810
800-227-1960

Dow Jones & Company, Inc.
P.O. Box 300
Princeton, NJ 08540
609-452-2000
800-257-5114

General Electric Information Services Company
401 North Washington Street
Rockville, MD 20850
301-340-4000

GTE Information Systems, Inc.
East Park Drive
Mount Laurel, NJ 08054
609-235-7300

Mead Data Central
200 Park Avenue
New York, NY 10017
212-883-8560

The New York Times Information Services, Inc.
1719-A Route 10
Parsippany, NJ 07054
201-539-5850

Quotron Systems, Inc.
5454 Beethoven Street
Los Angeles, CA 90066
213-398-2761

SDC Search Service
2500 Colorado Avenue
Santa Monica, CA 90406

203-820-4111
800-421-7229

I. P. Sharp Associates
145 King Street West
Toronto, Ontario, Canada M5H IJ8
416-364-5361

Source Telecomputing Corporation
1515 Anderson Road
McLean, VA 22102
703-734-7500X546
800-336-3366

TRW Information Services Division
1 City Boulevard
Orange, CA 92668
714-937-2700

United Telecom Computer Group
5454 West 110 Street
Overland Park, KA 66211
913-341-9161

How to Find Software Packages

The task of learning about software packages can seem staggering at first. The following section is a guide to reference material which will make this task much simpler. It describes sources of information which are available; which sources are the most useful; and how to make the best of them.

OVERCOMING THE TERMINOLOGY HURDLE

No matter which sources of information about software packages are used, understanding computer terminology is one of the first problems that those who are unfamiliar with computers will encounter. The evolution of computer science and its related fields has led to the proliferation of a special language with technical meanings that are often unfamiliar to the lay person. Some of these terms are heard quite often—for instance, almost everyone has been told at some time that he/she can't do something because "the computer is DOWN." Fortunately, many of these terms are becoming so common they are listed in recent dictionaries (for instance, the term "down time" is listed in *Webster's New Collegiate Dictionary*). In addition, there are a number of sources dealing

specifically with the technical language of computing which may be useful. Three of those sources are:

Computer Dictionary and Handbook, Charles J. Sippl, ed. [Howard W. Sams and Company, Inc.: 4300 West 62nd Street, Indianapolis, IN 46268].

Encyclopedia of Computer Science, Anthony Ralston, ed. [Van Nostrand Reinhold Company, Inc.: 135 West 50th Street, New York, NY 10020].

Dictionary for Information Processing [FIPS PUB 11-1, National Bureau of Standards].

The most important thing to remember when attempting to overcome the terminology hurdle is that the software to be purchased is intended to provide a service to its users. It should make life easier, not more complicated. The special terminology associated with computer technology need not have much impact upon the users of that technology. It is only in making sense of the available information on software packages and in dealing with vendors that understanding the special terminology is necessary.

INFORMATION SOURCES

A major problem encountered when attempting to select a software package is finding the information upon which to base a decision. At first, information is difficult to find, and then, when it is found, it may seem staggeringly com-

Source: Excerpted from *Introduction to Software Packages*, Sheila Frankel, editor. [NBS Special Publication 500-114], Systems and Software Technology Division, National Bureau of Standards, U.S. Department of Commerce.

plex—especially for a computer novice or a non-technical computer user.

There are numerous sources of information on applications software packages. The following sections discuss several of these sources and describe how to best use them. Many of the sources which are discussed here may be found in local public and university libraries or Federal agency libraries and reference rooms.

PERIODICALS

Periodicals are one of the most widely available sources of information on software packages; the problems which confront those who are attempting to computerize specific functions; and techniques to follow when computerizing. Computer journals are not the only periodicals which print useful articles. While computer trade magazines typically have more in-depth analyses of the technical aspects of software packages (e.g., process requirements and storage requirements), application area trade magazines typically are more oriented toward the procedures a package supports. Both sources are valuable in early evaluation of various packages. When evaluating software for a specific business application area, an evaluation team that is not particularly conversant with computers might find trade journals which concentrate on the specific application area useful. For instance, to automate an accounting system, accounting magazines are probably, initially at least, the best source of information.

Valuable information, such as how current users rate packages, is often available in computer periodicals. A good example of this is the magazine *Datamation*, which provides a yearly users' survey of software packages. In addition, some periodicals publish articles which give tips on where to buy software. Some of them also reference additional sources of software package information.

While trade journals are good sources of information on computerizing specific functions, they are unlikely to have articles on computing in each edition. Therefore, it is best to make use of periodical indexes. Two indexes which are especially useful are:

Business Index [Information Access Corporation: 404 6th Avenue, Menlo Park, CA 94025].

Business Index is provided on microfilm. Listings are filed alphabetically by subject headings and by magazine titles. *Business Index* includes listings from 640 periodicals (approximately 90,000 articles per year).

Business Periodicals Index [H. W. Wilson Company: 950 University Avenue, Bronx, NY 10452].

Business Periodicals Index is in book form. It lists magazines by subject headings followed by subheadings. In this index, which is less extensive than *Business Index*, but more readily available, articles on automation are usually under the heading Data Processing.

DIRECTORIES

There are several directories available which catalog software, often according to the hardware on which it is available. Because of the explosion in sales of personal computers, most such directories are for microcomputer applications. Examples of these directories follow:

The Apple Software Directory [WIDL Video: 5245 W. Diversey Ave., Chicago, IL 60639] Software for Apple Computers.

Commodore Software Encyclopedia [Commodore Business Machines, Computer Systems Division: 300 Valley Forge Sp., 681 Moore Rd., King of Prussia, PA 19046] Software for Commodore Computers.

Dataguide [Sentry Database Publishing: 5 Kane Industrial Dr., Hudson, MA 01749] Hardware, software and accessories.

Directory of Microcomputer Software [DATAPRO: 1805 Underwood Blvd., Delran, NJ 08075] Software, updated monthly, comes with telephone inquiry service.

International Microcomputer Software Directory [Imprint: 420 South Howes, Fort Collins, CO 80521] Software, vendor lists.

Software Directory [Digital Research: P.O. Box 579, Pacific Grove, CA 93950] Applications and system software.

Software Vendor Directory [Micro-Serve: P.O. Box 482, Nyack, NY 10960] Applications and system software, vendors. Also available on computer diskette.

TRS-80 Applications Software Sourcebook [Available at Radio Shack stores] Applications software for TRS-80 computers.

REFERENCE SERVICES

Services have been developed which aid in the process of sorting through the vast quantity of computer information which is available. Some of these services are computerized, while others are not. In general, they can be very useful.

Datapro is one such reference service that is well established and maintains a good reputation in the data processing community. *Datapro Reports* [Datapro Research Corporation: 1805 Underwood Blvd., Delran, NJ 08075] is published in a three-ring binder format and is updated monthly. The Datapro subscription fee not only includes the basic volumes of the service, but also includes updates and an inquiry service. Datapro covers a variety of subject areas related to computing. Two volumes of particular interest to software package research are the following:

Datapro Applications Software (part of the solutions series)—especially designed for those "with line or staff responsibilities in planning, designing, programming or maintaining applications software solutions to business problems." Includes "Software Development Concepts," "How to Buy Software Packages," "Make or Buy Tradeoffs," "Selection and Acquisition," "Reliability and Vendor Support" and "User Ratings." Software packages are identified by applications area and detailed descriptions of each package are provided. Vendor lists are also provided.

Datapro Reports on Minicomputers—provides "detailed coverage of all types of minicomputers." Includes "Software" (user's ratings) and "Computers" ("individual, detailed analyses of minicomputer and small business computer systems from all important suppliers"). These analyses include users' reactions and software information.

Another well established reference service similar to Datapro is Auerbach. *Auerbach Technology Reports* [Auerbach Publishers, Inc.: 6560 North Park Drive, Pennsauken, NJ 08109]. The Auerbach volume on applications software includes discussions of special problems involved in computerizing specific applications areas and lists available packages in each application area. Listings include the package price, hardware requirements, capabilities, the number of installations, date of first installation, and the address of the package developer. Some of the many application areas which are covered include:

Human resource management
Accounts receivable
Accounts payable
General ledger
Inventory control
Integrated accounting
General business management
Manufacturing
Banking
Transportation
Medical
Insurance
Utilities
Scientific/engineering

A third reference service is Data Sources. *Data Sources* [Ziff-Davis Publishing Co.: P.O. Box 5845, Cherry Hill, NJ 08034] is published quarterly. As with Auerbach, software packages are identified by application area and hardware compatibility. Application areas include those mentioned above and others, such as those listed below:

Project management
Legal
Bill of materials
Civil engineering
Health
Economic modeling
Financial analysis

Government (Federal)
Government (local and state)
Library services
Office automation
Professional time accounting
Research and survey analysis

One company which provides a customized search utilizing a computerized listing of software packages is SofSearch. SofSearch's data base includes some 30,000 software packages offered by 8,500 vendors. Provided with a description of the application, the target computer and operating system and the industry, SofSearch will perform a search and provide one page reports on each package which meets these briefly described requirements.

To help you locate the software you want, P.C. Telemart offers a free service in about 100 retail stores. To find the location of the nearest store, call 703-352-0721 or write: P.C. Telemart, 11787 Lee Jackson Highway Fairfax, VA 22033. Other sources of reference material are:

Directory of Systems Houses and Computer Distributors [Sentry Database Publishing: 5 Kane Industrial Drive, Hudson, MA 01749]

Computer Software Industry: A Financial and Strategic Analysis [Dun & Bradstreet Credit Services: New York, NY]

Software News [Sentry Database Publishing: 5 Kane Industrial Drive, Hudson, MA 01749]

Computerworld Software Buyer's Guide [C. W. Communications, Inc.: Box 880, 375 Cochituate Road, Framingham, MA 01701]

Microcomputer Software Letter [610 Fifth Avenue, Suite 706, New York, NY 10020].

PERIODICAL DESCRIPTIONS

The following section provides detailed descriptions of the periodicals.

Accountancy [The Institute of Chartered Accountants in England and Wales: 56/66 Goswell Road, London, England EL1B 7LD—American distributors: Expediters of the Printed Word LTD.: 527 Madison Avenue, Suite 1217, New York, NY 10022]. A British publication which often includes articles on the computerization of accounting practices. Articles are of high depth. One to two articles per issue are related to computerization. Published monthly.

Administrative Management [Geyer-McAllister Publications, Inc.: 51 Madison Avenue, New York, NY 10010]. This periodical contains an average of two computer articles and one article on new technologies per issue. Sample titles include: "A Buyer's Guide to Word Processing Software," by Alan Hoffberg, Contributing Editor; "What You Get with a '90-Day Trial,'" by Patrick Flanagan; "Superminis: In the Mainstream of Business DP," by Randi T. Sachs, Associate Editor; "Software for Sorts, Retrieval and Other Filing Tasks," by Bonnie Canning and Karen Michaels. Published monthly.

Byte [Byte Publications, Inc.: 70 Main St., Peterborough, NH 03458]. This monthly magazine is subtitled "The Small Systems Journal." Most articles are on computers (approximately 98%) with about half of the articles on hardware and half on software. About 60% of the advertisements are for hardware, 40% for software. Example articles are on how to select a text editor, and "Adapting Microcomputers to Wall Street." Issues are very long, averaging about 550 pages. Published monthly.

Chilton's Iron Age [Chilton Company: Wayne, PA 19089]. *Chilton's Iron Age* is subtitled "The Magazine for Metalworking Management." It contains some articles on computing and a few advertisements for computers. Articles are of low to medium depth. *Chilton's Iron Age* includes an advertisers' index. Free to qualified managers in US metal-working companies. Published every 10 days.

Computer Business News [C. W. Communications, Inc.: P.O. Box 880, 375 Cochituate Rd., Framingham, MA 01701]. This newspaper-format magazine is subtitled "The Newsweekly for the OEM Community." All articles are in some way related to computers. The focus is on marketing computers and computer industry investment information. A majority of articles and advertisements relate to hardware. Articles are of medium to low depth. A software applications directory is included annually. Published bi-monthly.

Computer Decisions [Hayden Publishing Co.: 50 Essex St., Rochelle Park, NJ 07662]. This magazine is subtitled "The Management Magazine of Computing." The magazine includes departments which appear in each issue such as "Snyder on Software" (including pros and cons of reviewed software), "Software" (write-ups by vendors) and an "Advertisers' Index." Example articles include: "Choosing the Right Turnkey Mini Supplier," by David Whieldon; "Office Automation Rolls Along," interview of Professor Howard Morgan; "How to Pick 'Friendly' Terminals," by David Whieldon; and "Don't Make—Buy! Support from Timesharing Services," by David Whieldon. There are many advertisements, both for hardware and business-applications software. Free subscriptions for executives of companies that deal with or use computers. Published monthly.

Computer Design [Computer Design Publishing Co.: 119 Russell St., Littleton, MA 01460]. Though a few useful articles are presented in this magazine on recent software developments, the orientation is toward hardware architecture issues and not business applications. Free subscriptions for engineers and those who manage engineers. Published monthly.

Computerworld [C. W. Communications, Inc.: P.O. Box 880, 375 Cochitaute Rd., Framingham, MA 01701]. This periodical, organized in a large newspaper format, is usually about 100 pages long. Many articles provide discussions of financial trends in the computer industry, while some discuss business applications. *Computerworld* includes many advertisements, including coupons for requesting specific information from vendors. It typically contains a software advertising section, often features special sections on software, and usually lists new product announcements. Published weekly.

Data Management [Data Processing Management Association: 505 Busse Highway, Park Ridge, IL 60068]. This magazine is business- and computer-oriented with a concentration on data management and processing. Most computer articles and advertisements are on software. Published monthly.

Datamation [Technical Publishing Company: 875 Third Avenue, New York, NY 10022]. This magazine has a business orientation and provides extensive information on all aspects of computing. User surveys of software are often included—for instance, the May 1982 issue included the "Applications Software Survey." Each edition includes an Advertisers' Index, which is an easy way to get a quick overview of what is available. Free subscriptions for qualified personnel. Published monthly.

Decision Sciences [American Institute for Decision Sciences: University Plaza, Atlanta, GA 30303]. *Decision Sciences* is designed for managers. On the average, one article per issue is concerned with computers. Articles contain in-depth analysis. Very few advertisements are included. Articles stress the use of behavioral, economic and quantitative methods of analysis for decision-making in public and private organizations. Published monthly.

Electronic Business [Cahners Publishing Co., Inc.: 270 Saint Paul Street, Denver, CO 80206]. *Electronic Business* has an electronic equipment orientation with an emphasis on text equipment. It occasionally provides application area articles.

Harvard Business Review [Subscription Service Department: P.O. Box 3010, Woburn, MA 01888]. This journal is published by Harvard Graduate School of Business Administration as part of a program in executive education. It is designed for a management audience. Approximately one article in each issue relates to computers. The depth of articles is medium to high, and the number of advertisements of any sort is low. Published bi-monthly.

IEEE Micro [IEEE, Inc., Computer Society: 445 Hoes Lane, Piscataway, NJ 08854]. All articles in this magazine are on computers. Few, however, address business applications. The technical level is high, as is the depth of articles. Published quarterly.

Infosystems [Hitchcock Publishing Companies, Inc.: Hitchcock Building, P.O. Box 3007, Wheaton, IL 60187]. This periodical is subtitled

"The Magazine for Information Systems Managers." It includes many advertisements, both for software and hardware, and some comparison articles. Example articles include: "Programming Tools: Impacting DP Productivity," by Carol Tomme Thiel; "Keys to Successful Office Automation: Company Strategies and User Needs," by Alan G. Rockhold, Senior Editor; "Bottom Line Report: Remote Computing Services: You've Got to Watch the Meter," by Wayne L. Rhodes, Jr., Senior Editor; and "Summer Bonanza: What's New in Software Packages," by Carol Tomme Thiel, Software Editor. Published monthly.

Interface: Data Processing Management [International Computer Programs, Inc.: 9000 Keystone Crossing, P.O. Box 40946, Indianapolis, IN 46240]. All articles are on computers and many are business related. Approximately 70% of the advertisements are for software, while the other 30% are for hardware and business services. A sample article is "In House Timesharing," by Ken Ross. Free subscription for qualified USA residents employed by one of the industries addressed by the publication. Published quarterly.

Interface Age [McPheters, Wolfe and Jones: 16704 Marquardt Ave., Cerritos, CA 90701]. This periodical is subtitled "Computing for Business." There are numerous advertisements, though more of them are for hardware than for software. All articles have something to do with computers, with about 40% pertaining to business applications. Many reviews of new hardware systems and software packages are provided. Some package comparisons, and useful articles on where to purchase software and how to negotiate for software packages are also provided. Published monthly.

Interfaces [The Institute of Management Sciences: 345 Whitney Avenue, New Haven, CT 06511]. This magazine is designed for managers and ADP specialists. Articles are of medium to high depth. Software advertisements and product comparisons are few. Published bi-monthly.

Journal of Accountancy [American Institute of Certified Public Accountants, Inc.: 1211 Avenue of the Americas, New York, NY 10036]. This magazine does not include articles on computing. However, it does include many advertisements for packages related to accounting. Published monthly.

Journal of Small Business Management [International Council for Small Business: West Virginia University, Bureau of Business Research, Morgantown, WV 26506]. This publication has an academic orientation and each edition has a particular theme. Only about one in five issues includes an article on computerization, although one entire issue was devoted to computerization with at least 60% of that issue's articles being on computers. No advertisements for either hardware or software are included.

Articles are of medium depth. Published quarterly.

Journal of Systems Management [Association for Systems Management: 24587 Bagley Road, Cleveland, OH 44138]. This journal is designed for managers. All articles are on computers. Articles are of medium depth and include such titles as "The V-Curve: A Road Map for Avoiding People Problems in Systems Changes" and "The Main-Frame Computer: A Glimpse into the Future." Published monthly.

Management Accounting [National Association of Accountants: 919 Third Ave., New York, NY 10022]. Computer advertisements are mostly for software (primarily accounting and financial packages). Only about one in five issues contains articles on computers, but one edition was a computer special and approximately 50% of its articles were on computing. The depth of these articles is from medium to high. Published monthly.

Management Review [American Management Associations: ARACOM Division, P.O. Box 319, Saranac Lake, NY 12983]. One in twelve issues includes an article on computing, and these articles are not directed toward the issues or audience addressed in this document. Articles are often very general. Published monthly.

Management Science [Institute of Management Sciences: 146 Westminister St., Providence, RI 02903]. This periodical is highly quantitative and academic. There are few advertisements. It is not recommended as a source for software package information. Published monthly.

Management Today [Management Publishing LTD.: 76 Dean Street, London, W1A 1BU]. *Management Today* is a British magazine. One in five issues includes an article on computers. Articles are of medium to high depth. Published monthly.

Merchandising [Gralla Publications: 1515 Broadway, New York, NY 10036]. This magazine has a large, glossy-newspaper format. While every issue has at least one article on computers, the orientation is not toward software packages, but on computer industry marketing information. Advertisements are also marketing-oriented. Published monthly.

Microcomputing [P.O. Box 997, Farmingdale, NY 11737]. All the articles in this magazine relate to microcomputers. Some articles address business concerns. An example article is "Meet the Monthly Billing Deadline," by Sam Davis. Monthly sections include descriptions of new products and software ratings. Most advertisements focus on hardware; however, some relate to software. Published monthly.

Mini-Micro Systems [Cahners Publishing Company, Inc.: 270 Saint Paul Street, Denver, CO 80206]. All articles in this magazine deal with computers. Articles are technically detailed and are rarely geared to business concerns. Articles do include comparisons, but the major emphasis is on hardware rather than software. This magazine provides articles directly related to a Government audience. Free subscriptions for qualified individuals. Published monthly.

Modern Office Procedures [Penton-IPC: Penton Plaza, 111 Chester Ave., Cleveland, OH 44114]. Approximately three articles per issue are on word processing. Occasionally, there are other articles on some type of computing. The articles concentrate on procedures rather than on types of software. The advertisements in this magazine are more often for hardware than for software. Published monthly.

The Office [Office Publications, Inc.: 1200 Summer St., Stamford, CT 06904]. This periodical is subtitled "Magazine of Management, Equipment, Automation." It contains many articles on office automation, word processing, etc. Articles are of medium depth. More articles are on procedures than on software, but some articles do include comparisons. Advertisements for software products are included. *The Office* has a business orientation. Published monthly.

Output [Technical Publishing: 1301 S. Grove Ave., Barrington, IL 60010]. This magazine is subtitled "The Information Systems Magazine for the General Management User." All of its articles are related in some way to computers and to business. Advertisements are for both software and hardware; however, the overall number of advertisements in these areas is low. Articles do include comparisons, such as in the article "Choosing a Vendor for the Automated Office," by Margaret Coffey. Published monthly.

Personal Computing [Hayden Publishing Company, Inc.: 50 Essex St., Rochelle Park, NJ 07662]. *Personal Computing* describes the uses of personal computers. Most articles are on how to use computers more effectively in the home. Some articles address the use of personal computers for business concerns as "When the Boss

Got into Computing," by Marvin Grosswirth. Articles are of medium depth. Approximately 20% of the advertisements are for software products. Published monthly.

Personnel Journal [A. C. Croft, Inc.: P.O. Box 2440, Costa Mesa, CA 92626]. One in three issues has an article on computerization. One such article is "A Guide for Building a Human Resource Data System," by Vincent R. Ceriello. Published monthly.

Personnel Management [Business Publications LTD.: Audit House, Field End Road, Ruislip, Middlesex HA4 9LT]. This magazine is a British publication. It includes advertisements for Personnel System Software packages. Most advertisements represent British products. Articles are of medium depth. Published monthly.

Purchasing [Cahners Publishing Company, Inc.: 270 Saint Paul Street, Denver CO 80206]. This periodical is business oriented. It does not include computer advertisements. Every issue has something on computers, but often the depth is low. An example article is "Computers in Purchasing: Part 30," by Robert Porter and Gilbert Trill. Published bi-monthly.

Software News [Sentry Database Publishing: 5 Kane Industrial Drive, Hudson, MA 01749]. All the articles in this periodical are concerned with computers; some also discuss business concerns. This periodical is designed like a newspaper. Articles are datelined, and are of medium depth. Sample articles include "Software and the Automated Office," by John A. Murphy and "Productivity Tools Mean Better Code," by Dave Ferris. Published monthly.

Today's Office [United Technical Publications, Inc.: 645 Stewart Ave., Garden City, NY 11530]. Most articles are on computers in business applications and comparisons are often included in these articles. Advertisements generally relate to office products while some (about 40%) are for computer software. Free to administrative executives and qualified Government offices. Published monthly.

Business Information Directory

Information Sources

GENERAL REFERENCES

The *United States Government Manual* is an annual publication. It describes the organization, purposes, and programs of most government agencies and lists top personnel. Available from the Superintendent of Documents, Government Printing Office, Washington, DC 20402.

Washington Information Directory is an annual publication listing, by topic, organizations and publications which provide information on a wide range of subjects. It also lists congressional committee assignments, regional federal offices, embassies, and state and local officials. Published by the Congressional Quarterly, Inc., 1414 22nd Street NW, Washington, DC 20037.

Statistical Abstracts of the United States, published annually, is the standard summary on the social, political, and economic statistics of the United States. It includes data from both government and private sources. Appendix II gives a comprehensive list of sources. (Available from the Superintendent of Documents, Government Printing Office, Washington, DC 20402)

Business Information Sources by Lorna M. Daniells ranks among the best general guides to business publications. It contains extensive references to U.S. business and economic data, including statistics, U.S. and foreign investment. Published by the University of California Press, Berkeley, CA.

Researcher's Guide to Washington Experts, Washington Researchers, 2612 P Street NW, Washington, D.C. 20007.

Population information on all aspects of national and world population is provided by the **Population Reference Bureau, Inc.**, 2213 M Street NW, Washington, DC 20037, or call 202–785–4664.

The **Washington Information Research Service** provides reports and guidance to information on a fee basis. Write Washington Researchers, 2612 P Street NW, Washington, DC 20007, or call 202–333–3499.

Information USA is a reference book with leads about how to tap the information mine of the federal government. Published by Penguin Books, 624 Madison Avenue, New York, NY 10022.

FEDfind explains how to get services and publications from the U.S. Government. Published by ICUC Press, P.O. Box 1447-NR, Springfield, VA 22151.

Professional and trade organizations and publications are a major source of contacts and information. Key directories to these sources are listed below:

Encyclopedia of Associations, published by Gale Research Co., Book Tower, Detroit, MI 48226.

The World Guide to Trade Associations gives a comprehensive national and international listing of associations. Published by R. R. Bowker Co., 205 East 42 Street, New York, NY 10017

Ulrich's International Periodical Directory covers both domestic and foreign periodicals. Published by R. R. Bowker Co., 205 East 42 Street, New York, NY 10017.

Standard Periodical Directory covers U.S. and Canadian periodicals. Published by Oxbridge Communications, Inc., 150 Fifth Avenue, New York, NY 10011.

The 1986 IMS Directory of Publications provides titles of trade newspapers and periodicals. Published by IMS Press, 426 Pennsylvania Avenue, Fort Washington, PA 19034.

Standard Rate and Data Service provides information on periodical circulation and advertising rates. Published by Standard Rates and Data Service, Inc., 5201 Old Orchard Road, Skokie, IL 60077–1021.

Encyclopedia of Information Systems and Services. Descriptions of U.S. organizations (and some foreign) that produce, process, store, and use bibliographic and non-bibliographic information. About 1500 data bases covered. Published by Gale Research Co., Book Tower, Detroit, MI 48226.

National Directory of Addresses and Telephone Numbers. A national business directory that lists all SEC registered companies, major accounting and law firms, banks, and financial institutions, associations, unions, etc. Available from Concord Reference Books, Inc., 830 Third Avenue Street, New York, NY 10022.

Encyclopedia of Business Information, a comprehensive single-volume source, is updated periodically. Available from Gale Research Co., Book Tower, Detroit, MI 48226.

Business Publications Index and Abstracts is a two volume set listing books, transaction proceedings, etc. with abstracts of each entry. Published by Gale Research Co., Book Tower, Detroit, MI 48226.

National Trade and Professional Associations of the United States. A comprehensive listing of professional trade and labor associations, including addresses, membership size, publications by the associations, and convention schedules. An annual published by Columbia Books, 777 14th Street NW, Washington, DC 20005.

Encyclopedia of Banking and Finance, is a comprehensive source on subjects indicated in title. Bankers Publishing Co., Boston, MA.

Listings of trade directories are given in the following:

Guide to American Directories, published by B. Klein Publications, Inc., P.O. Box 8503, Coral Springs, FL 33065.

Directory of Directories, distributed by Gale Research Co., Book Tower, Detroit, MI 48226.

BUSINESS AND ECONOMICS INFORMATION

Government publications referred to below may be obtained from the Government Printing Office (GPO), Washington, DC, 20402, unless other indicated.

Business and economic information is provided by the following key references.

Survey of Current Business is a major publication which is supplemented on a weekly basis with *Current Statistics.* The publication contains articles as well as comprehensive statistics on all aspects of the economy, including data on the GNP, employment, wages, prices, finance, foreign trade, and production by industrial sector. (GPO)

Business Conditions Digest is a monthly with an extensive collection of charts and tables on the national income and products, leading coincident and lagging cyclical indicators, foreign trade, prices, wages, analytical ratios, and international production and stock prices. (GPO)

Economic Indicators is a monthly summary-type publication prepared by the Council of Economic Advisers. It contains charts and tables on natural output, income, spending, employment, unemployment, wages, industrial production, construction, prices, money, credit, federal finance, and international statistics. (GPO)

Federal Reserve Bulletin is a monthly issued by the Federal Reserve System, containing articles and very extensive tabulated data on all aspects of the monetary situation, credit, mortgage markets, interest rates, and stock and bond yields. A monthly *Chart Book* is available which contains charts of financial and monetary data. Both are available from the Board of Governors, Federal Reserve System, Washington, DC 20551.

Monthly Labor Review. This monthly publication provides articles and statistics on employment, productivity, wages, earnings, prices, wage settlements, and work stoppages. (GPO)

U.S. Industrial Outlook is an annual providing evaluations and projections of all major industrial and commercial segments of the domestic economy. (GPO)

Quarterly Financial Report for Manufacturing, Mining, and Trade Corporations is issued by the Bureau of the Census of the U.S. Department of Commerce. It covers corporate financial statistics including sales, profits, assets, and financial ratios, classified by industry group and size. (GPO)

Current Industrial Reports are a series of over 100 monthly, quarterly, semiannual, and annual reports on major products manufactured in the United States. For subscription, contact the Bureau of the Census, U.S. Department of Commerce, Washington, DC 20233. (GPO)

Annual Survey of Manufacturers. General statistics of manufacturing activity for industry groups, individual industries, states, and geographical regions are provided. (GPO)

County Business Patterns is an annual publication on employment and payrolls, which include a separate paperbound report for each state. (GPO)

Foreign Trade is a Bureau of the Census publication giving monthly reports on U.S. foreign trade. (GPO)

Population: Current Report is a series of monthly and annual reports covering population changes and socioeconomic characteristics of the population. (GPO)

Retail Sales: Current Business Report is a weekly report which provides retail statistics. (GPO)

Wholesale Trade, Sales and Inventories: Current Business Report provides a monthly report on wholesale trade. (GPO)

Directory of Marketing Research Houses and Services is an annual available from the American Marketing Association, 420 Lexington Avenue, New York, NY 10022.

CORPORATE INFORMATION

The major sources of information on publicly held corporations (as well as government and municipal issues) are: *Moody's Investor Services, Inc.,* owned by Dun & Bradstreet, 99 Church Street, New York, NY 10007, and *Standard & Poor's Corp.,* owned by McGraw-Hill, 25 Broadway, New York, NY 10004.

Standard & Poor's *Corporate Records* and Moody's *Manuals* are large multivolume works published annually and kept up to date with daily (for Standard & Poor's) or semiweekly (for Moody's) reports. The services provide extensive coverage of industrials, public utilities, transportation, banks, and financial companies. Also included are municipal and government issues.

In addition, the above corporations provide computerized data services and magnetic tapes.

Compustat tapes, containing major corporate financial data, are available from Investor's Management Services, Inc., Denver, CO, a subsidiary of Standard & Poor's. Time-sharing access to Compustat and other financial data bases is available through Interactive Data Corporation, Waltham, MA (617) 890–1234.

DISCLOSURE II, available from Disclosure, Inc., (5161 River Road, Bethesda, MD 20816) provides an on line data base of corporate information for some 10,000 companies. Disclosure II can be used via the Dow Jones Retrieval Service, New York Times Information Service, Lockheed's DIALOG Information Services, Inc., ADP, CompuServe, among others.

Also available from Disclosure is MICRO/SCAN: Disclosure II, a monthly diskette service which provides information on dividends per share, 4-year growth rate in earnings per share, price/book value, etc. For information call 800–638–8076.

The 10-K and other corporate reports are filed with the Securities and Exchange Commission and are available at local SEC offices, investor relations departments of publicly traded companies, as well as various private services, such as Disclosure Inc. which provides a complete microfiche service. *The SEC News Digest*, formerly published by the government, is now available from Disclosure, Inc. (address above). Included in the *Digest* is a daily listing of 8K reports, a daily Acquisitions of Securities Report, as well as information about what's happening inside the SEC.

Disclosure Inc. has two additional services helpful for researching a corporation. Through the *SEC Watch Service* any report filed by a company with the SEC can be retrieved while corporate information such as prospective supplements and tender offers can be retrieved through the *SEC Research Service*.

Betchel Information Service located at 15740 Shady Grove Road, Gaithersburg, MD 20877 is another SEC document retrieval service.

How to Find Information About Companies, Washington Researchers, 2612 P Street NW, Washington, DC 20007.

Major trade directories include the annual *Thomas Register of American Manufacturers* (published by Thomas Publishing Company, 1 Pennsylvania Plaza, New York, NY 10005) and Dun & Bradstreet's *Reference Book of Manufacturers*.

Thomas Register includes in one volume an alphabetical listing of manufacturers, giving address, phone number, product, subsidiaries, plant location, and an indication of assets. Dun & Bradstreet's *Reference Book* covers similar information, including sales and credit. Dun & Bradstreet's *Million Dollar Directory* series provides data on U.S. companies whose net worth is $1,000,000 and up, including information on privately held corporations; also published is a companion volume the *Billion Dollar Directory* which tracks America's corporate families.

Directory of Wall Street Research, an annual published by Nelson Publishing, Rye, NY lists security analysts with a subject specialty, top corporate officers, and brokerage firms researching a given company.

Register of Corporations is published by Standard and Poor's Corp., 345 Hudson Street, New York, NY 10014.

Directory of Corporate Affiliations and International Directory of Corporate Affiliations are references to the structure of major domestic and international corporations. Published by NRPC, 3004 Glen View Road, Wilmette, IL 60091.

Sources of State Information on Corporations, provides information filed by companies with the state governments and also business related data collected by the states. Washington Researchers, 2612 P Street NW, Washington, DC 20007.

Future earnings projections of listed companies based on surveys by securities analysts is provided by Lynch, Jones, and Ryan, 325 Hudson Street, New York, NY 10013 (212-243-3137).

Information on foreign corporations is available from *World Trade Data Reports*, U.S. Department of Commerce, Washington, D.C. 20230 (202-377-4203).

TRACKING FEDERAL GOVERNMENT DEVELOPMENTS

Commerce Business Daily (CB). This daily provides information on contract awards and subcontract opportunities, Defense Department awards, and surplus sales. *CB* is available on-line from: United Communications Group, 8701 Georgia Avenue, Silver Springs, MD 20910; DIALOG Information Services, 3460 Hillview Avenue, Palo Alto, CA 94304; or Data Resources, Inc., 2400 Hartwell Avenue, Lexington, ME 02173. (GPO)

Federal Register. This daily provides information on federal agency regulations and other legal documents (GPO).

CQ Weekly Report. This major service follows every important piece of legislation through both houses of Congress and reports on the political and lobbying pressures being applied. Available from the Congressional Quarterly Service, 1414 22nd Street, Washington, DC 20037.

Daily Report for Executives. A daily series of reports giving Washington developments that affect all aspects of business operations. Available from the Bureau of National Affairs, Inc., 1231 25th Street NW, Washington, DC 20037. Call: 301-258-1033.

Two major services, the *Bureau of National*

Affairs, Inc. (address above) and the *Commerce Clearing House, Inc.* (4025 West Peterson Avenue, Chicago, IL 60646), publish a large number of valuable weekly loose-leaf reports covering developments in all aspects of law, government regulations, and taxation.

INDEX PUBLICATIONS

Indexes of a wide variety of articles appearing in periodicals, trade presses, and financial services dealing with corporations, industry, and finance are given in the following:

Business Periodicals Index published by H. W. Wilson Co., 950 University Avenue, Bronx, NY.

Funk and Scott Index of Corporations and Industries, published by Predicast, Inc., 11001 Cedar Street, Cleveland, OH 44141.

Major newspaper indexes are:

Wall Street Journal Index published by Dow Jones & Co. Inc., 22 Cortland Street, New York, NY 10007 (monthly).

New York Times Index published by the New York Times Company, 229 W. 43rd Street, New York, NY 10036 (semimonthly, cumulates annually).

TRACKING ECONOMIC INDICATORS

Composite Index of Leading Economic Indicators: Each month the Bureau of Economic Analysis compiles this data from the 12 leading economic indicators. This material appears each month in the *Bureau's Business Conditions Digest* (BCD) available by subscription from:

Superintendent of Documents
Government Printing Office
Washington, DC 20402

For current index values call: 202-523-0589.

Consumer Price Index (CPI) (changes in cost of goods to customers): For these monthly reports prepared by the Bureau of Labor Statistics write:

Bureau of Labor Statistics
Department of Labor
441 G Street NW
Washington, DC 20212

CPI 24 hour hotline: 202-523-1239.

Data from these reports is available within 24 hours of their release by subscription to the Consumer Price Index Mailgram Service. Contact:

National Technical Information Service
5285 Port Royal Road
Springfield, VA 22161
703-487-4630

Producer Price Index (PPI) (measures changes in prices received in primary markets by producers). For monthly reports write:

Bureau of Labor Statistics
Department of Labor
441 G Street NW
Washington, DC 20212

PPI 24 hour hotline: 202-523-1765.

Available from the Bureau of Labor Statistics are press releases on *State and Metropolitan Area Unemployment* (issued monthly), the *Employment Cost Index* (issued quarterly), and the *Employment Situation Study* (released monthly). For a sample copy call 202-523-1221. To subscribe write:

Bureau of Labor Statistics
Department of Labor
Washington, DC 20230

Unemployment Insurance Claims Weekly may be obtained by calling or by writing:

Employment and Training Administration
Department of Labor
601 D Street, NW
Washington, DC 20213

Releases on the *Money Supply* (Report H-6, issued weekly) and on *Consumer Credit* (Report G-19, issued monthly) may be obtained from the

Publications Services
Federal Reserve Board
Washington, DC 20551
202-452-3244

Personal Consumption Expenditure Deflator is prepared monthly by the Bureau of Economic Analysis of the Department of Commerce. This information appears in a press release *Personal Income and Outlays* and can be obtained in writing from the

Current Business Analysis
Bureau of Economic Analysis
Department of Commerce
Washington, DC 20230

For information on the above call 202-523-0777.

Monthly Trade Report (index of retail sales and accounts receivable) is compiled by the Bureau of the Census and published in *Current Business Reports* as part of what is known as the BR series. To subscribe contact the Superintendent of Documents (Address given above). For a sample copy call: 301-763-4100.

Survey of US Export and Import Merchandise (value of imports and exports) is available by subscription from:

Subscriber Services Section
Bureau of the Census
Washington, DC 20233

For a sample copy call: 301-763-4100.

Value of New Construction Put in Place is a Census Bureau monthly report (part of the C-30 Series) which charts the dollar amount of new construction. It is available on an annual subscription basis from the Superintendent of Documents, Government Printing Office, Washington, DC 20402. For a sample copy call: 301-763-4100.

Joint Economic Committee of Congress Reports

Reports on the economic issues studied by the Joint Economic Committee are available free of charge from:

Joint Economic Committee of Congress
Dirksen Senate Office Building
Washington, DC 20510
202-224-5321

FEDERAL INFORMATION CENTERS (FICs)

FICs located in key cities throughout the country are a joint venture of the U.S. General Services Administration and the U.S. Civil Services. Each center is a focal point for obtaining information about the federal government and often about state and local governments. A member of the center's staff can either provide information or direct inquiries to an expert who can. Some centers have specialists who speak foreign languages. The coordinator of the FICs is located at 18th and F Streets, NW, Washington, DC 20405. For a list of FICs write to: Consumer Information Center, Pueblo, CO 81009.

TRACKING CONGRESSIONAL ACTION

Congressional action information can be obtained from several sources. The Legis Office will provide information on whether legislation has been introduced, who sponsored it, and its current status. For House or Senate action, call 202-225-1772.

Cloakrooms of both houses will provide details on what is happening on the floor of the chamber. House cloakrooms: Democrat 202-225-7330; Republican 202-225-7350. Senate cloakrooms: Democrat 202-224-4691; Republican 202-224-6391.

BUSINESS ASSISTANCE FROM U.S. GOVERNMENT AGENCIES

The **Commerce Department's ombudsman** operates throughout the entire government complex to assist both business and consumers. Services include dissemination of information and reports such as *Outlook*. Write Office of Business Liaison, U.S. Department of Commerce, Washington, DC 20230, or call 202-377-3176. This office is also a focal point for handling inquiries for domestic business information.

European Community country information is available free from the European Community Information Service, 2100 M Street NW, Washington, DC 20037; or call 202-862-9500.

Industry experts in the International Trade Administration can provide specifics about an industry. A list of appropriate offices to call is given on page 614.

Country experts in the Department of State provide up to date economic and political information on countries throughout the world, as well as background reports on specific countries. For information contact:

Country Officers
U.S. Department of State
2201 C Street NW
Washington, DC 20520
Telephone: 202-647-4000

Major Bureau of Labor Statistics Indicators are available daily from a recorded message at 202-523-9658.

Economic news and highlights of the day are provided by phone from the Department of Commerce. For economic news call 202-393-4100. For news highlights call 202-393-1847.

The **Energy Information Center** will provide free information on energy and related matters. Write National Energy Information Center, Forrestal Building, 1000 Independence Avenue SW, Washington, DC 20585. Call 202-252-8800.

Industry information statistics and details on specific industries can be obtained from the Department of Commerce, Washington, DC 20230; or call 202-377-4356.

Technical and scientific information is provided by the **National Technical Information Service** of the Department of Commerce, 5285 Port Royal, Springfield, VA 22161, which handles requests about government-sponsored research of all kinds. The basic charge to research a subject is $125. For information call 703-487-4600. For orders call 703-487-4650. For rush orders within the local calling area call 703-487-4700. For rush order outside the local calling area call 800-336-4700.

With the close of the National Referral Center, questions on specific business subjects are now being handled at the **General Reading Room of the Library of Congress.** Call 202-287-5680 or write to the Library of Congress, General Reading Room Division, Washington, DC 20540.

The **Census Bureau** produces detailed statistical information for the Nation. Information is available on population, housing, agriculture, manufacturing, retail trade, service industries, wholesale trade, foreign trade, mining, transportation, construction, and the revenues and expenditures of state and local governments. The Bureau also produces statistical studies of many foreign countries.

Information Sources in the Bureau of the Census

User Services:

General Information .... (301) 763-4100
Data User Training 763-1510
Geographic Information...................... 763-5270
Product Information (print, map) 763-4100
Map Orders ....(812) 288-3212

Government, Commerce and Industry Subjects:

Agriculture Data........................ (301) 763-1113
Business Data (Retail, Wholesale,
Services)..763-7564
Construction Statistics........................ 763-7163
Government Data................................... 763-7366
Industry Data 763-7800
Manufacturers Data 763-7666

Population, Housing and Income Subjects:

Housing Data .... (301) 763-2881
International Statistics 763-2870
Neighborhood Statistics
(1980 Census)................................. 763-2358

Population Data (age, race, income,
education, etc.)................................. 763-5020
Special Demographic Studies............. 763-7720

Government, Commerce and Civic Relations:.................................(301) 763-2436

Regional Assistance:

Atlanta, Georgia........................ (404) 347-2274
Boston, Massachusetts..............(617) 223-0226
Charlotte, North Carolina .... (704) 371-6144
Chicago, Illinois ....(312) 353-0980
Dallas, Texas............................... (214) 767-0625
Denver, Colorado .... (303) 234-3924
Detroit, Michigan........................ (313) 226-7742
Kansas City, Kansas .... (913) 236-3731
Los Angeles, California..............(213) 209-6612
New York, New York .... (212) 264-3860
Philadelphia, Pennsylvania........(215) 597-8313
Seattle, Washington .... (206) 442-7080

For a detailed telephone
contact list............................. (301) 763-2436

Source: *Business Services Directory*, U.S. Department of Commerce, Office of Business Liason.

Information Sources in the U.S. Department of Commerce: Quick Reference List

Aeronautical Chart Sales .... (301) 436-6990
Business Assistance ....(202) 377-3176
Commerce Speakers.................(202) 377-1360
Copyright Information* .... (202) 287-8700
Consumer Information.............. (202) 377-5001
District Export Councils .... (202) 377-4767
Energy Related Inventions-
Evaluation................................(301) 921-3694

Export
Counseling............................. (202) 377-3181
Export Trading Company........(202) 377-5131
License/Application................ (202) 377-4811

Fish Exports/Imports .... (202) 634-7252
Fishery Management Plans........ (202) 634-7220
Foreign Trade Zones.................. (202) 377-2862
Freight Rates** ....(202) 426-5812
Industry/Products
Information............................(202) 377-1461
Metric Information .... (202) 377-0944
Micro Computer Information
Exchange................................(301) 948-5717
Minority Owned Business...........(202) 377-8015
Nautical Chart Sales .... (301) 436-6990
NTIS Sales Desk......................... (703) 487-4650
Overseas Customer Lists........... (202) 377-3022
Overseas Marketing ....(202) 377-3022
Overseas Trade Fairs................. (202) 377-8220
Patent & Trademark
Information............................(703) 557-3080
Productivity Enhancement
Information............................(202) 377-0940

Procurement
Bidder's List............................ (202) 377-3387
Commerce Buy List .... (202) 377-3387
MBDA Profile System .... (202) 377-2414

NOAA Opportunities...............(202) 377-1537
Small Business ....(202) 377-1472
Women Owned Business ....(202) 377-1472

Publications
"Business America"
Magazine............................. (202) 377-3251
Commerce Business Daily...... (202) 377-4868
Domestic Economic
Development........................(202) 377-5113
NBS Reference Materials .... (301) 921-2318
NTIA Publication
Information.......................... (202) 377-1551

Sea Grant Research ....(301) 443-8923

Small Business
Assistance...............................(202) 377-3176
Procurement/Set Asides........ (202) 377-1472

Standards & Codes for
Products...................................(301) 921-2587

Statistics
Business Cycles..................... (202) 523-0535
Capital Investment................. (202) 523-0874
Gross National Product.......... (202) 523-0669
Foreign Travelers to U.S. .... (202) 377-0140
Housing Starts........................ (301) 763-5731
Income Data .... (301) 763-5020
International Trade
Balance................................(202) 523-0620
Personal Income by
County.................................. (202) 523-0951
Population................................(301) 763-5020
Price Indexes.......................... (202) 523-0828
Retail Trade Data .... (301) 763-4100
Trade Statistics....................... (202) 377-2185

Technology
  International Joint
    Ventures............................ (202) 377-0944
  National Joint Ventures...........(202) 377-5914
  Small Business.......................(202) 377-8111
  Time of Day...........................(303) 499-7111

Travel
  "America, Catch the
    Spirit.".............................. (202) 377-4752
  Tourism Information
    (Inbound)............................(202) 377-4752

Weather
  Climate for Farming...............(301) 763-4690
  Forecast—
    U.S. Eastern Cities..............(301) 899-3244
  Forecast—
    U.S. Western Cities.............(301) 899-3249
  Past Conditions......................(202) 634-1822
  Tide & Water Levels...............(301) 443-8031

Women Owned Business...........(202) 377-1472

*Handled by the Library of Congress
**Handled by Maritime Commission

Source: *Business Services Directory*, U.S. Department of Commerce, Office of Business Liason.

ADDRESSES OF U.S. DEPARTMENT OF COMMERCE INFORMATION SOURCES

**Office of the Under Secretary
for Economic Affairs**
Rm. 4857, Main Commerce*
Telephone: (202) 377-2235

Bureau of the Census
Rm. 2705, Fed. Office Bldg. No. 3
Suitland, MD 20023
Telephone: (301) 763-4051

Bureau of Economic Analysis
Rm. 713, Tower Bldg.
1401 K Street, N.W.
Mailing Address:
U.S. Department of Commerce*
Telephone: (202) 523-0777

**Economic Development
Administration**
Rm. 7800B, Main Commerce*
Telephone: (202) 377-5113

**International Trade
Administration**
Rm. 4805, Main Commerce*
Telephone: (202) 377-3808

**Minority Business Development
Agency**
Rm. 5063, Main Commerce*
Telephone: (202) 377-1936

National Bureau of Standards
Rm. A903 Admin. Bldg.
Gaithersburg, Maryland
Mailing address:
National Bureau of Standards
Washington, D.C. 20234
Telephone: (301) 921-3112

**National Oceanic and
Atmospheric Admin.**
Rm. 5806, Main Commerce*
Telephone: (202) 377-4190

**National Technical Information
Service**
Room 1067, Main Commerce*
Telephone: (202) 377-0365

**National Telecommunications
and Information Administration**
Room 4889, Main Commerce*
Telephone: (202) 377-1551

-----
* 14th & Constitution Ave., N.W. Washington, D.C. 20230

Patent and Trademark Office
Rm. Id01, Crystal Plaza Building 3
2021 Jefferson Davis Highway
Arlington, VA 20231
Telephone: (703) 557-3428

Commodities: Sources of Government Information

Information on various commodities may be obtained by calling the following:

Office of Industries
International Trade Commission
701 E Street NW
Washington, DC 20436
Telephone: 292-523-0146

Bureau of Mines
2401 E Street NW
Washington, DC
The Bureau uses three basic classifications:
  Ferrous Metals
    Telephone: 202-634-1010
  Nonferrous Metals
    Telephone: 202-634-1055
  Industrial Minerals
    Telephone: 202-634-1202

Crops Branch
Department of Agriculture
1301 New York Avenue NW
Washington, DC 20005
Telephone: 202-786-1840

Federal and State Government Assistance Available to U.S. Businesses

Government support of technical innovation is growing rapidly both at the Federal and State levels. A helpful source for information regarding the transfer of Federal technology to the U.S. economy is the Center for the Utilization of Federal Technology (CUFT), which is part of the National Technical Information Service (NTIS) of the U.S. Department of Commerce, 5285 Port Royal Road, Springfield, VA 22161; (703) 487-4838. One of its major roles is to link U.S. businesses with federally developed technologies and resources having commercial or practical application. By working directly with U.S. Government agencies, CUFT has prepared a number of directories and catalogs to alert companies to these valuable Government resources.

Its most recent directory, *Directory of Federal and State business Assistance–A Guide for New and Growing Companies,* presents full descriptions to financial, management, innovation, and information programs and services established to help both large and small firms in their day-to-day operations. A listing of state services is given on page *561.*

A companion directory, *Directory of Federal Laboratory and Technical Resources–A Guide to Services, Facilities, and Expertise,* provides detailed descriptions of technology-oriented Federal resources. Especially notable are the entries describing 91 technical information centers offering information assistance in focused technology areas.

Also available are the *Federal Technology Catalogs–Guides to New and Practical Technologies* which annually offer full descriptions to more than 1,200 new technologies and R&D developments. Another annual catalog series, *Catalogs of Government Patents,* provides quick access to the more than 1,400 U.S. Government-owned inventions available for licensing (often exclusively).

For further information, write or call CUFT at the address given above or call (703) 487-4838.

Business Assistance Program: Commerce Department

The Business Assistance program is designed to shorten the time it takes a businessperson to track down information within the labyrinth of government bureaus and agencies. Business Assistance Program staffers can provide information or direct inquiries to the proper authority on such subjects as regulatory changes, government programs, services, policies, and even relevant government publications for the business community. For information call 203–377–3176 or write: Business Assistance Program Business Liason Office, Rm 5898-C, Department of Commerce, Washington, DC 20230.

U.S. General Services Administration: Business Service Centers

The Business Service Centers are a one stop, one point of contact for information on General Services Administration and other Government contract programs. The primary function is to provide advice on doing business with the Federal Government. The Centers provide information, assistance, and counseling and sponsor business clinics, procurement conferences, and business opportunity meetings.

Business representatives interested in selling products and services to the Government should contact the nearest Business Service Center given below.

Mailing Address and Telephone	Area of Service
Business Service Center General Services Administration John W. McCormack Post Office and Courthouse Boston, MA 02109 (617) 223–2868	Connecticut, Maine, Massachusetts, New Hampshire, Rhode Island, and Vermont
Business Service Center General Services Administration 26 Federal Plaza New York, NY 10007 (212) 264–1234	New Jersey, New York, Puerto Rico, and Virgin Islands
Business Service Center General Services Administration 7th and D Streets, SW., RM. 1050 Washington, DC 20407 (202) 472–1804	District of Columbia, nearby Maryland, Virginia
Business Service Center General Services Administration 9th and Market Streets Room 1300 Philadelphia, PA 19107 (215) 597–9613	Delaware, Pennsylvania, West Virginia, Maryland, Virginia

Mailing Address and Telephone	Area of Service
Business Service Center General Services Administration Richard B. Russell Federal Building and Court House 75 Spring Street Atlanta, GA 30303 (404) 221-5103	Alabama, Florida, Georgia, Kentucky, Mississippi, North Carolina, South Carolina, and Tennessee
Business Service Center General Services Administration 230 South Dearborn Street Chicago, IL 60604 (312) 353-5383	Illinois, Indiana, Ohio, Michigan, Minnesota, and Wisconsin
Business Service Center General Services Administration 1500 East Bannister Road Kansas City, MO 64131 (816) 926-7203	Iowa, Kansas, Missouri, and Nebraska
Business Service Center General Services Administration 819 Taylor Street Fort Worth, TX 76102 (817) 334-3284	Arkansas, Louisiana, New Mexico, Oklahoma, and Texas
Business Service Center General Services Administration Building 41, Denver Federal Center Denver, CO 80225 (303) 236-7409	Colorado, Montana, North Dakota, South Dakota, Utah, and Wyoming
Business Service Center General Services Administration 525 Market Street San Francisco, CA 94105 (415) 454-9000	California (northern), Hawaii, and Nevada (except Clark County)
Business Service Center General Services Administration 300 North Los Angeles Street Los Angeles, CA 90012 (213) 688-3210	Arizona, Los Angeles, California (southern), and Nevada (Clark County only)
Business Service Center General Services Administration 440 Federal Building 915 Second Avenue Seattle, WA 98174 (206) 442-5556	Alaska, Idaho, Oregon, and Washington

State Information Guide

Regional Directories

Central Atlantic States Manufacturing Directory, T. K. Sanderson Organization, 200 E. 25 Street, Baltimore, MD 21218

Daltons' Greater Philadelphia Industrial Directory, Dalton Corp., 2925 N. Broad Street, Philadelphia, PA 19132

Directory of Central Atlantic States Manufacturers, Manufacturers' News, Inc., 4 E. Huron Street, Chicago, IL 60611; George D. Hall Company, 20 Kilby Street, Boston, MA 02109

Directory of New England Manufacturers, The, George D. Hall Company, 20 Kilby Street, Boston, MA 02109

Eastern Manufacturers' and Industrial Directory, Bell Directory Publishers, Inc., 1995 Broadway, New York, NY 10023

MacRae's Blue Book, The National Industrial Directory, 87 Terminal Drive, Plainview, NY 11803

Midwest Manufacturers' and Industrial Directory, Industrial Directory Publishers, 1002 Park Avenue Building, Detroit, MI 48226

New England Apparel Directory, Register Publication, Inc., 99 Chauncey Street, Boston, MA 02111

New England Industrial Service Directory, George D. Hall Company, 20 Kilby Street, Boston, MA 02109

New England Manufacturers Directory, Manufacturers' News, Inc., 3 E. Huron Street, Chicago, IL 60611

State Executive Directory, Carroll Publishing Company, 1058 Thomas Jefferson NW, Washington, DC 20007

State Sales Guides, Dun & Bradstreet, Inc., 99 Church Street, New York, NY 10007

Survey of Industries in Texarkana (Arkansas-Texas), Texarkana Chamber of Commerce, Box 1468, Texarkana, AK 75501

State Business Assistance

Directory of Incentives for Business Investment and Development in the U.S., The Urban Institute Press, P.O. Box 19958 Hampden Station, Baltimore, MD 21211. State by state guide to economic business incentives. Included are descriptions of state assistance and financial assistance programs.

Monthly Checklist of State Publications, Superintendent of Documents. Washington, DC 20402. A monthly list of documents and publications received from the States.

STATE TECHNICAL ASSISTANCE CENTERS*

These centers offer assistance in business related matters. Such assistance includes information gathering, location of expert help, and guidance on new technologies. Most of these centers also are able to offer other types of assistance, such as market feasibility, or at least link businesses with appropriate contacts.

Alabama

Alabama Department of Agriculture and Industries, Post Office Box 3336, Montgomery, AL 36193. Contact (205) 261-2650. *Assistance:* Information/Technical

Alabama Department of Economic & Community Affairs–State Planning, 3465 Norman Bridge Road, P.O. Box 2939, Montgomery, AL 36105–0939. Contact Mr. Ned Butler at (205) 284-6706. *Assistance:* Business planning/information/Networking/Technical

Alabama Department of Economic and Community Affairs–Energy Division, 3465 Norman Bridge Road, P.O. Box 2939, Montgomery, AL 36105–0939. Contact Mr. Fred Braswell at (205) 284-8952. *Assistance:* Financial/Information/Networking/Technical

Alabama Department of Environmental Management, 1751 Federal Drive, Montgomery, AL 36130. Contact Ms. Marilyn Elliott at (205) 271-7715. *Assistance:* Information/Networking

Alabama Development Office, c/o State Capital, Montgomery, AL 36130. Contact (205) 263-0048. *Assistance:* Business planning/Financial/Information/Networking/Technical

Alabama High Technology Assistance Center, University of Alabama in Huntsville, 222 Morton Hall, Huntsville, AL 35899. Contact Dr. Edward F. Stafford at (205) 895-6409. *Assistance:* Business planning/Information/Networking/Technical

Alabama International Trade Center, P.O. Box 1996, Patton Building, University, AL 35486. Contact Mr. Nisa Bacon at (205) 348-7621. *Assistance:* Business planning/Information/Networking/Technical

Alabama Small Business Development Consortium, 1717 11th Avenue South, Medical Towers Building, Suite 419, Birmingham, AL 35294. Contact Mrs. Sherry Dilbeck at (205) 934-7260. *Assistance:* Business planning / Financial / Information /

* Source: *Directory of Federal and State Business Assistance: A Guide for New and Growing Companies*, National Technical Information Service, Center for the Utilization of Federal Technology, U.S. Department of Commerce. For further information call 703–487–4838.

Management / Networking / Technical. *Eligibility:* Smaller businesses

Auburn Technical Assistance Center, 202 Langdon Annex, Auburn University, AL 36849. Contact Mr. Henry Burdg at (205) 826-4659. *Assistance:* Management/Technical

Alabama State Department of Revenue. Research and Information Division, Administrative Building, 64 North Union Street, Montgomery, AL 36130. Contact Mr. William E. Crawford at (205) 261-3094 or 3366. *Assistance:* Information/Networking

Center for Economic Development & Business Research, Jacksonville State University, College of Commerce and Business Administration, 114 Merrill Hall, Jacksonville, AL 36265. Contact Ms. Pat W. Shaddix at (205) 435-9820 Ext: 324. *Assistance:* Business planning/Information/Technical

Economic Development Technical Assistance Unit, Tuskegee University Human Resources Development Center, P.O. Box 681, Tuskegee Institute, AL 36088. Contact (205) 727-8764. *Assistance:* Business planning/Information

Management Development Center, Jacksonville State University, Merrill Bldg., Room 113-A, Jacksonville, AL 36265. Contact Mr. David R. Copeland at (205) 435-9820 Ext: 342. *Assistance:* Business planning/Management

Alaska

Agricultural Loan Fund, Alaska Department of Natural Resources, Division of Agriculture, Pouch A, Wasilla, AL 99687. Contact (907) 376-3276. *Assistance:* Financial

Alaska Commercial Fishing and Agriculture Bank, P.O. Box Y-2070, Anchorage, AL 99509. Contact (907) 276-2007. *Assistance:* Financial/Networking/Technical

Alaska Industrial Development Authority, 1577 C Street, Suite 304, Anchorage, AL 99501–5177. Contact (907) 274-1651. *Assistance:* Financial/Networking

Economic Development Center, School of Business and Public Administration, University of Alaska-Juneau, 1108 F Street, Juneau, AK 99801. Contact Dr. Al Borrego at (907) 789-4402. *Assistance:* Business planning/Technical

Loan Fund Programs, Department of Commerce and Economic Development, Division of Investments, Pouch D, Juneau, AL 99811. Contact (907) 465-2510. *Assistance:* Financial

Arizona

Arizona Department of Commerce, 1700 West Washington, 4th Floor, Phoenix, AZ 85007. Contact Ms. Beth S. Jarman at (602) 255-5371. *Assistance:* Business planning/Financial/Information/Technical

Business and Trade Program, Arizona Department of Commerce, 1700 West Washington, 4th Floor, Phoenix, AZ 85007. Contact Ms. Beth S. Jarman at (602) 255-5371. *Assistance:* Business planning/Information/Networking/Technical

Development Finance Program, Arizona Department of Commerce, 1700 West Washington, 4th Floor, Pheonix, AZ 85007. Contact Ms Beth S. Jarman at (602) 255-5371. *Assistance:* Business planning/Financial/Information/Technical

Arkansas

Arkansas Industry Training Program, Education Building-West, #3 Capitol Mall, Little Rock, AR 72201. Contact Mr. Richard Cochran at (501) 371-2165. *Assistance:* Training

Arkansas Science and Technology Authority, 200 Main Street, Suite 201, Little Rock, AR 72201. Contact Dr. John Ahlen at (501) 371-3554. *Assistance:* Financial/Information/Networking/Technical

Business Development Services–University of Arkansas at Little Rock, 5th Floor, Library Building, UALR, 33rd and University Ave., Little Rock, AR 72204. Contact Mr. Paul McGinnis at (501) 371-5535. *Assistance:* Business planning/Financial/Information/Networking/Technical

Center for Technology Transfer–University of Arkansas at Little Rock, Department of Industrial Engineering, 309 Engineering Building, University of Arkansas, Fayetteville, AR 72701. Contact Dr. C. Robert Emerson at (501) 575-3156. *Assistance:* Information/Networking/Technical

Division of Finance–Arkansas Industrial Development Commission, One State Capital Mall, Little Rock, AR 72201. Contact Mr. Larry Patrick at (501) 371-1151. *Assistance:* Financial/Information/Networking/Technical

Energy Division–Arkansas Industrial Development Commission, One State Capitol Mall, Little Rock, AR 72201. Contact Ms. Cherry Duckett at (501) 371-1370. *Assistance:* Information/Networking/Technical

Marketing Division–Arkansas Industrial Development Commission, One State Capitol Mall, Little Rock, AR 72201. Contact Ms. Maria Haley at (501) 371-7678. *Assistance:* Information/Networking/Technical

Minority Business Division–Arkansas Industrial Development Commission, One State Capitol Mall, Little Rock, AR 72201. Contact Mr. James Hall at (501) 371-1060. *Assistance:* Business planning/Financial/Information/Networking/Technical. *Eligibility:* Minority businesses

California

Economic Adjustment Unit, Department of Commerce, 1121 L Street, Suite 600, Sacramento, CA 95814. Contact (916) 322-1515. *Assistance:* Training/Business planning/Information/Technical

Office of Business Development, Department of Commere, 1121 L Street, Sacramento, CA 95814. Contact (916) 322-5665. *Assistance:* Information

Office of Economic Research, Department of Commerce, 1121 L Street, Sacramento, CA 95814. Contact (916) 322-5853. *Assistance:* Information

Office of Small Business, Department of Commerce, 1121 L Street, Sacramento, CA 95814. Contact (916) 445-6545. *Assistance:* Business planning/Financial/Information/Technical. *Eligibility:* Smaller businesses

Urban University Center, Western Research Application Center, University of Southern California, 3716 South Hope Street, Los Angeles, CA 90007. Contact (213) 743-2371. *Assistance:* Business planning/Information/Technical

Colorado

Business Information Center, Office of Regulatory Reform, 1525 Sherman Street, #110, Denver, CO 80203. Contact (303) 866-3933. *Assistance:* Information

Colorado Housing Finance Authority, Commercial Programs, 500 E. 8th Ave., Denver, CO 80203. Contact (303) 861-8962. *Assistance:* Financial. *Eligibility:* Smaller businesses

Division of Commerce and Development, 1313 Sherman Street, #523, Denver, CO 80203. Contact (303) 866-2205. *Assistance:* Information/Networking/Technical

Minority Business Development Agency, 1525 Sherman Street, 7th Floor, Denver, CO 80203. Contact (303) 866-2077. *Assistance:* Information/Technical. *Eligibility:* Minority businesses

Small Business Assistance Center, 1690 38th Street, #101, Boulder, CO 80301. Contact (303) 444-5723. (800) 521-1243 in Colorado. *Assistance:* Business planning/Information/Technical. *Eligibility:* Smaller businesses

Connecticut

Connecticut Department of Economic Development–Business Services, 210 Washington Street, Hartford, CT 06106. Contact Mr. John J. Carson at (203) 566-3842. *Assistance:* Business planning/Information/Networking/Technical

Connecticut Department of Economic Development–Investment Incentives, 210 Washington Street, Hartford, CT 06106. Contact Mr. John J. Carson at (203) 566-3842. *Assistance:* Financial

Connecticut Department of Economic Development–Technical Assistance, 210 Washington Street, Hartford, CT 06106. Contact Mr. John J. Carson at (203) 566-3842. *Assistance:* Business planning/Information/Networking/Technical

Connecticut Development Authority, 217 Washington Street, Hartford, CT 06106. Contact Mr. Richard L. Higgins at (203) 522-3730. *Assistance:* Financial

Connecticut Product Development Corporation, 93 Oak Street, Hartford, CT 06106. Contact Mr. Jack Frazier at (203) 566-2920. *Assistance:* Financial

Connecticut Technology Assistance Center, Connecticut Department of Economic Development, 210 Washington Street, Hartford, CT 06106. Contact Mr. Eric Ott at (203) 566-4587 or 4862. *Assistance:* Training/Business planning/Financial/Information/Networking/Technical

Delaware

Delaware Development Office, Business Services Unit, 99 Kings Highway, P.O. Box 1401, Dover, DE 19903. Contact (302) 736-4271. *Assistance:* Financial/Information

Delaware Small Business Development Center, Suite 005 Purnell Hall, University of Delaware, Newark, DE 19716. Contact David Park at (302) 451-2747. *Assistance:* Business planning/Information/Management. *Eligibility:* Smaller businesses

District of Columbia

District of Columbia Department of Employment Services, 1350 Pennsylvania Avenue, N.W., Washington, DC 20004. Contact Ms Jackie Threadgill at (202) 639-1179. *Assistance:* Training/Information/Networking

Financial Services Division, Office of Business and Economic Development, 1350 Pennsylvania Avenue, N.W., Washington, DC 20001. Contact Ms. Pamela Vaughn Cooke Henry at (202) 727-6600. *Assistance:* Financial

Minority Business Opportunity Commission, 613 G Street, N.W., Washington, DC 20001. Contact Mr. William C. Jameson at (202) 727-3817. *Assistance:* Financial/Information/Networking. *Eligibility:* Minority businesses

Technical Services Division, Office of Business and Economic Development, 1350 Pennsylvania Avenue, N.W., Washington, DC 20004. Contact Mr. Kwasi Hulman at (202) 727-6600. *Assistance:* Information/Management/Networking/Technical

Florida

Business Service Program, Bureau of Business Assistance, Florida Department of Commerce, 107 West Gains Street, Tallahassee, FL 32301. Contact Mr. Leonard Elize at (904) 488-9357. *Assistance:* Information/Networking.

Financial Service, Bureau of Business Assistance, Florida Department of Commerce, 107 West Gains Street, Tallahassee, FL 32301. Contact Mr. Leonard Elize at (904) 488-9357. *Assistance:* Financial/Networking

Entrepreneurship Program, Bureau of Business Assistance, Florida Department of Commerce, 107 West Gains Street, Tallahassee, FL 32301. Contact Mr. Leonard Elize at (904) 488-9357. *Assistance:* Information

Florida Economic Development Center, 325 College of Business, Florida State University, Tallahassee, FL 32306-1007. Contact Mr. Roy Thompson at (904) 644-1044. *Assistance:* Business planning/Financial/Information/Networking/Technical

Florida Small Business Development Centers, University of West Florida, Pensacola, FL 32514. Contact Mr. Gregory L. Higgins at (904) 478-2820. *Assistance:* Business planning/Information/Management/Networking/Technical. *Eligibility:* Smaller businesses

NASA/Southern Technology Applications Center, University of Florida, 307 Weil Hall, Gainsville, FL 32611. Contact Mr. J. Ronald Thornton at (904) 392-0854. *Assistance:* Information/Networking/Technical

North Florida Entrepreneurial Network, Room 325, College of Business, Florida State University, Tallahassee, FL 32306–1007. Contact Mr. Greg Cardamone at (904) 644-1044. *Assistance:* Information/Networking/Technical

Production Innovation Center, University of North Florida, 4567 St. Johns Bluff Road, Jacksonville, FL 32216. Contact Mr. Richard L. Christian at (904) 646-2487. *Assistance:* Business planning/Information/Networking/Technical. *Eligibility:* Smaller businesses

Quest for Technology Program at Florida State University, 325 College of Business, Florida State University, Tallahassee, FL 32306–1007. Contact (904) 644-1044. *Assistance:* Business planning/Financial/Information/Networking/Technical

Georgia

Advanced Technology Development Center, 430 Tenth Street, Suite N-116, Atlanta, GA 30318. Contact (404) 894-3575. *Assistance:* Information/Networking/Technical

Georgia Department of Community Affairs, Room 800, 40 Marietta Street, N.W., Small Business Revitalization Program, Atlanta, GA 30303. Contact Mr. Steve Storey at (404) 656-6200. *Assistance:* Financial/Information/Networking/Technical

Georgia Productivity Center, Georgia Institute of Technology, Atlanta, GA 30332. Contact Dr. Bikram Garcha at (404) 658-4000. *Assistance:* Business planning/Information/Networking/Technical

Economic Development Division, Economic Development Laboratory, Georgia Tech Research Institute, Atlanta, GA 30332. Contact Mr. Arthur Brown at (404) 894-3858. *Assistance:* Business planning/Technical

Technical Assistance Center, Atlanta University, Inc., 223 Chestnut Street, S.W., Atlanta, GA 30314. Contact Mr. Thurmond Williams at (404) 681-0251. *Assistance:* Business planning/Technical. *Eligibility:* Minority businesses

The Small Business Development Center, College of Business Administration, Brooks Hall, The University of Georgia, Athens, GA 30601. Contact Mr. Lee Quarterman at (404) 658-3550. *Assistance:* Business planning/Information/Networking.

Financial Assistance Branch, Department of Planning and Economic Development, 250 South King Street, Honolulu, HI 96813. Contact (808) 548-4617. *Assistance:* Financial/Information/Networking. *Eligibility:* Smaller businesses

Hawaii

Department of Agriculture, State of Hawaii, 1428 South King Street, Honolulu, HI 96814. Contact (808) 548-7108. *Assistance:* Financial/Information/Networking/Technical

Industry and Product Promotion, Business Development Branch, Department of Planning and Economic Development, 250 South King Street, Honolulu, HI 96813. Contact (808) 548-3908. *Assistance:* Business planning/Information/Networking

International Services Branch, Department of Planning and Economic Development, 250 South King Street, Honolulu, HI 96813. Contact (808) 548-4621. *Assistance:* Business planning/Information/Networking

Pacific Business Center Program, College of Business Administration, 2404 Maile Way, Honolulu, HI 96822. Contact (808) 948-6286. *Assistance:* Business planning/Management. *Eligibility:* Smaller businesses

Small Business Information Service, Department of Planning and Economic Development, 250 South King Street, Honolulu, HI 96813. Contact (808) 548-7645. *Assistance:* Business planning/Information/Networking

Special Duty Attorney General for Small Business, 335 Merchant Street, Room 241A, Honolulu, HI 96813. Contact (808) 548-6744. *Assistance:* Information/Technical. *Eligibility:* Smaller businesses

Idaho

Idaho Business and Economic Development Center, 1910 University Drive, Boise State University, Boise, ID 83725. Contact Mr. Ronald R. Hall at (208) 385-1640. *Assistance:* Business planning/Information/Management/ Networking/Technical

Idaho Department of Commerce, Statehouse, Room 108, Boise, ID 83720. Contact Mr. Jay Engstrom at (208) 334-4719. *Assistance:* Business planning/Financial/Information/Networking/Technical

Idaho Small Business Development Center, 1910 University Drive, Boise State University, Boise, ID 83725. Contact (208) 385-1640. *Assistance:* Business planning/Information/Management/Networking/Technical. *Eligibility:* Smaller businesses

Region District Associations, Idaho Department of Commerce, Statehouse, Room 108, Boise, ID 83720. Contact Mr. Jay Engstrom at (208) 334-4719. *Assistance:* Financial

Illinois

Bond Programs, Illinois Department of Commerce and Community Affairs, 620 East Adams Street, Springfield, IL 62701. Contact (217) 782-6861. For the Chicago area, contact State of Illinois Center, 100 West Randolph Street, Suite 3-400; (312) 917-3133. *Assistance: Financial*

Center for Urban Economic Development, School of Urban Planning and Policy, The University of Illinois at Chicago, Box 4348, Chicago, IL 60680. Contact (312) 996-2178. *Assistance:* Business planning/Information/ Technical

Business Expansion Assistance, Illinois Department of Commerce and Community Affairs, 620 East Adams Street, Springfield, IL 62701. Contact (217) 782-6861. For the Chicago area, contact State of Illinois Center, 100 West Randolph Street, Suite 3-400; (312) 917-3133. *Assistance:* Information/Networking

Development Finance Unit, Illinois Department of Commerce and Community Affairs, 620 East Adams Street, Springfield, IL 62701. Contact (217) 782-6861. For the Chicago area, contact State of Illinois Center, 100 West Randolph Street, Suite 3-400; (312) 917-3133. *Assistance:* Technical

Export Assistance, Illinois Department of Commerce and Community Affairs, 620 East Adams Street, Springfield, IL 62701. Contact (217) 782-6861. For the Chicago area, contact State of Illinois Center, 100 West Randolph Street, Suite 3-400; (312) 917-3133. *Assistance:* Information/Networking/Technical

Export Financing, Illinois Department of Commerce and Community Affairs, 620 East Adams Street, Springfield, IL 62701. Contact (217) 782-6861. For the Chicago area, contact State of Illinois Center, 100 West Randolph Street, Suite 3-400; (312) 917-3133.

Illinois Enterprise Zone Program, Illinois Department of Commerce and Community Affairs, 620 East Adams Street, Springfield, IL 62701. Contact (217) 782-6861. For the Chicago area, contact State of Illinois Center, 100 West Randolph Street, Suite 3-400; (312) 917-3133. *Assistance:* Financial

Illinois Inventor's Council, Illinois Department of Commerce and Community Affairs, 620 East Adams Street, Springfield, IL 62701. Contact (217) 782-6861. For the Chicago area, contact State of Illinois Center, 100 West Randolph Street, Suite 3-400; (312) 917-3133. *Assistance:* Networking/Technical

Illinois Resource Network, Illinois Department of Commerce and Community Affairs, 620 East Adams Street, Springfield, IL 62701. Contact (217) 782-6861. For the Chicago area, contact State of Illinois Center, 100 West Randolph Street, Suite 3-400; (312) 917-3133.

Industrial Health and Safety Consultation, Illinois Department of Commerce and Community Affairs, 620 East Adams Street, Springfield, IL 62701. Contact (217) 782-6861. For the Chicago area, contact State of Illinois Center, 100 West Randolph Street, Suite 3-400; (312) 917-3133. *Assistance:* Technical

Illinois Software Association and Center, Illinois Department of Commerce and Community Affairs, 620 East Adams Street, Springfield, IL 62701. Contact (217) 782-6861. For the Chicago area, contact State of Illinois Center, 100 West Randolph street, Suite 3-400; (312) 917-3133. *Assistance:* Information/Networking

Large Business Development Program, Illinois Department of Commerce and Community Affairs, 620 East Adams Street, Springfield, IL 62701. Contact (217) 782-6861. For the Chicago area, contact State of Illinois Center, 100 West Randolph Street, Suite 3-400; (312) 917-3133. *Assistance:* Information/Management. *Eligibility:* Minority businesses

Minority Business Assistance, Illinois Department of Commerce and Community Affairs, 620 East Adams Street, Springfield, IL 62701. Contact (217) 782-6861. For the Chicago area, contact State of Illinois Center, 100 West Randolph Street, Suite 3-400; (312) 917-3133. *Assistance:* Information/Management. *Eligibility:* Minority businesses

One-Stop Permit Center, Illinois Department of Commerce and Community affairs, 620 East Adams Street, Springfield, IL 62701. Contact (217) 782-6861. For the Chicago area, contact State of Illinois Center, 100 West Randolph Street, Suite 3-400; (312) 917-3133. *Assistance:* Information

Procurement Assistance Program, Illinois Department of Commerce and Community Affairs, 620 East Adams Street, Springfield, IL 62701. Contact (217) 782-6861. For the Chicago area, contact State of Illinois Center, 100 West Randolph street, Suite 3-400; (312) 917-3133. *Assistance:* Technical

Sites, Buildings, and Community Profile Program, Illinois Department of Commerce and Community affairs, 620 East Adams Street, Springfield, IL 62701. Contact (217) 782-6861. For the Chicago area, contact State of Illinois Center, 100 West Randolph Street, Suite 3-400; (312) 917-3133. *Assistance:* Information

Small Business Development Centers, Illinois Department of Commerce and Community Affairs, 620 East Adams Street, Springfield, IL 62701. Contact (217) 782-6861. For the Chicago area, contact State of Illinois Center, 100 West Randolph Street, Suite 3-400; (312) 917-3133. *Assistance:* Business planning/Information/Networking/Technical. *Eligibility:* Smaller businesses

Small Business Development Program, Illinois Department of Commerce and Community Affairs, 620 East Adams Street, Springfield, IL 62701. Contact (217) 782-6861. For the Chicago area, contact State of Illinois Center, 100 West Randolph Street, Suite 3-400; (312) 917-3133. *Assistance:* Financial. *Eligibility:* Smaller businesses

Small Business Financing Funds, Illinois Department of Commerce and Community Affairs, 620 East Adams Street, Springfield, IL 62701. Contact (217) 782-6861. For the Chicago area, contact State of Illinois Center, 100 West Randolph Street, Suite 3-400; (312) 917-3133. *Assistance:* Financial. *Eligibility:* Smaller businesses

Small Business Growth Corporation, Illinois Department of Commerce and Community affairs, 620 East Adams Street, Springfield, IL 62701. Contact (217) 782-6861. For the Chicago area, contact State of Illinois Center, 100 West Randolph Street, Suite 3-400; (312) 917-3133. *Assistance:* Financial. *Eligibility:* Smaller businesses

Small Business Hotline, Illinois Department of Commerce and Community Affairs, 620 East Adams Street, Springfield, IL 62701. Contact 800-252-2930. *Assistance:* Information

Small Business Investment Companies, Illinois Department of Commerce and Community Affairs, 620 East Adams Street, Springfield, IL 62701. Contact (217) 782-6861. For the Chicago area, contact State of Illinois Center, 100 West Randolph Street, Suite 3-400; (312) 917-3133. *Assistance:* Financial. *Eligibility:* Smaller businesses

Small Business Energy Audit Assistance, Illinois Department of Commerce and Community Affairs, 620 East Adams Street, Springfield, IL 62701. Contact (217) 782-6861. For the Chicago area, contact State of Illinois Center, 100 West Randolph Street, Suite 3-400; (312) 917-3133. *Assistance:* Technical. *Eligibility:* Smaller businesses

Technology Commercialization Centers, Illinois Department of Commerce and Community Affairs, 620 East Adams Street, Springfield, IL 62701. Contact (217) 782-6861. For the Chicago area, contact State of Illinois Center, 100 West Randolph Street, Suite 3-400; (312) 917-3133. *Assistance:* Information/Networking/Technical

Training Programs, Illinois Department of Commerce and Community Affairs, 620 East Adams Street, Springfield, IL 62701. Contact (217) 782-6861. For the Chicago area, contact State of Illinois Center, 100 West Randolph Street, Suite 3-400; (312) 917-3133. *Assistance:* Training/Financial

Venture Capital and Direct Loan Programs, Illinois Development Finance Authority, Illinois Department of Commerce and Community Affairs, 620 East Adams Street, Springfield, IL 62701. Contact (217) 782-6861. For the Chicago area, contact State of Illinois Center, 100 West Randolph Street, Suite 3-400; (312) 917-3133. *Assistance:* Financial

Indiana

Agricultural Development Corporation, Division of Business and Financial Services, Indiana Department of Commerce, One North Capitol, Suite 700, Indianapolis, IN 46204. Contact (317) 232-8782. *Assistance:* Financial

Basic Industries Retraining Program, Division of Business and Financial Services, Indiana Department of Commerce, One North Capitol, Suite 700, Indianapolis, IN 46204. Contact (317) 232-8782. *Assistance:* Financial

Business and Industrial Development Center, Purdue University, Engineering Administration Building, West Lafayette, IN 47907. Contact (800) 821-8261. *Assistance:* Financial/Networking/Technical

Center for Entrepreneurial Resources and Applied Research, School of Continuing Education, Ball State University, Muncie, IN 47306. Contact (800) 541-9313. *Assistance:* Networking/Technical

Center for Research and Management Services, Indiana State University, School of Business, Terre Haute, IN 47809. Contact (812) 232-3232. *Assistance:* Information/Technical

Commercial/Industrial Liaison, Indiana University, Purdue University Indianapolis, 355 North Lansing, Indianapolis, IN 46202. Contact (317) 264-8285. *Assistance:* Networking

Division of Agriculture, Indiana Department of Commerce, One North Capitol, Suite 700, Indianapolis, IN 46204. Contact (317) 232-8770. *Assistance:* Information/Technical

Disadvantaged Business Enterprise Program, Equal Employment Opportunity Section, Indiana Department of Highways, Room 1313, State Office Building, Indianapolis, IN 46204.

Contact (317) 232-5093. *Assistance:* Technical. *Eligibility:* Minority businesses

Division of Continuing Studies and Community Services, Indiana University East, 2325 Chester Blvd., Richmond, IN 47374. Contact (317) 966-82621. *Assistance:* Training/Management

Division of Economic Analysis, Indiana Department of Commerce, One North Capitol, Suite 700, Indianapolis, IN 46204. Contact (317) 232-8959. *Assistance:* Information

Division of Energy Policy, Indiana Department of Commerce, One North Capitol, Suite 700, Indianapolis, IN 46204. Contact (317) 232-8940. *Assistance:* Financial/Information/Technical

Division of Industrial Development, Indiana Department of Commerce, One North Capitol, Suite 700, Indianapolis, IN 46204. Contact (317) 232-888. *Assistance:* Information/Networking

Division of Research, Graduate School of Business, Indiana University, Bloomington, IN 47405. Contact (812) 335-5507. *Assistance:* Information

Economic Development Administration University Center at IUPUI, 611 North Capitol Avenue, Indianapolis, IN 46204. Contact Mr. Frank Bivens at (317) 262-5052. *Assistance:* Business planning/Information/Networking/Technical

Enterprise Zone Program, Division of Business and Financial Services, Indiana Department of Commerce, One North Capitol, Suite 700, Indianapolis, IN 46204. Contact (317) 232-8782. *Assistance:* Financial

Entrepreneur in Residence, School of Business, Indiana University, Room 460A, Bloomington, IN 47405. Contact (812) 335-9200. *Assistance:* Business planning/Management/Networking. *Eligibility:* Smaller businesses

Indiana Contractors Educational Center, Inc., 617 Indiana Avenue, Suite 319, Indianapolis, IN 46204. Contact (317) 635-6364. *Assistance:* Technical. *Eligibility:* Smaller businesses and minority businesses

Innovators Forum, Rose-Hulman Institute of Technology, 5500 Wabash Avenue, Terre Haute, IN 47803. Contact Mr. Jim Eifert at (812) 877-1511. *Assistance:* Networking/Technical

Industrial Development Bond Program, Division of Business and Financial Services, Indiana Department of Commerce, One North Capitol, Suite 700, Indianapolis, IN 46204. Contact (317) 232-8782. *Assistance:* Financial

Indiana Technology Referral Network and Technology 2000 Program, EDA University Center at IUPUI, 611 North Capital Avenue, Indianapolis, IN 46204. Contact (800) 641-4434. *Assistance:* Information/Networking/Technical

Indiana Regional Minority Suppliers Development Council, 151 N. Delaware, Room 1560, Box 44801, Indianapolis, IN 46224. Contact (317) 634-2586. *Assistance:* Information/Networking. *Eligibility:* Minority businesses

Indiana Employment Development Commerce, Division of Business and Financial Services, Indiana Department of Commerce, One North Capitol, Suite 700, Indianapolis, IN 46204. Contact (317) 232-8782. *Assistance:* Financial

Institute for Molecular and Cellular Biology, Indiana University, Jordan Hall, Bloomington, IN 47405. Contact (812) 335-4183. *Assistance:* Technical

Institute of Transnational Business, College of Business, Ball State University, Muncie, IN 47302. Contact (317) 285-5207. *Assistance:* Information/Technical. *Elligibility:* Smaller businesses

Investment Incentive Program, Division of Business and Financial Services, Indiana Department of Commerce, One North Capitol, Suite 700, Indianapolis, IN 46204. Contact (317) 232-8782. *Assistance:* Financial

Materials Research Institute, Indiana University, Bloomington, IN 47405. Contact (812) 335-9127. *Assistance:* Technical

Inventors and Entrepreneurs Society of Indiana, Purdue University Calumet, Hammond, IN 46323. Contact Daniel Yovich at (219) 844-0520. *Assistance:* Information/Networking

McMillen Productivity and Design Center, Indiana Institute of Technology, 1600 East Washington Blvd., Fort Wayne, IN 46803. Contact (219) 422-5561. *Assistance:* Technical

Office of International Trade, Division of Business Expansion, Indiana Department of Commerce, One North Capitol, Suite 700, Indianapolis, IN 46204. Contact (317) 232-8845. *Assistance:* Information

Office of Industrial Training and Development, Indiana Vocational Technical College, One West 26th Street, P.O. Box 1763, Indianapolis, IN 46206. Contact (317) 929-4772. *Assistance:* Training/Technical

Office of Minority Business Enterprise, Division of Business Expansion, Indiana Department of Commerce, One North Capitol, Suite 700, Indianapolis, IN 46204. Contact (317) 232-8820. *Assistance:* Business planning/Information/Management/Technical. *Eligibility:* Minority businesses

Office of Research and Graduate Development, Indiana University, Bryan Hall 104, Bloomington, IN 47405. Contact (812) 335-9813. *Assistance:* Networking/Technical

Office of the Business Ombudsman, Division

of Business Expansion, Indiana Department of Commerce, One North Capitol, Suite 700, Indianapolis, IN 46204. Contact (800) 824-2476. *Assistance:* Technical

SBIR Proposal Assistance, Office of Research, Ball State University, 1825 Riverside Avenue, Muncie, IN 47306. Contact (317) 285-1600. *Assistance:* Technical. *Eligibility:* Smaller businesses

Small Business Development Centers, Indiana Economic Development Council, One North Capitol Street, Suite 200, Indianapolis, IN 46204. Contact (317) 634-6407. *Assistance:* Business planning/Information/Technical. *Eligibility:* Smaller businesses

Task Force on New Technologies, Purdue University Calumet, 2233 17th Street, Hammond, IN 46323. Contact William Robinson at (219) 844-0520. *Assistance:* Information/Networking/Technical

Technology Services Center, Indiana State University, School of Technology, Terre Haute, IN 47809. Contact Mr. Milton Woods at (812) 232-6311. *Assistance:* Technical

Training for Profit Program, Division of Business and Financial Services, Indiana Department of Commerce, One North Capitol, Suite 700, Indianapolis, IN 46204. Contact (317) 232-8782. *Assistance:* Training/Financial

Transportation Rate Service and Ombudsperson Program, Indiana Port Commission, 143 West Market Street, Room 204, Indianapolis, IN 46204. Contact (800) 232-PORT. *Assistance:* Information/Technical

Urban Technology Outreach Program, Purdue University Calumet, 2233 17th Street, Hammond, IN 46323. Contact William Robinson at (219) 844-0520. *Assistance:* Information/Networking/Technical

Vocational Technical Services Center, Indiana State University, Classroom Bldg., Room 206, Terre Haute, IN 47809. Contact (812) 232-6311. *Assistance:* Training

Iowa

Center for Industrial Research & Service, Iowa State University of Science and Technology, Ames, IA 50011. Contact (515) 294-3420. *Assistance:* Information/Management/Networking/Technical

Economic Development Set-Aside Program, Office for Planning and Programming, 523 East 12th Street, Des Moines, IA 50319. Contact (515) 281-3711. *Assistance:* Financial

Golden Circle Loan Guaranty Fund, Small Business Development Center, Drake University, 210 Aliber Hall, Des Moines, IA 50311. Contact (515) 271-2655. *Assistance:* Financial. *Eligibility:* Smaller businesses

Industrial New Jobs Training Program, Iowa

Development Commission, 600 East Court Avenue, Suite A, Des Moines, IA 50309. Contact (515) 281-8329. *Assistance:* Training

Iowa High Technology Council, Iowa Development Commission, 600 E. Court Street, Des Moines, IA 50309. Contact (515) 281-3251. *Assistance:* Financial

Iowa Product Development Corporation, 600 E. Court Ave., Suite C, Des Moines, IA 50309. Contact Mr. Doug Getter at (515) 281-3251. *Assistance:* Financial

Small Business Development Center, Iowa State University, Heady Hall, Ames, IA 50011. Contact Mr. Jan A. DeYoung at (515) 294-8069. *Assistance:* Business planning/Information/Networking/Technical. *Eligibility:* Smaller businesses

Small Business Loan Program, Iowa Finance Authority, 550 Liberty Building, 418 Sixth Avenue, Des Moines, IA 50309. Contact (515) 281-4058. *Assistance:* Financial

Kansas

Center for Entrepreneurship, 130 Clinton Hall, Wichita State University, Wichita, KS 67208. Contact Dr. Fran Jabarra at (316) 689-3000. *Assistance:* Management/Networking

Center for Productivity Enhancement, Room 100, Wallace Hall, Wichita State University, Wichita, KS 67208. Contact Dr. Richard Graham at (316) 689-3402. *Assistance:* Information/Management/Networking/Technical

Engineering Extension, Ward Hall 133, Kansas State University, Manhattan, KS 66506. Contact (913) 532-6026. *Assistance:* Information/Technical

Kansas Advanced Technology Commission, 503 Kansas Avenue, Topeka, KS 66603. Contact Dr. Phillips V. Bradford at (913) 296-5272. *Assistance:* Financial/Information/Networking

Small Business Development Centers, Clinton Hall, Room 021D, Wichita State University, Wichita, KS 67208. Contact Ms. Susan K. Osborne-Howes at (316) 689-3193. *Assistance:* Business planning/Information/Management/Networking. *Eligibility:* Smaller businesses

Kentucky

Center for Business Development, College of Business and Economics, University of Kentucky, Lexington, KY 40506. Contact Mr. James G. Owen at (606) 257-1751. *Assistance:* Business planning

Small Business Development Center, University of Kentucky, 18 Porter Building, Lexington, KY 40506–0205. Contact Mr. Jerry Owen at (606) 257-1751. *Assistance:* Business planning/Information/Technical. *Eligibility:* Smaller businesses

NASA/University of Kentucky Technology Applications Program, University of Kentucky, 109 Kinkead Hall, Lexington, KY 40506-0057. Contact (606) 257-6322. *Assistance:* Information/Technical

Office of Business and Technology, Kentucky Commerce Cabinet, 2400 Capital Plaza Tower, Frankfort, KY 40601. Contact Mr. Cary W. Blankenship at (502) 564-7670. *Assistance:* Business planning/Information/Networking/Technical. *Eligibility:* Smaller businesses

Louisiana

Center for Economic Development, College of Business Administration, University of New Orleans, New Orleans, LA 70122. Contact Dr. Ivan J. Miestochovitz at (504) 283-0663. *Assistance:* Business planning/Management/Technical

Department of Commerce, P.O. Box 94185, Baton Rouge, LA 70804–9185. Contact (504) 342-5361. *Assistance:* Financial/Information/Networking

Xavier University Economic Development Center, P.O. Box 71-B, New Orleans, LA 70126. Contact (504) 483-7675. *Assistance:* Business planning/Management/Technical

Maine

Maine Development Foundation, One Memoria Circle, Augusta, ME 04330. Contact (207) 622-6345. *Assistance:* Business planning/Information/Networking/Technical

Maine Growth Program, State Development Office, 193 State Street, State House Station 59, Augusta, ME 04333. *Contact* (207) 289-2656. *Assistance:* Financial

Maine State Development Office, 193 State Street, State House Station 59, Augusta, ME 04333. Contact (207) 289-5700. *Assistance:* Financial/Information/Networking

Small Business Development Center, Center for Research and Advanced Study, University of Southern Maine, 246 Deering Avenue, Portland, ME 04102. Contact Mr. Warren Purdy at (207) 780-4420. *Assistance:* Business planning/Information/Networking/Technical. *Eligibility:* Smaller businesses

The New Enterprise Institute, Center for Research and Advanced Study, University of Southern Maine, 246 Deering Avenue, Portland, ME 04102. Contact Dr. Richard J. Clarey at (207) 780-4420. *Assistance:* Business planning/Information/Management/Networking/Technical

Maryland

Development Credit Corporation of Maryland, Maryland Department of Economic and Community Development, 45 Calvert Street, Annapolis, MD 21401. Contact 1-800-654-7336. Those outside of Maryland should call (301) 269-3514.

Development Credit Fund, Inc., Maryland Department of Economic and Community Development, 45 Calvert Street, Annapolis, MD 21401. Contact 1-800-654-7336. Those outside of Maryland should call (301) 269-3514. *Assistance:* Financial. *Eligibility:* Minority businesses.

Maryland Energy Financing Administration, Maryland Department of Economic and Community Development, 45 Calvert Street, Annapolis, MD 21401. Contact 1-800-654-7336. Those outside of Maryland should call (301) 269-3514. *Assistance:* Financial

Maryland Business Assistance Center, Maryland Department of Economic and Community Development, 45 Calvert Street, Annapolis, MD 21401. Contact 1-800-654-7336. Those outside of Maryland should call (301) 269-3514. *Assistance:* Financial/Information/Networking

Maryland Office of Business and Industrial Development, Maryland Department of Economic and Community Development, 45 Calvert Street, Annapolis, MD 21401. Contact 1-800-654-7336. Those outside of Maryland should call (301) 269-3514. *Assistance:* Financial

Maryland Industrial Training Program, Maryland Department of Economic and Community Development, 45 Calvert Street, Annapolis, MD 21401. Contact 1-800-654-7336. Those outside of Maryland should call (301) 269-3514. *Assistance:* Technical

Maryland Industrial Development Financing Authority, Maryland Department of Economic and Community Development, 45 Calvert Street, Annapolis, MD 21401. Contact 1-800-654-7336. Those outside of Maryland should call (301) 269-3514. *Assistance:* Financial

Maryland Small Business Development Financing Authority, Maryland Department of Economic and Community Development, 45 Calvert Street, Annapolis, MD 21401. Contact 1-800-654-7336. Those outside of Maryland should call (301) 269-3514. *Assistance:* Financial. *Eligibility:* Smaller businesses

Technology Extension Service, University of Maryland, Engineering Research Center, College Park, MD. Contact Mr. W. Travis Walton at (301) 454-7941. *Assistance:* Information/Networking/Technical

Massachusetts

Center for Economic Development, 203 Hampshire House, University of Massachusetts, Amherst, MA 01003. Contact (413) 549-4930. *Assistance:* Business planning/Information/Networking/Technical

Community Development Finance Corporation, 131 State Street, Suite 600, Boston, MA 02109. Contact Mr. Charles T. Grigsby at (617) 742-0366. *Assistance:* Financial. *Eligibility:* Smaller businesses

Guaranteed Loan Program, Massachusetts Industrial Finance Agency, 400 Atlantic, Boston, MA 02210. Contact (617) 451-2477. *Assistance:* Financial. *Eligibility:* Smaller businesses

Massachusetts Business Development Corporation, One Liberty Square, Boston, MA 02109. Contact Mr. Kenneth J. Smith at (617) 723-7515. *Assistance:* Financial

Massachusetts Technology Development Corporation, 84 State Street, Suite 500, Boston, MA 02109. Contact Mr. John F. Hodgman at (617) 723-4920. *Assistance:* Financial

Massachusetts Industrial Finance Agency, 400 Atlantic, Boston, MA 02210. Contact (617) 451-2477. *Assistance:* Financial

Office of Training and Employment Policy, Executive Office of Economic Affairs, Office of Training & Employment Policy, Charles F. Hurley Bldg., 4th Floor, Government Center, Boston, MA 02114. Contact Ms. Catherine N. Stratton at (617) 727-2252. *Assistance:* Training/Financial

Site Inventory Tracking Exchange, Massachusetts Department of Commerce, 100 Cambridge Street, Boston, MA 02202. Contact (617) 727-3215. *Assistance:* Information

Spirit Line, Massachusetts Department of Commerce, 100 Cambridge Street, Boston, MA 02202. Contact (617) 727-3217 or (In State) 1-800-632-8181. *Assistance:* Information/Networking

Small Business Assistance Division, Massachusetts Department of Commerce, 100 Cambridge Street, Boston, MA 02202. Contact (617) 727-4005. *Assistance:* Business planning/Financial/Information/Networking. *Eligibility:* Smaller businesses

State Office of Minority Business Assistance, Massachusetts Department of Commerce, 100 Cambridge Street, 13th Floor, Boston, MA 02202. Contact (617) 727-8692. *Assistance:* Information/Networking. *Eligibility:* Minority businesses

The Office of Financial Development, Massachusetts Department of Commerce and Development, 100 Cambridge Street, Boston, MA 02202. Contact (617) 727-2932. *Assistance:* Information/Networking

Trade Development Program, Massport Foreign Trade Unite, 99 High Street, Boston, MA 02110. Contact (617) 973-5611. *Assistance:* Business planning/Financial/Information/Networking/Technical

Michigan

Center for Research on Integrated Manufacturing, University of Michigan College of Engineering, Chrysler Center, Ann Arbor, MI 48109. Contact Mr. Robert W. Schneider at (313) 763-5630. *Assistance:* Technical

Environmental Research Institute of Michigan, P.O. Box 8618, Ann Arbor, MI 48107. Contact Mr. George Peace at (313) 994-1200. *Assistance:* Technical

Food Industry Institute, 302 Food Science Building, Michigan State University, East Lansing, MI 48824. Contact Dr. Thayne Dutson at (517) 355-8295 or 355-8474. *Assistance:* Business planning/Information/Technical

Industrial Technology Institute, P.O. Box 1415, Ann Arbor, MI 48106. Contact (313) 769-4000. *Assistance:* Information/Technical

Industrial Development Institute, Michigan State University, 225 Administration Building, East Lansing, MI 48824. Contact Mr. Michael Martin at (517) 355-2180. *Assistance:* Business planning/Information/Networking/Technical

Institute of Science and Technology, The University of Michigan, 2200 Bonisteel Boulevard, Ann Arbor, MI 48109. Contact Mr. Larry R. Crockett at (313) 763-9000. *Assistance:* Business planning/Financial/Information/Networking/Technical

Metropolitan Center for High Technology, 2727 Second Avenue, Wayne State University, Detroit, MI 48201. Contact Mr. Bob Erlandson at (313) 963-0616. *Assistance:* Business planning/Information/Networking/Technical.

Michigan Biotechnology Institute, 276 Bessey Hall, Michigan State University, East Lansing, MI 48824. Contact Dr. Patrick Oriel at (517) 355-2277. *Assistance:* Business planning/Information/Networking/Technical

Michigan Department of Commerce–Technology Transfer Network, Hollister Building, #212, 106 West Allegan, Lansing, MI 48913. Contact (517) 373-7411. *Assistance:* Business planning/Financial/Information Networking/Technical

Michigan Energy and Resource Research Association, 328 Executive Plaza, 1200 Sixth Street, Detroit, MI 48226. Contact Mr. Todd Anuskiewicz at (313) 964-5030. *Assistance:* Information/Networking/Technical

Michigan Molecular Institute, 1910 West St. Andrews Road, Midland, MI 48640. Contact Mr. Gordon B. Carson at (517) 832-5553. *Assistance:* Technical

Michigan Strategic Fund, Michigan Department of Commerce, Hollister Building, #212, Lansing, MI 48913. Contact Mr. Gary Prince at (517) 373-7411. *Assistance:* Financial

Michigan Technology Deployment Service, Michigan Department of Commerce, Hollister Building, 106 West Allegan, Lansing, MI 48913. Contact Dr. Jack Russell at (517) 373-7411. *Assistance:* Financial/Information/Networking/Technical

Office of New Enterprise Services, Michigan Department of Commerce, Hollister Building, #212, 106 West Allegan, Lansing, MI 48913. Contact Mr. Gary Prince at (517) 373-7411. *Assistance:* Financial/Information/Networking

Minnesota

College of St. Thomas Entrepreneurial Enterprise Center, Peavey Center, 11 Peavey Road, Chaska, MN 55318. Contact (612) 448-3534. *Assistance:* Business planning/Information/Networking/Technical

Department of Energy and Economic Development, 900 American Center Building, 150 East Kellogg Boulevard, St. Paul MN 55101. Contact Mr. Mark Dayton at (612) 296-6424. *Assistance:* Business planning/Information/Networking/Technical

Department of Jobs and Training, 390 North Robert Street, St. Paul, MN 55101. Contact (612) 296-2536. *Assistance:* Information

Development Resources Program, 900 American Center Building, 150 East Kellogg Boulevard, St. Paul, MN 55101. Contact Mr. Harry Rosefelt at (612) 296-5010. *Assistance:* Financial/Information

Financial Management Division, Department of Energy and Economic Development Authority, 900 American Center Building, 150 East Kellogg Boulevard, St. Paul, MN 55101. Contact Mr. Edward J. Meyer at (612) 296-6616. *Assistance:* Financial

Inno-Media, 230 Tenth Avenue South, Minneapolis, MN 55415. Contact Mr. Gary Howe at (612) 342-4311. *Assistance:* Business planning/Information/Networking/Technical

Minneapolis Technology Enterprise Center, Inc., 1313 Fifth Street, S.E., Minneapolis, MN 55414. Contact (612) 623-7774. *Assistance:* Business planning/Information/Networking/Technical. *Eligibility:* Smaller businesses

Minnesota Cooperation Office, 965 Southgate Office Plaza, 5001 West 80th Street, Bloomington, MN 55437. Contact Mr. Theodore A. Johnson at (612) 830-1230. *Assistance:* Business planning/Information/Networking/Technical. *Eligibility:* Smaller businesses

Minnesota Office of Biomedical/Health Systems, 900 American Center Building, 150 East Kellogg Boulevard, St. Paul, MN 55101. Contact Mr. Michael C. O'Donnell at (612) 297-1388. *Assistance:* Information/Networking

Minnesota Project Innovation, 511 11th Avenue South, Minneapolis, MN 55415. Contact (612) 375-8084. *Assistance:* Financial/Information/Networking. *Eligibility:* Smaller businesses

Minnesota Trade Office, 90 West Plato Boulevard, St. Paul, MN 55107. Contact Mr. William C. Dietrich at (612) 296-4222 (Telex: 853610 MTOAG). *Assistance:* Information/Networking

Office of Project Management, 900 American Center Building, 150 East Kellogg Boulevard, St. Paul, MN 55101. Contact (612) 297-1160. *Assistance:* Financial

Office of Software Technology Development, 900 American Center Building, 150 East Kellogg Boulevard, St. Paul, MN 55101. Contact Ms. Rosemary T. Fruehling at (612) 297-1554. *Assistance:* Business planning/Financial/Information/Networking/Technical

Small Business Assistance Office, 900 American Center Building, 150 East Kellogg Boulevard, St. Paul, MN 55101. Contact Mr. Charles A. Schatter at (612) 296-3871. *Assistance:* Business planning/Information. *Eligibility:* Smaller businesses

University Research Consortium, Minneapolis Business and Technology Center, 511 11th Avenue South, Minneapolis, MN 55415. Contract Dr. Ellen Fitzgerald at (612) 341-0422. *Assistance:* Business planning/Information/Networking/Technical

Mississippi

Finance Division Department of Economic Development, P.O. Box 849, Jackson, MS 39205. Contact Mr. E. F. Mitcham at (601) 359-3437. *Assistance:* Financial

Industrial Division Department of Economic Development, P.O. Box 849, Jackson, MS 39205. Contact Mr. James W. Miller at (601) 359-3439. *Assistance:* Information/Networking

Institute for Technology Development, 3825 Ridgewood Rd., Jackson, MS 39211. Contact Neil Yawn at (601) 982-6456. *Assistance:* Information/Networking/Technical

Marketing Division Department of Economic Development, P.O. Box 849, Jackson, MS 39205. Contact Mr. Bill McGinnis at (601) 359-3607. *Assistance:* Technical

Mississippi Research and Development Center, 3825 Ridgewood Rd., Jackson, MS 39211. Contact Ms. Joyce Lewis at (601) 982-6231 (This is a toll free number within the state). *Assistance:* Business planning/Management/Networking/Technical

Missouri

Business and Industry Extension Service, 821 Clark Hall, University of Missouri-Columbia, Columbia, MO 65211. Contact Dr. Tom Henderson at (314) 882-4321. *Assistance:* Business planning/Information/Networking/Technical

Enterprise Zones Program, Missouri Division of Community and Economic Development, P.O. Box 118, Jefferson City, MO 65102. Contact Mr. Bill Blade at (314) 751-4241. *Assistance:* Financial/Technical

Existing Business Assistance, Missouri Division of Community and Economic Development, P.O. Box 118, Jefferson City, MO 65102. Contact Mr. Bill Blade at (314) 751-4241. *Assistance:* Information/Financial

Financial Programs, Missouri Division of Community and Economic Development, P.O. Box 118, Jefferson City, MO 65102. Contact Mr. Bill Blade at (314) 751-4241. *Assistance:* Financial

High Technology Program, Missouri Division of Community and Economic Development, P.O. Box 118, Jefferson City, MO 65102. Contact Mr. Bill Blade at (314) 751-4241. *Assistance:* Information/Technical

Industrial Development Time Deposit Program, Missouri Division of Community and Economic Development, P.O. Box 118, Jefferson City, MO 65102. Contact Mr. Bill Blade at (314) 751-4241. *Assistance:* Financial

Missouri Corporation for Science and Technology, P.O. Box 118, Jefferson City, MO 65102. Contact Mr. Jeffrey Coffey at (314) 751-3906. *Assistance:* Business planning/Financial/Information/Networking/Technical

On-the-Job Training, Division of Employment Security, P.O. Box 59, Jefferson City, MO 65104. Contact Mr. Bruce Carnet at (314) 751-3215. *Assistance:* Training

Montana

Advisory Council on Science & Technology, Department of Commerce, 1424 Ninth Avenue, Helena, MT 59620. Contact Mr. Frank Culver at (406) 444-5473. *Assistance:* Information/Networking/Technical

Agriculture Marketing Assistance, Department of Agriculture, Sixth & Roberts, Helena, MT 59620. Contact Mr. Steve Kalgaard at (406) 444-2402. *Assistance:* Information/Technical

Business Assistance Division, Department of Commerce, 1424 Ninth Avenue, Helena, MT 59620. Contact Mr. Gary Faulkner at (406) 444-4325. *Assistance:* Business planning/Information/Technical. *Eligibility:* Smaller businesses

Development Finance Technical Assistance, Business Assistance Division, Department of Commerce, 1424 Ninth Avenue, Helena, MT 59620. Contact Mr. Ron Preston at (406) 444-4323. *Assistance:* Business planning/Financial/Technical

Disadvantaged Business Enterprise and

Women Business Enterprise, Department of Highways, Capital Station, Helena, MT 59620. Contact Ms Peg M. Dolan at (406) 444-6332. *Assistance:* Technical

Industrial Start-Up Training Program, Job Service and Training Division, Department of Labor & Industry, P.O. Box 1728, Helena, MT 59624. Contact Mr. Gary Curtis at (406) 444-4500. *Assistance:* Training

International Export Assistance, Business Assistance Division, Department of Commerce, 1424 Ninth Avenue, Helena, MT 59620. Contact Mr. John J. Maloney at (406) 444-4380. *Assistance:* Technical. *Eligibility:* Smaller businesses

Product Marketing Assistance, Business Assistance Division, Department of Commerce, 1424 Ninth Avenue, Helena, MT 59620. Contact Mr. Gene Marcille at (406) 444-4392. *Assistance:* Information/Networking. *Eligibility:* Smaller businesses

Renewable Energy and Conservation Program, Grant & Loan Section, Department of Natural Resources & Conservation, 25 South Ewing, Helena, MT 59620. Contact Mr. Greg Mills at (406) 444-6774. *Assistance:* Financial/Information/Technical

Small Business Advocate and Business Licensing Center, Business Assistance Division, Department of Commerce, 1424 Ninth Avenue, Helena, MT 59620. Contact Mr. John W. Balsam at 1-800-221-8015. *Assistance:* Information. *Eligibility:* Smaller businesses

University Center for Business & Management Development, 445 Reid Hall, Montana State University, Bozeman, MT 59717. Contact Mr. Neal Nixon at (406) 994-2057. *Assistance:* Business planning/Information/Technical. *Eligibility:* Smaller businesses

Water Development Loan and Grant Programs, Water Development Bureau, Department of Natural Resources & Conservation, 28 South Rodney, Helena, MT 59620. Contact Ms. Caralee Cheney at (406) 444-6668. *Assistance:* Financial

Nebraska

Nebraska Food Processing Center, 134 Filley Hall, University of Nebraska-Lincoln, East Campus, Lincoln, NE 68583–0919. Contact Dr. Lowell D. Satterlee at (402) 472-2831. *Assistance:* Information/Networking/Technical

Nebraska Technical Assistance Center, W191 Nebraska Hall, University of Nebraska-Lincoln, Lincoln, NE 68588–0535. Contact Mr. Michael W. Riley, Director at (402) 472-5600. *Assistance:* Information/Networking/Technical

Nevada

City of Las Vegas Loan Program, 400 E. Stewart, Las Vegas, NV 89101. Contact Mr. Jack

Thomason at (702) 386-6551. *Assistance:* Financial

Commission on Economic Development, Capitol Complex, 600 E. William, Suite 203, Carson City, NV 89710. Contact Mr. Andrew P. Grose at (702) 885-4325. *Assistance:* Financial

Nevada Small Business Development Center, University of Nevada, College of Business Administration, Business Building, Room 411, Reno, NV 89557–0016. Contact Mr. Sam Males at (702) 784-1717. *Assistance:* Business planning / Information / Management / Technical. *Eligibility:* Smaller businesses

State Office of Community Services, Capitol Complex, Carson City, NV 89710. Contact (702) 885-4420. *Assistance:* Financial/Technical

White Pine County Loan Programs, P.O. Box 1002, Ely, NV 89301. Contact Ms. Karen Rajala at (702) 289-8841. *Assistance:* Financial

New Hampshire

New Hampshire Office of Industrial Development, Department of Resources and Economic Development, P.O. Box 856, Concord, NH 03301. Contact Mr. Paul H. Guilderson at (603) 271-2591. *Assistance:* Business planning / Financial / Information / Networking / Technical

New Hampshire Office of Industrial Development-Export Assistance Program, Department of Resources and Economic Development, P.O. Box 856, Concord, NH 03301. Contact Mr. Paul H. Guilderson at (603) 271-2591. *Assistance:* Business planning/Information/Networking/Technical

Office of Small Business Programs, 110 McConnell Hall, University of New Hampshire, Durham, NH 03824. Contact Mr. Craig R. Seymour at (603) 862-3556. *Assistance:* Business planning/Information/Technical

New Jersey

New Jersey Commission on Science and Technology, 225 W. State Street, CN 542, Trenton, NJ 08625. Contact Mr. Edward Cohen at (609) 984-1671. *Assistance:* Financial. *Eligibility:* Smaller businesses

New Jersey Economic Development Authority, 200 South Warren Street, Capital Place One, CN 990, 6th Floor, Trenton, NJ 08625. Contact Mr. James J. Hughes at (609) 292-1800. *Assistance:* Financial/Technical

New Jersey State Office of Minority Business Enterprise, Department of Commerce and Economic Development, 1 West State Street, Trenton, NJ 08625. Contact Mr. Lee L. Davis at (609) 292-0500. *Assistance:* Business planning/Financial/Information/Networking. *Eligibility:* Smaller businesses and minority businesses

Office of Business Advocacy, New Jersey Department of Commerce and Economic Development, New Jersey National Bank Building, Room 604, #1 West State Street, CN 823, Trenton, NJ 08625. Contact Paul Krane at (609) 292-0700. *Assistance:* Information/Networking/Technical

Office of Industrial Development, New Jersey Department of Commerce and Economic Development, 1 West State Street, CN 823, Trenton, NJ 08625. Contact Mr. Charles Connell at (609) 292-2462. *Assistance:* Financial/Information/Networking/Technical

Office of Small Business Assistance, New Jersey Department of Commerce and Economic Development, 1 West State Street, CN 823, Trenton, NJ 08625. Contact (609) 984-4442. *Assistance:* Business planning/Financial/Information/Networking/Technical. *Eligibility:* Smaller businesses and minority businesses

Rutgers University Technical Assistance Program, Rutgers University, 180 University Avenue, Newark, NJ 07102. Contact Ms. Patricia Johnson at (201) 648-5891. *Assistance:* Business planning/Technical. *Eligibility:* Smaller businesses

New Mexico

Agricultural Marketing Development Office, New Mexico Department of Agriculture, New Mexico State University, P.O. Box 5600, Las Cruces, NM 88003. Contact (505) 646-4929. *Assistance:* Technical

Business Assistance and Resource Center, 1920 Lomas, N.E., Albuquerque, NM 87131. Contact Mr. James T. Ray at (505) 277-3541. *Assistance:* Business planning/Information/Management/Technical

Center for Business Research and Services, New Mexico State University, Box 3CR, Las Cruces, NM 88003. Contact (505) 646-1434. *Assistance:* Business planning/Information/Technical

Development Training Programs, Economic Development and Tourism Department, Bataan Memorial Building, Santa Fe, NM 87503. Contact (505) 827-6200. *Assistance:* Training

Energy Research and Development Institute, 1220 South Street, Francis Drive #358, Santa Fe, NM 87501. Contact (505) 827-5886. *Assistance:* Financial

Industrial and Agricultural Finance Authority, Economic Development and Tourism Department, Bataan Memorial Building, Santa Fe, NM 87503. Contact (505) 827-6004. *Assistance:* Financial

New Mexico Solar Industry Development Corporation, 5301 Central N.E., Suite 705, Albuquerque, NM 87108. Contact (505) 262-2247. Contact (505) 262-2247. *Assistance:* Information/Networking/Technical

The Economic Incentive Loan Program, Economic Development and Tourism Department, Bataan Memorial Building, Room 201 EDB, Santa Fe, NM 87503. Contact (505) 827-6200.

Technology Innovation Centers, Anderson School of Management, University of New Mexico, Albuquerque, NM 87131. Contact (505) 277-2009. *Assistance:* Business planning/Financial/Information/Networking/Technical

New York

Centers for Advanced Technology Program, New York State Science and Technology Foundation, 99 Washington Avenue, Albany, NY 12210. Contact Mr. William J. Donohue at (518) 474-4347. *Assistance:* Information/Technical

Corporation for Innovation Development Program, New York State Science and Technology Foundation, 99 Washington Avenue, Albany, NY 12210. Contact (518) 474-4349. *Assistance:* Financial

Division for Small Business, New York State Department of Commerce, 320 Park Avenue, New York, NY 10169. Contact Mr. Raymond R. Norat at (212) 309-0400. *Assistance:* Business planning/Financial/Information/Management/Networking/Technical. *Eligibility:* Smaller businesses

Economic Development and Technical Assistance Center, State University of New York, Plattsburg, NY 12901. Contact Steven Hyde at (518) 654-2214. *Assistance:* Business planning/Information/Technical

Industrial Innovation Extension Service, New York State Science and Technology Foundation, 99 Washington Avenue, Albany, NY 12210. Contact Mr. H. Graham Jones at (518) 474-4349. *Assistance:* Information/Networking/Technical

New York State Small Business Development Center, State University of New York, State University Plaza, Albany, NY 12246. Contact Mr. James L. King at (518) 473-5398. *Assistance:* Business planning/Information/Management/Technical. *Eligibility:* Smaller businesses

New York State Small Business Innovation Research (SBIR) Promotion Program, 99 Washington Avenue, Albany, NY 12210. Contact Mr. H. Graham Jones at (518) 474-4349. *Assistance:* Financial/Information. *Eligibility:* Smaller businesses

Regional Technology Development Organization, New York State Science and Technology Foundation, 99 Washington Avenue, Albany, NY 12210. Contact Mr. H. Graham Jones at (518) 474-4349. *Assistance:* Information/Management/Networking/Technical

The Port Authority of New York and New Jersey, Economic Development Department, One World Trade Center-745, New York, NY 10048. Contact (800) 221-5468 or (212) 466-8848. *Assistance:* Financial

North Carolina

Center for Improving Mountain Living, Western Carolina University, Cullowhee, NC 28723. Contact Mr. Tom McClure at (704) 227-7492. *Assistance:* Technical

Minority Business Development Agency, 430 N. Salisbury Street, Raleigh, NC 27611. Contact Mr. Julian Brown at (919) 733-2712. *Assistance:* Business planning/Information/Networking/Technical. *Eligibility:* Minority businesses

National Minority Suppliers Development Council, P.O. Box 9156, Charlotte, NC 28299. Contact (704) 372-8732. *Assistance:* Business planning/Information/Networking/Technical. *Eligibility:* Minority businesses

North Carolina Small Business Development Centers, North Carolina Department of Community College, 20 Education Building, Raleigh, NC 27611. Contact Dr. Jean Overton at (919) 733-6385. *Assistance:* Business planning / Information / Networking / Technical. *Eligibility:* Smaller businesses

North Carolina Technological Development authority, 430 N. Salisbury Street, Raleigh, NC 27611. Contact Mr. Chilton Rogers at (919) 733-7022. *Assistance:* Financial/Information. *Eligibility:* Smaller businesses

Small Business and Technology Development Center, 820 Clay Street, Raleigh, NC 27605. Contact (919) 733-6343 or 1-800-258-0862. *Assistance:* Business planning/Financial/Technical

North Dakota

Bank of North Dakota, 700 East Main Avenue, Bismarck, ND 58501. Contact Mr. Herb Thorndal at (701) 224-5602. *Assistance:* Financial

Center for Economic Development, North Dakota State University, Fargo, ND 58102. Contact Dr. Robert L. Sullivan at (70) 237-8873. *Assistance:* Technical. *Eligibility:* Smaller businesses

Center for Innovation and Business Development, University of North Dakota, Engineering Experiment Station, Grand Forks, ND 58202. Contact Mr. Bruce Giovig at (701) 777-3132. *Assistance:* Business planning/Information / Networking / Technical. *Eligibility:* Smaller businesses

North Dakota Economic Development Commission, Liberty Memorial Building, Bismarck, ND 58505. Contact (701) 224-2810. *Assis-*

tance: Financial/Information/Networking/Technical

Small Business Development Division, North Carolina Department of Commerce, 430 North Salisbury Street, Raleigh, NC 27611. Contact Mr. Lewis Myers at (919) 733-7980. *Assistance:* Business planning/Financial/Information/Networking. *Eligibility:* Smaller businesses

State Development Credit Corporation, Box 1212, Bismarck, ND 58502. Contact Mr. William Smith at (701) 223-2288. *Assistance: Financial. Eligibility:* Smaller businesses

Ohio

Ohio Technology Transfer Organization, 1712 Neil Avenue, Columbus, OH 43210. Contact Dr. Robert E. Bailey at (614) 422-5485. *Assistance:* Business planning/Information/Networking/Technical

The Thomas Edison Program, P.O. Box 1001, Columbus, OH 43266-0413. Contact Mr. Christopher Coburn at (614) 466-3086. *Assistance:* Financial/Information/Technical

Urban Economic Development Center, Cleveland State University, Euclid Avenue at East 24th Street, Cleveland, OH 44115. Contact Mr. David Garrison at (216) 687-2134. *Assistance:* Business planning/Management/Networking/Technical

Oklahoma

Oklahoma Small Business Development Center, 517 West University Boulevard, Durant, OK 74701. Contact Mr. Lloyd Miller at (405) 924-0277. *Assistance:* Business planning/Financial/Information/Networking/Technical. *Eligibility:* Smaller businesses

Association of Central Oklahoma Governments, 4801 Classen, Suite 200, Oklahoma City, OK 73118. Contact Mr. Greg Wallace at (405) 848-8961. *Assistance:* Information/Networking/Technical

Central Oklahoma Economic Development District, 400 N. Bell, Shawnee, OK 74801. Contact (405) 273-6410. *Assistance:* Financial/Information

International Trade Services, 440 S. Houston, Room 205, Tulsa, OK 74127. Contact (918) 521-2865. *Assistance:* Information/Networking

Kerr Industrial Applications Center, Southeastern Oklahoma State University, Sta. A, Box 2584, Durant, OK 74701-2584. Contact Dr. Tom J. McRorey at (405) 924-6822. *Assistance:* Information/Technical

Oklahoma Industrial Finance Authority, 4042 N. Lincoln, Oklahoma City, OK 73105. Contact (405) 521-2182. *Assistance:* Financial

Rural Enterprises, 10 Waldron Drive, P.O. Box 1335, Durant, OK 74702-1335. Contact Mr. Lloyd Collins at (405) 924-5094. *Assistance:* Business planning/Financial/Information/Networking/Technical

South Western Oklahoma Development Authority, P.O. Box 569, Building 400, Clinton-Sherman Industrial Air Park, Burns Flats, OK 73624. Contact (405) 562-4884. *Assistance:* Financial/Information/Technical

Technology Transfer Center, 1515 West Main, P.O. Box 1713, Durant, OK 74702-1713. Contact (405) 920-0132. *Assistance:* Information/Networking

Training for Industrial Production Division, Oklahoma Department of Economic Development, State Vo-Tech Department, 4042 N. Lincoln Blvd., Oklahoma City, OK 73105. Contact (405) 521-2195. *Assistance:* Training

University Center of Oklahoma, East Central Oklahoma State University, Ada, OK 74820. Contact Mr. Thomas Beebe at (405) 332-8000. *Assistance:* Technical. *Eligibility:* Smaller businesses

Oregon

Business Information Division, Oregon Economic Development Department, 595 Cottage Street, N.W., Salem, OR 97310. Contact (503) 373-1200. *Assistance:* Financial/Information

The Oregon Productivity Center, School of Industrial and General Engineering, Oregon State University, Corvallis, OR 97331. Contact Dr. James Riggs at (503) 754-4645. *Assistance:* Business planning/Information/Technical

Oregon Small Business Development Network, 1059 Willamette St., Eugene, OR 97401. Contact Mr. Wendell Anderson at (503) 687-9125. *Assistance:* Business planning/Information/Networking/Technical. *Eligibility:* Smaller businesses

International Trade Division, Oregon Economic Development Department, 595 Cottage Street, N.W., Salem, OR 97310. Contact (503) 373-1200. *Assistance:* Business planning/Information

Pennsylvania

Appalachian Regional Commission Program, Department of Commerce, Bureau of Appalachian Development & State Grants, 467 Forum Bldg., Harrisburg, PA 17120. Contact Paul Hallacher at (717) 787-7120. *Assistance:* Financial/Technical

Ben Franklin Partnership–Challenge Grants/ Advanced Technology Centers, Department of Commerce, 463 Forum Building, Harrisburg, PA 17120. Contact Mr. Roger Tellefsen at (717) 787-4147. *Assistance:* Business planning / Financial / Information / Networking /Technical

Ben Franklin Partnership-Research "Seed" Grants, Department of Commerce, 463 Forum Building, Harrisburg, PA 17120. Contact Mr. Roger Tellefsen at (717) 787-4147. *Assistance:* Financial. *Eligibility:* Smaller businesses

Ben Franklin Partnership–Small Business Incubator Program, Department of Commerce, 463 Forum Building, Harrisburg, PA 17120. Contact Mr. Roger Tellefsen at (717) 787-4147. *Assistance:* Business planning/Financial/Information/Networking/Technical. *Eligibility:* Smaller businesses

Business Infrastructure Development Program, Department of Commerce, Bureau of Appalachian Development and State Grants, 467 Forum Building, Harrisburg, PA 17120. Contact Mr. William Logan at (717) 787-7120. *Assistance:* Financial

Customized Job Training Program, Department of Education, Bureau of Vocational and Adult Education, 6th Floor, 333 Market Street, Harrisburg, PA 17126-0333. Contact Mr. Bill Krash at (717) 787-5293. *Assistance:* Financial/Technical

Employee Ownership Assistance Program, Department of Commerce, Bureau of Economic Assistance, 405 Forum Building, Harrisburg, PA 17120. Contact Mr. Alan Welder at (717) 787-1909. *Assistance:* Financial/Technical

Office of Minority Business Enterprise, Department of Commerce, 491 Forum Building, Harrisburg, PA 17120. Contact Mr. Clarence Smith at (717) 783-1301. *Assistance:* Business planning/Financial/Information/Networking. *Eligibility:* Minority businesses

Pennsylvania Capital Loan Fund, Department of Commerce, Bureau of Economic Assistance, Room 405 Forum Building, Harrisburg, PA 17120. Contact: Mr. Alan Welder at (717) 787-1909. *Assistance:* Financial *Eligibility:* Smaller businesses

Pennsylvania Energy Development Authority, Department of Commerce, 462 Forum Building, Harrisburg, PA 17120. Contact Mr. Bill Roth at (717) 787-6554. *Assistance:* Financial

Pennsylvania Industrial Development Authority, Department of Commerce, Bureau of Economic Assistance, 405 Forum Building, Harrisburg, PA 17120. Contact Mr. Gerald Kapp at (717) 787-6245. *Assistance:* Financial

Pennsylvania Technical Assistance Program, The Pennsylvania State University, 501 J Orvis Keller Building, University Park, PA 16802. Contact Mr. Roy Marlow at (814) 865-0427. *Assistance:* Information/Technical

Revenue Bond and Mortgage Program, Department of Commerce, Bureau of Economic Assistance, Room 405 Forum Building, Harrisburg, PA 17120. Contact Mr. Alan Welder at (717) 787-1909. *Assistance:* Financial

Pennsylvania Minority Business Development Authority, Department of Commerce, 405 Forum Building, Harrisburg, PA 17120. Contact Mr. William Peterson at (717) 783-1127. *Assistance:* Business planning/Financial/Technical. *Eligibility:* Minority businesses

Seed "Venture" Capital Fund, Ben Franklin Partnership, Department of Commerce, 463 Forum Building, Harrisburg, PA 17120. Contact Mr. Roger Tellefsen at (717) 787-4147. *Assistance:* Financial

Small Business Action Center, Department of Commerce, 438 Forum Building, Harrisburg, PA 17120. Contact Ms. Jill Morrow at (717) 783-5700. *Assistance:* Business planning/Information/Networking/Technical. *Eligibility:* Smaller businesses

Rhode Island

Brown Venture Forum, Box 1949, Providence, RI 02912. Contact (401) 863-3528. *Assistance:* Business planning/Information/Networking

Export Trade Program, Rhode Island Department of Economic Development, 7 Jackson Walkway, Providence, RI 02903. Contact (401) 277-2601. *Assistance:* Information/Networking/Technical

Federal Procurement Program, Rhode Island Department of Economic Development, 7 Jackson Walkway, Providence, RI 02903. Contact (401) 277-2601. *Assistance:* Financial

Financing Program, Rhode Island Department of Economic Development, 7 Jackson Walkway, Providence, RI 02903. Contact (401) 277-2601. *Assistance:* Financial

Job Development and Training Division, Rhode Island Department of Economic Development, 7 Jackson Walkway, Providence, RI 02903. Contact (401) 277-2090. *Assistance:* Training

Marketing Division, Rhode Island Department of Economic Development, 7 Jackson Walkway, Providence, RI 02903. Contact (401) 277-2601. *Assistance:* Information/Technical

Minority Business Program, Rhode Island Department of Economic Development, 7 Jackson Walkway, Providence, RI 02903. Contact (401) 277-2601. *Assistance:* Information/Networking/Technical. *Eligibility:* Minority businesses

Opportunities Industrialization Center, 1 Hilton Street, Providence, RI 02905. Contact (401) 272-4400. *Assistance:* Financial/Information/Technical

Rhode Island Partnership for Science and Technology, Rhode Island Department of Economic Development, 7 Jackson Walkway, Providence, RI 02903. Contact Mr. Bruce R. Lang at (401) 277-2601. *Assistance:* Financial

Rhode Island Department of Environmental Management, 22 Hayes Street, Providence, RI 02908. Contact (401) 277-2781. *Assistance:* Information

Rhode Island Small Business Development Center, Bryant College, Smithfield, RI 02917. Contact (401) 232-6111. *Assistance:* Business planning/Information/Technical. *Eligibility:* Smaller businesses

University of Rhode Island Business Assistance Programs, University of Rhode Island, Kingston, RI. Contact (401) 792-4320. *Assistance:* Information/Technical

South Carolina

Agriculture Marketing Division, F & V Market News, P.O. Box 13531–0531, State Farmers Market, Columbia, SC 29201. Contact (803) 758–2293. *Assistance:* Information

Business Assistance and Services Information Center, State Development Board, 1301 Gervais Street, P.O. Box 927, Columbia, SC 29202. Contact (803) 758-3046 (or toll free in S.C. 800-922-6684). *Assistance:* Financial/Information/Networking/Technical

Economic Development and Technical Assistance Center, Benedict College, Harden & Blanding Streets, Columbia, SC 29204. Contact (803) 256-4220. *Assistance:* Business planning/Information/Technical

Job Creation Network–Incubators, Business Assistance and Services Information Center, South Carolina State Development Board, P.O. Box 927, Columbia, SC 29202. Contact Mr. P. M. Smurthwaite at (803) 758-3046 or 1-800-922-6684 (in-state). *Assistance:* Business planning/Financial/Information/Networking/Technical

Office of Small and Minority Business Assistance, 1205 Pendleton Street, Suite 305, Columbia, SC 29201. Contact (803) 758-5560. *Assistance:* Business planning/Information/Networking/Technical

Planning and Research Division, S.C. State Development Board, P.O. Box 927, Columbia, SC 29202. Contact (803) 758-2411. *Assistance:* Information

Small Business Development Center, College of Business Administration, University of South Carolina, Columbia, SC 29208. Contact Mr. William F. Littlejohn at (803) 777-4907. *Assistance:* Business planning/Information/Networking/Technical. *Eligibility:* Smaller businesses

The South Carolina Jobs Economic Development Authority, 1203 Gervais Street, Columbia, SC 29201. Contact (803) 758-2094. *Assistance:* Financial/Technical

South Dakota

Division of International Trade, University of South Dakota, School of Business, Vermillion, SD 57069. Contact Mr. John Huminiski at (605) 677-5455. *Assistance:* Information/Networking/Technical

Financing Assistance Program, Department of State Development, 711 Wells, Box 6000, Pierre, SD 57501. Contact (605) 773-5032. *Assistance:* Business planning/Financial/Information/Technical. *Eligibility:* Smaller businesses

Procurement Assistance Program, Department of State Development, 711 Wells, Box 6000, Pierre, SD 57501. Contact (605) 773-5032. *Assistance:* Business planning/Information/Networking/Technical

Tennessee

Office of Minority Business Enterprise, 7th Floor, 320 6th Avenue North, Nashville, TN 37219–5305. Contact (615) 741-2545. *Assistance:* Business planning/Financial/Information/Technical. *Eligibility:* Minority businesses

Regional Economic Development Center, 226 Johnson Hall, Memphis State University, Memphis, TN 38152. Contact (901) 454-2056. *Assistance:* Business planning/Information/Technical

The University of Tennessee Center for Industrial Services, Suite 401, Capitol Boulevard Building, Nashville, TN 37219. Contact (615) 242-2456. *Assistance:* Business planning/Financial/Technical

Tennessee Technology Foundation, P.O. Box 23184, Knoxville, TN 37933. Contact Dr. David A. Patterson at (615) 966-2804. *Assistance:* Financial/Information/Networking/Technical. *Eligibility:* Smaller businesses and minority businesses

Small Business Office, Department of Economic and Community Development, Rachel Jackson Building, 7th Floor, 320 6th Avenue North, Nashville, TN 37219–5308. Contact Mr. John E. Smith at (615) 741-2626. *Assistance:* Financial/Information/Networking/Technical. *Eligibility:* Smaller businesses

Texas

Center for Economic Development, University of Texas at San Antonio, San Antonio, TX 78285. Contact (512) 224-1945. *Assistance:* Business planning/Information/Management/Technical

Economic Development Center, Texas South University, School of Management, 3100 Cleburne Avenue, Houston, TX 77004. Contact (713) 52-7785. *Assistance:* Business planning/

Information/Technical. *Elibility:* Smaller businesses

Center for Technology Development and Transfer, EMS 103, University of Texas, Austin, TX 78712. Contact Dr. Helen Dorsey at (512) 471-7501. *Assistance:* Licensing inventions

Institute for Ventures in New Technology, Texas Engineering Experiment Station, The Texas A&M University System, College Station, TX 77843. Contact Mr. Franklin Sekera at (409) 845-0538. *Assistance:* Financial

Loan Programs, Texas Economic Development Commission, 410 East 5th Street, P.O. Box 12728, Capitol Station, Austin, TX 78711. Contact (512) 472-5059. *Assistance:* Financial

Small Business Loan Programs, Texas Economic Development Commission, Finance Department, 410 East 5th Street, P.O. Box 12728, Capitol Station, Austin, TX 78711. Contact (512) 472-5059. *Assistance:* Financial. *Eligibility:* Smaller businesses

Technology Training Board, Texas Economic Development Commission, P.O. Box 12728, Capitol Station, Austin, TX 78711. Contact Dr. Helen Dorsey at (512) 472-5059. *Assistance:* Information

Texas Research and Technology Foundation, Suite 345, 8207 Callaghan Road, San Antonio, TX 78230. Contact (512) 342-6063. *Assistance:* Financial/Information/Networking/Technical

Utah

Business Development Program, Utah Business and Economic Development Division, Room 6150, State Office Building, Salt Lake City, UT 84114. Contact (801) 533-5325. *Assistance:* Financial/Information/Networking/Technical. *Eligibility:* Smaller businesses

Utah Business Development Centers, University of Utah, Graduate School of Business, Room 410 BUC, Salt Lake City, UT 84112. Contact Mr. James Bean at (801) 581-7905. *Assistance:* Business planning/Financial/Information/Technical

Utah Innovation Center, 417 Wakara Way, Research Park, Salt Lake City, UT 84108. Contact Dr. Wayne S. Brown at (801) 584-2500. *Assistance:* Business planning/Financial/Information/Networking/Technical

Utah Technology Finance Corporation, 417 Wakara Way, Suite 150, Salt Lake City, UT 84108. Contact Mr. Grant Cannon at (801) 583-8832. *Assistance:* Financial. *Eligibility:* Smaller businesses

Vermont

Entrepreneurship Program, Division of Economic Development, Pavilion Building, 109 State Street, Montpelier, VT 05602. Contact Mr. Curt Carter at (802) 828-3221. *Assistance:* Business planning/Information/Networking/Technical

Export Development Program, Division of Economic Development, Pavilion Building, 109 State Street, Montpelier, VT 05602. Contact Mr. Graene Freeman at (802) 828-3221. *Assistance:* Business planning/Financial/Information/Networking/Technical

Small Business Resource and Referral Service, Division of Economic Development, Pavilion Building, 109 State Street, Montpelier, VT 05602. Contact Ms. Cindy Jones at (802) 828-3221. *Assistance:* Information/Networking. *Eligibility:* Smaller businesses

Vermont Business Expansion Program, Division of Economic Development, Pavilion Building, 109 State Street, Montpelier, VT 05602. Contact Mr. Steve Parsons at (802) 828-3221. *Assistance:* Business planning/Financial/Information/Networking/Technical

Vermont Trading Program, Division of Economic Development, Pavilion Building, 109 State Street, Montpelier, VT 05602. Contact Mr. Lou Dworshak at (802) 828-3221. *Assistance:* Training

Virginia

Center for Innovative Technology, P.O. Box 15373, Herndon, VA 22070–9998. Contact (703) 689-3000. *Assistance:* Financial/Information/Networking

Community Organization for Minority Economic Development, Planning and Community Services, 901 Main Street, Level B, Lynchburg, VA 24504. Contact (804) 846-2778. *Assistance:* Business planning/Management/Technical. *Eligibility:* Minority businesses

Division of Energy, Department of Mines, Minerals, and Energy, 2210 West Broad Street, Richmond, VA 23220. Contact (804) 257-0330. *Assistance:* Information

Export Development–International Marketing Division, Virginia Department of Economic Development, 1000 Washington Bldg., Richmond, VA 23219. Contact (804) 786-3791. *Assistance:* Information/Technical

George Mason Institute, George Mason University, 4400 University Drive, Fairfax, VA 22030. Contact Mr. Tom Ingram at (703) 323-2568. *Assistance:* Business planning/Information/Networking

Hampton University Business Assistance Center, P.O. Box 6148, Hampton, VA 23668. Contact (804) 727-5570. *Assistance:* Business planning/Information/Management/Technical

Norfolk Business Development Center, Plaza One Building, Suite 801, 1 Main Plaza East, Norfolk VA 23510. Contact (804) 627-5254. *Assistance:* Business planning/Information/

Management/Technical. *Eligibility:* Minority businesses

Office of Small Business and Financial Services. Virginia Department of Economic Development, 1000 Washington Building, Richmond, VA 23219. Contact Small Business Coordinator at (804) 786-3791. *Assistance:* Financial/Information/Management/Networking/Technical

The Metropolitan Business League, 214 East Clay Street, P.O. Box 26751, Richmond, VA 23261. Contact (804) 649-7473. *Assistance:* Business planning/Technical. *Eligibility:* Minority businesses

Tidewater Regional Minority Purchasing Council, Inc., 142 West York Street, Suite 308, Norfolk, VA 23510. Contact (804) 627-8471. *Assistance:* Information/Networking/Technical

Virginia Employment Commission, 703 East Main Street, P.O. Box 1358, Richmond, VA 23233. Contact (804) 786-8223. *Assistance:* Information/Technical

Virginia Port Authority, 600 World Trade Center, Norfolk, VA 23510. Contact (804) 623-8000. *Assistance:* Information/Technical

Virginia Regional Minority Supplier Development Council, 1214 Westover Hills Blvd., Suite 208, Richmond, VA 23225. Contact (804) 231-1023. *Assistance:* Technical. *Eligibility:* Minority businesses

Virginia State, Office of Minority Business Enterprise, Ninth Street Office Building, Room 1028, Richmond, VA 23219. Contact (804) 786-5560. *Assistance:* Information/Technical. *Eligibility:* Minority businesses

Washington

Business and Government Relations, Department of Trade and Economic Development, 101 General Administration Building, AX-13, Olympia, WA 98504. Contact Ms. Sandra Granger at 1-800-237-1233 (Toll free in the state) (206) 753-5634. *Assistance:* Information/Networking

Community Development Finance Program, Department of Community Development, 9th & Columbia Bldg., Olympia, WA 98504. Contact Mr. Chris Barada at 1-800-562-5677. *Assistance:* Financial

Department of Revenue, Department of Revenue, General Administration Building, Olympia, WA 98504. Contact (206) 753-5540. *Assistance:* Financial

Development Loan Fund, Department of Community Development, 9th & Columbia Bldg., Olympia, WA 98504. Contact Ms. Joan Machlis at (206) 754-8976. *Assistance:* Financial

Domestic and International Trade Development, Department of Trade and Economic Development, 312 First Avenue North, Seattle, WA 98109. Contact Mr. Paul Mastilak at (206) 464-6283. *Assistance:* Information/Networking/Technical

Job Skills Program, Commission for Vocational Education, Building 17, Airdustrial Park, Olympia, WA 98504. Contact Mr. Tom Lopp at 1-800-233-6267 (Toll free within the state) (206) 754-3321. *Assistance:* Training

Job Training Partnership Program, Department of Employment Security, 212 Maple Park, Olympia, WA 98504. Contact Mr. Gary Gallwas at 1-800-233-6267 (Toll free in the state) (206) 754-1024. *Assistance:* Training

License Information Service, Business License Center, Department of Licensing, Eastside Plaza, PB-01, 1300 Quince Street, Olympia, WA 98504. Contact 1-800-562-8203 (Toll free in the state) (206) 753-2784. *Assistance:* Information

Small Business Assistance Program, State Board for Community College Education, 319 East Seventh Avenue, Olympia, WA 98504. Contact Mr. Ron Fowler at (206) 753-2000. *Assistance:* Training. *Eligibility:* Smaller businesses

Small Business Development Center, College of Business and Economics, Pullman, WA 99164–4740. Contact Mr. Lyle M. Anderson at (509) 335-1576. *Assistance:* Business planning/Information/Networking/Technical

Office of Minority and Women's Business Enterprises, FK-11, 406 South Water, Olympia, WA 98504. Contact (206) 753-9693. *Assistance:* Technical. *Eligibility:* Smaller businesses and minority businesses

Small Business Export Finance Assistance Center, Department of Trade and Economic Development, 312 First Avenue North, Seattle, WA 98109. Contact Mr. Robert Sebastian at (206) 464-7123. *Assistance:* Business planning/Financial/Networking

West Virginia

Center for Regional Progress, Marshall University, Huntington, WV 25701. Contact Mr. Byron D. Carpenter at (304) 696-6797. *Assistance:* Business planning/Technical

West Virginia Division of Small Business, Governor's Office of Community and Industrial Development, State Capitol Complex, Charleston, WV 25305. Contact Ms. Eloise Jack at 1-800-225-5982. Those out of state should call (304) 348-2960. *Assistance:* Business planning/Financial/Information/Networking/Technical. *Eligibility:* Smaller businesses

Wisconsin

Bureau of Business Development Services, Department of Development, 123 West Washington Ave., P.O. Box 7970, Madison, WI 53707. Contact Mr. Mim Gruentzel at (608) 266-0165. *Assistance:* Business planning/Information/Networking/Technical

Permit Information Center, Department of Development, 123 West Washington Ave., P.O. Box 7970, Madison, WI 53707. Contact Mr. Phillip Albert at 1-800-435-7287. Those outside the state should call (608) 266-9869. *Assistance:* Information/Networking

Wyoming

Division of Manpower Planning, Barrett Building, 3rd Floor, Cheyenne, WY 82002. Contact Mr. David Griffin at (307) 777-7671. *Assistance:* Training/Financial/Technical

Economic Development and Stabilization Board, Herschler Building, Third Floor, Cheyenne, WY 82002. Contact (307) 777-7285. *Assistance:* Financial/Information/Technical

Wyoming Business Development Center, Casper College, 125 College Drive, Casper, WY 82601. Contact Mr. Mac Bryant at (307) 268-2552. *Assistance:* Business planning/Financial/Information/Management/Networking/Technical. *Eligibility:* Smaller businesses

Wyoming Community Development Authority, P.O. Box 634, Casper, WY 82602. Contact Mr. Mark Peterson at (307) 265-0603. *Assistance:* Financial/Networking/Technical

State Data Center Program of the Bureau of the Census

Access to the many statistical products available from the Bureau of the Census is provided through the services of the joint federal-state cooperative State Data Center Program. Through the Program, the Bureau furnishes statistical products, training in the data access and use, technical assistance, and consultation to states which, in turn, disseminate the products and provide assistance in their use.

Additional information on the State Data Program and a list of the State Data Centers can be obtained by contacting the User Services staff in any of the Bureau's regional offices or by calling the Data User Services Division of the Bureau of the Census at 301-763-1580.

Alabama*

STATE CAPITOL, MONTGOMERY, AL 36130 (205) 261-3599

---

* For Small Business Administration offices, see page 262.

INFORMATION OFFICES

Commerce/Economic Development
Alabama Development Office
135 S. Union Street
Montgomery, AL 36130
Department of Economic & Community Affairs
3465 Norman Bridge Road
Montgomery, AL 36105
Corporate
Secretary of State
State Capitol
Montgomery, AL 36130
Taxation
Department of Revenue
Administrative Building
64 N. Union Street
Montgomery, AL 36130
State Chamber of Commerce
Alabama Chamber of Commerce
468 S. Perry Street
P.O. Box 76
Montgomery, AL 36101
International Commerce
Department of International Trade
3465 Norman Bridge Road
P.O. Box 2939
Montgomery, AL 36105-0939
Banking
State Banking Department
651 Administrative Building
Montgomery, AL 36130
Securities
Alabama Securities Exchange Commission
100 Commerce Street
First Southern Towers
Montgomery, AL 36130
Labor and Industrial Relations
Department of Industrial Relations
649 Monroe Street
Montgomery, AL 36130
Alabama Department of Labor
Administrative Building
64 N. Union Street
Montgomery, AL 36130
Insurance
Department of Insurance
135 S. Union Street
Montgomery, AL 36130
Uniform Industrial Code
Alabama Development Office
State Capitol
Montgomery, AL 36130

INDUSTRIAL AND BUSINESS DIRECTORIES

Alabama Directory of Mining and Manufacturing, Alabama Development Office, State Capitol, Montgomery, AL 36130
Alabama Industrial Directory, Manufacturers' News, Inc., 3 E. Huron Street, Chicago, IL

60611; State Industrial Directories Corp., 2 Penn Plaza, New York, NY 10001

Alabama International Trade Directory, Office of State Planning and Federal Programs, State Capitol, Montgomery, AL 36130

Birmingham Industrial Directory, Birmingham Chamber of Commerce, 1914 6th Avenue, Birmingham, AL 35203

Alabama Metalworking Directory, Office of State Planning and Federal Programs, State Capitol, Montgomery, AL 36130

Alaska

STATE CAPITOL, JUNEAU, AK 99811
(907) 465–2111

INFORMATION OFFICES

Commerce/Economic Development
Department of Commerce & Economic Development
P.O. Box D
Juneau, AK 99811

Corporate
Department of Commerce & Economic Development
Corporation Section
P.O. Box D
Juneau, AK 99811

Taxation
Department of Revenue
P.O. Box S
Juneau, AK 99811

State Chamber of Commerce
Alaska State Chamber of Commerce
310 2nd Street
Juneau, AK 99801

International Commerce
Division of International Trade
Department of Commerce & Economic Development
3601 C Street
Anchorage, AK 99503

Banking
Division of Banking
Department of Commerce & Economic Development
P.O. Box D
Juneau, AK 99811

Securities
Division of Securities and Corporations
Department of Commerce and Economic Development
P.O. Box D
Juneau, AK 99811

Labor and Industrial Relations
Department of Labor
1111 W. 8th Street
Juneau, AK 99801

Insurance
Division of Insurance
Department of Commerce and Economic Development
P.O. Box D
Juneau, AK 99811

Uniform Industrial Code
Department of Natural Resources
Uniform Commercial Code
3601 C Street
Anchorage, AK 99503

INDUSTRIAL AND BUSINESS DIRECTORIES

Alaska Directory of Commercial Establishments, Manufacturers' News, Inc., 4 E. Huron Street, Chicago, IL 60611; State Industrial Directories Corp., 2 Penn Plaza, New York, NY 10001

Alaska Petroleum and Industrial Directory, 409 W. Northern Lights Boulevard, Anchorage, AK 99603

Arizona

STATE CAPITOL, PHOENIX, AZ 85007
(602) 255–4900

INFORMATION OFFICES

Commerce/Economic Development
Department of Commerce
1700 W. Washington Avenue
Phoenix, AZ 85007

Corporate
Arizona Corporation Commission
P.O. Box 6019
Phoenix, AZ 85005

Taxation
Department of Revenue
State Capitol
Phoenix, AZ 85007

State Chamber of Commerce
Arizona State Chamber of Commerce
3216 N. Third Street
Phoenix, AZ 85012

Banking
Banking Department
1601 W. Jefferson
Phoenix, AZ 85007

Insurance
Insurance Department
1601 W. Jefferson
Phoenix, AZ 85007

Securities
Arizona Corporation Commission
1200 W. Washington
Phoenix, AZ 85007

International Commerce
Department of Commerce

1700 W. Washington
Phoenix, AZ 85007
Labor and Industrial Relations
Industrial Commission
1601 W. Jefferson
Phoenix, AZ 85007

INDUSTRIAL AND BUSINESS DIRECTORIES

Arizona Directory of Industries, Manufacturers'
News, 3 E. Huron Street, Chicago, IL 60611
Arizona Directory of Manufacturers, Manufac-
turers' News, Inc., 3 E. Huron Street, Chi-
cago, IL 60611; State Industrial Directories
Corp., 2 Penn Plaza, New York, NY 10001
Arizona USA International Trade Directory, Ar-
izona State Department of Economic Plan-
ning and Development, 1700 W. Washington
Avenue, Phoenix, AZ 85007
Directory of Arizona Manufacturers, Phoenix
Chamber of Commerce, Phoenix, AZ 85001

Arkansas

STATE CAPITOL, LITTLE ROCK, AR 72201
(501) 371-1010

INFORMATION OFFICES

Commerce/Economic Development
Industrial Development Commission
Big Mac Building
One State Capital Mall
Little Rock, AR 72201
Corporate
Secretary of State
Corporation Department
State Capitol
Little Rock, AR 72201
Taxation
Division of Revenue Services
Department of Finance and Administration
7th and Wolfe Streets
Little Rock, AR 72201
State Chamber of Commerce
Arkansas State Chamber of Commerce
911 Wallace Building
Little Rock, AR 72201
International Commerce
Industrial Development Commission
Big Mac Building
One State Capitol Mall
Little Rock, AR 72201
Banking
Bank Department
323 Center
Little Rock, AR 72201
Securities
Securities Department
Heritage West Building

201 East Markham
Little Rock, AR 72201
Labor and Industrial Relations
Arkansas Department of Labor
1022 High Street
Little Rock, AR 72201
Insurance
Insurance Division
University Towers Building
Little Rock, AR 72204
Ombudsman
State Claims Commission
State Capitol
Little Rock, AR 72201

INDUSTRIAL AND BUSINESS DIRECTORIES

Arkansas Directory of Industries, Manufactur-
ers' News, 3 E. Huron Street, Chicago, IL
60611
Directory of Arkansas Manufacturers, Arkansas
Industrial Development Foundation, P.O.
Box 1784, Little Rock, AR 72203; State Indus-
trial Directories Corp., 2 Penn Plaza, New
York, NY 10001
State and County Economic Data (annual),
University of Arkansas Industrial Research
Center, University of Arkansas, Little Rock
College of Business Administration, 33rd and
University Avenue, Little Rock, AR 72204

Colorado

STATE CAPITOL, DENVER, CO 80203
(303) 866-5000

INFORMATION OFFICES

Commerce/Economic Development
Division of Commerce and Development
Department of Local Affairs
Centennial Building
1313 Sherman Street
Denver, CO 80203
Corporate
Secretary of State
Corporation Division
1560 Broadway
Denver, CO 80203
Taxation
Administrative Division
Department of Revenue
1375 Sherman Street
Denver, CO 80203
State Chamber of Commerce
Colorado Association of Commerce and In-
dustry
1390 Logan Street
Denver, CO 80203
International Commerce
Foreign Trade Office

Division of Commerce & Development
1313 Sherman Street
Denver, CO 80203
Banking
Division of Banking
303 W. Colfax Street
Denver, CO 80202
Securities
Division of Securities
1560 Broadway
Denver, CO 80202
Labor and Industrial Relations
Division of Labor
1313 Sherman Street
Denver, CO 80203
Insurance
Division of Insurance
303 W. Colfax Street
Denver, CO 80203
Uniform Industrial Code
Commercial Recordings Division
1560 Broadway
Denver, CO 80203
Business Ombudsman
Business Information Center
1525 Sherman Street
Denver, CO 80203

INDUSTRIAL AND BUSINESS DIRECTORIES

Directory of Colorado Manufacturers, Business Research Division, Graduate School of Business Administration, Campus Box 420, University of Colorado, Boulder, CO 80309

Connecticut

STATE CAPITOL, HARTFORD, CT 06106
(203) 566–4200

INFORMATION OFFICES

Commerce/Economic Development
Department of Economic Development
210 Washington Street
Hartford, CT 06106
Corporate
Secretary of State
Corporations Division
30 Trinity Street
Hartford, CT 06106
Taxation
Department of Revenue Services
92 Farmington Avenue
Hartford, CT 06106
State Chamber of Commerce
Connecticut Business and Industry Association
370 Asylum Street
Hartford, CT 06103

International Commerce
Department of Economic Development
210 Washington Street
Hartford, CT 06106
Banking
Department of Banking
44 Capitol Avenue
Hartford, CT 06106
Securities
Divisions of Securities & Business Investments
Department of Banking
44 Capitol Avenue
Hartford, CT 06106
Labor and Industrial Relations
Department of Labor
200 Folly Brook Boulevard
Wethersfield, CT 06109
Insurance
Department of Insurance
165 Capitol Avenue
Hartford, CT 06106
Uniform Industrial Code
Department of Economic Development
210 Washington Street
Hartford, CT 06106
Business Ombudsman
Department of Economic Development
210 Washington Street
Hartford, CT 06106

INDUSTRIAL AND BUSINESS DIRECTORIES

Classified Business Directory—State of Connecticut, Connecticut Directory Co., Inc., 322 Main Street, Stamford, CT 06901
Connecticut Classified Business Directory, Connecticut Directory Co., Inc., 322 Main Street, Stamford, CT 06901
Connecticut State Industrial Directory, Manufacturers' News, 3 E. Huron Street, Chicago, IL 60611; State Industrial Directories Corp., 2 Penn Plaza, New York, NY 10001
Directory of Connecticut Manufacturing Establishments, Connecticut Department of Labor, 200 Folly Brook Boulevard, Wethersfield, CT 06109

Delaware

LEGISLATIVE HALL, DOVER, DE 19901
(302) 736–4101

INFORMATION OFFICES

Commerce/Economic Development
Delaware Development Office
99 Kings Highway
P.O. Box 1401
Dover, DE 19903

Corporate
 Secretary of State
 Corporations Department
 P.O. Box 898
 Dover, DE 19903
Taxation
 Department of Finance
 Division of Revenue
 Carvel State Office Building
 820 N. French Street
 Wilmington, DE 19801
State Chamber of Commerce
 Delaware State Chamber of Commerce, Inc.
 One Commerce Center
 Wilmington, DE 19801
Banking
 State Bank Commission
 15 The Green
 Dover, DE 19901
Labor and Industrial Relations
 Division of Industrial Affairs
 Department of Labor
 Carvel State Office Building
 820 N. French Street
 Wilmington, DE 19801
Insurance
 State Insurance Commission
 21 The Green
 Dover, DE 19901

INDUSTRIAL AND BUSINESS DIRECTORIES

Delaware Directory of Commerce and Industry,
 Delaware State Chamber of Commerce, One
 Commerce Center, Wilmington, DE 19801
Delaware State Industrial Directory, State In-
 dustrial Directories Corp., 2 Penn Plaza, New
 York, NY 10001

Florida

STATE CAPITOL, TALLAHASSEE, FL 32301
(904) 488-1234

INFORMATION OFFICES

Commerce/Economic Development
 Department of Commerce
 Collins Building
 Tallahassee, FL 32301

 Division of Economic Development
 Department of Commerce
 Collins Building
 Tallahassee, FL 32301
Corporate
 Secretary of State
 Division of Corporations
 Capitol Building
 Tallahassee, FL 32304

Taxation
 Department of Revenue
 Carlton Building
 Tallahassee, FL 32301
State Chamber of Commerce
 Florida State Chamber of Commerce
 P.O. Box 11309
 Tallahassee, FL 32302
International Commerce
 Florida Department of Commerce
 Bureau of International Trade
 Collins Building
 Tallahassee, FL 32301
Banking
 Florida Department of Banking & Finance
 The Capitol
 Tallahassee, FL 32301
Securities
 Florida Department of Banking & Finance
 Division of Securities
 1402 Capitol
 Tallahassee, FL 32301
Labor and Industrial Relations
 Florida Department of Labor and Employ-
  ment Security
 Berkeley Building
 2590 Executive Center Circle, East
 Tallahassee, FL 32301
Insurance
 Florida Department of Insurance
 The Capitol
 Tallahassee, FL 32301
Uniform Commercial Code
 Florida Department of State
 Bureau of Uniform Commercial Code
 P.O. Box 5588
 Tallahassee, FL 32314
Business Ombudsman
 Florida Department of Commerce
 Bureau of Business and Community Develop-
  ment
 Collins Building
 Tallahassee, FL 32301

INDUSTRIAL AND BUSINESS DIRECTORIES

Directory of Florida Industries, Manufacturers'
 News, Inc., 4 E. Huron Street, Chicago, IL
 60611; Florida State Chamber of Commerce,
 P.O. Box 11309, Tallahassee, FL 32302; State
 Industrial Directories Corp., 2 Penn Plaza,
 New York, NY 10001
Florida Industries Guide, McHenry Publishing
 Co., Inc., Box 935, Orlando, FL 32802

Georgia

STATE CAPITOL, ATLANTA, GA 30334
(404) 656-2000

INFORMATION OFFICES

Commerce/Economic Development
Department of Industry and Trade
230 Peachtree Street NW
Atlanta, GA 30303
Corporate
Corporations Division
Secretary of State
2 Martin Luther King Jr. Drive, SE
Atlanta, GA 30334
Taxation
Department of Revenue
270 Washington Street, SW
Atlanta, GA 30334
State Chamber of Commerce
Business Council of Georgia
1280 S. Omni International
Atlanta, GA 30334
International Commerce
Department of Industry and Trade
230 Peachtree Street, NW
Atlanta, GA 30303
Banking
Department of Banking and Finance
2990 Brandywine Road
Atlanta, GA 30341
Securities
Securities Division
Secretary of State
2 Martin Luther King Jr. Drive, SE
Atlanta, GA 30334
Labor and Industrial Relations
Department of Labor
254 Washington Street, SW
Atlanta, GA 30334
Insurance
Office of Commissioner of Insurance
2 Martin Luther King Jr. Drive, SE
Atlanta, GA 30334

INDUSTRIAL AND BUSINESS DIRECTORIES

Georgia Manufacturing Directory, Department of Industry and Trade, 230 Peachtree Street, NW, Atlanta, GA 30303
Georgia World Trade Directory, Business Council of Georgia, 575 N. Omni International, Atlanta, GA 30335
Industrial Sites in Georgia, Georgia Power Company, Box 4545DJ, Atlanta, GA 30303
Georgia International Trade Directory, Department of Industry and Trade, 230 Peachtree Street NE, Atlanta, GA 30303
Georgia Directory of International Services, World Congress Institute, 1 Park Place S, Fulton Federal Building, Atlanta, GA 30303
International Companies with Facilities in Georgia. Department of Industry and Trade, 230 Peachtree Street, NW, Atlanta, GA 30303

Hawaii

STATE CAPITOL, HONOLULU, HI 96813
(808) 548-2211

INFORMATION OFFICES

Commerce/Economic Development
Department of Planning and Economic Development
250 S. King Street
Honolulu, HI 96813
Department of Commerce and Consumer Affairs
250 S. King Street
Honolulu, HI 96813
Corporate
Department of Commerce and Consumer Affairs
Business Registration Division
P.O. Box 40
Honolulu, HI 96810
Taxation
Department of Taxation
425 Queen Street
Honolulu, HI 96813
State Chamber of Commerce
Chamber of Commerce of Hawaii
735 Bishop Street
Dillingham Building
Honolulu, HI 96813
International Commerce
International Services Branch
State Department of Planning and Economic Development
P.O. Box 2359
Honolulu, HI 96804
Hawaii Foreign-Trade Zone No. 9, Pier 2
Honolulu, HI 96813
Banking
Division of Financial Institutions
State Department of Commerce and Consumer Affairs
1010 Richards Street
Honolulu, HI 96813
Securities
Division of Financial Institutions
State Department of Commerce and Consumer Affairs
1010 Richards Street
Honolulu, HI 96813
Labor and Industrial Relations
State Department of Labor and Industrial Relations
P.O. Box 3680
Honolulu, HI 96811
Insurance
Insurance Division
State Department of Commerce and Consumer Affairs

1010 Richards Street
Honolulu, HI 96813
Business Ombudsman
 Office of the Ombudsman
 465 S. King Street
 Honolulu, HI 96813

INDUSTRIAL AND BUSINESS DIRECTORIES

Directory of Manufacturers, State of Hawaii, Chamber of Commerce of Hawaii, Dillingham Building, 735 Bishop Street, Honolulu, HI 96813

Hawaii Business Directory, Hawaii Business Directory, Inc., 1164 Bishop Street, Honolulu, HI 96813

Hawaii Directory of Manufacturers, Manufacturers' News, Inc., 4 E. Huron Street, Chicago, IL 60611; State Industrial Directories Corp., 2 Penn Plaza, New York, NY 10001

Idaho

STATE CAPITOL, BOISE, ID 83720
(208) 334–2470

INFORMATION OFFICES

Mailing address for all state offices is:
 Statehouse
 Boise, ID 83720
Commerce/Economic Development
 Department of Commerce
 Capitol Building
 Boise, ID 83720
Corporate
 Secretary of State
 State Capitol
 Boise, ID 83720
Taxation
 Department of Revenue and Taxation
 Capitol Building
 Boise, ID 83720
State Chamber of Commerce
 Idaho Association of Commerce and Industry
 805 West Idaho
 Boise, ID 83702
International Commerce
 Department of Commerce
 Statehouse
 Boise, ID 83720
Banking
 Department of Finance
 700 W. State Street
 Boise, ID 83720
Securities
 Department of Finance
 700 W. State Street
 Boise, ID 83720
Labor and Industrial Relations
 Department of Labor and Industrial Services

317 Main Street
Boise, ID 83720
Insurance
 Department of Insurance
 700 W. State Street
 Boise, ID 83720
Uniform Industrial Code
 Department of Labor and Industrial Services
 317 Main Street
 Boise, ID 83720
Business Ombudsman
 Department of Commerce
 Statehouse
 Boise, ID 83720

INDUSTRIAL AND BUSINESS DIRECTORIES

Manufacturing Directory of Idaho, Center for Business and Research, University of Idaho, Moscow, ID 83843

Idaho Opportunities, Department of Commerce, Capitol Building, Boise, ID 83720

Illinois

STATE HOUSE, SPRINGFIELD, IL 62706
(217) 782–2000

INFORMATION OFFICES

Commerce/Economic Development
 Department of Commerce and Community Affairs
 620 E. Adams Street
 Springfield, IL 62701
Corporate
 Corporate Division
 Centennial Building
 Springfield, IL 62756
Taxation
 Department of Revenue
 101 W. Jefferson Street
 Springfield, IL 62708
State Chamber of Commerce
 Illinois State Chamber of Commerce
 20 N. Wacker Drive
 Chicago, IL 60606
International Commerce
 Department of Commerce & Community Affairs
 State of Illinois Center
 100 W. Randolph Street
 Chicago, IL 60601
Banking
 Department of Financial Institutions
 100 W. Randolph Street
 Chicago, IL 60601
Securities
 Secretary of State

840 S. Spring Street
Springfield, IL 62704
Labor and Industrial Relations
Department of Labor
100 N. 1st, Alzina Building
Springfield, IL 62706
Department of Commerce & Community Affairs
620 E. Adams Street
Springfield, IL 62701
Insurance
Department of Insurance
320 W. Washington Street
Springfield, IL 62767
Uniform Industrial Code
Department of Commerce & Community Affairs
620 E. Adams Street
Springfield, IL 62701
Business Ombudsman
Department of Commerce & Community Affairs
620 E. Adams Street
Springfield, IL 62701

INDUSTRIAL AND BUSINESS DIRECTORIES

Chicago Buyers' Guide, Chicago Association of Commerce and Industry, 130 S. Michigan Avenue, Chicago, IL 60603

Chicago Cook County and Illinois Industrial Directory, National Publishing Corp., 3150 Des Plaines Avenue, Des Plaines, IL 60018

Chicago Geographic Edition, Manufacturers' News, Inc., 4 E. Huron Street, Chicago, IL 60611; State Industrial Directories Corp., 2 Penn Plaza, New York, NY 10001

Guide to Illinois State Services, Department of Commerce and Community Affairs, 620 E. Adams, Springfield, IL 62701

Illinois Exporters Director, Department of Commerce and Community Affairs, State of Illinois Center, 100 W. Randolph Street, Chicago, IL 60601

International Business Services Directory, Department of Commerce and Community Affairs, State of Illinois Center, 100 W. Randolph Street, Chicago, IL 60601

Illinois Industrial Directory, Illinois Industrial Directories National Publishing Corp., 3150 Des Plaines Avenue, Des Plaines, IL 60018

Illinois Manufacturers Directory, Manufacturers' News, Inc., 3 E. Huron Street, Chicago, IL 60611; State Industrial Directories Corp., 2 Penn Plaza, New York, NY 10001

Illinois Services Directory, Manufacturers' News, Inc., 3 E. Huron Street, Chicago, IL 60611

Illinois Financial Sources Directory, Department of Commerce and Community Affairs, 620 E. Adams, Springfield, IL 62706

Indiana

STATE HOUSE, INDIANAPOLIS, IN 46204
State Information Center
(317) 232–3140

INFORMATION OFFICES

Commerce/Economic Development
Department of Commerce
1 N. Capitol Avenue
Indianapolis, IN 46204
Corporate
Secretary of State
Corporation Division
State House
Indianapolis, IN 46204
Taxation
Department of Revenue
State Office Building
Indianapolis, IN 46204
State Board of Tax Commissioners
201 State Office Building
Indianapolis, IN 46204
State Chamber of Commerce
Indiana State Chamber of Commerce, Inc.
1 N. Capitol Avenue, Ste 200
Indianapolis, IN 46204
International Commerce
International Trade Division
Indiana Department of Commerce
1 N. Capitol Avenue
Indianapolis, IN 46204-2243
Banking
Indiana Bankers Association
1 N. Capitol Avenue
Indianapolis, IN 46204-2243
Securities
Secretary of State
Securities Commission
1 N. Capitol Avenue
Indianapolis, IN 46204-2243
Labor and Industrial Relations
Indiana Industrial Board
State Office Building
100 N. Senate Avenue
Indianapolis, IN 46204
Insurance
Indiana Department of Insurance
State Office Building
100 N. Senate Avenue
Indianapolis, IN 46204
Uniform Industrial Code
Uniform Commercial Code Division
Secretary of State Office
State House
Indianapolis, IN 46204
Business Ombudsman
Office of Regulatory Ombudsman
Indiana Department of Commerce

1 North Capitol Avenue
Indianapolis, IN 46204-2243

INDUSTRIAL AND BUSINESS DIRECTORIES

Indiana Industrial Directory, Harris Publishing Co., 2057–2 Aurora Rd., Twinsburg, OH 44087 Indiana State Chamber of Commerce, 1 N. Capitol Avenue, Ste 200, Indianapolis, IN 46204

Iowa

STATE CAPITOL, DES MOINES, IA 50319
(515) 281–5011

INFORMATION OFFICES

Commerce/Economic Development
Development Commission
Capitol Center Building
600 E. Court Avenue
Des Moines, IA 50309
Corporate
Secretary of State
Corporation Division
Hoover Building
Des Moines, IA 50319
Taxation
Department of Revenue
Hoover Building
Des Moines, IA 50319
International Commerce
Iowa Development Commission
600 E. Court Avenue
Des Moines, IA 50309
Banking
Iowa Banking Department
530 Liberty Building
Des Moines, IA 50309
Iowa Housing Finance Authority
550 Liberty Building
Des Moines, IA 50309
Securities
Securities Division
Insurance Department of Iowa
Lucas Building
Des Moines, IA 50319
Labor
Industrial Commissioner
507 10th Street
Des Moines, IA 50309
Bureau of Labor
307 E. 7th Street
Des Moines, IA 50309
Insurance
Insurance Department
Lucas Building
Des Moines, IA 50319

INDUSTRIAL AND BUSINESS DIRECTORIES

Directory of Iowa Manufacturers, Iowa Development Commission, 600 E. Court Avenue, Des Moines, IA 50309
Doing Business in Iowa, Iowa Development Commission, 600 E. Court Avenue, Des Moines, IA 50309

Kansas

STATE HOUSE, TOPEKA, KS 66612
(913) 296–0111

INFORMATION OFFICES

Commerce/Economic Development
Department of Economic Development
400 W 8th Street
Topeka, KS 66603–3957
Corporate
Secretary of State
State House
Corporation Department
Topeka, KS 66612
Taxation
Department of Revenue
State Office Building
Topeka, KS 66612
State Chamber of Commerce
Kansas Chamber of Commerce and Industry
500 Bank IV Tower
534 Kansas
Topeka, KS 66603-3460
International Commerce
Department of Economic Development
400 West 8th Street
Topeka, KS 66603–3957
Banking
Banking Department
700 Jackson Street
Topeka, KS 66603
Securities
Securities Commissioner of Kansas
503 Kansas Avenue
Topeka, KS 66603
Labor and Industrial Relations
Department of Human Resources
401 Topeka Boulevard
Topeka, KS 66603
Insurance
Insurance Department
420 SW 9th Street
Topeka, KS 66612
Business Ombudsman
Department of Economic Development
400 West 8th Street
Topeka, KS 66603–3957

INDUSTRIAL AND BUSINESS DIRECTORIES

Directory of Kansas Manufacturers and Products, Kansas Department of Economic Development, 400 W. 8th Street, Topeka, KS 66603–3957; State Industrial Directories Corp., 2 Penn Plaza, New York, NY 10001

Directory of Manufacturers, Wichita, Kansas, Wichita Area Chamber of Commerce, 350 West Douglas, Wichita, KS 67202

Kansas Fortune 500 Companies, Kansas Department of Economic Development, 400 W. 8th Street, Topeka, KS 66603–3957

Kansas Manufacturing Firms in Export, Kansas Department of Economic Development, 400 W. 8th Street, Topeka, KS 66603–3957

Kansas Association Directory, Kansas Department of Economic Development, 400 W. 8th Street, Topeka, KS 66603–3957

Kentucky

STATE CAPITOL, FRANKFORT, KY 40601
(502) 564–3130

INFORMATION OFFICES

Commerce/Economic Development
Department of Economic Development
Capitol Plaza Office Tower
Frankfort, KY 40601
Corporate
Office of Secretary of State
Corporation Division
Capitol Building
Frankfort, KY 40601
Taxation
Revenue Cabinet
Capitol Annex
Frankfort, KY 40601
State Chamber of Commerce
Kentucky Chamber of Commerce
Versailles Road
P.O. Box 817
Frankfort, KY 40602
International Commerce
Kentucky Commerce Cabinet
Office of International Marketing
Capital Plaza Tower
Frankfort, KY 40601
Banking
Kentucky Department of Financial Institutions
Division of Banking and Thrift Institutions
911 Leawood Drive
Frankfort, KY 40601–3392
Securities
Kentucky Department of Financial Institutions
Division of Securities

911 Leawood Drive
Frankfort, KY 40601
Labor Industrial Relations
Kentucky Labor Cabinet
The 127 Building
Frankfort, KY 40601
Insurance
Kentucky Department of Insurance
P.O. Box 517
Frankfort, KY 40602
Uniform Industrial Code
Kentucky Department of Housing, Buildings, and Construction
U.S. 127 South
Frankfort, KY 40601
Business Ombudsman
Kentucky Department of Economic Development
Capital Plaza Tower
Frankfort, KY 40601

INDUSTRIAL AND BUSINESS DIRECTORIES

Kentucky International Trade, Kentucky Commerce Cabinet, Capitol Plaza Tower, Frankfort, KY 40601

Kentucky Directory of Manufacturers, Department of Economic Development, Capitol Plaza Tower, Frankfort, KY 40601; and from Manufacturers' News, 4 E. Huron Street, Chicago, IL 60611; State Industrial Directories Corp., 2 Penn Plaza, New York, NY 10001; Harris Publishing Co., 20572 Aurora Road, Twinsburg, OH 44087

Louisiana

STATE CAPITOL, BATON ROUGE, LA 70804
(504) 342–7015

INFORMATION OFFICES

Commerce/Economic Development
Department of Commerce
P.O. Box 44185
Baton Rouge, LA 70804
Corporate
Secretary of State
Division of Corporation
P.O. Box 44125
Baton Rouge, LA 70804
Taxation
Department of Revenue
P.O. Box 201
Baton Rouge, LA 70821
State Chamber of Commerce
Louisiana Association of Business and Industry
P.O. Box 3988
Baton Rouge, LA 70821

International Commerce
  Department of Commerce
  Office of International Trade,
    Finance and Development
  P.O. Box 94185
  Baton Rouge, LA 70804
Banking
  Department of Commerce
  Office of Financial Institutions
  P.O. Box 94185
  Baton Rouge, LA 70804–9185
Securities
  Louisiana Securities Commission
  315 Louisiana State Office Building
  New Orleans, LA 70112
Labor and Industrial Relations
  Department of Labor
  P.O. Box 94094
  Baton Rouge, LA 70804–9094
Insurance
  Office of Insurance Rating Commission
  P.O. Box 44157
  Baton Rouge, LA 70804
Uniform Industrial Code
  Department of Commerce
  P.O. Box 94185
  Baton Rouge, LA 70804–9185
Department of Labor
  P.O. Box 94094
  Baton Rouge, LA 70804–9094
Business Ombudsman
  Department of Commerce
  P.O. Box 44185
  Baton Rouge, LA 70804

INDUSTRIAL AND BUSINESS DIRECTORIES

Louisiana Directory of Manufacturers, Department of Commerce, State Land and Natural Resources Building, Baton Rouge, LA 70804; and from Manufacturers' News, Inc., 4 E. Huron Street, Chicago, IL 60611; State Industrial Directories Corp., 2 Penn Plaza, New York, NY 10001

Louisiana International Trade Directory, International House, New Orleans, LA 70150

Maine

STATE HOUSE, AUGUSTA, ME 04333
(207) 289–1110

INFORMATION OFFICES

Commerce/Economic Development
  State Development Office
  State House Station
  Augusta, ME 04333

Corporate
  Department of State
  Division of Corporations
  State House Station #101
  Augusta, ME 04333
Private Development Associations
  Maine Development Foundation
  1 Memorial Circle
  Augusta, ME 04330
Taxation
  Bureau of Taxation
  Department of Finance and Administration
  State House Station #24
  Augusta, ME 04333
State Chamber of Commerce
  Maine State Chamber of Commerce and Industry
  126 Sewall Street
  Augusta, ME 04330
International Commerce
  State Development Office
  State House Station #59
  Augusta, ME 04333
Banking
  Bureau of Banking
  State House Station #36
  Augusta, ME 04333
Securities
  Bureau of Banking
  Securities Division
  State House Station #36
  Augusta, ME 04333
Labor and Industrial Relations
  Department of Labor
  Bureau of Labor Standards
  State House Station #45
  Augusta, ME 04333
Insurance
  Bureau of Insurance
  State House Station #34
  Augusta, ME 04333
Business Ombudsman
  State Development Office
  State House Station #59
  Augusta, ME 04333

INDUSTRIAL AND BUSINESS DIRECTORIES

Maine Marketing Directory, State Development Office, State House Station #59, Augusta, ME 04333

Maine Register, Tower Publishing Company, Portland, ME 04101

Maryland

STATE HOUSE, ANNAPOLIS, MD 21404
(301) 269–3901

INFORMATION OFFICES

Commerce/Economic Development
Department of Economic and Community
   Development
45 Calvert Street
Annapolis, MD 21401
Corporate
State Department of Assessments and Taxation
301 W. Preston Street
Baltimore, MD 21201
Taxation
Comptroller of the Treasury
Louis L. Goldstein Treasury Building
P.O. Box 466
Annapolis, MD 21404
State Chamber of Commerce
Maryland State Chamber of Commerce
60 West Street
Annapolis, MD 21401
International Commerce
Department of Economic and Community
   Development
45 Calvert Street
Annapolis, MD 21401

Maryland Port Administrator
Office of Port Administration
World Trade Center
Baltimore, MD 21202
Banking
State Banking Commission
34 Market Place
Baltimore, MD 21202
Securities
Division of Securities
7 N. Calvert Street
Baltimore, MD 21201
Labor and Industrial Relations
Division of Labor and Industry
Department of Licensing and Regulations
501 St. Paul Place
Baltimore, MD 21202
Insurance
State Insurance Division
501 St. Paul Place
Baltimore, MD 21202
Business Ombudsman
Department of Economic and Community
   Development
45 Calvert Street
Annapolis, MD 21401

INDUSTRIAL AND BUSINESS DIRECTORIES

Directory of Maryland Manufacturers, Maryland Department of Economic and Community Development, 45 Calvert Street, Annapolis, MD 21401
Maryland State Industrial Directory, State Industrial Directories Corp., 2 Penn Plaza, New York, NY 10001

Massachusetts

STATE HOUSE, BOSTON, MA 02133
(617) 727–2121

INFORMATION OFFICES

Commerce/Economic Development
Governor's Office of Economic Development
Room 109
State House
Boston, MA 02133

Massachusetts Department of Commerce and
   Development
Division of Economic Development
100 Cambridge Street
Boston, MA 02202

Executive Office of Economic Affairs
2101 McCormack Building
1 Ashburton Place
Boston, MA 02108

Department of Commerce and Development
Leverett Saltonstall Building
100 Cambridge Street
Boston, MA 02202
Corporate
Secretary of State
1 Ashburton Place
Boston, MA 02108
Taxation
Accounting Bureau
Leverett Saltonstall Building
100 Cambridge Street
Boston, MA 02202
International Commerce
Office of International Trade and Investment
Executive Office of Economic Affairs
1 Ashburton Place
Boston, MA 02208
Banking
Division of Banks and Loan Agencies
100 Cambridge Street
Boston, MA 02202
Securities
Secretary of State
Securities Division
1 Ashburton Place
Boston, MA 02108
Labor and Industrial Relations
Executive Office of Labor
1 Ashburton Place
Boston, MA 02108

Department of Labor and Industries
Executive Office of Economic Affairs
100 Cambridge Street
Boston, MA 02202
Insurance
Division of Insurance
100 Cambridge Street
Boston, MA 02202

INDUSTRIAL AND BUSINESS DIRECTORIES

Directory of Directors in the City of Boston and Vicinity, Bankers Service Co., 14 Beacon Street, Boston, MA 02108
Directory of Massachusetts Manufacturers, George D. Hall Company, 20 Kilby Street, Boston, MA 02109
Massachusetts Directory of Manufacturers, Manufacturers' News, Inc., 4 E. Huron Street, Chicago, IL 60611
Massachusetts State Industrial Directory, State Industrial Directories Corp., 2 Penn Plaza, New York, NY 10001

Michigan

STATE CAPITOL, LANSING, MI 48913
(517) 373–1837

INFORMATION OFFICES

Commerce/Economic Development
Department of Commerce
525 W. Ottawa Street
P.O. Box 30225
Lansing, MI 48909
Corporate
Corporation and Securities Bureau
6546 Mercantile Way
P.O. Box 30054
Lansing, MI 48909
Taxation
Bureau of Collection
Department of Treasury
Treasury Building
Lansing, MI 48922
State Chamber of Commerce
Michigan State Chamber of Commerce
200 N. Washington Square
Lansing, MI 48910
International Commerce
Office of International Development
Department of Commerce
P.O. Box 30105
Lansing, MI 48909
Banking
Financial Institutions Bureau
Department of Commerce
Law Building
P.O. Box 30224
Lansing, MI 48909
Securities
Corporation and Securities Bureau
Department of Commerce
6546 Mercantile Way
P.O. Box 30222
Lansing, MI 48909
Labor and Industrial Relations
Bureau of Labor Relations

Department of Labor
State of Michigan Plaza Building
1200 Sixth Street
Detroit, MI 48226
Department of Labor
Lansing Plaza
309 North Washington
P.O. Box 30015
Lansing, MI 48909
Insurance
Insurance Bureau
Department of Licensing and Regulation
611 West Ottawa
North Ottawa Tower
P.O. Box 30220
Lansing, MI 48909

INDUSTRIAL AND BUSINESS DIRECTORIES

Directory of Michigan Manufacturers, Manufacturers' News, Inc., 4 E. Huron Street, Chicago, IL 60611; Manufacturers Publishing Co., 8543 Puritan Avenue, Detroit, MI 48238
Harris Michigan Marketers Industrial Directory, Harris Publishing Company, 33140 Aurora Road, Cleveland, OH 44139
Michigan State Industrial Directory, State Industrial Directories Corp., 2 Penn Plaza, New York, NY 10001
MacRae's Michigan State Industrial Directory, MacRae Publishing, 817 Broadway, New York, NY 10003
Economic Development Corporations Directory for the State of Michigan, Department of Commerce, Office of Business and Community Development, Lansing, MI 48909

Minnesota

STATE CAPITOL, ST. PAUL, MN 55155
(612) 296–6013

INFORMATION OFFICES

Commerce/Economic Development
Department of Energy and Economic Development
900 American Center Building
St. Paul, MN 55101
Minnesota Department of Commerce
Metro Square Building
7th and Robert Streets
St. Paul, MN 55101
Corporate
Corporation Division
180 State Office Building
St. Paul, MN 55155
Taxation
Department of Revenue

Centennial Office Building
St. Paul, MN 55145
State Chamber of Commerce
Minnesota Association of Commerce and Industry
Hanover Building
480 Cedar Street
St. Paul, MN 55101
International Commerce
Minnesota Trade Office
90 W. Plato Boulevard
St. Paul, MN 55107
Banking
Minnesota Department of Commerce
Banking Division
Metro Square Building
7th & Robert Streets
St. Paul, MN 55101
Securities
Minnesota Department of Commerce
Registration Unit
Metro Square Building
7th & Robert Streets
St. Paul, MN 55101
Labor and Industrial Relations
Minnesota Department of Labor and Industry
444 Lafayette Road
St. Paul, MN 55101
Insurance
Minnesota Department of Commerce
Policy Analysis Division
Metro Square Building
7th & Robert Streets
St. Paul, MN 55101
Business Ombudsman
Department of Energy and Economic Development
900 American Center Building
St. Paul, MN 55101

INDUSTRIAL AND BUSINESS DIRECTORIES

Minnesota Directory of Manufacturers, Manufacturers' News, Inc., 4 E. Huron Street, Chicago, IL 60611; State Industrial Directories Corp., 2 Penn Plaza, New York, NY 10001

Mississippi

NEW CAPITOL, JACKSON, MS 39205
(601) 359-3100

INFORMATION OFFICES

Commerce/Economic Development
Mississippi Department of Economic Development
P.O. Box 849
Jackson, MS 39205

Department of Agriculture and Commerce
1604 Sillers Building
Jackson, MS 39205
Corporate
Secretary of State
Corporation Division
P.O. Box 136
Jackson, MS 39205
Taxation
Tax Commission
102 Woolfolk Building
Jackson, MS 39201
State Chamber of Commerce
P.O. Box 1849
Jackson, MS 39205-1849
Banking
Department of Banking and Consumer Finance
1206 Woolfolk State Office Building
Jackson, MS 39205
Securities
Department of State
Securities Division
P.O. Box 136
Jackson, MS 39205
Labor and Industrial Relations
1520 W. Capitol Street
Jackson, MS 39205
Insurance
Department of Insurance
1804 Sillers Building
Jackson, MS 39205

INDUSTRIAL AND BUSINESS DIRECTORIES

Mississippi International Trade Directory, Mississippi Marketing Council, Box 849, Sillers State Office Building, Jackson, MS 39205
Mississippi Manufacturers' Directory, Manufacturers' News, Inc., 4 E. Huron Street, Chicago, IL 60611; Public Information Office, Mississippi Research and Development Center, Jackson, MS 39205; State Industrial Directories Corp., 2 Penn Plaza, New York, NY 10001

Missouri

STATE CAPITOL, JEFFERSON CITY, MO 65101
(314) 751-2151

INFORMATION OFFICES

Commerce/Economic Development
Department of Economic Development
Truman State Office Building
P.O. Box 1157
Jefferson City, MO 65102
Corporate
Secretary of State

Corporations Division
P.O. Box 778
Jefferson City, MO 65102
Taxation
Department of Revenue
Division of Taxation
Truman State Office Building
P.O. Box 629
Jefferson City, MO 65105
State Chamber of Commerce
Missouri Chamber of Commerce
428 East Capitol Avenue
P.O. Box 149
Jefferson City, MO 65102
International Commerce
International Business Development
Missouri Division of Community & Economic
  Development
Truman State Office Building
P.O. Box 1157
Jefferson City, MO 65102
Banking
Missouri Division of Finance
Truman State Office Building
P.O. Box 716
Jefferson City, MO 65102
Securities
Office of the Secretary of State
Securities Division
Truman State Office Building
P.O. Box 778
Jefferson City, MO 65102
Labor and Industrial Relations
Missouri Dept. of Labor & Industrial Rela-
  tions
421 E. Dunklin
Jefferson City, MO 65102
Insurance
Missouri Division of Insurance
Truman State Office Building
P.O. Box 690
Jefferson City, MO 65102
Uniform Industrial Code
Missouri Division of Labor Standards
P.O. Box 449
Jefferson City, MO 65102
Business Ombudsman
Office of the Lieutenant Governor
Missouri State Capitol
P.O. Box 563
Jefferson City, MO 65102

INDUSTRIAL AND BUSINESS DIRECTORY

*Contacts Influential: Commerce and Industrial
  Directory (for Kansas City Area),* Contacts
  Influential, Inc., 6347 Brookside Boulevard,
  Suite 204, Kansas City, MO 64113
*Missouri Directory of Manufacturing and Min-
  ing* (annual), Informative Data Co., 3546 Wat-
  son Road, St. Louis, MO 63139

Montana

STATE CAPITOL, HELENA, MT 59620
(406) 444–3111

INFORMATION OFFICES

Commerce/Economic Development
Department of Commerce
1424 9th Avenue
Helena, MT 59620
Economic Development and Research
Department of Commerce
1429 9th Avenue
Helena, MT 59620
Census and Economic Information Center
Department of Commerce
1429 9th Avenue
Helena, MT 59620
Corporate
Secretary of State
Corporation Bureau
State Capitol Building
Helena, MT 59620
State Chamber of Commerce
Montana Chamber of Commerce
P.O. Box 1730
Helena, MT 59601
International Commerce
International Export Officer
Montana Department of Commerce
1424 9th Avenue
Helena, MT 59620
Banking
Commissioner of Financial Institutions
Montana Department of Commerce
1424 9th Avenue
Helena, MT 59620
Securities
Securities Division
State Auditor's Office
Sam Mitchell Building
Helena, MT 59620
Labor & Industrial Relations
Commissioner's Office
Montana Department of Labor & Industry
Lockey and Roberts
Helena, MT 59620
Insurance
Insurance Division
State Auditor's Office
Sam Mitchell Building
Helena, MT 59620
Uniform Commercial Code
Secretary of State
Uniform Commercial Code Bureau
State Capitol Building
Capitol Station
Helena, MT 59620
Business Ombudsman
Small Business Advocate

Montana Department of Commerce
1424 9th Avenue
Helena, MT 59620

INDUSTRIAL AND BUSINESS DIRECTORIES

Montana Manufacturers and Products Directory, Department of Commerce, 1424 9th Avenue, Helena, MT 59620

Montana Business & Industrial Location Guide, Department of Commerce, 1424 9th Avenue, Helena, MT 59620

Nebraska

STATE CAPITOL, LINCOLN, NE 68509
(402) 471–3111

INFORMATION OFFICES

Commerce/Economic Development
Department of Economic Development
301 Centennial Mall South
P.O. Box 94666
Lincoln, NE 68509
Corporate
Secretary of State
Corporation Division
State Capitol
Lincoln, NE 68509
Taxation
Department of Revenue
P.O. Box 94818
Lincoln, NE 68509
State Chamber of Commerce
Nebraska Association of Commerce and Industry
P.O. Box 81556
Lincoln, NE 68501
International Commerce
Nebraska Department of Economic Development
International Division
Nebraska State Office Building
Lincoln, NE 68509
Banking
Department of Banking and Finance
Nebraska State Office Building
Lincoln, NE 68509
Securities
Department of Banking and Finance
Bureau of Securities
Nebraska State Office Building
Lincoln, NE 68509
Labor and Industrial Relations
Nebraska Department of Labor
550 South 16th Street
Lincoln, NE 68509
Insurance
Department of Insurance

Nebraska State Office Building
Lincoln, NE 68509
Uniform Industrial Code
Uniform Commercial Code Division
Nebraska State Office Building
Lincoln, NE 68509
Business Ombudsman
State Claims Board
Office of Risk Management
Nebraska State Office Building
Lincoln, NE 68509

INDUSTRIAL AND BUSINESS DIRECTORIES

Directory of Nebraska Manufacturers and Their Products, Manufacturers' News, Inc., 4 E. Huron Street, Chicago, IL 60611

Directory of Nebraska Manufacturers and Their Products, Nebraska State Department of Economic Development, Lincoln, NE 68509

Manufacturers and Wholesalers Directory, Lincoln Chamber of Commerce, 200 Lincoln Building, Lincoln, NE 68508

Directory of Manufacturers for the Omaha Metropolitan Area, Omaha Economic Development Council, 1606 Douglas, Omaha, NE 68102.

Directory of Major Employers for the Omaha Area, Omaha Economic Development Council, 1606 Douglas, Omaha, NE 68102.

Nevada

STATE CAPITOL, CARSON CITY, NV 89710
(702) 885–5627

INFORMATION OFFICES

Commerce/Economic Development
Department of Commerce
Nye Building
201 S. Fall Street
Carson City, NV 89710
Department of Economic Development
600 E. William Street
Capitol Complex
Carson City, NV 89710
Corporate
Secretary of State
Capitol Complex
Carson City, NV 89710
Taxation
Tax Commission
1340 S. Curry Street
Carson City, NV 89710
State Chamber of Commerce
Nevada Chamber of Commerce Association
P.O. Box 2806
Reno, NV 89505

International Commerce
Department of Commerce
201 S. Fall Street
Carson City, NV 89710
Banking
Financial Institutions Division
Department of Commerce
406 E. Second Street
Carson City, NV 89710
Securities
Office of Secretary of State
State Capitol Building
Carson City, NV 89710
Labor and Industrial Relations
Office of Labor Commission
Kinkead Building
505 E. King Street
Carson City, NV 89710

Department of Industrial Relations
1390 S. Curry Street
Carson City, NV 89710
Insurance
Insurance Division
201 S. Fall Street
Carson City, NV 89710

INDUSTRIAL AND BUSINESS DIRECTORIES

Nevada Industrial Directory, Department of Economic Development, Capitol Complex, Carson City, NV 89710
Nevada Directory of Business, Manufacturers' News, Inc., 4 E. Huron Street, Chicago, IL 60611

New Hampshire

STATE HOUSE, CONCORD, NH 03301
(603) 271–1110

INFORMATION OFFICES

Commerce/Economic Development
Department of Resources and Economic Development
Division of Economic Development
105 Loudon Road, Building #2
Prescott Park
Concord, NH 03301
Corporate
Secretary of State
Corporations Division
State House Annex
Concord, NH 03301
Taxation
Board of Taxation
61 S. Spring Street
Concord, NH 03301
Department of Revenue Administration

61 S. Spring Street
Concord, NH 03301
State Chamber of Commerce
Business and Industry Association of New Hampshire
23 School Street
Concord, NH 03301
International Commerce
Department of Resources & Economic Development
Division of Economic Development
105 Loudon Road, Building #2
Prescott Park—Concord, NH 03301
Banking
Banking Department
State of New Hampshire
97 N. Main Street
Concord, NH 03301

New Hampshire Banking Association
125 N. Main Street
Concord, NH 03301
Securities
Insurance Department, Securities Division
State of New Hampshire
169 Manchester Street
Concord, NH 03301
Labor and Industrial Relations
Department of Employment Security
State of New Hampshire
32 S. Main Street
Concord, NH 03301

Department of Labor
State of New Hampshire
32 S. Main Street
Concord, NH 03301
Insurance
Insurance Department
State of New Hampshire
169 Manchester Street
Concord, NH 03301
Standard Industrial Code
Department of Employment Security
State of New Hampshire
32 S. Main Street
Concord, NH 03301

INDUSTRIAL AND BUSINESS DIRECTORIES

Made in New Hampshire, New Hampshire Office of Industrial Development, Department of Resources, Concord, NH 03301
New Hampshire Register, Tower Publishing Company, 163 Middle Street, Portland, ME 04111

New Jersey

STATE HOUSE, TRENTON, NJ 08625
(609) 292–2121

INFORMATION OFFICES

Commerce/Economic Development
Department of Commerce and Economic
Development
CN 820, 1 W. State Street
Trenton, NJ 08625

Division of Travel and Tourism
CN 826, 1 West State Street
Trenton, NJ 08625

Economic Development Authority
200 S. Warren Street
CN 990, Capitol Place One
Trenton, NJ 08625

Corporate
Secretary of State
State House
CN 300
Trenton, NJ 08625

Taxation
Department of Treasury
Division of Taxation
CN 240, 50 Barrack Street
Trenton, NJ 08625

State Chamber of Commerce
New Jersey State Chamber of Commerce
240 W. State Street
Trenton, NJ 08625

International Commerce
Division of International Trade
744 Broad Street
Newark, NJ 07102

Banking
Department of Banking
CN 340, 36 W. State Street
Trenton, NJ 08625

Securities
Bureau of Securities
236 W. State Street
Trenton, NJ 08625

Labor and Labor Relations
Department of Labor and Industry
CN 110, John Fitch Plaza
Trenton, NJ 08625

Insurance
Department of Insurance
CN 325, 201 E. State Street
Trenton, NJ 08625

Business Ombudsman
Department of Public Advocate
25 Market Street, CN 850
Trenton, NJ 08625

INDUSTRIAL AND BUSINESS DIRECTORIES

New Jersey State Industrial Directory, Manufacturers' News, Inc., 4 E. Huron Street, Chicago, IL 60611; State Industrial Directories Corp., 2 Penn Plaza, New York, NY 10001

New Mexico

STATE CAPITOL, SANTE FE, NM 87503
(505) 827–4011

INFORMATION OFFICES

Commerce/Economic Development
Economic Development and Tourism
Bataan Memorial Building
Sante Fe, NM 87503

Corporate
State Corporation Commission
P.O. Drawer 1269
Sante Fe, NM 87501

Taxation
Bureau of Revenue
Manuel Lujan Sr. Building
Santa Fe, NM 87501

State Chamber of Commerce
Association of Commerce and Industry of
New Mexico
117 Quincy NE
Albuquerque, NM 87108

International Commerce
Department of International Trade
Bataan Memorial Building
Sante Fe, NM 87503

Banking
Lew Wallace Building
Sante Fe, NM 87503

Securities
Lew Wallace Building
Sante Fe, NM 87503

Labor and Industrial Commission
509 Camino de Los Marques
Sante Fe, NM 87501

Insurance
State Corporation Commission
P.O. Box 1269
Sante Fe, NM 87501

INDUSTRIAL AND BUSINESS DIRECTORIES

New Mexico Directory of Manufacturing, Manufacturers' News, Inc., 4 E. Huron Street, Chicago, IL 60611; New Mexico Commerce and Industry Department, Bataan Memorial Building, Santa Fe, NM 87503; State Industrial Directories Corp., 2 Penn Plaza, New York, NY 10001

New York

STATE CAPITOL, ALBANY, NY 12224
(518) 474–8390

INFORMATION OFFICES

Commerce/Economic Development
Department of Commerce
One Commerce Plaza
Albany, NY 12245
Division of Industrial and Corporate Development
One Commerce Plaza
Albany, NY 12245
Corporate
Secretary of State
162 Washington Avenue
Albany, NY 12231
Taxation
State Tax Commission
Department of Taxation and Finance
State Campus Building #9
Albany, NY 12227
State Chamber of Commerce
New York State Business Council
152 Washington Avenue
Albany, NY 12210
Small Business Advisory Board
Division of Small Business Services
230 Park Avenue
New York, NY 10169
International Commerce
Department of Commerce
230 Park Avenue
New York, NY 10169
Banking
Department of Banking
194 Washington Avenue
New York, NY 12210
Labor and Industrial Relations
Department of Labor
State Campus
Albany, NY 12240
Insurance
Department of Insurance
Empire State Plaza
Agency Building #1
Albany, NY 12257
Business Ombudsman
Department of Commerce
Small Business Services Division
230 Park Avenue
New York, NY 10169

INDUSTRIAL AND BUSINESS DIRECTORIES

New York and Surrounding Territory Classified Business Directory, New York Directory Co., Inc., 1440 Broadway, New York, NY 10018
New York Classified Business Directory, New York Directory Co., Inc., 1440 Broadway, New York, NY 10018
MacRae's New York State Industrial Directory, MacRae's Blue Book, Inc., 87 Terminal Drive, Plainview, NY 11803

New York State Industrial Directory, State Industrial Directories Corp., 2 Penn Plaza, New York, NY 10001; Manufacturers' News, Inc., 4 E. Huron Street, Chicago, IL 60611
Directory of Minority and Woman's Business, Minority and Woman's Business Division, New York State Department of Commerce, 230 Park Avenue, New York, NY 10169

North Carolina

STATE LEGISLATIVE BUILDING, RALEIGH, NC 27611
(919) 733–1110

INFORMATION OFFICES

Commerce/Economic Development
Department of Commerce
430 N. Salisbury Street
Raleigh, NC 27611
Corporate
Secretary of State
Corporation Division
300 N. Salisbury Street
Raleigh, NC 27611
Taxation
Department of Revenue
2 S. Salisbury Street
Raleigh, NC 22760
State Chamber of Commerce
North Carolina Citizens for Business and Industry
P.O. Box 2508
Raleigh, NC 27602
International Commerce
International Development
Department of Commerce
430 N. Salisbury Street
Raleigh, NC 27611
Banking and Securities
Banking Commission
Department of Commerce
430 N. Salisbury Street
Raleigh, NC 27611
Labor and Industrial Relations
Department of Labor
4 W. Edenton Street
Raleigh, NC 27611
Insurance
Department of Insurance
430 N. Salisbury Street
Raleigh, NC 27611
Business Ombudsman
Business Assistance
Department of Commerce
430 N. Salisbury Street
Raleigh, NC 27611

INDUSTRIAL AND BUSINESS DIRECTORIES

Directory of North Carolina Manufacturing Firms, North Carolina Department of Commerce, Raleigh, NC 27611; State Industrial Directories Corp., 2 Penn Plaza, New York, NY 10001; Manufacturers' News, Inc., 4 E. Huron Street, Chicago, IL 60611

North Dakota

STATE CAPITOL, BISMARCK, ND 58505
(701) 224–2000

INFORMATION OFFICES

Commerce/Economic Development
Economic Development Commission
Liberty Memorial Building
Bismarck, ND 58505
Corporate
Corporation Department
Office of the Secretary of State
Bismarck, ND 58505
Taxation
Tax Department
State Capitol
Bismarck, ND 58505
State Chamber of Commerce
Greater North Dakota Association—State Chamber of Commerce
P.O. Box 2467
Fargo, ND 58102
International Commerce
International Trade Department
Economic Development Commission
Liberty Memorial Building
Bismarck, ND 58505
Banking
State Banking Commission
State Capitol
Bismarck, ND 58505
Securities
Securities Commissioner
State Capitol
Bismarck, ND 58505
Labor and Industrial Relations
State Commissioner of Labor
State Capitol
Bismarck, ND 58505
Insurance
Insurance Commissioner
State Capitol
Bismarck, ND 58505
Uniform Industrial Code
Secretary of State
State Capitol
Bismarck, ND 58505
Business Ombudsman
Economic Development Commission

Liberty Memorial Building
Bismarck, ND 58505

INDUSTRIAL AND BUSINESS DIRECTORIES

North Dakota Manufacturers Directory, Economic Development Commission, Liberty Memorial Building, Bismarck, ND 58505; Manufacturers' News, Inc., 4 E. Huron Street, Chicago, IL 60611; State Industrial Directories Corp., 2 Penn Plaza, New York, NY 10001
Strictly Business, Frontier Directory Co., Inc., 515 E. Main Street, Bismarck, ND 58501

Ohio

STATE HOUSE, COLUMBUS, OH 43215
(614) 466–2000

INFORMATION OFFICES

Commerce/Economic Development
Ohio Department of Development
30 E. Broad Street
Columbus, OH 43266
Corporate
Secretary of State
Corporation Section
30 East Broad Street
Columbus, OH 43266
Taxation
Department of Taxation
30 E. Broad Street
Columbus, OH 43266
State Chamber of Commerce
Ohio Chamber of Commerce
35 E. Gay Street
Columbus, OH 43215
International Commerce
Ohio Department of Development
International Trade Division
30 E. Broad Street
P.O. Box 1001
Columbus, OH 43266
Banking
Ohio Department of Commerce
Division of Banks
Two Nationwide Plaza
Columbus, OH 43266
Securities
Ohio Department of Commerce
Division of Securities
Two Nationwide Plaza
Columbus, OH 43266
Labor and Industrial Relations
Ohio Department of Industrial Relations
2323 W. Fifth Avenue
P.O. Box 825
Columbus, OH 43266
Office of Collective Bargaining

Department of Administrative Services
375 S. High Street
Columbus, OH 43266
State Employment Relations Board
65 E. State Street
Columbus, OH 43215
Insurance
Ohio Department of Insurance
2100 Stella Court
Columbus, OH 43266
Uniform Industrial Code
Industrial Commission of Ohio
Division of Safety and Hygiene
246 N. High Street
Columbus, OH 43266
Business Ombudsman
Ohio Department of Development
Small and Developing Business Division
Minority Business Development Division
P.O. Box 1001
Columbus, OH 43266

INDUSTRIAL AND BUSINESS DIRECTORIES

Akron, Ohio Membership Directory and Buyers Guide, Akron Area Chamber of Commerce, P.O. Box 436, Crystal Lake, IL 60014
Directory of Manufacturers in the Toledo Area, Toledo Area Chamber of Commerce, 218 Huron Street, Toledo, OH 43604
Directory of Ohio Manufacturers, Harris Publishing Co., 2057-2 Aurora Road, Twinsburg, OH 44087; Manufacturers' News, Inc., 4 E. Huron Street, Chicago, IL 60611
Manufacturers Directory, Columbus Area Chamber of Commerce, 37 North High Street, Columbus, OH 43215
Ohio and International Trade, Division of International Trade, Department of Development, P.O. Box 1001, Columbus, OH 43266

Oklahoma

STATE CAPITOL, OKLAHOMA CITY, OK 73105
(405) 521-2011

INFORMATION OFFICES

Commerce/Economic Development
Department of Economic Development
4024 N. Lincoln
Oklahoma City, OK 73105
Department of Economic and Community Affairs
4545 Lincoln Boulevard
Oklahoma City, OK 73105
Corporate
Secretary of State

State Capitol
Oklahoma City, OK 73105
Taxation
Tax Commission
M. C. Connors Building
Oklahoma City, OK 73105
State Chamber of Commerce
Oklahoma State Chamber of Commerce
4020 North Lincoln
Oklahoma City, OK 73105
International Commerce
.International Export Services
P.O. Box 53424
Oklahoma City, OK 73152
Banking
Oklahoma Banking Services
4100 Lincoln Boulevard
Oklahoma City, OK 73105
Securities
Oklahoma Securities Commission
2915 Lincoln Boulevard
Oklahoma City, OK 73152
Labor and Industrial Relations
Oklahoma Labor Department
State Capitol
Oklahoma City, OK 73105
Insurance
Insurance Commission
408 Will Rogers Memorial Office Building
Oklahoma City, OK 73105
Uniform Industrial Code
Universal Commercial Code Division
County Clerk's Office
County Court House
Oklahoma City, OK 73102

INDUSTRIAL AND BUSINESS DIRECTORIES

Oklahoma Directory of Manufacturers and Products, Industrial Development Department, P.O. Box 53424, Oklahoma City, OK 73152

Oregon

STATE CAPITOL, SALEM, OR 97310
(503) 378-3131

INFORMATION OFFICES

Commerce/Economic Development
Department of Economic Development
595 Cottage Street, N.E.
Salem, OR 97310
Corporate
Corporation Commission
Commerce Building
158 12th Street N.E.
Salem, OR 97310

Taxation
Department of Revenue
Revenue Building
955 Center Street
Salem, OR 97310
International Commerce
Economic Development Department
International Trade Division
921 S.W. Washington
Portland, OR 97205
Banking
Department of Commerce
Banking Division
280 Court Street N.E.
Salem, OR 97310
Securities
Department of Commerce
Corporation Division—Securities Section
Commerce Building
158 12th Street N.E.
Salem, OR 97310
Labor and Industrial Relations
Bureau of Labor and Industries
1400 S.W. 5th Avenue
Portland, OR 97201
Insurance
Department of Commerce
Insurance Division
Commerce Building
158 12th Street N.E.
Salem, OR 97310
Uniform Industrial Code
Department of Commerce
Building Codes Division
401 Labor and Industries Building
Salem, OR 97310

INDUSTRIAL AND BUSINESS DIRECTORIES

Oregon Manufacturers Directory, Department of Economic Development, 595 Cottage Street, N.E., Salem, OR 97310; State Industrial Directories Corp., 2 Penn Plaza, New York, NY 10001; Manufacturers' News, Inc., 4 E. Huron Street, Chicago, IL 60611

Pennsylvania

MAIN CAPITOL BUILDING, HARRISBURG, PA 17120
(717) 787–2121

INFORMATION OFFICES

Department of Commerce
Department of Commerce
433 Forum Building
Harrisburg, PA 17120

Bureau of Domestic and International Commerce

Department of Commerce
453 Forum Building
Harrisburg, PA 17120

Bureau of International Commerce
Department of Commerce
450 Forum Building
Harrisburg, PA 17120

Bureau of Economic Assistance
Department of Commerce
405 Forum Building
Harrisburg, PA 17120

Small Business Action Center
Department of Commerce
494 Forum Building
Harrisburg, PA 17120
Corporate
Department of State
Bureau of Corporations
North Office Building
Harrisburg, PA 17120
Taxation
Department of Revenue
Information Service
P.O. Box 8056
Harrisburg, PA 17120
State Chamber of Commerce
Pennsylvania Chamber of Commerce
222 N. Third Street
Harrisburg, PA 17101
Banking
Banking
333 Market Street
Harristown II
Harrisburg, PA 17101-2290
Securities
Securities Commission
333 Market Street, Harristown II,
Harrisburg, PA 17101
Labor and Industrial Relations
Department of Labor & Industry
Labor & Industry Building
Harrisburg, PA 17120
Insurance
Insurance
Strawberry Square
Harrisburg, PA 17120

INDUSTRIAL AND BUSINESS DIRECTORIES

Industrial Directory of the Commonwealth of Pennsylvania, Department of General Services, Harris Publishing Company, 2057-2 Aurora Road, Twinsburg, OH 44087

Rhode Island

STATE HOUSE, PROVIDENCE, RI 02903
(401) 277–2000

INFORMATION OFFICES

Commerce/Economic Development
Department of Economic Development
7 Jackson Walkway
Providence, RI 02903
Taxation
Division of Taxation
Department of Administration
289 Promenade Street
CIC Complex
Providence, RI 02908
Corporate
Secretary of State
Corporation Department
270 Westminster Street
Providence, RI 02903
State Chamber of Commerce
Rhode Island Chamber of Commerce
91 Park Street
Providence, RI 02908
International Commerce
Rhode Island Department of Economic Development
European Office
Meir 24
2000 Antwerp
Belgium
Banking
Department of Business Regulation
Banking Division
100 N. Main Street
Providence, RI 02903
Securities
Department of Business Regulation
Banking Division
100 N. Main Street
Providence, RI 02903
Labor and Industrial Relations
Department of Labor
220 Elmwood Avenue
Providence, RI 02907
Insurance
Department of Business Regulation
Insurance Division
100 N. Main Street
Providence, RI 02903
Uniform Industrial Code
Department of Labor
220 Elmwood Avenue
Providence, RI 02907
Business Ombudsman
Business Action Center
Department of Economic Development
7 Jackson Walkway
Providence, RI 02903

INDUSTRIAL AND BUSINESS DIRECTORIES

Rhode Island Directory of Manufacturers, Department of Economic Development, 7 Jackson Walkway, Providence, RI 02903

Rhode Island State Industrial Directory, State Industrial Directories Corp., 2 Penn Plaza, New York, NY 10001

South Carolina

STATE HOUSE, COLUMBIA, SC 29211
(803) 758–0221

INFORMATION OFFICES

Commerce/Economic Development
South Carolina State Development Board
P.O. Box 927
1301 Gervais Street
Columbia, SC 29202
Taxation
Tax Commission
P.O. Box 125
John C. Calhoun Office Building
Columbia, SC 29214
Corporate
Secretary of State
P.O. Box 11350
Columbia, SC 29211
State Chamber of Commerce
South Carolina Chamber of Commerce
1301 Gervais Street
Columbia, SC 29202
International Commerce
South Carolina State Development Board
1301 Gervais Street
P.O. Box 927
Columbia, SC 29202
Labor and Industrial Relations
South Carolina Labor Department
Landmark Center, 3600 Forest Drive
P.O. Box 11329
Columbia, SC 29211
Insurance
South Carolina Department of Insurance
2711 Middleburg Drive
P.O. Box 4067
Columbia, SC 29240
Business Ombudsman
South Carolina State Development Board
1301 Gervais Street
P.O. Box 927
Columbia, SC 29202

INDUSTRIAL AND BUSINESS DIRECTORIES

Industrial Directory of South Carolina, South Carolina State Development Board, P.O. Box 927, 1301 Gervais Street, Columbia, SC 29202
South Carolina International Trade Directory, South Carolina State Development Board, P.O. Box 927, 1301 Gervais Street, Columbia, SC 29202

South Dakota

STATE CAPITOL, PIERRE, SD 57501
(605) 773-3011

INFORMATION OFFICES

Commerce/Economic Development
Department of State Development
711 Wells Avenue
Capitol Lake Plaza
Pierre, SD 57501
Department of Commerce and Regulation
910 E. Sioux
Pierre, SD 57501
Corporate
Secretary of State
Corporation Division
Capitol Building
Pierre, SD 57501
Taxation
Department of Revenue
Kniep Building
Pierre, SD 57501
State Chamber of Commerce
South Dakota State Chamber of Commerce
300 S. Highland
P.O. Box 548
Pierre, SD 57501
International Commerce
Department of State Development
P.O. Box 6000
Pierre, SD 57501
Banking
Department of Commerce and Regulation
Division of Banking
105 S. Euclid
Pierre, SD 57501
Securities
Department of Commerce and Regulation
Division of Securities
910 E. Sioux
Pierre, SD 57501
Labor and Industrial Relations
Department of Labor
Division of Labor and Management
Kneip Building
Pierre, SD 57501
Insurance
Department of Commerce and Regulation
Division of Insurance
910 E. Sioux
Pierre, SD 57501

INDUSTRIAL AND BUSINESS DIRECTORIES

Directory of South Dakota Industries, Manufacturers' News, Inc., 4 E. Huron Street, Chicago, IL 60611

South Dakota Manufacturers and Processors Directory, South Dakota Department of State Development, 711 Well Avenue, Capitol Lake Plaza, Pierre, SD 57501; State Industrial Directories Corp., 2 Penn Plaza, New York, NY 10001

South Dakota Export Directory, South Dakota Department of State Development, 711 Well Avenue, Capitol Lake Plaza, Pierre, SD 57501

Tennessee

STATE CAPITOL, NASHVILLE, TN 37219
(615) 741-2001

INFORMATION OFFICES

Commerce/Economic Development
Department of Economic and Community Development
Rachel Jackson Building
320 6th Avenue North
Nashville, TN 37219-5308
Corporate
Secretary of State
Records Division
James K. Polk Building
Nashville, TN 37219
Taxation
Department of Revenue
927 Andrew Jackson Building
Nashville, TN 37219
State Chamber of Commerce
State Chamber Division of the Tennessee Taxpayers Association
242 Doctors Building
Nashville, TN 37203
International Commerce
Department of Economic & Community Development
International Sales & Marketing
Rachel Jackson Building
320 6th Avenue North
Nashville, TN 37219-5308
Banking
Department of Financial Institutions
James K. Polk State Office Building
505 Deaderick Street
Nashville, TN 37219
Securities
Department of Commerce & Insurance
Securities Division
614 Tennessee Building
Nashville, TN 37219
Labor and Industrial Relations
Department of Labor
501 Union Building
Nashville, TN 37219
Insurance
Department of Commerce & Insurance

Insurance Division
1808 West End Building
Nashville, TN 37219
Business Ombudsman
Department of Economic & Community Development
Business & Industry Services Division
Rachel Jackson Building
320 6th Avenue North
Nashville, TN 37219–5308

INDUSTRIAL AND BUSINESS DIRECTORIES

Directory of Tennessee Industries, Manufacturers' News, Inc., 4 E. Huron Street, Chicago, IL 60611; State Industrial Directories Corp., 2 Penn Plaza, New York, NY 10001

Texas

STATE CAPITOL, AUSTIN, TX 78701
State Information: (512) 475–2323

INFORMATION OFFICES

Commerce/Economic Development
Texas Economic Development Commission
410 East 5th Street
Austin, TX 78711
Corporate
Secretary of State
P.O. Box 13701
Sam Houston Building
Austin, TX 78711
Taxation
Comptroller of Public Accounts
104 LBJ State Office Building
Austin, TX 78711
State Chamber of Commerce
Texas State Chamber of Commerce
77001 N. Lamar
Suite 302
Austin, TX 78752
Tourism Department
P.O. Box 12008
Austin, TX 78711
Lower Rio Grand Valley Chamber of Commerce
P.O. Box 975
Weslaco, TX 75896
South Texas Chamber of Commerce
6222 NW IH 19
San Antonio, TX 78201
East Texas Chamber of Commerce
P.O. Box 1592
Longview, TX 75601
West Texas Chamber of Commerce
P.O. Box 1516
Abilene, TX 79604

International Commerce
International Division
Texas Economic Development Commission
P.O. Box 12728, Capitol Station
Austin, TX 78711
Banking
Texas Department of Banking
2601 North Lamar
Austin, TX 78705
Securities
Securities Board
1800 San Jacinto St.
Austin, TX 78701
Labor and Industrial Relations
Texas Department of Labor and Standards
P.O. Box 12157, Capitol Station
Austin, TX 78711
Insurance
Texas State Board of Insurance
State Insurance Building
1110 San Jacinto
Austin, TX 78786
Uniform Industrial Code
Uniform Commercial Code Section
Secretary of State's Office
P.O. Box 13193, Capitol Station
Austin, TX 78711
Business Ombudsman
Governor's Office of Economic Development
P.O. Box 13561
Austin, TX 78711

INDUSTRIAL AND BUSINESS DIRECTORIES

Dallas Business Guide, Dallas Chamber of Commerce, Fidelity Tower, Dallas, TX 75201
Directory of Texas Manufacturers, Bureau of Business Research, University of Texas, Austin, TX 78712; State Industrial Directories Corp., 2 Penn Plaza, New York, NY 10001
Fort Worth Directory of Manufacturers, Fort Worth Area Chamber of Commerce, 700 Throckmorton Street, Fort Worth, TX 76102
Texas Exporter-Importer Directory, Gulf International Trades, Box 52717, Houston, TX 77052
Texas Manufacturers Directory, Manufacturers' News, Inc., 4 E. Huron Street, Chicago, IL 60611

Utah

STATE CAPITOL, SALT LAKE CITY, UT 84114
(801) 533–4000

INFORMATION OFFICES

Commerce/Economic Development
Department of Business Regulation

160 East 300 South Street
Salt Lake City, UT 84111-5802
Department of Community and Economic
  Development
6290 State Office Building
Salt Lake City, UT 84114
Office of Planning & Budget
Data Resources Section
116 Capitol Building
Salt Lake City, UT 84114
Corporate
  Division of Corporations
  Heber M. Wells Building
  160 E. 300 South
  Salt Lake City, UT 84111-5802.
Taxation
  Department of State Tax Commission
  Heber M. Wells Building
  160 E. 300 South
  Salt Lake City, UT 84134-4000
International Commerce
  International Business Development
  Division of Economic & Industrial Develop-
    ment
  6150 State Office Building
  Salt Lake City, UT 84114
Banking
  Department of Financial Institutions
  Heber M. Wells Building
  160 E. 300 South
  P.O. Box 89
  Salt Lake City, UT 84110-5802
Securities
  Division of Securities
  Heber M. Wells Building
  160 E. 300 South
  P.O. Box 89
  Salt Lake City, UT 84110-5802
Labor and Industrial Relations
  Industrial Commission of Utah
  Heber M. Wells Building
  160 E. 300 South
  Salt Lake City, UT 84110-5800
Insurance
  Department of Insurance
  Heber M. Wells Building
  160 E. 300 South
  Salt Lake City, UT 84110-5803
Uniform Industrial Code
  Employment Security/Job Service
  174 Social Hall Avenue
  Salt Lake City, UT 84147

INDUSTRIAL AND BUSINESS DIRECTORIES

Directory of Utah Manufacturers, Manufacturers' News, Inc., 4 E. Huron Street, Chicago,
IL 60611; Department of Employment Security, 1234 S. Main Street, Salt Lake City, UT
84147

Vermont

STATE HOUSE, MONTPELIER, VT 05602
(802) 828-2228

INFORMATION OFFICES

Commerce/Economic Development
  Agency of Development and Community Af-
    fairs
  Department of Economic Development
  109 State Street
  Montpelier, VT 05602
Corporate
  Secretary of State
  Corporation Department
  26 Terrace Street
  Montpelier, VT 05602
Taxation
  Department of Taxes
  Agency of Administration
  109 State Street
  Montpelier, VT 05602
State Chamber of Commerce
  Vermont State Chamber of Commerce
  P.O. Box 37
  Montpelier, VT 05602
Insurance
  Department of Banking and Insurance
  120 State Street
  Montpelier, VT 05602
Banking
  Department of Banking and Insurance
  120 State Street
  Montpelier, VT 05602

INDUSTRIAL AND BUSINESS DIRECTORIES

Vermont Directory of Manufacturers, Vermont
Agency of Development and Community Affairs, Montpelier, VT 05602
Vermont State Industrial Directory, Manufacturers' News, Inc., 4 E. Huron Street, Chicago, IL 60611; State Industrial Directories
Corp., 2 Penn Plaza, New York, NY 10001
Vermont Yearbook, The National Survey, Chester, VT 05143

Virginia

STATE CAPITOL, RICHMOND, VA 23219
(804) 786-0000

INFORMATION OFFICES

Commerce/Economic Development
  Department of Economic Development
  1000 Washington Building

Richmond, VA 23219
Department of Conservation and Historic Resources
1100 Washington Building
Richmond, VA 23219
Corporate
State Corporation Commission
1220 Bank Street
Richmond, VA 23209
Taxation
Department of Taxation
2200 W. Broad Street
Richmond, VA 23219
State Chamber of Commerce
Virginia State Chamber of Commerce
611 E. Franklin Street
Richmond, VA 23219
International Commerce
Department of Economic Development
1000 Washington Building
Richmond, VA 23219
Banking
State Corporation Commission
Bureau of Financial Institutions
701 E. Byrd Street
Richmond, VA 23205
Securities
State Corporation Commission
Division of Securities and Retail Franchising
11 S. 12th Street
Richmond, VA 23219
Labor and Industrial Relations
Department of Labor and Industry
205 N. 4th Street
Richmond, VA 23241
Insurance
State Corporation Commission
Bureau of Insurance
1220 Bank Street
Richmond, VA 23209
Uniform Industrial Code
Virginia Employment Commission
Research and Analysis Division
703 E. Main Street
Richmond, VA 23211
Business Ombudsman
Department of Agriculture and Consumer Services
Office of Consumer Affairs
1100 Bank Street
Richmond, VA 23219

INDUSTRIAL AND BUSINESS DIRECTORIES

Industrial Directory of Virginia, Chamber of Commerce, 611 E. Franklin Street, Richmond, VA 23219
Virginia Industrial Directory, Manufacturers' News, Inc., 4 E. Huron Street, Chicago, IL 60611; State Industrial Directories Corp., 2 Penn Plaza, New York, NY 10001

Washington

101 GENERAL ADMINISTRATION BUILDING, OLYMPIA, WA 98504
(206) 753–5630

INFORMATION OFFICES

Commerce/Economic Development
Department of Commerce and Economic Development
101 General Administration Building
Olympia, WA 98504
Corporate
Secretary of State
Corporate Division
Legislative Building
Olympia, WA 98504
Taxation
Department of Revenue
412 General Administration Building
Olympia, WA 98504
State Chamber of Commerce
Association of Washington Business
1414 S. Cherry Street
Olympia, WA 98501
Small Business Development Centers
441 Todd Hall
Washington State University
Pullman, WA 99164

180 Nickerson
Seattle, WA 98109

101 General Administration Building
Olympia, WA 98504

303 E. D Street
Yakima, WA 98901

705 W. 1st Street
Spokane, WA 99204

Western Washington University
Bellingham, WA 98225
International Commerce
Department of Commerce & Economic Development
Domestic & International Trade Development
312 First Avenue North
Seattle, WA 98109
Banking
General Administration Building
Banking & Small Loans
218 General Administration Building
Olympia, WA 98504
Securities
Department of Licensing Building
Att: Securities Division
1300 Quince Street SE
Olympia, WA 98504
Labor and Industrial Relations
Department of Labor & Industries

Employment Standards Division
General Administration Building
Olympia, WA 98504
Insurance
Insurance Commissioner's Office
Insurance Building
Olympia, WA 98504
Uniform Commercial Code
Department of Licensing
Business License Centre
1300 Quince Street SE
East Side Plaza
Olympia, WA 98504
Business Ombudsman
Department of Commerce & Economic Development
Office of Small Business
101 General Administration Building
Olympia, WA 98504

INDUSTRIAL AND BUSINESS DIRECTORIES

1984 Directory of Advanced Technology Industries in Washington State, Economic Development Partnership for Washington State, 1800 Pacific Highway South, Seattle, WA 98188

Business Assistance in Washington State, Washington State International Trade Directory, Department of Commerce and Economic Development, 101 General Administration Building, Olympia, WA 98504

Minority Women Business Enterprises, Office of Minority Women Business Enterprise, 406 S. Water Street, Olympia, WA 98504

Washington Manufacturers Register, Times Mirror Press, 1115 S. Boyle, Los Angeles, CA 90023

MacRae's Washington State Industrial Directory, 87 Terminal Drive, Plainview, NY 11803

Washington Forest Industry Mill Directory, Department of Natural Resources, Public Lands Building, Olympia, WA 98504

Directory of Washington Mining Operations, Department of Natural Resources, Olympia, WA 98504

West Virginia

STATE CAPITOL, CHARLESTON, WV 25305
(304) 348-0400

INFORMATION OFFICES

Commerce/Economic Development
Governor's Office of Community and Industrial Development
1900 Washington Street East

Building I
Charleston, WV 25305
Corporate
Secretary of State
Corporate Division
1900 Washington Street East
Building 1
Charleston, WV 25305
Taxation
Tax Department
1900 Washington Street East
Building 1
Charleston, WV 25305
State Chamber of Commerce
P.O. Box 2789
1101 Kanawha Valley Building
Charleston, WV 25330
International Commerce
Governor's Office of Community and Industrial Development
1900 Washington Street East
Building 6
Charleston, WV 25305
Banking
Department of Banking
1900 Washington Street East
Building 5
Charleston, WV 25305
Securities
Auditor's Office
1900 Washington Street East
Building 1
Charleston, WV 25305
Labor & Industrial Relations
Governor's Office of Community and Industrial Development
1900 Washington Street East
Building 6
Charleston, WV 25305
Insurance
Insurance Department
2100 Washington Street East
Charleston, WV 25305
Uniform Industrial Code
Governor's Office of the Secretary of State
1900 Washington Street East
Building 1
Charleston, WV 25305
Business Ombudsman
Governor's Office of Community and Industrial Development East
Building 6
Charleston, WV 25305

INDUSTRIAL AND BUSINESS DIRECTORIES

West Virginia Manufacturing Directory, Harris Publishing Company, Inc., 2057-2 Aurora Road, Twinsburg, OH 44087; State Industrial Directories Corp., 2 Penn Plaza, New York, NY 10001

Wisconsin

STATE CAPITOL, MADISON, WI 53702
(608) 266-2211

INFORMATION OFFICES

Commerce/Economic Development
Department of Development
123 W. Washington Avenue
Madison, WI 53702
Corporate
Secretary of State
Corporate Division
201 E. Washington Avenue
Madison, WI 53702
Taxation
Department of Revenue
125 S. Webster Avenue
Madison, WI 53702
State Chamber of Commerce
Wisconsin Association of Manufacturers and
Commerce
111 E. Wisconsin Avenue
Milwaukee, WI 53202
International Commerce
International Business Services
Department of Development
123 W. Washington Avenue
Madison, WI 53702
Banking
Banking, Office of the Commissioner
123 West Washington Avenue
Madison, WI 53702
Securities
Securities—Office of the Commissioner
111 West Wilson Avenue
Madison, WI 53703
Labor and Industrial Relations
Department of Industry, Labor, and Human
Relations
201 E. Washington Avenue
Madison, WI 53702
Insurance
Office of the Commissioner—Insurance
123 West Washington Avenue
Madison, WI 53702
Uniform Industrial Code
Department of Industry, Labor and Human
Relations
201 E. Washington Avenue
Madison, WI 53702
Business Ombudsman
Small Business Ombudsman
Department of Development
123 W. Washington Avenue
Madison, WI 53702

INDUSTRIAL AND BUSINESS DIRECTORIES

Classified Directory of Wisconsin Manufacturers, Wisconsin Association of Manufacturers

and Commerce, 111 E. Wisconsin Avenue,
Milwaukee, WI 53202; Sta e Industrial Directories Corp., 2 Penn Plaza, New York, NY
10001
Wisconsin Manufacturers Directory, Manufacturers' News, Inc., 4 E. Huron Street, Chicago, IL 60611
Wisconsin Local Development Organizations
(annual), Wisconsin Department of Development, 123 W. Washington Avenue, Madison,
WI 53702

Wyoming

STATE CAPITOL, CHEYENNE, WY 82002
(307) 777-7011

INFORMATION OFFICES

Commerce/Economic Development
Department of Economic Planning and Development
Herschler Building
Cheyenne, WY 82002
Corporate
Secretary of State
Corporate Division
State Capitol
Cheyenne, WY 82002
Taxation
Department of Revenue and Taxation
Herschler Building
Cheyenne, WY 82002
International Commerce
International Trade Office
State Planning Coordinator
Herschler Building
Cheyenne, WY 82002
Banking
State Examiner
Herschler Building
Cheyenne, WY 82002
Securities
Secretary of State
Securities Division
State Capitol
Cheyenne, WY 82002
Labor and Industrial Relations
Department of Labor and Statistics
Herschler Building
Cheyenne, WY 82002
Insurance
Insurance Commission
Herschler Building
Cheyenne, WY 82002
Uniform Industrial Code
Industrial Siting Commission
Boyd Building
1720 Carey Avenue
Cheyenne, WY 82002

Industrial Development Division
Department of Economic Planning and Development
Herschler Building
Cheyenne, WY 82002

INDUSTRIAL AND BUSINESS DIRECTORIES

Wyoming Directory of Manufacturing and Mining, Manufacturers' News, Inc., 4 E. Huron Street, Chicago, IL 60611; Department of Economic Planning and Development, Herschler Building, Cheyenne, WY 82002; State Industrial Directories Corp. 2 Penn Plaza, New York, NY 10001

Puerto Rico

CAPITOL, SAN JUAN, PR 00901
(809) 724–6040 (House of Representatives)
(809) 724–2030 (Senate)

INFORMATION OFFICES

Commerce/Economic Development
Puerto Rico Department of Commerce
P.O. Box S 4275
San Juan, PR 00905
Puerto Rico Economic Development Administration
G.P.O. Box 2350
San Juan, PR 00936
Puerto Rico Planning Board
P.O. Box 41119
San Juan, PR 00940
Government Development Bank
P.O. Box 42001
Minillas Station
Santurce, PR 00940
Taxation
Puerto Rico Department of Treasury
P.O. Box S-4515
San Juan, PR 00901
Office of Industrial Tax Exemption
P.O. Box 2121
Hato Rey, PR 00918–2121
Chamber of Commerce
Camara De Comercio de Puerto Rico
P.O. Box 3789
San Juan, PR 00904
Puerto Rico Manufacturers Association
P.O. Box 2410
Hato Rey, PR 00919
Securities
Puerto Rico Treasury Department

Office of the Commissioner of Financial Institutions
P.O. Box 4515
San Juan, PR 00905
Puerto Rico Labor Relations Board
P.O. Box 4048
San Juan, PR 00905
National Labor Relations Board
Federal Building
Charlos E. Chardon Street
Hato Rey, PR 00918
Insurance
Office of the Insurance Commissioner
P.O. Box 8330, Fdez Janoos Station
Santurce, PR 00910
Puerto Rico Insurance Companies Association, Inc.
Housing Investment Building
San Juan, PR 00918
Uniform Industrial Code
Department of Labor and Human Resources
505 Muñoz Rivera Avenue
Prudencio Rivera Martínez Building
Hato Rey, PR 00918
Business Ombudsman
Ombudsman Office
1205 Ponce de León Avenue
Banco de San Juan
Santurce, PR 00907–3995
International Commerce
Puerto Rico Department of Commerce
External Trade Promotion Program
P.O. Box S 4275
San Juan, PR 00905
US Department of Commerce
International Trade Administration
Charlos E. Chardon Street
Federal Building
Hato Rey, PR 00918
Puerto Rico Chamber of Commerce
International Trade Division
P.O. Box 3789
San Juan, PR 00904
Banking
Puerto Rico Bankers Association
Banco Popular Center
Hato Rey, PR 00918

INDUSTRIAL AND BUSINESS DIRECTORIES

Puerto Rico Official Industrial and Trade Directory, Witcom Group, Inc., P.O. Box 2310, San Juan, PR 00902
The Businessman's Guide to Puerto Rico, Puerto Rico Almanacs, Inc., P.O. Box 9582, Santurce, Puerto Rico 00908

International Information Sources

Foreign Trade Information

Business people seeking information about foreign commercial opportunities or sources of business contacts have available a number of government and private services that are described in this and subsequent sections. The extensive nature of these services is not always fully appreciated by members of the business community. Some of the most helpful services are provided by the International Trade Administration (ITA) 202–377–3808 of the Department of Commerce, described below. This agency is particularly helpful in establishing initial contacts and in evaluating foreign markets.

Business people traveling abroad will find the following services of help in initiating contacts:

1. Office of Export Counselling, U.S. Department of Commerce. Telephone: 202-377-3181.
2. Commercial offices at U.S. embassies or consulates.

Foreign credit information sources are provided at the end of this section.

DEPARTMENT OF COMMERCE

Address: Constitution and 14th Street NW, Washington, DC 20230. Information phone: 202–377–2000.

The central export information source within the Department of Commerce is the International Trade Administration (ITA), which promotes the growth of U.S. industry and commerce, both foreign and domestic. Several units with functions relevant to exporters are:

- U.S. and Foreign Commercial Service (below)
- International Economic Policy (page 614)
- Trade Development (page 614)
- Trade Administration (page 615)

• U.S. AND FOREIGN COMMERCIAL SERVICE

The U.S. and Foreign Commercial Service (US&FCS) offers the American exporter coordinated trade assistance, both in the United States and abroad. US&FCS can help new exporters enter their first overseas market; it also can help

Source: Excerpted from *Business America* and other Department of Commerce sources.

experienced exporters penetrate additional or harder-to-enter markets.

With offices in major foreign cities in countries that are the United States' principal trading partners US&FCS provides a full range of business, investment, and financial counseling services. These include political and credit risk analysis, advice on market entry strategy and source of financing, and major project identification, tracking and assistance. In addition, US&FCS overseas officers can make introductions to local business and government leaders, assist in trade disputes, and provide liaison between American and foreign business communities.

A major priority of the US&FCS is to help U.S. businesses exploit the trade opportunities resulting from the 1979 Multilateral Trade Negotiations (MTN).

Domestic Operations

The domestic side of the US&FCS operates District Offices in industrial and commercial centers throughout the nation. These offices offer a broad range of trade-related information, as well as one-on-one counseling by experienced trade specialists.

The District Offices can tell exporters and other prospective business people about trade and investment opportunities abroad; foreign markets for U.S. products and services; financing aid; insurance from the Foreign Credit Insurance Association (FCIA); tax advantages of exporting; international trade exhibitions; export documentation requirements; economic facts on foreign countries; and export licensing and import requirements.

In *Commerce Business Daily*, US&FCS publicizes proposed foreign government procurement actions and foreign trade leads, as well as information on U.S. Government procurement actions. For a sample, write US&FCS, Room 3012, U.S. Department of Commerce, Washington, D.C. 20230. To subscribe, call the Superintendent of Documents, U.S. Government Printing Office, Washington, D.C. 20402, on 202-783-3238.

The District Offices work closely with American business people experienced in all aspects of export trade through District Export Councils (DECs). DEC members counsel prospective exporters on the "how-to's" of international trade, cosponsor seminars and workshops with the District Offices, address business groups on international business opportunities, and promote awareness of the trade-assistance programs of the Department of Commerce.

Export Counseling Center: ITA also maintains an Export Counseling Center in Washington, D.C., to help U.S. firms develop or expand markets abroad. Counselors advise exporters on the choice of services and guide them in the use of export practices and procedures.

An important part of this program is an Export Information Reference Room where businesspeople can review a wide range of major foreign projects under consideration by international financial institutions—World Bank Group, Inter-American Development Bank, Asian Development Bank, and the United Nations Development Programme.

U.S. business executives wishing appointments with a Commerce Department program specialist and/or other agencies involved in international marketing, should contact the nearest District Office or the Export Counseling Center, US&FCS, Washington, D.C. 20230, telephone 202-377-3181.

Caribbean Basin Business Information Center (CBIC)

The Caribbean Basin Business Information Center (CBIC) is a specialized unit in US&FCS charged with facilitating investment and trade between entrepreneurs in the United States and the Caribbean Basin. A *CBI Starter Kit* is available from the Center at 202-377-2527.

Publications That Assist Exporters

A variety of publications are available to help exporters reach and expand foreign markets. The foremost of these is *Business America*, which is Commerce Department's principal periodical for domestic and international business news and covers a wide range of topics. Subscriptions are available from the Superintendent of Documents, General Printing Office, Washington, DC 20402. Other publications include:

Commercial News USA (CN) is the Department of Commerce export magazine. Several times a year it is devoted to the technology and products of a single industry to help firms in that particular industry reach overseas markets. Information is available at any Commerce Department District Office.

A Basic Guide to Exporting: This publication takes a step-by-step approach to exporting especially designed for firms with little or no export experience. Assessment of export potential is treated first, along with sources of export counseling and education. Other topics include: selecting markets, export strategies, pricing, financing, shipment, methods of payment, export documentation, and government regulations. A glossary of export terms and list of export-assistance groups is provided. Available from the Superintendent of Documents, General Printing Office, Washington, DC 20402.

A Summary of U.S. Export Administration

Regulations, prepared by the International Trade Administration, provides a brief introduction to export control licensing provisions contained in the Commerce Department's *Export Administration Regulations.*

Expand Overseas Sales With Commerce Department Help describes the various types of assistance available from the Commerce Department for small businesses seeking foreign markets. Available from International Trade Administration.

The U.S. Department of Commerce has discontinued publication of the *Export Promotion Calendar* due to budget cutbacks. However, the same information (e.g., listings of Commerce Department supported trade events in the U.S. and overseas, etc.) that was in the printed publication is now on-line at Department of Commerce District Offices around the country (see page 616).

Export Assistance Services

ITA offers many services to help U.S. companies begin exporting and to locate or expand foreign markets.

Many are provided by the U.S. and Foreign Commercial Service. Some are based on the Automated Information Transfer System (AITS), a linked system of small computers that has been installed in most ITA District Offices and overseas posts to make market-related information accessible worldwide.

AITS creates computer files of U.S. exporters and foreign importers, making them readily available at ITA District Offices and foreign posts. The system can match U.S. producers with overseas buyers interested in their products; retrieve trade leads, company contacts, and other information; and send messages from one ITA location to another.

Comparison Shopping Service, offered by the U.S. Department of Commerce, is a custom-tailored export assistance program for U.S. businesses. This service will provide information requested by a U.S. firm about a product's market potential and competition in a particular market overseas. It will also give names of interested agents, distributors, and buyers. For further information contact the nearest Commerce Department District Office (page 616), or write the U.S. Department of Commerce, Attention, Director, OIPDD, P.O. Box 14207, Washington, D.C. 20044.

Also of help to the business community are the recently expanded services of the Exporter Assistance Division of the Office of Export Administration.

The following are some useful telephone numbers:

Regulatory and Policy Information, and State of Emergency Cases, 202/377-4811

Status of all Pending Cases, 202/377–2752
Emergency Handling Requests, 202/377–2793,
  or 202/377–2799
Trade Fair Licenses, 202/377–2752
Publications, 202/377–2574
Seminars, 202/377–3856

Market Identification Information

Export Statistics Profiles (ESP) are tables of
U.S. exports for a specific industry which help
exporters locate best export markets. The *ESP*
analyze the industry's exports product-by-prod-
uct, country-by-country over each of the last
five years to date.

Custom Statistical Service (CSS) is a tailored
set of tables of U.S. export or import statistics.
The custom service allows an exporter to obtain
data for specific products or countries of interest, or for ones which may not appear in the
standard ESP country and product rankings.
Data can be supplied in other formats such as
quantity, unit quantity, unit value and percentages.

Country Trade Statistics (CTS) are a set of
four key tables that indicate which U.S. products are in the greatest demand in a specific
country over the most recent five-year period.

Market Assessment Information

*International Market Research Reports
(IMR)* cover single industries in selected countries or markets and are chosen according to
their potential for U.S. export sales. These reports are produced abroad under contract with
experienced local research analysts according
to detailed specifications prepared in Washington.

Country Market Surveys (CMS) are special
"bulletins" that point out unique market situations and new opportunities to U.S. exporters
in specific markets. Each *CMS* summarizes an
International and Market Research Report discussed above.

*Annual Worldwide Industry Reviews
(AWIR)* are a combination of country-by-country market assessments, export trends, and five-
year statistical tables of U.S. exports for a single
industry integrated into one report. They show
an industry's performance for the most recent
year in many countries.

*Product/Country Market Profiles (PMP-
CMP)* are single industry, multi-country or sin-
gle-country, multi-industry reports, including
trade contacts, specific trade leads, and statistical analyses.

Market Share Reports (MSR). These annual
reports provide a five-year record of U.S. participation in foreign markets for manufactured
products. Both country and product series are
available. For a free catalogue write:

National Technical Information Service
5285 Port Royal Road
Springfield, VA 22161

Market Contact Information

Export Mailing List Services (EMLs) are
mailing lists of prospective overseas customers
from the Commerce Department's automated
worldwide file of foreign firms. EMLs identify
manufacturers, agents, retailers, service firms,
government agencies, and other one-to-one
contacts. EMLs information is available in three
forms:

1. *Export Mailing Lists* are on-line, custom
retrievals based on the market criteria specified
by the exporter.

2. *Trade Lists* provide listings for all the
companies in the computer for a single country
across all product sectors, or all the companies
in a single industry across all countries.

3. Access to the Commerce Department's
worldwide file of foreign firms is also available
at a local Commerce Department District Office, or from the private sector DIALOG database.

Trade Opportunities Program (TOP) provides timely sales leads from overseas firms
seeking to buy or represent U.S. products and
services. U.S. Commercial Officers worldwide
gather leads through local channels. Lead details are telexed daily to a computer center in
Washington and then sent directly to the company requesting the information. Trade opportunity information is available in two forms:

1. *TOP Notice* daily searches the TOP computer and automatically sends only the leads
for those products and services for which the
subscriber is registered.

2. *TOP Bulletin* is a weekly publication of
all the leads received the previous week for
all products from all countries.

Agent Distributor Service (ADS) is a custom
overseas search for interested and qualified foreign representatives on behalf of a U.S. exporter. A report is prepared identifying up to
six foreign prospects that have examined the
U.S. firm's product literature and have expressed interest in representing or handling the
U.S. firm's products. Application forms (ITA-
424P) may be obtained from any Commerce
Department District Office.

World Traders Data Reports (WTDR) are
background reports on individual foreign firms,
containing information about each firm's business activities, its standing in the local business
community, its credit-worthiness, and its overall
reliability and suitability as a trade contact for
U.S. exporters. WTDRs are designed to help
U.S. firms evaluate potential foreign customers
before making a business commitment.

For additional information on any of the
above products and services call the ITA District Office in your area or a client service representative on 202-377-2432 or write Client Service, Trade Information Services, U.S.
Department of Commerce, P.O. Box 14207,
Washington, D.C. 20044.

Additional ITA Publications and Services

Many of the ITA publications listed below are provided by USFCS. Except as otherwise noted they may be ordered from:

Office of Trade Information Services
Room 1324
U.S. Department of Commerce
P.O. Box 1427
Washington, D.C. 20044

Foreign Traders Index: Information on more than 140,000 foreign importing organizations in 130 countries is stored in ITA's *Foreign Traders Index* (FTI), a computerized file. New information on listed firms and information on newly identified firms are constantly added to the index. The information in the file is collected and supplied to Commerce by the U.S. Foreign Service—Department of State.

Data Tape Service: U.S. firms with computer facilities may purchase magnetic tapes containing information on all firms in selected countries or in all countries covered in the *Foreign Traders Index*. This service makes it possible for users to retrieve various segments of data from the *Foreign Traders Index* through their own computer facilities.

Foreign Economic Trends (FET) present current business and economic developments and the latest economic indicators in more than 100 countries. They are prepared on an annual or semiannual basis by the U.S. Foreign Service and U.S. Foreign Commercial Service. Available from the Superintendent of Documents, U.S. Government Printing Office, Washington, D.C. 20402.

Overseas Business Reports (OBR) include current and detailed marketing information, trade outlooks, statistics, regulations, and market profiles. They are available from the Superintendent of Documents, U.S. Government Printing Office, Washington, DC 20402.

International Marketing Information are reports prepared by U.S. Embassies describing market opportunities or conditions within a country, but not in accordance with *International Market Research* specifications.

International Economic Indicators presents a wide variety of comparative economic statistics for the United States and seven major competitor nations for recent periods. This quarterly publication is available from the Superintendent of Documents, U.S. Government Printing Office, Washington, DC 20402.

Current International Trade Position of the United States is a free reference guide from the Department of Commerce on U.S. imports of petroleum, U.S. trading by type and area, balance of payments and U.S. share of world exports. Order from the U.S. Department of Commerce, Publications Sales Branch, Washington, DC 20230.

Prepared by the Census Department and available from the Government Printing Office, Washington, DC 20402, the *Foreign Trade Report FT 410: U.S. Exports Commodity by Country* is one of the best sources for locating export markets. These monthly publications provide a statistical record of the shipments of all merchandise from the United States to foreign countries.

New Product Information Service (NPIS)

This program provides worldwide publicity for new U.S. products available for immediate export. Promotional descriptions are published in *Commercial News USA* magazine. Information on selected NPIS products is also broadcast overseas by the U.S. Information Agency's "Voice of America" radio shows. For an application, contact a Trade Specialist at the nearest ITA District Office or write the Director, New Product Information Service, US&FCS, Room 2106, U.S. Department of Commerce, Washington, D.C. 20230.

International Trade Fairs and Commercial Exhibitions

ITA sponsors participation by U.S. firms in worldwide international trade fairs, assisting with many pre-show promotional services such as marketing, provision of exhibit space, design and construction of exhibits. For the latest calendar of scheduled events, write: Event Management and Support, US&FCS, Room 2806, U.S. Department of Commerce, Washington, D.C. 20230.

ITA has a program to certify qualified U.S. organizations to recruit and manage U.S. exhibits at international shows. The program is open to exposition management companies, trade fair operators, trade associations, and other qualified organizations with trade fair experience. For further information, call or write: Director, Trade Fair Certification, US&FCS, Room 2806, U.S. Department of Commerce, Washington, D.C. 20230.

Video Catalog Program

The Video Catalog Program Service to exporters combines individual company catalogs with video presentations of one or two of a firm's products in an exhibition at several US&FCS overseas posts. The technique is especially useful in countries where it is not cost effective to send actual products for display or company personnel. For information, contact: Event Management and Support Services, US&FCS, Room 2806, U.S. Department of Commerce, Washington, D.C. 20230; telephone 202-377-3973.

Industry-Organized Government-Approved (IOGA) Trade Missions

Trade missions of this type are export-oriented events planned and organized by nonfederal government groups such as local and state governments, industry trade associations, and chambers of commerce. For information, contact: Event Management and Support Services, US&FCS, Room 2806, U.S. Department of Commerce, Washington, D.C. 20230; telephone 202-377-4231.

CBI Business Bulletin

The CBI Business Bulletin features a complete Caribbean Basin Initiative calendar of events and a list of specific CBI import and investment opportunities. The Bulletin also includes information on technical aspects of doing business in the Caribbean Basin. Available at local U.S. Commercial Service District Offices of the U.S. and Foreign Commercial Service.

• INTERNATIONAL ECONOMIC POLICY

Another source of business counseling is International Economic Policy (IEP), which provides commercial and economic information on a country-specific or multilateral basis.

IEP country specialists can provide information on foreign market conditions, commercial policies, business practices, economic and political developments, tariffs and trade regulations, as well as statistical data and trends on imports and exports, production, and third-country competition.

IEP country specialists also assist in resolving problems that U.S. firms encounter overseas.

Working with US&FCS, specialists also assist in identifying agent/distributors, private overseas marketing specialists, and export opportunities.

IEP has sponsored a series of seminars on "Doing Business In . . ." and sponsors country or region-specific seminars to inform the business community whenever a country revises its trade policies. Assistance on marketing in specific countries may be obtained by dialing the following numbers:

Country	Telephone Number
Africa	(202) 377-2175
North Africa	-3752
Near East	-4441
South Asia	-2954
The People's Republic of China and Hong Kong	-3583
Japan	-4527
The Pacific Basin	-3857
Western Europe	-5341
European Community Affairs	-5276
Eastern Europe and Soviet Affairs	-1104
North America	-3101
Central America	-5324
Mexico and the Caribbean Basin	-5329
South America	-2436

IEP's Office of Multilateral Affairs (202-377-3227) handles questions U.S. firms may have regarding their rights and benefits under the OECD, the GATT and the other MTN codes. Businesses may refer problems with tariff or non-tariff barriers to the office for resolution through multilateral channels.

• TRADE DEVELOPMENT

Industry Sectors

Trade Development (TD) provides market analyses and assistance on an industry-specific basis. TD's sectoral programs integrate industries' identification of trade problems, issues, and opportunities with U.S. Government efforts to:

- Identify obstacles and opportunities by product, industry sector, and market by working with industry associations, individual firms, and advisory committees such as the President's Export Council and the Industry Sector Advisory Committees.

- Monitor foreign targeting practices and assess the impact of these practices on U.S. industry.

- Develop priorities for industry-specific programs and formulate strategies to advance trade in specific sectors. TD reviews these programs with industry, and pursues sector strategies through government-to-government discussions.

Assistance about marketing specific products or services may be obtained by contacting the following TD units:

- Aerospace, 202-377-8228
- Automotive Affairs, 377-0554
- Basic Industries, 202-377-0614
- Capital Goods and International Construction, 202-377-5023
- Consumer Goods, 377-0337
- Science and Electronics, 202-377-3548
- Services, 202-377-3575
- Textiles and Apparel, 202-377-3737
- Trade Adjustment Assistance, 202-377-0150
- Trade Information and Analysis, 202-377-1316

Export Trading Companies

The Office of Export Trading Company Affairs (OETCA) promotes the formation of export trading companies and is responsible for administering the antitrust preclearance program set up by the Export Trading Company Act of 1982.

For further information contact OETCA at 202-377-5131.

OETCA is also responsible for the Contact Facilitation Service, a clearinghouse for matching U.S. suppliers of exportable goods and services with firms that provide trade facilitation services. To register for this service, contact the nearest Commerce Department District Office. The *Contact Facilitation Service Directory*, giving the names of registered firms and their products and services, is available from Commerce District Offices or by writing ITA/OETCA, U.S. Department of Commerce, Washington, D.C. 20230.

The *Export Trading Company Guidebook*, published by the Department of Commerce, explains the Export Trading Company Act and the Certificate of Review program and offers guidance in setting up and operating various types of export trading companies. Available from the Superintendent of Documents, U.S. Government Printing Office, Washington, DC 20402.

- TRADE ADMINISTRATION

The Office of Export Administration (OEA) controls exports for national security and foreign policy reasons.

To assist the exporter, the following programs are available:

Fast Track: "Fast Track" is an accelerated license processing system to help U.S. exporters compete in the world markets. The average license processing time is 15 days for export licenses for commodities going to Free World countries that do not require interagency review or further internal OEA review. OEA's licensing officers conduct a substantive review of Free World cases and control over applications through tighter supervision for national security purposes.

Counseling for Exporters: Assistance for exporters is available from the Exporters Assistance Division at a walk-in Counselling Service in Room 10990 at the 14th Street and Pennsylvania Avenue entrance of the Department of Commerce.

Publication Program: For information on booklets/brochures for the business community call 202-377-2574. Recent publications include: *Export Licensing Information and Assistance* (telephone referral), *Introduction to the Export Administration Regulations, The Quick Reference Guide to the Export Administration Regulations,* and an updated copy of the *Denial Orders Currently Affecting Export Privileges.*

Telephone Information Service: Exporters can contact an Exporters Assistance Division telephone consultant by calling the number that most closely relates to a need or problem. Telephone assistance is available for: Regulations and Policy Information, 202-377-4811; Licensing and Status Cases, 202-377-2752; Emergency Handling Requests, 202-377-2793 or 202-377-2799.

Seminar Program: To help U.S. exporters better understand (and use) the Export Administration Regulations, the Office of Export Administration presents monthly "Introductory" and "Advanced" export control training seminars in major cities and high-technology centers around the country.

Call 202-377-8731 for additional information or to attend a seminar.

Multiple License Program: This unit handles five special licensing procedures: project license, distribution license, qualified general license, service supply procedure and aircraft and vessel repair station procedure. For information call 202-377-0808.

Control Commodity List (CCL): The Office of Export Administration will, upon request of the exporter, assist an export company determine the Export Control Commodity Number (ECCN) of the product/service it intends to export. However, OEA will only review a maximum of ten items per request. Such opinions may only be rendered in writing on the appropriate forms and/or stationery. It takes approximately four to six months to receive a classification. For further information or a written CCL determination write:

U.S. Department of Commerce
International Trade Administration
Exporters Assistance Division
Room 1099
Washington, D.C. 20230
Attn: CCL Determinations Request

Computer Systems Parameters: To assist the exporter in completing the required forms for export of electronic computers and related equipment to Bloc Country Groups call 202-377-4811 for assistance.

Trade Fair Applications: Information on trade fair applications may be obtained by calling 202-377-2525.

Technical Advisory Committees (TACs): The TACs are a voluntary joint industry-government mechanism through which the concerns of various industries can be discussed. For information, call 202-377-2583.

U.S. EXPORT DEVELOPMENT OFFICES (EDO'S)

The Department of Commerce provides worldwide opportunities for both new and established exporters to enter export markets through its trade promotion activities. These activities are coordinated by the Department's Export Development Offices (EDO's).

For information on the various event programs for a specific industry contact a local U.S. Department of Commerce District Office of the appropriate industry sector office of the International Trade Administration (ITA) of the Department of Commerce.

Department of Commerce International Trade Administration District Offices

District Office Assistance

Alabama, Birmingham	(205) 254-1331
Alaska, Anchorage	(907) 271-5041
Arizona, Phoenix	(602) 261-3285
Arkansas, Little Rock	(501) 378-5794
California, Los Angeles	(213) 209-6707
*California, Santa Ana	(714) 836-2461
*California, San Diego	(619) 293-5395
California, San Francisco	(415) 566-5860
*California, San Jose	(408) 291-7648
Colorado, Denver	(303) 844-3246
Connecticut, Hartford	(203) 722-3530
Florida, Miami	(305) 350-5267
*Florida, Clearwater	(813) 461-0011
*Florida, Jacksonville	(904) 791-2796
*Florida, Orlando	(305) 425-1247
*Florida, Talahassee	(904) 488-6469
Georgia, Atlanta	(404) 881-7000
Georgia, Savannah	(912)-944-4204
Hawaii, Honolulu	(808) 546-8694
*Idaho, Boise	(208) 334-2470
Illinois, Chicago	(312) 353-4550
*Illinois, Palantine	(312) 397-3000 Ext. 532
*Illinois, Rockford	(815) 987-8100
Indiana, Indianapolis.........	(317) 269-6214
Iowa, Des Moines	(515) 284-4222
*Kansas, Wichita..............	(316) 269-6160
Kentucky, Louisville	(502) 582-5066
Louisiana, New Orleans......	(504) 589-6546
*Maine, Augusta	(207) 622-8249
Maryland, Baltimore	(301) 962-3560
*Maryland, Rockville..........	(301) 251-2345
Massachusetts, Boston	(617) 223-2312
Michigan, Detroit	(313) 226-3650
*Michigan, Grand Rapids	(616) 456-2411
Minnesota, Minneapolis	(612) 349-3338
Mississippi, Jackson.........	(601) 960-4388
Missouri, Kansas City........	(816) 374-3142
Missouri, St. Louis	(314) 425-3302
Nebraska, Omaha...........	(402) 221-3664
Nevada, Reno	(702) 784-5203
New Jersey, Trenton	(609) 989-2100
New Mexico, Albuquerque ...	(505) 766-2386
New York, Buffalo	(716) 846-4191
New York, New York	(212) 264-0634
*New York, Rochester	(716) 263-6480
North Carolina, Greensboro ..	(919) 378-5345
*North Carolina, Raleigh	(919) 755-4687
Ohio, Cincinnati	(513) 684-2944
Ohio, Cleveland	(216) 522-4750
Oklahoma, Oklahoma City ...	(405) 231-5302
*Oklahoma, Tulsa	(918) 581-7650
Oregon, Portland	(503) 221-3001
Pennsylvania, Philadelphia ...	(215) 597-2866
Pennsylvania, Pittsburgh	(412) 644-2850
Puerto Rico, San Juan	(809) 753-4555

*Rhode Island, Providence	(401) 277-2605 Ext. 22
South Carolina, Columbia	(803) 765-5345
*South Carolina, Charleston ...	(803) 724-4361
*South Carolina, Greenville....	(803) 235-5919
*Tennessee, Memphis........	(901) 521-4826
Tennessee, Nashville........	(615) 251-5161
*Texas, Austin	(512) 472-5059
Texas, Dallas	(214) 767-0542
Texas, Houston	(713) 229-2578
Utah, Salt Lake City	(801) 524-5116
Virginia, Richmond	(804) 771-2246
*Virginia, Dunn Loring (Fairfax County)............	(703) 573-9460
Washington, Seattle	(206) 442-5616
*Washington, Spokane........	(509) 838-8202
West Virginia, Charleston	(304) 347-5123
Wisconsin, Milwaukee	(414) 291-3473

*Denotes Branch Office

U.S. Foreign-Trade Zones (FTZs)*

Firms involved in certain operations subject to significant customs duties should consider using Foreign Trade Zones (FTZs), which are now available in nearly 100 port of entry communities throughout the United States. The advantages of using an FTZ include the following:

1. Foreign and domestic merchandise may be moved into an FTZ for storage, exhibition, assembly, manufacture, or other processing free of duties and quotas;
2. Duties are payable and quotas are applied if and when the merchandise enters the U.S. market;
3. Domestic goods entering the FTZ for export are considered exported when they enter the zone.

Information on FTZs is available from the International Trade Administration at 202–377–2862.

Financing Exports*

Many sources of financial assistance are available to exporters. In addition to your own working capital or bank line of credit, the following are brief descriptions of some important sources of export financing assistance.

COMMERCIAL BANKS

A wide choice of financial institutions that provide marketing assistance, as well as interna-

* Source: Excerpted from *A Basic Guide to Exporting*, U.S. Department of Commerce and other sources.

tional financing is available to exporters. More than 250 U.S. banks have qualified international banking departments with specialists familiar with specific foreign countries and/or various types of commodities and transactions. These banks, located in all major U.S. cities, maintain correspondent relationships with smaller banks throughout the country. This banking network enables exporters to find export financing assistance for themselves or their foreign customers. Larger banks also maintain correspondent relationships with banks in most foreign countries or operate their own overseas branches, providing a direct channel to foreign customers.

Firms that are seriously interested in developing an export trade will probably wish to work directly with a bank that offers at least one full-time international banker. These specialists are generally well-informed about export matters, even in areas that fall outside the usual limits of international banking. If they are unable to provide direct guidance or assistance, they may be able to refer you to other specialists who can. In short, the international banker is a valuable source of expertise which beginning exporters should not overlook. Best of all, since they primarily derive income from loans to the exporter and from fees for special services, banks are able to provide consultation and guidance free of charge to their clients.

The variety of services and resources available from many commercial banks throughout the United States include: advice on export regulations, exchange of currencies, collection of foreign invoices, drafts, letters of credit, and other foreign receivables, transfer of funds to other countries, letters of introduction and credit, credit information on potential buyers overseas, and credit assistance to the exporter's foreign buyers.

FACTORING HOUSES

Certain companies, known as "factoring houses" or simply "factors" will purchase your export receivables (i.e., your invoices to foreign buyers) for a somewhat discounted price, perhaps 2 to 4 percent less than their face value. The actual amount of the discount will depend on the factoring house, the kind of product(s) involved, the customer, and the country. Factors offer two important advantages: (1) They enable you to receive immediate payment for your goods, freeing cash that could otherwise be tied up for months. (2) They relieve you of the burden of collection.

Arrangements with factoring houses are made either with or without "recourse." Arrangements "with recourse" leave you, the exporter, ultimately liable for repaying the factor if the foreign buyer defaults or other problems prevent payment within a reasonable period. Arrangements "without recourse" free you

from this responsibility. Naturally, factors that accept export receivables "without recourse" generally require a large discount.

EXPORT MANAGEMENT COMPANIES (EMCs)

Export management companies (EMCs) will not only act as your export representative but, in some cases, will carry the financing for your export sale, assuring you of immediate payment and removing from your firm any foreign credit risk. EMCs solicit and transact business in the name of the manufacturers they represent for a commission, salary, or retainer plus commission. Many EMCs will also carry the financing for export sales, ensuring immediate payment for the manufacturer's products.

An agreement with an EMC can be an especially advantageous arrangement for smaller firms that do not have the time, personnel, or money to develop foreign markets, but wish nonetheless to establish a corporate and product identity overseas. For a description of services rendered to exporters by EMCs (and suggestions for choosing an appropriate firm) request Commerce's pamphlet, *"The EMC— Your Export Department."* Commerce also publishes a *"U.S. Export Management Companies Directory"* listing the names, addresses, and industry specialties of more than 1,100 EMCs in the United States. A copy of the first publication may be requested from the Publications Sales Branch, International Trade Administration, U.S. Department of Commerce, Washington, D.C. 20230. The "EMC Directory" can be purchased from: Superintendent of Documents, U.S. Government Printing Office, Washington, D.C. 20402.

The Foreign Trade Market Place, edited by George J. Schults, contains a listing of export management companies with sections on export opportunities, trade shows, financing, etc. Published by Gale Research, Book Tower, Detroit, MI 48226.

Exporters Directory, U.S. Buyers Guide, The Journal of Commerce, 445 Marshall Street, Phillipsburg, 08865. Lists export firms, including export managers, export merchants, manufacturers (as well as products exports) and trade association.

CONFORMING

Designed to help exporters and importers expand their markets, improve cash flow, and create greater profit leverage, "conforming" is a financial service in which an independent company confirms an export order in the vendor's own country and makes payment for the goods in the currency of that country. This service can pay for and finance on terms the following items: The goods themselves, transportation (ocean or air), inland transportation at both ends, forwarding fees, customs brokerage fees, duties, etc. For the U.S. exporter, this means that the entire export transaction, from factory to end-user, can be fully coordinated and paid for with terms. Though common in Europe, conforming is still in its infancy in the United States. There are, however, U.S. firms that will provide such assistance. For further information, contact: Director, Office of Export Marketing Assistance, International Trade Administration, U.S. Department of Commerce, Washington, D.C. 20230.

EXPORT-IMPORT BANK

Address: 811 Vermont Avenue NW, Washington, DC 20571. Phone: 202–566–8990. Public Affairs Phone: 202–566–8860

Small Business Advisory Hotline Service
800–424–5201

In addition to its other export-related assistance, the U.S. Government participates in the financing of America's exports. The Export-Import Bank of the United States (Eximbank) offers direct loans for large projects and equipment sales that usually require longer-term financing. It cooperates with commercial banks in the United States and abroad in providing a number of financial arrangements to help U.S. exporters offer credit guarantees to commercial banks that finance export sales. Through the Foreign Credit Insurance Association it also provides insurance to U.S. exporters, enabling them to extend credit terms to their overseas buyers. In all cases, the Bank must find a "reasonable assurance of repayment" as a precondition of participating in the transaction.

Eximbank's support for short-term (up to 180 days) export sales rests exclusively with the export credit insurance program that it jointly operates with the Foreign Credit Insurance Association. The advantages of export credit insurance are significant. Most importantly, it offers protection in what is usually the riskiest part of an exporter's business—foreign sales receivables. In addition, prudent use of export credit insurance can:

- Protect exporters against political and commercial risks over which they have no control.
- Encourage exporters to make competitive offers by extending terms of payments.
- Broaden potential markets by minimizing exporter risks.
- Give leveraging possibility on exporter accounts receivable.

Three Eximbank programs are specifically designed to support medium-term (181 days–5 years) export sales:

- FCIA's medium-term export credit insurance.
- Discount Loan Program.
- U.S. Commercial Bank Guarantee Program.

For complete information on the above programs contact the Export-Import Bank at the phone numbers given above. Detailed information on Eximbank and FCIA programs and services is provided in the brochure *The Export-Import Bank: Financing for American Experts—Support for American Jobs*. For a free copy write: Office of Public Affairs, Export-Import Bank, Washington, D.C. 20571.

FOREIGN CREDIT INSURANCE ASSOCIATION (FCIA)

Address: 40 Rector Street, New York, NY 10006. Phone: 212–306–5000.

The export credit insurance offered by FCIA provides three basic incentives for American exporters when they do offer competitive terms to buyers. It enables them to (1) protect corporate assets as credit is extended; (2) maximize the rate of plant utilization as overseas competition is matched and orders won; and (3) improve corporate liquidity when insured foreign receivables are financed.

FCIA administers the U.S. export credit insurance program on behalf of its member insurance companies and the Export-Import Bank, an agency of the U.S. Government. The private insurers cover the normal commercial credit risks, primarily the insolvency of or protracted payment default by overseas buyers.

U.S. SMALL BUSINESS ADMINISTRATION [SBA]

Answer desk: 800–368–5855
Business publications: 202-653-6365

Through financial assistance programs, the SBA can promote small business participation in international trade by making funds available for export-oriented activities.

Funds may be used to purchase machinery, equipment, facilities, supplies, or materials needed to manufacture or sell products overseas, as well as for working capital. Working capital loans may be used to defray the costs of developing or penetrating foreign markets. Specifically, this can include costs for professional foreign marketing advice and services, foreign business travel, shipping sample merchandise abroad, shopping foreign markets, participating in overseas trade center shows and international fairs, foreign advertising and preparation of promotional materials, and other related purposes.

For information on the SBA financial assistance programs, policies and requirements, contact the nearest SBA field office (see page 262).

PRIVATE EXPORT FUNDING CORPORATION (PEFCO)

Address: 280 Park Avenue, New York, NY 10017. Telephone: 212–557–3100.

PEFCO, owned by 62 investors (mostly commercial banks), lends only to finance export of goods and services of U.S. manufacture and origin. PEFCO's loans generally have maturities in the medium-term area and all are unconditionally guaranteed by Eximbank as to payment of interest and repayment of principal. PEFCO's funds supplement the financing of U.S. exports available through commercial banks and Eximbank.

OVERSEAS PRIVATE INVESTMENT CORPORATION (OPIC)

Address: 1129 20th Street NW, Washington, DC. 20521. Information phone: 800–424–OPIC; in DC: 202–653–2800.

OPIC, established in 1971, is an independent agency of the U.S. government with the mission of reducing or eliminating private investment risks in the developing countries. OPIC insures U.S. investors against political risks of expropriation, inconvertability of local currency holdings, and damage from war, revolution, or insurrection. The agency offers lenders protection by guaranteeing payment of principal, interest, and loans.

The corporation offers investment information and counseling to business and participates in the cost of locating and developing projects.

Foreign Sales Corporation (FSC)*

A Foreign Sales Corporation (FSC) is a foreign chartered corporation through which exports can be made. A portion of the foreign income thus generated will be exempt from Federal taxation as of 1985.

In order to qualify as a FSC certain criteria must be met with respect to the management of the FSC and the exports made through it. Among the requirements are:

- The FSC must not have more than 25 shareholders.

- A statement of election to be treated as a FSC must be filed with the Internal Revenue Service.

- A bank account must be maintained in a foreign bank and accounting records kept in a foreign office.

There are two exceptions for small exporters. (1) Small exporters may use the FSC without meeting some of the export activities test or (2) small exporters may maintain their DISC (Domestic International Sales Corporation) by paying an annual interest charge on the DISC deferred tax liability.

Further information can be obtained by calling 202–377–4471.

Export Assistance from State Governments**

State development agencies, departments of commerce, and other departments within State governments often provide valuable assistance to exporters within the State. These groups may provide assistance in marketing, market development, and in arranging for trade shows and trade missions. The agencies in each state responsible for international trade and export assistance to local firms are given under each state in the State Information Guide section of the *Almanac,* page 561. Information is also obtainable from the National Association of State Development Agencies (NASDA), 444 N. Capitol Street, Washington, DC 20001. Telephone: 202–624–5411.

Private and Government Information Sources: International Commerce†

Advisory Council on Japan-U.S. Economic Relations (U.S. Section)[1]
Phone: (202) 659–3054

African Development Bank and Fund
B.P. No. 1387
Abijan, Ivory Coast

Asean-U.S. Business Council (U.S. Section)[1]
Phone: (202) 659–6117

Asian Development Bank
Roxas Blvd.
P.O. Box 789
Manila, Philippines

---

* Source: International Trade Administration, U.S. Department of Commerce.

** Source: International Trade Administration, U.S. Department of Commerce.

† Source: *Basic Guide to Exporting,* International Trade Administration, U.S. Department of Commerce.

[1] Address: Chamber of Commerce of the United States, International Division, 1615 H Street NW, Washington, DC 20062.

Association of American Chambers of Commerce in Latin America
1615 H Street, NW.
Washington, D.C. 20062
Phone: (202) 659–3055

Brazil-U.S. Business Council (U.S. Section)[1]
Phone: (202) 659–3055

Bulgarian-U.S. Economic Council (U.S. Section)[1]
Phone: (202) 659–2024

The Business Roundtable
200 Park Ave.
New York, N.Y. 10017
Phone: (212) 682–6370

Caribbean Development Bank
P.O. Box 408 Wildey
St. Michael, Barbados
West Indies

Chamber of Commerce of the United States
1615 H Street, NW.
Washington, D.C. 20062
Phone: (202) 659–6000

Committee for the Caribbean
1333 New Hampshire Ave., NW.
Washington, D.C. 20036
Phone: (202) 466–7464

Committee on Canada-United States Relations (U.S. Section)[1]
Phone: (202) 659–3054

Czechoslovak-U.S. Economic Council (U.S. Section[1]
Phone: (202) 659–2024

Department of Commerce International Trade Administration
14th Street and Constitution Ave., NW.
Washington, D.C. 20230
Phone: (202) 377–3808

Department of State Bureau of Economic and Business Affairs
2201 C Street, NW.
Washington, D.C. 20520
Phone: (202) 632–0354

East-West Trade Council
1700 Pennsylvania Ave., NW.
Suite 670
Washington, D.C. 20006
Phone: (202) 393–6240

Egypt-U.S. Business Council (U.S. Section)[1]
Phone: (202) 659–3058

Export-Import Bank of the United States
811 Vermont Ave., NW.
Washington, D.C. 20571
Phone: (202) 566–2117

FCIB (Foreign Credit Interchange Bureau/National Association of Credit Management Corporation)
475 Park Ave. South
New York, N.Y. 10016
Phone: (212) 725–1700

Federal Trade Commission
Pennsylvania Ave. at Sixth Street, NW.
Washington, D.C. 20580
Phone: (202) 523–3625

Foreign Credit Insurance Association
One World Trade Center
New York, N.Y. 10048
Phone: (212) 432–6200

Hungarian-U.S. Economic Council (U.S. Section)[1]
Phone: (202) 659–2024

India-U.S. Business Council (U.S. Section)[1]
Phone: (202) 659–3058

Inter-American Development Bank
308 17th Street, NW.
Washington, D.C. 20557
Phone: (202) 634–8152

International Advertising Association, Inc.
475 Fifth Ave.
New York, N.Y. 10017
Phone: (212) 684–1583

International Centre for Settlement of Investment Disputes
1818 H Street, NW.
Washington, D.C. 20433
Phone: (202) 676–1438

International Monetary Fund
700 19th Street, NW.
Washington, D.C. 20431
Phone: (202) 477–7000

International Trade Centre (UNCTAD/GATT)
4, Route des Morillons
CH-1211, Geneva 22
Switzerland

Israel-U.S. Business Council (U.S. Section)[1]
Phone: (202) 659–6116

National Association of Export Management Companies, Inc.
65 Liberty Street
New York, N.Y. 10005
Phone: (212) 766–1343

National Association of Manufacturers
1776 F Street, NW.
Washington, D.C. 20006
Phone: (202) 331–3700

The National Council for U.S.-China Trade
1050 17th Street, NW.
Washington, D.C. 20036
Phone: (202) 828–8300

National Foreign Trade Council, Inc.
10 Rockefeller Plaza, Room 530
New York, N.Y. 10020
Phone: (212) 581–6420

Office of the United States Trade Representative
1800 G Street, NW.
Washington, D.C. 20506
Phone: (202) 395–4647

Organization for Economic Cooperation and Development
1750 Pennsylvania Ave., NW.
Washington, D.C. 20006
Phone: (202) 724–1857

Overseas Private Investment Corporation
1129 20th Street, NW.
Washington, D.C. 20527
Phone: (202) 653–2920

Polish-U.S. Economic Council (U.S. Section)[1]
Phone: (202) 659–2024

President's Export Council
Washington, D.C. 20230
Phone: (202) 377–5719

Romanian-U.S. Economic Council (U.S. Section)[1]
Phone: (202) 659–2026

Small Business Administration Office of International Trade
1441 L Street, NW.
Washington, D.C. 20416
Phone: (202) 653–6600

Sudan-U.S. Business Council (U.S. Section)[1]
Phone: (202) 659–3057

U.S. Council of the International Chamber of Commerce
1212 Avenue of the Americas
New York, N.Y. 10036
Phone: (212) 354–4480

U.S.-European Community Conference on Agriculture[1]
Phone: (202) 659–2022

U.S.-German Democratic Republic Trade and Economic Council
40 Westminister Street
Providence, Rhode Island 02903
Phone: (401) 331–2400

U.S. International Trade Commission
701 E Street, NW.
Washington, D.C. 20004
Phone: (202) 523–0161

U.S.-Korea Economic Council
88 Morningside Drive
New York, N.Y. 10027
Phone: (212) 749–4200

U.S.-Republic of China Economic Council
200 Main Street
Crystal Lake, IL 60014
Phone: (815) 459–5875

U.S.-U.S.S.R. Trade and Economic Council
1211 Avenue of the Americas
New York, N.Y. 10036
Phone: (212) 840–5500

U.S.-Yugoslav Economic Council, Inc.
51 East 42nd Street
New York, N.Y. 10017
Phone: (212) 687–7797

DUN & BRADSTREET

Address: 99 Church Street, New York, NY. 10007 Phone: 212–312–6500.

Dun & Bradstreet provides a number of valuable services and publications in the area of international business, i.e., international credit reports on companies, international marketing guides and services, and directories of foreign firms. Dun & Bradstreet publishes the comprehensive annual, *Exporters Encyclopedia*, with monthly supplements. It details the rules and regulations in over 220 world markets and is arranged alphabetically by country and market area. *Principal International Businesses* is a useful marketing publication providing addresses, lines of business, sales figures, and other information on nearly 50,000 foreign firms.

INTERNATIONAL REPORTS

Address: 200 Park Avenue South, New York, NY 10003 Phone: 212–477–0003

International Reports publishes reports on sources of worldwide export credit insurance, foreign investment guarantees, and export financing under the title of *Insurance in International Finance*.

It also publishes the monthly *International Commercial Finance Service*, containing extensive information and data on financing and interest rates, surveys of credit ratings, and foreign payment records of individual countries.

BUSINESS INTERNATIONAL

Address: One Dag Hammarskjold Plaza, New York, NY 10017. Phone: 212-750-6300.

Business International publishes a series of weekly reports: *Business International* (a global view of business); *Business Europe; Business Latin America; Business Asia; Eastern Europe Report; Business China* (People's Republic); *Business International Money Report; Investing, Licensing, Trading Report;* and *Financing Foreign Operations.* It publishes a multivolume series, *Doing Business with Eastern Europe.*

COMMERCE CLEARING HOUSE

Address: 4025 West Peterson Avenue, Chicago, IL 60646. Phone 312-583-8500.

Commerce Clearing House publishes a number of widely used looseleaf series updated on a weekly or monthly basis. In the international field these include: *Euromarket News; Doing Business in Europe; Balance of Payment Reports; Common Market Reports;* and *Income Taxes World Wide.* It also publishes a number of detailed tax and legal guides for specific countries, i.e., Canada, Mexico, Australia, England, and Germany.

U.S. DEPARTMENT OF STATE

Address: New State Building, 2201 C Street, NW, Washington, DC 20520.
Information: 202-632-9884.

PUBLICATIONS

Background Notes of the Countries of the World gives profiles of foreign countries.

Key Officers of Foreign Service Posts lists the addresses and phone numbers of all American embassies and consulates and their key personnel.

Department of State Bulletin is a weekly publication devoted to the latest developments in international politics and trade agreements.

THE LIBRARY OF CONGRESS

The Library of Congress's international divisions provide overseas free research assistance on social, economic, and political topics. Call:

African and Middle East
Division 202-287-7937
Asian Division 202-287-5420
European Division 202-287-5413
Hispanic Division 202-287-5400

Write: Library of Congress, 10 First Street SE, Washington, D.C. 20540.

UNITED STATES INTERNATIONAL TRADE COMMISSION*

Address: 701 E Street NW, Washington, DC 20436. Information phone: 202-523-0161.

Formerly the U.S. Tariff Commission, the name was changed to the U.S. International Trade Commission in 1974.

The commission is given broad powers of investigation relating to the customs laws of the United States and foreign countries, the volume of importation in comparison with domestic production and consumption, the conditions, causes, and effects relating to competition of foreign industries with those of the United States and all other factors affecting competition between articles of the United States and imported articles.

Businesspersons who believe they have been injured by unfair trade methods from abroad may file a complaint with this commission.

Summaries of trade and tariff information may be obtained directly from the commission.

OTHER PUBLICATIONS

Europa Year Book is an annual two-volume work covering a wide range of commercial, economic, and political statistics and information about every country in the world. Volume I deals with international organizations and the countries of Europe, while Volume II covers Africa, the Americas, Asia, and Australia. It is published by Europe Publications, Ltd., 18 Bedford Square, London, England.

Jane's Major Companies of Europe is an annual providing extensive information about all major European companies. It is available from Jane's Yearbooks, 8 Shepherdess, London N1 7LW, England.

World Directory of Chambers of Commerce provides sources of contact in nearly 150 Chambers of Commerce offices around the world. Supplements are published periodically. Available from ISS Publishing, 156 Fifth Avenue, New York, NY 10010.

Foreign Commerce Handbook provides information on international trade and foreign markets. Included are addresses and phone numbers of organizations involved with foreign trade, a glossary of foreign commercial terms and a bibliography of indexes and periodicals. Available from the Chamber of Commerce of the United States, 1615 H Street NW, Washington, DC 20062.

---

* Source: *U.S. Government Organization Manual.*

International Marketing Handbook contains marketing profiles for over 130 countries, near term trade outlooks for major countries, as well as business guides to the Near East, North Africa and Eastern bloc countries Available in the U.S. from Gale Research Company, Book Tower, Detroit, MI 48226.

International Directory of Marketing Research Houses and Services (the "Green Book") is a directory of marketing research organizations in some 50 countries and includes descriptions of services, contact people, phone numbers, and addresses. Available from: American Marketing Association, 420 Lexington Avenue, New York, NY 10170.

Lambert's World Government Directory identifies government officials in 168 countries as well as officials in Inter-Governmental organizations. Published by International Executive Reports, 115 Massachusetts Avenue NW, Washington, DC 20005.

Country Experts in the Federal Government is a guide to U.S. government analysts for almost all countries. Published by Washington Researchers, 2612 P Street, NW, Washington, DC 20007.

International Research Center Directory edited by Anthony F. Kruzas and Kay Gill identifies 15,000 university-related, independent and government research organizations throughout the world. Available from Gale Research Company (address on p. 612).

Croner's Reference Book for World Traders is a three volume work covering basic data and hard-to-locate information for international traders and market researchers. Available from Croner Publications, 211-05 Jamaica Avenue, Queens Village, New York, 11428.

Incoterms is a booklet providing a set of international rules for interpreting the main terms used in foreign trade contracts. Available from the U.S. Council of the International Chamber of Commerce, Inc. 1212 Avenue of the Americas, New York, NY 10036. Also publishes other useful material.

Revised American Foreign Trade Definitions, is a compilation from the National Council of Importers, the Chamber of Commerce of the U.S., and the National Foreign Trade Council. Available from the National Foreign Trade Council at 100 E. 42nd Street, New York, NY 10017.

European Markets: A Guide to Company and Industry Information Sources is a three volume resource for accessing information on European companies and markets. Available from Washington Researchers, 2612 P Street NW, Washington, DC 20007.

Exporters' Encyclopaedia, Dun & Bradstreet International, 99 Church Street, New York, NY 10007. Gives country by country coverage of 220 world markets.

Sources of International Credit Information

International Trade Administration, U.S. Department of Commerce, Washington, DC.

Dun & Bradstreet, 99 Church Street, New York, NY 10007.

FCIB-NACM Corp., 475 Park Avenue South, New York, NY 10015.

Major Commercial Banks

U.S. Department of Agriculture, U.S. Foreign Agriculture Service, Export Credit Sales Program, Washington, DC 20250.

International Organizations

UNITED NATIONS (UN)

Address: New York, NY 10017. Information phone: 212-754-1234.

The UN and its affiliated organizations publish a large number of reports and statistical tables covering all member nations. Publications may be obtained by writing: Sales Section, United Nations Publications, New York, NY 10017. A periodic check list of UN publications is available on request.

PUBLICATIONS

Economic Survey of Europe.

Journal of Development Planning.

Guidelines for Contracting for Industrial Projects in Developing Countries.

World Economic Survey.

Annual Bulletin of Exports of Chemical Products.

Annual Bulletin of Coal Statistics for Europe.

Statistics of World Trade in Steel.

Annual Bulletin of Gas Statistics for Europe.

Annual Bulletin of Electric Energy Statistics for Europe.

Economic Bulletin for Europe.

Economic Bulletin for Asia and the Pacific.

Economic Bulletin for Africa.

Economic Bulletin for Latin America.

Quarterly Bulletin of Statistics for Asia and the Pacific.

Statistical Yearbook for Asia and the Pacific.

Demographic Yearbook.

Yearbook of International Trade Statistics Vol. I: Trade by Country; Vol. II: Trade by Commodity.

Monthly Bulletin of Statistics provides monthly statistics on 70 subjects from more than 200 countries and territories together with special tables illustrating important economic developments. Quarterly data for significant world and regional aggregates are also prepared regularly for the bulletin.

Statistical Yearbook is a comprehensive compilation of international statistics relating to: population and manpower; agricultural, mineral, and manufacturing production; construction; energy; trade; transport; communications; consumption; balance of payments; wages and prices; national accounts; finance; development assistance; health; housing; education; science and technology; and culture.

Population and Vital Statistics Reports (quarterly).
Yearbook of National Accounts Statistics.
Yearbook of International Trade Statistics.
Yearbook of Construction Statistics.
Commodity Trade Statistics (quarterly).
World Trade Annual.
The Growth of World Industry: Vol. I General Industrial Statistics; Vol. II Commodities Production Data.

INTERNATIONAL MONETARY FUND (IMF)

Address: 19th and II Streets NW, Washington, DC 20431. Phone: 202–477–7000.

The IMF was organized in 1945 with the purpose of promoting international monetary cooperation and consultation. The fund also seeks to facilitate the expansion of international trade and currency exchange stability. The fund issues Special Drawing Rights (SDR), a form of reserve currency used by central banks for settling balance of payment obligations.

PUBLICATIONS

The IMF issues a broad range of publications (some in conjunction with the World Bank Group) of interest to the business community.

Foreign Trade Statistics. Series A. This monthly bulletin provides a breakdown of overall trade by main commodity categories and available indices of foreign trade unit values and volumes. *Series B. Trade by Commodities. Analytical Abstracts* (quarterly). *Series C. Trade by Commodities. Market Summaries* (yearly). *Provisional Oil Statistics* (quarterly).

The Annual Report of the Executive Directors reviews the funds' activities, policies, organization, and administration and surveys the world economy, with special emphasis on international liquidity, payments problems, exchange rates, and world trade.

Annual Report on Exchange Restrictions reviews developments in exchange controls and restrictions and other measures that may have direct implications for the balance of payments of member countries.

International Financial Statistics (monthly) reports for most countries of the world current data needed for analyzing problems of international payments and inflation and deflation, i.e., data on exchange rates, international liquidity, money and banking, international trade, prices, production, government finance, interest rates, and other items. Information is presented in country tables for each country and in tables with area and world aggregates. Charts on each country page show recent changes in important series.

Balance of Payments Yearbook presents statistics in a standard form, expressed in a common unit of account, for countries that report information to the fund on their balance of payments transactions. In the tables that are designated as "standard presentations," these transactions are classified in terms of objective criteria; in the tables designated as "analytic presentations," they are regrouped to facilitate further analysis and certain cumulative balances are drawn.

Direction of Trade is published jointly by the International Monetary Fund and the International Bank for Reconstruction and Development. The monthly issues provide the latest available information on each country's direction of trade, with comparative data for the corresponding period of the preceding year.

The *IMF Survey* is a topical report of the fund's activities (including all press releases, texts of communiques and major statements, SDR valuations, and exchange rates) presented in the broader context of developments in national economics and international finance.

ORGANIZATION FOR ECONOMIC COOPERATION AND DEVELOPMENT (OECD)

Address: 2 Rue Andre Pascal 75775 Paris CEDEX16, France.
1750 Pennsylvania Avenue ՝NW, Washington, DC 20026. Phone: 202–724–1857.

The OECD, established in 1961, is an outgrowth of the Organization for European Economic Cooperation, set up under the Marshall Plan in 1948. It consists of 24 developed countries: Canada, United States, Japan, Australia, New Zealand, Austria, Belgium, Denmark, England, Finland, France, West Germany, Greece, Iceland, Italy, Luxembourg, Netherlands, Norway, Portugal, Spain, Sweden, Turkey, Switzerland, and Yugoslavia.

PUBLICATIONS

OECD Observer is intended for people who are interested in and concerned with economic and social planning in the broadest sense and who want to have relevant information in the most succinct form possible. It presents in readable fashion the entire range of OECD's work—in economic affairs, trade, manpower, social affairs, science and education, the environment, financial affairs, and development assistance. (Published bimonthly.)

The *OECD Economic Outlook* is a twice yearly, detailed survey of economic trends and prospects for the immediate future.

OECD Financial Statistics supplies complete, up-to-date, authoritative information on financial markets in 24 European countries, the United States, Canada, and Japan. (Published yearly with bimonthly supplements.)

OECD Economic Surveys is an annual analysis of the economic policy of each OECD country as seen by the others.

Main Economic Indicators, a monthly publication, is an essential source of statistics for the student of the international business cycle.

Indicators of Industrial Activity is a quarterly publication that provides an overall view of short-term economic developments in different industries for all OECD member countries.

Monthly Statistics of Foreign Trade includes a detailed regional analysis of trade of the main country groupings in the OECD area. Series are shown non-adjusted and seasonally adjusted.

Foreign Trade by Commodities is an annual publication with matrix tables showing trade between OECD countries and partner countries of commodity groups defined at 1- and 2-digit levels of the Standard International Trade Classification. Separate volumes are published for exports and imports.

GENERAL AGREEMENT ON TRADE AND TARIFFS (GATT)

Address: Centre William Rappard, 154 Rue de Lausanne, Geneva, Switzerland.

GATT is a multilateral trade treaty (entered into force in 1948) among 83 countries providing for the reduction of tariffs and other trade barriers, standardization of trade procedures, and the resolution of trade disputes. GATT publishes *Compilations of Basic Information on Export Markets; Guide to Sources of Foreign Trade Information; Analytical Bibliography: A Compendium of Sources: International Trade Statistics;* and *World Directory of Industry and Trade Associations.*

International Information Available in the U.S. by Country

This section lists helpful addresses in the United States for those doing business with countries where business practices may present certain problems.

JAPAN

Exporters and importers generally find it essential to use the services of the Japanese trading companies, which offer a wide range of services including negotiation of overseas deals, transportation, storage, finance, and marketing. The largest trading companies are listed below. The small exporter will often do better using smaller trading companies that specialize in one or two types of products. Exporters seeking an appropriate trading company should contact the local office of the Japan Trade Center:

Bank of America Tower*
555 S. Flower Street
Los Angeles, CA 90071

360 Post Street*
San Francisco, CA 94108

230 N. Michigan Avenue*
Chicago, IL 60601

1221 Avenue of the Americas*
New York, NY 10020

One World Trade Center
2100 Stemmons Freeway
Dallas, TX 75258

1221 McKinney Street*
One Houston Center
Houston, TX 77010

P.O. Box 3356
Marina Station
Mayaguez, PR 00708

* Problems and or inquiries concerning non-tariff barriers can be handled in the United States at the action desks at specific Japan Trade Centers indicated above by an asterisk. The inquiry will be directed to the proper authority in Japan at JETRO (Japan External Trade Organization). Inquiries can of course, be made directly to Japan at one of the following:

Ministry of Foreign Affairs
First International Organizations Division
Economic Affairs Bureau
Tokyo, Japan

Ministry of International Trade and Industry
Import Division, International
Trade and Administration
Bureau
Tokyo, Japan

Economic Planning Agency
First International Economic Affairs Division
Coordination Bureau
Tokyo, Japan

Ministry of Finance
Import Division
Customs and Tariffs Bureau
Tokyo, Japan

MAJOR TRADING COMPANIES (U.S. OFFICES)

Mitsubishi International Corporation
520 Madison Avenue
New York, NY 10022

Mitsui & Co. (USA), Inc.
200 Park Avenue
New York, NY 10017

Marubeni Corporation
200 Park Avenue
New York, NY 10017

C. Itoh & Co. (America), Inc.
270 Park Avenue
New York, NY 10017

Sumitomo Shoji America, Inc.
345 Park Avenue
New York, NY 10022

Nissho-Iwai American Corporation
1211 Avenue of the Americas
New York, NY 10036

Toyo Menka (America), Inc.
One World Trade Center
New York, NY 10048

Kanematsu-Gosho (USA), Inc.
One World Trade Center
New York, NY 10048

Itoman USA Inc.
1211 Avenue of the Americas
New York, NY 10036

Nichimen America, Inc.
1185 Avenue of the Americas
New York, NY 10036

Occidental Center
1150 S. Olive Street
Los Angeles, CA 90015

Chori New York, Inc.
350 Fifth Avenue
New York, NY 10001

TRADING WITH JAPAN

When U.S. firms encounter difficulty doing business with Japanese companies because of Japanese regulations contact the Japan desk of the International Trade Administration at 202-377-4527.

The following publications provide information on trading with Japan.

Country Market Profiles—Japan contains statistics on exports, information on some seven industries with export potential to Japan, developments in bilateral trade, and much more. Prepaid at $300, this book is available from the Office of Trade Information Services, Department of Commerce, P.O. Box 14207, Washington, DC 20044.

How to Find Information about Japanese Companies and Industries is an extensive guide to information sources both here and abroad helpful for doing business with Japan. Priced at $100, this volume is available from Washington Researchers Publishing, 2612 P Street NW, Washington, DC 20007.

THE PEOPLE'S REPUBLIC OF CHINA (PRC)

For information or advice on contacting the Chinese on commercial matters, call or write to:

U.S. Department of Commerce
International Trade Administration Office of
    PRC and Hong Kong
Washington, DC 20230
Telephone: 202-377-3583/4681

Commercial Office
Embassy of the People's Republic of China
2300 Connecticut Avenue, N.W.
Washington, DC 20008
For free publications on trade with China call 202-328-2520

Doing Business with China, prepared by the International Trade Administration (Department of Commerce) is available from the:

Superintendent of Documents
Government Printing Office
Washington, D.C. 20402

THE NATIONAL COUNCIL FOR U.S.-CHINA TRADE

Address: 1818 N Street NW, Suite 500. Washington, DC 20220. Phone: 202-429-0340.

The Council, a nonprofit, private organization maintaining close liaison with the U.S. government, serves as a forum for the discussion of trade policy and issues. It also serves as a focal point for business contact and the dissemination of information on marketing in the PRC. The council maintains a business counseling service; it also publishes the *China Business Review* bimonthly. The council facilitates the reciprocal arrangements of trade missions and trade exhibitions in the United States and China.

USSR AND EASTERN EUROPE*

USSR

USSR Affairs Division, International Economic Policy (202-377-4655). This division collects, analyzes, and disseminates current information on economic, commercial, and other

---

* Source: Excerpted from Department of Commerce Overseas Reports, "Trading with the USSR."

developments in the USSR and estimates their impact on the U.S. business community. The division develops policy guidance in our commercial relationship with the Soviet Union and provides staff support to and representation on the Joint Commercial Commission. It also maintains close contact with the U.S. Commercial Office in Moscow and with USSR commercial officials in the United States in order to initiate and pursue official representations on behalf of the American business community.

The U.S. Commercial Office (USCO), Moscow. The USCO should be a firm's first stop when visiting the USSR. Located next door to the U.S. Embassy, the USCO provides seminars, exhibit and reception facilities, commercial information, and other assistance to the business person.

It may also be to the company's advantage to touch base with the following USSR commercial organizations in the United States to try to obtain some indication of Soviet interest and to identify contacts in the Soviet Union:

The Trade Representation of the USSR in the U.S.A., 2001 Connecticut Avenue NW, Washington, DC 20008, telephone: 202–234–7170.

The Amtorg Trading Corporation, 750 Third Avenue, New York, NY 10017, telephone: 212–972–1220.

The staffs of both Amtorg and the Trade Representation include representatives of individual foreign trade organizations (FTOs).

The USSR Consulate General, 2790 Green Street, San Francisco, CA 94123, telephone: 415–922–6642, may have information conveniently available for companies on the West Coast.

Insurance Coverage

Insurance coverage for U.S.-USSR. trade is available from a number of U.S. insurance companies on a case-by-case basis in the areas of export insurance, transportation insurance, and insurance on fixed locations. No political or commercial credit risk coverage is currently available for the USSR from the Foreign Credit Insurance Association (FCIA) or the Export-Import Bank because of the 1974 Trade Act provisions. Many of the private U.S. companies, however, have established working and contractual relationships with the USSR State Insurance Company (Ingosstrakh) and with the wholly owned Soviet insurance companies, Black Sea and Baltic Company, Ltd., in London, Schwarzmeer und Ostee A.G. in Hamburg, and Garant A.G. in Vienna.

Private American insurers which write policies on some or all of the areas of standard property, casualty transportation, marine and war risk insurance, and more specialized insurance

for Soviet-American cooperative projects in the USSR or a third country are:*

Cigna World Wide Insurance Co.
110 William Street
New York, NY 10038
Telephone: 212–732–9070

Members of the American Institute of Marine Underwriters
14 Wall Street
New York, NY 10005
Telephone 212–233–0550

American International Underwriters Corporation
70 Pine Street
New York, NY 10005
Telephone: 212–770–5533

Chubb and Son, Inc.
International Department
100 William Street
New York, NY 10038
Telephone: 212–285–2850

Insurance Company of North America
International Insurance Section
2 INA Plaza
1600 Arch Street
Philadelphia, PA 19101
Telephone: 215–241–4000

EASTERN EUROPE

Commercial transactions with Bulgaria, Czechoslovakia, East Germany, Hungary, Poland, and Romania are similar to those with the USSR. Contracts are negotiated with the appropriate Foreign Trade Organization. For detailed information about trade shows, missions, export licenses, and FTOs, contact the Office of East-West Trade, Department of Commerce in Washington, or the Commerce Department Offices at the district level. Another key source of information is the U.S. East-West Trade Development Office in Vienna.

BULGARIA

Bulgarian Embassy
2100 16th Street NW
Washington, DC 20009

Bulgarian Commercial Counselor
121 E. 62nd Street
New York, NY 10021

CZECHOSLOVAKIA

Czechoslovakian Embassy
3900 Linnean Avenue NW
Washington, DC 20008

---

* This listing is not to be considered an endorsement by the Department of Commerce, the U.S. government or the *Business and Investment Almanac.*

Office of the Czechoslovakian Commercial
  Counselor
292 Madison Avenue
New York, NY 10016

EAST GERMANY
(German Democratic Republic)

Embassy of the German Democratic Republic
1717 Massachusetts Avenue NW
Washington, DC 20036

Permanent Mission of German Democratic
  Republic to the United Nations
58 Park Avenue
New York, NY 10016

U.S. banks with offices in Berlin
Citibank, New York NY

HUNGARY

Embassy of Hungary to the United States
2437 15th Street NW
Washington, DC 20009

Office of the Commercial Counselor of the Embassy of Hungary
2401 Calvert Street
Washington, DC 20008

Hungarian Consulate
8 E. 75th Street
New York, NY 10021

POLAND

Economic Counselor's Office
Embassy of the Polish People's Republic
2540 16th Street NW
Washington, DC 20008

Polish Consulate General
233 Madison Avenue
New York, NY 10016

Polish Commercial Counselor's Office
1 Daghammarskjold Plaza
New York, NY 10017

Office of Polish Commercial Consul
333 E. Ontario Street
Chicago, IL 60611

Polish Chamber of Foreign Trade
44 Montgomery Street
San Francisco, CA 94104

U.S. banks with offices in Warsaw
First National Bank, Chicago

ROMANIA

Romanian Embassy
1607 23rd Street NW
Washington, DC 20008

Romanian Office of the Economic Counselor
200 E. 38th Street
New York, NY 10016

Romanian Foreign Trade Promotion Office
100 W. Monroe Street
Chicago, IL 60603

Romanian Foreign Trade Promotion Office
22 Battery Street
San Francisco, CA 94111

U.S. banks with offices in Bucharest
Manufacturer's Hanover Trust, New York, NY

NEAR EAST AND NORTH AFRICA*

The Commercial Action Group for the Near
East (CAGNE) within the International Trade
Administration serves as the focal point for the
U.S. Department of Commerce response to the
changing economic situation and significant
business opportunities in the Near East and
North Africa. The group assembles, analyzes,
and disseminates to the U.S. business community information on economic conditions and
new opportunities in the area, provides counseling for and makes representations on behalf of
U.S. exporters, and plans promotional programs
to assist U.S. firms to take advantage of the expanded commercial potential. The Office of The
Near East also coordinates Department of Commerce participation in joint commission activities.

To take advantage of these programs call
202–377–5767 (Arab States); 202–377–4652
(Iran, Israel, Egypt, North Africa). For information concerning major projects call 202–377–
4441. The mailing address is Commerce Action
Group for the Near East, International Trade
Administration, Washington, DC 20230.

ALGERIA

Embassy of Algeria
2118 Kalorama Road NW
Washington, DC 20008
Telephone: 202–328–5300

BAHRAIN

Embassy of Bahrain
3502 International Drive NW
Washington, DC 20008
Telephone: 202–342–0741

ARAB REPUBLIC OF EGYPT

Embassy of the Arab Republic of Egypt
2310 Decatur Place NW
Washington, DC 20008
Telephone: 202–232–5400

Commercial and Economic Office
2232 Connecticut Avenue NW
Washington, DC 20008
Telephone: 202–234–1414

* Source: *A Business Guide to the Near East & North Africa*,
International Trade Administration, U.S. Department of
Commerce.

Egyptian Commercial Office
20 E. 46th Street
New York, NY 10017
Telephone: 212–286–0060

Permanent Economic Mission
500 Fifth Avenue
New York, NY 1010
Telephone: 212–398–9130

Consulate of the Arab Republic of Egypt
1110 Second Avenue
New York, NY 10022
Telephone: 212–759–7120

Consulate of the Arab Republic of Egypt
3001 Pacific Avenue
San Francisco, CA 94115
Telephone: 415–346–9700

IRAQ

Iraqi Interests Section
Indian Embassy
1801 P Street NW
Washington, DC 20008
Telephone: 202–483–7500

ISRAEL

Embassy of Israel
3514 International Drive NW
Washington, DC 20008
Telephone: 202–364–5500

Israel Consulates General
Atlanta, Boston, Chicago, Houston, Los
Angeles, New York City, Philadelphia, and
San Francisco

Investment Authority and Branches:
350 Fifth Avenue
New York, NY 10001
Telephone: 212–560–0610

174 N. Michigan Avenue
Chicago, IL 60601
Telephone: 312–332–2160

Israel Trade Center
350 Fifth Avenue
New York, NY 10001
Telephone: 212–560–0660

Israel Supply Mission
350 Fifth Avenue
New York, NY 10001
Telephone: 212–560–0680

6380 Wilshire Boulevard
Los Angeles, CA 90048
Telephone: 213–651–5700

JORDAN (HASHEMITE KINGDOM OF)

Embassy of Jordan
2319 Wyoming Avenue, NW
Washington, DC 20008
Telephone: 202–265–1606

Consulate General
866 U.N. Plaza
New York, NY 10017
Telephone: 212–752–0135

Consulates are also located in Houston, Chicago,
Scottsdale, and Palm Beach.

STATE OF KUWAIT

Embassy of Kuwait
2940 Tilden Street NW
Washington, DC 20008
Telephone: 202–966–0702

LEBANON

Embassy of Lebanon
2560 28th Street NW
Washington, DC 20008
Telephone: 202–462–8600

Consulate General
9 E. 76th Street
New York, NY 10021
Telephone: 212–744–7905

Consulate General
1300 Lafayette East
Detroit, Michigan 48207
Telephone: 313–963–0233

MOROCCO

Embassy of Morocco
1601 21st Street NW
Washington, DC 20009
Telephone: 202–462–7979/82

Consulate General
437 Fifth Avenue
New York, NY 10016
Telephone: 212–683–3062

OMAN

Embassy of the Sultanate of Oman
2342 Massachusetts Avenue NW
Washington, DC 20008
Telephone: 202–387–1980

Combined Consulate and Permanent Mission
to the United Nations
605 Third Avenue
Room 3304
New York, NY 10016
Telephone: 202–682–0447

QATAR

Embassy of Qatar
600 New Hampshire Avenue NW
Washington, DC 20037
Telephone: 202–338–0111

SAUDI ARABIA

Saudi Arabian Embassy
1520 18th Street NW
Washington, DC 20036
Telephone: 202–483–2100

Consulate General
866 United Nations Plaza
New York, NY 10017
Telephone: 212–752–2740

Consulate
5433 West Heimer, Suite 825
Houston, Texas 77056
Telephone: (713) 961–3351

Commercial Attache
1155 15th Street NW
Washington, DC 20005
Telephone: 202–331–0422

SYRIAN ARAB REPUBLIC

Embassy of the Syrian Arab Republic
2215 Wyoming Avenue NW
Washington, DC 20008
Telephone: 202–232–6313

TUNISIA

Embassy of Tunisia
2408 Massachusetts Avenue NW
Washington, DC 20008
Telephone: 202–234–6644

Tunisian Investment Promotion Agency
Tunisian National Tourist Office
2408 Massachusetts Avenue NW
Washington, DC 20008
Telephone: 202–234–6644

UNITED ARAB EMIRATES

Embassy of the United Arab Emirates
Suite 740
600 New Hampshire Avenue, N.W.
Washington, DC 20037
Telephone: 202–338–6500

YEMEN ARAB REPUBLIC

Embassy of the Yemen Arab Republic
600 New Hampshire Avenue, NW
Suite 860
Washington, DC 20037
Telephone: 202–965–4760

Consulate of the Yemen Arab Republic
211 East 43rd Street
Room 2402
New York, NY 10017
Telephone: 212–986–0990

FAST—MATCH

A quick, easy way to match your international business requirements to the appropriate Government programs or services designed to satisfy those needs

IF YOU ARE SEEKING INFORMATION REGARDING ➡

USE ⬇

	Potential Markets	Market Research *	Direct Sales Leads	Agents/Distributors	Licenses	Credit Analysis	Financial Assistance	Risk Insurance	Tax Incentives
Foreign Trade Statistics (FT-410)	•								
Global Market Surveys	•	•							
Foreign Market Reports	•	•							
Market Share Reports	•	•							
Foreign Economic Trends	•	•							
Business America	•	•	•	•	•				
Commercial Exhibitions	**	**	•	•	•				
Overseas Business Reports (OBR)		•							
Overseas Private Investment Corp.		•					•	•	
Commerce Business Daily			•						
New Product Information Service			•	•	•				
Trade Opportunity Program (TOP)			•	•	•				
Industry Trade Lists			•	•	•				
Special Trade Lists			•	•	•				
Export Mailing List Service (EMLS)			•	•	•				
Agent/Distributor Service (ADS)				•					
World Traders Data Reports (WTDR)						•			
Export—Import Bank							•	•	
Foreign Credit Insurance Assoc. (FCIA)								•	
Domestic Int'l. Sales Corp. (DISC)							•		•

* Foreign Trade Outlook Market Profiles; Industry Trends; Distribution and Sales Channels; Transportation Facilities; Local Business Practices and Customs; Investment Criteria; Import Procedures and Trade Regulations; and Industrial Property Rights.

** Research material developed regarding a planned exhibition and released to support promotional activities.

Cost of services may be obtained from Commerce District Offices.

Source: Industry and Trade Administration, U.S. Department of Commerce.

Index

A

Accounts payable, definition of, 311
Advance-Decline Index, 281
Aerospace industry
 stock market average for the, 284
 survey, 47–48
Agriculture Department, 40
Air Liquide acquisition of Big Three Industries, 41
Airlines industry
 stock market average for the, 284
 survey, 49–50
Akers, John, 28, 34
Alcoa Aluminum strike, 36
Allied-Signal to create spinoff companies, 10
Allied Stores purchases Gimbels, 33
Aluminum industry, stock market average for the, 285
American Depository Receipt (ADR), 511
American Medical International, 5
American Stock Exchange (Amex), 30, 36, 331, 449–51, 470
AMEX Commodities Corp., 470
Amoco, 7
Anderson Clayton takeover plan by Bear Stearns and Gruss & Co., 32–33
Annual reports, corporate, 329
Apparel industry survey, 51–56
Apple Computer, 3
Armacost, Samuel, 37
Armco losses, 39
A.S.E. Market Value Index, 281
Asian Wall Street Journal, The, address of, 360
Asset(s)
 annual rate of profit on total, 136
 financial, rise in value in the 1980s of, 267–69
 fixed, definition of, 311
 liquid, 196
 return on tangible, 267–69
 return on total, 45
 total, 311
 total current, 136
 turnover, 45
Associated Dry Goods
 acquisition by May Stores, 34–35
 earnings drop, 41
AT&T
 layoffs at, 7
 long-distance assignments of, 6
 long-distance rate cuts by, 27
 lower earnings in fourth quarter by, 17
 Net 1000 computer network abandoned by, 17

AT&T—*Cont.*
 preferred stock rating downgrade possible for, 2
Atlantic Richfield, 4, 6, 19
Auerbach Technology Reports, 548
Automobiles
 boost in prices of new, 1, 40
 earnings by manufacturers of U.S., 6
 financing incentives for, 3, 5–7, 9, 11–12, 14–15, 18, 21, 29, 32, 34, 40, 42
 manufacturing, 123
 parts and accessories for, 124
 production of, 33
 slow sales due to strong yen for Japanese, 36
 slow sales of new, 7, 9, 11, 13, 15, 18, 21–22, 24–25, 32, 38, 42
 stock market average for the, 284–85
 strong sales of imported, 25, 28, 32
 strong sales of new, 1–2, 4–5, 15, 21, 26, 28–29, 34, 36–37, 40
 voluntary export restraints for Japanese, 13, 15, 19

B

Baker, Treasury Secretary, 9, 20, 25, 29
Balance sheet ratios, 315–16; *see also* Financial statement (balance sheet and income statement).
Baldridge, Commerce Secretary, 23
Bank(s)
 bad debt reserves under new tax legislation, 505
 capital requirement increase sought by Fed for, 2
 deposit insurance for, 3
 failures, 22, 198–202
 farm problem loans by, 8, 22
 Federal Reserve, 435–36
 50 largest international, 234–36
 financing exports through commercial, 616–17
 fraud to be reported by outside auditors, 28
 holding companies' expansion into nonbanking businesses approved by the Fed, 34
 industry survey, 57–59
 Japanese international assets exceed those of U.S., 18
 liability insurance strongly preferred for companies seeking loans from, 23
 limited-service, 17
 mixed fourth quarter profit reports by holding, 17
 prime rate of, 22, 42, 173, 406
 special reserves required for loans to Peru by, 7